Between Malachi and Jesus

Writings from Maccabean and Roman Times

Evan and Marie Blackmore

Between Malachi and Jesus: Writings from Maccabean and Roman Times

P.O. Box 6259, Chillicothe, Ohio 45601
800.300.9778
www.deward.com

Cover design by Jonathan Hardin.

Cover illustration: A bronze coin issued by John son of Simon, the earliest known Judean leader to issue his own coinage. *Front cover:* The Hebrew inscription reads "John the high priest, head of the company of the Judeans." *Back cover:* A pomegranate (emblem of the high priest) between two horns of plenty.

All translations are by the authors, unless otherwise stated.

Printed in the United States of America.

ISBN: 978-1-936341-69-6

PREFACE

The Final Centuries Before Christ

The last three centuries before Christ are little known to Bible readers nowadays. Yet during that time God was doing wonderful works, amazing works, in order to prepare the world—and especially the nation of Israel—for the coming of His Son. He had already foretold through His prophets that He would do these things. And, step by step, piece by piece, every detail of the great plan came to pass. Not the tiniest jot or tittle went astray. All was fulfilled.

As the promised time drew near, the opposition by God's enemies became particularly intense. It was an age of terrible persecutions—some of the most terrible ever endured by God's people (Dan 8.23–25; 11.33; Maccabaica 1.64; 9.27). Those who remained faithful to the Lord were tortured and slaughtered (Heb 11.35), sometimes without even raising a hand to resist (Maccabaica 2.36–38).

And that was not the worst. The swords of unbelieving foreigners could have achieved little, had they not been helped by weapons even more dangerous (Jas 3.6)—by the tongues of those who professed to be believers and servants of God. Israelites went around corrupting their fellow Israelites, seducing them to live and behave like "the nations that are round about us" (Maccabaica 1.11–13). "Many people of Israel were well pleased" with that easy doctrine (1.43). The Law of God was set aside, while new forms of worship, more appealing to the people of the world, were introduced (1.43–52). By such methods, the worship that God had appointed was profaned and defiled (1.46; 2.12; Eighteen Psalms 1.8; 2.3). People whose hearts had "departed far from the Lord" gathered "in the council of the holy ones" (4.1), while those who truly "loved the assemblies of the holy ones" were driven out (17.18–20; Maccabaica 1.38–40; 2.27–30). Those who called themselves priests of God were foremost in corrupting and destroying the people of God (7.5–22); those who claimed to be worshipers practiced fornication openly and without shame (Epitome 6.4; Eighteen Psalms 2.12–15). In fact, "their transgressions exceeded the nations who had been before them" (1.8); "they did not leave any sin that they did not do more than the nations" (8.13; 17.21–22).

But it was also an age of shining lights amid the darkness (Dan 12.3), great examples worthy of remembrance, honor, and imitation (Heb 12.1). Many stood firm in spite of the persecutions, and laid down their lives gladly without reaping any visible reward for their labors (Dan 11.33, 35; Maccabaica 2.50; 13.3–6). They looked forward to the coming of a faithful Prophet as promised by Moses (Maccabaica 14.41; 4.46; Eighteen Psalms 17.23–51; 18.6–10; cf. Deut 18.15–19), even though they did not live to see how their own deeds were helping to pave the way for Him (Luke 10.24; Heb 11.13, 39–40).

In this book you will read their story—told not at second hand, but by some of the very people who remained faithful while most of their former brethren drifted into worldliness and corruption, Phariseeism and Sadduceeism and sometimes outright paganism.

The Contents of this Volume

Some periods of history are documented more fully than others.

Bible readers are well aware of that. We know much about the time when Israel had kings of its own (from Saul and David to the last kings of Judah). We know far less about the time of the judges, and some parts of the Persian period. How much can be said about Tola (who judged Israel for 23 years; Jdg 10.1–2), or about the governors of Persian Judah between Zerubbabel and Nehemiah?

The same principle applies to the time between the Persian period and Jesus. Much is known about some sections of that time—particularly the three major upheavals that God planned for Israel:

1. The change **from Persian rule to Greek rule** (around 330 BCE, in the time of Alexander the Great).
2. The change **from Greek rule to Judean independence** (around 175–135 BCE, in the Maccabean period).
3. The change **from Judean independence to Roman rule** (around 63 BCE, in the time of the Roman leader Pompey).

Far less is known about what happened in Israel during the century and a half after Alexander (about 320–180 BCE),[1] and during the half century leading up to the Roman conquest (about 130–70 BCE). Even the ancient Judaic historian Josephus, who tried to provide a continuous history of Israel from the beginning to his own day, had little reliable information about those periods (see Part Four of this book).

Therefore, this volume does not discuss all parts of the time between the Persian period and Jesus in equal detail. Instead, it concentrates mainly on the parts that are most solidly documented—which are the three upheavals listed above.

The volume is divided into five main parts:

- **Part One** briefly traces the history of Israel down to the time of Christ.
- **Part Two** contains complete translations of the two main Judean documents describing the events of the final centuries before Christ: the **Maccabean History** (often called "1 Maccabees") and the **Eighteen Psalms** of the Roman period

---

[1] "Apart from the uncertain references of Josephus and documents like the Elephantine Papyri, virtually nothing can be known of Jewish affairs to the end of the Persian period and on into the Hellenistic" (Merrill, *Historical Survey of the Old Testament,* 303). "Our information prior to the beginning of Seleucid rule (c. 200 B.C.) is slight" (Scott, *Jewish Backgrounds of the New Testament,* 75).

(often called "Psalms of Solomon"). Between them, these documents record all three of the great upheavals that happened to God's people in those days. The Maccabean History records the change **from Persian rule to Greek rule** and the change **from Greek rule to Judean independence.** The Eighteen Psalms record the change **from Judean independence to Roman rule.**

- **Part Three** provides, for further reference, the complete Greek or Syriac texts of those two documents, plus detailed commentaries on them.
- **Part Four** discusses the other ancient Jewish histories that deal with this period: the Ptolemaic History (often called "3 Maccabees"), the Epitome of the Acts of Judas Maccabeus (often called "2 Maccabees"), and the writings of Josephus.
- **Part Five** shows how these events fulfilled prophecies that God had previously given to Israel.

Readers looking for a concise overview of the period may wish to concentrate on Parts One and Two. Those investigating a specific point of detail may turn directly to the relevant section of Part Three.

It has been wisely said that "five words in an original source are worth a thousand words in a secondary source" (Ferguson, *Backgrounds of Early Christianity,* xvi–xvii); and this is especially true when the original source was written by someone with an "excellent and good heart" (cf. Luke 8.15). As will be seen later, the Maccabean History and the Eighteen Psalms are especially valuable because they were written by faithful brethren who continued "walking in all the commandments and ordinances of the Lord" (cf. Luke 1.6), and who "spoke and taught accurately the things about Jesus" even before He came (cf. Acts 18.25)—at a time when most of the people around them did "not know the Scriptures" (Mark 12.24) and/or "set aside the commandment of God" in order to keep rules that were merely of human origin, "traditions of Men" (Mark 7.8–9).[2] At the very least, therefore, these books are to be treated with the respect that we would give to any work done faithfully by faithful brethren in our own age, or in any other age (cf. 1 Thes 5.12–13).

Unless otherwise indicated, all English translations have been prepared by the present authors.

The Purpose of this Volume

Nowadays, books like the Maccabean History are most often consulted by Bible readers seeking to understand the background of the New Testament Scriptures and/or the fulfillment of Old Testament prophecies.

---

[2] This paragraph makes two fundamental assumptions: first, that it is possible to tell the difference between faithfulness to God and unfaithfulness (cf. Matt 7.15–27); and secondly, that the best and most edifying history of God's people is not written from a "neutral" or "non-partisan" viewpoint (there is no such thing: see, e.g., Wright, *The New Testament and the People of God,* 81–88), but is uncompromisingly partisan in the service of the Lord (cf. Josh 23.6–8; 24.15; Maccabaica 2.19–22; Eighteen Psalms 14.1–7).

Commentaries designed for that purpose have been published in several major European languages.[3] But in English, the only detailed commentaries on these books have been prepared by authors who rejected, at least in part, the truthfulness and historicity of the Scriptures. Some of their commentaries' presuppositions would naturally be unacceptable to many believers in the word of God.

The present volume is designed to fill that gap.

It is annotated throughout from the Scriptures, recognizing that all Scripture is the word of God (2 Tim 3.16) and that all His word is truth, without error or inconsistency (John 17.17; cf. Titus 1.2; Num 23.19; Rom 3.4).

It does not set out to "prove" the historicity of the Bible. It is simply provided as a resource for those who (on other grounds) accept the full historicity of the Bible.

Nor does it propose any new reading of the Maccabean and early Roman writings. Rather, it summarizes a very old way of looking at them. Even so, like all books, it is likely to be tainted with the passing novelties of its own day, and influenced too little by the eternal truths known from ancient times.

In annotating these books, there are two complementary dangers to be avoided.

1. It would be a mistake to treat these books only, or mainly, as sources of historical information.[4] Their main purpose was not to record history, but to glorify the Lord; and they recorded historical events simply because the Lord was glorified by those events (Maccabaica 3.19, 60; 4.55; 12.15; 16.2–3; Eighteen Psalms 8.7–8, 27–32).

   In preparing our commentaries, therefore, we have sought not merely to gather historical information, but above all to sit at the feet of the faithful brethren who wrote these books two thousand years ago, and to listen submissively to their wisdom.

2. But we must not fall into the opposite error, and treat the historical information in these books as unimportant. Every incident that happened to Israel during this period was vitally important, because it all contributed to the great design that God had planned before the foundation of the world (cf. Eph 1.4; 3.9, 11; 2 Tim 1.9–10; 2 Pet 1.2, 20; Rom 11.2; Rev 13.8) and had foretold by the mouth of His prophets (cf. Amos 3.7; Isa 42.9; John 13.19; 15.15).[5]

---

[3] In German, for instance, the famous Keil and Delitzsch Old Testament commentary was supplemented by Keil with a *Commentar über die Bücher der Makkabäer*. Unlike the rest of the series, that supplement was never translated into English.

[4] At first glance, readers sometimes feel that "as history, 1 Maccabees is very valuable and interesting to read, but it has less substantial devotional content"—in which respect it is felt to be "like the Book of Esther" (*The Apocrypha: The Lutheran Edition,* ed. Engelbrecht, 157). In reality, however, there is rich "devotional content" in every sentence of a faithful history of God's dealings with His people.

[5] Historical information is particularly crucial in matters foretold by prophets, because it is one of the means by which the true word of God can be recognized. The LORD who declares the

We have tried to annotate every point, large or small, that Bible readers might be likely to want explained—even if the answer involves technicalities. (For instance, some readers will want to know why different English translations of these books sometimes differ. That question often involves some discussion of Greek manuscripts or Greek grammar.) As far as possible, the main commentary is written in non-technical terms, reserving these technicalities for footnotes.

Most modern translations of the Maccabean History have been based either on Kappler's Göttingen edition (1936) or on Rahlfs's similar edition (1935, adapted from Kappler's preliminary draft). Most modern translations of the Eighteen Psalms have been based either on Gebhardt's edition (1895) or on Rahlfs's adaptation of Gebhardt (1935).

However, Kappler's edition of the Maccabean History has been one of the most severely criticized volumes in the Göttingen series,[6] and Gebhardt's edition of the Eighteen Psalms must be handled with even greater caution (it was prepared before the discovery of the Syriac version, and it also makes extensive use of conjectural emendation in a way no longer acceptable to most textual scholars).[7]

For the present volume, therefore, we have prepared new editions of the texts, and in the case of the Eighteen Psalms, we have printed the Greek and the Syriac in parallel.[8] We have been concerned solely with printing textual readings that actually exist in the ancient manuscripts, and seeking to understand those texts in forms that

---

end from the beginning (Isa 46.9–10) never issues false prophecies. "When a prophet speaks in the name of the LORD, and the word is not so, and does not come about, it is a word that the LORD has not spoken. The prophet has spoken it in insolence; you shall not be afraid of him" (Deut 18.22).

[6] In particular, Kappler has been criticized for attaching too little importance to the earliest Latin version and to the Greek manuscripts that most closely resemble it (Bogaert, "Septante et versions grecques," 611; Abel-Starcky 79–82; Kilpatrick, "I–III Maccabees," 418–33). Kappler conscientiously paid attention to de Bruyne's work on the Old Latin texts; but, for reasons that every researcher will understand, he had difficulty shifting from a frame of reference that he had established well before de Bruyne's publications appeared.

A less commonly noted limitation of Kappler's edition is his decision not to record the manuscripts' first/second person plural pronoun variants (e.g., *hēmas/humas*).

[7] Because of this lavish use of emendation, the section of Rahlfs adapted from Gebhardt is stylistically quite unlike the rest of his *Septuaginta*.

Wright's recent edition of the Eighteen Psalms (2007) helpfully corrects these flaws, but its own usefulness is impaired by misprints and other errors affecting its Greek text and apparatus as well as its English translation and introduction (cf. Werline, "Robert B. Wright, ed., *The Psalms of Solomon*," 203–07).

[8] In preparing this edition, the published textual collations of the following manuscripts have been checked against photographs: S, V, A, 64, 93, 236, 253, 260, 336, La^{109}, La^{146}, 7a1, 10h1, and 16h1.

were handed down by the ancient scribes and readers who copied and cherished them.[9]

Acknowledgements

For photographic images of manuscripts, we are indebted to the Biblioteca Nazionale Marciana (Gr. Z.1), the Bibliothèque Nationale Française (Gr. 2), the Biblioteca Apostolica Vaticana (Vat. Gr. 331), the Biblioteca Complutense (BH MSS 31), the Bibliothèque Municipale de Lyon (Ms. 430), the British Library (Royal MS 1 D II and Add MS 14538), and Robert B. Wright (the Greek manuscripts of the Eighteen Psalms and 16h1).[10]

Harry and Gwenda Blackmore, Warner and Erica Quarles, Peter Bowyer, Richard and Mary Greenwell, and Peter and Suzanne Dehne kindly assisted us by reading and commenting on parts of the material published in this volume. In addition, Warner provided valuable help during proofreading. We are also grateful to Nathan Ward for his assistance during the gestation of this project, and to Crystal Crawford for her exemplary copyediting.

For the errors that remain, we alone are responsible; and errors are particularly likely in a book containing much material that has not been presented before (at least in our language). "Who can recognize sins of ignorance? Cleanse me from hidden sins" (Psa 19.12). Readers are urged to search the Scriptures to determine what is so (Acts 17.11), and by that standard to test all things in the following pages, holding fast whatever is good, but rejecting whatever is evil (1 Thes 5.21–22).

---

[9] At points in the Eighteen Psalms where the existing Greek and Syriac texts differ significantly, we have sought to discover and explain the sense of each.

[10] For Greek codices Sinaiticus and Alexandrinus, and the Syriac manuscript 7a1, we have used the published photofacsimiles (see the Bibliography).

CONTENTS

List of Maps

On the maps, towns of **known** location are marked with a *solid circle,* and towns of **uncertain** location are marked with a *query inside a circle.*

Abbreviations and Other Symbols

†	second person singular (KJV "thou" or "thee"); contrast ^{pl}
§	section (e.g., of a reference grammar or lexicon entry)
≡	corresponds to
1QSb	Qumran Blessings document
58	Greek minuscule Vat. Regin. Gr. 10
64	Greek minuscule BNF Gr. 2
93	Greek minuscule BL Royal MS 1 D II
236	Greek minuscule Vat. Gr. 331
253	Greek minuscule Vat. Gr. 336
260	Greek minuscule Copenhagen GkS 6
336	Greek minuscule Athos Iveron 555
655	Greek minuscule Vat. Ottob. Gr. 60
659	Greek minuscule Vat. Ottob. Gr. 384
7a1	Syriac Codex Ambrosianus
7h7	Syriac manuscript BL Add MS 14446
8a1	Syriac manuscript BNF Syr. 341
10h1	Syriac manuscript BL Add MS 14538
16h1	Syriac manuscript Rylands Syr. Cod. 9
θ′	Greek version attributed to Theodotion
A	Greek Codex Alexandrinus
AAT	*Apócrifos del Antiguo Testamento,* ed. Díez Macho and Piñero Sáenz
ABD	*Anchor Bible Dictionary,* ed. Freedman
Abel	Abel, *Livres des Maccabées* (Études Bibliques)
Abel, *GP*	Abel, *Géographie de la Palestine*
Abel, *Grammaire*	Abel, *Grammaire du grec biblique*
Abel-Starcky	Abel and Starcky, *Livres des Maccabées* (Bible de Jérusalem, 3rd ed., 1961)
Amyzon	Robert, *Fouilles d'Amyzon en Carie*
AOT	*Apocryphal Old Testament,* ed. Sparks
APAT	*Apokryphen und Pseudepigraphen des Alten Testaments,* ed. Kautzsch
APOT	*Apocrypha and Pseudepigrapha of the Old Testament,* ed. Charles
Arayathinal	Arayathinal, *Aramaic Grammar*
ASV	American Standard Version
B	Greek Codex Vaticanus
Baars	"Psalms of Solomon," ed. Baars (Leiden Peshitta)
BCE	dates before the Common Era (equivalent to BC)
BDAG	Bauer, Arndt, and Gingrich, *Greek-English Lexicon of the New Testament,* revised by Danker (3rd ed., 2000)
BDB	Brown, Driver, and Briggs, *Hebrew and English Lexicon*

BDF	Blass and Debrunner, *Greek Grammar of the New Testament,* revised by Funk
Bergsträsser	Bergsträsser, *Hebräische Grammatik*
BGS	*Biblia Griega Septuaginta,* ed. Fernández Marcos and Spottorno Díaz-Caro
Brenton	*Septuagint Version,* tr. Brenton
Buttmann	Buttmann, *Grammar of the New Testament Greek,* tr. Thayer
Calmet	Calmet, *Maccabées*
CD	Cairo Damascus Document
CE	Common Era dates (equivalent to AD)
CIJ	*Corpus Inscriptionum Judaicarum,* ed. Frey
CM	Glassner, *Mesopotamian Chronicles*
Cotton	Cotton, *Five Books of Maccabees*
CPJ	*Corpus Papyrorum Judaicarum,* ed. Tcherikover and Fuks
D	Greek Codex Bezae Cantabrigiensis
DGE	*Diccionario Griego-Español,* ed. Adrados
Diodati	Bibbia Diodati (2nd ed., 1641)
Diodati Fr	Bible Diodati (French, 1644)
Dionysius	Dionysius Cartusianus, *Ennarrationes in Iob… II Machabaeorum*
DJPA	Sokoloff, *Dictionary of Jewish Palestinian Aramaic*
DRCV	Douai-Rheims-Challoner Version (1749–1750)
Drusius	Drusius, *Liber Hasmonaeorum*
DRV	Douai-Rheims Version (1609–1610)
Duval	Duval, *Traité de grammaire syriaque*
Dyserinck	*Apocriefe Boeken,* tr. Dyserinck
ed.	edition; edited by
ESV	English Standard Version
f^{19}	Family 19 (Antiochene Greek minuscules 19, 62, 93, and 542)
f^{64}	Family 64 (Antiochene Greek minuscules 64, 236, 381, 534, and 728)
f^{120}	Family 120 (Greek minuscules 29, 68, 71, 74, 98, 107, 120, 130, 134, 243, 379, and 731)
f^{253}	Family 253 (Greek minuscules 253, 655, and 659)
f^{260}	Family 260 (Greek minuscules 149, 260, 336, 471, 606, 629, 769, and 3004)
Fairweather-Black	Fairweather and Black, *First Book of Maccabees*
FGrH	*Fragmente der griechischen Historiker,* ed. Jacoby
Gebhardt	*Psalmen Salomo's,* ed. Gebhardt
Geneva	Geneva Bible
Gillet	Gillet, *Machabées*
GKC	Kautzsch, *Gesenius' Hebrew Grammar,* revised by Cowley
Grimm	Grimm, *Erste Buch der Maccabäer*
HALOT	Koehler, Baumgartner, and Stamm, *Hebrew and Aramaic Lexicon of the Old Testament*
Harris-Mingana	Harris and Mingana, *Odes and Psalms of Solomon* (1916–1920)
Hendin	Hendin, *Guide to Biblical Coins* (5th ed., 2010)

Hendin (1996)	Hendin, *Guide to Biblical Coins* (3rd ed., 1996)
Holm-Nielsen	Holm-Nielsen, *Psalmen Salomos*
ISBE	*International Standard Bible Encyclopedia,* ed. Bromiley (1979–1988)
Jastrow	Jastrow, *Dictionary of the Targumim, the Talmud Babli and Yerushalmi, and the Midrashic Literature*
JB	Jerusalem Bible (1966)
Jünemann	Versión Jünemann
KB	Kühner and Blass, *Ausführliche Grammatik der grieschischen Sprache,* Teil 1
Keil	Keil, *Commentar über die Bücher der Makkabäer*
KG	Kühner and Gerth, *Ausführliche Grammatik der grieschischen Sprache,* Teil 2
King	*The Old Testament,* tr. Nicholas King
KJV	King James Version
Knabenbauer	Knabenbauer, *Commentarius in duos libros Machabaeorum*
König 1–3	König, *Lehrgebäude der hebräischen Sprache,* vols. 1–3
König 4	König, *Stilistik, Rhetorik, Poetik*
La^{109}	Latin Codex Complutensis 1 (BUC 31)
La^{146}	Latin Codex Lugdunensis (Lyon 430)
Lapide	Cornelius a Lapide, *Commentarius in … Machabaeos*
LEH	Lust, Eynikel, and Hauspie, *Greek-English Lexicon of the Septuagint*
LSJ	Liddell and Scott, *Greek-English Lexicon,* revised by Jones (9th ed., 1940, with revised Supplement, 1996)
Luther	Lutherbibel 1545
Luther 1912	Lutherbibel 1912
LXX	Old Greek (including Septuagint)
LXX.D	Septuaginta Deutsch
LXX.DE	*Septuaginta Deutsch: Erläuterungen und Kommentare,* ed. Karrer and Kraus
mg	marginal note
Martin	Version Martin, revised by Roques (1744)
MHT	Moulton, Howard, and Turner, *Grammar of New Testament Greek*
MT	Masoretic text
Muraoka	Muraoka, *Greek-English Lexicon of the Septuagint*
NAB	New American Bible (1st ed., 1970)
NASB	New American Standard Bible (1st ed., 1971)
Nelis	Nelis, *I Makkabeeën*
NETS	New English Translation of the Septuagint
NIDB	*New Interpreter's Dictionary of the Bible,* ed. Sakenfeld
NIDNTT	Brown, *New International Dictionary of New Testament Theology*
NJB	New Jerusalem Bible
Nöldeke	Nöldeke, *Compendious Syriac Grammar,* tr. Crichton
NRSV	New Revised Standard Version
OGIS	*Orientis Graeci Inscriptiones Selectae,* ed. Dittenberger
OTP	*Old Testament Pseudepigrapha,* ed. Charlesworth
P. Cair. Zen.	Zenon Papyri
Pellicanus	Pellicanus, *Commentaria Bibliorum*
^{pl}	second person plural (KJV "you" or "ye"); contrast †

PG	Patrologia Graeca, ed. Migne
PL	Patrologia Latina, ed. Migne
Prigent	"Psaumes de Salomon," tr. Prigent (Pléiade)
Rahlfs	*Septuaginta,* ed. Rahlfs
REB	Revised English Bible
Ryle-James	Ryle and James, *Psalms of the Pharisees*
Robertson	Robertson, *Grammar of the Greek New Testament in the Light of Historical Research*
RST	Russian Synodal Version
RV	Revised Version (1881–1895)
S	Greek Codex Sinaiticus
SAAS	St. Athanasius Academy Septuagint
Sacy	Lemaistre de Sacy and du Fossé, *Machabées*
SC	Houghton and Lorber, *Seleucid Coins*
Schürer	Schürer, *History of the Jewish People in the Age of Jesus Christ,* tr. Macpherson, Taylor, and Christie (1890)
Schürer-Vermes	Schürer, *History of the Jewish People in the Age of Jesus Christ,* revised by Vermes, Millar, and Black (1973–1987)
Schwyzer	Schwyzer, *Griechische Grammatik*
Scío	Versión Scío de San Miguel, revised by Palau (1846)
SDB	*Smith's Dictionary of the Bible,* ed. Hackett (1868–1870)
SE	Seleucid Era dates
SEG	*Supplementum Epigraphicum Graecum*
SH	Sachs and Hunger, *Astronomical Diaries and Related Texts from Babylonia*
SIG^3	*Sylloge Inscriptionum Graecarum,* ed. Dittenberger (3rd ed., 1915–1924)
Simons	Simons, *Geographical and Topographical Texts of the Old Testament*
Sir	Ben Sira (Jesus son of Sirach)
SL	Sokoloff, *Syriac Lexicon*
Stone	Stone Tanach
SV	Statenvertaling
SyI	Common Syriac version of the Maccabaica
SyII	Revised Syriac version of the Maccabaica
Syr	Syriac
TDNT	Kittel and Friedrich, *Theological Dictionary of the New Testament*
TDOT	Botterweck, Ringgren, and Fabry, *Theological Dictionary of the Old Testament*
TEV	Today's English Version (Good News Bible)
Thackeray	Thackeray, *Grammar of the Old Testament in Greek*
Thayer	Grimm, *Greek-English Lexicon of the New Testament,* revised by Thayer
TLOT	Jenni and Westermann, *Theological Lexicon of the Old Testament*
tr.	translated by
Trafton	Trafton, *Syriac Version of the Psalms of Solomon*
Trench	Trench, *Synonyms of the New Testament*
TS	Payne Smith, *Thesaurus Syriacus*
v, vv	verse, verses

V	Greek Codex Venetus
Vg	Latin Vulgate
Viteau	Viteau, *Psaumes de Salomon*
Viteau, *Sujet*	Viteau, *Étude sur le grec...: Sujet, complément et attribut*
Viteau, *Verbe*	Viteau, *Étude sur le grec...: Le Verbe*
VRV	Versión Reina-Valera (1602)
Whiston	"Psaltery of Solomon," tr. Whiston
Winer	Winer, *Treatise on the Grammar of New Testament Greek,* tr. Moulton (3rd ed., 1882)
Wis	Wisdom (of Solomon)
Wright	*Psalms of Solomon,* ed. Wright
Wycl	Wycliffite Later Version
ZB	Zürcher-Bibel (1931)
ZEB	*Zondervan Encyclopedia of the Bible,* ed. Tenney, revised by Silva (2nd ed., 2009)
Zöckler	Zöckler, *Apokryphen*

Textual Symbols

The Greek and Syriac texts in this volume are accompanied by a textual apparatus, which uses the following symbols. (The **lemma** is the portion of text to which the textual variants apply.)

Swete and Kappler used the symbol V^1 both for alterations by the original scribe of V and for alterations by the manuscript's first corrector (Swete, *Old Testament in Greek,* 3.xvi). We have reserved the symbol V^1 for alterations by the original scribe himself (none of these appear in our textual apparatus). Therefore, alterations by the first corrector are now called V^a, and alterations by the second corrector are called V^b (not V^a, as in Swete and Kappler). The first corrector was apparently contemporary with the original scribe; the second worked much later.

>	the preceding lemma is omitted by the listed manuscripts
+	the following text is inserted after the lemma by the listed manuscripts
^	the following text inserted before the lemma by the listed manuscripts
~	the lemma is transposed by the listed manuscripts; within the lemma, the transposed sections are separated by the symbol /
( )	the bracketed letters are indicated by a contraction mark in the specified manuscript
[ ]	the bracketed manuscripts support the reading, but with minor variations (which are usually indicated inside the brackets)
=	identical except in spelling
???	illegible letters
1°, 2°, 3° ...	first, second, third ... occurrence of the word(s) within this particular verse
S*, V*, 253* ...	original text of manuscript S, V, 253 ...
S^1	alteration to S by the original scribe
S^{ca}	alteration to S by the Antiochene corrector
S^{cb1}	alteration to S by corrector b1
S^c	alteration to S by an unidentified corrector
V^a	alteration to V by the first corrector (Swete's V^1)
V^b	alteration to V by the second corrector (Swete's V^a)
A^c, 253^c ...	alterations to A, 253 ... by any corrector
$64^{+}236$, $La^{109+146}$	the manuscripts linked by the superscript $^{+}$ belong to the same family
|	separates alternate readings to the same lemma
•	marks the end of the apparatus to a lemma
< >	the text enclosed within the angle brackets differs from the reading found in the copytext (which is specified in the apparatus)

Terminology

Covenants and Scriptures

The **Old Covenant** (or **Old Testament**) was inaugurated through Moses at Mount Sinai (Heb 9.18–20) and continued until Christ died on the cross. Since that time the **New Covenant** (or **New Testament**) has been in operation (Heb 9.15).

Strictly speaking, therefore, there was never any "Intertestamental Period." The period between Malachi and Jesus was part of the Old Testament period.

In this volume, the Scriptures from Genesis through Malachi are called the **Hebrew Scriptures,** because they were written mainly or entirely in Hebrew. (Some of them—such as Job and Genesis—may have been written before the start of the Old Testament, and certainly describe events that happened prior to the Old Testament. Therefore, we have avoided the potentially confusing term "Old Testament Scriptures.")

Names of Books

Many of the historical works cited in this book have been known by several different names in ancient and/or modern times. This book uses whichever of the ancient names would be least likely to confuse a reader unfamiliar with the material:

- The **Maccabean History** (or **Maccabaica**) is the work often called "1 Maccabees."
- The **Epitome of the Acts of Judas Maccabeus** (or **Maccabean Epitome**) is the work often called "2 Maccabees."
- The **Ptolemaic History** (or **Ptolemaica**) is the work often called "3 Maccabees."
- The **Eighteen Psalms** is the collection often called "Psalms of Solomon."

In this volume, the book of Psalms in the Hebrew Scriptures is always called the **Hebrew Psalter,** to avoid confusion with the Eighteen Psalms.

Chapter and Verse Numbers

For Scripture books, chapter and verse numbers are always cited according to the system used in standard English versions (e.g., KJV, ASV, NASB, and ESV)—even when the reference is to a foreign language edition that normally uses a different numbering system.

It should be noted that all the chapter numbers, verse numbers, and book titles in standard editions of the Bible were inserted by uninspired people, and are not parts of the word of God. What the KJV calls "The First Epistle of Paul the Apostle to the Corinthians" was certainly not Paul's first epistle to the Corinthians; he had already written at least one other epistle to them (cf. 1 Cor 5.9). What the KJV calls "The Second Book of Samuel" is not about Samuel at all, and never even mentions him; he had already died before the events recorded in it (cf. 1 Sam 25.1; 28.3). Therefore, all references in the present commentary to "1 Cor," "2 Sam," etc., should be regarded merely as nominal symbols for sections of Scripture, not as abbreviated descriptions of their content.

In the **Eighteen Psalms,** two different systems of verse numbering are in common use. One system (introduced by La Cerda in 1626) has been used in all Syriac editions and some Greek ones. The other system (introduced by Gebhardt in 1895) has been used in other Greek editions. Neither system corresponds fully to the psalms' natural sense divisions (therefore, both systems require some verse numbers to be placed partway through a phrase or clause). Since this book discusses both the Greek and the Syriac versions of these psalms, it uses the numbering system that has been applied to both—La Cerda's system. In some sections of this book Gebhardt's verse numbers are also provided, inside square brackets, for ease of reference.

In the **Maccabean History,** the verse numbering corresponds to that in Kappler's Göttingen edition (1936), which sometimes differs from that found in other editions.

References to **Diodorus** use the numbering of Dindorf's Teubner edition. Where the new Budé numbering has been published (as of 2013) and is different, it is also provided, inside square brackets.

Judean, Judaic, Jewish, Hebraic, Hellenic, Hellenistic

We use the term **Judean** for a person from Judea, and the term **Judaic** for a believer in Judaism. The term **Jewish** describes people of Jewish ancestry (wherever they live, and whatever their beliefs). Something written in a Hebrew-like style (e.g., the Maccabean History) is called **Hebraic,** whereas something written in a more Greek-like style (e.g., the Ptolemaic History) is called **Hellenic.** The term **Hellenistic** refers to the period of history when parts of the Middle East were under Greek rule (from the conquest by Alexander the Great to the death of Cleopatra, i.e., about 330–30 BCE).

Dates

Two different systems of numbering years are used for events during the Greek and Roman periods:

- **BCE** (equivalent to BC) and **CE** (equivalent to AD). In the period covered by this book, the term BC ("before Christ") is potentially misleading. That term was based on an incorrect ancient estimate of the time of Christ's birth, which leads to paradoxical statements such as "Christ was probably born several years BC." To avoid confusion, this book uses instead the term BCE ("before the common era"—that is, before the timepoint chosen by common usage for the numbering of dates). For the same reason, later dates are designated CE ("common era") instead of AD.
- **SE** ("Seleucid Era"). This system—years "of the kingdom of the Greeks"—is used in the Maccabean History and Epitome. It apparently starts from the time when Seleucus I (one of Alexander the Great's successors) reckoned himself to be king. The year 1 SE would correspond to about 312–311 BCE (= BC). The year 170 SE (the end of Greek rule over Israel) would correspond to about 142 BCE (= BC).

Translation Policies

The translation of the **Maccabean History** has been adapted from the 1895 Revised Version. The translation of the **Eighteen Psalms** has been adapted from the version by William Whiston (1727). In both cases, the translation has been adjusted to match the Greek and Syriac texts printed in this volume, and the English has been modernized except for some terms that have no exact modern equivalents and would be familiar to most readers of the Scriptures.

The detailed commentary later in the volume includes different translations, which follow more precisely the wording and grammar of the Greek and Syriac texts (somewhat in the style of ancient translations of these books—which tended to be highly isomorphic). By adopting that approach, we have aimed to supplement rather than duplicate the English versions already in print.

The translations use various special policies, all of which have been employed in some standard English versions of the Scriptures:

Proper Names

Names of places and people are spelled in whatever way would be most familiar to readers of well-known English versions of the Scriptures (such as the KJV, ASV, NASB, and ESV). When the Hebrew and Greek forms of a name are likely to be about equally familiar (e.g., Ashdod and Azotus), we have used the Hebrew form. The names *Christos* and *Hadēs* in the Greek version of the Eighteen Psalms are rendered "Christ" and "Hades"; the corresponding names *Mšyḥ'* and *Šywl* in the Syriac version are rendered "Messiah" and "Sheol."

Capitalization

In accordance with DeWard house style, all pronouns referring to Deity are capitalized. This is highly appropriate in these books, which speak of the Lord with the utmost reverence even when (as often in the Maccabean History) only a pronoun is used to refer to Him.

Capitalization is also used to distinguish a few words that might otherwise be confusing or ambiguous. The word "Law" is capitalized when it refers to the Law of God. The word "Man" is capitalized when it refers generically to both male and female (Greek *anthrōpos*), but is printed in small letters, "man," when it refers specifically to males (Greek *anēr*).

The special Syriac form *MRY',* which is applied only to the true God (somewhat like Hebrew *YHWH,* "Jehovah"), is translated "LORD" in small capitals.

Second Person Singular and Plural

Words and phrases addressed to one person (KJV "thou" or "thee") are marked with a superscript dagger thus: you[†]. Words and phrases addressed to two or more people (KJV "you" or "ye") are marked with a superscript [pl] thus: you[pl]. Where the English rendering of a verb includes an English pronoun, the superscript is attached to that pronoun (e.g., "you[pl] will live"). Where it does not, the superscript is attached to the last of whatever English words are used to render it (e.g., "be zealous^{pl} for the Law").

Italics

As in the KJV, ASV, and NASB, *italics* mark material that does not correspond to anything in the original, but has been added by the translators for the sake of clarity. (In some contexts, "holy *places*" could possibly be rendered "holy *things*," and "*may* salvation *be* on Israel" could possibly be rendered "salvation *will be* on Israel" or "salvation *is* on Israel.")

Where Greek imperfects are rendered "*began* doing" or "*kept* doing" rather than "were doing," the words *began* and *kept* are italicized to distinguish them from the Greek verbs for "begin" and "keep."

Boldface

In the commentary sections of this volume, **boldface print** marks a direct quotation from the passage under discussion, whereas quotations from other sources are cited in quotation marks.

Square Brackets

The Greek text of the Maccabean History occasionally transliterates Hebrew words (e.g., geographical terms) rather than translating them. At those points, the English translation likewise transliterates the Hebrew word, but supplies an English rendering of it inside square brackets, e.g., "Shephelah [lowland]."

By contrast, curved brackets are used in the usual way, as marks of punctuation separating material within the text, e.g., "(as at other times)" (Maccabaica 3.30).

Between Malachi and Jesus

FROM THE CREATION TO THE PERSIAN PERIOD

God's word gives only a few glimpses of the world's early history, and those glimpses concentrate mainly on a handful of individuals: Adam and Eve, Noah, and especially Abraham and his family.

Some of Abraham's descendants—the nation of Israel—settled in the land of Egypt. Several centuries later, God brought that nation out of Egypt under the leadership of Moses, and made a covenant with them—the Old Covenant (or Old Testament).

From that time on, the Scriptures give much more detailed historical information. They provide a nearly continuous, generation-by-generation narrative of God's dealings with the nation of Israel during a period spanning almost a thousand years.

That narrative can be divided into several phases, in which different kinds of leaders were appointed by God to govern His people:

- **Before Moses:** By faith, Abraham left his original home and traveled to the land of Canaan. Several generations later, some of his descendants moved to Egypt, where they—the Israelites—became subject to the **Egyptian kings.**

  These events are described in the first part of the Law of Moses (Genesis).
- **Moses:** Under the leadership of God's mediator Moses, the Israelites journeyed from Egypt to Mount Sinai, and then through the wilderness to the verge of the promised land.

  These events are described in the last four-fifths of the Law of Moses (Exodus, Leviticus, Numbers, and Deuteronomy).
- **Joshua and the judges:** The Israelites entered the promised land and began to dwell there. At this time, they had no earthly king (Jdg 17.6; 18.1; 19.1; 21.25); their only king was the LORD (1 Sam 12.12; 8.7). On earth, they were governed first by Joshua (Josh 1.1–18), and then, after his death, by a succession of judges (Acts 13.20).

  These events are described mainly in the books of Joshua, Judges, and Ruth.
- **Israelite kings:** After they had been living in the land for several hundred years, the Israelites demanded to be ruled by an earthly king "like all the nations" (1 Sam 8.5, 19–20). The Lord therefore provided them with kings: first Saul, then David, then David's son Solomon (Acts 13.21–22; 1 Sam 10.21–26; 11.15; 15.1; 16.1, 13; Psa 78.70–72; 1 Kgs 1.29–40). After Solomon's death, the nation was divided: the southern kingdom of Judah continued to be ruled by David's descendants, whereas the northern tribes of Israel had various other Israelite rulers

(1 Kgs 11.31–32, 35–37; 12.16–20). Two and a half centuries later, the northern tribes were carried away into captivity by Assyria (2 Kgs 17.6–23), but the southern kingdom of Judah remained until its last king, Zedekiah, was removed by Nebuchadnezzar, king of Babylon (2 Kgs 25.1–21).

These events are described mainly in Samuel-Kings and Chronicles.

- **Foreign kings:** Eventually, because the Israelites had persistently disobeyed Him, the Lord ordained that they would be subject to a series of foreign kings (Deut 28.47–48; Neh 9.32–37). The earliest of those foreign rulers were **Babylonians** (Jer 27.1–17; Dan 2.37–38), three of whom are mentioned by name in the Scriptures: Nebuchadnezzar (2 Kgs 25.1; Dan 1.1), Evil-Merodach (2 Kgs 25.27), and Belshazzar (Dan 5.1; 7.1). After that, Israel was ruled by **Persians** (2 Kgs 36.20), including Cyrus (Ezra 1.1; Dan 6.28), Darius (Ezra 4.5), Ahasuerus (Ezra 4.6; Est 1.1), Artaxerxes (Ezra 4.7–8; 7.1), and a later Darius (Neh 12.22).

  These events are described mainly in Daniel, Ezra-Nehemiah, and Esther.

This brings us to the end of the Hebrew Scriptures—the part of God's word usually described as the "Old Testament."

But the story did not end at that point. On the contrary, the story was still only in its early stages. Everything that had happened so far, from the creation down to the Persian period, was just preliminary. It was all preparation for a great event that would take place hundreds of years later, when God would bless "all the nations of the earth" through a descendant of Abraham (Gen 22.16; Gal 3.8, 16).

This volume looks at the events that happened to Israel during the centuries after the end of the Hebrew Scriptures—the centuries that saw the final preparations for the blessing of all nations.

Dates

The length of time between Moses and the Babylonian empire can be approximately estimated from information provided in the Scriptures:

- **From Moses to the Israelite kings:** There were exactly 480 years between the departure from Egypt and the fourth year of King Solomon's reign (1 Kgs 6.1).
- **The Israelite kings:** The Scriptures tell us the length of each Israelite king's reign. Those figures cannot simply be added end to end, because one king sometimes began to reign before his predecessor had died (cf. 1 Kgs 1.29–40; 2 Kgs 15.5). Nevertheless, even allowing for all possible overlaps, there must have been something like 350 to 400 years between the start of Solomon's reign and the end of Zedekiah's.
- **The Babylonian kings:** The Israelites were subject to the Babylonians for 70 years (Jer 25.11–12; 2 Chr 36.20–22).

Thus the total time between the departure from Egypt and the end of the Babylonian empire would have been about 900 to 950 years.

The chart below outlines the history of Israel from Moses to the end of the Hebrew Scriptures. The dates on the chart are estimates based on the usually accepted assumption that Babylonian rule ended around 538 BCE.

Government of Israel	Historical records	Other books	Estimated date BCE
Egyptian rulers	Gen–Exod	? Job	1500
Moses	Exod–Deut		
Joshua and judges	Josh Jdg, Ruth		1400 1300 1200 1100
Israelite kings	1 Sam–2 Kgs 1–2 Chr	Psa Prov, Ecc, Song Jnh Isa, Hos, Amos, Mic Nah, Hab, Zep	1000 900 800 700
Babylonian rulers	Dan	Jer, Ezek Lam, Oba	600
Persian rulers	Ezra–Neh, Est	Hag, Zec, Mal ? Joel	500 400

FROM THE PERSIAN PERIOD TO JESUS

SOURCES OF INFORMATION

As we have just seen, the Hebrew Scriptures came to an end during the Persian period, about four centuries before the birth of Christ. But God did not stop working at that point (cf. John 5.17). Throughout the next four centuries, He continued to perform His will, carrying out what had been decreed (Dan 11.36), and preparing for His Son to be sent "when the completion of the time came" (Gal 4.4).

For the events of those centuries, we have various different sources of information:

1. Prophecies in the Hebrew Scriptures

The Hebrew Scriptures were written to describe not only the past, but also the future. "I am God, and there is no other; I am God, and there is no one like me, declaring from the beginning the end, and from former times things that have not yet been done," says the Lord (Isa 49.9–10; cf. 41.22–23; 42.9; 44.7; 45.21; Acts 15.18). To Him, the future is as definite as the past. Therefore His word can report accurately not only what has happened in the past, but also what will happen in the future.

God provided His people with various prophecies foretelling the events that would follow the Persian period.

- In the time of Moses, Balaam briefly foretold (Num 24.24) that an invader from the Mediterranean coastal regions (Kittim) would one day come and defeat peoples of the Middle East (Assyria and Eber).[11]
- Later prophets foretold that the people of Judah would be oppressed and taken captive by the Greeks, but would rise up and overthrow their oppressors (Zec 9.13–16; Joel 3.6–8).
- The most detailed prophecies of all were given by Daniel (especially in chapters 2; 7; 8; and 11). Daniel foretold that the Persian kingdom would be followed by a *Greek kingdom* (Dan 8.3–8, 20–21; 11.2–4). After many generations, one of the Greek rulers would severely oppress the Israelites and stop the sacrificial worship

---

[11] "Ships will come from the hand of Kittim, and they will afflict Assyria, and they will afflict Eber" (Num 24.24). Balaam uses only names that were familiar in very ancient times. **Kittim** was the term for the Mediterranean coastal regions (Gen 10.4–5; Jer 2.10; 1 Chr 1.7; Dan 11.30; Maccabaica 1.1). The **Assyria** mentioned by Balaam was the great Mesopotamian nation that took captive the Kenites (Num 24.21–22) and many other peoples in the region (2 Kgs 15.29; 16.9; 17.6; Isa 20.1, 4; 2 Chr 33.11). **Eber** was the ancestor of many Middle Eastern peoples (Gen 10.21, 24–25).

of God for several years (Dan 8.9–14, 23–25; 11.21–39), but the faithful Israelites would oppose him (Dan 11.32–35) and the sacrifices would be restored (Dan 8.14). Later, the Greek kingdom would be replaced by *another foreign kingdom* (Dan 2.33, 40–43; 7.7). In those days God would set up *His Kingdom,* which would last forever (2.34–35, 44; 7.13–14, 18).

These prophecies will be discussed in more detail in Part Five of this volume.

2. Later Israelite Writings

The most important later sources are two books written in Judea during the last two centuries before Christ:

- The **Maccabean History** (**Maccabaica;** now often called "1 Maccabees"), probably written around 110–70 BCE. It describes the period of *Greek* rule, beginning with the overthrow of the Persian empire by the Greek king Alexander the Great (about 330 BCE). It concentrates on the persecution of Judea by one of Alexander's successors, Antiochus Epiphanes, for several years (about 167–164 BCE), and the deliverance of Judea from Greek rule under the leadership of the Maccabean family (a process completed about 142 BCE).
- A collection of **Eighteen Psalms** (now often called the "Psalms of Solomon"), probably written at various times around 70–30 BCE. Several of these psalms describe the end of rule by the Maccabean family and the start of *Roman* rule in Judea (about 63 BCE).

The Maccabean History and the Eighteen Psalms will be printed in full and discussed in detail in Parts Two and Three.

Other ancient Israelite writings that refer to this period include the following:

- The **Ptolemaic History** (**Ptolemaica;** now often called "3 Maccabees"), a short book describing a brief but intense persecution of the Jews by the Greek ruler Ptolemy Philopator (late in the third century BCE). Despite its common name, it has no connection with the Maccabean History. It may have been written any time during the final two centuries BCE.
- The **Epitome of the Acts of Judas Maccabeus** (now often called "2 Maccabees"), which describes the persecution of the Judeans by Antiochus Epiphanes and the early stages of their deliverance. In its present form, it was probably compiled around 120–70 BCE. Its contents are not entirely reliable and should be treated with caution (for instance, it preserves two contradictory accounts of the death of Antiochus: 1.13–16 and 9.1–28). Despite its common name, it is not a sequel to the Maccabean History; instead, it is an independent account of part of the same period.
- The histories of Israel written by **Josephus** late in the first century CE. For the Greek and Roman periods, Josephus relied partly on the Maccabean History, and partly on several less reliable sources.

The Ptolemaic History, the Maccabean Epitome, and Josephus will be discussed further in Part Four.

3. Writings by Gentiles

Many ancient writings by non-Israelites are known to have mentioned aspects of Israel's history. However, only a small proportion of this material has survived.

- Various short inscriptions, letters, and other **contemporary documents** dating from Greek and Roman times have been discovered (especially in Egypt, where the dry climate has preserved even very fragile materials). None of these documents gives a connected history of the period, but some of them contain useful information about particular events or circumstances.
- **Polybius,** who lived during the second century BCE, wrote a detailed history of Greek and Roman activities, concentrating mainly on his own lifetime and the previous half century. Much of his history survives only in fragments. He was a generally careful historian, but he had no knowledge of God and his main sources of information tended to be anti-Israelite (he was a personal friend of the Greek ruler Demetrius son of Seleucus, one of the main adversaries of Israel).[12]
- Some material from Polybius and other lost sources was adapted by later Classical historians, especially **Diodorus Siculus** (first century BCE), **Livy** and **Strabo** (both of whom worked around the time of Christ's birth), **Appian** (second century CE), and **Cassius Dio** (third century CE). However, many of their works, like Polybius's, survive only in fragmentary form. The writings of **Plutarch** (second century CE) also contain valuable pieces of information about the period.

SUMMARY

From these various sources, the history of Israel from the Persian period to the birth of Jesus may be summarized as follows:

- **Start of Greek rule.** The Persian empire was ultimately conquered by the Greek king Alexander of Macedon (about 330 BCE; Dan 8.5–7, 20–21; 11.3; Maccabaica 1.1–4).
- **Division of the Greek kingdom.** Alexander died a few years later (about 323 BCE). His kingdom was then divided among his leading officers (Dan 8.8, 22; 11.4; Maccabaica 1.5–9).
- **Egyptian rule of Judea.** At first (until about 200 BCE), Judea was ruled by the Ptolemies, the kings living to the south of Israel, in Egypt (Dan 11.5–14).

---

[12] Grainger (*Roman War of Antiochos the Great,* 3) also points out that the writings of Polybius and his Classical successors were "Rome-centered," and considers that their accounts of the eastern Mediterranean may have been "often distorted" by this. That judgment may be too extreme, but clearly their discussions of matters potentially unfavorable to Rome must always be treated with caution (cf. Sherwin-White and Kuhrt, *From Samarkhand to Sardis,* 6).

- **Syrian rule of Judea.** After about 200 BCE, Judea was ruled by the Seleucids, the kings living to the north of Israel, in Syria (Dan 11.15–20).
- **Oppression under Antiochus Epiphanes.** One of the Seleucid kings, Antiochus Epiphanes, forbade the Judeans to worship God (about 167 BCE), and replaced the offerings appointed by the Law of Moses with forms of idolatry (Dan 8.9–14, 23–26; 11.21–32; Maccabaica 1.10–64).
- **Struggle for Judean independence.** The priest Mattathias, with his family[13] and other faithful Judeans, rebelled and refused to obey the new laws imposed by Antiochus (Dan 11.32–35; Maccabaica 2.1–30). The Judeans were led by three of Mattathias's sons in succession: Judas Maccabeus, Jonathan, and Simon. After three years of oppression (about 164 BCE) the appointed offerings were restored (Dan 8.13–14; Maccabaica 4.36–58). After many years of struggle (about 142 BCE) Judea became independent of Seleucid rule (Maccabaica 13.41–42).
- **Unauthorized kingship in Judea.** Shortly before 100 BCE, the descendants of Mattathias began to call themselves kings (Eighteen Psalms 17.6–8; Josephus, *Wars,* 1.70; Strabo 16.2.40). This was contrary to God's ordinance that only descendants of David could be kings in Israel (2 Sam 7.12–16; 1 Kgs 9.5; Psa 89.20–37; Eighteen Psalms 17.5).
- **Roman rule of Judea.** Around 63 BCE, the Roman leader Pompey was invited into Jerusalem (Eighteen Psalms 8.16–20), apparently because a dispute had broken out among Mattathias's descendants (Josephus, *Wars,* 1.120–132). Once inside the city, Pompey and his soldiers captured it (Eighteen Psalms 8.21–24; 2.1–6; Josephus, *Wars,* 1.141–151), and Judea was placed under Roman rule (Josephus, *Wars,* 1.155–157)—which was still continuing in the time of Jesus and His apostles (John 11.48; 19.15; Acts 28.17). Three of the Roman emperors are named in the New Testament Scriptures: Augustus (Luke 2.1), Tiberius (Luke 3.1), and Claudius (Acts 18.2).

---

[13] Josephus (*Antiquities,* 12.265; 14.490) and some later writers refer to Mattathias and his family as "Hasmoneans," supposedly because the family was derived from an ancestor called Heshmon, Hashmon, Hashmonah, or Hashmonay. However, the existence of that ancestor is doubtful (NIDB 2.740). No member of the family is known to have used the term "Hasmonean," and it has never been found in any contemporary document. A family name of that kind would be more likely in a Hellenic community than in a Hebraic one (ABD 3.67–68); it may therefore have arisen during the increasing Hellenization of Israel in post-Maccabean times.

THE MACCABEAN HISTORY (MACCABAICA)

Introduction

The final history books in the Hebrew Scriptures describe the period of Persian rule.

The Maccabean History continues from that point. It describes the period when Judea was ruled by "the kingdom of the Greeks" (1.10), until at last "the yoke of the nations was lifted up from Israel" (13.41).

Its history can be divided into seven stages, according to the successive rulers over Judea and leaders of the Judeans:

1. Alexander and his successors (1.1–9). Alexander of Macedon, king of Greece, defeated the final king of Persia, Darius, and replaced him as ruler over the nations (1.1–4). When Alexander died, his kingdom was divided among his servants (1.5–7). They and their descendants continued to reign for many years (1.8–9).

2. Antiochus Epiphanes (1.10–64). After more than a century of Greek rule, some Israelites rejected the Law of God and sought to live like the surrounding nations (1.10–15). The Greek king Antiochus Epiphanes not only gave them his official approval, but later desecrated and plundered the temple at Jerusalem (1.16–28) and commanded all Judeans to abandon God's Law and worship idols (1.29–64).

3. Mattathias (2.1–70). The priest Mattathias refused to obey the king's commands (2.1–26). He and his sons, with other people who sought to live righteously, fled into the wilderness and fought against the evildoers (2.27–48). Soon after, Mattathias died, appointing his son Judas Maccabeus to lead the continuing struggle (2.49–70).

4. Judas Maccabeus (3.1–9.22). Antiochus Epiphanes repeatedly sent officers and soldiers to destroy the rebellion in Judea, but without success (3.1–4.34). Led by Judas, the faithful Judeans regained control of the Jerusalem temple, cleansed it, and dedicated it, appointing a feast of the dedication to be held each year in commemoration (4.35–61). They delivered those who were being oppressed, not only in Judea, but also in Gilead and Galilee (5.1–68). Antiochus Epiphanes died in great misery (6.1–16), but hostilities against the Judeans continued under his successors Antiochus Eupator (6.17–63) and Demetrius son of Seleucus (7.1–49). To strengthen the position of his people, Judas made an alliance with Rome (8.1–32). He himself ultimately died in battle (9.1–22).

5. Jonathan (9.23–12.53). After the death of Judas, his brother Jonathan successfully continued the struggle (9.23–73). Alexander Epiphanes became king in opposition to Demetrius, and supported the Judeans (10.1–47). When the two rival kings met in battle, Demetrius died (10.48–66), but his son, a second Demetrius, renewed the war against the Judeans (10.67–89), and Alexander Epiphanes was killed by his enemies (11.1–18). The second Demetrius eventually made a treaty with the Judeans, but did not keep it (11.19–53). His armies were defeated several times by the Judeans, who received messages of support from Rome and Sparta, as well as from Demetrius's political rivals in Syria (11.54–12.38). However, one of those rivals, Trypho, captured Jonathan by deceit (12.39–53), and later killed him (13.12–30).

6. Simon (13.1–16.22). After Jonathan was captured, his brother Simon became leader of the Judeans (13.1–11). Under his leadership, Israel was finally freed from Greek rule, and Simon himself was appointed ruler of the Judeans (13.31–14.49). A few further attempts to oppose Judean independence took place during the reign of Antiochus son of Demetrius (15.1–16.10). Later, Simon was killed treacherously by one of his own relatives (16.11–22).

7. John (16.23–24). After Simon's death, Judea was governed by his son John (16.23–24).

The book's main narrative (1.10–16.22) covers a period of forty years, from the accession of Antiochus Epiphanes in the year 137 SE (1.10) to the death of Simon in the year 177 SE (16.14), as the following chart shows. In years BCE, this would probably be from about 175 BCE to about 135 BCE.

Kings of the Nations	Judeans	Year	Events
Alexander of Macedon			Alexander became king (1.1) Alexander reigned 12 years and he died (1.7)
....		Many years	His servants began to rule and their sons after them (1.8–9)
Antiochus Epiphanes		137	Antiochus became king (1.10)
		143	He went up against Israel (1.20)
		145	Abomination built on altar (1.54)
	Mattathias	146	Mattathias died (2.70)
	Judas	147	Antiochus crossed Euphrates (3.37)
		148	Holy places cleansed (4.52)
		149	Antiochus Epiphanes died (6.16)
Antiochus Eupator		150	Judas besieged the citadel (6.20)

Kings of the Nations	Judeans	Year	Events
	Judas	151	Demetrius came (7.1)
		152	Alcimus came; Judas died (9.3)
Demetrius son of Seleucus	Jonathan	153	Alcimus died (9.54)
			The land had rest two years (9.57)
		160	Alexander came (10.1)
			Jonathan was high priest (10.21)
Alexander Epiphanes		162	Alexander married Ptolemy's daughter (10.57)
		165	Demetrius came (10.67)
			Alexander & Ptolemy died (11.17–18)
Demetrius son of Demetrius		167	Demetrius became king (11.19)
Antiochus son of Alexander			Antiochus became king (11.54)
			Trypho captured Jonathan (12.48)
	Simon		Trypho became king (13.32)
Trypho		170	Yoke of the nations lifted (13.41)
		171	Simon cleansed the citadel (13.51)
		172	Demetrius captive in Media (14.1)
Antiochus son of Demetrius		174	Antiochus came (15.10)
			Trypho fled (15.37)
		177	Simon died (16.14)
	John		John became high priest (16.24)

Alexander and his successors (1.1–9)

Hundreds of years before the start of the Maccabean History, the Lord showed Daniel how the kingdom of the Persians and Medes would come to an end. In a vision, Daniel saw a ram with two horns. The ram was defeated by a he goat with "a visible horn between his eyes," who "came from the west" (Dan 8.3–8). The ram with two horns was the kingdom of Media and Persia. The he goat was the kingdom of Greece, and its great horn was its first king (Dan 8.20–21). No enemy would be able to stand before him (Dan 8.7–8); he would "rule a great realm, and do as he pleases" (Dan 11.3).

The beginning of the Maccabean History shows us the fulfillment of those prophecies. **Alexander,** the king of **Greece,** came **out of the land of Kittim** (the coastal regions of the Mediterranean, west of Israel). He conquered the **king of the Persians**

and Medes (Maccabaica 1.1), and became the ruler of **a multitude of nations** (1.2–4). Yet Daniel had also prophesied that the first king of Greece would be "broken" just when his kingdom "was powerful" (Dan 8.8, 21–22; 11.4). After that, "four kingdoms will stand from the nation, but not with his strength" (Dan 8.8, 22). "His kingdom will be broken. And it will be divided to the four winds of the heavens, and not to his descent; and it will not be like his realm which he ruled. For his kingdom will be uprooted, and will be for others apart from these" (Dan 11.4).

Everything that Daniel had prophesied happened. **After** all the triumphs described in the opening verses of the Maccabean History, Alexander **fell upon the bed** and **died.** He had ruled his empire for only **12 years** (Maccabaica 1.7). In his place, his **servants** governed the various parts of his realm (1.8). Eventually, some time **after he was dead,** they made themselves kings (**put on diadems**). Their separate kingdoms were handed down to their descendants (**sons**) and continued **for many years.** During this time many **evils** happened (1.9), just as Daniel had also prophesied (Dan 11.5–20).

Alexander the Macedonian becomes king

1.1 And it came about that Alexander *the* Macedonian, the *son* of Philip, came out of *the* land of Kittim and defeated Darius king of *the* Persians and Medes. And after he had defeated *him,* then he became king in place of him, *as he had* previously *been* over Greece.
1.2 And he fought many battles, and took possession of fortresses, and killed kings of the earth,
1.3 and went through to *the* ends of the earth, and took plunder from a multitude of nations. And the earth was quiet before him. And his heart was exalted and lifted up.
1.4 And he gathered together a very strong army, and ruled countries, nations, and monarchs; and they became tributary to him.

Alexander dies

1.5 And after these *things* he fell upon *his* bed, and he knew that he was dying.
1.6 And he called his servants, who *were* honored, who had been brought up with him from *his* youth; and he divided his kingdom among them, while he *was* still alive.
1.7 And Alexander reigned 12 years, and he died.

Alexander's servants begin to rule

1.8 And his servants began to rule, each *one* in his *own* place.
1.9 And they all put on diadems after he *was* dead, and *so did* their sons after them, for many years: and they multiplied evils in the earth.

Antiochus Epiphanes (1.10–64)

After **many years** (1.9) **Antiochus Epiphanes** became king. He is described here as a **sinful root** (1.10; cf. Heb 12.14), and by Daniel as a "despised" person (Dan 11.21).

In those days, **transgressors** arose in Israel. They wanted to make a **covenant with the nations** around them (Maccabaica 1.11), contrary to God's Law for Israel (Deut 7.1–4; 13.6–15). They wanted to do what **was good in their** own **eyes** (1.12), not what was good in the eyes of God (Prov 3.7; 12.15; 26.12; Isa 5.21; Rom 1.22; 12.16).

Antiochus sought to rule **two kingdoms:** his own northern kingdom based at Antioch, and the southern kingdom of **Egypt** (Maccabaica 1.16). So he **made war against Ptolemy king of Egypt** and defeated him (1.16–20). This too had been prophesied by Daniel: "He will rouse up his strength and his heart against the king of the South, with a great force. And the king of the South will stir himself up even to war, with a force that is great and extremely powerful; but he will not stand ... and many wounded will fall" (Dan 11.25–26). Antiochus returned home "with great possessions" (Dan 11.28), but **went up against Jerusalem,** entering the **holy place** (contrary to the Law of Moses, Num 18.1–7) and plundering the **treasures** of the temple (Maccabaica 1.20–24).

Two years later the king sent an officer who attacked Jerusalem, killing **many people** and plundering the city again (1.29–32, 37). Within Jerusalem the attackers built a **citadel,** in which they installed armed forces supporting the king (1.32–36). For twenty-five years this **citadel** remained one of the most troublesome problems for the Judeans (3.45; 4.2; 6.18ff.; 9.52–53; 11.20–22, 41; 12.36; 13.21, 49–52). The people of Jerusalem began to flee from the city (1.38).

Up to this time, worship of the true God, in accordance with His Law, had not been prohibited. But now Antiochus went further. He **wrote to his whole kingdom** that everyone should **sacrifice** to **idols** on **heathen altars** (1.41–49). Disobedience would be punished by death (1.50). This meant that God's people would no longer be allowed to bring Him the **offerings** that He had appointed or observe the **feasts** that He had appointed (1.45).

Many people from Israel gathered to obey the king, and **did evil things** (1.52), and **sacrificed** and **burned incense** in ways that God's word had not authorized (1.59, 55). Those who refused to submit either fled into **hidden places** (1.53) or else **died** for their disobedience (1.57, 60–63), as Daniel had foretold (Dan 8.24).

These calamities were not accidents. They were permitted by God because of his **very great wrath** against the evildoers in Israel (Maccabaica 1.64). "Does harm come about in a city, when the LORD has not done it?" (Amos 3.6; Isa 45.7).

Antiochus Epiphanes becomes king

1.10 And *there* came out of them a sinful root, Antiochus Epiphanes, son of Antiochus the king, who had been a hostage at Rome; and he became king in *the* 137th year of *the* kingdom of *the* Greeks.

Transgressors from Israel yoke themselves with the nations

1.11 In those days, *there* came out of Israel sons *who were* transgressors, and they persuaded many, saying, "Let us go and make a covenant with the nations that *are* round about us: for since we were separated from them, many evils have come upon us."

1.12 And the saying was good in their eyes.

1.13 And some of the people were eager *in this,* and went to the king; and he gave them authority to do the ordinances of the nations.

1.14 And they built a place of exercise in Jerusalem according to the laws of the nations;

1.15 and they made themselves uncircumcised, and forsook *the* holy covenant, and yoked themselves together to the nations, and sold themselves to do wickedness.

Antiochus attacks Egypt

1.16 And the kingdom was prepared in *the* sight of Antiochus, and he determined to become king over *the* land of Egypt, so that he might be king over the two kingdoms.

1.17 And he entered into Egypt with a great multitude, with chariots and elephants and horsemen and a great array;

1.18 and he made war against Ptolemy king of Egypt; and Ptolemy turned back before him, and fled; and many fell wounded.

1.19 And they took possession of the strong cities in *the* land of Egypt; and he took the plunder of *the* land of Egypt.

Antiochus plunders the temple in Jerusalem

1.20 And after *he* had defeated Egypt, Antiochus returned in the 143rd year, and went up against Israel. And he went up against Jerusalem with a great multitude,

1.21 and entered arrogantly into the holy place, and took the golden altar, and the lampstand of the light, and all its vessels,

1.22 and the table of the showbread, and the cups for drink offerings, and the bowls, and the golden incense vessels, and the veil, and the crowns, and the golden adornment that *was* on *the* face of the temple, and he scaled off everything.

1.23 And he took the silver and *the* gold and *the* precious vessels; and he took the hidden treasures that he found.

1.24 And when *he* had taken everything, he went away into his *own* land. And he made a great slaughter, and spoke very arrogantly.

The people of Israel mourn

1.25 And *there* came great mourning upon Israel, in every place *where* they *were;*

1.26 and *the* rulers and elders groaned, *the* virgins and young men became feeble, and the beauty of the women was changed.

1.27 Every bridegroom took up a lamentation; she who sat in the marriage chamber was mourning.

1.28 And the land quaked for its inhabitants, and all the house of Jacob was clothed with shame.

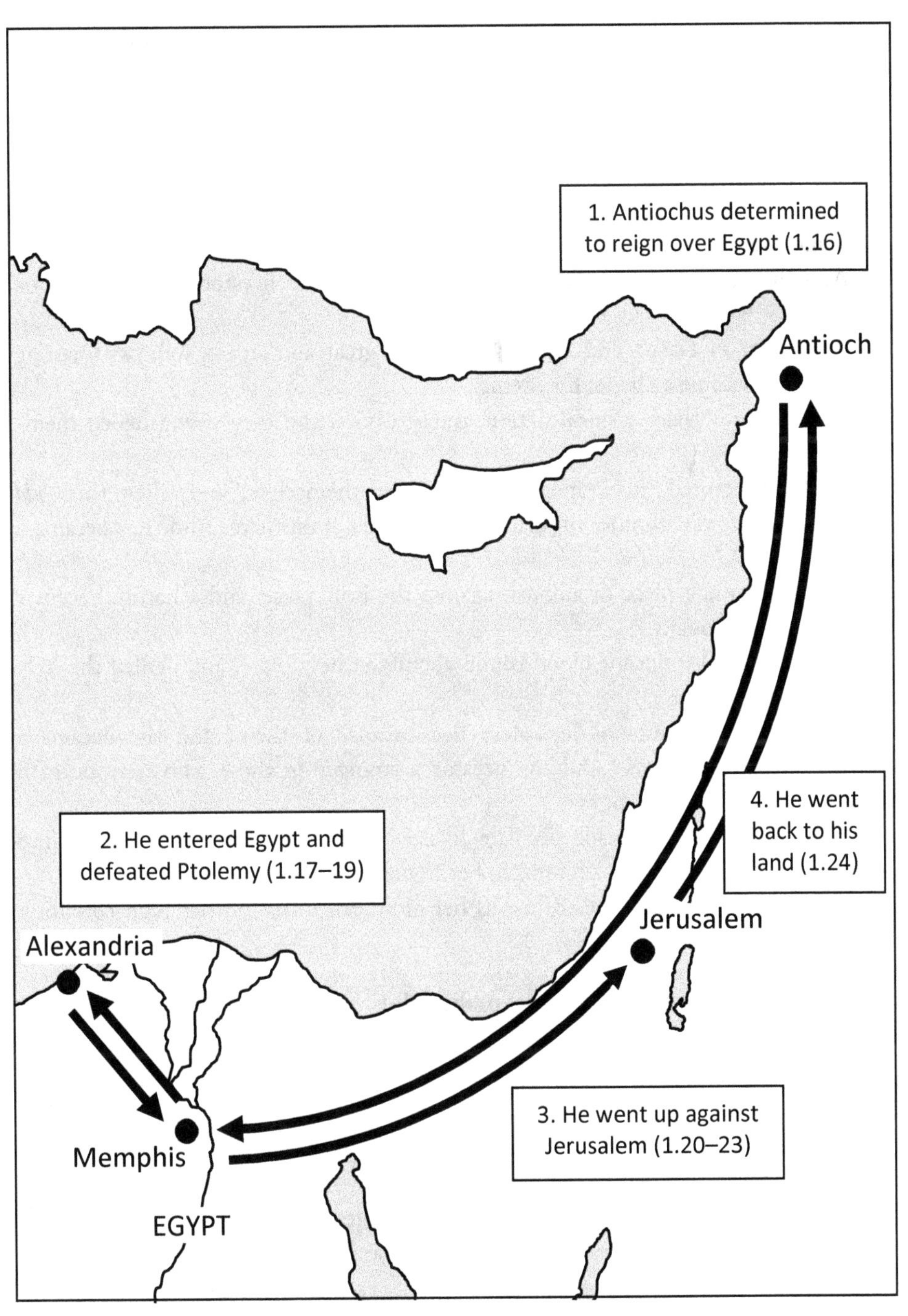

Map 1: Antiochus Epiphanes in Jerusalem (Maccabaica 1.16–23)

Jerusalem is attacked; the citadel is set up

1.29 And after two years, the king sent a chief collector of tribute into the cities of
Judah. And he came into Jerusalem with a great multitude,
1.30 and spoke words of peace to them deceitfully; and they believed him. And he fell
upon the city suddenly, and struck it with a great calamity, and destroyed many people out of Israel.
1.31 And he took the plunder of the city, and burned it with fire, and pulled down its
houses and the walls round about.
1.32 And they took captive the women and children and livestock. And they took
possession
1.33 of the city of David, and built *it* up with a great and strong wall, with strong
towers; and it became a citadel for them.
1.34 And they put there a sinful nation, transgressors, and they strengthened themselves in it.
1.35 And they stored up weapons and food for themselves; and when they *had*
gathered together the plunder of Jerusalem, they laid *it* up there. And they became a
great trap;
1.36 and it became a place of ambush against the holy place, and a harmful accuser
against Israel continually.
1.37 And they shed innocent blood round about the holy place, and defiled the holy
place.
1.38 And the inhabitants of Jerusalem fled because of them; and she became a
dwelling-place of strangers. And she became a stranger to those who were born in
her, and her children forsook her.
1.39 Her holy place was made desolate like a desert, her feasts were turned into
mourning, her Sabbaths into a reproach, her honor into contempt.
1.40 Her dishonor was multiplied just as her glory *had been,* and her high condition
was turned into mourning.

The king commands the people to worship idols

1.41 And the king wrote to his whole kingdom, that they should all be one people,
1.42 and that each should forsake his *own* laws. And all the nations agreed, according
to the king's word.
1.43 And many *people* of Israel were well pleased with his way of worship, and
sacrificed to idols and profaned the Sabbath.
1.44 And the king sent letters by *the* hand of messengers to Jerusalem and the cities of
Judah, that they should follow laws strange to the land,
1.45 and should forbid burnt offerings and sacrifices and drink offerings in the holy
place; and should profane *the* Sabbaths and feasts,
1.46 and pollute the holy place and those who *were* holy;
1.47 that they should build heathen altars and temples, and shrines for idols, and
should sacrifice swine's *flesh* and unclean beasts:

1.48 and that they should leave their sons uncircumcised, and that they should make their souls abominable with everything *that was* unclean and profane,
1.49 so as to forget the Law and change all the ordinances.
1.50 "And whoever shall not do according to the king's word will die."
1.51 In accord with all these words, he wrote to his whole kingdom; and he appointed overseers over all the people, and commanded the cities of Judah to sacrifice, city by city.

The king's commands are carried out

1.52 And many of the people gathered together to them—everyone who forsook the Law; and they did evil *things* in the land.
1.53 And Israel hid themselves in hidden *places*, in every place of refuge *that* they *had.*
1.54 And on the 15th day of Chislev, *in* the 145th year, they built an abomination of desolation on the sacrificial altar; and they built heathen altars *in* the cities of Judah round about.
1.55 And they burned incense at the doors of the houses and in the streets.
1.56 And they burnt the books of the Law that they found in *the* fire, *after* having torn them in pieces.
1.57 And wherever a book of *the* covenant was found with anyone, and if anyone delighted in the Law, the king's sentence put him to death.
1.58 They did *these things* in their strength to Israel, to *those* who were found month by month in the cities.
1.59 And on the 25th *day* of the month *they* sacrificed on the heathen altar that was on the sacrificial altar.
1.60 And the women who had circumcised their sons, they put to death according to the commandment
1.61 (and they hanged their babes from their necks), and their house*holds*, and those who had circumcised them.
1.62 And many in Israel were strong, and they determined within themselves not to eat unclean *things*.
1.63 And they chose to die, so that they might not be defiled with the foods, and might not profane *the* holy covenant; and they died.
1.64 And very great wrath came upon Israel.

Mattathias (2.1–70)

Deliverance does not always come from the direction that people might expect (John 1.46; 1 Cor 1.23–24). The chain of events that would lead, many years later, to the overthrow of "the yoke of the nations" (Maccabaica 13.41) began with a single act of opposition by a subsidiary priest, **Mattathias,** in a subordinate town, **Modein.**

Mattathias and his **five sons** (2.1–5) **mourned** over the evil deeds that were being done in the land (2.6–14). When **the king's officers** came to **Modein** and instructed the priest to **do the king's command** by offering **sacrifice** on a **heathen altar,**

Mattathias refused. He slew the evildoers, tore down the altar, and **fled into the mountains,** encouraging all those who supported God's **Law** and **covenant** to follow him (2.15–30).

Some of the refugees died because they refused to fight **on the Sabbath day** (2.31–38). **Mattathias and his friends,** however, believed that defending themselves against attack on the Sabbath was a good work and therefore permissible (2.39–41). They went through the land, tearing down the heathen altars, circumcising the uncircumcised, and fighting against the king's supporters. Even at this early stage, **the work prospered in their hand** (2.42–48).

The following year, Mattathias **died,** after encouraging his sons to **be zealous for the Law** and sacrifice their own **lives** for **the covenant of** the **fathers** (2.49–70).

Mattathias and his five sons

2.1 In those days, *there* rose up Mattathias *the* son of John, the *son* of Simeon, a priest of the sons of Joiarib, from Jerusalem; and he settled in Modein.
2.2 And he had five sons: John, who *was* called Gaddi;
2.3 Simon, who *was* called Thassi;
2.4 Judas, who *was* called Maccabeus;
2.5 Eleazar, who *was* called Avaran; Jonathan, who *was* called Apphus.

Mattathias mourns over the blasphemies in Judah

2.6 And he saw the blasphemies that were committed in Judah and in Jerusalem,
2.7 and he said, "Woe *is* me! Why was I born to see the destruction of my people, and the destruction of the holy city—and they sat there while it *was* given into *the* hand of *the* enemies, the holy place into *the* hand of strangers?
2.8 Her temple has become like a man without glory;
2.9 her vessels of glory have been carried away into captivity; her young children have been killed in her streets, her young men with *the* sword of *the* enemy.
2.10 What nation has not taken an inheritance in *her* kingdom, and taken possession of her plunder?
2.11 All her adornment has been taken away; instead of a free *woman,* she has become a slavewoman;
2.12 and, behold, our holy *place*s and our beauty and our glory have been made desolate, and the nations have profaned them.
2.13 Why *are* we still living?"
2.14 And Mattathias and his sons tore their clothes, and put on sackcloth, and mourned greatly.

Mattathias refuses to forsake the Law

2.15 And the king's *officers*, who were enforcing the rebellion, came into the city Modein, so that they should sacrifice.
2.16 And many *people* of Israel came to them. And Mattathias and his sons gathered together.

2.17 And the king's *officer*s answered and spoke to Mattathias, saying, "You† are a ruler and an honored and great *man* in this city, and strengthened with sons and brothers.
2.18 Now, come† first and do† the king's command, as all the nations have done, and the men of Judah, and *those* who remain in Jerusalem. And you† and your† sons will be *counted* among the king's Friends, and you† and your† sons will be honored with silver and gold and many gifts."
2.19 And Mattathias answered and said with a loud voice, "If all the nations that are in *the* house of the king's kingdom listen to him, *for* each to depart from his fathers' way of worship, and *if* they have made their choice *to walk* in his commands,
2.20 yet I and my sons and brothers will walk in the covenant of our fathers.
2.21 *Heaven be* gracious to us! To forsake *the* Law and *the* ordinances!
2.22 We will not listen to the king's word*s*, to go aside from our worship *to the* right or *the* left."
2.23 And when he stopped speaking these words, a Judean man came in *the* sight of everyone to sacrifice on the heathen altar that was at Modein, according to the king's command.
2.24 And Mattathias saw *it,* and he was filled with zeal, and his inner parts trembled, and he aroused *his* indignation justly, and ran, *and* killed him on the heathen altar.
2.25 And at that time he killed the king's *officer,* who *was* compelling *people* to sacrifice; and he pulled down the heathen altar.
2.26 And he was zealous for the Law, just as Phinehas did against Zimri the son of Salu.

Those who are seeking justice flee

2.27 And Mattathias cried out in the city with a loud voice, saying, "Whoever is zealous for the Law *and* maintains *the* covenant, let him come out after me."
2.28 And he and his sons fled into the mountains, and left everything *that* they had in the city.
2.29 Then many who were seeking justice and judgment went down into the desert, to settle there—
2.30 they and their sons and their wives and their livestock; because evils pressed hard upon them.

War on the Sabbath day

2.31 And it was told to the king's *officer*s, and the forces that were in Jerusalem, *the* city of David, that *certain* men had rejected the king's command *and* gone down into the hidden *place*s in the desert.
2.32 And many pursued after them and overtook them. And they camped against them, and prepared to make war against them on the Sabbath day,
2.33 and said to them, "Till this moment! When *you* come out[pl], do[pl] according to the king's word, and you[pl] will live."

2.34 And they said, "We will not come out, nor will we do the king's word, to profane the Sabbath day."
2.35 And they quickly made war against them.
2.36 And they did not answer them, or throw a stone at them, or block up the hidden *places*,
2.37 saying, "Let us all die in our innocence; Heaven and earth bear witness over us, that you[pl] are destroying us without justice."
2.38 And they rose up against them in battle on the Sabbath, and they died, they and their wives and their children and their livestock, to *the number of* 1,000 human souls.
2.39 And Mattathias and his friends knew *it,* and they mourned over them very much.
2.40 And *one* man said to another, "If we all do as our brothers have done, and do not make war against the nations for our lives and our ordinances, now they will quickly destroy us from the earth."
2.41 And they took counsel on that day, saying, "Let us make war against everyone who may come against us to make war on the Sabbath day; and let us certainly not die, as our brothers died in the hidden *places*."

The work prospers

2.42 Then *there* gathered with them a company of Hasidim—mighty *men* of valor from Israel—everyone who offered himself willingly for the Law.
2.43 And all those who fled from the evils were added to them, and became a support for them.
2.44 And they brought together an army, and struck down sinners in their anger, and transgressors in their wrath. And the rest fled to the nations for safety.
2.45 And Mattathias and his friends went round about, and pulled down the heathen altars,
2.46 and circumcised by force all the uncircumcised boys *that* they found within *the* borders of Israel.
2.47 And they pursued the sons of arrogance, and the work prospered in their hand.
2.48 And they took back the Law out of *the* hand of the nations and kings, and they did not allow the sinner *any* power.

Mattathias encourages his sons

2.49 And the days of Mattathias drew near *for him* to die; and he said to his sons, "Now arrogance and rebuke have grown strong, and a time of overthrow, and anger of indignation.
2.50 Now, *my* children, be zealous[pl] for the Law, and give[pl] your[pl] lives for *the* covenant of our fathers.
2.51 And call to mind[pl] *our* fathers' deeds, which they did in their generations; and receive[pl] great honor and a lasting name.
2.52 Was not Abraham found faithful in trial? and it was reckoned to him for righteousness.
2.53 Joseph in *the* time of his distress kept *the* command, and became lord of Egypt.

2.54 Phinehas our father, because he was zealous *with* zeal, obtained *the* covenant of an everlasting priesthood.
2.55 Joshua, by fulfilling the word, became a judge in Israel.
2.56 Caleb, by bearing witness in the assembly, received an inheritance.
2.57 David, by his mercy, inherited *the* throne of a kingdom for ever.
2.58 Elijah, by being zealous *with* zeal *for the* Law, was taken up into Heaven.
2.59 Hananiah, Azariah, Mishael, believed, *and* were saved out of *the* flame.
2.60 Daniel, by his innocence, was delivered from *the* mouth of lions.
2.61 And thus call to mind[pl], *from* generation to generation, that no *people* who put their trust in Him will become weak.
2.62 And do not be afraid[pl] of *the* words of a sinful man; for his glory *will become* dung and worms.
2.63 Today he will be lifted up, and tomorrow he shall certainly not be found, because he has returned into his dust, and his thought will perish.
2.64 *My* children, act valiantly[pl], and be strong[pl] on behalf of the Law; for in it you[pl] will be honored.
2.65 And, behold, Simon your[pl] brother—I know that he is a man of counsel; listen[pl] to him all *your* days; he will be a father to you.
2.66 And Judas Maccabeus, strong *and* mighty since his youth—he will be your[pl] army commander, and he will fight *the* war of *the* peoples.
2.67 And you[pl] will bring[pl] to yourselves[pl] all the doers of the Law. And take vengeance[pl] for *the* vengeance of your[pl] people.
2.68 Repay[pl] a repayment to the nations, and pay attention[pl] to the command of the Law."

Mattathias dies

2.69 And he blessed them, and was added to his fathers.
2.70 And he died in the 146th year, and was buried in the tomb of his fathers, at Modein. And all Israel made a great lamentation for him.

Judas Maccabeus (3.1–9.22)

THE DEEDS OF JUDAS MACCABEUS

> **Judas Maccabeus** arose after the death of his father Mattathias and successfully **pursued the transgressors,** so that **salvation prospered in his hand** and God's **wrath** against **Israel** was **turned away** (3.1–9).

3.1 And his son Judas, who *was* called Maccabeus, rose up in place of him.
3.2 And all his brothers helped him, and *so did* all *those* who had joined with his father. And they fought *the* war *of* Israel with gladness.
3.3 And he extended glory for his people, and put on a breastplate like a mighty man, and girded himself with his war equipment, and waged war, protecting *the* army with *his* sword.

3.4 And he was like a lion in his deeds, and like a young lion roaring for prey.
3.5 And he pursued *the* transgressors, seeking *them* out, and he burned in *the* flames those who were troubling his people.
3.6 And the transgressors were confined for fear of him, and all the workers of transgression were severely troubled; and salvation prospered in his hand.
3.7 And he angered many kings, and made Jacob glad with his acts; and his memory *is* a blessing for ever.
3.8 And he went around among *the* cities of Judah, and utterly destroyed irreverent *people* out of *the land,* and turned away wrath from Israel.
3.9 And he was renowned to *the* end of the earth. And he gathered together *those* who were ready to perish.

HIS FIRST BATTLES AGAINST THE NATIONS

Two of King Antiochus's officers—**Apollonius** and **Seron**—successively tried to oppose the **sons of Israel,** but both were defeated (3.10–24).

After this, **Antiochus** decided to gather a stronger army (3.25–28), but he was worried that he would not have enough **money** in his **treasuries** to keep paying them (3.29–30). Therefore, he himself departed for **Persia,** across the **Euphrates River,** hoping to get the necessary money there (3.31, 37). In the meantime, he left in charge **Lysias,** a member of the **royal** family. The king instructed Lysias **to send an army against** the people of Israel and **shatter** them (3.32–36).

The army **sent** by Lysias **camped near Emmaus** (3.38–41). The people of Israel **gathered** in **prayer** at **Mizpah** (3.44, 46–54); then they prepared for battle and pitched their camp **south of Emmaus** (3.55–60).

One of Lysias's commanders, **Gorgias,** set out to attack the **army of the Judeans** at **night** (4.1–2). However, the Judeans heard of this plan. They attacked the enemy **camp** at daybreak, while its forces were still depleted, before Gorgias and his company could return (4.3–4). Despite their small numbers and unsatisfactory weapons, the Judeans were victorious, and their opponents **fled** to **Idumea** and the land of the Philistines (4.6–15).

Meanwhile, **Gorgias** had **found no one** at all in the Judean **camp,** and thought that his opponents had run away (4.5). But when he and his company returned, they saw that **the Judeans were burning the camp** and were in possession of the field, so they too **fled** (4.16–22). The Judeans gained **great riches** from the **plunder** of the enemy camp, and gave thanks **to Heaven** for the victory (4.23–25).

In the next year, Lysias attacked the Judeans again. This time, his army **camped at Bethzur** (4.28–29). Again Judas and his companions prayed for help to the **Savior of Israel,** and were victorious in battle (4.30–34). **Lysias** returned **to Antioch,** planning yet another attack (4.35).

Apollonius is defeated and killed

3.10 And Apollonius gathered together *the* nations, and a great army from Samaria, to make war against Israel.

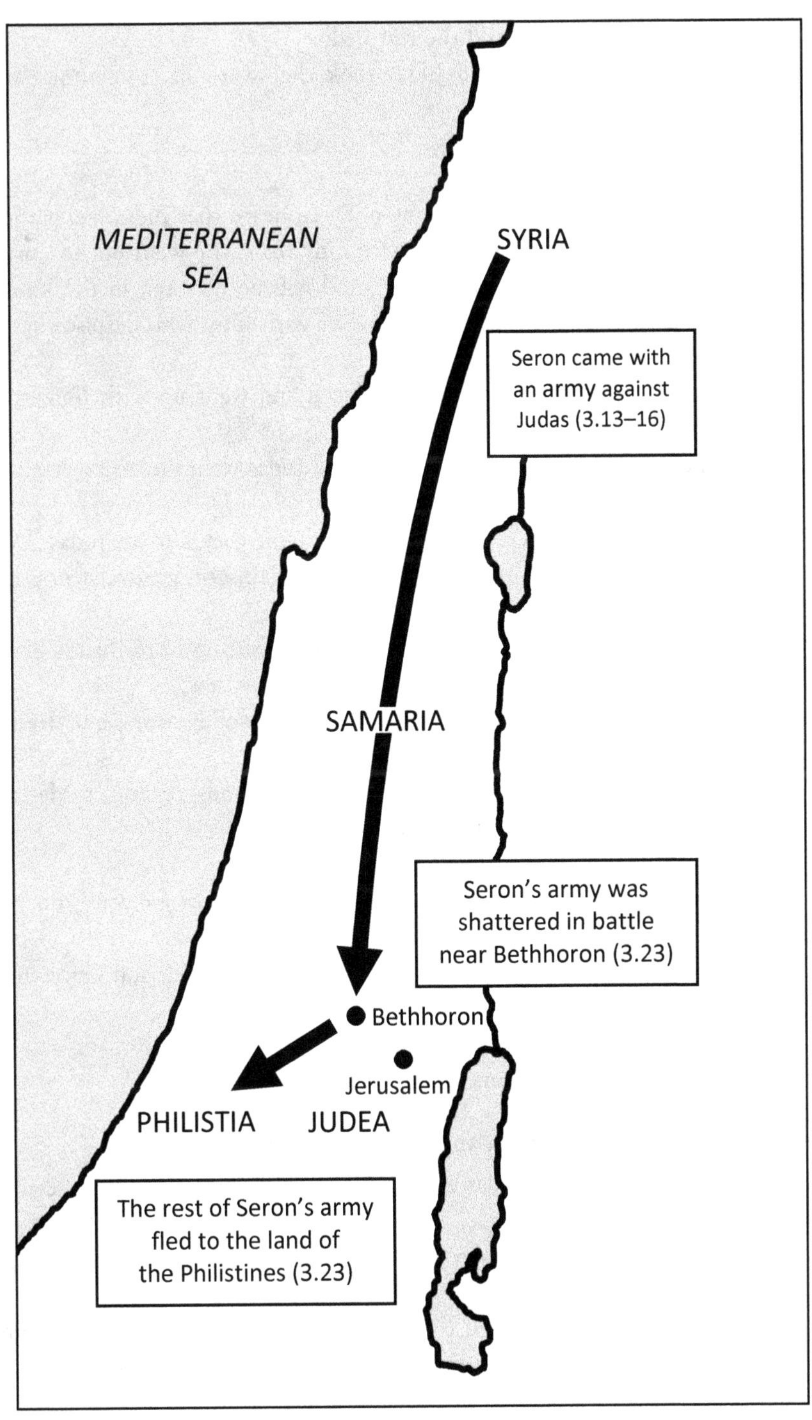

Map 2: The battle against Seron at Bethhoron (Maccabaica 3.13–23)

3.11 And Judas knew *it,* and he went out to meet him, and defeated him, and killed *him;* and many wounded *men* fell, and the rest fled;
3.12 and he took their plunder. And Judas took the sword of Apollonius, and he fought with it all *his* days.

Seron is defeated at Bethhoron

3.13 And Seron, the commander of the army of Syria, heard that Judas had gathered a gathering and an assembly of faithful *people* with him, *those* who went out to war;
3.14 and he said, "I will make myself a name, and will be honored in the kingdom; and I will make war against Judas and *those who are* with him, who despise the king's word."
3.15 And a strong army of irreverent *men* advanced and went up with him, to help him take vengeance on *the* sons of Israel.
3.16 And he came near *the* ascent of Bethhoron, and Judas went out to meet him *with* a small *company.*
3.17 But when he saw the army coming to meet them, they said to Judas, "What? Will we, being a small *company,* be able to make war against so great a strong multitude? And we are faint, having had no food today."
3.18 And Judas said, "It is an easy *thing* for many to be shut up in *the* hands of a few; and *there* is no difference with Heaven to save by many or by few:
3.19 for victory in battle does not depend on *the* multitude of an army; but strength *is* from Heaven.
3.20 They are coming against us full of ill-treatment and transgression, to destroy us and our wives and our children, to plunder us;
3.21 but we are making war for our lives and our laws.
3.22 And He Himself will shatter them before our face; but *as for* you^{pl}, do not be afraid^{pl} of them."
3.23 Now as he stopped speaking, suddenly he sprang upon them, and Seron and his army were shattered before him.
3.24 And they pursued them by the descent of Bethhoron to the plain, and about 800 men of them fell, and the rest fled into *the* land of *the* Philistines.

Antiochus leaves Lysias in charge, and departs for Persia

3.25 And the fear and dread of Judas and his brothers began to fall on the nations round about them.
3.26 And his name came near even to the king, and the nations were telling the battles of Judas.
3.27 But when King Antiochus heard these words, he became angry and indignant; and he sent and gathered together all the forces of his kingdom, an extremely strong army.
3.28 And he opened his treasury, and gave *his* forces pay for a year, and commanded them to be ready for every duty.

3.29 And he saw that the money from *his* treasures had failed, and *that* the tributes of the district were small, because of the divisions and the harm that he had brought upon the land *by* taking away the laws that had been from the first days.
3.30 And he feared that he would not have *enough* (as once or twice *before*) for the expense and the gifts that he had given previously with a lavish hand (and he had done *this* more profusely than the kings *who had been* before *him*).
3.31 And he was extremely perplexed in his mind, and he took counsel to go into Persia, and take the tributes of the districts, and gather much money.
3.32 And he left Lysias—an honored man, and *one* of royal descent—to be over the business of the king, from the River Euphrates to *the* borders of Egypt,
3.33 and to bring up his son Antiochus, until he returned.
3.34 And he delivered to him half of *his* forces, and the elephants, and gave him commands about everything that he wanted, and about those who dwelt in Judea and Jerusalem,
3.35 to send an army against them, to shatter and destroy the strength of Israel and the remainder of Jerusalem, and to take away their memory from the place,
3.36 and to make foreigners dwell in all their boundaries, and to give away their land as an inheritance.
3.37 And the king took the remaining half of the forces, and moved away from Antioch, his royal city, *in the* 147th year. And he crossed over the river Euphrates, and went through the upper districts.

Lysias sends an army into the land of Judah

3.38 And Lysias chose Ptolemy the *son* of Dorymenes, and Nicanor, and Gorgias, mighty men among the king's Friends;
3.39 and he sent with them 40,000 men and 7,000 horse, to go into *the* land of Judah and destroy it, according to the king's word.
3.40 And they moved away with all their army, and came and camped near Emmaus in the plain.
3.41 And the traders of the district heard the fame of them, and took very much silver and gold, and fetters, and came to the camp to take the sons of Israel for servants. And *there* were added to them force*s* from Syria and from *the* land of *the* foreigners.

Judas and his people pray and prepare for war

3.42 And Judas and his brothers saw that evils were multiplied, and *that* the forces were camping within their borders; and they knew the king's words, which he had commanded, to destroy the people and make an end *of them*.
3.43 And they said, each *man* to his neighbor, "Let us raise up the ruin of our people, and let us make war for our people and the holy *place*s."
3.44 And the assembly gathered together to be ready for war, and to pray and ask for mercy and compassion.

3.45 And Jerusalem was without inhabitants, like a desert; none of her offspring were going in or out. And the holy place *was* trodden down, and foreigners' sons were in the citadel—the nations *were* lodging there. And joy was taken away from Jacob, and *the* flute and lyre ceased.

3.46 And they gathered together and came to Mizpah, near Jerusalem; for a place of prayer for Israel had been in Mizpah previously.

3.47 And they fasted that day, and put on sackcloth, and *put* ash on their heads, and tore their clothes,

3.48 and opened the book of the Law, about which the nations were seeking the likenesses of their idols.

3.49 And they brought the priests' garments, and the firstfruits, and the tithes; and they stirred up the Nazirites who had accomplished *their* days.

3.50 And they cried out aloud toward Heaven, saying, "What should we do with these *people,* and where should we lead them away?

3.51 And Your[†] holy *place*s have been trodden down and profaned, and Your[†] priests are in mourning and humiliation.

3.52 And, behold, the nations are gathered against us to destroy us. You[†] Yourself[†] know what things they are planning against us.

3.53 How shall we be able to stand before them, unless You[†] Yourself[†] are our help[†]?"

3.54 And they trumpeted with the trumpets, and cried out with a loud voice.

3.55 And after this, Judas appointed leaders of the people: leaders of thousands, and leaders of hundreds, and leaders of fifties, and leaders of tens.

3.56 And he told those *who were* building houses, and betrothing wives, and planting vineyards, and fearful, to return, each *one,* to his own house, according to the Law.

3.57 And the army moved away, and camped on *the* south of Emmaus.

3.58 And Judas said, "Gird yourselves[pl], and be[pl] valiant sons, and be[pl] ready for *the* morning, to make war against these nations who *are* gathered against us to destroy us and our holy *place*s;

3.59 for *it is* better for us to die in the war, than to look on the evils of our nation and the holy *place*s.

3.60 But however *the* will in Heaven may be, so He will do."

Lysias's army is defeated at Emmaus

4.1 And Gorgias took 5,000 men, and 1,000 chosen horse, and the army moved away *by* night,

4.2 so as to fall upon the army of the Judeans and strike them down suddenly. And men of the citadel were his guides.

4.3 And Judas heard, and he and the valiant *men* moved away to strike down the king's army that *was* in Emmaus,

4.4 while the forces were still dispersed from the camp.

4.5 And Gorgias came into the camp of Judas *by* night, and found no one. And he sought them in the mountains; for he said, "These *men* are fleeing from us."

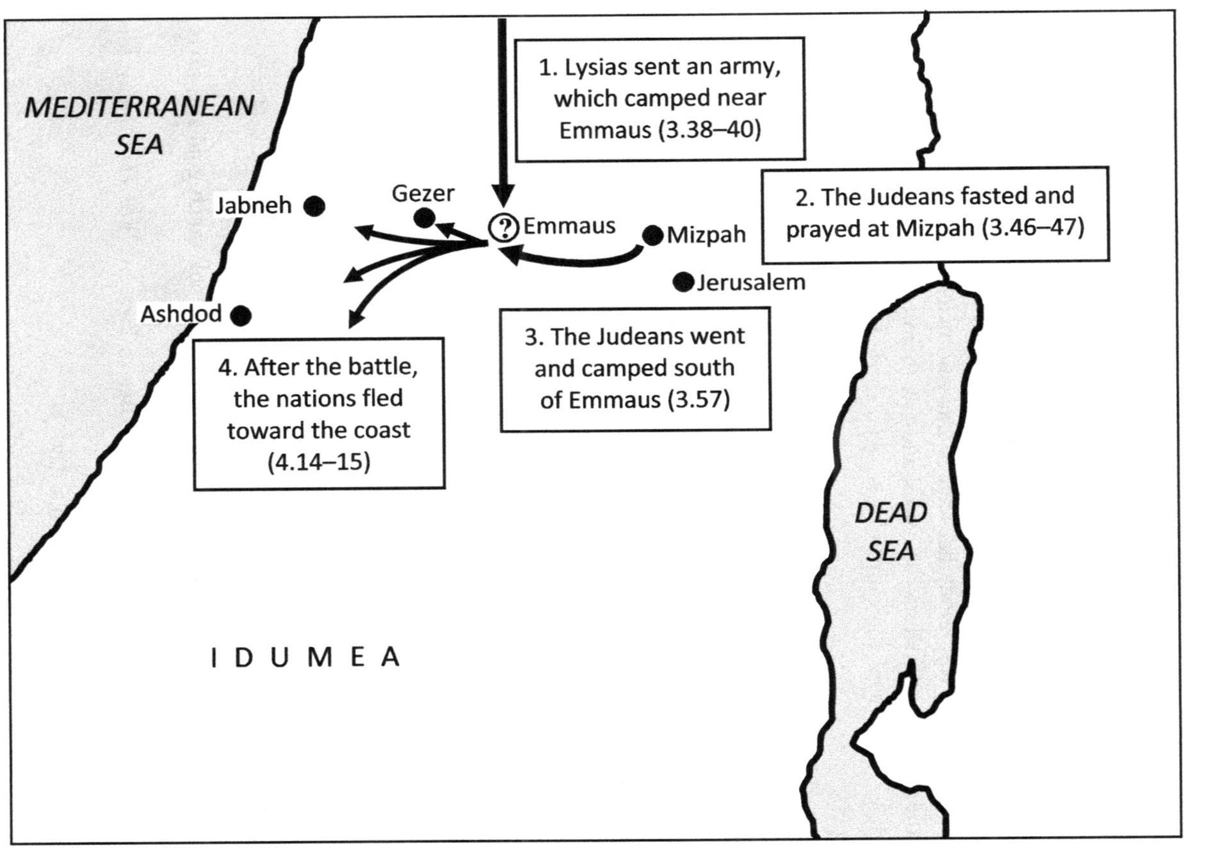
MEDITERRANEAN SEA
1. Lysias sent an army, which camped near Emmaus (3.38–40)
2. The Judeans fasted and prayed at Mizpah (3.46–47)
Jabneh
Gezer
Emmaus
Mizpah
Jerusalem
Ashdod
3. The Judeans went and camped south of Emmaus (3.57)
4. After the battle, the nations fled toward the coast (4.14–15)
DEAD SEA
I D U M E A

Map 3: The battle against Lysias at Emmaus (Maccabaica 3.38–4.15)

4.6 And as soon as it was day, Judas appeared in the plain with 3,000 men; however, they did not have armor or swords *such* as they wanted.
4.7 And they saw *the* camp of *the* nations, strong and fortified, and horse*men* going round about it; and these *were* expert in war.
4.8 And Judas said to the men who *were* with him, "Do not be afraid[pl] of their multitude, nor be terrified[pl] of their onslaught.
4.9 Call to mind[pl] how our fathers were saved in *the* Red Sea, when Pharaoh pursued them with *his* army.
4.10 And now, let us cry out to Heaven, if He will have mercy on us, and will be mindful of *the* covenant of *our* fathers, and destroy this army before our face today;
4.11 and all the nations will know that *there* is *One* who redeems and saves Israel."
4.12 And the foreigners lifted up their eyes, and saw them coming opposite *them;*
4.13 and they went out of the camp to war. And those *who were* with Judas sounded *their* trumpets,
4.14 and joined battle; and the nations were shattered, and fled into the plain,
4.15 but all those *who were coming* last fell by *the* sword. And they pursued them up to Gezer and the plains of Idumea and Ashdod and Jabneh. And about 3,000 of their men fell.
4.16 And Judas and his army turned back from pursuing them,
4.17 and he said to the people, "Do not desire the plunder, because *there is* a battle before us;
4.18 and Gorgias and *his* army *are* in the mountain near us. But stand[pl] now against our enemies, and make war[pl] against them; and afterwards, you[pl] will take the plunder with boldness."
4.19 While Judas was still finishing these *words*, a part *of them* was seen looking out from the mountain.
4.20 And he saw that they had been put to flight, and *the Judeans* were burning the camp; for the smoke that was seen revealed what had happened.
4.21 But when they saw these *things*, they were very much afraid; and also seeing the army of Judas in the plain, ready for battle,
4.22 they all fled into the land of the foreigners.
4.23 And Judas turned back to plunder the camp, and they took much gold and silver and blue and sea purple and great riches.
4.24 And they returned, *and* sang hymns and praises to Heaven, "For *He is* good, for His mercy endures for ever."
4.25 And Israel had a great deliverance that day.

Lysias's army is defeated at Bethzur

4.26 But all those of the foreigners who had escaped, went *and* told Lysias all the *things* that had happened.
4.27 And when *he* heard *it,* he was in turmoil and was discouraged, because the *things* that he had wanted *to happen* to Israel had not happened, and the *things* that the king had commanded him had not come to pass.

4.28 And in the next year, he gathered together 60,000 chosen men and 5,000 horse, so as to overcome them in war.
4.29 And they came into Idumea, and camped at Bethzur; and Judas met them with 10,000 men.
4.30 And they saw the strong army; and he prayed, and said, "You[†] are blessed, O Savior of Israel, who shattered the onslaught of the mighty *man* by *the* hand of Your[†] servant David, and delivered the camp of the foreigners into *the* hands of Jonathan *the* son of Saul, and of his armorbearer.
4.31 Shut[†] up this army in *the* hand of Your[†] people Israel, and let them be ashamed of their army and *their* horse*men*;
4.32 send[†] on them terror and melt away[†] *the* boldness of their strength, and let them quake at their destruction;
4.33 cast them down[†] with *the* sword of *those* who love You[†], and let all *those* who know Your[†] name praise You[†] with hymns."
4.34 And they joined battle; and *there* fell about 5,000 men from the army of Lysias, and they fell down opposite them.
4.35 But when Lysias saw that his *battle* array was put to flight, and the boldness of *those who were* with Judas, and how they were ready either to live or to die nobly, he moved away to Antioch. And he summoned foreigners, and an even greater *company,* who set out to go into Judea.

THE CLEANSING AND DEDICATION OF THE JERUSALEM TEMPLE

Judas and his companions now went up to Jerusalem in order to **cleanse** and **dedicate** the holy places of the temple (4.36–37). They found the temple **desolate** and desecrated (4.38–40), as previously described (1.37, 39, 46, 54, 59; 3.45, 51).

Faithful **priests** removed everything that had been polluted by practices contrary to God's Law. They restored the temple and all its furnishings to the condition required by the Law, with a **new altar of burnt offering** (4.42–53). Meanwhile, Judean soldiers guarded the temple workers from attack by the enemy's military base within Jerusalem (the **citadel,** 4.41; see 1.32–36).

The new altar was dedicated, and the daily offerings were restored, exactly three years after the temple began to be used for heathen sacrifices (4.52–58; cf. 1.59). The Israelites appointed the **days of the dedication** to be **kept** annually as a feast to the Lord (4.59)—a feast that was attended, less than two hundred years later, by Jesus Himself (John 10.22–23).

Judas and his companions also rebuilt the city's **walls** and **fortified** the city of **Bethzur,** on the border of the enemy province of **Idumea** (Maccabaica 4.60–61).

Judas and his companions go up to Mount Zion

4.36 But Judas and his brothers said, "Behold, our enemies have been shattered; let us go up to cleanse the holy *place*s and dedicate *them*."
4.37 And all the army gathered together, and went up to Mount Zion.

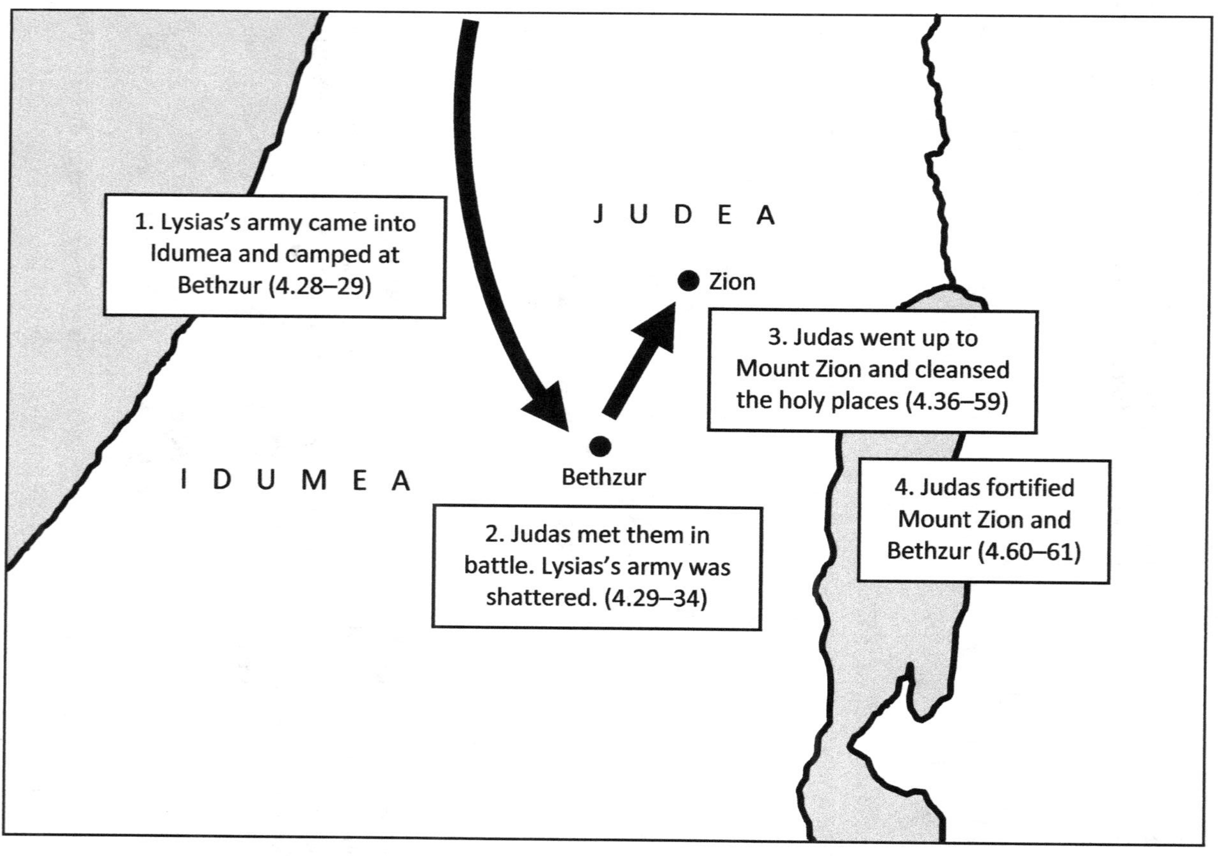
1. Lysias's army came into Idumea and camped at Bethzur (4.28–29)
J U D E A
Zion
3. Judas went up to Mount Zion and cleansed the holy places (4.36–59)
Bethzur
I D U M E A
2. Judas met them in battle. Lysias's army was shattered. (4.29–34)
4. Judas fortified Mount Zion and Bethzur (4.60–61)

Map 4: The battle against Lysias at Bethzur (Maccabaica 4.29–61)

4.38 And they saw the holy place desolate, and the altar profaned, and the gates burned down, and shrubs growing in the courtyards as *if* in a forest or on one of the mountains, and the chambers pulled down.
4.39 And they tore their clothes, and made a great lamentation, and put ash on their *heads,*
4.40 and fell on *their* faces to the ground. And they trumpeted with the trumpets of signaling, and cried out to Heaven.

They cleanse the holy places and dedicate the altar

4.41 Then Judas appointed *certain* men to make war against those *who were* in the citadel, until he had cleansed the holy *place*s.
4.42 And he chose unblemished priests, who were willing *to obey the* Law;
4.43 and they cleansed the holy *place*s, and took away the polluted stones into an unclean place.
4.44 And they took counsel about the altar of burnt offering, which had been profaned, *to decide* what they should do with it.
4.45 And *there* came to them a good counsel, that they should pull it down, lest it should become a reproach to them, because the nations had defiled it. And they pulled down the altar,
4.46 and laid aside the stones in the mountain of the house in a suitable place, until *there should* come a prophet to give an answer about them.
4.47 And they took whole stones according to the Law, and built a new altar like *the* previous *one.*
4.48 And they built the holy *place*s and the inner *parts* of the house; and they hallowed the courtyards,
4.49 and made new holy vessels, and brought the lampstand and the altar of incense and the table into the temple.
4.50 And they burned incense on the altar, and lit the lamps that *were* on the lampstand; and they were shining in the temple.
4.51 And they put loaves on the table, and spread out the curtains. And they finished all the works that they had done.

They offer sacrifice in accordance with the Law

4.52 And they rose up at dawn, early *in* the morning, on the 25th *day* of the ninth month, which *is* the month Chislev, *in* the 148th year,
4.53 and offered sacrifice according to the Law on the new altar of burnt offerings that they had made.
4.54 At the time and *on the* day on which the nations had profaned it, on that day it was dedicated, with songs and harps and lyres and cymbals.
4.55 And all the people fell on *their* faces, and bowed down, and gave blessings to Heaven, the *One* who had prospered them.

The feast of the dedication is established

4.56 And they kept the dedication of the altar *for* eight days, and offered burnt offerings with gladness, and sacrificed a sacrifice of deliverance and praise.
4.57 And they adorned the front of the temple with golden crowns and small shields, and dedicated the gates and chambers, and made doors for them.
4.58 And *there* was very great gladness among the people, and *the* reproach of *the* nations was turned away.
4.59 And Judas and his brothers, and the whole assembly of Israel, ordained that the days of the dedication of the altar should be kept in their seasons year by year *for* eight days, from the 25th *day* of the month Chislev, with gladness and joy.

Zion and Bethzur are fortified

4.60 And at that time they built up Mount Zion *with* high walls and strong towers round about, lest the nations should come *and* trample them down, as they had done previously.
4.61 And he set apart a force there, to guard them. And he fortified Bethzur, to guard it, *for* the people to have a fortress against Idumea.

WAR AGAINST THE NATIONS IN THE SOUTH, EAST, AND NORTH

The cleansing of the holy places in Jerusalem made the surrounding nations even more determined to oppose the Israelites (5.1–2).

Judas had to deal with trouble from the Edomites (**sons of Esau**) in the south (in **Idumea**) and from the **sons of Ammon** across the Jordan to the east (in the vicinity of **Jazer;** 5.3–8).

After his return to Judea, still greater problems arose: there were simultaneous urgent appeals for help from oppressed Israelites both across the Jordan (in **Gilead,** 5.9–13) and in the far north (in **Galilee,** 5.14–15). Judas and his brothers divided their forces and set out for both regions (5.16–20).

Simon rescued the oppressed families in **Galilee** and **brought them** to **Judea,** where they would be safer (5.21–23).

Judas and **Jonathan** crossed the Jordan (where they met one friendly nation, the **Nabateans**) and delivered the Israelites in **Gilead** from their enemies in many places, from **Bozrah** in the south to **Karnaim** in the north (5.24–44). These oppressed families were likewise brought to Judea (5.45–54).

While Judas and his brothers were away in Gilead and Galilee, **Joseph** and **Azariah,** who had been left in charge of the remaining forces in Judea, tried to attack their enemies at **Jabneh** (contrary to Judas's instructions, 5.18–19). However, Joseph and Azariah were defeated. Unlike Judas and his brothers, they were not members of the family (**seed**) of Mattathias, **by whose hands** God had chosen to give **deliverance ... to Israel** (5.55–62).

After **Judas and his brothers** returned to Judea, they fought further battles **in the land toward the south** against the **sons of Esau** (this time at **Hebron**) and in the **land of the foreigners** (Philistines), in the region of **Ashdod** (5.63–68).

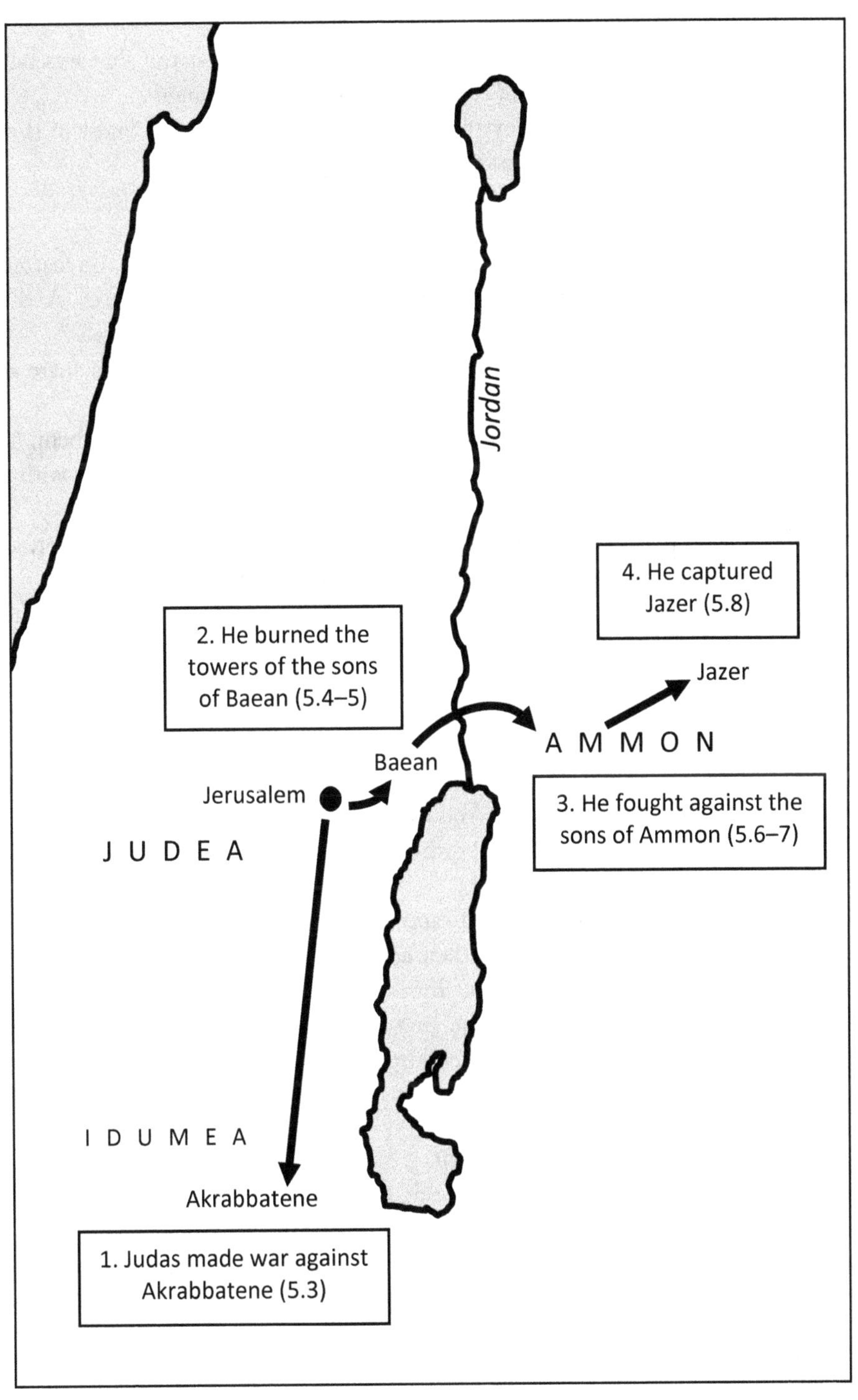

Map 5: Battles against Akrabattene and Ammon (Maccabaica 5.3-8)

The surrounding nations determine to kill the Israelites

5.1 And it came about, when the nations round about heard that the altar was built, and the holy place dedicated as *it had been* before, they were very angry.
5.2 And they took counsel to destroy the race of Jacob that was in *the* midst of them, and they began to kill and destroy among the people.

Judas defeats the Edomites and Ammonites

5.3 And Judas made war against the sons of Esau in Idumea—*against* Akrabattene, because they besieged Israel and struck them down *with* a great slaughter. And he confined them, and took their plunder.
5.4 And he called to mind the wickedness of *the* sons of Baean, who were a snare and a stumblingblock to the people, ambushing them on the paths.
5.5 And they were shut up by him in the towers; and he camped against them, and devoted them *to destruction.* And he burned its towers with fire, together with all those who were inside.
5.6 And he crossed over against the sons of Ammon, and found a mighty power, and many people, and a strong power, with Timothy *as* their leader.
5.7 And he fought many battles against them, and they were shattered before his face; and he defeated them,
5.8 and captured Jazer and its villages; and he turned back into Judea.

The Israelites in Gilead ask for help

5.9 And the nations in Gilead gathered together against the Israelites who were within their borders, to destroy them. And they fled into the fortress of Dathema,
5.10 and sent letters to Judas and his brothers, saying, "The nations round about us have gathered together to destroy us:
5.11 and they are preparing to come and capture the fortress into which we have fled for refuge, and Timothy is the leader of their army.
5.12 Now therefore, come[†] *and* deliver[†] us from their hand; for many of us have fallen;
5.13 and all our brothers who were in the *land* of Tubias have been put to death; and they have taken captive their wives and children and equipment; and they have destroyed there about 1,000 men."

The Israelites in Galilee also ask for help

5.14 *While* the letters were still being read, behold, other messengers came from Galilee, with *their* clothes torn, bringing a report similar to these words,
5.15 saying that *people* from Ptolemais and Tyre and Sidon, and all Galilee of the foreigners, *were* gathered against them, "to destroy us."

Judas divides his forces

5.16 Now when Judas and the people heard these words, a great assembly gathered together, to take counsel what they should do for their brothers who were in oppression and being attacked by them.

5.17 And Judas said to Simon his brother, "Choose[†] men, and go[†] and deliver[†] *your* brothers *who are* in Galilee; but I and Jonathan my brother will go into the land of Gilead."
5.18 And he left Joseph the *son* of Zechariah, and Azariah, a leader of the people, with the rest of the army, in Judea, to guard *it*.
5.19 And he commanded them, saying, "Direct[Pl] this people, and do not fight[Pl] *any* battle against the nations, until we return."
5.20 And 3,000 men were assigned to Simon, to go into Galilee; and to Judas 8,000 men, *to go* into the land of Gilead.

Simon delivers the people in Galilee

5.21 And Simon went into Galilee, and fought many battles against the nations. And the nations were shattered before him,
5.22 and he pursued them to the gate of Ptolemais. And about 3,000 men from the nations fell, and he took their plunder.
5.23 And he took those *who were* from Galilee and in Arbatta, with *their* wives and children, and all that they had, and brought them into Judea with great gladness.

Judas and Jonathan go to Gilead

5.24 And Judas Maccabeus and his brother Jonathan went over the Jordan, and went three days' journey in the desert,
5.25 and met with the Nabateans. And these *people* met them peacefully, and told them all the *things* that had happened to their brothers in the land of Gilead;
5.26 and that "Many of them are shut up inside Bozrah and Bezer, and in Alema, and Casphon, Maked, and Karnaim" (those cities *were* fortified and great),
5.27 "and they are shut up in the remaining cities of the land of Gilead, *and* tomorrow they have decided to camp against the fortresses and capture *them*, and to destroy all these *people* in one day."

They capture the cities from Bozrah to Karnaim

5.28 And Judas and his army turned away suddenly *on the* path into the desert to Bozrah. And he captured the city, and killed every male with *the* edge of *the* sword, and took all their plunder. And he burned it with fire.
5.29 And he moved away from there *by* night, and they went up near the fortress.
5.30 And the morning came, *and* they lifted up their eyes, and, behold, many people, who could not be numbered, carrying ladders and devices to capture the fortress; and they were making war against them.
5.31 And Judas saw that the battle had begun, and the outcry of the city went up to Heaven—the trumpet and great outcry;
5.32 and he said to the men of *his* army, "Make war[Pl] today for your[Pl] brothers."
5.33 And he went out from behind them, *divided* in three companies, and they trumpeted with *their* trumpets, and cried out in prayer.

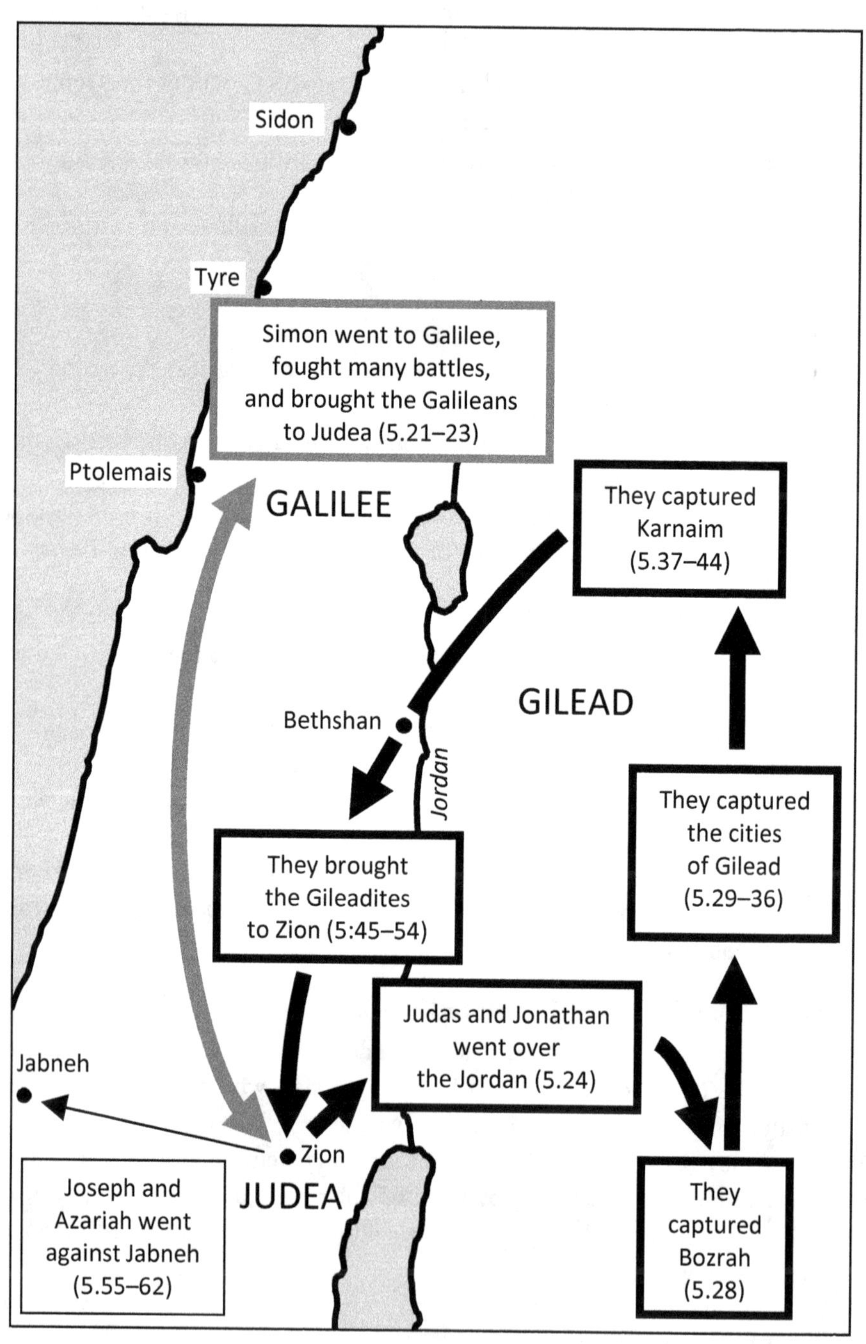

Map 6: Battles in Galilee and Gilead (Maccabaica 5.21–54)

5.34 And Timothy's army knew that it was Maccabeus, and they fled from before him.
And he struck them down *with* a great slaughter; and about 8,000 of their men fell on
that day.
5.35 And he turned aside to Maapha, and made war against it, and captured it, and
killed all its males, and took its plunder, and burned it with fire.
5.36 From there he moved away, and captured Casphon, Maked, and Bezer, and the
remaining cities of the land of Gilead.
5.37 Now after these things Timothy gathered another army, and camped against *the*
face of Raphon, beyond the storm-brook.
5.38 And Judas sent *men* to spy out the camp; and they reported to him, saying, "All
the nations round about us have gathered together to him—a very great army.
5.39 And they have hired Arabs to help them, and they are camping beyond the
storm-brook, ready to come against you[†] for war." And Judas went to meet them.
5.40 And Timothy said to the leaders of his army, when Judas and his army came near
the storm-brook of water, "If he should pass over first to us, we will not be able to
stand before him, for he will certainly be able *to stand* against us;
5.41 but if he should be afraid, and camp beyond the river, we will cross over to him
and we will be able *to stand* against him."
5.42 Now when Judas came near the storm-brook of water, he told the scribes of the
people to remain by the storm-brook, and commanded them, saying, "Do not allow[pl]
anyone to camp, but let them all come to the battle."
5.43 And he crossed over first against them, and all the people following him. And all
the nations were shattered before his face, and threw away their weapons, and fled
into the heathen temple at Karnaim.
5.44 And they captured the city, and burned the heathen temple with fire, together
with all those *who were* in it. And Karnaim was overthrown, and they were not able to
stand *any* longer against *the* face of Judas.

They capture Ephron and return to Jerusalem

5.45 And Judas gathered together all Israel who *were* in the land of Gilead, from *the*
littlest to *the* greatest, and their wives and children and equipment, a very great
company, to come into *the* land of Judah.
5.46 And they came as far as Ephron. And this city was great; *it was* on *their* path, *and*
fortified very much. He could not turn aside from it *to* right or left, but *he had* to go
through its midst.
5.47 And the *people* of the city shut them out, and blocked up the gates with stones.
5.48 And Judas sent to them with words of peace, saying, "We will go through your[†]
land to go into our *own* land, and no one will do you[pl] any evil; we will only pass by
on *our* feet." And they were not willing to open up to him.
5.49 And Judas commanded a proclamation to be made in the company to camp, each
man in *the* place where he was.

5.50 And the men of the army camped, and made war against the city all that day and all that night, and the city was delivered into his hand;
5.51 and he destroyed every male with *the* edge of *the* sword, and uprooted it, and took its plunder, and passed through the city over those who had been killed.
5.52 And they went over the Jordan into the great plain against *the* face of Bethshan.
5.53 And Judas gathered together those who were coming last, and encouraged the people all the way, until they came into *the* land of Judah.
5.54 And they went up to Mount Zion with gladness and joy, and offered burnt offerings, because not even one of them fell, until they returned in peace.

Joseph and Azariah are defeated in Judea

5.55 And in the days when Judas and Jonathan were in *the* land of Gilead, and Simon his brother *was* in Galilee against *the* face of Ptolemais,
5.56 Joseph the *son* of Zechariah, and Azariah, *the* leaders of the army, heard of *their* valiant deeds and the war, such *things* as they had done;
5.57 and they said, "Let us also make a name for ourselves, and let us go to make war against the nations that *are* round about us."
5.58 And he gave commands to the *men* of the army that *was* with them, and went against Jabneh.
5.59 And Gorgias and his men came out of the city to meet them in battle.
5.60 And Joseph and Azariah were put to flight, and were pursued to the borders of Judea; and on that day about 2,000 men of Israel fell.
5.61 And *there* was a great overthrow among the people, because they had not listened to Judas and his brothers, thinking to do valiant deeds.
5.62 But they were not from the seed of those men by whose hands deliverance was given to Israel.

Judas and his brothers are honored

5.63 And the man Judas and his brothers were honored very much in the sight of all Israel and all the nations where their name was heard;
5.64 and *people* gathered together to them, speaking good *of them*.

War in the south

5.65 And Judas and his brothers went out, and made war against the sons of Esau in the land toward the south. And he struck down Hebron and its villages, and pulled down its fortresses, and burned its towers round about.
5.66 And he moved away to go into *the* land of *the* foreigners; and he went through Mareshah.
5.67 In that day *some* priests, wanting to do valiant deeds, fell in warfare, when they went out to battle contrary to counsel.
5.68 And Judas turned aside to Ashdod, *the* land of *the* foreigners; and he pulled down their heathen altars, and burned down the carved images of their gods with fire, and took the plunder of *their* cities. And he returned into *the* land of Judah.

The Death of Antiochus Epiphanes

Some time earlier, **King Antiochus** had left for the **upper districts** of **Persia,** in the hope of finding riches that would enable him to pay for the upkeep of his army (3.29–37). There, in the region of **Elam,** he attacked a rich **city** but was defeated and **fled** (6.1–3).

While he was returning toward **Babylon** (6.4), he heard that his armies in **Judah** had been defeated, and that the **holy place** in **Jerusalem** had been restored to its previous condition (6.5–7). He fell ill and died in **great sorrow** (6.8–16), in accordance with Daniel's prophecy that "he will come to his end, and there will be no one helping him" (Dan 11.45). "I have seen a wicked violent man lifting himself up like a flourishing tree ... and I passed, and see! he was not there; and I sought him, and he was not found" (Psa 37.35–36).

Shortly before his death, Antiochus appointed a man named **Philip ... over all his kingdom** (Maccabaica 6.14–15).

Antiochus tries to plunder a city in Persia, but fails

6.1 And King Antiochus was journeying through the upper districts; and he heard that in Elam in Persia *there* was a city renowned for riches, for silver and gold;
6.2 and that the temple in it *was* extremely rich, and *in it* there *was* golden armor and breastplates and weapons, which Alexander, the *son* of Philip, the Macedonian king, who had reigned first among the Greeks, had left behind there.
6.3 And he came and sought to capture the city and pillage it; but he was not able, because the thing had become known to the *people* of the city,
6.4 and they rose up against him for battle, and he fled. And he moved away from there with great sorrow, to return to Babylon.

He hears what has happened in the land of Judah

6.5 And someone came into Persia, reporting to him that the armies that had gone into *the* land of Judah had been put to flight;
6.6 and Lysias had gone with a strong army in *the* first *place,* and had been put to flight before them; and *they had* become strong with weapons and power and much plunder, which they had taken from the armies that they had cut off;
6.7 and they had pulled down the abomination that they had built on the sacrificial altar in Jerusalem; and they had surrounded the holy place with high walls, just as *it had been* before, and Bethzur, his city.

He falls ill and dies

6.8 And it came about, when the king heard these words, he was astonished and very much shaken; and he fell on *his* bed, and fell into an illness from the sorrow, because it had not come about for him as he had desired.
6.9 And he was there many days, because *his* great sorrow was renewed upon him, and he realized that he was dying.
6.10 And he called for all his Friends, and said to them, "Sleep is departing from my eyes, and I am downcast with worry.

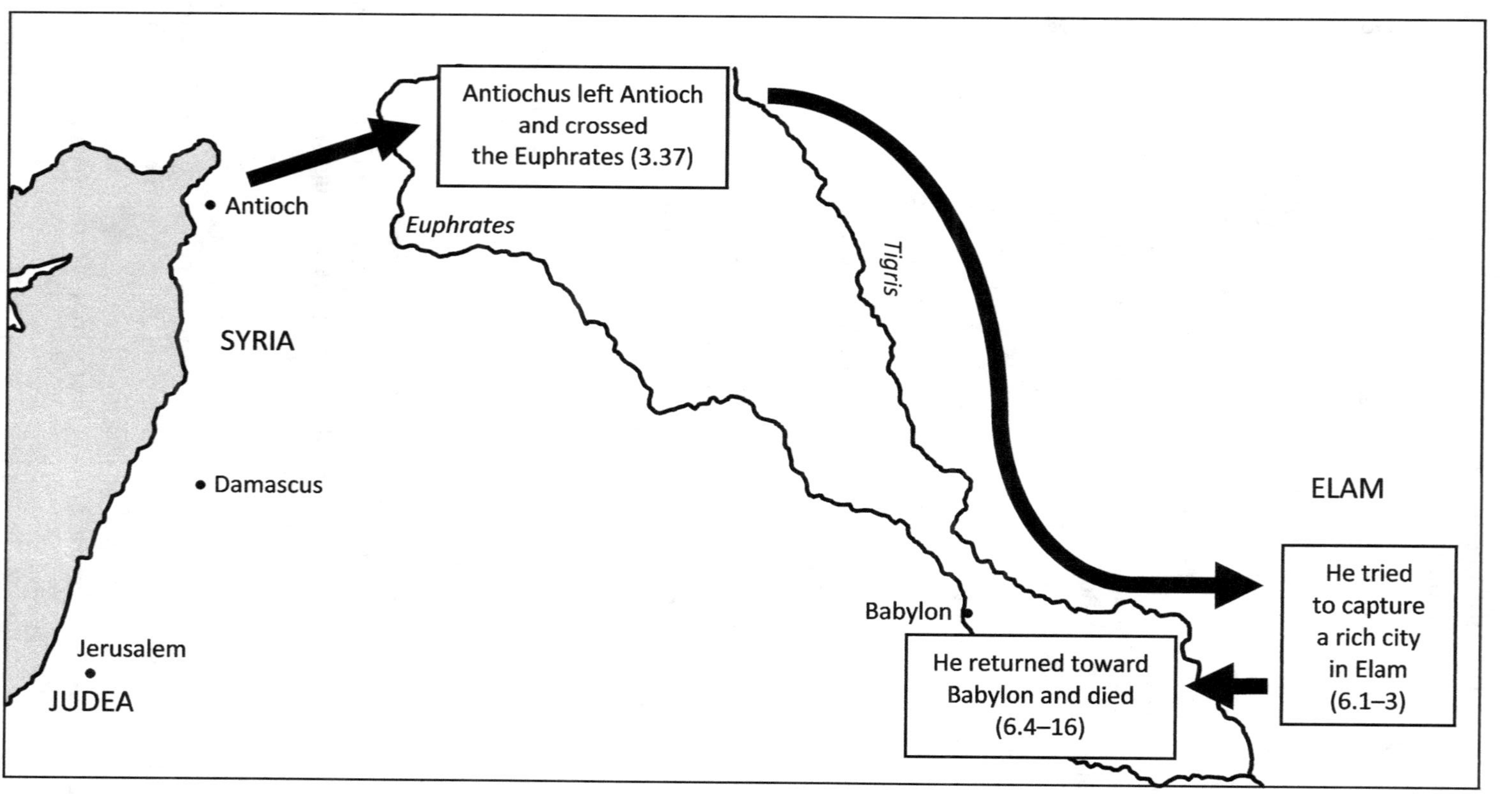
Antiochus left Antioch
and crossed
the Euphrates (3.37)
Antioch
Euphrates
Tigris
SYRIA
Damascus
ELAM
Babylon
Jerusalem
JUDEA
He tried
to capture
a rich city
in Elam
(6.1–3)
He returned toward
Babylon and died
(6.4–16)

Map 7: Antiochus Epiphanes' journey to Persia (Maccabaica 6.1–16)

6.11 And I said to my heart: To what affliction I have come, and how great a flood I am in now! for I was kind and *was* beloved in my authority.
6.12 But now I call to mind the evils that I did in Jerusalem, and *how* I took all the silver and golden vessels that *were* in it, and sent *people* to destroy the inhabitants of Judah without *any* cause.
6.13 I know that, because of this, these evils have come upon me, and, behold, I am perishing in great sorrow in a strange land."
6.14 And he called for Philip, one of his Friends, and set him over all his kingdom,
6.15 and gave him *his* diadem and his robe and signet-ring, to guide Antiochus his son and bring him up to be king.
6.16 And King Antiochus died there *in the* 149th year.

THE REIGN OF ANTIOCHUS EUPATOR

The dead king's **son** (likewise called **Antiochus**) was now **set up** in his place, and was given the name **Eupator** (6.17).

In the following year (the **150th**), **Judas determined** to besiege the **citadel** in Jerusalem (6.18–20). Some of the besieged people **came out**, and were **joined** by **irreverent** people **from Israel.** Together, they appealed to **the king** for **justice** and vengeance against their opponents, who had already **fortified the holy place** (Mount Zion) **and Bethzur,** and were now **camped ... against the citadel** (6.21–27).

The king gathered a very large army, and began to besiege **Bethzur** (6.28–31). Judas and his supporters fought against them near Bethzur, at **Bethzechariah** (6.32–42), but were unable to dislodge the king's forces (6.47). During this battle one of Judas's brothers, **Eleazar** (2.5), died. **He gave himself to deliver his people, and to get himself an everlasting name** (6.43–46), just as his father had urged (2.50–51). "Some of those who are wise will fall"; but they will "shine ... like the stars to lasting time and continuing time" (Dan 11.35; 12.3).

The king continued to besiege **Bethzur,** and started to besiege **Mount Zion** also. It was a **Sabbath** year, when the Israelites were forbidden to sow or reap crops (Lev 25.2–7). Both the besieged strongholds suffered for lack of **nourishment** (Maccabaica 6.49, 53), and so did the besiegers (6.57). The people of **Bethzur** surrendered (6.49–50), but the siege of Mount Zion was interrupted when the king learned that his father's commander **Philip** had returned and was trying to take control of the **government** (6.55–57). The king agreed to a peace settlement that would allow the Judeans **to go in their own laws** (6.58–61). But afterwards, when he entered **Mount Zion**, he ordered its **wall** to be torn down, contrary to his sworn agreement (6.62).

Returning **to Antioch,** the king defeated **Philip** (6.63). But a more dangerous enemy was about to appear (7.1–4).

Antiochus Eupator becomes king

6.17 And Lysias knew that the king was dead, and he set up Antiochus his son to be king, whom he had brought up *when he was* young; and he called his name Eupator.

Judas besieges the citadel

6.18 And those *who* were in the citadel were shutting up Israel round about the holy *places*, and always sought their harm and *the* strengthening of the nations.
6.19 And Judas determined to destroy them, and he assembled all the people to besiege them.
6.20 And they gathered together, and besieged it *in the* 150th year, and made towers for arrow-shooting, and *other* devices.

The evildoers appeal to the king

6.21 And *some* of them came out from *the* siege, and some of the irreverent *people* of Israel joined them.
6.22 And they went to the king, and said, "How long will you† not do justice and avenge† our brothers?
6.23 We were willing to serve your† father and walk according to his words and follow his commandments;
6.24 and because of this, the sons of our people have besieged it, and were estranged from us; but they have killed as many of us as *they* found, and plundered our inheritances.
6.25 And not against us only did they stretch out *their* hand, but also against all their boundaries.
6.26 And, behold, they are camped today against the citadel at Jerusalem, to capture it; and they have fortified the holy place and Bethzur.
6.27 And unless you† capture them quickly, they will do greater *things than* these; and you† will not be able to hold them back."

The king's army fights against the Judeans at Bethzechariah

6.28 And when the king heard *this,* he was angry, and gathered together all his Friends, and the leaders of his army, and those *who were* over the horse.
6.29 And bands of hired soldiers came to him from other kingdoms, and from islands of *the* seas.
6.30 And the number of his forces was 100,000 footsoldiers, and 20,000 horsemen, and 32 elephants trained for war.
6.31 And they went through Idumea, and camped against Bethzur, and made war against it many days, and made devices *of war*. And those *inside* came out, and burned them with fire, and made war valiantly.
6.32 And Judas moved away from the citadel, and camped at Bethzechariah, opposite the king's camp.
6.33 And the king rose at dawn, early *in* the morning, and moved his army away at full speed along the road to Bethzechariah; and *his* forces prepared for battle, and trumpeted with the trumpets.
6.34 And they showed the elephants *the* blood of grapes and mulberries, to prepare them for the battle.

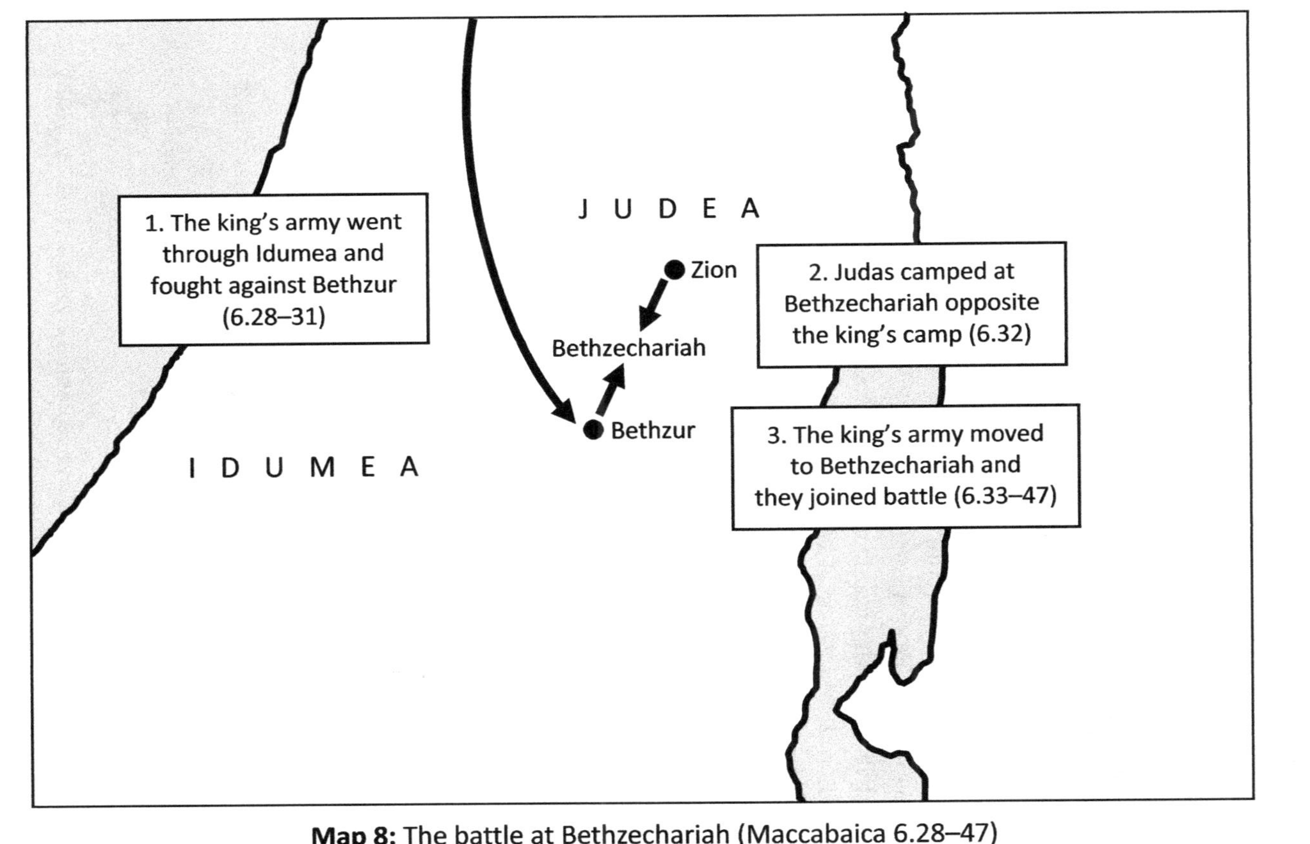
1. The king's army went through Idumea and fought against Bethzur (6.28–31)
J U D E A
Zion
Bethzechariah
Bethzur
2. Judas camped at Bethzechariah opposite the king's camp (6.32)
3. The king's army moved to Bethzechariah and they joined battle (6.33–47)
I D U M E A

Map 8: The battle at Bethzechariah (Maccabaica 6.28–47)

6.35 And they divided the animals among the phalanxes, and with each elephant they stationed 1,000 men breastplated in chain mail, and *with* bronze helmets on their heads; and 500 chosen horse *were* assigned to each animal.
6.36 These *were ready* beforehand; wherever the animal was, they were; and wherever it went, they went together; they never departed from it.
6.37 And wooden towers *were* on them, strong *and* covered, on each animal, girded on it with devices; and on each *animal were* 30 valiant men, who made war upon them, beside its Indian.
6.38 And the rest of *the* horse he set on this *side* and that, on the two sides of the army, striking terror, and enclosed in the phalanxes.
6.39 Now when the sun shone on the golden and bronze shields, the mountains shone with them, and blazed like lamps of fire.
6.40 And part of the king's army was spread out on the high mountains, and part *was* on the low *ground;* and they went ahead firmly and in order.
6.41 And all those who heard the noise of their multitude, and *the* marching of the multitude, and *the* rattling of the weapons, were trembling; for the army was very great and strong.
6.42 And Judas and his army drew near for battle, and 600 men of the king's army fell.
6.43 And Eleazar Avaran saw one of the animals, which was armed with *the* king's breastplates, and it was higher than all the animals, and the king was thought to be on it.
6.44 And he gave himself to deliver his people, and to get himself an everlasting name;
6.45 and he ran upon it confidently, into *the* midst of the phalanx, and killed right and left, and they parted from him this *side* and that.
6.46 And he crept under the elephant, and stabbed it from beneath, and killed it; and it fell on the ground upon him, and he died there.
6.47 And they saw the strength of the kingdom, and the onslaught of the armies; and they turned away from them.

The king captures Bethzur and besieges Mount Zion

6.48 But the *people* of the king's army went up to Jerusalem to meet them, and the king camped in Judea, and at Mount Zion.
6.49 And he made peace with the *people* of Bethzur; and they came out of the city, because they had no food there to endure *the* siege, because it was a Sabbath for the land.
6.50 And the king captured Bethzur, and appointed a garrison there to guard it.
6.51 And he camped against the holy place *for* many days; and he set there towers for arrow-shooting, and devices, and fire-throwers, and stone-throwers, and machines to shoot arrows, and slings.
6.52 And they also made devices against their devices, and made war *for* many days.

6.53 But there was no food in the containers, because it was the seventh year, and those who fled into Judea for safety from the nations had eaten up the rest of the store.
6.54 And few men remained in the holy *places*, because the famine had overpowered them, and they had been scattered, each *one* to his *own* place.

The king makes peace with the people of Zion

6.55 And Lysias heard that Philip—whom King Antiochus, while *he was* still alive, had appointed to bring up his son Antiochus to be king—
6.56 had returned from Persia and Media, and with him *were* the forces that had gone with the king; and that he was seeking to take over the business of government.
6.57 And he hastened, and agreed to depart; and he said to the king and the leaders of the army and the men, "We are perishing daily, and *there is* little food for us, and the place where we are camping is fortified, and the business of the kingdom is pressing upon us;
6.58 now therefore let us give *the* right *hand* to these Men, and let us make peace with them and all their nation.
6.59 And let us agree for them to go in their *own* laws, as *they did* before; for *it was* because of their laws, which we abolished, *that* they became angry and did all these *things*."
6.60 And *this* saying pleased the king and the leaders, and he sent them *an offer* to make peace; and they accepted *it*.
6.61 And the king and the leaders swore an oath to them. On these *conditions* they came out of the fortress.

The king destroys the wall of Zion and returns to Antioch

6.62 And the king came into Mount Zion; and he saw the fortress of the place, and set aside the oath that he had sworn, and commanded to pull down the wall round about.
6.63 And he moved away hastily, and returned to Antioch; and he found Philip lord over the city; and he made war against him, and captured the city by force.

THE FIRST CONFLICTS WITH DEMETRIUS SON OF SELEUCUS

Now a rival ruler appeared: **Demetrius,** the son of an earlier king, **Seleucus** (7.1–2). **Antiochus** Eupator and **Lysias** were killed, and for a while **Demetrius** reigned unchallenged (7.2–4).

All the **irreverent** Israelites appealed to the new king, led by a would-be high priest, **Alcimus** (7.5–7, 21). Demetrius sent an important official, **Bacchides,** with a large army to crush Judas and his allies (7.8–10).

Judas and his brothers did not trust Bacchides and Alcimus (7.10–11), but some other faithful Israelites did, including some of the **scribes** and **Hasidim** (a group mentioned in 2.42). As a result, **60** of them were **killed… in one day** (7.12–18).

After a while **Bacchides** returned **to the king;** but **Alcimus** remained (7.20). At first, he and his supporters **brought great harm on Israel** (7.21–23), but later he found that he did not have the power to oppose Judas, so he went and complained to the king (7.24–25).

In response, the king sent another commander, **Nicanor,** to **destroy** Judas and his allies (7.26). For a while Nicanor tried to deal with Judas **peaceably,** but his **deceit** was discovered (7.27–30), so he openly attacked the faithful Israelites near **Kaphar-salem.** Yet again Judas and his allies were victorious (7.31–32).

Nicanor visited the temple at **Mount Zion,** where he acted blasphemously and ill-treated the **priests,** even though they were presenting an offering **for the king** at that very time (7.33–35).

A new battle between **Nicanor** and **Judas** took place near **Bethhoron** (7.39–40). Just as God had punished previous blasphemers serving the Assyrian king Sennacherib (2 Kgs 19.6, 35), Judas prayed that He might **shatter** the army of the new blasphemer (Maccabaica 7.41–42). The prayer was answered. Not only were Nicanor's forces resoundingly defeated, but **he himself was the first to fall in the battle** (7.43–47).

The people of Israel **kept that day** with rejoicing, and determined to repeat the observance **each year** (7.48–49). For a while, **the land... was quiet** (7.50).

Demetrius son of Seleucus becomes king

7.1 *In the* 151st year Demetrius the *son* of Seleucus came out from Rome, and went up with a few men to a city by *the* sea, and became king there.

7.2 And it came about, as he was going into the house of *the* kingdom of his fathers, that the army captured Antiochus and Lysias, to bring them to him.

7.3 And the act became known to him; and he said, "Do not show[pl] me their faces."

7.4 And the army killed them. And Demetrius sat on *the* throne of his kingdom.

He sends Bacchides and Alcimus to take vengeance

7.5 And *there* came to him all *the* men of Israel *who were* transgressors and irreverent; and Alcimus was their leader, wanting to be priest.

7.6 And they accused the people to the king, saying, "Judas and his brothers have destroyed all your[†] friends, and have scattered us from our *own* land.

7.7 Now therefore send[†] a man whom you trust[†], and let him go *and* see all the ruin that he has done to us, and to the king's district, and *how* he has punished them and all those who helped them."

7.8 And the king chose Bacchides, one of the king's Friends, who was ruler in the *district* beyond the river, and *was* a great *man* in the kingdom, and faithful to the king.

7.9 And he sent him, and the irreverent Alcimus, and assigned the priesthood to him; and he commanded him to take vengeance on the sons of Israel.

Some who trust Bacchides and Alcimus are killed

7.10 And they moved away, and came with a great army into *the* land of Judah; and he sent messengers to Judas and his brothers with words of peace deceitfully.

7.11 And they did not pay attention to their words; for they saw that they had come with a great army.
7.12 And a company of scribes gathered together to Alcimus and Bacchides, to seek for justice.
7.13 And the Hasidim were *the* first among the sons of Israel *that* sought peace with them;
7.14 for they said, "A person *who is* a priest of *the* seed of Aaron has come with the forces, and he will not do *any* wrong to us."
7.15 And he spoke words of peace with them, and swore an oath to them, saying, "We will not seek evil for you[pl] or your[pl] friends."
7.16 And they believed him. And he captured 60 men of them, and killed them in one day, according to the word that He wrote,
7.17 "*The* flesh, *the* carcass of Your[†] saints, and their blood they shed round about Jerusalem; and *there* was no *one* to bury them."
7.18 And the fear and dread of them fell on all the people, for they said, "*There* is no truth or justice in them; for they have broken the agreement and the oath that they swore."
7.19 And Bacchides moved away from Jerusalem, and camped in Bethzeth. And he sent and took many of the deserters *who were* with him; and he slew some of the people into the great pit.
7.20 And he assigned the district to Alcimus, and left a force with him to help him. And Bacchides went away to the king.
7.21 And Alcimus strove for the high priesthood.
7.22 And all those who were troubling their people gathered to him, and they overpowered *the* land of Judah, and brought great harm on Israel.

Alcimus returns to the king

7.23 And Judas saw all the evil that Alcimus and those *who* were with him had done among *the* sons of Israel, beyond *what* the nations *had done.*
7.24 And he went out into all the borders of Judea round about, and took vengeance on the men who had deserted; and they were confined *from* going out into the district.
7.25 But when Alcimus saw that Judas and those *who* were with him had grown strong, and he knew that he was not able to stand before them, then he returned to the king, and brought harmful accusations against them.

The king sends Nicanor

7.26 And the king sent Nicanor, one of his honored leaders, and a *man* who hated and was hostile to Israel; and he commanded him to destroy the people.
7.27 And Nicanor came to Jerusalem with a great army; and he sent to Judas and his brothers deceitfully with words of peace, saying,
7.28 "Let *there* be no battle between me and you[pl]; I will come with a few men, so that I may see your[pl] faces in peace."

7.29 And he came to Judas, and they greeted one another peaceably. And the enemies were ready to seize Judas;
7.30 and the thing became known to Judas, that he had come to him in deceit; and he was afraid of him, and would not see his face *any* more.
7.31 And Nicanor knew that his counsel had been discovered; and he went out to meet Judas in battle opposite Kapharsalem;
7.32 and about 500 men of Nicanor's side fell; and they fled into the city of David.

Nicanor mocks the priests and elders

7.33 And after these things Nicanor went up to Mount Zion: and *some* of the priests came out of the holy *place*s, and *some* of the elders of the people, to greet him peacefully and show him the burnt offering *that was* being offered for the king.
7.34 And he mocked them, and laughed at them, and polluted them, and spoke arrogantly,
7.35 and swore an oath with indignation, saying, "Unless Judas and his army are delivered into my hands now, then it will be that, if I return in peace, I will burn down this house." And he went out with great indignation.
7.36 And the priests went in, and stood before the altar and the temple; and they wept, and said,
7.37 "You† Yourself† chose this house to be called by Your† name, to be a house of prayer and supplication for Your† people.
7.38 Take vengeance† on this Man and his army, and let them fall by *the* sword; be mindful† of their blasphemies, and do not let them live† *any* longer."

Nicanor is defeated and killed

7.39 And Nicanor went out from Jerusalem, and camped in Bethhoron; and a force *from* Syria met him.
7.40 And Judas camped in Adasa with 3,000 men. And Judas prayed and said,
7.41 "When those *who came* from the king blasphemed, Your† angel went out, and struck down 185,000 among them.
7.42 In the same way shatter† this army before us today, and let the rest know that he has spoken evil against Your† holy *place*s; and judge† him according to his wickedness."
7.43 And *on* the 13th *day* of the month Adar the armies joined battle; and Nicanor's army was shattered, and he himself was *the* first to fall in the battle.
7.44 Now when his army saw that Nicanor had fallen, they threw away *their* weapons, *and* fled.
7.45 And they pursued after them a day's journey from Adasa, as far as the approach to Gezer, and they trumpeted behind them with the trumpets of signaling.
7.46 And *people* came out of all the villages of Judea round about, and outflanked them; and these *one*s turned back against those *one*s, and they all fell by *the* sword, and *there* was not even one of them left.

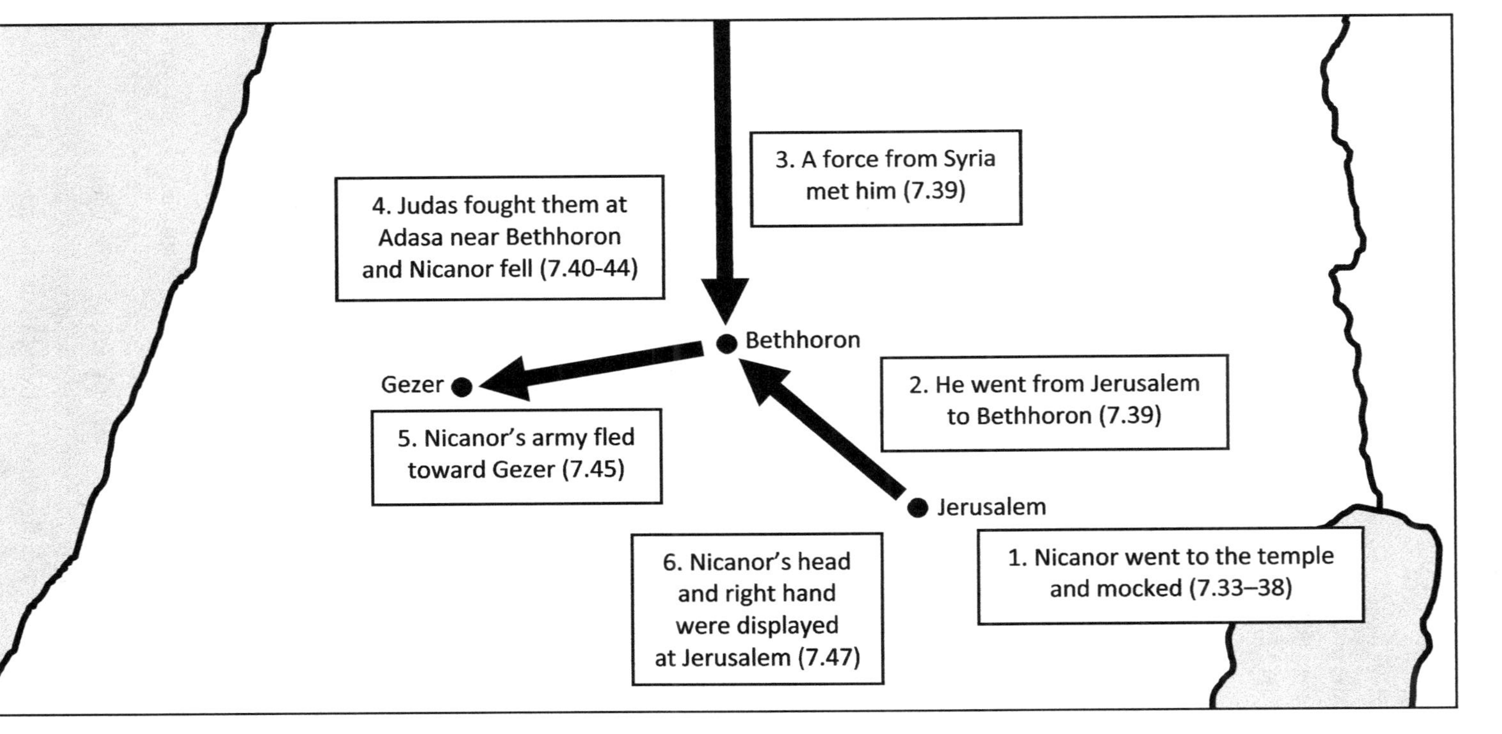

1. Nicanor went to the temple and mocked (7.33–38)
Jerusalem
2. He went from Jerusalem to Bethhoron (7.39)
Bethhoron
3. A force from Syria met him (7.39)
4. Judas fought them at Adasa near Bethhoron and Nicanor fell (7.40-44)
Gezer
5. Nicanor’s army fled toward Gezer (7.45)
6. Nicanor’s head and right hand were displayed at Jerusalem (7.47)

Map 9: The death of Nicanor (Maccabaica 7.33–48)

7.47 And they took the plunder and the pillage, and they cut off Nicanor's head, and his right hand, which he had stretched out arrogantly; and they brought *them*, and displayed *them* beside Jerusalem.
7.48 And the people were very glad, and they kept that day *as a day* of great gladness.
7.49 And they ordained to keep this day each year, the 13th *day* of Adar.
7.50 And the land of Judah had rest a few days.

THE ALLIANCE WITH ROME

Judas Maccabeus **heard** the **fame** of the **Romans** (8.1). His informants **told him** that the Romans had successfully **conquered** opponents in many places far and near (8.2–11), including the people of **Spain, Kittim** (the region around Macedonia, 1.1), and **Greece,** as well as the **Galatians** and even **Antiochus the Great,** who had been an earlier **king of Asia** (the kingdom now ruled by Demetrius; cf. 11.13; 12.39). They were also reputedly successful in defending their allies (8.12–13). They were said to have no king (wearer of a **diadem,** 11.54) or authoritative ruler (wearer of **purple,** 10.20), but to be governed by an assembly of three hundred counselors, under the leadership of someone chosen **every year** (8.14–16). Unlike the Greeks now ruling Judea, they were reputedly **well ordered,** not torn by internal divisions arising from **envy** or **jealousy** (8.15–16).

Hearing these reports, Judas **sent** two ambassadors to establish an **alliance** with the Romans, because Judea was being oppressed by **the kingdom of the Greeks** (8.17–20).

The Romans agreed to the alliance (8.21) and prepared a written agreement stating that the **Romans** and the **Judeans** would come to each other's aid in times of war, and would give no support to each other's enemies (8.22–29). The treaty could be modified in future if both parties (**these people and those people**) agreed to it (8.30). The Romans warned **Demetrius** that they would **make war against** him if the Judeans appealed to them again (8.31–32).

Judas hears about the Romans

8.1 And Judas heard of the fame of the Romans, that they were powerful *and* strong, and were well pleased with all *those* who joined them, and established friendship with all *those* who came to them,
8.2 and that they were powerful *and* strong. And they told him about their wars and valiant deeds which they had been doing among the Galatians, and that they had conquered them and made them subject to tribute;
8.3 and all *the things* they had done in *the* land of Spain, to get control of the mines of silver and gold *that were* there;
8.4 and they had conquered the whole place by their counsel and patience (and the place was very far away from them), and the kings who had come against them from *the* end of the earth, until they had shattered them and struck them down with a great slaughter; and the rest were giving them tribute every year;

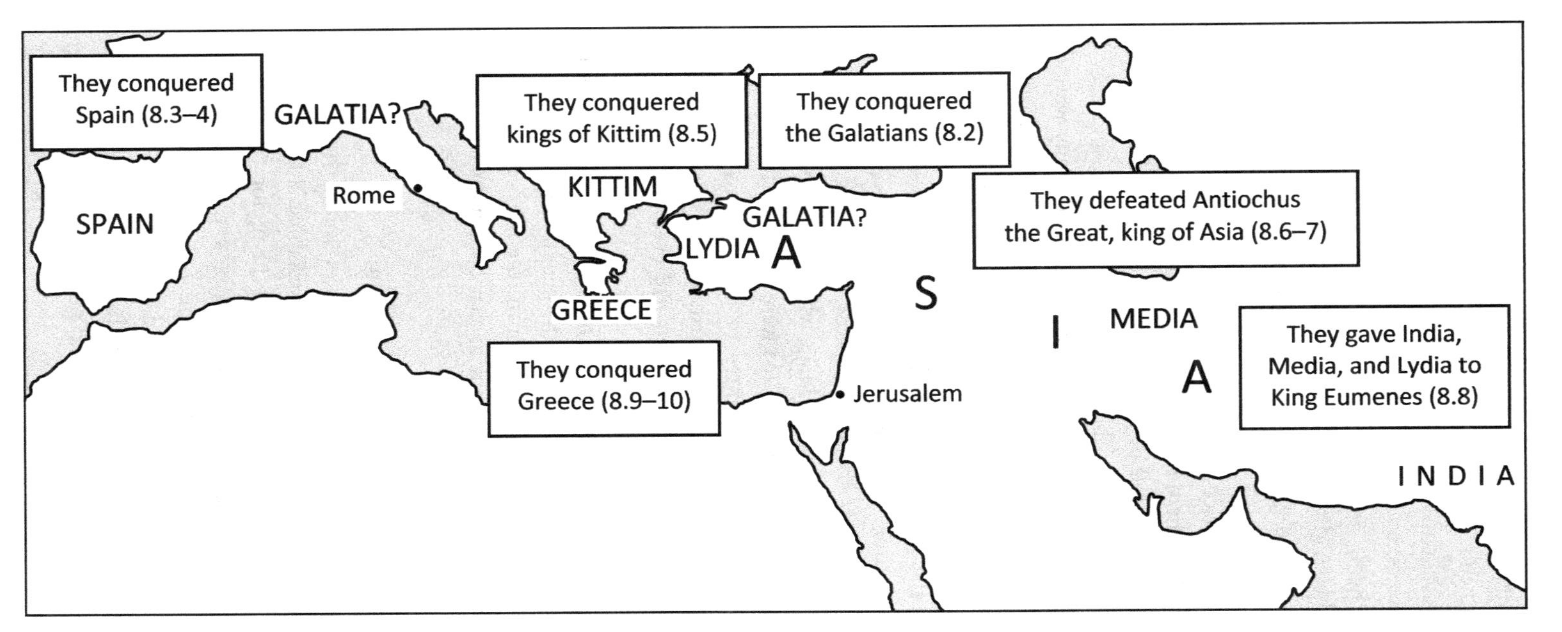

Map 10: What Judas heard about the Romans (Maccabaica 8.1–10)

8.5 and they had shattered in battle and conquered Philip, and Perseus king of Kittim, and those who lifted themselves up against them,

8.6 and Antiochus the Great, king of Asia, who had gone to war against them, having 120 elephants, and horse, and chariots, and a very great army; and he had been shattered by them,

8.7 and they had taken him alive, and established that both he and those who reigned after him should give them a great tribute, and should give *them* hostages, and a section *of land,*

8.8 even *the* district of India and Media and Lydia, *some* of their best districts; and they had taken them from him and given them to king Eumenes:

8.9 and that the *people* of Greece had taken counsel to come and destroy them,

8.10 and the thing had become known to them, and they had sent an army leader against them, and made war against them, and many wounded *men* of them fell; and they had taken captive their wives and children, and pillaged them, and conquered their land, and pulled down their fortresses, and pillaged them, and enslaved them, until this day;

8.11 and the rest of the kingdoms and islands—all *those* who had risen up against them at any time—they had destroyed and enslaved;

8.12 but with their friends and those who relied on them, they had kept friendship; and they had conquered the kings who were near and *those who were* far away; and all *those* who had heard of their fame were afraid of them;

8.13 and whomever they wanted to help and make king, they had made kings; and whomever they wanted, they deposed; and they were greatly exalted;

8.14 but for all this, none of them had ever put on a diadem or clothed himself in purple, to be magnified by it;

8.15 and they had made a council house for themselves, and every day 320 *men* sat in council, consulting at all *times* for the people, so that they might be well ordered;

8.16 and they entrusted one person to rule them every year, and be lord over all their land; and they were all obedient to that one, and there was no envy or jealousy among them.

Judas establishes an alliance with Rome

8.17 And Judas chose Eupolemos son of John, the *son* of Accos, and Jason son of Eleazar; and he sent them to Rome, to establish a friendship and alliance with them,

8.18 and to take the yoke away from them; for they saw *that* the kingdom of the Greeks *was* utterly enslaving Israel with slavery.

8.19 And they went to Rome, and the journey *was* very long; and they came into the council house, and answered and said,

8.20 "Judas Maccabeus and his brothers, and the people of the Judeans, have sent us to you[pl], to establish an alliance and peace with you, and to register ourselves as your[pl] allies and friends."

A copy of the alliance

8.21 And the thing was pleasing to them.

8.22 And this *is* a copy of the writing that they copied on bronze tablets and sent to Jerusalem, to be with them there *as* a memorial of peace and alliance:

8.23 "May *all* be well for *the* Romans, and for the nation of *the* Judeans, at sea and on dry *land,* for ever; and may *the* sword and *the* enemy be far from them.

8.24 But if war comes to Rome first, or any of their allies in all their dominion,

8.25 the nation of the Judeans will be *their* allies with all *their* heart, as the occasion may prescribe to them;

8.26 and to those who make war *on them* they will not give or supply *any* grain, weapons, money, *or* ships, as it has seemed *good* to *the* Romans; and they will keep their obligations without taking *anything in return.*

8.27 And in the same way, if war comes first to *the* nation of *the* Judeans, the Romans will be *their* allies with *all their* soul, as the occasion may prescribe to them;

8.28 and to *their enemies'* allies *there* will not be given *any* grain, weapons, money, *or* ships, as it has seemed *good* to *the* Romans; and they will keep these obligations, and *do so* without deceit.

8.29 According to these words *the* Romans have established *a treaty* thus with the people of the Judeans.

8.30 But if, hereafter, these *people* and those *people* take counsel to add or remove *anything,* they may do *it* at their pleasure; and whatever they may add or remove will be established.

8.31 And concerning the evils that king Demetrius is doing to them, we have written to him, saying, 'Why have you† made your† yoke heavy on our friends *and* allies the Judeans?

8.32 If therefore they appeal *any* more against you†, we will do justice for them, and make war against you† by sea and dry *land.*'"

THE DEATH OF JUDAS MACCABEUS

After the death of his army leader **Nicanor** (7.43–50), King **Demetrius** sent additional forces into Judea under the leadership of **Bacchides and Alcimus** (9.1).

When the Syrian army approached, most of Judas's forces became **very much afraid** and **slipped away,** leaving him with only **800 men** (9.4–6). Judas was disheartened and saw that he was likely to **die,** but he refused to **flee** and remained determined to **make war** for the sake of his **brothers** (9.7–10). In the battle, he managed to drive back the stronger **right wing** of the Syrian army (9.14–15), but the **left wing** attacked him from **behind,** and he was killed. The remainder of the Judean army **fled** (9.16–18).

Judas was **buried** in **Modein,** the home of his ancestors (9.19). **All Israel** mourned for him in words derived from the Scriptures: **How has the mighty fallen!** (9.20–21; cf. 2 Sam 1.19). His **valiant deeds** had been **very many,** more than have been recorded (Maccabaica 9.22), like those of Jesus (John 21.25).

Bacchides and Alcimus return to Judea

9.1 And Demetrius heard that Nicanor and his forces had fallen in battle; and he sent Bacchides and Alcimus again into *the* land of Judah, a second *time,* and the right wing *of his army* with them.
9.2 And they went *by the* way that *led* to Gilgal; and they camped against Mesaloth, which *is* in Arbela, and captured it, and destroyed many people.
9.3 And *in* the first month of the 152nd year they camped against Jerusalem.

Judas fights against them, but is killed

9.4 And they moved away, and went to Berea, with 20,000 men and 2,000 horse.
9.5 And Judas was camped at Elasa, and 3,000 chosen men with him.
9.6 And they saw the multitude of the forces, that they were many; and they were very much afraid. And many slipped away out of the army; none of them were left but 800 men.
9.7 And Judas saw that his army had slipped away, and the battle was pressing upon him; and he was greatly troubled in heart, for he had no time to gather them together,
9.8 and he became tired. But he said to those who were left, "Let us rise up, and go up against our enemies, if perhaps we may be able to make war against them."
9.9 And they tried to dissuade him, saying, "We should certainly not be able; but rather, let us save *our* own lives now; and *then* let us return, *we* and our brothers, and make war against them; but we *are* few."
9.10 And Judas said, "Far be it *from us* to do such a thing, to flee from them; and if our time has come, let us die valiantly for *the* sake of our brothers, and not leave a cause of reproach against our honor."
9.11 And the army moved away from the camp, and stood to encounter them. And the horse was parted into two companies, and the slingers and the archers were going ahead of the army, and all the powerful fighters *were* at *the* front.
9.12 But Bacchides was in the right wing; and the phalanx came near, on the two sides, and they blew *their* trumpets. And the men of Judas' side also trumpeted with their trumpets.
9.13 And the earth shook with the shout of the armies, and the battle was joined, *and continued* from morning until evening.
9.14 And Judas saw that Bacchides and the strength of his army *were* on the right *side,* and all those *who were* brave in heart went with him,
9.15 and the right wing was shattered by them, and he pursued behind them to *the* Ashdoth [slopes] of *the* mountains.
9.16 And those *who were* on the left wing saw that the right wing had been shattered; and they turned back on *the* heels of Judas and those *who were* with him, behind *them.*
9.17 And the battle was severe, and many wounded *men* fell on both sides.
9.18 And Judas fell, and the rest fled.

9.19 And Jonathan and Simon took Judas their brother, and buried him in the tomb of their fathers at Modein.
9.20 And all Israel wept *for* him and made great lamentation *for* him, and mourned many days, and said,
9.21 "How has *the* mighty fallen, *the* savior of Israel!"
9.22 And the additional acts of Judas, and his wars, and the valiant deeds that he did, and his greatness, have not been written down; for they were very many.

Jonathan (9.23–12.53)

JONATHAN ESTABLISHES PEACE IN ISRAEL

When Judas died, **those who did unrighteousness** reappeared in Israel and led the people in **the district** astray (9.23–24). This was a time of **great tribulation** for the faithful (9.26–27), who chose Judas's brother **Jonathan** (cf. 2.5) as their new leader (9.28–31).

At first, Jonathan and his companions **fled** from their oppressors **into the desert of Tekoa** in central Judah (9.33), but their enemies, again led by **Bacchides** (9.32), came after them. Bacchides traveled to the **Jordan** River (9.34, 43) because Jonathan and his companions had crossed the Jordan to take vengeance for the death of his brother **John,** who had been killed trying to place their **equipment** in safe keeping with their friends across the river (9.35–42). While Jonathan and his companions were returning toward Judea (9.42), they were trapped at the Jordan, with no means of escape, by the army of Bacchides (9.43–45). Jonathan and his companions looked to Heaven for help, and were granted a great victory over their enemies (9.46–49).

Bacchides then **fortified** the Jerusalem citadel and various other **cities in Judea . . . to oppose Israel** (9.50–53). His ally **Alcimus** the priest (cf. 7.5–25) tried to tear down some parts of the temple area (the **holy places**), but was stricken with paralysis and **died** (9.54–56).

When Bacchides no longer had the support of Alcimus, he **returned** to Antioch, and Judea had **rest for two years** (9.57). But then the **transgressors** persuaded Bacchides to return and attack the Judeans once more (9.58–60). However, the plot backfired: Jonathan and his companions were not snared, and some of the **main leaders** of the plot were killed instead (9.61).

Jonathan and his companions went into the Judean **desert** to fortify the city of **Bethbasi** (9.62). Bacchides came and besieged them there, but Jonathan divided his forces, so that his enemies found themselves under attack both from inside the city (under the leadership of Jonathan's brother **Simon**) and from outside (under the leadership of **Jonathan** himself; 9.63–67). Again Bacchides was defeated (**shattered,** 9.68), and again **many** of the people who had **counseled** Bacchides to return perished (9.69). Bacchides and his allies **took counsel to go away** (9.69), and Jonathan made **peace** with them. Bacchides promised never to return, and he kept his word (9.70–72).

During the following time of peace **Jonathan began to judge the people,** cleansing the nation of evildoers (9.73).

A time of great tribulation

9.23 And it came about, after the end of Judas's *life,* that the transgressors peered out in all the borders of Israel, and all those who did unrighteousness rose up
9.24 (in those days *there* was a very great famine), and the district deserted with them.
9.25 And Bacchides chose the irreverent men, and made them lords of the district.
9.26 And they sought and searched for the friends of Judas, and brought them to Bacchides; and he took vengeance on them, and scoffed at them.
9.27 And there was great tribulation in Israel, such as had not happened since the time when no prophet appeared among them.

Jonathan is appointed leader

9.28 And all the friends of Judas gathered together, and said to Jonathan,
9.29 "Since your† brother Judas ended *his life, there* is no man like him to go out against *our* enemies and Bacchides, and among those of our nation who are enemies.
9.30 Now therefore we have chosen you† today to be our ruler and leader in his place, to fight our battles."
9.31 And Jonathan accepted the leadership at that time, and rose up in place of Judas his brother.
9.32 And Bacchides knew *this;* and he sought to kill him.
9.33 And Jonathan, and Simon his brother, and all those *who were* with him, knew *it;* and they fled into the desert of Tekoa, and camped near the water of *the* pool Asphar.
9.34 And Bacchides knew *this,* on the Sabbath day; and he came, he and all his army, over to *the* other side of the Jordan.

The death of John

9.35 And *Jonathan* sent his brother *as* leader of the multitude, and asked his friends the Nabateans *for permission* to leave with them their equipment, *which was* a large amount.
9.36 And the sons of Jambri, *who were* from Medeba, came out and took John, and all that he had, and went away with *them.*
9.37 After these things, they reported to Jonathan and Simon his brother that *the* sons of Jambri were making a great wedding, and were bringing the bride from Nadabath, a daughter of one of the great noblemen of Canaan, with a great convoy.
9.38 And they called to mind the blood of John their brother, and went up, and hid under cover of the mountain.
9.39 And they lifted up their eyes, and saw; and, behold, a noisy gathering and a large amount of equipment; and the bridegroom and his friends and his brothers came out to meet them with drums and musicians and many weapons.
9.40 And they rose up against them from the ambush, and killed them. And many fell wounded, and the rest fled to the mountain. And they took all their plunder.
9.41 And the wedding was turned into mourning, and the voice of their musicians into lamentation.

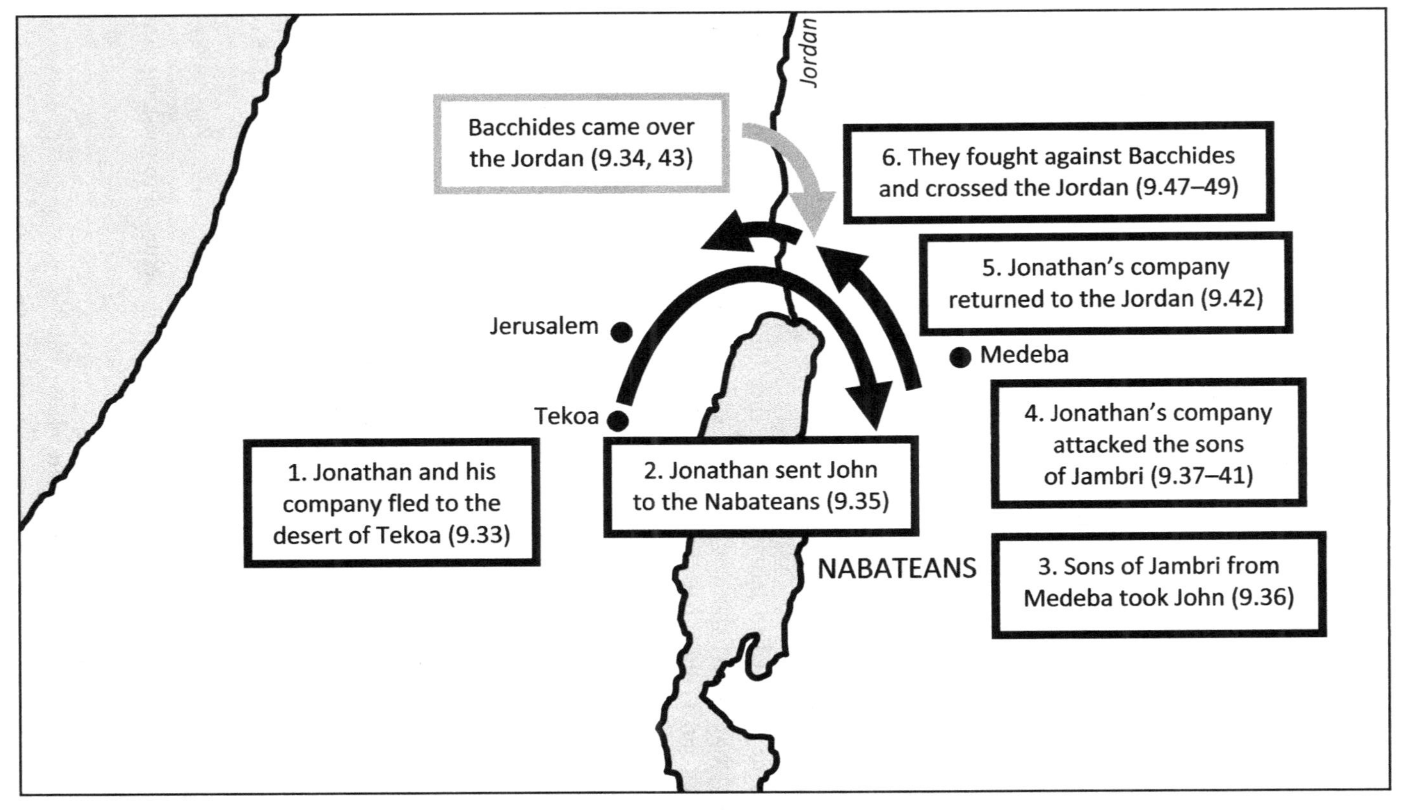
Jordan
Bacchides came over the Jordan (9.34, 43)
6. They fought against Bacchides and crossed the Jordan (9.47–49)
5. Jonathan's company returned to the Jordan (9.42)
Jerusalem
Medeba
Tekoa
4. Jonathan's company attacked the sons of Jambri (9.37–41)
1. Jonathan and his company fled to the desert of Tekoa (9.33)
2. Jonathan sent John to the Nabateans (9.35)
NABATEANS
3. Sons of Jambri from Medeba took John (9.36)

Map 11: The battle against Bacchides at the Jordan (Maccabaica 9.31–49)

9.42 And they fully avenged *the* blood of their brother, and returned to the marsh of the Jordan.

Bacchides is defeated at the Jordan

9.43 And Bacchides heard *it,* and he came on the Sabbath day to the banks of the Jordan, with a great army.
9.44 And Jonathan said to his company, "Let us rise up now and make war for our lives, for today is not like yesterday and *the* day before.
9.45 For, behold, the battle *is* in front and behind us, and the water of the Jordan is on this *side* and that *side,* and marsh and forest; *there* is no place to turn aside.
9.46 Now therefore cry out[pl] to Heaven, so that you[pl] may be delivered out of *the* hand of our enemies."
9.47 And the battle was joined, and Jonathan stretched out his hand to strike down Bacchides, and he turned away back from him.
9.48 And Jonathan and those *who were* with him leaped into the Jordan, and swam over to the other side. And they did not go over the Jordan against them.
9.49 And *there* fell from Bacchides' company, that day, about 1,000 men.

Bacchides fortifies Judea

9.50 And he returned to Jerusalem. And they built up fortified cities in Judea: the fortress *that was* in Jericho, and Emmaus, and Bethhoron, and Bethel, and Timnath, Pharathon, and Tephon, with high walls and gates and bars.
9.51 And he set a garrison in them, to oppose Israel.
9.52 And he fortified the city Bethzur, and Gezer, and the citadel, and put forces in them, and stores of food.
9.53 And he took the sons of the district's leaders *as* hostages, and put them under guard in the citadel at Jerusalem.

The death of Alcimus

9.54 And in the 153rd year, *in* the second month, Alcimus commanded to pull down the wall of the inner courtyard of the holy *place*s; and he pulled down the works of the prophets. And he began to pull *them* down.
9.55 At that time Alcimus was stricken, and his works were hindered; and his mouth was stopped, and he was paralysed, and he could not speak anything or give orders about his house *any* more.
9.56 And Alcimus died at that time in great torment.
9.57 And Bacchides saw that Alcimus was dead, and he returned to the king. And the land of Judah had rest *for* two years.

An unsuccessful plot against Jonathan

9.58 And all the transgressors took counsel, saying, "Behold, Jonathan and his companions are dwelling at ease, *and* confident. Now therefore, let us bring Bacchides, and he will capture them all in one night."

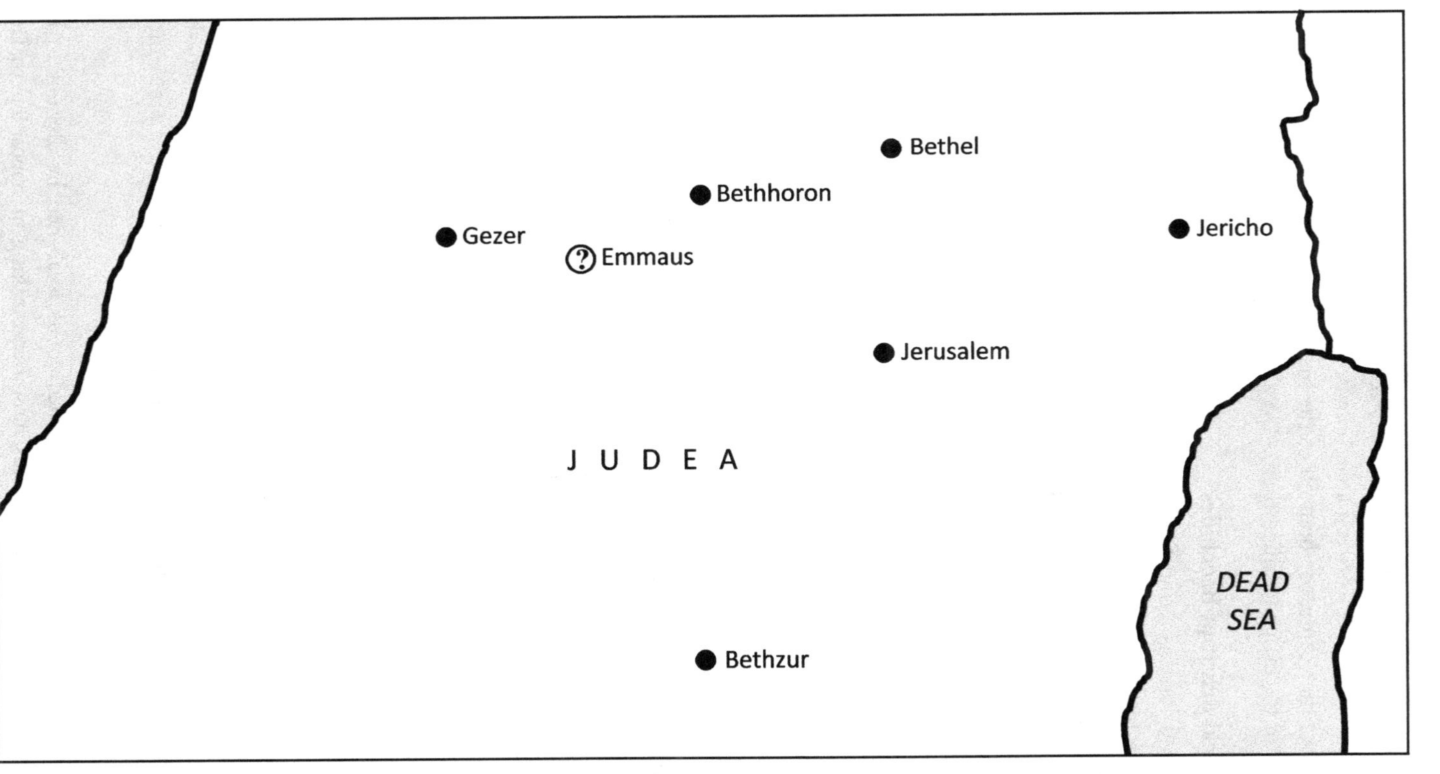

Map 12: Judean cities fortified by Bacchides (Maccabaica 9.50–53)

9.59 And they went *and* consulted with him.
9.60 And he moved away *and* came with a great army. And he sent letters privately to all his allies who *were* in Judea, *telling them* to capture Jonathan and those who *were* with him. And they were not able, because their counsel became known.
9.61 And they captured about 50 of the men of the district, *who were among* the main leaders of the evil, and killed them.

The final defeat of Bacchides

9.62 And Jonathan, and Simon, and those who *were* with him, departed to Bethbasi, which *is* in the desert. And he built up the *parts* of it that had been pulled down, and made it strong.
9.63 And Bacchides knew *this;* and he gathered together all his multitude, and sent orders to the *people* of Judea.
9.64 And he went *and* camped against Bethbasi, and made war against it many days, and made devices *of war.*
9.65 And Jonathan left his brother Simon in the city, and went out into the district. And he went with a few men.
9.66 And he struck down Odomera and his brothers, and the sons of Phasiron in their tent. And they began striking *them* down and going up with *their* forces.
9.67 And Simon and those *who were* with him went out of the city, and set the devices on fire,
9.68 and made war against Bacchides, and he was shattered by them; and they afflicted him severely; for his counsel and his coming had been in vain.

Peace with Bacchides

9.69 And they were angry *and* indignant with the transgressors who had counseled him to come into the district; and they killed many of them. And they took counsel to go away into his land.
9.70 And Jonathan knew of *this,* and sent ambassadors to him, to make peace with him, and so that he would give the captives back to them.
9.71 And he accepted *this,* and did according to his words. And they swore an oath to him not to seek evil for him all the days of his life.
9.72 And he gave back to him the captives whom he had taken captive previously from *the* land of Judah. And he returned *and* went away to his *own* land, and did not come into their borders *any* more.
9.73 And *the* sword ceased from Israel. And Jonathan dwelt at Michmash. And Jonathan began to judge the people; and he destroyed the irreverent *people* out of Israel.

ALEXANDER EPIPHANES OPPOSES DEMETRIUS

The kingdom of the Greeks continued to be weakened by divisions. **Alexander Epiphanes, the son of Antiochus,** now **became king** in opposition to Demetrius (10.1). Both **Demetrius** (10.3–6, 22–45) and **Alexander** (10.15–20) wrote letters **to**

Jonathan, trying to enlist his support, and promising the Judeans many **good things.** Jonathan and his people **did not believe** Demetrius, because his words were not consistent with his deeds (10.46), but they agreed to be **allies** of Alexander (10.47).

The rival kings' letters had two important effects. First, they gave Jonathan official **authority** to **gather** army **forces,** rebuild the defenses of **Jerusalem,** and free the **hostages** in the **citadel** (10.6–11, 21). And secondly, they **established** him as **high priest** (clothed **with the holy robe,** 10.20–21).

Demetrius **gathered together very great forces** to fight against Alexander (10.2). When the battle took place, **Demetrius** put the opposing army to flight—but he himself was the one who **fell** (10.48–50).

Alexander then made an alliance with **Ptolemy king of Egypt** and married Ptolemy's daughter (10.51–58). On that occasion, Alexander **honored** Jonathan greatly and forbad Jonathan's enemies to **appeal against him** for any reason (10.59–66).

Alexander becomes king

10.1 And in *the* 160th year Alexander Epiphanes, the *son* of Antiochus, went up and captured Ptolemais: and they accepted him, and he became king there.

Demetrius seeks an alliance with Jonathan

10.2 And king Demetrius heard, and he gathered together very great forces, and went out to meet him in battle.
10.3 And Demetrius sent letters to Jonathan with words of peace, so as to exalt him;
10.4 for he said, "Let us act first to make peace with them, before he makes *peace* with Alexander against us;
10.5 for he will call to mind all the evil *thing*s that we have done against him and his brothers and his nation."
10.6 And he gave him authority to gather forces and prepare weapons, and *for* him to be his ally; and he said that they should deliver up to him the hostages *who were* in the citadel.

Jonathan strengthens Jerusalem

10.7 And Jonathan came to Jerusalem, and read the letters in the hearing of all the people, and of those from the citadel;
10.8 and they were very much afraid, when they heard that the king had given him authority to gather forces.
10.9 And the *people* of the citadel delivered up the hostages to Jonathan, and he restored them to their parents.
10.10 And Jonathan dwelt in Jerusalem, and began to build and renew the city.
10.11 And he told the workers to build the walls and Mount Zion round about with square stones, for a fortification. And he did so.
10.12 And the foreigners who were in the fortresses that Bacchides had built, fled away;
10.13 and each *one* left his place, and went away to his *own* land.

10.14 Only in Bethzur *there* remained some of those who had forsaken the Law and the commandments; for it was a place of refuge *for them.*

Alexander seeks an alliance with Jonathan

10.15 And King Alexander heard the promises that Demetrius had sent to Jonathan; and they told him about the battles and the valiant deeds that he and his brothers had done, and the labors that they had endured.
10.16 And he said, "We shall not find such a man, even one, *shall we?* And now, let us make him our Friend and ally."
10.17 And he wrote letters, and sent *them* to him according to these words, saying,
10.18 "King Alexander to *his* brother Jonathan: Greeting.
10.19 We have heard about you[†], that you[†] are a mighty man of valor, and suitable to be our Friend.
10.20 And now, we have established you[†] today *as* high priest of your[†] nation, and to call yourself[†] the king's Friend" (and he sent him a purple *robe* and a golden crown), "and to favor our *interests* and keep friendship with us."

Jonathan becomes high priest

10.21 And Jonathan put on the holy robe *in* the seventh month of *the* 160th year, at *the* Feast of Tabernacles. And he gathered together forces, and prepared many weapons.

Demetrius seeks an alliance again

10.22 And Demetrius heard these things, and he was sorrowful, and said,
10.23 "What *is* this we have done, that Alexander has acted before us to establish friendship with the Judeans, to strengthen *himself?*
10.24 I myself will also write to them words of encouragement and honor and gifts, so that they may be with me to help *me.*"
10.25 And he sent to them according to these words:
"King Demetrius to the nation of the Judeans: Greeting.
10.26 Since you[pl] have kept *your* agreements with us and continued[pl] in our friendship, and have not departed[pl] to our enemies, we have heard and are glad.
10.27 And now, still continue[pl] to keep faith with us, and we will repay good *things* to you[pl], in return for your[pl] dealings with us,
10.28 and we will free many things for you[pl] and give you[pl] gifts.
10.29 And now I release you[pl], and free all the Judeans, from the tribute *payments* and salt duty, and from the crowns.
10.30 And instead of *taking* a third of the seed, and instead of *taking* half of the fruit from the trees, which are assigned for me to take, I release *them* from this day forward, *no longer* taking *them* from *the* land of Judah and from the three provinces that are added to it from the region of Samaria and Galilee, from this day and for all time.

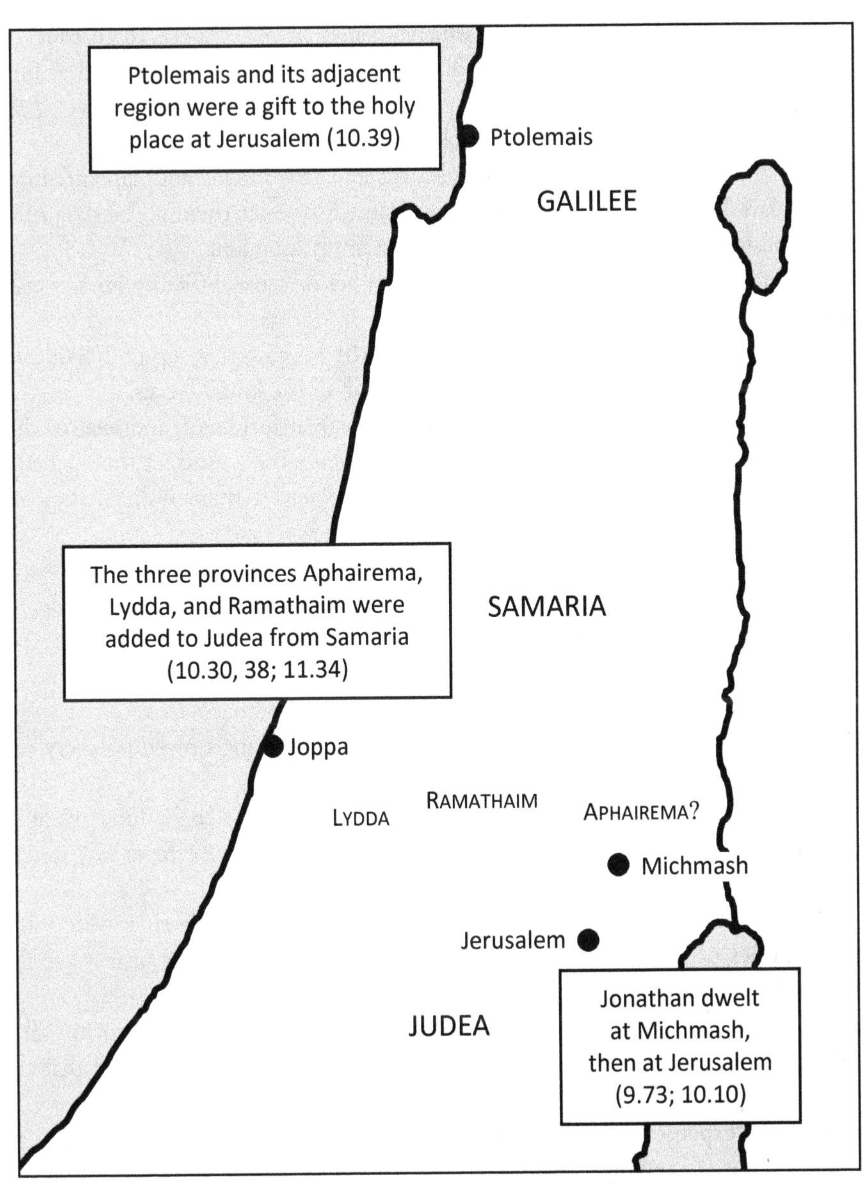

Map 13: Regions granted to Judea by Demetrius (Maccabaica 10.30–39)

10.31 And let Jerusalem be holy and free, and her borders. The tenths and the payments
10.32 I am setting free, and I am giving *my* authority over the citadel in Jerusalem to the high priest, so that he may appoint in it whichever men he may choose, to guard it.
10.33 And every soul of *the* Judeans who has been taken captive from *the* land of Judah into any part of my kingdom, I am setting free *as* a gift; and let them all leave *off their* tribute *payments* and *those* of their livestock.
10.34 And *as for* all the feasts, and the Sabbaths and new moons and appointed days, and three days before a feast and three *days* after a feast—let them all be days of exemption and freedom for all the Judeans who are in my kingdom.
10.35 And no one will have any authority at all to act or cause difficulty for any *one* of them about any matter.
10.36 And let *some* of the Judeans be enrolled in the king's forces, up to 30,000 men; and provisions will be given to them, as is fitting for all the king's forces.
10.37 And *some* of them will be placed in the king's great fortresses, and *some* of them will be placed over *the* duties of the kingdom that *require* trust. And let their superiors and their rulers be *chosen* from among themselves. And let them walk in their *own* laws, just as the king has commanded in *the* land of Judah.
10.38 And *as for* the three provinces that have been added to Judea from the district of Samaria—let them be added to Judea *and* reckoned to be under one *person,* not obeying *any* other authority than the high priest's.
10.39 Ptolemais and its adjacent *region* I have given *as* a gift to the holy *places* at Jerusalem, *to provide* for the expense*s* that are fitting for the holy *places*.
10.40 And I myself give 15,000 shekels of silver from the king's revenues every year, from the places that are fitting.
10.41 And all the additional *money*—which the *people* over the *king's* duties were not paying back *to you* as the former nations *had done*—they will give from now on, for the works of the house.
10.42 And in addition to this, *the* 5,000 shekels of silver—which they were taking from the duties of the holy *place* from the revenue every year—this also is set free, because it *is* fitting for the priests who are ministering.
10.43 And whoever may flee into the temple that *is* at Jerusalem, and within all its boundaries, owing *the* king's *taxes,* or *for* any *other* matter—let them, and all that they have in my kingdom, be released.
10.44 And the expense of building and renewing of the works of the holy *places* will also be given out of the king's revenue.
10.45 And the expense of building the walls of Jerusalem and fortifying *it* round about, and building the walls in Judea, will also be given out of the king's revenue."

The people of Judea favor Alexander

10.46 Now when Jonathan and the people heard these words, they did not believe or accept them, because they called to mind the great evil that they had done in Israel, and *that* he had afflicted them very much.

10.47 And they were well pleased with Alexander, because he had been *the* first *who spoke* words of peace to them; and they were allies with him all *his* days.

Demetrius is killed

10.48 And King Alexander gathered great forces, and camped opposite Demetrius.
10.49 And the two kings joined battle, and Alexander's army fled; and Demetrius pursued him, and overpowered them.
10.50 And he kept fighting very strongly until the sun set; and Demetrius fell that day.

Alexander marries Ptolemy's daughter

10.51 And Alexander sent ambassadors to Ptolemy king of Egypt according to these words, saying,
10.52 "Since I have returned to my kingdom and sat on *the* throne of my fathers, and have taken hold of the dominion, and have overthrown Demetrius, and gained power over our district—
10.53 and I joined battle with him, and he and his army were overthrown by us, and we sat on *the* throne of his kingdom—
10.54 now then, let us establish a friendship between *our*selves, and give[†] me your[†] daughter for *my* wife, and I will make a marriage alliance with you[†], and I will give you[†] and her gifts *that are* worthy of you[†]."
10.55 And Ptolemy the king answered, saying, "*It was* a good day when you[†] returned to *the* land of your[†] fathers and sat[†] on *the* throne of their kingdom.
10.56 And now I will do for you[†] what you[†] have written; but meet[†] me at Ptolemais, so that we may see one another; and I will make a marriage alliance with you[†], just as you[†] have said."
10.57 And Ptolemy went out of Egypt, he and Cleopatra his daughter, and came to Ptolemais *in the* 162nd year.
10.58 And King Alexander met him; and he gave him Cleopatra his daughter; and he celebrated her wedding at Ptolemais with great glory, just as kings *do.*

Alexander honors Jonathan

10.59 And King Alexander wrote to Jonathan to come to meet him.
10.60 And he went with glory to Ptolemais, and met with the two kings, and gave them and their Friends silver and gold and many gifts, and found favor in their sight.
10.61 And *some* men from Israel *who were* plague-bearers, men *who were* transgressors, gathered together against him, to appeal against him; and the king did not pay *any* attention to them.
10.62 And the king commanded, and they took off Jonathan's garments, and clothed him in purple. And they did so.
10.63 And the king seated him with him*self,* and said to *his* leaders, "Go out[pl] with him into *the* midst of the city, and proclaim[pl] that no one should appeal against him about any matter at all; and let no one cause him *any* difficulty for any reason."

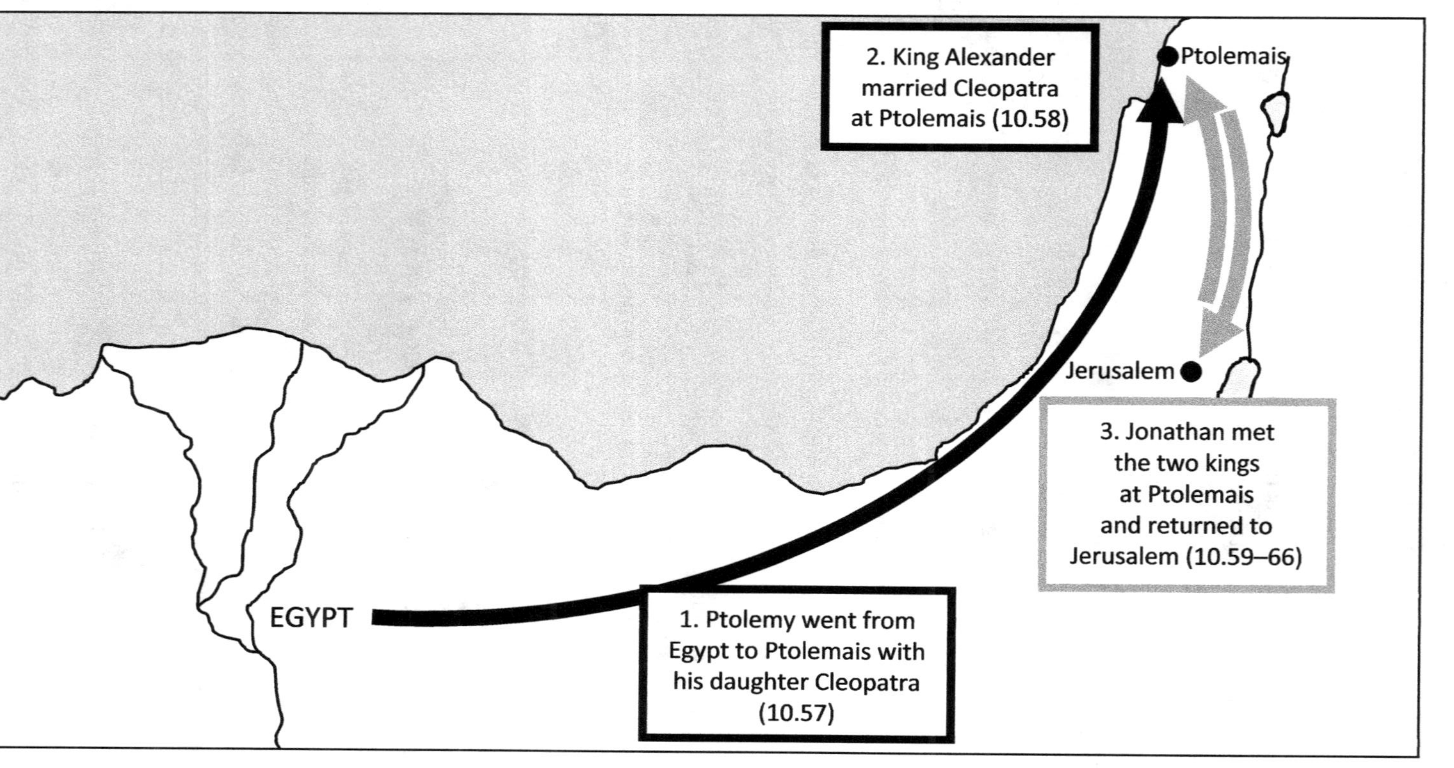
2. King Alexander married Cleopatra at Ptolemais (10.58)
Ptolemais
Jerusalem
3. Jonathan met the two kings at Ptolemais and returned to Jerusalem (10.59–66)
EGYPT
1. Ptolemy went from Egypt to Ptolemais with his daughter Cleopatra (10.57)

Map 14: The marriage of Alexander Epiphanes (Maccabaica 10.57–66)

10.64 And it came about, when those who were appealing against him saw his honor, just as *the king* had proclaimed, and *saw* him clothed in purple, they all fled away.
10.65 And the king honored him, and registered him among *his* Chief Friends, and made him an army commander and governor of a province.
10.66 And Jonathan returned to Jerusalem in peace and gladness.

DEMETRIUS SON OF DEMETRIUS OPPOSES ALEXANDER

Alexander Epiphanes did not reign undisturbed for long. Three years after his marriage to Ptolemy's daughter (10.57), he was opposed by a new rival, **Demetrius, son of** the previous **Demetrius** (10.67–68).

Apollonius, one of Demetrius's officers, now **gathered together a great army** and moved into the land of the Philistines, where he besieged the city of **Jabneh** and sent a message of defiance to **Jonathan** (10.69–73). **Jonathan** then moved through the land of the Philistines with his own army, subduing the enemy cities one after another (10.74). **Joppa** and **Ashkelon** surrendered to him (10.75–76, 86), but at **Ashdod** his army was surrounded by Apollonius's cavalry. Nevertheless, the Israelites stood firm until their enemies' horses **became weary** and the surrounding forces could be put to flight (10.77–83). After that, **Ashdod** and the nearby **cities** were **burned with fire** (10.84–85).

Alexander... honored Jonathan **still more** as a result of these successes, and assigned him another Philistine city, **Ekron** (10.88–89).

Demetrius son of Demetrius arrives

10.67 And in *the* 165th year, Demetrius son of Demetrius came out of Crete to the land of his fathers.
10.68 And King Alexander heard, and he was very sorrowful, and returned to Antioch.

Apollonius challenges Jonathan

10.69 And Demetrius appointed Apollonius, who was over Coele-Syria, and he gathered together a great army, and camped against Jabneh, and sent to Jonathan the high priest, saying,
10.70 "You† alone are lifting yourself† up against us, but I am an *object of* derision and reproach because of you†. And why are you† exercising authority against us in the mountains?
10.71 Now therefore, if you† are confident in your† forces, come down† to us, to the plain, and there let us judge *between our*selves; for with me is *the* power of the cities.
10.72 Ask† and learn† who I am, and the rest who help us. And they say, 'Your[pl] foot cannot stand before our face; for twice your† fathers have been put to flight in their *own* land.'
10.73 And now you† will not be able to stand before *my* horse*men* and such an army *as this* in the plain, where *there* is no stone or flint or place to flee."

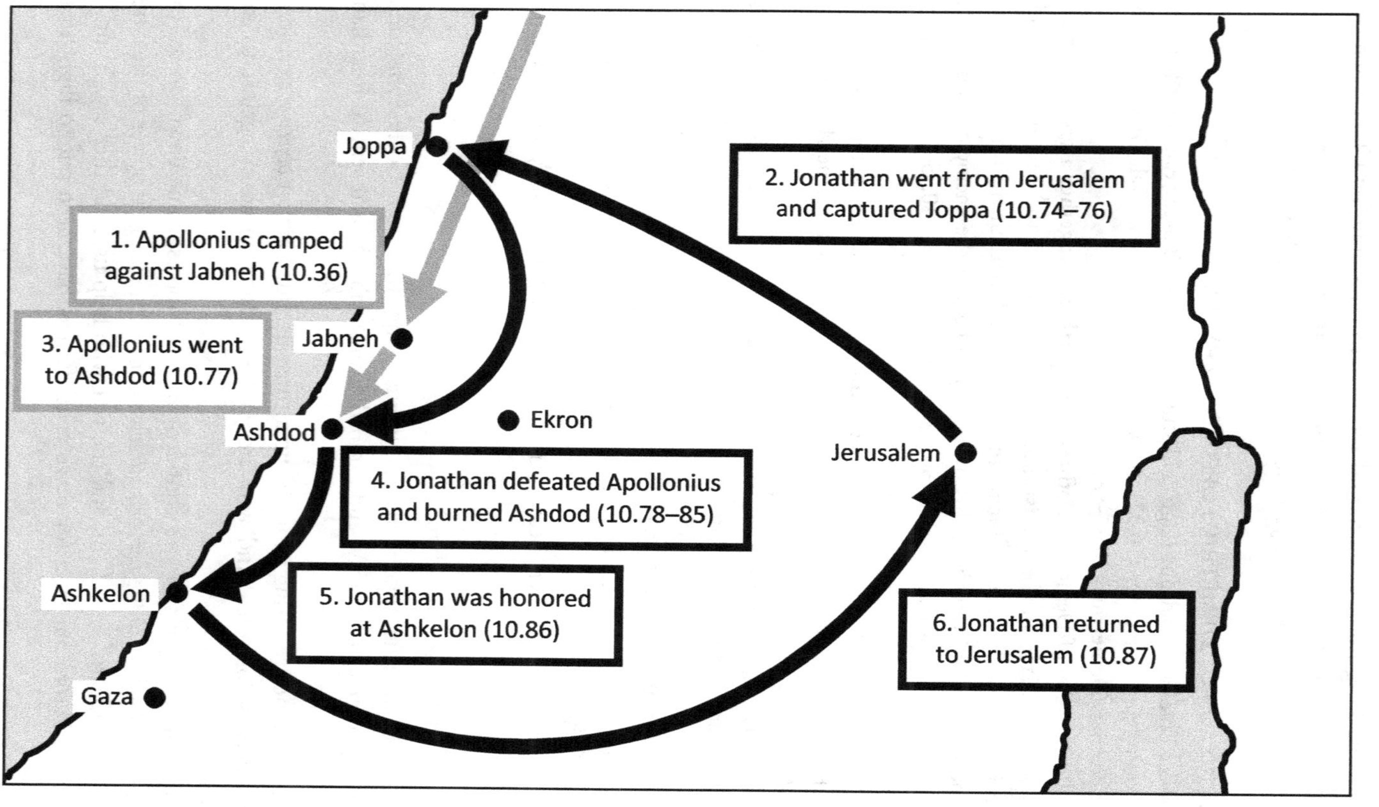
Joppa
1. Apollonius camped against Jabneh (10.36)
Jabneh
3. Apollonius went to Ashdod (10.77)
Ashdod
Ekron
Ashkelon
Gaza
2. Jonathan went from Jerusalem and captured Joppa (10.74–76)
4. Jonathan defeated Apollonius and burned Ashdod (10.78–85)
5. Jonathan was honored at Ashkelon (10.86)
Jerusalem
6. Jonathan returned to Jerusalem (10.87)

Map 15: Apollonius and the coastal cities (Maccabaica 10.69–89)

Joppa submits to Jonathan

10.74 Now when Jonathan heard the words of Apollonius, he was moved in *his* mind, and chose 10,000 men, and went out from Jerusalem; and Simon his brother met him to help him.
10.75 And he camped against Joppa; and the *people* of the city shut it, because Apollonius *had* a garrison in Joppa. And they made war against it.
10.76 And the *people* of the city were afraid, *and* opened *it* up; and Jonathan became master of Joppa.

Jonathan defeats Apollonius at Ashdod

10.77 And Apollonius heard, and he gathered an army of 3,000 horse, and a great force, and went for battle to Ashdod, as *though he was* passing through; and at *the* same *time* he went forward into the plain, because he *had* a multitude of horse and put *his* trust in it.
10.78 And he pursued after him for battle to Ashdod, and the armies joined battle.
10.79 And Apollonius had left 1,000 horse in hiding behind them.
10.80 And Jonathan knew that there was an ambush behind him. And they went around his army, and shot *their* arrows at the people, from morning until evening;
10.81 but the people stood *still,* just as Jonathan had commanded *them.* And their horses became weary.
10.82 And Simon brought out his army, and joined battle with the phalanx (because the horse had become weary), and they were shattered by him, and fled,
10.83 and the horse were scattered in the plain. And they fled into Ashdod, and entered into Beth-Dagon [the house of Dagon], their idol's temple, to save themselves.
10.84 And Jonathan burned Ashdod, and the cities round about it, and took their plunder. And the temple of Dagon, and those who had fled into it, he burned with fire.
10.85 And those who had fallen by *the* sword, together with those who were burned, came to about 8,000 men.

Ashkelon submits to Jonathan

10.86 And Jonathan moved away from there, and camped against Ashkelon; and the *people* of the city came out to meet him with great honor.
10.87 And Jonathan returned to Jerusalem, together with those *who were* with him, having much plunder.

Alexander honors Jonathan still more

10.88 And it came about, when King Alexander heard these things, he honored Jonathan *still* more,
10.89 and sent him a golden pin, as it is *the* custom to give to kings' relatives, and gave him Ekron and all its borders for an inheritance.

Ptolemy opposes Alexander

Ptolemy, not content with being **king of Egypt,** wanted to **add** Alexander's kingdom **to his own.** He traveled north through the Philistine cities (**Ashdod . . . Joppa**) to **Antioch.** Everywhere he went, he placed some of his army **forces for a garrison,** so that he became **master of the cities** (11.2–13). He did nothing that might alienate the people of Judea (11.5–6).

After a while he openly broke with **Alexander** (**their enmity was openly seen**). He took away **his daughter** (whom Alexander had married, 10.57–58), **and gave her to** Alexander's rival **Demetrius** instead. He began to wear **two diadems,** professing to be king not only of **Egypt** but also of the northern kingdom, **Asia** (11.12–13).

Alexander had been away dealing with a rebellion in a western region of his kingdom, **Cilicia** (11.14). Now he returned and met Ptolemy **in battle.** Ptolemy's forces were victorious, and **Alexander fled into Arabia,** where he was killed. But Ptolemy himself **died the third day afterwards** (11.15–18).

Ptolemy travels into Syria

11.1 And the king of Egypt gathered together many forces, like the sand *that is* by the sea shore, and many ships, and sought to overpower Alexander's kingdom by deceit and add it to his own kingdom.

11.2 And he went out into Syria with words of peace, and the *people* of the cities opened up to him, and met him; for it was King Alexander's command that they should meet him, because he was his father-in-law.

11.3 But as Ptolemy entered into the cities, he set apart *his* forces *for* a garrison in each city.

11.4 But when they came near Ashdod, they showed him the temple of Dagon that had been burned down, and Ashdod and its suburbs that had been pulled down, and the bodies that had been thrown away, and those who had been burned, whom he had burned in the battle, for they had made heaps of them in his path.

11.5 And they told the king what *things* Jonathan had done, so that they might discredit him. And the king kept silent.

11.6 And Jonathan met the king with honor at Joppa; and they greeted one another, and they slept there.

11.7 And Jonathan went with the king as far as the river that *is* called Eleutherus, and returned to Jerusalem.

Ptolemy makes an alliance with Demetrius

11.8 But King Ptolemy became master of the cities upon the sea coast, as far as Seleucia that *is* by the sea. And he planned harmful plans about Alexander.

11.9 And he sent ambassadors to King Demetrius, saying, "Come, let us make a covenant with one another, and I will give you[†] my daughter whom Alexander used to have, and you[†] will be king over your[†] father's kingdom:

11.10 for I regret that I gave him my daughter, because he has sought to kill me."

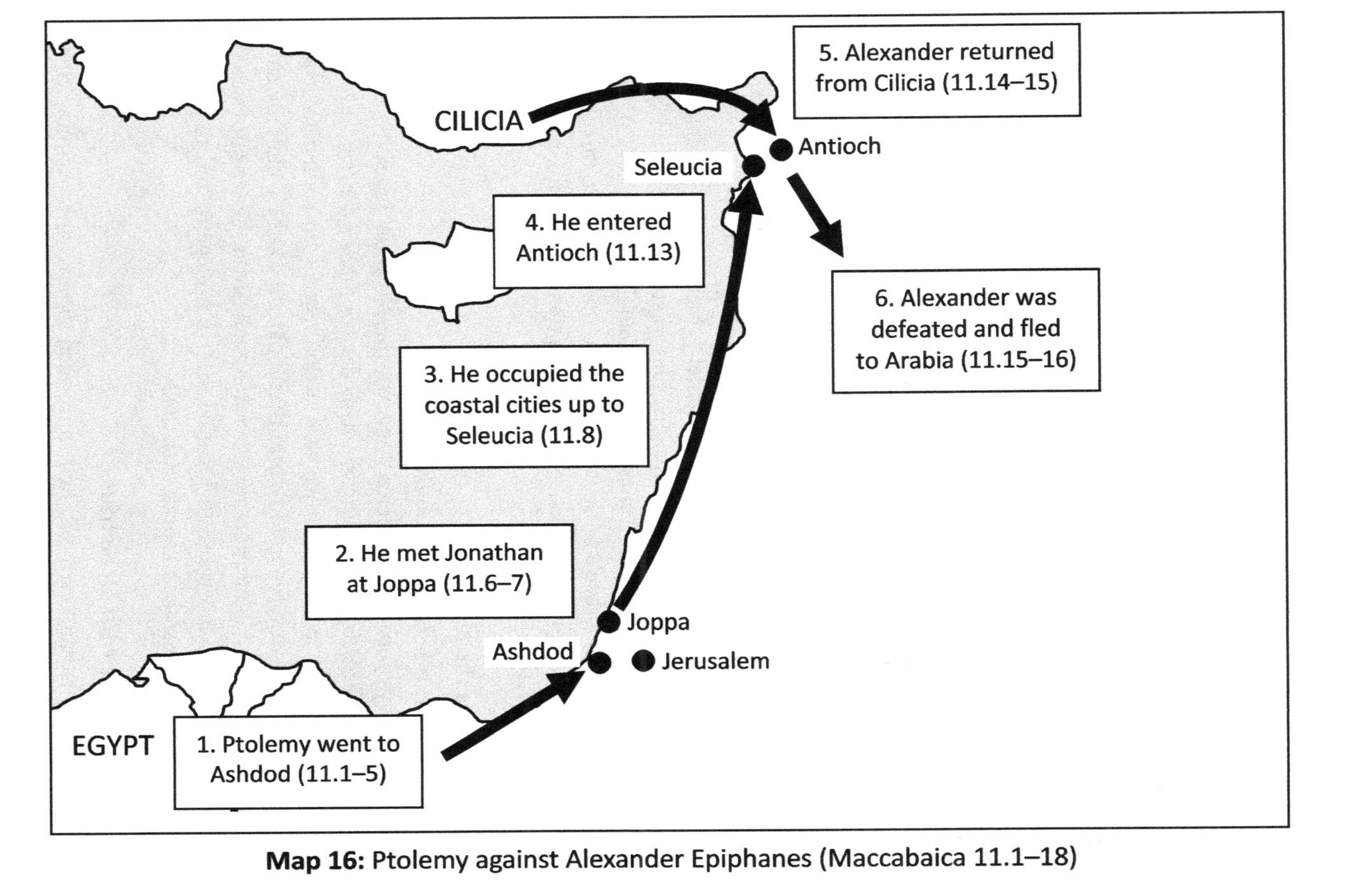

Map 16: Ptolemy against Alexander Epiphanes (Maccabaica 11.1–18)

11.11 And he discredited him, because he desired his kingdom.
11.12 And taking his daughter from him, he gave her to Demetrius. And he was estranged from Alexander, and their enmity was openly seen.
11.13 And Ptolemy entered into Antioch, and put on himself the diadem of Asia; and he put two diadems upon his head, the *diadem* of Egypt and *that* of Asia.

Deaths of Alexander and Ptolemy

11.14 But King Alexander was in Cilicia at that time, because the *people* of those places were in revolt.
11.15 And Alexander heard, and came against him in battle; and Ptolemy led out *his army,* and met him with a strong force, and put him to flight.
11.16 And Alexander fled into Arabia, so that he might be sheltered there; but King Ptolemy was exalted.
11.17 And Zabdiel the Arab cut off Alexander's head, and sent it to Ptolemy.
11.18 And King Ptolemy died the third day afterwards; and the *men* who were in his fortresses were killed by those *who were* in the fortresses.

Demetrius son of Demetrius becomes king

Now that the other two professed kings of Syria (Alexander and Ptolemy) were dead, **Demetrius became king** (11.19).

Jonathan began besieging the Jerusalem **citadel** (which was still occupied by Israel's enemies, 1.32–36). The king commanded him to stop, but Jonathan continued the siege and met the king **at Ptolemais,** where he **found favor** (11.20–24). The king officially confirmed Jonathan's previous **honors,** the transfer of **the three provinces** from the Samaritan region **to Judea,** and the exemption of Judea from various tribute **payments** (11.26–37).

Jonathan besieges the citadel

11.19 And Demetrius became king *in the* 167th year.
11.20 In those days Jonathan gathered together the *people* of Judea, to capture the citadel *that was* in Jerusalem; and he made many devices *to use* against it.
11.21 And some *people* who hated their *own* nation, men who committed transgression, went to the king, and reported to him that Jonathan was besieging the citadel.
11.22 And he heard, *and* became angry; but when he heard *it,* he set out immediately, *and* came to Ptolemais, and wrote to Jonathan not to besiege *it,* and to meet him at Ptolemais as soon as possible, to speak with *him.*

Jonathan finds favor with Demetrius

11.23 But when Jonathan heard *this,* he commanded *them* to *keep* besieging *it:* and he chose *some* of the elders of Israel and *some* of the priests, and put himself in danger,
11.24 and taking silver and gold and clothing and many other presents, he went to Ptolemais to the king. And he found favor in his sight.

11.25 And some transgressors, among *those who were* of *his* nation, were appealing against him.
11.26 And the king dealt with him just as his predecessors had dealt with him, and exalted him in the sight of all his Friends,
11.27 and confirmed the high priesthood for him, and all *the* other honors that he had previously had, and made him a leader among his Chief Friends.
11.28 And Jonathan entreated the king to make Judea and the three provinces, and the country of Samaria, free from tribute, and promised him 300 talents.
11.29 And the king was well pleased, and wrote letters to Jonathan about all these *things*, after this manner:
11.30 "King Demetrius to *his* brother Jonathan and *the* nation of *the* Judeans: Greeting.
11.31 *This* copy of the letter that we wrote to our relative Lasthenes about you[pl], we have written also to you[pl], so that you[pl] may see *it:*
11.32 'King Demetrius to *his* father Lasthenes: Greeting.
11.33 We have determined to do good to the nation of the Judeans—*who are* our friends and are doing what is right toward us—because of their good will toward us.
11.34 We have confirmed for them the borders of Judea and the three provinces—Aphairema and Lydda and Ramathaim (*these* have been added to Judea from the region of Samaria)—and all *the places* that belong to them, for all those who sacrifice at Jerusalem, in place of the king's *taxes* which the king received from them previously each year, from the produce of the land and the forest crops.
11.35 And as for the other things that belong to us—the tithes and payments that belong to us, and the saltpits, and the crowns that belong to us—from now *on,* we will bestow all these on them.
11.36 And not one of these *things* shall be annulled, from now *on* and for ever.
11.37 Now therefore, take care[pl] to make a copy of these *things*, and let it be given to Jonathan, and let it be set up on the holy mountain, in a conspicuous place.'"

Trypho Opposes Demetrius

King Demetrius saw that the land was quiet, and he decided to discharge nearly **all his** military **forces** (11.38). This was a serious error of judgment. Not only the discharged soldiers, but also many citizens of **Antioch** turned against him. Demetrius asked Jonathan for help, promising in exchange to **cast out** Israel's enemies from the Jerusalem citadel and to **honor** the Judeans in other ways. Jonathan sent him **3,000 men,** who **saved the king** (11.41–51). But Demetrius did not keep his promises; once his own position was secure again, he **afflicted** the Judeans **greatly** (11.52–53).

Meanwhile, **Trypho** (a previous supporter of **Alexander**) went to Arabia and brought back Alexander's young son **Antiochus** to be a rival king (11.39–40, 54). He gained support from **all the** military **forces that Demetrius had** dismissed (**sent to the crows**). **They made war against** Demetrius, who **fled,** and Trypho gained control of **Antioch** (11.55–56).

The young Antiochus confirmed the honors previously given to the Judeans (11.57–58) and also established Jonathan's brother **Simon** as **army leader** in his kingdom (11.59).

Trypho goes to Antiochus son of Alexander

11.38 And King Demetrius saw that the land was quiet before him, and *that there* was no opposition to him. And he sent away all his forces, each *one* to his own place, except for the foreign forces, which he had summoned from the islands of the nations. And all the forces who *had come* from his fathers hated him.
11.39 Now Trypho was *one* of those who had been on Alexander's side previously. And he saw that all the forces were grumbling against Demetrius, and he went to Imalcue the Arab, who was bringing up Antiochus the young child of Alexander.
11.40 And he kept urging him to deliver him to him, so that he might be king in place of his father. And he told him everything that Demetrius had commanded, and the hatred with which his forces hated him. And he remained there many days.

Jonathan sends military aid to Demetrius

11.41 And Jonathan sent to King Demetrius, in order that he would cast out of Jerusalem the *people* of the citadel, and those *who were* in the fortresses; for they *kept* fighting against Israel.
11.42 And Demetrius sent to Jonathan, saying, "Not only will I do these *things* for you† and your† nation, but I will greatly honor you† and your† nation, if I find a good opportunity.
11.43 Now therefore, you† will do well to send me men who will be my allies; for all my forces have departed."
11.44 And Jonathan sent 3,000 mighty men of valor to him at Antioch. And they came to the king, and the king was glad at their coming.

The Judeans rescue Demetrius

11.45 And the *people* of the city gathered together in *the* midst of the city, about 120,000 men; and they wanted to kill the king.
11.46 And the king fled into the courtyard; and the *people* of the city seized control of the streets through the city, and began to make war.
11.47 And the king called the Judeans to help *him,* and they gathered to him, all together; and they dispersed themselves in the city, and killed that day about 100,000.
11.48 And they set the city on fire, and took much plunder that day, and saved the king.
11.49 And the *people* of the city saw that the Judeans had overpowered the city as they wanted. And they became faint-hearted, and cried out to the king with supplication, saying,
11.50 "Give† us *your* right *hand,* and let the Judeans stop making war against us and the city."

11.51 And they threw away *their* weapons and made peace. And the Judeans were honored in the sight of the king, and in the sight of all those *who were* in his kingdom. And they returned to Jerusalem, having much plunder.

Demetrius is estranged from Jonathan

11.52 And King Demetrius sat on the throne of his kingdom, and the land was quiet before him.
11.53 And he lied *in* all *the things* that he had said; and he estranged himself from Jonathan, and did not repay *him* according to the good that he had done to him. And he afflicted him greatly.

Trypho and Antiochus overpower Antioch

11.54 Now after these *things* Trypho returned, and with him *the* young child Antiochus; and he became king, and put on a diadem.
11.55 And all the forces that Demetrius had sent to the crows gathered to him. And they made war against him, and he fled and was put to flight.
11.56 And Trypho took the *war* animals, and became master of Antioch.

Antiochus honors Jonathan

11.57 And the young Antiochus wrote to Jonathan, saying, "I confirm the high priesthood to you†, and appoint you† over the four provinces, and *appoint* you† one of the king's Friends."
11.58 And he sent him golden *vessels* and a *table* service, and gave him authority to drink from golden *vessels*, and to be *clothed* in purple, and to have a golden pin.
11.59 And he made his brother Simon army leader from the region of Tyre to the borders of Egypt.

Progress in Galilee and the Philistine Region

Jonathan now **besieged** the ancient Philistine city of **Gaza** till it sought peace as its neighbor **Ashkelon** had done (11.60–62). When he heard that some of Demetrius's officials were causing unrest **in Galilee,** he left his brother **Simon** in the south and went north to Galilee himself (11.63–64). In the south, **Simon** conquered the city of **Bethzur,** one of Judea's most important enemies (11.65–66). In the north, **Jonathan** attacked the opposing forces near **Hazor** in Galilee. At first Jonathan was deserted by almost all his men, but he put his trust in the Lord and was granted an outstanding victory (11.67–74).

Gaza submits to Jonathan

11.60 And Jonathan went out and passed through *the region* beyond the River and through the cities. And all *the* forces of Syria gathered to him to be his allies. And he came to Ashkelon, and the *people* of the city met him with honor.
11.61 And he went from there to Gaza. And the *people* of Gaza shut *him* out; and he besieged it, and burned its suburbs with fire, and plundered them.

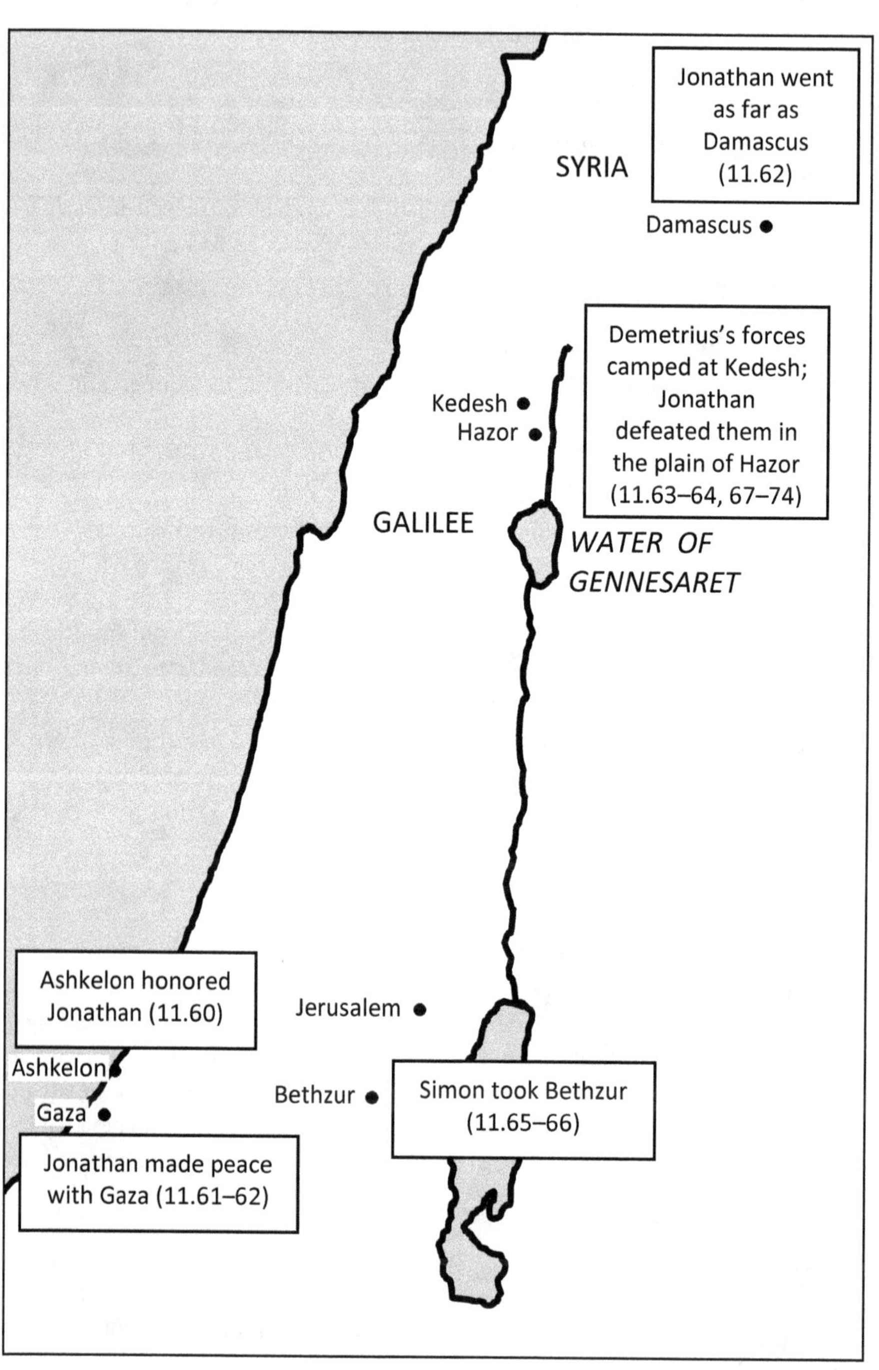

Map 17: Jonathan's activities from Gaza to Damascus (Maccabaica 11.60–74)

11.62 And the *people* of Gaza entreated Jonathan; and he gave them *his* right *hand,* and took the sons of their rulers for hostages, and sent them away to Jerusalem. And he passed through the district as far as Damascus.

Jonathan goes to Galilee

11.63 And Jonathan heard that Demetrius's leaders had come to Kedesh, which *is* in Galilee, with a great army, wanting to remove him from *his* office;
11.64 and he went to meet them, but he left his brother Simon in the country.

Bethzur submits to Simon

11.65 And Simon encamped against Bethzur, and made war against it many days, and shut them up.
11.66 And they presented a request to him that he would take *their* right *hands*; and he gave *his* to them, and he cast them out from there, and took possession of the city, and set a garrison over it.

Jonathan defeats the foreigners in Galilee

11.67 And Jonathan and his army camped near the water of Gennesaret. And they got up at dawn early *in* the morning *and* they went to the plain of Hazor.
11.68 And, behold, the foreigners' army met him in the plain; and they set an ambush against him in the mountains, but they themselves met *him* face to face.
11.69 But those *who lay* in ambush rose up out of their places, and joined battle.
11.70 And those *who were* on Jonathan's side fled; not one of them was left, except Mattathias the *son* of Absalom, and Judas the *son* of Chaphi, leaders of the forces.
11.71 And Jonathan tore his clothes, and put earth upon his head, and prayed.
11.72 And he returned against them in battle, and put them to flight, and they fled.
11.73 And the *people* on his side, who were fleeing, saw *this,* and returned to him, and pursued with him to Kedesh, to their camp; and they camped there.
11.74 And about 3,000 men of the foreigners fell on that day. And Jonathan returned to Jerusalem.

Renewed Alliances with Rome and Sparta

The Judeans had previously arranged a **friendship and alliance** with **Rome** (established by Judas, 8.17–32) and with **the Spartans** in Greece (established at an earlier time, when **Onias** was high priest of Israel and **Areus** was king of Sparta, 12.7–8, 19–23).

Now **Jonathan** decided that it was a suitable **time** to **renew** those alliances. He **sent** two men (**Numenius** and **Antipater**) **to Rome.** When they reached their destination, the Romans **gave them letters to the people in each place** that they would pass **on their way** home, so that they would return **to the land of Judah in peace** (12.1–4).

Numenius and **Antipater** also went to Sparta with **letters** of friendship from **Jonathan.** Jonathan's message of friendship **to the Spartans** is quoted (12.5–18). At the end of his letter, Jonathan attached a copy of the much earlier message from **Areus** of Sparta to **Onias** of Judea, establishing the alliance between the two nations (12.19–23).

Jonathan sends to Rome and Sparta

12.1 And Jonathan saw that the time was working to assist him, and he chose men, and sent *them* to Rome, to confirm and renew *their* friendship with them.
12.2 And he sent letters to the same effect to the Spartans and to other places.
12.3 And they went to Rome, and entered into the senate house, and said, "Jonathan the high priest, and the nation of the Judeans, have sent us to renew their friendship and alliance, as in previous times."
12.4 And they gave them letters to the *people* in each place, so that they would help them on their way to *the* land of Judah in peace.

Jonathan's letter to Sparta

12.5 And this *is* a copy of the letters that Jonathan wrote to the Spartans:
12.6 "Jonathan *the* high priest, and the eldership of the nation, and the priests, and the rest of *the* people of the Judeans, to *their* brothers *the* Spartans: Greeting.
12.7 Even before this time, letters were sent to Onias the high priest from Areus, who was king among you[pl], *saying* that you[pl] are our brothers, as the copy placed below states.
12.8 And Onias accepted with honor the man who was sent, and received the letters, in which *our* alliance and friendship was declared.
12.9 Therefore we—although *we* do not need these *things*, having *for our* encouragement the holy books that *are* in our hands—
12.10 we have tried to send *this* to renew *our* brotherhood and friendship with you[pl], so that we should not become altogether estranged from you[pl]: for much time has passed since you[pl] sent to us.
12.11 We therefore are mindful of you[pl] at all times without ceasing, in our feasts and on the other appointed days, in *the* sacrifices that we offer, and in our prayers, as it is right and fitting to be mindful of brothers.
12.12 And we are glad at your glory.
12.13 But *as for* ourselves, many afflictions and many wars have surrounded *us,* and the kings who *are* round about us have made war against us.
12.14 We were unwilling, therefore, to trouble you[pl], and the rest of our allies and friends, in these wars;
12.15 for we have the help *that is* from Heaven helping us, and we have been delivered from our enemies, and our enemies have been brought low.
12.16 We have chosen, therefore, Numenius *son* of Antiochus, and Antipater *son* of Jason, and we have sent *them* to *the* Romans, to renew *our* previous friendship and alliance with them.

12.17 We have commanded them, therefore, to go also to you[pl], and to greet you[pl] and deliver you[pl] *these* letters from us about *our* renewal *of friendship* and our brotherhood.
12.18 And now, you[pl] will do well to answer us about these *things*."

The Spartans' earlier letter to the high priest Onias

12.19 And this *is* a copy of the letters that they had sent to Onias:
12.20 "Areus, king of *the* Spartans, to Onias *the* chief priest: Greeting.
12.21 It has been found in writing, concerning the Spartans and Judeans, that they are brothers, and that they are from *the* race of Abraham.
12.22 And now, since this has come to our knowledge, you[pl] will do well to write to us about your[pl] welfare.
12.23 And we also are writing back to you[pl], *that* your[pl] livestock and possessions are ours, and ours are yours[pl]. We are commanding, therefore, that they may report to you[pl] to this effect."

FURTHER PROGRESS

The Judeans made further progress in the north and the Philistine region (continuing from the events reported in 11.60–74). **Demetrius' commanders ... returned ... to make war,** but Jonathan **met them** on the northern border between Syria and Israel, near **Hamath** (12.24–25). **The adversaries** planned a surprise attack **in the night,** but when they discovered that the Israelites were **ready for battle all night,** they were too **afraid** to attack them openly, and merely fled, leaving **fires burning in their camp** to cover their flight (12.26–30).

While he was still in the north, Jonathan defeated **the Arabs who are called Zabadeans** and passed through the district of **Damascus** (12.31–32).

In the Philistine region to the south, **Simon** revisited **Ashkelon and its neighboring fortresses.** He **set a garrison** in **Joppa** to prevent Demetrius' men from using it as a base (12.33–34). He also **fortified** the nearby city of **Hadid** (12.38).

In **Judea** itself, the people began to strengthen their **fortresses** and **make the walls of Jerusalem higher.** In particular, they built **a great mound in between the citadel and the city** (12.35–37). From this time on, the people in the citadel were no longer able to get any provisions (**buy** or **sell**), and began to starve (see 13.21–22, 49–51).

Jonathan on the Syrian border

12.24 And Jonathan heard that Demetrius's leaders had returned to make war against him, with a greater army than before.
12.25 And he moved away from Jerusalem, and met them in the region of Hamath; for he did not give them *any* opportunity to set foot in his *own* district.
12.26 And he sent spies into his camp; and they came back and reported to him that they had been planning to fall upon them *in* the night.
12.27 But when the sun was set, Jonathan commanded his *men* to keep watch and be armed, to be ready for battle all night; and he put out guards round about the camp.

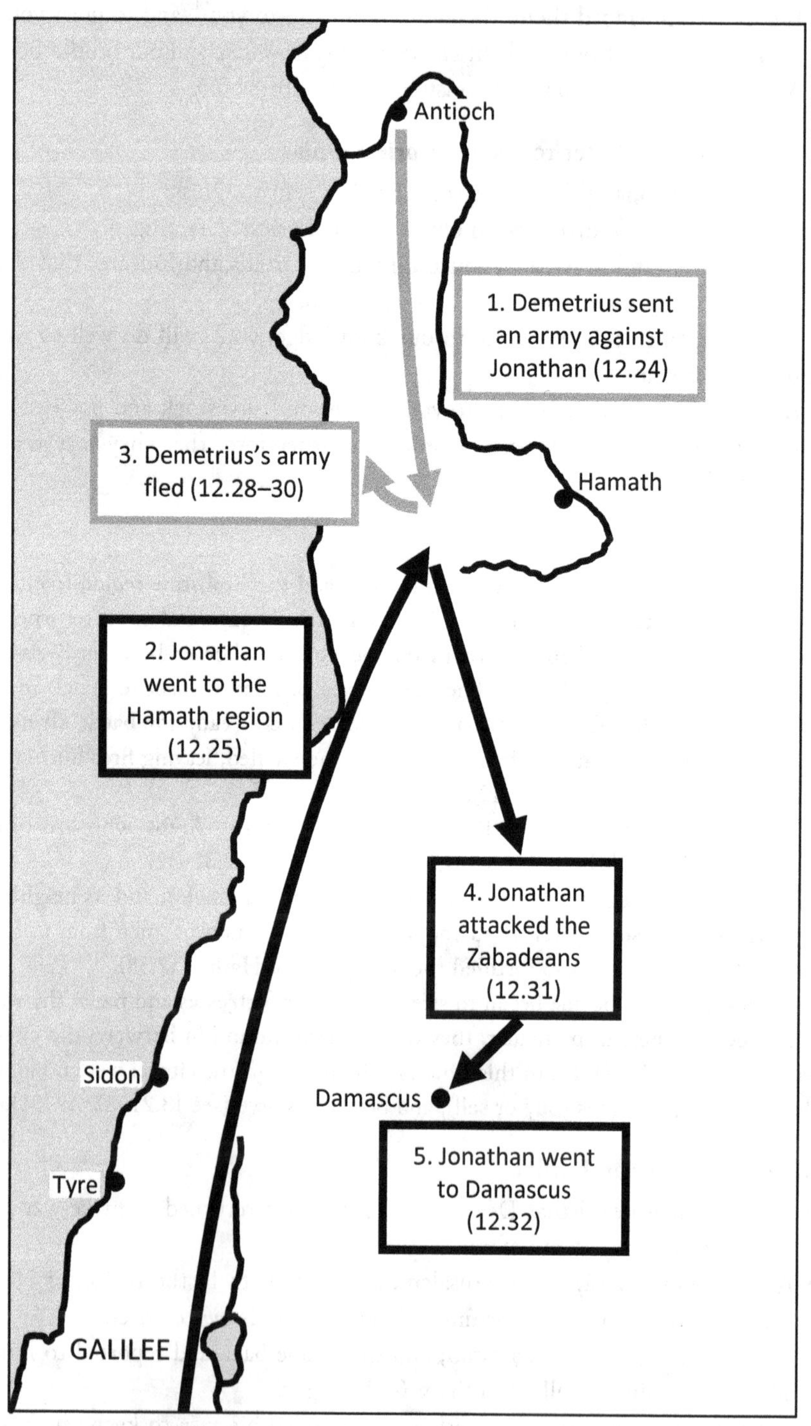

Map 18: Jonathan meets Demetrius's army at Hamath (Maccabaica 12.24–32)

12.28 And the adversaries heard that Jonathan and his *men* were ready for battle; and they were afraid, and terrified in their heart*s*, and they set up fires burning in their camp.
12.29 But Jonathan and his *men* did not know *it* till early morning; for they saw the lights burning.
12.30 And Jonathan pursued after them, but did not overtake them; for they had gone over the Eleutherus River.
12.31 And Jonathan turned aside against the Arabs who *are* called Zabadeans; and struck them down and took their plunder.
12.32 And he set out *from there and* came to Damascus, and traveled through all *that* district.

Simon in the Philistine region

12.33 And Simon went out, and traveled as far as Ashkelon, and *its* neighboring fortresses. And he turned aside to Joppa, and took possession of it;
12.34 for he had heard that they were wanting to deliver the fortress to the *men* of Demetrius. And he set a garrison there to guard it.

Building defenses in Judea

12.35 And Jonathan returned and summoned the elders of the people; and he took counsel with them to build fortresses in Judea,
12.36 and to make the walls of Jerusalem higher, and to raise a great mound in between the citadel and the city, to separate it from the city, so that it should be *all* alone, so that *people* would neither buy nor sell.
12.37 And they gathered together to build up the city; and *part* of the wall of the storm-brook on *the* east side had fallen; and he repaired the *place* that is called Chaphenatha.
12.38 And Simon built up Hadid in the Shephelah [lowland], and fortified it, and set up *its* gates and bars.

TRYPHO OPPOSES JONATHAN

Trypho had made the boy **Antiochus** king (11.54), but he himself now **sought to be king over Asia** (12.39). **He was afraid that Jonathan** might prevent him, so **he sought a way to capture** and **destroy** Jonathan (12.40).

Trypho went south toward Judea as far as **Bethshan** (12.40). **Jonathan came out to meet him** there with a large army, but Trypho **received him with honor** and told him that he had come peacefully to **give** Jonathan the city of **Ptolemais,** together with other **fortresses** and army **forces** (12.41–45). He persuaded Jonathan to send away nearly all **his forces,** taking only **1,000** men **with him,** and leaving another **2,000 in Galilee** (12.46–47).

When Jonathan reached **Ptolemais,** its **citizens… captured him** and **killed** the men who had come with him (12.48). **Trypho sent** military **forces** to kill the Judeans in **Galilee,** but his soldiers did not dare to attack them, and **turned back** (12.49–

51). Jonathan's men in Galilee returned to **Judah,** where they **mourned** over the loss of their leader and the others who had gone to Ptolemais (12.52). The surrounding **nations** thought that the Israelites now had no **ruler or helper,** and **sought to destroy them utterly** (12.53).

Trypho plans to capture Jonathan

12.39 And Trypho sought to be king over Asia and to put the diadem on himself, and to stretch out *his* hand against Antiochus the king.
12.40 And he was afraid that Jonathan might not allow him, and might make war against him; and he sought *a way* to capture him and destroy *him*. And he moved away, *and* came to Bethshan.

Jonathan meets Trypho at Bethshan

12.41 And Jonathan came out to meet him with 40,000 men chosen for battle, and came to Bethshan.
12.42 And Trypho saw that he had come with a great army. He was afraid to stretch out his hand against him,
12.43 and he received him with honor, and commended him to all his Friends, and gave him gifts, and commanded his Friends and his forces to obey him, as *him*self.

Jonathan sends away his forces

12.44 And he said to Jonathan, "Why have you† put all these people to trouble, when there is no war between us?
12.45 And now, send† them away to their homes; but choose† for yourself† a few men who will be with you†, and come† with me to Ptolemais, and I will give it over to you†, and the rest of *the* fortresses and the rest of *the* forces, and all the *people* who are over the duties. And I will turn back and depart; for this *is* why I have come."
12.46 And he trusted him, and did even as he said, and sent away his forces; and they departed into the land of Judah.
12.47 But he kept with himself 3,000 men, of whom he left 2,000 in Galilee, but 1,000 went with him.

Jonathan is captured

12.48 Now when Jonathan entered into Ptolemais, the citizens of Ptolemais shut the gates and captured him; and all the *men* who had come in with him they killed with *the* sword.
12.49 And Trypho sent forces and horse*men* to Galilee and the great plain, to destroy all Jonathan's *men*.
12.50 And they knew that he and his *men* had been taken and had perished; and they encouraged one another, and went on their way close together, ready for battle.
12.51 And *their* pursuers saw that they were ready *to fight* for their lives; and they turned back.

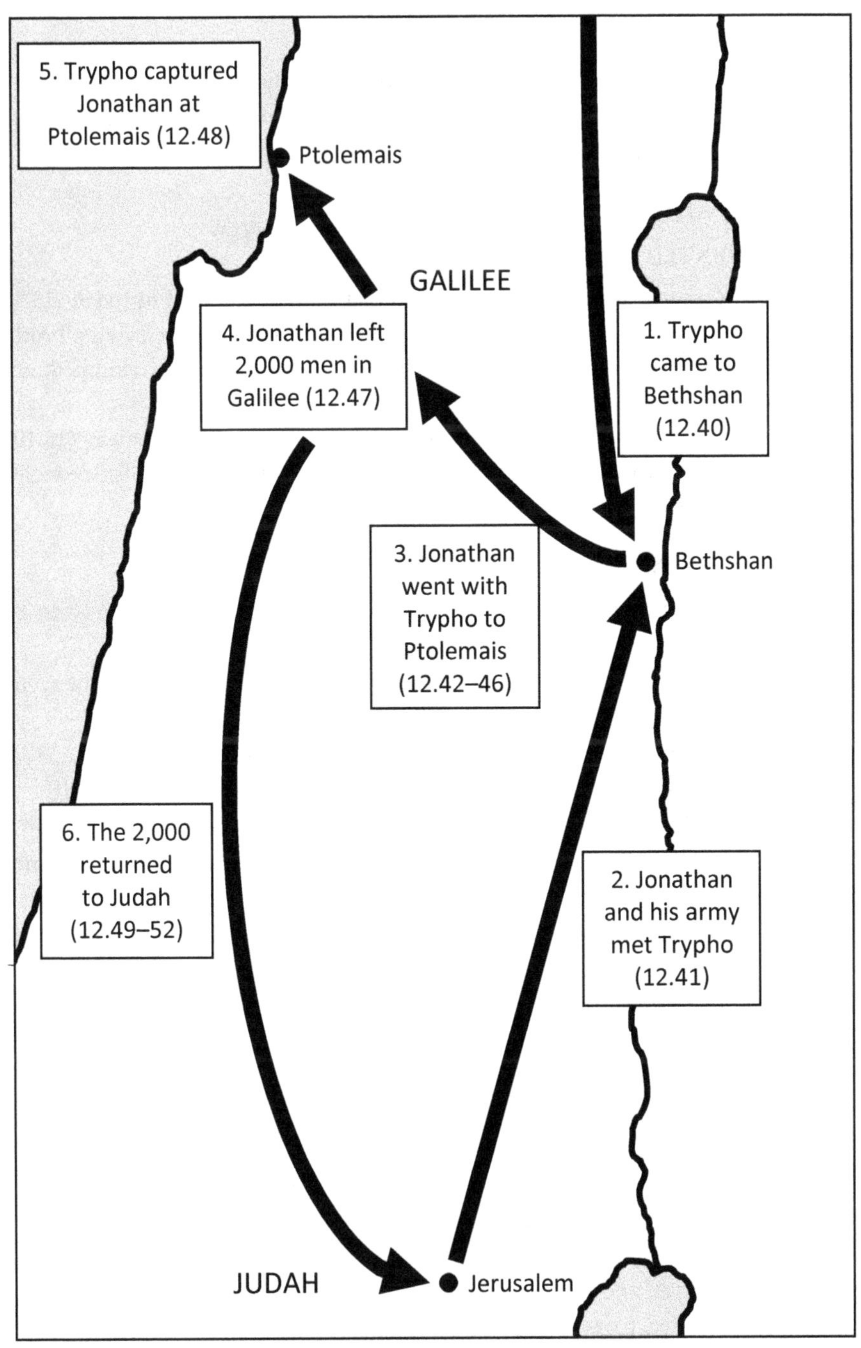
5. Trypho captured Jonathan at Ptolemais (12.48)
Ptolemais
GALILEE
4. Jonathan left 2,000 men in Galilee (12.47)
1. Trypho came to Bethshan (12.40)
3. Jonathan went with Trypho to Ptolemais (12.42–46)
Bethshan
6. The 2,000 returned to Judah (12.49–52)
2. Jonathan and his army met Trypho (12.41)
JUDAH
Jerusalem

Map 19: Trypho captures Jonathan (Maccabaica 12.39–53)

12.52 And they all came in peace into *the* land of Judah; and they mourned for Jonathan and those *who were* with him, and they were very much afraid; and all Israel mourned *with* a great mourning.
12.53 And all the nations *that were* round about them sought to destroy them utterly: for they said, "They have no ruler or helper; now therefore, let us make war against them, and take away their memory from among Men."

Simon (13.1–16.22)

SIMON IS APPOINTED LEADER

After he had captured Jonathan, **Trypho** planned to invade the **land of Judah** (13.1). The **people** of Judah were **very much afraid** (13.2), but Jonathan's remaining brother **Simon** encouraged them (13.3–6). **The spirit of the people was rekindled,** and they chose Simon to be their new **leader** (13.7–9).

Simon **hastened** to strengthen the land's defenses, fortifying **Jerusalem** (13.10), and installing a **great army** in **Joppa** (13.11), one of the cities in the Philistine region that had recently surrendered to the Judeans (cf. 10.75–76; 12.33–34).

Simon encourages the people

13.1 And Simon heard that Trypho had gathered together a mighty army to come into *the* land of Judah, and destroy it utterly.
13.2 And he saw that the people trembled and were very much afraid; and he went up to Jerusalem, and gathered the people together;
13.3 and he encouraged them, and said to them, "You[pl] *your*selves know all *the things* that I and my brothers and my father's house have done for the laws and the holy *place*s, and the battles and the distresses that we have seen.
13.4 Because of this, all my brothers have perished for Israel's sake, and I alone am left.
13.5 And now be it far from me to spare my *own* life in any time of affliction; for I am not better than my brothers.
13.6 But I will take vengeance for my nation, and for the holy *place*s, and for your wives and children; because all the nations have gathered to destroy us, because of *their* hatred."

The people choose Simon as their leader

13.7 And the spirit of the people was rekindled when they heard these words.
13.8 And they answered with a loud voice, saying, "You[†] are our leader instead of Judas and Jonathan your[†] brother.
13.9 Fight[†] our battles; and all that you[†] say to us, we will do."
13.10 And he gathered together all the men of war, and hastened to finish the walls of Jerusalem, and fortified it round about.
13.11 And he sent Jonathan the *son* of Absalom, and with him a great army, to Joppa. And he cast out those who were there, and he remained there in it.

TRYPHO AND SIMON

Trypho moved south along the coast from Syria toward the **land of Judah. Jonathan** was still his prisoner (13.12).

Simon camped at **Hadid** in the coastal lowland (cf. 12.38), blocking Trypho's way (13.13). Avoiding **battle,** Trypho claimed that he was **holding** Jonathan only because some **taxes** had not been paid. If Simon sent a large sum of money (**100 talents of silver**) and **two of** Jonathan's **sons as hostages,** Trypho promised that he would **set** Jonathan **free** (13.14–16).

Simon knew that Trypho could not be trusted, but he still **sent the children and the 100 talents,** in order to avoid stirring up **great enmity among the people** of Judea. Nevertheless, Trypho **utterly lied, and did not set Jonathan free** (13.17–19).

Trypho tried **to invade the land** of Judea by a different route, but wherever he went, **Simon and his army** kept blocking his way (13.20). **The people of the citadel** in Jerusalem were being besieged (cf. 12.36), and they asked Trypho **to send them food,** but he was not able to come because at the crucial time there was **very much snow** (13.21–22).

In the end Trypho merely **moved away** through **the land of Gilead** back to **his** own **land,** Syria. On the way, **he killed Jonathan** (13.23–24).

Simon **buried** Jonathan **at Modein, the city of his fathers** (cf. 2.1), where he extended **the tomb** of his family as a memorial (13.25–30).

Trypho continued with his plan (cf. 12.39). He killed **the young king Antiochus,** and **became king over** the Seleucid kingdom (**Asia**) himself (13.31–32).

Trypho asks for money and hostages

13.12 And Trypho moved away from Ptolemais with a mighty army to enter into *the* land of Judah, and Jonathan *was* with him under guard.
13.13 But Simon camped at Hadid, opposite the plain.
13.14 And Trypho knew that Simon had risen up in place of his brother Jonathan, and was going to join battle with him. And he sent ambassadors to him, saying,
13.15 "*It is* for *the* money that Jonathan your[†] brother owed for the king's *taxe*s, because of *the* duties he had, *that* we have been holding him.
13.16 And now, send[†] 100 talents of silver, and two of his sons *as* hostages, so that when he is set free he may not rebel against us, and we will set him free."

Simon sends them

13.17 And Simon knew that they spoke to him deceitfully; and he sent for the money and the children, lest he should arouse great enmity among the people,
13.18 *who might be* saying, "Because I did not send him the money and the children, he perished."
13.19 And he sent the children and the 100 talents. And he utterly lied, and did not set Jonathan free.

Trypho seeks to destroy Judea

13.20 And after this Trypho came to invade the land and destroy it. And he went round about *by the* way that *goes* to Adora. And Simon and his army went opposite him to every place where he went.
13.21 Now the *people* of the citadel sent ambassadors to Trypho, hurrying him to come to them through the desert, and to send them food.
13.22 And Trypho got all his horse ready to come. And in that night *there* was very much snow; and because of the snow, he did not come. And he moved away, and went into the land of Gilead.

Trypho kills Jonathan

13.23 But when he came near Baskema, he killed Jonathan; and he was buried there.
13.24 And Trypho turned back, and went away into his *own* land.
13.25 And Simon sent, and took the bones of Jonathan his brother, and buried him at Modein, *the* city of his fathers.
13.26 And all Israel made a great lamentation for him, and mourned for him many days.

The tomb raised by Simon

13.27 And Simon built upon the tomb of his father and brothers, and raised it high to the sight, with polished stone behind and in front.
13.28 And he set up seven pyramids, one opposite another, for *his* father and mother and four brothers.
13.29 And he made devices for these, placing great pillars around *them;* and on the pillars he made all *kinds of* weaponry for a lasting memorial; and beside all the *kinds of* weaponry, carved ships, to be seen by all those who sail the sea.
13.30 This *is* the tomb that he made at Modein, *and it is there* to this day.

Trypho becomes king of Asia

13.31 Now Trypho dealt deceitfully with the young king Antiochus; and he killed him,
13.32 and became king in place of him, and put on himself the diadem of Asia. And he brought great harm on the land.

JUDEA IS FREED FROM THE NATIONS

Simon continued to fortify **Judea** (13.33), and began negotiating with Trypho's opponent, **King Demetrius** (13.34). **Demetrius** agreed to **make a great peace** with the Judeans and **grant** them **freedom** from their taxes and other obligations toward him. He also authorized the Judeans to build and possess their own **fortresses** (13.35–40).

At last **the yoke of the nations was lifted up from Israel,** and the people began dating their records by the years of their own **leader,** Simon, instead of by the years of any foreign king (13.41–42).

In the Philistine region, Simon besieged and recaptured the enemy city of **Gaza.** He **cleansed** the city from **all** forms of **uncleanness,** and **settled it with** faithful Israelites who **would keep** God's **Law** (13.43–48).

In Jerusalem, the people inside the besieged **citadel** eventually became so **hungry** that they surrendered. Simon **cast them out . . . and cleansed the citadel from its pollutions.** A **great enemy** of Israel had been overcome at last (13.49–52).

When Simon's son **John** became a **man,** his father **made him leader of all the** army **forces** (13.53).

Demetrius now **went into** the land of **Media,** hoping to gather **help** for a **war against** his rival king, **Trypho** (14.1). But his attempt to improve his position ruined it. Forces sent by **Arsaces,** the current **king** of Media, captured Demetrius and kept him **under guard** (14.2–3).

Demetrius makes peace with Simon

13.33 And Simon built up the fortresses of Judea, and walled *them* around with high towers and great walls, and gates and bars; and he stored food in the fortresses.
13.34 And Simon chose men, and sent *them* to King Demetrius, to grant freedom to the district, because all that Trypho did was to plunder.
13.35 And King Demetrius sent to him according to these words, and answered him, and wrote him a letter like this:
13.36 "King Demetrius to Simon, high priest and kings' Friend, and to the elders and nation of the Judeans: Greeting.
13.37 We have received the golden crown and palm branch that you^{pl} sent; and we are ready to make a great peace with you^{pl}, and to write our officers to grant freedom to you^{pl}.
13.38 And whatever things we have confirmed to you^{pl}, they are confirmed; and the fortresses that you^{pl} have built, let them be your^{pl} *own.*
13.39 But we forgive *any* oversights and faults *committed* before this day, and the crowns that you^{pl} owed *us;* and if any other *thing* was being taxed in Jerusalem, let it be taxed no longer.

The yoke of the nations is removed

13.40 And if any of you^{pl} *are* suitable to be enrolled among our attendants, let them be enrolled, and let *there* be peace between us."
13.41 *In the* 170th year, the yoke of the nations was lifted up from Israel.
13.42 And the people began to write in *their* writings and contracts: "*In the* first year of Simon, great high priest and army commander and leader of *the* Judeans."

Gaza submits to Simon

13.43 In those days he camped against Gaza, and surrounded it with camps; and he made a siege engine, and brought *it* up to the city, and attacked a tower and took possession of *it.*
13.44 And those *who were* in the siege engine leaped out into the city; and *there* was a great uproar in the city.

13.45 And the *men* of the city tore their clothes, and went up on the wall with *their* wives and children, and cried out with a loud voice, asking Simon to give them *the* right hand.
13.46 And they said, "Do not treat[†] us according to our wickedness, but according to your[†] mercy."
13.47 And Simon was reconciled to them, and did not make war against them. And he cast them out of the city, and cleansed the houses in which the idols had been; and so he entered into it *with* hymns and blessings.
13.48 And he cast out of it all uncleanness, and settled it with men who would keep the Law. And he made it stronger *than it was before,* and built in it a dwelling-place for *him*self.

The citadel is cleansed

13.49 But the *people* of the citadel in Jerusalem were hindered from going out and going into the district, and buying and selling. And they were very hungry, and a great *number* of them were perishing through hunger.
13.50 And they cried out to Simon to take *their* right *hand*s; and he gave *his* to them. And he cast them out from there, and cleansed the citadel from *its* pollutions.
13.51 And he entered into it on the 23rd *day* of the second month *in the* 171st year, with praise and palm branches, and with lyres and cymbals and harps and hymns and songs: because a great enemy had been destroyed out of Israel.
13.52 And he ordained that they should keep that day every year with gladness. And he made the temple mountain alongside the citadel stronger *than it was before,* and there he dwelt, he and his *men.*

John son of Simon

13.53 And Simon saw that John his son was a man, and he made him leader of all the forces; and he dwelt in Gezer.

Demetrius is captured in Media

14.1 And in *the* 172nd year King Demetrius gathered his forces together, and went into Media, to get help for *him*self, so that he might make war against Trypho.
14.2 And Arsaces, the king of Persia and Media, heard that Demetrius had come into his borders; and he sent one of his commanders to take him alive.
14.3 And he went and defeated the army of Demetrius, and captured him, and brought him to Arsaces; and he put him under guard.

ISRAEL AND THE NATIONS

At this point the Maccabean History provides an overview of **the days of Simon** (14.4–15), mirroring its overview of the days of Judas Maccabeus (placed in a similar position near the start of the book, 3.1–9).

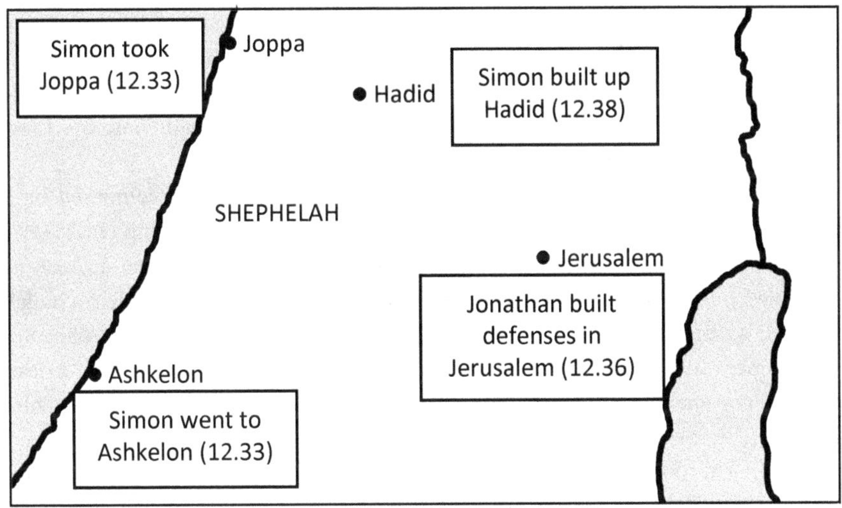

Map 20: Fortresses built by Jonathan and Simon (Maccabaica 12.33–38)

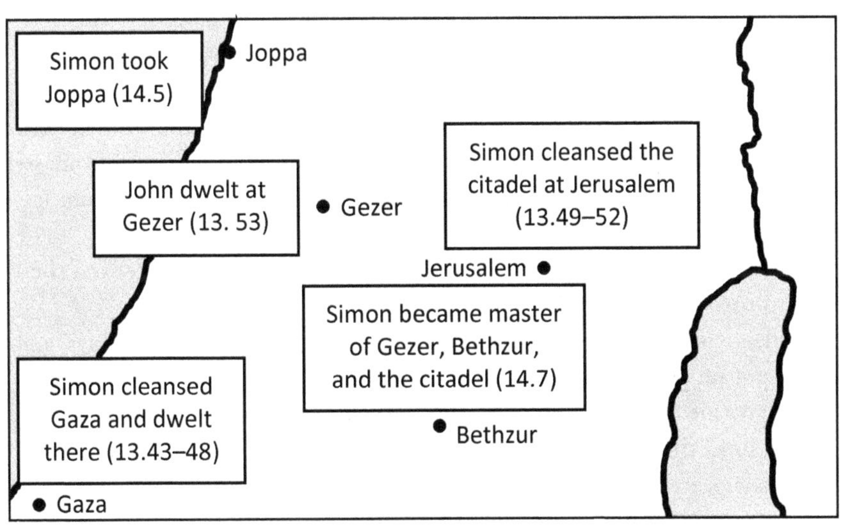

Map 21: Activities of Simon (Maccabaica 13.43–14.7)

The time of Simon was a time of **peace** and prosperity (14.4, 8, 10–12), when no one **made war against** Israel (14.7, 13). Simon **sought the good,** not of himself, but **of his nation** (14.4). He **enlarged** its **boundaries** and captured the last remaining enemy strongholds in the region (including **Joppa, Gezer, Bethzur,** and the Jerusalem **citadel;** 14.5–7). He cleansed the land of **uncleannesses** and **wicked** people (14.7, 14). He cared for **people who had been brought low, sought out the Law,** and **glorified** the temple (**the holy places;** 14.14–15).

Additional testimony to these facts is preserved in a document composed by **a great assembly** of the nation during the **third year** of Simon's leadership (14.25–49). The document tells how Simon and his family **glorified their nation** and drove away its **enemies** (including those in **Bethzur, Joppa, Gezer,** and the Jerusalem **citadel,** 14.29–37), so that even foreign rulers treated the Judeans **with honor** (14.38–40). The document also records that Simon had been appointed as **leader, high priest,** and **army commander** of Judea, and that no one had authority to oppose him (14.41–45). Simon and his subjects were alike **well pleased** with these decisions (14.46–47). The document was preserved on **bronze tablets . . . in a conspicuous place** in Mount Zion (14.26, 48–49).

Simon was appointed as leader and high priest **until a faithful prophet should rise up** (14.41; cf. Deut 18.15–18; Acts 3.22–23).

Meanwhile, hearing that Simon had replaced Jonathan, the Judeans' allies at **Rome** and **Sparta** wrote to renew their **friendship and alliance** (Maccabaica 14.16–24).

Israel in the time of Simon

14.4 And the land of Judah had rest all the days of Simon; and he sought *the* good of his nation; and his authority and his glory pleased them, all *his* days.

14.5 And with all his glory, he took Joppa for a harbor, and made an entrance to the islands of the sea;

14.6 and he enlarged the borders of his nation, and gained possession of the district,

14.7 and gathered together a great number of captives. And he became master of Gezer, and Bethzur, and the citadel, and he put away the uncleannesses from it. And *there* was no one who resisted him.

14.8 And they farmed their land in peace; and the land gave its produce, and the trees of the plains their fruit.

14.9 *The* elders sat in the streets; all *of them* together spoke about good *things*, and the young men put on glory and robes of war.

14.10 They provided food for the cities, and furnished themselves with implements of fortification, until the name of his glory was named to *the* end of *the* earth.

14.11 He made peace in the land, and Israel rejoiced *with* great joy.

14.12 And everyone sat under his vine and his fig tree, and *there* was no one to terrify them;

14.13 and those who made war against them in the land ceased; and the kings were shattered in those days.

14.14 And he strengthened all those of his people *who had been* brought low; he sought out the Law, and put away everyone who was committing transgression and wicked.
14.15 And he glorified the holy *place*s, and multiplied the vessels of the holy *place*s.

Messages from Rome and Sparta

14.16 And it was heard at Rome that Jonathan was dead; and as far as Sparta, and they were very sorrowful.
14.17 But when they heard that his brother Simon had become high priest in place of him, and held power over the district and its cities,
14.18 they wrote to him on bronze tablets, to renew with him *the* friendship and alliance that they had established with Judas and Jonathan his brothers.
14.19 And they were read before the congregation at Jerusalem.

A letter from the Spartans

14.20 And this is a copy of the letters that the Spartans sent:
"*The* rulers of *the* Spartans, and the city, to Simon *the* chief priest, and to the elders and priests and the rest of the Judean people *our* brothers: Greeting.
14.21 The ambassadors who were sent to our people told us about your[pl] glory and honor; and we were glad at their coming.
14.22 And we recorded the things said by them in the records of the people, as follows: 'Numenius *son* of Antiochus, and Antipater *son* of Jason, ambassadors of *the* Judeans, came to us to renew *their* friendship with us.
14.23 And it pleased the people to accept the men with honor, and to place a copy of their words in the books available to the people, so that the people of the Spartans would have a memorial *of it;* and they wrote a copy of these things to Simon the high priest.'"

Another mission to Rome

14.24 After this, Simon sent Numenius to Rome with a great golden shield weighing 1,000 minas, to confirm the alliance with them.

The people's inscription in Zion

14.25 But when the people heard these *thing*s, they said, "What thanks shall we give to Simon and his sons?
14.26 for he and his brothers and his father's house have remained steadfast; and he has fought Israel's enemies *away* from them; and they have established freedom for it." And they wrote on bronze tablets, and set *them* on pillars in Mount Zion;
14.27 and this *is* a copy of the writing:
"*On the* 18th *day* of Elul *in the* 172nd year (and this *is the* third year of Simon *the* great high priest), in Hasar-am-el [*the* courtyard of *the* people of God],
14.28 in a great assembly of priests and people and leaders of *the* nation and elders of the district, he made *this* known to us:

14.29 'Since *there* have often been wars in the district, but Simon the son of Mattathias, priest of the sons of Joiarib, and his brothers, put themselves in danger, and stood against the enemies of their nation, so that their holy *place*s and the Law would be established; and they glorified their nation with great glory;
14.30 and Jonathan gathered together his nation, and became their high priest, and was added to his people;
14.31 and their enemies wanted to invade their district and stretch out *their* hands against their holy *place*s;
14.32 then Simon rose up against them and made war for his nation; and he spent much money of *his* own, and armed the valiant men of his nation, and gave them wages;
14.33 and he fortified the cities of Judea, and Bethzur (which *is* on the borders of Judea, where the weapons of *their* enemies had previously been), and he set there a garrison of Judean men;
14.34 and he fortified Joppa (which *is* near the sea) and Gezer (which *is* on the borders of Ashdod, where *their* enemies had previously been dwelling), and he settled Judeans there, and placed in them all *the thing*s that were suitable for restoring them;
14.35 and the people saw Simon's faithfulness, and the glory that he determined to provide for his nation, and they made him their leader and high priest, because he *had* done all these *thing*s, and the righteousness and faithfulness that he kept toward his nation, and *how* he sought out every way to exalt his people:
14.36 and in his days it prospered in his hands *for* the nations to be put away out of their district, and those *who were* in the city of David, in Jerusalem (who had made themselves a citadel, out of which they had gone and polluted *the* surroundings of the holy *place*s, doing great harm to *their* purity);
14.37 and he settled Judean men in it, and fortified it for *the* security of the district and city, and raised high the walls of Jerusalem;
14.38 and King Demetrius confirmed the high priesthood for him according to these *thing*s,
14.39 and made him *one* of his Friends, and honored him with great honor;
14.40 for he had heard that the Judeans had been publicly declared friends and allies and brothers by the Romans, and that they had met the ambassadors of Simon with honor;
14.41 and that the Judeans and priests had been well pleased *for* Simon to be their leader and high priest for ever, until a faithful prophet *should* rise up,
14.42 and to be their army commander, and that he should take care of the holy *place*s, and *would* set *people* over their works, and over the district and the weapons and the fortresses;
14.43 and that he should take care of the holy *place*s, and that he should be obeyed by everyone, and that all *the* writings in the district should be written in his name, and that he should be clothed in purple and wear gold;
14.44 and it would not be lawful for anyone of the people or priests to set aside any of these *thing*s or contradict his words, or to gather an assembly in the district without him, or to be clothed in purple or wear a golden pin;

14.45 but whoever should do anything beyond this, or set aside any of these things, would be held for punishment.
14.46 And all the people were well pleased to assign Simon *the right* to do according to these words;
14.47 and Simon accepted, and was well pleased to be high priest and army commander and governor of the Judeans and of *the* priests, and to protect all *of them*."
14.48 And they commanded to place this writing on bronze tablets and set them up within the surroundings of the holy *place*s, in a conspicuous place;
14.49 and to place copies of them in the storage-place, so that Simon and his sons might have *them*.

Antiochus son of Demetrius

While Demetrius was still in captivity (14.2–3), another member of the Seleucid royal family, **Antiochus son of Demetrius,** came from **the islands of the sea** to take possession of the kingdom. He wrote to Simon beforehand, approving the **remissions** and **gifts** that had been granted to Judea by his predecessors, and promising to **honor** the nation **with great honor** (15.1–9).

When **Antiochus** arrived in Syria, **all the** military **forces** supported him and deserted **Trypho,** who **fled** into the city of **Dor,** on the coast (15.10–12). Antiochus besieged him there (15.13–14).

Meanwhile, Simon had sent Numenius to Rome (14.24). **Numenius** now returned with **letters** from Rome, which strongly supported the Judeans and warned many **kings and... districts** in the eastern Mediterranean **not** to **make war against them** or assist their enemies in any way (15.15–24).

Simon **sent... allies** and **equipment** to help **Antiochus** against **Trypho** (15.25–26). However, Antiochus now **set aside all the things that he had** promised the Judeans (15.27). He sent one of his officers, **Athenobius,** with a message accusing the Judeans of seizing land that belonged to Antiochus and was **outside the boundaries of Judea.** In particular, he told the Judeans either to **deliver up** the cities of **Joppa and Gezer,** or else pay a very large amount of **silver** for them (15.28–31). Athenobius **was amazed** to see how Simon was prospering (15.32).

Simon replied that the Judeans had taken nothing that belonged to other nations (**strangers**). They had merely regained Israelite land (part of their **fathers' inheritance**) that had been seized by their enemies. Even so, Simon generously offered to pay a large amount (**100 talents**) for the cities of **Joppa and Gezer** (15.33–35).

Athenobius reported this answer to King Antiochus, who became **extremely angry** (15.36) and sent an army leader, **Cendebeus,** to **make war against the people** of Judea (while Antiochus himself continued his campaign against **Trypho;** 15.37–39).

Cendebeus installed his military **forces** in the nearby cities of **Jabneh** and **Kedron,** and began to capture and **kill** some of the Judeans (15.40–41).

Simon's son **John** now came from his home at **Gezer** (13.53) to warn **his father** about the activities of **Cendebeus** (16.1). Simon appointed John and another son, **Judas,** to **fight for** their **nation** (16.2–3).

Near the city of **Modein,** the Judean army encountered Cendebeus and his **great army** (16.4–7). In the battle, **Cendebeus and his army were put to flight;** many **fell,** and the rest **fled** (16.8). **John pursued after them,** and destroyed many of them by burning the **towers** into which they had **fled.** Once more there was **peace** in **Judea** (16.9–10).

Antiochus son of Demetrius writes to Simon

15.1 And Antiochus son of Demetrius the king sent letters from the islands of the sea to Simon, high priest and governor of the Judeans, and to all the nation;
15.2 and their contents were like this:
"King Antiochus to Simon, chief priest and governor, and to the nation of the Judeans: Greeting.
15.3 Since some plague-bearers have overpowered the kingdom of our fathers, but I want to take action against *them* for the kingdom, so that I may restore it as it was previously; and I have summoned a multitude of foreign forces, and have prepared warships;
15.4 and I want to go through the district, so that I may pursue those who have destroyed our district, and those who have made many cities in my kingdom desolate;
15.5 now therefore, I confirm to you[†] all the remissions that the kings before me released for you[†], and whatever other gifts they released for you[†];
15.6 and I permit you[†] to make *your* own coinage *as* legal tender for your[†] district,
15.7 and *for* Jerusalem and the holy *places* to be free. And *as for* all the weapons that you[†] have prepared, and the fortresses that you[†] have built and are holding—let them remain yours[†].
15.8 And *as for* everything that is owed to *the* king, or will be *owed* to *the* king from now *on* and for ever—let it be released for you[†].
15.9 And when we have established our kingdom, we will honor you[†] and your[†] nation and the temple with great honor, so that your[pl] honor *will* be visible in all the earth."

Antiochus expels Trypho

15.10 *In the* 174th year, Antiochus came out into the land of his fathers; and all the forces came together to him, so that *there were* few left with Trypho.
15.11 And Antiochus pursued him; and, as *he* fled, he came to Dor, *which is* near the sea:
15.12 for he knew that evils had gathered against him, and *his* forces had forsaken him.
15.13 And Antiochus camped against Dor, and with him 120,000 men of war and 8,000 horse.
15.14 And he surrounded the city, and the ships joined battle from *the* sea. And he oppressed the city by land and sea, and did not allow anyone to go out or in.

Letters from Rome

15.15 And Numenius and his *company* came from Rome, having letters to the kings and to districts, in which these things were written:
15.16 "Lucius, consul of *the* Romans, to King Ptolemy: Greeting.
15.17 The Judean ambassadors have come to us *as* our friends and allies, renewing *our* earlier friendship and alliance, having been sent by Simon the high priest, and by the people of the Judeans.
15.18 And they brought a golden shield *weighing* 1,000 minas.
15.19 Therefore it has pleased us to write to the kings and districts, so that they may not seek evil *thing*s for them, nor make war against them and their cities and their district, nor be allies with those who make war against them.
15.20 And it has seemed good to us to receive the shield from them.
15.21 Therefore, if any plague-bearers have fled from their district to you[pl], deliver them to Simon the high priest, so that he may take vengeance *on* them according to their law."
15.22 And he wrote these *thing*s to Demetrius the king, and to Attalus and Ariarathes and Arsaces,
15.23 and to all the districts, and to Sampsaces and *the* Spartans, and to Delos and Myndus and Sicyon and Caria and Samos and Pamphylia and Lycia and Halicarnassus and Rhodes and Phaselis and Cos and Side, and to Arvad and Gortyna and Cnidus and Cyprus and Cyrene.
15.24 And they wrote a copy of these *thing*s to Simon the high priest.

Antiochus is estranged from Simon

15.25 But Antiochus the king camped against Dor, in *its* outer *district,* bringing *his* powers near it continually, and making devices *of war.* And he shut Trypho up *from* going in or out.
15.26 And Simon sent him 2,000 chosen men to be his allies, and silver and gold and much equipment.
15.27 And he was not willing to receive them, but set aside all *the thing*s that he had previously agreed with him; and he was estranged from him.
15.28 And he sent to him Athenobius, one of his Friends, to confer with him, saying, "You[pl] have overpowered Joppa and Gezer and the citadel that *is* in Jerusalem, cities of my kingdom.
15.29 You[pl] have made their borders desolate, and done[pl] great harm in the land, and gained dominion[pl] over many places in my kingdom.
15.30 Now therefore, deliver up[pl] the cities that you[pl] have taken, and the tributes of the places where you[pl] have gained dominion, outside the borders of Judea;
15.31 or else give[pl] *me* 500 talents of silver for them; and 500 other talents for the harm that you[pl] have done, and *for* the tributes of the cities; or else we will come and overpower you[pl] in battle."

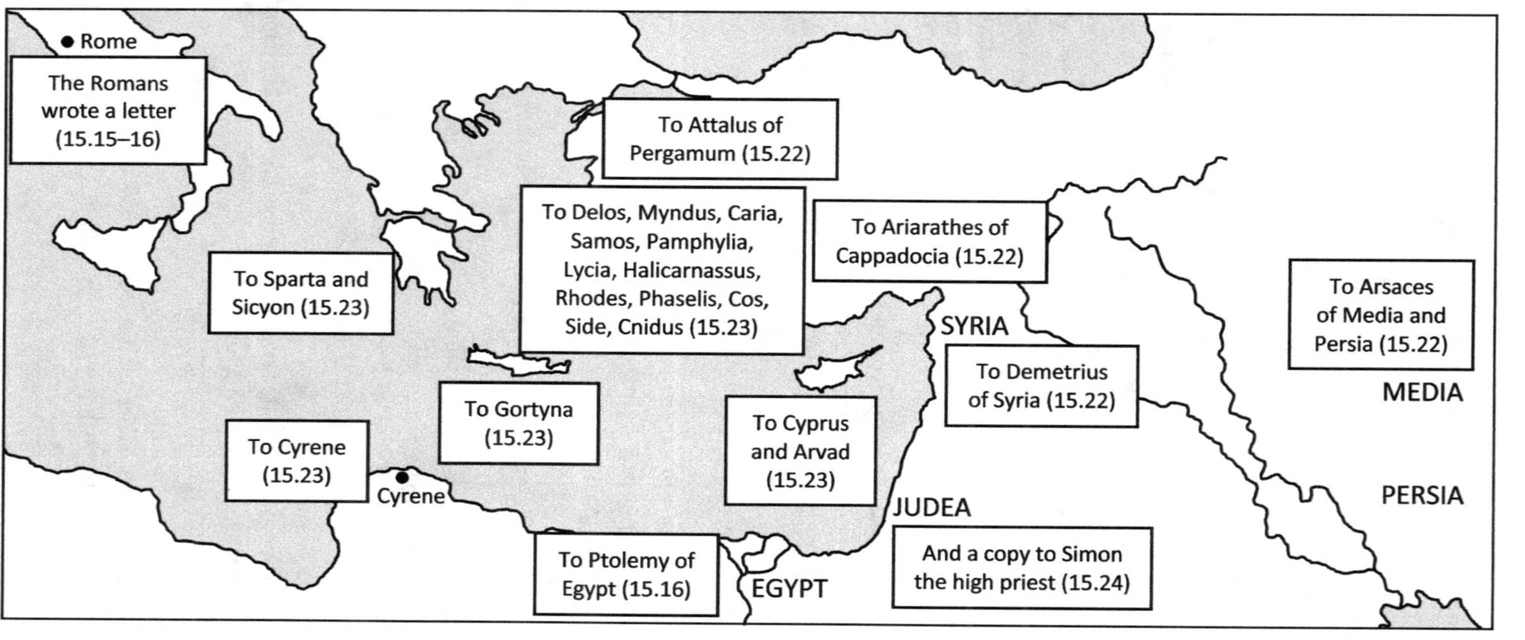

Map 22: Places receiving letters from Rome (Maccabaica 15.15–24)

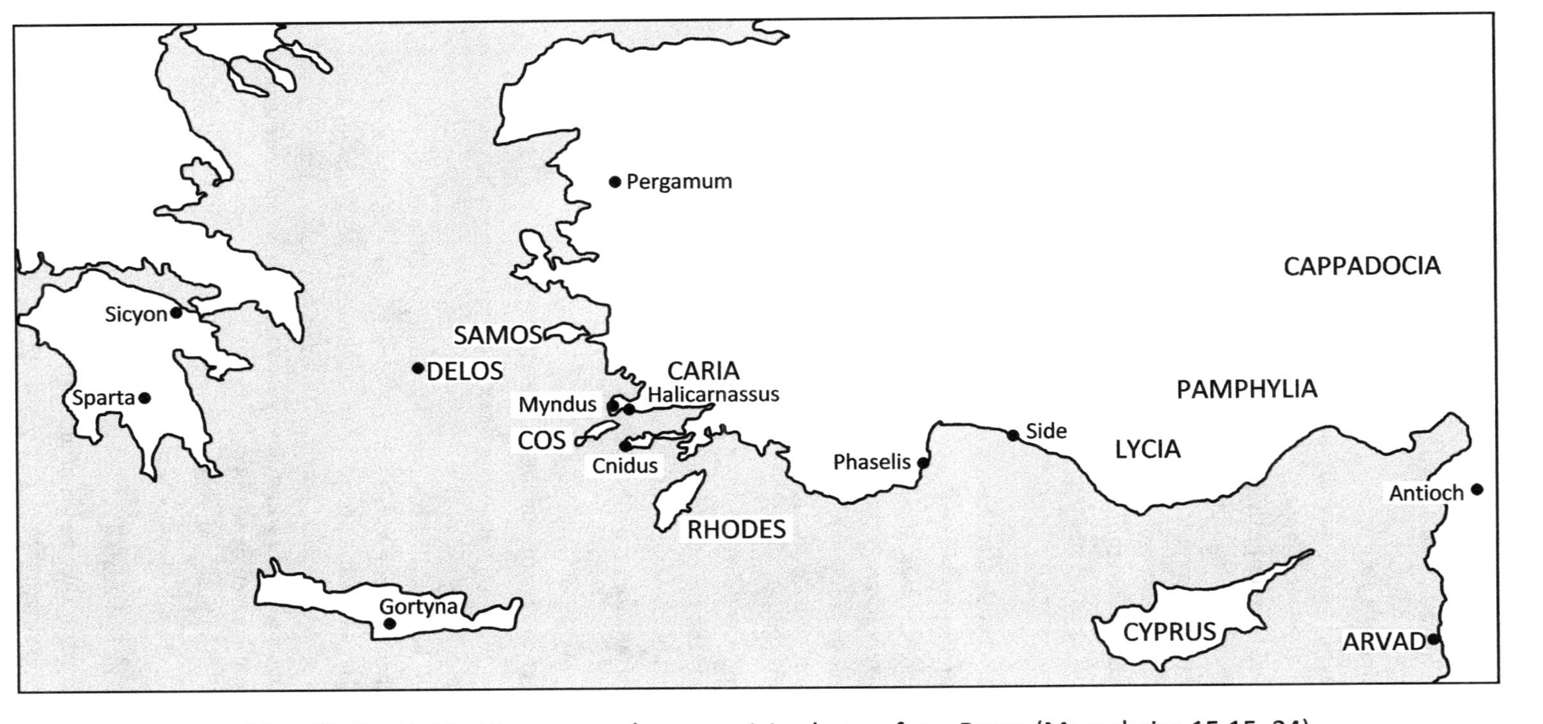

Map 23: North Mediterranean places receiving letters from Rome (Maccabaica 15.15–24)

15.32 And Athenobius the king's Friend came to Jerusalem; and he saw the glory of Simon, and *his* cabinet *with* gold vessels and silver vessels, and *the* mighty state *that he kept;* and he was amazed. And he told him the king's words.

Simon defends Judea

15.33 And Simon answered, *and* said to him, "We have neither taken strangers' land nor held strangers' *property,* but *only that* of our fathers' inheritance. But for some time it had been unjustly possessed by our enemies.
15.34 But we, having opportunity, are holding our fathers' inheritance.
15.35 But concerning Joppa and Gezer, which you[†] are asking for, they did great harm among the people and *in* our district; we will give 100 talents *for* them." And he did not answer him anything,
15.36 but returned in a rage to the king, and told him these words, and the glory of Simon, and everything that he had seen. And the king was extremely angry.

Antiochus sends Cendebeus against Judea

15.37 But Trypho boarded a ship *and* fled to Orthosia.
15.38 And the king appointed Cendebeus *as* chief army commander of the seaside, and gave him forces *of* footsoldiers and horse.
15.39 And he commanded him to camp opposite Judea, and commanded him to build up Kedron and fortify the gates, and to make war against the people. But the king pursued Trypho.
15.40 And Cendebeus came to Jabneh, and began to stir up the people and invade Judea and take the people captive and kill them.
15.41 And he built up Kedron, and set apart horsemen and forces there, so that, when *they* went out, they would depart *on* the pathways of Judea, just as the king had commanded him.

Simon sends his sons against Cendebeus

16.1 And John went up from Gezer, and told Simon his father what Cendebeus had been doing.
16.2 And Simon called his two older sons, Judas and John, and said to them, "I and my brothers and my father's house have fought the battles of Israel from our youth until today; and it has prospered in our hands to deliver Israel many times.
16.3 But now I am old, but you[pl], by *His* mercy, you are of a sufficient age. Be[pl] in place of me and my brothers, and go out[pl] *and* fight[pl] for our nation; and may the help *that is* from Heaven be with you[pl]."
16.4 And he chose out of the district 20,000 men of war and horsemen, and they went against Cendebeus, and slept at Modein.

Cendebeus is defeated

16.5 And when they had risen up early *in* the morning, they went into the plain; and, behold, a great army *came* to meet them—footsoldiers and horsemen; and *there* was a

storm-brook between them.
16.6 And he and his people camped opposite them. And he saw that the people were afraid to cross over the storm-brook; and he crossed over first, and the men saw him, and crossed over behind him.
16.7 And he divided the people, and *set* the horsemen in *the* midst of the footsoldiers; but *the* enemies' horse were very many.
16.8 And they trumpeted with the sacred trumpets; and Cendebeus and his army were put to flight. And many of them fell wounded; but those who were left fled into the fortress.
16.9 Then Judas, John's brother, was wounded. But John pursued after them till he came to Kedron, which he had built up.
16.10 and they fled into the towers *that were* in the fields of Ashdod. And he burned it with fire, and about 2,000 of their men fell. And he returned to Judea in peace.

The Death of Simon

A **relative by marriage** of Simon (**the high priest**), named **Ptolemy the son of Abubus,** plotted to gain control of the **district** of Judea by destroying **Simon and his sons** (16.11–13). He invited them to a **banquet** in a **little fortress** near **Jericho** (16.14–15). **When Simon and his sons were full of drink, Ptolemy and his men** attacked them and **killed** them (16.16–17).

Nevertheless, Simon's son **John** was not slain, because he was at **Gezer.** Ptolemy **sent** some men **to do away with** him (16.18–20), but John was warned about them beforehand, and they themselves perished (16.21–22).

Ptolemy son of Abubus

16.11 And Ptolemy the *son* of Abubus had been appointed army commander for the plain of Jericho, and he had much silver and gold;
16.12 for he was the high priest's relative by marriage.
16.13 And his heart was exalted, and he wanted to overpower the district; and he took counsel deceitfully against Simon and his sons, to do away with them.

Ptolemy kills Simon and his sons

16.14 Now Simon was coming through the cities that *were* in the district, and attending to the care of them. And he came down to Jericho, he and Mattathias and Judas his sons, *in the* 177th year, in *the* eleventh month (this *is* the month Shebat).
16.15 And the *son* of Abubus received them deceitfully into the little fortress *that is* called Dok, which he had built. And he made a great banquet for them, and hid men in there.
16.16 And when Simon and his sons were full of drink, Ptolemy and his *men* rose up and took their weapons, and came in upon Simon, into the banquet, and killed him and his two sons and some of his servants.
16.17 And he committed a great act of treachery, and returned evil for good.

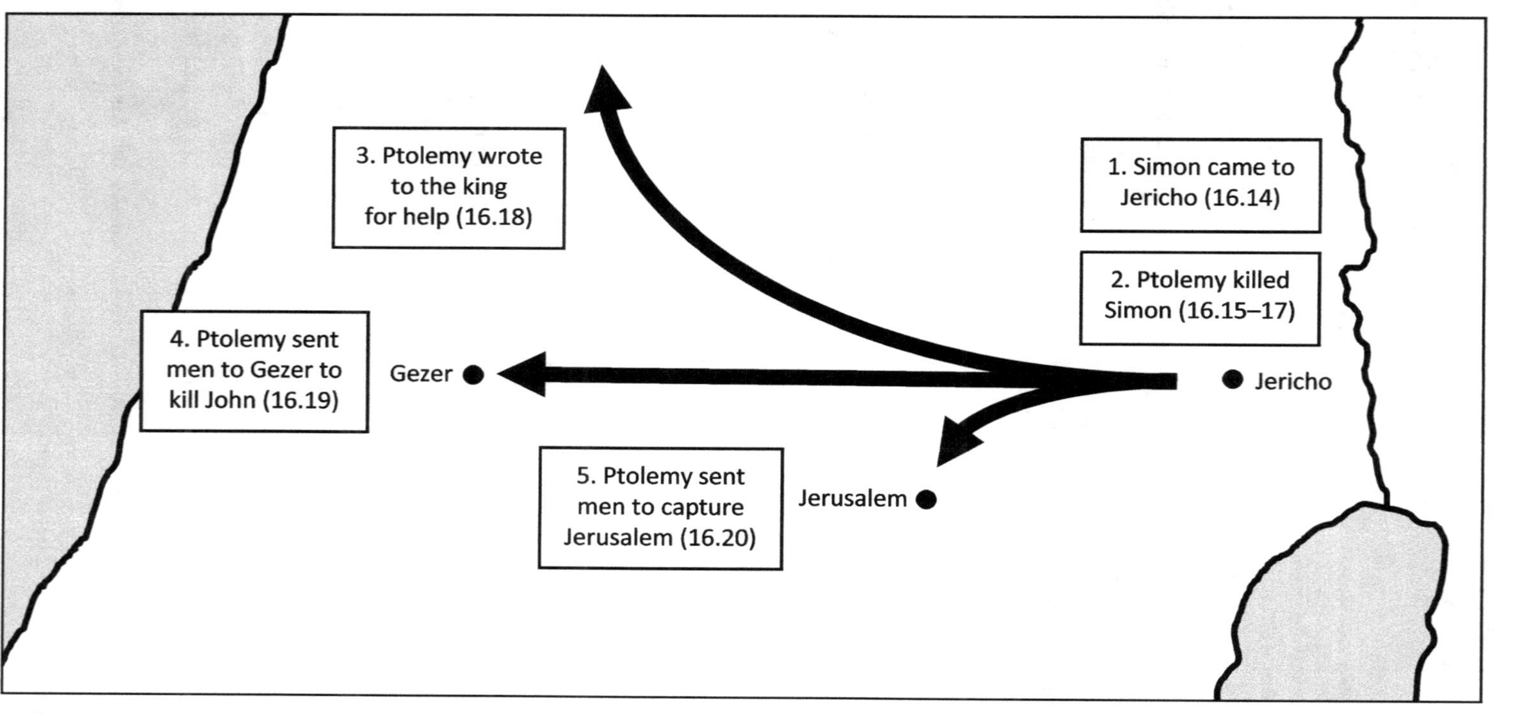
1. Simon came to Jericho (16.14)
2. Ptolemy killed Simon (16.15–17)
Jericho
3. Ptolemy wrote to the king for help (16.18)
Gezer
4. Ptolemy sent men to Gezer to kill John (16.19)
Jerusalem
5. Ptolemy sent men to capture Jerusalem (16.20)

Map 24: The death of Simon (Maccabaica 16.11–22)

Ptolemy seeks control of the district

16.18 And Ptolemy wrote *about* these *things*, and sent to the king, so that he should send him forces to help *him,* and deliver the cities and district to him.
16.19 And he sent others to Gezer, to do away with John. And he sent letters to the commanders of thousands, *for them* to come to him, so that he might give them silver and gold and gifts.
16.20 And he sent others to capture Jerusalem and the mountain of the temple.

Ptolemy's plan to kill John fails

16.21 And a certain *man* ran ahead, *and* told John at Gezer that his father and brothers had perished, and that "he has sent to kill you† also."
16.22 And when *he* heard, he was very much amazed. And he captured the men who came to destroy him, and killed them; for he knew that they were seeking to destroy him.

John son of Simon (16.23–24)

> After the death of his father, **John** became **high priest.** He too carried out **wars, valiant deeds,** and **building** programs, which were recorded in the chronicles (the **book of the days**) **of his high priesthood** (16.23–24).

16.23 And the rest of the acts of John, and his wars and his valiant deeds that he did, and the building of the walls that he built, and his activities,
16.24 behold, they are written in *the* book of *the* days of his high priesthood, from *the time* when he became high priest after his father.

EIGHTEEN PSALMS OF THE ROMAN PERIOD

Introduction

The Maccabean History recorded the history of Judea down to the time of the high priest John son of Simon, who died about a century before the birth of Christ.

The Eighteen Psalms describe the major event of that final century: the start of Roman rule in Jerusalem. They also look ahead to the coming of the promised Messiah and the establishment of God's kingdom, in accordance with Daniel's prophecies.

The Maccabean History is a narrative book. Reading it is like reading the life of David in Samuel-Kings. By contrast, the Eighteen Psalms is a songbook. Reading it is like reading the life of David in the Psalter. It records the crucial events, and the prayers that were prayed by faithful brethren when those events happened. But it does not link the events together in a narrative sequence. It sets us down, right in the midst of the turmoil, at the very outset: "I cried out to the Lord when I was afflicted to the uttermost, to God when the sinners set on me. A cry of war was suddenly heard before me" (1.1–2). Only later, as we continue to read, do we gradually learn which war this is, and what it is all about.

The three largest psalms are placed near the beginning (2), middle (8), and end (17) of the collection. Each of them is flanked by smaller supplementary psalms on the same subjects (1; 7; 9; 18). These three groups of psalms (1–2; 7–9; 17–18) are the ones that speak about a foreign invader in Jerusalem, and look ahead to the coming of the Messiah.

Putting together what the various psalms tell us, the following sequence of events emerges:

1. Before the War. The people of Jerusalem had been sinning greatly (1.8; 8.14; 17.20–21). They had a king—but even that king was transgressing God's Law (17.22). Only descendants of David had been authorized by God to be kings of Israel (2 Sam 7.16: Psa 89.3–4, 29, 35–37; Jer 33.20–21). But at this time, people who were not descendants of David, and who were not promised the kingship by God, had seized it "by force" (Eighteen Psalms 17.5–11).

2. The War. Because of Jerusalem's sins, the Lord allowed foreign nations, led by an arrogant man "from the end of the earth" (8.16), to enter Jerusalem. The rulers of Judea welcomed him and opened the gates for him to come in peacefully (8.18–20). But once he was inside, he besieged part of the city, broke down its walls (2.1; 8.21), slaughtered some of its inhabitants (8.23; 17.13), carried others away into exile "far to the west" (17.14; 2.6; 8.24), and defiled the temple, which was trampled by the feet of foreigners (2.2).

3. After the War. The sinners who had presumptuously seized the kingship would vanish from the earth (17.8–11), and the arrogant foreigner would himself be slain "near the mountains of Egypt," where his unburied body would be left drifting in the waves (2.30–31).

The Eighteen Psalms do not name this new invader, but later historians do. They reveal that, after the death of the high priest John son of Simon about 104 BCE (cf. Maccabaica 16.23–24), his heirs declared themselves kings, even though they were not descended from David (Josephus, *Antiquities,* 13.301; Strabo 16.2.40). About thirty years later, a dispute arose between two rival claimants to the throne (Josephus, *Antiquities,* 14.4). Each of them appealed to the Roman leader Pompey, who entered Jerusalem peacefully, but then attacked the temple area, killed or exiled various opponents, entered the temple itself, and made Judea a Roman province (about 63 BCE; Josephus, *Antiquities,* 14.30–78). Pompey himself was later (about 48 BCE) killed on the coast of Egypt at Mount Cassius, and his body was left drifting in the waves (Plutarch, *Pompey,* 77.4–80.1; Cassius Dio 42.4–5).

In some respects, this new time of tribulation resembled the one that had happened a century earlier, during the reign of Antiochus Epiphanes. Again there was widespread corruption in Judea. Again some of the people supported a foreign ruler. Again the foreign ruler defiled the temple, tore down the city's walls, and killed some of the inhabitants.

But this time, there was a notable difference. When Antiochus Epiphanes oppressed the Judeans, God raised up deliverers who overcame the enemy by the sword (Maccabaica 5.62; 3.1–9), as Joshua and Gideon and David had done. But now, when this new foreign ruler was oppressing the Judeans, God would raise up a deliverer who would overcome the enemy in a new way—not by earthly war (Eighteen Psalms 17.37), but by "the word of His mouth" (17.39). The Eighteen Psalms describe this forthcoming deliverer as the Anointed One (Christ), the Son of David, and the King of Israel (17.23, 36, 47; 18.6, 8). He would reprove sinners (17.27), breaking them in pieces, like a potter's vessel, with a rod of iron (17.26). He would gather together a holy people (17.28), who would be sons of God (17.30), whom He would cleanse (17.33), and the nations would serve under His yoke (17.32). He would smite the earth with the word of His mouth (17.39). He would be pure from sin (17.41) and powerful in the Holy Spirit (17.42), shepherding the flock of the Lord (17.45).

The Eighteen Psalms exist in both Greek and Syriac versions. The Greek version is translated below, as the known copies of the Syriac version are slightly incomplete. Both versions are printed and translated in the commentary section of this volume.

Psalm 1

The speaker is Jerusalem (a city **abounding in children,** v 3), as in Lamentations 1.12–22; 2.20–22. **Suddenly** there was **a cry of war** in her presence. **Sinners** attacked her (**set on** her), and she was **afflicted** greatly (**to the uttermost**). So she **cried out to the Lord** to help her (v 1).

In verses 3–8, Jerusalem confesses the sins of her people. At the time when the enemy attacked, the city had seemed to be **filled with righteousness.** It was **well off;** it was **abounding in** inhabitants (**children**), who were rich, glorious, and **exalted** (vv 3–5).

Yet secretly (**in hidden places**) the inhabitants of Jerusalem were committing **sins** and **transgressions** (vv 7–8). In spite of their **possessions** (their **riches** and **glory,** v 4), they were doing **exorbitant wrong** (v 6), even beyond **the nations** who had lived in the land of Canaan **before** Israel (v 8).

Jerusalem calls out to the Lord in wartime

1.1 I cried out to the Lord when I was afflicted to *the* uttermost,
to God when the sinners set on *me.*
1.2 A cry of war was suddenly heard before me.

She had thought herself righteous

He will hear me, because I am filled with righteousness:
1.3 I reasoned in my heart that I was filled with righteousness,
when I was well off and abounding in children.
1.4 Their riches were distributed throughout the whole earth,
and their glory to *the* end of the earth.
1.5 They were exalted to the stars;
they said they would never fall.

Her children sinned greatly

1.6 And while *they had* their possessions, they did exorbitant wrong,
and they brought no *offering.*
1.7 Their sins were in hidden *place*s,
and I myself did not know *it.*
1.8 Their transgressions exceeded the nations *who had been* before them;
they profaned the Lord's holy *place*s with profaneness.

Psalm 2

The Lord allowed an **arrogant** sinner to attack Jerusalem's **fortified walls** with a **battering ram** (v 1); He allowed foreign (**strange**) **nations** to trample His **altar** (v 2) and to take Jerusalem's inhabitants (her **sons** and **daughters**) captive, with their necks sealed, a **notable** sign of their punishment (v 6; cf. vv 20–23).

These terrible **judgments** from the Lord were **righteous** (vv 12, 16–19), because He was repaying Jerusalem's inhabitants **according to their sins** (vv 7, 17). They were doing **wicked things;** they were staining and profaning not only **themselves,** but also the Jerusalem temple (**the holy places of the Lord**) and the **offerings** offered there (vv 3, 9–15). The Lord does not show favoritism; **He will not be impressed by anyone's face** (v 19), and therefore no one who sins can hope to be exempt from His judgment.

Now the psalmist entreats the Lord for mercy, saying that Jerusalem has been punished **enough** (v 24). The conquering **nations** cannot long hold power over her, because they too have sinned: they acted in **anger,** not **in zeal** for the Lord, and merely followed their own **desire** (vv 25–29).

And, before **long,** the Lord shows the psalmist the **reproach** that comes to the evildoer (**the dragon**). The arrogant sinner is **wounded near the mountains of Egypt,** where **his dead body** is left unburied, tossing about on the **waves** (vv 29–31). He thought he himself would **be lord of earth and sea,** but he did not take account of **God,** who is **King over** even the world's mightiest **kings and rulers,** and destroys all those who are **arrogant** (vv 32–35).

This judgment is a warning to all other **great men of the earth** (v 36), and it is one of the reasons why **those who fear the Lord with understanding** bless Him. He is both merciful and **righteous** in judgment: in every age, He will **have mercy on the righteous man,** and He will **repay the sinner** (vv 37– 41).

Foreign nations trampled the Lord's altar

2.1 When the sinful *man became* arrogant, he cast down *the* fortified walls with a *battering* ram,
and You† did not hinder.
2.2 Strange nations went up on Your† altar;
they trampled *it* arrogantly with their feet,
2.3 because the sons of Jerusalem defiled the holy *place*s of *the* Lord;
they profaned the offerings of God by *their* transgressions.

Jerusalem's children were taken captive

2.4 Therefore He said, "Cast[pl] them far away from Me."
He did not make the beauty of His glory to prosper for them;
2.5 it was brought to nothing before God;
it was dishonored to *the* uttermost.
2.6 *Her* sons and daughters *were* in harmful captivity;
their neck *had* a seal, a notable *impression*, among the nations.

God judged them for their sins

2.7 He did to them according to their sins,
because He left them in *the* hands of *those* who were powerful.
2.8 For He turned away His face from *showing* mercy to them,
the young *man* and *the* old *man* and their children all alike,
2.9 because they did wicked *things* all alike, *and would* not listen.
2.10 And the heaven was greatly indignant, and the earth abhorred them,
2.11 because no one on it had done as much as these *people* did.
2.12 And the earth will know all Your† righteous judgments, O God.
They set up the sons of Jerusalem for a reproach, because of *the* harlots *who were* in there;
2.13 everyone who went past went in *there,* right in front of the sun.
They mocked at their transgressions, **2.14** *which were* just as they themselves did.
They openly published their unrighteous *deeds* before the sun.
And *the* daughters of Jerusalem *were* profane, in accordance with Your† judgment,
2.15 because they had defiled themselves in a mixed intermingling.

His judgments were righteous

I grieve *in* my belly and my inward parts, on account of these *things*.
2.16 I will acknowledge You† to be righteous, O God, in uprightness of heart,
because in Your† judgments *is* Your† righteousness, O God.
2.17 Because You† have repaid the sinners in accordance with their works,
and in accordance with their sins, *which were* very wicked.
2.18 You† have uncovered their sins, so that Your† judgment may be seen;
2.19 You† have blotted out their memory from the earth.
God *is* a righteous judge, and will not be impressed by *anyone's* face.

The nations dishonored Jerusalem

2.20 For *the* nations reproached Jerusalem by treading *her* down;
He threw down her beauty from *the* throne of glory.
2.21 She girded herself with sackcloth, instead of a garment of beauty;
a cord *was* around her head, instead of a crown.
2.22 She took off *the* headdress of glory that God had put on her;
2.23 her beauty was cast down on the earth in dishonor.

Let it be enough, Lord

And I myself saw *this,* **2.24** and entreated the Lord's face, and said,
"Let *it* be enough, Lord—*the* heavy hand You† have laid on Israel by bringing *the* nations against *it,*
2.25 because they mocked *us* and did not spare, in anger and indignation with wrath;

2.26 and they will be completely destroyed unless You†, Lord, reprove them in Your† anger;
2.27 because they did not act from zeal, but from *the* desire of *their* soul,
2.28 to pour out their anger upon us, by plundering.
And do not wait† a long time, O God, to repay them upon *their* heads,
2.29 to say *that* the arrogance of the dragon *is* in dishonor."

The arrogant one is destroyed

2.30 And I did not wait a long time until God showed me his disgrace,
when he was wounded near the mountains of Egypt
on behalf of *the* least *person*, *when he was* despised on land and sea,
2.31 *when* his dead body *was* carried about on *the* waves with great disgrace,
and *there* was no *one* to bury *him*, **2.32** because he treated him as nothing, in dishonor.

He did not know the greatness of God

He did not consider that he was *only* a Man,
and did not consider *his* end.
2.33 He said, "I will be lord of earth and sea,"
and he did not know that *it is* God *who is* great,
and mighty in His great power.
2.34 He *is* King over the heavens,
and judges kings and rulers,
2.35 the *One* who raises me up to glory,
and lays *the* arrogant asleep to eternal destruction in dishonor,
because they have not known Him.

See the Lord's judgment, and bless Him

2.36 And now, O great men of the earth, behold[pl] the Lord's judgment:
because *He is* a great King, and righteous, judging what *is* under heaven.
2.37 Bless[pl] God, *you* that fear the Lord with understanding,
because the Lord's mercy *is* upon those who fear Him with judgment,
2.38 to make a distinction between *the* righteous *man* and *the* sinner,
to repay sinners for ever, according to their works,
2.39 and to have mercy on *the* righteous *man* from *the* humiliation of *the* sinner;
and to repay *the* sinner because of *what* he did to *the* righteous *man,*
2.40 because the Lord *is* gracious to *those* who call on Him with endurance,
to do according to His mercy to His holy *ones*,
that they might stand before Him continually with power.
2.41 Blessed *be the* Lord for ever in *the* presence of His servants.

Psalm 3

The psalmist urges his **soul** to wake from sleep (**be watchful**) and bless the Lord in a **psalm** (vv 1–2).

A **righteous** person is **mindful of the Lord continually**. When he is **disciplined by the Lord,** he justifies **the Lord** (acknowledges the Lord's righteousness; vv 3–4) and does not persist in doing evil (**sin upon sin does not dwell** in his house, vv 5–7). He makes **atonement** for his sins of **ignorance,** and is cleansed by the Lord (vv 8–10).

A **sinner,** by contrast, **curses his life** when he stumbles (v 11) and continues doing evil (adds **sins upon sins,** v 12). He will never get back on his feet (**will not rise again** after his **fall**); he will be punished with **destruction . . . for ever** (vv 13, 15), whereas **those who fear the Lord will rise again to eternal life . . . in the light of the Lord** (v 16).

Sing to the Lord

3.1 Why are you† sleeping, *my* soul, and not blessing† the Lord?
3.2 Sing[pl] a new hymn to God, *who is* worthy to be praised.
Sing† and be watchful† to be watchful with Him,
because a good psalm to God *is* out of a good heart.

The righteous one looks to God and is cleansed from sin

3.3 *The* righteous will be mindful of the Lord continually;
with open acknowledgement and justification *they will be mindful of* the Lord's judgments.
3.4 A righteous *man* will not despise *it* when he is disciplined by the Lord;
his good pleasure *is* continually before *the* Lord.
3.5 The righteous *man* has stumbled, and has justified the Lord;
he has fallen, and he is looking for what God will do for him;
3.6 he is watching *to see* where his salvation will come from.
3.7 *The* faithfulness of the righteous *is* from God their Savior.
Sin upon sin does not dwell in the house of a righteous *man.*
3.8 The righteous *man* watches over his house continually,
to take away unrighteousness in his transgression.
3.9 He has made atonement for *his* ignorance with fasting, and will humble his soul;
3.10 and the Lord cleanses every man *who is* holy, and his house*hold.*

The sinner stumbles and is destroyed for ever

3.11 *The* sinner has stumbled, and he curses his life,
the day of his birth, and *his* mother's birthpangs.
3.12 He has added sins upon sins to his life.
3.13 He has fallen. Because his fall *is* ruinous, then he will not rise *again.*
The destruction of the sinner *will be* for ever,
3.14 and He will not be mindful of *him*, when He watches over *the* righteous.

Eternal destruction and eternal life

3.15 This *will be* the sinners' portion for ever,
3.16 but *those* who fear the Lord will rise *again* to eternal life,
and their life *will be* in *the* light of *the* Lord, and will not cease *any* more.

Psalm 4

This psalm is concerned with **profane** people who are **living hypocritically with the holy** (vv 1, 7). They speak **the Law with deceit** (v 10), pretending to be **innocent** (v 6), and **among the first** in **condemning sinners** (vv 2–3). But in reality they themselves are sinning secretly (**in hidden places,** v 5) and are **filled with transgression** (vv 15, 1, 27). They have **deceived** the **innocent** (v 25), and are **destroying** and making **desolate** whole households (**houses**) of the people around them (vv 11–15, 23, 27).

Jesus denounced hypocrites in the severest possible terms, declaring that "the blood of all the righteous" would come upon them (Matt 23.13–38; 15.7–9). This psalm, similarly, asks the Lord to **take away those who are living hypocritically** (vv 7–9, 25) and render to them the **dishonor** that they have inflicted on **many** others (vv 16–25).

The Lord will deliver those who **fear** Him from the snares of the **transgressor** (vv 26–29).

The hypocrite among the holy ones

4.1 Why are you† sitting, you† profane *man*, in *the* council of *the* holy *ones*,
while your† heart has departed far from the Lord,
provoking the God of Israel by *your* transgressions?
4.2 More profuse in words, more profuse in sign*s* than all *people,*
harsh in words, condemning sinners in judgment,
4.3 and his hand *is* among the first upon him, as *if* in zeal,
while he himself *is* held for punishment with a variety of sinners in excesses.
4.4 His eyes *are* upon every woman without distinction;
his tongue *is* lying in *the* agreement *that* he has sworn to.
4.5 He sins in the night and in hidden *places*, as *if he is* not seen;
he speaks with his eyes to every woman, with an assignation of wickedness;
4.6 *he is* quick in entering into every house with joy, as *if he is* innocent.

May God take away the hypocrites

4.7 May God take away those *who* live hypocritically with *the* holy;
may He take away his life in the corruption of his flesh, and *in* poverty.
4.8 May God uncover the works of Men-pleasers;
may He uncover his works with laughter and derision.
4.9 And may *the* holy *ones* justify the judgment of their God,
when sinners are taken away before the face of *the* righteous *man*—

The hypocrite's deceitful words

4.10 a Man-pleaser, who speaks *the* Law with deceit.
4.11 And their eyes *are* on a man's house *that is* secure—like *the* serpent,
destroying each other's wisdom by *the* words of transgressors.
4.12 His words *are* deceitful words, for *the* practice of *the* unrighteous *man*'s desire;
4.13 he did not leave until he had conquered *so as* to scatter *them*, as *if* with *the* loss of children,
and he made *their* house desolate for *the* sake of *the* transgressor's desire;
4.14 he deceived with his words, *saying* that *there* is no *one* who sees and judges.
4.15 He became filled with transgression by this,
and his eyes *were* upon another house,
to overthrow *it* by words of flight.
His soul, like Hades, is not satisfied with all these *things*.

May he fall in dishonor

4.16 Lord, may his portion be in dishonor before You†;
may his going out *be* with groans, and his coming in with a curse;
4.17 *may* his life *be* with sorrows, and poverty, and distress;
Lord, *may* his sleep *be* with sorrows, and his awaking with distresses.
4.18 May sleep be taken away from his temples at night;
may he fall away from every work of his hands in dishonor.
4.19 May he enter his house with his hands empty,
and *may* his house lack any*thing* by which his soul might be satisfied.
4.20 *May* his old age *be* in solitude lacking children, until he *is* taken away.
4.21 May *the* flesh of Men-pleasers be torn to pieces by wild beasts,
and *may the* bones of transgressors *be torn in pieces* before the sun in dishonor.
4.22 May *the* ravens pick out *the* eyes of hypocrites,
4.23 because they have made many people's houses desolate in dishonor,
and have dispersed *them* at *their own* desire,
4.24 and they have not been mindful of God,
and have not feared God in any of these *things*,
4.25 and they have provoked God to anger,
and He has been exasperated *so as* to take them away from the earth,
because they have played *the* hypocrite with deceitful words to *the* souls of *the* innocent.

God will deliver those who fear Him

4.26 Blessed *are those* who fear the Lord in their innocence,
4.27 and the Lord will deliver them from deceitful people and sinners,
and will deliver us from every stumblingblock of *the* transgressor.
4.28 May God take away those who do all unrighteousness in *their* arrogance,
because a great and mighty judge **4.29** in righteousness *is the* Lord our God.
Lord, may Your† mercy be on all those who love You†.

Psalm 5

God's people **praise** His **name with gladness** (vv 1, 21) **because** He is **kind and merciful** (vv 2, 21). Those who are **afflicted** (v 7)—such as those who are **poor** or **hungry** (vv 2, 10, 13)—can **call on** Him **for help,** in the confidence that He **will give** what they need (vv 7, 10), because of His **kindness** (vv 14–17) to all creatures (vv 11–12) and all people (vv 13). Indeed we could **take** nothing **unless** He should **give** it to us (vv 4–6). He gives in a way that is **great with kindness, and rich** (vv 16–17; unlike human kindness, vv 14–15). If He gives us **a moderate measure of contentment,** that, **with righteousness,** is **enough . . . for satisfaction** (vv 18–20). **Too great an abundance** might lead us to sin (v 19).

Lord, You are kind and merciful

5.1 O Lord God, I will praise Your† name with gladness,
in *the* midst of *those* who know Your† righteous judgments,
5.2 because You† *are* kind and merciful, the refuge of the poor *one.*
5.3 When I have cried out to You†, do† not be silent from me.

Who will take from You, unless You give?

5.4 For no one *can* take plunder from a powerful man,
5.5 and who *can* take from all *the things* that You† have made, unless You† Yourself† give *it?*
5.6 Because a person and his portion *are weighed out* from You† in a balance;
he *can*not increase *it* beyond Your† judgment, O God.

We will call on You when we are afflicted

5.7 We will call on You† for help when we *are* afflicted,
and You† will not turn away our entreaty,
because You† are our God.
5.8 Do not lay Your† hand heavily† on us,
so that we may not sin because of necessity.
5.9 And if You† do not turn us away, we will not be far away,
but to You† we will come.
5.10 For if I should be hungry, I will cry out to You†, O God,
and You† will give me *food.*

You nourish all creatures

5.11 You† feed the birds and the fishes
when You† give rain in *the* desert for *the* growth of plants,
to prepare food in *the* desert for every living *thing,*
5.12 and if they should be hungry, they will lift up their faces to You†.
5.13 You†, O God, feed the kings and rulers and peoples,
and who is the hope of *one who is* poor and needy, except You†, Lord?

The kindness of God

5.14 And You† will hear *them,* because who *is* kind and gentle except You†,
making *the* humble soul rejoice, when You† open Your† hand in mercy?
5.15 A Man's kindness *is done* sparingly and tomorrow,
and if he does *it* twice without grumbling, then You† might wonder at it.
5.16 But what You† give *is* great with kindness, and rich,
and *there* is no hope in You† when a *person* is sparing with a gift.
5.17 Your† mercy is upon all the earth, Lord, with kindness.

A moderate measure is enough

5.18 Blessed *is the one* of whom God is mindful with a moderate measure of contentment;
5.19 if a person has too great an abundance, he sins.
5.20 A moderate *portion*, with righteousness, *is* enough;
and in this *is* the Lord's blessing for satisfaction with righteousness.

Your kindness is on Israel

5.21 Those who fear *the* Lord have rejoiced in good *things*;
and Your† kindness *will be* upon Israel in Your† kingdom.
5.22 Blessed *be* the glory of *the* Lord, because He *is* our King.

Psalm 6

The man who prepares his heart **to call on the Lord's name ... will be saved** (vv 1–2); the **Lord** will direct **his paths** and guard his **works** (v 3). Even in times of distress (**bad dreams; passing through rivers** and **stormy seas**), he **will not be terrified;** instead, he will bless the Lord in **security** of **heart** (vv 4–7).

The Lord will fulfill **every entreaty** of **everyone** who fears and loves Him **in truth** (vv 8–9).

The man who calls on the Lord's name will be saved

6.1 Blessed *is the* man whose heart *is* prepared to call on the Lord's name;
6.2 when he is mindful of the Lord's name, he will be saved.
6.3 His paths are directed by *the* Lord,
and *the* works of his hands *are* guarded by *the* Lord his God.

His soul will not be terrified

6.4 He will not be disturbed by *the* sight of his bad dreams;
6.5 his soul will not be terrified when *he is* passing through rivers or stormy seas.
6.6 He has arisen from his sleep and blessed the name of *the* Lord;
6.7 in *the* security of his heart he has sung hymns to the name of God,

The Lord fulfills every entreaty of those who fear Him

and he has entreated the Lord's face for all his house,
6.8 and *the* Lord has heard *the* prayer of every*one who is* in *the* fear of God,
and the Lord fulfills every entreaty of *the* soul who hopes in Him.
6.9 Blessed *be the* Lord, who shows mercy to those who love Him in truth.

Psalm 7

This psalm refers to a time when there was a danger that Israel might be attacked by enemies (**those who have hated us for nothing**). At this time, therefore, the foreign invasion and defilement of the temple described in the next psalm (8.16–24; cf. 2.1–2) had not yet happened. The people appeal to God **not** to remove His dwelling place (His **tabernacle**) from them, and not to allow the enemy to **tread down** His temple (**holy place**; vv 1–2). Nevertheless, they are willing to accept **discipline** and even **death** from the Lord, because He is **merciful** and would **not ... consume** them (vv 3–6).

The closing lines look forward to the **time of Your help**—the **day** that the Lord had **promised,** when He would have **mercy on the house of Jacob** and **direct** His people (v 9). Less than a century later, those promises were fulfilled through Jesus (Luke 1.54–55, 68–79).

Do not let our enemies tread down Your holy place

7.1 Do not remove† Your† tabernacle from us, O God,
lest those who have hated us for nothing fall upon us;
7.2 because You† have rejected them, O God;
do not let their foot tread down *the* inheritance of Your† holy place.

Discipline us mercifully

7.3 Discipline† us by Your† *own* will,
and do not give† *us* to *the* nations;
7.4 for if You† send death,
You† Yourself† will command it concerning us;
because You† are merciful,
and will not be angry† *so as* to consume us.
7.5 We will obtain mercy, while Your† name dwells in our midst,
7.6 and no nation will have power against us,
because You† hold a shield over us,

We will call on You, and You will hear us

7.7 and we will call upon You†, and You† will hear us,
7.8 because You† will have mercy on the race of Israel for ever,
and will not reject† *us*,

and we *will be* under Your† yoke for ever,
and *under* the rod of Your† discipline.
7.9 You† will direct us in *the* time of Your† help,
having mercy on the house of Jacob for *the* day that You† have promised them.

Psalm 8

A sound has been **heard... in Jerusalem** (v 4). It is **the voice of war ... the voice of a great people,** a sound of **slaughter and destruction** (vv 1–2). It is a terrifying sound (vv 5–6). Where **will God judge** this destroyer (v 3)?

At first it might seem that Jerusalem's inhabitants would **order their path aright in righteousness** (v 7). But God **uncovered** all kinds of **sins** that were being done secretly in the city, **in underground hidden places:** the people were committing fornication and **adultery,** plundering God's **holy places,** and defiling His **sacrifices** (vv 8–14, 26). **Because of this,** God brought an enemy **against Jerusalem** from a distant place (**the end of the earth**). That enemy struck the land **severely** and decisively (**he decided the war;** vv 15–17). At first, the **rulers** of Jerusalem had welcomed him into the city **with joy** (vv 18–19). But once he was established in the city (v 20), he **seized** possession of Jerusalem's **towers** and **walls** (v 21). **He destroyed** the city's **rulers** and **poured out** the **blood** of its inhabitants (v 23). Others **he carried away** into captivity (v 24). All these things happened because the inhabitants, **who had been fathered** by sinners, had sinned **just as their fathers had done** (vv 24–26).

God was **justified in** these **judgments** against Israel, as even the surrounding **nations** could see (vv 7, 27–32). Now the psalm asks Him to **have compassion on** His people and **gather together** those who had been scattered (v 33–34). The people humbly confess their sins (**we have hardened our neck,** v 35), and put their **hope** solely **on** Him (v 37), promising **never** to **be shaken any more** (vv 38–39).

The Lord is to be praised for **His judgments** by His **holy ones** (vv 29 40), and they will be **blessed** by Him **for ever** (v 41).

The voice of war in Jerusalem

8.1 My ear heard affliction and *the* voice of war,
the voice of a resounding trumpet, slaughter and destruction,
8.2 *the* voice of a great people, like *that* of a very great wind,
like a stormwind of a mighty fire carried through *the* desert.
8.3 And I said to my heart,
"Where then will God judge him?"
8.4 I heard a voice in Jerusalem, *the* city of *the* holy place;
8.5 my loins were shaken by hearing *it*,
my knees were weakened, **8.6** my heart was afraid,
my bones were disordered, like flax.
8.7 I said, "They will order their paths aright in righteousness."

God has uncovered the people's sins

I considered God's judgments from *the* creation of heaven and earth;
I justified God in His judgments that have been from eternity.
8.8 God has uncovered their sins before the sun;
the whole earth has known God's judgments *to be* righteous.
8.9 Their transgressions *were* in underground hidden *places*, provoking *Him* to anger.
8.10 *The* son intermingled with *the* mother, and *the* father with *the* daughter;
8.11 every*one* committed adultery with his neighbor's wife.
They made an agreement among them*selves* with an oath **8.12** concerning these *things*.
They plundered the holy *places* of God,
as *if there* were no heir who redeemed.
8.13 They trod down the Lord's altar from every *kind of* uncleanness,
and they defiled the sacrifices, like profane meats, with menstruation of blood.
8.14 They did not leave *any* sin that they did not do more than the nations.

Because of this, God brought war on them

8.15 Therefore God mixed for them a spirit of going astray;
He made them drink a cup of unmixed wine, to *the point of* drunkenness.
8.16 He brought from the end of the earth *one* who strikes severely;
8.17 he decided the war against Jerusalem and her land.
8.18 The rulers of the land met him with joy;
they said to him, "Blessed *is* your[†] path; come, enter[pl] with peace."
8.19 They smoothed *the* rough paths away from his entrance;
they opened *the* gates near Jerusalem; they crowned her walls.
8.20 He entered like a father into *the* house of his sons, with peace;
he set up his feet with great security.
8.21 He seized Jerusalem's towers and wall,
8.22 because God led him securely, as they *had* gone astray.
8.23 He destroyed their rulers and every*one who was* wise in counsel;
he poured out the blood of Jerusalem's inhabitants like water of uncleanness.
8.24 He carried away their sons and daughters who had been fathered in profaneness.
8.25 They did in accordance with their impurities, just as their fathers *had done.*
8.26 Jerusalem also defiled the *things* that had been sanctified to the name of God.

God judges in righteousness

8.27 God was justified in His judgments among the nations of the earth,
8.28 and God's holy *ones were* like innocent lambs in *the* midst of them.
8.29 Worthy of praise *is the* Lord, who judges all the earth in His righteousness.

8.30 Behold, now, O God, You† have shown us Your† judgment in righteousness;
8.31 our eyes have seen Your† judgments, O God.
We have justified Your† honorable name for ever,
8.32 because You† *are* the God of righteousness, judging Israel with discipline.

God, have compassion on us

8.33 Restore Your† mercy to us, O God,
and have compassion† on us.
8.34 Gather† together the dispersion of Israel with mercy and kindness,
8.35 because Your† faithfulness *is* with us,
and we have hardened our neck,
and You† are *the One* who disciplines us.
8.36 Do not overlook† us, O our God,
lest *the* nations swallow us up, as *if there* were no *one* to redeem *us.*

We will not keep away from You

8.37 And You† *are* our God from *the* beginning,
and our hope *is* on You†, Lord.
8.38 And we will not keep away from You†,
because Your† judgments *are* kind toward us.
8.39 *Your* good pleasure *will be* to us and to our children for ever;
Lord our Savior, we will never be shaken *any* more.
8.40 Worthy of praise *is the* Lord in His judgments in *the* mouth of *His* holy *ones*,
8.41 and blessed *be* Israel by *the* Lord for ever.

Psalm 9

Having **departed from the Lord,** the people of Israel **were cast out from** their **inheritance** (the land of Canaan) and **led away in captivity into a strange land,** so that they were scattered **in every nation** (vv 1–2). This happened **in accordance with the word of God,** who had warned His people that such punishments would happen if they disobeyed Him (vv 1–2). It was a righteous judgment (vv 3–4, 10), because no human deeds, good or bad, are ever **hidden from** God's **knowledge** (vv 5–6). If we do **righteous deeds,** we are treasuring up **life ... with the Lord;** if we do **unrighteousness,** we shall receive **destruction.** The choice is ours (vv 7–9).

In His **kindness,** God will **forgive** and **cleanse** those **who have sinned,** if they **repent** of their sins, make an open **confession** of them, and **call upon the Lord** for forgiveness, in the way He has prescribed (vv 11–15). So, confessing that they have done **iniquities** (v 3), and promising to **repent** from sin and set their **hope** on God, the psalm appeals to Him to **have compassion** on His people, whom He has **loved** and **chosen,** and for whom He made His **covenant with** their **fathers** (vv 16–20).

Israel was led away in captivity because of its sins

9.1 When Israel was led away in captivity into a strange land,
when they departed from *the* Lord who had redeemed them,
9.2 they were cast out of *the* inheritance that *the* Lord had given them.
Israel *was* dispersed in every nation, in accordance with the word of God,
9.3 so that You†, O God, might be justified in Your† righteousness, by our iniquities,
9.4 because You† *are the* righteous judge over all the peoples of the earth.

No one is hidden from Your knowledge

9.5 For no *one* who does unrighteous *deeds* will be hidden from Your† knowledge,
9.6 and the righteous deeds of Your† holy *ones are* before You†, Lord;
and where will a person be hidden from Your† knowledge, **9.7** O God?

Our soul can choose to do righteousness or unrighteousness

Our works *are* in *the* choice and power of our soul
to do righteousness or unrighteousness by *the* works of our hands;
9.8 and in Your† righteousness You† watch over *the* sons of Men.
9.9 The *one* who does righteousness treasures up life for him*self* with *the* Lord,
and the *one* who does unrighteousness—he *himself* causes *the* destruction of *his* soul,
9.10 for the Lord's judgments *are* in righteousness on every man and *his* house.

God will be merciful to those who call on Him

9.11 To whom will You† be merciful, O God, except to those who call on the Lord?
9.12 He will cleanse *the* soul *that is* in *its* sins, by confession, by public declarations,
9.13 because shame *belongs* to us and to our faces, on account of all *things*.
9.14 And to whom will He forgive sins, except to those who have sinned?
9.15 You† will bless *the* righteous, and will not punish† *them* for their sins;
and Your† kindness *is* toward *those* who sin *and* repent.

Have compassion, because You have chosen Israel

9.16 And now, You† *are* God, and we *are* Your† people whom You† have loved;
see†, and have compassion†, O God of Israel, because we are Yours†,
and do not take Your† mercy away† from us, so that they may not fall upon us,
9.17 because You† have chosen the seed of Abraham above all the nations,
9.18 and You†, Lord, have put Your† name upon us;
and You† will not rest for ever.
9.19 You† made a covenant with our fathers concerning us,
and we will hope in You†, in *the* returning of our soul.
9.20 *May* the Lord's mercy *be* upon *the* house of Israel for ever and ever.

Psalm 10

A person who is disciplined by the Lord **with reproof** and afflictions (**a scourge**) is **blessed,** because he is **cleansed from sin** and **shielded from the wicked path** (vv 1–2a).

The Lord is kind and merciful to **those who love Him in truth** and **who endure** when they are disciplined (vv 2b–4). The **Law** of God testifies to that (v 5). His people will **praise** His **name, openly acknowledge it** in public, and **glorify** it. They will receive the Lord's **mercy, salvation,** and an **eternal** life of **soundness of mind** in **straight paths** (vv 6–9).

Blessed is the man whom the Lord scourges

10.1 Blessed *is the* man of whom the Lord has been mindful with reproof,
and he has been shielded from *the* wicked path with a scourge,
so that he may be cleansed from sin, so that it may not multiply.
10.2 He who prepares *his* back for scourges will also be cleansed,

The Lord is kind to those who love Him

for the Lord *is* kind to those who endure under discipline.
10.3 For He will make *the* paths of *the* righteous straight,
and will not turn *them* aside by discipline,
10.4 and the Lord's mercy *will be* upon those who love Him in truth;
and *the* Lord will be mindful of His servants in mercy,
10.5 for *His* testimony *is* in *the* Law of *the* eternal covenant—
the Lord's testimony upon *the* paths of Men in *His* watching over *them.*
10.6 Our Lord *is* righteous and holy in his judgments for ever,
and Israel will praise the Lord's name with gladness,
10.7 and the holy *ones* will openly acknowledge *it* in *the* congregation of *the* people;
and the Lord will have mercy on *the* poor, in *the* gladness of Israel,
10.8 because God *is* kind and merciful for ever,
and *the* assemblies of Israel will glorify the name of *the* Lord.
10.9 *May* the Lord's salvation *be* upon *the* house of Israel, for eternal soundness of mind.

Psalm 11

God's people **in Jerusalem (Zion)** are here instructed to **proclaim ... the voice of the one who brings good news.** This proclamation is to be accompanied by the **trumpet of signaling** appointed on such occasions under the old covenant. The proclamation is to be made **because** God has been **watching over** Israel and **has had mercy on** them (vv 1–2) by preparing to bring back **Jerusalem**'s inhabitants (**children**) from the places where they have been scattered: **from the east**, the **west**, the **north,** and the **islands** (vv 3–4). He is smoothing the way for them, clearing away all obstacles (**high mountains ... hills**), shading them from the heat of the sun, and blessing their path with **fragrant trees** (vv 5–7). In preparation, **Jerusalem** is told to **clothe** herself with **glory** and holiness (v 8).

All these things had been prophesied long ago (e.g., in Psa 107.1–3). The present psalm prays that they may now happen: **may the Lord do what He has spoken** (v 9). As we know today, that prayer was answered only a few decades later, when the good news (gospel) of Jesus was proclaimed, gathering together the spiritual Israel from all nations (Luke 24.47; 1 Pet 1.1–4), and bringing them all to the heavenly Jerusalem (Heb 12.20).

Proclaim the good news of God's mercy on Israel

11.1 Sound *the* trumpet[pl] in Zion with *the* saints' trumpet of signaling;
11.2 proclaim[pl] in Jerusalem *the* voice of *the one* who brings good news;
because God has had mercy on Israel, in watching over them.

The Lord is gathering Israel together

11.3 Stand† on high, Jerusalem, and see† your† children
gathered together from *the* east and west all alike by *the* Lord.
11.4 They come from *the* north to the gladness of their God;
from *the* islands far away God has gathered them together.
11.5 He has laid low *the* high mountains into a plain for them;
11.6 the hills have fled away from their entrance.
The forests have given them shade as they *were* passing;
11.7 God has made every fragrant tree to grow for them,
so that Israel might pass on as *the* glory of their God was watching over *them*.

God has spoken good things for Israel

11.8 Put on†, *O* Jerusalem, the clothes of your† glory;
prepare† the robe of your† holy place,
because God has spoken good *things* for Israel, for ever and ever.

May the Lord raise up Israel

11.9 May *the* Lord do what He has spoken concerning Israel and Jerusalem;
may *the* Lord raise up Israel by *the* name of His glory;
may the Lord's mercy *be* on Israel for ever and ever.

Psalm 12

This psalm prays for deliverance from the person who utters **lies and deceits** (v 1). Such a person's speech is crooked and shifty (**in various twistings**), and it burns people **like a fire** (v 2), seeking to harm both the righteous (**trees of gladness,** whose joy provokes him—**sets** him **on fire**) and the unrighteous (**transgressors' houses;** vv 3–4a).

The psalm prays that the evil talkers may be removed **from the innocent** and **perish** (vv 4b–5), and, conversely, that the Lord may **preserve** and **direct** the righteous (**the soul that is quiet . . . the man who makes peace in his house**) so that they receive **the Lord's salvation** and **inherit the Lord's promises** (vv 6–8).

Lord, deliver my soul from a lying tongue

12.1 Lord, deliver[†] my soul from a man *who is* a transgressor and wicked;
from a transgressing and whispering tongue,
which speaks lies and deceits.
12.2 The words of a wicked man's tongue *are* in various twistings,
like a fire among a people, burning its beauty.
12.3 His visit *will* fill houses with *his* lying tongue,
to cut down *the* trees of *the* gladness that sets on fire *the* transgressors,
12.4 *and* to set in turmoil *the* transgressors' houses by warfare with whispering lips.
May God remove from *the* innocent *the* lips of transgressors with perplexity,
and may *the* bones of whisperers be scattered from *those* who fear the Lord;
12.5 may *the* whispering tongue perish from *the* holy *ones*, in a flaming fire.
12.6 May *the* Lord preserve *the* soul *that is* quiet, *and* hates *the* unrighteous;
and may *the* Lord direct *the* man who makes peace in *his* house.
12.7 *May* the Lord's salvation *be* upon Israel His servant for ever,
12.8 and may the sinners perish from *the* face of *the* Lord once *for all*,
and may *the* Lord's holy *ones* inherit *the* Lord's promises.

Psalm 13

The Lord has sent against Jerusalem four judgments: the **sword that passes by, famine, death,** and **harmful wild beasts** (just as He did in Babylonian times: Ezek 14.13–22). But His **right hand** and His **arm** have **covered, spared, saved,** and **delivered** some of the people from **all these** judgments (vv 1–3).

Surviving transgressors (**ungodly** people) were **disturbed,** fearing that they might **be taken** (v 4) **together with the sinners** who had already been destroyed (vv 2–3). But **nothing of all** God's judgments **will touch the righteous one** (v 5). **Sinners,** in spite of their fine outward garb (**finery**), are overthrown and **taken away to destruction** (vv 5–7, 10), but **the righteous** are lovingly **disciplined** by the Lord (to rid them of the **offences** they commit in **ignorance**), and are granted everlasting **life** (vv 6–9).

The arm of the Lord has saved us

13.1 *The* right hand of *the* Lord has covered me;
the right hand of *the* Lord has spared us;
13.2 the arm of *the* Lord has saved us from *the* sword that passed by,
from famine and *the* death of sinners.
13.3 Harmful wild beasts ran upon them;
with their teeth they tore their flesh,
and with *their* grinders they crushed their bones.
And from all these things *the* Lord has delivered us.

The ungodly man was disturbed

13.4 The ungodly *man* was disturbed because of his offences,
lest he should be taken together with the sinners,
13.5 because the overthrow of the sinner *will be* terrible,

The righteous are disciplined but spared

and nothing of all these *things* will touch *the* righteous *one;*
13.6 because the disciplining of *the* righteous in *their* ignorance *is* not like
the overthrow of the sinners **13.7** in *their* finery.
The righteous *one* is disciplined so that the sinner may not rejoice over the righteous *one*;
13.8 because He will admonish *the* righteous *one* as the son of *His* love,
and his disciplining *will be* like *that* of *the* firstborn,
13.9 because *the* Lord will spare His holy *ones*,
and will blot out their offences by discipline;

The righteous will live for ever, but sinners will be destroyed

for the life of the righteous *will be* for ever,
13.10 but *the* sinners will be taken away to destruction,
and their memorial will not be found *any* more.
13.11 But the Lord's mercy *will be* upon those *who are* holy,
and His mercy *will be* upon those who fear Him.

Psalm 14

Those who **love** the Lord **in truth,** who **endure under His disciplining,** and who **walk in** His commands, are **trees of life,** because they **will live . . . for ever** and will never be **uprooted.** They are **God's portion and inheritance,** and He **is faithful to** them, blessing them by giving them His **Law,** in which they will continue to live **for ever** (vv 1–3).

The **sinners and transgressors** are **not** like that. Instead, they **have loved** a little time (a **day**) participating in **sin** and **worthlessness** (v 4). **They have not been mindful** that God **understands the secrets of the heart,** and that He knows all the **paths of Men** (v 5). Therefore sinners will inherit death (**Hades**) and **destruction,** whereas **the Lord's holy ones will inherit life in gladness** on the **day** when He has **mercy** on them (vv 6–7).

The Lord is faithful to those who love Him in truth

14.1 *The* Lord *is* faithful to those who love Him in truth,
to those who endure under His disciplining,
to those who walk in *the* righteousness of His commandments.

They will never be uprooted

In *the* Law, He has commanded us for our life;
14.2 *the* Lord's holy *ones* will live in it for ever.
His holy *ones are* the Paradise of the Lord, the trees of life;
14.3 their plant *is* rooted for ever;
they will not be uprooted *in* all the days of heaven,
because Israel is God's portion and inheritance.

Not so are the sinners

14.4 But not so are the sinners and transgressors,
who have loved a day in *the* participation of their sin.
Their desire *is* in the littleness of worthlessness,
14.5 and they have not been mindful of God,
that *the* paths of Men *are* always known before Him,
and *that* He understands *the* secrets of *the* heart before they exist.

The inheritance of the sinners and the righteous

14.6 Therefore their inheritance *will be* Hades and darkness and destruction,
and they will not be found in *the* day of mercy for *the* righteous;
14.7 but the Lord's holy *ones* will inherit life in gladness.

Psalm 15

God is the **hope and refuge** of those who are **poor** and suffering **affliction** (vv 1–2). Therefore our **strength** should be used to **acknowledge** His mercy, offering Him **from** the **heart** a **psalm** as the **fruit of** our **lips** (vv 3–5). The person who does this will never **be shaken** or touched, when the **flame** of the Lord's **wrath** goes out **to destroy** the sinners (vv 6–7). Instead, **the righteous** will be marked with a **sign … for salvation** (v 8), so that the various judgments pursuing the wicked—such as **famine and the sword and death—will be far from the righteous,** and will even **flee from** them (v 9).

Sinners will leave no **inheritance … for their children;** instead, their **houses** will be **desolate,** and their only **inheritance will be destruction and darkness,** with no **escape** from **the Lord's judgment,** even in the realm of the dead (**Hades;** vv 9–14). But **in** that day, **those who fear the Lord will receive mercy** from Him, and **will live** (v 15).

God is the hope of the poor

15.1 When I *was* in affliction, I called on the name of *the* Lord;
I hoped for *the* help of the God of Jacob, and was delivered,
15.2 because You†, O God, *are the* hope and refuge of the poor.

Those who openly acknowledge God will never be shaken

15.3 For who has strength, O God, except to openly acknowledge You† in truth?
15.4 and why *does* a person *have* power, except to openly acknowledge Your† name?
15.5 A new psalm with a song in gladness of heart,
the fruit of lips with *the* matched instrument of *the* tongue,
the firstfruits of lips from a holy and righteous heart—
15.6 he who does these *things* will never be shaken by evil;
the flame of fire and *the* wrath of *the* unrighteous will not touch him,
15.7 whenever it comes upon sinners from *the* Lord's face
to destroy every foundation of sinners,
15.8 because the sign of God *will be* upon *the* righteous for salvation;
famine and the sword and death *will be* far from *the* righteous,
15.9 because they will flee from *the* holy *ones*, like those who are pursued by famine,

Sinners will perish in the day of judgment

but they will pursue after sinners and take hold of *them,*
and those who commit transgression will not escape the Lord's judgment;
they will be laid hold of, as *if* by skillful warriors,
15.10 because the sign of destruction *is* on their forehead.
15.11 And the inheritance of the sinners *will be* destruction and darkness,
and their transgressions will pursue them even to Hades below.

15.12 Their inheritance will not be found for their children,
15.13 for sins will make *the* houses of *the* sinners desolate,
and *the* sinners will perish in *the* day of *the* Lord's judgment for ever,
15.14 when God watches over the earth in His judgment;
15.15 but those who fear the Lord will receive mercy in it,
and will live by the merciful deeds of their God;
and *the* sinners will perish for ever.

Psalm 16

My soul nearly **slipped** into the **sleep** of being **carried away from the Lord,** and was nearly **poured out to death** (the **death** that the **sinner** will face when he has passed through the **gates of Hades** into the realm of the dead). But **the Lord ... helped me** (vv 1–3). **He pierced me** (as an animal is pierced with a **spur**) to rouse me from that **sleep** into the watchfulness that He requires. In this way, He **saved me** from sin (v 4). The psalm **openly acknowledges** that God has **helped me for salvation,** and has **not counted me** among the **sinners** (v 5).

Salvation can be obtained only by God's **help** (vv 3–5)—only if He does **not remove** His **mercy from me** (v 6), if He **preserves** me from all forms of **sin** (vv 7–8), and if He keeps **my steps** and **words,** so that I do not slip into **anger,** or into **grumbling** when I face **oppression** (vv 9–11).

God can **make my soul steadfast** and **strengthen** it, so that I can **bear discipline in poverty** with **gladness** and **good pleasure,** knowing that **what has been given** by God **will satisfy me** (vv 12–13). **When** anyone faces the **affliction of poverty,** God is **testing** him, and his **soul is disciplined by means of** the **worthlessness** that he suffers (v 14). If he **endures** during **these** sufferings, he will receive **mercy** from **the Lord** (v 15).

I almost slipped, but God helped me

16.1 When my soul slumbered from *the* Lord,
I almost slipped in *the* corruption of sleep;
16.2 when *it was* far from God,
my soul was almost poured out to death
near *the* gates of Hades, with *the* sinner,
16.3 when my soul was carried away from *the* Lord God of Israel,
if the Lord had not helped me by His mercy, *which is* for ever.
16.4 He pierced me like *the* spur of a horse, to make *me* watchful with Him;
my Savior, and He who helps me at all times, saved me.
16.5 I will openly acknowledge You†, O God, because You† have helped me for salvation,
and You† have not counted me among the sinners for destruction.

Keep me from sin

16.6 Do not remove† Your† mercy from me, O God,
nor the mindfulness of You† from my heart until death.
16.7 Preserve† me, O God, from harmful sin,
and from every harmful woman who causes *the* unwise to stumble,
16.8 and do not let *the* beauty of a transgressing woman deceive me,
or of any*thing* that is in subjection from unprofitable sin.
16.9 Direct† the works of my hands in Your† place,
and keep† my steps in the mindfulness of You†.
16.10 Array† my tongue and my lips in words of truth;
put† anger and unreasoning wrath far away from me;
16.11 remove† far from me grumbling and faintheartedness in oppression;
if I should sin, when You† discipline *me, it is* for *my* conversion.

The righteous one is disciplined and endures

16.12 But make my soul steadfast† in good pleasure with gladness;
when You† strengthen my soul, what has been given *me* will satisfy me;
16.13 because unless You† Yourself† strengthen *us,*
who *can* bear discipline in poverty?
16.14 When a soul is disciplined by means of his worthlessness,
it is Your† testing in his flesh, and in *the* affliction of poverty.
16.15 When the righteous *man* endures these things, he will be shown mercy by *the* Lord.

Psalm 17

The time of a person's life on the earth is brief, and **his hope** is as brief as **his time** (v 2). But **we will hope in God,** because His **power** and His **kingdom** endure **for ever,** both in showing **mercy** and in exercising **judgment** over all **nations** (vv 3–4).

God **chose David** to be **king over Israel,** and promised him that **his seed** would have **kingship** over Israel **for ever** (v 5). But now, **sinners** to whom God **made no promise** of kingship (i.e., who are not descended from David) have risen up in **arrogance,** have driven out the faithful, and have seized the **kingship** by **force—in place of** the exalted position that God had already given them (vv 6–8).

Nevertheless, God **will cast... out** these sinners and their **seed** by means of a foreigner who is **strange to our race** (vv 8–11), **estranged from our God,** and a **transgressor.** This enemy has already **destroyed** some inhabitants of the land, **sent** others **away far to the west,** and set the arrogant **rulers for a mockery** (vv 13–15). **In Jerusalem,** he has dared to behave just the same way as **the nations** do in other **cities to their** false **gods** (v 16).

God has also **restrained the falling of rain on the land, because** all the inhabitants of **Jerusalem,** from the unauthorized **king** to **those who were least,** were involved in **every sin** (vv 17, 21–22).

Yet the faithful Israelites (**sons of the covenant**) have not been overcome by the foreign **mingled nations.** Instead, the faithful have **had power over them** and have been **saved... from evil** by fleeing from **Jerusalem** into the **deserts** (vv 17–20).

The psalm prays that God will **raise up** the rightful **King, the Son of David** (also called **Christ,** v 36), **to make Him reign over Israel** at the **time** which God **has seen** to be right (vv 23, 51). The psalm describes this Son of David accurately, in terms consistent with the earlier prophecies of Scripture. By His God-given **power,** the Son of David would **beat down the unrighteous rulers, cleanse Jerusalem, driving away sinners,** and **destroying the transgressing nations** (vv 24–27). **He will gather together a holy people, all** of whom are **sons of their God** and **holy;** He **will not allow** any **unrighteousness** among them (vv 28–30, 36). **Nations** will **come from the end of the earth to see His glory.** He **will judge** them **in the wisdom of His righteousness;** they will serve **Him under His yoke** (vv 31–34), and **He will have mercy on all** those **nations** who approach Him **in fear** (v 38), so that they are **sanctified** (v 49) just as the faithful Israelites are **sanctified** (v 48). **He will lead them all in equality,** and none among them will be **weak** (vv 45–46).

The Son of David will be **righteous** (v 35) and **pure from sin** (v 41). He will be **powerful in the Holy Spirit,** and no one will be **able to oppose Him** (vv 42–44). Yet He will defeat His enemies **by the word of His mouth** (vv 27, 39, 41), not by any earthly power (**horse, rider, bow, gold, silver,** or **multitudes** of warriors, v 37).

Those who live **in** the **days** of this Son of David will be **blessed** (v 50).

We will hope in God

17.1 Lord, You† Yourself† *will be* our King for ever and ever;
because in You†, O God, our soul will boast.
17.2 And what *is* the time of a person's life on the earth?
As *is* his time, *so* also his hope *is* upon him.
17.3 But we will hope in God our Savior,
because the power of our God *will be* for ever, with mercy,
17.4 and the kingdom of our God *will be* for ever over the nations, in judgment.

You swore that David's kingship would not cease

17.5 You†, Lord, chose David *as* king over Israel,
and You† swore to him concerning his seed for ever,
that his kingship would not cease before You†.

But sinners, to whom You made no promise, took the kingship by force

17.6 But in our sins, sinners rose up against us;
they—*those* to whom You† made no promise—fell upon us and drove us out;
they took *it* away by force,
17.7 and they did not glorify Your† honorable name with glory.
They put kingship in place of their exaltation;
17.8 in *the* arrogance of *that* exchange, they made the throne of David desolate.

You will cast them down when a foreigner arises

But You†, O God, will cast them down and take† their seed from the earth;
17.9 when a person strange to our race rises up against them,
17.10 You† will repay them, O God, in accordance with their sins,
so that it will come upon them in accordance with their works.
17.11 God will not have mercy on them;
He has sought out their seed, and has not left one of them.
17.12 The Lord *is* faithful in all His judgments which He does on the earth.

The transgressor made our land desolate

17.13 The transgressor made our land desolate from its inhabitants;
they destroyed *the* young *man* and *the* old *man* and their children together.
17.14 In *the* wrath of his beauty he sent them away far to *the* west,
and *he set* the rulers of the land for a mockery, and did not spare.
17.15 The enemy acted arrogantly in *his* estrangement,
and his heart *was* estranged from our God,
17.16 and all *the thing*s that he did in Jerusalem
were just as the nations *did* in the cities to their gods.

Those who were faithful fled

17.17 But the sons of the covenant had power over them in *the* midst of *the* mingled nations.
There was no *one* in the midst of them, in Jerusalem, who did mercy and truth.
17.18 Those who loved *the* assemblies of the holy *one*s fled from them;
like birds they flew away from their bed.
17.19 They wandered in the deserts to save their souls from evil,
and a soul *that was* saved from them *was* precious in *the* eyes of *the* sojourners.
17.20 They were dispersed by *the* transgressors into all the land,
because heaven restrained the falling of rain on the land;
17.21 *the* eternal wellsprings were restrained, from *the* depths, from *the* high mountains,
because there was no *one* among them who did righteousness and judgment.
From their ruler to *those who were* least, *they were* in every sin:
17.22 the king *was* in transgression, and the judge *was* in disobedience, and the people in sin.

Raise up the Son of David to be King over Israel

17.23 Behold†, Lord, and raise up† for them their King, *the* Son of David,
for the time which You†, O God, have seen, to make Him reign over Israel, Your† servant,
17.24 and gird† Him with power to beat down *the* unrighteous rulers,
17.25 to cleanse Jerusalem from *the* nations who tread *it* down in destruction,

by wisdom *and* by righteousness **17.26** driving away sinners from *the* inheritance,
breaking in pieces *the* arrogance of *the* sinner like a potter's vessels,
with a rod of iron breaking down all their foundation,
17.27 destroying *the* transgressing nations with *the* word of His mouth,
making *the* nations flee from His face at His rebuke,
and reproving sinners in *the* word of their heart.

He will lead a holy people

17.28 And He will gather together a holy people whom He will lead in righteousness,
and will judge *the* tribes of *the* people that is made holy by *the* Lord His God.
17.29 And He will not allow unrighteousness to abide in their midst *any* more,
and no one who knows wickedness will dwell with them;
17.30 for He will know them, that they are all sons of their God,
and He will divide them in their tribes over the land,
17.31 and *the* sojourner and *the* foreigner will not sojourn with them *any* longer. Selah.

He will rule the nations in righteousness

He will judge *the* peoples and nations in *the* wisdom of His righteousness,
17.32 and He will have *the* peoples of *the* nations serving Him under His yoke,
and He will glorify the Lord in a conspicuous *place* of all the earth,
17.33 and He will cleanse Jerusalem by sanctification, just as *it was* at the beginning,
17.34 so that *the* nations may come from *the* end of the earth to see His glory,
bringing *as* gifts her sons who have become weak,
17.35 and to see the Lord's glory *with* which God has glorified her.
And He *is* a righteous King taught by God over them,
17.36 and *there* will be no unrighteousness in His days in their midst,
because all *of them will be* holy, and Christ *the* Lord *will be* their King.

He will not wage war by earthly power

17.37 For He will not trust in *the* horse and *the* rider and *the* bow,
nor will He multiply for Himself gold or silver for war,
and He will not gather together hopes by multitudes for *the* day of battle.

He will smite the earth with His word

17.38 *The* Lord Himself *is* His King, *the* hope of the *One who is* mighty in *the* hope of God,
and He will have mercy on all the nations *who are* before Him in fear.
17.39 For He will smite *the* earth with the word of His mouth for ever;
17.40 He will bless *the* Lord's people in wisdom with gladness.
17.41 And He *will be* pure from sin, so that He may rule over a great people,

reproving rulers and destroying sinners by *the* power of *His* word.
17.42 And He will not be weak in His days on His God,
because God has made Him powerful in *the* Holy Spirit
and wise in *the* counsel of understanding with power and righteousness,
17.43 and *the* Lord's blessing *will be* with Him in power,
and He will not be weak;
17.44 His hope *will be* on *the* Lord,
and who will be able *to* oppose Him?
Powerful in His deeds, and strong in *the* fear of God,
17.45 shepherding the flock of *the* Lord in faithfulness and righteousness,
and He will not allow *any* among them to be weak in their pasture.
17.46 He will lead them all in equality,
and there will not be *any* arrogance among them, so that none of them will be overpowered.
17.47 This *will be* the excellence of the King of Israel whom God has known,
to raise Him up over *the* house of Israel, to instruct them.
17.48 His words *will be* refined by fire more than the most precious gold;
in *the* assemblies He will judge *the* tribes of *the* sanctified people;
17.49 His words *will be* like *the* words of *the* holy *ones*, in *the* midst of *the* sanctified peoples.

May God hasten His mercy

17.50 Blessed *are* those who will live in those days,
to see the good *things* of Israel, which God will do when *he* gathers *their* tribes.
17.51 May God hasten His mercy on Israel;
He will deliver us from *the* impurity of *our* profane enemies.
The Lord Himself *will be* our King for ever and ever.

Psalm 18

The Lord shows **mercy** to **all the earth,** but especially He lavishes His **kindness** and **love** on His people (**Israel,** the **seed of Abraham;** vv 1–4). If they are **poor,** he hearkens to their **entreaty** and sees that they do not **lack anything** they need (vv 2–3). He treats them **as a firstborn, an only son,** giving them His **discipline** to **turn** them **back** from sins of **ignorance** (vv 4–5).

May God cleanse Israel . . . for the day of His choosing, when He will bless His people and show **mercy** on them by raising up **His Christ** (v 6), who will govern them with a **rod of discipline** in **wisdom** and the **fear of His God** (v 8), so that they walk **in works of righteousness** (vv 9–10). Those who live **in those days** will be **blessed** (v 7).

Great is our God and glorious (v 11). The **lights** in the heavens (the sun, moon, and stars) have never **gone astray from the path that** He **commanded them** (vv 12–13). Yet even they have altered their paths at the **order** of God's **servants** such as Joshua (v 14).

Lord, your mercy will be on Israel

18.1 Lord, Your† mercy *will be* upon the works of Your† hands for ever;
18.2 Your† kindness *will be* with a rich gift on Israel.
Your† eyes look on them, and none of them will lack *anything*;
18.3 Your† ears hearken to *the* poor *man*'s entreaty in hope.
Your† judgments *will be* on all the earth with mercy,
18.4 and Your† love *will be* on *the* seed of Abraham, *on the* son of Israel.
Your† discipline *will be* on us, as on a firstborn, an only son,
18.5 to turn back a receptive soul from being unlearned in ignorance.

May God cleanse Israel for the day of His Christ

18.6 May God cleanse Israel for *the* day of mercy by *His* blessing,
for *the* day of *His* choosing in *the* raising up of His Christ.
18.7 Blessed *are* those who will live in those days,
to see the Lord's good *things*, which he will do for the generation to come,
18.8 under *the* rod of discipline of Christ *the* Lord in *the* fear of His God,
in *the* wisdom of *the* Spirit and of righteousness and of power,
18.9 to direct a man in works of righteousness in *the* fear of God,
to establish them all in *the* sight of *the* Lord
18.10 *as* a good generation in *the* fear of God, in *the* days of mercy. Selah.

Great is our God, who has commanded the lights

18.11 Great *is* our God and glorious, dwelling in *the* highest *places*,
18.12 who ordained *the* lights in *their* journey for *the* times of hours from days to days,
and they have not gone astray from *the* path that You† commanded them.
18.13 Their path *has been* in *the* fear of God every day,
from *the* day *when* God created them, and for ever.
18.14 And they have not wandered from *the* day *when* He created them;
from ancient generations they have not forsaken their paths,
except *when* God commanded them by *the* order of His servants.

COMMENTARY ON THE MACCABEAN HISTORY

Introduction

The book known in ancient times as the *Makkabaika* ("the Maccabean History") describes the period when Judea was ruled by "the kingdom of the Greeks" (1.10), until at last "the yoke of the nations was lifted up from Israel" (13.41).

The Maccabean History reports the fulfillment of some of Daniel's visions, and describes the origin of the "feast of the dedication" attended by Jesus (John 10.22). Its summary of the life of Judas Maccabeus was taken by the Holy Spirit as the basis for His summary of the life of Jesus:

> "And the additional acts of Judas, and the wars and manly good deeds that he did, and his greatness, have not been written down: for they were very many" (Maccabaica 9.22).

> "And there are also many other things that Jesus did, which, if they were written one by one, I suppose not even the world itself would contain the books that would be written" (John 21.25).

In this way, the Scriptures themselves have drawn a parallel between the "very many" good deeds of Judas Maccabeus and the even more numerous good deeds of Jesus Christ.

Structure

The death of Judas Maccabeus is placed almost exactly at the midpoint of the book, dividing it into two approximately equal halves (1.1–9.22 and 9.23–16.24)—a division that has been noticed ever since ancient times.[1] Some blocks of material in the first half symmetrically balance similar blocks in the second half. For instance, the praise of Judas's achievements in 3.1–9 balances the praise of Simon's achievements in 14.4–15; Mattathias's forward-looking commemoration of the faithful and commission to his family in 2.49–68 balances the nation's backward-looking commemoration of the family in 14.25–49.

---

[1] Some ancient copies divided the Maccabean History into two "books" at that point (de Bruyne and Sodar, *Anciennes Traductions latines des Machabées,* lvii–lviii).

Within those two halves, the narrative may be divided into seven stages, according to the successive rulers over Judea and leaders of the Judeans:

1. Alexander and his successors (1.1–9).
2. Antiochus Epiphanes (1.10–64).
3. Mattathias (2.1–70).
4. Judas Maccabeus (3.1–9.22).
5. Jonathan (9.23–12.53).
6. Simon (13.1–16.22).
7. John (16.23–24).

The brief opening and closing sections (1.1–9; 16.23–24) act in effect as a frame for the narrative. Its main action starts when the oppression of Judea begins in the days of Antiochus Epiphanes, and ends when the deliverance of Judea is completed in the days of Simon.

The arrangement is mainly chronological, but as in the Law of Moses, Judges, Samuel-Kings, Ezra-Nehemiah, and the Gospels, some of the material is organized on the basis of subject matter rather than chronology. This means that a later incident may sometimes be discussed before an earlier one. For instance, Jonathan's message to the Spartans (12.5–18) is recorded before the Spartans' much earlier message to Onias (12.19–23).

Rulers

The Maccabean History starts with Darius, the last king of the **Medo-Persian** empire, who was overthrown by Alexander of **Macedon.** On Alexander's death, his empire was divided. The Maccabean History then concentrates mainly on the Seleucids ruling **Asia** (to the north of Israel) and the Ptolemies ruling **Egypt** (to the south): these are the "kings of the North" and "kings of the South" described in Daniel 11.5–45.

The chart on the following page provides modern identifications of the principal foreign rulers and Judean leaders mentioned in the Maccabean History, with their professed lines of descent, and with modern estimates of the approximate dates of their reigns.

One ruler of Syria—Trypho, who reigned from about 142 to about 138 BCE—does not appear on the chart, as he did not claim descent from the Seleucid royal family.

Names that are not given in the Maccabean History are printed in square brackets. Unofficial names (nicknames) are presented in quotation marks. John son of Simon, a great opponent of Greek rule, would probably not have wanted to be called by the Hellenic name "Hyrcanus"—and Ptolemy VIII would certainly not have wanted to be remembered as "Physcon" ("Fatso").

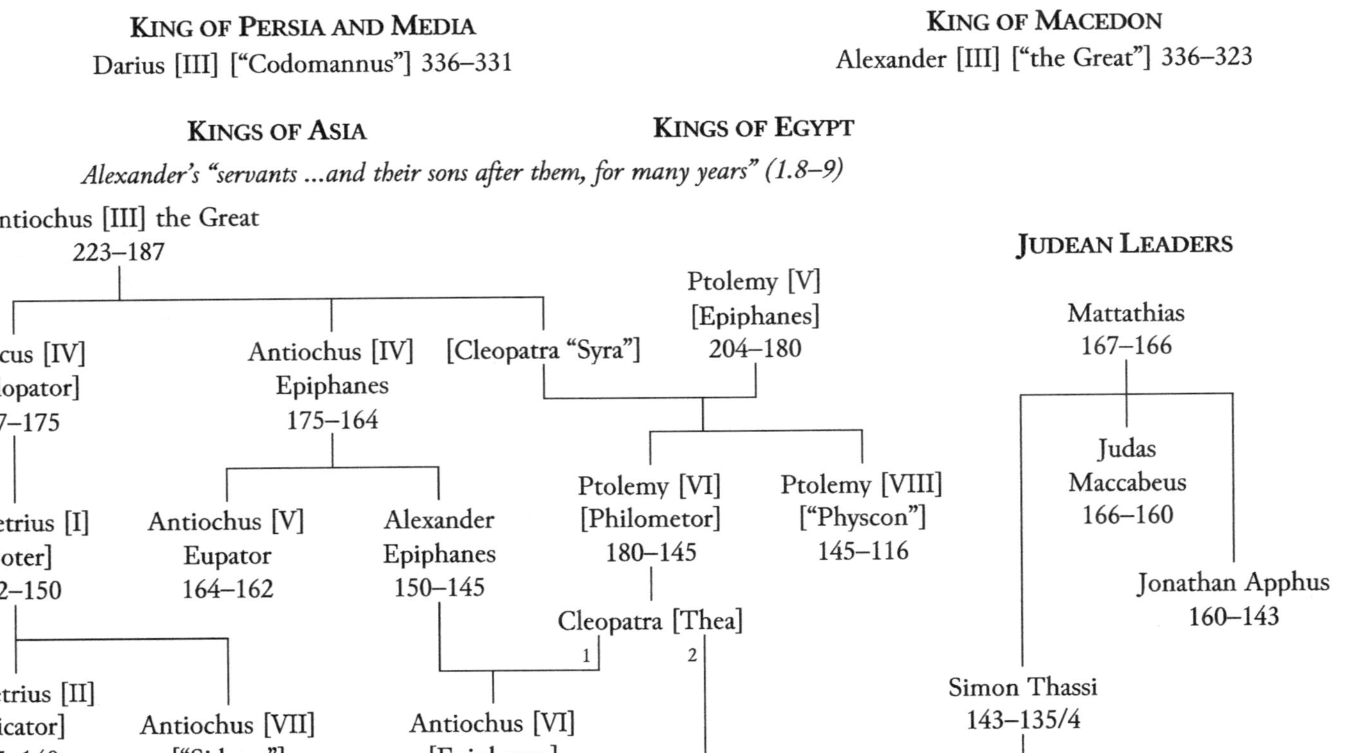

King of Persia and Media
Darius [III] ["Codomannus"] 336–331
King of Macedon
Alexander [III] ["the Great"] 336–323
Kings of Asia
Kings of Egypt
Alexander's "servants ...and their sons after them, for many years" (1.8–9)
Antiochus [III] the Great 223–187
Judean Leaders
Ptolemy [V] [Epiphanes] 204–180
Mattathias 167–166
Seleucus [IV] [Philopator] 187–175
Antiochus [IV] Epiphanes 175–164
[Cleopatra "Syra"]
Judas Maccabeus 166–160
Ptolemy [VI] [Philometor] 180–145
Ptolemy [VIII] ["Physcon"] 145–116
Demetrius [I] [Soter] 162–150
Antiochus [V] Eupator 164–162
Alexander Epiphanes 150–145
Jonathan Apphus 160–143
Cleopatra [Thea]
1
2
Demetrius [II] [Nicator] 145–140, 129–125
Antiochus [VII] ["Sidetes"] 139–129
Antiochus [VI] [Epiphanes] 145–142
Simon Thassi 143–135/4
John ["Hyrcanus"] 135/4–104

The chart shows only two portions of Alexander the Great's former empire—the portions governed by the Seleucids and Ptolemies. Other territories that had been ruled by Alexander passed into the hands of other kings, and six of those kings are mentioned in passing in the Maccabean History:

KINGS OF MACEDON
Philip [V] [221–179 bce]
Perseus [179–168 BCE]

KINGS OF PERGAMUM
Eumenes [II] [197–159 BCE]
Attalus [II] [159–138 BCE]

KING OF CAPPADOCIA
Ariarathes [V] [163–130 BCE]

KING OF PERSIA AND MEDIA [PARTHIAN]
Arsaces [VI, Mithridates I] [171–138 BCE]

Dates

The system for numbering **months** appears to be the same throughout the Maccabean History, but the system for numbering **years** may possibly vary in different sections of the book.

Months. When God brought the Israelites out of Egypt, He commanded them to reckon the month of the Passover as the first month of the year (Exod 12.2). The Maccabean History appears to use the same numbering system. It numbers the month Chislev as the ninth month of the year (Maccabaica 4.28), just as the Hebrew Scriptures do (Zec 7.1), and it reckons the Feast of Tabernacles as occurring in the seventh month of the year (Maccabaica 10.21), just as the Hebrew Scriptures do (Lev 23.34; Neh 8.14).

Years. The Maccabean History dates events in years "of the kingdom of the Greeks" (1.10). It is generally believed that this refers to some form or forms of the Seleucid Era (SE) reckoning, which was the standard system in territories ruled by Seleucid kings. According to this system, years were counted from the start of the reign of Seleucus I (Josephus, *Antiquities,* 13.213). Year 1 SE was about 312–311 BCE; year 2 SE was about 311–310 BCE; and so on.

Many areas under Seleucid control reckoned each year as beginning in the fall. In Israel, however, each year was often reckoned as beginning in the springtime, at the month of the Passover. Spring-start years might start either six months earlier or six months later than fall-start years. Consequently, there might be three different ways of numbering years SE (see the chart on the facing page).

Season	Month	Year		
		Fall start	Spring start	
Spring	1		Year 1 SE	
	2			
	3			
Summer	4			
	5			
	6			
Fall	7	Year 1 SE		
	8			
	9			
Winter	10			
	11			
	12			
Spring	1		Year 2 SE	Year 1 SE
	2			
	3			
Summer	4			
	5			
	6			
Fall	7	Year 2 SE		
	8			
	9			
Winter	10			
	11			
	12			

The following year-numbers are specified in the Maccabean History:

Year 137: Antiochus Epiphanes becomes king (1.10).
Year 143: He marches against Israel (1.20).
After two years: His tribute collector attacks Jerusalem (1.29).
Year 145, month Chislev, day 15: An abomination of desolation is built (1.54).
Year 145, month Chislev, day 25: Sacrifices on the heathen altar begin (1.59).
Year 146: Mattathias dies (2.70).
Year 147: Antiochus crosses the Euphrates (3.37).
In the coming year: His general Lysias gathers a new army (4.28).
Year 148, month 9 (Chislev), day 25: The new altar is dedicated (4.52).
Year 149: Antiochus Epiphanes dies (6.16).
Year 150: Judas besieges the citadel (6.20).

Year 151: Demetrius son of Seleucus comes from Rome (7.1).
Year 151, month Adar, day 13: Nicanor dies (7.43).
Year 152, month 1: Bacchides and Alcimus attack Jerusalem (9.3).
Year 153, month 2: Alcimus dies (9.54).
For two years: The land of Judah is quiet (9.57).
Year 160: Alexander Epiphanes becomes king (10.1).
Year 160, month 7: Jonathan becomes high priest (10.21).
Year 162: Ptolemy meets Alexander (10.57).
Year 165: Demetrius son of Demetrius arrives (10.67).
Year 167: He becomes king (11.19).
Year 170: The yoke of the nations is lifted from Israel (13.41).
Year 171, month 2, day 23: Simon cleanses the citadel (13.51).
Year 172: Demetrius goes into Media (14.1).
Year 172, month Elul, day 18: Stelae are set up to honor Simon (14.27).
Year 174: Antiochus son of Demetrius arrives (15.10).
Year 177, month 11 (Shebat): Simon dies (16.14).

Nowadays it is usually believed that the Maccabean History's year-numbers for most or all events *outside Judea* use the *fall-start* reckoning.

However, there is disagreement about the book's year-numbers for most or all events *within Judea.* Some researchers believe that the book uses the *fall-start* system for these dates as well. Other researchers believe that it uses a *spring-start* system beginning six months *before* the fall-start system. And still others believe that it uses a *spring-start* system beginning six months *after* the fall-start system.[2]

In practice, the possibility of different year-numberings is important to remember when comparing dates in the Maccabean History with those in other ancient documents (such as the Maccabean Epitome or Babylonian historical documents)—and even when comparing dates in one part of the Maccabean History with those in another. For instance, the dedication of the altar (dated 148 SE in Maccabaica 4.52) may *possibly* have been very close in time to the death of Antiochus Epiphanes (dated 149 SE in Maccabaica 6.10).

However, it is futile to speculate about the system(s) of reckoning used for most of the year-numbers in the Maccabean History. The book itself tells us very little about most of its dates, and rarely do we have any other reliable source of information about them. No amount of scholarly research has ever altered or is ever likely to alter that.

---

[2] Bringmann, *Hellenistische Reform und Religionsverfolgung in Judäa,* 15–40, argued that all year-dates in the Maccabean History use the fall-start system.

Grabbe, "Maccabean Chronology," 59–74, argued that its Judean year-dates use a spring-start system beginning six months before the fall-start system.

Bickerman, *God of the Maccabees,* 155–58, argued that its Judean year-dates use a spring-start system beginning six months after the fall-start system.

Teachings

The Maccabean History describes times when "arrogance was established, and reproof, and a period of overturning" (2.49), and when "those who were opposed to the Law peered out in all the appointed boundaries of Israel, and all those who were working unrighteousness rose up . . . and great oppression came about in Israel" (9.23, 27). Many who had previously been living among God's people departed from the Lord and lived like the worldly people around them (1.11–15, 41–59). What should have been the city of God and the temple of God were put to uses that were contrary to God's word (2.7–12).

The book acknowledges that Israel had incurred the wrath of God (1.64), and that the nation was delivered from foreign rule, not by superior military force or skill, but solely by the power of God. Success comes only by seeking help from Heaven (2.61; 4.10, 55; 9.46; 12.15; 16.3), never by any human source of strength (3.18–19). Nothing can ever be accomplished unless it is the Lord's will for it to happen (3.53, 60; 5.62). "If the LORD does not build a house, those who build it have toiled in vain" (Psa 127.1).

Under the old covenant, when this book was written, God often revealed His will not only through His written word (Maccabaica 1.57; 3.48; 13.9), but also through living prophets (Amos 3.2). However, in a time of oppression, while Israel was suffering under the wrath of God, the Lord might refuse to speak to them (1 Sam 28.6; Prov 1.28), so that they no longer received any prophecies (Lam 2.9; Psa 74.9; Ezek 7.26). So it was during the oppression described in this book (9.27). But the Lord is merciful. His wrath is only for a moment (Psa 30.5; 103.9, 17; Isa 54.7–8; 57.16); when people return to Him, He restores His blessings at the earliest possible moment, "at the turn of the morning" (Psa 46.5; Luke 18.7–8). Therefore, under the old covenant, whenever Israel returned to the Lord, He resumed the continual sending of His prophets, "daily rising up early and sending them" (Jer 7.25; 2 Chr 36.15; Neh 9.30; Matt 21.34–36). And so it would be after the oppression described in this book (Matt 11.13; Luke 2.36; 1.76). Looking still further ahead, the Maccabean History foresaw the coming of a "faithful Prophet" who would be able to change the leadership of Israel (Maccabaica 14.41) and reveal what would be done with the stones of the temple (4.46).

In this time of trouble, Mattathias and his sons were "those men through whose hands salvation was given to Israel" (5.62). They could lead the people, and they could even be appointed high priests (10.20–21, 69; 13.42; 14.17, 30, 35), for they were descended from Aaron (2.1). But they were not kings, and their leadership could pass away when the faithful Prophet came (14.41).

The Maccabean History abundantly illustrates the importance of standing firm and keeping faithfully to the commands of God, even in an age when almost everyone else is departing from the Lord and living a worldly life (2.19–22). God's people should look to His word for guidance (3.48; 13.9), not to the people of the world. "In every season unceasingly" they should pray for those around them and (under the old covenant) offer the appointed sacrifices (12.11). They should help those who are weak or suffering (3.9; 5.16, 53–54), and they should never return evil for good (16.17).

The book does not pretend that those who serve God will have an easy or comfortable life. On the contrary, they suffer many hardships and setbacks (14.29). "Through many tribulations we must enter into the kingdom of God" (Acts 14.22). Some of the Lord's servants are even required to give up their lives in service to him (Maccabaica 2.50; 9.10). A good work may be accomplished only after many years, and after the death of most of those who toiled for it (cf. Dan 11.33, 35).

The accuracy of the book's historical information needs no defense. The Maccabean History has been subjected to more intense critical scrutiny than most documents, because it has been diligently assailed from two sides: by skeptics striving to undermine its testimony to the fulfillment of Daniel's prophecies, and by certain Protestants fearing that anyone who acknowledged its merits would be in effect submitting to the Papacy. Yet none of the book's critics has detected any historical error in it—except by arguments that would also find fault with the Gospels, the book of Acts, and the historical books in the Hebrew Scriptures. Here a point often made about the book of Acts is relevant. Even setting aside the question of divine inspiration, the book of Acts is a historical document of such consistently demonstrable reliability that its testimony should be accepted even in the (very few) instances where other ancient documents appear to disagree with it. The same can be said about the Maccabean History.[3]

The time when the book was written—during or after the leadership of John son of Simon—is the very time when the divisions between Phariseeism and Sadduceeism are reported to have become prominent (Josephus, *Antiquities,* 13.288–298). Yet it is evident that the writer of the Maccabean History did not belong to either of those denominations.

The Pharisees supplemented the Scriptures with many unwritten "traditions of the elders" (Mark 7.1–13 ≡ Matt 15.1–9). Nor were they alone in doing so; many other ancient Judaic writers (e.g., Philo and the writers of most of the Dead Sea Scrolls) did the same. (Indeed, Mark 7.3 says that "all the Jews" did so.) But there is not the slightest trace of such supplements in the Maccabean History.

The Sadducees did not accept such teachings of Scripture as the existence of angels and the resurrection from the dead (Acts 23.8; Mark 12.18, 24). The author of the

---

[3] Of course, some of the statements *quoted* in these books are incorrect. Ananias and Sapphira certainly lied in what they said to the apostle Peter (Acts 5.1–11), but the book of Acts is not at fault for recording those lies accurately. Some of the statements *quoted* in the Maccabean History may likewise be incorrect, e.g., the stories told to Judas Maccabeus about the Romans, the Spartans' claim to be descendants of Abraham, and (especially) the claims made by some of the Seleucid kings. But even in these cases, there is good reason to think that the statements have been *reported* faithfully, i.e., that Judas's informants, the Spartans, and the Seleucid kings did indeed say or write such things. See the commentary below for details.

Maccabean History was no Sadducee either: for instance, he states without any ambiguity or reservation that Sennacherib's army was destroyed by an angel sent from God (Maccabaica 7.41).[4]

In an age when most of those around him seem to have been siding with one denominational faction or the other, the author of the Maccabean History did not. He simply held to the doctrines of Scripture, neither adding to them nor taking away from them.

The Maccabean History has special value in our own time. The period since the late nineteenth century has itself been a kind of Maccabean age, in which the church—which ought to be "Mount Zion … the city of the living God, the heavenly Jerusalem" (Heb 12.22)—has progressively been defiled and ruined by enemies both from outside and from inside, who have "departed from the holy covenant, and yoked themselves with the nations, and sold themselves to do wickedness" (Maccabaica 1.15), by seeking to introduce the world's beliefs and ways of living into the Israel of God (cf. 1 Jn 2.15–17; 2 Cor 6.14–7.1; Eph 4.17–20). Indeed, those who call themselves priests of God are often leaders in corrupting and destroying the nation of God (Maccabaica 7.5–22). The earthly war waged by Judas Maccabeus, his brothers, and his companions is therefore a model to be treasured by all who follow in their steps in the great spiritual war today.[5]

Names

In ancient times the book was sometimes called "the [Book] of Maccabaica" (*to tōn Makkabaikōn;* Clement of Alexandria, *Stromata,* 1.21.123), or, more briefly, "the Maccabaica" (*ta Makkabaika;* Origen in Eusebius, *History,* 6.25). The term "Maccabaica" means "Maccabean Matters," i.e., matters related to Judas Maccabeus—what we would call in modern English "Maccabean History."[6]

---

[4] Sadducean tendencies have sometimes been seen in the fact that the author "does not refer to the resurrection of the dead, not even when great leaders have fallen" (ZEB 3.15). But "mention of this belief is almost completely absent from the [Hebrew] Bible and various other purely Jewish works (such as III Maccabees) which were not suspected of Sadducee bias" (Efrón, *Studies on the Hasmonean Period,* 18). What reference to the resurrection is there after the death of Jonathan, or Josiah, or Samson, or Joshua, or David? That topic was not part of the books' subject matter. A Biblical history book speaks of resurrection only if people were raised from the dead during the time period covered by the history (e.g., in the days of Elijah and Elisha). Indeed it is noteworthy that the Maccabean History specifically mentions the ascension of Elijah (Maccabaica 2.58). No true Sadducee (as described in the New Testament) could have accepted the authority of the Elijah and Elisha narratives, with their resurrections (1 Kgs 17.17–24; 2 Kgs 4.32–37; 13.21) and angelic hosts (2 Kgs 6.16–17).

[5] This point seems to have first been made by Wordsworth, in his sermons on *The Church and the Maccabees;* see also his *Holy Bible,* 6.xvi–xxi.

[6] In ancient Greek, a history was often described by a plural name ending in *-ika,* e.g., *Hellēnika* ("Greek History," Thucydides 1.97); *Ptolemaika* ("Ptolemaic History"); *Argonautika*

The same name—"Maccabaica"—was sometimes applied to a different book, the one known more fully as the Epitome of the Acts of Judas Maccabeus. To distinguish them, the present book was sometimes called "the First Book of Maccabaica," i.e., "the First Book of Maccabean History" (Hippolytus, *Daniel,* 4.3.8).

Later, the form "the First Book of the Maccabees" developed (Eusebius, *Preparation,* 8.72). It is still current today. However, this name is both misleading and incorrect. It is misleading, because the book is complete in itself and has no sequel. And it is incorrect, because there is only one "Maccabee" in the book—Judas Maccabeus.[7]

Therefore, the older, simpler, and more accurate term "Maccabaica" ("Maccabean History") has been preferred in the present work.

In Hebrew or Aramaic, the Maccabean History was reportedly known by a name that was transliterated into Greek as *sar beth sabanaiel* (Origen in Eusebius, *History,* 6.25). Many scholars have attempted to decipher that phrase.[8] Its first components most likely referred either to Judas Maccabeus ("the leader [*śar*] of the house [*bêt*]," Hebrew) or to the book itself ("the book [*s^e^par*] of the house [*bêt*]," Aramaic). Its second half *(sabanaiel)* remains a mystery. Some suggestions have been:

śr byt š bnh 'l, "the leader of the house that God has built";
śr byt š bny 'l, "the leader of the house that [are] sons of God";
spr byt š bnh 'l, "the book of the house that God has built";
spr byt š bny 'l, "the book of the house that [are] sons of God";
spr byt śr bny 'l, "the book of the house of the leader of the sons of God";
spr byt srbny 'l, "the book of the house of the rebels of God."

The last four of those suggestions assume that *sar* stands for Greek *sphar* (≡ Aramaic *s^e^par*). The last two also assume that *sabanaiel* stands for *sarbanaiel.* The final sugges-

---

("Argonautic History"). Schwartz (*2 Maccabees,* 58), misled by the plural form *Makkabaika,* thinks that Origen could have been referring to a plurality of Maccabean books. In fact the name is plural simply because the history consists of a plurality of things (KG 2.1.268, §403aẟ). The equally plural name *Ptolemaika* was assigned in Greek manuscripts to a single book—and a very short one at that (see Part Four). Moreover, Clement of Alexandria undoubtedly had in mind a single book when he referred to "the [Book] of Maccabaica" (using the article *to* [singular]: *Stromata,* 1.21.123).

The *Makkabaika* listed by Origen was one of the Hebrew writings preserved by the Jews (Eusebius, *History,* 6.25). Other Maccabean books were certainly in existence, but none of them was written in Hebrew, so the Hebrew work called *Makkabaika* was undoubtedly the present book and only the present book.

[7] Uninformed writers occasionally refer to Judas Maccabeus's brothers as "Jonathan Maccabeus," "Simon Maccabeus," etc. This is a mistake of the same kind as calling Simon Peter's brother "Andrew Peter." "Maccabeus," like "Peter," was not a family name. It was a name given to one particular member of the family (Maccabaica 2.4).

[8] Various proposed interpretations are discussed by Grimm xvii; Keil 22; Fairweather-Black 39–40; André, *Apocryphes de l'Ancien Testament,* 61–62; Abel iv–v; Bartlett, *1 Maccabees,* 18.

tion is by far the least likely: *srbny* is a rare word, and would more naturally be applied to God's enemies than to those who were delivering His people.

In one respect all of the suggestions listed above are suspect. All of them assume that the final syllable represents Hebrew or Aramaic *'l* ("God")—but in Greek, that was usually transliterated *ēl* (with a long *eta*), seldom *el* (with a short *epsilon*).

Authorship and Date of Composition

The Maccabean History is written with the same strict anonymity as Joshua, Judges, Samuel-Kings, Chronicles, and Esther. As in those books, the author never speaks in the first person and makes no allusion to identity or personal situation.

The last events reported in the Maccabean History are the wars, building programs, and other activities that took place during the high priesthood of John son of Simon (16.23–24), who is believed to have been high priest between about 134 and 104 BCE.[9] The book must have been written some time within the following century and a half, because Josephus, who was a contemporary of the apostles, used its Greek version extensively as source material for his *Antiquities.*

Attempts have frequently been made to date the book more precisely, but none of the proposed arguments is conclusive.

1. It is occasionally argued that the book must have been written very early during John's high priesthood, because its author must have been "an eye-witness of the battles of Ammaus and Beth Zacharia" (Bar-Kochva, *Judas Maccabeus,* 152–68), and therefore must already have been adult around 147 SE ≡ 165 BCE (cf. Maccabaica 3.37–4.25). Yet detailed, accurate histories do not need to be written by eyewitnesses (especially if they are based on eyewitness testimony: Luke 1.1–4). Probably, like the Gospel of Luke, the Maccabean History is largely composed of eyewitness testimony; but its final compiler need not have been an eyewitness.
2. It is occasionally argued from 4.46; 9.27; 14.41 that the book must have been written before the return of prophecy to Israel—which happened well before the birth of Jesus (Luke 2.26, 36).[10] However, the Maccabean History's statements

---

[9] When the Maccabean History was written, John's activities had already been recorded in a "book of the days" (16.23–24), but this does not necessarily indicate that John was dead by that time. In the ancient world, books containing the events of rulers' reigns were often compiled—and sometimes consulted—while the rulers were still alive (Est 6.1–2).

The year of John's death is not certain. The date usually given, 104 BCE, derives only from information in Josephus—whose figures for the period do not tally, and whose manuscripts also vary at one point in their estimates of the length of John's high priesthood (see Schürer-Vermes 1.200–01, n. 1).

[10] Indeed, prophecy may have returned more than a century before the birth of Jesus. Josephus (*Antiquities,* 13.299–300, 321–322) reports some apparent true prophecies made by John son of Simon (who probably died about 104 BCE; see the preceding footnote); cf. Gray, *Prophetic Figures in Late Second Temple Jewish Palestine,* 16–23; VanderKam, *From Joshua to Caiaphas,* 304–07. Josephus is not a reliable witness for this period (see Part Four), but on this particular

about the lack of prophecy refer only to the previous period of tribulation between Antiochus Epiphanes (4.46) and Simon (14.41), not to the time when the book itself was written. (In the same way, the statement "There is no longer a prophet" in Psalm 74.9 refers only to the period of tribulation described in that psalm, not to the time when the psalm itself was written; its author was himself a prophet: 2 Chr 29.30; Matt 13.35.)

3. It is occasionally argued that the book must have been written before the city of Pergamum came under Roman rule (about 130 BCE), because it makes no reference to that event when listing the achievements of the Romans (Maccabaica 8.1–16).[11] However, that passage reports only what Judas Maccabeus heard about the Romans (8.1). Judas could not possibly have heard anything about the takeover of Pergamum, because it happened 30 years after his death. Moreover, some even later events do appear to be mentioned elsewhere in the Maccabean History: John's notable "wars" and "the walls that he built" (16.23) could scarcely have begun until some time after the death of Antiochus son of Demetrius around 129 BCE (cf. Josephus, *Antiquities,* 13.247, 254–257; Diodorus 34/35.1.5).
4. It is often argued that the book must have been written before Judea came under Roman rule and the Jerusalem temple was defiled (about 63 BCE), because it makes no reference to those events and speaks positively about the Romans. But Biblical writers often speak positively about Roman and other rulers authorized by the Lord, even when those rulers were persecuting His people (cf. Matt 22.17–21; Rom 13.1–7; 1 Pet 2.17; Jer 27.1–22). And many books written well after the final destruction of the Jerusalem temple in 70 CE continued to speak as if it was still standing and in active use (e.g., Josephus, *Against Apion,* 2.77, 193–196; *Antiquities,* 3.231–233, etc.; "Barnabas" 7.3–8.7; Diognetus 3.2–5).

Style

The Maccabean History is written in a markedly Hebraic style comparable to that of the histories in the Hebrew Scriptures (Joshua, Judges, Samuel-Kings, Chronicles, Ezra-Nehemiah, Esther, and the historical narratives in the Law of Moses). In many respects, its phrasing, syntax, and word order are closer to Hebrew than to standard practice in Greek of this period. For instance:

- As in Hebrew but not in standard Greek, nearly all sentences are linked by "and" (Greek *kai,* corresponding to Hebrew *w-*).
- As in Hebrew, the verb generally precedes the other elements of the sentence (in standard Greek, the word order is much more varied).

---

point, his testimony would be consistent with the Lord's dealings with Israel under the old covenant. At every other time when prophecy was taken away during a period of tribulation, it was restored very soon after the tribulation ended.

[11] Momigliano, "Date of the 1st Book of Maccabees," 561–66; Schwartz, "Israel and the Nations Roundabout," 16–38.

- As in Hebrew, part of a group may be described simply as "from" or "out of" that group, where standard Greek would require a noun or pronoun as well (*exēlthon apo tōn hiereōn,* "there came out [some] from the priests," 7.33; *katastathēsetai ex autōn,* "there will be established [some] out of them," 10.37).
- As in Hebrew, a resumptive pronoun may be inserted where none would be necessary in standard Greek (*ton logon hon egrapsen auton,* "the word that He wrote it," 7.16).
- In addition, many turns of phrase are close imitations of Hebrew idioms, e.g., "and they became to him for tribute" (*kai egenonto autō eis phoron* ≡ Hebrew *wyhyw lw lmm*, 1.4); "there has found us many evil things" (*heuren hēmas kaka polla* ≡ *m*ʹʹ*ny rʿyt rbwt*, 1.11); "and the kingdom was made ready" (*kai ētoimasthē hē basileia* ≡ *wtkn mlkyt*, 1.16); "after two years of days" (*meta duo etē hēmerōn* ≡ *lšntym ymym*, 1.29); "for a harmful accuser" (*eis diabolon ponēron* ≡ *lšṭn rʿ*, 1.36).

Its narrative procedures are also comparable to those of the histories in the Hebrew Scriptures. It begins with a form of statement familiar from those earlier books: "And it came about, after . . . that" (Maccabaica 1.1; cf. Jdg 1.1). Its successive stages are introduced with forms of statement familiar from those earlier books, e.g., "In those days there rose up.... And ... rose up in place of him" (Maccabaica 2.1; 3.1; cf. Jdg 3.31). And it ends with a form of statement familiar from those earlier books: "And the rest of the accounts of... and his wars ... behold, they are written in the book of the days of..." (Maccabaica 16.23–24; cf. 1 Kgs 14.19).

In most respects the history books in the Hebrew Scriptures share a common style, but in a few respects each of them has its own distinctive stylistic features. The Maccabean History likewise has some distinctive stylistic features, two of which are remarkable enough to deserve special discussion.

1. From time to time, the book repeats a phrase or clause—either exactly or with slight modifications—after an interval: "The smiting by Alexander . . . and he smote" (1.1). "A mighty hand ... and a strong hand" (5.6). "The outcry ... and great outcry" (5.31). "That they were powerful with strength ... and that they were powerful with strength" (8.1–2). "And they had pillaged them ... and they had pillaged them" (8.10). "And Bacchides knew this, on the Sabbath day; and he came, he and all his army, over to the other side of the Jordan .... And Bacchides heard it, and he came on the Sabbath day up to the banks of the Jordan" (9.34, 43). "I have shattered Demetrius ... and he himself and his company were shattered by us" (10.52–53). "And that he should take care of the holy places ... and that he should take care of the holy places" (14.42–43). It will be seen that these repetitions are not random. They occur only in one particular context: they always stress the power of a group of people and/or its leader, whether for evil or for good. The repetition emphasizes the inexorability and inescapability of what is being repeated (cf. "the dream was repeated ... because the

thing is established by God," Gen 41.32; "as we have said before, now also I say again," Gal 1.8–9).[12]

2. Like the book of Esther, the Maccabean History avoids naming God even at various points where it might seem most appropriate to do so (cf. Est 4.14):[13] "He Himself will shatter them" (3.22); "You Yourself know" (3.52); "however the will in Heaven may be, thus He will do" (3.60); "let us cry out to Heaven, if He will have mercy on us" (4.16); "the word that He wrote" (7.16); "You Yourself chose this house" (7.32); "by the mercy" (16.3); "may the help from Heaven be with you" (16.3). If anything, this technique has the remarkable effect of making Him all the more conspicuous: it forces the reader to pause and ponder who the unnamed Subject might be. The One whose name is a marvel (Jdg 13.18) and whose mind can never be plumbed (Isa 40.28; Rom 11.33–34) stands out infinitely beyond the many humans who pass busily across the scene, with names and minds that are always within easy reach. Matthew Henry famously declared, when introducing the book of Esther, "Though the name of God be not in it, the finger of God is." In the Maccabean History not only His finger, but also His mighty hand and outstretched arm are everywhere manifest.

Language

Ever since ancient times, it has generally been believed that the Maccabean History was originally written in Hebrew. The main evidence for this is as follows:

- Perhaps the strongest evidence is found in 7.13–17, which says that a passage of Scripture about God's "lovingkind ones" is talking about the "Hasidim." In Greek, as in English, there is no apparent connection between the terms "Hasidim" (Ασειδαιοι) and "lovingkind ones" (οσιων). But in Hebrew, those terms would have been forms of the same word (*ḥsdym* and *ḥsydyk*). Therefore, at least this section of the Maccabean History must derive, directly or indirectly, from a Hebrew source.[14]

---

[12] Modern editors and translators have often treated these repetitions as textual errors, and deleted them. To that policy there are several objections: (i) In most of these places the repetition is attested by every existing manuscript. (ii) As noted above, the repetitions do not occur randomly, but always when the text is stating the power of those who are mentioned in the repetition. (iii) If such repetitions are textual errors, they should be seen about as often in manuscripts of some other narrative books. But they are not—not even in those books that shared most of their textual history with the Maccabaica (e.g., Esther, Tobit, and the Maccabean Epitome).

[13] Most manuscripts of the Maccabean History (including S, V, and 64*236) do designate Him as *theos* ("God") and/or *kurios* ("Lord"), but only very sparingly (e.g., at 3.18). Manuscript A does not apply the terms "God" or "Lord" to Him anywhere.

[14] Even this has been challenged, however. Nodet ("*Asidaioi* and Essenes," 78–79) argues that 7.13 (the verse that mentions the Hasidim) must have been originally written in Greek and by

- Early in the third century CE, Origen reported that the Maccabean History was circulating among the Jews along with the Hebrew Scriptures, and quoted a Hebrew or Aramaic name for it (Eusebius, *History,* 6.25). However, this might simply indicate that the book had been translated into Aramaic by that time (as some other books written in Greek undoubtedly were).
- Jerome, two centuries later, wrote: "The First Book of Maccabees I have found [*repperi*] in Hebrew; the Second is Greek, as can be proved from its very style" (*Prologus in libro Regum*). Jerome may mean that he had seen a copy of the "First Book" (the Maccabean History) written in Hebrew. However, he may mean merely that he had deduced from its style that it was written in Hebrew—just as he deduced the "Second" book (the Epitome of the Acts of Judas Maccabeus) to be written in Greek.
- As noted above, the book's phrasing, syntax, and word order are strongly Hebraic. This point too is not conclusive, because people writing in one language may closely reproduce the idioms of another—especially if the latter is their native tongue. Many Hebraic characteristics (including some of those listed above) can be found in some New Testament books that were undoubtedly written in Greek, not Hebrew.
- A few researchers have claimed that certain turns of phrase in the Maccabean History are mistranslations, which arose because the Greek translator misunderstood the sense of the Hebrew original. However, none of the alleged "mistranslations" has been generally accepted.[15] Moreover, even if the book did use Greek words in ways that would normally be permissible only in Hebrew, this would not prove that the book had been written in Hebrew. It might mean only that the writer customarily thought in Hebrew, and therefore naturally wrote Greek in Hebraic ways.

Any Hebrew form of the Maccabean History must have been extremely rare and hard to obtain, even in ancient times. In practice, the book circulated almost entirely in Greek.

No fragment of an ancient Hebrew text of the Maccabean History has ever been discovered. The vast body of Rabbinic literature contains no quotation from it in Hebrew. When Josephus and ancient Syriac translators were dealing with some books of the Hebrew Scriptures, they seem to have worked partly from the Greek versions, and partly from the original Hebrew text. But when they turned to the Maccabean History, there is no tangible evidence that they made even the slightest use of any Hebrew text. As far as can be determined, they relied entirely on the Greek.

---

a writer who did not make any connection between "Hasidim" and "lovingkind ones" (as the use of two different Greek words shows).

[15] Similar "mistranslations" have been perceived in some very strange places. Some have claimed that the existing Greek text of Paul's letters to churches in Greece and Macedonia contains errors caused by mistranslation of Paul's supposed Aramaic original text.

In some of these respects, the Maccabean History may be compared to the First Gospel. There was a widespread ancient belief that this Gospel was originally written by Matthew in Hebrew; some ancient writers even reported seeing copies in that language; and its Greek text contains various Hebraic-looking idioms and sentence constructions (cf. Tregelles' comments in SDB 4.3381–82). But all these matters are of little practical relevance nowadays. No Hebrew form of the book now exists. We have it only in Greek, and in versions translated from the Greek.

Text

The text of the Maccabean History has been preserved in excellent condition. Most of the variations between the existing ancient and medieval Greek manuscripts affect only minor details, such as whether the leader of a group did something (third person singular aorist) or the whole group did it (third person plural aorist)—generally in contexts where both statements would be true, e.g., εποιηϲεν ("he made" a murderous killing) or εποιηϲαν ("they made" a murderous killing), 1.24; ωκοδομηϲαν ("they built" the city) or ωκοδομηϲεν ("he built" the city), 1.33.

Greek manuscripts containing the Maccabean History include:[16]

- Codex Sinaiticus (S), believed to date from the fourth century CE—the oldest known manuscript of the Maccabean History. Where the original text of this manuscript was subsequently altered, S* designates the original reading; S^1 designates an alteration by the original scribe (Scribe A); S^{ca} designates an alteration by a reviser who modified the text (probably during the seventh century) in ways that bring it closer to the Antiochene text (see below); S^{cb1} designates an alteration by a later reviser; S^c designates alterations by unidentified hands.
- Codex Alexandrinus (A), believed to date from the fifth century.
- Codex Venetus (V), believed to date from the eighth century. V^a and V^b designate alterations by two revisers.
- The Antiochene text preserved in five medieval manuscripts (64, 236, 381, 534, and 728, collectively designated f^{64}). (In Kappler's Göttingen edition, the collective symbol for this family is *L*.)
- Various medieval manuscripts containing mixed texts, with both Antiochene and non-Antiochene features. These include 19, 62, 93, and 542 (collectively designated f^{19}; in Kappler's edition, the collective symbol for this family is *l*), as well as 58 and 311.

---

[16] To avoid confusion, the present book avoids the textual symbol *L* (it has been applied both to the Greek Antiochene text and to one of the Old Latin texts). The tendentious term "Lucianic" is also avoided (there is no clear evidence that Lucian ever did any work on the text of the Maccabaica). The type of text sometimes called "Lucianic" is described in this book as "Antiochene," a more factual and less theory-dependent term. Whether or not this type of text originated at Antioch, it was demonstrably used there.

- A further family of medieval and post-medieval manuscripts (29, 68, 71, 74, 98, 107, 120, 130, 134, 243, 379, and 731, collectively designated f^{120}), which contains a distinctive text of a non-Antiochene type. (In Kappler's edition, the collective symbol for this family is *q*.)

Josephus's *Antiquities* (first century CE) contains a paraphrase of much of the Maccabean History. This shows that the text circulating in the time of the apostles was essentially identical with that of the manuscripts listed above (at least in the sections used by Josephus). However, his adaptation substantially rephrases the original, so it is rarely possible to reconstruct the exact wording of the Greek text used by him. More precise Greek quotations from the Maccabean History have been preserved in the works of Hippolytus (third century) and later writers.

Ancient manuscripts of excellent Latin and Syriac translations also exist. The oldest known **Latin** version of the Maccabean History has been most fully preserved in two manuscripts believed to date from about the ninth century: Complutensis I (La^{109}) and Lugdunensis (La^{146}).[17] The text found in those manuscripts closely resembles the quotations from the Maccabean History in the ancient Latin writers Cyprian (third century) and Lucifer of Caligari (fourth century), so this form of text was evidently in use at that time. Several later revisions of it have been preserved in Latin manuscripts; one of these revisions is printed in editions of the Latin Vulgate. (None of the Latin versions is by Jerome; he did no translational work on the Maccabean History.)

Two main **Syriac** renderings of the Maccabean History have been preserved:[18]

- The common version (designated SyI), which is preserved in all known Syriac manuscripts except the first nine-tenths (1.1–14.25) of Codex Ambrosianus (7a1).
- A revised version (designated SyII), which is preserved only in the first nine-tenths (1.1–14.25) of 7a1.

For the Greek text printed in the following pages, the copytext is Codex Sinaiticus (S), in the form in which its original scribe left it after completing his last alterations.

---

[17] The symbols La^{109} and La^{146} are those assigned by the Beuron Vetus Latina project. The symbols used in de Bruyne's edition are X and L respectively. Other, more fragmentary, texts of a similar kind have been published by Cañas Reillo (*Glosas marginales de Vetus Latina;* "Un testimonio inédito de Vetus Latina," 57–82).

The Armenian version of the Maccabaica may have been derived from a Greek text somewhat similar to that used for the Latin version (Bévenot, "Armenian Text of Maccabees," 268–83); but no textually satisfactory edition of it has yet been published (Cowe, "Versión armenia," lxxi–lxxii), and the degree of variation in its manuscripts requires further investigation.

[18] Schmidt, "Die beiden Syrischen Übersetzungen des 1. Maccabäerbuches," 1–47, 233–62. Penna's Leiden edition uses 7h7 as the copytext of SyI in 1.1–14.25, and 7a1 in 14.26–16.24; Lagarde's edition uses 7h7 as the copytext throughout. Our textual apparatus lists 7a1 and 7h7 as members of the same family in 14.26–16.24, but separately in the earlier parts of the book.

(Thus, at points where he altered what he himself had written, the copytext is S^1 rather than S*.)

There is, of course, no uniquely "right" way to edit an ancient text, especially in details of spelling, punctuation, and typography. Different styles of presentation suit different purposes.

In general, modern editors are tending to make fewer and fewer silent alterations to their copytexts in such matters, because this reduces the danger that the sense might unwittingly be distorted. We have followed a set of principles used by many recent editors of ancient Greek texts:

- No **punctuation** or **accentuation** is introduced. (There is none in Sinaiticus, and there would almost certainly have been none in the first Greek manuscript of the Maccabean History.)
- Only one form of the letter **sigma** is used (c—not σ and ς, as seen in modern Greek books). (Again, this is the situation in Sinaiticus, and would have been the situation in the first Greek manuscript of this work.)
- **Spelling** has not been standardized. In ancient times, Greek spelling was flexible. Different scribes might spell the same word in different ways, and even a single scribe might spell the same word differently on different occasions. For instance, the scribe of Sinaiticus sometimes treats ε as interchangeable with αι, and often treats η as interchangeable with ει or ι (Milne and Skeat, *Scribes and Correctors of Codex Sinaiticus,* 51–55). Indeed, in 3.41 every known Greek manuscript spells "fetters" with -αι- (exactly like "servants"). Inflected forms (e.g., verb-augments and case-endings) are particularly liable to appear in diverse spellings: both ωκοδομηcεν (9.62, etc.) and οικοδομηcεν (10.12, etc.) occur repeatedly (cf. Thackeray §16.2), and a dative plural usually spelled with -αιc may be spelled with -οιc if other -οιc endings are in the vicinity (13.33; 14.25; cf. Thackeray §10.26). It is impossible to reconstruct the spelling of the first Greek manuscript of the Maccabean History,[19] and there is no reason to imagine that its spelling would have been rigorously consistent throughout. (For instance, there is no reason to imagine that it consistently used Ιουδου for the genitive of "Judas" and Ιουδα for the genitive of "Judah," or consistently used πρεcβευτ- for "ambassador" and πρεcβυτ- for "elder," as twentieth-century editors of the Maccabean History invariably did.)[20]

[19] Nevertheless, at least some of the seemingly idiosyncratic spellings in Sinaiticus were not unique to that manuscript, but were circulating in the oldest form of text that can be determined (that current in the third century CE), since they appear also in the earliest Latin versions (see, e.g., the footnote on 13.43).

[20] In the uncial era, the textual differences ο/ω and λλ/λ may sometimes have been mere spelling variants (cf. Threatte, *Grammar of Attic Inscriptions,* 1.385–87), but may sometimes have marked differences in meaning (Thackeray §§6.28–31), and are therefore routinely

- The text is printed throughout as **prose.** Some sections of the Maccabean History (such as 1.26–28, 36–40; 2.8–13; 3.3–9, 45; 7.17) consist of parallel clauses, and are often printed as verse in modern editions—although it is not always clear where those sections should begin and end (some modern editions also print 1.24–25; 2.7, 51–64; 3.50–53; 7.37–38; 14.4–15 as verse, whereas others do not). In all the ancient manuscripts, the text is presented throughout as prose; none of the above passages is distinguished in any way, either by lineation or by punctuation, from the rest of the material.
- Scribal **contractions** (indicated in Sinaiticus by a bar above the contracted form) have been expanded inside curved brackets: cυ´- is expanded cυ(ν)-, δαδ´ is expanded Δα(υι)δ, and the Sinaiticus scribe's idiosyncratic form ιηλμ´ is expanded Ι(ερουcα)λημ.
- For ease of reading, **spaces** have been introduced between words, and the text is printed in a **lowercase** Greek font except for the first letters of proper names, which are printed in **uppercase.** (Sinaiticus has no spaces between words and makes no distinction between uppercase and lowercase; neither would the first Greek manuscript of the Maccabean History have done.)
- Except for the points listed above, all **changes** to the copytext have been placed inside subscript angle brackets ⸤thus⸥ (the reading of the copytext being recorded underneath in a brief textual apparatus).

Like every manuscript, S was written by a fallible human being and contains errors. In the places where S has *impossible* readings, the manuscript that most consistently has correct readings is La^{109}, nearly always supported by V and/or f^{64}—for instance:

2.8 αδοξος (the temple has become "inglorious") 58 La^{109} | ενδοξος (the temple has become "glorious") S V A 64^{+}236 La^{146} 7h7 7a1

4.49 το θυcιαcτηριον των θυμιαματων ("the altar of incense") 64^{+}236 La$^{109+146}$ 7h7 7a1 | το θυcιαcτηριον των ολοκαυτωματων και θυμιαματων ("the altar of burnt offering and of incense") S V A

6.49 εξηλθον ("they [the people of Bethzur] came out" of the city) 64^{+}236 La^{109} 7h7 7a1 | εξηλθεν ("he [the king besieging Bethzur] came out" of the city) S V A La^{146}

14.27 οκτωκαιδεκατη Ελουλ ετουc ("the eighteenth of Elul in the year . . .") V A 64^{+}236 La^{109} 7h7 7a1 | οκτωκαιδεκατη ετουc ("the eighteenth in the year . . .") S La^{146}

The principles established from such passages can be applied in places where all the manuscripts have possible readings. Since the combination of La^{109} plus V and/or f^{64} nearly always has a correct text at points where the alternate option is impossible, it is

---

recorded in the textual apparatus. That situation had changed by medieval times (see the introduction to the commentary on the Eighteen Psalms).

most likely to have a correct text also at points where either reading would theoretically be possible:[21]

1.54 ωκοδομηcαν βδελυγμα ("they built an abomination") S^{ca} V A 64^{+}236 La^{109} | ωκοδομηcε βδελυγμα ("he built an abomination") S* La^{146}

2.46 εν οριοιc Ιcραηλ ("in the appointed boundaries of Israel") V A 64^{+}236 La$^{109+146}$ | εν υιοιc Ιcραηλ ("among the sons of Israel") S

2.50 πατερων ημων ("our fathers") A 64^{+}236 La$^{109+146}$ | πατερων υμων ("your fathers") S V

2.60 εκ cτοματοc λεοντων ("out of the mouth of lions") V A La$^{109+146}$ | εκ cτοματοc λεοντοc ("out of the mouth of the lion") S 64^{+}236

2.63 οτι επεcτρεψεν ("for he will have turned back") V A 64^{+}236 La$^{109+146}$ | και επεcτρεψεν ("and he will have turned back") S

2.66 εκ νεοτητοc αυτου ("from the time of his youth") V A 64^{+}236 La$^{109+146}$ | εκ νεοτητοc ("from the time of youth") S

3.12 ελαβεν τα cκυλα αυτων ("he took their plunder") V 64 La^{109} | ελαβον τα cκυλα αυτων ("they took their plunder") S A 236 La^{146}

In the Maccabean History, Codex Alexandrinus (A) has a slightly atypical text, not closely related to any other known early form of the book.[22] Its text is readily available in Swete's edition of *The Old Testament in Greek.*

The Antiochene text (f^{64}) has undergone a considerable amount of expansion (especially by the addition of names, titles, and pronouns) and other stylistic revisions.[23] For instance, in 1.5, where S, La$^{109+146}$, and A have επεcεν επι την κοιτην ("he fell on the bed"), 64^{+}236 add αυτου ο Αλεξανδροc (so that the statement becomes "Alexander fell on his bed"). The Old Latin version preserved in La$^{109+146}$

[21] A small number of errors were clearly present in a common ancestor of La$^{109+146}$ and S, as they are found in all three copies. In 10.37, S and La$^{109+146}$ omit almost the whole clause και καταcταθηcεται εξ αυτων εν τοιc οχυρωμαcιν του βαcιλεωc τοιc μεγαλοιc ("and some of them will be established in the great fortresses of the king"), preserving only its last two Greek words (which S* and La$^{109+146}$ construed in different ways). Thus the text of La^{109} cannot always be regarded as correct where it lacks support from such manuscripts as V, 64^{+}236, and 58.

[22] De Bruyne, "Texte grec des deux premiers livres des Machabées," 53; Bogaert, "Septante et versions grecques," 611. Many of the variations appear to be stylistic—e.g., in 1.10, εν S V 64^{+}236 > A; τριακοcτω / και / εβδομω S V 64^{+}236 ~ A; in 1.20, Ι(ερουcα)λημ S V 64^{+}236 | Ιεροcολυμα A. Hippolytus, who quoted those verses early in the third century, has the same text as S V 64^{+}236 at each of the points cited. (Another unique text form, not closely related to that found in the majority of either early or later manuscripts, is preserved in minuscule 55.)

[23] Fernández Marcos, *Septuagint in Context,* 230–31; ibid., "Antiochene Edition in the Text History of the Greek Bible," 64–65; de Bruyne and Sodar, *Anciennes Traductions latines des Machabées,* v; Fischer, "Lukian-Lesarten in der Vetus Latina der vier Königsbücher," 175–76; Bogaert, "Septante et versions grecques," 573–75.

appears to have been translated from a Greek text that closely resembled the Antiochene form, but did not have these stylistic revisions.

Those textual phenomena are not unique to the Maccabean History; the Antiochene and Old Latin texts of most historical books in the Hebrew Scriptures have the same characteristics.

The final section of La[109] (approximately 11.48–16.24) is translated in a more paraphrastic (less isomorphic) style, with many abridgements;[24] but where the underlying Greek text can still be determined with confidence, it appears to retain its excellence (as the example cited above from 14.27 shows).

The common Syriac version (SyI) was translated from a Greek text of Antiochene type (including the characteristic Antiochene stylistic revisions: in 1.5, 7h7 reads *npl ʾlksndrws ʿl ʿrsh,* "Alexander fell on his bed").

The SyII text found in 7a1 is probably a revision of SyI. Some of the distinctive Antiochene features have been preserved, but others have been altered (apparently to match a Greek text resembling that of S).[25]

In summary, our aim has been to prepare a Greek text composed entirely of readings that seem to have been current in third- or fourth-century manuscripts, without retaining any reading that is unique to a single manuscript. (Such a reading might never have existed in any other manuscript; it might have been merely an error of one particular scribe on one particular occasion.)

Any reading found in S obviously existed in the fourth century. The evidence of Cyprian and Lucifer of Caligari shows that most readings of La[109] and La[146] also existed by that date, and the probability is especially high if they are also found in the Antiochene text (the common source of the Antiochene and Old Latin texts must have existed by then) and/or in V (which has a text more closely akin to S than any other existing Greek manuscript).

The main relationships between these manuscripts and their closest relatives may be charted as follows:[26]

---

[24] Therefore, the textual apparatus lists La[109] and La[146] as members of the same family up till 11.48, but separately thereafter.

[25] Occasionally 7a1 agrees with S (or even S*) against almost all other known witnesses—e.g., in reading the plural αρχοντας in 1.29, ωc in 4.4, ηλθεν in 4.29, and Ονια Αρηc in 12.19–20.

[26] This chart is not a genealogical diagram (stemma) in the strict sense. Scribes often altered one manuscript by checking it against a different manuscript (as the changes to Sinaiticus show), so that a considerable amount of textual cross-fertilization took place, even in the earliest centuries.

The chart does not include less closely related manuscripts (such as A, 55, and *f*[120]) because, when textual variations are so numerous and extensive cross-checking of manuscripts is likely to have occurred, even the main relationships can no longer be traced; the observed differences could have arisen in many different ways.

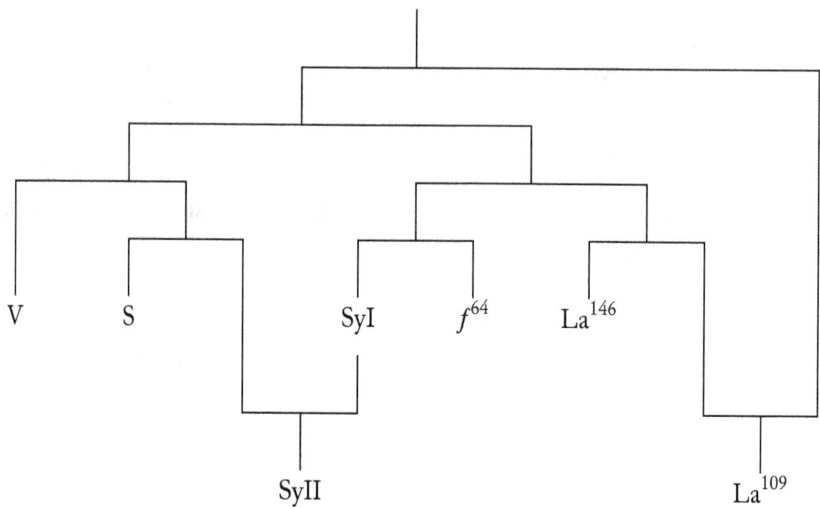

Unlike the twentieth-century editors (Rahlfs, Kappler, and Abel) we have not introduced any reading that does not exist in the known Greek manuscripts. Nor have we tried to reconstruct a hypothetical state of text earlier than that accessible in the existing manuscripts. We do not believe that would be possible—any more than it would be possible to reconstruct (say) a hypothetical source text of the Law of Moses or one of the Gospels. Our concern is limited to the texts that exist.

The **textual apparatus** printed underneath the Greek text on the following pages is also a limited one. At every point where our text departs from S, the apparatus records the readings of S, V, A, 64, 236, and (where they can be deduced) the Greek texts underlying La^{109} and La^{146}.

Syriac manuscripts have been cited only at points of special interest or importance—especially where SyI's f^{64}-like source apparently had a reading not found in any known manuscript of f^{64}, or where SyII's S-like Greek source apparently had a reading not found in S itself.

A few noteworthy readings from the semi-Antiochene Greek manuscripts 58 and 93 are also cited.[27] Readings of 58 have been taken from Kappler's Göttingen edition, and of 7h7 from Penna's Leiden edition; all other readings have been checked against photofacsimiles.

In the footnotes to the commentary, a small number of textual variants are discussed because they help to explain the differences between standard English translations of the Maccabean History. Often, the variant in question will not have been mentioned in our textual apparatus (because we have not departed from the text of Codex Sinaiticus at that point).

---

[27] 55 and f^{120} have not been cited, because we have found no evidence that they contain any correct readings not preserved in the manuscripts listed above.

The Maccabean History

Alexander and his successors (1.1–9)

Alexander the Macedonian becomes king

1.1 και εγενετο μετα το παταξαι	**1.1** And it came about, after the smit-
Αλεξανδρο(ν) τον Φιλιππου	ing by Alexander the *son* of Philip,
Μακαιδονα ος εξηλθε(ν) εκ γηc	*the* Macedonian—who came out of
Χεττιειμ κ(αι) επαταξεν τον Δαρειον	*the* land of Kittim, and smote Darius
βαcιλεα Περcω(ν) και Μηδων και	king of *the* Persians and Medes—that
εβαcιλευcεν αντ αυτου	he became king in place of him,
προτερον επι τη(ν) Ελλαδα	*as he had* previous*ly been* over Greece.

1.1 Many ancient books (including some books of Scripture: cf. Luke 1.1–4; Acts 1.1–5) begin with an unusually long and complicated sentence. This forces the reader to stop at the outset and read carefully—perhaps more than once—to grasp the sense. That is certainly so here. The main thread of the sentence is: **And it came about after the smiting by Alexander ... that he became king.** It has the same structure as the first sentence of Judges: "And it came about after the death of Joshua, that the children of Israel asked ..." (Jdg 1.1).[28] But in the midst of the sentence, an additional clause is inserted to explain the nature of the **smiting:** Alexander **came out ... and smote Darius.** This additional clause disrupts the smooth course of the sentence, as Alexander himself disrupted the course of the Persian empire.[29]

The last **king of the Persians and Medes** was named **Darius,** like several previous Medo-Persian kings (Dan 5.31; Ezra 4.5; Hag 1.1; Zec 1.1; cf. Neh 12.22).

---

[28] **And** (Greek *kai* ≡ Hebrew *w-*) at the start of a narrative book generally indicates that the book is not a fresh start but a continuation from past events (Keil 28; Bergsträsser 2.§8a*; cf. Ezra 1.1 ≡ 2 Chr 36.22). In the present verse, the point of connection with the past is explicitly specified (**And it came about after the smiting by Alexander ...**), as often elsewhere: "And it came about after the death of Moses ..." (Josh 1.1); "And it came about after the death of Joshua ..." (Jdg 1.1); "And it came about in the days when the judges judged ..." (Ruth 1.1).

In Greek and Hebrew, when a section begins **And it came about** *(kai egeneto ≡ wyhy),* most of the subsequent clauses can be placed on an equal footing by starting each of them with *kai* ≡ *w-* (cf. Thackeray 50–52; Viteau, *Sujet,* §105A). But in English, one of those clauses must be singled out as the conclusion (apodosis) of the sentence. In the present case, most English versions find this concluding clause later in verse 1: **And it came about ... that** [*kai*] **he became king** (cf. KJV, RV, APOT, NAB, ESV). A few versions find the concluding clause in verse 2: "And it came about ... that [*kai*] he carried out many wars" (cf. DRCV, SAAS). There have occasionally been suggestions to place the concluding clause still further down, e.g., in verse 5 ("And it came about ... that [*kai*] after these things he fell on the bed") or even verse 10 ("And it came about ... that [*kai*] there came out from them a sinful root"). See Robertson 1042–43; BDF §442.5.

[29] Nearly all modern translations simplify the construction of this opening sentence.

Kittim was a general term for the "coastal regions" of the northern Mediterranean (Gen 10.2–5; Jer 2.10; Ezek 27.6; Num 24.24). **Macedonia** is a more specific term: it refers to the region around Philippi, where Paul would later preach the gospel (Acts 16.12). In that area, **Alexander** was already king, not only of **Macedonia,** but also of **Greece** (the land next to Macedonia: Acts 20.1–2).[30] But when he **came out of** the coastal regions ("came from the west," Dan 8.5), he became a much more powerful monarch. He defeated **(smote)** Darius and **became king in place of him** over a **multitude of nations,** in a vast empire that eventually extended **to the ends of the land** (v 3).

1.2 και cυνεcτηcατο πολεμουc πολλουc και εκρατηcεν οχυρωματων και εcφαξεν βαcιλειc τηc γηc	**1.2** And he carried out many wars, and took hold of fortresses, and slew kings of the earth,
1.3 και διηλθε(ν) εωc ακρων τηc γηc και ελαβεν cκυλα ‹πληθουc› εθνων και ηcυχαcεν η γη ενωπιον αυτου ‹και› ‹υψωθη κ(αι) επηρθη η καρδια αυτου›	**1.3** and went through to *the* ends of the earth, and took plunder of a multitude of nations. And the earth was quiet in his sight. And his heart was exalted and lifted up.

1.3 πληθουc V A 64⁺236 La[109+146] | πληθοc S • και 4° A 64⁺236 La[146] | > S V La[109] • υψωθη κ(αι) επηρθη η καρδια αυτου V A 64⁺236 La[146] | > S La[109] •

1.3 The earth was quiet, just as it had been when the Persian empire was at its greatest (Zec 1.11). Alexander had no remaining opponents anywhere on earth: even the mightiest rulers could not "stand before his face" or "rescue . . . from his hand" (Dan 8.7). Indeed, after his conquest of Darius, not one of the **districts, nations, and monarchs** subjugated by him is even named. They are of no account compared to him.

His heart was exalted and lifted up.[31] Alexander had become "great" and "mighty," as Daniel had prophesied (Dan 8.8, 21; 11.3). To this day, in popular speech, he and his greatness are so inseparable that he is never called anything except "Alexander the

---

[30] English translations vary slightly at this point, because of a one-letter variation in the Greek manuscripts. The statement that Alexander **had previously been** *(proteron)* king of Greece is the reading of S, A, and 64⁺236 (supported by La[109+146]). Some other Greek manuscripts (including V and 93) say instead that Alexander was "the first" *(proteros)* king of Greece (cf. Dan 8.21).

[31] English versions of **and his heart was exalted and lifted up** vary for two reasons. (i) In the Greek, that statement could also be construed "and he was exalted, and his heart was lifted up" (as in RV). Elsewhere, however, the **heart** is often the subject of **exalted** (*hupsōthē;* cf. Ezek 28.2; 2 Chr 26.16; Dan 5.20; 8.25), suggesting that the same is true in this passage also. (ii) The placement of **and his heart was exalted and lifted up** also varies. In V, A, and 64⁺236 (supported by La[146]), it is placed after **quiet in his sight** (as indicated above). In La[109], it is placed after **a very strong force** (v 4). In S and V, it is placed after **nations and monarchs** (v 4). (Thus V has this statement in two places.)

Great." The Scriptures provide many warnings against exalting oneself when things are going well (Deut 8.11–14; 17.20; 2 Chr 26.16; 32.25; Ezek 28.2, 6–9, 17; Dan 5.22–23; 1 Tim 3.6). All blessings have been given by God, not gained by ourselves (Deut 8.17–18; 1 Chr 29.12–16; 1 Cor 4.7), and are to be used for His glory (Psa 115.1; Jer 9.23–24; 1 Cor 1.31). "A person's exaltation will bring him low" (Prov 29.23), because "God sets Himself against the arrogant, but He gives favor to the lowly. Make yourselves low, therefore, under the mighty hand of God" (1 Pet 5.5–6). "The haughty eyes of humanity will be brought low, and the loftiness of man will be bowed down, and the LORD alone will be exalted" (Isa 2.11–17; Matt 23.11–12).

1.4 και cυνηξεν δυναμιν ιcχυραν cφοδρα και ηρξεν χωρων εθνω(ν) και τυραννων ‹› και ‹εγενοντο› αυτω εις ‹φορον›	**1.4** And he gathered together a very strong force, and ruled districts, nations, and monarchs; and they became *payers of* tribute to him.

1.4 και 4º A 64⁺236 La109+146 | ^ και υψωθη και επηρθη η καρδια αυτου S V • εγενοντο … φορον V A 64⁺236 La109+146 | εγενετο … φοβερον S •

1.4 Districts, nations, and monarchs[32] **. . . became payers of tribute to him.** More precisely, the Greek says that they "became for tribute [*phoron*] to him." The ancient Greek translations of Judges apply the same term to the Canaanites, who "became for tribute" to the Israelites (Jdg 1.30, LXX). The **districts, nations, and monarchs** in Alexander's empire were subservient to him, just as the subjected Canaanites had been to the Israelites. Later, under Roman rule, the Judeans were similarly required to pay "tribute [*phoron*] to Caesar" (Luke 20.22–25).

Alexander dies

1.5 και μετα ταυτα επεcεν επι την κοιτην και εγνοι οτι αποθνηcκι	**1.5** And after these *things*, he fell on the bed, and knew that he was dying.
1.6 και εκαλεcεν τουc παιδαc αυτου τουc ενδοξουc τουc cυνεκτροφουc αυτου εκ νεοτητοc και διειλεν ‹αυτοιc› την βαcιλειαν αυτου ετι αυτου ζωντοc	**1.6** And he called his servants—the honored *ones* who *had been* brought up with him from youth—and he divided his kingdom among them while he *was* still living.

1.6 αυτοιc Sca V A 64⁺236 La109+146 | -του S* •

1.6 He called his servants . . . and he divided his kingdom among them. Many different accounts of Alexander's final days were circulating in ancient times.[33]

[32] **Monarchs** *(turannōn)* is the reading of S and 64⁺236 (supported by La109+146, 7h7, and 7a1). V and A read "monarchies" *(turanniōn)* instead. English translations vary accordingly.

[33] All the surviving Classical accounts were written late and were compiled in part from untrustworthy sources. (For instance, the so-called "Royal Diary," used by Arrian and Plutarch at least, was demonstrably either invented or altered some time after Alexander's death: Pearson, "Diary and Letters of Alexander the Great," 429–39.)

According to some, the dying king expected his subordinates to compete among themselves for his kingdom, and said that he left it to whoever was "mightiest" *(kratistō;* Arrian 7.26.3; Diodorus 17.117.4; Quintus Curtius 10.5.5; Justin 12.15.8). According to others, he gave his signet ring to Perdiccas, the leader of his bodyguard—which was taken by some to indicate that Perdiccas had authority to determine the disposition of the kingdom (Diodorus 17.117.3; Quintus Curtius 10.5.4; Justin 12.15.12–13). According to still others, Alexander left behind a written will dividing his kingdom among his generals (Quintus Curtius 10.10.5; *Alexander Romance,* A, 3.32.8–3.33.25).

The Maccabean History is the earliest surviving source of information on this subject. It states that the dying Alexander authorized some of those who had been his subjects (**servants**)[34] and companions (**who had been brought up with him from youth**) to govern divisions of **his kingdom.** But it says nothing either about any written will, or about Alexander authorizing those servants to be kings.[35] Rather, it declares that they themselves assumed the kingship (**they** put diadems on themselves) **after** Alexander **was dead** (v 9).

1.7 κ(αι) εβασιλευσεν Αλεξανδρος ετη ιβʹ και απεθανεν	**1.7** And Alexander was king twelve years; and he died.

1.7 Alexander was king twelve years; and he died. "Here ended all the designs of this great and vainglorious prince. Never had any man a greater run of success than he had for twelve years and a half together .... But God having ordained him to be His instrument, for the bringing to pass of all that was by the prophet Daniel foretold concerning him, He did by His providence bear him through in all things for the accomplishing of it, and when that was done, did cast him out of His hand" (Prideaux, *Historical Connection of the Old and New Testaments,* 1.443).

"The Most High rules in the kingdom of men, and gives it to whom He wishes" (Dan 4.17, 32). "He takes away kings, and sets up kings" (Dan 2.21; cf. 1 Sam 2.7–8;

---

[34] **Servants.** The term used *(paidas)* places the emphasis not on their authority ("chief ministers," APOT; "officers," ESV) but on their subservience (cf. Matt 14.2; 8.6; Luke 12.45). BGS has the apt Spanish rendering *criados.*

[35] Drusius 5–6. Alexander probably did not assign particular provinces to particular **servants.** If that had happened, Ptolemy would surely have mentioned it in his (now lost) history of the period—which apparently he did not (Arrian 7.26.3). Rather, the statement that Alexander **divided his kingdom among them** must mean simply that he instructed them to divide it (Hrabanus Maurus, PL 109.1131)—just as the statement that Solomon "built" the temple means that Solomon instructed his subjects to build it (1 Kgs 6.1–2, 9, 12, 14). The widely reported remark that Alexander expected his servants to compete for the kingdom, with "the mightiest" prevailing, would fit well in such a context. At his death he left about 20 semi-autonomous provinces (cf. Bosworth, *Legacy of Alexander,* 5); according to the Hellenistic and Roman historians, the final assignment of those provinces was worked out over the following two decades, and only after many disputes.

Psa 113.7–8; Luke 1.51–52). At whatever moment God has appointed, even the mighty die and leave their earthly possessions behind (Jas 1.10–11; Luke 12.16–21; Psa 37.35–36; 49.16–20; Ecc 5.15–16; Heb 9.27). "So teach us to number our days, and we will bring a heart of wisdom" (Psa 90.12).

Alexander's servants begin to rule

1.8 και επεκρατηcαν οι παιδεc αυτου εκαcτοc εν τω τοπω αυτου	**1.8** And his servants took hold of *the* power, each in his place.
1.9 και επεθεντο πα(ν)τεc διαδηματα μετα το αποθανιν αυτον και ‹οι› υιοι αυτω(ν) οπιcω αυτων ετη πολλα και επληθυναν κακα εν τη γη	**1.9** And they all put on diadems after he *was* dead, and *so did* their sons after them, for many years; and they multiplied evil *things* in the earth.

1.9 οι V A 64⁺236 | > S •

1.9 The descendants of Alexander's successors **multiplied evil things in the earth.** This too is what Daniel had prophesied: he had spoken of deceit, violence, and recurrent wars between the kings of the south (the Ptolemies) and the kings of the north (the Seleucids) during that long period of time (Dan 11.5–20).

Antiochus Epiphanes (1.10–64)

Antiochus Epiphanes becomes king

1.10 και εξηλθεν ‹απ› αυτω(ν) ρειζα αμαρτωλοc Αντιοχοc Επιφανηc υιοc Αντιοχου του βαcιλεωc οc η(ν) ομηρα εν Ρωμη και εβαcιλευcεν εν ετι εκατοcτω και τριακοcτω και εβδομω βαcιλειαc Ελληνων	**1.10** And *there* came out from them a sinful root, Antiochus Epiphanes, son of Antiochus the king, who had been a hostage in Rome; and he became king in *the* hundred and thirty-seventh year of *the* kingdom of *the* Greeks.

1.10 απ V 64⁺236 | εξ S A •

1.10 There came out[36] **from them a sinful root, Antiochus Epiphanes.** A **root** (Greek *rhiza* ≡ Hebrew *šrš*), like a branch, is something that grows out from a plant (2 Kgs 19.30; cf. Isa 11.1). In the Scriptures, therefore, an offshoot of a family can be called either a root or a branch of that family. Jesus is called "the root of Jesse" (Rom 15.12 ≡ Isa 11.10) and "the root and the offspring of David" (Rev 22.16) as well as the "righteous branch" of David (Jer 23.5; 33.15), because he was the offspring of Jesse and David (Matt 1.5–6; Luke 3.31–32). **Antiochus Epiphanes**[37] was the opposite of a

---

[36] As Alexander **came out** from the west to gain his kingdom (v 1), so did **Antiochus,** and so, later, would other rulers (7.1; 10.67)—but not always with the same result. God raises up some rulers to conquer for Him (Isa 45.1–3), others to be conquered by Him (Rom 9.17).

[37] **Epiphanes** means "made visible." On some of his coins (e.g., SC 2.1476) the title is expanded to *Antiochou Theou Epiphanous:* "Antiochus, god made visible." (In those days, coinage "was the

righteous branch: he was a **sinful root,** corrupt itself (Deut 29.18–20) and corrupting others (Heb 12.15).

In modern histories, Epiphanes is reckoned as **Antiochus** IV. He ruled from the city of Antioch (3.37), north of Judea (Acts 15.22–23; 11.19–27). Therefore he is called a "king of the North" by Daniel (Dan 11.21, 40). He **had been a hostage in Rome** (cf. Maccabaica 8.7), and Daniel indicated that he would gain his kingship deceitfully: the people themselves would "not give him the honor of kingship," but he would "come at ease, and take the kingship strongly by smooth words" (Dan 11.21).

Law-breakers from Israel yoke themselves with the nations

1.11 εν ταιc ημεραιc εκειναιc εξηλθον ‹εξ› Ιc(ραη)λ υιοι παρανομοι και ανεπιcαν πολλουc λεγοντεc πορευθωμεν και ‹διαθωμεθα› διαθηκην μετα των εθνων των κυκλω ημων οτι αφ ηc εξωριcθημε(ν) απ αυτων ευρεν ημαc κακα πολλα	**1.11** In those days, *there* came out of Israel sons *who were* Law-breakers, and they convinced many, saying: "Let us go, and let us covenant a covenant with the nations that *are* round about us: for since we have been separated from them, many evil *things* have found us."

1.11 εξ S^{ca} V A $64^{+}236$ $La^{109+146}$ | > S* • διαθωμεθα V A $64^{+}236$ | -με(ν) S* | -με(ν)θα S^{1} • εξωριcθημε(ν) S* = εχω- S^{c} V A $64^{+}236$ •

1.11 Many evil things had indeed been happening (v 9)—but not for the reason that the **Law-breakers**[38] said. "Many evils and troubles" had come upon the people of Israel (**found** them, cf. 6.13), not because they had been too faithful to the Lord, but because they had not been faithful enough (Deut 31.16–18). If "you have sinned against the LORD ... know that your sin will find you" (Num 32.23; cf. Prov 13.21). Like the people in Jeremiah's day, the Law-breakers in the time of Antiochus blamed obedience for problems that had really been caused by disobedience (Jer 44.15–18; cf. Isa 5.20).

1.12 και ηγαθυνθη ο λογοc εν οφθαλμοιc αυτων	**1.12** And the word was good in their eyes.

most effective way of reaching the largest number of people with the messages the government wanted to convey": Ferguson, *Backgrounds of Early Christianity,* 91.) The term *epiphanēs* ("made visible") is applied in Acts 2.20 (≡ Joel 2.31) to the coming of the Lord Jesus (like the similar forms *epiphainō* and *epiphaneia:* His first coming, 2 Tim 1.10; Titus 2.11; 3.4; His second coming, 2 Thes 2.8; 2 Tim 4.1, 8; Titus 2.13; cf. NIDNTT 3.317–20). Daniel had prophesied that Antiochus would "exalt himself, and magnify himself above every god" (Dan 11.36–37).

[38] Throughout the Maccabaica, the term **Law-breakers** *(paranomoi;* v 34; 10.61; 11.21; "transgressors of the law," RV; "lawless," RSV) refers to those who break God's Law, not human laws. Compare Acts 23.3, where Paul was accused of doing so. See also the notes on "men opposed to the Law" (2.44).

1.13 και προεθυμωθηςαν τινες ‹απο› του λαου και επορευθηςαν προς τον βαςιλεα και εδωκεν αυτοις εξουςιαν ποιηςαι τα δικαιωματα τω(ν) εθνων	**1.13** And some of the people were eager, and went to the king; and he gave them authority to do the nations' ordinances.

1.13 απο V A La[109+146] 7h7 7a1 | > S 64[+]236 •

1.13 Ordinances are, more precisely, "rules for righteousness" (*dikaiōmata;* BDAG 249, §1). The term is elsewhere applied mainly to God's rules for righteousness (including those that He gave to Israel under the old covenant: Luke 1.6; Rom 8.4; Heb 9.1, 10), which were far more righteous than anything that the Gentile nations could offer (Deut 4.8; Psa 19.9; Rom 7.12; 2 Tim 3.16). But the people described here "did not subject themselves to the righteousness [*dikaiosunē*] of God" (Rom 10.3). Instead, they eagerly submitted to **the nations' ordinances**—the nations' "rules for righteousness."

1.14 και ωκοδομηςαν γυμναςιον εν Ιεροςολυμοις κατα ‹τα› νομιμα των εθνων	**1.14** And they built a training-place in Jerusalem, in accordance with the laws of the nations,
1.15 και εποιηςαν εαυτοις ακροβυςτιας και απεςτηςαν απο διαθηκης αγιας και εζευγιςθηςαν εν τοις εθνεςιν και επραθηςαν του ποιηςαι το πονηρον	**1.15** and they made themselves uncircumcised, and departed from *the* holy covenant, and yoked themselves with the nations, and sold themselves to do wickedness.

1.14 *τα* S[ca] V A 64[+]236 | > S* •

1.15 They made themselves uncircumcised (contrary to God's old covenant Law for Israel: Acts 7.8; John 7.22), **and departed from the holy covenant** (which God had given them: Deut 31.16), **and yoked themselves with the nations** (instead of keeping their ways separate from those of the nations, as God had commanded: Jer 10.2; Lev 18.3; 20.23; Ezek 20.32), **and sold themselves to do wickedness** (like those whom God had previously punished: 1 Kgs 21.25–26; 2 Kgs 17.17).

It is the same in our own age. God's people today are "a holy nation" (1 Pet 2.9), dwelling spiritually in "the city of the living God, the heavenly Jerusalem," and sanctified under a "new covenant" (Heb 12.22–24). At the time when they were buried with Christ in baptism, they were "circumcised with a circumcision not made with hands" (Col 2.11–12)—not the circumcision "that is outward in the flesh," but "that of the heart" (Rom 2.28–29; Phil 3.3). Since their hearts have been purified in that way, they cannot be "unequally yoked with unbelievers," because they can have nothing in common with unbelievers (2 Cor 6.14–16). They cannot **sell themselves** into slavery under sin (Rom 7.14; 6.16–23) and remain slaves of God. They cannot **depart** from God's **holy covenant** (Heb 10.29) and remain the people of God. The Spirit of God commands them: "Do not be fashioned in accordance with this world" (Rom 12.2). Instead of training themselves at some worldly **training-place** *(gumnasion)* to live like **the nations,** they must "have their senses trained [*gegumnasmena*] to discern both good and evil" (Heb 5.14), no longer walking as the nations walk (Eph 4.17).

Antiochus attacks Egypt

1.16 και ητοιμασθη ‹η› βασιλεια ενωπιον Αντιοχου και υπελαβεν βασιλευσαι γης Αιγυπτου οπως βασιλευση επι τας δυο βασιλειας	**1.16** And the kingdom was ready in *the* sight of Antiochus, and he undertook to become king of *the* land of Egypt, so that he might be king over the two kingdoms.
1.17 και εισηλθεν εις Αιγυπτον εν οχλω βαρει εν αρμασιν και ελεφασι(ν) και εν ιππευσιν κ(αι) στολω μεγαλω	**1.17** And he came into Egypt with a heavy crowd, with chariots and elephants and with horsemen and a great array,
1.18 και συνεστησατο πολεμον προς Πτολεμαιον βασιλεα Αιγυπτου και ‹ενετραπη› Πτολεμαιος απο προσωπου αυτου και εφυγεν και ‹επεσον› τραυματιαι πολλοι	**1.18** and he made war against Ptolemy king of Egypt. And Ptolemy turned around from his face, and fled; and many wounded *ones* fell.
1.19 και κατελαβοντο τας πολεις τας οχυρας εν ‹γη› Αιγυπτω και ελαβεν τα σκυλα ‹γης› Αιγυπτου	**1.19** And they took hold of the fortified cities in *the* land of Egypt; and he took the plunder of *the* land of Egypt.

1.16 η S^{ca} V A 64^{+}236 | > S* • **1.18** ενετραπη S^{ca} V A 64^{+}236 | απεστραφη S* • επεσον S^{ca} V 64^{+}236 La$^{109+146}$ | -σαν A | εφυγον S* • **1.19** γη V A 64^{+}236 La$^{109+146}$ | τη S • γης A 64^{+}236 La^{146} | της S | > V •

1.16–19 The kingdom was ready (*ētoimasthē;* "prepared," SAAS). Kingdoms do not rise and fall by chance; they are made **ready** (1 Kgs 2.12, LXX; 2 Sam 7.12; Matt 25.34), just as meals and lodgings are made ready (Matt 22.4; Luke 17.8; Phm 22). Yet someone who has everything **ready** in his sight may still not be given the opportunity to make use of it (Luke 12.20). The king whose realm was flourishing so much at this time would see most of his prosperity disappear even before his death (Maccabaica 3.29–30; 6.11, 13).

Antiochus ... undertook to become king of the land of Egypt. Daniel's prophecies record a first expedition against Egypt, in which Antiochus was completely victorious (Dan 11.25–26), and a second expedition, in which he was not so successful because "ships of Kittim" came against him (Dan 11.29–30). The account in the Maccabean History obviously describes the first, more triumphant expedition: Antiochus **made war against Ptolemy king of Egypt,** who **turned around from his face, and fled** (v 18),[39] so that Antiochus gained control of **the fortified cities in the land of Egypt** and

[39] **Many wounded ones** [*traumatiai*] **fell.** The term **wounded** *(traumatiai)* does not necessarily mean "wounded to death" (KJV); cf. 16.9, 14; Epitome 11.12.

took its **plunder** (v 19), as described in Daniel 11.28. (The second, less successful expedition against Egypt, which is not discussed in the Maccabean History, is mentioned briefly in Epitome 5.1.)

In ancient times, **Egypt** had been one of the most powerful kingdoms in the world. Its strength had "no limit" (Nah 3.8–9; cf. Ezek 31.2). But the Lord declared that, after the Babylonian era, haughty Egypt would become "a lowly kingdom... and it will not lift itself up any more above the nations: and I will make them small, so that they will not rule over the nations" (Ezek 29.14–15). The defeat of Egypt by Antiochus Epiphanes was one step in that gradual decline and diminution. Like ancient Egypt, "every high thing that is raised up against the knowledge of God" will inevitably be cast down (2 Cor 10.5). In that way, "the loftiness of humanity will be bowed down, and the haughtiness of men will be made low; and the LORD alone will be exalted" (Isa 2.11–17).

1.17 Antiochus **came into Egypt with a heavy crowd, with chariots and elephants and with horsemen**[40] **and a great array.** During Hellenistic times **elephants** were often used in warfare, as described more fully in 6.30, 34–37 (cf. 3.34; 8.6; 11.56). The term **array** (Greek *stolos*) is often elsewhere applied specifically to an array of ships (as in Epitome 12.9), an "armada" (Muraoka 638), although nothing in the present context explicitly indicates that. In itself, the word might also refer to an array of soldiers (an "army," SAAS) or of equipment ("gear for military force," LEH 571).

Antiochus plunders the temple in Jerusalem

1.20 και επεστρεψεν Αντιοχος μετα το παταξαι Αιγυπτον εν τω ρ´ και μ´ και γ´ ‹ετι› και ανεβη επι Ι(σρα)ηλ και ‹ανεβη› επι Ι(ερουσα)λημ εν οχλω βαρει	**1.20** And Antiochus turned back after *he* had smitten Egypt, in the hundred and forty-third year, and went up against Israel. And he went up against Jerusalem with a heavy crowd,

1.20 ετι S^{ca} V A 64^{+}236 La$^{109+146}$ | > S* • ανεβη 2° 64^{+}236 La^{109} | > S V A La^{146} •

1.21 και εισηλθεν εις το αγιασμα εν υπερηφανια και ελαβεν το θυσιαστηριον το χρυσουν και τη(ν) λυχνιαν του φωτος και παντα τα σκευη αυτης	**1.21** and came into the holy place in arrogance, and took the golden sacrificial altar, and the lampstand of the light, and all its vessels,
1.22 και την τραπεζαν της προθεσεως και τα σπονδια και τας φιαλας και τας θυισκας τας χρυσας	**1.22** and the table of presentation, and the drink-offering cups, and the bowls, and the golden incense-bowls,

[40] **And with horsemen** *(kai en hippeusin)* is the reading of S, V, and A (supported by 7h7 and 7a1); the phrase is omitted by 64^{+}236 (supported by La$^{109+146}$). English translations vary accordingly.

και το καταπεταϲμα και τουϲ ϲτεφανουϲ και το(ν) κοϲμον τον χρυϲουν τον κατα προϲωπον του ναου και ελεπιϲεν πα(ν)τα	and the curtain, and the crowns, and the golden adornment that *was* against *the* face of the sanctuary; and he scaled off all *things*;
1.23 και ελαβεν ‹το αργυριον και το χρυϲιον› και τα ϲκευη τα επιθυμητα και ελαβεν τουϲ θηϲαυρουϲ τουϲ αποκρυφουϲ ουϲ ευρεν	**1.23** and he took the silver and gold and desirable vessels; and he took the hidden treasures that he found.

1.23 το αργυριον / και / το χρυσιον V A $64^{+}236$ La$^{109+146}$ | ~ S •

1.20–23 Antiochus . . . went up against Jerusalem after his expedition against Egypt **and came into the holy place**—the temple, which the LORD appointed as His own dwelling place among His people during the old covenant era (Exod 15.17). The temple contained two chambers separated by a curtain (Heb 9.1–5). The outer chamber contained three main objects (Exod 40.4–6, 22–27; 1 Kgs 7.48–49):

- A **golden sacrificial altar,** used exclusively to offer incense (Exod 30.1–5; 37.25–28; Luke 1.11).
- A golden **lampstand**[41] with seven lamps and various accessory gold **vessels** (Exod 25.31–39; 37.17–24).
- A gold-overlaid **table,** on which the bread of **presentation** (traditionally translated "showbread")[42] was presented to the LORD (Exod 25.23–30; 37.10–16). Also stored on this table were various golden **cups, bowls,** and other utensils used in the sacrificial service (Exod 25.29; 37.16; Num 4.7). Some of them were used to carry the **drink offering** that was poured out before the LORD when many of the animal offerings were presented (Num 15.2–16; 28.7–8). Others were used to carry the **incense** that was burned on the golden altar (Exod 30.1, 6–8, 34–36).

The inner chamber originally contained the ark of the covenant (Exod 26.33; 40.21), but there is no record that the ark existed in the temple after the Babylonian captivity; perhaps it was destroyed when the Babylonians burned the temple (2 Kgs 25.9). At any rate, there is no indication in this passage that Antiochus found any treasures inside the inner chamber.

The term **curtain** ("veil," KJV; Greek *katapetasma,* BDAG 524) is applied both to the outer curtain at the entrance of the original tabernacle (Exod 26.36–37) and to the inner curtain separating the two chambers (the "second curtain," Heb 9.3, ESV;

---

[41] The KJV rendering "candlestick" is not strictly accurate. The **lampstand** carried oil lamps (Lev 24.2–4), not candles.

[42] In the Hebrew Scriptures this bread is called the "bread of the face" (*leḥem pānîm,* Exod 25.30); in the Greek Scriptures it is called "the bread of presentation" (*hoi artoi tēs protheseōs,* Matt 12.4). Both names indicate that the bread was presented before the face of the LORD (Lev 24.6). In Spanish and French it is customarily called bread of *proposición* (VRV) ≡ *proposition* (Martin), i.e., bread of "placing" *(posición)* "before" *(pro-)* the LORD.

Exod 26.31–33). Each curtain was woven of precious materials (Exod 26.31, 36).

The **crowns** taken by Antiochus were presumably sculptured motifs, part of the temple's outer **adornment** mentioned in the immediately following context. (This is certainly the meaning in 4.57.) Other suggestions are (i) that they were gifts given to the treasury by the rich (Luke 21.1; cf. the crowns sent as gifts or tribute items in Maccabaica 10.20, 29; 11.35; 13.37, 39), and (ii) that they were the capitals of precious metal on top of the temple's pillars (cf. Exod 36.38; 38.17, 19, 28; 1 Kgs 7.16–20).

Antiochus removed the **adornment** on the outer façade (**against the face**) of the temple, and even scraped off (**scaled off**) anything valuable on its surface. He was a lavish spender (more so than his predecessors; see 3.30), and he was not afraid of desecrating temples (see 6.1–3), because he had no reverence either for the true God or for any of the other gods worshiped by his vassals (Dan 11.36–37). In spite of all the treasures that he had obtained from Egypt (v 19), he would want to collect as much additional wealth from Jerusalem as he could. "He who loves silver will not be satisfied with silver; nor whoever loves abundance, with increase" (Ecc 5.10).[43]

1.24 και λαβων παντα απηλθεν εις την γην αυτου και εποιηςεν φονοκτονιαν και ελαληςεν υπερηφανιαν μεγαλην	**1.24** And when *he* had taken all *the things*, he went away into his land. And he made a murderous killing, and spoke great arrogance.

1.24 He made a murderous killing, and spoke great arrogance—both of which had been prophesied by Daniel (Dan 8.24–25; 11.36–37). This statement need not refer specifically to Antiochus's behavior at the time when he entered the temple (vv 21–23). It might be the start of the general summary in verses 25–28, and therefore might encompass deeds that were done at various times (including some of those described later in this chapter, e.g., in vv 41–51).[44]

The people of Israel mourn

1.25 και εγενετο πενθος μεγα επι Ι(ςρα)ηλ εν παντι τοπω αυτων	**1.25** And *there* came great mourning upon Israel, in every place *where* they *were,*
1.26 και εςτεναξαν αρχοντες και πρεςβυτεροι παρθενοι και νεανιςκοι ηςθενηςαν και το καλλος των γυναικων ηλλοιωθη	**1.26** and rulers groaned, and elders; virgins and young men became weak, and the beauty of the women was changed;

[43] Antiochus's entrance into the temple and plundering of its treasures are reported also in the Maccabean Epitome 5.15–21.

[44] The unusual term **murderous killing** *(phonoktonia)* is a combination of "murder" (*phonos,* as in Mark 7.21; Rom 1.29) and "kill" (*kteinō,* as in Ptolemaica 1.2; a more familiar form is *apokteinō,* e.g., Matt 10.28; Mark 3.4). This rare double word catches the eye and ensures that the reader does not pass lightly over an act of great evil.

1.27 πας νυμφιος ανελαβεν θρηνον καθημενη εν παστω επενθει	**1.27** every bridegroom took up a lamentation; *the bride* sitting in *the* wedding chamber was mourning;

1.25–27 There came great mourning upon Israel,[45] as at the times of the Babylonian destruction of Jerusalem (see, especially, Lam 2.10; 1.6; Jer 7.34), the threatened slaughter of the Jews under Ahasuerus (Est 4.3), and the Roman destruction of Jerusalem (Luke 21.23–24). All kinds of people—old and young, male and female—were affected. The **young,** who would normally be strong, **became weak** (Isa 40.30); and the **bridegroom** and **bride,**[46] who would normally be joyful, lamented (Jer 7.34; Rev 18.23).

1.28 και εcιcθη η γη επι τουc κατοικουνταc αυτην και παc ‹ο› οικοc Ιακωβ ενεδυcατο εcχυνην	**1.28** and the land quaked on account of its dwellers, and all the house of Jacob was clothed with shame.

1.28 ο V A 64*236 | > S •

1.28 The land quaked on account of its dwellers. The Scriptures describe the **land** bearing witness, as a living thing, to the evil done by **its dwellers** (Deut 4.26), and quaking (as if in an earthquake) at the sight of their sins (Amos 8.8; Jer 2.12–14).

And all the house of Jacob was clothed with shame. The Lord brings low those who are proud (Luke 18.14), and He clothes with **shame** those who magnify themselves against Him (Psa 35.26; 109.28–29; 132.18). People who were not ashamed to rebel in His sight (Jer 6.15) were shamed by their humiliation in the sight of the nations (Ezek. 5.14–15). During the oppression of Antiochus Epiphanes, the nation of Israel (**the house of Jacob**) was **clothed with shame** because its people had opposed the Lord and "departed from the holy covenant" (vv 11–15, 43, 52). But later, when the nation turned back to God, its "young men clothed themselves with glory" (14.9).

Jerusalem is attacked; the citadel is set up

1.29 ‹κ(αι) μετα› δυο ετη ημερων απεcτιλεν ο βαcιλευc ‹αρχοντα› φορολογιαc ειc ταc πολειc Ιουδα και ηλθεν ειc Ι(ερουcα)λημ εν οχλω βαρει	**1.29** And after two years of days, the king sent a commander of tribute-collection into the cities of Judah. And he came into Jerusalem with a heavy crowd,
1.30 και ελαληcεν αυτοιc λογουc ιρηνικουc εν δολω και ενεπιcτευcαν αυτω και επεπεcεν επι την πολιν	**1.30** and spoke peaceful words to them in deceit; and they had faith in him. And he fell on the city

[45] **There came great mourning upon Israel.** The wording is remarkable: **mourning** is depicted as coming **upon** *(epi)* the land, in the way that a calamity comes (Jer 6.26; Amos 8.10).

[46] The one **sitting in the wedding chamber** is feminine *(kathēmenē),* and must therefore be the **bride** (not the bridegroom, as in SAAS).

εξαπινα και επαταξε(ν) αυτην πληγην μεγαλην και απωλεσεν λαον πολυ(ν) εξ Ις(ραη)λ	suddenly, and smote it *with* a great injury, and destroyed many people out of Israel.
1.31 και ελαβεν τα cκυλα τηc πολεωc και ενεπρηcεν αυτην πυρι και καθειλεν τουc οικουc αυτηc και τα τειχη κυκλω	**1.31** And he took the plunder of the city, and set it on fire with fire, and pulled down its houses and the walls round about.

1.29 κ(αι) μετα S^{ca} 64^{+}236 La^{109} | μετα δε V | μετα S* A La^{146} • αρχοντα S^{ca} V A 64^{+}236 La^{109} | -ταc S* La^{146} •

1.29 After two years of days[47] **the king sent a commander of tribute-collection into the cities of Judah.** Any province ruled by a nation was required to pay **tribute** to it (v 4; Luke 20.22–25), and we have already seen Antiochus's eagerness to increase his revenues (see on vv 20–23). Now he sent out a **commander of** his **tribute-collection.**[48]

1.30 The officer **spoke peaceful words to them in deceit; and they had faith in him,** as Daniel had prophesied (Dan 11.32). "By their kind words and blessings" deceivers may "deceive the hearts of the innocent" (Rom 16.17–18). The Scriptures warn us not to believe all the words we hear, but to investigate and test them (Prov 14.15; 1 Jn 4.1). "He who hates disguises himself with his lips, and in his inside he places deceit; when he shows favor with his voice, do not believe in him, for seven abominations are in his heart" (Prov 26.24–25). We can discern these people by their fruits (Matt 7.16–20; 12.33), as the present book illustrates (Maccabaica 7.10–11).

Those who have faith in deceivers' words will assuredly suffer for it (1 Kgs 13.21–22; Titus 1.10–11; Jer 17.5–6). The officer whom the people of Jerusalem had trusted **fell on the city suddenly, and smote it with a great injury, and destroyed many people.**

---

[47] **Two years of days** is a characteristic Hebrew expression (the same wording is found in Gen 41.1; cf. NETS). It is usually interpreted as "two full years" (KJV), but the Scripture usage need not require anything more specific than "two years' time" (see the evidence cited in BDB 399, §6b; and cf. GKC §131*d*).

[48] **A commander of tribute-collection** *(archonta phorologias)*. A somewhat similar term (*architelōnēs,* "leading tax collector" or "commander of tax collectors") is applied to Zaccheus in Luke 19.2. But the **commander** in the present passage wielded much greater power than Zaccheus. The Maccabean Epitome gives his name as Apollonius (cf. Maccabaica 3.10–12), and calls him a *musarchēs* (Epitome 5.24)—a term that could mean either "commander of the Mysians" or "commander of pollutions" (or, indeed, both at the same time; cf. APOT 139; RV mg; Schwartz, *2 Maccabees,* 265). Mysia was one of the provinces in what is now Turkey (Acts 16.7–8), and its people would probably have been within Antiochus's kingdom (Polybius 31.3;. Grainger, *Seleukid Prosopography and Gazetteer,* 809). In Hebrew, "commander of the Mysians" would presumably be *śr hmwsym,* while **commander of tribute-collection** would be *śr hmsym* (as in Exod 1.11), so the latter title may be designed in mockery of the former, indicating that the man's true role was less honorable than his official title (cf. Luke 5.29–30; 18.10–11)—just as Antiochus Epiphanes was mockingly known as "Epimanes" ("insane"; Polybius 26.1.1).

1.32 και ηχμαλωτιcα(ν) ταc γυναικαc και τα τεκνα και τα κτηνη ‹κ(αι)› ‹εκληρονομηcαν›	**1.32** And they took captive the women and the children and the live- stock. And they took *as* an inheritance
1.33 και ωκοδομηcαν την πολιν Δα(υι)δ τειχει μεγαλω και οχυρω πυργοιc οχυροιc και εγενετο αυτοιc ειc ακραν	**1.33** the city of David, and built *it* up with a great and fortified wall, with fortified towers; and it became a citadel for them.
1.34 και εθηκαν εκι εθνοc αμαρτωλο(ν) ανδραc ‹παρανομουc› και ενιcχυcαν εν αυτη	**1.34** And they placed there a sinful nation, men *who were* Law-breakers; and they strengthened themselves in it.
1.35 και παρεθε(ν)το οπλα και τροφην και cυναγαγοντεc τα cκυλα Ι(ερουcα)λημ απεθεντο εκει και ‹εγενοντο› ειc μεγαλην παγιδα	**1.35** And they laid up for themselves weapons and nourishment; and when they *had* gathered the plunder of Jerusalem, they put *it* aside there. And they became a great snare.
1.36 και εγενετο ειc ενεδρον τω αγιαcματι και ειc διαβολο(ν) πονηρον τω Ιc(ραη)λ δια παντοc	**1.36** And it became an ambush to the holy place, and a harmful accuser to Israel, at all *times*.
1.37 και εξεχεαν αιμα αθωον κυκλω του αγιαcματοc και εμολυναν το αγιαcμα	**1.37** And they poured out guiltless blood round about the holy place, and defiled the holy place.

1.32 κ(αι) 4° S^{ca} $64^{+}236$ La^{109} | > S* V A La^{146} • εκληρονομηcαν S^{ca1} V A $64^{+}236$ $La^{109+146}$ | -cεν S^{ca*} | > S* • **1.34** παρανομουc V A $64^{+}236$ $La^{109+146}$ | παρανουc S • **1.35** εγενοντο V $La^{109+146}$ 7a1 | εγενετο S A $64^{+}236$ 7h7 •

1.32–36 And they took as an inheritance the city of David, and built it up[49] **with a great and fortified wall, with fortified towers; and it became a citadel for them.** When David captured Jerusalem from the Jebusites, he dwelt in one particular part of the city, "the stronghold of Zion … and he called it the city of David" (2 Sam 5.7–9). That was the part of Jerusalem now **built up** and **fortified** by Antiochus's forces as a **citadel.**[50] Evildoers (**a sinful nation, men who were Law breakers**) were installed in

[49] In verses 32–33, $64^{+}236$ and S^{ca} (supported by La^{109} and 7h7) read **And they took captive the women and the children and the livestock. <u>And</u> they took as an inheritance the city of David, and built it up.** V and A (supported by La^{146} and 7a1) do not have the underlined **And** *(kai)*. In those texts, the sense is: "And they took captive the women and the children; and the livestock they took as an inheritance. And they built up the city of David." S* is faulty at this point, altogether omitting the phrase **And they took as an inheritance** (a mistake that is easiest to explain if its source contained the underlined **And**).

[50] **Citadel.** The Greek term *(akra)* indicates that it was built on a high point (cf. the "top" [*akron*] of Jacob's staff, Heb. 11.21; DGE 1.149, §II.1), perhaps a "rocky outcrop" (Muraoka 22; *rocca,* Diodati). It was located somewhere close to the temple area (Maccabaica 13.52; 1.36;

it, and they were provided with supplies of **weapons and nourishment.** The **plunder** taken from Jerusalem was also stored there. The citadel must have been a particularly strategic site, because the Israelites took a quarter of a century to dislodge the foreign forces from it—from 145 SE (1.20, 29, 54) to 171 SE (13.49–52)—even though they had gained control of the rest of Jerusalem much earlier—by 148 SE (4.52).

In the meantime, the citadel and its occupants were persistently (**at all times**) a force for evil:

- A **snare** (*pagis,* a trap to catch people unexpectedly, as in Luke 21.34–35; in French, an *occasion … de ruine,* Martin). Joshua had warned the Israelites that, if they associated with foreign nations, those nations "will be a snare and a trap to you, and a scourge in your sides, and thorns in your eyes, until you perish from this good land" (Josh 23.13).
- An **ambush** (*enedron,* as in 9.40; 10.80; 11.68–69) from which surprise raids could be made against **the holy place** (as described in 14.36; cf. 6.18).
- A **harmful accuser,**[51] seeking to bring injurious accusations against the people of **Israel** (as described in 6.18–27; cf. Ezra 4.6; Dan 6.4–13; Mark 15.3–4; Acts 25.18–19).

1.38 και εφυγον οι κατοικοι Ι(ερουϲα)λημ δι αυτουϲ και εγενετο κατοικια αλλοτριων και εγενετο αλλοτρια τοιϲ γενημαϲιν αυτηϲ και τα τεκνα αυτηϲ ενκατελιπον αυτην	**1.38** And the dwellers in Jerusalem fled because of them, and she became a dwelling-place of strangers; and she became a stranger to her offspring, and her children left her.

1.38 The dwellers in Jerusalem fled because of the evildoers in the citadel. The city's own **children left her;** instead, **she became a dwelling-place of strangers**—foreigners who were enemies of Israel (2.7). Similar things had happened when the Babylonians conquered the city: "Our inheritance has been turned over to strangers, our houses to aliens …. The mountain of Zion … has been desolate; foxes have walked in it" (Lam 5.2, 18).

4.41; 6.18). Josephus says that the descendants of Mattathias eventually demolished it completely and leveled the ground on which it stood (*War,* 5.137–139; 1.50; *Antiquities,* 13.215–217). His accounts appear to be at least partly inaccurate (see Schürer-Vermes 1.192, n. 10), but the citadel may indeed have been razed to the ground: no clear archeological trace of it has ever been detected, and therefore its exact position remains unknown (ABD 3.758; ZEB 3.550–51; Schürer-Vermes 1.154–55, n. 39).

[51] **A harmful accuser** *(diabolon ponēron).* The Greek term *diabolos* is applied to the great accuser—the devil (Rev 12.9–10)—and to people who accuse as the devil does (2 Tim 3.3). In this passage, *ponēros* is usually taken to mean "evil" (KJV), but the context would suggest rather the meaning "harmful and injurious" (Muraoka 576, §2; see the footnote to Eighteen Psalms 2.6): the phrase is concerned not with what the citadel was in itself, but with what it was doing **to Israel** (cf. 14.36).

1.39 το αγιαϲμα αυτηϲ ηρημωθη ωϲ ερημοϲ αι εορται αυτηϲ ‹εϲτραφηϲα(ν)› ειϲ πενθοϲ τα ϲαββατα αυτηϲ ‹ειϲ ονιδιϲμον η τιμη αυτηϲ› ειϲ εξουδενωϲιν	**1.39** Her holy place was made desolate like a desert; her feasts were turned into mourning, her Sabbaths into a reproach, her honor into despising.

1.39 εϲτραφηϲα(ν) S^{ca} V A $64^{+}236$ $La^{109+146}$ | -φη S* • ειϲ ονιδιϲμον η τιμη αυτηϲ S^{ca} V [A] $64^{+}236$ $La^{109+146}$ | > S* •

1.39 Her holy place was made desolate like a desert. The temple was not destroyed, but it was desecrated and neglected (2.12; 4.38). The temple worship included regular **feasts** and **Sabbaths** that had been appointed by the Lord under the Law of Moses (Lev 23.2–43). But now all these appointed times were abandoned (vv 43, 45; contrast 10.34), and became a cause of **mourning** and **reproach,** as also happened after the Babylonian conquest (Lam 1.4; 2.6).

1.40 κατα την δοξα(ν) αυτηϲ ‹επληθυνθη η› ατιμια αυτηϲ και το υψοϲ αυτηϲ εϲτραφη ειϲ πε(ν)θοϲ	**1.40** Her dishonor was multiplied as her glory *had been,* and her high condition was turned into mourning.

1.40 επληθυνθη η S^{ca} V A $64^{+}236$ $La^{109+146}$ | επληϲθη η γη S* •

1.40 Jerusalem's **dishonor was multiplied as her glory had been:** that is, her **dishonor** became as great as her previous **glory** (**high condition**) had been. In this respect too, the city had suffered similarly after the Babylonian conquest: "How she has sat alone, the city that was great with people; she has become like a widow, the great one among the nations; the princess among the provinces, she has been put to menial tasks.... All of her honor has gone away from the daughter of Zion" (Lam 1.1, 6).

The king commands the people to worship idols

1.41 και εγραψεν ο βαϲιλευϲ παϲη τη βαϲιλεια αυτου ειναι πανταϲ λαον ενα	**1.41** And the king wrote to all his kingdom, *for it* to be all one people,
1.42 και ενκαταλιπει(ν) εκαϲτον τα νομιμα αυτου και επεδεξατο παντα τα εθνη κατα τον λογον του βαϲιλεωϲ	**1.42** and *for* each to leave his laws. And all the nations accepted *it,* in accordance with the king's word.
1.43 και πολλοι απο Ι(ϲρα)ηλ ευδοκηϲαν τη λατρια αυτου και εθυϲαν τοιϲ ιδωλοιϲ και εβεβηλωϲαν το ϲαββατον	**1.43** And many *people* from Israel were well pleased with his way of worship, and sacrificed to idols and profaned the Sabbath.

1.41–43 The king[52] **wrote to all his kingdom . . . for each to leave his laws.** Age after age there have been enticements for God's people to **leave** the **laws** of their Mas-

[52] S, V, and A (supported by $La^{109+146}$) read **the king;** $64^{+}236$ read **King Antiochus.**

ter, and to become **one people** with those around them. That was a danger against which Joshua warned the people of Israel: "Be very strong... to keep and do all that is written in the book of the Law of Moses, so that you may not turn aside from it to the right or to the left, so that you may not go together with these nations ... nor make mention of the name of their gods, nor swear an oath, nor serve them, nor bow down to them. But to the LORD your God you shall cling, as you have done until this day" (Josh 23.6–8). The New Testament Scriptures warn us today against the same danger: "Do not become unequally yoked with unbelievers; for what fellowship have righteousness and iniquity ... or what portion has a believer with an unbeliever? ... Come out of their midst and be separate, says the Lord, and do not touch any unclean thing, and I will accept you" (2 Cor 6.14–7.1).

All the nations accepted it .... And many people from Israel were well pleased with his way of worship.[53] Similarly, in John's vision, "all the nations" were deceived by "the great city that reigns over the kings of the earth" (Rev 18.23; 17.18). Even today, many historians basically approve of Antiochus's policies.[54] But even if all the nations accept something that is evil, God's people are not to accept it (see the notes on 2.19–22). "You shall not follow a multitude to do evil" (Exod 23.2).

1.44 και απεστιλεν ο βασιλευc βιβλια εν χειρι αγγελων ειc Ι(ερουcα)λημ και ταc πολειc Ιουδα πορευθηναι οπιcω νομιμω(ν) αλλοτριων τηc γηc	**1.44** And the king sent scrolls by *the* hand of messengers to Jerusalem and the cities of Judah, *for them* to go after laws strange to the land,
1.45 και ‹κωλυcαι› ολοκαυτωματα και θυcιαν και cπονδη(ν) εκ του αγιαcματοc και βεβηλωcαι caββατα και εορταc	**1.45** and to prevent whole burnt offerings and sacrifice and drink offering from the holy place, and to profane Sabbaths and feasts,
1.46 και μιαναι αγιαcμα και αγιουc	**1.46** and to pollute *the* holy place and *the* holy *people*,
1.47 οικοδομηcαι βωμουc και τεμενη και ειδωλια και θυειν υεια και κτηνη ‹κοινα›	**1.47** to build heathen altars and heathen temples and idol- shrines, and to sacrifice swine's *flesh* and unholy livestock,

1.45 κωλυcαι V A 64⁺236 La[109+146] | κυκλωc- S • **1.47** κοινα S[ca] V A 64⁺236 La[109+146] | πολλα S* •

[53] Antiochus required not only Israelites, but also people of other **nations** within **his kingdom,** to adopt Greek practices. This is independently attested in letters of the period between Antiochus and the Samaritans (Josephus, *Antiquities,* 12.258–263; cf. Kasher, *Jews and Hellenistic Cities in Eretz-Israel,* 56–57). But most nations had little trouble conforming to this policy. It had significant consequences only for Israelites (cf. Epitome 6.1–2; Tacitus, *Histories,* 5.8).

[54] So, e.g., Mørkholm, *Antiochus IV of Syria,* 55–63; Mittag, *Antiochos IV Epiphanes,* 260, 281, 334–35. The world will accept Barabbas more readily than Jesus (Luke 23.18–19; Acts 3.14).

1.48 και αφειναι τους υιους αυτων απεριτμητους ‹και› βδελυξαι τας ψυχας αυτων εν ‹παντι› ακαθαρτω και βεβηλωσει	**1.48** and to leave their sons uncircumcised, and to make their souls abominable with every unclean *thing* and profaneness,
1.49 ωστε επιλαθεσθε του νομου και ‹αλλαξαι› παντα τα δικαιωματα	**1.49** so as to forget the Law and change all the ordinances.

1.48 και 2° 64^{+}236 La^{109} | > S V A La^{146} • παντι S^{ca} V A 64^{+}236 La$^{109+146}$ | πνι΄ S* • **1.49** αλλαξαι V A 64^{+}236 La$^{109+146}$ | -ξασθαι S •

1.44–49 To become **one people** (v 41) with the nations around them, the Israelites would have to **forget the Law** of God (Hos 4.6; Psa 119.109) **and change all the ordinances** that God had ordained.

Under the old covenant, God's Law required His people to present various offerings regularly at His temple (**the holy place**)—including **whole burnt offerings** (which had to be offered at least twice every day: Num 28.3–8; Exod 29.38–42), **sacrifices** (peace offerings,[55] presented as acts of thanksgiving to God, or in fulfillment of vows, or simply as acts of free will: Lev 7.11–18; 22.21–23), and **drink offerings** (which had to accompany all animal burnt offerings and peace offerings: Num 15.2–16).

God's old covenant Law also required His people to circumcise their **sons** (Gen 17.10–14; Exod 12.48; Lev 12.3; John 7.22–23), to observe the appointed **Sabbaths and feasts** (Lev 23.2–43; Ezek 20.12–13), and to avoid contact with everything that was designated by the Law as an **unclean thing** *(akathartos)* and a **profaneness** *(bebēlōsis),* such as various foods (vv 62–63; Lev 11.2–47; Acts 10.14).

Any Israelites who wanted to become **one people** with other nations would have to abandon all the above requirements of the Law. Instead, those Israelites would have to worship **idols** as the other nations did (v 43), **build heathen altars and heathen temples**[56] **and idol-shrines** (v 47), and sacrifice there the kinds of animals that the

---

[55] **Sacrifice** (Greek *thusia* ≡ Hebrew *zebaḥ:* Matt 9.13 ≡ Hos 6.6; Heb 10.5 ≡ Psa 40.6) has both a broad and a narrow meaning in the Scriptures. In the broad sense it applies to every offering in which an animal was slain (including burnt offerings, Exod 20.24). In the narrow sense, **sacrifice** refers solely to peace offerings (Lev 3.1; 17.5; 1 Kgs 8.62–64), as distinct from burnt offerings (Exod 18.12; Lev 17.8; Psa 40.6 ≡ Heb 10.5).

In the present passage the term **sacrifice** must be used in the latter sense, since it is distinguished from **burnt offerings** (v 45).

[56] The terms here translated **heathen altar** (*bōmos,* vv 47, 54, 59; 2.23–25, 45; 5.68; Acts 17.23) and **heathen temple** (*temenos,* v 47; 5.43–44) are applied in this book solely to places for the worship of false gods (Trench 364–66; Muraoka 124, 676), whereas the altar of the true God is always called a **sacrificial altar** (*thusiastērion,* "sacrifice-place"; vv 21, 54, 59; 4.38–56; 5.1; 6.7; 7.36; Luke 1.11; Matt 5.23–24). Jünemann and BGS preserve the distinction by consistently using Spanish *ara* to translate Greek *bōmos,* and Spanish *altar* to translate Greek *thusiastērion.* Diodati consistently uses Italian *altare* (lowercase) for the former, and *Altare* (with a capital letter) for the latter.

other nations sacrificed, including **swine** and other **unholy livestock** (v 47), the offering of which was never permitted by the old covenant Law (Lev 1.1–7.38; 22.18–19).

Under the new covenant, there has been a change of the law (cf. Heb 7.12; 8.6–13). Christ "declared all foods clean" (Mark 7.19), and His death did away with the animal sacrifices (Heb 10.11–18) and the feasts and Sabbaths appointed by the old covenant (Col 2.14–17). Yet God still commands His people not to walk as the nations around us walk (Eph 4.17–20). We are to "cleanse ourselves from all defilement of flesh and spirit" (2 Cor 7.1), avoiding all uncleanness (Eph 5.3, 5; 1 Thes 4.7; 2 Cor 6.17) and profaneness (1 Tim 6.20; 4.7; Heb 12.16). We are to circumcise our hearts (Rom 2.28–29; Phil 3.3) and offer, not animal sacrifices, but our own lives as living sacrifices to our God (Rom 12.1; 1 Pet 2.5; Heb 13.15–16). We are to "flee from idolatry" (1 Cor 10.14; 1 John 5.21) and to worship the true God only (Matt 4.10; 1 Cor 8.5–6; John 17.3).

1.50 και οc α(ν) μη ποιηcη κατα τον λογον του βαcιλεωc αποθανιται	**1.50** "And whoever may not do in accordance with the king's word will die."
1.51 κατα παντας τουc λογουc τουτουc εγραψεν παcη τη βαcιλεια αυτου και εποιηcεν επιcκοπουc ‹επι› παντα τον λαο(ν) και ‹ενετειλατο› ταιc πολεcιν Ιουδα θυcιαζειν κατα πολι(ν) και πολιν	**1.51** According to all these words, he wrote to all his kingdom; and he made overseers over all the people, and commanded the cities of Judah to be sacrificing, city by city.

1.51 επι V A 64⁺236 La$^{109+146}$ | κατα S • ενετειλατο A 64⁺236 La$^{109+146}$ | -λαντο S V •

1.50–51 And whoever may not do in accordance with the king's word will die. The evildoing was no longer optional; from now on, it was **commanded** by the king.[57] Every person had now to choose between the wrath of their king on earth and the wrath of their King in Heaven. "Do not be afraid of those who kill the body, and after that have no more that they can do. But I will warn you whom you shall fear: Fear Him, who after He has killed has power to cast into hell; yes, I say to you, Fear Him" (Luke 12.4–5).

The king wrote to all his kingdom **according to** the **words** of verses 44–50. That is, his message was not necessarily put in those particular words, but it was consistent with (in accord with, *kata*) them.[58] The expression **according to** is used in the same sense in 5.14; 10.17, 25, 51; 13.35.

---

[57] A and 64⁺236 (supported by La$^{109+146}$) read **he commanded** *(eneteilato)*. S and V read "they commanded" *(enet[e]ilanto)*.

[58] Many examples of this use of *kata* are listed in BDAG 513, §5b, and Muraoka 365, §7a.

The king's commands are carried out

1.52 και ϲυνηθροιϲθηϲαν απο του λαου πολλοι προϲ αυτουϲ ‹παϲ ο› ενκαταλιπων τον νομον και εποιηϲαν κακα εν τη γη	**1.52** And many from the people drew together to them— every*one* who *was* leaving the Law; and they did evil *things* in the land.
1.53 και εθεντο τον Ι(ϲρα)ηλ εν ‹κρυφιοιϲ› εν πα(ν)τι φυγαδευτηριω αυτων	**1.53** And Israel placed themselves in hidden *places*, in every place of flight *that* they *had*.

1.52 παϲ ο S^{ca} A 64^{+}236 La$^{109+146}$ | και S* | και παϲ ο V • **1.53** κρυφιοιϲ S^{ca} V A 64^{+}236 | -φοιϲ S* •

1.53 Israel placed themselves in hidden places, in every place of flight that they had. Because of the evils around them (v 52), many of the faithful Israelites fled from the cities and **placed themselves**[59] **in hidden places**[60] (described in more detail in 2.27–31, 42–43), just as happened in other times of great distress (1 Sam 13.6; Matt 24.15–18; cf. Heb 11.38). "A prudent man sees the evil, and hides himself" (Prov 22.3 ≡ 27.12; Isa 26.20).

1.54 και τη πεντεκαιδεκατη ημερα Χαϲαλευ τω ε´ και μ´ και ρ´ ετει ‹ωκοδομηϲαν› βδελυγμα ερημωϲεωϲ επι το θυϲιαϲτηριον και εν πολεϲιν Ιουδα κυκλω ωκοδομηϲαν βωμουϲ	**1.54** And *on* the fifteenth day of Chislev of the hundred and forty- fifth year, they built an abomination of desolation on the sacrificial altar. And in *the* cities of Judah round about, they built heathen altars.

1.54 ωκοδομηϲαν 1° S^{ca} V A 64^{+}236 La^{109} | -ϲεν S* La^{146} •

1.54 On the fifteenth day of Chislev . . . they built an abomination of desolation on the sacrificial altar. They began sacrificing on it ten days later (v 59). The **sacrificial altar**—the altar of burnt offering (4.44) appointed by God's Law (Exod 27.1–8)—was not taken away. Its stones were left in place (4.44–46), and an **abomination of deso-**

[59] This sentence is generally taken to mean, not that the Israelites **placed themselves** in hiding, but that the evildoers "drove" (KJV) or "forced" (ESV) them into hiding. However, that is not a possible meaning of the verb **placed** (*ethento,* aorist middle), which never describes an unintended consequence, but always an act of deliberate placement—either by other people ("he placed him in safekeeping," 14.3; "he placed a garrison there," 12.34; "he placed him as commander," 13.53; cf. 9.51–53; 10.65; 11.66; 13.33; 14.26, 33–35; Luke 1.66; Acts 1.7; 4.3; 5.18; 12.4; 19.21; 20.28; 27.12; 1 Cor 12.18, 28; 1 Thes 5.9) or by oneself (Peter, "placing himself on his knees" [*puesto de rodillas,* VRV], Acts 9.40). In the present sentence **Israel** takes a plural verb, as on most of its occurrences in the Maccabean History (2.70; 9.20; 13.26).

[60] V, A, 64^{+}236, and a corrector of S have the adjective *kruphiois* (**hidden places**); S* has the noun *kruphois* ("hiding places"). This is little more than a spelling variation. Similar variations are found at 2.31, 36, 41.

lation (described in v 59 as a **heathen altar**) was simply erected on top of it.[61] This is a significant point, because it posed a problem for the Israelites several years later, when they came to cleanse the temple: after they had removed the heathen altar, could they reuse the old **sacrificial altar** underneath it to worship God (4.44–47)?

Chislev was the ninth month of the Israelite year (4.52; Zec 7.1), in the winter (Jer 36.22; cf. Ezra 10.9).

Abomination of desolation. Every false god (2 Kgs 23.13), and everything set up to worship such a god (Jer 7.30), is described in the Scriptures as an **abomination** (Greek *bdelugma,* Matt 24.15 ≡ Hebrew *šqwṣ,* Dan 9.27), because God's people are to "abominate" *(šqṣ)* it (Deut 7.26). "What is exalted among Men is an abomination in the sight of God" (Luke 16.15). The abomination set up on this occasion was called an abomination **of desolation** (Greek *erēmōseōs* ≡ Hebrew *šmm)* because it was something that made the holy place desolate ("like a desert," v 39; 2.12; 4.38; cf. Dan 9.26, 18; 8.13; Luke 21.20; Matt 23.38).

Daniel had prophesied that an **abomination of desolation** would be set up (a) during the Greek kingdom (Dan 11.31) and (b) at a time when Jerusalem and its sanctuary would be destroyed (Dan 9.27). These prophecies clearly refer to two different times, because neither the sanctuary nor Jerusalem was destroyed during the Greek kingdom (Dan 8.13–14). The first prophecy was fulfilled when Antiochus's subjects set up the **abomination of desolation** on the occasion described in the present passage. The second prophecy was fulfilled when Jerusalem was destroyed by the Romans, within the lifetime of the generation that heard Jesus (Matt 24.15, 34 ≡ Luke 21.20, 32; cf. Luke 19.41–44; John 11.48).

Other **heathen altars** were built in other **cities of Judah** (including Modein, 2.23).

1.55 και επι των θυρων των οικιων και εν ταις πλατιαις εθυμιω(ν)	**1.55** And at the doors of the houses, and in the broad *places*, they were burning incense.

1.55 At the doors of the houses, and in the broad places, they were burning incense. Under God's Law for Israel, **incense,** like all other offerings, could be burned only to Him, only at His appointed sanctuary, and only by His appointed priests—the descendants of Aaron (Deut 33.10; Num 16.40).

The broad places *(plateia)* were the widest streets or other outdoor open spaces within the city (cf. Luke 14.21; Acts 5.15; Rev 21.21)—suitable places for any act that was meant to be seen by people in general (Matt 6.5).

1.56 και τα βιβλια του νομου α ευρον ‹ενεπυρισαν εν πυρι κατασχισαντες›	**1.56** And the books of the Law that they found, they set on fire with fire, having split *them* in pieces.

1.56 ενεπυρισαν εν πυρι / κατασχισαντες A 64⁺236 La$^{109+146}$ | ~ S [V] •

---

[61] The heathen worship in the Jerusalem temple is described in the Maccabean Epitome 6.2–6.

1.57 και οπου ευρισκετο παρα τινι βιβλιον διαθηκης και ει τις συνευδοκει τω νομω το συνκριμα του βασιλεως ‹εθανατου› αυτον	**1.57** And where a book of *the* covenant was found alongside anyone, or if anyone was well pleased with the Law, the king's judgment put him to death.

1.57 εθανατου [θ- V] A 64*236 La[109+146] | -ουν S •

1.56 The books of the Law that they found, they set on fire with fire, having split them in pieces. The evildoers were doubly zealous to destroy God's word: not only did they burn it **with fire,** but they also cut it **in pieces** (as Jehoiakim did, Jer 36.22–25). Yet the word of the Lord cannot be destroyed by any power on earth. It "will stand to lasting time," and those who try to destroy it will themselves be destroyed (Isa 40.8 ≡ 1 Pet 1.23–25).

1.58 εν ισχυι αυτων εποιουν τω Ις(ραη)λ τοις ευρισκομενοις εν παντι μηνι και μηνι εν ταις πολεσιν	**1.58** In their strength they were acting against Israel, against *those* who were found month by month in the cities,
1.59 και πεμπτη και εικαδι του μηνος θυσιαζοντες επι τον βωμον ος ην επι του θυσιαστηριου	**1.59** and, on *the* twenty-fifth of the month, sacrificing on the heathen altar that was on the sacrificial altar.
1.60 και τας γυναικας τας περιτετμηκυιας τα τεκνα αυτων εθανατωσαν κατα το προσταγμα	**1.60** And the women who had circumcised their children, they put to death in accordance with the decree
1.61 και εκρεμασαν τα βρεφη εκ των τραχηλων αυτω(ν) και τους οικους αυτων και τους περιτετμηκοτας αυτους	**1.61** (and they hanged the babies from their necks), and their house*hold*s, and the *people* who had circumcised them.
1.62 και πολλοι εν Ις(ρα)ηλ εκραταιωθησαν και οχυρωθησαν εν αυτοις του μη φαγειν κοινα	**1.62** And many in Israel remained strong, and were fortified in *them*selves not to eat unholy *things*.

1.58–62 In their strength they were acting against Israel[62]—and yet **many in Israel remained strong** (as Daniel had prophesied, Dan 11.32), **and were fortified in themselves not to eat unholy things.** Those who are "strong in the Lord, and in the strength of His might" (Eph 6.10–18), "can do all things in Him" (Php 4.13), and can withstand whatever strength this world may bring against them (2 Tim 4.17).

The ruler of this world, Satan, is strong; but there is One who is even stronger, and who has the power to bind him (Luke 11.20–22). All the **strength** of the city that

[62] The sentence construction here is **they were acting** [imperfect tense] **against Israel ... and ... sacrificing** [participle] **on the heathen altar** (vv 58–59). There is a similar construction in, e.g., "we are not again commending [present tense] ourselves ... but giving [participle] you ..." (2 Cor 5.12; MHT 3.343, §3*d;* BDF §468.1; cf. Thackeray 24, §3).

reigns over the kings of the earth (Rev 17.18) cannot protect that city against the strength of the God who judges her (Rev 18.10, 8).

1.60–61 The women who had circumcised their children, they put to death . . . and their households, and the people who had circumcised them.[63] Anyone who might have assisted the forbidden act in any way was punished. Under the Law of Moses, those who had "committed a sin worthy of death" might be put to death and then hanged (Deut 21.22–23)—but these women were put to death for keeping the Law. And even if the mothers had been worthy of death, it was contrary to the Law to put to death their babies (Deut 24.16).

1.63 και επεδεξαντο αποθανιν ινα μη μιανθωϲιν τοιϲ βρωμαϲιν και μη βεβηλωϲωϲι(ν) διαθηκην αγιαν και απεθανον	**1.63** And they accepted death, in order that they should not be polluted with the foods and should not defile *the* holy covenant; and they died.

1.63 Those who remained strong (v 62) **accepted death . . . and they died.** In the eyes of the world, an act of disobedience to God's Law might seem a trivial thing. Did it really matter so much whether someone ate a forbidden food, or burned incense in a place that had not been authorized (v 55)? (Nowadays there are many who profess belief in God yet would rather break some of His commands than incur a raised eyebrow or a murmur of social disapproval.) Nevertheless, those who remained faithful were so firmly determined not to **be polluted**[64] or **defile the holy covenant** (cf. Dan 1.8) that they chose to die rather than sin. Jesus said: "Whoever would save his life will lose it; and whoever will lose his life for My sake and the gospel's will save it" (Mark 8.35–36; cf. Rev 12.11; 2.10; Acts 20.24).

1.64 και εγενετο οργη μεγαλη επι Ιϲ(ραη)λ ϲφοδρα	**1.64** And *there* came to be very great anger upon Israel.

[63] **The women who had circumcised their children** and **the people who had circumcised them** are usually taken to be two different groups. This is possible; but repetition of a statement after a small interval is one of the Maccabean History's most distinctive mannerisms (compare, e.g., 8.1–2: "Judas heard the name of the Romans, that they were powerful with strength . . . and that they were powerful with strength"). Those who believe that the two groups were different have not been able to agree as to the nature of the difference. According to Grimm (33), the first group were those who arranged for the circumcision, the second those who performed it. According to Knabenbauer (63), the first group were those who circumcised their own children (cf. Exod 4.25), the second those who circumcised others' children (cf. 2.46; Acts 16.3). Abel (27) is undecided.

The incidents described in this passage are reported also in Epitome 6.10.

[64] Being **polluted** *(miainō)* is the opposite of being pure (Titus 1.15; cf. 2 Pet 2.20, 10; Heb 12.15).

1.64 And there came to be very great anger upon Israel. "The anger of God is revealed from heaven against all irreverence and unrighteousness of people" (Rom 1.18; John 3.36; Eph 5.6). In this respect also, Israel's sufferings at the hands of Antiochus Epiphanes resembled her earlier sufferings at the hands of the Babylonians (Jer 7.20; Zec 7.12) and her later sufferings at the hands of the Romans (Luke 21.23).

These things happened to God's people in the past partly in order to warn future generations about the **very great anger** that will come on them at the last day if they disobey His commands (Rom 2.5–9). "Who can stand before His indignation? and who can abide in the fierceness of His anger?" (Nah 1.6; Psa 2.12; 76.7; Jer 10.10; Rev 6.16–17).

Mattathias (2.1–70)

Mattathias and his five sons

2.1 εν ταιϲ ημεραιϲ εκιναιϲ ανεϲτη Ματταθιαϲ υιοϲ Ιωαννου του Cυμεων ιερευϲ των υιων ‹Ιωαριβ› απο Ι(ερουϲα)λημ και εκαθιϲεν εν Μωδει(ν)	**2.1** In those days, *there* rose up Mattathias son of John the *son* of Simeon, a priest of the sons of Joiarib, from Jerusalem; and he settled in Modein.

2.1 Ιωαριβ V La[109+146] [ܝܘܝܪܒ 7h7 7a1] | -ριμ S A 64[*]236 •

2.1 There rose up Mattathias son of John the son of Simeon,[65] **a priest of the sons of Joiarib, from Jerusalem.** The **sons of Joiarib**[66] were the very first division of the priests descended from Aaron (1 Chr 24.7; cf. 1 Chr 9.10; Neh 11.10). Two of Mattathias's sons (Jonathan and Simon), and his grandson John, eventually became high priest (10.20–21, 69; 12.3; 13.36, 42; 14.17, 30, 35, 41, 47; 16.24).

The work of a **priest** involved teaching the Law faithfully (Deut 33.10; Lev 10.11; Mal 2.6–7), judging (Deut 17.9–11; 2 Chr 19.8), blessing the people (Num 6.23–26; 1 Chr 23.13), and offering the appointed offerings (Deut 33.10; Num 16.40; 1 Sam 2.28; Luke 1.8–9). Therefore, many of the priests lived where the place of sacrifice was located, at **Jerusalem** (Ezra 6.18), although some priests lived and taught elsewhere in Israel (Josh 21.4, 13–19; 1 Chr 6.57–60; 2 Chr 17.9).

The statement that Mattathias **rose up** (*anestē;* like Deborah, Jdg 5.17) begins a series that runs through the book. After him, "Judas who was called Maccabeus, his

---

[65] The translation "Mattathias the son of John of the tribe of Simeon" (SAAS) is incorrect. The **sons of Joiarib,** like all old covenant priests, belonged to the tribe of Levi (1 Chr 24.1–7). Therefore, the **Simeon** mentioned in this verse cannot have been the founder of the tribe, and must have been a descendant of Levi (just as the Simeon in Jesus' genealogy was a descendant of Judah, Luke 3.30, 33).

[66] **Joiarib.** Also spelled "Jehoiarib" in the Hebrew Scriptures (Ginsburg, *Introduction to the Massoretico-Critical Edition of the Hebrew Bible,* 372, §8).

son, rose up [*anestē*] in place of him" (3.1). Next "Jonathan… rose up [*anestē*] in place of Judas his brother" (9.31). Later, "Simon had risen up [*anestē*] in place of Jonathan his brother" (13.14), completing Israel's deliverance. Finally the book looks beyond Simon to the time when "a faithful prophet should rise up [*anastēnai*]" (14.41). All these deliverers **rose up** because God raised them up (Jdg 2.16; 3.9; Acts 3.22).[67]

He settled in Modein, a town somewhere west of central Judea (between that region and the Philistine city Ashdod: 15.41–16.10).[68] Mattathias's ancestors had already lived there, and the family's burial place was there (see 2.70; 9.19; 13.25–30).

2.2 και αυτω υιοι πε(ν)τε Ιωαννηc ⸤ο⸥ επικαλουμενοc Γαδδει	**2.2** And he had five sons: John, who *was* called Gaddi;
2.3 Cιμων ⸤ο⸥ καλουμενοc Θαccει	**2.3** Simon, who *was* called Thassi;
2.4 Ιουδαc ο καλουμενοc ⸤Μακκαβεοc⸥	**2.4** Judas, who *was* called Maccabeus;
2.5 ⸤Ελεαζαροc⸥ ⸤ο⸥ καλουμενοc Αυαραν Ιωναθηc ο καλουμενοc ⸤Απφουc⸥	**2.5** Eleazar, who *was* called Avaran; Jonathan, who *was* called Apphus.

2.2 ο S^{ca} V A La$^{109+146}$ | > S* 64^{+}236 • **2.3** ο V A La$^{109+146}$ | > S 64^{+}236 • **2.4** Μακκαβεοc S^{ca} V A 64^{+}236 La$^{109+146}$ | > S* • **2.5** Ελεαζαροc S^{ca} [-ρ V] A 64^{+}236 La$^{109+146}$ | Ιελ- S* • ο 1° S^{ca} V A La$^{109+146}$ | > S* 64^{+}236 • Απφουc V 64^{+}236 La$^{109+146}$ | Cα- S A •

2.2–5 He had five sons. All five had common Israelite names: **John, Simon** (Simeon, v 65), **Judas** (Judah), **Eleazar,** and **Jonathan.** Each of them also had an alternate

---

[67] The statement that Mattathias **rose up** is sometimes connected with **from Jerusalem** (he "rose up from Jerusalem and settled in Modein," SAAS; "moved from Jerusalem and settled in Modein," ESV). However, that is not consistent with the usage of the term in this book (see the passages cited above). Moreover, never in the Scriptures is anyone said to go **up** *(ana-)* from Jerusalem to any place. Travel from Jerusalem is always "down" (Luke 10.30). In the present verse, therefore, **in those days** refers to the time when Mattathias **rose up,** but not necessarily to the time when he left Jerusalem and **settled in Modein.** That might have happened at the same time, or it might have happened previously; the Greek text does not specify. "It was in those days that… Mattathias… came on the scene. He was a priest of the Joarib family from Jerusalem, now settled at Modin" (REB).

[68] **Modein.** The location of the town is no longer known, and has been the subject of much debate (Scolnic, "Mattathias and the Jewish Man of Modein," 463–83); "any one of… many" sites would fit (Stanley, *Sinai and Palestine,* 162). The notion that it was visible from the sea derives from a misreading of 13.29 (see the notes there). Modein is placed south of Bethhoron on the ancient Medeba map (Avi-Yonah, *Madaba Mosaic Map,* 58); Eusebius states that it was near Lydda (*Onomasticon,* 132.16); the Babylonian Talmud puts it fifteen Roman miles from Jerusalem (*Pesahim,* 93b); but all those testimonies date from several centuries after the Roman destruction of Jerusalem, and therefore may not be reliable guides.

name[69] (just as Andrew's brother Simon was given the alternate name Cephas ≡ Peter, John 1.42).

Mattathias mourns over the city

2.6 και ιδε(ν) τας βλαcφημιας τας ‹γινομενας› εν Ιουδα και εν Ι(ερουcα)λημ	**2.6** And he saw the blasphemies that had come about in Judah and Jerusalem,
2.7 και ειπεν οιμμοι ινα τι τουτο εγεννηθην ιδει(ν) το cυντριμμα του λαου μου ‹κ(αι)› το cυντριμμα της αγιας πολεως και εκαθιcαν εκι εν τω δοθηναι αυτην ε(ν) χειρι εχθρων το αγιαcμα εν χειρι αλλοτριων	**2.7** and he said: "Woe *is* to me! Why *is* this, *that* I was born to see the shattering of my people, and the shattering of the holy city—and they sat there while she *was* given in*to* *the* hand of enemies, the holy place in*to the* hand of strangers?

2.6 γινομενας V^b A 64^+236 [*fiebant* $La^{109+146}$] | γεινουμ- V* | γενομ- S • **2.7** κ(αι) 2° S^{ca} V A 64^+236 $La^{109+146}$ | > S* •

2.6 He saw the blasphemies that had come about. Any words that revile or denigrate the Lord and His ways are **blasphemies** *(blasphēmias)* in the Scripture sense of the term (7.38, 41; Rev 13.5–6; Rom 2.24; 2 Pet 2.2; 1 Cor 10.30; 1 Pet 4.4; TDNT 1.621–25; BDAG 178).

2.7 Woe is to me! Why is this, that I was born to see the shattering of my people, and the shattering of the holy city? Mattathias responds to the distresses around him as Jeremiah did: "Why is this, that I came out from the womb to see toil and sorrow?" (Jer 20.18). When we contemplate "the tears of the oppressed" who have "no one to comfort them," better than either the dead or the living "is the one who has not yet been, who has not seen the evil work that is done under the sun" (Ecc 4.1–3).

---

[69] The meanings of most of these alternate names cannot be identified; there are inconclusive discussions in Abel (ii–iii, 31–32), Nelis (74–76), Calmet (26–28), and Grimm (35). The names appear to have been given while Mattathias was still alive (v 66) and therefore would not refer to the sons' actions after his death. **Gaddi** presumably represents *gdy* (as in Num 13.11), which could mean "fortunate" or "[God is] my fortune" or "my troop" (cf. Gen 30.11; 49.19). For **Thassi** (spelled *Thassis* in A, supported by La^{109}) there are many possibilities. It could represent *tršyš* (as in 1 Chr 7.10; "jewel," cf. Exod 28.20) or Aramaic *tsys* ("boiling," cf. Jastrow 1683; DJPA 587) or *tšyš* ("weak," cf. Jastrow 1704–05; DJPA 593–94). Alternatively, it could represent a *t*-prefixed form, e.g., *tʿṣy* ("counselor," cf. v 65; Isa 9.6) or *tʿśy* ("made [by God]," cf. 1 Chr 27.21; Gen 1.26). **Maccabeus** might perhaps represent *mkby* ("quenching," cf. Isa 43.17) or *mqby* ("hammer," cf. Jdg 4.21), although both these suggestions have been much criticized (cf. Schürer 1.1.212–13; Schürer-Vermes 1.158). **Avaran** could represent *ʿwrn* ("awake," "stirred up," cf. Jdg 5.12; Hag 1.14) or *ḥwrn* ("white," cf. Est 1.6). **Apphus** could represent *ḥpwṣ* ("delighted in," cf. Psa 18.19). No conclusions can be drawn from the spellings in the Syriac versions, as they have simply been transliterated from the Greek.

Shattering (*suntrimma;* "destruction," RV; "ruin," NRSV) is a term also applied to the shattering of pots (Rev 2.27; Mark 14.3) and chains (Mark 5.4).[70] Shattering is a result of all sin (Rom 3.16). It will ultimately happen to Satan himself (Rom 16.20).

Mattathias's compatriots (**my people**) **sat there**[71] **while** the holy city **was given into the hand of enemies.** When the calamity happened, the people sat motionless and did nothing to stop it, like those rebuked by Deborah: "Gilead remained beyond the Jordan; and Dan, why did he stay with the ships? Asher kept sitting by the coast of the sea, and remained by his inlets" (Jdg 5.17).

2.8 εγενετο ο ναος αυτηc ωc ανηρ ⸢αδοξοc⸣	**2.8** Her sanctuary has become like a man *who is* inglorious;
2.9 τα cκευη τηc δοξηc αυτηc αιχμαλωτα ⸢⸣ απηχθη απεκτανθη τα νηπια αυτηc εν ταιc πλατιαιc αυτηc οι νεανιcκοι αυτηc εν ρομφαια εχθρου	**2.9** the vessels of her glory have been carried away captive. Her young children have been killed in her broad *place*s, her young men with *the* sword of *the* enemy.

2.8 αδοξοc 58 La^{109} | ενδ- S V A 64^{+}236 La^{146} • **2.9** απηχθη S^{ca} V A 64^{+}236 La$^{109+146}$ | ^ α S* •

2.8–9 Mattathias continues to describe the condition of the holy city: **Her**[72] **sanctuary has become like a man who is inglorious.**[73] The city's **sanctuary** (the temple, *naos,* as in Matt 23.35; 27.5, 51) had been defiled and misused (as described in v 12; 4.38; 1.37, 46). It had lost its own glory, and had been robbed of its glorious **vessels** (as described in 1.21–23). Even the city's **young children** had been slain in its **broad places** (see the notes on 1.55; and cf. Rev 11.8; Lam 2.21).

---

[70] **Shattering.** Spanish *quebranto* (Jünemann) ≡ *quebrantiomento* (VRV) and Dutch *verbrijzeling* (Dyserinck) capture the sense of the word well.

[71] S, V, and 64^{+}236 (supported by La$^{109+146}$) read **to see the shattering of my people . . . and they sat there** *(ekathisan)*. (ESV's ". . . and they lived there" misunderstands the idiom: see Jdg 5.17; Isa 30.7; Jer 8.14.) A reads "to see the shattering of my people . . . and to sit there" *(kathisai)*.

[72] **Her.** As usual, the **city** (v 7; Greek *polis* [feminine] ≡ Hebrew *'yr* [feminine]) is compared to a woman (cf. 1.38; Lam 1.1). In the present context, this leads logically to the comparison of the **sanctuary** (Greek *naos* [masculine] ≡ Hebrew *hykl* [masculine]) to a **man** (cf. Psa 19.5).

[73] **Inglorious** (*adoxos,* i.e., "without honor," DRCV; *infame,* Diodati) is the reading of a few Greek manuscripts (notably 58), supported by La^{109}. The impossible reading "glorious" *(endoxos)* is found in S, V, A, and 64^{+}236, supported by La^{146}, 7h7, and 7a1. Alone among English versions, RV attempted to make sense of the latter reading, and rendered the verse: "Her temple is become as a man that was glorious." But the second half of this verse must describe the state of the temple after "is become" *(egeneto),* not before (compare the passages listed in Muraoka 131, §3; BDAG 198, §5). 7a1, uniquely, omits that verb, adding *ḥlṣw* at the end of the verse ("Her sanctuary like a glorious man has been plundered").

2.10 ποιον εθνος ουκ εκληρονομησεν εν βασιλια και ουκ εκρατησεν των σκυλων αυτης	**2.10** What nation has not taken an inheritance in *her* kingdom, and has not taken hold of her plunder?

2.10 What nation has not taken an inheritance in[74] **her kingdom,**[75] **and has not taken hold of her plunder?** The royal forces were drawn from various different nations (3.41; 4.35; 11.38; 15.3; cf. Epitome 8.9), all of whom participated in the **plunder** and in the allotment of Judean land (1.38; 3.36, 45; 10.12).

2.11 πας ο κοσμος αυτης αφηρεθη αντι ελευθερας εγενετο εις δουλην	**2.11** All her adornment has been removed; in place of a free *woman,* she has become a slavewoman.

2.11 In place of a free woman, the city **has become a slavewoman,** just as happened during the Babylonian conquest: "The princess among the provinces, she has been put to menial tasks" (Lam 1.1).

2.12 και ιδου τα αγια ημων και η καλλονη ημων και η δοξα ημων ηρημωθη και εβεβηλωσαν αυτα τα εθνη	**2.12** And see! our holy *places* and our beauty and our glory have been made desolate, and the nations have profaned them.
2.13 ινα τι ημιν ετι ζωη	**2.13** Why *is there* still *any* life for us?"

2.12 The **holy places** *(hagia)* were the various components of the LORD's house, the temple at Jerusalem (4.36–38, 43, 48; 9.54; 14.48; Jer 51.51; Heb 9.2–3).[76] In times of great distress, God's people sometimes wonder **why** their Master **still** continues to give them **life** (Num 11.14–15; 1 Kgs 19.4). Yet if He does grant them continuing life, it is because He still has use for them (cf. Php 1.24–25)—as He was about to use Mattathias and his sons.

2.14 και διερρηξεν Ματταθιας και οι υιοι αυτου τα ιματια αυτων	**2.14** And Mattathias and his sons tore their clothes,

---

[74] **Taken an inheritance in** *(eklēronomēsen en)* indicates the location where the inheritance is obtained (see the LXX of Num 32.19; Jdg 11.2; Sir 45.22). Therefore, "what nation has not possessed her in its kingdom" (ESV; similarly NETS) is not a possible translation.

[75] The ancient manuscripts vary at this point. Some read **taken an inheritance in her kingdom** (*en basileia,* S; *en basileia autēs,* 64[+]236, supported by 7h7). Others read "taken [her] royal palaces [as] an inheritance" (*hē basileia,* V; *basileia,* A, supported by La[109+146]). (For *basileia* meaning "royal palaces," see Luke 6.25; the sense "royal prerogatives" [NJB] does not occur anywhere in the Greek Scriptures.)

[76] **Holy places.** The Greek could also be rendered "holy things" (RV), although that would not suit most of the other occurrences of the term in this book (see the passages cited above). See also the notes on Eighteen Psalms 1.8.

και περιεβαλοντο σακκους και ‹επενθησαν› σφοδρα	and wrapped themselves in sackcloth, and mourned very much.

2.14 επενθησαν S^{ca} V A 64^{+}236 La$^{109+146}$ | -σεν S* •

2.14 Mattathias and his sons tore their clothes, and wrapped themselves in sack-cloth, and mourned very much. This is one of the signs by which God's people can be distinguished: unlike other people, they sigh and weep over the abominations that are done around them (Ezek 9.4–6; Psa 119.136; 1 Cor 5.2; 2 Pet 2.7–8).

Mattathias refuses to forsake the Law

2.15 και ‹ηλθον οι› παρα του βασιλεως οι καταναγκαζοντες την αποστασιν εις ‹Μωδεειν› την πολιν ινα θυσιασωσιν	**2.15** And the *people* from the king— the *one*s who were compelling the rebellion—came to the city Modein, in order that they should sacrifice.
2.16 και πολλοι απο Ισ(ραη)λ προς αυτους προσηλθο(ν) και Ματταθιας και οι υιοι αυτου συνηχθησαν	**2.16** And many *people* from Israel came to them. And Mattathias and his sons gathered together.
2.17 και απεκριθησα(ν) οι παρα του βασιλεως και ειπον τω Ματταθια λεγοντες αρχων κ(αι) ενδοξος και μεγας ει εν τη πολι ταυτη και εστηρισμενος υιοις και αδελφοις	**2.17** And the *people* from the king responded and said to Mattathias, saying: "You† are a ruler and an honored and great *man* in this city, and supported by sons and brothers.
2.18 νυν προσελθε πρωτος και ποιησον το προσταγμα του βασιλεως ‹› ως ‹εποιησαν› πα(ν)τα τα εθνη και οι ανδρες Ιουδα και οι καταλιφθεντες εν Ι(ερουσα)λημ και εση συ και οι υιοι ‹σου των φιλων του βασιλεως κ(αι) συ κ(αι) οι υιοι› σου ‹δοξασθησεσθ(αι)› αργυριω και χρυσιω και αποστολαις πολλαις	**2.18** Now, come† first and do† the king's decree, as all the nations have done, and the men of Judah, and *those* who are left in Jerusalem. And you† and your† sons will be among the king's Friends; and you† and your† sons will be honored with silver and gold and many presents."

2.15 ηλθον οι S^{ca} V A 64^{+}236 La$^{109+146}$ | ηλλοιωθη S* • Μωδεειν S^{ca} V A 64^{+}236 La$^{109+146}$ | Μωλειν S* • **2.18** ως S^{ca} V A 64^{+}236 La$^{109+146}$ | ^ και S* • εποιησαν V A La$^{109+146}$ | -σεν S 64^{+}236 • σου των φιλων του βασιλεως κ(αι) συ κ(αι) οι υιοι S^{ca} V A 64^{+}236 La$^{109+146}$ | > S* • δοξασθησεσθ(αι) S^{ca} V A 64^{+}236 La^{109} | -ασθηση S* La^{146} •

2.15–18 The people from the king . . . came to . . . Modein, in order that they should sacrifice.[77] They went to Mattathias **first,** trying to win him with praise (**you are . . . an**

[77] **In order that they should sacrifice.** In Greek, such a clause could mean either "in order that the people from the king should sacrifice" (cf. RV) or "in order that the people of Modein should sacrifice" (cf. KJV). For the first type of sentence construction, cf. 1.63; for the second, cf. 11.41. The context here (vv 17–18) favors the second.

honored and great man) and promises (**you and your sons will be among the king's Friends, and... will be honored with silver and gold and many presents**). The same methods were tried even with Jesus (praise: "Teacher, we know that you say and teach rightly," Luke 20.20–21; promises: "To you I will give all this authority and glory," Luke 4.5–8). "A man who says smooth things to his neighbor is spreading a net for his steps" (Prov 29.5). Whatever may be offered, "if sinners entice you, do not consent" (Prov 1.10). No sin is worth it (Luke 9.24–26; cf. 1 Thes 2.4–6; Gal 1.10).

Rebellion *(apostasia)* consists of turning away from *(apo-)* a steadfast position (*stasis,* as in 7.18; 10.72). Elsewhere in this book, the term is applied to those who are rebelling against a king (11.14; 13.16). Here it is applied to those who are obeying the king but rebelling against that king's superior—the King of kings (cf. 2 Thes 2.3).

The king's Friends occupied positions of special honor in the kingdom (3.38; 6.14; 7.8; 10.16, 20, 60; 11.57; 14.39; cf. 1 Kgs 4.5; 1 Chr 27.33).

2.19 και απεκριθη Ματταθιας και ειπεν φωνη μεγαλη ει παντα τα εθνη τα εν οικω της βαcιλιας του βαcιλεως ακουουcιν αυτου αποcτηναι εκαcτος απο λατριας πατερων αυτου και ηρετιcαντο εν ταις εντολαις αυτου	**2.19** And Mattathias responded and said with a great voice: "If all the nations that are in *the* house of the kingdom of the king hear him, *for* each to depart from his fathers' way of worship, and *if* they have made their choice *to walk* in his commands,
2.20 καγω και οι υιοι μου και οι αδελφοι μου πορευcομεθα εν διαθηκη π(ατε)ρων ημων	**2.20** yet I and my sons and my brothers will go in *the* covenant of our fathers.
2.21 ειλεως ημιν καταλιπειν νομον και δικαιωματα	**2.21** *Let Him be* gracious to us! To leave *the* Law and ordinances!
2.22 τον λογον του βαcιλεως ουκ ακουcομεθα παρελθιν την λατριαν ημων δεξιαν η αριcτεραν	**2.22** We will not hear the king's word, to go beyond our way of worship *to the* right or *to the* left."

2.19–22 Mattathias refused **to leave the Law and ordinances.** Whatever **all the nations** might do, he and his family would serve the Lord (like Joshua, Josh 24.15; cf. Mic 4.5; 1 Kgs 22.13–14). Even if we live when "most people's love will grow cold," we are not to be shaken; "the one who endures to the end, he shall be saved" (Matt 24.12–13; cf. Jer. 35.5–6, 13–19). Nothing should entice the Lord's people to **go beyond** His requirements in any respect (2 Jn 9; 1 Cor 4.6). Those who keep His commands are on the narrow path of life (Matt 7.14), and must not turn aside from it: "You shall be careful to do as the LORD your God has commanded you; you shall not turn aside to the right or the left" (Deut 5.32; Josh 23.6; Prov 4.27; Isa 30.21).

The Law and the ordinances. The **Law** (Greek *nomos* ≡ Hebrew *trh,* Gal 3.10 ≡ Deut 27.26) is the teaching of God (Deut 17.11), recorded in the Scriptures (1.56–57; 3.48). The **ordinances** *(dikaiōmata)* are God's rules for righteousness (see the notes on

1.13), which are expressed in the Law (Rom 8.4). Some of the ordinances in the Law concern the right **way of worship** (*latreia,* as in Heb 9.1; Rom 12.1). Under the old covenant, the right way of worship included the offering of animal sacrifices (Heb 9.6, 9), but only to the Lord (Matt 4.10). Under the new covenant, the right way of worship includes the offering of ourselves as spiritual sacrifices (Rom 12.1), again only to the Lord (Heb 12.28–29).

Let him be gracious [*hileōs*] **to us!** The wording is similar to that in Luke 18.13 ("Lord, be merciful [*hilasthētai*] to me"; cf. Matt 16.22). Mattathias seeks first God's grace and mercy; he knows full well that God would not be gracious to him if he and his house should ever leave His law and His ordinances.

2.23 και ωc επαυcατο λαλων ⸂τουc λογουc τουτουc⸃ προcηλθε(ν) ανηρ Ιουδαιοc εν οφθαλμοιc παντων θυcιαcαι επι του βωμου εν ⸂Μωδεειν⸃ κατα το προcταγμα του βαcιλεωc	**2.23** And as he stopped speaking these words, a Judean man came in *the* eyes of all to sacrifice on the heathen altar in Modein, in accordance with the king's decree.
2.24 και ειδεν Ματταθιαc και εζηλωcεν και ετρομηcαν οι νεφροι αυτου και ανηνεγκεν θυμον κατα το κριμα και δραμων εcφαξεν αυτον επι τον βωμον	**2.24** And Mattathias saw, and he was jealous, and his kidneys trembled; and he lifted up an indignation *that was* in accordance with justice. And, having run, he slew him on the heathen altar.
2.25 και τον ανδραν του βαcιλεωc τον αναγκαζοντα θυειν απεκτινεν εν τω καιρω εκεινω και το(ν) βωμον ⸂καθειλε(ν)⸃	**2.25** And the man of the king, who *was* compelling *them* to sacrifice, he killed at that period of time; and the heathen altar he pulled down.
2.26 και ⸂εξηλωcεν⸃ τω νομω καθωc εποιηcεν Φινεεc τω Ζαμβρει υιω Cαλωμ	**2.26** And he was jealous for the Law, just as Phinehas did against Zimri son of Salu.

2.23 τουc λογουc τουτουc S[cb1] V A 64[+]236 La[109+146] | > S* • Μωδεειν S[ca] La[109] [-ιμ V A 64[+]236 La[146]] | Βωδειν S* • **2.25** καθειλε(ν) S[ca] V A 64[+]236 La[109+146] | -λο(ν) S* • **2.26** εξηλωcεν S[ca] A 64[+]236 La[109] | -cαν V La[146] | εδωκαν S* •

2.23–26 A Judean man came . . . to sacrifice on the heathen altar. Under the old covenant Law, anyone who served another god had to be punished by death; the Law permitted no other course of action ("your eye shall not pity him, nor shall you spare," Deut 13.6–11). So, when Mattathias **slew** the man, his act of **indignation** was **in accordance with justice,** and was exactly what faithful servants of the Lord in earlier times had done (1 Kgs 18.40; 2 Kgs 10.25–28; 2 Chr 23.16–17). That command is not repeated under the new covenant; God has not given His servants today any authority to execute worshipers of false gods. Yet Mattathias's action remains an example for us to imitate. "We do not war according to the flesh," but we are still fighting a war in the spirit, and "the weapons of our warfare are not of the flesh, but mighty before

God to the casting down . . . of every high thing that is raised up against the knowledge of God" (2 Cor 10.3–5; Eph 6.12). We must put to death every evil desire in ourselves as zealously as Mattathias put to death this idolater (Rom 8.13; Col 3.5).

Mattathias's indignation at this sin was like the great indignation that God Himself has every day (Psa 7.11). Just as surely as Mattathias slew the idolater, God will slay those who presume on His patience and do not repent of their sins (Luke 19.27; 2 Thes 2.8). His eye will not spare, nor will He have pity (Ezek 5.11).

Mattathias **was jealous** *(zēloō)* **for the Law** (vv 26, 27, 50). Today our language distinguishes "jealous" from "zealous," but the two were originally the same word even in English, and are certainly not distinguished in Scripture: anyone who is passionately devoted to something is passionately opposed to whatever may threaten it. The LORD "is a jealous God" (Exod 20.4–5; 34.14; Deut 4.23–24; 6.14–15; 32.16), and regards the worship of anyone other than Himself as a husband regards adultery in the wife he loves (Hos 2.1–20; Ezek 16.32, 38; 23.37; Isa 54.5–8). His people are to be jealous on His behalf (Num 25.11; 1 Kgs 19.10; 2 Cor 11.2–3), just as Jesus was (John 2.17).

Mattathias's jealousy for the Law closely resembled that of his ancestor **Phinehas** (v 54). Phinehas "was jealous for his God, and made atonement for the children of Israel" by slaying an Israelite man (**Zimri son of Salu**) who had allied himself with idolaters (Num 25.1–13); "and it was accounted to him for righteousness, for generation after generation, to the ages" (Psa 106.30–31). "Those who leave the law praise a wicked one; but those who keep the law contend with them" (Prov 28.4–5).

Those who are seeking righteousness flee

2.27 και ανεκραξεν Ματταθιας εν τη πολι φωνη μεγαλη λεγων πας ο ζηλων τω νομω ιστων διαθηκη(ν) εξελθετω οπισω μου	**2.27** And Mattathias cried out in the city with a great voice, saying: "Every *one* who is jealous for the Law, who is establishing *the* covenant, let him come out after me."

2.27 Mattathias appealed for support to **every one who is jealous for the Law** and **who is establishing the covenant** (i.e., who is working for the covenant to be established, 14.29). So Moses had summoned support against worshipers of idols: "Whoever is on the LORD's side, let him come to me" (Exod 32.26). Every day, the wisdom of God is calling (Prov 1.20). His sheep hear His voice and follow Him (John 10.27; cf. Psa 119.74, 79); but the others will not (Matt 22.4–5).

2.28 και εφυγον αυτος και οι υιοι αυτου εις τα ορη και ενκατελιπον οσα ειχον ε(ν) τη πολει	**2.28** And he and his sons fled into the mountains; and they left all *that* they had in the city.

2.28 He and his sons fled into the mountains;[78] **and they left all that they had in the city,** as Jesus instructed His disciples to do in a similar time: "When therefore you see

[78] This flight **into the mountains** is reported also in Epitome 5.27.

the abomination of desolation, which was spoken of by Daniel the prophet, standing in the holy place . . . then let those who are in Judea flee to the mountains" (Matt 24.15–21; cf. Matt 10.23). Those who are oppressed by the persecutions of the devil may always flee for refuge to the Lord, who is a high rock and a defense against the enemy (Psa 61.2–3; 27.5; 40.2; 62.2). To do so, like Abraham (Gen 12.1; Heb 11.8–10), Moses (Heb 11.24–27), and Paul (Php 3.4–8), they must leave all that they have (Luke 14.33; Matt 13.44–46; Mark 10.28–30).

2.29 τοτε κατεβηcαν πολλοι ζητουντεc δικαιοcυνην και κριμα ειc την ερημο(ν) καθιcαι εκει	**2.29** Then many who were seeking righteousness and justice came down into the desert, to settle there—
2.30 αυτοι και οι υιοι αυτων και αι γυναικεc αυτων και τα κτηνη αυτω(ν) οτι εcκληρυνθη επ αυτουc ‹› τα κακα	**2.30** they and their sons and their wives and their livestock: for the evil *thing*s pressed hard upon them.

2.30 αυτουc V A 64⁺236 La[109+146] | + επληθυνθη S* | + κ(αι) επ- S[ca] •

2.29 Many who were seeking righteousness and justice came down into the desert, although not necessarily where Mattathias was (see vv 31–39; and cf. 1 Sam. 22.1–2). Everyone who is **seeking** God's kingdom and His **righteousness** in preference to the things that the Gentiles seek will be blessed by Him (Matt 6.32–33).

War on the Sabbath day

2.31 και ανηγγελλη τοιc ανδραcιν του βαcιλεωc και ‹ταιc δυναμεcιν› αι ηcαν εν Ι(ερουcα)λημ πολει Δα(υι)δ οτι κατεβηcαν ‹› ανδρεc οιτινεc διεcκεδαcαν την ‹εντολην› του βαcιλεωc ειc τουc κρυφιουc εν τη ερημω	**2.31** And it was declared to the king's men, and to the forces that were in Jerusalem *the* city of David, that men—whoever repudiated the king's command— had come down into the hidden *place*s in the desert.
2.32 και εδραμον οπιcω αυτων πολλοι και κατελαβοντο αυτουc και ‹παρενεβαλον› ‹επ› αυτουc και cυνεcτηcαντο προc αυτουc πολεμον εν τη ημερα των cαββατων	**2.32** And many ran after them and overtook them. And they camped against them, and prepared to make war against them on the Sabbath day,
2.33 και ειπον προc αυτουc εωc του νυν εξελθο(ν)τεc ‹ποιηcαται› κατα τον λογον του βαcιλεωc κ(αι) ζηcεcθε	**2.33** and said to them: "Till now! When *you* have come out[pl], do[pl] in accordance with the king's word, and you[pl] will live."

2.31 ταιc δυναμεcιν V A 64⁺236 La[109] | αι δυναμειc S La[146] • ανδρεc V A 64⁺236 | ^ οι S • εντολην V A 64⁺236 La[109+146] | βουλην S • **2.32** παρενεβαλον S[cb1] V A 64⁺236 | -λοντο S* • επ S[cb1] V A 64⁺236 La[109+146] | προc S* • **2.33** ποιηcαται S[ca] V A 64⁺236 La[109+146] | -cωμεν S* •

2.31–33 The king's men . . . said to those in the **hidden places** (1.53) in the desert: **Till now!** The wording is uniquely clipped and abrupt; **till now** is a very common phrase (Mark 13.19; Ezra 5.16; etc.), but never elsewhere is it found in blunt isolation like this.[79]

The brusque tone continues in the next sentence: **When you have come out, do in accordance with the king's word, and you will live.** The king's men do not ask or command their opponents to come out ("Come out and do what the king commands," NRSV); instead, they *presume* that it will happen.

You will live. Any promise of life that depends on disobeying the law of God is a lie, and comes from the father of lies (Gen 3.4). Those who heed such a promise are dead even while they live (1 Tim 5.6; Eph 2.1, 5); those who reject such a promise live forever even if they die (John 11.25–26; 5.24; Rom 8.10–13).

2.34 και ειπον ουκ εξελευcομεθα ουδε ποιηcομεν τον λογον του βαcιλεωc βεβηλωcαι την ημεραν των cαββατων	**2.34** And they said: "We will not come out, nor will we do the king's word, to profane the Sabbath day."

2.34 The people in the hidden places refused to take any action, on the grounds that it would **profane the Sabbath day.**[80] To understand their position, we must remember that they were living under the old covenant Law (vv 20–21, 27); therefore, the ordinances that applied to them—both in regard to the Sabbath day (cf. Col 2.13–17) and in regard to warfare (cf. 2 Cor 10.3–5)—were different from those that apply to us who live under the new.

In the old covenant Law, God forbade the Israelites to "do any work" on the Sabbath day (Exod 20.8–11; 16.23–30). On that day each week, they could not kindle a fire (Exod 35.3), gather sticks (Num 15.32–36), trade (Neh 10.31; 13.15–22), or carry

[79] **Till now** (Greek *heōs tou nun* ≡ Hebrew *'d hnh,* Jdg 16.13, etc.). Even in ancient times, copyists and translators were troubled by the brevity of the phrase and sought to expand it, although they could not agree about the kind of supplement to be provided. The Antiochene copies add *hikanon* ("Let that which ye have done hitherto suffice," KJV), and many modern versions still insert an "enough" or something similar. The Latin Vulgate has *Resistitis et nunc adhuc?* ("Do ye still resist?", DRCV). Some commentators have suggested that the context implies "Till now [you have disobeyed, but now] come out and obey" (Grimm 42; Keil 62)—however, in that case some word indicating the contrast would be expected (cf. Polybius 1.78.14). Others expand in an opposite way: "There is still time" for you to obey (REB; теперь еще можно, RST)—but no ancient reader seems to have understood it thus. There would be the same objection if the phrase were construed with *poiēsate* ("Up till now obey," i.e., "Obey by this very moment"). "Now, come out and do . . ." (SAAS) overlooks the *heōs.* Perhaps it is wisest not to smooth out or spell out what the text leaves surprising and unstated. Among English renderings, "Thus far" (RV—no doubt one of Scrivener's audacities) is unique in matching the unexpectedness and economy of the Greek.

[80] This incident is also reported in Epitome 6.11.

loads (Jer 17.21–22). Nevertheless, He did not forbid them to good on the Sabbath; someone who did good on the Sabbath was not breaking any command of the old covenant Law (Matt 12.10–12; Luke 13.14–17).

The old covenant Law also allowed Israel to wage war against its earthly enemies (Num 10.9; 31.3). God appointed Mattathias and his family to deliver Israel by that means (Dan 11.32–33; Maccabaica 5.62). Therefore, that was a good work—something that could lawfully be done on the Sabbath.[81] As Mattathias and his friends recognized, they would prevent good being done if they *refused* to defend themselves on the Sabbath (vv 39–41).

But the old covenant Law did not authorize any Israelite at all to wage war against Israel's enemies in any situation at all. In some situations, and for some Israelites, an attempt to do so was an act of disobedience to God (Deut 1.41–44). That too was seen in the days of Mattathias and his sons: war could not lawfully be waged in all situations. For instance, some people were authorized to wage war under the leadership of the family appointed by God (Maccabaica 5.18–19), but when they sought to do the same deed on their own initiative, they were disobeying God (5.56–62).

Therefore, people who lived under the old covenant had to discern when war was a good work and when it was not. This was not to be done by trial and error—by going out to battle and seeing whether you were still alive at the end of it. On the contrary, it was to be determined beforehand by counsel (5.67; 2.41; cf. 4.44–45).

We today have very little information about the particular group of people who sheltered in these hidden places. Consequently, we cannot say in precisely which circumstances it would have been right or wrong for them to fight. That is not our business. Our task today is not to determine what would have been right or wrong for them under the old covenant, but to determine what is right and wrong for ourselves under the new. "Each one of us shall give an account to God concerning himself" (Rom 14.10–12). But we do know that their decision not to defend themselves in this specific situation was a considered one, and that it was based on a singleminded adherence to what is good ("wholeheartedness"; see on v 37).

As for ourselves, our situation under the new covenant is laid out clearly for us in God's word. Under this covenant, no law of God restricts work on any day of the week (Col 2.16–17). Therefore, God's people are not committing transgression if they choose to do any permissible task on the Sabbath or any other day (cf. Rom 14.5–6; Gal 4.9–11). And under this covenant, we are fighting a spiritual war, not an earthly one (2 Cor 10.3–5; 1 Tim 6.12; 2 Tim 2.3–4; 4.7; see also the comments on vv 23–26). Every one of us must fight in this war; and in this war, every one of us must defend ourselves against the enemy constantly, every day of our lives, "at all times" (Eph 6.11–17; 1 Pet 5.8–9; cf. Luke 21.36).

---

[81] When the Israelites led by Joshua marched around the city of Jericho for seven successive days (Josh 6.3–4), they must necessarily have done that good work on a Sabbath (Tertullian, *Adversus Judaeos,* 4.8–9).

2.35 και ‹εταχυναν› επ αυτους πολεμον	**2.35** And they quickly made war against them.
2.36 και ουκ απεκριθηcαν αυτοιc ου λιθον ενετιναξαν αυτοιc ουδε ενεφραξαν τουc ‹κρυφιουc›	**2.36** And they did not respond to them; not a stone did they shake against them, nor did they close up the hidden *place*s,
2.37 λεγοντεc αποθανωμεν παντεc εν τη απλοτητι ημων μαρτυρι ‹εφ ημαc› ο ου(ρα)νοc και η γη οτι ακριτωc απολλυτε ημαc	**2.37** saying: “Let us all die in our wholeheartedness; Heaven and earth are bearing witness over us, that you^{pl} are destroying us without justice.”
2.38 και ανεcτηcαν ‹επ› αυτουc εν ‹τω› πολεμω ‹τοιc› cαββαcι(ν) και απεθανον αυτοι και αι γυναικεc αυτων και τα τεκνα αυτων και τα κτηνη αυτων εωc ‹χιλιων› ψυχω(ν) αν(θρωπ)ων	**2.38** And they rose up against them in battle on the Sabbath, and they died, they and their wives and their children and their livestock, up to a thousand souls of persons.
2.39 και εγνω Ματταθιαc και οι φιλοι αυτου και επενθηcαν ‹επ› αυτουc cφοδρα	**2.39** And Mattathias and his friends knew; and they mourned over them very much.
2.40 και ειπε(ν) ανηρ τω πληcιο(ν) αυτου εαν παντεc ποιηcωμεν ωc οι αδελφοι ημω(ν) εποιηcαν και μη πολεμηcωμεν προc τα εθνη υπερ ‹των ψυχων› ημων και των ‹δικαιωματων› ημων νυν ταχιον ολοθρευcουcιν ημαc απο τηc γηc	**2.40** And *each* man said to his neighbor: “If we all should do as our brothers have done, and not make war against the nations on behalf of our souls and our ordinances, now they will destroy us quickly from the earth.”
2.41 και εβουλευcαντο ‹τη ημερα εκεινη› λεγοντεc παc αν(θρωπ)οc οc εαν ελθη εφ ημαc ειc πολεμον τη ημερα των cαββατων πολεμηcωμεν κατεναντι αυτου και ου μη αποθανωμεν παντεc ‹καθωc› απεθανον οι αδελφοι ημων εν τοιc κρυφιοιc	**2.41** And they took counsel on that day, saying: “Every person whoever who may come on us to make war on the Sabbath day— let us make war against him, and let us certainly not die as our brothers died in the hidden *places*.”

2.35 εταχυναν V A 64^{+}236 La$^{109+146}$ \| -υνεν S • **2.36** κρυφιουc S^{ca} V 64^{+}236 \| -φουc A \| κυφρουc S* • **2.37** εφ ημαc S^{ca} V A 64^{+}236 La$^{109+146}$ \| > S* • **2.38** επ V A 64^{+}236 La$^{109+146}$ \| προc S • τω V A 64^{+}236 \| > S • τοιc S^{ca} V A 64^{+}236 \| > S* • χιλιων S^{ca} V A 64^{+}236 La$^{109+146}$ \| > S* • **2.39** επ V A 64^{+}236 La$^{109+146}$ \| > S • **2.40** των ψυχων 64^{+}236 La$^{109+146}$ \| τηc ψυχηc S V A • δικαιωματων S^{ca} V A 64^{+}236 La$^{109+146}$ \| διωμ- S* • **2.41** τη ημερα εκεινη V A 64^{+}236 [*in die illa* La^{146}] \| την ημεραν εκεινην S • καθωc V A 64^{+}236 \| ωc S •

2.37 Let us all die in our wholeheartedness. The term **wholeheartedness** *(haplotēs)* involves both “simplicity” (NETS) and “innocence” (KJV): it describes a singleminded, undivided adherence to what is good (contrasted with evil, Matt 6.22–23; 2 Cor 11.3), which comes “from the heart” (Eph 6.5–6) and is absolutely unreserved (Maccabaica 8.25; 2 Cor 8.2; 9.11, 13). The **wholeheartedness** of these souls who chose to **die** rather than submit (1.63) “condemns in every age the astounding ease with which people so often set aside the indispensable ordinances of the law of Jesus Christ—not merely to save their lives, but even for very trivial reasons, and sometimes with no other excuse than that of custom or human whim” (Sacy 40).

Heaven and earth are bearing witness over us, that you are destroying us without justice. Even if there were no human observers of the injustice, **Heaven and earth** were present and witnessed it (as in Deut 4.26; 30.19; 31.28; cf. Isa 1.2; Mic 1.2). God’s people, including Jesus Himself, have often been hated, persecuted, and destroyed without cause and **without justice** (1 Sam 24.9–11; Psa 59.4; John 15.25; 19.4; Acts 25.10–11).

2.41 After this, Mattathias and his friends resolved to defend themselves, if necessary, when attacked **on the Sabbath day;** see on v 34 above. Subsequent enemies did indeed attack the Judeans at least once on the Sabbath day, but were defeated (9.43–49).

The work prospers

2.42 τοτε cυνηχθηcαν προc αυτουc ‹› cυναγωγη ‹Αcιδαιων› ιcχυροι δυναμει απο Ι(cρα)ηλ πac ο εκουcιαζομενοc τω νομω	**2.42** Then *there* gathered with them a gathering of Hasidim—strong *people* with power from Israel, every *one* who was offering himself willingly for the Law.

2.42 cυναγωγη A 64⁺236 La[109+146] | ^ παcα S | + παcα V • Αcιδαιων A 64⁺236 [*in auxilia eorum* La[146]] | Ιουδαιων S V La[109] •

2.42 There gathered with them a gathering of Hasidim.[82] The Hebrew term **Hasidim** *(ḥsdym)* means “lovingkind ones”—people who practice lovingkindness (*ḥsd;* Mic 7.2) and to whom the Lord shows lovingkindness (Psa 18.25).[83] It is applied in

[82] **Hasidim** *([H]asidaiōn)* is the reading of A and 64⁺236. It is indirectly supported by La[146]—whose reading, *in auxilia eorum,* must have arisen from *Asilaiōn* (*d* and *l* are easily confused in Greek uncial script)—and also by the Syriac copies: *’syry’* (7h7), *’ysr’yl* (7a1), *’srly’* (8a1 and apparently almost all later manuscripts); *d* and *r* are easily confused in all Syriac scripts. The reference in 7.13 appears to be an allusion to a group already mentioned (“the [*hoi*] Hasidim”), and therefore also supports the reading **Hasidim** here. By contrast, S and V (supported by La[109]) have “Judeans” *(Ioudaiōn)* here. (Kappler’s textual apparatus does not accurately represent the readings of the Syriac manuscripts at this point.)

[83] “Lovingkind ones”: the meaning of the term is discussed in TLOT 2.462–64, §IV.6; TDOT 1.305–07; Kirkpatrick, *Book of Psalms,* 3.835–36.

the Scriptures to Jesus (Psa 16.10 ≡ Acts 2.27) and to all those who serve the Lord faithfully (Psa 50.5; 12.1), who are protected and set apart by Him (Prov 2.8; 1 Sam 2.9; Psa 97.10; 37.28; 4.3). "Love the LORD, all His lovingkind ones [*ḥsdyw*] .... Be strong, and let Him make your heart firm" (Psa 31.23–24). In this book (here and at 7.13) the name is applied to certain people within **Israel** who were **strong ... with power** in their defense of **the Law.**[84]

2.43 και πα(ν)τες οι φυγαδευοντες απο των κακων προσετεθηcαν αυτοιc και εγενοντο αυτοιc ειc cτηριγμα	**2.43** And all the *people* who were fleeing from the evil *things* were added to them; and they became a support for them.

2.43 They became a support [*stērigma*] **for them,** just as Peter was instructed to support *(stērizō)* his fellow disciples (Luke 22.32), and just as God Himself supports *(stērizō)* His people (1 Pet 5.10) by providing them with His word (Rom 16.25; 2 Pet 1.12; cf. 1 Thes 3.2).

2.44 και cυνεcτηcαντο δυναμιν και ‹επαταξαν› αμαρτωλουc εν οργη αυτω(ν) και ανδραc ανομουc εν θυμω αυτων και οι λοιποι εφυγον ειc τα εθνη cωθηναι	**2.44** And they brought together a force, and smote sinners in their anger, and men opposed to *the* Law in their indignation. And the rest fled into the nations to save themselves.

2.44 επαταξαν S^c V A 64$^+$236 | -ξαντο S* •

2.44 They brought together a force (that is, a military force, as in 1.4; 2.31; 3.10), **and smote sinners in their anger, and men opposed to *the* Law**[85] **in their indignation.** Although **anger** *(orgē)* and **indignation** *(thumos)* are nearly always sinful (Eph 4.31; Gal 5.20; Jas 1.20), both are also characteristics of God (v 49; Rev 14.10; 16.19; 19.15; Rom 2.8) and—very occasionally—of righteous people who are devoted to God's interests rather than their own (Mark 3.5; cf. Eph 4.26). Nevertheless, this point should not be misconstrued. Everyone who is angry believes their anger to be

[84] Outside the Maccabean History, the only definite ancient reference to a subgroup of Israelites called **Hasidim** is in the Epitome 14.6; but that is a quotation from someone who is opposing them, so its information may not be accurate (Schwartz, *2 Maccabees,* 471). It is not clear whether the term **Hasidim** was applied to one group or to a diversity. There is no significant evidence for the oft-repeated claim that the Hasidim were forerunners of the Pharisees (see Kampen, *Hasideans and the Origin of Pharisaism;* Schwartz, "Hasidim in 1 Maccabees 2:24?").

[85] **Opposed to the Law** ("lawless," RV; 3.5, 6; 7.5; 9.23, 58, 69; 11.25; 14.14). The Greek term *(anomous)* describes those who are in a state of opposition *(a-)* to law *(nomos).* As with "breakers of the Law" (*paranomoi,* 1.11), in this book the reference is always to God's Law, not human laws. "Sin is opposition to the Law" (1 Jn 3.4). The Law was made for the very people who oppose it (1 Tim 1.9).

justified—but believing something to be right does not make it right (1 Cor 4.4; Prov 14.12). In the Scriptures, praiseworthy human anger is extremely rare (Jas 1.20; Psa 37.8; Col 3.8).

2.45 και ‹εκυκλωcεν› Ματταθιαc και οι φιλοι αυτου και καθιλον τουc βωμουc	**2.45** And Mattathias and his friends went round about, and pulled down the heathen altars,
2.46 και περιετεμον τα πεδαρια τα απεριτμητα οcα ευρον εν ‹οριοιc› Ic(ραη)λ εν ιcχυι	**2.46** and circumcised by force all the uncircumcised boys *that* they found in *the* appointed boundaries of Israel.

2.45 εκυκλωcεν V A $La^{109+146}$ ܐܬܟܪܟ ܗܘ 7h7 | -cαν $64^{+}236$ 7a1 | εκελευcεν S • **2.46** οριοιc V A $64^{+}236$ $La^{109+146}$ | υιοιc S •

2.45–46 Mattathias and his friends … pulled down the heathen altars, and circumcised by force all the uncircumcised boys. Under the old covenant, absolutely no uncircumcision and absolutely no alternate objects of worship were tolerated: the Law was emphatic and unambiguous on both points. "The uncircumcised male who is not circumcised in the flesh of his foreskin, that soul will be cut off from his people; he has broken My covenant" (Gen 17.14). "Destroying, you shall destroy all the places where the nations that you are dispossessing served their gods … and you shall break down their altars and shatter their pillars" (Deut 12.2–3).

Correcting those errors was therefore urgent and vitally important (2 Chr 34.2–7).

2.47 και εδιωξαν τουc υιουc τηc υπερηφανιαc κ(αι) κατευοδωθη το εργον εν χιρι ‹αυτων›	**2.47** And they pursued the sons of arrogance, and the work prospered in their hand.
2.48 και αντελαβοντο του νομου εκ χιροc των εθνω(ν) και των βαcιλεω(ν) και ουκ εδωκαν κεραc τω αμαρτωλω	**2.48** And they took back the Law out of *the* hand of the nations and kings, and did not give a horn to the sinner.

2.47 αυτων S^{ca} V A $64^{+}236$ $La^{109+146}$ | -του S* •

2.48 They **did not give a horn to the sinner.** An animal's **horn** is the part with which it overpowers its opponents (Deut 33.17; Ezek 34.21; Exod 21.28–29; Dan 8.5–7). In the Scriptures, to remove a **horn** from people is to remove their power, their might (Jer 48.25; Lam 2.3; Dan 8.8, 22; Zec 1.18–21).

When the kings of Judah "left the Law of the Most High … their horn was given to others, and their glory to a foreign nation" (Sir 49.4–5). In the days of Mattathias and his sons, that process was reversed: the people of Israel began to prosper (cf. v 47), and their enemies were no longer given a **horn.** "God is the Judge; He makes this one low, and He raises this one aloft . . . . All the horns of the wicked [He] cuts off; the horns of the righteous one are raised aloft" (Psa 75.4–10).

Mattathias encourages his sons

2.49 και ηγγιcαν αι ημεραι ‹του› Ματταθιου αποθανιν και ειπεν τοιc υιοιc αυτου νυν εcτηριcθη υπερηφανια και ελεγμοc και καιροc καταcτροφηc και οργη θυμου	**2.49** And the days of Mattathias came near *for him* to die; and he said to his sons: "Now has arrogance been established, and reproof, and a period of overturning, and anger of indignation.

2.49 του V A 64^{+}236 | > S •

2.49 Mattathias gives his final instructions **to his sons.** They were living in a time of great distress, when four things had become **established:**

- **Arrogance** *(huperēphania),* the opposite of humility or lowliness (Jas 4.6; 1 Pet 5.5). Judea was suffering from the arrogance of Antiochus (1.21, 24) and his servants (v 47; 7.34, 47).
- **Reproof** *(elegmos),* the experience of being rebuked for one's sins (1 Tim 5.20; Jas 2.9; Luke 3.19; 2 Pet 2.16). Reproof is painful; yet it is a sign of God's love (Heb 12.5–6; Rev 3.19).
- **Overturning** *(katastrophē),* as Jesus overturned the tables of the money changers (Mark 11.15). The nation's obedience to the law (1.45–52), its peace, and its glory (2.8–9) had all been overturned.
- **Anger of indignation** *(orgē thumou).* Just as Mattathias and his friends displayed anger and indignation against the sinners around them (see the notes on v 44), so did the Lord (see the notes on 1.64).

The Scriptures contain similar descriptions of several other times when great sufferings were inflicted on Judea: by the Assyrians under Sennacherib ("This day is a day of distress, and rebuke, and rejection," Isa 37.3), by the Babylonians under Nebuchadnezzar ("The day … is coming …. Arrogance has blossomed; violence has risen to a rod for wickedness," Ezek 7.10–11), and by the Romans ("These are days of vengeance …. There will be great distress on the land, and anger to this people," Luke 21.22–23). Similar will be the final "day of anger and revelation of the righteous judgment of God," when there will be "anger and indignation, tribulation and anguish, on every soul of humanity that does evil, of the Jew first, and also of the Greek" (Rom 2.5–9).

2.50 νυν τεκνα ζηλωcατε τω νομω και δοτε ταc ψυχαc υμων υπερ διαθηκηc πατερω(ν) ‹ημων›	**2.50** Now, children, be jealous[pl] for the Law, and give[pl] your[pl] souls on behalf of *the* covenant of our fathers,
2.51 και μνηcθηται τα εργα των πατερων α ‹εποιηcα(ν)› εν ταιc γενεαιc αυτων και δεξαcθαι δοξαν μεγαλην και ονομα αιωνιον	**2.51** and be mindful[pl] of the fathers' works, which they did in their generations; and receive[pl] great honor and a lasting name.

2.50 ημων A 64^{+}236 La$^{109+146}$ | υμ- S V • **2.51** εποιηcα(ν) S^{ca} V A 64^{+}236 La$^{109+146}$ | -cε(ν) S* •

2.50 Mattathias exhorts his sons to give their **souls** ("lives," KJV; Greek *psuchas*) **on behalf of the covenant** (cf Epitome 7.20–23). Jesus said, "Whoever would save his soul [*psuchēn*] will lose it; and whoever will lose his soul for My sake and the gospel's will save it" (Mark 8.35; cf. Acts 20.24). All five of Mattathias's sons would ultimately be killed. No two of them would die in the same way; yet each death would arise, directly or indirectly, from the struggle to establish God's **covenant** in the land (6.43–46; 9.5–21, 35–42; 12.39–48; 13.3–5, 23; 16.13–16).

2.51 Be mindful of the fathers' works, which they did in their generations. We are to be "imitators of those who, by faith and patience, inherit the promises" (Heb 6.12; 13.7), who are surrounding us in a great "cloud of witnesses" (Heb 12.1).

Those who are **mindful** of their example will **receive great honor.** The term **honor** *(doxa)* encompasses both splendor ("glory," NAB; cf. vv 9, 12) and respect (cf. vv 17–18). The glory promised here is not the glory that the king's supporters offered Mattathias (v 18), and not even the glory of "all the kingdoms of the world" (Luke 4.5–6), but the glory that comes from God (John 17.22), "praise and glory and honor, at the revelation of Jesus Christ" (1 Pet 1.7; Rom 2.7, 10). The **name** of God's servants will be **lasting** (*aiōnios,* enduring age after age), just as their glory will never fade away (1 Pet 5.4; 1.4; 2 Tim 2.10). They "will shine ... as the stars to lasting time and continuing time" (Dan 12.3).

In the following verses (vv 52–60), Mattathias describes some of the **works** done by **the fathers** when they were faced with distresses similar to those now facing Judea. (The list has a strong resemblance to Heb 11.1–12.1.)

2.52 Αβρααμ ουχι εν πιραcμω ευρεθη πιcτοc και ελογιcθη αυτω ειc δικ(αι)οcυνην	**2.52** Was not Abraham found faithful in trial? and it was counted to him for righteousness.

2.52 The age of Antiochus Epiphanes was not the only time of **trial** ("temptation," KJV; Greek *peirasmos*) in the history of the world. Indeed all God's people must expect to suffer trials (1 Pet 1.6; 4.12; Jas 1.2; 1 Cor 10.13; Jesus Himself did, Luke 22.28; 4.2–13). **Abraham** underwent a great **trial** when he was commanded to sacrifice his own son (Gen 22.1–18; Heb 11.17). Nevertheless, **he was found faithful ... and it was counted to him for righteousness** (Jas 2.21–23).

2.53 Ιωcηφ εν καιρω cτενοχωριαc αυτου εφυλαξεν εντολην και εγενετο κ(υριο)c Αιγυπτου	**2.53** Joseph in *the* period of his oppression kept *the* command, and he became lord of Egypt.

2.53 Joseph too underwent a period of **oppression** (*stenochōria,* as in Rom 8.35; 2 Cor 6.4; 12.10). Because he **kept the command** (even when put under the authority of foreigners and exhorted to sin, Gen 39.7–10), **he became lord of Egypt** (Acts 7.10; Psa 105.17–21).

2.54 Φινεες ο πατηρ ημων εν τω ζηλωσαι ζηλο(ν) ελαβεν ‹διαθηκην› ‹ιερωσυνης αιωνιας›	**2.54** Phinehas our father, by being jealous *with* jealousy, received *the* covenant of a lasting priesthood.

2.54 διαθηκην V A 64^{+}236 La$^{109+146}$ | κληρον διαθηκης S • ιερωσυνης / αιωνιας V [A] 64^{+}236 La$^{109+146}$ | ~ S •

2.54 Phinehas, like Mattathias, was **jealous with jealousy** (see the notes on vv 23–26), and therefore **received the covenant of a lasting priesthood** (Num 25.13).

2.55 Ιηcουc εν τω πληρωcαι λογον εγενετο κριτηc εν Ι(cρα)ηλ	**2.55** Joshua, by fulfilling the word, became a judge in Israel.

2.55 Joshua "fully followed the LORD" (Num 32.12) and faithfully carried out the **word** that the Lord gave him (Josh 1.7–8), so that by the end of his life "not one word has failed, of all the good words that the LORD your God spoke concerning you; all of it has come to you" (Josh 23.14). He cleansed the land of foreign nations and exhorted Israel to shun the practices of those nations, remaining steadfast to God's word (Josh 23.6–8; 24.14–24).

Because of his faithfulness, God chose him to be a **judge in Israel.** In the Scriptures, a **judge** (Greek *kritēs* ≡ Hebrew *špt:* Acts 13.20 ≡ Jdg 2.16) was not a person who sat in a law court, but a person appointed over the people (2 Sam 7.11; 1 Chr 17.6)—as Joshua was (Num 27.15–23; Josh 1.2–9)—to provide them with judgments (*mšpt,* Deut 16.18; 2 Chr 19.6)—as Joshua did (Josh 24.25).

2.56 Χαλεβ εν τω ‹επιμαρτυραcθαι› εν τη εκκληcια ελαβεν την κληρονομιαν	**2.56** Caleb, by bearing witness in the assembly, received *his* inheritance.

2.56 επιμαρτυραcθαι V A 64^{+}236 | μαρ- S •

2.56 Caleb, like Joshua, bore **witness in the assembly** and encouraged Israel to oppose foreign nations without fear, when the spies had returned from the land of Canaan (Num 14.6–9). He therefore **received his inheritance** in the land (Num 14.24; Josh 14.6–14).

2.57 Δα(υι)δ εν τω ελεει αυτου εκληρονομηcεν θρονον βαcιλιαc ειc αιωναc	**2.57** David, by his mercy, inherited *the* throne of a kingdom to lasting times.

2.57 David showed **mercy** during his conflict both with the house of Saul (2 Sam 9.1–6) and with foreign nations (2 Sam 10.2). (The sons of Mattathias would likewise show mercy during their struggles against their Israelite and foreign enemies; cf. 13.46–47.) The Lord therefore dealt mercifully with David (2 Sam 7.15; 22.51), and granted him **the throne of a kingdom to lasting times** (2 Sam 7.16; Psa 89.24–37; cf. Isa 55.3).

2.58 ‹Ηλιας› εν τω ζηλωσαι	**2.58** Elijah, by being jealous
‹ζηλον νομου›	*with* jealousy *for the* Law,
ανελημφθη εις τον ‹ου(ρα)νον›	was taken up into Heaven.

2.58 Ηλιας S^{c} V A 64^{+}236 La$^{109+146}$ | Ιλ- S* • ζηλον νομου V A 64^{+}236 La$^{109+146}$ | νομον ζηλους S • ου(ρα)νον S^{ca} V A 64^{+}236 La$^{109+146}$ | ουνον S* •

2.58 Elijah was **jealous with jealousy for the Law** (1 Kgs 19.10; like Phinehas and Mattathias, vv 23–26, 54) at a time when no one around him would speak a word in favor of the Lord (1 Kgs 18.21–22). As a result, he **was taken up into Heaven**[86] (2 Kgs 2.11).

2.59 Ανανιας Αζαριας Μισαηλ	**2.59** Hananiah, Azariah, Mishael,
πιστευσα(ν)τες	having believed,
εσωθησαν εκ φλογος	were saved out of *the* flame.

2.59 Hananiah, Azariah, and **Mishael** (Dan 1.6–7) were cast into a fiery furnace because they refused to worship a foreign king's idol (Dan 3.13–18), but they **were saved out of the flame** because they **believed** (Dan 3.28).

2.60 Δανιηλ εν τη απλοτητι αυτου	**2.60** Daniel, by his wholeheartedness,
ερρυσθη	was delivered
εκ στοματος ‹λεοντων›	out of *the* mouth of lions.

2.60 λεοντων V A La$^{109+146}$ 7h7 7a1 | -τος S 64^{+}236 •

2.60 Daniel displayed **wholeheartedness** (singleminded adherence to what is good: see the notes on v 37), when he continued to worship the Lord faithfully in opposition to a foreign king's command (Dan 6.6–13). Therefore he **was delivered out of the mouth of lions** (Dan 6.20–23).

2.61 και ουτως εννοηθηται	**2.61** And thus have in mind^{pl},
κατα γενεαν και γενεαν	generation by generation,
οτι παντες οι ελπιζοντες επ αυτον	that all *those* who are hoping on Him
ουκ ασθενησουσιν	will not become weak.

2.61 All those who are hoping on Him will not become weak. They will "not be weary" in spirit, but will "renew their strength" (Isa 40.30–31; Gal 6.9). God's people are to "be strong in the Lord, and in the strength of his might" (Eph 6.10). Most of the earthly strength may be on the side of their opponents (3.15–19); but earthly strength cannot deliver (Psa 33.16; 52.7; 1 Sam 2.9).

---

[86] **Was taken up into Heaven** is the reading of S (supported by La$^{109+146}$). V and A have "was taken up as if [*hōs*] into Heaven" (cf. the visions "as if" of Heaven in Exod 24.10; Ezek 1.22). Comparable textual variations occur in 2 Kgs 2.1, 11, where some copies (e.g., B) have "as if," but others (e.g., A) do not. (Both in the Maccabaica and in 2 Kgs, the Antiochene copies are divided on this issue.)

2.62 και απο λογων ανδρος αμαρτωλου μη φοβηθητε οτι η δοξα αυτου εις κοπρια και ει σκωληκας	**2.62** And do not be afraid[pl] from *the* words of a sinful man: for his glory *will become* dung and grubs.
2.63 σημερον επαρθησεται και αυριον ου μη ευρεθη ⸢οτι⸣ επεστρεψεν εις τον χουν αυτου και ο διαλογισμος αυτου απολιται	**2.63** Today he will be lifted up, and tomorrow he shall certainly not be found: for he will have returned into his dust, and his reasoning will be destroyed.

2.63 οτι V A 64⁺236 La[109+146] \| και S •

2.62–63 God's people are **not** to **be afraid from the words of a sinful man,** even one with as much power as Antiochus Epiphanes, because **his glory will become dung and grubs:**[87] even an Antiochus Epiphanes "will come to his end, and no one will help him" (Dan 11.45; Maccabaica 6.8–16; cf. Herod, Acts 12.21–23). "Do not fear the reproach of men, or be dismayed at their revilings. For the moth will eat them like a garment, and the worm will eat them like wool" (Isa 51.7–8, 12; cf. Psa 37.35–36; 146.3–4; Isa 14.11).

2.64 τεκνα ανδριζεσθε και ισχυσατε εν τω νομω οτι εν αυτω δοξασθησεσθαι	**2.64** Children, act manfully[pl], and be strong[pl] in the Law: for in it you[pl] will be honored.

2.64 The command to **act manfully and be strong** is repeated in the New Testament Scriptures (1 Cor 16.13).[88] To **act manfully** *(andrizesthe)* is to be the opposite of a child (1 Cor 13.11; 14.20; Eph 4.13–14). Those who serve the Lord in that way **will be honored** (*doxasthēsesthe;* "glorified," NAB, cf. v 51)—not with the glory *(doxa)* of a sinner (v 62), but with the glory that the Lord bestows on those who are **strong in** his **Law** (Rom 8.30; John 17.22; 1 Thes 2.12; 2 Thes 1.10, 12; 2.14).

2.65 και ιδου Συμεων ο αδελφος υμω(ν) οιδα οτι ανηρ βουλης εστιν αυτου ακουετε πασας τας ημερας αυτος εσται υμων πατηρ	**2.65** And see! Simeon your[pl] brother—I know that he is a man of counsel; hear[pl] him, all the days; he himself will be a father to you[pl].

2.65 "Each one has his own gift from God, one in this way, and another in that" (1 Cor 7.7). Mattathias's son **Simeon** (Simon, v 3) was already **a man of counsel** *(boulē),* someone who could give wise advice like a **father** (Prov 1.8; 6.20; 13.1). The others

[87] **Will become** [*eis*] **dung and grubs.** Greek *eis* here marks the predicate (as in 1 Cor 4.3; cf. BDAG 291, §8a) and/or indicates the result (as in Col 2.22; cf. BDAG 290, §4). In this passage, as very often elsewhere (e.g., 1.4, 36; 10.70; Rev 8.11; Luke 13.19), there is little or no difference between those two options (Abel, *Grammaire,* §42*d*).

[88] In the LXX, "be strong and act manfully" often translates the Hebraic expression "be strong and of good courage" (e.g., in Deut 31.6–7).

were therefore to heed his counsel at all times (**all the days**). Good counsel is to be heeded not only when it suits us, but "continually" (Prov 6.21–22).

2.66 και Ιουδας ⸤ο⸥ Μακκαβαιος ισχυρος ⸤δυναμει⸥ εκ νεοτητος ⸤αυτου⸥ αυτος εσται υμιν αρχων στρατιας και πολεμησει πολεμον λαων	**2.66** And Judas who *is* Maccabeus, strong with power from *the time* *of* his youth—he himself will be a commander of *the* army for you[pl], and he will war *the* war of *the* peoples.

2.66 ο V A 64^{+}236 \| > S • δυναμει V A 64^{+}236 \| -μιν S • αυτου V A 64^{+}236 La$^{109+146}$ \| > S •

2.66 Judas had been **strong with power from his youth,** and would therefore be able to lead the **army** in **war** (as outlined in 3.2–5).[89] Mattathias is not here appointing Judas as head of the whole army (the term **commander of the army** is applied elsewhere to subordinate commanders: 11.70; 5.56). He is simply saying that Judas will be a good leader in battle (just as, in v 65, he is simply saying that Simon will be a good counselor).

Both **counsel** and **war** will succeed only when God grants success (Psa 127.1). Simon, the man of **counsel** (v 65), was nevertheless overcome by counsel (16.13); Judas, the man of **war** (v 66), was nevertheless overcome by war (9.17–18).

Jesus combines both roles: He is the "Wonderful Counselor" (Isa 9.6), and also the leader of "the armies that are in heaven" (Rev 19.11, 14–15).

2.67 και υμεις προσαξετε προς υμας παντας τους ποιητας του νομου και εκδικησαται εκδικησιν του λαου υμων	**2.67** And you[pl] yourselves[pl] will bring near to you[pl] all the doers of the Law. And take vengeance[pl] for *the* vengeance of your[pl] people;
2.68 ανταποδοται ανταποδομα τοις εθνεσιν και προσεχετε εις προσταγμα του νομου	**2.68** repay[pl] a repayment to the nations, and pay attention[pl] to *the* decree of the Law."

2.67–68 Mattathias tells his sons to **take vengeance for the vengeance of your people** and **repay a repayment to the nations** (i.e., render to the nations as they have rendered to Israel; cf. Rev 18.6). Under the old covenant, God's servants were sometimes commanded to **take vengeance** for wrongs (Num 31.2; see the notes on 7.24). Under the new covenant, they are always to leave vengeance to Him (Rom 12.19).

Pay attention to the decree of the Law. Just before his death, Moses instructed the

---

[89] Does **the war of the peoples** *(polemon laōn)* mean "the war on behalf of the peoples of Israel" (cf. Geneva; ESV mg) or "the war against the foreign nations" (cf. NAB; ESV)? In Greek, **the war of** someone (genitive) is generally a war on behalf of them (9.30; 13.9; Num 21.14; 2 Chr 32.8), though in Hebrew it sometimes means a war against them (Jdg 3.1). On the other hand, the **peoples** (plural) are usually the foreign nations (Deut 7.16; Josh 24.18; 2 Sam 22.48; Psa 47.3), though there is at least one unambiguous reference to "the peoples of Israel" (Acts 4.27).

Israelites: "Set your heart to all the words that I am testifying to you this day, that you shall command your children to be careful to do all the words of this law" (Deut 32.46). The same command is given to everyone under the new covenant: "Become doers of the word, and not only listeners .... The one who has peered down into the complete law of freedom and continued in it, being not a listener of forgetfulness but a doer of work—this one will be blessed in what he does" (Jas 1.22–25; John 14.15; 15.10). "Not the hearers of the law are righteous before God, but the doers of the law will be held righteous" (Rom 2.13).

Mattathias's last words, like Moses' (Deut 33.1–29) and David's (2 Sam 23.1–7), are all the more powerful because they are consistent with the speaker's own past deeds (2.6–28, 45–48). They are advice of "the best kind"—the kind "that is preceded by a good example: 'not in word or tongue, but in deed and truth' [1 Jn 3.18]" (Barotti, *Lezioni sacre,* 2.103–04).

Mattathias dies

2.69 και ευλογηϲεν αυτουϲ και προϲετεθη προϲ τουϲ πατεραϲ ‹αυτου›	**2.69** And he blessed them, and was added to his fathers,
2.70 και απεθανεν εν τω ‹ζ΄› και μ΄ και ‹› ρ΄ ετει και εταφη εν ταφοιϲ π(ατε)ρων αυτου εν Μωδειν και εκοψαντο αυτον παϲ Iϲ(ραη)λ κοπετον μεγαν	**2.70** and he died in the hundred and forty-sixth year, and was buried in *the* burial-places of his fathers, at Modein. And all Israel beat themselves for him *with* a great beating.

2.69 αυτου S^{ca} V A $64^{+}236$ $La^{109+146}$ | -των S* • **2.70** ζ΄ S^{ca} V A $64^{+}236$ $La^{109+146}$ | γ΄ S* • ρ΄ S^{ca} V A $64^{+}236$ $La^{109+146}$ | ^ ε S* •

2.69–70 Having **blessed** his sons (cf Gen 27.4; Deut 33.1; Heb 11.21; Luke 24.51), Mattathias **died in the hundred and forty-sixth year,** only a year after the enforcement of heathen sacrifice in Judea began (cf. 1.20, 29, 45).

All Israel beat themselves for him with a great beating, a customary sign of grief (9.20; Luke 18.13; 23.48; Nah 2.7).

Judas Maccabeus (3.1–9.22)

The Deeds of Judas Maccabeus

3.1 και ανεϲτη Ιουδαϲ ο καλουμενοϲ Μακκαβαιοϲ υιοϲ αυτου αντ ‹αυτου›	**3.1** And Judas who *was* called Maccabeus, his son, rose up in place of him.

3.1 αυτου 2° S^{ca} V A $64^{+}236$ $La^{109+146}$ | αρτ- S* •

3.1 Judas ... rose up as his father had done (see the notes on 2.1).

3.2 και εβοηθου(ν) αυτω παντεϲ οι αδελφοι αυτου	**3.2** And all his brothers helped him,

κ(αι) παντες οι εκολληθηcαν τω π(ατ)ρι αυτου και ‹επολεμουν τον› πολεμο(ν) Ι(cρα)ηλ μετ ευφροcυνηc	and all *those* who had joined themselves to his father. And they were warring *the* war *of* Israel with gladness.

3.2 επολεμουν τον S^{ca} V A $64^{+}236$ $La^{109+146}$ | επολεμουντο S* •

3.2 All his brothers helped him, and all those who had joined themselves to his father. The Lord not only helps His faithful servants Himself (Heb 13.6; 2 Cor 6.2), but sometimes also provides them with companions to help and encourage them (Acts 16.9; Php 2.2; 1 Tim 1.16–18).

They were warring the war of Israel with gladness. Whatever troubles God's people may face in the world, they "always" have reason to "rejoice in the Lord" (Php 4.4; Isa 51.11) and "serve the LORD with joy" (Ps 100.2). "The LORD has done great deeds for us; we have been joyful" (Psa 126.4–6; 4.7–8). In all things we have reason to rejoice—even in those that are very painful or dangerous for us: "in our tribulations" (Rom 5.3), "in weaknesses, in injuries, in necessities, in persecutions, in distresses, for Christ's sake" (2 Cor 12.10).

3.3 και επλατυνεν δοξαν τω λαω αυτου και ενεδυcατο θωρακα ωc γιγαc και cυνεζωcατο τα cκευη τα πολεμικα αυτου και cυνεcτηcατο πολεμουc cκεπαζων παρεμβολην εν ρομφαια	**3.3** And he was spreading glory wide for his people. And he clothed himself with a breastplate like a mighty man, and girded himself with his war equipment; and he waged wars, covering *the* camp with *his* sword.

3.3 He was spreading glory wide for his people. "Righteousness raises a nation aloft; but sin is a disgrace to any peoples" (Prov 14.34). In earlier times, when Israel had disobeyed, the Lord had declared that "the glory of Jacob will wane, and the fatness of his flesh will become lean" (Isa 17.4; Hos 4.7). But now the reverse was happening: people in Israel were serving the Lord faithfully, and therefore its **glory** was being extended (cf. Isa 62.2).

He clothed himself with a breastplate like a mighty man,[90] **and girded himself with his war equipment,**[91] as the Lord Himself does (Isa 59.16–17), and as, in the spirit, all His servants must do, to defend themselves against "the spiritual forces of wickedness" (Eph 6.10–17).

Covering the camp with his sword. The **camp** of the Lord's people is to be protected, not only with walls and fortifications, but also with the active use of the **sword** (cf. Eph 6.17; Rev 2.16; 19.15). The prophets had already foretold the deeds of Judas and his companions: "I will rouse up your sons, Zion, over against your sons, Greece, and I will set you as a sword of a mighty man" (Zec 9.13; see Part Five).

---

[90] Greek *gigas* ("giant," KJV) is here equivalent to Hebrew *gbwr*, **mighty man** (as often in the LXX: Ezek 32.12; Isa 3.2; etc.).

[91] **Equipment** *(skeuē)* is a broad term, applicable to implements of all kinds (cf. 14.10), including both "armor" (NRSV) and "weapons" (NAB).

3.4 και ωμοιωθη λεοντι εν τοιc εργοιc ⸂αυτου⸃ και ωc cκυμνοc ⸂ερευγομενοc⸃ ειc θηραν	**3.4** And he was like a lion in his deeds, and like a young lion that is calling out for prey.

3.4 αυτου V A 236 La$^{109+146}$ | -των 64 | > S • ερευγομενοc V A 64*236 La$^{109+146}$ | ορ- S •

3.4 He was like a lion in his deeds, and like a young lion that is calling out for prey (cf. Isa 5.29; 1 Chr 12.8). In these respects also, Judas acted as the Lord Himself does: "As the lion and the young lion growls over his prey, if a multitude of shepherds are summoned against him, he will not be dismayed at their voice . . . so the LORD of hosts will come down to fight on Mount Zion" (Isa 31.4–5).

3.5 και εδιωξεν ανομουc εξερευνω(ν) και τουc ταραcco(ν)ταc τον λαον αυτου εφλογιcεν	**3.5** And he pursued *those who were* opposed to *the* Law, searching *them* out; and those who were unsettling his people, he burned in *the* flames.
3.6 και cυνεcταληcαν ανομοι απο του φοβου αυτου και παντεc οι εργαται τηc ανομιαc cυνεταραχθηcαν και ευοδωθη cωτηρια εν χιρι αυτου	**3.6** And *those* opposed to *the* Law were confined for fear of him, and all the workers of opposition to *the* Law were utterly unsettled; and salvation prospered in his hand.

3.5–6 Those who were unsettling [*tarassontas*] **his people . . . were utterly unsettled** [*sunetarachthēsan*] by Judas: as they themselves had done, so God requited them (2.68; cf. Jdg 1.7; 1 Sam 15.33). "With whatever measure you measure, it will be measured to you" (Matt 7.2). In the Scriptures, the people of this world were often **unsettled** *(tarassō)* by the works of God (Matt 2.3; Acts 12.18; 17.8; 19.23). But the people of God need not be unsettled by what unsettles their opponents. "Do not fear their fear, nor be unsettled [*tarachthēte*]; but sanctify in your hearts Christ as Lord" (1 Pet 3.14–15; John 14.1, 27).

Not only were the evildoers unsettled by Judas, but they **were confined**[92] because of their **fear of him:** their activities were limited (5.3; 7.23–24), as, on a much larger scale, the activities of Satan were limited by Christ (Matt 12.29; Heb 2.14–15; Rev 20.1–3).

---

92 The term **confine** *(sustellō)* is applied to the binding up of a corpse (Acts 5.6) and the restriction of a period of time (1 Cor 7.29). Thus the point here is not simply that the evildoers "were humbled" (SAAS), or that they "shrank back" (ESV; the form here is passive, *sunestalēsan,* not active), but that they were held back, restricted, bound up. The classic Spanish and French renderings (*fueron bueltos atràs,* VRV; *compelidos fueron,* Jünemann; *furent réprimés,* Martin) express the sense of forcible constraint more vividly than most English versions. Compare the use of *anastellō* in 7.24: because of Judas's activities, the evildoers "were confined [*anestalēsan*] from going out into the surrounding district."

Some of them **he burned in the flames** (see 5.5, 44), as the Lord sometimes required under the old covenant (Josh 7.15), and as He Himself will ultimately do to all those who do not bear good fruit (Matt 3.10–12).

Salvation prospered in his hand, as it had prospered in the days of his father (2.47). When a man refuses to walk with the wicked, "all that he does will prosper" (Psa 1.3).

3.7 και επικρανεν βαϲιλιϲ πολλουϲ και ευφρανεν τον Ιακωβ εν τοιϲ εργοιϲ αυτου και εωϲ του αιωνοϲ το μνημοϲυνο(ν) αυτου ‹› ειϲ ευλογιαν	**3.7** And he embittered many kings, and made Jacob glad with his deeds; and until lasting time his memory *is* a blessing.

3.7 ειϲ S^{ca} V A 64^{+}236 La$^{109+146}$ | ^ και S* •

3.7 He embittered[93] **many kings, and made Jacob glad with his deeds.** The success and prosperity of God's servants embitters some (Gen 37.4–5, 11; Psa 112.10; Dan 6.3–4), yet it makes others glad (1 Sam 18.5–16; Psa 35.26–27; Acts 13.48–50). The servants of God are not to be envious or bitter (Eph 4.31; 1 Pet 2.1; 1 Cor 3.3), but are to rejoice when their brethren are elevated or honored (John 3.29–30; 1 Cor 12.26; cf. Num 11.29; 1 Sam 23.16–18) and when the work of the Lord prospers in someone's hands (Acts 11.21–24; Php 1.18).

Judas **embittered many kings,** including Antiochus Epiphanes (v 27; 6.8–13), his son Antiochus Eupator (6.28), and Demetrius son of Seleucus (7.8–9, 26).

Until lasting time his memory is a blessing, like the remembrance of Jesus Himself (Psa 72.17; 1 Cor 11.24–26), His mother Mary (Luke 1.48), and the woman who anointed His feet (Mark 14.9). "The memory of a righteous one is a blessing; but the name of wicked people rots" (Prov 10.7; cf. the comments on Seron, v 13 below).

3.8 και διηλθεν εν ‹πολεϲιν› Ιουδα και εξωλεθρευϲεν αϲεβειϲ εξ αυτηϲ και απεϲτρεψεν οργην απο Ιϲ(ραη)λ	**3.8** And he went through among *the* cities of Judah, and utterly destroyed *the* irreverent *people* from it; and he turned away anger from Israel.

3.8 πολεϲιν V A 64^{+}236 La$^{109+146}$ | -λι S •

3.8 Irreverent people (v 15; 6.21; 7.5, 9; 9.25, 73) are those who do not revere God.[94] It was for the irreverent that Christ died (Rom 5.6). "The anger of God is revealed from heaven against all irreverence" (Rom 1.18), and therefore His **anger** had lately been manifested against **Israel** because of the irreverent deeds committed in the land (see the notes on 1.64; 2.49), but Judas **turned away** that anger—just as "Moses his

---

93 **Embittered** *(epikranen).* The mouth of the sinner "is full of cursing and bitterness [*pikrias*]" (Rom 3.14).

94 **Irreverent** ("ungodly," KJV) translates Greek *asebēs,* the opposite *(a-)* of *sebomai,* "revere" (as in Mark 7.7; Acts 18.7, 13). God's people are to be *eusebēs,* "reverent" (2 Pet 2.9; 1.3, 6; 3.11; 1 Tim 2.2).

chosen one stood before His face . . . to turn away His anger from destroying" (Psa 106.23) and "Phinehas . . . turned [the LORD's] anger away from the children of Israel" (Num 25.11), and just as "we shall be saved from the [Lord's] anger through" Jesus (Rom 5.9).

3.9 και ωνομασθη εως εσχατου γης και συνηγαγεν απολλυμενους	**3.9** And he was named even to *the* end of *the* earth. And he gathered together *those* who were being destroyed.

3.9 He was named even to the end of the earth. "The nations were telling about the battles of Judas" (v 26); he was known at least as far away as Rome (8.17–32). Once again, what is here said about Judas is said elsewhere, on an infinitely vaster scale, about the Lord Himself: "All the ends of the earth have seen the salvation of our God" (Isa 52.10; Psa 22.27; 45.17; 72.17; Mal 1.11; Luke 3.6; Matt 28.19; Mark 16.15; Acts 1.8; 13.47).

He gathered together those who were being destroyed *(apollumenous).* "The Lord is . . . not wanting any to be destroyed [*apolesthai*]" (2 Pet 3.9); He therefore sent His Son and His servants "to seek and save what was lost [*apolōlos*]" (Luke 19.10; John 3.16; Matt 10.6).

HIS FIRST BATTLES AGAINST THE NATIONS

Apollonius is defeated and killed

3.10 και συνηγαγεν Απολλωνιος εθνη και απο Σαμαριας δυναμι(ν) μεγαλην του πολεμησαι προς το(ν) Ισ(ραη)λ	**3.10** And Apollonius gathered together *the* nations, and a great force from Samaria, to make war against Israel.

3.10 Apollonius may or may not be the "commander of tribute-collection" mentioned in 1.29 (see the notes there). He **gathered together the nations:** Antiochus ruled over a diversity of **nations** (1.41–42) and drew his forces from many different peoples (see the notes on 2.10). In addition to the other nations, **a great force from Samaria** came **to make war against Israel.** The Samaritans were already allied with Israel's enemies in the time of Nehemiah (Neh 4.1–3), and the two nations continued to be at enmity in the time of Jesus (John 4.9; 8.48).

3.11 και εγνω Ιουδας και εξηλθεν εις συναντησιν αυτω και επαταξεν αυτο(ν) και απεκτινεν και επεσον τραυματιαι πολλοι και οι επιλοιποι εφυγον	**3.11** And Judas knew, and he came out to meet him, and smote him, and killed *him.* And many wounded *one*s fell, and the rest fled;
3.12 και ‹ελαβεν› τα σκυλα αυτων και την μαχαιραν Απολλωνιου ελαβεν Ιουδας και ην πολεμων εν αυτη πασας τας ημερας	**3.12** and he took their plunder. And Judas took the sword of Apollonius; and he was making war with it all *his* days.

3.12 ελαβεν 1° V 64 93 La[109] | -βον S A 236 La[146] •

3.11–12 This was the first of Judas's recorded victories. Apollonius and **many** of his soldiers were **killed . . . and the rest fled.** Judas **took**[95] **their plunder,** including **the sword of Apollonius,** which he used thereafter in the service of the LORD (as David, in at least one situation, used the sword of Goliath: 1 Sam 21.8–9). The weapons that are prepared for use against God are turned against His enemies in the end (Psa 37.14–15; 64.3, 8; Isa 54.17).

Seron is defeated

3.13 και ηκουcεν Cηρων ο αρχων της δυναμεως Cυριας οτι ηθροιcεν Ιουδας αθροιcμα και εκκληcιαν πιcτων μετ αυτου ‹› εκπορευομενων εις πολεμον	**3.13** And Seron, the commander of the force of Syria, heard that Judas had drawn together a gathering and an assembly of faithful *people* with him, *those* who were going out to war;
3.14 και ειπεν ποιηcω εμαυτω ονομα κ(αι) ‹δοξαcθηcομαι› εν τη βαcιλια και πολεμηcω τον ‹› Ιουδαν και τους cυν αυτω τους εξουδενουντας τον λογον του βαcιλεως	**3.14** and he said: "I will make a name for myself, and I will be honored in the kingdom. And I will make war against Judas and the *people* with him who are despising the king's word."

3.13 αυτου 64⁺236 La[109] | + και S V A La[146] • **3.14** δοξαcθηcομαι V A 64⁺236 | ενδ- S • Ιουδαν S[ca] V A 64⁺236 La[109+146] | ^ υιον S* •

3.13–14 Seron commanded part of Antiochus's army (the part from **Syria;** cf. v 41; see the notes on 11.2). He now saw an opportunity to **make a name for** himself and to **be honored** (*doxasthēsomai;* "be glorified," DRCV) **in the kingdom,** by succeeding where Apollonius had failed. In the same way, the people of Babel sought to **make a name** for themselves (Gen 11.4). But "it is not the one who commends himself who is approved, but the one whom the Lord commends" (2 Cor 10.18). No fame can ever be achieved by human effort, and it is foolish to seek one's own glory *(doxa)* instead of God's (John 7.18; 5.44; Prov 25.27). "Many plans are in a man's heart, but the counsel of the LORD, it will stand" (Prov 19.21). The **name** of Seron has long been forgotten by the world; today it is known only by those who remember him with *dis*honor. His "glory" *(doxa)* has now become "dung and grubs" (2.62–63; compare the comments on Judas, v 7 above).

3.15 και προcεθετο και ανεβη μετ αυτου παρεμβολη αcεβων ιcχυρα βοηθηcαι αυτω ποιηcαι την εκδικηcιν εν υιοις Ic(ραη)λ	**3.15** And a strong company of irreverent *people* proceeded and went up with him, to help him to take vengeance among *the* sons of Israel.

[95] In verse 12, V, 64, and 93 (supported by La[109]) read **and he took** [*elaben*] **. . . and Judas took** (a construction resembling, e.g., "and He called . . . and the LORD said," Ezek 9.3–4; Lev 1.1). S, A, and 236 (supported by La[146]) read "and they took [*elabon*] . . . and Judas took."

3.15 Many **irreverent people proceeded and went up**[96] **with him, to help him.** Those who seek to do evil in this world have no shortage of helpers (Psa 83.5–8; Acts 4.25–27; Rev 19.19; 20.7–9; Ezek 38.15–16); but those who have the Lord on their side need not be concerned about the lack of any other help (Heb 13.6; Psa 118.7–9).

They sought **to take vengeance among the sons of Israel**—and therefore the Lord took vengeance on them (2.67). "Because Edom has worked against the house of Judah by taking vengeance . . . I will place My vengeance on Edom by the hand of My people Israel" (Ezek 25.12–17).

3.16 και ηγγιcεν εωc αναβαcεωc Βαιθωρων και εξηλθεν Ιουδαc ειc cυναντηcιν αυτω ολιγοcτοc	**3.16** And he came near, up to *the* ascent of Bethhoron; and Judas came out to meet him *with* very few.

3.16 Seron **came near, up to the ascent of Bethhoron. Bethhoron** consisted of two cities (2 Chr 8.5), upper (the **ascent**) and lower (the **descent,** v 24; cf. Abel, *GP,* 2.274–75; ABD 1.688–89). They were located north of Judah, on the border between Ephraim (Josh 16.3, 5) and Benjamin (Josh 18.14–15). Thus they were on the way from **Syria** (v 13) to Judah. Bethhoron was appointed as one of the Levitical cities (Josh 21.22), and both upper and lower Bethhoron were fortified by Solomon "with walls, gates, and bars" (2 Chr 8.5), so they were evidently towns of some size. The region had been the setting for part of Joshua's battle against the five kings (Josh 10.10–11) and part of Saul's battle against the Philistines at Michmash (1 Sam 13.18[97]). Judas Maccabeus would later fight another battle in the region, against Nicanor (7.39).

3.17 ωc δε ειδεν την παρεμβολην ερχομενην ειc cυναντηcιν αυτων ειπον τω Ιουδα τι δυνηcομεθα ολιγοcτοι οντεc πολεμηcαι προc πληθοc τοcουτο ιcχυρο(ν) και ημιc εκλελυμεθα αcιτου(ν)τεc cημερον	**3.17** But when he saw the company that was coming to meet them, they said to Judas: "What? Will we be able, being very few, to make war against so great a strong multitude? And we ourselves are tired, having had no food today."
3.18 και ειπεν Ιουδαc ευκοπον εcτιν cυ(ν)κλιcθηναι πολλουc εν χερcιν ολιγων και ουκ εcτιν διαφορα εναντιον ‹› του ουρανου cωζειν ‹› εν πολλοιc η εν ολιγοιc	**3.18** And Judas said: "It is easy for many to be shut up in *the* hands of few; and *there* is no difference before Heaven to save by many or by few:

96 **Proceeded and went up** *(prosetheto kai anebē)*. A strikingly Hebraic construction; compare, e.g., "proceeded and touched" (Dan 10.18; *prosetheto kai hēpsato,* θ'). In ordinary Greek, "proceeded to go up" would be more usual (cf. 9.1; 10.88; Luke 19.11; Acts 12.3).

97 Cf. also the Egyptian and Antiochene texts of 1 Sam 14.23.

3.19 οτι ουκ εν πληθει δυναμεωc νικη πολεμου εcτι(ν) αλλ εκ του ουρανου η ιcχυc	**3.19** for conquest of war is not in *the* multitude of *the* force; but strength *is* from Heaven.

3.18 εναντιον A 93 $\text{La}^{109+146}$ [7h7] 7a1 | + του θ(εο)υ S V $64^{+}236$ • cωζειν V A $64^{+}236$ $\text{La}^{109+146}$ | + η S •

3.17–19 Judas's soldiers were **very few** (v 16), **tired,** and lacking **food,**[98] whereas Seron's army was **so great a strong multitude.** But Judas said: **There is no difference before Heaven**[99] **to save by many or by few: for conquest of war is not in the multitude of the force; but strength is from Heaven.** The battle is not necessarily to the **strong** (Ecc 9.11; Psa 33.16). "There is no hindrance to the LORD to save by many or by few" (1 Sam 14.6; 2 Chr 14.11), and it is **easy . . . for many to be shut up in the hands of few,** when **Heaven** is supporting those few. That is what Joshua had promised the Israelites: "One man of you shall chase a thousand; for the LORD your God, He is the One who fights for you" (Josh 23.10; Lev 26.8). If God is for His people, no one can overcome them (Rom 8.31; 1 Cor 1.25)—not even "the principalities . . . the powers . . . the world rulers of this darkness . . . the spiritual forces of wickedness" (Eph 6.10–17), "because greater is He who is in you than he who is in the world" (1 Jn 4.4). "Give us help against the oppressor; for worthless is the salvation of humanity. In God we shall do powerfully; for He Himself will tread underfoot our oppressors" (Psa 60.11–12).

3.20 αυτοι ερχονται εφ ημαc εν πληθει υβρεωc και ανομιαc του εξαραι ημαc και ταc γυναικαc ημων κ(αι) τα τεκνα ημων του cκυλευcαι ημαc	**3.20** They themselves are coming against us with a multitude of ill- treatment and opposition to *the* Law, to put us away, and our wives and our children, to plunder us;
3.21 ημειc δε πολεμουμεν περι των ψυχων ημω(ν) και των νομιμω(ν) ‹ημω(ν)›	**3.21** but we ourselves are making war for our souls and our laws.

3.21 ημω(ν) 2° S^{ca} V A $64^{+}236$ $\text{La}^{109+146}$ | > S* •

[98] The tiredness and lack of **food** might have been caused by military hardships (2 Sam 16.2, 14; 17.29); but in addition, the Israelites prepared for battle by fasting and prayer (see vv 46–50). They did not need their own strength for victory; they were willing to reduce it in order to obtain help from a greater Strength (Psa 33.16–19; Jer 17.5–8).

[99] A (supported by $\text{La}^{109+146}$ and 7a1) reads **Heaven** *(tou ouranou)*. 7h7 has "the Inhabitant of Heaven" *('mwr' dšmy')*. (Despite the statement in Kappler's textual apparatus, this did not derive from a longer Greek text; it is simply a standard Syriac translation of "Heaven": see TS 2.2920.) Manuscript 93 reads "the Heavenly One" (*tou ou[ra]niou)*. S, V, and $64^{+}236$ read "the God of Heaven" *(tou theou tou ouranou)*. Saying that "Heaven rules" is equivalent to saying that God rules (Dan 4.26, 32); saying that people have "sinned against Heaven" is equivalent to saying that they have sinned against God (Luke 15.18; Psa 51.4).

3.20–21 Judas points out the difference between the two armies. Seron's forces **are coming against us with a multitude of ill-treatment**[100] **and opposition to the Law, to put us away, and our wives and our children, to plunder us**—whereas **we** (the Israelites) **are making war for our souls and our laws** ("for our people and the holy places," v 43). Seron's forces are fighting to destroy and cast down; the Israelites are fighting to have life, and to build up (John 10.10; 2 Cor 13.10). The difference is as great as that between Goliath and David: "You come to me with a sword and a spear and a javelin; but I come to you in the name of the LORD of hosts" (1 Sam 17.45). What does a believer have in common with an unbeliever (2 Cor 6.14–16)?

3.22 και αυτος cυντριψει αυτουc προ προcωπου ημων υμειc δε μη φοβειcθε απ αυτων	**3.22** And He Himself will shatter them before our face; but *as for* you[pl], do not be afraid[pl] of them."

3.22 Do not be afraid of them. Just as we are not to be afraid of sinners' words (2.62), so we are not to be afraid of their deeds (see the notes on vv 5–6). "The fear of humanity brings a snare" (Prov 29.25). There is One whom we should fear; and the fear of Him casts out the fear of humanity (Luke 12.4–5; Heb 11.27; Dan 3.16–18).

3.23 ωc δε επαυcατο λαλων ενηλατο ειc αυτουc αφνω και cυνετριβη Cηρων και η παρεμβολη αυτου ενωπιον αυτου	**3.23** But as he stopped speaking, suddenly he *began* springing into them; and Seron and his company were shattered in his sight.
3.24 και εδιωκο(ν) αυτον εν τη καταβαcι Βαιθωρων εωc του παιδιου και επεcον απ αυτων ειc ανδραc οκτακοcιουc οι δε λοιποι εφυγον ειc γην Φυλιcτιειμ	**3.24** And they *kept* pursuing him by the descent of Bethhoron to the level place; and up to eight hundred men of them fell, and the rest fled into *the* land of *the* Philistines.

3.23–24 The battle was like Joshua's battle on the same terrain: on both occasions the Israelites attacked **suddenly** (cf. Josh 10.9) and the enemy was driven down the slope (**they kept pursuing him**[101] **by the descent of Bethhoron;** cf. Josh 10.11).

Those who were not slain **fled into the land of the Philistines.** The Philistines inhabited the coastal plain west of Judea (Zep 2.4–7; Josh 13.2–3; Isa 11.14). They were

---

[100] **Ill-treatment** *(hubreōs):* see on Eighteen Psalms 1.6; 2.30–31. Classically educated translators naturally tend to render the word as "pride" (ESV) or "arrogance" (NETS), but "it is remarkable that … the abstract use of *hybris* in the sense of pride is completely absent from the NT," where "the word clearly means ill-treatment" (and, in the passive sense, the result of ill-treatment: "hardship, damage and disaster"). "Similarly the vb. *hybrizō* regularly has the meaning of ill-treat" (NIDNTT 3.27–28). The same is likely in this passage: its emphasis is on the fact that the foes **are coming against us … to put us away, and our wives and children, to plunder us.**

[101] S and 64[+]236 (supported by La[109+146]) read **him** *(auton).* V and A read "them" *(autous).*

powerful enemies of Israel from the time of the judges (Jdg 14.4) to the time of David (2 Sam 8.1; 19.9). Later they had less power, but the region remained a land of foreigners hostile to Israel (2 Chr 21.16–17; 26.6–7; Amos 1.6–8). At least three of their principal cities—Ashdod, Ashkelon, and Gaza—became major centers of opposition to Judas Maccabeus and his brothers (5.68; 10.78–86; 11.4, 61–62; 13.43–48; 14.34).

Antiochus leaves Lysias in charge, and departs for Persia

3.25 και ηρξατο ο φοβος Ιουδας και τω(ν) αδελφων αυτου και η πτοη επεπιπτεν επι τα εθνη τα κυκλω αυτων	**3.25** And *there* began the fear of Judas and his brothers; and *its* terror *began* falling on the nations round about them.

3.25 There began the fear of Judas and his brothers; and its terror began falling on the nations round about them. Similar **fear** spread when Israel's enemies were defeated in the days of Moses ("This day I will begin to put the dread of you and the fear of you on the peoples that are under the whole heaven," Deut 2.25), David ("The name of David went out into all lands; and the LORD put the fear of him on all nations," 1 Chr 14.17), and Jehoshaphat ("The fear of God was on all the kingdoms of the countries, when they heard that the LORD fought against the enemies of Israel," 2 Chr 20.29). Such fear also comes on those against whom Christ wages war under the new covenant (Isa 2.10; Rev 11.13; 18.9–10, 15).

3.26 και ηγγισεν εως του βασιλεως το ονομα αυτου και υπερ των παραταξεων Ιουδα εξηγειτο τα εθνη	**3.26** And his name came near up to the king; and the nations were telling about the battles of Judas.

3.26 His name came near up to [*ēggisen heōs*] **the king.** The Greek wording emphasizes just how far the news traveled.[102]

3.27 ως δε ηκουσεν ⸂Αντιοχος ο βασιλευς⸃ τους λογους τουτους ωργισθη θυμω και απεστιλεν και συνηγαγεν τας δυναμις πασας της βασιλιας αυτου ⸂παρεμβολην ισχυραν σφοδρα	**3.27** But when Antiochus the king heard these accounts, he became angry with indignation; and he sent and gathered all the forces of his kingdom, an extremely strong company;
3.28 και ηνοιξεν το γαζοφυλακιον αυτου⸃ και εδωκεν οψωνια ταις δυναμεσιν εις ενιαυτον και ενετιλατο αυτοις ειναι ετοιμους εις πασαν χριαν	**3.28** and he opened his treasury, and gave the forces pay for a year, and commanded them to be ready for any duty.

3.27 Αντιοχος / ο βασιλευς V A 64^{+}236 La^{109} | ~ S • **3.27–28** παρεμβολην ισχυραν σφοδρα και ηνοιξεν το γαζοφυλακιον αυτου S^{ca} V A 64^{+}236 La$^{109+146}$ | > S* •

[102] *Eggizō heōs* is used similarly in Sir 37.30; 51.6.

3.29 και ειδεν οτι εξελιπεν το αργυριον εκ τω(ν) θηcαυρων και οι φοροι τηc χωραc ολιγοι χαριν τηc διχοcταcιαc και πληγηc ηc κατεcκευαcεν εν τη γη του αραι τα νομιμα α ηcαν αφ ημερων των πρωτων	**3.29** And he saw that the money out of the treasuries had ceased; and the tribute-offerings of the district *were* small, on account of the divisions and *the* injury that he had prepared in the land *by* taking away the laws that had been from the first days.
3.30 και ευλαβηθη μη ουκ εχη ωc απαξ και διc ειc ταc δαπαναc και τα δοματα α εδιδου εμπροcθεν δαψιλη χειρει και επεριccευcεν υπερ τουc βαcιλειc τουc εμπροcθεν	**3.30** And he feared he might not have *enough* (as *had happened* once or twice) for the expense and the gifts that he had been giving before with a lavishly-spending hand (and he overflowed *in this* beyond the kings *who had been* before *him*).

3.27 The king . . . became angry with indignation and **gathered all** his **forces** against the cause of the trouble (see the comments on 6.28). But all those who become enraged against the purposes of God "shall be put to shame and confounded"; they "shall be as nothing, and shall perish" (Isa 41.11; Psa 124.2–8).

3.28–30 He opened his treasury, and gave the forces pay for a year. Antiochus Epiphanes was famous for his **lavish** expenditure, in which **he overflowed** (see the footnote on 9.22) **beyond the kings who had been before him.** As Daniel had prophesied, "he will do what his fathers have not done, or his fathers' fathers; and he will scatter among [his people] plunder and loot and goods . . . . He will rule over the treasures of gold and silver, and over all the desirable things of Egypt" (Dan 11.24, 43; cf. Maccabaica 1.19–24). "A rich man's sufficiency is his strong city, and as a high wall in his imagination" (Prov 18.11; Psa 49.6).

But now Antiochus **saw** that his **treasuries** were depleted. Moreover, he had taken **away the laws that had been** in the land of Judea previously; as a result, there were **divisions** (cf. 1.52–53) and hardships (**injury,** 1.30) among the people, and he was receiving fewer **tribute-offerings** from **the district.**[103] Riches "make themselves wings, like an eagle that flies toward heaven" (Prov 23.5; 27.24).

3.31 και ηπορειτο τη ψυχη αυτου cφοδρα και εβουλευcατο του πορευθηναι ειc την Περcιδα και	**3.31** And he was very much perplexed in his soul; and he took counsel to go into Persia, and to take

[103] **He might not have enough (as had happened once or twice).** Some translations take this to mean "he might not have as much as he usually had" (NETS); others take it to mean "as had happened once or twice before, he might be short of money" (REB). Either would fit the Greek syntax.

Once or twice: cf. Neh 13.20.

λαβειν τους φορους των χωρω(ν) και συναγαγειν αργυριον πολυ	the tribute-offerings of the districts, and to gather much money.

3.31 So Antiochus **took counsel to go into Persia, and to take the tribute-offerings of** that region. Great treasures had supposedly been left there by Alexander (6.1–2).

3.32 και ‹κατελιπεν› Λυσιαν αν(θρωπ)ον ενδοξον και απο γενους της βασιλειας επι των πραγματων του βασιλεως απο του ποταμου Ευφρατου και εως οριων Αιγυπτου	**3.32** And he left Lysias—a person *who was* honored and from *the* race of the kingdom—over the affairs of the king, from the River Euphrates even up to *the* appointed boundaries of Egypt,
3.33 και τρεφειν Αντιοχον τον υιον αυτου εως του επιστρεψαι αυτον	**3.33** and to bring up Antiochus his son, until he returned.

3.32 κατελιπεν S^{ca} V A 64^{+}236 La$^{109+146}$ \| απελυσεν S* •

3.32 To govern the country in his absence, he appointed **Lysias,** a member of the royal family (**from the race of the kingdom;** cf. Jer 41.1). The Greek word applied to him here (*endoxon,* **honored**) is used in Jesus' saying: "Those who are dressed in glorious [*endoxō*] clothing and live in luxury are in kings' courts" (Luke 7.25).

3.33 Antiochus his son would later become king under the name Antiochus Eupator (see 6.17).

3.34 και παρεδωκεν αυτω τας ημισεις των δυναμεων και τους ελεφαντας και ενετιλατο αυτω περι παντω(ν) ων ηβουλετο και περι των κατοικουντων την Ιουδαιαν και Ι(ερουσα)λημ	**3.34** And he gave over to him half of *his* forces, and the elephants, and he commanded him about all *the things* that he was wanting, and about the *people* dwelling in Judea and Jerusalem,
3.35 αποστιλαι επ αυτους δυναμιν ‹› του εκτριψαι και εξαραι την ισχυν Ι(σρα)ηλ και το καταλιμμα Ι(ερουσα)λημ και αραι το μνημοσυνον αυτων απο του τοπου	**3.35** to send a force against them, to utterly shatter and do away with the strength of Israel and the remainder of Jerusalem, and to take away their memory from the place,
3.36 και κατοικισαι ‹υιους› αλλογενεις εν πασι(ν) τοις οριοις αυτω(ν) και κατακληροδοτησαι την γην αυτων	**3.36** and to make foreign sons dwell in all their appointed boundaries, and to give away their land as an inheritance.

3.35 δυναμιν V A La$^{109+146}$ \| + και S 64^{+}236 • **3.36** υιους S^{ca} V A 64^{+}236 La$^{109+146}$ \| απ αυτων S* •

3.34–35 The king commanded Lysias **to utterly shatter and do away with the strength of Israel and the remainder of Jerusalem** ("for their destruction and their complete end," v 42). That was what God had done to Babylon: "I will rise up against them ... and will cut off from Babylon name and remnant" (Isa 14.22). But His purpose for Israel was different (2 Kgs 14.27; Rom 11.2–7).

3.36 As Daniel had prophesied (Dan 11.39), the king was also hoping to **give away** Israel's **land as an inheritance**[104] to **foreign sons** (in the way that the northern tribes' land had been given to foreigners, 2 Kgs 17.24). But eventually his successors would do just the opposite: they would give land from foreign nations as an inheritance to Israel (10.89).

3.37 και ο βαcιλευc παρελαβεν ταc ημιcειc των δυναμεων ταc καταλιφθιcαc και απηρεν απο Αντιοχιαc απο πολεωc βαcιλειαc αυτου ετουc ζ´ και μ´ και ρ´ και διεπεραcεν τον Ευφρατην ποταμο(ν) και διεπορευετο ταc επανω χωραc	**3.37** And the king took the remaining half of the forces, and moved away from Antioch, from *the* city of his kingdom, *in the* hundred and forty-seventh year. And he crossed over the Euphrates River, and passed through the upper districts.

3.37 Taking **half** the army with him, the king left **Antioch,** his capital (the **city of his kingdom**), and **crossed over the Euphrates River** (v 32) to reach the Persian highlands (the **upper districts,** 6.1). He never returned (6.16).

Lysias sends an army into the land of Judah

3.38 και επελεξεν Λυcιαc Πτολεμαιον τον Δορυμενουc και Νικανορα και Γοργιαν ανδραc δυνατουc των φιλων του βαcιλεωc	**3.38** And Lysias chose Ptolemy the *son* of Dorymenes, and Nicanor, and Gorgias, powerful men among the king's Friends;
3.39 και απεcτιλεν μετ αυτων τεccερακοντα χιλιαδαc ανδρων και επτακιcχιλιαν ιππον του ελθιν ‹ειc› γην Ιουδα και καταφθιραι ‹αυτην› κατα τον λογο(ν) του βαcιλεωc	**3.39** and he sent with them forty thousand men and seven thousand horse, to come into *the* land of Judah and ruin it, in accordance with the king's word.

3.39 ειc S^{ca} V A $64^{+}236$ $La^{109+146}$ | > S* • αυτην S^{ca} V A $64^{+}236$ La^{109} | > S* La^{146} •

3.38 To lead the army against the Judeans, **Lysias chose** three **powerful men** who were **among the king's Friends** (an honor that Mattathias had rejected, 2.18). The first of the three men—**Ptolemy the son of Dorymenes**—is not named again in the

---

[104] **To give away ... as an inheritance** *(kataklērodotēsai)* combines forms of *klēros* (an allotted **inheritance,** as in Col 1.12) and *didōmi* (**give,** as in Acts 7.5). Compare the wording in 10.89: *edōken ... eis klērodosian* ("gave ... for an inheritance").

Maccabean History, but battles against **Gorgias** (4.1–25; 5.59–60) and **Nicanor** (7.26–43) are described in detail.[105]

3.40 και ‹απηραν›	**3.40** And they moved away,
συν παcη τη δυναμι αυτων	together with their entire force.
και ηλθον και παρενεβαλον	And they came and camped
πληcιον Αμμαου εν τη γη τη πεδινη	near Emmaus, in the level land.

3.40 απηραν V A 64⁺236 La[109] | -ρεν S* La[146] •

3.40 The army[106] **camped near Emmaus,**[107] in **level** country. This battle would be fought under very different conditions from that at Bethhoron (vv 16–24). In a **level place,** there would be less cover, and the greater numbers of the Syrian army would be more of an advantage (10.70–73). Like those who lived in Syria before them (1 Kgs 20.23), they trusted in the lie of the land, not in the LORD (Prov 21.30–31).

3.41 και ηκουcαν οι εμποροι τηc	**3.41** And the traders of the district
χωραc το ονομα αυτων	heard the name of them,
και ελαβον αργυριον και χρυcιον	and took very much silver and gold,
πολυ cφοδρα και παιδαc και ‹ηλθον›	and fetters, and came
ειc την παρεμβολην του λαβειν	to the camp to take the sons of Israel
τουc υιουc Ic(ραη)λ ειc παιδαc	for servants. And *there* were added
και προcετεθηcα(ν) προc αυτουc ‹›	to them a force from Syria
δυναμιc Cυριαc και γηc αλλοφυλων	and from *the* land of *the* foreigners.

3.41 ηλθον S[ca] V A 64⁺236 La[109+146] | -θεν S* • αυτουc V A 64⁺236 La[109+146] | + και S •

3.41 Traders arrived, bringing **silver and gold** (to buy Israelite captives **for servants**) and **fetters**[108] (to chain them). The prophet Joel rebuked the enemies of Israel who

[105] This expedition of **Ptolemy, Nicanor,** and **Gorgias** against the Judeans is reported also in Epitome 8.8–27. Elsewhere (4.45–46) the Epitome describes **Ptolemy the son of Dorymenes** as a counselor of Antiochus Epiphanes.

[106] V, A, and 64⁺236 (supported by La[109]) read **they moved away** *(apēran).* S (supported by La[146]) reads "he moved away" *(apēre),* and this reading has been accepted by two English versions (NETS and SAAS), but it cannot be right; Lysias himself did not go with the army (4.26).

[107] This **Emmaus** may or may not have been the village of that name close to Jerusalem (Luke 24.13). "Many places bore the name in antiquity" (ABD 2.497).

[108] **Fetters** is spelled *paidas* here in all the ancient Greek manuscripts. This is not a mistake for *pedas,* but an alternate spelling. In Greek, as in most other languages, spelling used to be much more flexible than it is today, and *ai* and *e* were frequently interchanged in Greek manuscripts of the early centuries after Christ; S, for instance, has *Makaidona* at 1.1, where V has *Makedona.* Many other examples are listed in Thackeray, 77–78, §6.11; 69, §5(3).

"sold sons of Judah and sons of Jerusalem to the sons of the Greeks" (Joel 3.2–8; cf. Rev 18.11–13). But God's people, who "were sold for nothing . . . shall be redeemed without money" (Isa 52.3; 1 Pet 1.18). And the treasures brought by the traders on this occasion would be used for a greater purpose than they intended (4.23, 57).

The army was joined by forces not only **from Syria** (cf. v 13), but also **from** another **land of the foreigners.** The term **foreigners** *(allophuloi)* can be applied to non-Israelites of any kind, including Syrians (v 45; 4.12; etc.), but in this context the reference is presumably to "the land of the Philistines" (v 24; cf. 4.30; 5.68).

Judas and his people pray and prepare for war

3.42 και ειδεν Ιουδας και οι αδελφοι αυτου οτι επληθυνθη τα κακα και αι δυναμις παρεμβαλλουςιν εν τοις οριοις αυτων και επεγνωςαν τους λογους του βαςιλεως ους ενετιλατο ποιηςαι τω λαω εις απωλιαν και ςυντελειαν	**3.42** And Judas and his brothers saw that the evil *thing*s had been multi- plied, and the forces were camping in their appointed boundaries; and they knew the words of the king, which he had commanded to do to the people for *their* destruction and *their* complete end.
3.43 κ(αι) ειπαν εκαςτος προς τον πληςιο(ν) αυτου ‹αναςτηςωμεν› την καθαιρεςιν του λαου ημων και ‹πολεμηςωμεν› περι του λαου ημων και των αγιων	**3.43** And they said, each to his neighbor: "Let us raise up the downcast condition of our people, and make war for our people and the holy *place*s."

3.43 αναςτηςωμεν A 64^{+}236 La$^{109+146}$ | -ςον S* | -ςομεν S^{ca} V •
πολεμηςωμεν 64^{+}236 La$^{109+146}$ | -ςομε(ν) S •

3.42–43 Judas and his allies said: **Let us raise up the downcast condition of our people.** God Himself delights in raising up what has been cast down (1 Sam 2.8; Psa 113.7–8; Luke 1.52; Amos 9.11 ≡ Acts 15.16; Isa 40.4 ≡ Luke 3.5), including above all His own Son (Php 2.8–11). Therefore, when Judas and his allies decided to raise up what was downcast, they were deciding to imitate God (2 Cor 10.8; 1 Cor 8.1; 1 Thes 5.14).

Judas and his companions were fighting not for themselves, but **for our people and the holy places** (see the notes on 2.12), just as their ancestors had done ("for our people, and for the cities of our God," 2 Sam 10.12).

3.44 και ηθροιςθη η ςυναγωγη του ειναι ετοιμους εις πολεμον και του προςευξαςθαι και αιτηςαι ελεος και οικτιρμους	**3.44** And the gathering drew together, to be ready for war, and to pray and ask for mercy and compassions.

3.44 The Israelites in the days of Ezra "fasted and besought our God" for help against their enemies, rather than trusting to human strength for deliverance (Ezra 8.20–23). So did those in the days of Judas: they gathered not simply **to be ready for war,** but especially **to pray and ask for mercy and compassions.** We today have equal reason to pray, "Give us help against the oppressor; for worthless is the salvation of humanity." Only God, by His **mercy and compassions,** has the power to "tread underfoot our oppressors" (Psa 60.11–12), including the devil (Jas 4.7) and the spiritual forces of wickedness (Eph 6.10–18).

3.45 και Ι(ερουϲα)λημ ην ανοικητοϲ ωϲ ερημοϲ ουκ ην ο ειϲπορευομενοϲ ⸂κ(αι) εκπορευομενοϲ⸃ εκ των γενηματων αυτηϲ και το αγιαϲμα καταπατουμενο(ν) και υιοι αλλογενω(ν) εν τη ακρα καταλυμα τοιϲ εθνεϲιν και εξηρθη τερψιϲ εξ Ιακωβ και εξελιπεν αυλοϲ και κινυρα	**3.45** And Jerusalem was without dwellers, like a desert; *there* was no *one* of her offspring going in and going out. And the holy place *was* being trampled down, and sons of foreigners *were* in the citadel, a lodging for the nations. And delight was put away out of Jacob, and *the* flute and lyre ceased.

3.45 κ(αι) εκπορευομενοϲ S^{ca} A $64^{+}236$ $La^{109+146}$ | > S* V •

3.45 The Israelites gathered near **Jerusalem** (v 46), and the condition of the city is now summarized. At this time it was largely desolate, **like a desert** (see the notes on 1.38–39); its **holy place** was desecrated (1.39; 2.12), and **foreigners** were dwelling in its **citadel** (1.32–36). There were no longer any signs of **delight** (1.39–40; cf. Jer 7.34; 25.10–11; 33.10–11), such as the sound of the **flute and lyre** (cf. Isa 24.8–12; Ezek 26.12–14; Rev 18.22–23).

3.46 και ϲυνηχθηϲαν και ηλθοϲαν ειϲ Μαϲϲηφα κατεναντι Ι(ερουϲα)λημ οτι τοποϲ προϲευχηϲ ην εν Μαϲϲηφα το προτερον τω Ι(ϲρα)ηλ	**3.46** And they gathered together, and came to Mizpah, opposite Jerusalem: for a place of prayer for Israel had been in Mizpah previous*ly*.

3.46 They gathered at **Mizpah,** a town in Benjamin (Josh 18.26) on or near the route from the north to Jerusalem (Jer 41.5–6). It was close to Jerusalem (*katenanti,* **opposite** it; "across from" it, NETS; cf. Abel, *GP,* 2.389), and a **place of prayer** had been located there **previously** (as described in 1 Sam 7.5–6).

3.47 και ενηϲτευϲαν τη ημερα εκεινη και περιεβαλοντο ϲακκουϲ και ϲποδον επι την κεφαλην αυτων και διερρηξαν τα ιματια αυτων	**3.47** And they fasted on that day, and wrapped themselves in sackcloth, and *put* ash on their head, and tore their clothes.

3.47 As in Samuel's time (1 Sam 7.5–6, 8), the Israelites **fasted** (see the comments on Eighteen Psalms 3.9) and called out to Heaven (v 50) in prayer. Like Daniel (Dan 9.3), the repentant people of Nineveh (Jnh 3.5–10), and the Jews in Esther's time (Est 4.1, 3), they accompanied their prayer and fasting with signs of mourning (v 51): wearing **sackcloth,** putting **ash on their head,** and tearing **their clothes** (11.72; Gen 37.34; 2 Sam 13.19; Jer 6.26; 36.24; Matt 11.21; Acts 14.14).

3.48 και ‹εξεπετασαν›	**3.48** And they spread out
το βιβλιον του νομου	the book of the Law,
περι ων εξηρευνων τα εθνη	about which the nations were
τα ομοιωματα των ειδωλων αυτων	searching the likenesses of their idols.

3.48 εξεπετασαν V A 64^{+}236 La$^{109+146}$ | -σεν S •

3.48 They spread out *(exepetasan)* **the book of the Law.** That is, they "unrolled" it (NAB); the book was a scroll (cf. Luke 4.17). The book of the Law is profitable for the instruction of anyone who will search it (12.9; 2 Tim 3.15–17; Acts 17.11).

About which the nations were searching the likenesses of their idols is a strange-looking statement. Three main explanations have been advocated:

1. "In which the Gentiles searched for the likeness of their idols" (DRCV). According to this view, the nations were looking for Scripture passages that supported their idolatry (Lapide 22; Gillet 71). But there is no other evidence that Antiochus's foreign supporters were doing that. They sought copies of God's word to destroy it, not to consult it (1.56). Moreover, this view presupposes either that Gentiles (people of the **nations**) in the second century before Christ could read Hebrew, or else that the Scriptures were already circulating within Judea at that time in Greek.
2. "For which the heathen had sought diligently to paint in them the pictures of their idols" (Cotton). According to this view, the nations were trying to deface copies of the Scriptures by painting images of idols in them (Grimm 62–63; Keil 81–82). But this derives from an inferior Greek text;[109] and again there is no other evidence that it happened (1.56 describes not defacement but destruction—which would have been both simpler and more effective).
3. "Seeking there the guidance which the Gentiles seek from the images" of their idols (REB). On this view, the sentence states that Judas and his companions opened **the book of the Law about** [the things about] **which the nations were searching the likenesses of their idols.**[110] In matters that might cause **the nations** to seek guidance from **idols** (Ezek 21.21; cf. 2 Kgs 1.2; Hos 4.12), the Lord's people sought guidance from the living word of their living Master (see the notes on 4.45; 12.9; 2.19–22; Psa 119.105). In particular, verse 56 shows that

---

[109] After the statement **the nations were searching,** the words "to paint in them" *(tou epigraphein ep' autōn)* are inserted by f^{120}. That addition is not present in S, V, A, 64^{+}236, or La$^{109+146}$.

[110] Such a construction would be more natural in Biblical Greek than it is in modern English. For the unstated antecedent of the pronoun **which** *(hōn),* see "in exchange for [the things] which [*hōn*] you are doing with us" (10.27); "he learned obedience from [the things] which [*hōn*] he suffered" (Heb 5.8); cf. Robertson 719–21. For the omission of the second preposition (**about**), see "for the work [for] which I have called them" (Acts 13.2); cf. BDF §294(3). For both these features together, see "I might have grief from [the ones from] whom [*hōn*] I ought to have joy" (2 Cor 2.3).

Judas read out the Law's instructions about armies preparing for war (Deut 20.1–9) on the present occasion.[111]

3.49 και ηνεγκαν τα ιματια της ιερωςυνης ‹και τα› πρωτογενηματα και τας δεκατας και ηγειραν τους Ναζειραιους οι επληρωςαν τας ημερας	**3.49** And they brought the clothes of the priesthood, and the firstfruits, and the tenths; and they roused the Nazirites who had fulfilled *their* days.
3.50 και εβοηςαν φωνη εις τον ουρανον λεγοντες τι ποιηςωμεν τουτοις και που αυτους απαγαγωμεν	**3.50** And they called out with *their* voice to Heaven, saying: "What should we do with these *people*, and where should we lead them away?
3.51 και τα αγια ςου καταπεπατηνται και βεβηλωνται και οι ιερις ςου εν πενθει και ταπινωςει	**3.51** And Your† holy *places* have been trampled down, and are being profaned; and Your† priests *are* in mourning and humiliation.

3.49 και τα V A La$^{109+146}$ | τα S | τα τε 64*236 •

3.49–50 Having opened the book of the Law (v 48), they immediately set out to obey it (contrast Acts 7.53; Rom 2.23). They wanted to use the **clothes** that the Law prescribed for the **priesthood** (Exod 28.40–43). They wanted to present the **firstfruits** and **tenths** (tithes) that the Law prescribed (Deut 26.2; Num 18.12–13; Lev 27.30). And they wanted to fulfill **Nazirite** vows in the way prescribed by the Law (Num 6.13–21).

But the Law required that each of those commands had to be carried out at "the place that the LORD your God shall choose" (Exod 28.43; Deut 14.22–26; 26.2–4; Num 6.13, 18): the temple at Jerusalem (1 Kgs 9.3). How could that be done while the Jerusalem temple was in the hands of unbelievers (vv 45, 51; 1.54; 2.12)? Therefore the faithful Israelites brought all these matters before the Lord, and asked Him **what** they **should . . . do.** In the absence of the Jerusalem temple, **where should** they take the people who were ready to carry out those commands?

---

[111] A view especially popular among modernist Roman Catholics holds that Judas and his companions practiced a kind of *sortes Virgilianae,* opening the Scriptures at random and superstitiously allowing themselves to be guided by whatever they happened to find there (Bévenot, *Beiden Makkabäerbücher,* 70; Abel 69–70; Nelis 105–06; NJB mg). That view is inconsistent with the evidence of v 56 and 4.45: on both of those occasions, Israel was guided by Scripture passages so directly pertinent that they could only have been selected deliberately, not at random. Nor is it supported by anything elsewhere in either the Maccabean History or the Epitome (which says that the Israelites "read aloud the sacred book" on this occasion, but does not indicate how the passage for reading was chosen; Epitome 8.23). Historical evidence would suggest that the *sortes Virgilianae* developed among pagan nations; no trace of such a practice in ancient Israel has ever been documented.

3.51 The **priests** were **in mourning and humiliation** because the holy places were desolate and the people were put to shame (2.1, 6–14; cf. Neh 1.2–4; Lam 1.4; Joel 1.9).

3.52 και ιδου τα εθνη cυνηκται εφ ημαc του εξαραι ημαc cυ οιδαc α λογιζο(ν)ται εφ ημαc	**3.52** And see! the nations are gathered against us to put us away. You Yourself† know† *the things* that they are planning against us.
3.53 πωc δυνηcομεθα υποcτηναι κατα προcωπον αυτω(ν) εαν μη cυ βοηθηcηc ημιν	**3.53** How will we be able to stand against their face, if You Yourself† should not help† us?"

3.52–53 Judas and his companions based their prayer on the fact that the Lord knows His people's needs even before they ask (Matt 6.8; Psa 38.9; cf. Isa 65.24): **You Yourself know the things that they are planning against us.** (Cf. Psa 69.19; Jer 18.23; Acts 4.26–30.) None of us would **be able to stand against** our adversaries, if He did **not help us** (see the notes on vv 17–18; Psa 94.17; 124.1–8; 2 Chr 20.12).

3.54 και εcαλπιcαν ταιc cαλπιγξιν και εβοηcαν φωνη μεγαλη	**3.54** And they trumpeted with the trumpets, and called out with a great voice.

3.54 They trumpeted with the trumpets (4.40) appointed by the old covenant Law for use in worship to God and in preparation for battle (Num 10.9–10).

3.55 και μετα τουτο κατεcτηcεν Ιουδαc ηγουμενουc του λαου χιλιαρχουc και εκατονταρχουc ‹ κ(αι) πεντηκονταρχουc› και δεκαταρχουc	**3.55** And after this, Judas established commanders of the people: commanders of thousands, and commanders of hundreds, and commanders of fifties, and commanders of tens.

3.55 κ(αι) πεντηκονταρχουc S[ca] V A 64⁺236 La[109+146] | > S* •

3.55 Judas established commanders of the people, also in accordance with the old covenant Law (Deut 20.9; cf. Exod 18.21; Num 31.48; 2 Sam 18.1).

3.56 και ειπεν τοιc οικοδομουcιν οικιαc και μνηcτευομενοιc γυναικαc και φυτευουcιν αμπελωναc και δειλοιc αποcτρεφειν εκαcτον ειc τον οικον αυτου κατα τον νομον	**3.56** And he said to those *who were* building houses, and betrothing themselves to wives, and planting vineyards, and terrified, to return each *one* to his house, in accordance with the Law.

3.56 He sent away **those who were building houses, and betrothing themselves to wives, and planting vineyards, and terrified.** This too was **in accordance with the Law,** which required that people who were fearful or currently involved in unfinished business should be sent away from the army (Deut 20.5–8). A soldier entangled in the affairs of this life cannot "please the one who enrolled him as a soldier" (2 Tim 2.4). Similarly, soldiers of Christ must disentangle themselves from worldly affairs in order to be pleasing and useful to Him (Luke 8.14; 9.59–62; 14.16–24, 26, 33).

3.57 και απηρεν η παρεμβολη και παρενεβαλον κατα νοτον Αμμαους	**3.57** And the company moved away, and camped against *the* south of Emmaus.
3.58 και ειπεν Ιουδας περιζωcαcθε ‹και› γεινεcθε εις υιους ‹δυνατους› και γεινεcθε ετοιμοι εις πρωι του πολεμηcαι εν τοις εθνεcιν τουτοις τοις επιcυνηγμενοις εφ ημας εξαραι ημας και τα αγια ημω(ν)	**3.58** And Judas said: "Gird your- selves[pl], and become[pl] powerful sons, and be[pl] ready for early morning, to make war against these nations that *are* gathered against us to put away us and our holy *places*:
3.59 οτι κριccον ημας αποθανιν εν τω πολεμω η εφιδειν επι τα κακα του εθνους ημων και των αγιων	**3.59** for *it is* better for us to die in the war, than to look on the evils of our nation and of the holy *places*.
3.60 ωc δ αν η θεληµα εν ουρανω ουτωc ποιηcει	**3.60** But however *the* will in Heaven may be, thus He will do."

3.58 και 2° V A 64*236 La$^{109+146}$ | > S • δυνατους V A 64 La$^{109+146}$ | -αμεως S 236 •

3.59 It would be **better . . . to die in the war, than to look on the evils** prevalent in the land. When "the righteous perishes," he "is taken away from evil" and "enters into peace" (Isa 57.1–2). "To depart and be with Christ . . . is very far better" than life in this evil world (Php 1.23; cf. Psa 63.3; Ecc 4.1–3).

3.60 How ever the will in Heaven may be, thus He will do. "He does in accordance with His will in the army of heaven, and among the inhabitants of the earth; and no one can restrain His hand" (Dan 4.35; cf. Matt 6.10; Luke 22.42; Acts 21.14). His people are simply to do what is right, leaving the outcome to Him (Dan 3.17–18).

Lysias's army is defeated at Emmaus

4.1 κ(αι) παρελαβεν Γοργιας πεντακιcχιλιους ανδρας και χιλιαν ιππον εκλεκτην και απηρεν η παρεμβολη νυκτος	**4.1** And Gorgias took five thousand men, and a thousand chosen horse, and the company moved away *by* night,
4.2 ωcτε επιβαλειν επι την παρεμβολην τω(ν) Ιουδαιων και παταξαι αυτους αφνω και υιοι της ακρας ηcαν αυτω οδηγοι	**4.2** so as to set on the camp of the Judeans and smite them suddenly. And sons of the citadel were guides for him.

4.1–2 Gorgias (3.38) proposed to attack the Judean **camp** at **night,** using **five thousand** footmen and **one thousand** horsemen (a force amounting to one-eighth of the infantry and one-seventh of the cavalry currently stationed at Emmaus, 3.39–40). They were guided by **sons of the citadel**—that is, "men from the citadel" (NRSV),[112] the Jerusalem fortress that was a "harmful accuser to Israel at all times" (see the notes on 1.32–36).

4.3 και ηκουcεν Ιουδαc και απηρε(ν) αυτοc και οι δυνατοι παταξαι την δυναμιν του βαcιλεωc την εν ‹Εμμαουν›	**4.3** And Judas heard; and he moved away, he and the powerful *men,* to smite the king's force that *was* in Emmaus,
4.4 ‹εωc› ετι εcκορπιcμεναι ηcαν αι δυναμιc απο τηc παρεμβοληc	**4.4** while the forces were still scattered from the camp.

4.3 Εμμαουν S[ca] [Αμμαουμ V] [Εμμαουμ A 64[+]236] [*ammau* La[109] La[146]] | Ναμμ- S* • **4.4** εωc V A 64[+]236 | ωc S •

4.3–4 Judas heard of the plan. Avoiding Gorgias's smaller force, he attacked the major part of the enemy army in the **camp** at Emmaus.

This approach was typical of him. In other battles, he sprang decisively into the midst of the enemy, aiming straight at its strongest part, never waiting for others to make the first move (3.23; 5.40–43; 9.14–15). He was a man "prompt [*mhyr*] in his work" (Prov 22.29), "bold as a lion" (Prov 28.1), who "hastened and did not delay" to obey God (Psa 119.60).

4.5 και ηλθεν Γοργιαc ειc την παρεμβολην Ιουδα νυκτοc και ουδενα ευρεν και εζητει αυτουc εν τοιc ορεcιν οτι ειπεν φευγουcιν ουτοι αφ ημων	**4.5** And Gorgias came to the camp of Judas *by* night, and found no one. And he *began* seeking them in the mountains, for he said: "These *people* are fleeing from us."

4.5 Gorgias . . . found no one in the Judean camp and proceeded to search for his opponents **in the mountains**—thus further delaying his return to his own camp at Emmaus (v 19).

4.6 και αμα ημερα ωφθη Ιουδαc εν τω πεδιω εν τριcχιλιοιc ανδραcιν πλην καλυμματα και μαχαιραc ουκ ειχον ωc η βουλοντο	**4.6** And as soon as it was day, Judas was seen in the level place, with three thousand men; nevertheless, they did not have *such* protective armor and swords as they were wanting.
4.7 και ειδον παρεμβολη(ν) εθνων ιcχυραν και ‹τεθωρακειcμενην›	**4.7** And they saw *the* camp of *the* nations, strong and breastplated,

[112] In the Scriptures, the term **sons of** a place often refers to people from that place. "Sons of Zion" (Lam 4.2) are people from Zion; "sons of the province" (Ezra 2.1) are people from that province. (Further examples are given in TDNT 8.346, §4b.)

και ιππον κυκλουcαν αυτη(ν)	and horse*men* going round about it;
και ουτοι διδακτοι πολεμου	and these *people had been* taught war.

4.7 τεθωρακειcμενην S^{ca} V A $64^{+}236$ $La^{109+146}$ | -κειμ- S* •

4.6–7 As soon as it was day[113] Judas and his companions prepared for battle on the plain (**the level place**) at Emmaus (3.40). Even without Gorgias's contingent, the enemy camp was still well guarded (its **horsemen** were **going round about it**), well equipped (**breastplated**), experienced (its soldiers **had been taught war**), and **strong:** the numbers already given (3.39–40; 4.1) show that it must have contained about thirty-five thousand footmen and six thousand horsemen.

Judas, by contrast, had only **three thousand men,** who did not have adequate **protective armor**[114] **and swords.** But the Lord does not require good weapons in order to conquer. The Israelites who set out to fight the Philistines in the time of Saul had been similarly disadvantaged, and had still been granted the victory (1 Sam 13.19–22; 14.14). "The name of the LORD of hosts" is mightier than sword, spear, and javelin (1 Sam 17.45; Psa 44.5–7).

4.8 και ειπεν Ιουδαc τοιc ανδραcιν τοιc μετ αυτου μη φοβειcθαι το πληθοc αυτων και το ορμημα αυτω(ν) μη ‹δειλωθητε›	**4.8** And Judas said to the men who *were* with him: "Do not be afraid[pl] of their multitude, and do not be terrified[pl] of their onslaught.
4.9 μνηcθητε ωc εcωθηcαν οι π(ατε)ρεc ημω(ν) εν θαλαccη ερυθρα οτε εδιωκεν αυτουc Φαραω ε(ν) δυναμει	**4.9** Be mindful[pl] how our fathers were saved in *the* Red Sea, when Pharaoh was pursuing them with *his* force.

4.8 δειλωθητε V $64^{+}236$ $La^{109+146}$ | εδεcθ- S | διωθηται A •

4.8–9 Just as he had done before the battle against Seron (3.22), Judas encouraged his men **not** to **be afraid** of the enemy's numbers (**multitude**) or the sheer force of its **onslaught.**[115] The Savior of Israel (v 11) **saved** His people from the might of an Egyptian **force** at the **Red Sea** (Exod 14.30), and has the power to deliver His people from all their enemies (cf. 7.41–42; 1 Sam 17.34–37; 2 Cor 1.9–10; 2 Pet 2.4–9).

---

[113] **As soon as it was day.** The Greek wording is *hama hēmera,* "together with day."

[114] **Protective armor** *(kalummata),* "coverings" (cf. 2 Cor 3.13; Luke 8.16; 23.30; Matt 8.24)—in this context, coverings used for defense (*defensas,* Jünemann; *Schutzwaffen,* Zöckler). See also the notes on 6.2.

[115] **Onslaught** (*hormēma,* as in Rev 18.21, "thrown down with violence," BDAG 724). The term indicates an intensely forceful onrush (*Ansturm,* ZB). It is applied in the LXX to the swoop of an eagle (Deut 28.49) and the surge of a torrent (Hos 5.10; Psa 46.4; cf. *hormē,* Prov 21.1). The verbal form *(hormaō)* is applied to the rush of the Gadarene swine (Matt 8.32) and to that of the Ephesian mob (Acts 19.29).

4.10 και νυν ‹βοηcωμεν› εις ουρανον ει ‹ελεηcη› ημας και μνηcθηcεται διαθηκηc π(ατε)ρων και cυντριψει την παρεμβολην ταυτην κατα προcωπον ημω(ν) cημερον	**4.10** And now, let us call out to Heaven, if He will have mercy on us, and will be mindful of *the* covenant of *the* fathers, and shatter this company before our face today;
4.11 και γνωcονται παντα τα εθνη οτι εcτιν ο λυτρουμενοc ‹ κ(αι) cωζω(ν)› τον Ι(cρα)ηλ	**4.11** and all the nations will know that *there* is *One* who releases and saves Israel."

4.10 βοηcωμεν V A 64*236 La[109+146] | -cομεν S • ελεηcη 64*236 La[109+146] | θεληcει S V A • **4.11** κ(αι) cωζω(ν) S[ca] V A 64*236 La[109+146] | > S* •

4.10–11 The Israelites appealed **to Heaven** to **have mercy on** them and to **be mindful of the covenant of the fathers,** as He had been mindful of it when previous generations had appealed to Him (Exod 6.5; Lev 26.40–45; Psa 106.45).

In the same way, God was mindful of his holy covenant when He prepared the way of salvation through His Son (Luke 1.68–72). All those who **call out to** Him in truth will be heard and saved (Psa 145.18–19; Rom 10.12–13). And when that happens, **all the nations will know that** He is indeed God (Isa 37.20; 49.26; 52.10; Psa 59.13; Rev 2.23). "We shall all stand before the judgment seat of God"; and on that occasion, "every knee shall bow, and every tongue shall confess to God" (Rom 14.10–11; Php 2.10–11).

4.12 και ηραν οι αλλοφυλοι τουc οφθαλμουc αυτων και ειδον αυτουc ερχομενουc εξ εναντιαc	**4.12** And the foreigners lifted up their eyes, and saw them coming from opposite *them,*
4.13 και εξηλθον εκ τηc παρεμβοληc ειc πολεμον και εcαλπιcαν οι παρα ‹Ιουδα›	**4.13** and they came out of the camp for war. And the *men* from alongside Judas trumpeted,
4.14 και cυνηψα(ν) και cυνετριβηcα(ν) τα εθνη και εφυγον ειc το παιδιον	**4.14** and they made contact; and the nations were shattered, and fled to the level place,
4.15 οι δε εcχατοι παντεc επεcον εν ρομφαια και εδιωξαν αυτουc εωc Γαζηρων και εωc των παιδιων τηc Ιδουμαιαc και Αζωτου και Ιαμνειαc και επεcαν εξ αυτων ειc ανδραc τριcχιλιουc	**4.15** but all those *who were* last fell by *the* sword. And they pursued them up to Gezer, and up to the level places of Idumea and Ashdod and Jabneh. And up to three thousand men of them fell.

4.13 Ιουδα S[c] V 64*236 La[109+146] | Ιουλου A | του Δαν S* •

4.14–15 The two armies **made contact,**[116] and the forces from the **nations** again fled

[116] **They made contact** (*sunēpsan;* LEH 588), i.e., they "touched" (*aptomai,* as in Matt 8.3, 15; 9.20, etc.) "together" *(sun-),* "joined together" (Geneva), *griff an* (Luther), *kwamen aan elkander*

for safety to the land of the Philistines (see the notes on 3.24). In the book of the Law, God had promised the Israelites that "if you walk in my assigned instructions, and keep my commandments, and do them ... you will chase your enemies, and they will fall before you by the sword; and five of you will chase a hundred, and a hundred of you will chase ten thousand" (Lev 26.3–8).

Gezer (Gazera or Gazara), **Ashdod** (Azotus), and **Jabneh** (Jamnia or Jabneel) were situated near the Mediterranean coast, on or near the border between Ephraim and Judah (Josh 15.11, 46–47; 16.3, 10). All three had been Philistine cities (Josh 13.3; 1 Chr 20.4; 2 Chr 26.6) and were centers of opposition to Israel during the Maccabean period (10.83–84; 14.34; 15.40).

Idumea[117] (Mark 3.8) was apparently a Greek form of "Edom" (see 1 Kgs 11.14–17, LXX, where the forms *Idoumaia* and *Edōm* used interchangeably). In later times it was also applied to the south central region within the land of Israel (5.3, 65; bordering on Bethzur, vv 29, 61; 6.31)—perhaps because many Edomites were now living in that region (5.3, 65; cf. ABD 3.382). Thus it lay immediately east of (and inland from) the land of the Philistines.

4.16 και απεστρεψεν Ιουδας και η δυναμιc ‹αυτου› απο του διωκειν οπιcθε(ν) αυτων	**4.16** And Judas and his force turned back from pursuing behind them;
4.17 και ειπεν προc τον λαον μη επιθυμηcητε των cκυλων οτι πολεμοc εξ εναντιαc ημων	**4.17** and he said to the people: "Do not desire^{pl} *any* of the plunder: for *there is* war opposite us,
4.18 και Γοργιαc και η δυναμιc εν τω ορι εγγυc ημων αλλα cτητε νυν εναντιον των εχθρων ημων και πολεμηcατε αυτουc και μετα ταυτα ‹ληψεσθε› τα cκυλα μετα παρρηcιαc	**4.18** and Gorgias and *his* force *are* in the mountain near us. But stand^{pl} now before our enemies, and make war^{pl} against them; and after these *things* you^{pl} will take the plunder with open confidence."

4.16 αυτου 64^{+}236 La$^{109+146}$ | > S V A • **4.18** ληψεσθε 64^{+}236 La^{109} | λαβετε S V A | *summentes* La^{146} •

4.16–18 The battle was not yet finished: the troops in the enemy's camp had been defeated, but **Gorgias and his force,** who had gone out to raid the Judean camp (vv 1–2), were still **in the mountain** country nearby (v 5). Therefore Judas exhorted his followers not to be enticed from their vigilance by a **desire** for **plunder.** Judas had the attitude of Joshua (Josh 10.17–22) rather than the Amalekites (1 Sam 30.16–17). The

---

(SV). In this book the term is usually applied to armies that made contact in battle (5.7, 19, 21, etc.), although once it describes a naval blockade (15.14).

[117] **Idumea** *(Idoumaias)* is the reading of S, V, and 64^{+}236 (supported by La$^{109+146}$). A reads "Judea" *(Ioudaias).*

enemy army was a "strong man" still at liberty; and that strong man needed to be bound, before his possessions could be plundered (cf. Mark 3.27).

Those who pursue immediate wealth may lose permanent wealth (1 Tim 6.8–10; Luke 12.16–21; 16.19–25; Acts 5.1–11). Nevertheless, "the laborer is worthy of his wages" (Luke 10.7; 1 Tim 5.18); when Judas's men had completed their work, they would receive the **plunder** they had earned.

4.19 ετι πληρουντος Ιουδα ταυτα ‹ωφθη μερος τι› εκκυπτω(ν) εκ του ορους	**4.19** While Judas *was* still completing these *words*, a certain part *of them* was seen peering out from the mountain.
4.20 και ειδεν οτι τετροπω(ν)ται και εμπυριζουςιν την παρεμβολην ο γαρ καπνος ο θεωρουμενος ενεφανιζεν το γεγονος	**4.20** And he saw that they had been turned back, and they were setting on fire the camp: for the smoke that was seen was showing what had come about.
4.21 οι δε ταυτα συνειδοντες εδειλωθησαν σφοδρα συνιδοντες δε ‹και› τη(ν) Ιουδα παρεμβολην εν τω πεδιω ετοιμην εις παραταξιν	**4.21** And the *people*, perceiving these *things*, were extremely terrified; and also perceiving the company of Judas in the level place, ready for battle,
4.22 εφυγον παντες εις γην αλλοφυλων	**4.22** they all fled into *the* land of *the* foreigners.

4.19 ωφθη / μερος τι A 64⁺236 La[109+146] | ~ S V • **4.21** και V A 64⁺236 La[109+146] | > S •

4.20–22 Gorgias and his soldiers **saw**[118] that their companions had been **turned back** ("put to flight," KJV), and that their **camp** was **on fire** (as happened at Ai, Josh 8.20); so they too **fled.**

4.23 και Ιουδας ανεστρεψεν επι την σκυλιαν της παρεμβολης και ελαβον χρυσιον πολυ και αργυριον και υακινθον ‹και› πορφυραν θαλασσιαν και πλουτον μεγα(ν)	**4.23** And Judas turned back for the plundering of the camp; and they took much gold and silver and blue and sea purple and great riches;
4.24 και επιστραφεντες υμνουν και ευλογουν εις ουρανον οτι καλον οτι εις τον αιωνα το ελεος αυτου	**4.24** and, having returned, they were singing hymns and blessings to Heaven: "For *He is* good: for His mercy *is* to lasting time."

4.23 και 5° S[ca] V A 64⁺236 La[109+146] | > S* •

4.23 Solomon, who did not ask for riches, was rewarded with the riches that he had

[118] **He saw** *(eiden)* is the reading of S and A (supported by La[109+146]). "They saw" *(eidon)* is the reading of V and 64⁺236.

not asked for (1 Kgs 3.11–13); **Judas** and his companions, who resisted the temptation to pursue riches (vv 16–18), were rewarded by finding **great riches.** Traders, in their eagerness to buy Israelite slaves, had brought much **gold and silver** to the enemy **camp** (3.41). There were also valuable fabrics of **blue and sea purple** *(huakinthon kai porphuran),* which were used as signs of exalted rank (8.14; 10.20, 62; 14.43–44; Ezek 27.7, LXX) and were appointed by God as materials for His tabernacle (Exod 25.4; 26.1, 31, 36, LXX) and temple (2 Chr 3.14, LXX). These things were not given by chance: they provided the Israelites with resources for a task that they would soon be in a position to accomplish—the restoration of the temple (v 57). An enemy of God may "heap up silver like the dust, and prepare clothing like the clay; he may prepare it, but the righteous shall put it on, and the innocent shall divide the silver" (Job 27.16–17; cf. Prov 28.8; Ecc 2.26).

On the other hand, Antiochus Epiphanes, who had gone out in search of riches (3.31; 6.1–3), would not only fail to gain them, but would lose even his life (6.4–16).

4.24 Judas and his companions returned **singing hymns and blessings to Heaven** from the book of Psalms: **For He is good: for His mercy is to lasting time** (Psa 106.1; 107.1; 118.1; 136.1; cf. 2 Chr 7.3, 6; Ezra 3.11). They gave the glory to Him, not to any human effort (Psa 115.1).

4.25 και εγενηθη cωτηρια μεγαλη εν τω Ι(cρα)ηλ εν τη ημερα εκεινη	**4.25** And *there* was a great salvation in Israel in that day.

4.25 There was a great salvation in Israel in that day. The Scriptures use the same word—**salvation** *(sōtēria)*—for deliverance from earthly enemies (2 Sam 23.10) and for deliverance from spiritual enemies (Heb 2.3).

Lysias's army is defeated at Bethzur

4.26 οcοι δε των αλλοφυλων διεcωθηcα(ν) παραγενηθεντες απηγγιλαν τω Λυcια παντα τα cυμβεβηκοτα	**4.26** But all those of the foreigners who got safely through, when *they* came, reported to Lysias all the *things* that had happened.
4.27 ο δε ακουcαc cυνεχυθη και ηθυμει οτι ουχ οια ηθελε(ν) τοιαυτα εγεγονει τω Ιc(ραη)λ και ‹ουχ› οια αυτω ενετιλατο ο βαcιλευc ‹› εξεβη	**4.27** And when *he* heard, the *man* was in turmoil, and was discouraged: for the *things* that he had been wanting *to* *happen* to Israel had not come about, and the *things* that the king had com- manded him had not come to pass.

4.27 ουχ 2° V A 64*236 La109+146 | > S • εξεβη V A 64*236 La109+146 | ^ ουκ S •

4.26–27 Lysias . . . was in turmoil (*sugcheō,* like the crowd at Ephesus, Acts 19.32), **and was discouraged** (*athumeō,* as in Col 3.21). "The wise men have been put to shame, they have been dismayed and captured; behold, they have rejected the word of the LORD; and what wisdom is theirs?" (Jer 8.9). Things had not worked out as he himself **had been wanting,** and as his **king had commanded him.** "Many plans are in a man's heart, but the counsel of the LORD, it will stand" (Prov 19.21; Psa 33.10–11).

4.28 και εν τω ‹εχομενω› ενιαυτω ‹συνελοχησεν› ανδρω(ν) επιλεκτων εξηκοντα χιλιαδας και πεντακισχιλιαν ιππον ωστε ‹εκπολεμησαι› αυτους	**4.28** And in the next year, he numbered together sixty thousand chosen men and five thousand horse, so as to overcome them in war.

4.28 εχομενω 64^{+}236 La$^{109+146}$ | ερχ- S V A • συνελοχησεν S^{ca} V A 64^{+}236 La$^{109+146}$ | συνευδο- S* • εκπολεμησαι A 64^{+}236 La^{109} [*debellarent* La^{146}] | π- S V •

4.28 The following year,[119] **he numbered together** *(sunelochēsen)* an even larger army (**sixty thousand chosen** footmen and **five thousand** horsemen; cf. 3.39). This time, he himself led his forces (v 35; and see the notes on 6.6). Understanding that "salvation belongs to the LORD" (Prov 21.31), Judas had given Him the praise for it (4.24). But Lysias had not learnt that lesson; he still looked to an abundance of men and horses for his salvation (Psa 33.16–17). "These commemorate chariots, and these horses; but we will commemorate the name of the LORD our God" (Psa 20.7).

4.29 και ‹ηλθον› εις τη(ν) ‹Ιδουμαιαν› και ‹παρενεβαλον› εν Βεθσουροις και συνηντησεν αυτοις Ιουδας ‹εν δεκα χιλιασιν› ανδρω(ν)	**4.29** And they came into Idumea, and camped at Bethzur. And Judas met them, with ten thousand men.

4.29 ηλθον V A 64^{+}236 La$^{109+146}$ | -θεν S • Ιδουμαιαν V A 64^{+}236 La$^{109+146}$ | Ιουδαιαν S • παρενεβαλον S^{ca} V A 64^{+}236 La$^{109+146}$ | -βαλλον S* • εν δεκα χιλιασιν V A 64^{+}236 7h7 7a1 | δεκα χειλιαδας εχων S | *undecim milia habens* [≡ ενδεκα χιλιαδας εχων] La$^{109+146}$ •

4.29 The army camped on the border of **Idumea** (v 15), at **Bethzur** (a city in the hill country of Judah, Josh 15.58; 2 Chr 11.5–7), one of the most intensely contested centers of opposition to Israel during the Maccabean period (v 61; 6.7, 49–50; 9.52; 10.14; 11.65–66; 14.7, 33; cf. Abel, *GP,* 2.283; ABD 1.701–02). Judas's victories (and perhaps the "great riches" gained from his last battle, v 23) had increased the size of his army considerably ("people were gathering together to them," 5.64), from three thousand (v 6) to **ten thousand.** Even so, his forces were still greatly outnumbered.

4.30 και ειδον την παρεμβολην ισχυραν και ‹προσηυξατο› και ‹ειπεν›	**4.30** And they saw the strong company. And he prayed, and said:

[119] **Next** (*echomenō,* 64^{+}236 La$^{109+146}$), as in Acts 21.26 (BDAG 422, §11bβ; Muraoka 311, II.2b); synonymous with "coming" (*erchomenō,* S V A; BDAG 394, §4a; Muraoka 292, §1b) when used with the article (as in this passage). Manuscripts of Josephus (*Antiquities,* 12.313) have the same textual variation (despite the statement in Abel 79).

ευλογητος ει ο c(ωτ)ηρ Ι(cρα)ηλ ο cυντριψαc το ορμημα του δυνατου εν χιρι του δουλου cου Δα(υι)δ και παρεδωκαc την παρεμβολην τω(ν) αλλοφυλων ειc χιραc Ιωναθου υιου Cαουλ και του αιροντοc τα cκευη αυτου	"Blessed are You†, O Savior of Israel, who shattered the onslaught of the powerful *man* by *the* hand of Your† slave David; and You† gave over the camp of the foreigners into *the* hands of Jonathan son of Saul, and of the *man* who was bearing his armor.

4.30 προcηυξατο V A 64*236 La$^{109+146}$ | -αντο S • ειπεν V A 64*236 La$^{109+146}$ | -πον S •

4.30 Seeing[120] the strength of the enemy, again Judas **prayed** to the **Savior of Israel** for deliverance, recalling how He had overcome the **onslaught** (v 8) of the **powerful man** (1 Sam 17.4, LXX) Goliath by means of the youth **David**[121] (1 Sam 17.4–51), and had overthrown a whole garrison of Philistines (**foreigners;** see the notes on 3.41) by means of **Jonathan** and his **armor** bearer (1 Sam 14.1–14).

4.31 cυνκλιcο(ν) την παρεμβολην ταυτην εν χιρι λαου cου Ι(cρα)ηλ και αιcχυνθητωcαν επι τη δυναμι και τη ιππω αυτων	**4.31** Shut up† this company in *the* hand of Your† people Israel, and let them be ashamed of their power and horse;
4.32 δοc αυτοιc διλιαν και τηξον θραcοc ιcχυοc αυτων και cαλευθητωcαν τη cυντριβη αυτων	**4.32** give† them terror, and melt away† *the* confidence of their strength, and let them be shaken in their shattering.
4.33 καταβαλε αυτουc ρομφαια αγαπωντω(ν) cε και αινεcατωcαν cε παντεc οι ειδοτεc το ονομα cου εν υμνοιc	**4.33** Pull them down† with *the* sword of *those* who love You†; and let all *those* who know Your† name praise You† with hymns."

4.31 Shut up this company in the hand of Your people. When the Lord shuts, no one can open (Rev 3.7–8); and even the mightiest of His enemies has been **shut up** by the hand of His servant (Rev 20.1–3).

Let them be ashamed of their power and horse. The **horse** was considered to be a crucial source of "great power" and "strength" in ancient warfare (Psa 33.17; 147.10; Prov 21.31). But "the nations will . . . be ashamed of all their might" (Mic 7.16). In spite of their **power,** "they will be ashamed` and confounded . . . they will be as nothing, and will perish" (Isa 41.11).

---

[120] **They saw** *(eidon)* is the reading of S (supported by La$^{109+146}$). V, A, and 64*236 read "he saw" *(eiden).*

[121] **David** is described here as the Lord's **slave** (*doulos* ["servant," KJV], the term frequently applied to Christians in the New Testament Scriptures: Acts 2.18; 4.29; 1 Pet 2.16; Rev 1.1). See the comments on Eighteen Psalms 18.14.

4.32 Give them terror, and melt away the confidence of their strength, as happened to the Canaanites when the Israelites arrived in the time of Joshua (Josh 5.1). The Lord can give (Psa 138.3; Acts 4.29, 31) or take away (Lev 26.36; Deut 28.65; 2 Kgs 7.6–7) boldness and confidence, as it pleases Him.

4.34 και cυνεβαλλον αλληλοιc και επεcον εκ τηc παρεμβοληc Λυcιου ειc πεντακιcχιλιουc ανδραc και επεcον εξ εναντιαc αυτων	**4.34** And they drew together to one another; and *there* fell from the company of Lysias up to five thousand men; and they fell opposite them.

4.34 When the troops **drew together,** the large size of Lysias's army led only to large numbers of casualties: **five thousand** of them **fell,** mainly in close hand-to-hand combat (while they were placed **opposite** their opponents[122]—unlike those described in verse 15 and 3.24, who died while being pursued).

4.35 ειδων δε Λυcιαc τη(ν) γενομενην τροπην τηc αυτου cυ(ν)ταξεωc τηc δε Ιουδα το γεγενημενο(ν) θαρcοc και ωc ετοιμοι ειcιν ει ζη(ν) η τεθνηκεναι γενεωc απηρεν ειc Α(ν)τιωχιαν και εξενολογει και πλεοναcτον παλιν γενηθεντα παραγειν εcθαι ειc την Ιουδαιαν	**4.35** But when Lysias saw the overturning of his battle array— and the confidence of Judas's *array,* and how they were ready either to live or die in a true-born way— he moved away to Antioch. And he *began* calling strangers, and an increased *number* again, who started to come to Judea.

4.35 The reaction of **Lysias** is described in two of the book's few convoluted sentences (appropriate for a person "in turmoil," v 27). In view of three things—**the overturning of his battle array,** and **the confidence of Judas's** (battle array, unstated), and the fact that **they** (Judas's battle array) **were ready either to live or die in a true-born way**[123]—Lysias decided to withdraw **to Antioch.**

But, like his master Antiochus (3.31–33) and their ultimate master the devil, he intended to withdraw only "for a time" (Luke 4.13). All too often, people are not dissuaded by the failure of evil schemes; instead of repenting, they struggle to do wrong with even greater determination (2 Chr 28.22; Hos 11.2; Rev 9.18–21; see also the notes on 5.37). So it was with Lysias. He had fewer financial resources for military expeditions than ever (cf. v 23; 3.29–30); he had less ability to win the confidence of his people (cf. vv 11, 32); and he had fewer soldiers (cf. vv 15, 34). Yet **he began**

---

[122] The expression **opposite them** *(ex enantias autōn)* indicates that they were in close proximity (as the centurion at the cross was in close proximity to Jesus, Mark 15.39; cf. Muraoka 233, §I.1b). There may possibly be an implication that they fell because they were hemmed in by the sheer numbers around and behind them, and were unable to maneuver or escape.

[123] **In a true-born way** *(gennaiōs).* God's people are born of Him (John 1.13), and are to live in accordance with their birth (John 3.6; 8.41–42; 1 Jn 3.9).

calling strangers,[124] **and an increased number again, who started to come to Judea.** The unusual Greek phrasing suggests much laborious effort,[125] but not much immediate result. Those who fight against the truth never travel along ways of pleasantness and paths of peace (Prov 3.17; Isa 57.20–21), nor do they travel with an easy yoke and a light burden (Matt 11.28–30).

THE CLEANSING AND DEDICATION OF THE JERUSALEM TEMPLE

Judas and his companions go up to Mount Zion

4.36 ειπεν δε Ιουδας κ(αι) οι αδελφοι αυτου ιδου συνετριβηςα(ν) οι εχθροι ημων ‹αναβωμεν καθαριςαι› τα αγια και ε(ν)καινιςαι	**4.36** But Judas and his brothers said: "See! Our enemies have been shattered. Let us go up to cleanse the holy *place*s and dedicate *them*."

4.36 αναβωμεν καθαριςαι V A La[109+146] | -βαται καθαριςαται S* | -βωμεν κ(αι) καθαριςωμεν S[ca] 64[+]236 •

4.36 Judas and his brothers now resolved **to cleanse** and **dedicate** the **holy places** of the Jerusalem temple (Jer 51.51), which had been defiled by the nations (2.12; 3.51).[126] (In the same way, Hezekiah had cleansed the temple after it was defiled by Ahaz, 2 Chr 29.1–36.) This was one of the most urgent goals of the current war (3.43): until the temple was cleansed, the Lord's commands could not be fully obeyed (see the notes on 3.49–50).

The modern world does not think of a successful military leader as a zealous holy man. But in old covenant times, all three of the leaders under whom Israel gained

---

[124] **He began calling strangers** *(exenologei)*—that is, people of other nations (1.38; 2.7; 15.33). Hellenistic kings might hire mercenaries from remote regions (e.g., the "strangers' forces ... from the islands of the sea" in 11.38), especially if they could not obtain enough soldiers among their own subjects.

[125] **Who started to come** is more repetitive and even more laborious in the Greek (*genēthenta paraginesthai,* "having become to come," "having come-about to come"). That is the text of S, V, and A, supported by La[109+146]. (A has the aorist infinitive, *paragenesthai,* instead of the present infinitive, but the sense is not significantly affected.) La[109+146] construe **again** *(palin)* with the following verb (" ... an increased number, who again started to come into Judea"), which is possible (the Greek word order is against it, but there cannot be much reason to expect that so unconventional a sentence should obey conventions of word order). Alternatively, **again** could be construed with the preceding term, **an increased number**—which could indicate either that Lysias was assembling another large army, like the previous one ("becoming numerous again," NETS), or possibly even that he was assembling "a much larger army" (REB) than the previous one. As usual where syntax is complex, the Antiochene manuscripts (*f*[64+19] and their allies) modify it substantially.

Nearly all modern English versions translate texts of verse 35 that have no manuscript support (many modern texts omit *kai;* some omit *genēthenta;* cf. Abel 80–81).

[126] The cleansing and dedication of the temple are reported also in Epitome 10.1–8.

their greatest victories—Joshua, David, and Judas Maccabeus—were also outstanding examples of devotion to the Lord (cf. Josh 24.14–15; 1 Chr 29.10–19).

Dedicate *(egkainisai).* "Make new" (Wycl) would be a more accurate rendering, but the term "Feast of the Dedication" (*egkainia,* John 10.22) has become so familiar in English that any other translation would be confusing. The word does not necessarily mean "renew" (SAAS) or "rededicate" (NETS); it can be applied to anything "new made," even if nothing preceded it. So the first covenant was "dedicated" or "new made" *(egkekainistai)* at Sinai (Heb 9.18). The second covenant was "dedicated" or "new made" *(enekainisen)* "by the blood of Jesus" (Heb 10.19–20). What Judas did in Jerusalem on a small scale, his Lord is now doing on a universal scale: He has said, "I am making all things new" (*kaina,* Rev 21.5).

4.37 και συνηχθη η παρεμβολη πασα και ανεβησαν εις ορος Σιων	**4.37** And all the company gathered together, and went up to Mount Zion.
4.38 και ειδον το αγιασμα ηρημωμενον και το θυσιαστηριον βεβηλωμενον και τας ‹πυλας› κατακεκαυμενας και εν ταις αυλαις φυτα πεφυκοτα ως εν δρυμω η ως ενι των ορεων και τα παστοφορια καθειρημενα	**4.38** And they saw the holy place desolate, and the sacrificial altar profaned, and the gates burned down, and in the courtyards, plants grown up as *if* in a forest, or as *if* on one of the moun- tains, and the chambers pulled down.

4.38 πυλας V A 64⁺236 La[109+146] | θυρας S •

4.38 The temple was neglected, overgrown with **plants** (like the field of a lazy man, Prov 24.30–31), and partly destroyed (Psa 74.3–7; like Jerusalem in the days of Nehemiah, Neh 2.13–14).

4.39 και ‹διερρηξαν› τα ιματια αυτων και εκοψαντο κοπετον μεγαν και επεθεντο σποδο(ν)	**4.39** And they tore their clothes, and beat themselves *with* a great beating, and put ash on themselves,
4.40 και επεσαν επι προσωπον επι την γην και εσαλπισαν ταις σαλπιγξιν των ‹σημασιων› και εβοησαν εις ουρανον	**4.40** and fell on *their* face on the ground. And they trumpeted with the trumpets of signals, and called out to Heaven.

4.39 διερρηξαν V A 64⁺236 | ερρ- S • **4.40** σημασιων V A 64⁺236 | σημιων S •

4.39–40 They **tore their clothes, beat themselves, put ash** on their heads (all of which were signs of mourning: see the notes on 2.14, 70; 3.47), and **fell on their face on the ground** (a sign of abject submission to someone superior, Gen 44.14; Ruth 2.10; 2 Sam 14.4, 22; especially submission to the Lord, v 55; 2 Chr 20.18; 1 Cor 14.25; Rev 4.10).

They trumpeted with the trumpets of signals:[127] see the notes on 3.54 and 5.31. The trumpets were **signals** not only to people (e.g., to prepare themselves for battle, Ezek 33.3–6; 1 Cor 14.8) but also, as on the present occasion, **to Heaven,** praising Him (2 Chr 5.12–13; Psa 98.4–6; Eighteen Psalms 11.1), so that the people would "be remembered before the LORD your God" (Num 10.9–10).

They cleanse the holy places and dedicate the altar

4.41 τοτε επεταξεν Ιουδας ανδραcιν πολεμειν τουc εν τη ακρα εωc καθαριcη τα αγια	**4.41** Then Judas appointed men to make war against those *who were* in the citadel, until he had cleansed the holy *place*s.

4.41 Judas and his followers did not have complete control of Jerusalem. **The citadel** was still in enemy hands (see the notes on 1.32–36), and therefore some of his men had **to make war against** the forces in it, while their companions **cleansed the holy places** (compare the situation in the days of Nehemiah, when everyone who was building up Jerusalem had to work "with his sword girded by his side," Neh 4.18). The people of God in every age must resist those who try to tear down the work of God while it is being done (Acts 13.45; 19.9; Rom 16.17; 1 Thes 2.14–16).

4.42 και επελεξατο ιεριc αμωμουc θεληταc νομου	**4.42** And he called out unblemished priests, willing *to obey the* Law;
4.43 και εκαθαριcαν τα αγια και ηραν τουc λιθουc του μιαcμου ειc τοπον ακαθαρτον	**4.43** and they cleansed the holy *place*s, and took away the stones of the pollution into an unclean place.

4.42 Unblemished priests were those who kept themselves from iniquity (Psa 18.23), "walking in all the commandments and ordinances of the Lord" (Luke 1.6).[128] During the Maccabean period, not all of the priests remained **unblemished;** some of them were "opposed to the Law and irreverent" (7.5, 9), doing evil "beyond what the nations had done" (7.23).

4.43 They cleansed the holy places, removing the **stones** that were polluted by the recent idolatry (1.46–47, 54, 59), and disposing of them in an **unclean place** (a place of the kind described in Lev 14.40–41, 45; 2 Chr 29.16; 2 Kgs 23.4, 6, 12; the opposite of the "clean places" where the ashes of sacrifices were poured out, Lev 4.12; 6.11; Num 19.9, and where the appointed portions of sacrifices were eaten, Lev 10.14).

---

[127] In relation to trumpets, LXX **signals** *(sēmasiōn)* corresponds to Hebrew *trw'h* (Num 31.6; 2 Chr 13.12), "resounding." "With trumpets ... resound [*rw'*] before the King, the LORD" (Psa 98.6).

[128] The same principle applies under the new covenant. Our great High Priest is "holy, guileless, undefiled" (Heb 7.26–27); His people must likewise be a "holy priesthood" (1 Pet 2.5), unblemished and undefiled (2 Pet 3.14; Eph 5.27; 2 Cor 7.1).

4.44 και εβουλευcαντο περι του θυcιαcτηριου τηc ολοκαυτωcεωc του βεβηλωμενου τι ‹αυτω› ποιηcωcιν	**4.44** And they took counsel about the sacrificial altar of whole burnt offering that had been profaned, *to decide* what they should do with it.
4.45 και επεcε(ν) ‹αυτοιc› βουλη αγαθη καθελειν αυτο μηποτε γενητε αυτοιc ειc ονιδοc οτι εμιαναν ‹αυτο τα εθνη› και καθειλον το θυcιαcτηριον	**4.45** And *there* fell to them a good counsel, to take it down, lest it should become a reproach to them: for the nations had polluted it. And they took down the sacrificial altar,
4.46 και απεθεντο τουc λιθουc εν τω ορει του οικου εν τοπω επιτηδιω μεχρι του παραγενηθηναι προφητην του αποκριθηναι περι αυτων	**4.46** and put aside the stones in the mountain of the house in a suitable place, until the coming *of* a prophet to respond about them.
4.47 και ελαβον λιθουc ολοκληρουc κατα τον νομον και ‹ωκοδομηcαν› θυcιαcτηριον καινον κατα το προτερον	**4.47** And they took whole stones, in accordance with the Law, and built a new sacrificial altar in accordance with *the* previous *one.*

4.44 αυτω V A La$^{109+146}$ | αυτο S 64^{+}236 • **4.45** αυτοιc S^{ca} V A 64^{+}236 La$^{109+146}$ | -τοc S* • αυτο / τα εθνη 64^{+}236 La$^{109+146}$ | ~ S V A • **4.47** ωκοδομηcαν S^{ca} V 64^{+}236 La$^{109+146}$ | -cεν S* A •

4.44–47 The **sacrificial altar of burnt offering** had been **profaned** and **polluted,** because the **nations** had built a heathen altar on top of it (see the notes on 1.54, 59). This altar needed to be "most holy"; it sanctified whatever touched it (Exod 30.28–29; Matt 23.19). Therefore, Judas and his companions decided **to take it down** and replace it with a **new sacrificial altar** made of unhewn stones (**whole stones**), **in accordance with** the requirements of God's **Law** (Exod 20.25; cf. Deut 27.5–6).[129] Worship must always be **in accordance with** the pattern that God has laid down in His word (Heb 8.5; Exod 25.9). No worship that deviates from His commands is acceptable to Him (Matt 15.3–9; 7.21–27).

What should be done with the **stones** from the old altar? Judas and his companions **put** them **aside** temporarily **in a suitable place** on Mount Zion (**the mountain of the** Lord's **house:** cf. Isa 2.2), **until** a **prophet** should arise and **respond about them** (i.e., "tell what to do with them," NRSV). No **prophet** was available during those days, just as no prophet was available at other times when the Lord had punished His people by leaving them in the hand of their enemies (9.27; 14.41; 1 Sam 28.6; Psa 74.9; Lam 2.9; cf. Ezra 2.63).

---

[129] If the old altar had been left standing, it might have become a **reproach** (*oneidos,* cf. v 58; 1.39; 10.70), a term describing rebukes issued either by God (Matt 11.20; Mark 16.14; Wis 2.12) or by His enemies (Rom 15.3 ≡ Psa 69.9; 44.13; 79.4; Neh 4.4). God's people are to be careful to give no just cause for reproach (Neh 5.9; 1 Pet 4.14–15; cf. 1 Tim 5.14; Titus 2.5, 8).

When Judas and his companions made these decisions, **there fell to them**[130] **a good counsel.**[131] The wording deserves careful attention. This **good counsel** did not originate in their own minds; it **fell to them** from an outside Source (which, as usual, this book does not explicitly name; cf. Est 4.14). Nor are we to conclude that it came into their minds by direct revelation from God. There was no **prophet** among them at the time. No, they found their **counsel** in the place where they customarily looked for it—in God's written word (3.48; 12.9). That written word describes how Zerubbabel had decreed that people should not serve as priests if they could not be demonstrated to meet the requirements of the Law. Instead, they were to be reckoned unclean and set aside until some revelation about them was received from the Lord (Ezra 2.61–63). The rule applied in that passage to people is applied here to stones.

The similarity between the two incidents cannot be coincidental. Judas and his companions cannot have happened by chance to hit on a procedure so closely matching Zerubbabel's. Nor can they have found it by opening the Scriptures randomly and clutching at the first thing that met their eyes. They must have searched through God's word for guidelines fitting their own situation, until they found the incident in Ezra 2. **Counsel** like this—which is decided by the testimony of God's word, not by mere human opinion or the inward prompting of some subjective impulse—is always **good** (Neh 9.13; Heb 6.5; Rom 7.12; 2 Tim 3.16–17).

Two centuries later, a **prophet**—Jesus of Nazareth (Luke 4.24; 13.33; 24.19; Acts 3.22–23)—did indeed arise and **respond,** not only about these particular **stones,** but about all the other stones of the temple as well: "There shall not be left here one stone upon another, that shall not be thrown down" (Matt 24.2). A new covenant was at hand; and under that covenant, the Lord would be worshiped by "living stones" (1 Pet 2.5) "in every place," not only at the temple in Jerusalem (John 4.21–24; Mal 1.11; 1 Cor 1.2; 1 Tim 2.8).

4.48 και ωκοδομηcα(ν) τα αγια και τα εντοc του οικου και ταc αυλαc ηγιαcαν	**4.48** And they built the holy *place*s, and the inside *part*s of the house. And they hallowed the courtyards,
4.49 και εποιηcαν cκευη αγια καινα και ειcηνεγκαν την λυχνιαν και το θυcιαcτηριον των ‹› θυμιαματων και την τραπεζαν ειc τον ναον	**4.49** and made new holy vessels, and brought the lampstand and the sacrificial altar of incense and the table into the sanctuary,

4.49 των 64*236 93 La[109+146] | + ολοκαυτωματων και S V A •

[130] **There fell to them** (in German, *da fiel ihnen,* LXX.D). Compare Ruth 3.18: "Sit still, my daughter, until you know how the matter will fall." Presumably the image derives from the casting of a lot into the lap (Prov 16.33).

[131] **A good counsel.** The wording indicates that the **counsel** was indeed **good**—not merely that Judas and his companions believed it to be good, as most modern translations suggest ("they thought it best," ESV; "it seemed to them the best plan," SAAS).

4.50 και εθυμιαcαν επι το θυcιαcτηριον και εξηψαν τουc λυχνουc τουc επι τηc λυχνιαc και εφαινον ε(ν) τω ναω	**4.50** and burned incense on the sacrificial altar, and lit the lamps that *were* on the lampstand; and they were shining in the sanctuary.
4.51 και επεθηκαν επι την τραπεζαν αρτουc και εξεπεταcαν τα καταπεταcματα και ετελεcαν παντα τα εργα α εποιηcαν	**4.51** And they put loaves on the table, and spread out the curtains. And they completed all the works that they had done.

4.48–51 Everything pertaining to the temple was prepared in accordance with the Law: the **holy places** and other **inside parts** of the temple (Exod 26.33; 1 Kgs 6.5–10, 15–22; Heb 9.2–3), the **courtyards** around it (Exod 27.9–18; 2 Chr 4.9; 1 Kgs 6.36; 7.12), the **holy vessels,** the **sacrificial altar of incense**[132] (where **incense** was **burned** inside the temple), the **table** of showbread with its **loaves,** the **lampstand** with its **lamps,** and the **curtains** (all described in the notes on 1.20–23).[133]

The Law required most of these objects to be made of gold, silver, and precious fabrics, including blue and purple (Exod 25.3–8, 29–39; 26.31–36; etc.)—the very materials that the Israelites had found in the Syrian camp (v 23). Like David when he gathered the materials for the first temple, they were simply giving back to God what He had given to them (1 Chr 29.11–16).

Even in the time of Hezekiah, it took sixteen days to cleanse the temple (2 Chr 29.17). On the present occasion, the work must have taken much longer: the temple had been much more severely desecrated, so that much more extensive restoration was required (as the preceding verses show), and the work was constantly being hindered by the opponents in the citadel (v 41; 1.36).

They offer sacrifice in accordance with the Law

4.52 και ωρθριcαν το πρωι τη πεμπτη και εικαδι του μηνοc ‹του ενατου› ουτοc ο μην Χαcαλευ του η΄ και μ΄ και ρ΄ ‹ετουc›	**4.52** And they got up at dawn *in* the early morning, on the twenty-fifth *day* of the ninth month (this *is* the month Chislev) of the hundred and forty-eighth year,

---

[132] This **sacrificial altar** is called an altar "of burnt offering and incense" *(holokautōmatōn kai thumiamatōn)* in S, V, and A, but that cannot be correct; burnt offerings were presented on a different altar, outside the temple (Exod 40.5–6; 1 Chr 6.49). The main Antiochene copies, including 64*236 and 93 (supported by La[109+146]), rightly describe this altar simply as one **of incense** *(thumiamatōn).*

[133] The last clause of verse 51, **And they completed all the works that they had done,** acts both as a summary of the preceding section ("Thus they finished all the work they had undertaken," NRSV; cf. Knabenbauer 104) and as an introduction to the following section ("And when they had completed all the works that they had done, then they got up at dawn ..."; cf. Grimm 74).

4.53 και ανηνεγκαν θυcιαν κατα τον νομον επι το θυcιαcτηριον των ολοκαυτωματων το κενον ο εποιηcαν	**4.53** and offered up sacrifice, in accordance with the Law, on the new sacrificial altar of whole burnt offerings that they had made.
4.54 κατα τον καιρον και κατα την ημερα(ν) εν η εβεβηλωcαν αυτο τα εθνη εν εκεινη τη ημερα ενεκενιcθη εν ωδαιc και κιθαραιc και κινυραιc και κυμβαλοιc	**4.54** In accordance with the period and day on which the nations had profaned it, on that day it was dedicated, with songs and harps and lyres and cymbals;
4.55 και επεcεν παc ο λαοc επι προcωπον και προcεκυνηcα(ν) και ευλογηcαν ειc ουρανον τον ευοδωcαντα αυτοιc	**4.55** and all the people fell on *their* face, and bowed down, and gave blessings to Heaven, the *One* who had prospered them.

4.52 του ενατου V A 64[+]236 La[109+146] | > S • ετουc V A La[109+146] | > S 64[+]236 •

4.52–54 They offered up sacrifice, in accordance with the Law, exactly three years after **the nations had profaned** the altar—on the very same **day** of the year: **the twenty-fifth day of the ninth month,** the month **Chislev** (1.54, 57). Events in the history of Israel did not happen randomly, or at chance intervals, but "by the appointed counsel and foreknowledge of God" (cf. Acts 2.23). The Israelites left the land of Egypt on "the same day" of the year that they had entered it four hundred and thirty years earlier (Exod 12.40–41). Jerusalem suffered three and a half years of oppression by a "little horn" during the time of Antiochus Epiphanes (Dan 8.8–14, 23–26; see below) and another three and a half years of oppression by a "little horn" during the Roman period (Dan 7.8–11, 24–25).

The offerings began in the **early morning,** when the old covenant Law required a continual burnt offering to be presented daily (Exod 29.38–42; Num 28.3–8; 2 Chr 13.11; Ezra 3.3).

The new altar **was dedicated with songs and harps and lyres and cymbals.** Like the animal sacrifices, the instrumental music was specifically commanded as a part of worship under the old covenant (2 Chr 29.25–30), but not under the new covenant (when the only authorized sacrifices are "spiritual sacrifices," 1 Pet 2.5; Rom 12.1, and only the human voice and heart are authorized to make melody during worship, Eph 5.19; Col 3.16).

4.55 All the people fell on their face, and bowed down (see the notes on v 40), **and gave blessings to Heaven,** as His servants, then, now, and forever, have reason to do "at all times… continually" (Psa 34.1; Luke 24.53; cf. Rev 5.13–14; 7.11–12; 4.8–11).

Heaven had **prospered** [*euodōsanta*] them (cf. 2 Chr 26.5), and they were giving to Him as they had prospered (see the notes on vv 48–51), just as "each one" of us today is commanded to give "as he may prosper [*euodōtai*]" (1 Cor 16.2).

The feast of the dedication is set up

4.56 και εποιηςα(ν) τον ενκαινιcμο(ν) του θυcιαcτηριου ημεραc οκτω και προcηνεγκαν ολοκαυτωματα μετα ευφροcυνηc και εθυcαν θυcια(ν) cωτηριου και αινεcεωc	**4.56** And they made the dedication of the sacrificial altar *for* eight days; and they offered up whole burnt offerings with gladness, and sacrificed a sacrifice of salvation and of praise.

4.56 The dedication of the sacrificial altar lasted for **eight days,** during which time **whole burnt offerings** and peace offerings (**sacrifice**) were presented (see the notes on 1.45). Under the old covenant Law, both of these kinds of offering could be presented at any time, as freewill offerings to the Lord (Lev 7.16; 22.18). Both kinds were presented during Solomon's dedication of the first temple and its altar (2 Chr 7.7–10).

4.57 και κατεκοcμηcαν το κατα προcωπον του ναου cτεφανοιc ‹χρυcοιc› και αcπιδιcκαιc και ενεκαινιcαν ταc πυλαc και τα παcτοφορια και ‹εθυρωcαν› αυτα	**4.57** And they adorned the *part* on *the* face of the sanctuary with golden crowns and small shields; and they dedicated the gates and the chambers, and made doors for them.

4.57 χρυcοιc S[ca] V A 64[+]236 La[109+146] \| > S* • εθυρωcαν S[ca] V A 64[+]236 La[109+146] \| εθυcαν S* •

4.57 The façade (the **face of the sanctuary**) was now **adorned … with golden crowns and small shields** (cf. Luke 21.5), replacing what Antiochus had taken away (1.22).

4.58 και εγενηθη μεγαλη ευφροcυνη εν τω λαω cφοδρα και απεcτραφη ονιδιcμοc εθνων	**4.58** And *there* was very great gladness among the people; and *the* reproach of *the* nations was turned away.

4.58 The reproach of the nations was turned away. Israel suffered **reproach** from the **nations** (Neh 5.9; Joel 2.19; Ezek 36.15) when she became an object of "scoffing and derision" in their eyes (Psa 79.4; 44.13; Neh 4.4; Ezek 22.4)—for instance, when foreigners entered the holy places of the LORD's house (Jer 51.51). At last that reproach had been reversed. Instead of mocking, the **nations** were now in fear and terror of the Israelites (3.25) and would soon be starting to honor them (5.63).

4.59 και εcτηcεν Ιουδαc και οι αδελφοι αυτου και παcα η εκκληcια Ιc(ραη)λ ινα αγω(ν)ται αι ημεραι του ε(ν)καινιcμου του θυcιαcτηριου εν τοιc καιροιc αυτων ‹ενιαυτον› κατ ενιαυτον ημεραc οκτω απο τηc πεμπτηc και εικαδοc του μηνοc Χαcελευ μετ ευφροcυνηc και χαραc	**4.59** And Judas and his brothers, and all the assembly of Israel, established that the days of the dedication of the sacrificial altar should be kept in their periods of time year by year: eight days, from the twenty-fifth of the month Chislev, with gladness and joy.

4.59 ενιαυτον 1° S[ca] V A 64[+]236 La[109+146] \| -του S* •

4.59 The whole **assembly of Israel** ordained (**established**) that this feast of **the dedication of the sacrificial altar should be kept** every **year** for **eight days,** starting on **the twenty-fifth of the month Chislev.** Jesus Himself attended it (John 10.22–23).

Zion and Bethzur are fortified

4.60 και ωκοδομηcαν εν τω καιρω εκινω το οροc Cιων κυκλοθεν τιχη υψηλα και πυργουc ‹οχυρουc› μηποτε παραγενηθε(ν)τα τα εθνη καταπατηcουcιν αυτα ωc εποιηcαν το προτερον	**4.60** And at that period of time they built up Mount Zion round about, *with* high walls and fortified towers, lest the nations, coming, should trample them down as they had done previous*ly*.
4.61 και απεταξεν εκει δυναμι(ν) τηριν αυτα και ωχυρωcεν ‹αυτο› τηριν την ‹Βαιθcουρα› του εχειν τον λαον οχυρωμα κατα προcωπον τηc Ιδουμαιαc	**4.61** And he set apart a force there, to keep them. And he fortified Bethzur, to keep it, *for* the people to have a fortress against *the* face of Idumea.

4.60 οχυρουc S^{ca} V [-ροιc 64^{+}236] La$^{109+146}$ | υψηλουc S* | ιcχυρουc A | + και S • **4.61** αυτο S^{ca} V A | -του S* | -την 64^{+}236 • Βαιθcουρα V A La$^{109+146}$ | Βαθ- S | Βεθcουρ 64^{+}236 •

4.60–61 Jerusalem's walls had been broken down by the king's commander three and a half years earlier (1.31; cf. vv 52–54), just as had happened previously when Judah was defeated by the northern kingdom of Israel (2 Chr 25.23) and by Babylon (Jer 52.14). Now Judas and his companions **built up Mount Zion** with **high walls** on all sides (**round about**) and with **fortified towers** (cf. 2 Chr 32.5; Ezra 9.9; Neh 1.3; 2.17; 6.15), and they appointed a military **force** to guard it against further trouble from **the nations.** When God gives His people a time of peace and prosperity, it is an opportunity for building (2 Chr 14.6; Acts 9.31). See also the notes on 10.10–11; 12.35–37.

Judas also **fortified Bethzur**[134] against their enemies in **Idumea** (see on v 29).

War against the Nations in the South, East, and North

The surrounding nations determine to kill the Israelites

5.1 ‹κ(αι) εγενετο› οτε ηκουcαν τα εθνη κυκλοθεν οτι ‹οικοδομηθη› το θυcιαcτηριον και ενεκενιcθη το αγιαcμα ωc το προτερον και ωργιcθηcαν cφοδρα	**5.1** And it came about, when the nations round about heard that the sacrificial altar was built, and the holy place was dedicated as *it had been* pre- vious*ly*, that they became very angry;

5.1 κ(αι) εγενετο S^{ca} V 64^{+}236 La$^{109+146}$ | το S* • οικοδομηθη S^{ca} V* [ωκ- V^{b} A 64^{+}236] La$^{109+146}$ | -μη S* •

---

[134] **He fortified Bethzur, to keep it.** Not "he fortified it [Mount Zion] to hold Beth-zur" (ESV); Judas did indeed hold and fortify Bethzur itself at this time, as 6.26 shows.

5.2 και ‹εβουλευcαντο› του αραι το γενος Ιακωβ τουc ονταc ‹εν μεcω αυτων› και ηρξαντο του θανατουν εν τω λαω κ(αι) εξαιρειν	**5.2** and they took counsel to do away with the race of Jacob that was in *the* midst of them; and they began to put to death among the people and do away with *them.*

5.2 εβουλευcαντο S[ca] [-ευον- V] A 64[+]236 La[109+146] | ωργιcθηcαν S* • εν μεcω / αυτων V A 64[+]236 La[109+146] | ~ [-τω S*] S[ca]

5.1–2 The restoration of Jerusalem had the same effect as it did in the time of Nehemiah (Neh 4.1, 7–8): **the nations round about** became **angry,** and fought against the revival of Israel (**the race of Jacob**). Opponents specifically mentioned in the following verses include Edomites (vv 3, 65), Ammonites (v 6), Phoenicians (v 15), and Arabs (v 39). Thus the words of Asaph the prophet were being fulfilled: "Your enemies [including Edom, Ammon, and Philistia] . . . take clever counsel against Your people . . . . They have said, Come, and let us efface them from being a nation, and the name of Israel will no longer be remembered" (Psa 83.2–7).

They began to put to death among the people. Daniel had prophesied that deliverance from the Gentiles would not be won easily; Israelites would continue to perish for "many days" during the struggle (Dan 11.33). In this world, all those who serve the Lord must be prepared to suffer tribulation (John 16.33; 2 Tim 3.12; Acts 14.22; 1 Thes 3.4; 1 Pet 5.9).

Judas defeats the Edomites and Ammonites

5.3 και επολεμει Ιουδαc προc τουc υιουc Ηcαυ εν τη Ιδουμαια την Ακραβαττηνη(ν) οτι περιεκαθηντο τον Ιc(ραη)λ και επαταξαν αυτουc πληγην μεγαλην και cυνεcτιλεν αυτουc και ελαβεν τα cκυλα αυτω(ν)	**5.3** And Judas made war against the sons of Esau in Idumea— *against* Akrabattene; for they were besieging Israel, and they smote them *with* a great injury. And he confined them, and took their plunder.

5.3 Esau (Edom, Gen 25.30; 36.1, 43) was the twin brother of Jacob (**Israel**), but their descendants were rarely at peace. "Edom . . . pursued his brother with the sword, and he destroyed his own compassions, and his anger tore perpetually, and he kept his anger constantly" (Amos 1.11).

At this particular time the Edomites were **besieging** the Israelites[135] **in Idumea** (see the notes on 4.15). Judas therefore **made war against** them, and **confined** them—that

[135] S (supported by La[109]) reads **they smote** [*epataxan*] **them with a great injury,** describing the Edomites' activities against the Israelites (cf. v 2, "they began putting to death among the people and doing away with them"). V, A, and 64[+]236 (supported by La[146]) read "he smote [*epataxen*] them with a great injury," so that the clause describes Judas's activities against the Edomites.

is, he "drove them to straits" (Geneva), forced them back, restricted their activities (as in 3.6: see the notes there).

That incident was part of the LORD's appointed judgment against Edom, which had been foretold by His prophets: "Because an age-old enmity was yours, and you gave over the sons of Israel to the hands of the sword in the time of their calamity ... I will appoint you for blood, and blood will pursue you: since you have not hated blood, therefore blood will pursue you" (Ezek 35.5–6; Mal 1.4).

Akrabattene: there was an "ascent of Akrabbim" in the territory of Judah near the border of Edom and the south end of the Dead Sea (Josh 15.1–3; Num 34.4).[136]

5.4 και εμνηcθη τηc κακιαc υιων Βαιαν οι ηcαν τω λαω ειc παγιδα και ‹ειc› cκανδαλον εν τω ενεδρευειν αυτουc εν ταιc οδοιc	**5.4** And he was mindful of the evil- doing of *the* sons of Baean, who were a trap and an obstacle to the people by ambushing them on the paths.

5.4 ειc 2° A 64⁺236 La[109] | > S V La[146] •

5.4 The expression **sons of Baean** means "people of Baean" (see the notes on 4.2). **Baean** may have been Bohan on the border between Judah and Benjamin, just west of the Dead Sea (Josh 15.6; 18.17).[137] These people were a **trap** and an **obstacle,** and so Judas **was mindful** of their **evildoing.** God's people today are likewise commanded to "watch out for those who causing the divisions and occasions of stumbling" (Rom 16.17), and to "support the weak" brethren (1 Thes 5.14) who could be deceived by them (cf. Titus 1.10–11).

5.5 και cυνεκλιcθηcαν υπ αυτου ειc τουc πυργουc και παρενεβαλεν επ αυτουc και ανεθεματιcεν αυτουc και ενεπυριcε τουc πυργουc αυτηc εν πυρι cυν παcιν τοιc ενουcιν	**5.5** And they were shut up by him into the towers, and he camped against them, and devoted them *to* *destruction.* And he set its towers on fire with fire, together with all the *people* who were within.

---

[136] Josephus also mentions a region with a similar name in Samaria (*War,* 2.235; 4.551); but this is much too far north to be called **in Idumea** (Simons §1120*bis*).

The syntax has puzzled some commentators, but is fully consistent with Greek usage. **Akrabattene** (*tēn Akrabattēnēn,* accusative) stands in apposition to **the sons of Esau** (*tous huious Ēsau,* likewise accusative), giving further information about those who were **made war against** (Viteau, *Sujet,* §285*a*). As usual in such cases (MHT 3.206; Winer §20.3a), the apposed **Akrabattene** has the article *(tēn)* to distinguish this group from other **sons of Esau in Idumea.** (Cf. also Viteau, *Sujet,* §290*b*.) Judas **made war against the sons of Esau in Idumea**—specifically, the *(tēn)* **Akrabattene** people.

[137] Simons §1121. Judas was still on the Judean side of the Jordan (cf. v 6) when he besieged **Baean** (v 5). Therefore, it could not have been Beon (Baal-meon) on the other side of the Jordan, in the territory of Reuben (Num 32.3, 38).

5.5 Judas besieged the evildoers (**shut** them **up**) in the towers of Baean,[138] and **devoted them to destruction,**[139] as the Law required when a city within Israel was taken over by idolaters (Deut 13.12–18; 20.16–18). The towers were **set . . . on fire,** and the people **within** them perished. The LORD has often sent a fire to consume His adversaries (Gen 19.24–25; Isa 29.6; Hos 8.14; Amos 1.4, 7, 10, 12; 2.2, 5; Ezek 39.6), as He did here by the hand of Judas (cf. v 44; 10.84–85; 16.10), and as He will one day do to all who defy Him (Matt 13.41–42; 2 Thes 1.7–8; 2 Pet 3.7). Truly "our God is a consuming fire" (Heb 12.29).

5.6 και διεπερασεν επι τους υιους Αμμων και ευρεν χειρα κραταιαν και λαον πολυ(ν) και χειρα ισχυρα(ν) και Τιμοθεον ηγουμενον αυτω(ν)	**5.6** And he crossed over against the sons of Ammon, and found a mighty hand and a large group of people and a strong hand, and Timothy their leader.

5.6 Another nation closely related to Israel were the **sons of Ammon** (descendants of Abraham's nephew Lot, Gen 19.36, 38; Deut 2.19), who lived across the Jordan from Judea (Jdg 10.9). They too had long been enemies of Israel (Deut 23.3–4; Jdg 3.13; 10.7; 1 Sam 14.47; 2 Chr 20.1; Neh 4.7). In the time of Judas Maccabeus, a **large group** of them were opposing Israel, **their leader** being **Timothy** (vv 11, 37).

A mighty hand. That is, a mighty company (cf. 2 Kgs 11.7, where two military companies are called "two hands," KJV mg). In the Scriptures, the term **hand** is often equivalent to "power" or "force" (Deut 8.17; Neh 1.10; Isa 50.2; 1 Pet 5.6), so that calling an army a **hand** is similar to calling it a "force" (*dunamis,* as in vv 11, 18, 38; 1.4; 3.27–28). In this verse there is a highly expressive example of the Maccabean History's most distinctive stylistic feature—repetition after an interval (see the introduction to this commentary): **a mighty hand and a large group of people and a strong hand.**[140]

5.7 και συνηψεν προς αυτους πολεμους πολλους	**5.7** And he made contact against them with many battles.

---

[138] **Its** [*autēs,* feminine] **towers** means "Baean's towers" (cf. v 4). Cities are customarily treated as feminine (v 8; 1.38; 2.8, 11; cf. Rev 21.2), and there is no other possible feminine antecedent in this context. (The NRSV marginal note to this verse is misplaced. The pronoun *autēs* is attached to the second instance of **towers** in the verse, not the first.)

[139] Greek *anethematisen* (cf. Luke 21.5) ≡ Hebrew *ḥrm,* **devoted** (in this context, **to destruction,** as in Exod 22.20; Lev 27.29); cf. TDOT 5.182, §I.2. Judas "placed them under the curse of destruction" (NJB; cf. German *Vernichtungsweihe,* LXX.DE 1.1360). The same condemnation is appointed, under the new covenant, for all those who preach a different gospel (Gal 1.8–9; cf. 1 Cor 16.22).

[140] **And a strong hand** *(kai cheira ischuran)* is present in S, V, and 64[+]236, but not in A (or in La[109+146]).

και συνετριβησαν προ προσωπου αυτου και επαταξεν αυτους	And they were shattered before his face, and he smote them,
5.8 και προκατελαβετο την Ιαζηρ κ(αι) τας θυγατερας αυτης και ‹ανεστρεψεν› εις την Ιουδαιαν	**5.8** and took hold of Jazer and its daughters; and he turned back into Judea.

5.8 ανεστρεψεν V A 64⁺236 La[109+146] | -ψαν S •

5.7 In the resulting **battles,** the Ammonites **were shattered.** The LORD had warned them that they (like the Edomites; cf. v 3) would be punished for their evil deeds—especially their evil deeds against Israel (Ezek 25.2–7; Jer 49.2–5; Amos 1.13–15). Those prophecies (like the prophecies against Edom) were now being fulfilled.

5.8 By defeating the Ammonites, Judas gained control of **Jazer,** a city in the territory of Gad, near the land of Ammon (Josh 13.24–25).[141] It had been chosen as one of the Levitical cities (Josh 21.39), and was evidently a large and prosperous settlement (Num 32.1), surrounded by attendant villages (**its daughters**—a common Hebrew expression; cf. Neh 11.25–31; BDB 123, §4).

The Israelites in Gilead ask for help

5.9 και επισυνηχθησαν ‹› τα εθνη τα εν τη Γαλααδ επι τον Ις(ραη)λ τους οντας ‹εν› τοις οριοις αυτων του εξαραι αυτους και εφυγον εις Δαθαιμα το οχυρωμα	**5.9** And the nations in Gilead gathered together against Israel—the *ones* who were in their appointed boundaries—to do away with them. And they fled into Dathema the fortress,
5.10 και απεστιλαν γραμματα προς Ιουδαν και τους αδελφους αυτου λεγοντες επισυνηγμενα εστι(ν) ‹εφ ημας› τα εθνη κυκλω ημων του εξαραι ημας	**5.10** and sent writings to Judas and his brothers, saying: “The nations round about us are gathered together to do away with us;
5.11 και ετοιμαζονται ελθειν και προκαταλαβεσθαι το οχυρωμα εις ο ‹κατεφυγομεν› και Τιμοθεος ηγειτε της δυναμεως αυτων	**5.11** and they are getting ready to come and take hold of the fortress into which we have fled; and Timothy is the leader of their force.
5.12 νυν ουν ελθω(ν) εξελου ημας εκ χιρος αυτων οτι πεπτωκεν εξ ημων πληθος	**5.12** Now therefore, coming†, take us away† out of their hand: for a multitude of us have fallen;

5.9 τα 1° V A 64⁺236 La[109+146] | ^ εις S • εν 2° V 64⁺236 | επι S A • **5.10** εφ ημας V A 64⁺236 La[109+146] | > S • **5.11** κατεφυγομεν S[ca] V A 64⁺236 La[109+146] | -γον S* • **5.13** οντες S[ca] V A 64⁺236 La[109+146] | > S* • αυτων V A 64⁺236 La[109+146] | > S •

[141] The precise location of **Jazer** remains uncertain (ABD 3.650–51).

5.13 κ(αι) παντες οι αδελφοι ημων οι ‹οντες› εν τοις Τουβιου τεθανατωνται και ηχμαλωτικασιν τας γυναικας ‹αυτων› και τα τεκνα και την αποσκευην και απωλεσαν εκει ωσι μιαν χιλιαρχιαν ανδρων	**5.13** and all our brothers who are in the *regions* of Tubias have been put to death; and they have taken captive their wives and children and equipment; and they have destroyed there about one thousand men."

5.9–12 The region where the battles of verses 6–8 had been fought—the Israelite territory immediately north of the land of Ammon—was the land of **Gilead** (Num 32.1; Deut 3.16). After Judas returned to Judea (v 8), conflict in that region broke out again—this time involving not only the Ammonites but a plurality of **nations.** Again the enemy **leader** was **Timothy** (v 6).[142] Many of the oppressed Israelites in the region now fled into **Dathema,** a fortress near Bozrah in Moab (see the notes on vv 26–35), and wrote **to Judas and his brothers** for help (as formerly the men of Jabesh in Gilead had sent for help when the Ammonites threatened them, 1 Sam 11.3).

5.13 The regions of Tubias *(tois Toubiou)* could perhaps be either "the land of Tob" (ESV), an area elsewhere associated with the Ammonites (2 Sam 10.6; Jdg 11.3, 5), or "the territory of the Tobiads" (NAB), an area east of the Jordan mentioned in Hellenistic papyri (*tē Toubiou,* CPJ 1.2d).[143]

The Israelites in Galilee also ask for help

5.14 ετι ‹αι› επιστολαι ανεγιγνωσκοντο και ιδου αγγελοι ετεροι παρεγενοντο εκ της Γαλιλαιας διερρηχοτες τα ιματια απαγγελλοντες κατα τα ρηματα ταυτα	**5.14** The letters were still being read, and, see! other messengers came out of Galilee, having torn the*ir* clothes, reporting in accordance with these words,
5.15 λεγοντες επισυνηχθαι επ αυτους εκ Πτολεμαιδος και Τυρου και Σειδωνος και ‹πασης Γαλιλαιας› αλλοφυλων του εξαναλωσαι ημας	**5.15** saying *that* against them *were* gathered *people* from Ptolemais and Tyre and Sidon and all Galilee of *the* foreigners, "to utterly consume us."

5.14 αι V A 64⁺236 | > S • **5.15** πασης Γαλιλαιας 64⁺236 La[109+146] | πασα Γαλιλαια S | πασα(ν) Γαλιλαιαν V A •

5.14–15 At the same time, **messengers** from **Galilee** came in mourning (**having torn**

[142] This war in **Gilead** against the nations led by **Timothy** is reported also in Epitome 12.10–28.

[143] Epitome 12.17 mentions in this context a group of Jewish people called *Toubianous*—which might mean either "men of Tob" (RV mg) or "Tobiads" (cf. Schwartz, *2 Maccabees,* 428–29). According to non-Biblical sources the Tobiads were an influential Israelite family east of Jordan (CPJ 1.1–2, 4–5; Josephus, *Antiquities,* 12.229–232), possibly further south than the Biblical land of Tob (NIDB 5.612); they may have had Ammonite connections (cf. Neh 2.10).

their clothes: see on 2.14; 3.47) with the news[144] that the Israelites there were being attacked by people from the Phoenician coastal cities (**Ptolemais, Tyre,** and **Sidon**) as well as by **foreigners** from within **Galilee** itself (Isa 9.1 ≡ Matt 4.15).[145]

Tyre and **Sidon** were major ancient seaports in the vicinity of Lebanon (Ezek 27.3–8; Ezra 3.7; Luke 6.17), bordering on Zebulun (Gen 49.13) and therefore close to Galilee (Mark 7.31). The LORD's prophets had foretold that they would be punished because they had "sold the children of Judah ... to the sons of the Greeks" (Joel 3.4–6). **Ptolemais** was a coastal city south of Tyre and north of Caesarea (Acts 21.7–8).

The letters[146] were still being read. God's people are sometimes "afflicted on every side" all at once (2 Cor 7.5; 4.8; 11.28; "while he was still speaking, there came also another ...", Job 1.14–19).

Judas divides his forces

5.16 ωϲ δε ηκουϲεν Ιουδαϲ και ο λαοϲ τουϲ λογουϲ τουτουϲ επιϲυνηχθη εκκληϲια μεγαλη ‹βουλευϲαϲθ(αι)› τι ποιηϲωϲιν τοιϲ αδελφοιϲ αυτων τοιϲ ουϲιν εν θλιψι και πολεμουμενοιϲ υπ αυτων	**5.16** And when Judas and the people heard these words, a great assembly gathered together, to take counsel what they should do for their brothers who were in oppression and being attacked by them.
5.17 και ειπεν Ιουδαϲ Ϲιμωνι τω αδελφω αυτου επιλεξον ϲεαυτω ανδραϲ και πορευου και ρυϲαι τουϲ αδελφουϲ τουϲ εν τη Γαλιλαια εγω δε και ‹Ιωναθαν› ο αδελφοϲ ‹μου› πορευϲομεθα ειϲ την Γαλααδειτιν	**5.17** And Judas said to Simon his brother: "Choose† men for yourself†, and go† and deliver† the brothers *who are* in Galilee. But I and Jonathan my brother, we will go into the Gilead region."
5.18 και κατελιπεν Ιωϲηπον τον του Ζαχαριου και Αζαριαν ηγουμενον του λαου μετα τω(ν) επιλοιπων τηϲ δυναμεωϲ εν τη Ιουδαια ειϲ τηρηϲι(ν)	**5.18** And he left Joseph the *son* of Zechariah, and Azariah, a leader of the people, with the rest of the force, in Judea, to keep *it*;

5.16 βουλευϲαϲθ(αι) S^{cb1} V [-λευεϲθαι A] 64^{+}236 La$^{109+146}$ | > S* • **5.17** Ιωναθαν V A 64^{+}236 La$^{109+146}$ | Ιωαναθαϲ S • μου S^{ca} V A 64^{+}236 La$^{109+146}$ | αυτου S* •

---

[144] The messengers' report was **in accordance with** *(kata)* certain **words** (consistent with them, similar to them: see the notes on 1.51). This could mean either (a) that it resembled the preceding **words** from Gilead in vv 10–13 ("messengers arrived from Galilee . . . bearing similar news," NJB; cf. 1.51), or (b) that it resembled the following **words** in v 15, which summarize its content ("messengers [came] from Galilee . . . bringing a report to the following effect," APOT; cf. 10.51).

[145] **Against them were gathered people ... "to consume us."** The narrative increases in urgency as it unfolds, moving from indirect speech to direct speech (like Acts 1.4).

[146] The plural form **letters** *(epistolai)* often designates a single document (12.5, 7, 19; 14.20).

5.19 και ενετιλατο αυτοιϲ λεγων προϲτητε του λαου τουτου και μη ϲυναψηται πολεμον προϲ τα εθνη εωϲ του επιϲτρεψαι ημαϲ	**5.19** and he commanded them, saying: "Direct[pl] this people, and do not make contact[pl] in battle against the nations, until we have returned."
5.20 κ(αι) εμεριϲθηϲαν ‹Cιμωνι› ανδρεϲ τριϲχιλιοι του πορευθηναι ειϲ την Γαλιλαιαν Ιουδα δε ανδρεϲ ‹‚η´› ειϲ την Γαλααδειτι(ν)	**5.20** And three thousand men were apportioned to Simon, to go into Galilee; and to Judas eight thousand men, *to go* into the Gilead region.

5.20 Cιμωνι V A 236 La[109+146] | -ν S • ‚η´ S[ca] V A 236 La[109+146] | η´ ϛ´ η´ γ´ S* •

5.16–20 A great assembly gathered together to take counsel, just as other important decisions were made by the whole **assembly** under both the old covenant (2 Chr 30.23) and the new (Acts 6.5; 15.22).

To take counsel what they should do for their brothers who were in oppression. They did not think of their own security, but of what they could **do** "on behalf of [their] brothers" (v 32; cf. Luke 3.11; 2 Cor 8.13–14). "Whoever has the world's means of life, and sees his brother in need and closes his bowels against him, how does the love of God remain in him? Little children, let us not love with word or tongue, but in deed and truth" (1 Jn 3.17–18). "One who shuts his ear from the outcry of the weak will likewise call out and not be answered" (Prov 21.13; cf. Matt 25.31–46).

The forces were divided as follows:

- **Judas** took his brother **Jonathan,** with **eight thousand men,** to rescue the people in **Gilead.**
- At the same time, their brother **Simon** went with another **three thousand men** into **Galilee.**
- The **rest of the force** was left **in Judea** under the leadership[147] of **Joseph the son of Zechariah** and **Azariah** (who were not related to Judas and his brothers; v 62).

Compare the division of the Lord's forces on other occasions for earthly or spiritual battle (1 Sam 13.2; 2 Sam 10.9–12; Mark 6.7; Luke 10.1; cf. 1 Thes 3.1–2; Acts 15.39–41). Notice also Judas's generosity: he himself took the task that appeared to require the larger army, but he gave his brother the first choice of men (as Abraham had given his nephew the first choice of land, Gen 13.8–9).

Simon delivers the people in Galilee

5.21 και επορευθη Cιμων ειϲ την Γαλιλαιαν και ϲυνηψεν πολεμουϲ	**5.21** And Simon went into Galilee, and he made contact in many battles

147 S, V, and A (supported by La[109+146]) describe Azariah as **a leader** *(hēgoumenon)* of the people. 64+236 describe both Joseph and Azariah as "among the leaders" *(tōn hēgoumenōn)* of the people. Other manuscripts have still other readings.

πολλους προς τα εθνη και cυνετριβη τα εθνη απο προcωπου αυτου	against the nations. And the nations were shattered before his face,
5.22 και εδιωξεν αυτους εως της πυλης Πτολεμαιδος και επεcον εκ των εθνων εις τριcχιλιους ανδρας και ελαβον τα cκυλα αυτων	**5.22** and he pursued them up to the gate of Ptolemais. And up to three thousand men from the nations fell; and they took their plunder.
5.23 και ‹παρελαβεν› τους εκ της Γαλιλαιας και εν Αρβανοις cυν ταις γυναιξιν και τοις τεκνοις και παντα οcα ην αυτοις και ηγαγεν εις τη(ν) Ιουδαιαν μετ ευφροcυνης μεγαλης	**5.23** And he took the *men* from Galilee and *those* in Arbatta, together with the women and the children, and all *the things* that were theirs; and he brought *them* into Judea with great gladness.

5.23 παρελαβεν A 64⁺236 La[109+146] | -βον S V •

5.21–23 Simon defeated the **nations** in **Galilee,** and **brought** the oppressed Israelite families (**men, women,** and **children,** with **all** their possessions,[148] cf. 1 Sam 30.18–19) to safety in **Judea** (cf. v 45) with **great gladness** (cf. Psa 126.1–3).

Arbatta (spelled variously in the manuscripts[149]) cannot be definitely identified.[150] The context shows it to be a region (or, less probably, a town) near but not in Galilee.

Judas and Jonathan go to Gilead

5.24 και Ιουδας ο Μακκαβαιος και Ιωναθαν ο αδελφος αυτου διεβηcα(ν) τον Ιορδανην και επορευθηcαν οδον τριων ημερω(ν) εν τη ερημω	**5.24** And Judas Maccabeus and Jonathan his brother went over the Jordan, and *for* three days they went *on the* path in the desert;

[148] **All the things that were theirs.** The Greek is *panta hosa ēn autois:* "all [thing]s, as many as [there] were to them."

[149] The customary English form **Arbatta** derives from *Arbattois,* the spelling found in f^{120} (supported by Vg). Other attested spellings include *Arbanois,* S*; *errabant,* La[109]; *Arbaktois,* S[ca] and A; *Arbatnois,* V*; *Arbatanois,* V[b]; *Adrabuttois,* 64⁺236; *'rdbt,* 7h7; *Nhrbtn,* 7a1; *Grabbatis,* La[146]. Some copyists appear to have confused this name with Akrabattene (v 3) and/or with the Nabateans (v 25).

[150] Elitzur, *Ancient Place Names in the Holy Land,* 77, n. 7. If the form **Arbatta** *(Arbattois)* is correct—which is improbable—it might conceivably be either the "Aruboth" of 1 Kgs 4.10 (a place of unspecified location somewhere in Israel; cf. ABD 1.465–67) or else a transliteration of the Hebrew word *'rbwt,* "plains" (as in 2 Kgs 25.5), which in this context would refer to the plain near the Jordan south of the Sea of Galilee (Chinneroth; Josh 11.2; Deut 3.17). Cf. Knabenbauer 112. But when the Scriptures refer to that plain, they always use the singular form of the word, *'rbh* ("Arabah"; cf. HALOT 2.880, §2). The form *Arbanois,* which has stronger textual support (S* and La[109]), might suggest Arabbuna west of Bethshan (Abel, *GP,* 2.176, 248)—but that is a town, whereas the present passage is apparently referring to a region. Josephus elsewhere mentions a Narbata near Caesarea (*War,* 2.291, 509; cf. Simons §1132).

5.25 και συνηντησαν τοις ‹Ναβαταιοις› και απηντησαν αυτοις ‹ιρηνικως› και διηγησαντο αυτοις παντα τα συνβαντα τοις αδελφοις αυτων εν τη Γαλααδειτι	**5.25** and they met with the Nabateans. And they met them peacefully, and they told them all the *things* that had happened to their brothers in the Gilead region;
5.26 και οτι πολλοι εξ αυτων συνιλημμενοι εισιν εις Βοσορα και Βοσορ ‹και› εν Αλεμοις κ(αι) Κασφω Μακεδ κ(αι) ‹Καρναειν› αυται αι πολεις οχυραι και μεγαλαι	**5.26** and that "Many of them are shut inside Bozrah and Bezer, and in Alema, and Casphon, Maked, and Karnaim" (these cities *were* fortified and great),
5.27 και εν ταις ‹λοιπαις› πολεσιν της Γαλααδειτιδος εισιν συνειλημμενοι εις αυριον τασσονται παρεμβαλλειν επι τα οχυρωματα και καταλαβεσθε και εξαραι παντας τουτους εν ημερα μια	**5.27** "and they are shut up in the remaining cities of the Gilead region. Tomorrow they have assigned to camp against the fortresses and take hold of *them*, and to do away with all these *people* in one day."

5.25 Ναβαταιοις A [-ττ- 64⁺236] La[109] 7h7 | Αναβαταις οι S | Αναβατταιοις V | *ascensoribus* La[146] • ιρηνικως S[ca] V A 64⁺236 La[109+146] | -κοις S* • **5.26** και 3° 64⁺236 La[109] | > S V A La[146] • Καρναειν [-νειν A] 64⁺236 La[109[+146]] | -ναιδ S V • **5.27** λοιπαις V A 64⁺236 La[109+146] | αλλαις S •

5.24–25 Judas Maccabeus and Jonathan, leading their forces into Gilead (**over the Jordan**), were met **peacefully** by the **Nabateans,** people who lived in the southern region across the Jordan from Judea (9.33, 35). The Nabateans are not mentioned in the Hebrew Scriptures, so they were apparently recent arrivals in the region, and there is no reason to think that they were as closely related to the Israelites as many of the older neighboring nations; yet, unlike the others, they treated the Israelites as friends (9.35). "There is a friend who is more attached than a brother" (Prov 18.24; cf. Mark 10.28; John 7.5).

5.26–27 The Nabateans reported that **many** of Israel's enemies[151] in **the Gilead region** were in various **fortified cities.**

Bozrah, a city of Moab (Jer 48.24), was probably the one closest to the Jordan, since it was the one that Judas and his companions attacked first (v 28).[152]

---

[151] **Them** (the people who were **inside Bozrah and Bezer . . . and Casphon, Maked, and Karnaim**) were not the Israelites but their enemies (as vv 28, 36, 41 show). The Israelites were in the fortress of Dathema (vv 9, 29, 31–32).

[152] **Bozrah** was also the name of two other cities. One was south of the Dead Sea in Edom (Jer 49.13, 22; Isa 63.1; 34.6; Amos 1.12); but the Judeans would not have crossed the Jordan (v 24) to reach that. The other was far north in Bashan (it is not mentioned in the Hebrew Scriptures, but flourished during Roman times: Abel, *GP,* 2.286–87; ISBE 1.538–39, §3; ABD 1.775–76, §3). But it is most unlikely that Judas would go first (v 28) to a city so far north,

Bezer, in the territory of Reuben, was a city large enough to have accompanying villages, and had been chosen as both a city of refuge and a Levitical city (Deut 4.43; Josh 20.8; 21.36).[153]

Alema,[154] **Casphon,**[155] and **Maked** have not been identified. **Casphon** and **Maked** were located somewhere near Bezer (v 36).

The name "Ashteroth-karnaim" (Gen 14.5) suggests that **Karnaim** was either the same as, or near, the city of Ashtaroth still further north (in the territory of Manasseh), which had been a principal city of the pre-Israelite kingdom of Bashan, and was one of the appointed Levitical cities (Deut 1.4; Josh 12.4; 1 Chr 6.71). Judas and his companions, moving from south to north, would reach Karnaim last (vv 43–44).

They capture the cities from Bozrah to Karnaim

5.28 και απεστρεψεν Ιουδας και	**5.28** And Judas and his company
η παρεμβολη αυτου οδο(ν)	suddenly turned away *on the* path
εις την ερημον Βοσορα ‹αφνω› και	into the desert to Bozrah. And he
κατελαβετο την πολιν και απεκτινε	took hold of the city, and killed every
παν αρσενικο(ν) εν στοματι ρομφαιας	male with *the* mouth of *the* sword,
και ελαβεν παντα τα σκυλα αυτων	and took all their plunder.
και ‹ενεπρησεν› αυτην πυρι	And he set it on fire with fire.

5.28 αφνω S^{cb1} A 64^{+}236 La$^{109+146}$ | αφων S* V • ενεπρησεν V A 64^{+}236 La$^{109+146}$ | -σαν S •

5.28 Judas and his company acted **suddenly** to deliver their brethren. First they captured **Bozrah** in Moab. In the case of a hostile foreign city like this, the commands of the old covenant Law required **every male** to be **killed** and the city to be plundered (Deut 20.10–15).

---

then double back to places that he had already passed before reaching it (e.g., to Bezer, v 36), and finally proceed north once again (to Karnaim, vv 43–44); cf. SDB 1.319, 322, §2.

[153] **Bezer** in Reuben is sometimes identified with the Bozrah in Moab (Abel, *GP,* 2.287, "Boṣra (3)"), but the present passage shows that there were indeed two separate cities with these names in this general region.

[154] **Alema** might possibly be the Helam mentioned in 2 Sam 10.16–17 (it too was a place east of the Jordan). **And in Alema** is the reading of 64^{+}236 and La^{109}, whereas S, V, and A (supported by La^{146}) read simply "in Alema." In the former text, **Alema** is undoubtedly separate from Bezer; in the latter text, it might be either separate from Bezer or else the region in which Bezer was located ("Bosor in Alema," REB).

[155] **Casphon.** The name occurs only in vv 26 and 36. The principal manuscripts spell its ending sometimes as *-ōn* (S in v 36 and V in v 36, supported by La^{109} in both verses), sometimes as *-ō* (S* in v 26 and V in v 26, supported by La^{146} in both verses). This suggests that the Hebrew name may have ended in *-ōh* (which often becomes *-ōn* in Greek; "Solomon" is a familiar example). Spellings in other manuscripts include *-ōr* (64 in both verses; S^{ca} in v 26 and A in v 26) and *-ōth* (A in v 36).

5.29 κ(αι) απηρεν εκειθεν νυκτος και επορευοντο εως επι το οχυρωμα	**5.29** And he moved away from there *by* night, and they went up until *they were* close to the fortress.
5.30 και εγενετο εωθινη ηραν τους οφθαλμους αυτων και ιδου λαος πολυς ‹ου ουκ ην αριθμος› αιροντες κλιμακας και μηχανας καταλαβεσθαι το οχυρωμα και επολεμουν αυτους	**5.30** And daybreak came. They lifted up their eyes, and, see! a large group of people, who could not be numbered, lifting up ladders and devices to take hold of the fortress; and they were making war against them.
5.31 και ειδεν Ιουδας οτι ηρκται ο πολεμος και η κραυγη της πολεως ανεβη εως ουρανου η σαλπιγξ και κραυγη μεγαλη	**5.31** And Judas saw that the battle had begun, and the outcry of the city went up to Heaven—the trumpet and great outcry;
5.32 και ειπεν τοις ανδρασιν της δυναμεως πολεμησατε σημερον υπερ των αδελφω(ν) υμων	**5.32** and he said to the men of *his* force: "Make war^{pl} today on behalf of your^{pl} brothers."
5.33 και εξηλθεν εν τρισιν αρχαις εξοπισθεν αυτων και εσαλπισαν ταις σαλπιξιν ‹› κ(αι) εβοησαν εν προσευχη	**5.33** And he went out from behind them, *divided* under three commands; and they trumpeted with the trumpets, and called out in prayer.

5.30 ου ουκ ην αριθμος S^{cb1} V [ους ουκ ην αρ- A] La$^{109+146}$ | ουκ ην αυτοις αρ- 64^{+}236 | > S* • **5.33** σαλπιξιν S^{ca} V A 64^{+}236 La$^{109+146}$ | + και εβοησαν ταις σαλπιγξιν S* •

5.29–30 Still traveling in haste (at **night,** like Joshua: Josh 10.6–9), Judas and his companions reached **the fortress** mentioned in verse 9 (where its name was given as Dathema). They found that it was already being actively assaulted, with scaling **ladders** and **devices to take hold of the fortress.** In this book, the term **devices** *(mēchanai)* often refers specifically to engines of war used against besieged cities (6.20, 31, 51–52; 9.64, 67; 11.20; 15.25)—although the word is also employed in other senses (6.37; 13.29). Compare the Babylonians' siege engines against Jerusalem (Ezek 21.22).

5.31 The outcry of the city went up to Heaven—the trumpet[156] and great outcry. As elsewhere (v 33; 3.54; 4.40), **the trumpet** summoned to war not only the people (1 Cor 14.8), but also the Lord in **Heaven** (Num 10.9–10). "The LORD is near ... to all those who call on Him in faithfulness ... and He hears their cry for help, and He saves

[156] **The trumpet** *(hē salpigx)* is the reading of S* (a simple nominative in apposition to **the outcry** earlier in the verse; cf. Robertson 399). V and A read "with trumpets" *(salpigxin);* S^{ca} and 64^{+}236 read "and a trumpet" *(kai salpigx).* The rendering in La$^{109+146}$ is "as a trumpet" *(sicut tuba),* but that is probably a translator's decision to turn a (supposed) metaphor into a simile (no known Greek manuscripts have an "as" at this point). At any rate, the Latin translator certainly worked from a Greek text in which **trumpet** was singular and was not preceded by "and."

them" (Psa 145.18–19). And He does so without delay, "speedily" (Luke 18.8), "at the turning of the morning" (Psa 46.5).

5.33 Judas and his companions[157] likewise **trumpeted with the trumpets and called out in prayer**—just as brethren in Christ "strive together" in prayer with those who are praying (Rom 15.30; 2 Cor 1.10–11; Eph 6.18–19; Col 4.12).

5.34 και επεγνω η παρεμβολη Τιμοθεου οτι Μακκαβαιος εστιν και εφυγον απο προσωπου αυτου και επαταξεν αυτους πληγην μεγαλην και επεσον εξ αυτων εν εκινη τη ημερα εις ‹οκτακισχιλιους› ανδρας	**5.34** And Timothy's company knew that it was Maccabeus, and they fled from his face. And he smote them *with* a great injury; and up to eight thousand men of them fell in that day.

5.34 οκτακισχιλιους S[cb1] V A 64[+]236 La[109+146] \| τρισχ- δεκα S* •

5.34 The enemy **fled** because they **knew that it was Maccabeus.** His very name was becoming a terror to the nations (3.25–26), as the name of David had been (1 Chr 14.17), and as the name of Jesus will be (Php 2.9–10).

5.35 και απεκλινεν εις Μαφα και επολεμησε(ν) αυτην και κατελαβετο αυτην και απεκτινεν πα(ν) αρσενικον αυτης και ελαβεν τα σκυλα αυτης και ενεπρησεν αυτην εν πυρι	**5.35** And he turned aside unto Maapha, and made war against it and took hold of it. And he killed every male of it, and took its plunder, and set it on fire with fire.

5.35 Next Judas and his company **turned aside to Maapha,** a place not previously mentioned (unless it was Alema, v 26).[158] It was treated like Bozrah (v 28): **every male** was **killed** and the **plunder** was taken, after which the city was **set … on fire.**

5.36 εκειθεν απηρεν και προκατελαβετο την Χασφων Μακεδ και Βοσορ και τας λοιπας πολεις της Γαλααδειτιδος	**5.36** From there he moved away, and took hold of Casphon, Maked, and Bezer, and the remaining cities of the Gilead region.

---

[157] **Divided under three commands.** The Greek text has *en trisin archais* ("in three rulerships").

[158] In verse 26 all the ancient manuscripts have "Alema" or something similar, but the name given in verse 35 varies considerably. S, V, and A have *Maapha* (spelled *Mapha* in S). La[146] has *Masfa.* La[109] has *Mala,* and 7a1 has *M'l.* Among the Antiochene manuscripts, 93 has *Lema,* 19 has *Alema,* and 64[+]236 have *Salema* (the *s* being derived from the end of the previous word, *eis*); 7h7 has *'lym.* Some manuscripts of Josephus (*Antiquities,* 12.340) have *Maaphēn;* others have *Malla* or *Mella.* In ancient Greek uncial script, *M* looked like *LL* or *LA* or *AL* or *AA;* a word containing any sequence of such letters could easily be misread. Mizpeh in Gilead (Jdg 11.29) was too far north to be the place mentioned at this particular point. It might just possibly have been Mephaath near Bezer, which was originally in the territory of Reuben (1 Chr 6.78–79) but was later reckoned as a city of Moab and was destined for judgment (Jer 48.20–24).

5.36 Apparently moving north, they captured (among other **cities**) **Casphon, Maked,** and **Bezer**—by which time they were certainly within the borders of Israel (cf. v 26).

5.37 μετα δε τα ρηματα ταυτα	**5.37** But after these things
συνηγαγεν Τιμοθεος παρεμβολην	Timothy gathered another company,
αλλην και παρενεβαλεν	and camped
κατα προcωπον Ραφων εκ	against *the* face of Raphon, across
‹περαν› του χιμαρρου	*the* other side of the storm-brook.

5.37 περαν V A 64^{+}236 La$^{109+146}$ | προcωπου S •

5.37 Like Lysias (see the notes on 4.35), **Timothy** learned nothing from his previous defeats (vv 6–7, 34). He **gathered another company** and opposed the Israelites again. "If you pound a fool in a mortar with a pestle in the midst of the crushed grain, his foolishness will not turn aside from him" (Prov 27.22; cf. Isa 1.5; Jer 13.23).

This time, Timothy **camped** opposite (**against the face of**) **Raphon** (a place not mentioned elsewhere), just **across** a **storm-brook**[159] from Judas and his company.

5.38 και απεcτιλεν Ιουδαc	**5.38** And Judas sent *men*
καταcκοπευcαι την παρεμβολην	to spy out the camp;
και απηγγειλαν αυτω λεγοντεc	and they reported to him, saying:
επιcυνηγμενα ειcιν προc αυτον	"All the nations round about us
παντα τα εθνη τα κυκλω ημων	are gathered to him—
δυναμιc πολλη cφοδρα	a very great force.
5.39 και Αραβαc μεμιcθωνται ειc	**5.39** And they have hired Arabs to
βοηθιαν αυτοιc και ‹παρενβαλλουcιν›	help them, and they are camping
περαν του χιμαρρου	*on the* other side of the storm-brook,
ετοιμοι του ελθειν επι cε	ready to come over against you[†]
ειc πολεμον και επορευθη Ιουδαc	for war." And Judas went
ειc cυναντηcιν αυτω(ν)	to meet them.

5.39 παρενβαλλουcιν S^{ca} V* A La$^{109+146}$ | -αλου- S* V^{b} | -ενεβαλον 64^{+}236 •

5.39 They have hired Arabs to help them. Arabs had also been among the enemies of Israel in the time of Nehemiah (Neh 4.7; 2.19; 6.1). At a later time, however, Arabs (either Jews or proselytes) would be among the "devout men" who gathered in Jerusalem on the Day of Pentecost (Acts 2.5, 11).

5.40 και ειπεν Τιμοθεοc	**5.40** And Timothy said
τοιc αρχουcιν τηc δυναμεωc αυτου	to the commanders of his force,

---

[159] A **storm-brook** (*cheimarro[u]s,* John 10.22) is a wadi (REB)—a stream that flows *(rheō)* only at the times of year when there are storms (*cheimōn,* Acts 27.20; Matt 16.3); in German, a *Giessbach* (Zöckler). The Hebrew equivalent is *nḥl,* which can be anything from an overflowing stream to a dry riverbed, depending on the recent weather (Job 6.15; Gen 26.19; 1 Kgs 17.7; 2 Kgs 3.16–17; Jer 47.2; Psa 78.20; 104.10); cf. Stanley, *Sinai and Palestine,* 505–07, §38.

εν τω εγγιζει(ν) Ιουδαν και την παρεμβολην αυτου επι τον χιμαρρουν του υδατος εαν διαβη προς ημας προτερος ου δυνηcομεθα υποcτηναι αυτον οτι δυναμενος δυνηcεται προς ημας	when Judas and his camp *were* coming near the storm-brook of water: "If he should go over to us first, we will not be able to stand before him: for, being able, he will be able *to stand* against us;
5.41 εαν δε δειλανθη και παρενβαλη περαν του ποταμου διαπεραcομεν προς αυτον και δυνηcομεθα προς αυτο(ν)	**5.41** but if he should be terrified and camp *on the* other side of the river, we will cross over to him, and we will be able *to stand* against him."
5.42 ωc δε ηγγιcεν Ιουδας επι τον χιμαρρουν του υδατος εcτηcεν τουc γραμματειc του λαου επι του χιμαρρου και ενετιλατο αυτοιc λεγων μη αφητε παντα αν(θρωπ)ον παρεμβαλλειν αλλα ερχεcθωcα(ν) παντες ειc τον πολεμον	**5.42** But as Judas came near the storm-brook of water, he stood the scribes of the people at the storm-brook, and commanded them, saying: "Do not allow[pl] any person to camp, but let them all come to the battle."
5.43 και διεπεραcεν επ αυτουc προτερος και πας ο λαος οπιcθεν αυτου και cυνετριβηcαν προ προcωπου αυτων ‹παντα› τα εθνη και ερριψα(ν) τα οπλα αυτων και εφυγον ειc το τεμενος εν Καρναιν	**5.43** And he crossed over first against them, and all the people behind him. And all the nations were shattered before their face, and threw away their weapons, and fled into the heathen temple in Karnaim.

5.43 παντα V A 64*236 La^{109} \| > S La^{146} •

5.40–43 Timothy hoped that he might be able to defeat the Israelites if they were **terrified** and remained **on the other side of the river.** But Judas himself **crossed over** the storm-brook **first,** with **all** his army **behind him;** none of them were allowed to stay behind the brook. In our conflict with our great adversary the devil, we are not to "shrink back to destruction" (Heb 10.39), but to resist him actively (Jas 4.7; 1 Pet 5.8–9) and "fight the good fight of the faith" (1 Tim 6.12; 1.18; cf. 1 Cor 9.26–27).

Again Timothy's forces **were shattered** and **fled**—this time into a **heathen temple** (cf. 1.47)[160] in the city of **Karnaim** (see the notes on v 26). But false gods cannot deliver even themselves (Isa 46.2), let alone those who trust in them (Isa 28.15–17).

5.44 και προκατελαβοντο την πολιν και το τεμενος ενεπυριcαν εν πυρι cυν παcιν τοιc εν αυτω και ετροπωθη Καρναιν	**5.44** And they took hold of the city, and set fire to the heathen temple with fire, together with all the *people* in it. And Karnaim was overturned,

[160] The Maccabean Epitome states that it was a temple of the goddess Atargatis (Epitome 12.26), a Syrian equivalent of Ashtoreth (cf. ISBE 1.348). The name "Ashteroth-karnaim" (Gen 14.5) confirms that Ashtoreth (1 Kgs 11.5) was indeed worshiped in this region.

και ουκ ηδυναντο ετι υποστηναι κατα προσωπον Ιουδα	and they were not able to stand *any* more against *the* face of Judas.

5.44 Judas and his men captured **the city** and **set fire to the heathen temple . . . together with all the people in it,** in accordance with the Law (see the notes on v 5).

They were not able to stand any more against the face of Judas. The LORD had promised the Israelites that, "if, keeping, you will keep all this command . . . to do it, to love the LORD your God, to walk in all His ways . . . no one will be able to stand before you" (Deut 11.22–25; 7.24; Josh 1.5).

They capture Ephron and return to Jerusalem

5.45 και συνηγαγεν Ιουδας παντα Ις(ραη)λ τους εν ⸤τη⸥ Γαλααδειτιδι απο μικρου εως μεγαλου και τας γυναικας αυτω(ν) και τα τεκνα αυτω(ν) και την αποσκευην παρεμβολην μεγαλην σφοδρα ελθειν εις γην Ιουδα	**5.45** And Judas gathered together all Israel who *were* in the Gilead region, from little up to great, and their wives and their children and equipment, a very great company, to come into *the* land of Judah.

5.45 τη S^{ca} V A $64^{+}236$ | τω S* •

5.45 As Simon did in Galilee (v 23), **Judas gathered together all** the endangered Israelites **in the Gilead region**—men, women, and **children,** with their belongings (**equipment**)—to bring them to safety in the **land of Judah.**

5.46 και ηλθον εως Εφρων και αυτη η πολις μεγαλη επι της οδου ⸤οχυρα⸥ σφοδρα ουκ η(ν) εκκλιναι απ αυτης δεξιαν η αριστερα(ν) αλλ η δια μεσου αυτης πορευεσθαι	**5.46** And they came up to Ephron. And this city *was* great, on the path, fortified very much. He was not *able* to turn aside from it *to* right or left, but rather, *he had* to go through its midst.
5.47 και απεκλειcαν αυτους οι εκ της πολεως και ενεφραξαν τας πυλας λιθοις	**5.47** And the *people* from the city shut them out, and closed up the gates with stones.
5.48 και απεστιλεν προς αυτους Ιουδας λογοις ιρηνικοις λεγω(ν) διελευcομεθα δια της γης cου ⸤του⸥ απελθειν εις την γην ⸤ημων⸥ και ουδις κακοποιηcει υμας πλην τοις ποσιν παρελευcομεθα και ουκ ηβουλοντο ανοιξαι αυτω	**5.48** And Judas sent to them with peaceful words, saying: "We will go through your† land, to go away into our land, and no one will do *any* evil to you[pl]; we will only go past on *our* feet." And they were not willing to open up to him.
5.49 και ⸤επεταξεν⸥ Ιουδας ⸤⸥ κηρυξαι εν τη παρεμβολη του παρεμβαλειν εκαστον εν ω εστιν ⸤τοπω⸥	**5.49** And Judas ordered a proclamation to be made in the company to camp, each in *the* place in which he was.

5.50 και παρενεβαλον οι ανδρες της δυναμεως κ(αι) ˻επολεμηcαν˼ την πολιν ολην την ημεραν εκεινην και ολην την νυκτα και παρεδοθη η πολις εν χιρι αυτου	**5.50** And the men of the force camped, and made war against the city, that whole day and the whole night. And the city was given up in*to* his hand;
5.51 και απωλεςε(ν) παν αρcενικον εν cτοματι ρομφαιας και εξεριζωcεν αυτην και ελαβεν τα cκυλα αυτης και διηλθεν δια της πολεως επανω των απεκτανμενων	**5.51** and he destroyed every male with *the* mouth of *the* sword; and he uprooted it, and took its plunder, and went through the city over the *people* who had been killed.

5.46 οχυρα S^{ca} V $64^{+}236$ $La^{109+146}$ | -ας S | ιcχυρα A • **5.48** του V A $64^{+}236$ | > S • ημων S^{ca} V A $64^{+}236$ $La^{109+146}$ | υμ- S* • **5.49** επεταξεν S^{ca} V A $64^{+}236$ $La^{109+146}$ | επατ- S* • Ιουδας V A $64^{+}236$ | + του S • τοπω S^{cb1} V A $64^{+}236$ $La^{109+146}$ | τρο- S* • **5.50** επολεμηcαν V A $64^{+}236$ La^{109} | -cεν S La^{146} •

5.46–51 Ephron,[161] a city that could not be bypassed, “did not remember to do lovingkindness” to those in need (Psa 109.16). It would not let the Israelites continue on their journey—in spite of the **peaceful words** that Judas had sent to its inhabitants. Therefore it was treated like Bozrah (v 28) and Maapha (v 35): **every male** was **destroyed,** and the city was plundered. Sihon, king of Heshbon, had responded similarly to Moses’ peaceful words many hundreds of years earlier, and had similarly perished (Deut 2.26–35).

The Lord’s judgments are designed to warn others who rebel against Him, in order that they might be brought to repentance (Deut 13.11; 17.13; 19.20; cf. Josh 2.9–13). Yet the cities successively attacked by Judas did not heed those warnings. Each of them seemed to think it could escape the fate of its predecessors (Isa 47.6–7; Ezek 23.10–11; Jer 3.8). But none of them did (cf. Luke 13.1–5; Rom 11.20–22).

5.52 και διεβηcα(ν) τον Ιορδανην εις το παιδιον το μεγα κατα προcωπο(ν) Βαιθcαν	**5.52** And they went over the Jordan into the great level place against *the* face of Bethshan.

5.52 Crossing the **Jordan,** the Israelites reached the **great level place** opposite (**against the face of**) **Bethshan** (Bethshean), a city in the lowland regions of western Manasseh, not far from Megiddo and Jezreel (Josh 17.11, 16; Jdg 1.27; 1 Chr 7.29). Thus they were still in northern Israel, and would have a considerable distance to travel before they could reach the land of Judah (v 53).[162]

---

[161] Little can be said about the location of this **Ephron** except that it was somewhere east of the Jordan (cf. v 52). There was at least one other Ephron, which was west of the Jordan, on the border of Judah (Josh 15.9; cf. 2 Chr 13.19; John 11.54).

[162] The return via Bethshan to Jerusalem is reported also in Epitome 12.29–31 (where Bethshan is called by its Hellenic name, Scythopolis).

5.53 και ην Ιουδας επισυναγων τους εσχατιζοντας και παρακαλων τον λαον κατα πασαν την οδον εως ‹ηλθον› εις γην Ιουδα	**5.53** And Judas *kept* gathering together those who were coming last, and encouraging the people on all the path, until they came into *the* land of Judah.
5.54 και ανεβησαν εις ορος Σιων εν ευφροσυνη και χαρα και προσηγαγον ολοκαυτωματα οτι ουκ επεσεν εξ αυτων ουθεις εως του επιστρεψαι εν ιρηνη	**5.54** And they went up to Mount Zion with gladness and joy, and presented whole burnt offerings: for no one at all of them fell, until they *had* returned in peace.

5.53 ηλθον 64[+]236 La[109] | -θεν S V A La[146] •

5.53–54 Judas kept **encouraging the people** and **gathering together those who were coming last,** so that **no one at all of them fell,** and they all reached **Mount Zion** safely **with gladness and joy.** Our Shepherd does not want even one star, or one sheep, to be lost (Isa 40.26; Luke 15.4–7). He "wants all people to be saved" (1 Tim 2.4), "not wanting any to perish, but all to make room for repentance" (2 Pet 3.9). Jesus "guarded" his disciples during his time on earth, "and not one of them perished, except the son of destruction" (John 17.12; cf. 1 Cor 15.8–9). Those who are in the church are commanded to "encourage those who are fainthearted, support those who are weak, be longsuffering toward all" (1 Thes 5.14), so that they might all enter the heavenly city together: "Make the weak hands strong, and make the unsteady knees firm. Say to those who are faint of heart, Be strong . . . . And the ransomed of the LORD will return, and come to Zion with singing, and age-long joy will be on their head; gladness and joy will reach them, and sorrow and sighing will flee away" (Isa 35.3–4, 10).

If God's people endure their long journey without falling (Isa 5.27), all the thanks are due to Him, not to themselves (Psa 37.24; 94.18; 145.14). Moses' officers made a freewill offering to the LORD when they found that not one of them had fallen in battle (Num 31.48–50), and Judas's people **presented whole burnt offerings** to the LORD because not one of them had fallen on their long journey (cf. Psa 107.22).

Joseph and Azariah are defeated in Judea

5.55 και εν ταις ημεραις ‹› αις ην Ιουδας και Ιωναθαν εν γη Γαλααδ και Σιμων ο αδελφος αυτου εν τη Γαλιλαια κατα προσωπον Πτολεμαιδος	**5.55** And in the days when Judas and Jonathan were in *the* land of Gilead, and Simon his brother *was* in Galilee against *the* face of Ptolemais,
5.56 ηκουσεν Ιωσηφ ο του Ζαχαριου και ‹Αζαριας› αρχοντες της δυναμεως των ανδραγαθιων και του πολεμου οια εποιησαν	**5.56** Joseph the *son* of Zechariah, and Azariah, *the* commanders of the force, heard of the manly good deeds and the war, such *things* as they had done.

5.57 και ειπον ποιηcωμεν και αυτοι εαυτοιc ονομα ‹και› πορευθωμεν πολεμηcαι προc τα εθνη τα κυκλω ημω(ν)	**5.57** And they said: "Let us ourselves also make a name for *our*selves; and let us go to make war against the nations that *are* round about us."

5.55 αιc V A La^{109} | > 64^{+}236 | ^ εν S La^{146} • **5.56** Αζαριαc V 64 La$^{109+146}$ 7h7 7a1 | Ζαχαριαc S A 236 • **5.57** και 3° V A 64^{+}236 La$^{109+146}$ | > S •

5.55–57 Mattathias had exhorted his children to "act manfully"—that is, to act maturely, not childishly (see the notes on 2.64). Judas, Jonathan, and Simon were now doing what their father had asked: they were doing **manly good deeds** (9.22; 10.15).

Joseph and **Azariah,** who had been left as **commanders of the force** in Judea (vv 18–19), now decided to do the same thing ("to do manly good deeds," v 61). But they chose to imitate only the outward action (**war against the nations**), not the heart. Judas, Jonathan, and Simon made war to "deliver [their] brothers" (vv 17, 32), whereas Joseph and Azariah made war to **make a name for** themselves (as the Syrian commander Seron had sought to do, 3.14). And it is by the heart that God judges (1 Sam 16.7; Luke 16.15). "Everyone who exalts himself will be humbled, and the one who humbles himself will be exalted" (Luke 14.11).

5.58 και παρηγγιλεν τοιc απο τηc δυναμεωc τηc μετ αυτων και επορευθηcαν επι ‹Ιαμνειαν›	**5.58** And he instructed the *men* of the force that *was* with them, and went against Jabneh.
5.59 και εξηλθεν Γοργιαc εκ τηc πολεωc και οι ανδρεc αυτου ειc cυνα(ν)τηcιν αυτοιc ειc πολεμον	**5.59** And Gorgias and his men came out of the city to meet them in battle.

5.58 Ιαμνειαν S^{ca} V A 64^{+}236 La^{109} | Αμ- S* | *Saminiam* La^{146} •

5.58–59 They **instructed**[163] their army to attack the old Philistine city of **Jabneh** (see the notes on 4.15), where one of the enemy commanders, **Gorgias** (3.38), was currently based. (The last mention of Gorgias described him fleeing into "the land of the foreigners" in the neighborhood of Jabneh, 4.22, 15.)

5.60 και ετροπωθη ‹Ιωcηφοc› και Αζαριαc και εδιωχθηcαν εωc τω(ν) οριων τηc Ιουδαιαc και επεcον εν τη ημερα εκεινη εκ του λαου Ι(cρα)ηλ ειc διcχιλιουc ανδραc	**5.60** And Joseph and Azariah were turned back, and were pursued up to the appointed boundaries of Judea; and on that day up to two thousand men of the people of Israel fell.

5.60 Ιωcηφοc [-ποc S^{ca}] V A 64^{+}236 | -φωc S* •

5.60 In the battle, **Joseph and Azariah** were put to flight, and **up to two thousand men of the people of Israel fell.** A sin committed by one or two people may have

[163] S and V (supported by La$^{109+146}$) read **he instructed** *(parēggeilen)*. A and 64^{+}236 read "they instructed" *(parēggeilan)*.

consequences that affect many others. "Did not Achan the son of Zerah commit a transgression … and there was wrath on all the congregation of Israel? and he was not the only one to die in his iniquity" (Josh 22.20). Similarly, when King Zedekiah disobeyed the Lord, the city of Jerusalem was destroyed, and its people were carried away into captivity—whereas if Zedekiah had obeyed, the whole city would have been spared (Jer 38.17–23; 27.12–13).

5.61 και εγενηθη τροπη μεγαλη εν τω λαω οτι ουκ ηκουϲαν Ιουδα και τω(ν) αδελφων αυτου οιομενοι ανδραγαθηϲαι	**5.61** And *there* was a great *over*turning among the people, for they had not listened to Judas and his brothers, thinking to do manly good deeds;
5.62 αυτοι δε ουκ ηϲαν εκ του ϲπερματοϲ των ανδρων εκεινω(ν) οιϲ εδοθη ϲωτηρια Ιϲ(ραη)λ δια χιροϲ αυτων	**5.62** but they themselves were not from the seed of those men through whose hands salvation was given to Israel.

5.61 The people were turned back and destroyed because Joseph and Azariah **did not listen to Judas and his brothers** (who had instructed them not to wage war against the nations: v 19), just as the Israelites in the wilderness were turned back and destroyed because they went into battle contrary to Moses' instructions (Num 14.40–45; Deut 1.41–44)—and just as, in the present age, "every soul that will not listen to" our own leader (Jesus of Nazareth) "will be utterly destroyed" (Acts 3.23).

5.62 Joseph and Azariah had attempted a task that God had not appointed them to do: they **were not from the seed of those men through whose hands salvation was given to Israel.** Different works of God are **given** through the hands of different people. Under the old covenant, a king was not to do a priest's appointed work (2 Chr 26.16–20), and one king was not to do another king's appointed work (1 Kgs 8.17–19). In the present age, most of God's people are not given the tasks of being elders (1 Tim 3.2–7) or teachers (Jas 3.1). Each of us is not to seek anything for himself (1 Cor 10.24, 33; Php 2.4, 21), and is "not to think more highly of himself than he ought to think" (Rom 12.3).

This incident was a reminder that the victories of Judas and his brothers had not been achieved by their own efforts, but had been **given** them by the grace of God. "Not by their sword did they possess the land, and their arm did not save them; for it was Your right hand and Your arm and the light of Your face: for You were pleased with them" (Psa 44.3).

Judas and his brothers are honored

5.63 και ο ανηρ Ιουδαϲ και οι αδελφοι αυτου εδοξαϲθηϲαν ϲφοδρα ⸤εναντιον⸥ παντοϲ Ιϲ(ραη)λ και των εθνων παντων ου ηκουετο το ονομα ⸤αυτων⸥	**5.63** And the man Judas and his brothers were honored very much in front of all Israel and all the nations *in* which their name was being heard;

5.64 και επιcυνηγοντο προς αυτους ευφημου(ν)τες	**5.64** and *people* were gathering together to them, speaking good *of them.*

5.63 εναντιον V A $64^{+}236$ | -τι S • αυτων S^{ca} V A $64^{+}236$ $La^{109+146}$ | > S* •

5.63 Judas and his brothers were honored very much, not only within **Israel** but in **all the nations** who **heard** of them. People in other countries feared them (3.25) and talked about them (3.9, 26); no longer did the nations treat Israel with reproach (4.58). Later, Judas and his brothers were honored as far away as Rome (8.17–32; 12.1–4; 14.16–19, 40; 15.15–24) and Sparta (14.16–23). "An overseer . . . must have good testimony from those outside" (1 Tim 3.2, 7).

5.64 Within Israel, **people were gathering together**[164] **to them** and **speaking good** *(euphēmountes)* of them. Success attracts many friends (cf. Prov 14.20); "great multitudes" sometimes followed Jesus (Matt 13.2; 20.29; 21.8–11)—but a "great multitude" also came against Him (Matt 26.47). The Lord's servant may expect to be the subject of both "evil speech" and "good speech" (*euphēmias,* 2 Cor 6.8).

War in the south

5.65 και εξηλθεν Ιουδας και οι αδελφοι ⸤αυτου⸥ και επολεμου(ν) τους υιους Ηcαυ ε(ν) τη γη ⸤τη⸥ προς νοτον και επαταξεν την Χεβρων και τας θυγατερας αυτης και καθειλεν τα οχυρωματα αυτης και τους πυργους αυτης ενεπυριcεν κυκλοθεν	**5.65** And Judas and his brothers went out; and they were making war against the sons of Esau in the land that *was* to the south. And he smote Hebron and its daughters, and pulled down its fortresses, and set its towers on fire round about.

5.65 αυτου S^{cb1} V A $64^{+}236$ $La^{109+146}$ | > S* • τη 2° S^{ca} A $64^{+}236$ $La^{109+146}$ | > S* V •

5.65 The Lord's service requires work continually, "without ceasing" (Acts 5.42; 20.31; 1 Thes 5.17; 2 Tim 1.3; 4.2). **Judas and his brothers** did not end their labors on their return from Gilead and Galilee; they **went out** to fight **against the sons of Esau** in yet another part of the land.

Hebron was a prominent city with attendant villages (**daughters;** cf. v 8), in the hill country (Josh 11.21) **to the south** of Judea. It had been part of the territory of Judah (Josh 20.7) and had once been its capital (2 Sam 2.11), but it was now part of the province of Idumea (see the notes on 4.15), where the **sons of Esau** had been troubling Israel (v 3). Just as the fortifications of God's people had to be built up (4.60–61; cf. Psa 51.18), so those of His enemies had to be **pulled down** (cf. 2 Chr 26.6). Both tasks are also important in the Lord's spiritual warfare today (building up, 1 Pet 2.5; pulling down, 2 Cor 10.4–5).

---

[164] **People were gathering together** *(episunēgonto).* The verb has an indefinite subject; "they [unspecified] were gathering together" (cf. the examples listed in MHT 3.292–93, §2).

5.66 και απηρεν του πορευθηναι εις γην αλλοφυλων και διεπορευετο την ‹Μαρισαν›	**5.66** And he moved away to go into *the* land of *the* foreigners; and he was passing through Mareshah.

5.66 Μαρισαν ≡ *Marisan* La$^{109+146}$ | Σαμαριαν S V A 64^{+}236 •

5.66 Going from Hebron to the **land of the foreigners,** Judas passed **through Mareshah,**[165] a city in lowland Judah (listed next to the Philistine cities, Josh 15.44–47).

5.67 εν τη ημερα εκεινη επεσον ιερεις εν πολεμω βουλομενοι ‹› ανδραγαθησαι εν τω ‹αυτους› εξελθει(ν) εις πολεμον αβουλευτως	**5.67** In that day *some* priests fell in war, wanting to do manly good deeds, when they *were* going to battle contrary to counsel.

5.67 βουλομενοι S* 64^{+}236 La^{109} | -νου S^{ca} V A La^{146} | + αυτου S V A La^{146} • αυτους 64^{+}236 La^{109} | -τον S V A La^{146} •

5.67 At that time **some priests** erred in the same way as Joseph and Azariah (vv 55–62): because they wanted **to do manly good deeds**[166] (v 61) and went **to battle contrary to counsel** *(abouleutōs)*. "The Pharisees and the Law-teachers rejected for themselves the counsel [*boulēn*] of God" (Luke 7.30). "With counsel, plans are established; and with guidance, make war" (Prov 20.18).

5.68 και εξεκλινεν Ιουδας εις Αζωτον γην αλλοφυλων ‹και› καθιλεν τους βωμους αυτων και τα γλυπτα των θεων αυτων ‹› κατεκαυσεν πυρι και εσκυλευσεν τα σκυλα των πολεων και επεστρεψεν εις γην Ιουδα	**5.68** And Judas turned aside to Ashdod, *the* land of *the* foreigners; and he pulled down their heathen altars, and burned down the carved images of their gods with fire, and plundered the plunder of the cities. And he returned into *the* land of Judah.

5.68 και 2° S^{ca} V A 64^{+}236 La$^{109+146}$ | > S* • αυτων 2° V A 64^{+}236 La$^{109+146}$ | + και S •

---

[165] La$^{109+146}$ read **Mareshah** *(Marisan),* and this is also the name given in Josephus's paraphrase of the Maccabean History (*Antiquities,* 12.353). (Moreover, it appears in 7a1 at 9.4.) Here, however, all known Greek and Syriac copies read "Samaria" *(Samarian),* which cannot be right (see Keil 110). Judas and his army were in the south, traveling from Hebron (v 65) to **the land of the foreigners** (including Ashdod, v 68), and had not yet reached the land of Judah (v 68)—whereas Samaria was directly north of Judah (on the way to Galilee, John 4.3–4, and Phoenicia, Acts 15.3). Even if Judas had wished to make a detour (as argued by Grimm 90–91), which the text does not suggest (he was seeking out and dealing with trouble spots, not avoiding them), he would not have had to go as far afield as that.

[166] **Wanting to do manly good deeds, when they were going to battle** *(boulomenoi andragathēsai en tō autous…)* is the reading of 64^{+}236 (supported by La^{109}). S^{ca}, V, and A (supported by La^{146}) have "as he [Judas] wanted to do manly good deeds, when he was going to battle" *(boulomenou autou andragathēsai en tō auton . . .).* S* reads "wanting to do manly good deeds there, when he was going to battle" *(boulomenoi autou andragathēsai en tō auton…).*

5.68 After passing through Mareshah (v 66), **Judas turned aside to Ashdod.** Ashdod was the name both of a city (10.83–84; see on 4.15) and of the surrounding region (14.34; cf. Neh 13.24; Simons §1118). Here the reference is to the region (**land**).

Ashdod was an old stronghold of **the foreigners** (the Philistines; see on 3.41) and a center of idolatry (its city contained a famous temple of the Philistine god Dagon, 10.83–84; 1 Sam 5.1–5). Judas destroyed its **heathen altars** and burned its **carved images of gods,** in accordance with the Law ("You shall burn the carved images of their gods with fire: you shall not desire the silver or gold that is on them, nor shall you take it for yourself, lest you are snared by it; for it is an abomination to the LORD your God," Deut 7.25). After he had done so, he returned to the **land of Judah.**

THE DEATH OF ANTIOCHUS EPIPHANES

Antiochus tries to plunder a city in Persia, but fails

6.1 και ο βαcιλευc Αντιοχοc διεπορευετο ταc επανω χωραc κ(αι) ηκουcεν οτι εcτι(ν) εν ‹Ελυμαιc› εν τη Περcιδι πολιc ενδοξοc πλουτω αργυριω και χρυcιω	**6.1** And King Antiochus was passing through the upper districts; and he heard that in Elam in Persia *there* was a city glorious for riches, for silver and gold,
6.2 και το ιερον το εν αυτη πλουcιον cφοδρα και ‹εκει› καλυμματα χρυcα και θωρακεc και οπλα α κατελιπεν εκει Αλεξανδροc ο του Φιλιππου ο βαcιλευc ο Μακαιδονων οc εβαcιλευcε(ν) πρωτοc εν ‹τοιc Ελληcι›	**6.2** and the temple in it *was* extremely rich, and *in it* there *was* golden protective armor and breastplates and weapons, which Alexander the *son* of Philip, the Macedonian king, who had been king first among the Greeks, had left there.

6.1 Ελυμαιc A 64^{+}236 La^{109} | Λ- S V La^{146} • **6.2** εκει 1° V A 64^{+}236 La$^{109+146}$ | εχει S • τοιc Ελληcι V A 64^{+}236 La$^{109+146}$ | αυτοιc S •

6.1 Meanwhile, Antiochus Epiphanes had led his army across the Euphrates River to the Persian highlands (the **upper districts,** 3.37). He heard stories of a rich city **in Elam,**[167] the province that contained the Persian capital Shushan (Dan 8.2; cf. Jer 49.38) and that was closely associated with Media (Isa 21.2; Jer 25.25; Acts 2.9).

---

[167] **In** *(en)* is present in S, V, and A, but not in 64^{+}236 or La^{109} (in those texts, **Elam** would seem to be the name of the **city**). La^{146} has *eum,* which might or might not correspond to Greek *en.* The spelling of the name **Elam** also varies somewhat (*Elumes,* A ≡ *Elumais,* 64^{+}236 ≡ *'ylm,* 7h7 and 7a1; but *Lumais,* S and V). No city with any such name is mentioned elsewhere, whereas Elam the province is familiar (see above) and is also named by Polybius as the site of this incident (*eis tēn Elumaida,* 31.9.1). None of the Classical historians names the city itself; the Epitome of the Acts of Judas Maccabeus states that it was Persepolis (Epitome 9.2), but Polybius's statement that the temple was one of "Artemis" (31.9.1) has led many modern historians to think that the city may have been Shushan (the site of the most famous such temple in the region: Pliny, *Natural History,* 6.31.135).

6.2 The city's **temple** reputedly contained great treasures[168] left by **Alexander . . . the Macedonian** (1.1). Alexander now lay in a place where his great riches were no use to him (Psa 49.17; 1 Tim 6.7), while his distant successor Antiochus Epiphanes would lose his life in trying to obtain them. "Surely a man walks in a mere shadow; surely they are in a tumult in vain: he heaps up riches, and does not know who will gather them" (Psa 39.6).

6.3 και ηλθεν και εζητει καταλαβεcθαι την πολιν κ(αι) προνομευcαι αυτην και ουκ ηδυναcθη οτι ‹› εγνωcθη ο λογοc τοιc εκ τηc πολεωc	**6.3** And he came, and he *began* seeking to take hold of the city and pillage it; and he was not able: for the account had become known to the *people* from the city,
6.4 και αντεcτηcαν αυτω ειc πολεμον και εφυγε(ν) και απηρεν εκειθε(ν) μετα λυπηc μεγαληc αποcτρεψαι ειc Βαβυλωνα	**6.4** and they stood up against him for battle, and he fled. And he moved away from there in great sorrow, to return to Babylon.

6.3 οτι S^{ca} V A $64^{+}236$ $La^{109+146}$ | + ουκ S* •

6.3–4 Antiochus sought to **pillage** the city, its inhabitants fought against him and put him to flight, so he **moved away** in the direction of **Babylon.** As so often, the pursuit of riches had led only to **sorrow** (Prov 23.5; Ecc 5.10–12; cf. Jas 5.1–5).

He hears what has happened in the land of Judah

6.5 κ(αι) ηλθεν τιc απαγγελλων ‹αυτω› ειc την Περcιδα οτι τετροπω(ν)ται αι παρεμβολαι αι πορευθιcαι ειc ‹γην› Ιουδα	**6.5** And someone came into Persia, reporting to him that the companies that had gone into *the* land of Judah had been turned back,
6.6 και επορευθη Λυcιαc δυναμι ιcχυρα εν πρωτοιc και ενετραπη απο προcωπου αυτων και ‹επιcχυcαν› οπλοιc και δυναμει και cκυλοιc πολλοιc ‹οιc› ελαβον απο τω(ν) παρεμβολων ‹ων› εξεκοψαν	**6.6** and Lysias had gone with a strong force in *the* first *place*, and had been overturned from their face; and *they had* become strong with weapons and power and much plunder that they had taken from the companies that they had cut off;
6.7 και καθειλον το βδελυγμα ‹ο› ‹ωκοδομηcαν› επι το θυcιαcτηριον το εν Ι(ερουcα)λημ και το αγιαcμα ‹καθωc› το προτερον	**6.7** and they had taken down the abomination that they had built on the sacrificial altar in Jerusalem; and they had surrounded the holy

[168] In this context, the term **protective armor** (*kalummata,* as in 4.6) could include any "coverings" (KJV) for protection in war. "Shields" (NRSV) and "helmets" (NAB) are both too specific.

εκυκλωcαν τιχεcιν υψηλοιc και την Βαιθcουραν ‹πολιν αυτου›	place with high walls, just as *it had been* previous*ly,* and Bethzur his city.

6.5 αυτω V A 64^{+}236 La$^{109+146}$ \| > S • γην V A 64^{+}236 La$^{109+146}$ \| την S • **6.6** επιcχυcαν V A 64^{+}236 \| ενι- S • οιc V A 64^{+}236 La$^{109+146}$ \| οι S • ων V A 64^{+}236 La$^{109+146}$ \| κ(αι) S • **6.7** ο V A 64^{+}236 La$^{109+146}$ \| και S • ωκοδομηcαν V La^{109*} \| -μουν S La$^{109c+146}$ \| -μηcεν A \| -μηθη 236 • καθωc S^{ca} V A 64^{+}236 La$^{109+146}$ \| και S* • πολιν αυτου S^{ca} V A [-ων 64^{+}236 7h7] La$^{109+146}$ 7a1 \| > S* •

6.5–7 A messenger arrived in **Persia** with recent news from the **land of Judah,** including the defeat of **Lysias** (4.27–35),[169] the removal of the **abomination**[170] of desolation (4.43; see on 1.54), and the fortification of **the holy place** (Mount Zion, 4.60) and **Bethzur** (4.61).

Bethzur was ruled by Antiochus and is therefore called **his city.** (In the same way, cities ruled by Sihon are called "his cities," Deut 2.34.)[171]

He falls ill and dies

6.8 και εγενετο ωc ηκουcεν ο βαcιλευc τουc λογουc τουτουc εθαμβηθη και εcαλευθη cφοδρα και επεcεν επι την κοιτην και ‹ενεπεcεν› ειc αρρωcτιαν απο τηc λυπηc οτι ουκ εγενετο αυτω καθωc ενεθυμειτο	**6.8** And it came about, when the king heard these words, he was astonished, and was very much shaken. And he fell on *his* bed, and fell into an illness from the sorrow: for *this* had not come about for him as he had desired.
6.9 και ην εκει ημεραc πλιουc οτι ανεκαινιcθη επ αυτον λυπη μεγαλη και ελογιcατο οτι αποθνηcκει	**6.9** And he was there many days, because *his* great sorrow was renewed upon him; and he took account that he was dying.

6.8 ενεπεcεν V A 64^{+}236 \| επεcεν S •

6.8–9 Antiochus **was astonished** (*ethambēthē,* as in Mark 10.24, 32) and **was very much shaken** (*esaleuthē,* as in 2 Thes 2.2; Acts 2.25) by the news. He **fell into an**

[169] **Lysias** went **in the first place** *(en prōtois),* a term that can describe position in time ("at first," Deut 13.9; 1 Kgs 20.17; 1 Chr 11.6; 2 Sam 20.18), position in space ("at the front," Gen 33.2), or importance ("foremost," cf. 1 Cor 15.3; 1 Sam 9.22). The present passage has been taken to mean either (a) that Lysias went out mightily "at first" (NAB) but was subsequently turned back, or (b) that he went "at the head" of his army (APOT)—leading it himself (4.28, 35), no longer merely sending subordinates as he had previously done (3.38–39).

[170] **The abomination that they had built** is the reading in S *(ōkodomoun)* and V *(ōkodomēsan),* supported by La$^{109+146}$. "The abomination that he had built" is the reading in A *(ōkodomēsen).*

[171] The SAAS rendering, "Beth-zur his hometown," is therefore incorrect. **His** [*autou*] **city** is the reading of S^{ca}, V, and A (supported by La$^{109+146}$). 64^{+}236 read "their [*autōn*] city," i.e., the Judeans' city. S* omits the phrase, no doubt by accident (it is present in 7a1, which is not simply copying SyI at this point).

illness that lasted for **many days,** during which time **his great sorrow was renewed** [*anekainisthē,* as in Heb 6.6] **upon him**—that is, it returned, it came back and could not be brushed aside.[172] The same term is used in the LXX to translate "my sorrow was stirred"—it was stirred up, was revived (Psa 39.2).

6.10 και εκαλεcεν παντας τουc φιλουc αυτου και ειπεν προc αυτουc αφιcταται ο υπνοc απο των οφθαλμων μου και cυνπεπτωκα ⸂τη καρδια⸃ ⸂απο τηc μεριμνηc⸃	**6.10** And he called all his Friends, and said to them: "Sleep is departing from my eyes, and I am downhearted from worry.
6.11 και ειπα τη καρδια ⸂μου⸃ εωc τινοc θλιψεωc ηλθα κ(αι) κλυδωνοc μεγαλου εν ω νυν ειμι οτι χρηcτοc κ(αι) αγαπωμενοc ημην εν τη εξουcια μου	**6.11** And I said to my heart: To what oppression have I come, and in what a great flood am I now! for I was kind and *was* loved in my authority.

6.10 τη καρδια A 64^{+}236 La$^{109+146}$ | > S V • απο τηc μεριμνηc V A 64^{+}236 La$^{109+146}$ | + τη καρδια S • **6.11** μου 1° 64^{+}236 La$^{109+146}$ | > S V A •

6.11 The king who had commanded the oppression *(thlipsis)* of so many others (5.16) was now suffering **oppression** *(thlipsis)* himself, as though he was being overwhelmed by a **great flood** (cf. Lam 3.54; Psa 69.1–2, 14–15).

Antiochus could claim to have been **kind** (*chrēstos;* he was famous for the generosity of his gifts, 3.30), and to have been **loved** by those who were under his **authority** (Lysias, for instance, subsequently praised him by calling his son "well-fathered," v 17). Even today, he still has no shortage of admirers (see the footnote to 1.42–43). "Those who love a rich person are many" (Prov 14.20; 19.4).

But kindness and lovability are not enough to commend us in the sight of God. People who are popular, giving with amazing generosity (1 Cor 13.3) and uttering "kind words" *(chrēstologias),* may nevertheless "serve not our Lord Christ, but their own belly" (Rom 16.18; Matt 7.21–23). To be loved by the world is in fact a bad sign (John 15.19), because the world loves "darkness rather than light" (John 3.19). Not the world's love, but the Father's love is to be sought (1 Jn 3.1); not the kindness that the world practices, but the kindness that is a fruit of the Spirit (Gal 5.22; Col 3.12).

6.12 νυν δε μνηcκομαι ⸂των κακων ω(ν) εποιηcα⸃ εν Ιερουcαλημ και ελαβον παντα τα cκευη	**6.12** But now I am mindful of the evil *things* that I did in Jerusalem, and I took all the silver and golden

[172] **Was renewed** (*anekainisthē,* aorist) describes something that "revert[s] to [a] former condition" (see Muraoka 40), a recurrence (possibly even "recurrent fits," NJB). Antiochus was stricken by **sorrow** when he heard the news (v 8), and that **sorrow** recurred later (v 9). The term does not necessarily imply increase ("grief mounted in him," NETS) or persistence ("grief continually gripped him," ESV; that would more naturally be expressed by the imperfect).

τα αργυρα και τα χρυcα τα εν αυτη και εξαπεcτιλα εξαραι τουc κατοικουνταc Ιουδα δια κενηc	vessels that *were* in it, and I sent out *people* to do away with those who were dwelling in Judah, for nothing.

6.12 μνηcκομαι S A = μιμν- V 64*236 • των κακων ω(ν) εποιηcα V A [των κακων μου ων ε- 64*236] La[109+146] | ων εποιηcα κακων S •

6.12 His kindness had not restrained Antiochus from doing **evil things** to the people of Judah **for nothing.**[173] He had contended for nothing with those who had done him no evil (Prov 3.29–30; cf. Psa 7.4).

6.13 εγνων οτι χαρι(ν) τουτων ευρεν με τα κακα ταυτα και ιδου απολλυμαι λυπη μεγαλη εν γη αλλοτρια	**6.13** I know that, on account of these *things,* these evil *thing*s have found me, and see! I am being destroyed in great sorrow in a strange land."

6.13 Not only on the last day, but also in the present life, God's judgments fall on people—both for their good deeds (Mark 10.29–30; 2 Cor 9.8–11) and for their bad deeds (2 Sam 12.9–14; 1 Kgs 11.6–10, 14, 23; 2 Chr 16.9; Jer 20.1–4). Antiochus recognized that his present distress was a punishment for his sins against the people of Judah, as Joseph's brothers recognized that their distress in Egypt was a punishment for their treatment of Joseph twenty years earlier (Gen 42.21).

6.14 και εκαλεcεν Φιλιππον ενα των φιλων αυτου και κατεcτηcεν αυτον επι παcηc τηc βαcιλειαc αυτου	**6.14** And he called Philip, one of his Friends, and established him over all his kingdom,
6.15 και εδωκεν αυτω το διαδημα και τη(ν) cτοληv αυτου και τον δακτυλιον του αγαγειν Αντιοχο(ν) τον υιον αυτου κ(αι) εκθρεψαι αυτον του βαcιλευειν	**6.15** and gave him the diadem and his robe and the finger-ring, to guide Antiochus his son, and to bring him up to be king.

6.14–15 Lysias had already been appointed "over the affairs of the king, from the River Euphrates ... to the appointed boundaries of Egypt" (3.32); now the dying king appointed **one of his Friends** (see the notes on 2.18), **Philip,** over **all his kingdom.** Philip received the traditional signs of authority: the royal **diadem** (1.9), the royal **robe,** and the **finger-ring** (like Joseph when he was "set ... over all the land of Egypt," Gen 41.42–43).

From now on, therefore, both Lysias and Philip could claim that their rule had been authorized by Antiochus Epiphanes (cf. vv 55–56, 63). The kingdom that opposed God's Law was becoming divided against itself (cf. Matt 12.25).

---

[173] **For nothing.** More precisely, the Greek text reads *dia kenēs,* "because of emptiness" (as in Psa 25.3, LXX; cf. Muraoka 395, §3b).

6.16 κ(αι) απεθανεν εκει Αντιοχος ο βαcιλευc ετουc θ΄ και μ΄ και ρ΄	**6.16** And Antiochus the king died there *in the* hundred and forty-ninth year.

6.16 Antiochus Epiphanes **died,** still in the place where he had fallen ill "many days" earlier (v 9), **in the hundred and forty-ninth year.**[174]

The reign of Antiochus Eupator

Antiochus Eupator becomes king

6.17 ‹κ(αι)› επεγνω Λυcιαc οτι τεθνηκεν ο βαcιλευc και κατεcτηcεν βαcιλευειν Αντιοχο(ν) τον υιον αυτου ον εξεθρεψεν νεωτερον και εκαλεcεν το ονομα αυτου Ευπατωρ	**6.17** And Lysias knew that the king had died; and he established Antiochus his son to be king, whom he had brought up *when he was* young; and he called his name Eupator.

6.17 κ(αι) 1° S^{ca} V A 64^{+}236 La$^{109+146}$ | > S* •

6.17 Like his father, the new king bore the name **Antiochus** (v 15; 3.33). (In modern histories, he is reckoned as Antiochus V.) Lysias gave him the additional name **Eupator** ("well-fathered"; see the notes on v 11).

The citadel is besieged

6.18 και οι εκ τηc ακραc ηcαν cυνκλιοντεc τον Ιc(ραη)λ κυκλω των αγιων και ζητουντεc κακα δι ολου και cτηριγμα τοιc εθνεcιν	**6.18** And the *people* from the citadel were shutting up Israel round about the holy *places*, and *the* whole *time they were* seeking evil *things*, and support for the nations.

6.18 The enemy **citadel** in Jerusalem was "an ambush to the holy place, and a harmful accuser to Israel, at all times" (see on 1.32–36). Its occupants were now **shutting up**

[174] A fragmentary entry in the Babylonian Hellenistic Royal Chronicle states that, some time during the month of Chislev, "it was heard that Antiochus the king" was dead (CM §4.29); and an astronomical diary reports that his body was brought to Babylon the following month (SH 3.18–19, §-163). The year date is not preserved in either document, but planetary observations in the diary show that the king's death occurred in the final months of 164 BCE.

The Maccabean History states that the new altar was dedicated in Chislev 148 SE (4.52), and that Antiochus died in 149 SE. This probably means that Antiochus died almost a year after the dedication of the altar. However, some theorists have suggested that the date in 4.52 might be calculated on a spring-start system 6–12 months behind the system used in 6.16 (see the introduction to this commentary)—in which case, the dedication of the altar would have occurred at almost the same time as Antiochus's death. If so, the messenger who reached the king during his final illness (vv 5–7) would have brought news of only Judas's initial operations in Jerusalem: the removal of the abomination (no doubt the very first action when the temple was reached) and the building of fortifications. At that time, the full cleansing and dedication of the temple would have still been some weeks in the future (cf. the comments on 4.51).

Israel round about the holy places—that is, "confining the Israelites to the neighbourhood of the temple" (REB). More generally, they were constantly **seeking evil things** (cf. Psa 40.14). But "one who seeks evil, it will come to him" (Prov 11.27).

6.19 και ελογιcατο Ιουδαc εξαραι αυτουc και εξεκκληcιαcε πα(ν)τα τον λαον του περικαθιcαι επ αυτουc	**6.19** And Judas determined to do away with them; and he assembled all the people to besiege them.
6.20 και cυνηχθηcα(ν) αμα και περιεκαθιcαν επ αυτην ετουc ν′ και εκατοcτου και ‹εποιηcαν› βελοcταcειc ‹κ(αι)› μηχαναc	**6.20** And they gathered together, and besieged it *in the* hundred and fiftieth year. And they made towers for arrow-shooting, and *other* devices.

6.20 εποιηcαν V $\mathrm{La}^{109+146}$ 7h7 7a1 | -cεν S A $64^{+}236$ • κ(αι) 5° S^{ca} V A $64^{+}236$ $\mathrm{La}^{109+146}$ | > S* •

6.19–20 Therefore **Judas determined**[175] to remove the troublemakers (**do away with them**). He **assembled** his **people to besiege** the citadel's occupants. This involved the use of various siege engines (**towers for arrow-shooting . . . devices;** cf. v 51; 2 Chr 26.14–15), as described in 5.30.

The evildoers appeal to the king

6.21 και εξηλθον εξ αυτων εκ του cυνκλιcμου και εκολληθηcαν αυτοιc τινεc των αcεβων εξ ‹Ι(cρα)ηλ›	**6.21** And *some* of them came out from *the* siege, and some of the irreverent *ones* from Israel joined them;

6.21 Ι(cρα)ηλ V A $64^{+}236$ $\mathrm{La}^{109+146}$ | Ιηλμ′ S •

6.21 A number of the enemies besieged in the citadel managed to escape (**came out**). Most (if not all) of them would have been "sons of foreigners" (3.45), but they found willing supporters among the **irreverent** people **from Israel.** Some of Israel's worst enemies were Israelites (1.11; 3.15). "They are not all Israel, that are from Israel . . . . That is, it is not the children of the flesh that are children of God; but the children of the promise" (Rom 9.6–8). Jesus was betrayed by a familiar friend who had eaten His bread and walked in the house of God with Him (Psa 41.9; 55.13–14; Luke 22.21; Matt 26.50); His followers have likewise suffered at the hands of their countrymen and kinsfolk (Luke 21.16; 2 Cor 11.26; Matt 10.35–36).

6.22 και επορευθηcαν προc τον βαcιλεα κ(αι) ειπαν εωc ποτε ου ποιηcη κριcιν και εκδικηcειc τουc αδελφουc ημων	**6.22** and they went to the king, and said: "How long will you† not do justice and take vengeance† for our brothers?

[175] **Determined.** He "reckoned," "calculated," or "accounted" to do this (Greek *elogisato,* as in 2 Cor 10.2; Muraoka 433, §2; Thayer 379, §3c). The word generally implies not a hasty thought but a result of calculation or deliberation (cf. 2 Chr 5.6, LXX; Heb 11.19; 2 Cor 10.7, 11).

6.23 ημειc ευδοκουμεν δουλευειν τω πατρι cου και πορευεcθαι τοιc υπ αυτου λεγομενοιc και κατακολουθιν τοιc προcταγμαcιν αυτου	**6.23** We ourselves were well pleased to be enslaved to your[†] father, and to walk in the *thing*s that were said by him, and to follow his orders;
6.24 και περιεκαθη(ν)το επ ‹αυτην› οι υιοι του λαου ημων χαριν τουτου και ηλλοτριουντο αφ ημων ‹πλην οcοι ηυριcκοντο αφ ημων› εθανατου(ν)το και αι κληρονομιαι ημων ‹διηρπαζοντο›	**6.24** and on account of this, the sons of our people have been besieging it, and becoming estranged from us. Nevertheless, they have been putting to death as many of us as *they* found, and they have been plundering our inheritances;
6.25 και ουκ εφ ημαc μονον εξετιναν χειρα αλλα και επι παντα τα ορια αυτων	**6.25** and not against us only have they stretched out *their* hand, but also against all their appointed boundaries.
6.26 και ιδου παρεμβεβληκαcι cημερο(ν) επι την ‹ακραν› εν Ι(ερουcα)λημ του καταλαβεcθαι αυτην κ(αι) το αγιαcμα και τη(ν) Βαιθcουρα ωχυραcαν	**6.26** And, see! they are camped today against the citadel in Jerusalem, to take hold of it; and they have fortified the holy place and Bethzur.
6.27 και αν μη προκαταλαβητε ‹αυτουc› δια ταχουc μειζονα τουτων ποιηcουcιν και ου δυνηcη του καταcχειν αυτων	**6.27** And if you[pl] do not take hold of them quickly, they will do greater things than these; and you[†] will not be able to hold them back."

6.24 αυτην S[cb1] V La[109] | -τον S* | την ακραν 64[+]236 | > La[146] • πλην οcοι ηυριcκοντο αφ ημων S[ca] V A 64[+]236 La[109+146] | και S* • διηρπαζοντο S[ca] V A 64[+]236 La[109+146] | > S* • **6.26** ακραν S[ca] V A 64[+]236 La[109+146] | ακραcια(ν) S* • **6.27** αν S = εαν V A 64[+]236 • αυτουc S[ca] V A 64[+]236 La[109+146] | -τη(ν) S* •

6.22–27 The evildoers entreated **the king** for **justice,** on the grounds that they had faithfully obeyed his **father** (Antiochus Epiphanes) and were losing their lives and **inheritances** as a result. They urged him to **take hold of**[176] the rebels **quickly.** Otherwise, Judas and his supporters would **do greater things,** and it would no longer be possible **to hold them back.** Indeed God's work (5.62) can never be held back (Dan 4.35; Isa 43.13; Prov 21.30), as even Gamaliel recognized (Acts 5.39).

[176] S, V, 64[+]236, and La[109+146] envisage this task as done by the king's forces in general (**you**[pl] **do not take hold of them,** *mē prokatalabēte,* plural), whereas A envisages it as done by the king himself ("you[†] do not take hold of them," *mē prokatalabē,* singular). The prefix *pro-* is sometimes taken to mean "beforehand" ("unless you quickly forestall them," NAB), but that would not fit most of the other instances of *prokatalambanō* in this book (5.8, 36, 44; 9.2; 12.33; further examples where "the meaning probably [is] just *to seize, capture*" are listed in Muraoka 587, §1).

Notice how the urgency of the complaint disrupts the speech of the complainants. The siege is so dominant in their minds that they speak of it first, out of sequence, and without even explaining what is being besieged (**the sons of our people have been besieging it,** v 24), reiterating the point after an interval, more fully and in its proper place (**they are camped today against the citadel,** v 26). In a book constructed with such tidiness, disruption of sequence and/or omission of material essential to the sense do not occur at random; always they mark an urgent crisis (1.1; 2.33; etc.).[177]

This appeal to act **quickly** ("How long will you not do justice and take vengeance for our brothers?", v 22) elicited a quick response from an unrighteous king (vv 27–28). The righteous King of kings is more longsuffering (2 Pet 3.9), yet He too will respond "quickly" to the appeal of His faithful subjects: "How long, O Master, the holy and true, do You not judge and avenge our blood on those who dwell on the earth?" (Rev 6.10). "Will not God avenge His chosen ones, who cry to Him day and night? … I say to you, that He will avenge them quickly" (Luke 18.7–8).

The king's forces fight against the Judeans at Bethzechariah

6.28 και ωργιcθη ο βαcιλευc ‹οτε› ηκουcεν και cυνηγαγεν παντας τουc φιλουc ‹αυτου και τουc› αρχοντας δυναμεωc αυτου και τουc επι των ηνιω(ν)	**6.28** And when the king heard, he became angry, and gathered together all his Friends, and the commanders of his force, and those over the horse;
6.29 και απο βαcιλειω(ν) ετερων και απο νηcων θαλαccω(ν) ηλθον προc αυτο(ν) ‹δυναμιc› μιcθωται	**6.29** and hired forces came to him from other kingdoms and from islands of *the* seas.
6.30 και ην ο αριθμοc των δυναμεων αυτου εκατον χιλιαδεc πεζων και εικοcι χιλιαδεc ιππεων και ελεφα(ν)τεc δυο και τριακο(ν)τα ιδοτεc πολεμο(ν)	**6.30** And the number of his forces was a hundred thousand footsoldiers, and twenty thousand horsemen, and thirty-two elephants that knew war.

6.28 οτε A 64 La[109+146] | οτι S V 236 • αυτου και τουc 1° 64[+]236 La[109+146] | αυτου S A[c] | αυτουc A* | και V • **6.29** δυναμιc S[ca] V A 64[+]236 La[109+146] | -μι S* •

6.28–30 The king … became angry, and gathered together a very large army, including **hired forces … from other kingdoms.** "The fury of a king is messengers of

---

[177] As would be expected, some ancient copyists sought to regularize the clause **the sons of our people have been besieging it** (v 24) by one means or another. 64[+]236 specified the object of the siege (*tēn akran,* "the citadel"); A omitted the clause entirely. Similar techniques can be seen in many modern translations.

In their heat, the complainants distorted the truth. "The garrison was besieged not for their obedience to Antiochus, but because they molested those going out and in from the Temple" (Fairweather-Black 136).

death" (Prov 16.14); in the same way, Satan, the ruler of this world, is perpetually **angry** against God's people and wages war against them (Rev 12.17); and so do the kings who serve Satan (Dan 3.19–22; Matt 2.16). The armies invading Judea had increased from 40,000 men and 7,000 horse (3.39), to 60,000 men and 5,000 horse (4.28), and now to **100,000** men, and **20,000** horse—so many that even the sound of them made people tremble (vv 38, 41). But, as on previous occasions, the size of the force did not achieve victory. "There is no king who is saved by the abundance of his force" (Psa 33.16).

Judas and his companions would outlive both Antiochus and Lysias (7.2–4).

6.31 και ηλθον δια της Ιδουμαιας και παρενεβαλον επι Βεθσουρα και ‹επολεμησαν› ημερας πολλας και ‹εποιησαν› μηχανας και εξηλθον και ενεπυριcα(ν) αυτας πυρι και ‹επολεμησαν› ανδρωδως	**6.31** And they came through Idumea, and camped against Bethzur, and made war many days, and made devices *of war.* And they came out and set them on fire with fire, and made war manfully.
6.32 και απηρεν Ιουδας απο της ακρας και παρενεβαλε(ν) εις Βαιθζαχαρια απεναντι της παρεμβολης του βασιλεως	**6.32** And Judas moved away from the citadel and camped at Bethzechariah, opposite the king's camp.

6.31 επολεμησαν 1° V A $64^{+}236$ La^{109} | -cεν S La^{146} • εποιησαν V A $64^{+}236$ La^{109} | -cεν S La^{146} • επολεμησαν 2° V A La^{109} | -cεν S $64^{+}236$ La^{146} •

6.31–32 The forces took the same route as those led by Lysias two years earlier: they **came through Idumea, and camped against Bethzur** (see 4.29), which Judas had fortified since their previous visit (4.61; 6.26). In response, **Judas** moved his forces **from** the Jerusalem **citadel** to **Bethzechariah** near Bethzur (**opposite the king's camp**).[178]

6.33 και ωρθριcε(ν) ο βαcιλευc το πρωι και απηρεν την παρεμβολην εν ορμηματι αυτης κατα την οδον ‹› Βαιθζαχαρια και διεcκευαcθηcαν αι δυναμιc ειc τον πολεμον και ‹εcαλπιcαν› ταιc cαλπιγξιν	**6.33** And the king got up at dawn *in* the early morning, and moved the company away in its headlong rush, on the Bethzechariah path; and the forces equipped themselves for war, and trumpeted with the trumpets.
6.34 και τοιc ελεφαcιν ‹εδειξαν› αιμα cταφυληc και μορων του παραcτηcαι αυτουc ειc τον πολεμον	**6.34** And they showed the elephants blood of grapes and of mulberries, to set them in readiness for the battle.

[178] **Bethzechariah,** like most ancient places in the Middle East, can no longer be located exactly (ISBE 1.480). Josephus (*Antiquities,* 12.369) puts it about 70 stadia (about 8 miles = 13 km.) from Bethzur, but modern "Beit Skâriā" is only 6 miles = 10 km. from modern "Burj eṣ-Ṣur." Either or both lines of evidence could be in error (Josephus was no expert on the location of small places; and, as time passes, place names can be reassigned or used more than once).

6.35 και διειλον τα θηρια εις τας φαλαγγας και ‹παρεστησαν› εκαστω ελεφαντι χιλιους ανδρας τεθωρακισμενους εν αλυσιδωτοις και περικεφαλαιαι χαλκαι επι των κεφαλω(ν) αυτων και πεντακοσια ιππος διατεταγμενη εκαστω θηριω εκλελεγμενη	**6.35** And they divided the animals among the phalanxes; and nearby each elephant they set in readiness a thousand men breastplated in chain mail and *with* bronze helmets on their heads, and five hundred chosen horse, assigned to each animal.
6.36 ουτοι προ καιρου ου αν η το θηριον ησαν και ου εαν επορευετο επορευοντο ‹αμα› ουκ αφισταντο ‹απ αυτου	**6.36** These *were there* beforehand: whichever *way* the animal might be, they were; and whichever *way* it was going, they were going together; they would never depart from it.
6.37 κ(αι) πυργοι› ξυλινοι επ αυτους ‹οχυροι› σκεπαζομενοι ‹εφ εκαστου› θηριου εζωσμενοι ‹επ› αυτου μηχαναις και εφ εκαστου ανδρες δυναμεως τριακοντα οι πολεμουντες επ ‹αυτους› και ο Ινδος αυτου	**6.37** And wooden towers *were* on them, fortified covering *one*s, on each animal, girded on it with devices; and on each *one were* thirty men of power, making war on them, and *also* its Indian.

6.33 οδον V A 64^{+}236 La$^{109+146}$ | + αυτης S • εσαλπισαν A 64^{+}236 La$^{109+146}$ | -ισεν S V • **6.34** εδειξαν V A 64^{+}236 La$^{109+146}$ | -ξεν S • **6.35** παρεστησαν V A 64 La$^{109+146}$ | -ησεν S • **6.36** αμα S^{ca} V A 64 La$^{109+146}$ | αλα S* | και 236 • **6.36–37** απ αυτου κ(αι) πυργοι S^{ca} V [επ A] 64^{+}236 La$^{[109+]146}$ | αλγοι S* • **6.37** οχυροι S^{ca} V A 64^{+}236 La$^{109+146}$ | ??ροι S* • εφ εκαστου 1° S^{ca} V A La$^{109+146}$ | εκεφαιστου S* | εφ εκατερου 64^{+}236 • επ 2° V A 64^{+}236 La$^{109+146}$ | υπ S • αυτους 2° V A La$^{109+146}$ | -τοις S | -του 64^{+}236 •

6.35 Here and elsewhere in this book (vv 38, 45; 9.12; 10.82), divisions of an army are termed **phalanxes.**[179]

6.34 The king's soldiers **showed the elephants blood of grapes and of mulberries,** supposing that this would **set them in readiness for the battle.**[180] The term **blood of grapes** refers to the juice of the vine (Gen 49.11; Deut 32.14).

---

[179] In 9.12 all the ancient copies read **phalanx** *(phalagx),* but in each of the other verses some copies read forms of "valley" *(pharagx):* S* in 10.82; V in 6.38 and 10.82; A in 6.35, 45; 64^{+}236 in 6.38; and La^{146} in 6.38, 45.

[180] The soldiers' reasoning is not explained, and may be nothing more than a superstition (like the modern superstition that the color red will enrage a bull). Perhaps they fancied that the elephants would be roused to anger by being able to see but not taste the drinks (Grimm 99), or that the sight of bloodlike liquids would accustom the animals to the sight of blood (Calmet 91–92). In other ancient contexts there are reports of attempts to intoxicate elephants (Ptolemaica 5.2, 10, 43; Aelian, *Natura animalium,* 13.8), but before a battle (when the whole force would have to move "securely and in order," v 40) that would obviously be foolish.

6.37. There were "thirty-two elephants" (v 30) and a similar number of soldiers riding them, **thirty men of power.** "Thirty" can mean "about thirty" (David's "thirty chief men" were "thirty-seven in all," 2 Sam 23.13, 39), so the present text does not indicate whether there were slightly more soldiers than elephants, an equal number, or slightly fewer (improbably; in that case, not all of the elephants would have been used simultaneously).[181]

Each animal **also** had **its Indian** attendant.[182] By this time India had regular commerce with the Mediterranean world (8.8; Est 1.1; 8.9).

6.38 και την ‹επιλοιπον› ιππον	**6.38** And the rest of *the* horse
ενθεν και ενθεν ‹› εϲτηϲεν	he established here and *t*here,
επι τα δυο μερη τηϲ παρεμβοληϲ	on the two sides of the company,

---

[181] S and $64^{+}236$, supported by $La^{109+146}$, read **thirty** *(triakonta),* whereas V and A read "thirty-two" *(duo kai triakonta)*—in which case the number of **men of power** would exactly equal the number of elephants. The alteration may have been introduced by a copyist who was troubled by the apparent discrepancy in numbers.

The plurals in this verse have sometimes been misunderstood. **Wooden towers were . . . on each animal . . . and on each one were thirty men of power.** The statement that there were **wooden towers** (plural) **on each** *(eph' hekastou)* elephant does not imply more than one wooden tower per elephant. In the same way, the statement that there were soldiers (plural) **on each** *(eph' hekastou)* elephant does not imply more than one soldier per elephant. **Each** *(hekastos),* in a sentence of this kind, means simply that "*every one* has or does someth[ing], but one does one thing, another someth[ing] else" (BDAG 298). "Each [*hekastos*] one of you says, I am of Paul; and I of Apollos: and I of Cephas; and I of Christ" (1 Cor 1.12) does not mean that every individual was saying all four of those things (instead, one individual said one of those things, another said another). In the same way, **on each one were thirty men** does not mean that every animal had all thirty of those men (instead, one animal had one of those men, another had another). In fact, it is usual for *eph' hekastou* to take a plural subject distributed singly, as in this verse (similarly "the gatekeepers at each gate," 1 Esdras 1.16; 7.9; there was normally one gatekeeper per gate: 2 Sam 18.26)—whereas *hekastō* takes a singular subject (as it does in v 35).

The modern conjectual emendations "two or three" (Michaelis, *Erste Buchs der Maccabäer,* 139–40), "three" (Abel 120–21; NAB), "four" (Rahlfs, "Kriegselephanten im I. Makkabäerbuche," 78–79; NRSV), and "two officers" (≡ Hebrew *šny šlšym;* Tedesche and Zeitlin, *First Book of Maccabees,* 130–31), are therefore based on a grammatical misunderstanding. (Even when ancient scribes sought to alter the number, they still understood its grammar: see the first paragraph of this note.) Those who suppose a textual error here would logically also need to suppose an equivalent error involving the plural **towers** in the analogous preceding clause. And two successive errors of the kind, neither of which is attested in any known manuscript, would be extraordinarily unlikely.

[182] The shift from plural (**towers . . . men of power**) to singular (**Indian**) is necessary to avoid an ambiguity ("their Indians" might have been misconstrued as "the soldiers' Indians"), and also highlights the personal relationship between individual elephant and individual Indian.

καταςειοντες και καταφραςςομενοι εν ταις ‹φαλαγξιν›	making *people* quake, and being enclosed in the phalanxes.
6.39 ως δε εςτιλβεν ο ηλιος επι τας χρυςας ‹κ(αι) χαλκας› αςπιδας εςτιλβεν τα ορη ‹απ› αυτων και κατηυγαζεν ως λαμπαδες ‹πυρος	**6.39** And when the sun was sparkling on the golden and bronze shields, the mountains were sparkling with them, and were shining out like lamps of fire.
6.40 κ(αι) εξεταθη μερος τι της› παρεμβολης του βαςιλεως επι τα ‹υψηλα› ορη και τινες επι τα ταπινα και ηρχοντο αςφαλως και τεταγμενως	**6.40** And a certain part of the king's company was stretched out on the high mountains, and certain *men* on the lowly *places*; and they were begin- ning *to advance* securely and in order.
6.41 και εςαλευοντο παντες οι ακουοντες της φωνης πληθους αυτων και οδοιποριας του πληθους ‹και› ςυνκρουςμου των οπλων ην γαρ η παρεμβολη μεγαλη ςφοδρα και ιςχυρα	**6.41** And all the *people* were trem- bling—*those* who were hearing the voice of their multitude, and *the* trav- eling of the multitude, and *the* knock- ing together of the weapons: for the company was very great and strong.

6.38 επιλοιπον S^{ca} V A 64^{+}236 La$^{109+146}$ | επιτοι- S* • ενθεν 2° V A 64^{+}236 La$^{109+146}$ | + και S • φαλαγξιν S^{ca} [-λαξ- S*] A La^{109} 7h7 7a1 | φαραγξιν V 64^{+}236 La^{146} • **6.39** κ(αι) / χαλκας S^{ca} V 64^{+}236 La^{146} | ~ S* • απ S^{ca} A 64^{+}236 La$^{109+146}$ | υπ S* V • **6.39–40** πυρος κ(αι) εξεταθη μερος τι της S^{ca} V A [κ(αι) κατεταθη 64] [και κατεςταθη 236] La$^{109+146}$ | > S* • **6.40** υψηλα S^{ca} V A 64^{+}236 La$^{109+146}$ | > S* • **6.41** και 3° S^{ca} V A 64^{+}236 La$^{109+146}$ | > S* •

6.38 On this occasion the army **company** was in **two sides**—an expression used again in 9.11–16 to describe an army that was "parted in two parts" ("horns" or "wings"). Many of **the horse** had been assigned to accompany the elephants (v 35), but **the rest** were placed on these wings, in order to terrify the enemy (**making** them **quake,** cf. v 41). The "great power" of the horse (Psa 33.17; 147.10) and the terror of its approach are vividly described in Job 39.19–25 (cf. Jer 8.16; Rev 9.9). But if enemy armies go to battle on horses (2 Kgs 6.14–15), there are far greater equestrian armies to oppose them (2 Kgs 6.16–17; Rev 19.11, 14, 19, 21).

The **horse** on these wings were **enclosed in the phalanxes.** Whatever the precise meaning of this expression,[183] it shows that the horse and their accompanying in-

[183] **Being enclosed in the phalanxes.** Elsewhere forms of *phrassō* clearly mean "close" (2.36; 5.47; 9.55; Heb 11.33; Rom 3.19). The particular form here is passive (*kataphrassomenoi,* **being enclosed**) and is followed by the preposition *en* (**in** or "by"). Thus the cavalry was not "enclosing" the two sides of the army ("covering their flanks," Cotton; "as guards for the phalanxes," NETS). Rather, it was **enclosed in** them. This is usually taken to mean that it was "protected by the phalanxes" (NRSV). However, such a rendering weakens the force of *phrassō* ("close") considerably (see the passages just cited). No other ancient instance of *kataphrassō* has been

fantry were moving and acting together (just as the elephants and their accompanying forces were moving and acting together, v 36). The whole company was proceeding "securely and in order" (v 40), with impressive power (v 41).

6.42 και ηγγιcεν Ιουδας και η παρεμβολη αυτου εις παραταξιν και επεcον απο της παρεμβολης του βαcιλεως εξακοcιοι ανδρεc	**6.42** And Judas and his company came near for battle; and six hundred men from the king's company fell.
6.43 και ειδεν Ελεαζαροc ο ‹Αυαραν› εν τω(ν) θηριων τεθωρακιcμενον θωραξιν βαcιλικοιc και ην υπεραγων πα(ν)τα τα θηρια και ωηθη οτι εν αυτω εcτιν ο βαcιλευc	**6.43** And Eleazar Avaran saw one of the animals, which was breastplated with *the* king's breastplates, and was raised up above all the animals; and it was thought that the king was on it.
6.44 και εδωκεν εαυτον του cωcαι τον λαον αυτου και περιποιηcαι εαυτω ονομα αιωνιον	**6.44** And he gave *him*self to save his people, and to gain possession for *him*self of a lasting name.
6.45 και επεδραμεν αυτω θραcει εις μεcον της φαλαγγοc και εθανατου(ν) ‹δεξια› και ευωνυμα και εcχιζοντο απ αυτου ενθα και ενθα	**6.45** And he ran on it confidently, into *the* midst of the phalanx; and he was putting to death *to* right and left; and they were parting from him here and *t*here.
6.46 και ειcεδυ υπο τον ελεφαντα και υπεθηκεν αυτω και ανειλεν αυτον και επεcε(ν) επι την γην επανω αυτου και απεθανεν εκει	**6.46** And he *began* going in under the elephant, and he stabbed it underneath, and did away with it; and it fell on the ground upon him, and he died there.
6.47 κ(αι) ‹ειδον› την ιcχυ(ν) της βαcιλειαc και ‹το ορμημα των δυναμεων› ‹και› ‹εξεκλιναν› απ αυτων	**6.47** And they saw the strength of the kingdom, and the onslaught of the forces; and they turned aside from them.

---

traced, but the prefix *kata-* is often used with "verbs naming that with which anything is covered, concealed, overshadowed" (examples are listed in Thayer 329, §III.3; e.g., *katakaluptō* ["cover up," 1 Cor 11.6–7]; *kataskiazō* ["overshadow," Heb 9.5]), and if anything it would intensify the main verb (e.g., by "bringing the action of the verbal root to a definite result," MHT 2.316). Thus if *kataphrassomenoi* means anything other than merely **being enclosed,** it would be likely to mean "being completely enclosed" or "being tightly enclosed"—which seems to be how the early Latin translators understood it (*constipati,* La[109+146]). Compare the description of a later army: "the horsemen were in the midst of the footsoldiers" (16.7), perhaps to protect them for use in the later stages of the battle (Abel 279). Vg omits the preceding **and,** so that **being enclosed** becomes a description of the infantry (the cavalry was stationed "to hasten them forward that stood thick together [≡ *kataphrassomenoi*] in the legions," DRCV). But in the Greek text, those who are **enclosed** are unambiguously the **horse.**

6.43 Αυαραν V A 64⁺236 [*sabaram* La^{109}] | Αυρ- S La^{146} • **6.45** δεξια S^{ca} V A 64⁺236 | -αν S* • **6.47** ειδον V A La^{146} [*diuiderunt* La^{109}] 7a1 | ιδεν S^{ca*} 64⁺236 7h7 | ιδοντες S* S^{ca1} • το ορμημα / των δυναμεων V [A] 64⁺236 La$^{109+146}$ | ~ S • και 3° V A 64⁺236 La$^{109+146}$ | > S • εξεκλιναν S^{ca} V A La$^{109+146}$ 7a1 | -ινεν S* 64⁺236 7h7 •

6.43–46 Eleazar Avaran, the last of Mattathias's sons listed in 2.2–5, was the first who **gave himself** in the way that his father had urged: "Give your souls on behalf of the covenant of our fathers . . . and receive great honor and a lasting name" (2.50–51). **It was thought that the king was on** one of the elephants, so Eleazar slew it at the cost of his own life. Even though the king escaped (v 50), Eleazar's deed is highly praised because it was done **to save his people, and to gain possession for himself of a lasting name** (see the notes on 2.51). What is precious to God is not the visible consequences of a deed but the heart of the doer (Luke 16.15; Rev 2.23; 1 Pet 3.4; 2 Chr 6.30). Eleazar's death may have had less practical consequence than Samson's ("the dead that he killed at his death were more than those that he killed in his life," Jdg 16.30), and Samson's than Christ's (He "gave Himself a ransom for all," 1 Tim 2.6, "so that He might deliver us out of the present evil age," Gal 1.4)—but all three of them **gave** themselves **to save** their **people,** and therefore all three acts are to be honored: "Whoever wants to save his own life will lose it; and whoever will lose his life for My sake and the gospel's will save it" (Mark 8.34–38).

God's servants are to seek a **lasting name.** They are to "seek glory and honor and immortality" (Rom 2.7)—not human glory, but "the glory that comes from the only God" (John 5.44).[184] "Seek the things that are above, where Christ is, seated at the right hand of God" (Col 3.1; cf. Matt 6.33; Luke 13.24). And if they are faithful unto death (Rev 2.10; 12.11), they **gain possession of** that **name**—a name that has "been written in the book of life from the foundation of the world" and will never be blotted out of it (Rev 17.8; 3.5; 13.8; cf. 2 Tim 4.7–8; Dan 12.1)—just as Christ Himself, by being faithful unto death, gained possession of a name that "will be to lasting time" and is "remembered in every generation" (Psa 72.17; 45.17; Phil 2.8–10).[185]

After the death of Eleazar, the Judeans **turned aside**[186] **from** their opponents. God's

---

[184] Cf. the last words of Judas Maccabeus (9.10). Judas and Eleazar, "seeing themselves as defenders of the glory of their God, did not at all separate His glory from theirs" (Sacy 121–22).

[185] Eleazar's act was not a suicide; it was done not to end his own life, but to attack **the king** and to **save his people** (Sacy 122–23; Calmet 97–98). Certainly, like everyone who takes active part in a battle, he was risking death; but, as Sacy remarks, he might seem to have been in more danger earlier, when he "ran . . . confidently, into the midst of the phalanx, and he was putting to death to right and left" (v 45), than when he stabbed the elephant. "Righteous ones are confident as a lion" (Prov 28.1), whether or not they die as a result (see on 9.10).

[186] **They turned aside** *(exeklinan).* The term indicates a change of direction (5.68; 12.31, 33) and sometimes a retreat (9.47), as it presumably does here ("they retreated from them," NAB; *retiráron se,* VRV ≡ *se retirèrent,* Martin; *se apartaron de ellos,* BGS; уклонились от них, RST).

people cannot expect to be resoundingly victorious in every conflict. In many situations their enemies can be overcome only "little by little," over an extended period of time (Exod 23.28–29; Deut 7.22; Jdg 3.1–4). Some will not be fully eradicated until the final harvest (Matt 13.28–30; 1 Cor 15.25–26).

The king captures Bethzur and besieges Mount Zion

6.48 οι δε εκ της παρεμβολης του βασιλεως ανεβαινον εις συναντησιν αυτω(ν) εις Ιερουσαλημ και παρενεβαλεν ο βασιλευς εις τη(ν) Ιουδαιαν και εις το ορος Σιων	**6.48** But the *people* from the king's camp were going up to Jerusalem to meet them; and the king camped in Judea and at Mount Zion.
6.49 και εποιησεν ειρηνην μετα των εκ Βεθσουρων και ‹εξηλθον› εκ της πολεως οτι ουκ ην αυτοις εκει διατροφη του συνκεκλισθε εν αυτη οτι σαββατον ην τη γη	**6.49** And he made peace with the *people* from Bethzur; and they came out of the city: for *there* was no nourishment for them there, to be besieged in it: for it was a Sabbath for the land.
6.50 και κατελαβετο ο βασιλευς την Βαιθσουραν κ(αι) επεταξεν εκει φρουραν τηριν αυτην	**6.50** And the king took hold of Bethzur, and appointed a garrison there to keep it.

6.49 εξηλθον 64*236 La[109] | -θεν S V A La[146] •

6.49 It was a **Sabbath** year (a seventh year, v 53), when no sowing or reaping could be done under the old covenant law (Lev 25.2–7). After a time, the **besieged** inhabitants of **Bethzur** (v 31) ran out of **nourishment,** and were forced to come **out of the city** and make **peace** with the king. The Lord had promised Israel that, if they served Him faithfully, they would never lack food during the Sabbath Year (Lev 25.6–7, 20–22), whereas if they disobeyed Him, they might suffer dearth during any year (Lev 26.19–20, 26; Ezek 4.16–17; 14.13; Hag 1.6–11), especially when besieged by their enemies (Deut 28.47–48, 52–53; 2 Kgs 6.24–25; Jer 52.4–6). In this respect, as in so many others, the Israelites who lived during the Maccabean era were suffering the consequences of the nation's sins (1.64; cf. Dan 11.33, 35).

6.51 και παρενεβαλεν επι το αγιασμα ημερας πολλας κ(αι) εστησεν εκει βελοστασιας και μηχανας και πυροβολα και λιθοβολα	**6.51** And he camped against the holy place *for* many days. And he established there stands for arrow-shooting, and devices, and fire-throwers, and stone-

The addition "in flight" (ESV) is authorized by nothing in either the verb itself or its present context. The account of the same incident in the Epitome (13.16) says that the Judeans departed *euēmerountes* (perhaps "with good success" [RV; LEH 248], perhaps "in good cheer" [Muraoka 299])—which is certainly not a description of a flight.

και σκορπιδια εις το βαλλεσθαι βελη και σφενδονας	throwers, and shooting-machines to shoot arrows, and slings.
6.52 και εποιησαν και αυτοι μηχανας προς τας μηχανας αυτων και επολεμησαν ημερας ‹πολλας›	**6.52** And they themselves also made devices against their devices; and they made war *for* many days.
6.53 βρωματα δε ουκ ην εν τοις ‹αγγειοις› δια το εβδομο(ν) ετος ειναι και οι ανασωζομενοι εις την Ιουδαιαν απο των εθνων κατεφαγον το υπολιμμα της παραθεσεως	**6.53** But there were no foods in the containers, because it was the seventh year, and those who went to Judea for safety from the nations had eaten up the rest of the store.
6.54 και υπελιφθησαν εν τοις αγιοις ανδρες ολιγοι οτι κατεκρατησεν αυτων ο λειμος και εσκορπισθησαν εκαστος εις τον τοπον αυτου	**6.54** And few men remained in the holy *place*s: for the famine had overpowered them, and they had been scattered, each *one* to his place.

6.52 πολλας A 64^{+}236 La$^{109+146}$ | > S V • **6.53** αγγειοις V^{a} La^{109} | αγιοις S A 64^{+}236 La^{146} | αγειοις V* •

6.51–54 The king also **camped against the holy place** at Mount Zion (v 48),[187] and the **famine** that had caused the fall of Bethzur happened here as well: **it was the seventh year,** and the place's **store** of food was **eaten up** by those who had taken refuge there, until **no foods** remained **in the containers.**[188]

The king makes peace with the people of Mount Zion

6.55 και ηκουσεν Λυσιας οτι Φιλιππος ον κατεστησεν ο	**6.55** And Lysias heard that Philip—whom King Antiochus,

[187] This passage contains the book's most detailed list of siege engines. Nearly all their names are self-explanatory, at least in the Greek. The term **stands for arrow-shooting** *(belostasias)* is used in the LXX most often to translate Hebrew *dyq* ("bulwarks," "siege walls," Ezek 17.17; 21.22), so these may have been not "towers" (NRSV) but protective "mounds" (RV) or "emplacements" (REB) for the use of the following **devices** (*mēchanas,* a general term: see on 5.30). A **stone-thrower** *(lithobolos)* was a machine that did what people did when they stoned *(lithoboleō)* a criminal (Num 15.35–36; Acts 7.58–59). The comparable term **fire-thrower** *(purobolos)* describes a similar machine that hurled burning projectiles (cf. Prov 26.18; Eph 6.16). A **shooting-machine** (*skorpidion,* "scatterer") scattered *(skorpizō)* **arrows** *(belē)* against the enemy (Psa 18.14). A **sling** *(sphendonē)* was a device for hurling stones against an enemy (cf. Jdg 20.16; 1 Sam 17.40, 49). The LORD had promised His people success against such missiles: "I will rouse up your sons, O Zion, against your sons, O Greece… The LORD of hosts will shelter them; and they will devour, and will tread underfoot the sling stones" (Zec 9.13–15).

[188] V^{a} and 58, supported by La^{109}, say that there were no foods in the **containers** (*aggeiois),* a term applied to "vessels" (KJV), e.g., for oil (Matt 25.4) or fish (Matt 13.48 D ≡ *aggē* B and S). The word does not elsewhere mean "storerooms" (NAB). S, V*, A, and 64^{+}236, supported by La^{146}, say that there were no foods in the **holy places** *(hagiois).*

βασιλευϲ Αντιοχοϲ ετι ζωντοϲ αυτου εκθρεψαι Αντιοχον τον υιον αυτου ειϲ το βαϲιλευϲαι αυτον	while still living, had established to bring up Antiochus his son to be king—
6.56 απεϲτρεψεν απο τηϲ Περϲιδοϲ και Μηδειαϲ και ⸤αι⸥ δυναμιϲ αι πορευθιϲαι μετα του βαϲιλεωϲ μετ αυτου και οτι ζητει παραλαβειν τα των ⸤πραγματων⸥	**6.56** had returned from Persia and Media, and with him *were* the forces that had gone with the king; and that he was seeking to take over the business of government.
6.57 και κατεϲπευδεν και επενευϲεν του απελθειν και ειπεν προϲ τον βαϲιλεα και τουϲ ηγεμοναϲ τηϲ δυναμεωϲ και τουϲ ανδραϲ εκλιπομεν καθ ημεραν και η τροφη ημιν ολιγη και ο τοποϲ ου παρεμβαλλομεν εϲτιν ⸤οχυροϲ⸥ και επικειται ημι(ν) τα τηϲ βαϲιλιαϲ	**6.57** And he *began* hurrying, and agreed to go away; and he said to the king, and the leaders of the force, and the men: "We are coming to an end each day, and *there is* little nourish- ment for us, and the place where we are camping is fortified; and the *thing*s of the kingdom are pressing upon us.
6.58 νυ(ν) ουν δωμεν δεξιαν τοιϲ αν(θρωπ)οιϲ τουτοιϲ και ποιηϲωμεν ⸤μετ αυτων⸥ ιρηνην και μετα παντοϲ εθνουϲ αυτων	**6.58** Now therefore, let us give *the* right *hand* to these persons, and let us make peace with them, and with all their nation.
6.59 κ(αι) ⸤ϲτηϲωμεν αυτοιϲ⸥ του πορευεϲθαι τοιϲ νομιμοιϲ αυτων ωϲ το προτερον χαριν γαρ των νομιμων αυτω(ν) ων διεϲκεδαϲαμεν ωργιϲθηϲαν και εποιηϲαν ⸤παντα ταυτα⸥	**6.59** And let us establish for them to go in their *own* laws, as previous*ly*: for *it was* on account of their laws, which we abolished, *that* they became angry and did all these *things*."
6.60 και ηρεϲε(ν) ο λογοϲ εναντιον του βαϲιλεωϲ και των αρχοντων και απεϲτιλεν προϲ αυτουϲ ειρηνευϲε και επεδεξαντο	**6.60** And the word pleased the king and the commanders; and he sent them *an offer* to be at peace; and they accepted.
6.61 και ⸤ωμοϲεν⸥ αυτοιϲ ο βαϲιλευϲ και οι αρχο(ν)τεϲ επι τουτοιϲ εξηλθον εκ του οχυρωματοϲ	**6.61** And the king and the commanders swore an oath to them. On these *condition*s they came out of the fortress.

6.56 αι 1° V A 64^{+}236 La$^{109+146}$ | > S • πραγματων S^{ca} V A [-τα 64^{+}236] La$^{109+146}$ | προϲταγ- S* • **6.57** οχυροϲ V A 64^{+}236 La^{146} [*minutus* La^{109}] | ιϲχ- S • **6.58** μετ αυτων V A 64^{+}236 La$^{109+146}$ | > S • **6.59** ϲτηϲωμεν αυτοιϲ V A 64^{+}236 La$^{109+146}$ | ϲτηϲομεν αυτουϲ S • παντα / ταυτα V 64 La$^{109+146}$ | ~ S A 236 • **6.61** ωμοϲεν S^{ca} V A 64^{+}236 La$^{109+146}$ | ωμολογηϲεν S* •

6.55–61 However, the king's forces could not continue the siege of Mount Zion long enough to force a surrender there, in the way that had happened at Bethzur. The

LORD now intervened almost as He had done when Sennacherib besieged Jerusalem ("he will hear a report, and return to his land; and I will cause him to fall by the sword in his land," 2 Kgs 19.7) and when Saul's men had surrounded David's ("a messenger came to Saul, saying, 'Hasten and come; for the Philistines have raided the land'," 1 Sam 23.27). News arrived that **Philip** (whom Antiochus Epiphanes had "established . . . over all his kingdom," v 14) had now **returned from Persia and Media,** and was trying **to take over the business of government.** Moreover, the lack of **nourishment** was affecting the king's forces, as well as their opponents. The king therefore agreed to **make peace** with the people in Mount Zion, so that he could leave to deal with Philip. The peace terms would allow the Judeans **to go in their own laws, as previously**—an official reversal of the contrary decree issued by Antiochus Epiphanes five years earlier (1.41–51). The terms were confirmed with an **oath.**[189]

Let us give the right hand to these persons. A mark of fellowship (11.50, 62, 66; 13.45, 50; 2 Kgs 10.15; Gal 2.9).

The king destroys the wall of Zion and returns to Antioch

6.62 και ‹εισηλθεν› ο βασιλευς εις ορος Σιων και ειδε(ν) το οχυρωμα του τοπου και ηθετησεν τον ‹ορκισμον› ον ωμοσεν και ενετιλατο καθελει(ν) το τιχος κυκλοθε(ν)	**6.62** And the king came into Mount Zion, and saw the fortress of the place, and he set aside the oath that he had sworn, and commanded to pull down the wall round about.

6.62 εισηλθεν S^{ca} V A 64^{+}236 La$^{109+146}$ | -θον S* • ορκισμον S^{ca} V A La$^{109+146}$ | ορισ- S* | ορκον 64^{+}236 •

6.62 But those who proposed the peace terms did not keep them. When they saw the fortifications that Judas had constructed in **Mount Zion** (v 57; "high walls and fortified towers," 4.60), the king **set aside the oath** and ordered the **wall** to be pulled down. Very soon afterwards, he who broke the oath would himself be repaid with treachery (7.2–4; cf. Ezek 16.59; 17.13–18). God's enemies may often use deceit and treachery in their dealings (cf. 1.30; 7.13–18; 11.53; 12.42–48; 16.11–17), but He requires His people to be truthful in all their dealings (Lev 19.11; Zep 3.13; Col 3.9; Jas 5.12; cf. John 8.44), as He Himself is (2 Tim 2.13).

6.63 και απηρεν κατα σπουδην και απεστρεψεν εις Αντιοχιαν και ευρεν Φιλιππον κυριευο(ν)τα της πολεως και επολεμησε(ν) προς αυτον και κατελαβετο την πολιν βια	**6.63** And he moved away with diligence, and returned to Antioch; and he found Philip lord over the city. And he made war against him, and took hold of the city by force.

6.63 The king now **took hold of** *(katelabeto)* Antioch and overcame the opposition of **Philip**—though he had not been able to "take hold of" Judas and his supporters (v

[189] The news of Philip's rebellion and the king's oath are mentioned briefly in Epitome 13.23.

27). He could defeat a rival human **lord,** but against the Lord of lords he was powerless (Rev 17.14; Job 40.9–14; 1 Cor 10.22; 2 Kgs 19.22–23; see also on v 27).

The first conflicts with Demetrius son of Seleucus

Demetrius son of Seleucus becomes king

7.1 ετουϲ α′ και ⸂ν′ και ρ′⸃ εξηλθεν	**7.1** *In the* hundred and fifty-first year,
Δημητριοϲ ⸂ο⸃ του Ϲελευκου	Demetrius the *son* of Seleucus came
εκ Ρωμηϲ και ανεβη ⸂ϲυν ανδραϲιν⸃	out from Rome. And he went up,
ολιγοιϲ ⸂ειϲ πολιν παραθαλαϲϲιαν⸃	with a few men, to a city beside *the*
και εβαϲιλευϲεν εκει	sea, and became king there.

7.1 ν′ / και / ρ′ V 64^{+}236 La$^{109+146}$ | ~ S | πεντηκοστου A | + και S V • ο S^{ca} V A 64^{+}236 | > S* • ϲυν ανδραϲιν S^{ca} V A 64^{+}236 La$^{109+146}$ | εν ανδραϲιν εν S* • ειϲ πολιν παραθαλαϲϲιαν S^{ca} V A 64^{+}236 La$^{[109+]146}$ | παραθαλαϲϲαν S* •

7.1 Rome had defeated Antiochus the Great, and had required him and his successors to give them hostages (8.6–7). Antiochus Epiphanes himself "had been a hostage in Rome" before he became king (1.10). Now the pattern was repeated: **Demetrius . . . came out of Rome** and **became king.**[190] Demetrius was a descendant of the previous kings of Syria (they were "his fathers," v 2), and therefore he had a claim to the Seleucid throne.[191]

7.2 και ⸂εγενετο⸃ ωϲ ειϲεπορευετο	**7.2** And as he was going into *the*
ειϲ οικον βαϲιλειαϲ πατερω(ν) αυτου	house of *the* kingdom of his fathers,
⸂ϲυνελαβον⸃ αι δυναμειϲ	it came about *that* the forces
τον Αντιοχον και το(ν) Λυϲιαν	took hold of Antiochus and Lysias,
αγαγειν αυτουϲ αυτω	to bring them to him.

7.2 εγενετο S^{ca} V A 64^{+}236 La$^{109+146}$ | επονειτο S* • ϲυνελαβον S^{ca} V A 64^{+}236 La$^{109+146}$ | -οντο S* •

7.2 When he reached Syria, Demetrius proceeded to enter **the house of the kingdom** (a term for the royal palace, as in Est 1.9), which had belonged to the previous kings, **his fathers.** The army **forces** decided to support him, and so they **took hold of Antiochus and Lysias.**

---

[190] According to his personal friend Polybius, **Demetrius** was being held in Rome as a hostage; the Roman senate refused him permission to return to Syria, but he escaped (31.11–15).

[191] Other historical sources report that Antiochus the Great had been succeeded as king by his son **Seleucus** (Appian, *Syriaca,* 45.232; Epitome 3.3; cf. Dan 11.20) and then by the latter's brother Antiochus Epiphanes (CM §4.23–25; Epitome 4.7; cf. Dan 11.21). **Demetrius** was a **son of Seleucus;** his rival Antiochus Eupator was a son of Antiochus Epiphanes (see 6.17). Both of them, therefore, were sons of previous kings. However, Demetrius's father had been the earlier of those kings, and his rival's father had not been "given" the kingdom but had "taken" it "by smooth words" (Dan 11.21).

7.3 και εγνωcθη αυτω το πραγμα και ειπεν μη μοι διξηται τα προcωπα αυτων	**7.3** And the act became known to him; and he said: "Do not show^{pl} me their faces."
7.4 και απεκτιναν αυτουc αι δυναμειc και εκαθιcεν Δημητριοc επι θρονου βαcιλειαc αυτου	**7.4** And the forces killed them. And Demetrius sat on *the* throne of his kingdom.

7.3–4 Demetrius told the army: **Do not show me their faces**—an ambiguous instruction, which could mean merely "Do not let them enter my presence" (as in 2 Sam 14.24). But the soldiers carried out the command in a different way (cf. Est 7.8). They **killed** Antiochus and Lysias, leaving Demetrius the uncontested ruler of the **kingdom**—until the next upheaval (which would happen less than a decade later: 10.1–2). "Not from the east or from the west or from the desert does raising come; but God is the Judge: He puts this one down, and He raises that one up" (Psa 75.6–7; Dan 2.21).

He sends Bacchides and Alcimus to take vengeance

7.5 και ηλθον προc αυτον παντεc ανδρεc ανομοι και αcεβειc εξ Ιc(ραη)λ και ‹Αλκιμοc› ηγειτο αυτων ‹› βουλομενοc ιερατευειν	**7.5** And *there* came to him all *the* men out of Israel *who were* opposed to *the* Law and irreverent; and Alcimus was leading them, wanting to do *the* work of a priest.

7.5 Αλκιμοc V 64^{+}236 La$^{109+146}$ | -ιcμοc S | -ινοc A • αυτων V A 64^{+}236 La$^{109+146}$ | + ηγουμενοc S •

7.5 All the **irreverent** (see on 3.8) people in **Israel** now turned to Demetrius for help, just as they had recently turned to his rival (6.21–22). Among them was **Alcimus,** who was a descendant of Aaron (v 14) and was therefore authorized under the old covenant law to be a **priest** (Exod 29.9; 40.14–15; Num 16.40; 2 Chr 26.18).[192] But a priest should fear God, speak truth, turn people away from iniquity, and teach the Law (Mal 2.4–7). These things Alcimus did not do.

7.6 και ‹κατηγορηcαν› του λαου προc τον βαcιλεα λεγοντεc απωλεcεν Ιουδαc και οι αδελφοι αυτου πανταc τουc φιλουc cου και ημαc εcκορπιcεν απο τηc γηc ημων	**7.6** And they spoke publicly against the people to the king, saying: "Judas and his brothers have destroyed all your† friends; and us he has scattered from our land.

7.6 κατηγορηcαν S^{cb1} V A 64^{+}236 La$^{109+146}$ | -cαι S* •

---

[192] Epitome 14.3 states that **Alcimus** had previously been high priest (at some unspecified time). This is possible but not certain (Doran, *2 Maccabees,* 266–67).

7.7 νυν ουν αποστιλον α(ν)δρα ω ‹πιστευεις› και πορευθεις ειδετω ‹την εξολοθρευσιν πασαν› ην εποιησεν ημιν και τη χωρα του βασιλεως και εκολασατο αυτους και πα(ν)τας τους επιβοηθου(ν) τας αυτοις	**7.7** Now therefore, send† a man whom you† trust; and when *he has* gone, let him see all the utter destruction that he has done to us and to the district of the king, and *that* he has punished them and all those who helped them."

7.7 πιστευεις S^{ca} V A 64^{+}236 La^{109} | -ευσεις S* La^{146} • την εξολοθρευσιν / πασαν V A 64^{+}236 La$^{109+146}$ | ~ S •

7.6–7 Judas and his brothers had **destroyed** some of the king's Israelite supporters and **scattered** others **from** their **land** (as described in 2.44; 3.8), in accordance with the teachings of the old covenant: "A person who works deceit will not dwell inside my house .... I will destroy all the wicked ones of the land, to cut off from the city of the LORD all those who do iniquity" (Psa 101.7–8). In this way, Judas had **punished** the king's loyal subjects[193] **and all those who helped them.** "Whatever a person sows, this he shall also reap" (Gal 6.7). The LORD's enemies were now reaping the very things that they had previously sown among the faithful (destruction, 1.30; 2.38; 3.8; scattering, 1.38, 53; 2.28–30, 43).

7.8 και επελεξεν ο βασιλευς τον Βαχχιδην τω(ν) φιλων του βασιλεως κυριευοντα εν τω περαν του ποταμου και μεγαν εν τη βασιλεια και πιστο(ν) τω βασιλει	**7.8** And the king chose Bacchides, *one* of the king's Friends, who was lord on the other side of the River, and a great *man* in the kingdom, and faithful to the king;
7.9 και απεστιλεν αυτον και ‹› Αλκιμον τον ασεβην ‹και› εστησεν αυτω την ιερωσυνην και ενετιλατο αυτω ποιησαι την εκδικησιν εν τοις υιοις Ισ(ραη)λ	**7.9** And he sent him, and the irreverent Alcimus, and established the priesthood for him; and he commanded him to take vengeance among the sons of Israel.

7.9 και 2° V A 64^{+}236 | + τον S • και 3° S^{ca} V A 64^{+}236 La$^{109+146}$ | > S* •

7.8–9 The king **established Alcimus** in the **priesthood.**[194] In the Maccabean period, foreign kings often assumed that they had some say in the appointment of Israelite priests (although the old covenant Law nowhere gave kings any role in that process). For instance, Simon's appointment as high priest was determined by the Israelites' choice (14.35) and his own acceptance (14.47), but the current king also officially "established" him in the position (14.38). Jonathan's appointment, too, evidently involved both Israelites and foreign kings (see the footnote to 10.20; cf. 11.27, 57).

---

[193] S, V, and A, supported by La$^{109+146}$, read **he has punished them** *(ekolasato autous)*. 64^{+}236 read "let him punish them" *(kolasato autous)*.

[194] Perhaps even the high priesthood; cf. v 21 ("priest" can sometimes mean specifically "high priest": 2 Kgs 12.7–9).

Against Israel the king **sent** an army ("a great force," v 10) under the leadership of **Bacchides,** who was **a great man in the kingdom,** being **one of the king's Friends** (as Mattathias and his sons might have been, 2.18) and governor of the region **on the other side of the River**—a term applied sometimes to districts east of the Euphrates (Josh 24.2–3), but here to districts west of the Euphrates, such as Samaria and Israel (as in Ezra 4.10–11, 16–17, 20).

Some who trust Bacchides and Alcimus are killed

7.10 και απηρον και ηλθον μετα δυναμεωϲ πολληϲ ειϲ γην Ιουδα και απεϲτιλεν αγγελουϲ προϲ Ιουδαν και τουϲ αδελφουϲ αυτου λογοιϲ ειρηνικοιϲ μετα δολου	**7.10** And they *began* moving away, and they came with a great force into *the* land of Judah. And he sent messengers to Judas and his brothers with peaceful words in deceit.
7.11 και ου προϲεϲχον τοιϲ λογοιϲ αυτων ειδον γαρ οτι ηλθα(ν) μετα δυναμεωϲ πολληϲ	**7.11** And they did not pay attention to their words: for they saw that they had come with a great force.

7.10–11 Bacchides sent **peaceful words in deceit** (cf. 1.30) to Judas and his brothers, but **they did not pay attention,** because his deeds were not in accordance with his words (cf. 1 Jn 3.18; Titus 1.16): despite his **peaceful** talk, he had brought **a great force** with him. "A person who hates disguises himself with his lips, and places deceit in his heart; when he shows favor with his voice, do not believe him, for there are seven abominations in his heart" (Prov 26.24–25). So Jeremiah was warned not to believe the people around him, "though they speak good words to you" (Jer 12.6), and Jesus "did not entrust Himself to" the people around Him, "because He knew all people" (John 2.24–25). "Someone who is open to enticement believes every word; but a prudent person understands his going" (Prov 14.15). It is no virtue to "believe every spirit" (1 Jn 4.1).

7.12 και επιϲυνηχθηϲαν προϲ Αλκιμον και ‹Βακχιδην› ϲυναγωγη γραμματεων εκζητηϲαι ‹δικαια›	**7.12** And a gathering of scribes gathered to Alcimus and Bacchides, to seek for *thing*s that were righteous.
7.13 και πρωτοι οι Αϲειδαιοι ηϲαν εν υιοιϲ Ιϲ(ραη)λ και επεζητουν παρ αυτων ειρηνην	**7.13** And the Hasidim [lovingkind *one*s] were first among *the* sons of Israel, and they were seeking peace from them;
7.14 ειπον γαρ ανθρωποϲ ιερευϲ εκ ϲπερματοϲ Ααρων ηλθεν εν ταιϲ δυναμεϲιν και ουκ αδικηϲει ημαϲ	**7.14** for they said: "A person *who is* a priest from *the* seed of Aaron has come with the forces, and he will not do *any* unrighteousness to us."

7.12 Βακχιδην S^{ca} V [Κακχ- A] $64^{+}236$ $La^{109+146}$ | -ηϲ S* • δικαια S^{ca} V A $64^{+}236$ $La^{109+146}$ | -αιοι S* •

7.12–14 Others, however, were more easily deceived ("good words and blessings" may "deceive the hearts of the innocent," Rom 16.18). Some of the **scribes** went **to Alcimus and Bacchides** to ask for **things that were righteous.**[195] And the group known as the **Hasidim** ("lovingkind ones": see the notes on 2.42) reasoned that a **priest**[196] **from the seed of Aaron** would not do them any harm (cf. Isa 63.8).[197] "A priest's lips should keep knowledge, and they should seek the law at his mouth; for he is the messenger of the LORD of hosts"—but all too often, Israel's priests had "turned aside out of the law" (Mal 2.1–9; Ezek 22.26; Ezra 9.1; 10.18–19), as they would do again in the time of the Messiah (Mark 14.55). "They are not all Israel, who are of Israel" (Rom 9.6); in fact, some of them are "enemies" of Israel (Mic 7.5–6 ≡ Matt 10.35–36).

7.15 και ελαληcεν μετ αυτω(ν) λογουc ιρηνικουc και ωμοcεν αυτοιc λεγων ουκ εκζητηcομεν υμιν κακον και τοιc φιλοιc υμων	**7.15** And he spoke peaceful words with them, and swore an oath to them, saying: "We will not seek evil for you[pl] or your[pl] friends."
7.16 και ‹ενεπιcτευcαν› αυτω και cυνελαβεν εξ αυτω(ν) εξηκοντα ανδραc και απεκτινεν αυτουc εν ημερα μια κατα τον λογον ον εγραψεν αυτον	**7.16** And they had faith in him. And he took hold of sixty men from them, and killed them in one day, in accordance with the word that He wrote:
7.17 cαρκαc κρεαc οcιων cου και αιμα αυτων εξεχεαν κυκλω Ιερουcαλημ και ουκ η(ν) αυτοιc ο θαπτων	**7.17** "*The* flesh, *the* carcass of Your[†] lovingkind *one*s, and their blood, they have poured out round about Jerusalem, and *there* was no *one* burying for them."

7.16 ενεπιcτευcαν S[ca] V A 64[+]236 La[109+146] | -ευcεν S* •

7.15–17 Bacchides and Alcimus "cried peace . . . and prepared war" (Mic 3.5; cf. 2 Sam 20.9–10; Psa 28.3; 12.1–2). One of them[198] **swore an oath** that those who trusted

---

[195] **Things that were righteous:** *dikaia,* like the laws and judgments of God Himself (Deut 4.8; Eighteen Psalms 2.12; Phil 4.8).

[196] **A person [who is] a priest.** The Greek wording is *anthrōpos hiereus,* as in Lev 21.9, LXX.

[197] The statement that the Hasidim **were first among the sons of Israel, and they were seeking peace** means simply that they were the first "who sought peace" (Cotton); cf. Keil 128–29; Abel 132–33. Such idioms are common in Hebrew (BDB 253, §1k) and in the LXX (Abel, *Grammaire,* §78*b,* 3°).

[198] The shift from third person plural (**them,** v 13) to third person singular (**he spoke . . . and swore an oath,** v 15) may not have any special significance (such shifts are characteristic of the book's style). The individual discussed in the immediately preceding context (v 14) is Alcimus; yet Bacchides, the military leader of the expedition (v 8), is more likely to have authorized the killing described in v 16 (cf. v 19).

him would not be harmed, but afterwards killed **sixty men from** among **them . . . in one day.**

This deed was **in accordance with** Asaph's prophecy[199] of the evils that would come upon Jerusalem: "God, nations have come into Your inheritance; they have made unclean the temple of Your holiness; they have set Jerusalem in ruins. They have given the corpse of Your servants as food to the flying creature of the heavens, the flesh[200] of Your Hasidim [*ḥsydyk,* Your lovingkind ones] to the beast of the land. They have poured out their blood like waters round about Jerusalem, and there was no one that buried" (Psa 79.1–3).[201]

Asaph's prophecy is framed throughout in general terms, which are applicable to each and all of the disasters that would befall Jerusalem. Some have argued that its reference to Hasidim *(ḥsydyk)* is applicable only to the Maccabean period (cf. Lapide 39; Truchet 113), but all God's faithful people in every age have been Hasidim, "lovingkind ones" (Psa 31.23); Jesus Himself was a *Ḥsyd* (Psa 16.10 ≡ Acts 13.35–37). Others have argued that the psalm's reference to Jerusalem being "in ruins" is applicable only to the Babylonian period (cf. Keil 130), but Jerusalem was certainly also left in ruins by Antiochus Epiphanes, whose agents "took the plunder of the city, and set it on fire with fire, and pulled down its houses and the walls round about" (1.31), leaving "the holy place desolate, and the sacrificial altar profaned, and the gates burned down, and in the courtyards, plants grown up . . . and the chambers pulled down"

---

[199] S* and V, supported by La[146], describe this prophecy as **the word that He wrote** (*ton logon hon egrapsen auton,* S*; *ton logon hon egrapsen,* V)—meaning not that "the psalmist" (RV) **wrote** it but that the LORD did (King). (In this book, an unnamed person with no true grammatical antecedent is always the LORD, never a human; cf. 3.22, 60; 4.16.) A reads "the words that He wrote" *(tous logous hous egrapsen).* As elsewhere in the book, many copyists and translators tended to adapt the unexpressed subject in various ways. La[109] and 7a1 have "the word that is written" *(verbum quod scriptum est ≡ mlt' dktyb).* S[ca] and 64[+]236 (supported by 7h7) read "the word that the prophet wrote" *(ton logon hon egrapsen ho prophētēs).* The supplementary *auton* in S* is a familiar Semitic idiom (compare *hon arithmēsai auton,* Rev 7.9; BDF §297).

[200] The term **carcass** *(kreas)* is usually applied to the flesh of a dead animal (Rom 14.21; 1 Cor 8.13; not necessarily a portion to be eaten, Exod 29.14, LXX etc.), but occasionally to the flesh of a person (Deut 32.42, LXX)—in which case it is often derisive or comic (Zenobius, *Proverbs,* 4.85; LSJ 992, §2; Muraoka, 411, §1c), although not always (Job 10.11, LXX). **The flesh, the carcass** (*sarkas kreas,* S* V La[109+146]) is either a condensation of two clauses from the psalm ("the corpse . . . the flesh" [*nblt . . . bśr*], Psa 79.2), or else a double rendering of *bśr.* Double renderings of a single word are frequent in ancient Greek, Syriac, and Aramaic translations of Hebrew (e.g., *polutelē eklekton* [Isa 28.16, LXX], a double rendering of *bḥn* [Isa 28.16, MT] ≡ *eklekton* [1 Pet 2.6]).

[201] "Asaph the seer" lived in the time of David and Solomon (1 Chr 16.7; 25.6; 2 Chr 5.12; 29.30), centuries before any slaughter of God's people at Jerusalem by the nations. His prophecy is phrased as though the foretold events had already been completed (like many other Scripture prophecies; e.g., Isa 53: "He was led as a sheep to the slaughter . . ."; cf. Acts 8.32–35).

(4.38). The truth is that people in any age when Jerusalem was despoiled and ruined—whether in Babylonian, Maccabean, or Roman times—could have sung every syllable of that psalm as being fulfilled in their own generation.[202] It can still be sung today, when the church—which ought to be "Mount Zion . . . the city of the living God, the heavenly Jerusalem" (Heb 12.22)—is being defiled by enemies both from outside and from inside, who seek to impose the world's beliefs and ways of living on the Israel of God (cf. 1 Jn 2.15–17; 2 Cor 6.14–7.1; Eph 4.17–20), while the body of Christ, the *Ḥsyd* who died for all, is trodden underfoot even by those who call themselves His priests, and His blood is rejected as an unholy thing (Heb 10.29).

7.18 και επεπεσεν αυτων ο φοβος και	**7.18** And fear of them and trembling
ο τρομος εις παντα τον λαον οτι	fell on all the people; for they said:
ειπον ουκ εστιν εν αυτοις αληθια και	"*There* is no truth and justice in them;
κρισις παρεβησαν γαρ	for they have turned away from
τη(ν) στασιν	the established agreement
και τον ορκον ον ωμοσαν	and the oath that they swore."

7.18 Fear of them and trembling fell on all the people. It is a shocking thing when someone who professes to be a servant of God proves to be a servant of the devil. Such a person is condemned in the most vehement language ever recorded from the mouth of Jesus (e.g., Matt 23.13–36), and is treasuring up wrath for himself in the day of judgment (Rom 2.5). "Will he prosper? Will he who does such things escape? And will he break the covenant and escape?" (Ezek 17.12–18; Hos 10.4). The LORD Himself never breaks His word (Psa 89.33–34; Jer 33.20–21), "for He cannot deny Himself" (2 Tim 2.13); and He cannot endure those who do so.[203]

There is no truth and justice in them. A tree is known by its fruit, and, even in sheep's clothing, a wolf can be recognized by its behavior (Matt 7.15–18). When a person lies (John 3.21; 8.44) or seeks to kill any servant of God (John 8.40), he shows that he is not of God.

7.19 και απηρεν Βακχιδης απο	**7.19** And Bacchides moved away from
Ι(ερουσα)λημ και παρενεβαλεν εν	Jerusalem, and camped in Bethzeth.
Βηθζαιθ και απεστιλεν	And he sent,
και ‹συνελαβεν› πολλους απο τω(ν)	and took many of the men who
μετ αυτου αυτομοληςαντων ανδρω(ν)	had deserted, *who were* with him;
και τινας του λαου εθυσεν	and some of the people he himself
αυτος εις το φρεαρ το μεγα	sacrificed into the great well-hole.
7.20 και κατεστησεν τη(ν) χωραν	**7.20** And he established the district
‹τω Αλκιμω› και αφηκεν μετ αυτου	for Alcimus, and left a force

[202] Geier, *Commentarius in Psalmos,* 1453.

[203] The word that was broken is called an **established agreement** *(stasin).* Compare Matt 18.16 ("by the mouth of two witnesses or three, every word may be established"); Heb 10.9.

δυναμιν του βοηθειν αυτω	with him to help him.
και απηλθε(ν) Βακχιδηc	And Bacchides went away
προc το(ν) βαcιλεα	to the king.

7.19 cυνελαβεν S^{ca} V A 64⁺236 $La^{109+146}$ | cυνεβαλεν S* • **7.20** τω Αλκιμω S^{cb1} V A 64⁺236 $La^{109+146}$ | των -μων S* •

7.19 Bacchides now moved from Jerusalem to **Bethzeth** (a place not otherwise mentioned), where he seized and slaughtered a number of people. At least some of Bacchides' victims were **men who had deserted** from Judas and were now **with him,**[204] so he was killing the very people who had put their trust in him (cf. vv 16, 34). The Scriptures contain many warnings against those who "speak peace with their companions, and evil is in their hearts" (Psa 28.3; 12.2; 55.21; Jer 9.8), and against making any agreement with them to do evil (2 Cor 6.14; Prov 1.10–19), as these people had done with Bacchides.

The term used for the slaughter is a remarkable one: Bacchides **sacrificed** *(ethusen)* his victims, as if offering them to a god (1.43, 47; 2.25; 4.56).[205]

7.21 και ηγωνιcατο Αλκιμοc	**7.21** And Alcimus strove
περι τηc ‹αρχιερωcυνηc›	for the high priesthood.
7.22 και cυνηχθηcαν προc αυτον	**7.22** And all those who were unset-
παντεc οι ταραccοντεc τον λαον	tling their people gathered to him,
αυτων και κατεκρατηcαν γην Ιουδα	and they overpowered *the* land
και εποιηcα(ν) πληγην μεγαλην	of Judah, and did a great injury
εν Ιc(ρα)ηλ	in Israel.

7.21 αρχιερωcυνηc V A 64⁺236 $La^{109+146}$ | ιερ- S •

7.21 After Bacchides returned to the king, **Alcimus strove for the high priesthood** ("put up a strong fight for" it, REB): he pursued it with the fervor and commitment that God's people today are commanded to expend when striving for the eternal heavenly prize (Luke 13.24; 1 Cor 9.25; 1 Tim 6.12).[206]

---

[204] S, V, and A, supported by $La^{109+146}$, describe these as people who had deserted **[who were] with him** *(met' autou)*. 64⁺236 describe them as people who had deserted "from him" *(ap' autou)*.

[205] In the Scriptures, forms of *thuō* are almost always used of sacrifices to a deity (TDNT 3.180–83); the nearest analogy to the present passage is John 10.10. **Some of the people he himself sacrificed** *(... ethusen autos)* is the wording in S*, supported by $La^{109+146}$, whereas V, A, and 64⁺236 read "some of the people, and he sacrificed them" *(... kai ethusen autous)*. S^{ca} altered S* partway toward the form found in 64⁺236, resulting in ... *kai ethusen autos.*

[206] **Strove** *(ēgōnisato)* **for the high priesthood.** The wording does not indicate whether he was already high priest ("struggled to maintain his high priesthood," NRSV) or whether he was trying to become so ("struggled to gain the high priesthood," NETS). In the Scriptures, forms of *agōnizomai* always indicate intense effort and exertion (*kämpfte,* Zöckler); see the passages cited above and in BDAG 17; TDNT 1.134–40.

To serve God as high priest was a good work (Heb 5.1–4), and it is not wrong to seek a good work (cf. 1 Tim 3.1). But Alcimus was not seeking to serve God (v 9).

Alcimus returns to the king

7.23 και ειδεν Ιουδας πασαν την κακιαν ην εποιηcεν Αλκιμος και οι μετ αυτου εν υιοις Ιc(ραη)λ υπερ τα εθνη	**7.23** And Judas saw all the evil that Alcimus and those with him had done among *the* sons of Israel, beyond *what* the nations *had done.*

7.23 Like King Manasseh (2 Kgs 21.9), **Alcimus** enticed people to do more **evil** than **the nations** had done. When "from among your own selves men [arise], speaking twisted things, to draw away the disciples after them" (Acts 20.30), it is worse than when outsiders do so. Unlike outsiders, God's people are called by His name (so that, if they dishonor Him and profane His holy name, they may cause Him to be blasphemed: Ezek 36.20–23; Rom 2.23–24; 2 Pet 2.1–2), and are entrusted by Him with holy things (which therefore they have greater opportunities to despise and treat as unholy, Heb 10.29—just as Manasseh did, 2 Kgs 21.4–5, 7). Such people will be more severely punished than those who never knew the way of righteousness (2 Pet 2.20–22; Luke 12.47–48; cf. Matt 11.21–24). See also on Eighteen Psalms 1.8; 8.14.

7.24 κ(αι) εξηλθεν εις παντα τα ορια της Ιουδαιας κυκλοθεν και εποιηcεν εκδικηcιν εν τοις ανδραcι(ν) τοις αυτομοληcαcι(ν) και ανεσταληcαν του εκπορευεcθαι εις την χωραν	**7.24** And he went out into all the appointed boundaries of Judea round about, and took vengeance on the men who had deserted; and they were confined *from* going out into the district.

7.24 To oppose Alcimus, Judas **took vengeance on the men who had deserted** (cf. v 19), and **confined** them (see the notes on 3.6), preventing them from **going out** to other places (**the district,** as in 13.49). **Vengeance** *(ekdikēsis)* belongs to the Lord, and we must always leave it in His hands rather than attempting to take it into ours (Rom 12.19), but again and again in the history of the world He performed that vengeance by raising up appointed leaders who were specifically authorized by Him to carry it out (Rom 13.1–4; 1 Pet 2.14)—leaders such as Moses (Num 31.1–3; Acts 7.24), Jephthah (Jdg 11.36), "the kings of the Medes" (Jer 51.11; 50.15), and those whom He appointed to execute vengeance on Edom (Ezek 25.14). Judas's God-given authority to bring salvation to Israel (5.62; 9.21) necessarily involved a God-given authority to overturn and confine those who were in opposition (3.6; 2.67). Jesus, similarly, has authority to bring not only salvation to His people, but also vengeance *(ekdikēsis)* to His adversaries (2 Thes 1.7–9).

7.25 ως δε ειδεν Αλκιμος οτι ενιcχυcεν Ιουδας και οι μετ αυτου και εγνω οτι ου δυναται υποcτηναι αυτους και επεcτρεψεν	**7.25** But when Alcimus saw that Judas and those with him had grown strong, and he knew that he was not able to stand before them, then he returned

προc τον βαcιλεα και κατηγορηcεν αυτων πονηρα	to the king, and spoke harmful *things* publicly against them.

7.25 Being **unable to stand before** Judas and his supporters (cf. Deut 7.24; 11.25; Josh 1.5), **Alcimus . . . returned to the king, and spoke harmful things publicly against them,** like his master, "the accuser of our brothers … who accuses them before our God day and night" (Rev 12.10), and like the wicked person rebuked by the LORD: "Your tongue binds together deceit…. Against your brother you speak, against your mother's son you set blame" (Psa 50.19–20; cf. Jer 9.4). Nevertheless God's eternal promise to His people is: "No weapon that is formed against you will prosper; and every tongue that rises against you in judgment you will condemn" (Isa 54.17; under the new covenant: Isa 54.13 ≡ John 6.45).

The king sends Nicanor

7.26 και απεcτιλεν ο βαcιλευc Νικανορα ενα των αρχοντων ₍₎ αυτου των ενδοξων και μιcουντα και εκχθραινοντα τω Ic(ραη)λ και ενετιλατο αυτω εξαραι τον λαον	**7.26** And the king sent Nicanor, one of his honored commanders, and who was hating and at enmity with Israel; and he commanded him to do away with the people.
7.27 κ(αι) ηλθεν Νικανωρ ειc I(εροuca)λημ δυναμι πολλη και απεcτιλεν προc Ιουδαν κ(αι) τουc αδελφουc αυτου μετα δολου λογοιc ιρηνικοιc λεγω(ν)	**7.27** And Nicanor came to Jerusalem with a great force, and sent to Judas and his brothers in deceit, with peaceful words, saying:
7.28 μη εcτω μαχη ανα μεcον εμου κ(αι) υμων ηξω εν ανδραcιν ολιγοιc ινα ειδω υμων τα προcωπα μετ ειρηνηc	**7.28** "Let *there* be no fight between me and you^{pl}; I will come with a few men, so that I may see your^{pl} faces in peace."
7.29 και ηλθεν προc Ιουδαν και ηcπαcαντο αλληλουc ειρηνικωc και οι πολεμιοι ετοιμοι ηcαν εξαρπαcαι τον Ιουδαν	**7.29** And he came to Judas, and they greeted one another peacefully. And the warring *people* were ready to seize Judas;
7.30 και εγνωcθη ο λογοc τω Ιουδα οτι μετα δολου ηλθεν επ αυτον και εптοηθη απ αυτου και ουκ εβουληθη ετι ειδιν το προcωπον αυτου	**7.30** and the account became known to Judas, that he had come to him in deceit; and he was terrified of him, and did not want to see his face *any* more.

7.26 αυτου S^{ca} V A 64^{+}236 | ^ των S* •

7.26–29 The king now sent another officer, **Nicanor,** to Jerusalem.[207] Like Bacchides

[207] Nicanor's expedition against the Judeans is also reported in Epitome 14.12–15.36.

(see the notes on vv 10–11), Nicanor came **with a great force** but spoke **peaceful words** to Judas and his brothers in **deceit.**

7.30 However, the deceit **became known** to Judas. After that, **he was terrified of** Nicanor, and would not **see his face any more**—just as Nehemiah refused to see those who sought to harm him (Neh 6.2–4).

Judas was not afraid to meet Nicanor in battle (vv 31–32, 39–43), but he was afraid to entrust himself to Nicanor's deceitful assurances. "A wise person sees the evil, and hides himself; but those who are open to enticement pass on, and are punished for it" (Prov 22.3)—as had happened to those who were deceived by Bacchides and Alcimus (vv 12–14). Knowledge is a defense against any enemy (Ecc 7.12), even the strongest enemy of all (2 Cor 2.11).

7.31 και εγνω Νικανωρ οτι απεκαλυφθη η βουλη αυτου και εξηλθεν εις συναντησιν τω Ιουδα εν πολεμω κατα Χαφαρσαλαμα	**7.31** And Nicanor knew that his counsel had been revealed; and he came out to meet Judas in battle opposite Kapharsalem.
7.32 και επεσον τω(ν) παρα Νικανορος ωσει πεντακοσιοι ανδρες και εφυγον εις την πολιν Δα(υι)δ	**7.32** And about five hundred men of *those* alongside Nicanor fell. And they fled into the city of David.

7.31–32 Nicanor's first battle against Judas occurred in the vicinity of **Kapharsalem,** a place not otherwise mentioned (Simons §1143). Evidently it was near Jerusalem, because when Nicanor's forces were defeated,[208] **they fled into the city of David** (a stronghold of Israel's enemies: see the notes on 1.33).

Nicanor mocks the priests and elders

7.33 και μετα τους λογους τουτους ανεβη Νικανωρ εις ορος Σιων και ‹εξηλθον› απο τω(ν) ιερεων εκ των αγιω(ν) και απο των πρεσβυτερων του λαου ασπασασθαι αυτο(ν) ιρηνικως και διξαι αυτω την ολοκαυτωσιν την ‹προσφερομενην› υπερ του βασιλεως	**7.33** And after these things, Nicanor went up to Mount Zion; and *some* of the priests came out of the holy *places*, and *some* of the elders of the people, to greet him peacefully and show him the whole burnt offering being offered on behalf of the king.

7.33 εξηλθον V [-θαν A] 64⁺236 La[109+146] | -θεν S • προσφερομενην S[ca] V A 64⁺236 La[109] | προφ- S* La[146] •

7.33 Inside Jerusalem, **Nicanor** went to see the temple region (**Mount Zion,** 4.37–38;

[208] About **five hundred** *(pentakosioi)* of Nicanor's men were slain, according to S and 64⁺236, supported by La[109+146], 7h7, and 7a1. Other manuscripts give the number as "five thousand" (*pentakischilioi,* V; *pentakischilious,* A).

5.54), where he was shown **the whole burnt offering being offered on behalf of the king.**[209] Under the old covenant law, burnt offerings could lawfully be presented as freewill offerings on any occasion (Lev 22.18; 1.2–17), in addition to being required "every morning and evening" (2 Chr 13.11; Exod 29.38–42; Num 28.3–8) and at other appointed times (Num 28.9–29.39). Judas and his friends were not seeking to overthrow a **king** whose rule had been authorized by God (Dan 2.37–39); on the contrary, they were entreating the LORD to favor him—just as their fathers had entreated the LORD's favor for the authorized Babylonian and Persian kings (Jer 29.7; Ezra 6.10). In the same way, under the new covenant the apostle Paul instructed Timothy "that supplications, prayers, intercessions, thanksgivings, be made … for kings and all who are in a high position" (1 Tim 2.1–2), even in an age when those rulers would assuredly punish some of the very people who were praying for them (Luke 21.12; Mark 13.9). "If possible, as far as it depends on you, be at peace with all people" (Rom 12.18), and "pray for those who persecute you" (Matt 5.44).

7.34 και εμυκτηρισεν αυτους και κατεγελασεν αυτων και εμιανεν αυτους και ελαλησεν υπερηφανως	**7.34** And he mocked them, and laughed at them, and polluted them, and spoke arrogantly,
7.35 και ωμοσεν μετα θυμου λεγω(ν) εαν μη παραδοθη Ιουδας και η παρεμβολη αυτου εις χιρας μου το νυν και εσται εαν επιστρεψω εν ιρηνη ενπυριω τον οικον τουτον και εξηλθεν μετα θυμου μεγαλου	**7.35** and swore an oath with indignation, saying: "If Judas and his company are not given over into my hands now, then it will be, if I return in peace, I will set this house on fire." And he went out with great indignation.
7.36 και εισηλθον οι ιερεις και εστησαν κατα προσωπον του θυσιαστηριου και του ναου και εκλαυσαν και ειπον	**7.36** And the priests went in, and stood before *the* face of the sacrificial altar and of the sanctuary; and they wept, and said:
7.37 συ εξελεξω τον οικον τουτον επικληθηναι το ονομα σου επ ‹αυτον› ειναι οικον προσευχης και δεησεως τω λαω σου	**7.37** "You† Yourself† have chosen this house, for Your† name to be called on it, to be a house of prayer and request for Your† people.
7.38 ποιησον εκδικησιν ‹εν› τω αν(θρωπ)ω τουτω και εν τη παρεμβολη αυτου κ(αι) πεσετωσαν εν ρομφαια μνησθητι των δυσφημιων αυτων και μη δως αυτοις μονην	**7.38** Take vengeance† on this person, and on his company, and let them fall by *the* sword. Be mindful† of their blasphemies, and do not give† them an abode."

7.37 αυτον V A 64*236 | -του S • **7.38** εν 1° V A 64*236 La[109+146] | > S •

[209] **The whole burnt offering.** Notice the article **the** *(tēn)*. This was not just "an" offering for the king; it was "the" offering for the king—i.e., the familiar, well-known one (Winer 134). It was no isolated occurrence.

7.34 Nicanor not only **mocked** the priests who were offering sacrifice for the king, but even **polluted**[210] **them**—that is, he made them unclean in some unspecified way. Priests could present offerings only when they were free from defilement in terms prescribed by the old covenant law (Lev 22.3–9), so Nicanor was effectively preventing the priests whom he encountered from doing anything else that day to intercede for their ruler.

Similarly, God's messengers had been mocked by previous generations of scoffers (2 Chr 30.10; 36.16); and a few generations later the great High Priest would Himself "be mocked, and shamefully treated, and spat upon" by the very people for whom He was preparing to offer His sacrifice (Luke 18.32; Matt 27.29–31).

7.35–38 The temple was a **house of prayer,** which the Lord had **chosen** (1 Kgs 8.28–30; 9.3; cf. Mark 11.17), so the priests stood there and prayed to Him, entreating Him to spare it, and to **take vengeance** on those who were blaspheming it (speaking evil of it, v 42). "The temple of God is holy" (1 Cor 3.17). The stones of the temple under the old covenant were holy (Psa 79.1; Matt 23.17). The "living stones" of the temple under the new covenant are also holy (1 Cor 3.17; Eph 2.19–22; 1 Pet 2.5). Those who serve Him cannot stand idly by when they see His house threatened and His goodness blasphemed. They must appeal to Him to take action. "Spare Your people, O Lord, and do not give Your inheritance to be a reproach" (Joel 2.17). "How long, O Sovereign, the holy and true One, will You not judge and avenge our blood from those who dwell on the earth?" (Rev 6.10). "Will not God avenge His chosen ones, who cry to Him day and night? . . . I say to you, that He will avenge them speedily" (Luke 18.7–8). On this occasion, He did indeed hear their prayer and avenge them speedily.

Jesus promised His faithful disciples an **abode** with His Father (in whose house are "many abodes," John 14.2, 23; Heb 10.34; 13.14; cf. Psa 23.6). The counterpart is seen in the present passage: the Father will **not give** His enemies any lasting **abode.**[211] They may be present for a little while, but they will not abide; they will pass away (Psa 37.9–10, 35–38).

Nicanor is defeated and killed

7.39 και εξηλθεν Νικανωρ	**7.39** And Nicanor went out
εξ Ι(ερουςα)λημ	of Jerusalem,
και παρενεβαλεν εν Βαιθωρων	and camped in Bethhoron;
και ςυνηντηςεν αυτω δυναμις Cυριας	and a force *from* Syria met him.

[210] **Polluted:** *emianen,* the word used in John 18.28.

[211] A *monē* (**abode**) is a place of abiding ("do not give them any dwelling," LEH 407; *no les des mansión,* Jünemann; BDAG 658, §2) and/or a condition of abiding ("do not give to them that they abide," Wycl; не дай им оставаться долее, RST; BDAG 658, §1). Those who do not have an **abode** *(monē)* are those who do not abide (*menō;* John 15.6).

7.40 και Ιουδας παρενεβαλεν εν Αδασα εν τριςχιλιοις ανδρασιν και προσηυξατο Ιουδας και ‹ειπεν›	**7.40** And Judas camped in Adasa, with three thousand men. And Judas prayed, and said:
7.41 οι παρα του βασιλεως οτε εδυσφημησαν εξηλθεν ο αγγελος σου και επαταξεν εν αυτοις εκατον ογδοηκοντα πεντε χιλιαδας	**7.41** "When the *people* from the king spoke blasphemy, Your† angel came out; and he smote a hundred eighty-five thousand among them.
7.42 ουτως συντριψον την παρεμβολην ταυτην ενωπιον ημων σημερον και γνωτωσαν οι επιλοιποι οτι κακως ελαλησεν επι τα αγια σου και κρινον αυτον κατα την κακιαν αυτου	**7.42** In the same way shatter† this company in our sight today, and let the rest know that he has spoken evil against Your† holy *places*; and judge† him in accordance with his evildoing."

7.40 ειπεν S^{ca} V A $64^{+}236$ $La^{109+146}$ | -πον S* •

7.39 Nicanor now pitched his camp at **Bethhoron** (where Seron had unsuccessfully fought against Judas several years earlier, 3.16–24). He was joined by army reinforcements from **Syria.**

7.40 Judas pitched his own camp at **Adasa,** near Bethhoron (v 39), and about a day's journey from Gezer in the land of the Philistines (v 45).[212] As always (3.44, 50–54; 4.10; 30–33; 5.33), he did not trust to his own power but sought help from the Lord.

7.41–42 Just as Nicanor had blasphemed the LORD, so **people from** an earlier **king** (Sennacherib of Assyria) had spoken **blasphemy** against the LORD in the days of Hezekiah (2 Kgs 19.6). On that occasion, the LORD's **angel** had slain **a hundred eighty-five thousand** of Sennacherib's soldiers in a single night (2 Kgs 19.35). Judas now prayed that Nicanor's company might be struck down **in the same way,** so that everyone else might **know** that Nicanor's utterances had been **evil** (2 Kgs 19.19; 20.28; 2 Chr 20.29; 1 Sam 17.46; Psa 83.17–18). By that means, all nations might fear God's holy name (Psa 9.20; Mal 1.11, 14). Like his father before him (2.24), Judas was jealous for the LORD, that His name should be honored and not despised. And, like his father (2.51–61), Judas was constantly "mindful of the fathers' works," and of the LORD's deliverance of the faithful in past generations (see on 4.9).

7.43 και συνηψαν αι παρεμβολαι εις πολεμο(ν) τη τρισκεδεκατη του μηνος Αδαρ και συνετριβη	**7.43** And the companies made contact for war *on* the thirteenth of the month Adar. And Nicanor's

[212] **Adasa** might perhaps be Hadashah, a town in the lowland of Judah (Josh 15.37, 33). As in many other cases, the evidence provided by Josephus, Eusebius, and similar-sounding modern place names is contradictory and inconclusive (ABD 1.70).

η παρεμβολη Νικανορος και ‹επεσεν› αυτος πρωτος εν τω πολεμω	company was shattered, and he himself fell first in the battle.
7.44 ως δε ειδεν η παρεμβολη αυτου οτι επεσεν Νικανωρ ριψαντες τα οπλα εφυγον	**7.44** But when his company saw that Nicanor had fallen, they fled, having thrown away *their* weapons.

7.43 επεσεν V A $64^{+}236$ | επεπεσεν S •

7.43–44 The battle occurred **on the thirteenth** day of the twelfth month, **Adar** (the day of the year when the LORD had delivered the Jews from their adversaries in the time of Esther, Est 9.1–18). Its outcome was swift and sudden. Nicanor had shot evil words at God's servants (Psa 64.3–4); now God shot a sudden arrow at him (Psa 64.7). **He himself** was slain **in the battle;** and **when his company saw** that, they **fled.** Thus the Lord answered the prayer of His servants (v 38); and, as so often happens, His answer went even beyond what had been asked (cf. Eph 3.20). Not only did Nicanor fall in the battle, but he was the **first** to fall.

7.45 και κατεδιωκον αυτους οδον ‹ημερας μιας› απο Αδασα εως του ελθειν εις Γαζηρα και εσαλπιζον οπισω αυτων ταις σαλπιγξιν των σημασιων	**7.45** And they pursued after them *on the* path one day*'s journey* from Adasa, up to the approach to Gezer; and they *kept* trumpeting behind them with the trumpets of signals.
7.46 και εξηλθον εκ πασων τω(ν) κωμων της Ιουδαιας κυκλοθεν και υπερεκερων αυτους και απεστρεφον ουτοι προς τουτους και επεσον παντες ρομφαια και ‹ου κατελιφθη› εξ αυτων ουδε εις	**7.46** And *people* came out of all the villages of Judea round about, and they were outflanking them; and these *one*s were turning back against those *one*s, and they all fell by *the* sword; and *there* was no *one* left from them, not even one.

7.45 ημερας / μιας V A $64^{+}236$ $La^{109+146}$ | ~ S • **7.46** ου κατελιφθη S^{ca} V A $64^{+}236$ | ουκ απελ- S* •

7.45–46 The Israelites' enemies fled toward **Gezer** in the land of the Philistines (see the notes on 4.15). Judas and his men **pursued after them,**[213] and in addition, **people came out of all the** nearby **villages of Judea** to help Judas, **outflanking** the fugitives. Trying to flee both from the soldiers behind and from the villagers ahead, the Syrian soldiers began **turning back** on one another, and **not even one** of them escaped (cf. Josh 8.21–22; Jdg 7.20–24; 1 Sam 14.20–23), just as no none will escape the sudden destruction on the last day (1 Thes 5.3).

7.47 και ελαβον τα σκυλα και την προνομην και την κεφαλην	**7.47** And they took the plunder and the pillage; and the head of Nicanor

[213] The **trumpets of signals** are discussed in the notes on 4.40.

Νικανορος αφιλον και τη(ν) δεξιαν αυτου ην εξετινεν υπερηφανως και ηνεγκαν και εξετιναν παρα τη Ι(ερουςα)λημ	they removed, and his right *hand* that he had stretched out arrogantly, and they brought *them,* and stretched *them* out beside Jerusalem.

7.47 Nicanor's **head** and **right hand** were set up[214] **beside** (i.e., "just outside," NRSV) **Jerusalem,** to bear witness to the result of his blasphemies (cf. 1 Sam 17.54). Inside the city there were still many enemies of Israel (cf. 10.7–8) who might take warning and "fear, and never again do any such wickedness as this" (Deut 13.11).

7.48 και ηυφρανθη ο λαος ϲφοδρα και ηγαγο(ν) την ημεραν εκινη(ν) ‹› ευφροϲυνηϲ ‹μεγαληϲ›	**7.48** And the people were very glad; and they kept that day *as one* of great gladness.
7.49 και εϲτηϲαν του αγει(ν) κατ ενιαυτον τη(ν) ημεραν ταυτην τη τριϲκεδεκατη του Αδαρ	**7.49** And they established to keep this day each year, the thirteenth of Adar.

7.48 εκινη(ν) $64^{+}236$ $La^{109+146}$ | + ημεραν S V A • μεγαληϲ S^{ca} V $64^{+}236$ $La^{109+146}$ | -λην S* A •

7.48–49 The **day** of the deliverance was **kept** that year as a day **of great gladness** (see 3.2; 5.23). Moreover, the people agreed to continue observing the same day (**the thirteenth of Adar**) **each year,** just as the Jews in Esther's time had agreed to observe the day when their deliverance was completed (the fourteenth of Adar; Est 9.18–22, 27), and just as Judas and his companions had agreed to observe the days when the altar was dedicated (4.59).[215] Indeed, on every day of the year we have reasons to bless the LORD (Psa 34.1; 1 Thes 5.18) and not to forget any of His merciful dealings toward us (Psa 103.2; 2 Pet 1.9).

7.50 και ηϲυχαϲεν η γη Ιουδα ημεραϲ ολιγαϲ	**7.50** And the land of Judah was quiet a few days.

7.50 As after other occasions when Israel's enemies had been resoundingly defeated (Josh 11.23; Jdg 8.28), **the land . . . was quiet.** Nevertheless, the period of peace would last only a very short time (**a few days**).[216] In this life the devil never departs permanently, but, at most, merely "for a season" (Luke 4.13).

---

[214] The hand that had been **stretched out** *(exetinen)* against God's people was now **stretched out** (the same word) by God's people.

[215] The Day of Nicanor continued to be observed by the Jews in the time of the apostles (Josephus, *Antiquities,* 12.412; *Megillat Ta'anit,* 32). The Maccabean Epitome notes that it was "the day before the day of Mordecai" (15.36).

[216] Nicanor was slain halfway through the twelfth month of 151 SE (7.1, 43, 49). The next enemy army attacked Jerusalem before the end of the next month—the first month of 152 SE (9.1–3).

The Alliance with Rome

Judas hears about the Romans

8.1 και ηκουσεν Ιουδας το ονομα των Ρωμαιων οτι ειcιν δυνατοι ιcχυι και αυτοι ευδοκουcιν εν παcιν τοιc προcτιθεμενοιc αυτοιc και οcοι αν προcελθωcιν αυτοιc ιcτωcιν αυτοιc φιλιαν	**8.1** And Judas heard the name of the Romans, that they were powerful with strength, and they themselves were well pleased with all *those* who joined them, and they would establish friendship with everyone who would come to them,
8.2 και οτι ειcιν δυνατοι ιcχυι και διηγηcαντο αυτω τουc πολεμουc αυτω(ν) και ταc ανδραγαθιαc αc ποιουcιν εν τοιc Γαλαταιc και οτι κατεκρατηcαν αυτων και ηγαγον αυτουc υπο φορον	**8.2** and that they were powerful with strength. And they declared to him their wars, and the manly good deeds that they had been doing among the Galatians, and that they had overpowered them and made them subject to tribute;
8.3 και οcα εποιηcαν εν χωρα Cπανιαc του κατακρατηcαι των μεταλλων του αργυριου και του χρυcιου του εκει	**8.3** and all *the things* they had done in *the* district of Spain, to get control of the mines of silver and of gold *that were* there;
8.4 και κατεκρατηcαν του τοπου παντοc τη βουλη αυτω(ν) και τη μακροθυμια και ο τοποc η(ν) απεχων μακραν απ αυτων cφοδρα και των βαcιλεω(ν) των επελθοντω(ν) επ αυτουc απ ακρου τηc γηc ‹εωc› cυνετριψαν αυτουc και επαταξαν εν αυτοιc πληγην μεγαλην και οι επιλοιποι διδοαcιν αυτοιc φορον κατ ενιαυτο(ν)	**8.4** and they had overpowered all the place by their counsel and patience (and the place was very far away from them), and the kings who had come against them from *the* end of the earth, until they had shattered them and smitten them *with* a great injury; and the rest were giving them tribute each year;
8.5 και τον Φιλιππον και τον Περcεα Κιτιεων βαcιλεα και τουc επηρμενουc επ αυτουc cυνετριψαν αυτουc εν πολεμω και κατεκρατηcαν αυτων	**8.5** and *as for* Philip, and Perseus king of Kittim, and the *people* who lifted themselves up against them— they had shattered them in battle and overpowered them,
8.6 και Αντιοχον τον μεγαν βαcιλεα τηc Αcιαc τον πορευθε(ν)τα επ αυτουc ειc πολεμον εχοντα εκατον εικοcι ελεφανταc και ιππον και αρματα και δυναμιν πολλην cφοδρα και cυνετριβη ‹απ› ‹αυτων›	**8.6** and Antiochus the Great, king of Asia, who had gone to war against them, having a hundred twenty elephants, and horse, and chariots, and an extremely great force; and he had been shattered by them,

8.7 και ελαβο(ν) αυτον ζωντα και εστηcαν αυτοιc ‹διδοναι› αυτον τε και τουc βαcιλευονταc μετ αυτον φορον μεγαν ‹και› διδοναι ‹ομηρα› και διαcτολην	**8.7** and they had taken him alive, and had established *for* both him and those who were king after him to give them a great tribute, and to give *them* hostages and a section *of territory,*
8.8 και χωραν την Ινδικην και Μηδιαν και Λυδια(ν) απο των καλλιcτω(ν) χωρων αυτων και λαβοντεc αυταc παρ αυτου εδωκαν αυταc Ευμενει τω βαcιλει	**8.8** even *the* district of India and Media and Lydia, *some* of their best districts; and, when *they* had taken them from him, they had given them to Eumenes the king;
8.9 και οτι οι εκ τηc Ελλαδοc εβουλευcαντο ελθι(ν) και εξαραι αυτουc	**8.9** and that the *people* from Greece had taken counsel to come and do away with them,
8.10 και εγνωcθη ο λογοc αυτοιc και απεcτιλαν επ αυτουc cτρατηγον ενα και επολεμηcαν προc αυτουc και επεcο(ν) εξ αυτων τραυματιαι πολλοι και ηχμαλωτιcαν ταc γυναικαc αυτων και τα τεκνα αυτω(ν) και ‹επρονομευcα(ν)› αυτουc και ‹κατεκρατηcαν› τηc γηc και ‹καθειλαν› τα οχυρωματα αυτων και επρονομευcαν αυτουc και κατεδουλωcαντο αυτουc εωc τηc ημεραc ταυτηc	**8.10** and the thing had become known to them, and they had sent against them one army commander, and made war against them; many wounded *one*s of them had fallen; and they had taken captive their wives and children, and had pillaged them, and overpowered the land, and pulled down their fortresses, and pillaged them, and utterly enslaved them, until this day;
8.11 κ(αι) ταc επιλοιπουc βαcιλειαc και ταc νηcουc ‹οcοι› ποτε ‹αντεcτηcαν› αυτοιc κατεφθειραν και εδουλωcαν αυτουc	**8.11** and *as for* the rest of *the* king- doms, and the islands—all *those* who had stood against them at *any* time— they had ruined and enslaved them;

8.4 εωc V A La$^{109+146}$ | ωc S | > 64^{+}236 • **8.6** απ S^{ca} A La$^{109+146}$ | υπ S* V | > 64^{+}236 • αυτων S^{ca} V A La$^{109+146}$ | -του S* | -τον 64^{+}236 • **8.7** διδοναι 1° S^{ca} V A 64^{+}236 | δουναι S* • και 4° A 64^{+}236 La$^{109+146}$ | > S V • ομηρα V A 64^{+}236 La$^{109+146}$ | -ρον S • **8.10** επρονομευcα(ν) 1° S^{ca} A [προενομ- V 64^{+}236] La$^{109+146}$ | -cε(ν) S* • κατεκρατηcαν S^{ca} V A 64^{+}236 La$^{109+146}$ | -cεν S* • καθειλαν S^{ca} [-λον V A 64^{+}236] La$^{109+146}$ | -λεν S* • **8.11** οcοι V A 64 | οι S • αντεcτηcαν 64 La$^{109+146}$ | ανε- S V A •

8.1–11 To hear someone's **name** (3.41) is to hear their "reputation" (NAB), to hear "reports"[217] about them (REB)—which may be either accurate ("King Herod heard"

[217] In the LXX, **name** *(onoma)* translates both Hebrew *šm* ("name," 1 Chr 14.17; Neh 6.13; Gen 11.4) and Hebrew *šmʿ* (a "thing heard," a "report," Gen 29.13; Deut 2.25; 1 Kgs 10.1).

the mighty deeds of Jesus, "for His name had become known," Mark 6.14) or inaccurate ("You have a name that you are living; and you are dead," Rev 3.1). So **Judas heard the name of the Romans** (v 1)—in other words (as the rest of vv 1–16 show), he heard **that** *(hoti)* the Romans were reported to be various things and to have done various things. Thus verses 1–16 of this chapter do not tell us what the Romans *were.* They tell us what Judas **heard** about the Romans—what the Romans were *reported* to be.[218] This is an elementary point, but it is often neglected by commentators on the Maccabean History.

Notice, too, that the book does not say *when* in Judas's career the negotiations with Rome took place. It is obviously convenient to discuss all his successes within Judea first, and the full story of his foreign negotiations after that. There is no implication that they all happened in that order.[219]

The Romans had undergone some of "the same kinds of sufferings" as the Judeans (cf. 1 Pet 5.9). **People from Greece had taken counsel to come and do away** [*exarai*] **with them,** just as other Greeks had taken counsel to **do away with** the Judeans (the same word: Maccabaica 3.20, 35; 6.12; 7.26). But God was giving the Romans power to withstand their enemies (cf. Jer 27.5–7), just as He was giving the Judeans (Maccabaica 3.19).

The book stresses the power of the Romans in its characteristic way, by means of repetition after an interval (see the introduction to this commentary): Judas heard **that they were powerful with strength, and** [something else], **and** [something else], **and that they were powerful with strength** (vv 1–2); and that they **pillaged** their adversaries, **and** [did other deeds], **and pillaged them** (v 10). In particular, Judas's informants **declared to him** (v 2) the successful wars that the Romans had reportedly fought in many parts of the Mediterranean world, overpowering:

- **the Galatians** (v 2);[220]
- the **district of Spain** (vv 3–4), further west even than Rome (Rom 15.24, 28);[221]

---

218 Pellicanus 5.308r. Jesus was *reported* to be a Samaritan, a drunkard, and a demoniac (John 8.48; 10.20; Matt 11.19), but this does not mean that He *was* any of those things (Lapide 41).

219 "The author does not follow chronological sequence but brings together in a single place everything concerning the Romans, so as to arrange his history in the best order" (Girbau, *Macabeus,* 114). No more than a month and a half, at most, elapsed between 7.48–49 and 9.3; the expedition to Rome described in this chapter would have taken much longer (v 19).

220 The term **Galatians** (or Gauls) describes not a place but a people. Thus it could refer either to Galatians living in the region east of Greece (Acts 16.6; 18.23; 1 Pet 1.1) or to those living in the region northwest of Rome (near **Spain,** the next place mentioned in the present context, v 3). Classical historians report that both groups had been defeated by Rome before this time: the eastern Galatians in 189 BCE (Livy 38.12–27), and the western Gauls of the Po valley in 222 BCE (Polybius 2.18–35).

221 According to Classical historians, Rome conquered **Spain** in 206–195 BCE (Polybius 11.20–34; Livy 28.12–38; 34.8–21; cf. Curchin, *Roman Spain,* 24–39). The term **place** *(topos)* refers

- **Philip** and **Perseus** the king of **Kittim** (the coastal regions of the northern Mediterranean—in this book, the term is applied especially to Macedonia: see 1.1), with their supporters (**people who had lifted themselves up against** the Romans, v 5);[222]
- **Antiochus the Great** (vv 6–8; presumably the "Antiochus the king" mentioned in 1.10), the king of **Asia**[223] (the Seleucid kingdom: see 11.13; 12.39), who had ruled lands as far east as **India** (Est 1.1) and **Media** (2 Kgs 17.6; Acts 2.9), and as far west as **Lydia;**[224]
- **the people from Greece** (vv 9–10; see the notes on 1.1);[225]
- **all** the other **kingdoms** and **islands . . . who had stood against them** (v 11).

---

here to a province or country (as in 1 Sam 12.8; Jer 16.2–3), not to the whole Iberian peninsula.

[222] Classical historians report that the kings of Macedonia **Philip** V and **Perseus** were defeated by Rome in 197 BCE and 168 BCE respectively (Polybius 18.19–27; Livy 33.3–13; 44.17–45; Plutarch, *Aemilius,* 7–24).

[223] **Asia,** in this context, is the continent east of Europe (from Phrygia in the west to the region beyond the Indus in the east: Appian, *Syriaca,* 55.281).

[224] The title "great king" had been adopted by Assyrian and Persian kings (2 Kgs 18.19; Aristophanes, *Plutus,* 170 and its scholia) and by both of the previous Seleucid kings named Antiochus (SH 2.6–7, §-260; CM §4.10, 13) before being used by Antiochus III (*basileuontōn Antiochou megalou,* Amyzon §14; cf. Muccioli, "Antioco III e la politica onomastica dei Seleucidi," 88–89). In subsequent usage, however, the term **Great** was customarily applied specifically to Antiochus III, in order to distinguish him from the other kings of the same name (e.g., Antiochus Epiphanes [Maccabaica 1.10] and Antiochus Eupator [6.17]); compare "James the Less" (Mark 15.40), used to distinguish him from the other disciples of the same name.

Rome's eventual victory over Antiochus the Great (about 190 BCE, after a long struggle) was famous in ancient times (Livy 37.37–44; the final treaty is recorded in Polybius 21.43 ≡ Livy 38.38). Antiochus is said to have brought back 150 **elephants** (v 6) from his expedition to India (Polybius 11.34.12). After his defeat, members of his family were taken to Rome as **hostages** (including, at different times, Antiochus Epiphanes [see 1.10] and Demetrius son of Seleucus [see 7.1]). Many of his former territories were given to Rome's ally **Eumenes** II of Pergamum (Polybius 21.45; cf. Luke 19.24; 1 Sam 15.28; 1 Kgs 11.11).

His successors—Seleucus, Antiochus Epiphanes, and their descendants—inherited a kingdom substantially reduced in size, though it still extended from the "upper districts" east of the Euphrates "to the appointed boundaries of Egypt" (3.37, 32).

No other ancient writer mentions **India** (the neighborhood of the Indus River) among the regions given to Eumenes; Judas's informants may have been mistaken on that point.

[225] Classical historians report that **people from Greece** had supported both Philip V and Antiochus III against Rome and had incurred defeat themselves (Livy 35.33; 36.24). The conflict between Rome and Greece intensified during the following decades, and after about 146 BCE Greece was totally under Roman control (which remained the situation at the time when the Maccabean History was written—**until this day,** v 10).

8.12 μετα δε των φιλω(ν) αυτων και των επαναπαυομενω(ν) αυτοις συνετηρησαν φιλιαν και κατεκρατησαν των βασιλεων των εγγυς και των μακρα(ν) και οσοι ηκουον το ονομα αυτων εφοβουντο απ αυτων	**8.12** but with their friends, and the *one*s who were relying on them, they had kept friendship; and they had overpowered the kings *who were* near and *those who were* far away; and all *those* who had heard their name were afraid of them;
8.13 οις δ αν βουλωνται βοηθειν και βασιλευειν ‹› βασιλευουσιν ους δ αν βουλωνται μεθιστωσιν και υψωθησαν σφοδρα	**8.13** and whomever they wanted to help and make king, were becoming kings, but whomever they wanted, they took away; and they had been raised very high;
8.14 και εν πασιν τουτοις ουκ επεθεντο αυτων ουδε εις διαδημα ουδε ‹περιεβαλλετο› πορφυραν ωστε αδρυ(ν)θηναι ‹επ αυτη›	**8.14** and *along* with all these *thing*s, not even one of them had put on a diadem or wrapped himself in purple, so as to be exalted by it;
8.15 και βουλευτηριον εποιησαν εαυτοις και καθ ημεραν εβουλευο(ν)το τριακοσιοι και εικοσι βουλευομενοι δια παντος περι του πληθους του ευκοσμειν αυτους	**8.15** and they had made a council house for *them*selves, and each day three hundred and twenty *people* who counseled were taking counsel at all *times* about the multitude, for them to be well ordered;
8.16 και πιστευουσιν ενι ανθρωπω αρχειν αυτων κατ ενιαυτον και ‹κυριευειν› πασης της γης αυτων και παντες ακουουσιν του ενος και ουκ εστιν φθονος ουδε ζηλος εν αυτοις	**8.16** and they *kept* trusting one person to rule them each year, and to be lord over all their land; and they all *kept* listening to the one *person*, and there was no envy or jealousy among them.

8.13 βασιλευειν S^{ca} V A 64^{+}236 La$^{109+146}$ | + και S* • **8.14** περιεβαλλετο 64 [-βαλετο 236] La^{109} | -βαλοντο S V A La^{146} • επ αυτη S^{ca} [εν α- V] A 64^{+}236 La$^{109+146}$ | > S* • **8.16** κυριευειν S^{ca} V A 236 La$^{109+146}$ | -ευει 64 | > S* •

8.12–13 At this time the Romans were not yet rulers of the whole Mediterranean world (Demetrius, for instance, had no allegiance to them). But they were on the way to becoming so (Dan 7.23; Luke 2.1; Rev 17.18; 18.3). Already **they had been raised very high.**[226] Already they had gained power over peoples who were **near** them and **far away** from them (vv 12, 4). They had a reputation for successfully shattering their enemies but successfully supporting their **friends.** If they decided to **help** a man and **make** him **king,** so it was said, that man would become king; if they decided to **take** him **away,** he would be taken away. Less than two centuries later, a Roman governor

[226] **They had been raised very high** *(hupsōthēsan),* as Alexander had formerly been (1.3), and as the people of God will ultimately be (1 Pet 5.6).

would be telling a man born **far away** in Judea: "I have authority to release you, and I have authority to crucify you" (John 19.10–11; cf. 1 Pet 2.13–14; Rom 13.1–2).

Of course, those who possess such authority do not possess it by their own ability. They possess it only because God has given it to them for a period of time (Dan 5.19). He, and He alone, "removes kings, and sets up kings" (Dan 2.21).

8.14–16 Yet, so it was said, the Romans had no king or emperor. No one among them had **put on a diadem** (a mark of kingship, 11.54) like the Ptolemies and Seleucids who were causing so much trouble to Israel (1.9; 6.15; 11.13, 54; 12.39; 13.32). No one among them had **wrapped himself in purple** (a mark of high position, though not necessarily kingship, 10.20).

Instead, their **counsel** was reportedly determined each day by an assembly of **three hundred and twenty people,** led by a person who was chosen **each year.**[227] Their government was said to be **well ordered** (cf. 1 Cor 14.40; Exod 18.19–22), with **no envy or jealousy among them** (cf. Psa 106.16–17; 1 Cor 3.3–4).[228]

Judas establishes an alliance with Rome

8.17 και επελεξατο Ιουδας τον Ευπολεμον υιον Ιωαννου του Ακκως και Ιασονα υιον Ελεαζαρου και απεστιλεν αυτους εις Ρωμη(ν) στησαι ‹αυτοις› φιλιαν κ(αι) συμμαχιαν	**8.17** And Judas chose Eupolemos son of John the *son* of Accos, and Jason son of Eleazar; and he sent them to Rome, to establish a friendship and a military alliance with them,
8.18 και του αραι τον ζυγο(ν) απ αυτων οτι ‹ιδον› την βασιλιαν τω(ν) Ελληνων καταδουλουμενους το(ν) Ισ(ραη)λ δουλια	**8.18** and to lift the yoke up from them: for they saw *that* the kingdom of the Greeks *was* utterly enslaving Israel with slavery.

8.17 αυτοις S[ca] V A 64[+]236 La[109+146c] | > S* La[146*] • **8.18** ιδον V A 64[+]236 La[109+146] | ειδε(ν) S •

[227] Classical historians report that Rome was governed during this era by about three hundred senators (who met at regular times and also on any other day when the need arose), together with ten curule magistrates and ten tribunes of the people, under the leadership of two consuls chosen annually. The division of authority between the two consuls was more complex than is often assumed (and the surviving documents leave many aspects of it uncertain: see, e.g., Pina Paolo, *The Consul at Rome,* 5–6, 19, 193–194). At any given time, only one consul bore the fasces and therefore the ultimate responsibility of government (Livy 2.1.8). Moreover, each consul generally had distinct responsibilities; at least during this phase of Rome's history, only one at any given time handled foreign diplomacy and was called the "highest of the Romans" in that area (Maccabaica 15.16; Josephus, *Antiquities,* 13.260; 14.233). This may be what Judas's informants meant when they said that there was **one person** governing at Rome **each year.**

[228] During the Maccabean period, no significant internal dissensions at Rome are reported by Classical historians (Polybius 6.11–18)—in striking contrast to the many intrigues and insurrections among the Ptolemies and Seleucids of the eastern Mediterranean (Maccabaica 6.55–56; 7.1–4; 10.1–2, 48–50, 67–68; 11.1–3, 8–19, 39–40, 54–56; 13.31–32; 14.1–3; 15.10–14).

8.19 και επορευθηςαν εις Ρωμην και η οδος πολλη ςφοδρα και ειςηλθοςαν εις το βουλευτηριον και απεκριθηςαν και ειπον	**8.19** And they went to Rome, and the journey *was* very long; and they came into the council house, and responded and said:
8.20 Ιουδας ο ‹› Μακκαβαιος και οι αδελφοι αυτου και το πληθος τω(ν) Ιουδαιων ‹απεςτειλαν› ημας προς υμας ςτηςαι μεθ υμων ςυμμαχιαν και ειρηνην και γραφηναι ημας ςυμμαχους και φιλους ‹υμων›	**8.20** "Judas Maccabeus and his brothers, and the multitude of the Judeans, have sent us to you^{pl}, to establish a military alliance and peace with you^{pl}, and to inscribe ourselves *as* your^{pl} military allies and friends."

8.20 ο V 64^{+}236 La$^{109+146}$ | + και S A • απεςτειλαν V A 64^{+}236 La$^{109+146}$ | -τιλεν S • υμων S^{ca} V^{b} A 64^{+}236 La$^{109+146}$ | ημ- S* V* •

8.17–18 Judas **sent** two ambassadors (**Eupolemos** and **Jason**) **to establish a friendship and a military alliance with** the Romans. (Compare the covenants established between Abram and the Amorites, Gen 14.13, and between Solomon and Hiram of Tyre, 1 Kgs 5.12.)

Ever since the time of Alexander, **the kingdom of the Greeks** (1.10) had been ruling **Israel.** The Israelites were suffering under a **yoke** of **slavery** (v 31), just as God had warned them would happen if they persisted in disobeying Him: "Because you did not serve the LORD your God with joy... then you will serve your enemies whom the LORD will send against you ... and He will put a yoke of iron on your neck" (Deut 28.47–48). The LORD had already freed their nation from a yoke of slavery when He delivered them from Egypt (Lev 26.13) and from Assyria (Isa 10.24–27). Therefore, He might also free them from their current yoke (as indeed He later did, 13.41). In fact, little more than a century after the Maccabean period, He would free them from a still greater yoke of slavery (Gal 5.1) by sending the Prince of Peace to rule His people (Isa 9.1–7).

Under the old covenant Law, the Israelites were forbidden to make any alliances with the nations in the land that God had given them (Exod 23.31–33; 34.12–16; Deut 7.1–5; Jdg 2.2). But they were permitted to make alliances with distant nations (cf. Deut 20.10, 15; Josh 9.3–27). Thus Judas could lawfully seek aid from Rome in his efforts **to lift the yoke of the Greeks** from his people.[229] Faced with enmity not only from the nations immediately around him, but even from among his fellow Israelites, he accepted some who were further off but were willing to receive him—just

[229] During that process, Israel was seeking deliverance not by the power of Rome but by the power of God (as 12.14–15 indicates). Never once, in even the worst times of trouble, did Judas Maccabeus, Jonathan, or Simon appeal to Rome (or to any earthly power) for military aid. They simply made use of the fact that Rome could legitimately command its subordinates and neighbors to be at peace with Judea (8.31–32; 12.4; 15.19–23).

as Jesus did in the realm of the spirit (Acts 13.46–47; 28.25–28; Rom 10.19–21; 11.19–22).[230]

The development of ties with Rome also had another significance: although Judas could scarcely have foreseen this, he was laying a foundation for Rome to become his nation's next overlord. Because of the Israelites' sins, God had taken the kingship away from them and made them subject to foreign kings (Jer 27.12–13). When He freed them from one such king, it was to make them subject to another (Dan 2.37–40). So, in the present situation, God would indeed free Israel from the **yoke** of the **Greeks** (13.41); but He would subsequently require them to "render to Caesar the things that are Caesar's" (Matt 22.21).

A copy of the alliance

8.21 και ηρεσε(ν) ο λογος εναντιο(ν) αυτων	**8.21** And the word pleased them.
8.22 και τουτο το αντιγραφον της ‹γραφης› ης αντεγραψαν επι δελτοις χαλκαις και απεστιλαν εις Ι(ερουσα)λημ ειναι παρ αυτοις εκει μνημοσυνον ιρηνης και συμμαχιας	**8.22** And this *is* a copy of the writing that they copied on bronze slabs and sent to Jerusalem, to be *kept* beside them there, a memo- rial of peace and military alliance:
8.23 καλως γενοιτο Ρωμαιοις και τω εθνι Ιουδαιω(ν) εν τη θαλασση και επι της ξηρας εις τον αιωνα και ρομφαια και εκχθρος μακρυνθιη απ αυτων	**8.23** "May *all* be well for *the* Romans and for the nation of *the* Judeans, at sea and on dry *land,* to lasting time; and may *the* sword and *the* enemy be kept far from them.
8.24 εαν δε ενστη πολεμος Ρωμη προτερα η πασιν τοις συμμαχοις αυτων εν παση ‹› κυρια αυτων	**8.24** But if war should come to Rome first, or to any of their military allies in all their dominion,
8.25 συμμαχησει το εθνος τω(ν) Ιουδαιων ως αν ο καιρος υπογραφη αυτοις καρδια πληρη	**8.25** the nation of the Judeans will be *their* military ally wholeheartedly, how- ever the time may inscribe for them;
8.26 και τοις πολεμουσιν ‹ου δωσουσιν› ουδε επαρκεσουσιν σιτον οπλα αργυριο(ν) ‹πλοια› ως εδοξε(ν) ‹Ρωμαιοις› και φυλαξο(ν)ται τα φυλαγματα αυτων ουθεν λαβοντες	**8.26** and to those who make war they will not give or provide *any* grain, weapons, money, ships, as it has seemed *right* to *the* Romans; and they will keep their obligations without taking *anything in return.*

8.22 γραφης V A La$^{109+146}$ | επιστολης S 64^{+}236 • **8.24** κυρια V A 64^{+}236 | ^ τη S • **8.26** ου δωσουσιν S^{ca} V A 64^{+}236 La$^{109+146}$ | > S* • πλοια S^{ca} V A 64^{+}236 La$^{109+146}$ | -οιον S* • Ρωμαιοις S^{ca} 64^{+}236 La$^{109+146}$ | Ρωμη S* V A •

[230] Cf. Calmet 133 (cited in our comments on 9.22).

8.27 κατα τα αυτα δε εαν εθνει Ιουδαιων ϲυμβη προτεροιϲ πολεμοϲ ϲυνμαχηϲουϲιν οι Ρωμαιοι εκ ψυχηϲ ωϲ αν αυτοιϲ ο καιροϲ υπογραφη	**8.27** And in accordance with those *things*, if war should come to *the* nation of *the* Judeans first, the Romans will be military allies from *the* soul, however the time may inscribe for them;
8.28 και τοιϲ ϲυμμαχουϲι(ν) ου δοθηϲεται ϲειτοϲ οπλα αργυριο(ν) πλοια ωϲ εδοξεν Ρωμαιοιϲ ‹κ(αι) φυλαξονται› τα φυλαγματα ταυτα και ου μετα δολου	**8.28** and to the military allies *there* will not be given *any* grain, weapons, money, ships, as it has seemed *right* to *the* Romans; and they will keep these obligations, and without deceit.
8.29 κατα τουϲ λογουϲ τουτουϲ ουτωϲ εϲτηϲαν Ρωμαιοι τω δημω των Ιουδαιων	**8.29** In accordance with these words, *the* Romans have established *a treaty* thus for the people of the Judeans.
8.30 εαν δε μετα τουϲ λογουϲ τουτουϲ βουλευϲονται ουτοι η ουτοι προϲθειναι η αφελειν ποιηϲωνται εξ αιρεϲεωϲ αυτων και ο αν προϲθωϲιν η αφελωϲιν εϲται κυρια	**8.30** But if, after these words, these *people* and those *people* take counsel to add or remove *anything,* they may do *it* from their *own* choice; and however they may add or remove, it will be authoritative.
8.31 και περι των κακων ων ο ‹βαϲιλευϲ› Δημητριοϲ ϲυντελειται ειϲ αυτουϲ εγραψαμεν αυτω λεγοντεϲ δια τι εβαρυναϲ τον ζυγον ϲου επι τουϲ φιλουϲ ημων τουϲ ϲυμμαχουϲ ‹› Ιουδαιουϲ	**8.31** And concerning the evil *things* that King Demetrius is doing to them, we have written to him, saying: 'Why have you† weighed your† yoke down on our friends, the Judean military allies?
8.32 εαν ουν ετι εντυχωϲιν κατα ϲου ποιηϲομεν ‹αυτοιϲ› την κριϲιν κ(αι) πολεμηϲομεν ‹ϲε› δια τηϲ θαλαϲϲηϲ και δια τηϲ ξηραϲ	**8.32** If therefore they appeal *any* more against you†, we will do justice for them, and will make war against you† by sea and dry *land*.'"

8.28 κ(αι) φυλαξονται [-ξωνται S^{ca} La^{146}] V A 64^{+}236 La^{109} \| φυλαϲϲουϲιν S* • **8.30** αν S = εαν V A 64^{+}236 • **8.31** βαϲιλευϲ S^{ca} V A 64^{+}236 \| > S* • ϲυμμαχουϲ V A La$^{109+146}$ \| + ημων S 64^{+}236 • **8.32** αυτοιϲ V A 64^{+}236 \| εαυ- S • ϲε S^{cb1} V A 64^{+}236 La$^{109+146}$ \| υπερ ϲου S* •

8.21–22 The Romans were **pleased** with Judas's proposal, and **sent** the Israelites a lasting record (**memorial**) of the **alliance,** which was written on **bronze slabs** (14.18, 27, 48), enabling it to be preserved longer (cf. Jer 15.12).

8.23–32 The alliance treaty contained four main parts:

- If **Rome** or Rome's **military allies** became involved in a war, the **Judeans** would assist them fully (**wholeheartedly**), and would not provide aid for Rome's opponents: vv 24–26.

- If **the Judeans** became involved in a war, **Rome** would assist them fully (**from the soul**), and would not provide aid for the Judeans' opponents:[231] vv 27–28.
- If[232] the Romans and the Judeans (**these people and those people**) agreed to modify the treaty at a later date (**after these words**), they were at liberty to do so:[233] v 30.
- The Romans issued a rebuke to **King Demetrius,** and warned him that if the Judeans made any further complaints about his actions, Rome would **do justice**[234] for the Judeans, and would **make war against** him: vv 31–32.

Somewhat similar agreements to help one another had been made by the tribes of Judah and Simeon (Jdg 1.3), by David and Jonathan (1 Sam 20.4–17), and by Joab and Abishai (2 Sam 10.9–11). God's people today are likewise military allies in a spiritual war (2 Cor 10.3–5); they are bound to assist each other in whatever ways may be needed (Rom 16.1–2; 3 Jn 5–8; 2 Cor 8.13–14; 1 Jn 3.16–17), and not to provide any aid for their opponents (2 Jn 10–11; cf. Rom 16.17).

THE DEATH OF JUDAS MACCABEUS

Bacchides and Alcimus return to Judea

9.1 και ηκουσεν Δημητριος	**9.1** And Demetrius heard
οτι ‹επεσεν› Νικανωρ και η δυναμις	that Nicanor and his force had fallen

[231] Some older commentators construed the treaty as saying: "Rome will not pay the costs of [Judean] soldiers sent to help her [v 26], and Rome will not pay the costs of [her] soldiers sent to help Judea [v 28]"—and/or: "the Judeans will do only what Rome thinks fit [v 26] and the Romans will do only what Rome thinks fit [v 28]" (so that "the Romans practically left themselves free to do as they pleased," Fairweather-Black 164–65). However, no ancient parallel for such a strange treaty has ever been found (Täubler, *Imperium Romanum,* 243–47). Moreover, the document is presented as something extremely beneficial to Judea (v 23). In reality the two clauses **as it has seemed right to the Romans** (vv 26, 28) indicate nothing more than "this part of the treaty has been approved by the Romans" ("thus has Rome decided," NJB).

[232] **If** [*ean*] they **take counsel** [*bouleusontai,* future indicative] ... **however** [*ho an*] **they may add** [*prosthōsin,* subjunctive] **or remove** [*aphelōsin,* subjunctive]. *Ean* is used not only with the subjunctive but also, at times, with the future indicative (BDAG 267, §1bα; MHT 3.115–16; BDF §372(1*a*)). Alternatively, *bouleusontai* (S V*) might be a variant spelling of the subjunctive *-sōntai* (V^{a} A $64^{+}236$); but in manuscripts of this period, that is less likely (Thackeray §6.28), especially in view of the tendency to use a future indicative in an opening clause with subjunctives in later clauses (Thackeray §6.31). Ancient copyists often treated *ean* and *an* as interchangeable forms (Thackeray §§5(4), 6.49; cf. Maccabaica 6.27).

[233] The modifications would be **authoritative** (Greek *kuria,* "lordly," having the authority of a lord; Muraoka 420, §4; LEH 361; BDAG 576). Contrast the laws issued by the Medes and Persians, which could never be modified, even by a king (Dan 6.8, 12, 15; Est 1.19).

[234] To **do justice** is to ensure that justice is done, and that people are not treated unjustly (Deut 10.18; Jer 7.5–6; 1 Kgs 3.28). The LORD loves to **do justice** (Psa 37.28; 140.12).

αυτου πολεμω και προcεθετο τον Βαχχιδην και τον Αλκιμον εκ δευτερου αποcτιλαι ειc γην Ιουδα και το δεξιον κεραc μετ αυτω(ν)	in battle; and he proceeded to send Bacchides and Alcimus a second *time* into *the* land of Judah, and the right flank with them.
9.2 και επορευθηcαν οδον την ειc Γαλγαλα και παρενεβαλον επι Μαιcαλωθ την εν Αρβηλοιc και προκατελαβοντο ‹αυτην› και απωλεcαν ‹› ψυχαc ανθ(ρωπ)ων πολλαc	**9.2** And they went *on the* path that *led* to Gilgal; and they camped against Mesaloth, which *is* in Arbela, and took hold of it, and destroyed many souls of persons.
9.3 και του μηνοc του πρωτου ετουc του δευτερου και ν´ και ρ´ παρενεβαλο(ν) επι Ι(ερουcα)λημ	**9.3** And *in* the first month of the hundred and fifty-second year, they camped against Jerusalem.

9.1 επεcεν S^{ca} V A $64^{+}236$ $La^{109+146}$ | επιc- S* • **9.2** αυτην S^{ca} V A $64^{+}236$ $La^{109+146}$ | αυτουc S* • ψυχαc V A $64^{+}236$ $La^{109+146}$ | ^ ειc S •

9.1–2 After the death of Nicanor, **Demetrius . . . proceeded to send**[235] **Bacchides** (7.8) and **Alcimus** (7.5) back to Judea with additional forces (reckoned as **the right flank** of the Syrian army; see the notes on 6.38). Their route is described in detail, but none of the places named can be identified. They set out on the road toward **Gilgal.** There was evidently more than one Gilgal. One was situated between the Jordan and Jericho (Josh 4.19); another was close to Jerusalem (Josh 15.7; Neh 12.29); and other passages (including the present one[236]) may refer to still others (cf. Josh 12.23; ZEB 2.765, §2). At any rate the forces were clearly traveling from Syria toward Jerusalem (v 3). They reached **Arbela,** a place of uncertain location,[237] where they gained a victory.

Judas fights against them, but is killed

9.4 και απηραν και επορευθηcαν ειc Βερεαν εν εικοcι χιλιαcιν α(ν)δρων και ‹,β´› ‹ιππω›	**9.4** And they moved away, and went to Berea, with twenty thousand men and two thousand horse.

---

[235] **Proceeded to send.** The Greek is *prosetheto . . . apost(e)ilai,* "added to send."

[236] Bartlett, *First and Second . . . Maccabees,* 114. The question is complicated by the fact that different manuscripts have different readings, here and in other passages (including Josh 12.23); see ISBE 2.470–72. In the present verse, S, V, and A (supported by $La^{109+146}$) read **Gilgal** *(Galgala),* whereas $64^{+}236$ read "Gilead" *(Galaad).* Josephus (*Antiquities,* 12.421) has "Galilee" (was this once a variant reading in the Greek text of the present verse, or is it the result of a misreading by Josephus himself or one of his early copyists?).

[237] The name **Arbela** may have been given to sites in Galilee, in Gilead, in Samaria, near Jezreel, and near Aijalon (Elitzur, *Ancient Place Names in the Holy Land,* 57–60; ISBE 1.234). Nothing in the context shows which one is meant here. **Mesaloth** (≡ Hebrew *mslwt*) might either be a town or refer to "highways" at Arbela (Simons §1148; Num 20.19, etc.; cf. "Ashdod" in v 15).

9.5 και Ιουδας ην παρενβεβληκως εν Ελαςα και ‹‚γʹ› ανδρες ‹εκλεκτοι μετ αυτου›	**9.5** And Judas was camped at Elasa, and three thousand chosen men with him.

9.4 ‚βʹ S^{ca} V A $64^{+}236$ $La^{109+146}$ | βʹ S* • ιππω $64^{+}236$ [*equitum* $La^{109+146}$] | ιππο(ν) S | ιππων V A • **9.5** ‚γʹ S^{ca} V A $64^{+}236$ $La^{109+146}$ | γʹ S* • εκλεκτοι / μετ αυτου A $64^{+}236$ La^{109} | ~ S V La^{146} •

9.4–5 The Syrian army proceeded to **Berea,**[238] near Judas's camp at **Elasa.** Both places are unrecorded elsewhere, and therefore cannot be identified (Simons §1149; Schürer-Vermes 1.173).

9.6 και ειδο(ν) το πληθος των δυναμεων οτι πολλοι ειςιν και εφοβηθηςαν ςφοδρα και εξερυηςαν πολλοι απο της παρεμβολης ου κατελιφθηςαν εξ αυτων αλλ η οκτακοςιοι ανδρες	**9.6** And they saw the multitude of the forces, that they were many; and they were very much afraid. And many melted away from the camp; none of them were left but eight hundred men.
9.7 κ(αι) ειδεν Ιουδας οτι απερρυη η παρεμβολη αυτου και ο πολεμος εθλιβεν αυτον κ(αι) ςυνετριβη τη καρδια οτι ουκ ειχεν κ(αι)ρον ςυναγαγειν αυτους	**9.7** And Judas saw that his company had melted away, and the war was oppressing him; and he was shattered in heart: for he had no time to gather them together,
9.8 και εξελυθη κ(αι) ειπεν τοις καταλιφθειςιν αναςτωμεν και αναβωμε(ν) επι τους υπεναντιους ημων εαν αρα δυνωμεθα πολεμηςαι προς αυτους	**9.8** and he became tired. And he said to the *one*s who were left: "Let us rise up, and go up against our opponents, if perhaps we may be able to make war against them."
9.9 κ(αι) απεςτρεφον ‹αυτον› λεγοντες ου μη δυνωμεθα αλλ η ‹ςωζωμεν› τας εαυτων ψυχας το νυν ‹και› επιςτρεψωμεν και οι αδελφοι ημων και πολεμηςωμεν προς αυτους ημις δε ολιγοι	**9.9** And they *began* turning him away, saying: "We should certainly not be able; but rather, let us save *our* own souls now; and *then* let us return, and our brothers, and make war against them. But we *are* few."

9.9 αυτον S^{ca} V A $64^{+}236$ $La^{109+146}$ | αυτους S* • ςωζωμεν A $64^{+}236$ $La^{109+146}$ | ςωζομεν S* V| ςωςομεν S^{ca} • και 2° $64^{+}236$ $La^{109+146}$ | > S V A •

9.6–8 Most of Judas's army now became **very much afraid** and **melted away** (cf. Deut 20.8; 1 Sam 13.5–7; Jer 49.23–24), even though they had faced greater numbers on

[238] **Berea** *(Berean)* is the reading of S, V, and A. In most other copies the final syllable includes a *-t-: Bereatim* (La^{109}), *Berethin* (La^{146}), *Beērthaz* ($64^{+}236$), *Beērzath* (93, supported by 7h7: cf. "Bethzeth," 7.19), *Byrt* (most medieval and later Syriac manuscripts). 7a1 has *M'ršʾ* ("Mareshah"; cf. 5.66). Manuscripts of Josephus (*Antiquities,* 12.422) also have diverse readings.

previous occasions (cf. 3.39; 4.28; 6.30). He was left with only **eight hundred men** to face **twenty thousand** infantry and **two thousand** cavalry. In this situation he himself became disheartened (**shattered in heart**) and **tired** (and therefore all the more vulnerable to attack, like David in 2 Sam 21.15–17). Yet he was determined to **rise up and go up against** the enemy nonetheless. God's people are to fight for their Master not only "in season," but also "out of season" (2 Tim 4.2); when they are weary and their feet are failing, they are to lift up their limbs and press forward along "straight paths" without faltering, for that is the way to be healed (Heb 12.3, 11–12). "The LORD is near to those who are shattered in heart; and those who are crushed in spirit He saves. Many are the evils of the righteous one; but from them all, the LORD brings him to safety" (Psa 34.18–19; 147.3).

9.10 κ(αι) ειπεν Ιουδας	**9.10** And Judas said:
μη γενοιτο ποιηcαι το πραγμα ⸂τουτο⸃	"May it not come about *for us* to do
φυγιν απ αυτων	this act, to flee from them;
και ει ηγγικεν ο καιροc ημων	and if our time has come near,
αποθανωμεν ⸂εν ανδρεια⸃ χαριν	let us die in a manly *way*, on account
των αδελφων ⸂ημω(ν)⸃ και μη	of our brothers; and let us not leave
καταλιπωμεν αιτιαν τη δοξη ημων	an accusation against our honor."

9.10 τουτο V A $64^{+}236$ $La^{109+146}$ | > S • εν ανδρεια $64^{+}236$ $La^{109+146}$ | ανδριωc S V | ανδρια A • ημω(ν) 2° S^{c} V A $64^{+}236$ $La^{109+146}$ | > S* •

9.10 Judas was well aware that his **time**—the time for him to **die**—might have **come near** (cf. Jas 4.14). He was no prophet (v 27; 4.46), so he could not foretell his death, as Jesus and Paul foretold theirs ("My time has come near," Matt 26.18; "The time of my release is standing near," 2 Tim 4.6). Yet even **if** it was time for him to die, he was determined to die **in a manly way** (*en andreia,* cf. v 22)—that is, not just "bravely" (NRSV) but in the way of a grownup person as opposed to a child.[239] To **flee,** and think only of oneself (v 9), would be childish. A mature adult would act on behalf of his **brothers** rather than himself (just as Jesus did, Php 2.3–5; cf. 1 Cor 10.24; Rom 12.10). It would be better to die than to look on the surrounding evils and do nothing to oppose them (3.59).

Judas was determined not to **leave an accusation against** his **honor** (or "glory," RV; Greek *doxa,* as in 2.51, 64: "act manfully, and be strong in the Law: for in it you will be honored"). God's people are to keep their "way of life good among the nations, so that, in a matter where they speak against you as evildoers, they may, by seeing your good works, glorify God" (1 Pet 2.12). Again Jesus is the model: at His death, no **accusation** could be found against Him (John 18.38).

---

[239] In expressions of this kind, **man** is contrasted with "child," not with "woman" (as 1 Cor 13.11 shows). A responsible, trustworthy woman is *andreios* (Prov 31.10, LXX; Sir 26.2), no less than a responsible, trustworthy man.

9.11 και απηρεν η δυναμις απο της παρεμβολης και εστησαν ‹αυτοις εις συναντησιν› και εμερισθη η ιππος εις δυο μερη και οι σφενδονηται και οι τοξοται ‹προεπορευοντο› της δυναμεως και οι πρωταγωνισται παντες οι δυνατοι	**9.11** And the force moved away from the camp, and stood to meet them. And the horse was parted into two parts, and the slingers and the bowmen were going ahead of the force, and all the powerful fighters *were* at *the* front.
9.12 Βακχιδης δε ην ε(ν) τω δεξιω κερατι κ(αι) ηγγισεν η φαλαγξ εκ των δυο μερω(ν) και εφωνουν ταις σαλπιγξιν και εσαλπισαν οι παρα Ιουδα και αυτοι ταις σαλπιγξιν	**9.12** But Bacchides was with the right flank; and the phalanx came near, from the two sides; and they *kept* calling with the trumpets. And the *men* alongside Judas trumpeted, they also, with the trumpets.
9.13 και εσαλευθη η γη απο της φωνης των παρεμβολων και εγενετο ο πολεμος συνημμενος απο πρωιθεν ‹εως› εσπερας	**9.13** And the earth shook from the voice of the companies; and the battle came about, making contact from early morning until evening.
9.14 και ειδεν Ιουδας οτι Βακχιδης και το στερεωμα της παρεμβολης ‹εν› τοις δεξιοις και συνηλθον αυτω παντες οι ευψυχοι τη καρδια	**9.14** And Judas saw that Bacchides and the strength of the company *were* in the right *ranks*; and all those *who were* strong in heart came with him,
9.15 και συνετριβη το δεξιο(ν) μερος απ αυτων και εδιωκεν οπισω αυτων εως Αζωτου ορους	**9.15** and the right wing was shattered by them; and he *began* pursuing behind them, up to *the* Ashdoth [slopes] of *the* mountains.

9.11 αυτοις / εις συναντησιν 64⁺236 La[109+146] | ~ S V A • προεπορευοντο S[ca] A 64⁺236 La[109+146] | προσεπ- S* V • **9.13** εως V A 64⁺236 | μεχρι S • **9.14** εν V A 64⁺236 La[109+146] | > S •

9.11–15 As usual, Judas was not afraid to attack where the enemy's greatest **strength** lay, in its **right wing;** and his attack was successful. When faced with opposition from God's people, even the strongest enemy will flee (Josh 23.10; Jas 4.7; Rev 12.11).

Trumpets were used to summon the forces to battle, as often described in the Scriptures (1 Cor 14.8; Neh 4.20; Amos 3.6).

The right wing fled **up to the Ashdoth of the mountains**—that is, the "as far as the mountain slopes" (NAB; Greek *Azōtou* here represents Hebrew *'šdwt,* "slopes"; cf. Deut 3.17; Josh 10.40).[240]

[240] A country's geographical terms often tend to be transliterated rather than translated: narratives written in modern English often refer to Israel's south as the Negev (Hebrew *ngb,* "south"), its western plains as the Shephelah (see 12.38; Hebrew *šplh,* "lowland"), etc. Cf. also 14.27. Thus there is no need to assume that the book's writer or translator made an error here

9.16 και οι εις το αριστερον κερας ειδον οτι συνετριβη το δεξιον κερας ‹κ(αι)› ‹επεστρεψαν› ‹κατα ποδας› Ιουδα και των μετ αυτου εκ των οπισθεν	**9.16** And the *ones* in the left flank saw that the right flank had been shattered; and they turned back against *the* feet of Judas and those *who were* with him, behind *them*.
9.17 και εβαρυνθη ο πολεμος και επεσον τραυματιαι πολλοι εκ τουτων ‹και εκ τουτων›	**9.17** And the battle became heavy; and many wounded *ones* fell, from these *ones* and those *ones*;
9.18 και Ιουδας επεσεν και οι λοιποι εφυγον	**9.18** and Judas fell, and the rest fled.

9.16 κ(αι) 2° S^{ca} V A $64^{+}236$ $La^{109+146}$ | κατα προσωπον και S* • επεστρεψαν S^{ca} A $64^{+}236$ $La^{109+146}$ | -ψεν S* V • κατα ποδας S^{ca} V A $64^{+}236$ | > S* $La^{109+146}$ • **9.17** και εκ τουτων V A 64 $La^{109[+146]}$ 7h7 7a1 | > S 236 •

9.16–18 Nevertheless, the less strong **left flank** attacked Judas and his forces from behind. **Judas** was killed, and **the rest** of his army **fled.** Satan is losing the war (Rev 20.10), but he is permitted to win individual skirmishes (Rev 2.10)—when that suits God's purposes (John 19.11; Job 1.12; 2.6; 2 Cor 12.7). And for those purposes, while greater enemies are put to flight, lesser ones are sometimes allowed a moment of success. The One who conquered even the devil (Heb 2.14; 1 Jn 3.8; Rev 12.9) was successfully betrayed by someone subject to the devil's power (John 13.2, 27; Luke 22.3).

Each of the Lord's warriors has an appointed lifespan (Psa 139.16). As long as the Lord still has work for him to do, he will remain alive (Php 1.24–25). When his work is done, God's predetermined plan is that he will die—in some cases, at the hands of his enemies (as happened to Jesus, Acts 2.22–23; 4.27–28; Luke 24.7; to Stephen, Acts 7.58–60; to Peter, John 21.18–19; and to Paul, 2 Tim 2.8–9; 4.4–7). Sometimes one of God's people will be slain by the enemy, yet another will be spared. Jonathan the son of Saul died when David was spared (1 Sam 31.2; 2 Sam 1.17, 25–26); James the brother of John died when Peter was spared (Acts 12.1–11). Often, the person who starts a great work does not live to see it completed. The surpassingness of the power is not his, but God's; and not he, but God, is to be glorified for it (cf. Isa 48.11; Zec 4.6; 2 Cor 4.7). Moses led the Israelites to the promised land, but did not enter it (Deut. 34.1–5); David gathered the materials for the temple, but did not build it (1 Chr 28.1–21).

At whatever age God's people die, and in whatever circumstances, their assigned death is not a sign that their Lord has deserted them: for all those who die in Him are blessed (Rev 14.13), are taken away from the evil in the world (Isa 57.1–2), and receive a crown of righteousness (2 Tim 4.8).

(Abel 162–63) or was referring to the Philistine city Ashdod (which was located not in a mountainous region but on the coastal plain, Josh 15.46–47) or to an otherwise unknown "Mount Azotus" (KJV).

The mourning for Judas

9.19 και ‹ηραν› Ιωναθαν και Cιμων Ιουδαν τον αδελφον αυτων και εθαψαν αυτο(ν) εν τω ταφω των πατερων αυτων εν Μωδαειν	**9.19** And Jonathan and Simon took Judas their brother, and they buried him in the burial-place of their fathers, at Modein.
9.20 και εκλαυcαν αυτον και εκοψαντο αυτον παc Ιc(ραη)λ κοπετον μεγαν και επενθουν ημεραc πολλαc και ‹ειπον›	**9.20** And all Israel wept *for* him and beat themselves *for* him *with* a great beating; and they were mourning many days; and they said:
9.21 πωc επεcεν δυνατοc cωζων τον Ιc(ραη)λ	**9.21** "How has *the* powerful *one* fallen, *the one* who was saving Israel!"

9.19 ηραν V A 64*236 [*tulerunt* La[109+146]] | ηρεν S • **9.20** ειπον V [-παν A] 64*236 La[109+146] | -πεν S •

9.19–20 Judas was **buried** with his **fathers** in their home town, **Modein** (see on 2.1). **All Israel** mourned for him and **beat themselves . . . with a great beating** *(kopeton megan),* as they had done for his father Mattathias (see the notes on 2.70), and as they would do for his brother Jonathan (13.25–26). So too, in a later age, "devout men buried Stephen, and made a great beating [*kopeton megan*] over him" (Acts 8.2).

9.21 Judas had been a savior of **Israel.** In that respect, he was like the saviors given to Israel by God in the days of the judges and kings (Jdg 3.9, 15; 2 Kgs 13.5; Neh 9.27), and like the great Savior given to Israel a century and a half later (Luke 1.69–71; Acts 13.23; 5.31).

The Israelites mourned his death much as David had mourned the death of Saul and Jonathan: "How have the powerful ones fallen!" (2 Sam 1.17, 19). Compare also the mourning over the death of Jesus ("We were hoping that He Himself was the One who was going to redeem Israel," Luke 24.21).

9.22 και τα περιccια τω(ν) λογων Ιουδα και των πολεμων κ(αι) των ανδραγαθιων ων εποιηcεν και τηc μεγαλωcυνηc αυτου ου κατεγραφη πολλη γαρ ην cφοδρα	**9.22** And the overflow of the accounts of Judas, and of the wars and manly good deeds that he did, and his greatness, have not been written down: for they were very many.

9.22 Judas did **very many** other good deeds, an **overflow**[241] of them beyond what has **been written down.** In that respect too he resembled the great Savior of Israel who

[241] **The overflow** *(ta perissa).* Not only the "rest" of the deeds (RV), but the oversufficiency of the deeds (cf. "the abundant acts," SAAS)—the opposite of insufficiency (2 Cor 8.14; Php 4.12). What Antiochus Epiphanes was in wastefulness (*eperisseusen*, 3.30), Judas was in doing good. Indeed all God's people are to be "overflowing [*perisseuēte*] in every good work" (2 Cor 9.8), just as God Himself is, in His dealings with us (Eph 1.8; Rom 5.15, 17).

was shortly to come (John 21.25). Seed that is sown in good ground brings forth abundantly (Mark 4.8; Acts 9.36; John 15.8; 1 Cor 15.58).[242]

"There can scarcely be found in the whole Old Testament a hero with more of the outstanding qualities that make people holy and great. Few warriors can be found who are temperate, devout, self-controlled, free from ambition and pride, shunning pleasure, and above vainglory. Judas had all the characteristics of a hero: courage, boldness, power, counsel, wisdom—all this without impulsivity, violence, or ostentation. Beyond that, he had everything that ought to mark a priest of the Lord and a devout ruler: zeal for religion, purity of heart, and love of his people. He was pious, without superstition; devoted to worship, without baseness; zealous to observe the commandments, but with a zeal governed by knowledge and maintained by love. How clearly his profound knowledge of God's commandments and the principles of right living are shown in his speeches arousing his troops for battle, encouraging them in times of humiliation, and teaching them to scorn the greatest dangers! How wholehearted and pure are his prayers! How humbly and penitently he bows before the Almighty when preparing for battle! With what determination he ascends to the temple surrounded by enemies, in order to cleanse it from the defilement of the Gentiles! With what vigor he opposes the irreverent, and avenges wrongs done to the Lord! Finally, how attentively he cares for his people's interests, promoting their glory and advancement—both spiritual and earthly: 'he was spreading glory wide for his people' (3.3).

"If we were to compare this great man with the One who was the model and template for all holy people—with Jesus Christ, the Savior of the world—how many remarkable similarities would we notice! Judas, chosen among his brethren to save his people and be their head and ruler, in the blackest era of the Hebrew nation, when religion seemed certain to perish—isn't he an image of Jesus Christ, who came in these last days to draw the world out of the deep darkness in which it was immersed, to scatter superstition and idolatry by the bright light of His teaching, and to correct corrupt morals by the purity of His wholly divine morality? When we contemplate Judas at odds with all Israel's enemies, winning notable victories over them though he was almost alone and without human aid—when we see him almost constantly persecuted and wandering from place to place, and, as he was rejected by most of Israel, forced to seek alliance with foreigners and Gentiles—when we think of him devoted to cleansing the temple of its abominations, raising a new altar, and restoring the appointed sacrifices—lastly, when we envisage him in his ultimate battle, overcome by the power and number of his enemies, generously giving his life for his brethren in his prime—may we not also see, as if in a mirror, Jesus Christ persecuted in Himself and in the members of His body, not only by foreigners, but even more by His own brethren the Jews, willing to stretch out His hands to an unfaithful people, and to

---

[242] "There are many wars and manly good deeds done by holy people—or rather, by the Lord in them—the full sum of which no human can know, but they remain known to their Author alone" (Hrabanus Maurus, PL 109.1131).

accept in His church the Gentiles who by nature had no right to the inheritance of sons? Jesus Christ in the temple and on the cross—driving out of the former those who were profaning the holiness of His Father's house, and yielding himself up on the latter for the salvation of His people—isn't He likewise the perfect Original, of whom Maccabeus was the living copy?" (Calmet 132–33).

Jonathan (9.23–12.53)

JONATHAN ESTABLISHES PEACE IN ISRAEL

A time of oppression

9.23 και εγενετο μετα την τελευτην Ιουδου εξεκυψαν οι ανομοι εν πασιν τοις οριοις Ις(ραη)λ και ανετιλαν παντες οι εργαζομενοι την αδικια(ν)	**9.23** And it came about, after the completion of Judas*'s life*, those *who were* opposed to *the* Law peered out in all the appointed boundaries of Israel, and all those who were working unrighteousness rose
9.24 εν ταις ημεραις εκειναις εγενηθη λιμος μεγας σφοδρα και αυτομολησεν η χωρα μετ αυτων	**9.24** (in those days a very great famine came about); and the district deserted with them.

9.23–24 When "the one who is restraining" is taken "out of the midst ... the one who is opposed to the Law will be revealed" (2 Thes 2.7–8). So it was after the deaths of God's judges (Jdg 2.19), after the death of Jehoiada the priest (2 Chr 24.2, 15–18), and after the departure of the apostle Paul (Acts 20.29–30). So it was also **after the completion of Judas's life.**[243] While he had been alive, "those opposed to the Law were confined from fear of him" (3.5–6); but when he was taken out of the midst of Israel, **those who were opposed to the Law** and **who were working unrighteousness** reappeared. They had not been eliminated; they had merely been in hiding, and now they **peered out** once more (like the timid soldiers described in 4.19–22).[244] This was also a time of **very great famine,** and the people in Judea (the **district**)[245] **deserted** their Lord. Troubles of any kind should make us seek help from Him (1 Kgs 8.37–40; Psa 50.15), yet they cause many to forsake Him (Jer 44.17–18; Matt 13.21; 24.12). Few are those who persist in serving Him faithfully, not only when they are filled, but also when they are hungry (Php 4.12; cf. Matt 6.25; John 6.26–27).

---

243 **The completion of Judas' life.** Like Paul, Judas had "fought the good fight" and "completed the course" (2 Tim 4.7). He had accomplished the work that God had given him to do (John 17.4). "The day of death is better than the day of birth .... The end of a thing is better than its beginning" (Ecc 7.1, 8).

244 **Peered out** (*exekupsan;* "put forth their heads," RV; *mostrarono il viso,* Diodati), as if from behind a mountain (4.19) or a lattice (Song 2.9, LXX; cf. LEH 183; Muraoka 210).

245 The term **district** *(chōra)* refers in this context specifically to Judea (as e.g., in 13.20; 14.6); cf. 12.25.

9.25 και εξελεξε(ν) Βακχειδης τουϲ αϲεβειϲ ανδραϲ και κατεϲτηϲεν αυτουϲ κυριουϲ τηϲ χωραϲ	**9.25** And Bacchides chose the irreverent men, and established them *as* lords of the district;
9.26 και εξεζητουν και ηρευνουν τουϲ φιλουϲ Ιουδου και ηγον αυτουϲ προϲ Βακχιδην και ‹εξεδικει› αυτουϲ και ενεπαιζεν αυτοιϲ	**9.26** and they were seeking out and searching for the friends of Judas, and leading them to Bacchides; and he was taking vengeance *on* them, and scoffing at them.

9.26 εξεδικει V [-δικα A] 64⁺236 La[109+146] | -διωκε S • ηρευνουν S = ηρευνων V | εξηρευνων A = εξηρευνουν 64⁺236 •

9.25 During this time of trouble **Bacchides** appointed **irreverent men . . . as lords of the district.** When a ruler gives heed to evil, all the officials whom he appoints are wicked likewise (Prov 29.12; 2 Chr 13.6–7).

9.26 Bacchides **was taking vengeance on** the friends of Judas, **and scoffing at them.** God alone has authority to take vengeance (Rom 12.19; see the notes on 7.24). Those who take vengeance without His authorization will themselves experience His vengeance (Ezek 25.12–17; Lam 3.59–62); those who scoff at His servants (2 Chr 36.16) will themselves be scoffed at by Him (Prov 3.34; 1.26; Psa 2.4; 37.13).

9.27 και εγενετο θλιψιϲ μεγαλη εν τω Ιϲ(ραη)λ ητιϲ ουκ εγενετο αφ ηϲ ημεραϲ ουκ ωφθη προφητηϲ αυτοιϲ	**9.27** And great oppression came about in Israel, which had not come about since the day *when* no prophet was seen among them.

9.27 So, after the death of Judas, there was **great oppression . . . in Israel**—greater than at any time since they had last **seen** a **prophet** (cf. Dan 12.1; Joel 2.2). Similarly, Jesus foretold a time after His own death when there would be a "great oppression such as has not come about from the beginning of the world until now, no, nor ever will come about" (Matt 24.21). Like the period after Judas's death, it would be a time when "they shall deliver you up to be afflicted, and shall kill you" (Matt 24.9). These things happened to faithful servants of God who had "not forgotten" Him or "done falsehood in [His] covenant" (Psa 44.17), and yet were "killed all the day long" for His sake (Rom 8.36). God will sometimes inflict extraordinarily severe trials on the people He loves (Rev 13.7; 1 Cor 4.11–13; 2 Cor 11.23–33; Heb 11.36–38), but they have His unshakeable promises that they will "be able to bear it" (1 Cor 10.13) and that if they faithfully "endure to the end" (Matt 24.13), they are "more than conquerors" (Rom 8.37), and will ultimately receive "the crown of life" (James 1.12; Rev 2.10).

Under the old covenant, one of the punishments that God inflicted on His people, when they persistently disobeyed Him, was to deprive them of His prophetic word. When King Saul persisted in disobedience, "the LORD did not answer him, either by dreams, or by Urim, or by prophets" (1 Sam 28.6). During the Babylonian captivity, Jerusalem's "prophets found no vision from the LORD" (Lam 2.9; Psa 74.9; Ezek

7.26). And during the Greek period, when "there came to be very great anger upon Israel" (1.64; Dan 11.33), there was **no prophet . . . among** the people (Maccabaica 4.46; 14.41).[246] Only later, after those opposing the Law had been put away (14.14), did people in Israel again receive prophecies from the Lord (Luke 2.36; 1.67; Matt 11.9, 13).

Today, under the new covenant, "we have the prophetic word more firmly established" (2 Pet 1.19), and that word will never pass away (1 Pet 1.25). But if we persistently shut our eyes to it (Matt 13.15), the Lord may deprive us of it (cf. Amos 8.11–12) by Himself shutting our eyes so that we no longer have the capacity to see it (John 12.40; Rom 11.8). "Because I called, and you refused, I stretched out My hand, and there was no one who attended . . . then they will call on Me, and I will not answer; they will seek Me at dawn, and they will not find Me" (Prov 1.24–32).

Jonathan is appointed leader

9.28 και ηθροιcθηcαν παντες οι φιλοι Ιουδου και ειπο(ν) ‹τω› Ιωναθαν	**9.28** And all the friends of Judas drew together, and said to Jonathan:
9.29 αφ ου ο αδελφος cου Ιουδας τετελευτηκεν και ανηρ ομοιος αυτω ουκ εcτιν εξελθειν ‹› προς τους εχθρους και Βακχιδην και εν τοις εχθραινουcιν του εθνους ημων	**9.29** "Since *the day* when your† brother Judas completed *his life*, *there* is no man like him to come out against the enemies and Bacchides, and among those of our nation who are at enmity;
9.30 νυν ουν cε ηρετιcαμεθα cημερον του ειναι αντ αυτου ημιν εις αρχοντα και ηγουμενον του πολεμηcαι τον πολεμον ημων	**9.30** now therefore, we have chosen you† today, to be a ruler and leader for us in his place, to war our warfare."
9.31 και επεδεξατο Ιωναθαν ε(ν) τω καιρω εκεινω την ηγηcιν και ανεcτη αντι Ιουδου του αδελφου αυτου	**9.31** And Jonathan accepted the leadership at that period of time; and he rose up in place of Judas his brother.

9.28 τω S[ca] V A 64*236 | > S • **9.29** εξελθειν A 64*236 La[109+146] | + και ειcελθει(ν) S V •

9.28–31 All the friends of Judas now chose **Jonathan** to be their **leader,** just as the people of Gilead had chosen Jephthah in a much earlier time of oppression (Jdg 10.18;

[246] "We cannot state on the basis of these passages . . . when the period of prophecy was believed to have ended," but the wording indicates that it was not a recent event (Steinmann, *Oracles of God,* 57); Israel had been deprived of prophets at least as long as Judas had been leader (cf. 4.46), and probably at least since the earliest stages of the persecution under Antiochus Epiphanes (no prophets are mentioned even in 1.25–28; 2.6–13). Prophecy returned after the time of Simon (14.41) but well before the birth of Christ (Luke 2.36–37)—possibly as much as a century or more beforehand (see the introduction to this commentary).

11.6–11). So Jonathan **rose up in place of Judas his brother** (cf. 3.1). Like Jephthah, he was chosen by the people, but he was raised up by God (Jdg 2.16; see on 2.1).

9.32 και εγνω Βακχιδης και εζητει αυτον αποκτειναι	**9.32** And Bacchides knew *this;* and he was seeking him, to kill *him.*
9.33 και εγνω Ιωναθαν και Σιμων ο αδελφος αυτου και παντες οι μετ αυτου και εφυγον εις την ερημον Θεκωε και παρενεβαλον επι το υδωρ λακκου Ασφαρ	**9.33** And Jonathan, and Simon his brother, and all those with him, knew *it;* and they fled into the desert of Tekoa, and camped close by the water of *the* pit Asphar.
9.34 και εγνω Βακχιδης τη ημερα τω(ν) σαββατων και ηλθεν αυτος και παν το στρατευμα αυτου περαν του Ιορδανου	**9.34** And Bacchides knew *this,* on the Sabbath day; and he came, he and all his army, over to *the* other side of the Jordan.

9.32–34 Knowing that Jonathan had been appointed, **Bacchides** sought **to kill him.** The narrative alternates between the movements of Jonathan and those of Bacchides:

- **Jonathan ... and all those with him ... fled into the desert of Tekoa**[247] (a town of Judah, 2 Chr 11.5–6, situated in the desert not far from Jerusalem, 2 Chr 20.5, 17–20): v 33.
- **Bacchides ... and all his army** came[248] to the **Jordan:** v 34.
- Meanwhile, Jonathan and his companions moved from the Tekoa region to "the marsh of the Jordan" (which explains why Bacchides went to the Jordan, not to the desert near Jerusalem[249]): vv 35–42.

---

[247] Their camp was located near **the waters of the pit Asphar,** a place that cannot be identified (cf. Simons §1152).

[248] **He came** [*ēlthen*] **... over to the other side of** [*peran*] **the Jordan** (v 34). In other words, he crossed the Jordan (cf. John 6.17, where the same Greek construction occurs: "they were coming [*ērchonto*] over to the other side of [*peran*] the sea"). In this verse, all Greek manuscripts (supported by La[109+146]) state that **Bacchides knew** about Jonathan's movements **on the Sabbath day; and he came** to the Jordan. Vg has a slightly different word order: "Bacchides knew [this], and on the Sabbath day he came" to the Jordan (as in v 43).

[249] Thus "the narrative vv 35–42 ... showing how the Jews went from the desert of Tekoa east to the Jordan region ... chronologically precedes [Bacchides' arrival at the Jordan in] v 34, and the statement in v 34 is to be read as a kind of glance ahead or anticipation [*quasi praeoccupatione seu anticipatione*]; afterwards, v 43 takes up the story again" (Knabenbauer 168; Fillion, *La Sainte Bible,* 6.724). When he reached v 34, "the historian obviously wanted to narrate the clash between Bacchides and Jonathan at the Jordan (vv 43ff.). However, he recognized that he had not yet explained how Jonathan had come with his troops to the Jordan; so he presented the incident that had brought him there in the form of an insert, or rather a parenthesis" (Keil 158). Keil goes on to point out that all the aorist and imperfect tenses of vv 35–42 are past in relation to those of v 34, and therefore correspond to German (or English) pluperfects: "he had sent his brother ... and he had encouraged the Nabateans ..." and so on (cf. BDF §324). There

- Finally the narrative returns to Bacchides at the Jordan,[250] where the two armies meet in battle: vv 43–49.

When Jonathan and his companions escaped from their enemies into the Judean desert, they were doing what David had done centuries earlier (1 Sam 22.1–2; 23.13–15; Psa 63.0–1; 55.2–7).

The death of John

9.35 και απεστιλεν τον αδελφον	**9.35** And he sent his brother
αυτου ηγουμενον του οχλου	*as* leader of the crowd,
και παρεκαλεσεν τους Ναβαταιους	and he encouraged the Nabateans
φιλους αυτου του παραθεσθαι αυτοις	his friends *for him* to place with them
την ‹αποσκευην αυτων› την πολλη(ν)	their large amount of equipment.

9.35 αποσκευην αυτων V A 64⁺236 \| παρασκευην αυτου S •

9.35 Jonathan and his men had a **large amount of equipment,** so **he sent his brother** (John, vv 36, 38; cf. 2.2) to ask their **friends** across the Jordan, the **Nabateans** (see 5.24–25), to care for it (just as David, while he was in danger from Saul in Israel, took his family across the Jordan and left them with the king of Moab, 1 Sam 22.3–4).

9.36 και εξηλθον οι υιοι ‹Ιαμβρι›	**9.36** And the sons of Jambri, *who were*
οι εκ Μηδαβα κ(αι) συνελαβον	from Medeba, came out and took
Ιωαννην και παντα οσα ειχεν	John, and all *the things* that he had; and
και απηλθο(ν) εχοντες	when *they* had *them,* they went away.

9.36 Ιαμβρι V [-ειν A] La[109] \| Αμ- S 64⁺236 \| Μαμ- La[146] •

9.36 However, **John** and **all** the equipment were seized by **the sons of Jambri,** (foreigners **from Medeba,** an ancient town in Moab, Isa 15.2, on or near the border of Reuben, Josh 13.16). John was slain either at the time or soon afterwards (vv 38, 42).

9.37 μετα τους λογους τουτους	**9.37** After these things, they reported
‹απηγγειλαν› Ιωναθαν κ(αι) Σιμωνι	to Jonathan and Simon his brother
τω αδελφω αυτου οτι υιοι Ιαμβρι	that *the* sons of Jambri were making
ποιουσι(ν) γαμον μεγαν και αγουσιν	a great wedding, and were bringing
την νυμφην απο ‹Ναδαβαθ› θυγατερα	the bride from Nadabath, a daughter
ενος τω(ν) μεγαλων μεγιστανων	of one of the great*est* of *the* great men
Χαναan μετα παραπομπης μεγαλης	of Canaan, with a great convoy.

9.37 απηγγειλαν V A 64⁺236 \| -γγιλεν S • Ναδαβαθ A La[109] \| Ναβαδαθ V \| Γαβαδαν S \| Ναβατ 64⁺236 7h7 \| ܢܠܒܬ 7a1 •

---

is no need to suppose that anything in the narrative has been misplaced (and no textual evidence of any such misplacement).

[250] Note the use of repetition after an interval in vv 34, 43, as often elsewhere in the Maccabean History when describing a foreign power (see the introduction to this commentary).

9.37 Later, John's two remaining brothers—**Jonathan and Simon**—heard that there would be **a great wedding** among the **sons of Jambri,** because one of their men was marrying a woman from one of the **greatest** Canaanite families (cf. Matt 15.22), who would be coming **with a great convoy.**[251]

9.38 και εμνηςθηςαν του αιματος Ιωαννου του αδελφου ‹αυτων› κ(αι) ανεβηςαν και εκρυβηςαν υπο τη(ν) ςκεπην του ορους	**9.38** And they were mindful of the blood of John their brother; and they went up, and hid under the cover of the mountain.
9.39 και ηραν τους οφθαλμους αυτω(ν) και ιδον και ιδου θρους και η αποςκευη πολλη και ο νυμφιος εξηλθεν και οι φιλοι αυτου και οι αδελφοι αυτου εις ‹ςυναντηςιν› αυτων μετα τυμπανων και μουςικω(ν) και οπλων πολλω(ν)	**9.39** And they lifted up their eyes, and saw; and see! a hubbub, and a large amount of equipment; and the bridegroom and his friends and his brothers came out to meet them, with drums and musicians and many weapons.
9.40 και εξανεςτηςα(ν) επ αυτους απο του ενεδρου και ‹απεκτιναν› αυτους κ(αι) επεςον τραυματιαι πολλοι και οι επιλοιποι εφυγο(ν) εις το ορος και ελαβον παντα τα ςκυλα ‹αυτων›	**9.40** And they rose up against them from the ambush, and killed them. And many wounded *one*s fell, and the rest fled to the mountain. And they took all their plunder.
9.41 και μετεςτραφη ο γαμος εις πενθος και φωνη μουςικων αυτω(ν) εις θρηνον	**9.41** And the wedding was turned into mourning, and *the* voice of their musicians into lamentation.
9.42 και ‹εξεδικηςαν› την εκδικηςιν αιματος αδελφου ‹αυτων› και απεςτρεψαν εις το ελος του Ιορδανου	**9.42** And they took vengeance *with* vengeance for *the* blood of their brother; and they returned to the marsh of the Jordan.

9.38 αυτων S^{ca} A $64^{+}236$ \| -του S* V • **9.39** ςυναντηςιν V A $64^{+}236$ \| υπαντ- S • **9.40** απεκτιναν S^{ca} V A $64^{+}236$ $La^{109+146}$ \| -ινεν S* • αυτων S^{ca} V A $64^{+}236$ $La^{109+146}$ \| -του S* • **9.42** εξεδικηςαν S^{ca} V A $64^{+}236$ $La^{109+146}$ \| -ςεν S* • αυτων S^{ca} V A $64^{+}236$ \| -του S* •

9.38–42 Jonathan and his companions **hid** in **ambush** and attacked the large wedding party, killing **many** and plundering them of their **large amount of equipment.** In this

[251] The bride was coming from a place whose name is variously spelled: *Nadabath,* A (supported by La^{109}); *Nabadath,* V; *Gabadan,* S; *Nabat,* $64^{+}236$ (supported by 7h7); *Nḥlbt,* 7a1. Manuscripts of Josephus (*Antiquities,* 13.18) read *Nabatha* or *Gabatha.* It appears to be otherwise unrecorded (unless it is a form of Nodab, 1 Chr 5.19, or Nebo, Deut 32.49).

way **they took vengeance with vengeance**[252] **for the blood of their brother** John.

As the historical books of the Hebrew Scriptures often do with such episodes, the Maccabean History simply reports the deeds, and does not give us enough information to determine whether they were right or wrong. Certainly Jonathan was raised up by God as an instrument of His **vengeance** under the old covenant Law (see the notes on 2.67; 3.15; 7.24; cf. 13.6). But someone who was appointed by God to take vengeance might still be rebuked by Him for doing so in an evil way (Isa 10.5–19). Whether that happened on the present occasion can be known only to the One who searches the hearts (1 Kgs 8.39; 1 Sam 16.7; 1 Chr 28.9; Jer 17.10; Rev 2.23). For instance, the old covenant Law that authorized Jonathan to take vengeance also forbad him to "put out his hands against those who were at peace with him" (Psa 55.20; 7.4; Prov 3.29–30).

Was this wedding party at peace with the Israelites, or at enmity with them?[253] We do not have enough information to tell. We must never condemn others on inadequate evidence, for the standard by which we judge them is the standard by which our Lord will one day judge us (Matt 7.1–2; Jas 2.13).

Nothing in the Scriptures entitles God's people under the new covenant, who (unlike Jonathan) have been given no authority by Him as instruments of His vengeance, to inflict any harm on others (Rom 12.17–21; 1 Thes 5.15; 1 Pet 3.9).

As a result of this attack, **the wedding was turned into mourning, and the voice of their musicians into lamentation**—that is, an occasion that should have been entirely joyful was turned suddenly to grief (cf. 2 Sam 19.2; Isa 24.7–8; Jer 7.34; Lam 5.15; Amos 8.10).

This incident had taken place across the Jordan, in or near the region of Moab (vv 35–36). Afterwards, Jonathan and his companions **returned** toward Judea, and reached **the marsh of the Jordan,** where Bacchides was preparing to attack them (vv 34, 43).

Bacchides is defeated at the Jordan

9.43 και ηκουϲεν Βακχειδηϲ και ηλθεν τη ημερα των ϲαββατων εωϲ των ‹κρηπιδων› του Ιορδανου εν δυναμι πολλη	**9.43** And Bacchides heard *it,* and he came on the Sabbath day up to the banks of the Jordan, with a great force.

9.43 κρηπιδων S[ca] V A 64[+]236 La[109+146] | -ινων S* •

9.43 Now the narrative returns to **Bacchides,** in the place where he was last left. Knowing, on the Sabbath day, about Jonathan's movements (v 34), **he came on** that **day** to **the banks of the Jordan, with** his whole army (v 34), **a great force.** After their

[252] **They took vengeance with vengeance** *(exedikēsan tēn ekdikēsin).* Similar terms are applied to vengeances executed by God Himself (Ezek 16.38), by righteous people acting in obedience to Him (Num 31.2), and by unrighteous people acting in disobedience to Him (Ezek 25.12).

[253] None of the earlier or later battles involving Judas and his brothers raises such a question.

early successes **on the Sabbath day** (2.32–38), Israel's enemies would naturally tend to choose that day for their attacks.[254]

9.44 και ειπεν Ιωναθαν τοις παρ αυτου αναστωμεν δη κ(αι) πολεμησωμεν περι των ψυχων ημων ου γαρ εστι(ν) σημερον ως εχθες και τριτην ημερα(ν)	**9.44** And Jonathan said to the *people* alongside him: "Let us rise up indeed and make war for our souls: for today it is not like yesterday and *the* third day *ago;*
9.45 ιδου γαρ ο πολεμος εξ εναντιας και εξοπισθεν ημων το δε υδωρ του Ιορδανου ενθεν και ενθεν και ελος κ(αι) δρυμος ουκ εστιν τοπος του εκκλειναι	**9.45** for, see! the battle *is* opposite *us* and behind us, and the water of the Jordan *is* here and there, and marsh and forest; *there* is no place to turn aside.
9.46 νυν ουν κεκραξατε εις τον ου(ρα)νον οπως διασωθητε εκ χιρος ‹› εχθρω(ν) ημων	**9.46** Now therefore, cry out[pl] to Heaven, so that you[pl] may be brought safely through, out of *the* hand of our enemies."

9.46 εχθρω(ν) V A 64[+]236 | ^ των S •

9.44–46 Jonathan and his companions had **no place to turn aside:** in every direction they were confronted either with their enemies or with natural obstacles (**the water of the Jordan ... and marsh and forest**), which had not been so in their previous battles (**yesterday and the third day ago**[255]). As they had done in the past, they cried out **to Heaven** to save them from their enemies. When we are "afflicted on every side—fightings outside, fears inside"—we can trust in "the One who encourages the lowly" (2 Cor 7.5–6; Psa 34.17–18), for He is the only source of help in any time of trouble (Psa 121.1–2; 146.3–5; 60.11–12). In no other direction can we find any salvation (Acts 4.12).

9.47 και συνηψε(ν) ο πολεμος και εξετινεν Ιωναθαν την χειρα αυτου παταξε τον Βακχιδην και εξεκλινεν απ αυτου εις τα οπισω	**9.47** And the battle made contact; and Jonathan stretched out his hand to smite Bacchides; and he was turning aside from him, *and going* behind.
9.48 και ενεπηδησεν Ιωναθαν και οι μετ αυτου εις τον Ιορδανην και διεκολυμβησαν εις το περαν	**9.48** And Jonathan and the *men* with him leaped into the Jordan, and swam through to the other side.

[254] One text of the Eighteen Psalms of the Roman period describes Pompey as breaking down the walls of Jerusalem "at a feast" (Eighteen Psalms 2.1, 16h1), and this testimony is supported by Josephus ("on the day of the fast," *Antiquities,* 14.66), who also says that Pompey chose the Sabbath days for preliminary military operations (*War,* 1.146 ≡ *Antiquities,* 14.63–64).

[255] **Yesterday and the third day ago** ("yesterday and the day before," RV) is a common phrase in the Hebrew Scriptures (Gen 31.2, 5; Exod 5.7–8; Josh 4.18; 1 Sam 4.7; 2 Kgs 13.5; etc.).

και ου διεβηcαν επ αυτουc τον Ιορδανην	And they did not go over the Jordan against them.
9.49 επεcον δε παρα Βαχχιδου τη ημερα εκεινη ειc ‹χιλιουc› ανδραc	**9.49** But *there* fell from Bacchides' side, that day, up to a thousand men.

9.49 χιλιουc A 64⁺236 La[109+146] | ‚γ´ S[ca] V | γ´ S* •

9.47–49 In the **battle,** Bacchides' forces were decisively defeated, and he himself barely escaped with his life (**Jonathan stretched out his hand to smite** him, but Bacchides turned **aside** and retreated—went **behind**). **Jonathan** and his companions were able to swim across **the Jordan** into Judea (v 50), and their opponents did not follow them (**did not go over the Jordan against them**).

Bacchides fortifies Judea

9.50 και επεcτρεψεν ειc Ι(ερουcα)λημ και ωκοδομηcα(ν) πολειc οχυραc εν τη Ιουδαια το οχυρωμα το εν Ιεριχω και την Αμμαου και την Βαιθωρω(ν) και την Βαιθηλ και την Θαμναθα ‹Φαραθων κ(αι) την Τεφω(ν) εν τιχεcιν› υψηλοιc και ‹πυλαιc› και μοχλοιc	**9.50** And he returned to Jerusalem. And they built up fortified cities in Judea: the fortress *that was* in Jericho, and Emmaus, and Bethhoron, and Bethel, and Timnath, Pharathon, and Tephon, with high walls and gates and bars;
9.51 και εθετο φρουρα(ν) εν αυταιc του εκχθραινιν τω Ιc(ραη)λ	**9.51** and he placed a garrison in them, to be at enmity with Israel.
9.52 και ωχυρωcεν τη(ν) πολιν την Βεθcουραν και Γαζαρα και την ακραν και εθετο εν αυταιc δυναμιc και παραθεcιc βρωματων	**9.52** And he fortified the city Bethzur, and Gezer, and the citadel; and he placed in them forces, and stores of foods.
9.53 και ελαβεν τουc υιουc τω(ν) ηγουμενων τηc χωραc ομηρα και εθετο αυτουc εν τη ακρα εν Ι(ερουcα)λημ εν φυλακη	**9.53** And he took the sons of the leaders of the district *as* hostages, and placed them in the citadel in Jerusalem, in safekeeping.

9.50 Φαραθων κ(αι) την Τεφω(ν) εν τιχεcιν S[ca] V A 64 [κ- την Τεφ- εν τειχ- 236] La[109+146] | Φαcιν S* • πυλαιc V A 64⁺236 La[109+146] | θυροιc S •

9.50–53 Bacchides and his allies returned **to Jerusalem,** and began to fortify various **cities in Judea:**

- **Jericho,** an important city near the Jordan (Num 22.1; Josh 3.16), opposite the land of Moab (Deut 32.49).
- **Emmaus** (see the notes on 3.40).
- **Bethhoron** (see the notes on 3.16).
- **Bethel,** an important city near Jericho, on the former border between Benjamin and Ephraim (Josh 7.2; 16.1–2; 18.13; Neh 11.31); long a center of idolatry (1 Kgs 12.27–33; Amos 3.14; 4.4).

- **Timnath, Pharathon,**[256] and **Tephon,** which cannot be definitely identified with any cities mentioned elsewhere.[257]
- **Bethzur** (see the notes on 4.29).
- **Gezer** (see the notes on 4.15).

They also fortified **the citadel in Jerusalem** (see the notes on 1.32–36), and in it they placed some **sons** of their opponents as **hostages** (see 10.6–9).

Yet "if the LORD does not build the house, in worthlessness its builders have toiled in it; if the LORD does not keep the city, in worthlessness the watchman has been vigilant" (Psa 127.1). Nothing that is raised against Him or His people will prosper (2 Cor 10.4–5; Isa 54.15–17; Mal 1.4; Jer 51.53; 5.17). The cities that were now being fortified **to be at enmity with Israel** would later be fortified to defend it (14.33–34).

The death of Alcimus

9.54 και εν ετι γ΄ κ(αι) ν΄	**9.54** And in the hundred and fifty-
και ρ΄ τω μηνι τω δευτερω	third year, *in* the second month,
επεταξεν Αλκιμος καθαιρει(ν)	Alcimus ordered to take down
το τιχος της αυλης	the wall of the inside courtyard
των αγιων της εσωτερας και καθειλεν	of the holy *places*; and he took down
τα εργα των προφητων	the works of the prophets.
και ενηρξατο του καθαιρειν	And he began to take *them* down.

9.54 Alcimus, the irreverent priest (7.9), now made modifications to the temple, starting to tear down **the wall of the inside courtyard** (1 Kgs 6.36; 7.12; 2 Kgs 21.5; Ezek 8.16) and **the works of the prophets** (perhaps those authorized by Haggai and Zechariah, as recorded in Ezra 5.1–2).

"All things" in the LORD's temple are to be made in accordance with His instructions (Heb 8.5). His people are to "keep all its design, and all its decrees, and do them"; those who seek to add their own human works to it, placing "their threshold with My threshold, and their doorpost next to My doorpost," are defiling His holy name (Ezek 43.7–11; cf. 2 Cor 6.16).

---

[256] Many Latin and Syriac manuscripts read "Timnath and Pharathon," but the "and" is not present in any Greek manuscript or in the most trustworthy Latin text (La[109]). Yet this does not prove that we are dealing with a single compound name ("Timnath-pharathon," REB), because distinct names in a list of this kind are not necessarily separated by "and" ("Cush, and Mizraim, Put, and Canaan," 1 Chr 1.8; "Philip, and Thomas, Bartholomew, and Matthew," Acts 1.13; etc.). Josephus treats Timnath and Pharathon as different places (*Antiquities,* 13.15).

[257] Finkelstein, "Territorial Extent and Demography of Yehud/Judea in the Persian and Early Hellenistic Periods," 47–48. All the cities in this list were **in Judea,** so **Pharathon** cannot be the Pirathon much further north in the hill country of Ephraim (Jdg 12.15; ISBE 3.822, 873), and **Tephon** cannot be the Tappuah even further north on the border of Manasseh (Josh 17.8). For similar reasons **Timnath** cannot be Timnath-seres in the hill country of Ephraim (Josh 19.50). There were evidently at least two cities in Judah named Timnah (Josh 15.10, 57).

9.55 εν τω καιρω εκεινω ‹› επληγη Αλκιμος και ενεποδισθη τα εργα αυτου και απεφραγη το στομα αυτου και παρελυθη και ουκ ηδυνατο ετι λαλησαι λογον και εντιλασθαι περι του οικου αυτου	**9.55** At that period of time, Alcimus was smitten, and his works were hobbled; and his mouth was closed, and he was paralysed, and he was not able to speak a word or give a command about his house *any* more;
9.56 και απεθανεν Αλκιμος εν τω καιρω εκινω μετα βασανου ‹μεγαλης›	**9.56** and Alcimus died at that period of time in great torment.
9.57 και ειδεν Βακχιδης οτι απεθανε(ν) Αλκιμος και επεστρεψεν προς τον βασιλεα και ησυχασεν η γη Ιουδα ετη δυο	**9.57** And Bacchides saw that Alcimus had died; and he returned to the king. And the land of Judah was quiet two years.

9.55 επληγη V A 64^{+}236 La$^{109+146}$ | ^ και S • **9.56** μεγαλης V A 64^{+}236 = -λου S •

9.55–56 But the man who sought to destroy part of God's temple—both in earthly matters (v 54) and in spiritual matters (7.22)—was himself destroyed (1 Cor 3.17). **Alcimus was smitten,** like others who had tried to defile the LORD's holy things (Uzzah, 2 Sam 6.6–7; Jeroboam, 1 Kgs 13.4; Jehoram, 2 Chr 21.11–19; Uzziah, 2 Chr 26.16–21), and **died.**[258]

An unsuccessful plot against Jonathan

9.58 και εβουλευσα(ν)το παντες οι ανομοι λεγοντες ιδου Ιωναθαν ‹και› οι παρ αυτου εν ησυχια κατοικουσιν πεποιθοτες νυν ουν ‹αναξωμεν› τον Βακχιδην και συλλημψεται αυτους παντας εν νυκτι μια	**9.58** And all the *people* opposed to *the* Law took counsel, saying: "See! Jonathan and the *people* alongside him are dwelling in quietness, *and* confident. Now therefore, let us bring up Bacchides, and he will take hold of them all in one night."
9.59 και πορευθεντες συνεβουλευσαντο αυτω	**9.59** And, going, they consulted with him.

9.58 και 2° V A 64^{+}236 La$^{109+146}$ | > S • αναξωμεν V^{b} La$^{109+146}$ | -ξον S | -ξομεν V* | αξομεν A | αγαγωμεν 64^{+}236 •

9.58–59 After two years (verse 57) of **quietness** and apparent security, **the people opposed to the Law** began plotting with **Bacchides** to seize **all** their enemies **in one night.** The Lord's people can never relax their vigilance (Luke 21.34–36; 1 Cor 10.12; 1 Pet 5.8).

---

[258] **Torment** *(basanou)* is construed as masculine in S (taking an adjective in *-ou*), but as feminine in V, A, and 64^{+}236 (taking an adjective in *-ēs*). Grammatical gender, like spelling, was less fixed in ancient times (cf. Thackeray §10.11). A similar phenomenon is seen in 11.8.

9.60 κ(αι) ‹απηρεν› του ελθει(ν) μετα δυναμεως πολλης και απεστιλε(ν) λαθρα επιστολας πασιν τοις συμμαχοις αυτου τοις εν τη Ιουδαια οπως ‹συλλαβωσιν› τον Ιωναθαν και τους μετ αυτου και ουκ ηδυναντο οτι εγνωσθη η βουλη ‹αυτω(ν)›	**9.60** And he moved away to come with a great force; and privately he sent letters to all his military allies who *were* in Judea, *telling them* that they should take hold of Jonathan and the *people* who *were* with him. And they were not able: for their counsel was known.
9.61 και ‹συνελαβον› απο των ανδρων της χωρας των αρχηγων της κακιας και απεκτινεν αυτους	**9.61** And they took hold of *some* of the men of the district, *who were among* the first leaders of the evildoing; and they killed them.

9.60 απηρεν S^{ca} V A $64^{+}236$ $La^{109+146}$ | απηλθεν S* • συλλαβωσιν [-ιμ V] A $64^{+}236$ $La^{109+146}$ | -βουσιν S • αυτω(ν) V A $64^{+}236$ $La^{109+146}$ | -του S • **9.61** συνελαβον [-ελλα- V] A $64^{+}236$ $La^{109+146}$ | -εβαλον S •

9.60–61 But the plot against Jonathan and his companions became **known,** and failed. An evil intent, however closely concealed, cannot be hidden forever. It may not be discovered in time to prevent great harm (cf. 12.40–52; 16.13–17), but it will certainly be brought to light one day (Ecc 12.14; 1 Cor 4.5; 1 Tim 5.24–25). "All things are naked and exposed to the eyes of Him with whom is our account" (Heb 4.13).

As a result of the discovery of the plot, those who perished were not Jonathan and his allies, but some of **the first leaders of the evildoing.**[259] They had dug a pit, and they themselves were caught in it (Psa 9.15; 57.6; Prov 26.27).

The final defeat of Bacchides

9.62 και εξεχωρησεν ‹› Ιωναθα(ν) και Σιμων και οι μετ αυτου εις Βαιθβαισσει την εν τη ερημω και ωκοδομησεν τα καθειρημενα αυτης και εστερεωσαν αυτην	**9.62** And Jonathan, and Simon, and the *people* who *were* with him, departed to Bethbasi, which *is* in the desert. And he built up the *part*s of it that had been pulled down, and made it strong.

9.62 Ιωναθα(ν) V A $64^{+}236$ $La^{109+146}$ | ^ απ αυτων S •

9.62 Now **Jonathan** and his allies went **to Bethbasi,** a city (v 65) not mentioned elsewhere, which was situated **in the desert.**[260] It had evidently been walled or fortified in the past, but currently needed restoring, because **parts of it . . . had been pulled down.** Jonathan used even short periods of respite from warfare as opportunities to fortify his nation against further attack (a good example for us: 1 Thes 5.11; Heb 10.24–25).

---

[259] After **first leaders of the evildoing,** many manuscripts (including V, A, and $64^{+}236$, but not S or $La^{109+146}$) give an estimate of the number: *eis pentkonta andras* ("up to fifty men").

[260] There is a modern "Khirbet Beit Baṣṣi" northeast of Tekoa (Abel, *GP,* 2.269).

9.63 και εγνω Βακχιδης και συνηγαγεν πα(ν) το πληθος αυτου και ‹τοις› εκ της Ιουδαιας παρηγγειλεν	**9.63** And Bacchides knew *this;* and he gathered together all his multitude, and sent instructions to the *people* from Judea.
9.64 και ελθων παρενεβαλεν επι Βαιθβασσει και επολεμησεν αυτην ημερας πολλας και εποιησεν μηχανας	**9.64** And when *he* had come, he camped against Bethbasi, and he made war against it many days, and made devices *of war.*
9.65 και απελιπεν Ιωναθαν Σιμωνα τον αδελφον αυτου εν τη πολει και εξηλθεν εις την χωραν και ηλθεν αριθμω	**9.65** And Jonathan left Simon his brother in the city, and came out into the district. And he came with a *small* number.
9.66 και επαταξεν Οδομηρα και τους αδελφους αυτου και τους υιους Φασειρων εν τω σκηνωματι αυτων και ηρξαντο τυπτειν και ανεβαινον εν ταις δυναμεσιν	**9.66** And he smote Odomera and his brothers, and the sons of Phasiron in their tent; and they began to strike *them,* and *began* going up with *their* forces.
9.67 και Σιμων και οι μετ αυτου εξηλθον εκ της πολεως και ενεπυρισαν τας μηχανας	**9.67** And Simon and the *people* with him came out of the city, and set the devices on fire,
9.68 και επολεμησαν προς τον Βακχιδη(ν) και συνετριβη υπ αυτων και εθλειβον αυτον σφοδρα οτι ην η βουλη αυτου και η εφοδος αυτου καινη	**9.68** and made war against Bacchides; and he was shattered by them; and they were oppressing him extremely: for his counsel had been empty, and *so had* his visit.

9.63 τοις S^{ca} V A $64^{+}236$ $La^{109+146}$ \| τοι S* •

9.63–68 Hearing of these activities, **Bacchides** and **all his multitude** besieged the city for **many days,** using **devices of war** ("siege-engines," REB; see the notes on 5.30). In response, the faithful Israelites divided their forces (cf. 5.17):

- **Jonathan** himself, **with a small number** of men, went out of the **city** into the surrounding **district,** where their **forces** attacked some of the enemies (**Odomera and his brothers, and the sons of Phasiron**).[261]
- Meanwhile, **Simon** and the rest of the people were **left . . . in the city,** from which they sallied out to attack their besiegers and **set on fire** the siege engines.

---

[261] Neither **Odomera** nor **Phasiron** is mentioned elsewhere. Nearly all manuscripts (including S, A, and $64^{+}236$, supported by $La^{109+146}$) state that Jonathan **smote** *(epataxen)* Odomera and Phasiron. V states that he "ordered" *(epetaxen)* them, which has occasionally been construed as an indication that he "summoned" them (ISBE 3.579), but no form of *epitasso* has any such meaning elsewhere (4.41; 5.49; 10.81; 12.27, 43; cf. LEH 236; Muraoka 283–84; BDAG 383).

Thus **Bacchides** and his **multitude** were being assailed in two different ways at the same time. His intentions (**counsel,** v 69) and actions (**visit,** cf. 11.44) proved futile (**empty,** as in Acts 4.25), and he was again defeated (**shattered**). Counsel (1 Cor 3.19; Prov 21.30; Jer 19.7; Isa 19.11) and action (Psa 33.16–17; Isa 31.1–3; Jer 17.5–6) are alike powerless against God.

Peace with Bacchides

9.69 και ωργιcθηcα(ν) θυμω τοιc ανδραcι(ν) τοιc ανομοιc τοιc cυμβουλευcαcιν αυτω ελθειν ειc τη(ν) χωραν και απεκτιναν εξ αυτων πολλουc και εβουλευcα(ν)το του απελθειν ειc την γην αυτου	**9.69** And they became angry with indignation with the men who *were* opposed to *the* Law, who had counseled him *for him* to come into the district; and they killed many out of them. And they took counsel to go away to his land;
9.70 και επεγνω Ιωναθα(ν) και ‹απεcτιλεν› προc ‹αυτον› πρεcβειc του cυνθεcθαι προc αυτον ειρηνην και αποδουναι αυτοιc την αιχμαλωcιαν	**9.70** and Jonathan knew *this,* and sent ambassadors to him, to agree with him *on* a peace, and *for him* to give back to them the group of captives.
9.71 και επεδεξατο και εποιηcεν κατα τουc λογουc ‹αυτου› και ωμοcαν αυτω μη εκζητηcαι αυτω κακον παcαc ταc ημεραc τηc ζωηc αυτου	**9.71** And he accepted *this,* and did in accordance with his words. And they swore an oath to him not to seek evil for him all the days of his life.
9.72 και ‹απεδωκεν› αυτω την αιχμαλωcια(ν) ην αιχμαλωτευcε(ν) το προτερον εκ ‹γηc› Ιουδα και αποcτρεψαc απηλθεν ειc την γην αυτου και ου προcεθετο ετι ελθειν ειc τα ορια αυτων	**9.72** And he gave back to him the group of captives that he had taken captive previous*ly* from *the* land of Judah. And, returning, he went away to his land; and he did not proceed to come into their appointed boundaries *any* more.

9.70 απεcτιλεν S^{ca} V A 64^{+}236 La$^{109+146}$ | -λαν S* • αυτον 1° V A 64^{+}236 La$^{109+146}$ | -τουc S • **9.71** αυτου 1° S^{ca} V A 64^{+}236 La$^{109+146}$ | -τω S* • **9.72** απεδωκεν S^{ca} V A 236 | επεδωκαν S* | *reddiderunt* La$^{109+146}$ • γηc V A 64^{+}236 La$^{109+146}$ | τηc S •

9.69 **Many** of **the men opposed to the Law,** who had **counseled** Bacchides to come back to Judea, were **killed.**[262] Now Bacchides listened to a different kind of **counsel,**

[262] In this verse, manuscripts disagree as to which of the verbs are plural and which (if any) are singular. According to S* and A (supported by La^{109}), **they** [Jonathan and his companions] **became angry** *(ōrgisthēsan)* and **they** [Jonathan and his companions] **killed** *(apektinan)* many of those opposed to the Law. According to 64^{+}236, "he [Bacchides] became angry" *(ōrgisthē)* and "he [Bacchides] killed" *(apekteinen)* many of those opposed to the Law. According to V and S^{ca} (supported by La^{146}), "he [Bacchides] became angry" *(ōrgisthē)* and "they [presumably Bacchides

which advised him **to go away** from Judea **to his** own **land.** In that counsel he would remain (v 72).

9.70–72 Jonathan seized this opportunity to make **peace** with Bacchides and to deliver those who were still being held captive by him (cf. Psa 82.4; Prov 24.11). Bacchides and his allies **swore an oath** to do no **evil** to Jonathan ever again (**all the days of his life**). The Judean captives who had been **taken captive previously** were released (cf. 2 Chr 28.8–15; Luke 4.18 ≡ Isa 61.1; Zec 9.9–12). In the past Israel's enemies had sworn oaths and promptly broken them (see the notes on 6.61–62; 7.15–18). But this time Bacchides **did in accordance with his words:** he **went away** from the land and never returned.[263]

9.73 και κατεπαυcεν ρομφαια εξ Ιc(ραη)λ και ωκηcεν Ιωναθαν εν Μαχμαc και ηρξατο Ιωναθαν κρινιν το(ν) λαον και ηφανιcε(ν) τουc αcεβειc εξ Ιc(ραη)λ	**9.73** And *the* sword rested from Israel. And Jonathan dwelt at Michmash. And Jonathan began to judge the people; and he made the irreverent *one*s disappear out of Israel.

9.73 Again, there was period of peace (cf. v 57) when **the sword rested from Israel** (cf. Lev 26.6). **Jonathan** made his home at **Michmash** (a short distance north of Jerusalem in the territory of Benjamin, Neh 11.31, near Bethel, 1 Sam 13.2). He **began to judge the people,** like the previous human judges whom God had raised up, including Moses (Exod 18.13), Deborah (Jdg 4.4–5), Jephthah (Jdg 12.7), Samson (Jdg 15.20; 16.31), Samuel (1 Sam 7.6, 15–17), and the nation's kings (1 Sam 8.20; 1 Kgs 3.9; cf. 2 Kgs 15.5; Prov 29.14).

The task of judging the people is described by Moses: "When they have a matter, it comes to me, and I judge between a man and his neighbor, and I make known to them God's decrees and His laws" (Exod 18.16). God Himself is the great Judge over all the earth (2 Tim 4.8; Psa 7.11, 8; 75.7; Gen 18.25; Heb 10.30; 12.23). He always judges righteously (Psa 9.8; 96.13; Acts 17.31), and He requires His servants to do the same (Deut 1.16; 16.18; Lev 19.15; John 7.24), declaring righteous the righteous, and declaring wicked the wicked (Deut 25.1; Prov 17.15), in accordance with His laws (Ezek 44.24). Thus, when Jonathan judged the people, **he made the irreverent ones disappear out of Israel,** as Christ also has done and will do (Isa 11.3–4; Rev 19.11, 15; Psa 101.2–8).

---

and his companions] killed" *(apekteinan)* many. There is also a less significant variation at the end of the verse, where S (supported by La[109+146]) has a plural verb (Bacchides and those with him **took counsel,** *ebouleusanto*) but V, A, and 64*236 have a singular verb (Bacchides took counsel, *ebouleusato*).

[263] **He did not proceed to come ... any more.** The Greek wording is *ou prosetheto eti elthein,* "he did not add any more to come."

Alexander Epiphanes opposes Demetrius

Alexander becomes king

10.1 και εν ετι ξ´ και ρ´ ανεβη Αλεξανδρος ο του Αντιοχου ο Επιφανης και κατελαβετο Πτολεμαιδα και ‹απεδεξαντο› αυτον και εβασιλευσεν εκει	**10.1** And in *the* hundred and sixtieth year, Alexander Epiphanes, the *son* of Antiochus, went up and took hold of Ptolemais. And they accepted him, and he became king there.

10.1 απεδεξαντο V La$^{109+146}$ | επεξα(ν)το S* | απεδεξατο S^{ca} [επ- A 64^{+}236] •

10.1 Demetrius had gained the throne by dislodging Antiochus Epiphanes' primary heir, Antiochus Eupator, in 151 SE (7.1–4). But nine years later (in 160 SE) a new heir of Antiochus, **Alexander Epiphanes,**[264] arrived at **Ptolemais** (on the coast, Acts 21.7, in the region of Galilee, Maccabaica 5.55), where he was **accepted** as **king.**

Demetrius seeks an alliance with Jonathan

10.2 και ηκουσεν Δημητριος ο βασιλευς κ(αι) συνηγαγεν δυναμις πολλας σφοδρα και εξηλθεν εις συναντησιν αυτω εις πολεμον	**10.2** And Demetrius the king heard; and he gathered together a very great force, and came out to meet him for battle.

---

[264] **Son of Antiochus.** Several Classical historians claimed that Alexander was an impostor called Balas, and was not really the son of Antiochus Epiphanes (Diodorus 31.32a [31.47]; Appian, *Syriaca,* 67.354; Justin 35.1.6–7). However, that story "may reflect only the propaganda of the [rival] Seleucid line of Demetrius I" (Goldstein, *I Maccabees,* 398; Bevan, *House of Seleucus,* 2.300–01); all the historians in question seem to have derived the story from Polybius, who was a personal friend of Demetrius.

Other ancient writers did accept Alexander's claim (he "equalled the Macedonian kings in ancestry," Livy, *Periochae,* 50) or were undecided (he was "of uncertain ancestry," Livy, *Periochae,* 52). Moreover, even the Demetrians admitted that Alexander had the physical appearance of a son of Antiochus Epiphanes (to an extraordinary degree: *kath' huperbolēn,* Diodorus 31.32a [31.47]).

Still, the description **son of Antiochus** does not necessarily imply a close biological relationship; anyone who inherited what had belonged to Antiochus Epiphanes could be described as a "son of" him (cf. Rom 8.14–15; Gal 4.5–6; see also Steinmann, *Daniel,* 261–62). Ancient writers referred to Jehu as Omri's "son" (Grayson, *Assyrian Rulers (858–745 BC),* 54, 60, 149) and Sennacherib as Shalmaneser's "son" (Tobit 1.15). In both cases the later king occupied the place of the earlier, but was not descended from him. (Compare also v 72, where Jonathan's "fathers" are certainly not his biological ancestors.) If Alexander was indeed a biological son of Antiochus Epiphanes, he was presumably either born after Antiochus Eupator or else the son of a lesser wife.

Coins show that the title **Epiphanes** was also adopted by many later Seleucid kings who claimed the throne by descent either from Alexander or from his rival Demetrius—including Antiochus VI (SC 2, §1996), Alexander II (SC 2, §§2215, 2239), Antiochus VIII (SC 2, §2278), Seleucus VI (SC 2, §2403), Antiochus XI (SC 2, §2440), and Antiochus XII (SC 2, §2471).

10.2 Demetrius . . . came out to meet Alexander **for battle.** Both sides attempted beforehand to establish a military alliance with Jonathan (vv 3–47). The battle itself is described in verses 48–50.

10.3 και απεστιλεν Δημητριος προς Ιωναθαν επιστολας λογοις ιρηνικοις ωστε ‹μεγαλυναι› αυτον	**10.3** And Demetrius sent letters to Jonathan with words of peace, so as to increase his greatness:
10.4 ειπεν γαρ προφθασωμεν του ειρηνην θειναι μετ αυτων πριν η θειναι αυτον μετα Αλεξανδρου καθ ημων	**10.4** for he said: "Let us act beforehand, making peace with them, before he makes *peace* with Alexander against us:
10.5 μνησθησεται γαρ παντων τω(ν) κακων ων συνετελεσαμεν προς αυτον και εις τους αδελφους αυτου και εις το εθνος	**10.5** for he will be mindful of all the evil *things* that we carried out against him, and toward his brothers and the nation."
10.6 και εδωκεν αυτω εξουσιαν συναγαγειν δυναμις και κατασκευαζειν οπλα κ(αι) ειναι αυτον συμμαχον αυτου και τα ομηρα τα εν τη ακρα ειπεν παραδουναι αυτω	**10.6** And he gave him authority to gather forces and prepare weapons, and *for* him to be his military ally; and he said to give up to him the hostages *who were* in the citadel.

10.3 μεγαλυναι V A 64*236 La[109+146] | -υνθηναι S •

10.3–6 Demetrius sent letters[265] **to Jonathan,** lest Jonathan should **be mindful of all the evil things that we carried out against him.** So Demetrius sent **words of peace** allowing Jonathan **to gather** an army (**forces** and **weapons**), and ordering the release of the Judean **hostages** placed under guard in **the citadel** by Bacchides (see 9.53).

These decrees would place the Judean leader in a much stronger and more powerful position (**increase his greatness**).

Nevertheless, not all **words of peace** are to be trusted. There are those "who speak peace with their companions, and evil is in their heart" (Psa 28.3; Prov 27.6; 29.5; Jer 9.8). Kings had given assurances and sent **words of peace** to the Judeans before, but had broken their word (6.57–62; 1.29–30).

Jonathan strengthens Jerusalem

10.7 και ηλθεν Ιωναθαν εις Ι(ερουσα)λημ και ανεγνω τας επιστολας εις τα ωτα παντος του λαου και τω(ν) εκ της ακρας	**10.7** And Jonathan came to Jerusalem, and read the letters to the ears of all the people, and of those from the citadel.

---

[265] In this book, the plural form **letters** (*epistolas)* often designates a single document (12.5, 7, 19; 14.20).

10.8 και εφοβηθηcαν φοβο(ν) μεγαν οτε ηκουcα(ν) οτι εδωκεν αυτω ο βαcιλευc εξουcιαν cυναγαγειν ⸤δυναμειc⸥	**10.8** And they were afraid *with* great fear when they heard that the king had given him authority to gather forces.

10.8 δυναμειc S^{ca} A $64^{+}236$ $La^{109+146}$ | -μιν S* V •

10.7–8 The king's forces in the Jerusalem **citadel** (1.32–36) **were afraid with great fear when they heard that the king had given** Jonathan **authority to gather forces.** God had promised Israel that, if they served Him faithfully, "all the peoples of the land . . . will be afraid of you" (Deut 28.1, 10; cf. 1 Sam 18.12, 15; Mark 6.20). By contrast, those who have done good have no need to be "afraid of the king's commandment" (even if it is an unjust commandment, Heb 11.23, 27; Isa 8.11–12; Rom 13.3–4).

10.9 και παρεδωκαν οι εκ τηc ακραc Ιωναθαν τα ομηρα και ⸤απεδωκεν⸥ αυτουc τοιc γονευcιν ⸤αυτων⸥	**10.9** And the *people* from the citadel gave up the hostages to Jonathan; and he gave them back to their parents.

10.9 απεδωκεν V $64^{+}236$ $La^{109+146}$ | εδ- S | απεδωκαν A • αυτων S^{ca} V A $64^{+}236$ $La^{109+146}$ | -του S* •

10.9 The people from the citadel gave up the hostages, as the king had now commanded (v 6), and **Jonathan . . . gave them back to their parents.** "The LORD releases those who have been bound" (Psa 146.7; 147.2). In earthly terms, He released a small group of people through Jonathan; in spiritual terms, He released the whole world through Jesus (Luke 4.18; Isa 42.6–7) when it was held in captivity by the devil—someone far stronger than Demetrius or his soldiers (2 Tim 2.26; Isa 49.24–25; Matt 12.29 ≡ Luke 11.21–22; Col 1.13).

10.10 και ωκηcεν Ιωναθαν εν Ι(ερουcα)λημ και ηρξατο οικοδομειν και κενιζειν την πολιν	**10.10** And Jonathan dwelt in Jerusalem. And he began to build and renew the city,
10.11 και ειπεν προc τουc ποιουνταc τα εργα οικοδομειν τα τιχη και ⸤το⸥ οροc Cιων κυκλοθε(ν) εκ λιθων τετραποδων ⸤⸥ ειc οχυρωcιν και εποιηcεν ουτωc	**10.11** and he said to the *people* doing the works to build the walls and Mount Zion round about, with foursquare stones, for a fortification. And he did so.

10.11 το S^{cb1} V A $64^{+}236$ | > S* • ειc S^{cb1} V A $64^{+}236$ $La^{109+146}$ | ^ και S* •

10.10–11 Jonathan now moved his home from Michmash (9.73) to **Jerusalem,** which he fortified by building up its **walls** and **Mount Zion** (the temple area, 4.37–38; 5.54)

with foursquare[266] **stones.**[267] Fortifications had previously been undertaken in that area by Judas (4.60), but had been torn down by Antiochus Eupator (6.62).

"The LORD builds Jerusalem" (Psa 147.2; 102.16). He built the earthly city of Jerusalem through Solomon (1 Kgs 3.1) and Cyrus (Isa 44.28), as well as Jonathan; He built the heavenly city of Jerusalem through Jesus Christ (Heb 11.10; 12.22–24; Rev 21.10–27).

See also the notes on 12.35–37.

10.12 και εφυγον οι αλλογενεις οι οντες εν τοις οχυρωμασιν οις οικοδομησεν ‹ο› Βακχιδης	**10.12** And the foreigners who were in the fortresses that Bacchides had built fled,
10.13 και κατελιπεν εκαστος τον τοπον αυτου και απηλθεν εις την γην αυτου	**10.13** and each *one* left his place and went away to his *own* land.
10.14 πλην εν Βαιθσουροις υπελιφθησαν τινες των καταλιποντων τον νομον και τα προσταγματα ην γαρ εις φυγαδευτηριον	**10.14** Nevertheless, in Bethzur *there* remained some of the *people* who had left the Law and the decrees: for it was a place of flight.

10.12 ο S^{ca} V A 64^{+}236 | > S* •

10.12–14 The **foreigners ... fled** from Bacchides' **fortresses** (9.50–52) **and went away** from Judea. Only **Bethzur** continued to be a **place of flight**[268] for people disobedient to God's Law. That problem would not be eradicated until the time of Jonathan's successor Simon (11.65–66; 14.7, 33).

In the recent past, it had been God's people who had **fled** from their enemies (9.33) and had sought a **place of flight** (1.53). But now the situation was reversed: those enemies were fleeing from them. Similarly, there was a time when Jesus and His family had to flee from His enemies (Matt 2.13); yet one day those enemies will vainly seek to flee from Him (Rev 6.15–17; Matt 23.33). We ourselves, if we flee from evil (1 Cor 6.18; 10.14; 1 Tim 6.11; 2 Tim 2.22; Heb 6.18), will find that evil is forced to flee from us (Jas 4.7).

---

[266] **Foursquare.** The forms *tetrapodōn* (S* and V) and *tetrapedōn* (S^{ca} and 64^{+}236) are simply spelling variants. The meaning is presumably "square-cut" (SAAS) rather than "four-foot" (NETS), in view of Scripture usage (in 2 Chr 34.11, LXX *tetrapedous* ≡ Hebrew *mḥṣb,* "hewn"; Thackeray §6.27(1); Muraoka 677).

[267] S and V (supported by La$^{109+146}$ and the majority of Western Syriac manuscripts) read: **And he began to build .... And he did** [*epoiēsen*] **so.** (Cf. v 62: "And they clothed him .... And they did so.") In A and 64^{+}236 (supported by 7h7 and 7a1), the final clause reads: "And they did [*epoiēsan*] so."

[268] A **place of flight** (*phugadeutērion,* v 14) is a place for people who have **fled** (*ephugon,* v 12). The Dutch SV expresses the connection neatly: *vloden* (v 12) ... *toevlucht* (v 14).

Alexander seeks an alliance with Jonathan

10.15 και ηκουσεν Αλεξανδρος ο βασιλευς τας επαγγελιας ‹ας› απεστιλεν Δημητριος τω Ιωναθα(ν) και ‹διηγησαντο› αυτω τους πολεμους και τας ανδραγαθιας ας εποιησεν αυτος και οι αδελφοι αυτου και τους κοπους ‹ους εσχον›	**10.15** And Alexander the king heard the promises that Demetrius had sent to Jonathan. And they told him the wars and the manly good deeds that he had done, he and his brothers, and the labors that they had had.

10.15 ας 64$^+$236 La$^{109+146}$ | οσας S V A • διηγησαντο S^{ca} V A 64$^+$236 La$^{109+146}$ | -ατο S* • ους εσχον S^{ca} V [-χοσαν A] 64$^+$236 La$^{109+146}$ > S* •

10.15 Alexander ... heard the promises that Demetrius had sent—and he also heard about the **wars** and **manly good deeds** done by **Jonathan ... and his brothers.** Those things had not been done in a corner. Many years earlier the news had already spread "to the end of the land" (3.9); it had become the talk of the nations (3.26). Compare the reports of Joshua (Josh 6.27), David (1 Chr 14.17), Solomon (1 Kgs 4.31), and Mordecai (Est 9.4). Then, as now (cf. Acts 26.26; Col 1.6, 23), "all the ends of the land have seen the salvation of our God" (Psa 98.3).

10.16 και ειπεν μη ευρησομεν ανδρα τοιουτον ενα και νυν ‹ποιησωμεν› αυτον φιλον και συνμαχο(ν) ημων	**10.16** And he said: "We shall not find such a man, *even* one, *shall we*? And now, let us make him our Friend and military ally."
10.17 και εγραψεν επιστολας και απεστιλεν ‹αυτω› κατα τους λογους τουτους λεγων	**10.17** And he wrote letters, and sent to him in accordance with these words, saying:
10.18 βασιλευς Αλεξανδρος ‹τω› ‹αδελφω› Ιωναθαν χαιρειν	**10.18** "King Alexander to *his* brother Jonathan: Rejoice.
10.19 ακηκοαμεν περι σου οτι ανηρ δυνατος ισχυι και επιτηδιος ‹ει του› ειναι ημω(ν) φιλος	**10.19** We have heard about you[†], that you[†] are a man *who is* powerful with strength, and suitable to be our Friend.
10.20 και νυν κατεστακαμεν σε σημερον αρχιερεα του εθνους σου και φιλον ‹› βασιλεως ‹καλεισθαι› σε και απεστιλεν αυτω πορφυραν και στεφανο(ν) χρυσουν και φρονι(ν) τα ημων και συντηριν φιλιας προς ημας	**10.20** And now, we have established you[†] today *as* high priest of your[†] nation, and to call yourself[‡] a Friend of *the* king" (and he sent him a purple *robe* and a golden crown), "and to set *your* mind on our *interests*, and to keep friendship toward us."

10.16 ποιησωμεν V^b A 58 93 La$^{109+146}$ | -σομεν S V* 64$^+$236 • **10.17** αυτω S^{ca} V A La$^{109+146}$ | -του S* • **10.18** τω S^{cb1} V A 64$^+$236 | > S* • αδελφω V A 64$^+$236 | + τω S • **10.19** ει του A La$^{109+146}$ | εις το V | του S^{ca} 64$^+$236 | > S* • **10.20** φιλον V A 64$^+$236 | + του S • καλεισθαι S^{ca} V A 64$^+$236 La$^{109+146}$ | κεισθαι S* •

10.16–20 Alexander concluded that he would never **find such a man** (cf. Gen 41.38; 1 Sam 10.24; Php 2.20; John 7.46), and wrote letters appointing Jonathan as a **Friend of the king,** with **a purple robe and a golden crown** (cf. Dan 5.29; Est 8.15; Mark 15.17). In the past, Jonathan could have become a king's Friend only if he had become the LORD's enemy (see 2.18). But now, he was given the opportunity to be both a king's **Friend** and the LORD's **high priest**[269] at the same time.

King Alexander to his brother Jonathan: Rejoice. The letter begins in the customary way: the sender is named first, then the receiver, after which comes a greeting, **Rejoice**[270] (as in v 25; 11.30, 32; 12.6, 20; 13.36; 14.20; 15.2, 16; Acts 15.23; 23.26; Jas 1.1). The term **brother,** like **Friend** and **military ally,** acknowledges a bond of alliance (as in 14.40) and may also treat Jonathan as a relative (cf. v 89; 12.7, 21).

Jonathan becomes high priest

10.21 και ενεδυcατο Ιωναθαν	**10.21** And Jonathan clothed himself
την αγιαν cτολην	with the holy robe *in* the seventh
τω εβδομω μηνι ετουc ‹ξ´› και ρ´	month of *the* hundred and sixtieth
εν εορτη cκηνοπηγιαc	year, at *the* Feast of Tabernacles.
και cυνηγαγεν δυναμιc	And he gathered together forces,
και κατεcκευαcεν οπλα πολλα	and prepared many weapons.

10.21 ξ´ S^{ca} V A $64^{+}236$ $La^{109+146}$ | ζ´ S* •

10.21 In the **seventh month** of the year when Alexander arrived (v 1), **at the Feast of Tabernacles** (Lev 23.34), **Jonathan clothed himself with** the high priest's **holy robe** in accordance with the ordinance of the Law ("You shall put upon Aaron the holy robes ... and he shall act as priest to Me," Exod 40.13–15). Under the old covenant Law, only descendants of Aaron could be appointed as high priests (Num 3.10). Jonathan was fully qualified to be such a priest, because he was descended from Aaron's

---

[269] Someone from Israel must have advised Alexander to establish Jonathan **as high priest;** otherwise, the king would not have known anything about the subject. (Who, outside Israel, would have known that Jonathan was qualified to be high priest? And how many would even have been aware that the position was vacant?) Thus the term **established** means, not that Alexander "appointed [Jonathan] to be the high priest" (ESV), but that he gave his support and authorization to an appointment that had already been proposed in Israel (cf. 11.27, 57; 12.1; 14.38; 15.5—in all of which a ruler "established" something that was already in existence). See also the notes on 7.9.

[270] **Rejoice** (*chairein,* as in the passages cited above) expresses a wish that the receiver may be free from sorrows and in a joyful condition (cf. "May the God of hope fill you with all joy [*charas*]," Rom 15.13). The word carries meaning, and is not merely an empty token (as the connection of ideas in Jas 1.1–2 shows: "James ... to the twelve tribes that are in the dispersion: Rejoice [*chairein*]. Regard it as all joy [*charan*], my brothers ..."). "If anyone comes to you and does not bring this teaching ... do not say to him 'Rejoice' [*chairein*], for the one who says to him 'Rejoice' is sharing in his evil works" (2 Jn 10–11).

descendant Jehoiarib (Maccabaica 2.1), whose family was chosen to serve as the first course of priests at the temple (1 Chr 24.7).[271]

Under the new covenant, again priests can be appointed only in accordance with God's law (Heb 5.4). Yet there has now been a change in that law and a change in the priesthood (Heb 7.12): the High Priest today is Jesus (Heb 3.1; 4.14; 6.20), who was not descended from Aaron (Heb 7.14), and all those who are cleansed from sin by His blood are made priests by Him (Rev 1.5–6; 1 Pet 2.9), regardless of their descent in the flesh (Gal 3.28; Col 3.11).

Jonathan also **gathered together forces, and prepared many weapons,** as even Demetrius had now permitted him to do (v 6). He was arming the earthly Israel for an earthly fight; the spiritual Israel today is to be armed spiritually (in the ways described in Eph 6.11–18) for a spiritual fight.

Demetrius seeks alliance again

10.22 και ηκουςεν Δημητριος τους λογους τουτους και ελυπηθη και ειπεν	**10.22** And Demetrius heard these things, and he was sorrowful, and said:
10.23 τι τουτο ‹εποιηcαμεν› οτι προεφθαcεν ημαc Αλεξανδρος του φιλιαν καταλαβεcθαι	**10.23** "What *is* this we have done, that Alexander has acted before us to gain *the* friendship

[271] Josephus states that one of the Pharisees later objected to the high priesthood of John son of Simon, asserting that his mother had been a captive (*Antiquities,* 13.292). But according to Josephus himself, that story was false *(pseudēs);* and even if it had been true, it would not have been any Scriptural reason for refusing the high priesthood; and even if there had been a Scriptural reason for refusing the high priesthood, it would have affected only the high priesthood of Simon himself, not any of his relatives or descendants (cf. Lev 21.13–14).

O'Brien ("Between the Testaments," 364) says that the appointment of Mattathias's descendants as high priests overturned a command in the Law of Moses "that the high priest should be of the line of Phinehas (Numbers 25:12–15)." There are two errors here. In the first place, Mattathias was indeed apparently of the line of Phinehas (Maccabaica 2.54); and in the second place, the ordinance cited by O'Brien referred only to priesthood, not to high priesthood (Pomykala, "The Covenant with Phinehas in Ben Sira," 23).

O'Brien's further statement that the appointment overturned "the tradition that can be traced back to the time of David that only the line of Zadok out of all the line of Phinehas was the rightful high priestly line" is similarly mistaken. No such tradition can be traced back to the time of David (1 Sam 2:30–36 and 1 Kgs 2.27, 35 did not require all high priests to be sons of Zadok) or to anything anywhere else in Scripture (Ezek 44.15 speaks of priests, not high priests, and does not refer to the old covenant). And the common assumption that all high priests between Solomon and the Seleucid period were descendants of Zadok is supported neither by Scripture nor by other records (Hunt, *Missing Priests,* 41). "The view that the high priestly line was the exclusive Zadokite line, and in this way differed from other priests, is nowhere attested by our sources" (Grabbe, "Were the Pre-Maccabean High Priests 'Zadokites'?" 208–14).

τοις Ιουδαιοις εις στηριγμα	of the Judeans for a support?
10.24 γραψω ‹καγω αυτοις› λογους παρακλησεως και υψους και ‹δοματων› οπως ωσιν συν εμοι εις βοηθιαν	**10.24** I myself will also write to them words of encouragement and of high position and of gifts, so that they may be with me *as* a help."

10.23 εποιησαμεν V A 64⁺236 La[109+146] \| -ησας S • **10.24** καγω / αυτοις V A 64⁺236 La[109+146] \| ~ S • δοματων V A 64⁺236 La[109] \| -τος S •

10.22–24 Distressed by the fact that **Alexander** had gained **the friendship of the Judeans,** Demetrius decided to **write to them** again, with **words** that would promise the Judeans several enticements to help him: **encouragement, high position** (cf. 1.40; 8.13; "advancement," NJB), and **gifts.** But the people of Judah neither believed nor accepted them (v 46). Such enticements might indeed appeal to those who seek glory from men—but not to those who seek the glory of God (Matt 4.8–10).

10.25 και ‹απεστειλεν› αυτοις κατα τους λογους τουτους βασιλευς Δημητριος τω εθνι των Ιουδαιων χαιρει(ν)	**10.25** And he sent to them in accordance with these words: "King Demetrius to the nation of the Judeans: Rejoice.
10.26 επι συνετηρησατε ‹τας προς ημας› συνθηκας και ‹ενεμιναται› τη φιλια ημων και ου προσεχωρησατε τοις εχθροις ημων ηκουσαμεν και εχαρημεν	**10.26** Since you[pl] have kept *your* agreements toward us, and have continued[pl] in our friendship, and have not departed[pl] to our enemies, we have heard *of it* and rejoiced.

10.25 απεστειλεν A 64⁺236 La[109+146] \| επεστιλεν S V • **10.26** τας προς ημας S[ca] V A 64⁺236 La[109+146] \| τα προς εμας S[1] [τα π- τας ε- S*] • ενεμιναται S[ca] V A 64⁺236 La[109+146] \| ενετιλατο S* •

10.26 In the opening clauses of his letter, Demetrius claims to **have heard** that the Judeans **have continued in . . . friendship** with him, **and have not departed to** his **enemies.** In reality, he had heard exactly the opposite: that the Judeans had established **friendship** with his enemy Alexander (see v 23). At this point, therefore, Demetrius is demonstrably "conceiving and uttering from the heart words of falsehood" (Isa 59.13). That is an important observation, because it shows the unreliability of the lavish promises that follow (see the notes on v 46).

10.27 ‹και› νυν ενμινατε ετι συντηρησαι ‹› προς ημας πιστιν και ανταποδωσομεν υμι(ν) αγαθα ανθ ων ποιειτε μεθ ημων	**10.27** And now, still continue[pl] to keep *your* faith toward us, and we will repay good *things* to you[pl] in exchange for *the things* that you[pl] are doing with us,
10.28 και αφησομεν υμιν αφεματα πολλα και δωσομεν υμιν δοματα	**10.28** and we will free many free things for you[pl], and will give you[pl] gifts.

10.27 και 1° V A 64⁺236 La[109+146] \| > S • προς V A 64⁺236 La[109+146] \| ^ τι S •

10.29 και νυ(ν) απολυω υμας και αφιημι παντας τους Ιουδαιους απο τω(ν) φορων και της τιμης του αλος και απο των στεφανω(ν)	**10.29** And now I am releasing you[pl], and I am freeing all the Judeans from the tribute *payment*s and the honor of the salt, and from the crowns.
10.30 και αντι του τριτου της σπορας και αντι του ημισους του καρπου του ξυλινου του επιβαλλοντος μοι λαβειν αφιημι απο της σημερον και επεκεινα του λαβειν απο γης Ιουδα και απο τω(ν) τριων νομων των προστιθεμενων αυτη απο της Σαμαριτιδος και Γαλιλαιας απο της σημερον ημερας και εις τον απαντα χρονον	**10.30** And instead of *taking* the third of the seed, and instead of *taking* the half of the fruit of the trees that are assigned for me to take, I am freeing *them* from today and beyond, *no longer* taking *them* from *the* land of Judah and from the three legal provinces that are added to it from the Samaritan region and Galilee, from today's day and for all time.
10.31 και ‹› Ι(ερουσα)λημ εστω ‹› αγια και αφιμενη και τα ορια αυτης ε δεκαται και τα τελη	**10.31** And let Jerusalem be holy and free, and its appointed bounda- ries; the tenths and the payments
10.32 αφιημι και την εξουσιαν της ‹ακρας› ‹της› εν Ι(ερουσα)λημ διδωμι τω αρχιερει ‹› οπως αν καταστηση εν αυτη ανδρας ους αν αυτος εκλεξηται του φυλασσειν αυτην	**10.32** I am freeing, and *the* authority of the citadel in Jerusalem I am giving to the high priest, so that he may establish in it whichever men he himself may choose, to keep it.
10.33 και πασα(ν) ψυχην Ιουδαιω(ν) την εχμαλωτισθισαν απο γης Ιουδα εις πασαν βασιλιαν μου αφιημι ελευθεραν δωρεαν και παντες αφιετωσα(ν) τους φορους και των κτηνων αυτω(ν)	**10.33** And every soul of *the* Judeans who has been taken captive from *the* land of Judah into any *part* of my kingdom, I am freeing *as* a gift; and let them all leave *off their* tribute *payment*s and *those* of their livestock.
10.34 και πασαι αι εορται και τα σαββατα και ‹νουμηνιαι› και ημεραι ‹› αποδεδιγμεναι και τρις ημεραι προ εορτης και τρις μετα εορτην εστωσαν πασαι αι ημεραι ατελιας και αφεσεως πασιν τοις Ιουδαιοις τοις ουσιν εν τη βασιλια μου	**10.34** And *as for* all the feasts, and the Sabbaths and new moons and appointed days, and three days before a feast and three after a feast— let them all be days of exemption and freedom for all the Judeans who are in my kingdom.
10.35 και ουκ ‹εξει› εξουσιαν ουδεις πρασσει(ν) και παρενοχλειν τινα αυτων περι ‹παντος› πραγματος	**10.35** And no one will have any authority at all to act or cause difficulty for any *one* of them about any act.
10.36 και προγραφητωσαν των Ιουδαιω(ν)	**10.36** And let *some* of the Judeans be inscribed beforehand

εις τας δυναμις του βασιλεως εις τριακοντα χιλιαδας α(ν)δρων και δοθηcεται αυτοις ξενια ως καθηκει παcαις ταις δυναμεcι(ν) του βασιλεως	in the king's forces, up to thirty thousand men; and provisions for strangers will be given to them, as is fitting for all the king's forces.
10.37 ⸤και καταcταθηcεται εξ αυτων εν τοις οχυρωμαcιν του βασιλεως⸥ τοις μεγαλοις και ⸤εκ τουτων⸥ καταcταθηcονται επι χριων της βασιλιας των ουcων εις πιcτιν και οι επ αυτων και οι αρχοντες εcτωcα(ν) ⸤εξ αυτων⸥ και πορευεcθωcαν τοις νομοις ⸤αυτων⸥ ⸤καθα και⸥ προcεταξε(ν) ο βασιλευς εν γη Ιουδα	**10.37** And *some* of them will be established in the great fortresses of the king, and *others* of these will be established over *the* duties of the kingdom—the *thing*s that are *requiring* trust. And let their superiors and commanders be *chosen* from among them*selves*. And let them walk in their *own* laws, just as the king has decreed in *the* land of Judah.
10.38 και τους τρις νομους τους προcτεθε(ν)τας τη Ιουδαια απο της χωρας Cαμαριας προcτεθητω τη Ιουδαια προς ⸤το⸥ λογιcθηναι του γενεcθαι υφ ενα του μη ⸤υπακουcαι⸥ αλλ η εξουcια αλλ η του αρχιερεως	**10.38** And *as for* the three legal provinces that have been added to Judea from the district of Samaria— let them be added to Judea, *so that this* *is* accounted to be under one *person*, not obeying *any* other authority but *that* of the high priest.
10.39 Πτολεμαιδα και τη(ν) προcκυρουcαν αυτη δεδωκα δομα τοις αγιοις τοις εν Ι(ερουcα)λημ εις την καθηκουcαν δαπανη(ν) τοις αγιοις	**10.39** Ptolemais, and the *region* adjacent to it, I have given *as* a gift to the holy *place*s *that are* in Jerusalem, *to provide* for the expense that is fitting for the holy *place*s.
10.40 καγω διδωμι κατ ενιαυτο(ν) δεκα πεντε χιλιαδας cικλων αργυριου απο των λογω(ν) του βασιλεως απο των τοπων των ανηκοντων	**10.40** And I myself am giving each year fifteen thousand shekels of silver from the accounts of the king, from the places that are fitting.

10.31 και 1° V A $64^{+}236$ \| + η S • αγια S^{ca} V A $64^{+}236$ \| ^ η S* • **10.32** ακρας S^{ca} V A $64^{+}236$ $La^{109+146}$ \| cαρρας S* • της 2° S^{ca} A $64^{+}236$ $La^{109+146}$ \| την S* V • αρχιερει S^{ca} V A $64^{+}236$ $La^{109+146}$ \| + ανδρας S* • **10.34** νουμηνιαι S^{ca} V A $64^{+}236$ $La^{109+146}$ \| νουμηνια S* • ημεραι 1° V A $La^{109+146}$ \| + αι S $64^{+}236$ • ημεραι 1° V A $64^{+}236$ $La^{109+146}$ \| + εcτωcαν S • **10.35** εξει A $64^{+}236$ $La^{109+146}$ \| εχει S V • παντος V^{a} [-των V*] A $64^{+}236$ $La^{109+146}$ \| τινος S • **10.37** και καταcταθηcεται εξ αυτων εν τοις οχυρωμαcιν του βασιλεως V A [-θηcονται $64^{+}236$ 7h7 7a1] \| > S $La^{109+146}$ • εκ τουτων V A $64^{+}236$ $La^{109+146}$ \| κριται S • εξ αυτων V [A] $64^{+}236$ $La^{109+146}$ \| εαυτων S • αυτων 4° V A $64^{+}236$ \| εαυτων S • καθα και V A $64^{+}236$ \| καθως S • **10.38** το V A $64^{+}236$ \| > S • υπακουcαι S^{ca} V A $64^{+}236$ \| επ- S* •

10.41 και παν το πλεοναζο(ν) ο ουκ απεδιδοςα(ν) οι απο των χρειω(ν) ωϲ εν τοιϲ πρωτοιϲ εθνεϲιν απο του νυν δωϲουϲιν ειϲ τα εργα του οικου	**10.41** And all the additional *money*— which the *people* over the duties were not giving back *to you,* as *had been done* by the former nations— from now *on* they will give *it* for the works of the house.
10.42 και επι τουτοιϲ πεντακιϲχιλιουϲ ϲικλουϲ αργυριου οϲα ελαμβανον απο των χρειων του αγιου απο του λογου κατ ενιαυτο(ν) και ταυτα αφιται δια το ανηκιν αυτα τοιϲ ιερευϲιν τοιϲ λιτουργουϲι(ν)	**10.42** And in addition to these *things,* *the* five thousand shekels of silver— which they were taking from the duties of the holy *place* from the account each year—these also are set free, because they *are* fitting for the priests who are ministering.
10.43 και οϲοι εαν φυγωϲιν ειϲ το ιερον το εν Ιεροϲολυμοιϲ και εν παϲιν τοιϲ οριοιϲ αυτου οφιλω(ν) βαϲιλεικα και πα(ν) πραγμα απολελυϲθωϲαν και ‹πα(ν)τα› οϲα εϲτι(ν) αυτοιϲ ‹› εν τη βαϲιλια μου	**10.43** And whoever may flee into the temple that *is* in Jerusalem, and in all its appointed boundaries, owing *the* king's *taxe*s or *for* any *other* act— let them and all *thing*s that are theirs in my kingdom be released.
10.44 και του οικοδομηθηναι ‹και› επικαινιϲθηναι τα εργα των αγιων και η δαπανη δοθηϲεται εκ του λογου του βαϲιλεωϲ	**10.44** And the expense of building and renewing the works of the holy *place*s will also be given out of the king's account;
10.45 και του οικοδομηθηναι τα τιχη Ι(ερουϲα)λημ και ‹οχυρωϲαι› κυκλοθεν και η δαπανη δοθηϲεται εκ του λογου του βαϲιλεωϲ και του οικοδομηϲαι τα τιχη ‹εν› τη Ιουδαια	**10.45** and the expense of building the walls of Jerusalem, and fortifying *it* round about, will also be given out of the king's account; and *that* *of* building the walls in Judea."

10.43 πα(ν)τα S^{ca} V A 64^{+}236 La$^{109+146}$ \| πα(ν) πραγμα S* • αυτοιϲ V A [-ταιϲ 64^{+}236] La$^{109+146}$ \| + απολελυϲθωϲαν S • **10.44** και 2° S^{ca} V A 64^{+}236 La$^{109+146}$ \| > S* • **10.45** οχυρωϲαι V A 64^{+}236 La$^{109+146}$ \| ωχυρωϲεν S • εν V A 64^{+}236 La$^{109+146}$ \| ιηλμ´ S •

10.27–45 If the Judeans **continue** in **friendship** with him, Demetrius promises that he would **repay** it in **many good** ways.

- He would set them **free** from **many** duties (v 28). They would no longer have to send him **tribute payments** (vv 29; cf. 1.4), **salt** (v 29),[272] **crowns** (v 29),[273] one-

[272] The **salt** levy is called an **honor** *(timē),* i.e., something paid to honor the king ("Give back to all what is owed to them: tribute to whom tribute . . . honor to whom honor," Rom 13.7).

[273] The Judeans had been sending **crowns** to their kings (cf. 13.37)—but now they were starting to receive crowns from them (v 20).

third of their **seed** (v 30), **half of the fruit of** their **trees** (v 30), or **five thousand shekels of silver from** the temple (the **holy places,** v 42). All **captive Judeans** in every part of the **kingdom** would be set free, and no **tribute payments** (even ones that involved **their livestock**) would be required of them (v 33). In addition, the **Sabbaths** and various other specified **days** would **be days of exemption and freedom** from unspecified duties (v 34). And if people **owing** any debt fled **into the temple in Jerusalem,** they would **be released** from their obligations (v 43).

- He would give them various **gifts** (v 28). They would be given **three** additional **legal provinces from the district of Samaria** (v 38, 30),[274] **Ptolemais and the region adjacent to it** (the resources from which would be used specifically for the expenses of the **holy places,** v 42),[275] **fifteen thousand shekels of silver from the accounts of the king** every year (v 40), plus—also **out of the king's account**—the necessary **expense** for the **building and renewing** of the **holy places,** the city's **walls,** and **walls** in other parts of **Judea** (vv 44–45). Some **additional money,** which was **not** being given **back** to the Judeans, would be given **from now on... for the works of the house** (v 41).[276]
- The city of **Jerusalem** would be given a special status: it would be **holy and free,** and would no longer have to send **tenths**[277] and other **payments** to the king (vv 31–32).
- The **authority of the citadel in Jerusalem** would be given entirely to the Judean leader (the **high priest,** v 32)—a most important change, as the citadel had been the enemy's stronghold (see the notes on 1.33).
- **Up to thirty thousand Judeans** would be enlisted **in the king's forces,** under **commanders** of their own nation, and with permission to **walk in their own laws** (vv 36–37).

---

[274] The **three legal provinces** are listed by name in 11.34. In 10.30 their district is described as **the Samaritan region and Galilee** *(tēs Samaritidos kai Galilaias),* both of which are reckoned as parts of a single district ("Samaria-Galilee," NJB), elsewhere called simply "the Samaritan region" (11.28, 34). All three of the assigned provinces belonged to the Samaritan part of the district, not the Galilean part (see the notes on 11.34).

[275] Demetrius was giving away some things that he did not have. **Ptolemais** was under the control of his opponent (v 1).

[276] This **additional money** had lately been withheld by **the people over the duties** (the "revenue officials," REB), but it had been given **by** unspecified previous regimes (cf. Neh 5.15; Dan 7.23; Num 21.26; Jer 34.5; 50.17), **the former nations** (*ethnesin*, S* and 64[+]236, supported by La[109+146]; the reading of V, S[ca], and A, supported by 7a1, is *etesin,* "in the former years").

The **works of the house** are the various activities that involved the temple (Ezra 3.8; 1 Chr 23.4; 2 Chr 35.2; Neh 10.33), which is the **house** mentioned in the immediate context (vv 39, 43–44).

[277] As the name indicates, **tenths** *(dekatai)* are payments of one-tenth (the same proportion that was to be given to God under the old covenant Law, Lev 27.30, 32).

In the spirit, our King provides His people with far more **good things** (Heb 9.11; 10.1; Matt 7.11; Jas 1.17) than Demetrius ever offered in the flesh.

- He frees them from the immense debt that they owed (Matt 18.23–27), from the curse of the Law (Gal 3.13; Col 2.13–14), from sin and death (Rom 8.2; 6.18, 22), and from all spiritual captivity (Luke 4.18; see the notes on v 9).
- He gives them "all things" (Rom 8.32; 1 Tim 6.17; 1 Cor 1.5), "greater riches than the treasures of Egypt" (Heb 11.26), the "unsearchable riches" (Eph 3.8) of God's grace (Eph 1.7–8; 2.7), glory (Eph 1.18; 3.16; Col 1.27; Rom 9.23), salvation (Titus 3.5–6), wisdom (1 Cor 1.30; Col 2.3), and an inheritance not of a few provinces only, but of "a new heaven and a new earth" (Rev 21.1–7).
- Their city is "the heavenly Jerusalem" (Heb 12.22), which is holy (Rev 21.2, 10) and free (Gal 4.26) forever (Heb 13.14).
- "All authority . . . in heaven and on earth" is given to their High Priest (Matt 28.18; Heb 8.1; 7.26; 1.3–4), and nothing unclean can ever come into any part of His city (Rev 21.27; 22.15).
- Every one of them is enlisted in a spiritual army (2 Cor 10.3–5) where the leader is their own King (Rev 19.11–16; 17.14) and the laws are those of their own nation (Php 3.20).

The people of Judea favor Alexander

10.46 ωc δε ηκουcεν Ιωναθαν και ο λαοc τουc λογουc τουτουc ουκ ⸂επιcτευcαν⸃ αυτοιc ουδε ⸂επεδεξαντο⸃ οτι εμνηcθηcαν τηc κακιαc τηc μεγαληc ηc εποιηcαν εν Ιc(ραη)λ και εθλιψεν αυτουc cφοδρα	**10.46** But when Jonathan and the people heard these words, they did not believe or accept them: for they were mindful of the great evildoing that they had done in Israel, and *that* he had oppressed them very much.

10.46 επιcτευcαν S^{ca} V $64^{+}236$ $La^{109+146}$ | -τευcεν S* A • επεδεξαντο S^{ca} V A $64^{+}236$ $La^{109+146}$ | επεταξ- S* •

10.46 Jonathan and the people . . . did not believe or accept the words of Demetrius, because they saw that his words were not consistent with his deeds: **they were mindful of the great evildoing that** he and his supporters **had done**[278] **in Israel.** "Good words and blessings" cannot always be trusted (Rom 16.18; Col 2.4). Demetrius could be known by his fruits: what he was professing in his words, he had denied by his deeds (cf. Titus 1.16; 1 Jn 3.18; see also the notes on v 26). A corrupt tree will not bring forth good fruit; thistles and thornbushes will not bear grapes or figs (Matt 7.16–18).

10.47 και ευδοκηcαν εν Αλεξανδρω οτι αυτοc εγενετο	**10.47** And they were well pleased with Alexander: for he himself had been *the*

[278] **They had done** *(epoiēsan)* is the reading of S* (supported by $La^{109+146}$). The reading of V, S^{ca}, A, and $64^{+}236$ is **he had done** *(epoiēsen).*

αυτοις αρχηγος λογων ιρηνικω(ν) και συνεμαχουν αυτω πασας τας ημερας	first leader of peaceful words to them; and they were military allies to him all *his* days.

10.47 By contrast, the Judeans **were well pleased with Alexander**, whose **peaceful words** were consistent with his deeds (vv 59–66);[279] and they became Alexander's **military allies.**

Demetrius is killed

10.48 και συνηγαγεν ‹Αλεξανδρος ο βασιλευς› ‹δυναμεις μεγαλας› και παρενεβαλεν εξ εναντιας ‹Δημητριου›	**10.48** And Alexander the king gathered great forces and camped opposite Demetrius.

10.48 Αλεξανδρος / ο βασιλευς V A 64^{+}236 La$^{109+146}$ | ~ S • δυναμεις μεγαλας V A 64^{+}236 La$^{109+146}$ | πασας τας δυναμις S* [-μεις S^{cb1}] • Δημητριου S^{ca} V A 64^{+}236 | -ος S* •

10.48 The narrative has already reported that "Demetrius gathered together a very great force, and came out to meet [Alexander] for battle" (v 2). Now it returns to that subject. **Alexander** likewise **gathered great forces and camped opposite Demetrius.**

10.49 και συνηψαν πολεμον οι δυο βασιλεις και εφυγεν η παρεμβολη Αλεξανδρου και εδιωξεν αυτον ο Δημητριος και ισχυσεν επ αυτους	**10.49** And the two kings made contact in battle; and Alexander's company fled, and Demetrius pursued him, and overpowered them,
10.50 και εστερεωσεν τον πολεμον σφοδρα εως ‹εδυ ο ηλιος› και επεσεν ο Δημητριος εν τη ημερα εκεινη	**10.50** and kept the battle very strong until the sun set. And Demetrius fell on that day.

10.50 εδυ / ο ηλιος V A 64^{+}236 La$^{109+146}$ | ~ S •

10.49–50 The **battle** was close and prolonged (it remained **very strong until the sun set**).[280] **Alexander's company fled, and Demetrius pursued him.**[281] However, it was

---

[279] Alexander had been **the first leader** [*archēgos*] **of peaceful words to them.** The prefix *arch-* could mean either first in time ("the first that spake" peaceful words to them, RV) or first in importance ("the chief promoter" of peaceful words to them, DRCV; cf. Num 14.4, LXX). Choice between these options is often difficult (cf. TDNT 1.487–88; NIDTT 1.165, §5; 1.168, §4). In the present context v 23 might favor the former, vv 3–4 the latter (see also Sacy 204; Keil 179–80; Gutberlet, *Erste Buch der Makkabäer,* 172–73). Christ is the **first leader** *(archēgos)* of life (Acts 3.15), of faith (Heb 12.2), of salvation (Heb 2.10); and He is a "King of peace" (cf. Heb 7.2; Isa 9.6), whose words promise His subjects a greater peace than any earthly king could offer (Eph 2.15–16; Acts 10.36; John 14.27; 16.33).

[280] The closeness of the struggle is also attested by Classical sources (e.g., Justin 35.1.9–10; Josephus, *Antiquities,* 13.58–61, whose information is here drawn from those sources rather than from the Maccabean History).

Demetrius who **fell.** "The battle is not to the strong . . . for time and circumstance happen to them all" (Ecc 9.11). God alone determines the result, "taking away kings, and setting up kings" (Dan 2.21; Luke 1.52).

Alexander marries Ptolemy's daughter

10.51 και απεστιλεν Αλεξανδρος προς Πτολεμαιον βασιλεα Αιγυπτου πρεcβειc κατα τουc λογουc τουτουc λεγων	**10.51** And Alexander sent ambassa- dors to Ptolemy king of Egypt, in accordance with these words, saying:
10.52 επι ανεcτρεψα ειc την βαcιλιαν μου και ‹εκαθειcα› επι ‹θρονου› π(ατε)ρων μου και ‹εκρατηcα› τηc αρχηc και cυνετριψα τον Δημητριο(ν) και ‹επεκρατηcα› τηc χωραc ημω(ν)	**10.52** "Since I have returned to my kingdom and sat on *the* throne of my fathers, and have taken hold of the commandership, and have shattered Demetrius and gained power over our district—
10.53 και cυνηψα προc αυτον μαχην κ(αι) cυνετριβη αυτοc και η παρεμβολη αυτου υφ ημω(ν) και εκαθιcαμεν επι θρονου βαcιλιαc αυτου	**10.53** and I made contact with him *in* battle, and he himself and his company were shattered by us, and we have sat on *the* throne of his kingdom—
10.54 και νυ(ν) ‹cτηcωμεν› προc ‹εαυτουc› φιλιαν κ(αι) δοc μοι την θυγατεραν cου ειc γυναικα και επιγαμβρευcω cοι και δωcω cοι δοματα και αυτη αξια cου	**10.54** now then, let us establish a friendship between *our*selves, and give† me your† daughter for *my* wife, and I will become related by marriage to you†; and I will give you† and her gifts *that are* worthy of you†."

10.52 εκαθειcα V* [-θηcα V^{b}] A 64^{+}236 | ενεκ- S • θρονου S^{ca} V A 64^{+}236 La$^{109+146}$ | -νω(ν) S* • εκρατηcα S^{ca} V A 64^{+}236 La$^{109+146}$ | -cαc S* • επεκρατηcα S^{ca} V A 64^{+}236 La$^{109+146}$ | -cεν S* • **10.54** cτηcωμεν V [A] 64^{+}236 La$^{109+146}$ | -ηcομ- S • εαυτουc V 64^{+}236 | αυτουc S | αυτον A •

10.51–54 Alexander sent ambassadors to Ptolemy king of Egypt,[282] proposing to **establish a friendship between** them and to marry Ptolemy's **daughter.**[283] Compare

---

[281] **Alexander's company fled, and Demetrius pursued him** is the reading of S*, A, and 93 (supported by La^{109}), whereas V, S^{ca}, and 64^{+}236 (supported by La^{146}) have the names in the reverse order: "Demetrius's company fled, and Alexander pursued him" (which is the reading that a reader would naturally expect: cf. NETS 478).

[282] **Ptolemy king of Egypt.** According to Egyptian and Classical sources, this king was still Ptolemy Philometor (reckoned as Ptolemy VI by most modern historians)—the king who had been defeated by Antiochus Epiphanes many years earlier (1.18).

[283] **Daughter** (*thugateran).* Accusatives of third declension nouns ending in *-a* are often spelled *-an* in Sinaiticus (Thackeray §10.12). In V, A, and 64^{+}236 the spelling is *thugatera.*

the marriage alliances between Saul and David (1 Sam 18.17–27), between Solomon and Pharaoh (1 Kgs 3.1), between Hadad and Pharaoh (1 Kgs 11.19), and between earlier Ptolemaic and Seleucid kings (Dan 11.6).

10.55 και απεκριθη Πτολεμαιος ο βαcιλευc λεγων αγαθη ημερα εν η επεcτρεψαc ειc γη(ν) πατερων ‹cου› και εκαθιcαc επι θρονου βαcιλειαc ‹αυτων›	**10.55** And Ptolemy the king responded, saying: "*It was* a good day when you† returned into *the* land of your† fathers and sat† on *the* throne of their kingdom.
10.56 και νυν ποιηcω cοι α εγραψαc αλλα απαντηcον ειc Πτολεμαιδα οπωc ειδωμεν αλληλουc και επιγαμβρευcω cοι καθωc ειρηκαc	**10.56** And now I will do *the things* for you† that you† have written; but meet† *me* at Ptolemais, so that we may see one another; and I will become related by marriage to you†, just as you† have said."
10.57 και εξηλθεν Πτολεμαιοc εξ Αιγυπτου αυτοc και Κλεοπατρα η θυγατηρ αυτου και ηλθεν ειc Πτολεμαιδα ετουc δευτερου και ξ΄ και εκατοcτου	**10.57** And Ptolemy came out of Egypt, he and Cleopatra his daughter, and he came to Ptolemais *in the* hundred and sixty-second year.
10.58 ‹και› απηντηcεν αυτω Αλεξανδροc ο βαcιλευc και εξεδετο αυτω Κλεοπατρα(ν) την θυγατερα αυτου και εποιηcεν τον γαμον αυτηc εν Πτολεμαιδι καθωc οι βαcιλειc ε(ν) δοξη μεγαλη	**10.58** And Alexander the king met him; and he gave him Cleopatra his daughter; and he made her wedding at Ptolemais, just as kings *do*, with great glory.

10.55 cου S^{ca} V A 64^{+}236 La$^{109+146}$ | > S* • αυτων S^{ca} V A 64 La$^{109+146}$ | -του S* 236 • **10.58** και 1° V A 64^{+}236 La$^{109+146}$ | > S • εξεδετο S* A = -δοτο S^{ca} V 64^{+}236 •

10.55–58 Ptolemy ... responded by accepting **the things** that Alexander had **written.** The kings met **at Ptolemais,** where Ptolemy **gave** Alexander **Cleopatra**[284] **his daughter** in marriage. The **wedding** took place in the manner customary among **kings, with great glory.**

[284] There were many Hellenistic queens named **Cleopatra.** This one is called Cleopatra Thea ("Cleopatra the Goddess") on her coins (e.g., SC 2.2271) and by modern historians (e.g., Hölbl, *History of the Ptolemaic Empire,* 192–93, 200–01). After marrying Alexander (v 58) and Demetrius (11.12), Classical historians report that she married the latter's brother Antiochus (cf. 15.1), and claim that she later had both Demetrius and her eldest son Selecus murdered, finally perishing herself from poison that she had destined for her second son Antiochus Grypus (Appian, *Syriaca,* 68.360–69.363; Justin 39.1.9; 32.2.7–8). She is perhaps most widely known nowadays as the villainess of Corneille's tragedy *Rodogune.*

Alexander honors Jonathan

10.59 και εγραψεν Αλεξανδρος ο βασιλευς Ιωναθα ελθιν εις συναντησιν αυτω	**10.59** And Alexander the king wrote to Jonathan to come to meet him.
10.60 και επορευθη μετα δοξης εις Πτολεμαιδα και απη(ν)τησεν τοις δυσιν βασιλευσι και εδωκεν αυτοις αργυριον και χρυσιο(ν) και τοις φιλοις αυτων και δοματα πολλα και ευρεν χαριν ‹εναντιον› αυτων	**10.60** And he went with glory to Ptolemais, and met with the two kings, and gave them and their Friends silver and gold, and many gifts; and he found favor before them.
10.61 και επισυνηχθησαν προς αυτον ανδρες λοιμοι εξ Ις(ραη)λ ανδρες ‹παρανομοι› εντυχει(ν) κατ αυτου και ου προσεσχεν αυτοις ο βασιλευς	**10.61** And men from Israel *who were* plague-bearers, men *who were* Law- breakers, gathered together against him, to appeal against him. And the king did not pay *any* attention to them.
10.62 και προσεταξεν ο βασιλευς και εξεδυσαν Ιωναθαν τα ιματια αυτου και ενεδυσαν αυτον πορφυραν και εποιησα(ν) ουτως	**10.62** And the king decreed, and they unclothed Jonathan of his clothes, and clothed him in purple. And they did so.
10.63 και ‹εκαθισεν› αυτον ‹ο βασιλευς› μετ ‹αυτου› και ‹ειπεν› τοις αρχουσιν εξελθαται μετ αυτου εις μεσον της πολεως και κηρυξατε του μηδενα εντυγχανιν κατ αυτου περι μηδενος πραγματος και μηδεις αυτω παρενοχλειτω περι παντος λογου	**10.63** And the king seated him with him*self*, and said to *his* commanders: "Go out[pl] with him into *the* midst of the city, and proclaim[pl] *for* no one to appeal against him about any act at all; and let no one cause *any* difficulty for him on any account."
10.64 και εγενετο ως ειδον οι εντυγχανο(ν)τες την δοξαν αυτου καθως εκηρυξεν και περιβεβλημενον αυτον πορφυραν ‹› εφυγο(ν) παντες	**10.64** And it came about, when those who were appealing saw his honor, just as he had proclaimed, and *saw* him wrapped in purple, they all fled.
10.65 και εδοξασεν αυτον ο βασιλευς και εγραψε(ν) αυτον των πρωτων φιλων και εθετο αυτον στρατηγον και μεριδαρχην	**10.65** And the king honored him, and inscribed him among *his* First Friends, and placed him *as* army commander and province commander.
10.66 και επεστρεψεν Ιωναθαν ‹εις Ιερουσαλημ› μετ ειρηνης και ευφροσυνης	**10.66** And Jonathan returned to Jerusalem in peace and gladness.

10.60 εναντιον V A $64^{+}236$ | ενωπιον S • **10.61** παρανομοι V A $64^{+}236$ $La^{109+146}$ | αν- S • **10.63** εκαθισεν V A $64^{+}236$ $La^{109+146}$ | -σαν S • ο βασιλευς V A $64^{+}236$ $La^{109+146}$ | οι -λεις S • αυτου 1° S^{ca} V A $64^{+}236$ $La^{109+146}$ | -τω(ν)

S* • ειπεν S^{ca} V A 64^{+}236 La$^{109+146}$ | -παν S* • **10.64** εφυγο(ν) V 64^{+}236 La^{109} | ^ και S A La^{146} • **10.66** εις Ιερουςαλημ V A 64^{+}236 La$^{109+146}$ | > S •

10.59–65 Alexander invited **Jonathan** to the wedding at **Ptolemais,** where Jonathan **found favor**[285] in the sight of **the two kings** (Alexander and Ptolemy) **and gave them and their Friends . . . many gifts** (a sign of alliance, vv 20, 54, 88–89; 11.58; 12.43; 13.37; 14.24; 15.26; 16.19; 2.18). Alexander accorded Jonathan exceptionally high status (**among his First Friends;** cf. 11.27), ordered him to be **clothed . . . in purple** (a sign of exalted rank: see the notes on v 20 and on 4.23), and forbad anyone **to appeal against him about any act at all.**[286] This was a significant milestone, as it would have been the first official approval given in public to the new government of Judea.

Faced with these tributes, Jonathan's opponents (**Law-breakers** and **plague-bearers**[287] **from Israel) fled.** God's people are accused before Him day and night (Rev 12.10; Zec 3.1; cf. Job 1.9), but He is a righteous judge; in the end it will be the false accusers, not the falsely accused, who will be put to shame (Psa 71.13; 109.17–20, 29; Zec 3.2).

Demetrius son of Demetrius opposes Alexander

Demetrius son of Demetrius becomes king

10.67 και ‹εν› ‹ετι ε΄› και ξ΄ και ρ΄ ηλθεν Δημητριος υιος Δημητριου εκ Κρητης εις τη(ν) γην των π(ατε)ρων αυτου	**10.67** And in *the* hundred and sixty-fifth year Demetrius son of Demetrius came out of Crete to the land of his fathers.
10.68 και ηκουςεν Αλεξανδρος ο βαςιλευς και ελυπηθη ςφοδρα και υπεςτρεψεν εις Αντιοχιαν	**10.68** And Alexander the king heard, and he was very sorrowful, and returned to Antioch.

10.67 εν S^{ca} V A 64^{+}236 La^{146} | > S* • ετι / ε΄ V A 64^{+}236 La^{146} | ~ S •

10.67 Several years later a second **Demetrius,** the **son of** the first, arrived in the land from **Crete.** Yet again the kingdom was divided against itself (Matt 12.25).

Apollonius challenges Jonathan

10.69 και κατεςτηςεν Δημητριος Απολλωνιον το(ν) οντα επι Κοιλης Cυριας και ςυνηγαγεν	**10.69** And Demetrius established Apollonius, the *person* who was over Coele-Syria; and he gathered

[285] Similarly, Joseph (Gen 39.21), Samuel (1 Sam 2.26), Daniel (Dan 1.9), Esther (Est 2.15), and Jesus (Luke 2.52) **found favor** *(heuren charin)* in the sight of those around them.

[286] Compare the honors bestowed on Mordecai (Est 6.7–11), Joseph (Gen 41.42–43), and Daniel (Dan 2.48; 5.29).

[287] **Plague-bearers** *(loimoi)*. The term is applied both to diseases (Luke 21.11) and to people who are living embodiments of disease (15.3, 21; Psa 1.1, LXX; cf. Acts 24.5)—in German, *verdorbene* (LXX.D).

δυναμιν μεγαλην και ‹παρενεβαλεν› επι Ιαμνιαν και απεστιλεν προς Ιωναθαν τον αρχιερεα λεγων	a great force and camped against Jabneh. And he sent to Jonathan the high priest, saying:
10.70 cυ μονωτατοc επαιρη εφ ημαc εγω δε εγενηθην ειc καταγελωτα και ειc ονιδιcμον δια cε και δια τι cυ εξουcιαζη εφ ημαc εν τοιc ορεcι	**10.70** “You† may be *the* only *one* lifting yourself† up against us, but I myself have come to be an *object of* laughter and reproach because of you†. And why are you† yourself† exercising authority against us in the mountains?
10.71 νυν ουν ‹ει πεποιθαc› επι ταιc δυναμεcι(ν) cου καταβηθι προc ημαc ειc το πεδιον και cυνκριθωμεν εαυτοιc εκει οτι ‹μετ εμου εcτι(ν)› δυναμιc τω(ν) πολεων	**10.71** Now therefore, if you† are con- fident in your† forces, come down† to us, to the level place, and we shall judge *between our*selves there: for with me is *the* power of the cities.
10.72 ερωτηcον και μαθε τιc ειμι και οι λοιποι οι βοηθουντεc ημιν και λεγουcιν ουκ εcτιν ‹υμιν› cταcιc ‹ποδοc› κατα προcωπον ημω(ν) οτι ‹διc ετροπωθηcαν› οι πατερεc cου εν τη γη αυτων	**10.72** Ask† and learn† who I am, and the rest who are helping us. And *people* are saying: ‘Your[pl] foot cannot stand against our face: for twice your† fathers have been turned back in their *own* land.’
10.73 και νυν ου δυνηcη υποcτηναι την ιππον ‹και› δυναμιν τοιαυτην εν τω παιδιω οπου ουκ εcτιν λιθοc ουδε κοχλαξ ουδε τοποc του φυγειν	**10.73** And now you† will not be able to stand before *my* horse*men* and such a force in the level place, where *there* is no stone or flint or place to flee.”

10.69 παρενεβαλεν S^{ca} V A 64^{+}236 La$^{109+146}$ \| -λον S* • **10.71** ει πεποιθαc V A 64^{+}236 La$^{109+146}$ \| επιπεποιθαc S • μετ εμου εcτι(ν) S^{ca} V A 64^{+}236 La$^{109+146}$ \| ουκ εcτι(ν) ετι S* • **10.72** υμιν S^{ca} V A 64^{+}236 La$^{109+146}$ \| ημ- S* • ποδοc V A 64^{+}236 La$^{109+146}$ \| -δων S^{ca} \| > S* • διc ετροπωθηcαν V A 64^{+}236 La$^{109+146}$ \| διετ- S • **10.73** και 2° V A 64^{+}236 La^{109} \| > S La^{146} •

10.69–73 Apollonius, the governor of **Coele-Syria,**[288] now besieged the old Philistine city of **Jabneh** (4.15; 5.58; 15.40; 2 Chr 26.6) and openly defied **Jonathan** to fight against him **in the level place, where there is not a stone or a flint or a place to**

[288] The term **Coele-Syria** *(Koilē Suria)* was applied in Hellenistic and Roman times to a region of variable extent (Cohen, *Hellenistic Settlements in Syria, the Red Sea Basin, and North Africa,* 37–45), sometimes apparently extending from the Euphrates to the border of Egypt (Josephus, *Antiquities,* 14.79), sometimes apparently limited to the territory north of Samaria (Josephus, *War,* 1.213) and inland from Phoenicia (Epitome 3.5). Its name has been construed either as Greek, “hollow Syria,” comparable to “hollow Argos” (*koilon Argos,* Sophocles, *Oedipus at Colonus,* 378; cf. Jnh 1.5, LXX; LEH 345; Bickerman, “Coelè-Syrie,” 256–68), or as Aramaic, “all Syria,” comparable to “all [the region] beyond the River” (*kl 'br nhrh,* Ezra 4.20; cf. Sartre, “Syrie-Creuse n'existe pas,” 15–40).

flee.[289] Like some earlier Syrians (1 Kgs 20.23), he seems to have thought that Israel's forces were strong only **in the mountains.** But the LORD who created heaven and earth fills heaven and earth; no matter where we go, we are never beyond His power (Jer 23.24; 1 Kgs 8.27; Psa 139.7–12; Amos 9.2–4).

Apollonius complained that he had **come to be an object of laughter and reproach because of** Jonathan. Only a few years earlier the Judeans were the ones who were laughed at (7.34) and suffered reproach (1.39; 4.58)—as would happen later to Christ Himself (Rom 15.3; Luke 8.53; Mark 15.29–32) and His followers (Matt 5.11). But in the end it is always the LORD's enemies who incur His laughter (Psa 2.4; 37.13; 59.8; Prov 1.26) and a "lasting reproach" (Psa 78.66; Jer 49.13).

Twice in the past Jonathan's predecessors (**fathers;** cf. v 1) had **been turned back in their own land.** The tone of Apollonius's challenge does not suggest that he was taking pains to be historically precise (or linguistically precise[290]). A Syrian leader would recall the death of Judas (9.17–18) and would be aware that the Israelites had suffered some earlier defeats or retreats (cf. 2.28, 38; 5.60; 6.47), although he might not know the exact details (unless he had Israelite advisers, cf. v 20). If he was particularly well informed, he might just possibly refer to events in the more remote past, such as Israel's two major defeats by the Philistines (1 Sam 4.10–11; 31.1–6) or the victories of Necho (2 Chr 35.20–24) and Nebuchadnezzar (2 Kgs 24.1–25.11). In fact the Israelites had been defeated by their enemies not just **twice,** but many times—in accordance with the LORD's repeated warnings (Lev 26.17, 36; Deut 28.25; Isa 30.17).

You will not be able to stand. One of the stratagems of the enemy of mankind is to try to discourage the hearts of the faithful by undermining their confidence in God's salvation (Num. 13.31–14.3; Psa 3.2; 22.7–8; 2 Sam 16.8).

Joppa submits to Jonathan

10.74 ωc δε ηκουcεν Ιωναθαν τω(ν) λογων Απολλωνιου εκεινηθη τη διανοια και επελεξεν δεκα χιλιαδαc ανδρων και εξηλθεν ‹εξ› Ι(ερουcα)λημ και cυνηντηcεν αυτω Cιμων ο αδελφοc αυτου επι βοηθιαν αυτω	**10.74** But when Jonathan heard the words of Apollonius, he was moved in *his* mind, and he chose ten thousand men, and came out of Jerusalem; and Simon his brother met with him to help him.
10.75 και παρενεβαλεν επι Ιοππην και απεκλιcαν αυτη(ν) οι εκ τηc πολεωc οτι ‹φρουρα› Απολλωνιου εν Ιοππη ‹› και επολεμηcαν αυτην	**10.75** And he camped against Joppa; and the *people* from the city shut it: for a garrison of Apollonius *was* in Joppa. And they made war against it.

10.74 εξ S^{cb1} V A $64^{+}236$ $La^{109+146}$ | ειc S* • **10.75** φρουρα V A $64^{+}236$ $La^{109+146}$ | -αν S • Ιοππη V A $64^{+}236$ La^{109} | + ευρον S •

[289] **Your foot cannot stand.** The wording of the Greek is *ouk estin humin stasis podos* ("there is no standing of foot for you^{pl}").

[290] In such a message, **twice** might perhaps mean simply "more than once" (cf. 1 Thes 2.18).

10.76 και φοβηθεντες ηνυξαν οι εκ της πολεως και ‹εκυριευcεν› Ιωναθαν Ιοππης	**10.76** And the *people* from the city, being afraid, opened up; and Jonathan became lord over Joppa.

10.76 εκυριευcεν S^{ca} V A 64^{+}236 La$^{109+146}$ | -cαν S* •

10.74–76 Jonathan[291] first besieged the **city** of **Joppa** (on the coast, 14.5, 34; Jnh 1.3; Acts 10.5–6; in the Philistine region, 12.33; cf. Josh 19.46), where there was **a garrison of Apollonius.** The people of the city were **afraid** (cf. 3.6, 25; Deut 2.25; 11.25), and surrendered (**opened up**) to him.

Jonathan defeats Apollonius at Ashdod

10.77 και ηκουcεν Απολλωνιος και παρενεβαλεν τριcχιλιαν ιππο(ν) και δυναμιν πολλην και επορευθη εις Αζωτον ως διοδευων και αμα προηγεν εις το πεδιον δια το εχιν αυτον πληθος ιππου και πεποιθεναι επ αυτη	**10.77** And Apollonius heard; and he encamped three thousand horse and a great force, and went for battle to Ashdod, like a *man* who is traveling through; and together *with this* he *began* going forward to the level place, because he *had* a multitude of horse, and *was* confident in it.

10.77 Apollonius . . . went for battle to Ashdod (also in the Philistine region; 4.15; 5.68), and led his troops **to the level place** there, being **confident** that his **multitude of horse** would be victorious in such terrain (vv 71–73). But "the horse is a false thing for salvation, and with the abundance of his power he will not deliver" (Psa 33.17; 147.10). "The horse is established for the day of battle, but to the LORD belongs the salvation" (Prov 21.31; Isa 31.1; Psa 20.7). We may surround ourselves with every earthly advantage (Dan 4.30–31; Luke 12.19–20), but our times are in God's hands, not ours (Psa 31.15; 139.16), and He will do with us whatever He chooses (Psa 135.6; Dan 4.35).

10.78 και κατεδιωξεν οπιcω αυτου εις πολεμον εις Αζωτον και cυνηψαν αι παρεμβολαι ‹› εις πολεμον	**10.78** And he pursued after him for battle to Ashdod, and the companies made contact for battle.
10.79 και απελιπε(ν) Απολλωνιος χιλιαν ιππον κρυπτως καθοπισθε(ν) αυτων	**10.79** And Apollonius had left a thousand horse in hiding behind them,
10.80 και εγνω Ιωναθαν οτι εστι(ν) ενεδρον κατοπισθεν αυτου και εκυκλωcαν αυτου τη(ν) παρεμβολην και εξετιναξαν τας cχιζας εις τον ‹λαο(ν)› εκ πρωιθεν εως διλης	**10.80** and Jonathan knew that there was an ambush behind him; and they went round about his company, and shot *their* arrows into the people, from early morning until late afternoon,

[291] Jonathan took action because **he was moved** [*ekeinēthē;* "roused," NJB] **in his mind** (like the whole city of Ephesus in Acts 21.30; cf. Maccabaica 13.44; Dan 2.3, LXX).

10.81 ο δε λαος ιcτηκι καθωc επεταξε(ν) Ιωναθαν και εκοπιαcαν οι ιπποι αυτων	**10.81** but the people stood *still,* just as Jonathan had ordered. And their horses became weary.
10.82 και ειλκυcε(ν) Cιμων την δυναμιν αυτου και ‹cυνηψεν› προc την ‹φαλαγγα› η γαρ ιπποc εξελυθη και cυνετριβηcαν υπ αυτου και εφυγαν	**10.82** And Simon brought out his force and made contact against the phalanx: for the horse had become weary. And they were shattered by him, and fled,
10.83 και η ιπποc εcκορπιcθη εν τω πεδιω κ(αι) ‹εφυγον› ειc Αζωτο(ν) και ειcηλθον ειc ‹Βηθδαγων› το ιδωλιον αυτων του cωθηναι	**10.83** and the horse were scattered in the level place. And they fled into Ashdod, and went into Beth- Dagon [the house of Dagon], their idol-shrine, to save themselves.
10.84 και ενεπυριcεν Ιωναθαν την Αζωτον και ταc πολιc ταc κυκλω αυτηc και ελαβεν τα cκυλα αυτω(ν) και το ιερον Δαγω(ν) και τουc ‹cυνφευγονταc› ειc αυτο ενεπυριcεν πυρι	**10.84** And Jonathan set on fire Ashdod and the cities round about it, and he took their plunder. And the temple of Dagon, and the *people* who had fled into it, he set on fire with fire.
10.85 και ‹εγενοντο› οι πεπτωκοτεc μαχαιρα cυν τοιc εμπυριcθιcιν ειc ανδραc οκτακιcχιλιουc	**10.85** And the *people* who had fallen by *the* sword, together with the *one*s who were set on fire, came to be up to eight thousand men.

10.78 παρεμβολαι 64^{+}236 La$^{109+146}$ | + οπιcω αυτου S V A • **10.80** λαο(ν) S^{ca} V A 64^{+}236 La$^{109+146}$ | ναο(ν) S* • **10.82** cυνηψεν V A 64^{+}236 La$^{109+146}$ | -ψαν S • φαλαγγα S^{cb1} A 64^{+}236 La$^{109+146}$ | φαραγγα S* V • **10.83** εφυγον V A 64^{+}236 La$^{109+146}$ | -γεν S • Βηθδαγων S^{ca} V A 64^{+}236 | Βοδ- S* • **10.84** cυνφευγονταc S^{ca} V A La$^{109+146}$ | cυνφυτου(ν)τουνταc S* • **10.85** εγενοντο S^{ca} V A 64^{+}236 La$^{109+146}$ | εγενετο S* •

10.78–82 Jonathan pursued after him, but **Apollonius had left a thousand horse in hiding behind them,** so that Jonathan's **company** found themselves surrounded.[292]

[292] The statement **Jonathan knew that there was an ambush behind him** is usually taken to mean merely that Jonathan knew it when it happened ("Jonathan perceived that there was an ambushment behind him, for they had compassed in his host," Cotton; "Not until then did Jonathan realize that he was caught in an ambush," TEV). If so, why make the statement at all? Anyone caught in an ambush would know they were caught in an ambush. Elsewhere in this book, however, a statement that people **knew** about a plan always means that they knew about it before it was carried out (7.30; 9.33, 60; etc.). Compare "the king of Ai… did not know that there was an ambush for him behind the city" (Josh 8.14), which means that he did not know it beforehand (he certainly did know it when it happened). Therefore, the present statement must mean that Jonathan **knew** about the ambush beforehand, before the **horse** emerged from

Yet the plan did not work as Apollonius had intended. Jonathan ordered his company to stand still, and they held their position **from early morning to late afternoon,** until their opponents' **horses became weary.** Then **Simon brought out** his troops (**his force**) and **shattered** the weary enemy.[293]

It might almost be said that Apollonius's plan was its own undoing. A direct charge might have put the Israelites to flight. But by surrounding them on a "level place where there is not a stone or a flint or a place to flee" (v 73), he gave them the opportunity to wear his forces down. "A wicked one is trapped by the work of his own hands" (Psa 9.15–16).

More than once in old covenant times, God's people had only to stand still faithfully, and their enemies were defeated (Exod 14.13; 2 Chr 20.17); but when they sinned against Him, they were no longer able to stand before their enemies (Josh 7.11–12). So it is today in the spirit. "If indeed you abide in the faith well founded and firmly fixed [*edraioi*], and not moved away from the hope of the gospel" (Col 1.23; Josh 23.6; 2 Cor 1.24; 1 Pet 5.12), then, standing firm, "you will be able to quench all the fiery arrows of the evil one" (Eph 6.13–16); he and all his forces will "weary themselves for nothing" (cf. Hab 2.13; Isa 40.30–31).

10.83–84 The Israelites, who had no "place to flee," did not need one; their opponents, who found a place to flee, were destroyed by it. **They fled into Ashdod, and went into Beth-Dagon,**[294] **their idol-shrine, to save themselves.** Jonathan **set** the building **on fire with fire** (see the notes on 5.5), and the people who had sought salvation in it perished. Dagon himself did nothing—as always (cf. Jdg 16.23–30; 1 Sam 5.2–4; Psa 115.4–8; Hab 2.18).

Ashkelon submits to Jonathan

10.86 και απηρεν ‹εκειθεν› Ιωναθαν και παρενεβαλεν επι Αcκαλωνα και εξηλθον οι εκ τηc πολεωc ειc cυναντηcι(ν) αυτω εν δοξη μεγαλη	**10.86** And Jonathan moved away from there, and he camped against Ashkelon; and the *people* from the city came out to meet him, with great honor.

hiding. Knowing about it beforehand, he was able to prepare his company to deal with it. (Cf. Geneva: "Jonathan knew that there was an ambushment behind him, and though they . . . compassed in his host, and shot darts at the people from morning to evening, yet the people stood still, as Jonathan had commanded them.")

[293] **They went round about his company** *(parembolēn).* On the cross, Christ's enemies "surrounded" Him (Psa 22.12, 16) yet were defeated (Psa 118.10–13). Similarly, in John's prophecy "Gog and Magog . . . surrounded the camp [*parembolēn*] of the holy ones," yet perished by fire (Rev 20.8–9).

[294] **Dagon** was the god of the Philistines (Jdg 16.23); his temple at Ashdod was "the house of Dagon" (Hebrew *byt Dgwn,* **Beth-Dagon,** 1 Sam 5.2; 1 Chr 10.10).

10.87 και επεστρεψεν Ιωναθαν ις Ι(ερουσα)λημ συν τοις παρ αυτου ‹εχοντες› σκυλα πολλα	**10.87** And Jonathan returned to Jerusalem, together with the *people* alongside him, having much plunder.

10.86 εκειθεν A 64⁺236 La[109+146] | ενθε(ν) S | > V • **10.87** εχοντες S[ca] V A La[109+146] | εχοντι S* | -τει S[1] | εχων 64⁺236 •

10.86 Next, **Jonathan . . . camped against Ashkelon,** another of the principal cities of the Philistines (Josh 13.3; 1 Sam 6.17; 2 Sam 1.20; Amos 1.8). Its people did not oppose him, but **came out to meet him,** showing him **great honor,** just as their kings were now doing (Alexander, v 65, 88; Demetrius, 11.27, 44).[295]

Alexander honors Jonathan still more

10.88 και εγενετο ως ηκουσεν Αλεξανδρος ο βασιλευς τους λογους τουτους και προσεθετο ετι δοξασαι τον Ιωναθαν	**10.88** And it came about, when Alexander the king heard these things, that he proceeded to honor Jonathan *still* more,
10.89 και απεστιλε(ν) αυτω πορπην χρυσην ως εθος εστι(ν) διδοσθαι τοις συγγενεσιν των βασιλεων και εδωκεν αυτω την ‹Ακκαρων› και παντα τα ορια αυτης εις κληροδοσιαν	**10.89** and sent him a golden pin, as it is *the* custom to give to kings' relatives, and gave him Ekron and all its appointed boundaries for an inheritance.

10.89 Ακκαρων S[ca] V A 64⁺236 La[109+146] | -ρω S* •

10.88–89 After these successors, **Alexander . . . proceeded to honor Jonathan still more,** in the way that **kings' relatives** were honored (see the notes on "brother," v 18), and he assigned him yet another of the principal Philistine cities, **Ekron** (Josh 13.3; 1 Sam 7.14; Amos 1.8).[296]

The kinds of honors here bestowed on Jonathan by his earthly king are similar to those bestowed on His people by their heavenly King. "To everyone who has, it shall be given." Those whom He finds faithful in a few things He will set "over many things" (Matt 25.14–30; "over ten cities," Luke 19.17), and He will acknowledge them as His relatives (1 Jn 3.1; Heb 2.11). Indeed, all honors are from Him (1 Chr 29.12). He can give us "all things"; we can give Him nothing except what He has already given to us (Rom 11.35–36; 1 Cor 8.6; 1 Chr 29.14).

---

295 In this context *doxē megalē* (cf. 2.51) presumably means **great honor** (Geneva; *de grandes honneurs,* Martin; *vielen Ehren,* Zöckler), not "great pomp" (KJV and most other English versions). People whose besieger has just slain thousands of their closest compatriots (vv 84–85) are much more likely to fling themselves on his mercy timidly (v 76) and with a display of homage than with a display of pomp. Indeed many of the versions that have "pomp" here have "honor" in the almost identical context at 11.60 ("paid him honor," NRSV; "honored him," SAAS).

296 **He gave him Ekron,** just as an earlier king had given David the city of Ziklag (1 Sam 27.6).

Ptolemy opposes Alexander

Ptolemy travels into Syria

11.1 και βαcιλευc Αιγυπτου ηθροιcεν δυναμιc πολλαc ωc η αμμοc ‹η› παρα το χιλοc τηc θαλαccηc και πλοια πολλα και εζητηcε ‹κατακρατηcε› τηc βαcιλειαc Αλεξανδρου δολω και προcθειναι αυτην τη βαcιλεια αυτου	**11.1** And *the* king of Egypt drew together many forces, like the sand *that is* alongside the lip of the sea, and many ships; and he sought to overpower Alexander's kingdom by deceit, and to add it to his *own* kingdom.

11.1 η 2° S^{ca} V A La$^{109+146}$ | > S* • κατακρατηcε S^{ca} V A La$^{109+146}$ | και κατεκρ- S* | κρατηcαι 64^{+}236 •

11.1 Ptolemy **king of Egypt** now **sought to overpower Alexander's kingdom by deceit, and to add it to his own kingdom.**[297] He already controlled many men (like the grains of **sand alongside the lip of the sea** in number), as well as **many ships**. But his was a soul that was not satisfied with the abundance of his possessions (Ecc 5.10; 6.3, 7; cf. Luke 12.16–21).

11.2 και εξηλθεν ειc Cυριαν ‹λογοιc ειρηνικοιc› και ηνυγο(ν) αυτω οι απο ‹των πολεων› και cυνηντου(ν) αυτω οτι εντολη ην Αλεξανδρου του βαcιλεωc cυνανταν αυτω δια το πενθερον αυτου ειναι	**11.2** And he came out into Syria with peaceful words, and the *people* from the cities were opening up to him and meeting with him: for it was a command of Alexander the king *for them* to meet with him, because he was his father-in-law.
11.3 ωc δε ειcεπορευετο ειc ταc πολειc Πτολεμαιοc απεταccε ταc δυναμειc φρουραν εν εκαcτη πολει	**11.3** But as Ptolemy was going into the cities, he *kept* setting apart forces *as* a garrison in each city.

11.2 λογοιc ειρηνικοιc V A 64^{+}236 La$^{109+146}$ | λεγων λογουc ιρηνικουc S • των πολεων V A 64^{+}236 La$^{109+146}$ | τηc -εωc S • cυναντου(ν) S = -των V A 64^{+}236 |

11.2–3 Ptolemy traveled **into Syria**[298] **with peaceful words** (1.30; 5.48; 7.10, 15, 28; etc.) but contrary deeds (**he kept setting apart forces ... in each city**). Because he was

[297] In an earlier generation the king of Syria had tried to become king also of Egypt (1.16); now the situation was reversed (v 13). Ptolemy's initial support of Alexander and subsequent plot against him are also described by Diodorus (32.9c [32.32]).

[298] The term **Syria** was used in various senses (like Coele-Syria: see on 10.69). Here it includes the Philistine region (v 4), as often in Classical historians (e.g., Herodotus 1.105; 2.106). In other passages it is limited to the region north of Palestine (Gal 1.21; Acts 15.23, 41; so, probably, in Maccabaica 3.41).

the **father-in-law** of **Alexander** (10.57–58), the **cities** under Alexander's authority met him in peace.[299]

11.4 ωϲ δε ηγγειϲα(ν) Αζωτου εδειξαν αυτω το ιερον Δαγων ενπεπυριϲμενον και Αζωτον και τα περιπολια αυτηϲ καθειρημενα και ‹τα› ϲωματα ερριμμενα και τουϲ εμπεπυριϲμενουϲ ουϲ ενεπυριϲεν ε(ν) τω πολεμω εποιηϲαν γαρ θειμωνιαϲ αυτων εν τη οδω αυτου	**11.4** But when they came near Ashdod, they showed him the temple of Dagon that had been set on fire, and Ashdod and its city-surroundings that had been pulled down, and the bodies that had been thrown away, and those that had been set on fire, which he had set on fire in the battle: for they had made piles of them in his path.
11.5 και διηγηϲα(ν)το τω βαϲιλει α εποιηϲεν Ιωναθαν ειϲ το ‹ψογιϲαι› αυτον και εϲιγηϲεν ο βαϲιλευϲ	**11.5** And they told the king *the things* that Jonathan had done, to discredit him. And the king was silent.

11.4 τα 2° V A 64⁺236 | > S • 11.5 ψογιϲαι V A 64⁺236 | ψεξαι S •

11.4–5 Near Ashdod, people sought **to discredit**[300] Jonathan by telling Ptolemy what **Jonathan had done,** and showing him the burned **temple of Dagon,** the parts of **Ashdod and its city-surroundings that had been pulled down,** and the dead **bodies** (10.84–85). Ptolemy **was silent,** and did not condemn either side (cf. Acts 18.17; 1 Kgs 18.21; 2 Sam 13.22). He had spoken "peaceful words" to the people of Ashdod (v 2), and he would likewise accept Jonathan (v 6).

11.6 και ϲυνηντηϲεν Ιωναθαν τω βαϲιλει ειϲ Ιοππην μετα δοξηϲ και ηϲπαϲαντο αλληλουϲ και εκοιμηθηϲαν εκει	**11.6** And Jonathan met with the king at Joppa, with honor; and they greeted one another, and they slept there.
11.7 και επορευθη Ιωναθα(ν) μετα του βαϲιλεωϲ εωϲ του ποταμου του καλουμενου Ελευθερου και επεϲτρεψεν ειϲ Ι(ερουϲα)λημ	**11.7** And Jonathan went with the king up to the river that *is* called Eleutherus, and returned to Jerusalem.

11.6–7 Jonathan met with the king at Joppa (10.75–76) and traveled with him as far as **the river that is called Eleutherus** (apparently the northern boundary of Judean territory, 12.30).

---

299 **As Ptolemy** [*Ptolemaios*] **was going into the cities** is the reading of S[1] and 64⁺236 (supported by La[109+146]). The reading of V, S[ca], and A is "as he was going into the cities of Ptolemais [*Ptolemaidos*]."

300 **Discredit** *(psogisai)*. "I have heard the slander [*dbh,* Hebrew ≡ *psogon,* LXX] of many… when they are set together against me" (Psa 31.13).

Ptolemy makes an alliance with Demetrius

11.8 ο δε ‹βασιλευς Πτολεμαιος› εκυριευσεν των πολεων της ‹παραλιας› εως Σελευκιας της παραθαλασσιας και διελογιζετο περι Αλεξανδρου λογισμους πονηρους	**11.8** But king Ptolemy became lord over the cities of the seaside, up to Seleucia that *is* beside the sea. And he was planning harmful plans about Alexander.

11.8 βασιλευς Πτολεμαιος V A 64^{+}236 \| Πτολεμαιος ο βασιλευς S \| *rex* La$^{109+146}$ • παραλιας V A 64^{+}236 = -λιου S •

11.8 In each of the cities that **Ptolemy** visited, "he was setting apart forces as a garrison" (v 3). In this way he **became lord over the cities of the seaside,** even as far north as **Seleucia** (on the coast near Antioch, Acts 13.1, 4). All the time, **he was planning harmful plans**[301] **about Alexander,**

11.9 κ(αι) απεστιλεν πρεσβεις προς Δημητριον τον βασιλεα λεγων δευρο συνθωμεθα προς εαυτους διαθηκη(ν) και δωσω σοι τη(ν) θυγατεραν μου η(ν) ειχεν Αλεξανδρος ‹κ(αι)› βασιλευσεις ‹της βασιλειας› του πατρος σου	**11.9** And he sent ambassadors to Demetrius the king, saying: "Come, let us agree *in* a covenant between *our*selves. And I will give you† my daughter whom Alexander used to have; and you† will become king of your† father's kingdom.
11.10 ‹μεταμεμελημε γαρ› δους αυτω τη(ν) θυγατερα μου εζητησεν γαρ ‹με αποκτειναι›	**11.10** For I regret having given him my daughter: for he has sought to kill me."
11.11 και ‹εψογισε(ν)› αυτον χαριν του επιθυμησαι αυτον της βασιλιας αυτου	**11.11** And he discredited him, because he *was* desiring his kingdom.
11.12 κ(αι) αφελομενος αυτου την θυγατερα εδωκεν αυτην ‹τω› Δημητριω και ‹ηλλοιωθη› τω Αλεξανδρω και εφανη η εχθρα αυτων	**11.12** And when *he* had removed *his* daughter from him, he gave her to Demetrius. And he was estranged from Alexander, and their enmity became visible.

11.9 κ(αι) 3° S^{ca} V A 64^{+}236 La$^{109+146}$ \| > S* • της βασιλειας V A 64^{+}236 \| την -ειαν S • **11.10** μεταμεμελημε γαρ S^{ca} V A 64^{+}236 La$^{109+146}$ \| μετα γαρ εμε S* • με αποκτειναι A 64^{+}236 La$^{109+146}$ \| αποκτιναι με S V • **11.11** εψογισε(ν) S^{ca} V* [-γης- V^{b}] A 64^{+}236 La$^{109+146}$ \| εψεξε(ν) S* • **11.12** τω 1° V A 64^{+}236 \| > S • ηλλοιωθη V A 64^{+}236 La$^{109+146}$ \| εδηλωθη S •

11.9–12 Ptolemy sought a **covenant** with Alexander's opponent **Demetrius** (10.67), promising him that **you will become king of your father's kingdom** (though in fact

---

[301] **He was planning harmful plans.** The wording of the Greek is *dielogizeto . . . logismous ponērous,* "he was reasoning harmful reasonings."

Ptolemy's aim was to become king of that kingdom himself: vv 1, 11, 13). He also put asunder those whom God had joined together (Mark 10.9; cf. 1 Sam 25.44) by removing **his daughter from Alexander** (10.57–58), and giving **her to Demetrius.** And he accused Alexander of crimes that he himself was contemplating: **he has sought to kill me.** Those who do evil sometimes accuse others of the very evils that they themselves desire (Gen 39.7–18; Num 16.3, 7).[302]

11.13 και ‹εισηλθεν› Πτολεμαιος εις Α(ν)τιοχιαν και περιεθετο το διαδημα της Ασιας και περιεθετο δυο διαδηματα περι την κεφαλην αυτου το της Αιγυπτου και Ασιας	**11.13** And Ptolemy came into Antioch, and placed on himself the diadem of Asia. And he placed two diadems on his head: the *one* of Egypt and *that* of Asia.

11.13 εισηλθεν S^{ca} V A $64^{+}236$ $La^{109+146}$ | εξη- S* •

11.13 At last, reaching the kingdom's capital, **Antioch** (3.37), Ptolemy was able to crown himself with **two diadems:** that **of Egypt and that of Asia** (the Seleucid kingdom: see the notes on 8.6).

Deaths of Alexander and Ptolemy

11.14 Αλεξανδρος δε ο βασιλευς ην εν Κιλικια κατα τους καιρους εκεινους εκινους οτι απεστατουν οι απο των τοπων εκεινω(ν)	**11.14** But Alexander the king was in Cilicia during those times: for the *people* from those places were rebelling.
11.15 και ηκουσεν Αλεξανδρος και ‹ηλθεν› επ αυτον ‹› πολεμω και εξηγαγεν Πτολεμαιος και απηντησεν αυτω εν χιρι ισχυρα και ετροπωσατο αυτον	**11.15** And Alexander heard, and came against him in battle. And Ptolemy led out *his army,* and met him with a strong hand, and turned him back.

11.15 ηλθεν S^{ca} V A $64^{+}236$ $La^{109+146}$ | -θον S* • πολεμω S^{c} V A $64^{+}236$ $La^{109+146}$ | ^ πο S* •

11.14–15 Alexander, at that time, was away in **Cilicia** (the coastal region to the west, Acts 15.23, 41; 27.5; 21.39), because **the people from those places were rebelling.** He returned and **came against** Ptolemy **in battle,** but was put to flight (**turned ... back**).

11.16 και εφυγε(ν) Αλεξανδρος εις τη(ν) Αραβιαν	**11.16** And Alexander fled into Arabia,

[302] Diodorus also reports that Ptolemy "pretended [*prospoiētheis*] that there was a plot" against him (32.9c [32.32]). Josephus says that Alexander had indeed plotted to kill Ptolemy (*Antiquities,* 13.106–107), but his information is presumably derived either from a less reliable source, or else from a hasty reading of the present passage supplemented with details from the same source as Diodorus.

του σκεπασθηναι ‹αυτον› εκι ο δε βασιλευς Πτολεμαιος υψωθη	to be protected there; but king Ptolemy was exalted.
11.17 και αφιλε(ν) Ζαβδιηλ ο Αραψ τη(ν) κεφαλην Αλεξανδρου και απεστιλεν τω Πτολεμαιω	**11.17** And Zabdiel the Arab took off Alexander's head, and sent *it* to Ptolemy.
11.18 κ(αι) ‹ο› βασιλευς Πτολεμαιος απεθανεν ‹εν› τη ημερα τη τριτη και οι οντες εν τοις οχυρωμασιν αυτου απωλοντο υπο τω(ν) εν τοις οχυρωμασι(ν)	**11.18** And King Ptolemy died on the third day. And the *men* who were in his fortresses were destroyed by those in the fortresses.

11.16 αυτον S^{ca} V A $64^{+}236$ \| > S* • **11.18** ο S^{cb1} V A $64^{+}236$ \| > S* • εν 1° V A $64^{+}236$ $La^{109+146}$ \| > S •

11.16–18 Alexander fled into Arabia (5.39; Neh 4.7; Gal 1.17), seeking protection, but he found only death.[303] **Ptolemy was exalted;** yet his exaltation was worthless (cf. Psa 75.4–7). He won the battle but lost his life (cf. Matt 16.26). After his death, the people in the cities **destroyed** the garrisons that he had left in their **fortresses** (v 3). Thus the hopes of both sides alike came to nothing. Where now were the things they had prepared (Luke 12.20; Rev 18.14)?

Demetrius son of Demetrius becomes king

Jonathan besieges the citadel

11.19 και εβασιλευσεν Δημητριος ετους ζ´ και ξ´ και ρ´	**11.19** And Demetrius became king *in the* hundred and sixty-seventh year.

11.19 Now that both Alexander and Ptolemy were dead, for a short time there was again only one king in Syria: **Demetrius.**

11.20 εν ταις ημεραις εκειναι συνηγαγεν Ιωναθαν τους εκ της Ιουδαιας του ‹εκπολεμησαι› τη(ν) ακραν την εν Ι(ερουσα)λημ και εποιησεν ‹επ› ‹αυτην› μηχανας πολλας	**11.20** In those days Jonathan gathered the *people* from Judea, to overcome in battle the citadel *that was* in Jerusalem; and he made many devices *to use* against it.

11.20 εκπολεμησαι V $64^{+}236$ $La^{[109+]146}$ \| πολ- S \| εποιησαν A • επ S^{cb1} V A $64^{+}236$ $La^{109+146}$ \| εν S* • αυτην S^{ca} V A $La^{109+146}$ \| -τη S* $64^{+}236$ • εκειναις συνηγαγεν V A $64^{+}236$ = εκειναισυνηγαγεν S •

11.20 Jonathan made war against the main remaining trouble spot in Jerusalem, the **citadel** (1.32–36), using **many devices** (5.30; "siege engines," NETS) **against it.** He was not satisfied with cleansing the parts of God's city that were easy to deal with; he was determined to cleanse every part. "Every high thing raised against the knowledge

---

303 He "was put to death by his friends," according to Diodorus (32.10.1 [32.33]).

of God . . . every thought . . . all disobedience" must be overcome (2 Cor 10.5–6), for even a single point of corruption can destroy a whole person or a whole community (1 Cor 5.6–8; 2 Tim 2.16–17; Jas 2.10). God requires His people to be "wholly clean" (John 13.10), "not having a spot or a wrinkle or any one of such things" (Eph 5.27).

11.21 και ⸂επορευθηcαν⸃ τινεc μιcουντεc το εθνοc αυτων ανδρεc παρανομοι προc το(ν) βαcιλεα και απηγγιλα(ν) αυτω οτι Ιωναθαν περικαθητε την ακραν	**11.21** And some *people* who were hating their nation, men *who were* Law-breakers, went to the king, and reported to him that Jonathan was besieging the citadel.
11.22 και ακουcαc ωργιcθη ωc δε ηκουcε(ν) ευθεωc αναζευξαc ηλθεν ειc Πτολεμαιδα και εγραψεν Ιωναθαν του μη περικαθηcθε και του απαντηcαι αυτον αυτω cυνμιcγιν ειc Πτολεμαιδα την ταχιcτη(ν)	**11.22** And when *he* heard, he became angry; but as he heard, straightaway *he* set off *and* came to Ptolemais; and he wrote to Jonathan not to besiege *it,* and to meet him at Ptolemais to negotiate most quickly.

11.21 επορευθηcαν S^{ca} V A 64^{+}236 La$^{109+146}$ | -ημεν S* •

11.21–22 Some **Law-breakers** (1.11) from Israel went to **the king** (cf. 10.61), who ordered **Jonathan not to besiege** the citadel, **and to meet him at Ptolemais** (10.1). The servants of God should not be surprised if they encounter opposition. Similar enemies hindered the Lord's work during the Persian period (Ezra 4.1–6) and in the days of the apostles (Acts 17.5–9; 21.27–30; 1 Thes 2.14–16).

Jonathan finds favor with Demetrius

11.23 ωc ⸂δε⸃ ηκουcεν Ιωναθαν εκελευcεν περικαθηcθαι και ⸂επελεξεν⸃ των πρεcβυτερων Ι(cρα)ηλ και των ⸂ιερεων⸃ και εδωκε(ν) εαυτον τω κινδυνω	**11.23** But when Jonathan heard, he instructed *them* to *keep* besieging *it;* and he chose *some* of the elders of Israel, and *some* of the priests; and he gave *him*self to the danger,
11.24 και λαβων αργυριον και χρυcιον κ(αι) ιματιcμον και ετερα ξενια ⸂πλειονα⸃ και επορευθη προc το(ν) βαcιλεα ειc Πτολεμαιδα και ευρεν χαριν εναντιον αυτου	**11.24** and, having taken silver and gold and clothing and many other provisions for strangers, then he went to the king, to Ptolemais. And he found favor before him.
11.25 και ενετυγχανον κατ αυτου τινεc ανομοι των εκ του εθνουc	**11.25** And some *people* opposed to *the* Law, *some* of *those* from *his* nation, were appealing against him.

11.23 δε S^{ca} V A 64^{+}236 | > S* • επελεξεν V A 64^{+}236 | εξελ- S • ιερεων V A 64^{+}236 La$^{109+146}$ | Ιουδαιων S • **11.24** πλειονα S^{ca} V A 64^{+}236 La$^{109+146}$ | -ν S* •

11.26 και εποιηcε(ν) αυτω ο βαcιλευc καθωc εποιηcαν ‹αυτω οι προ αυτου› και υψωcεν αυτον ενα(ν)τιον των φιλω(ν) αυτου παντων	**11.26** And the king dealt with him just as the *one*s before him had dealt with him. And he exalted him in front of all his Friends,
11.27 κ(αι) εcτηcεν αυτω τη(ν) αρχιερωcυνην κ(αι) οcα αλλα ειχεν τιμια το προτερον κ(αι) εποιηcεν αυτον ‹των› πρωτων φιλων ηγειcθαι	**11.27** and established the high priesthood for him, and all *the* other honors that he had been having previous*ly*. And he made him a leader among the First Friends.

11.26 αυτω / οι προ αυτου V A 64⁺236 La$^{109+146}$ | ~ S • **11.27** των S^{ca} V A 64⁺236 | > S* •

11.23 On receiving the two commands specified in verse 22, Jonathan disobeyed one and obeyed the other. **He instructed** his forces **to keep besieging** the citadel in spite of the king's prohibition. It was a work that God required him to do (see on v 20), and so he had to "obey God rather than human beings" (Acts 5.29; 4.19; cf. Dan 6.10). At the same time, he obeyed the king's command to meet him at Ptolemais (v 24). He **gave himself** ("exposed himself", NAB) **to the danger** (like the dangers described in 2 Cor 11.26; Luke 8.23), as he and his brothers often did (14.29). It was dangerous because his siege of the citadel had provoked the king to anger (v 22), and "the fury of a king is messengers of death" (Prov 16.14). But we cannot disobey someone in authority simply because obedience would be dangerous (1 Pet 2.18–20).

11.24–27 Jonathan met Demetrius at **Ptolemais** (v 22) and **found favor before him.** Demetrius **dealt with him just as** his predecessors (his father, 10.3–6, 22–45; Alexander, 10.15–20, 59–65, 88–89; Ptolemy, 10.60) had done, confirming **the high priesthood . . . and all the other honors that** Jonathan **had been having previously.** The leader of Judea was becoming a more and more important person in the eyes of the surrounding nations. Alexander had appointed him as "a Friend of the king" (10.9–20), and later as one of the "First Friends" (10.65); now Demetrius **made him a leader among the First Friends.**[304] "When a man's ways are pleasing to the LORD, He makes even his enemies to be at peace with him" (Prov 16.7). The Law-breakers had intended to do evil to Israel by their accusations, but God turned it to good (cf. Gen 50.20; Rom 8.28), so that His faithful people might be still further exalted.

11.28 και ηξιωcε(ν) Ιωναθαν τον βαcιλεα	**11.28** And Jonathan presented a request to the king,

[304] **Made him a leader** [*hēgeisthai*] **among the First Friends** ("bestowed on him the rank of head of the first class of king's Friends," REB; cf. Muraoka 318, §3) is sometimes translated "made him to be regarded as one of his chief friends" (ESV; cf. Muraoka 318, §4). However, the usage of *hēgeomai* elsewhere in the book supports the former rendering (3.55; 5.18; 7.5; 9.35, 53; 13.53; etc.).

ποιηcαι την ‹Ιουδαιαν› αφορολογητον και ‹τας τριc τοπαρχιαc› και την Cαμαρειτιν και επηγγειλατο αυτω ταλα(ν)τα τριακοcια	to make Judea and the three ruled provinces, and the Samaritan region, free from tribute, and promised him three hundred talents.
11.29 και ευδοκηcεν ο βαcιλευc και εγραψεν τω Ιωναθαν επιcτολαc περι παντων τουτων εχουcαc το(ν) τροπον τουτον	**11.29** And the king was well pleased, and wrote letters to Jonathan about all these *thing*s, in this way:
11.30 βαcιλευc Δημητριοc Ιωναθαν τω αδελφω χαιρειν και εθνει Ιουδαιων	**11.30** “King Demetrius to Jonathan *his* brother and to *the* nation of *the* Judeans: Rejoice.
11.31 ‹το› α(ν)τιγραφον τηc επιcτοληc ηc εγραψαμε(ν) Λαcθενει τω cυνγενει ‹ημων› περι υμων γεγραφαμε(ν) και προc υμαc οπωc ιδητε	**11.31** *This* copy of the letter that we wrote to Lasthenes our relative about you^{pl}, we have written also to you^{pl}, so that you^{pl} may see *it:*
11.32 βαcιλευc Δημητριοc Λαcθενι τω πατρι χεριν	**11.32** ‘King Demetrius to Lasthenes *his* father: Rejoice.
11.33 τω εθνι των Ιουδαιω(ν) φιλοιc ‹ημων› και cυ(ν)τηρουcιν τα προc ημαc δικαια εκριναμεν αγαθον ποιηcαι χαριν τηc εξ αυτων ευνοιαc προc ημαc	**11.33** To the nation of the Judeans, *who are* our friends, and are keeping the *things* that are right toward us, we have determined to do good, on account of their good will toward us.
11.34 ‹εcτακαμεν› αυτοιc τα τε ορια τηc Ιουδαιαc και τουc τριc νομουc Αφαιρεμα και Λυδδα κ(αι) Ραθαμειν προcετεθηcαν τη Ιουδεα απο τηc Cαμαριτιδοc και παντα τα cυνκυρουντα αυτοιc παcιν τοιc θυcιαζουcιν ιc Ιεροcολυμα αντι των βαcιλικων ων ελαμβανεν ο βαcιλευc παρ αυτων το προτερον κατ ενιαυτο(ν) απο των γενηματων τηc γηc και τω(ν) ακροδρυων	**11.34** We have established for them both the appointed boundaries of Judea and the three legal provinces— Aphairema and Lydda and Ramathaim (they have been added to Judea from the Samaritan region)— and all the *place*s that belong to them, for all the *people* who are sacrificing at Jerusalem, in place of the king’s *taxe*s that the king was receiving from them previous*ly* each year, from the produce of the land and the forest crops.

11.28 Ιουδαιαν S^{ca} V A | -δαια S* | Ιδουμαιαν 64^{+}236 • ταc τριc τοπαρχιαc S^{ca} V A 64^{+}236 $La^{109+146}$ | τριc τριηραρχιαc S* • **11.31** το V A 64^{+}236 | > S • ημων S^{ca} V A 64^{+}236 $La^{109+146}$ | υμ- S* • **11.33** ημων V A 64^{+}236 $La^{109+146}$ | ουcιν S • **11.34** εcτακαμεν V A $La^{109+146}$ | -κιμ- S | -τηcαμ- 64^{+}236 •

11.35 και τα αλλα τα ανηκοντα ημιν απο του νυ(ν) των δεκατων κ(αι) των τελων ‹› τω(ν) ανηκοντων ημι(ν) και ‹τας› του αλος ‹λιμνας› και τους ανηκοντας ημιν στεφανους ‹ παντα› επαρκεσωμεν αυτοις	**11.35** And from now *on,* the other *things* that belong to us—of the tenths and of the payments of the *things* that belong to us, and the lakes of salt, and the crowns that belong to us—all *these* we will provide for them.
11.36 κ(αι) ουκ ‹αθετηθησεται› ουδε εν τουτων απο του νυν ‹και› εις τον απαντα χρονο(ν)	**11.36** And not even one of these *things* shall be set aside at all, from now *on* and for all time.
11.37 νυν ουν επιμελεσθαι του ποιησε τουτων αντιγραφον και δοθητω Ιωναθαν και τεθητω ε(ν) τω ορι τω αγιω εν ‹› τοπω ‹› επισημω	**11.37** Now therefore, take care^{pl} to make a copy of these *things*, and let it be given to Jonathan; and let it be set in the holy mountain, in a conspicuous place.'"

11.35 τελων S^{ca} V A 64^{+}236 La$^{109+146}$ | + και S* • τας S^{ca} V A 64^{+}236 | το S* • λιμνας S^{ca} V A 64^{+}236 | -μνων S* • παντα V A 64^{+}236 | παντας S • **11.36** αθετηθησεται V 64^{+}236 La$^{109+146}$ | αθετησετε S A • και 2° S^{ca} 64^{+}236 La$^{109+146}$ | > S* V A • **11.37** εν 2° V A 64^{+}236 | + τω S • τοπω 64^{+}236 La$^{109+146}$ 7a1 | + επιτηδιω [-ηνιω S*] S^{ca} V A •

11.28–37 Jonathan asked the king **to make Judea and the three ruled provinces** (the **Samaritan region**)[305] **free from tribute** (as his father had decreed, 10.29–30), promising the king **three hundred talents** (a generous offer; see the footnote to 13.16). This request was granted (**the king was well pleased**). The decision was recorded in **letters** addressed not only **to Jonathan . . . and to the nation of the Judeans,** but also to a certain official named **Lasthenes.**[306] The main points were the following:

- The king had **determined**[307] **to do good** to the **Judeans** because of their **good will toward** him: they were his **friends** and were **keeping the things that are right toward** him. God's people are to "do good to all" (Gal 6.10; 1 Thes 5.15), to "walk with proper decency [*euschēmonōs*] toward those who are outside" (1 Thes 4.12), and, if possible, to "be at peace with all people" (Rom 12.18). Even

[305] **And the three ruled provinces, and the Samaritan region.** The second phrase restates the first in slightly different terms (**the three ruled provinces** were components of **the Samaritan region:** v 34; 10.38). Compare, e.g., "and the woman who is unmarried, and the virgin" (1 Cor 7.34). There is no textual authority for the emendation "and the three districts of Samaria" (ESV); and if that had been the original reading, how and why would it have been altered to the existing one?

[306] **Lasthenes** is described as the king's **relative** and his **father.** These terms must indicate Lasthenes' official position, not his biological connections (the king's biological father was the previous Demetrius: 10.67). Jonathan too had been reckoned among the "kings' relatives" (10.89), and Joseph was called "father to Pharaoh" (Gen 45.8; cf. 2 Kgs 6.21).

[307] **We have determined.** The Greek word is *ekrinamen,* "we have judged."

in the time of Judas, when relations with their rulers had been far more troubled, faithful priests on Mount Zion still greeted the enemy leader peacefully and offered burnt offerings on behalf of the king who was persecuting them (7.33).

- **The three legal provinces . . . from the Samaritan region** are now named as **Aphairema**[308] **and Lydda** (near the coastal city of Joppa, Acts 9.38) **and Ramathaim** (in the hill country of Ephraim, 1 Sam 1.1). **Previously,** the king had been **receiving taxes from** those three provinces **each year (from the produce of the land and from the forest crops)**. But **in place of** that arrangement, the three provinces were now **added to Judea.**
- There were various **payments** that used to **belong to** the king, including **tenths** (see on 10.31) and **salt** and **crowns** (see on 10.29). But **from now on,** these would be provided **for them** (the **Judeans**) instead.
- A **copy of these** decrees would **be set in the holy mountain** (Mount Zion: Zec 8.3; Dan 9.16), **in a conspicuous place.**

The second Demetrius does not make such lavish promises in this letter as his father had done in 10.25–45. He does not give Ptolemais to Judea (he really is in control of Ptolemais, v 38, whereas his father was not, 10.1). He does not promise to pay for building programs in Judea (the programs that were actively being carried out seven years earlier, 10.10–11, might well be finished by now). He does not assign the Judeans positions in his army (at this stage he is trying to reduce his military forces, v 38, whereas his father was trying to increase them, 10.2). But his father's letter was demonstrably false and not to be trusted (see the notes on 10.26, 46), whereas every clause of the present letter might possibly be sincere: only time would tell (cf. v 53).

TRYPHO OPPOSES DEMETRIUS

Trypho goes to Antiochus son of Alexander

11.38 και ειδεν Δημητριος ο βαcιλευc	**11.38** And Demetrius the king saw
οτι ηcυχαcεν η γη ενωπιο(ν) αυτου	that the land was quiet in his sight,
και ουδεν αυτω ανθεcτηκι και	and nothing stood against him. And
απελυcεν ‹παcαc› ταc δυναμιc αυτου	he released all his forces,
εκαcτον ειc τον ιδιον τοπο(ν)	each *one* to his own place,
πλην των ξενων ‹δυναμεων›	apart from the strangers' forces
ων εξενολογηcεν απο των νηcων	that he had called from the islands
των εθνων και ηχθραινον αυτω	of the nations. And all the forces
παcαι αι δυναμιc	that *had come* from his fathers
αι απο τω(ν) π(ατε)ρων ‹αυτου›	were at enmity with him.

11.38 παcαc A 64*236 La[109+146] | > S V • δυναμεων V A 64*236 La[109+146] | -μενων S • αυτου 3° 64*236 La[109+146] | > S V A • ηχθραινον S = -αναν V 64*236 | -αcαν A •

[308] **Aphairema.** Cf. Ephron (near Bethel, 2 Chr 13.19), Ophrah (in Benjamin, Josh 18.23), and the city Ephraim (2 Sam 13.23; John 11.54); all of these might possibly refer to the same place.

11.38 Demetrius the king saw that he had no opponents (**nothing stood against him**). Therefore, **he released all his** military **forces,** except for some foreigners (**strangers) from the islands of the nations.** (Demetrius had lived on one of those **islands**—Crete—before his arrival in Syria: 10.67.) The soldiers who had served previous Seleucid kings (**his fathers;** see the notes on 10.1) had been discarded (see notes on v 55), and were now **at enmity with him.**

11.39 Τρυφων δε η(ν) των παρα Αλεξανδρου το προτερον και ειδεν οτι παcαι αι δυναμιc καταγο(ν)γυζουcιν κατα του Δημητριου και επορευθη προc Ιμαλκουε τον Αραβα οc ‹ετρεφεν› Αντιοχον το παιδαριον τον του Αλεξανδρου	**11.39** But Trypho was *one* of those *who had been* alongside Alexander previous*ly*. And he saw that all the forces were grumbling against Demetrius; and he went to Imalcue the Arab, who was bringing up Antiochus the boy, the *son* of Alexander.
11.40 κ(αι) προcηδρευεν αυτω οπωc ‹παραδω αυτον αυτω οπωc› βαcιλευcη αντι του π(ατ)ρ(ο)c αυτου και απηγγειλεν αυτω οcα cυνεταccεν ο Δημητριοc κ(αι) την εχθραν ην εχθρενουcιν αυτω αι δυναμιc αυτου και εμινεν εκει ημεραc πολλαc	**11.40** And he *kept* urging him, so that he might give him over to him, so that he might become king in place of his father. And he told him all the *thing*s that Demetrius had ordered, and the enmity with which his forces were at enmity with him. And he remained there many days.

11.39 ετρεφεν V A 64^{+}236 La$^{109+146}$ | εθρεψεν S^{1} [ετρ- S*] • **11.40** παραδω αυτον αυτω οπωc V [-δοι A] La$^{109+146}$ | αυτον π- αυτω ινα 64^{+}236 | > S •

11.39–40 Trypho,[309] who had **previously** been a supporter of **Alexander,** now saw an opportunity. **Demetrius** had little military support: he had discharged most of his soldiers, and they had turned **against him.** Consequently, Trypho thought it would be possible to set up a different **king**—Alexander's son **Antiochus,** who was being reared by **Imalcue**[310] **the Arab.** (Alexander had fled to Arabia shortly before his death: v 16.)

---

[309] **Trypho** *(Truphōn)*. The ancient Greek name-ending *-ōn* customarily becomes **-o** in English usage: *Platōn* ≡ Plato, *Galliōn* ≡ Gallio, etc. The form "Tryphon" was adopted in KJV and RV, and is still used by some modern historians (e.g., Grainger, *Seleukid Prosopography and Gazetteer,* 69), but NAB, NJB, NRSV, REB, NETS, ESV, SAAS, ISBE, ABD, NIDB, ZEB, and most modern historians use the form **Trypho.** According to Classical sources, Trypho's original name was Diodotus (Diodorus 33.4a; Appian, *Syriaca,* 68.357); he had been appointed by Alexander to govern Antioch (Diodorus 33.3), but had later assisted Ptolemy against Alexander (Diodorus 32.9a [32.32]).

[310] **Imalcue** (*Imalkoue,* S and V; *Eimalkoue,* 64^{+}236; *Ymlk,* 7a1; *Mlkw,* 7h7) is presumably analogous to the Israelite name "Jamlech" (*Ymlk,* 1 Chr 4.34). Trypho's dealings with him are reported also by Diodorus (33.4a).

Trypho **went to Imalcue** and for a long time (**many days**) **kept urging him** to hand over custody of the boy.

Jonathan sends military aid to Demetrius

11.41 και απεςτιλεν Ιωναθαν προς Δημητριον τον βαςιλεα ινα εκβαλη τους εκ της ακρας εξ Ι(ερουςα)λημ και τους εν τοις οχυρωμαςιν ηςαν γαρ πολεμουντες τον Ις(ραη)λ	**11.41** And Jonathan sent to Demetrius the king, in order that he would cast out of Jerusalem the *people* from the citadel, and the *people* in the fortresses: for they *kept* making war against Israel.
11.42 και απεςτιλεν Δημητριος προς Ιωναθαν λεγων ου ταυτα μονον ποιηςω σοι και τω εθνι σου ⸤αλλ η⸥ ⸤δοξη⸥ δοξαςω σε και το εθνος σου αν ευκεριας τυχω	**11.42** And Demetrius sent to Jona- than, saying: "Not only will I do these *thing*s for you† and for your† nation, but I will honor you† and your† nation with honor, if I may find a good time.

11.42 αλλ η S^{ca} A $64^{+}236$ \| αλλα S* V • δοξη S^{ca} V A [^ και $64^{+}236$] \| δοξα S* •

11.41–42 The people in the **citadel** and other enemy strongholds (**fortresses**) kept **making war against Israel** (cf. v 20)—even though their new master **Demetrius** had acknowledged the Judeans as his friends (v 33). **Jonathan** therefore asked Demetrius to **cast** the troublemakers **out of Jerusalem.** The king agreed, promising to **honor you and your nation with honor, if I may find a good time.** Those who wait for a **good time** to do a good work (cf. Acts 24.25) may never **find** it. Demetrius never did (v 53).

Nor did Demetrius keep even his first promise: he never cast out the people from the citadel. Those people left the citadel only much later, and not because of anything done by Demetrius (13.49–52).

11.43 νυν ουν ορθως ποιηςις αποςτιλας μοι ανδρας οι ςυμμαχηςουςιν μοι οτι απεςτηςαν παςαι αι δυναμεις μου	**11.43** Now therefore, you† will do uprightly *by* sending me men who will be military allies for me: for all my forces have departed."
11.44 κ(αι) απεςτιλεν Ιωναθαν ανδρας ⸤͵γ´⸥ δυνατους ιςχυι αυτω εις Α(ν)τιοχιαν και ηλθο(ν) προς τον βαςιλεα και ηυφρανθη ο βαςιλευς επι τη εφοδω αυτων	**11.44** And Jonathan sent three thousand men *who were* powerful with strength to him at Antioch. And they came to the king, and the king was glad at their visit.

11.44 ͵γ´ S^{ca} V A $64^{+}236$ $La^{109+146}$ \| γ´ S* •

11.43–44 By now, Demetrius was in need of **military allies** (for reasons revealed in v 45). **Jonathan sent three thousand men** to help him. Demetrius had responded to Jonathan's request for help with words; Jonathan responded to Demetrius's request for help with deeds (1 Jn 3.18; Jas 2.15–16).

The Judeans rescue Demetrius

11.45 και επιϲυνηχθηϲαν οι απο τηϲ πολεωϲ ειϲ μεϲον τηϲ πολεωϲ ειϲ ανδρων δωδεκα μυριαδαϲ και ηβουλοντο ανελι(ν) τον βαϲιλεα	**11.45** And the *people* from the city gathered in *the* midst of the city, up to a hundred and twenty thousand men. And they were wanting to do away with the king.
11.46 και εφυγεν ο βαϲιλευϲ ειϲ την αυλην και κατελαβοντο οι εκ τηϲ ‹πολεωϲ› ταϲ διοδουϲ τηϲ πολεωϲ και ηρξαντο πολεμι(ν)	**11.46** And the king fled into the courtyard; and the *people* from the city took control of the traveling paths through the city, and began to make war.

11.46 πολεωϲ 1° V A 64⁺236 La[109+146] | οικιαϲ S •

11.45–46 Demetrius was faced with trouble within the very center of his kingdom (3.37), **the city** of Antioch (v 44). A huge number of people, **up to a hundred and twenty thousand men,** had **gathered in the midst of the city** and were seeking to kill him. All the roads **through** the city (**traveling paths**) were under the rebels' **control,**[311] so **the king** had no way of escape.

11.47 και εκαλεϲεν ο βαϲιλευϲ τουϲ Ιουδαιουϲ επι βοηθιαν και επιϲυνηχθηϲαν παντεϲ προϲ αυτο(ν) αμα και διεϲπαρηϲαν εν τη πολι και απεκτιναν εν τη ημερα εκινη ειϲ μυριαδαϲ δεκα	**11.47** And the king called the Judeans for help; and they gathered to him, all together; and they scattered themselves in the city, and killed on that day up to a hundred thousand.
11.48 και ενεπυριϲαν την πολιν και ελαβον ϲκυλα πολλα εν εκινη τη ημερα κ(αι) εϲωϲαν τον βαϲιλεα	**11.48** And they set the city on fire, and took much plunder on that day, and saved the king.
11.49 και ειδον οι απο τηϲ πολεωϲ οτι κατεκρατηϲαν οι Ιουδαιοι τηϲ πολεωϲ ‹ωϲ εβουλοντο› και ηϲθενηϲαν ταιϲ διανοιαιϲ αυτων και ‹εκεκραξαν› προϲ τον βαϲιλεα μετα δεηϲεωϲ λεγοντεϲ	**11.49** And the *people* from the city saw that the Judeans had overpowered the city as they wanted. And they weakened in their minds, and cried out to the king with supplication, saying:
11.50 δοϲ ημιν δεξιαν και παυϲαϲθωϲαν οι Ιουδαιοι πολεμουντεϲ ημαϲ και την πολι(ν)	**11.50** "Give† us *the* right *hand,* and let the Judeans stop making war against us and the city."
11.51 και ερριψαν τα οπλα και εποιηϲαν ιρηνην	**11.51** And they threw away *their* weapons and made peace.

[311] **Took control of.** The Greek word is *katelabonto,* "took hold of" (not necessarily "seized," RV: cf. v 66; Rom 9.30; 1 Cor 9.24; Php 3.12).

και εδοξαcθηcαν οι Ιουδαιοι	And the Judeans were honored
εναντιον του βαcιλεωc και ενωπιο(ν)	in front of the king, and in front
‹παντω(ν)› των εν τη βαcιλεια αυτου	of all the *people* in his kingdom.
‹› κ(αι) ‹επεcτρεψαν› ειc Ι(εpουcα)λημ	And they returned to Jerusalem,
εχοντεc cκυλα πολλα	having much plunder.

11.49 ωc εβουλοντο S^{ca} V A 64^{+}236 La^{109} La^{146} | > S* • εκεκραξαν V A 64^{+}236 | εκρ- S^{ca} | εκρατηcαν S* • **11.51** παντω(ν) S^{ca} V A 64^{+}236 La^{109} La^{146} | > S* • αυτου S^{ca} V A 64^{+}236 La^{109} | + και ωνομαcθηcαν εν τη βαcιλεια αυτου S* La^{146} • επεcτρεψαν S^{ca} V A [απ- 64^{+}236] La^{109} La^{146} | -ψεν S* •

11.47–51 The Judeans . . . saved the king and **killed** most of his enemies in a single **day.**[312] No one in the **city** was able to withstand them: although they were outnumbered forty to one, they did **as they wanted** (in the way that a potter does with a pot, Jer 18.4). The LORD had raised up His people immensely since the time of Antiochus Epiphanes, when the people of Judea were shattered (2.7) and when the king was the one who had power to "do as was his good pleasure," not only in Antioch but throughout his kingdom (Dan 11.36).

The rebels then **weakened in their minds** (the opposite of standing firm and being strong: cf. Heb 11.34; 1 Cor 16.13; Dan 11.32). They threw away their **weapons** and pleaded for **peace,** saying **"Give us the right hand"** (see the notes on 6.58).

Demetrius is estranged from Jonathan

11.52 και εκαθιcεν	**11.52** And Demetrius
Δημητριοc ο βαcιλευc	the king sat
επι θρονου τηc βαcιλιαc αυτου	on *the* throne of his kingdom,
και ηcυχαcεν η γη ενωπιον αυτου	and the land was quiet in his sight.
11.53 κ(αι) ‹εψευcατο› παντα	**11.53** And he lied *in* all *the things* that
οcα ειπεν και ‹ηλλοτριωθη	he had said; and he became estranged
τω› Ιωναθαν και ουκ ‹ανταπεδωκεν	from Jonathan, and did not repay *him*
κατα ταc ευνοιαc	in accordance with the good will
αc ανταπεδωκεν› αυτω	that *Jonathan* had repaid to him; and
και εθλιβεν αυτον cφοδρα	he *began* oppressing him very much.

11.53 εψευcατο S^{ca} V A 64^{+}236 La^{109} La^{146} | εcπευ- S* • ηλλοτριωθη τω S^{ca} V A 64 [ηλλωτ- 236] La^{109} La^{146} | ηλλοτριωθηcαν S* • ανταπεδωκεν κατα ταc ευνοιαc αc ανταπεδωκεν V [κατα > A] 64^{+}236 La^{109} La^{146} | απεδωκεν S •

11.52–53 Very often people will beg help when they are in trouble, but forget to "render again according to the benefit done to" them (2 Chr 32.25; Luke 17.17–18). **Demetrius,** when **the land was quiet in his sight . . . became estranged from Jonathan, and did not repay him in accordance with the good will that Jonathan had**

[312] On that day **up to a hundred thousand** were slain by three thousand (v 44; for similar incidents, cf. 1 Kgs 20.29; 2 Chr 28.6). The incident is recorded also by Diodorus (33.4a).

repaid to him. He had promised to remove oppression from Judea (vv 41–42), yet now he began **oppressing . . . very much** those who had saved him (v 48). Those who, like Jesus, do good, will sometimes be repaid with evil, as He was (Psa 109.4–5; 35.12–16; 38.20; Jer 18.20). Nevertheless, "one who returns evil in return for good, evil will not be removed from his house" (Prov 17.13).

Trypho and Antiochus overpower Antioch

11.54 μετα δε ταυτα	**11.54** But after these *things*
απεστρεψεν Τρυφων και Αντιοχος ‹›	Trypho returned, and Antiochus
μετ αυτου παιδαριον νεωτερον	*the* young boy with him.
και εβασιλευσεν	And he became king,
και επεθετο διαδημα	and put on a diadem.
11.55 και ‹επισυνηχθησαν› προς αυτον	**11.55** And all the forces that Deme-
πασαι αι δυναμις ας απεσκορακισεν	trius had sent to *the* crows gathered to
Δημητριος ‹› και ‹επολεμησαν› προς	him. And they made war against him,
αυτον κ(αι) εφυγεν και ‹ετροπωθη›	and he fled, and was turned back.
11.56 και ελαβεν Τρυφων τα θηρια	**11.56** And Trypho took the animals,
κ(αι) κατεκρατησεν της Αντιοχιας	and overpowered Antioch.

11.54 μετ V A $64^{+}236$ La^{109} La^{146} | ^ και S • **11.55** επισυνηχθησαν S^{ca} [επε-V] A $64^{+}236$ La^{109} La^{146} | επισυνησαν S* • Δημητριος S^{ca} V A $64^{+}236$ La^{109} La^{146} | + ος S* • επολεμησαν A $64^{+}236$ La^{109} La^{146} | -σεν S V • ετροπωθη V A $64^{+}236$ La^{109} La^{146} | -θησαν S •

11.54–56 Trypho now **returned** from Arabia with young[313] **Antiochus** the son of Alexander (vv 39–40), who **became king** and received support from **all the forces that Demetrius had sent to the crows**[314] (i.e., had released from service and sent away, vv 38, 43). **They made war against** Demetrius, who **fled.** Trypho gained possession of **the animals** (the war elephants, 6.35–37), **and overpowered Antioch,** the capital city of the kingdom (3.37).

Antiochus honors Jonathan

11.57 και εγραψεν Αντιοχος	**11.57** And the young Antiochus wrote
ο νεωτερος Ιωναθαν λεγων ιστημι	to Jonathan, saying: "I am establishing
σοι την αρχιερωσυνη(ν)	the high priesthood for you[†];
και καθιστημι σε	and I am establishing you[†]

[313] **Young** *(neōteron)* is comparative in form, but here, as often elsewhere (BDF §244, §2; MHT 3.30, §4; BAGD 669, §§3aβ, 3bβ), means simply **young,** not comparatively "younger" than some other person. Livy (*Periochae,* 52) gives his age as two at this time (cf. Diodorus 33.4a; Appian, *Syriaca,* 68.357).

[314] People who have been **sent to the crows** *(apeskorakisen)* have been sent to the realm of creatures that scavenge the dead (Prov 30.17; Eighteen Psalms 4.22). They have not merely been sent away; they have been sent to the garbage dump.

επι των τεσσαρω(ν) νομων	over the four legal provinces, and *for*
⸤και⸥ ειναι σε των φιλων του βασιλεως	you[†] to be *one* of the king's Friends."
11.58 και απεστιλεν αυτω χρυσωματα	**11.58** And he sent him gold *vessels*
και διακονιαν και εδωκεν αυτω	and a *table* service, and gave him
εξουσιαν πινι(ν) εν χρυσωμασιν	authority to drink from gold *vessels*,
και ειναι εν πορφυρα	and to be in purple,
και εχειν πορπην χρυσην	and to have a golden pin.

11.57 και 3° S^{ca} V A $64^{+}236$ La^{109} La^{146} | > S* •

11.57–58 The new king **Antiochus**[315] **wrote to Jonathan,** confirming the honors that previous rulers had granted or acknowledged: **the high priesthood** (10.20), authority over **the four legal provinces** (Judea plus three provinces from the Samaritan region, v 34), status as **one of the king's Friends** (10.20), and the right **to drink from gold vessels** (a sign of great prosperity, 1 Kgs 10.21; Est 1.7; Dan 5.2–3), **and to be in purple** (a sign of authority, 10.20; 8.14), **and to have a golden pin** (a sign that he was ranked among the king's "relatives," 10.89).

11.59 και Σιμωνα τον αδελφο(ν)	**11.59** And he established Simon
αυτου κατεστησε(ν) στρατηγον	his brother *as* army commander
απο ⸤του κλιματος⸥ Τυρου	from the region of Tyre up to
εως των οριων Αιγυπτου	the appointed boundaries of Egypt.

11.59 του κλιματος $64^{+}236$ La^{109} La^{146} | της Κλιμακος S V A •

11.59 The king also assigned Jonathan's brother **Simon** a very important military post, as **army commander** over the whole of Syria-Palestine, **from the region of Tyre**[316] in the north (5.15; Josh 19.29) **to the appointed boundaries of Egypt** in the south (Josh 15.4; 1 Kgs 4.21). This was either the position held, or a position even broader than that held, by Apollonius, the Judeans' most recent military opponent (see the notes on 10.69). Israel was now treading on the high places of its enemies (Deut 33.29; Josh 10.24–25)—as Israel's King will Himself do on the last day (Psa 110.1–2; Heb 10.13; 1 Cor 15.25).

---

[315] **The young** [*neōteros*] **Antiochus.** The LXX.D treats the adjective as a title, *Antiochos die Jüngere* ("Antiochus the Younger"), distinguishing this **Antiochus** from other kings of the same name (Antiochus the Great, 8.6; Antiochus Epiphanes, 1.10; Antiochus Eupator, 6.17). However, the same Greek adjective three verses earlier (v 54) cannot be read in that way.

[316] **The region** [*klimatos*] **of Tyre** is the reading of $64^{+}236$ (supported by La^{109}, La^{146}, 7h7, and 7a1), whereas S, V, and A read "the Ladder [*klimakos*] of Tyre," reputedly referring to a ladder-like feature of the landscape near Tyre, although its identity is disputed (ISBE 3.60; ABD 4.128; NIDB 5.694–95). At this point all known manuscripts of Josephus (*Antiquities*, 13.146) read *klimatos* (yet nearly all modern editions of Josephus print *klimakos*). Very likely the two similar-sounding Greek words were used interchangeably in ancient times to identify the Tyrian region.

Progress in Galilee and the Philistine region

Gaza submits to Jonathan

11.60 και εξηλθεν Ιωναθαν κ(αι) διεπορευετο περα(ν) του ποταμου και ε(ν) ταις πολεςιν και ηθροιςθηςαν προς αυτον παςα δυναμις Cυριας εις ςυμμαχιαν και ηλθεν εις Αςκαλωνα και απηντηςαν αυτω οι εκ της πολεως ενδοξως	**11.60** And Jonathan came out and passed through *on the* other side of the River and among the cities. And all *the* force of Syria drew together to him for a military alliance. And he came to Ashkelon, and the *people* from the city met him with honor.

11.60 Jonathan traveled through the district **on the other side of the River** (a term used since Persian times to describe Syria-Palestine: Ezra 4.10, 16, 17, 20), from the Philistine region (**Ashkelon;** Gaza, v 61) to Damascus (v 62). **All the** military **force of Syria** was now in **alliance** with him—exactly the reverse of the situation when the Judeans first began to rebel (3.10, 13–14). The people of **Ashkelon . . . met him with honor,** just as they had done a few years earlier (10.86).

11.61 και απηλθεν εκειθεν εις Γαζαν και απεκλιςαν οι απο Γαζης και περιεκαθιςεν περι αυτην και ενεπυριςε(ν) τα περιπολια αυτης () πυρι και εςκυλευςεν αυτας	**11.61** And he went away from there to Gaza. And the *people* from Gaza shut *him* out; and he besieged it, and set its city-surroundings on fire with fire, and plundered them.
11.62 και ηξιωςαν οι απο Γαζης Ιωναθαν κ(αι) εδωκεν αυτοις δεξιαν και ελαβεν τους υιους των αρχοντω(ν) αυτων εις ομηρα και εξαπεςτιλεν αυτους εις Ι(ερουςα)λημ κ(αι) διηλθεν την χωραν εως Δαμαςκου	**11.62** And the *people* from Gaza presented a request to Jonathan; and he gave them *his* right *hand,* and took the sons of their rulers for hostages, and sent them away to Jerusalem. And he went through the district up to Damascus.

11.61 πυρι V 64⁺236 | ^ εν S A •

11.61–62 However, not everyone honored him. Even during their times of greatest prosperity, God's people must expect to face opposition ("Woe to you whenever all people speak well of you," Luke 6.26; John 15.19). Although Ashkelon and the Syrian army accepted Jonathan, **the people from Gaza shut him out.** Gaza was a southern coastal city near the border of Egypt (Gen 10.19; Acts 8.26). Like Ashkelon, it was one of the principal cities of the Philistines (Josh 13.3; 1 Sam 6.17; Amos 1.8). Now Jonathan **besieged it, and set its city-surroundings on fire,** until its inhabitants surrendered and sought his favor (**presented a request to** him,[317] as in vv 66, 28). Then he made peace with them (**gave them the right hand,** cf. 6.58), taking **as hostages** the

[317] **Presented a request to** [*ēxiōsan*] **him** (cf. Acts 28.22), as something that would be "worthy" *(axios)* for him to do (cf. Rom 16.1–2; 1 Cor 16.4; 3 Jn 6; Acts 15.38; BDAG 94, §2b).

sons of some of the city's **rulers.** Even so, this was not the last time that Gaza would cause trouble for Israel (13.43).

Jonathan goes to Galilee

11.63 και ηκουcεν Ιωναθαν οτι παρηcα(ν) οι αρχοντεc Δημητριου ειc ˻Κεδεc˼ τη(ν) εν τη Γαλιλαια μετα δυναμεωc πολληc βουλομενοι μεταcτηcαι αυτο(ν) τηc χριαc	**11.63** And Jonathan heard that Demetrius's commanders were present at Kedesh that *is* in Galilee, with a great force, wanting to shift him away from *his* duty.
11.64 και ˻cυνη(ν)τηcεν αυτοιc˼ ˻τον δε˼ αδελφον αυτου Cιμωνα ˻κατελειπεν˼ εν τη χωρα	**11.64** And he met with them; but he left his brother Simon in the district.

11.63 Κεδεc V 64^{+}236 | Κηδεc S A • **11.64** cυνη(ν)τηcεν αυτοιc S^{ca} V A 64^{+}236 La^{109} La^{146} | -cαν εαυ- S* • τον δε V A 64^{+}236 La^{109} La^{146} | κ(αι) κατελιπεν τον S • κατελειπεν V A 64^{+}236 La^{109} La^{146} | > S •

11.63–64 Antiochus's rival king, **Demetrius,** had fled the region (v 55), but **Jonathan heard that** Demetrius's **commanders** were **at Kedesh,** a city in the hill country of Naphtali **in Galilee** (Josh 20.7; Jdg 4.6, 9–10), **wanting to shift him away from his duty**[318] of subjugating the Judean region (vv 60–62). To deal with this threat, Jonathan divided his forces (just as Judas had previously done when there were problems in different parts of the land at the same time, 5.9–20). He himself went to meet the enemies in Galilee, while **his brother Simon** was **left… in the district** where they had just been (vv 60–62), so that the **duty** there would still be carried out (vv 65–66).

Bethzur submits to Simon

11.65 και παρενεβαλεν Cιμω(ν) επι Βεθcουρα και επολεμει αυτην ημεραc πολλαc και cυνεκλιcεν ˻αυτουc˼	**11.65** And Simon camped against Bethzur, and made war against it many days, and shut them in.
11.66 και ηξιωcαν αυτο(ν) του ˻δεξιαc˼ λαβειν και εδωκεν αυτοιc και εξεβαλεν αυτουc εκειθεν και κατελαβετο την πολιν και εθετο επ αυτην φρουρα(ν)	**11.66** And they presented a request to him to take *their* right *hands*; and he gave *his* to them, and cast them out from there, and took hold of the city, and placed a garrison over it.

11.65 αυτουc 64^{+}236 La^{109} La^{146} | -τη(ν) S V A • **11.66** δεξιαc S^{ca} A 64^{+}236 La^{109} La^{146} | -αν S* V •

---

318 **To shift him away from his duty** *(chr[e]ias).* The sense is not "to remove him from office" (ESV)—which would require the plural "duties" (as in 10.37, 41; 12.45; 13.15, 37; cf. Epitome 7.24)—but "to divert him from his mission" (JB), his "business" (*Geschäfte,* Zöckler), his task of overcoming opposition in and around Judea. (Cf. Epitome 8.20: the Israelites "went to the duty [*chreian*]" of fighting their enemies; Muraoka 735, §2.) **Duty** *(chr[e]ias)* is the reading of S, V, A, and 64^{+}236 (supported by La^{109} and La^{146}), whereas f^{120} has "region" *(chōras).*

11.65–66 The city of **Bethzur** (see on 4.29) was one of the last remaining centers of opposition on the boundaries of Judea (10.14; 14.33). **Simon** now besieged it[319] until its inhabitants sought peace (**presented a request to him to take their right hands,** cf. v 62), which he accepted (**he gave his** right hand **to them**). He then **cast . . . out** the enemies and **placed** an Israelite **garrison** to rule **over** the city. The conquest of this persistent source of trouble was an important step forward for Israel, and is listed repeatedly among Simon's major achievements (14.7, 33).

Jonathan defeats the foreigners in Galilee

11.67 και Ιωναθαν και η παρεμβολη αυτου ‹› παρενεβαλον επι το υδωρ του ‹Γεννηcαρ› και ωρθριcαν το πρωι ειc το παιδιον Αcωρ	**11.67** And Jonathan and his company camped close by the water of Gennesaret. And they got up at dawn *in* the early morning, *and went* to the level place of Hazor.

11.67 αυτου V A 64⁺236 La[109] La[146] | + και S • Γεννηcαρ S[ca] A 64⁺236 La[109] [La[146]] | -cαι S* •

11.67 While Simon was besieging Bethzur, **Jonathan and his company** went to Galilee (v 64), where they **camped close by the water of Gennesaret** (the Sea of Galilee, Luke 5.1; Mark 6.53) and proceeded **to the level place of Hazor** (near Kedesh, Josh 19.36–37; 2 Kgs 15.29).

11.68 και ιδου η παρεμβολη αλλοφυλων απηντα αυτω εν τω παιδιω και ‹εξεβαλον› ‹επ αυτον ενεδρον› εν τοιc ορεcιν αυτοι δε ‹απηντηcαν› εξ ενα(ν)τιαc	**11.68** And, see! the company of *the* foreigners *began* meeting him in the level place. And they set an ambush against him in the mountains; but they themselves met *him* face to face.
11.69 τα δε ενεδρα εξανεcτηcαν εκ τω(ν) τοπων αυτων κ(αι) cυνηψαν πολεμο(ν)	**11.69** But those *who were* in ambush rose up out of their places, and made contact in battle.
11.70 ‹κ(αι) εφυγον› οι παρα Ιωναθαν παντεc ουδε ειc κατελιφθη απ αυτων πλην Ματταθιαc ‹ο› του ‹Αψαλωμου› και Ιουδαc ο του Χαφει αρχοντεc τηc cτρατιαc των δυναμεω(ν)	**11.70** And the *men* alongside Jonathan all fled; not even one of them was left, apart from Mattathias the *son* of Absalom, and Judas the *son* of Chaphi, commanders of the army of the forces.

11.68 εξεβαλον S[ca] A 64⁺236 La[109] La[146] | -λεν S* V • επ αυτον / ενεδρον 64⁺236 La[109] La[146] | ~ S [-τοιc V] A • απηντηcαν V A 64⁺236 | παριcτηκιcαν S • **11.70** κ(αι) εφυγον S[ca] V A 64⁺236 La[146] [*fugerunt* La[109]] | > S* • ο 1° V A 64⁺236 | > S • Αψαλωμου V A La[109] [Αβεσσαλ- 64⁺236 La[146]] | Ψαλμωδου S •

---

319 **Shut them** [*autous*] **in** is the reading of 64⁺236 (supported by La[109], La[146], 7h7, and 7a1), whereas S, V, and A read "shut it [*autēn*] in."

11.68–70 While some of the **foreigners** met Jonathan's army **face to face . . . in the level place**, others ambushed them from the **mountains** nearby. **All** of those on Jonathan's side **fled,** except for two army leaders. Moses had scarcely more supporters left when the congregation turned against him at Kadesh in the wilderness (Num 14.10). Elijah on Mount Carmel, Jesus on the night when He was betrayed, and Paul at his first defense, had no human support of any kind (1 Kgs 18.21–22; 19.10; John 16.32; 2 Tim 4.16). Many who joyfully receive the word at first wither away when trouble or persecution comes (Matt 13.20–21). Those who walk by sight and not by faith (cf. 2 Cor 5.7), who set their minds on the things of earth and not the things above (cf. Col 3.2), and who forget that He who is with them is greater than he who is in the world (cf. 1 Jn 4.4), will turn back in the day of attack (cf. Psa 78.9). But there are a faithful few who will continue steadfastly through every trial (Prov 17.17; Php 2.19–22). Two **leaders of the forces—Mattathias the son of Absalom, and Judas the son of Chaphi**[320]—still remained with Jonathan.

11.71 και διερρηξεν Ιωναθαν τα ιματια αυτου και επεθετο γην επι την κεφαλην αυτου και προcηυξατο	**11.71** And Jonathan tore his clothes, and put earth on his head, and prayed.

11.71 Like Joshua after the defeat at Ai (Josh 7.6), **Jonathan tore his clothes, and put earth on his head** (in distress, 3.47; Job 2.12; 2 Sam 13.19), **and prayed.** "Is anyone among you suffering? let him pray . . . . A righteous person's request, working, has much strength" (Jas 5.13, 16).

11.72 και ‹υπεcτρεψεν› προc αυτουc πολεμω και ετροπωcατο αυτουc και εφυγον	**11.72** And he returned against them for battle, and turned them back, and they fled.
11.73 και ειδον οι φευγοντεc παρ αυτου και επεcτρεψαν επ αυτον και εδιωκαν μετ αυτου εωc Κεδεc εωc τηc παρεμβοληc αυτω(ν) και παρενεβαλον εκει	**11.73** And the *people* from alongside him, who were fleeing, saw *this,* and turned back to him, and *began* pursuing with him up to Kedesh, up to their camp. And they camped there.
11.74 και επεcον εκ των αλλοφυλων ε(ν) τη ημερα εκεινη ειc ανδραc τριcχιλιουc και επεcτρεψεν Ιωναθαν ειc Ι(ερουcα)λημ	**11.74** And up to three thousand men from the foreigners fell on that day. And Jonathan returned to Jerusalem.

11.72 υπεcτρεψεν S^{ca} V [επ- A] 64^{+}236 La^{109} La^{146} | -ρεφον S* •

11.72–74 When Jonathan, having prayed to the Lord, **returned against** his enemies, he **turned them back, and they fled.** It may sometimes take more than one attempt

[320] **Chaphi** *(Chaphei)* is the spelling in S and 64^{+}236 (supported by La^{109} and La^{146}) ≡ Hebrew *Ḥpwy* or Aramaic *Ḥpy,* whereas V and A have *Chalphei* ≡ Aramaic *Ḥlpy.*

to achieve success (Josh 7.4–5; 8.1; 2 Sam 6.1–17), but one man can put to flight a thousand when the LORD his God fights for him (Josh 23.10; Deut 32.30). This success caused the **fleeing** Israelites to turn back and assist Jonathan. The **foreigners** were pursued all the way back to **their camp** at **Kedesh** (v 63)—and the Israelites themselves **camped there.** The LORD causes His people to inherit what has belonged to their enemies (Psa 105.44; 78.55; 37.10–11; Acts 13.19; Josh 24.13).

RENEWED ALLIANCES WITH ROME AND SPARTA

Jonathan sends to Rome and Sparta

12.1 και ειδεν Ιωναθαν οτι ο καιροϲ αυτω ϲυνεργει και επελεξατο ανδραϲ και απεϲτιλεν ειϲ Ρωμην ϲτηϲαι και ανανεωϲαϲθαι την προϲ αυτουϲ φιλιαν	**12.1** And Jonathan saw that the time was working to assist him; and he chose men, and sent *them* to Rome, to establish and renew the*ir* friendship with them.
12.2 και ‹προϲ Σπαρτιαταϲ› και ειϲ τοπουϲ ετερουϲ απεϲτιλεν επιϲτολαϲ κατα ταυτα	**12.2** And he sent letters to the Spartans and to other places, in accordance with these *things*.
12.3 και επορευθηϲαν ειϲ Ρωμην και ειϲηλθον ειϲ το βουλευτηριον και ειπον Ιωναθαν ο αρχιερευϲ και το εθνοϲ των Ιουδαιων απεϲτιλεν ημαϲ ανανεωϲαϲθαι την φιλιαν εαυτοιϲ και την ϲυμμαχιαν κατα το προτερον	**12.3** And they went to Rome, and came into the council house, and said: "Jonathan the high priest, and the people of the Judeans, have sent us to renew for *them*selves the*ir* friendship and military alliance, in accordance with *the* previous *time.*"
12.4 και εδωκαν ‹αυτοιϲ επιϲτολαϲ› προϲ αυτουϲ κατα τοπον οπωϲ προπεμπωϲιν αυτουϲ ειϲ γην Ιουδα μετ ειρηνηϲ	**12.4** And they gave them letters to the *people* in each place, so that they would help them on their way to *the* land of Judah in peace.

12.2 προϲ Σπαρτιαταϲ S[ca] V A 64[+]236 = προϲπαρτιαταϲ S* • **12.4** αυτοιϲ / επιϲτολαϲ 64[+]236 La[109] La[146] | ~ S V A •

12.1–4 Jonathan saw that the time was working to assist him.[321] Not all times are helpful for all purposes (Ecc 3.1–8). Jonathan and his brothers knew that the Lord's work had to be done "in season [*eukairōs*], out of season [*akairōs*]" (2 Tim 4.2), whether the **time** *(kairos)* was assisting or hindering (cf. 9.10). When the time did

[321] **The time was working to assist** [*sunergei*] **him.** "The time helped him" (DRV; *le ayudaba,* VRV), by collaborating with *(sun-)* him in the work he had to do *(ergei)*. (Zöckler puts it deftly in German: the time *ihm förderlich war.*) The same Greek word is used to describe how the Lord collaborated together with His disciples in their work (Mark 16.20), how faith and works collaborated together in the life of Abraham (Jas 2.22), and how all things collaborate together for good to those who love God (Rom 8.28); cf. BDAG 969; TDNT 7.871–76.

assist them, they were eager to make the most of it, "redeeming" it, buying it up for their own use (Eph 5.16; Col 4.5). The same principle applies today. "As we have time [*kairon*], let us work good for all" (Gal 6.10). Jesus said: "We must work the works of the One who sent Me, while it is day; night is coming, when no one is able to work" (John 9.4).

Therefore Jonathan **sent** two men (Numenius and Antipater, v 16) **to Rome, to establish and renew** the alliance that Judas had established at a **previous time** (8.17–32), and also **to the Spartans**[322] **and to other places,** with messages of the same kind (**in accordance with these things**).

When Numenius and Antipater had reached Rome, the Romans provided them with **letters** instructing **the people in each place** to **help** the Judeans **on their way** back **to the land of Judah in peace.** Jesus' disciples are to provide their allies in the work of the Lord with similar help (3 Jn 5–8; Acts 15.33). Paul, for instance, wrote instructing the church at Corinth: "If Timothy should come ... send him forward on his way in peace" (1 Cor 16.10–11).

Jonathan's letter to Sparta

12.5 και τουτο το α(ν)τιγραφον των επιcτολων ων εγραψεν Ιωναθαν τοιc Cπαρτιαταιc	**12.5** And this *is* a copy of the letters that Jonathan wrote to the Spartans:
12.6 Ιωναθαν αρχιερευc και η γερουcια του εθνουc και οι ιερειc και ο λοιποc δημοc τω(ν) Ιουδαιων Cπαρτιαταιc τοιc αδελφοιc χαιρειν	**12.6** "Jonathan *the* high priest, and the eldership of the nation, and the priests, and the rest of *the* people of the Judeans, to *the* Spartans *their* brothers: Rejoice.

12.5–6 Jonathan's **letters ... to the Spartans** show how the Israel of God was structured at that time: **the priests and the rest of the people** were governed by their **high priest** (cf. 14.35) and by their **eldership** (v 35; 13.36; under the high priest's authority, cf. 10.38; Acts 5.21). The Israel of God today is similarly structured. We have "a great high priest ... Jesus the Son of God" (Heb 4.14), under whose authority are "elders in every church" (Acts 14.23; Titus 1.5). The only significant difference is that, in the church today, all the people are priests (Rev 1.6; 5.10; 1 Pet 2.5, 9).

The Israelites addressed the **Spartans** as **brothers,** just as their forefathers had been on terms of brotherhood with some of the peoples around them (Gen 29.4; 1 Kgs 9.13; cf. Gen 19.7; Ezek 16.48; Amos 1.9; and see v 21 below).

12.7 ετι προτερο(ν) απεcταληcαν επιcτολαι προc Ονιαν τον αρχιερεαν	**12.7** Letters have already been sent previous*ly* to Onias the high priest

[322] **To the Spartans** *(pros Spartiatas)*. In S* a single *s* does double duty as both the last component of the preposition and the first component of the noun (Thackeray §9.1); cf. 11.20 and the footnote to Eighteen Psalms 10.9.

παρα δ Αριου του βασιλευοντος εν υμιν οτι εσται αδελφοι ημω(ν) ‹ως› το αντιγραφον υποκειται	and from Areus, the *one* who was king among you[pl], *saying* that you[pl] are our brothers, as the copy placed below states.
12.8 και επεδεξατο ο Ονιας τον ανδρα τον απεσταλμενον ενδοξως και ελαβεν τας επιστολας εν αις διεσαφειτο περι συμμαχιας και φιλιας	**12.8** And Onias accepted with honor the man who was sent, and he received the letters, in which the *matter* concerning military alliance and friendship was made clear.

12.7 ως S^{ca} V A $64^{+}236$ La^{109} La^{146} | ω S* •

12.7–8 The alliance with Rome had been established in the time of Judas (8.17–32). The alliance with Sparta had been established at an even earlier time, when **Onias** had been **the high priest** of Israel.[323] At that time, **Areus**[324] (who was then **king among** the Spartans) had written **to Onias** establishing a **military alliance and friendship** between their two nations. A **copy** of the letter from Areus is **placed** at the end of (**below**) Jonathan's current letter (see vv 19–23).[325]

12.9 ημεις ουν απροσδεεις τουτων οντες παρακλησιν εχοντες τα βιβλια τα αγια τα εν ταις χερσιν ημων	**12.9** We ourselves, therefore— while *we* are in no need of these *things*, having *for our* encouragement the holy books that *are* in our hands—
12.10 επιραθημεν αποστιλαι την προς υμας αδελφοτητα και φιλιαν ανανεωσασθαι προς το μη εξαλλοτριωθηναι υμων πολλοι γαρ καιροι διηλθον αφ ου απεστιλατε προς ημας	**12.10** we have tried to send *this* to renew the brotherhood and friendship toward you[pl], *so as* not to become utter strangers from you[pl]: for much time has gone past since *the time* when you[pl] sent to us.

---

[323] **Onias** (Greek *Onias* ≡ Hebrew *Ywḥnn,* "Johanan") was the name of several high priests. The identity of the one named here is uncertain (ISBE 3.605). He might possibly be the Onias mentioned by Ben Sira (Sir 50.1). Josephus (*Antiquities,* 12.225–227) identified him with the Onias mentioned in the Maccabean Epitome, but this is certainly wrong (that Onias lived at a later time; Epitome 3.1; 15.12).

[324] Ancient Greek manuscripts had no distinction between uppercase and lowercase letters, and no spaces between the words. Therefore *para d Ariou* (**and from Areus;** cf. v 20) tended to be misread, even in ancient times, as *para Dariou* ("from Darius," KJV)—a much more familiar name, but a Medo-Persian one (1.1; Dan 5.31; Ezra 4.5), not a Greek one. Classical historians list two kings of Sparta named Areus, the first of whom reportedly reigned 44 years and died around 265 BCE (Diodorus 20.29.1); the second, a child, reigned for a short time around 255 BCE (Pausanias 3.6.6). Cf. Schürer-Vermes, 1.184–85.

[325] **As the copy placed below states.** The wording of the Greek is *hōs to antigraphon hupokeitai,* "as the copy is placed below."

12.9–10 Much time had now **gone past since** the letter from Areus was **sent.** Therefore, Jonathan and his people were writing **to renew** their **brotherhood and friendship** with Sparta—even though they did not **need** any human assistance (cf. vv 14–15), **having for our encouragement the holy books**[326] **that are in our hands.** "It is better to seek refuge in the LORD than to be confident in humanity" (Psa 118.8), and in the **holy books** of His word we have no shortage of such **encouragement** from Him: "Whatever was written formerly was written for our learning, so that, through patience and the encouragement of the Scriptures, we might have hope" (Rom 15.4; 2 Tim 3.16–17; 1 Cor 10.11).

12.11 ημειc ουν εν παντι καιρω	**12.11** We ourselves, therefore,
αδιαλιπτωc εν ‹› ταιc εορταιc	are mindful of you^{pl} on every occasion
και ‹εν› ταιc λοιπαιc καθηκουcαιc	without ceasing, in the feasts
ημεραιc μνηcκομεθα υμων	and on the rest of *the* appropriate days,
εφ ω(ν) προcφερομεν ‹θυcιων›	in *the* sacrifices that we are offering,
και εν ταιc προcευχαιc	and in *our* prayers,
ωc δεον εcτι(ν) και πρεπον	as it is binding and fitting
μνημονευειν αδελφω(ν)	to be mindful of brothers.
12.12 ευφρενομεθα δε	**12.12** And we are glad
επι τη δοξη υμων	at your^{pl} glory.

12.11 ταιc 1° V A $64^{+}236$ La^{109} La^{146} | ^ τε S • εν 3° V A $64^{+}236$ La^{109} La^{146} | > S • μνηcκομεθα S = μιμν- V A $64^{+}236$ • θυcιων A $64^{+}236$ La^{109} La^{146} | -ιαν S V •

12.11 The Israelites were **mindful of** the Spartans in their **sacrifices** and **prayers,** during the **feasts** and other **appropriate days** appointed by the old covenant law (Num 28.2–29.39).[327] (Compare the "whole burnt offering being offered on behalf of the king" in 7.33.) And they did this not only once or twice, but **on every occasion without ceasing**—just as we today are to offer prayers without ceasing (Eph 6.18; 1 Thes 5.17; 1.2–3; 3.9–10; 2 Tim 1.3; Rom 1.9) and for all people (1 Tim 2.1–2).

12.12 We are glad at your glory. Despite their own adversities ("many oppressions and many wars," v 13), the Judeans rejoiced that their Spartan allies were prospering, as John the Baptist rejoiced in the greater glory of Jesus (John 3.29–30), and as Paul in prison rejoiced in the steadfast faith of his brethren at liberty (Col 2.5; Php 4.1). If one member of a body is honored, all the members rejoice with it (1 Cor 12.26–27; cf. Rom 12.15).

---

[326] **The holy books.** God's word was given by the Holy Spirit (2 Pet 1.21) through holy men (2 Pet 3.2); it is **holy** itself (Rom 1.2); and it is able to make holy (sanctify, John 17.17; Eph 5.26; Acts 20.32; 1 Tim 4.5).

[327] To do this was not only **fitting** (appropriate, *prepon;* compare 1 Tim 2.10; Eph 5.3) but also **binding** (obligatory, *deon;* compare Heb 2.1; Matt 16.19). "It is necessary [binding, *dei*] to obey God" (Acts 5.29): that is, we cannot do otherwise (*ou dunametha … mē,* Acts 4.19–20).

12.13 ημας δε εκυκλωσα(ν) πολλαι θλιψις και πολεμοι πολλοι κ(αι) επολεμησαν ημας οι βασιλεις οι κυκλω ημων	**12.13** But *as for* us, many oppressions and many wars have surrounded *us,* and the kings who *are* round about us have made war against us.
12.14 ουκ ηβουλομεθα ουν παρενοχλησαι υμιν και ‹τοις λοιποις συμμαχοις και φιλοις› ημων εν τοις πολεμοις τουτοις	**12.14** We were unwilling, therefore, to cause *any* difficulty for you[pl], and for the rest of our military allies and friends, in these wars:
12.15 εχομεν γαρ την εξ ουρανου βοηθεια(ν) βοηθουσαν ημιν και ερρυσθημεν απο των εχθρων ‹ημων› και εταπινωθησαν οι εχθροι ημων	**12.15** for we have the help *that is* from Heaven helping us; and we have been delivered from our enemies, and our enemies have been made low.
12.16 επελεξαμεν ουν Νουμηνιον Αντιοχου και Αντιπατρον Ιασονος και απεσταλκαμεν προς Ρωμαιους ανανεωσασθαι την προς αυτους φιλιαν και συμμαχιαν την προτερον	**12.16** We have chosen, therefore, Numenius *son* of Antiochus, and Antipater *son* of Jason, and we have sent *them* to *the* Romans, to renew *our* previous friendship and military alliance with them.
12.17 ενετιλαμεθα ουν αυτοις και προς υμας πορευθηναι και ασπασασθαι υμας και αποδουναι υμιν τας παρ ημων επιστολας περι της ανανεωσεως και της αδελφοτητος ημων	**12.17** We have commanded them, therefore, to go also to you[pl], and to greet you[pl] and give you[pl] *these* letters from us concerning the renewal and our brotherhood.
12.18 και νυν καλως ποιησεται αντιφωνησαντες ημιν προς ταυτα	**12.18** And now, you[pl] will do well *by* replying to us *as* to these *things*."

12.14 τοις λοιποις συμμαχοις και φιλοις 64⁺236 La[109] La[146] | τους λοιπους συμμαχους και φιλους S V A • **12.15** ημων 1° V* A 64⁺236 La[109] | > S V[a] La[146] •

12.13–15 During their **many oppressions and many wars,** the Judeans had relied on **the help that is from Heaven** (cf. Acts 26.22) rather than on any human power (even that of their **military allies and friends** in Sparta and Rome). Ezra, similarly, "was ashamed to ask from the king a force and horsemen to help us against the enemy in the way, for we had spoken to the king, saying, 'The hand of our God is for good on all those who seek Him . . . .' And we fasted and besought our God about this, and He was indeed entreated by us" (Ezra 8.22–23). God's people "have the power to do all things through the One who strengthens" them (Php 4.13). If "the LORD is for me, I will not fear; what will humanity do to me?" (Psa 118.6; Rom 8.31; cf. 1 Jn 4.4).

As a result, **we have been delivered from our enemies.** When the Israelites first left Egypt, the LORD "saved them from the hand of the one who hated, and redeemed them from the hand of the enemy" (Psa 106.10; Exod 14.30). Then, under the old covenant, He promised His people that, when they served Him faithfully, "I will give peace in the land, and you will lie down, and there will be no one who terrifies you... and the sword will not pass through in your land, and you will pursue your enemies, and they will fall before you" (Lev 26.6–7). "The LORD made a covenant, and commanded them, saying... The LORD your God you shall fear, and He will deliver you out of the hand of all your enemies" (2 Kgs 17.35, 39). In accordance with that promise, "many times He delivered them" (Psa 106.43; Josh 21.44; Jdg 2.16; 1 Sam 12.11; Neh 9.27). And, looking further ahead, He promised them an even greater "salvation from our enemies, and from the hand of all those who hate us... to grant us to serve Him without fear, having been delivered out of the hand of our enemies" (Luke 1.71–74). "Israel will be saved by the LORD, a lasting salvation; you will not be put to shame and will not be disgraced, to ages of continuing time" (Isa 45.17; 35.9–10). Those prophecies have finally been fulfilled through Jesus (Zec 9.9–10 ≡ Matt 21.4–5; Rom 11.26; 1 Cor 15.25–26; Heb 2.15; 2 Cor 1.10). "Thanks be to God, the One who gives us the victory through our Lord Jesus Christ" (1 Cor 15.57).

And our enemies have been made low. "Everyone who exalts himself will be made low" (Luke 14.11) by the LORD: "With the arm of Your strength You have scattered Your enemies" (Psa 89.10).

The Spartans' earlier letter to the high priest Onias

12.19 και τουτο το αντιγραφον των επιcτολων ων απεcτιλαν Ονια	**12.19** And this *is* a copy of the letters that they had sent to Onias:
12.20 Αρηc βαcιλευc Cπαρτιατων Ονεια ιερει μεγαλω χαιρειν	**12.20** "Areus, king of *the* Spartans, to Onias *the* great priest: Rejoice.
12.21 ευρεθη εν γραφη περι τε των Cπαρτιατων και Ιουδαιων οτι ειcιν αδελφοι και οτι ειcιν εκ γενουc Αβρααμ	**12.21** It has been found in writing, concerning both the Spartans and Judeans, that they are brothers, and that they are from *the* race of Abraham.

12.20–21 The **Spartans** said[328] they had **found in writing** (cf. Ezra 6.2; Est 6.2), **concerning both the Spartans and Judeans, that they are brothers, and that they are from the race of Abraham.** The **writing** consulted by the Spartans no longer survives (very few Spartan documents have been preserved); therefore, it is impossible to know exactly what it said, or how reliable it may have been.[329]

---

[328] The end of v 19 (**... to Onias**) and the start of v 20 (**Areus the king...**) are correctly given by S[1]: *Onia Arēs basileus* (supported by 7a1). Most Greek manuscripts (including V, S[ca], A, and 64[+]236, supported by 7h7) merge the two names into one, and read *On[e]iarēs basileus.* In all known Latin manuscripts, that name's last syllable has been further conflated with the next word, *rex* ("the king"), so that the text is reduced to such forms as *Onia rex* (La[109]). (The text printed in Clementine editions of Vg, *Onias. Arius rex,* has no Latin manuscript authority.)

[329] The Maccabean History merely quotes what the Spartans said, and neither supports nor opposes it. A belief that Spartans and Jews were closely related is independently reported by the Maccabean Epitome, in a different context (Epitome 5.9). Various ancient Greek writings

12.22 και νυν αφ ου εγνωμεν ταυτα καλωc ποιηcετε γραφοντεc ημιν περι τηc ειρηνηc υμω(ν)	**12.22** And now, since we have come to know these *things*, you[pl] will do well *by* writing to us concerning your[pl] peace.
12.23 και ˏημειcˎ δε ˏαντιγραφομενˎ υμιν τα κτηνη υμων κ(αι) η υπαρξιc υμων ημι(ν) εcτιν και τα ημων υμιν εcτιν εντελλομεθα ουν οπωc απαγγειλωcιν υμι(ν) κατα ταυτα	**12.23** And we ourselves also are writing back to you[pl] *that* your[pl] livestock and your[pl] possessions are for us, and ours are for you[pl]. We are commanding, therefore, that they may report to you[pl] in accordance with these *things*."

12.23 ημειc S[ca] V A 64[+]236 La[109] La[146] | υμ- S* • αντιγραφομεν S[ca] V A 64[+]236 La[109] La[146] | -ονμεν S* •

12.23 The Romans were a prominent military power (8.1–13), and their treaty was mainly concerned with military assistance (8.24–32). The Spartans by this time had little military power; instead, their treaty offered help mainly with property and resources: **your livestock and your possessions are for us, and ours are for you.** Similar agreements were often made by nations in ancient times (cf. 1 Kgs 22.4; 2 Kgs 3.7), and the same attitude should exist today in the church: "The heart and soul of the multitude who believed was one; and not one was saying that any of the things belonging to him was his own, but all things were common among them" (Acts 4.32), "as anyone had need" (Acts 2.44–45).[330]

---

state—rightly or wrongly—that some of the Spartans' ancestors had been Cadmean Phoenicians from the eastern shores of the Mediterranean (cf. Herodotus 5.57–61; 4.149; Pausanias 3.15.8; 4.7.8; Diodorus, 11.3.2; Pindar, *Pythian* 5.75–76; *Isthmian* 7.17–18). This may have led the Spartans to think that they were related to the Israelites. (Indeed, if Areus and his counselors had any detailed information about Semitic genealogies, they might possibly have connected their ancestors with Abraham's offspring by Keturah or Hagar; Gen 25.1–6, 12–18: see VanderKam, *From Joshua to Caiaphas,* 135–36.) Calmet's carefully balanced conclusions remain valid: "Neither the materials that remain today in the holy Scriptures of the Jews, nor the writings of Greek or foreign authors, yield us sufficiently clear and substantial proofs … to persuade us that these two nations were offshoots of the same stock, and that Abraham had been the father of both …. But as [the Spartans] could have known on that subject many things unknown to us today, we cannot unreservedly accept the view that this genealogy was fictitious and imaginary. We cannot judge what is beyond our knowledge" (Calmet xvi–xxii; cf. Barotti, *Lezioni sacre,* 2.276).

In Hellenistic times, claims of kinship between distant nations were not uncommon. The people of Lampsacus said that they were related to the Romans (SIG[3] 2.591); there were reports of kinship between the Sidonians and the people of Thebes in Greece (Moretti, *Iscrizioni agonistiche greche,* 41), and, apparently, between the Tyrians and those of Delphi (SEG 2.330).

[330] In its current form, "this letter is not a verbatim copy of the official treaty, but simply a resumé of its substance" (Keil 206). It has obviously been converted from the Spartans' original Greek into Hebrew, and then back into the Maccabean History's Hebraic Greek; the interme-

FURTHER PROGRESS

Jonathan on the Syrian border

12.24 και ηκουcε(ν) Ιωναθαν οτι επεcτρεψαν ‹οι› αρχοντεc Δημητριου μετα δυναμεωc πολληc υπερ το προτερον του πολεμηcαι προc αυτο(ν)	**12.24** And Jonathan heard that Demetrius's commanders had returned with a great force, more than previous*ly*, to make war against him.

12.24 οι S[ca] V A 64[+]236 \| > S* •

12.24 Jonathan had previously driven **Demetrius' commanders** away from Kedesh in Galilee (11.63–74). But an evil is seldom repelled permanently by a single victory. Now he **heard that** they **had returned with a great force, more than previously, to make war against him.**

12.25 και απηρεν εξ Ι(ερουcα)λημ και απηντηcεν αυτοιc ειc την ‹Αμαθιτιν χωραν› ου γαρ εδωκε(ν) αυτοιc ανοχην του εμβατευcε ειc την χωραν αυτου	**12.25** And he moved away out of Jerusalem, and met them in the Hamath-region district: for he did not give them *any* oppor- tunity to go into his *own* district.

12.25 Αμαθιτιν / χωραν V A 64[+]236 La[109] La[146] \| ~ S •

12.25 Jonathan **did not give** the evildoers **any opportunity to go into** the land of Judea (**his own district**). Before they could get that far, he **met them** on the northern boundary between Israel and Syria, **in the Hamath-region district**[331] (Num 34.7–8; Zec 9.1–2; cf. 1 Kgs 8.65; 2 Kgs 14.25). An evil is best stopped in its very earliest stages (cf. 1 Cor 5.6–8; Gal 2.5).

12.26 και απεcτιλεν καταcκοπουc ειc την παρεμβολη(ν) αυτου και επεcτρεψαν και απηγγιλαν αυτω οτι ουτωc ταccονται επιπεcιν επ αυτουc την νυκτα	**12.26** And he sent spies into his camp; and they returned and reported to him that they had been designing this: to fall on them *in* the night.

---

diate Hebrew stage can still be glimpsed in such places as the inquiry **concerning your peace** (v 22)—which is a Hebrew, not a Classical Greek expression (cf. 1 Sam 17.18, 22; 2 Sam 8.10; 11.7). Claims that the letter is a forgery have no foundation. Its current wording is Hebraic, but its content has abundant parallels with other Hellenistic documents at every point (Keil 204–06; Rawlinson, "I Maccabees," 502; Gillet 170–71)—even the most unlikely-looking point, the Spartans' claim of kinship with Israel.

[331] **The Hamath-region district** *(tēn Hamathitin chōran).* The Greek wording emphasizes doubly that the reference is not to the city itself *(Hamath),* but to the general district (*chōran,* as in 3.29, 37; 7.24; 8.3; Matt 2.12) of its region (*-itin,* as in 5.17; 10.30; John 4.9). Compare "the Trachon-region district" (*Trachōnitidos chōras,* Luke 3.1).

12.27 ωc δε εδυ ο ηλιοc επεταξεν Ιωναθαν τοιc παρ αυτου γρηγορειν και ειναι επι τοιc οπλοιc ετοιμαζεcθαι ειc πολεμον δι ολης της νυκτος και εξεβαλεν προφυλακας κυκλω της παρεμβολης	**12.27** But when the sun set, Jonathan ordered the *people* alongside him to keep alert, and to be over *their* weapons, to be ready for battle through the whole night; and he put out guards round about the camp.
12.28 και ηκουcαν οι υπεναντιοι οτι ητοιμαcται Ιωναθαν και οι ‹παρ› αυτου ειc πολεμον κ(αι) εφοβηθηcαν και επτηξαν τη καρδια αυτων και ανεκαυcαν πυραc εν τη παρεμβολη αυτων	**12.28** And the opponents heard that Jonathan and the *people* alongside him were ready for battle. And they were afraid and terrified in their heart; and they set up fires burning in their camp.
12.29 Ιωναθαν δε και οι παρ αυτου ουκ εγνωcαν εωc πρωι εβλεπον γαρ τα φωτα κ(αι)ομενα	**12.29** But Jonathan and the *people* alongside him did not know until early morning: for they *kept* looking at the lights burning.
12.30 και κατεδιωξεν Ιωναθαν οπιcω αυτων και ου κατελαβεν αυτουc διεβηcαν γαρ τον Ελευθερον ποταμον	**12.30** And Jonathan pursued after them, and did not take hold of them: for they had gone over the Eleutherus River.

12.28 παρ V A 64⁺236 La[109] La[146] | πατερεc S •

12.26–30 The enemies were planning to attack the Judeans stealthily **in the night,** but were too **afraid and terrified** to face them in **battle** (after their previous experience, when the merest handful of Judeans had been enough to drive them back, 11.72). So this time the Judeans did not need even to draw a sword. All they had to do was **to be ready for battle through the whole night** (cf. Neh 4.8–9, 22–23), and their opponents fled, leaving **fires burning in their camp**[332] to give them time to escape undetected. By the time **Jonathan pursued after them . . . they had** already **gone over the Eleutherus River.**[333] At the LORD's rebuke, the nations "will flee far away and will be pur-

[332] **They set up fires burning in their camp** *(anekausan puras en tē parembolē autōn)* is the reading of S, V, and A (supported by La[109] and La[146]). 64⁺236 add explicitly: " . . . and they departed" *(kai anechōrēsan)*. In itself *anakaiō* can mean simply "set burning" (DGE 2.242), but in the present context the prefix *ana-* may emphasize the piling **up** of the fire (see Ezek 24.10; Hos 7.6; cf. *anabainō, anatellō,* etc.).

[333] The exact location of the **Eleutherus River** is unknown (ABD 2.465), but since it apparently marked the limit of Israelite control (cf. 11.7), it may have been quite near Hamath (which was a long-standing border of Israel, Num 34.7–8; 1 Kgs 8.65; 2 Kgs 14.25; Ezek 47.15–17). Either Jonathan's opponents had camped south of the Eleutherus (although still within the **Hamath-region district**), and they now fled north across the river (Abel 225), or else they had camped inland from the Eleutherus, and now fled coastwards across the river (Bartlett, *First and Second . . . Maccabees,* 171).

sued like the chaff of the mountains before the wind, and like a rolling thing before a storm" (Isa 17.13).

The spiritual forces of wickedness are likewise terrified of the power of God (Jas 2.19; cf. Matt 8.29) and will flee when resisted (Jas 4.7), provided the resistance is steadfast ("let us not sleep, as the rest do, but let us keep awake and be sober," 1 Thes 5.6; Rev 3.2; Luke 12.35–40; Mark 13.35–37). Those who are "established in righteousness ... will be far from oppression, for you will not be afraid; and from terror, for it will not come near you" (Isa 54.14).

12.31 και εξεκλινε(ν) Ιωναθαν επι τουϲ Αραβαϲ τουϲ καλουμενουϲ Ζαβαδαιουϲ και επαταξεν αυτουϲ και ελαβε(ν) τα ϲκυλα αυτων	**12.31** And Jonathan turned aside against the Arabs who *are* called Zabadeans; and he smote them and took their plunder.
12.32 κ(αι) αναζευξαϲ ηλθε̣ν ειϲ Δαμαϲκον και διωδευϲεν εν παϲη χωρα	**12.32** And when *he* had set off, he came to Damascus, and traveled through all *that* district.

12.31–32 While he was still in the north, **Jonathan turned aside** to defeat **the Arabs who are called Zabadeans,**[334] and passed through the region of **Damascus,** the ancient capital of Syria (1 Kgs 15.18; 2 Kgs 8.7; near Hamath, Jer 49.23; Ezek 48.1).

Simon in the Philistine region

12.33 και Cιμω(ν) εξηλθεν και διωδευϲεν εωϲ Αϲκαλωνοϲ και τα πληϲιον οχυρωματα και εξεκλινεν ειϲ Ιοππην και προκατελαβετο αυτην	**12.33** And Simon went out, and traveled through up to Ashkelon and the neighboring fortresses. And he turned aside to Joppa, and took hold of it:
12.34 ηκουϲεν γαρ οτι βουλονται το οχυρωμα παραδουναι τοιϲ παρα Δημητριου κ(αι) εθετο εκει φρουρα(ν) οπωϲ φυλαϲϲωϲι(ν) αυτην	**12.34** for he had heard that they were wanting to give the fortress up to the *men* from Demetrius. And he placed a garrison there, so that they should keep it.

12.33–34 Simon revisited the Philistine cities that had recently surrendered to Judea (10.74–86), including **Ashkelon** and **Joppa,** where **he placed a garrison,** because **he had heard that** the people had been **wanting to give** their **fortress up** to the forces of **Demetrius** (cf. v 24). We would be wise to pursue the same policy in our own lives.

---

[334] **Zabadeans** *(Zabadaious)*. Josephus (*Antiquities,* 13.179) has "Nabateans" *(Nabatēnous),* which cannot be correct; the Nabateans were friends of the Judeans and lived much further south (5.25; 9.35). The name **Zabadeans** is not definitely known elsewhere, although it is sometimes compared with "Zabdiel the Arab" (11.17), or with "Beth-Zabdi" *(byt Zbdy),* apparently a place in Syria where Gentiles rose up against Israelites at an unspecified time, according to Rabbinic tradition (*Megillat Ta'anit,* 35).

When the Lord's great enemy has been expelled from his previous stronghold, we must fill the place with our new Master's forces instead. Otherwise, the old enemy may return worse than ever (Matt 12.43–45; 13.20–21; Eph 4.14–16).

Building defenses in Judea

12.35 και επεστρεψεν Ιωναθαν και εξεκκλησιασεν τους πρεσβυτερους του λαου και εβουλευετο μετ αυτω(ν) του οικοδομησαι οχυρωματα εν τη Ιουδαια	**12.35** And Jonathan returned and assembled the elders of the people, and he *began* taking counsel with them to build fortresses in Judea,
12.36 και προσυψωσαι τα τειχη Ι(ερουσα)λημ και υψωσαι ‹υψος› ‹μεγα› ανα μεσον της ακρας και της πολεως ‹εις το διαχωρισαι αυτην της πολεως› ινα η αυτη κατα μονας ‹οπως μητε αγορασωσιν μητε πωλωσιν›	**12.36** and to heighten the walls of Jerusalem, and to raise a great height in *the* midst *between* the citadel and the city, to separate it from the city, in order that this *place* should be *all* alone, so that *people* should neither buy nor sell.
12.37 και συνηχθησαν ‹του› οικοδομειν την πολι(ν) και ‹επεπεσεν› του ‹τειχους› του χειμαρρου του εξ απηλιωτου και επεσκευασεν ‹το› καλουμενον Χαφεναθα	**12.37** And they gathered together to build up the city; and *part* of the wall of the storm-brook on *the* east had fallen. And he repaired the *place* that is called Chaphenatha.

12.36 υψος S^{ca} V A 64^{+}236 La^{109} La^{146} | μεως S* • μεγα V A 64^{+}236 | μεγαν S • εις το διαχωρισαι αυτην της πολεως S^{ca} V A 64^{+}236 La^{109} La^{146} | > S* • οπως μητε αγορασωσιν μητε πωλωσιν [πωλησωσιν S^{ca}] V [αγοραζωσιν A 64^{+}236] La^{109} La^{146} | > S* • **12.37** του 1° S^{cb1} V A 64^{+}236 | τω S* • επεπεσεν V [επεσεν A 64^{+}236] La^{109} La^{146} | επεπεσαν S • τειχους S^{ca} V A 64^{+}236 La^{109} La^{146} | χειους S* • το V A 64^{+}236 La^{109} La^{146} | τον S •

12.35–37 Jonathan began **to build fortresses in Judea, and to heighten the walls of Jerusalem** (see the notes on 4.60; 10.10–11), repairing **the place that is called Chaphenatha** (not mentioned elsewhere), and restoring a fallen **part of the wall of the storm-brook on the east.**[335]

In old covenant times it was important to "build the walls of Jerusalem"; this was a sign that God was well pleased with His people (Psa 51.18; Isa 58.8–12; cf. Lam 2.8–9) and that their reproach was removed (Neh 2.17; Psa 89.40–41; 80.12). Yet the prophets also looked ahead to an even greater building of Jerusalem's walls under the new covenant, when all nations would come to God's city (Mic 7.11–17). That time has

[335] **The wall of the storm-brook on the east.** On the **east** side of Jerusalem was the wadi (**storm-brook:** see on 5.37) Kidron (Jer 31.40), between the city and the Mount of Olives (John 18.1 ≡ Luke 22.39; Zec 14.4); one of the gates on that side of the city was called the "Water Gate" (Neh 12.37; 3.26).

now arrived (Amos 9.11–12 ≡ Acts 15.14–17). "You have come to Mount Zion, and to the city of the living God, the heavenly Jerusalem" (Heb 12.22), whose wall is "great and high" (Rev 21.12) and very precious (made of jasper, and adorned with other precious stones, Rev 21.18–20; Isa 54.11), "having twelve foundations, and on them twelve names of the twelve apostles of the Lamb" (Rev 21.14; cf. Heb 11.10). That wall, which provides salvation for her people (Isa 60.18; 26.1), is the LORD Himself; she has no need of any other (Zec 2.4–5).

Life was becoming ever more difficult for Israel's opponents in **the citadel** (1.32–36; 10.7–9; 11.20–24, 41–42). Jonathan now set out **to separate** the citadel **from the city** by building **a great height in the midst between** the two, **in order that** the citadel **should be all alone, so that** its **people should neither buy nor sell.** This would be the strategy that would eventually cause the enemies to surrender (13.21–22, 49–51).

12.38 και Cιμων οικοδομηcεν την Αδειδα εν τη Cεφηλα ‹› και ωχυρωcεν αυτην και επεcτηcεν θυραc και μοχλουc	**12.38** And Simon built up Hadid in the Shephelah [lowland], and fortified it, and established *its* gates and bars.

12.38 και 2° S^{ca} A 64^{+}236 La^{109} La^{146} | ^ πεδεινη S* V •

12.38 The **Shephelah** was Judah's western plain, as distinct from her southern region (Negev) and central "hill country" (Jer 32.44; Jdg 1.9; 2 Chr 28.18). As occasionally elsewhere (9.15; 14.27), the Maccabaica simply transliterates the Hebrew name.[336]

The Shephelah included the Philistine cities (Josh 15.33–47), which had lately been causing so many problems for the Judeans. In that area, **Simon built up** and **fortified** (with **gates and bars**) the city of **Hadid**[337] near Lydda (Ezra 2.33 ≡ Neh 7.37), which would be on or near the route taken by an army traveling south along the coast from Syria to Judea (13.13). As that last verse shows, this was a wise precaution.

TRYPHO OPPOSES JONATHAN

Trypho plans to capture Jonathan

12.39 και εζητηcεν Τρυφων βαcιλευcαι τηc Αcιαc κ(αι) περιθεcθαι το διαδημα και ‹εκτειναι› χειρα επ Αντιοχον τον βαcιλεα	**12.39** And Trypho sought to become king of Asia, and to place the diadem on himself, and to stretch out *his* hand against Antiochus the king.

12.39 εκτειναι V A 64^{+}236 La^{146} | εξετινε(ν) την S •

---

[336] **Shephelah** transliterates Hebrew *šplh* ("lowland"), a feminine form of *špl* ("make low," as in Isa 40.4). Like the Maccabean History, most English versions of the Hebrew Scriptures sometimes transliterate its name (the NASB has "Shephelah" twice, and the ESV ten times). Cf. ISBE 4.473–74; Stanley, *Sinai and Palestine,* 485–86, §8; Smith, *Historical Geography,* 201–03.

[337] **Hadid.** Greek *Hadida* ≡ Hebrew *Ḥdyd.* Quite a number of place names in this region acquired a final (Aramaizing) *-a* in Hellenistic times. Hebrew *Lwd* (Lod) became Greek *Lydda;* Hebrew *Gzr* (Gezer) became Greek *Gazēra.*

12.39 Trypho had set up Alexander's son **Antiochus** as **king** in opposition to Demetrius (11.39–40, 54). But this was not enough for him (cf. the notes on 11.1). He **sought… to stretch out his hand against** his king (cf. Luke 21.12; 2 Sam 1.14; Est 2.21), and **to become king of Asia** himself. The eventual accomplishment of Trypho's scheme is recorded in 13.31–32.

12.40 και ευλαβηθη μηποτε ουκ εαση αυτον Ιωναθαν και μηποτε πολεμηση προς αυτον και εζητει συλλαβειν αυτον ⸂και⸃ απολεσαι και απαρας ηλθεν εις Βαιθσαν	**12.40** And he was afraid that Jonathan might not allow him, and might make war against him. And he *began* seeking *a way* to take hold of him and destroy *him*. And, having moved away, he came to Bethshan.

12.40 και 4° V La^{109} | του S A 64^{+}236 La^{146} •

12.40 Sins lead to other sins (2 Tim 3.13; 2.16); Trypho's desire to commit one act of treachery (v 39) led him to another. He **was afraid that Jonathan might not allow him** to carry out his scheme. Therefore, Trypho **began seeking a way to take hold of** Jonathan **and destroy him.** As a first step, he went **to Bethshan** in the lowlands of Manasseh (see the notes on 5.52), between Syria and Judea.

Jonathan meets Trypho at Bethshan

12.41 και εξηλθεν Ιωναθαν εις απαντησιν αυτω εν μ´ χιλιασι(ν) ανδρων επιλελεγμεναις εις παραταξιν και ηλθεν εις Βαιθσαν	**12.41** And Jonathan came out to meet him, with forty thousand men that had been chosen for battle, and came to Bethshan.
12.42 και ειδεν Τρυφων οτι ηλθεν μετα δυναμεως πολλης εκτιναι χειρας επ αυτον ευλαβηθη	**12.42** And Trypho saw that he had come with a great force. He was afraid to stretch out *his* hands against him,
12.43 και επεδεξατο αυτον ⸂ενδοξως⸃ και ⸂συνεστησεν⸃ αυτον πασιν τοις φιλοις αυτου ⸂κ(αι) εδωκεν αυτω δοματα⸃ ⸂κ(αι) επεταξεν τοις φιλοις αυτου⸃ και ταις δυναμεσιν αυτου υπακουειν αυτου ως αυτου	**12.43** and he accepted him with honor, and commended him to all his Friends, and gave him gifts, and ordered his Friends and his forces to obey him as *him*self.

12.43 ενδοξως S^{ca} V A 64^{+}236 La^{109} La^{146} | ευλογως S* • συνεστησεν S^{ca} A 64^{+}236 La^{109} La^{146} | συνεταξεν S* | συνηντησεν V • κ(αι) εδωκεν αυτω δοματα S^{ca} A 64^{+}236 La^{109} La^{146} | > S* V • κ(αι) επεταξεν τοις φιλοις αυτου S^{ca} A La^{109} La^{146} 7h7 | > S* V 64^{+}236 7a1 •

12.41–43 Jonathan came out to meet Trypho at **Bethshan… with a great force (forty thousand** trained soldiers). Like the enemies in the Hamath region (see the notes on vv 26–28), **Trypho… was afraid to stretch out his hands against** Jonathan under such circumstances. Instead, he concealed the evil plans in his heart with words that were softer than oil (cf. Psa 55.20–21; Prov 26.23–26). He **accepted** Jonathan **with honor,** as those who are faithful and diligent should be accepted (cf. 3 Jn 8–10). He **commended him to all his Friends,** as such people should be commended (cf. Rom 16.1; 2 Cor 12.11). He **gave him gifts,** as is only fitting for those to whom we owe much (cf. 1 Cor 9.10–11; Rom 15.27). He **ordered his Friends and his forces to obey him,** as faithful leaders should be obeyed (cf. Heb 13.17; 1 Tim 5.17). "Satan transforms himself into an angel of light," and "his servants also transform themselves as servants of righteousness" (2 Cor 11.14–15).

Jonathan sends away his forces

12.44 και ειπεν τω Ιωναθαν ινα τι ⸂εκοπωcας⸃ ⸂παντα⸃ τον λαο(ν) τουτον ⸂πολεμου μη ενεcτηκοτος ημιν⸃	**12.44** And he said to Jonathan: "Why have you† wearied all this people, when there is no war among us?
12.45 και νυν αποcτιλον αυτουc ειc τουc οικουc αυτων επιλεξε δε cεαυτω ανδραc ολιγουc οιτινεc εcονται μετα cου και δευρο μετ εμου ειc Πτολεμαιδα και παραδωcω cοι αυτην και τα λοιπα οχυρωματα και τας δυναμιc τας λοιπας κ(αι) παντας τουc επι των χρειων και επιcτρεψας απελευcομαι τουτου γαρ χαριν παρειμι	**12.45** And now, send† them to their houses. But choose† for yourself† a few men who will be with you†, and come† with me to Ptolemais, and I will give it over to you†, and the rest of *the* fortresses, and the rest of *the* forces, and all the *people who are* over the duties. And when *I* have returned, I will go away: for this *is* the reason I am here."

12.44 εκοπωcαc V 64^{+}236 La^{109} La^{146} | εκοψαc S A • παντα A 64^{+}236 La^{109} La^{146} | > S V • πολεμου / μη ενεcτηκοτοc ημιν V A La^{109} La^{146} | ~ S 64^{+}236 •

12.44–45 Trypho told **Jonathan** that they were both on the same side (the side opposed to, and opposed by, Demetrius; 11.52–74): **there is no war among us.** Therefore, Jonathan had simply **wearied** his forty thousand men (**all this people**) by bringing them. The **reason** why Trypho had come was merely to **give … over to** Jonathan the city of **Ptolemais** (which had been promised to the Israelites at least once before, 10.39), **and the rest of the fortresses, and the rest of the** military **forces** (cf. 11.59), **and all the people who** were in charge of (**over**) **the duties** (cf. 10.41). In all of this, there is no hint of what was really in Trypho's heart.

12.46 και εμπιcτευcας αυτω εποιηcεν καθωc ειπεν και ⸂εξαπεcτιλεν⸃ τας ⸂δυναμειc και⸃ απηλθον ειc γη(ν) Ιουδα	**12.46** And he trusted him, and did just as he said, and sent away his forces; and they departed into the land of Judah.

12.46 εξαπεcτιλεν S^{ca} V A 64^{+}236 La^{109} La^{146} | -λαc S* • δυναμειc και [δ- Ιωναθαν κ- S^{ca}] V A 64^{+}236 La^{109} La^{146} | δυναμαι S* •

12.47 κατελιπεν δε μεθ εαυτου ανδρας τριςχιλιους ‹ων› διςχιλιους αφηκεν εν ‹τη› Γαλιλαια χιλιοι δε ςυνηλθον αυτω	**12.47** But he left with *him*self three thousand men, of whom he left two thousand in Galilee, but a thousand came with him.

12.47 ων V 64⁺236 La[109] La[146] | κ(αι) ως ανδρας S | ως A • τη S[ca] V A 64⁺236 | > S* •

12.46–47 Jonathan **trusted** Trypho, **and sent away his forces . . . into the land of Judah,** apart from **two thousand** whom he left **in Galilee,** and **one thousand** who **came with him** to Ptolemais.

Many commentators "find fault with Jonathan for trusting his enemy too easily.... He erred in believing so readily what a traitor was telling him."[338] But who at that stage knew—or could have known—that Trypho was an enemy or a traitor? He came as the trusted representative of the king, with whom Jonathan was at peace (11.57–59). Up till this moment, Trypho had made no move against his king, or Jonathan, or any of the other Judeans. His first perceptible step in that direction was still in the future (v 48).

"If possible, in what comes from you, be at peace with all people" (Rom 12.18). Certainly we are to be on our guard constantly, even in our dealings with those nearest to us (Jer 9.4–5; Mic 7.5–6). But if people show no sign of evil—as Trypho, up to this point, had shown no sign of what was in his heart—how can we not be at peace with them? "You will not contend with a person for nothing, if he has not dealt evil with you" (Prov 3.30). Inevitably that will sometimes cause us to trust people who later prove untrustworthy. Not all sins are evident beforehand (cf. 1 Tim 5.24), and it would be presumptuous to imagine that we are able to discern the thoughts and intentions of the hearts around us (only God has the power to do that: 1 Sam 16.7; 1 Kgs 8.39; Heb 4.12–13). Jesus told His disciples that some of them would be betrayed and killed, like Jonathan, by people whom they had befriended—and yet that they would really suffer no harm at all: "You will be delivered up even by parents and brothers and relatives and friends, and some of you they will put to death... and a hair out of your head will certainly not be destroyed" (Luke 21.16–18). "It is better, if the will of God should will it, to suffer for doing good" (1 Pet 3.17; 2.20)—even to die for doing good, as not only Jonathan and those disciples but also Jesus Himself did (1 Pet 2.21–24)—than to survive by withholding our kindness when we have no authority to withhold it (Eph 4.32; Luke 6.35; 1 Cor 13.4–7).

Jonathan is captured

12.48 ως δε ειςηλθεν Ιωναθαν εις Πτολεμαιδαν απεκλιςαν οι Πτολεμαις τας πυλας	**12.48** But when Jonathan came into Ptolemais, the citizens of Ptolemais shut the gates

[338] Sacy 241; cf. Hrabanus Maurus (PL 109.1199).

κ(αι) συνελαβον αυτον και παντας τους συνεισελθοντας ‹μετ αυτου› ‹απεκτιναν› εν ρομφαια	and took hold of him. And all the *men* who had come in with him they killed with *the* sword.

12.48 μετ αυτου V A 64[+]236 La[109] La[146] | αυτου S* | αυτω S[1] • απεκτιναν S[ca] A V 64[+]236 | -ινον S* •

12.48 The citizens of Ptolemais had been among Israel's early enemies during the Maccabean struggle (5.15). Now, **when Jonathan came into Ptolemais,** the townspeople **shut the gates and took hold of him,** and **killed** the men who were with him.

12.49 και απεστιλεν Τρυφω(ν) δυναμις και ιππο(ν) εις την Γαλιλαιαν και το παιδιον το μεγα του απολεσαι πα(ν)τας τους παρα Ιωναθαν	**12.49** And Trypho sent forces and horse to Galilee and the great level place, to destroy all the *men* from alongside Jonathan.
12.50 ‹› και επεγνωσαν ‹οτι› συνελημφθη και απολωλεν και οι μετ αυτου και παρεκαλεσαν εαυτους και επορευοντο συνεστραμμενοι ετοιμοι εις πολεμο(ν)	**12.50** And they knew that he and the *men* with him had been taken hold of and destroyed. And they encouraged one another, and *kept* going, gathered *closely* together, ready for battle.
12.51 και ειδον οι διωκο(ν)τες οτι περι ψυχης αυτοις εστιν και επεστρεψαν	**12.51** And the pursuers saw that it was *a matter* of *their* soul for them; and they turned back.

12.50 και 1° V A 64[+]236 La[146] | ^ ους S • οτι V A 64[+]236 La[109] La[146] | οτε δε S •

12.49–51 Trypho sent infantry and cavalry (**forces and horse**) **to Galilee ... to destroy** the two thousand men whom Jonathan had left there (v 47). But Trypho's men did not obey their instructions. Like Trypho himself (v 42) and others who had recently tried to oppose the Israelites (vv 24–30), they were too afraid of them to meet them in open conflict. When they saw that the Judeans were **ready for battle** and were willing to fight to the death (**it was a matter of their soul for them;** cf. 2.50; 3.21; 9.44), **they turned back.**[339] The Judeans, on the other hand, **encouraged one another** and **gathered closely together,** so that **all** of them **came in peace into Judah** (cf. Ecc 4.9–12; Php 1.27; Col 2.19).

12.52 και ηλθον παντες μετ ειρηνης εις γην Ιουδα και επενθησαν	**12.52** And they all came in peace into *the* land of Judah; and they mourned

[339] The Judeans **knew that** Jonathan **had been taken hold of and destroyed** *(apolōlen)*. This does not necessarily indicate that they believed him to be already dead; compare "I have found my sheep that was destroyed [*apolōlos*]" (Luke 15.6), and see also the footnote to 13.49. In fact, Trypho kept Jonathan alive till some time later (13.23).

τον Ιωναθαν και τουc μετ αυτου	for Jonathan and the *men* with him,
και εφοβηθηcαν cφοδρα	and they were very much afraid.
και επενθηcεν παc Ιc(ραη)λ	And all Israel mourned
πενθοc μεγα	*with* a great mourning.

12.52 All Israel mourned for the loss of **Jonathan and the men with him . . . with a great mourning,** as they had mourned for his father Mattathias (2.70) and his brother Judas (9.20).

And they were very much afraid. The people who had seen God's mighty works during the plagues in Egypt nevertheless became "very much afraid" when they could see no escape at the Red Sea (Exod 14.10–13). But they did not need to fear, because God delivered them (Exod 14.19–31). The people who had seen God's mighty works through both Judas and Jonathan nevertheless became **very much afraid** when Jonathan too was taken away. But they did not need to fear, because God would remain with them as long as they remained with Him (2 Chr 15.2; Psa 94.14). We, who have seen God's mighty works toward His people through the ages in the Scriptures (Psa 44.1–3; Rom 15.4; Heb 11.1–12.3), have no excuse to fear anything that may happen (Rom 5.8–10; 8.32) while the Lord is our helper (Psa 27.1–3; 56.3–4; Heb 13.5–6; Luke 12.4, 32; John 14.27; Rom 8.28).

12.53 και ‹εζητηcα(ν)› παντα τα εθνη	**12.53** And all the nations *that were*
τα κυκλω αυτων εκτριψαι αυτουc	round about them sought to shatter
ειπο(ν) γαρ	them utterly: for they said:
ουκ εχουcιν αρχοντα και βοηθουντα	"They do not have a ruler and a help;
νυν ουν πολεμηcωμεν αυτουc	now therefore, let us make war against
και εξαρωμεν εξ ανθρωπων	them and do away with their memory
το μνημοcυνον αυτων	from among humanity."

12.53 εζητηcα(ν) S^{ca} V A 64^{+}236 La^{109} La^{146} | εζητηcε S* •

12.53 As had happened after the death of Judas (9.23–27), **all the nations that were round about** the Judeans **sought to shatter them utterly** (cf. 3.35, 42; Exod 15.9; Psa 83.2–4; Zec 12.3; Acts 4.25–26), thinking that they did **not have a ruler** [*archonta*] **and a help** [*boēthounta*]. But in fact God's people never lack a ruler or a help. They have "the help that is from Heaven helping" them (v 15; Heb 13.6); and He is the ruler over the whole earth (Psa 47.2; Rev 1.5). In addition, He has always sent His people whatever earthly rulers and helps they needed. Moses was a **ruler** sent by Him (Acts 7.35); Jesus was a **help** sent by Him (Luke 1.54). He had just taken away from them one great ruler and help—Jonathan—but He was about to send them another (13.8; 14.4–15).

Their enemies hoped to **do away with their memory from among humanity.** But "the memory of the righteous one is for a blessing" (see on 3.7; Prov 10.7; Psa 112.6). His enemy is the one whose memory will be cut off (Psa 34.16, 21), "because he did not remember to do lovingkindness, and he persecuted the afflicted and needy man, and one who was smitten of heart, to put him to death; and he loved a curse, and it will come to him" (Psa 109.15–17).

Simon (13.1–16.22)

SIMON IS APPOINTED LEADER

Simon encourages the people

13.1 κ(αι) ηκουcεν Cιμων οτι cυνηγαγεν Τρυφων δυναμιν πολλην του ελθειν ειc γην Ιουδα και εκτριψαι αυτην	**13.1** And Simon heard that Trypho had gathered a great force to come into *the* land of Judah, and to shatter it utterly.

13.1 Now that he had captured Jonathan, **Trypho** planned **to come into the land of Judah, and to shatter it utterly** (vv 12, 20; see on 12.53).

13.2 και ειδε(ν) τον λαον οτι εντρομοc εcτιν και εκφοβοc και ανεβη ˻ειc˼ Ι(εροuca)λημ και ηθροιcεν τον λαον	**13.2** And he saw the people, that they were trembling and utterly fearful; and he went up to Jerusalem and drew the people together.
13.3 και παρεκαλεcεν αυτουc και ειπεν αυτοιc αυτοι οιδατε οcα εγω και οι αδελφοι μου και ο οικοc του π(ατ)ρ(ο)c μου παντεc εποιηcαμε(ν) χαριν των νομων και των αγιων ˻και˼ τουc πολεμουc ˻κ(αι) ταc cτενοχωριαc˼ ˻αc ιδομεν˼	**13.3** And he encouraged them, and said to them: "You^{pl} *your*selves know all *the thing*s that I and my brothers and my father's house have done for the laws and the holy *place*s, and the wars and the oppressions that we have seen.

13.2 ειc S^{ca} V A 64^{+}236 La^{109} | > S* • **13.3** και 6° A S^{ca} 64^{+}236 La^{109} La^{146} | > S* V • κ(αι) ταc cτενοχωριαc S^{ca} A 64^{+}236 La^{109} La^{146} | > S* V • αc ιδομεν S^{cb1} 64^{+}236 La^{109} La^{146} | > S* V A •

13.2–3 The people . . . were trembling and utterly fearful (see the notes on 12.52). But Simon gathered them together in **Jerusalem**, and **encouraged them** (cf. 1 Thes 5.14) by reminding them of **all the things that I and my brothers and my father's house have done for the laws and the holy places**—just as Moses, Joshua, and Jesus encouraged those around them by reminding them of all the things that had happened in their own times (Deut 29.2–8; Josh 23.3; Mark 8.17–21; Luke 7.22). "We also, having so great a cloud of witnesses lying around us . . . with patient endurance let us run the contest that is set before us" (Heb 12.1; 13.7).

13.4 ˻τουτου˼ χαριν απωλοντο παντεc οι αδελφοι μου χαριν του Ιc(ραη)λ και κατελιφθη(ν) εγω μονοc	**13.4** For this reason all my brothers have been destroyed, for *the* sake of Is- rael, and I myself have been left alone.

13.4 τουτου A [και τ- 64^{+}236 7h7] La^{109} La^{146} 7a1 | ων και S V •

13.5 και νυν μη μοι γενοιτο φειcαcθαι μου τηc ψυχηc εν παντι καιρω θλιψεωc ου γαρ ειμι κριccων των αδελφων μου	**13.5** And now, may it not be for me to spare my soul in any period of oppression: for I am not better than my brothers.

13.4–5 In this struggle **all** Simon's **brothers** had **been destroyed for the sake of Israel** (Eleazar, 6.43–46; Judas, 9.10–18; John, 9.35–36; Jonathan, 12.40–48). Simon was **left alone,** like Elijah (1 Kgs 18.22; 19.10 ≡ Rom 11.3) and Jesus (John 16.32)—although no one who serves the Lord is ever completely alone, because the Lord is with him (Deut 31.6; Psa 37.28; John 16.32; 8.29; 14.18; cf. Matt 18.20). Again like Elijah (1 Kgs 19.4), Simon knew that he was **not better than** those who had gone before him in the faith, and that he could not expect to have any special privileges. If they had not spared their souls (2.50) in times of **oppression,** he would not spare his. That was Paul's attitude also: "Nor do I make my soul of any account as valuable to myself, so that I may finish my course and the task of serving which I received from the Lord Jesus" (Acts 20.24). "For us He laid down His soul, and we ourselves ought to lay down our souls for the brothers" (1 Jn 3.16; cf. Rev 12.11; Rom 16.4; Php 2.30).

13.6 πλην εκδικηcω περι του εθνουc μου και περι των αγιω(ν) και των γυνεκων και τεκνων υμω(ν) οτι cυνηχθηcαν παντα τα εθνη εκτριψαι ημαc εχθραc χαριν	**13.6** Nevertheless, I will take vengeance concerning my nation, and concerning the holy *place*s and your wives and children: for all the nations have gathered together to shatter us utterly, because of enmity."

13.6 Simon was determined to do what his father had instructed him to do: **I will take vengeance concerning**[340] **my nation, and concerning the holy places and your wives and children** (see the notes on 2.67).

The people choose Simon as their leader

13.7 και ανεζωπυρηcεν το πν(ευμ)α του λαου αμα του ακουcαι των λογων τουτων	**13.7** And the spirit of the people was rekindled while *they were* hearing these words.

13.7 Simon's **words** encouraged the fainthearted (cf. 1 Thes 5.14), so that **the spirit of the people was rekindled** (cf. Gen 45.27). The LORD works "to revive the spirit of the lowly" (Isa 57.15).

---

[340] To **take vengeance concerning** *(peri)* something (Muraoka 206, §1, construction *m*) is not to "avenge" it (KJV) or take vengeance "for" it (NETS); the Greek of this period would express that in other ways (see, e.g., 9.42). Instead, to **take vengeance concerning** something is to take vengeance "in regard to" it (BDAG 797, §1e), as the context here shows. The **holy places** did not need avenging; they needed defending (cf. v 3; 14.29, 42; 3.43). Thus the meaning is "I shall take up the cause of my nation…" (REB), "I will fight to defend my nation…" (TEV).

13.8 και απεκριθηcαν φωνη μεγαλη λεγοντεc cυ ει ημω(ν) ηγουμενοc αντι Ιουδου και Ιωναθου του αδελφου cου	**13.8** And they responded with a great voice, saying: "You† yourself† are our leader in place of Judas and Jonathan your† brother.
13.9 πολεμηcον τον πολεμον ημων και παντα οcα αν ειπηc ημιν ποιηcομεν	**13.9** War† our warfare, and all *things* that you† may say to us, we will do."

13.8–9 The people chose Simon as their **leader** [*hēgoumenos*] **in place of Judas and Jonathan,** instructing him to **war our warfare** (cf. 2 Chr 32.8), and promising to do **all things that you may say to us** (as earlier generations had promised to earlier leaders of Israel: Exod 19.8; Deut 5.27; Josh 1.16–17). We likewise are to obey and submit to our own leaders *(hēgoumenois)* in the Israel of God today (Heb 13.17).

13.10 και cυνηγαγεν πανταc τουc ανδραc τουc πολεμιcταc και εταχυνε(ν) του τελεcαι τα τιχη Ι(εροUcα)λημ και ωχυρωcεν αυτην κυκλοθεν	**13.10** And he gathered together all the men *who were* warriors; and he acted quickly to complete the walls of Jerusalem, and fortified it round about.

13.10 Simon proceeded **to complete** the work of fortifying **Jerusalem,** which Jonathan had begun (12.35–37). What one had planted, another was now watering (cf. 1 Cor 3.6); the Lord would give the increase (Psa 127.1). In this task Simon **acted quickly.** It is never wise to delay in obeying the Lord (Psa 119.60; Acts 22.16), for the enemy may strike at any moment (1 Pet 5.8), and we do not know how much time or opportunity we may have to prepare our defenses (1 Thes 5.3–8).

13.11 και απεcτιλεν Ιωναθα(ν) τον του Αψαλωμου και μετ αυτου δυναμιν ικανην ειc Ιοππην και εξεβαλεν τουc ο(ν)ταc εκει και εμινεν ‹εκι› εν αυτη	**13.11** And he sent Jonathan the *son* of Absalom, and with him a considerable force, to Joppa. And he cast out the *people* who were there, and he remained there in it.

13.11 εκι S[ca] A 64[+]236 La[109] La[146] | > S* V •

13.11 Simon also continued the work in the Philistine region, sending **Jonathan the son of Absalom ... with ... a considerable force** to cast some troublemakers out of **Joppa,** which had previously been an enemy stronghold but had submitted to Jonathan (see the notes on 10.75–76; 12.33–34).

Trypho and Simon

Trypho asks for money and hostages

13.12 και απηρεν Τρυφων απο Πτολεμαιδοc μετα δυναμεωc πολληc ελθειν ειc γην Ιουδα και Ιωναθα(ν) μετ αυτου εν φυλακη	**13.12** And Trypho moved away from Ptolemais with a great force to come into *the* land of Judah, and Jonathan *was* with him in safekeeping.

13.12 Trypho now **moved away from Ptolemais** (where Jonathan had been captured, 12.48) **to come into the land of Judah** with a large army (**a great force**). **Jonathan** was still his prisoner (**in safekeeping,** the same expression as in Matt 14.3).

13.13 Σιμων δε παρενεβαλεν εν ‹Αδειδοις› κατα προςωπον του παιδιου	**13.13** But Simon camped at Hadid, opposite *the* face of the level place.
13.14 και επεγνω Τρυφων οτι ανεςτη Σιμω(ν) αντι Ιωναθου του αδελφου αυτου και οτι ςυναπτειν αυτω μελλει πολεμον και απεςτιλεν προς αυτον πρεςβεις λεγω(ν)	**13.14** And Trypho knew that Simon had risen up in place of Jonathan his brother, and that he was going to make contact with him in battle. And he sent ambassadors to him, saying:
13.15 περι αργυριου ου ωφειλεν Ιωναθαν ο αδελφος ςου εις το βαςιλικον δι ας ειχεν χριας ςυνειχομεν αυτον	**13.15** "*It is* for *the* money that Jonathan your† brother was owing for the king's *taxes*, because of *the* duties that he was having, *that* we have been holding him.
13.16 και νυν αποςτιλον αργυριου ταλαντα ρ´ και δυο των υιων αυτου ομηρα οπως μη αφεθεις αποςτατηςη αφ ημων και αφηςομεν αυτον	**13.16** And now, send† a hundred talents of silver, and two of his sons *as* hostages, so that when *he is* set free he may not rebel from us; and we will set him free."

13.13 Αδειδοις S[ca] A [-δα 64*236] La[146] | Αδεινοις S* | Αλιμοις V •

13.13–14 But Trypho found that the Judeans were not defenseless (12.53). **Simon had risen up in place of Jonathan his brother.** He **camped at Hadid,** facing the plain (**level place**) in the coastal lowland (see on 12.38), and prepared for **battle** with Trypho.

13.15–16 Again (see 12.42) Trypho did not choose to meet the Judeans in open conflict but took refuge in deceit. He claimed that he was holding Jonathan because of **money that Jonathan . . . was owing for the king's taxes, because of the duties that he was having.** Trypho promised to **set** Jonathan **free** if Simon paid **a hundred talents of silver**[341] and sent **two of** Jonathan's **sons**[342] **as hostages.** If Jonathan really did owe anything (which is doubtful; we have only Trypho's word for it), he would have owed it not to Trypho, but to Trypho's opponent Demetrius (cf. v 39).

[341] **A hundred talents of silver.** A talent (Greek *talanton* ≡ Hebrew *kkr*) was a measure of weight (cf. Rev 16.21). Two **talents of silver** were enough to buy the hill of Samaria (1 Kgs 16.24). **A hundred talents of silver** was therefore a very large sum, but not too large to be demanded from a subjugated nation (2 Kgs 23.33; 2 Chr 27.5).

[342] **Two of his sons** unambiguously indicates that Jonathan had at least one other son (Greek *tōn huiōn* ≡ Hebrew *mbnyw*). Assertions to the contrary (e.g., by Goldstein, *I Maccabees,* 473) are not supported by Hebrew and Greek usage (see Lev 13.2; Jdg 17.5).

Simon sends them

13.17 και εγνω Cιμων οτι δολω λαλουcιν προc αυτον και πεμπει του λαβειν το αργυριο(ν) και τα παιδαρια μηποτε εχθραν αρη μεγαλην προc το(ν) λαον	**13.17** And Simon knew that they were speaking to him in deceit; and he *began* sending to get the silver and the boys, lest he should raise great enmity among the people,
13.18 λεγοντεc οτι ουκ ⸢απεcτιλα⸣ αυτω το αργυριον και τα παιδαρια ⸢απωλετο	**13.18** *who might be* saying, "Because I did not send him the silver and the boys, he was destroyed."
13.19 και απεcτειλεν τα παιδαρια⸣ και τα ρ΄ ταλαντα και διεψευcατο και ουκ αφηκεν τον Ιωναθαν	**13.19** And he sent the boys and the hundred talents. And he utterly lied, and did not set Jonathan free.

13.18 απεcτιλα S^{ca} V A $64^{+}236$ La^{109} La^{146} | επ- S* • **13.18–19** απωλετο και απεcτειλεν τα παιδαρια [-δρια V*] V^{b} A $64^{+}236$ La^{109} La^{146} | > S •

13.17–19 Simon knew[343] that Trypho's ambassadors **were speaking to him in deceit.** A rotten tree does not produce good fruit (Matt 7.16–20); someone who had done what Trypho had recently done could not be trusted now. "One who hates disguises himself with his lips, but in his inside he places deceit. When he shows favor with his voice, do not believe him, for seven abominations are in his heart" (Prov 26.24–25). Nevertheless, Simon was not absolutely free to follow his own judgment. He had to think of **the people** also. He was concerned that he might provoke **great enmity among the people** if he **did not send** Trypho **the silver and the boys.** When God has given a command, we must obey Him rather than any **people** (Acts 5.29); but in matters of this kind, where we have no specific command from God either way, "let us pursue the things of peace, and the things for building up one another" (Rom 14.19; 12.18; Heb 12.14). A fool and oppressor, like Rehoboam, would simply have done what he himself preferred, without heeding **the people** (cf. 1 Kgs 12.13–15). But Simon, unlike Rehoboam, was "a man of counsel" and "a father to" his people (2.65); all his days "he sought good things for his nation ... and strengthened all the lowly ones of his people" (14.4, 14). Therefore in this situation he did what would preserve peace among the people, and **sent the boys** and the money.[344] Predictably, the evildoer continued to do evil (cf. Prov 6.14), **and did not set Jonathan free.**

---

[343] **Knew** *(egnō)* is the reading of S, A, and $64^{+}236$ (supported by La^{146}), whereas V (supported by La^{109}) reads "did not know" *(ouk egnō)*. The former option is supported by what follows. Simon accepted Trypho's demands **lest he should raise great enmity among the people**—which shows that his own personal preference would have been otherwise.

[344] "At first glance it would seem that he would have done better not to expose those poor boys to the fury of a deceiver, and not to despoil the nation of that sum of money, which would be useless in saving Jonathan's life. But . . . he could not set his own opinion, however well founded, above the great stumblingblock that he would have caused among the people" (Sacy 259–61; cf. Dionysius 199v; Lapide 67).

Trypho seeks to shatter Judea

13.20 και μετα ταυτα ηλθεν Τρυφω(ν) ‹› του εμβατευcαι εις την χωραν και εκτριψαι αυτην και ‹εκυκλωcεν› οδον την εις Αδωρα και Cιμων και η παρεμβολη αυτου ‹αντιπαρηγεν› αυτω εις παντα τοπον ου αν επορευετο	**13.20** And after these *things* Trypho came to move into the district and shatter it utterly. And he went round about, *by the* path that *goes* to Adora. And Simon and his company *kept* going opposite him to every place wherever he was going.

13.20 Τρυφω(ν) S[ca] V A 64[+]236 La[109] La[146] | + νυν S* • εκυκλωcεν A 64[+]236 La[109] | -cαν S V La[146] • αντιπαρηγεν V A 64[+]236 La[109] | -ηγαγεν S •

13.20 After these things Trypho tried **to move into the district** of Judea. Instead of pressing ahead on the coastal route, where Simon's forces were ready and waiting for battle (vv 13–14), **he went round about** by a different route, using **the path that goes to Adora.**[345] But in **every place** where he tried to go, **Simon and his company kept going opposite him.**

13.21 οι δε εκ της ακρας απεcτελλον προς Τρυφωνα πρεcβευτας καταcπευδοντας αυτον του ελθειν προς αυτους δια της ερημου και αποcτιλαι αυτοις τροφας	**13.21** But the *people* from the citadel were sending ambassadors to Trypho, hurrying him to come to them through the desert, and to send them nourishment.
13.22 και ητοιμαcεν Τρυφων παcαν την ιππον αυτου ελθειν και ε(ν) τη νυκτι εκεινη ην χειων πολλη cφοδρα και ουκ ηλθεν δια ‹την› χιονα και απηρεν και ηλθεν εις την Γαλααδειτιν	**13.22** And Trypho got all his horse ready to come. And in that night *there* was very much snow, and he did not come because of the snow. And he moved away, and came to the Gilead region.

13.22 την 2° S[cb1] V A 64[+]236 | τον S* •

13.21–22 By this time, the Judeans' attempts to blockade the enemy **citadel** within Jerusalem (11.20–23; 12.36) were starting to take effect. **The people in the citadel** sent messengers (**ambassadors**) asking **Trypho ... to send them nourishment**—a need that would become steadily greater as the siege continued (v 49). **Trypho** prepared **to come to them through the desert** of Judea one **night** with **all** his horsemen; but that night **there was very much snow,** and therefore **he did not come.**[346] The LORD does "all

[345] **Adora** might perhaps be the Adoraim mentioned as one of the cities of defense in Judah (2 Chr 11.9), but this is uncertain. In ancient Israel, identical or similar names were often given to more than one place.

[346] "Only someone who has witnessed one of these massive snowfalls (such as the one during the night of February 10–11, 1920) can tell what havoc they cause in a land unused to them" (Abel 238).

that He has pleased, in the heavens and in the land" (Psa 135.6), and He does not send His snow at random; among other things, He "has reserved [it] for the time of oppression, for the day of battle and war" (Job 38.22–23; cf. Josh 10.11; Exod 9.24). In the end Trypho merely **moved away** from Judea and crossed over **into the Gilead region** on the other side of the Jordan, which would allow him to return north to Syria (v 24) without disturbance. During all these maneuvers, he persistently avoided any battle—even though he had brought "a great force" with him (vv 12, 22; see the notes on 12.42).

Trypho kills Jonathan

13.23 ωc δε ηγγιcεν τηc Βαcκαμα απεκτινεν τον Ιωναθαν και εταφη ‹εκει›	**13.23** But when he came near Baskama, he killed Jonathan; and he was buried there.
13.24 και επεcτρεψε(ν) ‹› Τρυφων και απηλθεν ειc τη(ν) ‹γην αυτου›	**13.24** And Trypho turned back, and went away into his *own* land.

13.23 εκει V A 64^{+}236 La^{109} La^{146} | > S • **13.24** Τρυφων V A 64^{+}236 La^{109} La^{146} | ^ εκει S • γην αυτου S^{ca} V A 64^{+}236 La^{109} La^{146} | αυτου οικιαν S* •

13.23–24 Passing through the Gilead region (v 22), Trypho **killed Jonathan** near an otherwise unknown place called **Baskama,** and then **went away into his own land** (the region where the Seleucid kings ruled, vv 31–32, i.e., the vicinity of Antioch, 3.37; cf. 6.63; 10.68; 11.13, 56). In Israel it was customary not to kill captives (2 Kgs 6.22; cf 1 Kgs 20.31); sometimes, indeed, they were shown very great kindness (2 Chr 28.8–15). Trypho killed one who had done him no harm; Simon, on the other hand, extended mercy even to enemies (vv 47, 50).

13.25 και απεcτιλεν Cιμων και ελαβεν τα οcτα Ιωναθαν του αδελφου αυτου και εθαψεν αυτο(ν) εν Μωδειν πολι των πατερων αυτου	**13.25** And Simon sent and took the bones of Jonathan his brother, and buried him at Modein, *the* city of his fathers.
13.26 και εκοψα(ν)το αυτον παc Ιc(ραη)λ κοπετον μεγαν και επενθηcαν αυτον ημεραc πολλαc	**13.26** And all Israel beat themselves for him *with* a great beating, and mourned for him many days.

13.25–26 Jonathan's **bones** were taken back to be buried at **Modein,** where **his fathers** had lived (see the notes on 2.1), and again **all Israel . . . mourned for him** (see the notes on 12.52).

"For Jonathan, it was a very slight harm to fall into the snare of a treacherous man, whose cruelty could do nothing worse than advance a little the death of someone who had long dedicated himself (like his brothers) to dying for the defense of his people and the glory of the God of Israel [2.50]. Indeed it was safer and better for him to die in that way, by the hand of his enemies, than to enjoy in peace all the honors associated with his rank—in which case there could always be some fear that his heart might be corrupted [cf. Deut 8.11–17]. After all, the true portion of those who are Israelites according to the spirit has always been suffering, contempt, and persecution; and if they do seek any 'encouragement' in this life, they do so in the way that these noble Maccabees did, 'in the holy books' [12.9], reading which gives them support from God against all kinds of afflictions, and strengthens them in perseverance" (Sacy 242–43).

The burial-place raised by Simon

13.27 και ωκοδομηcεν Cιμων επι τον ταφον του π(ατ)ρ(ο)c αυτου και τω(ν) αδελφων αυτου και υψωcεν αυτο(ν) τη οραcει λιθω ξεcτω εκ των ‹οπιcθεν και εμπροcθεν›	**13.27** And Simon built upon the burial-place of his father and his brothers, and he raised it high to the sight, with polished stone behind and in front.
13.28 και εcτηcε(ν) επτα πυραμιδαc ‹μιαν› κατεναντι τηc μιαc τω πατρι και τη μητρι κ(αι) τοιc ‹τεccαρcιν› αδελφοιc	**13.28** And he established seven pyramids, one opposite another, for *his* father and mother and four brothers,
13.29 κ(αι) ‹ταυταιc› εποιηcεν μηχανηματα περιθειc cτυλουc μεγαλουc και εποιηcεν επι τοιc cτυλοιc ‹πανοπλιαc› ειc ονομα αιωνιον και παρα ταιc πανοπλιαιc πλοια ενγεγλυμμενα ειc το θεωριcθαι υπο πα(ν)των των πλεοντων την θαλαccαν	**13.29** and he made devices for these, placing around *them* great pillars; and on the pillars he made all *kinds of* weaponry, for a lasting name; and beside all the *kinds of* weaponry, carved ships, to be seen by all those who sail the sea.
13.30 ουτοc ο ταφοc ον εποιηcεν εν Μωδειν εωc τηc ημεραc ταυτηc	**13.30** This *is* the burial-place that he made at Modein, until this day.

13.27 οπιcθεν / και / εμπροcθεν V La[146] | ~ S [εμ- κ(αι) εκ των οπ- 64⁺236] | οπ- και εκ των οπ- A • **13.28** μιαν V A 64⁺236 | μια S • τεccαρcιν S[ca] V A 64⁺236 La[109] La[146] | > S • **13.29** ταυταιc V A 64⁺236 La[146] | ταυτα S • πανοπλιαc V A 64⁺236 La[109] La[146] | -λιαν S •

13.27–30 Simon extended (**built upon**) his family's **burial-place** at **Modein** (v 30), so that it was **raised … high.**[347] The tomb was adorned with **seven pyramids** (two for his parents, **four** for **his brothers,** and one for himself) flanked with **great pillars** that were carved with pictures of **weaponry** (the whole family had been "warring the war of Israel with gladness," 3.2) and **ships**[348] (one of Simon's most important achievements

---

[347] The monument had a front and a back, both of which were surfaced **with polished stone** (therefore, it was not a tomb cut into the rock, like that described in Matt 27.60).

[348] The **ships** were designed **to be seen by all those that sail the sea.** This does not mean that they were "visible to those at sea" (REB); no tomb carvings, however enormous, could fit that description! Rather, it means that **all** sailors (**those who sail the sea**) visiting the monument **at**

was that "he took Joppa for a harbor," so that Israel had its own "entrance to the islands of the sea" and was no longer forced to rely on foreign seaports: 14.5). In that way, the tomb devised by Simon commemorated his family's achievements by both land and sea (cf. 8.23).

The righteous receive a **lasting name** (Rev 3.12; Isa 56.5; Luke 10.20; in contrast to the wicked, Prov 10.7). An earthly tomb designed **for a lasting name** is an earthly reflection of that.

The tomb raised by Simon was still in existence at the time when the book was written (**until this day:** cf. Gen 35.20; Deut 34.6; 2 Sam 18.18).[349]

Trypho becomes king of Asia

13.31 ο δε Τρυφων επορευετο δολω μετα Αντιοχου του βαcιλεωc του νεωτερου και απεκτινεν αυτον	**13.31** But Trypho was proceeding in deceit with Antiochus the young king; and he killed him.
13.32 και εβαcιλευcεν αντ αυτου και περιεθετο το διαδημα τηc Αcιαc και εποιηcεν πληγην μεγαλην επι τηc γηc	**13.32** And he became king in place of him, and placed on himself the diadem of Asia. And he did a great injury on the land.

13.31–32 Eventually **Trypho** succeeded in carrying out his plan (first described in 12.39). Proceeding as deceitfully as ever, **he killed . . . Antiochus the young king** and **became king in place of him,** wearing the royal **diadem** (1.9) as king **of Asia** (the Seleucid kingdom: 8.6; cf. 11.13).[350] Like many of the earlier Seleucid kings, **he did a great injury on the land** (see the comments on 1.30): "all the activities of Trypho were plunderings" (v 34).

Modein would **see** the carved **ships** and remember how much they personally owed to the family of Mattathias (Saulcy, *Histoire de l'art judaïque,* 377). Cf. "every shipmaster, and everyone who sails to any place, and as many as work the sea" (Rev 18.17–19); "all those who handle an oar, mariners, all sailors of the sea" (Ezek 27.29–30): in both of those passages too, the sailors are on land at the time when they are described.

[349] The phrase **until this day** does not provide much help in dating the book; it can mark a lapse of time as short as a few months (1 Sam 29.3) or as long as ten centuries (Acts 2.29). "In the present case, the writer is merely indicating that the monument is still intact at the time of writing, despite the battles in the region after its completion," especially 16.4–8 (Grandclaudon, *Macchabées,* 11). The phrase would therefore suit any date after the start of John's high priesthood (cf. 16.24).

[350] Trypho's murder of Antiochus and usurpation of the kingdom are also reported by Classical historians (Diodorus 33.28–28a; Appian, *Syriaca,* 68.357). The successive steps in this process are discussed together in vv 31–32 for the sake of clarity, without any implication that they all happened chronologically between v 30 and v 33.

Judea is freed from the nations

Demetrius makes peace with Simon

13.33 και ωκοδομηcε(ν) Cιμων τα οχυρωματα της ‹Ιουδαιας› και περιετιχιcεν πυργοις υψηλοις και τιχεcιν μεγαλοις και πυλοις και μοχλοις και εθετο βρωματα εν τοις οχυρωμαcιν	**13.33** And Simon built up the fortresses of Judea, and walled *them* around with high towers and great walls, and gates and bars; and he placed foods in the fortresses.

13.33 Ιουδαιας S[ca] V A 64[+]236 La[109] La[146] | Ιδουμαιας S* • πυλοις S V = -λαις A 64[+]236 •

13.33 Simon continued the program of building and strengthening **the fortresses of Judea** (already described in 12.35, 38). **He placed** provisions (**foods**) **in the fortresses,** in case they were besieged (6.53; 9.52). Simon "sought good things for his nation" (14.4), giving himself (v 5) and his money (14.32) to build up his people—whereas Trypho did the opposite, injuring the land (v 32) and robbing its people (v 34).

13.34 και επελεξεν Cιμω(ν) ανδρας και απεcτιλεν προς Δημητριον τον βαcιλεα του ποιηcαι αφεcιν τη χωρα οτι παcαι αι πραξεις Τρυφωνος ‹ηcαν αρπαγαι›	**13.34** And Simon chose men and sent *them* to Demetrius the king, to make a free release for the district: for all the activities of Trypho were plunderings.

13.34 ηcαν αρπαγαι S[ca] V [-παcαι A] 64[+]236 La[109] La[146] | απαγαι S* •

13.34 All the activities of Trypho were plunderings (i.e., "all that Trypho did was to plunder," RV; cf. v 32). Therefore, **Simon** saw an opportunity to offer an alliance to Trypho's opponent **Demetrius the king** (who had fled, 11.55–56, but whose forces had been trying to reenter the land, 11.63; 12.24), on the condition that he would grant **the district** of Judea **a free release** (so that it would no longer have any obligations to the king: see vv 37–39).

13.35 και απεcτιλεν αυτω Δημητριος ο βαcιλευς κατα τους λογους τουτους και απεκριθη αυτω και εγραψεν αυτω επιcτολην τοιαυτην	**13.35** And Demetrius the king sent to him in accordance with these words, and responded to him, and wrote him such a letter:
13.36 βαcιλευς Δημητριος Cιμωνι αρχιερει και φιλω βαcιλεων και πρεcβυτεροις και εθνει Ιουδαιων χαιρειν	**13.36** "King Demetrius to Simon, high priest and kings' Friend, and to *the* elders and *the* nation of *the* Judeans: Rejoice.
13.37 τον cτεφανον τον χρυcουν και την ‹βαιν› ην απεcτιλατε κεκομιcμεθα και ετοιμοι εcμεν του ποιειν υμιν ειρηνην μεγαλην	**13.37** The golden crown and the palm-branch that you[pl] sent, we have received. And we are ready to make a great peace with you[pl], and

και γραφειν τοιc επι των χρειων του αφειναι υμιν τα αφεματα	to write to the *people* over the duties, to set free the free things for you[pl].
13.38 και οcα εcτηcαμεν προc υμαc εcτηκεν και τα οχυρωματα α οικοδομηκατε υπαρχετω υμιν	**13.38** And whatever things we have established for you[pl], they are estab- lished; and the fortresses that you[pl] have built, let them be yours[pl].
13.39 αφειεμεν δε αγνοηματα και τα αμαρτηματα εωc τηc cημερο(ν) ημεραc και τον cτεφανον ον ωφειλετε και ει τι αλλο ετελωνειτο εν Ι(ερουcα)λημ μηκετι τελωνειcθω	**13.39** But we forgive *all the* deeds of ignorance and the sins until today's day, and the crown that you[pl] were owing. And if any other *thing* was being taxed in Jerusalem, let it be taxed no longer.
13.40 και ει τινεc επιτηδειοι υμων γραφηναι ειc τουc περι ημαc ενγραφεcθωcα(ν) και ˻γινεcθω˼ ανα μεcον ημω(ν) ειρηνη	**13.40** And if some of you[pl] *are* suitable to be inscribed in the *people* around us, let them be inscribed; and let *there* be peace between us."

13.37 βαιν V A La^{146} | βαινην S $64^{+}236$ • **13.40** γινεcθω S^{*,c} V A $64^{+}236$ La^{109} La^{146} | -ωcαν S^{1} •

13.36–40 Demetrius accepted the offer and agreed to **a great peace** with the people of Judea (**you,** plural). He instructed **the people over the duties** (his "revenue officers," REB, as 10.41 shows) **to set free** the Judeans' obligations to pay taxes and tributes of **any** kind (vv 37, 39), including the requirement to send the king tribute payments in the form of a **crown** (see 10.29). He officially acknowledged the Judeans' right to build and possess their own **fortresses** (v 38). And he authorized any **suitable** Judeans to be **inscribed** in his "retinue" (REB; **the people around us,**[351] v 40).

The yoke of the nations is removed

13.41 ετουc ο΄ και εκατοcτου ηρθη ο ζυγοc των εθνω(ν) απο του Ι(cρα)ηλ	**13.41** *In the* hundred and seventieth year, the yoke of the nations was lifted up from Israel,
13.42 και ηρξατο ο λαοc γραφειν εν ταιc cυγγραφαιc και ˻cυναλλαγμαcιν˼ ετουc α΄ επι Cιμωνοc αρχιερεωc μεγαλου και cτρατηγου και ηγουμενου Ιουδαιων	**13.42** and the people began to write in *their* writings and agreements: "*In the* first year of Simon, *the* great high priest and army com- mander and leader of *the* Judeans."

13.42 cυναλλαγμαcιν S^{ca} V A $64^{+}236$ | -ματα S* •

13.41–42 Demetrius's treaty did not put an absolute end, once and for all, to all Seleucid claims of authority over **Israel** (at a later date, Antiochus son of Demetrius

[351] **The people around us** *(tous peri hēmas)*. The wording is more general than in 10.36 (where Judeans are to be inscribed specifically "in the king's forces").

would still call "the citadel that is in Jerusalem" part of "my kingdom," 15.28). But it entitled the Israelites to reckon themselves free from **the yoke of the nations** (cf. the notes on 8.18). Instead of dating **their writings** by the years of a foreign king (e.g., "in the second year of Darius the king," Hag 1.1; Zec 1.1; "in the twelfth year of king Ahasuerus," Est 3.7; "in the seventh year of Artaxerxes the king," Ezra 7.7), they were able to date them by the years of their own leader: **in the first year of Simon, the great high priest and army commander and leader of the Judeans.** That year corresponded to the **hundred and seventieth year** of the kingdom of the Greeks (cf. 1.10).

Under the old covenant Law, the Israelites had been warned that, if they did not serve the LORD with joy, they would be forced to serve their enemies and wear "a yoke of iron on your neck" (Deut 28.47–48). That warning finally came to pass in the days of the Babylonians, when the LORD declared: "I have put a yoke of iron on the neck of all these nations to serve Nebuchadnezzar king of Babylon" (Jer 28.14; 27.6–12). Since that time, Israel had been subject successively to the Babylonians, the Medes and Persians (Dan 5.30–31; 8.3–4, 20), and the Greeks (1.1, 10; 8.18; Dan 8.5–7, 21).

Nevertheless the LORD had promised His people that there would come a time when "I will break his yoke from over your neck, and I will tear off your bonds, and strangers will no longer enslave him; and they will serve the LORD their God" (Jer 30.8–9). That process was not finally completed in the days of Simon—there still lay ahead a "fourth kingdom on earth" to which Israel would become subject for a while (Dan 7.23; 2.40; cf. Matt 22.17–21). But the freedom that came about in the time of Simon was one further step in the series of events that the LORD's prophets had revealed, leading to the time when His own King would come and set His people free once and for all from all yokes of slavery (Gal 5.1) to serve Him under a yoke that is easy and a burden that is light (Matt 11.29–30).

Gaza submits to Simon

13.43 εν ταιϲ ημεραιϲ εκειναιϲ παρενεβαλλεν επι Γαζαν και εκυκλωϲεν αυτην παρεμβολαιϲ και εποιηϲεν ελεοπολιν και προϲηγαγεν τη πολει και επαταξεν πυργον ενα και κατελαβετο	**13.43** In those days he camped against Gaza, and surrounded it with camps, and made a city-taker, and brought *it* near the city. And he smote one tower and took hold of *it*,
13.44 και εξηλλοντο οι εν τη ελεοπολι ειϲ την πολιν και εγενετο κινημα ‹μεγα εν τη πολι›	**13.44** and the *men* in the city-taker *began* springing out into the city; and *there* came to be a great commotion in the city.

13.44 μεγα / εν τη πολι A 64[+]236 La[109] La[146] | ~ S V •

13.43–44 Simon also continued the military activities in and around the Philistine region (already described in 10.69–87; 11.60–62, 65–66; 12.33–34, 38; 13.11). **He**

camped against Gaza.[352] It had already been captured by the Israelites once (11.61–62), but now the process had to be repeated—as with various other cities in the neighborhood (e.g., Joppa, 10.75–76; 12.33–34; 13.11; Bethzur, 6.26; 11.65–66). Something that has once been saved from an enemy will not necessarily stay saved; it may again fall into enemy hands and need to be recaptured (cf. Jas 5.19–20; Gal 6.1; Matt 18.15). Constant vigilance, and constant readiness to repel the enemy, are always needed (cf. 1 Cor 9.24–27).

The Judeans **surrounded** Gaza **with** their army **camps,** and constructed a **city-taker.**[353] The detailed description here shows that this was a kind of "siege machine" (NAB), which could be **brought near the city** at a height that would enable some of the besieging soldiers to attack and capture a **tower** and so get **into the city.** NJB suggests that the city-taker was a "mobile tower."

13.45 και ανεβηcαν οι εν τη πολι cυν γυναιξιν κ(αι) τοιc τεκνοιc επι το τειχοc διερρηχοτεc τα ιματια αυτων κ(αι) εβοηcαν φωνη μεγαλη ‹αξιουντεc› Cειμωνα ‹δεξιαc› αυτοιc δουναι	**13.45** And the *men* in the city went up on the wall *with* their clothes torn, together with *the* women and the children; and they called out with a great voice, presenting a request for Simon to give right *hand*s to them,
13.46 και ειπαν μη ημιν χρηcη κατα ταc πονηριαc ημων αλλα κατα το ελεοc cου	**13.46** and they said: "Do not use† us in accordance with our wickedness, but in accordance with your† mercy."

13.45 αξιουντεc S^{ca} V A 64^{+}236 | > S* La^{146} • δεξιαc S^{ca} V A [-αν 64^{+}236] La^{146} | δει ιδιαc S* •

[352] **Gaza** *(Gazan)* is the reading of all ancient manuscripts in any language (Greek, Latin, and Syriac). Many modern editors emend to *Gazara* ("Gezer"), but nothing in the context favors such a change. Neither Gaza nor Gezer is explicitly stated to have been in enemy hands immediately before this episode, but both had certainly been enemy cities during earlier stages of the Maccabean struggle, and either or both of them might therefore need capturing now. Josephus is no help here, because about half the documented manuscripts of his paraphrase (*Antiquities,* 13.215) read *Gazan* at this point, while the other half read *Gazara.* Besides, he or his assistants or copyists misread or misconstrued a significant amount of what they adapted from the Maccabean History (see the chapter on Josephus in this book); where they wrote something that differs from all known manuscripts of their source, the simplest explanation is generally error.

[353] **A city-taker** *(heleopolin),* a device for taking (*helein*, second aorist of *haireō*) a city *(polis);* in Spanish, a *conquistadora de ciudades* (DGE 7.1444, §2). As Joshua had taken the cities *(poleis hairōn)* of Canaan (Josephus, *Antiquities,* 5.67), Simon now took *(hairei)* the cities of the Philistines (Josephus, *War,* 1.50; cf. LSJ 41, §A.II; DGE 1.115, §A.III.1). S has *heleopolin,* and the transcriptions in La^{109} and La^{146} show that the Old Latin version was also prepared from manuscript(s) with that spelling, whereas 64^{+}236 and all modern editions have the now customary spelling *helepolin.* V has the plural *helepoleis;* A omits the word entirely.

13.45–46 The people **in the city** entreated **Simon** to make peace (**give right hands,** as in 6.58; 11.50, 62, 66), saying: **Do not use us in accordance with our wickedness, but in accordance with your mercy.** Their position before Simon was similar to ours before God. We have done **wickedness** before Him (Isa 64.6), and cannot claim that we deserve forgiveness; we can base our plea for peace only on His mercy: "We are not casting down our supplications before You on account of our righteousnesses, but on account of Your great mercies" (Dan 9.18; Jer 14.7, 20–21; Psa 103.10–11; Ezra 9.13).

13.47 και cυνελυθη ‹αυτοιc Cιμων› και ουκ επολεμηcεν αυτουc και εξεβαλεν αυτουc ‹εκ› τηc πολεωc και εκαθαριcεν ταc οικιαc εν αιc ην τα ειδωλα και ουτωc ειcηλθεν ειc αυτην υμνων και ευλογων	**13.47** And Simon was restored to harmony with them, and did not make war against them. And he cast them out of the city, and cleansed the houses in which the idols had been; and thus he came into it *with* hymns and blessings.
13.48 και εξεβαλεν εξ αυτηc παcα(ν) ακαθαρcιαν κ(αι) κατωκηcεν εν αυτη ανδραc οιτινεc τον νομον ποιηcωcι(ν) και προcωχυρωcεν αυτην και ωκοδομηcε(ν) εαυτω εν αυτη οικηcιν	**13.48** And he cast out of it all uncleanness, and he settled it with men, whoever would do the Law. And he made it more fortified, and built in it a dwelling-place for *him*self.

13.47 αυτοιc / Cιμων S^{ca} V A [~ $64^{+}236$] La^{109} La^{146} | Cιμων S* • εκ V A $64^{+}236$ La^{109} La^{146} | εξω S •

13.47–48 Simon was merciful to his enemies. He himself had received undeserved mercy from a far greater Master; how then could he be unmerciful to those around him (Matt 18.33; 6.15; Jas 2.13)? He **was restored to harmony with them,** and, in spite of their wickedness (v 46), he **did not make war against them.** Nevertheless, **he cast them out of the city** and destroyed their works (cf. 2 Cor 10.3–5), cleansing **the houses in which the idols had been. All** forms of **uncleanness** could have no place in God's earthly cities under the old covenant, just as they can have no place in God's heavenly city under the new covenant (Rev 21.27; 22.15; 1 Cor 6.9–10; Gal 5.19–21).

Instead, Simon **came into** the city **with hymns and blessings** (cf. v 51; 4.24, 54–55)—the very opposite of **uncleanness** in word or deed (see Eph 5.3–5). **He settled**[354] the city with people **who would do the Law** (as the heavenly city is settled: Rev 22.14; 21.27), provided **himself** with a **dwelling-place** there, and **fortified** the city against the enemy (as the heavenly city is fortified: Rev 21.12).

The citadel is cleansed

13.49 οι δε εκ τηc ακραc ‹› εν Ι(ερουcα)λημ εκωλυοντο	**13.49** But the *people* from the citadel in Jerusalem were being prevented

[354] **He settled it with men.** Greek *katōkēsen en autē andras,* "he caused to dwell in it men."

εκπορευεcθαι και ειcπορευεcθαι ειc	from going out and going into
την χωραν ‹και› αγοραζειν και πωλιν	the district, and buying and selling.
και επιναcα(ν) cφοδρα	And they were very hungry;
και απωλοντο εξ αυτων ικανοι	and considerable *numbers* out of them
τω λειμω	were destroyed with hunger.

13.49 εν V A La^{109} La^{146} | ^ οι S 64^{+}236 • και 2° A 64^{+}236 La^{109} La^{146} | > S V •

13.49 The long struggle against **the people from the citadel in Jerusalem** was also nearing its end. The siege described in 11.20–23 and 12:35–36 was taking its toll. The people inside could not go **out** of the citadel and **into the** surrounding **district** (Judea, as in vv 34, 20, etc.). Nor could they buy or sell. They were desperately short of food (cf. v 21), **and considerable numbers out of them were destroyed**[355] **with hunger.**

13.50 και εβοηcαν προc Cιμωνα	**13.50** And they called out to Simon
δεξιαc λαβειν και εδωκεν αυτοιc	to take *their* right *hands*; and he gave
και εξεβαλεν αυτουc εκειθεν	*his* to them. And he cast them
και εκαθαριcεν	out from there, and cleansed
την ακραν απο των μιαcματων	the citadel from *its* pollutions.

13.50 As at Gaza (see the notes on vv 47–48), **Simon** mercifully accepted their plea for peace and did not take vengeance for all the harm they had done to the Judeans ("they poured out guiltless blood round about the holy place," 1.32–37; "the whole time they were seeking evil things," 6.18)—but he did not let them continue their evil works: **he cast them out from there, and cleansed the citadel from its pollutions** (cf. 14.7).

13.51 και ‹ειcηλθεν› ειc αυτην τη	**13.51** And he came into it on
τριτη και εικαδι του ‹δευτερου μηνοc›	the twenty-third of the second month
ετουc πρωτου ‹και› εβδομηκοcτου	of *the* hundred and seventy-first year,
και εκατοcτου μετα αινεcεωc	with praise
και ‹βαιω(ν)› και εν κινυραιc	and palm-branches, and with lyres
και εν κυμβαλοιc και εν ‹ναβλαιc›	and cymbals and harps and
και εν υμνοιc και εν ωδαιc οτι	hymns and songs: for a great enemy
cυνετριβη εχθροc μεγαc εξ Ιc(ραη)λ	had been shattered out of Israel.

13.51 ειcηλθεν V A La^{109} 7a1 | -θον S 64^{+}236 La^{146} 7h7 • δευτερου μηνοc V A La^{109} La^{146} | μηνοc του δευτερου S 64^{+}236 • και 3° V A 64^{+}236 | > S • βαιω(ν) S^{ca} V A 64^{+}236 | βαεω(ν) S* • ναβλαιc S^{ca} V A 64^{+}236 La^{146} | αβλ- S* •

---

355 **Were destroyed** *(apōlonto)* does not necessarily mean "died" (NAB): see the footnote to 12.50, and compare Rogland, *Alleged Non-Past Uses of Qatal,* §3.4.5 (the destruction is "as good as done"); Joosten, *Verbal System of Biblical Hebrew,* 206 (it "seems an inevitable end"); see also Num 17.12; Isa 6.5; Jer 4.13; Lam 3.54. A somewhat similar use of the term to express severe deprivation may be heard in Irish ("we're after forgetting his bit of bread . . . and it's destroyed he'll be going till dark night, and he after eating nothing since the sun went up": Synge, *Riders to the Sea*).

13.51 The Israelites finally entered the citadel in the **hundred and seventy-first year,** at least 35 years after it was set up (1.20, 29, 32–33). **A great enemy** (1.33–36) **had been shattered.** Of all those faithful servants who had fought and prayed and negotiated so long to overcome it, how many lived to see the final success? (Mattathias and four of his five sons did not.) But steadfast labor in the Lord is never wasted, even if we ourselves do not see the result in this life (1 Cor 15.58).

The victors entered the place **with praise and palm-branches** (used to accompany praise, John 12.12–13; Rev 7.9) and **hymns and songs,** as well as with the musical instruments (**lyres and cymbals and harps**) commanded by God under the old covenant Law (2 Chr 29.25). "When there is good for righteous ones, a town exults; and when wicked ones are destroyed, there is shouting" (Prov 11.10). See also on verse 47.

13.52 και εστησεν κατ ενιαυτον του αγειν την ημεραν ταυτην μετα ευφροσυνης και προσοχυρωσεν το ορος του ιερου το παρα την ακραν και ωκει εκει αυτος και οι παρ αυτου	**13.52** And he established each year to keep this day with gladness. And he made more fortified the mountain of the temple *that was* alongside the citadel; and he *began* dwelling there, he and the *people* alongside him.

13.52 The **day** when the citadel was entered ("the twenty-third of the second month," v 51) was to be kept **each year . . . with gladness.** Even after this triumph, Simon remained vigilant ("let the one who thinks himself to stand watch that he does not fall," 1 Cor 10.12). In spite of the fact that the enemies had now been cast out, he still protected **the mountain of the temple** from **the citadel** by strengthening the fortifications at that point "for the security of the district and of the city" (14.37), and by **dwelling there** himself with some of his helpers (cf. the notes on v 53).

John son of Simon

13.53 και ειδεν Σιμω(ν) τον Ιωαννην υιον αυτου οτι ανηρ εστιν και εθετο αυτον ηγουμενον των δυναμεων πασων και ωκει εν Γαζαροις	**13.53** And Simon saw John his son, that he was a man; and he placed him *as* leader of all the forces; and he *began* dwelling in Gezer.

13.53 This is the first mention of **John,** the **son** and eventual successor (16.23–24) of **Simon.** When he became **a man,** his father **placed him as leader of all the** military **forces:** the work of the Lord was starting to be handed down from Simon's generation (cf. v 42) to the next (16.2–3; cf 2 Tim 2.2). Like his father, John chose to dwell in a potential trouble spot, a place of longstanding opposition to Israel. His father had dwelling places at Gaza (v 48) and in or next to the citadel (v 52); John **began dwelling**[356] **in** another old Philistine city, **Gezer** (see the notes on 4.15).

[356] **He began dwelling at Gezer** refers to John, not to Simon. The next time we hear of John, he is at Gezer, and Simon is not (16.1).

Demetrius is captured in Media

14.1 και εν ετι δευτερω και ‹εβδομηκοστω› και ρ΄ συνηγαγεν Δημητριος ο βασιλευς τας δυναμις αυτου και επορευθη εις Μηδειαν του επισπασασθαι βοηθιαν αυτω οπως πολεμηση τον Τρυφωνα	**14.1** And in *the* hundred and seventy-second year, Demetrius the king gathered his forces and went into Media, to draw together help for *him*self, so that he might make war against Trypho.

14.1 εβδομηκοστω V A 64⁺236 La[109] La[146] | -μω S •

14.1 In the hundred and seventy-second year[357] (the year after the citadel was cleansed, 13.51), **Demetrius the king . . . went into Media** to gather **help** for a **war against Trypho.** The land of **Media** had long been closely allied with Persia (v 2; 1.1; Dan 5.28; 8.20; Est 1.3). It had been part of the Seleucid kingdom in the time of Antiochus the Great (8.8) and was among the "upper districts" across the Euphrates River, where Antiochus Epiphanes had sought to restore his finances (6.56; compare 3.31, 37).

14.2 και ηκουσεν ‹Αρσακης› ο βασιλευς της Περσιδος και Μηδιας ‹οτι› εισηλθεν Δημητριος εις τα ορια αυτου και απεστιλεν ενα των αρχοντων αυτου συνλαβιν αυτον ζω(ν)τα	**14.2** And Arsaces, the king of Persia and Media, heard that Demetrius had come into his appointed boundaries; and he sent one of his commanders to take him alive.
14.3 και επορευθη και επαταξεν την παρεμβολην Δημητριου και συνελαβεν αυτον και ηγαγεν αυτον προς Αρσακην ‹κ(αι) εθετο αυτον εν φυλακη›	**14.3** And he went and smote the company of Demetrius, and took hold of him, and brought him to Arsaces; and he placed him in safekeeping.

14.2 Αρσακης V A 64⁺236 La[109] La[146] | Αρσικης S • οτι V A 64⁺236 La[109] La[146] | οτε S* • **14.3** κ(αι) εθετο αυτον εν φυλακη S^ca V A 64⁺236 La[109] La[146] | > S* •

14.2–3 But the Seleucids were no longer in control of this region. When Demetrius advanced toward Media, he came within the **appointed boundaries** ruled by **Arsaces,**[358] who was now **king of Persia and Media** (cf. 15.22). Arsaces **sent one of his commanders,** who defeated (**smote,** as in 1.1) the army of **Demetrius, and took hold**

[357] 172 SE would probably be equivalent to about 140–139 BCE.

[358] **Arsaces** was the customary name (Strabo 15.1.36) for Parthian kings of this family (the Arsacid dynasty). The Arsaces mentioned here is generally called Mithridates I (Arsaces VI) by modern historians. The Median expedition of Demetrius and his capture by Arsaces are also recorded in historical documents of the period (SH 3.160–61, §-137A) and by Classical historians (Appian, *Syriaca,* 67.356; Justin 36.1.2–6; 38.9.2–3).

of him. Arsaces then **placed** Demetrius **in safekeeping.**[359] This left Trypho without a rival as ruler of the Seleucid kingdom—until the arrival of the next Antiochus (15.10).

ISRAEL AND THE NATIONS

Israel in the time of Simon

14.4 και ηϲυχαϲεν η γη Ιουδα παϲαϲ ταϲ ημεραϲ Ϲιμωνοϲ και εζητηϲεν αγαθα τω εθνι αυτου και ηρεϲεν αυτοιϲ η εξουϲια αυτου και η δοξα αυτου παϲαϲ ταϲ ημεραϲ	**14.4** And the land of Judah was quiet all the days of Simon; and he sought good *things* for his nation; and his authority pleased them, and his glory, all *his* days.

14.4 The account of Simon's deeds in this section (vv 4–15) mirrors the account of Judas's deeds near the start of the book (3.1–9). Judas "pursued those who were opposed to the Law, searching them out" (3.5); Simon "sought out the Law, and put away every one who was opposed to the Law and wicked" (14.14). When Judas led the people, "he made Jacob glad with his deeds . . . and he was named even to the end of the earth" (3.7–9). When Simon led them, "the name of his glory was named up to the end of the earth . . . and Israel was glad with great gladness" (14.10–11). Thus the brothers were one in mind and spirit (as we are to be, Php 1.27; 2.2; Rom 15.5–6; 1 Cor 1.10; 2 Cor 13.11). Yet, laboring at different times and in different situations, they had different tasks to perform. In the time of Judas, the main task was the achievement of victory: "They were warring the war of Israel with gladness . . . and he girded himself with his war equipment, and waged wars . . . and he turned away anger from Israel" (3.2–3, 8). In the time of Simon, the main task was the maintenance of peace: "The land of Judah was quiet all the days of Simon . . . . He made peace in the land . . . and those who were making war against them in the land ceased" (14.4, 11–13). During the days of Judas (and Jonathan) there had been repeated wars, and the land had been quiet only for brief periods ("a few days," 7.50; "two years," 9.57). But now that her great enemies were cast out (v 7; cf. 13.50–51), **the land of Judah was quiet all the days of Simon** (as described more fully in vv 11–13). In the same way, the wars in the time of David (1 Kgs 5.3; 1 Chr 22.8; 28.3) had led to the peace in the time of Solomon (1 Chr 22.9; 1 Kgs 4.24–25; 5.4)—and the "war in heaven" in the time of Jesus (Rev 12.1–17; Luke 10.18; John 12.31) led to the peace of the gospel (Isa 9.6–7; Psa 72.7; Luke 2.14; Eph 2.14–18).

Simon **sought good things for his nation** (cf. Est 10.3). That is what God Himself does (Luke 1.53; Matt 7.11; Rom 8.28; Jas 1.17); and "the one who does good is of God" (3 Jn 11; Luke 6.35). (Contrast the earlier high priest Alcimus, who had sought evil for his people: Maccabaica 7.15–18). **His authority pleased** his nation (as the great inscription recorded in vv 25–49 shows), and so did **his glory** *(doxa)*—not the

---

[359] Classical historians report that Demetrius remained in captivity for about ten years, but that he was treated favorably and even married Arsaces' daughter (Justin 36.1.6; 38.9.3).

glory "of a sinful man" (which "will become dung and grubs," 2.62), but the glory (honor) that comes from keeping the Law (see the notes on 2.51–52, 64), and the glory that Simon also "took counsel to provide for his nation" (v 35).[360]

14.5 κ(αι) μετα παϲηϲ τηϲ δοξηϲ αυτου ελαβε(ν) την ‹Ιοππην› ειϲ λιμενα και εποιηϲεν ειϲοδον ταιϲ νηϲοιϲ τηϲ θαλαϲϲηϲ	**14.5** And with all his glory, he took Joppa for a harbor, and made an entrance to the islands of the sea.
14.6 και επλατυνεν τα ορια τω εθνι ‹αυτου› και εκρατηϲεν τηϲ χωραϲ	**14.6** And he was broadening the appointed boundaries of his nation, and took hold of the district,
14.7 και ϲυνηγαγεν αιχμαλωϲιαν πολλην και ‹εκυριευϲεν› Γαζαρων και Βεθϲουρων και τηϲ ακραϲ και εξηρεν ταϲ ακαθαρϲιαϲ εξ αυτηϲ και ουκ ην ο αντικειμενοϲ αυτω	**14.7** and gathered a great group of captives. And he became lord over Gezer and Bethzur and the citadel, and put away the uncleannesses from it. And no one was setting himself against him.

14.5 Ιοππην S^{ca} V A 64^{+}236 La^{109} La^{146} | ιππον S* • **14.6** αυτου S^{ca} V A 64^{+}236 La^{109} La^{146} | τουτω S* • **14.7** εκυριευϲεν V A 64^{+}236 La^{109} La^{146} | ϲυνηγαγεν S •

14.5–7 Simon's activities in strengthening and stabilizing the land are here summarized. **He took Joppa for a harbor** (see 12.33–34; 13.11), so that Judea now had its own **entrance to the islands of the sea** (6.29; 15.1), a place like Tyre in Phoenicia (Ezek 27.3); see the notes on 13.29. Zephaniah had prophesied that "the region of the sea ... the land of the Philistines ... will be for the remnant of Judah" (Zep 2.5–7). The old covenant Israel had now taken possession of that region—which paved the way for the new covenant Israel to take possession of it also (Acts 9.36–43; 10.5–6; cf. Smith, *Historical Geography of the Holy Land,* 136–38).

Simon **was broadening**[361] **the appointed boundaries of his nation** (v 33), not by taking land "outside the appointed boundaries of Judea" (as the Judeans' enemies accused them of doing, 15.30), but by regaining land that had belonged to the nation in the days of their ancestors (15.33–34).

He took hold of the district (in this context—as in v 17; 9.24; 13.20—the word refers specifically to **the district** of Judea; cf. 12.25), **and gathered a great group of captives** who had been in the power of the enemy (as Judas and Jonathan had also

---

[360] So Simon's **glory** did not consist only in "the magnificence of his court" (Abel 250), though it certainly included that (15.32).

[361] **He was broadening** *(eplatunen).* The imperfect tense emphasizes that this was not just one isolated event (cf. 3.1–2; 5.53; 11.3; 13.20; see also the passages listed in MHT 3.66–67; Robertson 883–84; BDF §§325, 327). Simon did not do good on one occasion only. He persisted in it (Rom 2.7; Gal 6.9).

done, 5.13, 53–54; 9.70–72). Again the parallel with the spiritual work of Jesus is striking (Psa 68.18 ≡ Eph 4.8; Luke 4.18; 2 Tim 2.26).

He became lord over Gezer ("in which the warring people had previously been dwelling," v 34; 13.53) **and Bethzur** (v 33; 11.65–66) **and the citadel,** which he cleansed from its **uncleannesses** (see the notes on 13.50–51).

And no one was setting himself against [*antikeimenos*] **him** (as described in vv 11–12). Jesus promised His apostles: "I myself will give you a mouth and wisdom, which none of those who set themselves against [*antikeimenoi*] you will be able to stand against or speak against" (Luke 21.15).

14.8 και ηcαν γεωργουντεc την γην	**14.8** And they were farming their land
αυτω(ν) μετ ειρηνηc και η γη εδιδου	in peace; and the land was giving
τα γενηματα αυτηc κ(αι) τα ξυλα ‹›	its produce, and the trees
των πεδιων ‹› τον καρπον αυτων	of the level places their fruit.

14.8 ξυλα V A $64^{+}236$ La^{109} La^{146} | + αμα S • πεδιων S^{ca} V A $64^{+}236$ La^{109} La^{146} | + και S* •

14.8 The Judeans **were farming their land in peace; and the land was giving its produce, and the trees of the level places their fruit.** Under the old covenant, all these things were among the blessings that God promised His people if they obeyed Him faithfully (Lev 26.4–6; Deut 28.5, 11–12). The prophets had foretold that comparable blessings would later come to pass under the new covenant (Ezek 37.25–28; Zec 8.11–12; Isa 2.4), and those prophecies have now been fulfilled spiritually through Christ (Col 1.20, 6; Matt 13.23; Rev 22.2).

14.9 πρεcβυτεροι	**14.9** *The* elders were sitting
εν ταιc ‹πλατιαιc› εκαθηντο	in the broad *places*; all *of them* shared
παντεc περι αγαθων εκοινολογουντο	in speaking about good *things*;
και οι νεανιcκοι ενεδυcαντο	and the young men clothed them-
δοξαν και cτολαc πολεμου	selves with glory and robes of war.

14.9 πλατιαιc S^{ca} V A $64^{+}236$ La^{109} La^{146} | εκκληcιαιc S* •

14.9 The elders were sitting in the broad places, the most public areas of the city (Matt 6.5), where the people could gather (Ezra 10.9; 2 Chr 29.4; 32.6) in times of peace (Zec 8.4–5)—but where their dead bodies would lie in times of war (Jer 9.21; 49.26). When the nation was corrupt, it might be impossible to find in the broad places anyone "who is doing judgment, who is seeking truth" (Jer 5.1). But in the days of Simon, **all** the elders were there **speaking about good things,** in accordance with the commands of the Law (the words of God "shall be on your heart . . . and you shall speak of them when you sit in your house, and when you walk in the way, and when you lie down, and when you rise up," Deut 6.6–7; "all the day," Psa 119.97). "Whatever things are true, whatever things are honorable, whatever things are righteous, whatever things are pure, whatever things are worthy of love, whatever things are well spoken of, if there is any excellence, and if there is any praise, think on [*logizesthe*] these things" (Php 4.8).

The young men clothed themselves with glory[362] **and robes of war.** The Lord comes from the slaughter of His enemies "splendid in His clothing" (Isa 63.1–6); His people, though they may suffer and be "clothed with shame" for a while (1.28), will also wear glorious clothing (Isa 52.1; 61.10) and armor ("armor of light," Rom 13.12).

14.10 ταιc πολεcιν εχορηγηcαν βρωματα και εταξαν εαυτουc εν cκευεcιν ‹οχυρωcεωc› εωc οτου ωνομαcθη το ονομα τηc δοξηc αυτου εωc ακρου γηc	**14.10** To the cities they supplied foods, and they provided themselves with implements of fortification, until the name of his glory was named up to *the* end of *the* earth.

14.10 οχυρωcεωc S[ca] V A 64[+]236 La[109] | -ρωματω(ν) S* La[146] •

14.10 To the cities they supplied foods, and they provided themselves[363] **with implements of fortification.** A few years earlier, when Israel was disobedient to God, their **cities** did not always have enough **foods** (6.53–54), and the people did not always have the weapons and defenses that they needed (1.31; 4.6; 6.62). That was what God had warned them would happen if they failed to trust in Him (Lev 26.14–33; Deut 28.15–63). But in the prosperous days of Simon, the Judeans were blessed with **foods** for their **cities** and with **implements of fortification** (13.33).[364]

The name of his glory was named up to the end of the earth, like his brother Judas earlier (see the notes on 3.9) and Jesus later (Psa 72.19; Php 2.9–11).

14.11 εποιηcεν ιρηνη(ν) επι τηc γηc και ευφρανθη Ι(cρα)ηλ ευφροcυνην μεγαλην	**14.11** He made peace in the land, and Israel was glad *with* great gladness.
14.12 και εκαθιcεν εκαcτοc υπο την αμπελον αυτου ‹και την cυκην αυτου› και ουκ ην ‹ο› εκφοβω(ν) αυτουc	**14.12** And each *one* sat under his vine and his fig-tree, and *there* was no one to make them utterly afraid.

14.12 και την cυκην αυτου V A [κ- υποκατω τηc cυκηc α- 64[+]236] La[109] La[146] | > S • ο S[ca] V A 64[+]236 | > S* •

[362] **Clothed themselves with glory** [*doxan*]. "Glorious [*endoxō*] clothing" is a mark of high status (Luke 7.25; cf. Maccabaica 10.62). **Glory** *(doxan)* is the reading of S (supported by La[109] and 7h7), whereas V, A, and 64[+]236 (supported by La[146] and 7a1) read "glories" *(doxas)*.

[363] **They supplied** [*exorēgēsan*] **foods, and they provided themselves** [*etaxan heautous*] is the reading of S (supported by La[109] and La[146]), whereas V, A, and 64[+]236 (supported by 7h7) read "he supplied [*exorēgēsen*] foods, and he provided them [*etaxen autas*]," and 7a1 reads "he supplied foods, and they provided themselves."

[364] **Implements** *(skeuesin)* is a very broad term (*objetos,* BGS); see BDAG 927, §1; LSJ 1607, §§1–2. It could encompass "weapons" (REB, as in 4.30), "fortifications" (NJB, cf. 13.33), and/or food containers (*vasos,* Jünemann, cf. v 15).

14.11–12 He made peace in the land (Psa 37.11; Matt 5.9; Rom 14.19), so that everyone could sit **under his vine and his fig-tree** (in safety, 1 Kgs 4.25; applied to the spiritual blessings of the new covenant, Mic 4.4), **and there was no one to make them utterly afraid.** When God gives His people peace, they have no reason to fear anyone on earth (John 14.27; Isa 41.10–14; Jer 1.8).

14.13 και εξελιπεν πολεμων αυτουϲ επι τηϲ γηϲ και οι βαϲιλειϲ ϲυνετριβηϲαν εν ταιϲ ημεραιϲ εκειναιϲ	**14.13** And *those who were* making war against them in the land ceased; and the kings were shattered in those days.

14.13 Those who were making war against them in the land ceased; and the kings were shattered in those days. The LORD "makes wars to cease to the end of the land" (Psa 46.9; 8.2), and shatters all kings who rise up against Him and His people (Psa 2.1–12; 110.5). "All those who burn with anger against [Israel] will be put to shame and confounded ... the men who make war against [Israel] shall be as nothing and ended" (Isa 41.11–12).

14.14 και εϲτηριϲεν πανταϲ τουϲ ταπινουϲ του λαου αυτου τον νομον ‹εξεζητηϲεν› και εξηρεν παντα ανομο(ν) και πονηρον	**14.14** And he strengthened all the lowly *one*s of his people; he sought out the Law, and put away every *one who was* opposed to *the* Law and wicked.

14.14 εξεζητηϲεν V A 64 [εζητηϲε 236] La[109] La[146] | -ϲαν S •

14.14 Those who had been in high places were shattered (v 13), but **Simon strengthened all the lowly ones of his people,** again like Jesus (Psa 72.4; cf. Luke 1.52–53).

He sought out the Law (Psa 119.45, 94), like Ezra (Ezra 7.10). Under the old covenant, priests such as Simon and Ezra were expected to be sources of instruction in God's Law (Mal 2.7); under the new covenant, all God's people are priests (Rev 1.5), and all know His law (Heb 8.11; 5.12–14). "If you seek [the wisdom of God] as silver, and search for her as hidden things, then you will understand the fear of the LORD, and the knowledge of God you will find" (Prov 2.4–5).

Because Simon sought the Law, he **put away every one who was opposed to the Law and wicked** (see the notes on 13.47–48, 50; 3.5–6). Where God's law is truly honored, everything **opposed to** it must be rejected (2 Cor 6.14–16; 10.5; 1 Cor 5.1–13; Psa 17.3–4; 101.1–8).

14.15 ‹και› ‹τα αγια εδοξαϲεν› και ‹επληθυνεν› τα ϲκευη των αγιων	**14.15** And he glorified the holy *place*s, and he was multiplying the vessels of the holy *place*s.

14.15 και 1° 64*236 La[109] La[146] | > S V A • τα αγια εδοξαϲεν V A 64*236 La[109] La[146] | > S • επληθυνεν V A 64*236 La[109] | > S •

14.15 He glorified the holy places, and he was multiplying the vessels of the holy places, like David and Solomon (1 Kgs 7.48–51) and their faithful successors (1 Kgs 15.15; 2 Chr 24.14; 29.19). These things were earthly copies (Heb 8.5; 9.23) of the spiritual glory of God's spiritual holy place (Rev 21.22–23; cf. Hag 2.9; 2 Cor 3.9–11).

Messages from Rome and Sparta

14.16 και ηκουϲθη εν Ρωμη οτι απεθανεν Ιωναθαν και εωϲ Ϲπαρτηϲ και ελυπηθηϲαν ϲφοδρα	**14.16** And it was heard at Rome that Jonathan had died, and as far as Sparta; and they were very sorrowful.

14.16 When Israel's allies at **Rome** and **Sparta** (8.17–32; 12.1–23) **heard . . . that Jonathan had died . . . they were very sorrowful.** If one member of a body suffers, all the other members suffer also (1 Cor 12.26; Rom 12.15; 2 Cor 11.29).

14.17 ωϲ δε ηκουϲαν οτι Ϲειμων ο αδελφοϲ αυτου γεγονεν αρχιερευϲ αντ αυτου και αυτοϲ επικρατει τηϲ χωραϲ και των πολεω(ν) των εν αυτη	**14.17** But when they heard that Simon his brother had become high priest in place of him, and he himself was holding power over the district and the cities that *were* in it,
14.18 εγραψαν προϲ αυτον δελτοιϲ χαλκαιϲ του ανανεωϲαϲθαι προϲ αυτον φιλιαν και ϲυμμαχιαν ην εϲτηϲαν προϲ Ιουδαν και Ιωναθαν τουϲ αδελφουϲ αυτου	**14.18** they wrote to him on bronze slabs, to renew toward him *the* friendship and military alliance that they had established toward Judas and Jonathan his brothers.

14.17–18 The Romans and Spartans now **wrote to** Simon, **to renew . . . the friendship and military alliance that they had established** in the past with Onias, Judas, and Jonathan (8.17–32; 12.1–23).

14.19 και ανεγνωϲθηϲαν ενωπιον τηϲ εκκληϲιαϲ εν Ι(ερουϲα)λημ	**14.19** And they were read in *the* sight of the assembly in Jerusalem.

14.19 The letters from Rome and Sparta **were read** before **the assembly in Jerusalem** (cf. 1 Thes 5.27; Col 4.16).

A letter from the Spartans

14.20 και τουτο το αντιγραφον των επιϲτολων ων απεϲτιλαν οι Ϲπαρτιαται Ϲπαρτιατων αρχοντεϲ και η πολιϲ ⸂Ϲιμωνι⸃ ιερει μεγαλω και τοιϲ πρεϲβυτεροιϲ και τοιϲ ιερευϲιν και τω λοιπω δημω των Ιουδαιων αδελφοιϲ χαιρειν	**14.20** And this *is* a copy of the letters that the Spartans sent: "*The* rulers of *the* Spartans, and the city, to Simon *the* great priest, and to the elders and to the priests and to the rest of *the* people of the Judeans *our* brothers: Rejoice.

14.20 Ϲιμωνι S^{c} V A 64^{+}236 La^{109} La^{146} | -ν S* •

14.20 The narrative now quotes **a copy of the letters**[365] **that the Spartans sent.** The writers describe themselves as the people (the **city**) of Sparta and its **rulers,**[366] and address the **Judeans** as their **brothers** (see 12.21).

14.21 οι ⸤πρεσβευται⸥	**14.21** The ambassadors
⸤οι⸥ αποσταλεντες προς τον δημον	who were sent to our people
ημω(ν) απηγγειλαν ημι(ν)	told us
περι της δοξης ⸤υμων⸥ και τιμης και	about your[pl] glory and honor;
ηυφρανθημε(ν) επι τη εφοδω αυτων	and we were glad at their visit.
14.22 και ανεγραψαμεν	**14.22** And we have written down
τα υπ αυτω(ν) ειρημενα	the *thing*s said by them in the counsel
εν ταις βουλαις του δημου ουτως	*record*s of the people, thus: 'Numenius
Νουμηνιος Αντιοχου και Αντιπατρος	*son* of Antiochus, and Antipater *son*
Ιασονος πρεσβυται Ιουδαιων	of Jason, ambassadors of *the* Judeans,
ηλθον προς ⸤ημας⸥	came to us,
ανανεουμενοι την προς ⸤ημας⸥ φιλιαν	renewing *their* friendship toward us.
14.23 και ηρεσε(ν) τω δημω	**14.23** And it pleased the public
επιδεξασθε τους ανδρας ενδοξως	to accept the men with honor,
και του θεσθε το αντιγραφον τω(ν)	and to place a copy
λογων αυτων εν τοις αποδεδιγμενοις	of their words in the books shown
τω δημω βιβλιοις ⸤του⸥ μνημοσυνον	to the people, *for* the people
εχειν τον δημον ⸤των⸥ Σπαρτιατων	of the Spartans to have a memorial;
το δε αντιγραφον τουτων ⸤εγραψαν⸥	and they wrote a copy of these *thing*s
Σιμωνι τω αρχιερει	for Simon the high priest.'"

14.21 πρεσβευται A 64^{+}236 La^{109} La^{146} 7a1 | -βυτεροι S V 7h7 • οι 2° S^{ca} V^{a} A 64^{+}236 La^{109} La^{146} | > S* V* • υμων S^{ca} V A 64^{+}236 La^{109} La^{146} | ημ- S* • **14.22** πρεσβυται S V = -βευται A 64^{+}236 • ημας 1° S^{cb1} V A 64 [ημου 236] La^{109} La^{146} | υμ- S* • ημας 2° V A 64 [ημου 236] La^{109} La^{146} | υμ- S • **14.23** του μνημοσυνον εχειν V A [το μν- εχ- S] La^{146} | του εχ- το μν- 64^{+}236 • των 2° S^{ca} V A 64 La^{109} La^{146} | τον S* | > 236 • εγραψαν A 64^{+}236 La^{109} La^{146} | -ψα S* | -ψαμεν V •

14.21–23 In the **records** of their **counsel** sessions, the Spartan public preserved a **memorial** of the **visit** by Judea's **ambassadors** Numenius and Antipater (who had been sent by Jonathan, 12.1–2, 16), testifying that the ambassadors renewed the **friendship** between the two nations and were received by the Spartans **with honor.**

Another mission to Rome

14.24 μετα ταυτα απεστιλεν	**14.24** After these *things*,
Σιμω(ν) τον Νουμηνιον εις Ρωμην	Simon sent Numenius to Rome,

365 **Letters** *(epistolōn)*. As elsewhere (see on 10.3), the plural form describes a single document.

366 **Rulers** *(archontes)*. In earlier times, Sparta had been ruled by kings (12.7, 20), but Classical sources (e.g., Livy 35.35.1–35.37.3) indicate that the kingship was abolished by about 192 BCE.

εχοντα αϲπιδα χρυϲην μεγαλην	bearing a great golden shield *with* a
ολκην μνων ⸂͵α´⸃ ειϲ το ϲτηϲαι	weight of a thousand minas, to estab-
προϲ αυτουϲ τη(ν) ϲυμμαχιαν	lish the military alliance with them.

14.24 ͵α´ S^{ca} V A $64^{+}236$ La^{109} La^{146} | α´ S* •

14.24 Later, **Simon sent Numenius** again **to Rome,** to confirm their **military alliance** (v 18). He sent the Romans a present of **a great golden shield with a weight of a thousand minas.**[367] The result of this visit will be recorded in 15.15–24.

The people's inscription in Zion

14.25 ωϲ δε ηκουϲεν	**14.25** But when the people
ο δημοϲ των λογων τουτων ειπαν	heard these things, they said:
τινα χαριν αποδωϲομεν Ϲιμωνι ⸂⸃	"What thanks will we give back
και τοιϲ υιοιϲ αυτου	to Simon and his sons?
14.26 ⸂εϲτηριϲεν⸃ γαρ αυτοϲ	**14.26** for he has kept steadfast—he
και οι αδελφοι αυτου και ο οικοϲ	and his brothers and the house
του πατροϲ αυτου και επολεμηϲεν	of his father; and he has warred the
τουϲ εχθρουϲ Ιϲ(ραη)λ απ αυτων	enemies of Israel *away* from them; and
και εϲτηϲαν αυτω ελευθεριαν	they have established freedom for it."
και κατεγραψαν εν δελτοιϲ χαλκοιϲ	And they wrote on bronze slabs, and
και εθεντο ε(ν) ϲτηλαιϲ εν ορι Ϲιω(ν)	placed *them* on stelae in Mount Zion;

14.25 και S^{ca1} V A $64^{+}236$ | ^ ται S* | ^ τε S^{ca*} • **14.26** εϲτηριϲεν V A [*statuit* La^{109} La^{146}] | -ιϲται S | -ιξαν $64^{+}236$ • χαλκοιϲ S* = -καιϲ S^{ca} V A $64^{+}236$ •

14.25 In response to Simon's deeds, the **people** of Judah asked: **What thanks**[368] **will we give back to Simon and his sons?** God's people constantly find themselves asking that question, both in regard to their Lord ("What will I give back to the LORD for all his dealings toward me?", Psa 116.12; 1 Thes 3.9) and in regard to His faithful servants (we are commanded to "know those who labor among you, and are over you in the Lord, and admonish you; and to esteem them very highly in love for their work's sake," 1 Thes 5.12–13; cf. 1 Tim 5.17).

14.26 Simon had **kept steadfast,** along with **his brothers and the house of his father.** God's people are to keep themselves steadfast (Jas 5.8; 2 Pet 1.12; Rev 3.2); they are to keep one another steadfast (1 Thes 3.2; Luke 22.32); and the Lord will enable them to keep steadfast (Rom 16.25; 1 Thes 3.13; 2 Thes 2.17; 3.3; 1 Pet 5.10).

---

[367] The **mina** (Greek *mna* ≡ Hebrew *mnh,* BDB 584; HALOT 2.599; BDAG 654) was a unit of weight, used for measuring gold and silver (1 Kgs 10.17; Neh 7.71–72; Ezek 45.12; Luke 19.12–26).

[368] **Thanks** renders Greek *charin* ("favor," "grace"), as in 2 Cor 9.15, etc. (BDAG 1080, §5). The connection of sense is easier to express in Spanish (*¿Con qué acciónes de gracias pagarémos á Simón?,* Scío) and French (*Quelles grâces rendrons-nous à Simon?,* Diodati Fr) than in English.

He had **warred the enemies of Israel away from** the nation (**them**), a remarkably forceful compression of sense—as though the very act of waging **war** with those enemies inevitably shifted them **away** [*ap'*], and no further steps were needed (or, at least, those further steps—defeat and flight—were so inevitable that they did not need to be specified). "Resist the devil, and he will flee from [*ap'*] you" (Jas 4.7).[369]

Like other rulers whom God raised up to set His people free (Pharaoh, Psa 105.20; Cyrus, Isa 45.13; Jesus, Isa 61.1 ≡ Luke 4.18), Simon and his family had **established freedom for** Israel (**it**).

To show their thankfulness for their deliverance (v 25), the people **wrote** a record of it **on bronze slabs** (which would not easily be destroyed, Jer 15.12; 1.18–19), and set this up **on stelae**[370] for public view "in the surroundings of the holy places, in a prominent place" (v 48).

14.27 και τουτο το αντιγραφον της γραφης οκτωκαιδεκατη ‹Ελουλ› ετους β´ και ο´ και ρ´ ‹και τουτο› τριτον ετος επι Σιμωνος αρχιερεως μεγαλου εν Ασαραμελ	**14.27** and this *is* a copy of the writing: "*On the* eighteenth of Elul *in* *the* hundred and seventy-second year (and this *is the* third year in *the time* of Simon *the* great high priest), in Hasar- am-el [*the* court of *the* people of God],
14.28 επι συναγωγης μεγαλης ιερεων και λαου και αρχοντων εθνους και των πρεσβυτερων της χωρας εγνωρεισεν ημιν	**14.28** in a great gathering of priests and people and commanders of *the* nation and the elders of the district, he made *this* known to us:

14.27 Ελουλ V A 64 [-υμ 236] La[109] | > S La[146] • και τουτο 2° V A La[109] | τουτο 64⁺236 | το S La[146] •

[369] **He has warred the enemies of Israel away from them** *(epolemēsen tous echthrous Israēl ap' autōn)* is a more startling construction than the standard English renderings might suggest. By itself, *epolemēsen tous echthro`us Israēl* would be a perfectly normal sentence, "he has made war with the enemies of Israel" (cf. 3.14; 4.18, 41; etc.), but the additional *ap' autōn* has no close parallel in the Greek Scriptures. "The preposition contains the notion of a [further] verb, extending the sense of the expressed verb" (Abel, *Grammaire,* §82*e;* Winer §66.2d)—as in "He will save me into [*sōsei eis*] His heavenly kingdom" (2 Tim 4.18). Such constructions are especially common in the Eighteen Psalms, where we find, e.g., "he has been surrounded from the bad path" (10.1) and particularly "He will not become weak on His God" ≡ "He will not become weak; His hope is on the Lord" (17.42–44).

He has warred *(epolemēsen)* is the reading of S and V (supported by La[109] and La[146]), whereas A and 64⁺236 read "they have warred" *(epolemēsan).*

[370] **Stelae** *(stēlai)* are "perpendicular blocks" (Muraoka 636), "pillars" (KJV), which could be inscribed with a message (Ptolemaica 2.27). The word is applied in the LXX to the "pillar of salt" that Lot's wife became (Gen 19.26), and to the pillar set up by Jacob over Rachel's grave (Gen 35.20).

14.27–28 The document is dated **on the eighteenth** day of the month **Elul** (Neh 6.15) **in the hundred and seventy-second year** of the kingdom of the Greeks (v 1), equivalent to **the third year in the time of Simon** (see on 13.42). It records[371] **a great gathering** of the assembly of Israel, including **priests and people and commanders of the nation and the elders of the district** (Judea: see on 12:6), in a place called **Hasar-am-el,**[372] which in Hebrew would mean "the court of the people of God."

14.29 επι πολλακις ‹εγενηθηcα(ν)› πολεμοι εν τη χωρα Cιμων δε ο υ(ιο)c Ματταθιου ‹› ιερευc των υιων Ιωαρειβ και οι αδελφοι αυτου εδωκαν αυτουc τω κινδυνω και αντεcτηcαν τοιc υπεναντιοιc του εθνουc ‹αυτων› οπωc cταθη τα αγια αυτων και ο νομοc και δοξη μεγαλη εδοξαcαν το εθνοc αυτω(ν)	**14.29** 'Since *there* have often been wars in the district, but Simon the son of Mattathias, priest of the sons of Joiarib, and his brothers, gave *them*selves to the danger, and stood against the opponents of their nation, so that their holy *place*s and the Law would be established; and they glorified their nation with great glory;
14.30 ‹και ηθροιcεν Ιωναθαν το εθνοc› ‹αυτου› και εγενηθη αυτοιc αρχιερευc και προcετεθη προc τον λαον αυτου	**14.30** and Jonathan drew together his nation, and became their high priest, and was added to his people;

14.29 εγενηθηcα(ν) S^{ca} V A La^{109} La^{146} | -θημε(ν) S* | εγενοντο 64^{+}236 • ιερευc S V La^{109} La^{146} | υιοc A 64^{+}236 7a1 | ܒܪ 7h7 | ^ υιοc υιων S V • αυτων 1° V A 64^{+}236 La^{146} | > S • **14.30** και ηθροιcεν Ιωναθαν το εθνοc V A 64^{+}236 La^{109} La^{146} | > S • αυτου 1° V A La^{109} La^{146} | -των 64^{+}236 | > S •

[371] **He made this known to us** *(egnōr[e]isen hēmin)* is usually interpreted as equivalent to an impersonal passive ("it was made known to us," NETS). This is possible but would be unusual Greek (in such cases, the third person plural would be expected, as in v 48: see BDF §130.2). There are two other options: (i) In the present context, the obvious subject is Simon (v 27): after the inscription had been prepared (v 46), it was approved by him (v 47) and he is now presenting it to the people (**to us**). (ii) Alternatively, the clause might have an unexpressed subject, i.e., the Lord: He has **made . . . known** to His people the blessings described in the following verses (cf. "He has made known [*egnōrisen,* LXX] . . . to the sons of Israel His actions," Psa 103.7; 77.14).

[372] **Hasar-am-el** (Greek *[H]asaramel* ≡ Hebrew *Ḥṣr-ʿm-ʾl,* "the court of the people of God"), a place for "the assembly of the people [*ʿm*] of God" (cf. Jdg 20.2; 2 Sam 14.13). Compare the "great court [*ḥṣr*]" near Jerusalem's first temple (1 Kgs 7.12). *[H]asaramel* is the reading of S, V, and 64 (supported by La^{109} and La^{146}), whereas A reads *Saramel.* In theory the latter might correspond to Hebrew *Śr-ʿm-ʾl,* "the ruler of the people of God," but in the present context that would not fit the preceding **in** *(en)*. "The solemn assembly of the people of God" has been suggested, too, but in Hebrew its first component would be *ʿṣrt-* (as in Jer 9.2), not *ʿṣr-*. *[H]asar-* is also the LXX rendering of Hebrew *Ḥṣr-* in Gen 10.26 (Abel 256).

14.31 και εβουληθηcαν οι εχθροι αυτων εμβατευcε ειc την χωραν αυτων και ‹εκτιναι› χιραc επι τα αγια αυτω(ν)	**14.31** and their enemies wanted to go into their district and stretch out *their* hands against their holy *place*s;
14.32 τοτε αντεcτη Cιμων και επολεμηcε περι του εθνουc αυτου και εδαπανηcεν χρηματα πολλα των εαυτου και οπλοδοτηcεν ‹› τουc ανδραc τηc δυναμεωc του εθνουc αυτου και εδωκεν αυτοιc οψωνια	**14.32** then Simon rose up against them, and made war for his nation; and he spent much money of *his* own, and gave weapons to the men of the force of his nation, and gave them payments;
14.33 και οχυρωcεν ταc πολιc τηc Ιουδαιαc και τη(ν) Βαιθcουραν την επι των οριων τηc Ιουδαιαc ου ην τα οπλα των πολεμιω(ν) ‹το› προτερον και εθετο εκει φρουραν ανδραc Ιουδαιουc	**14.33** and he fortified the cities of Judea, and Bethzur (which *is* on the appointed boundaries of Judea, *in* which the weapons of the warring *people* had previous*ly* been), and he placed there a garrison of Judean men;
14.34 και Ιοππην ωχυρωcεν την επι τηc θαλαccηc και την ‹Γαζαραν› την επι των οριων Αζωτου εν η ωκουν οι πολεμιοι το προτερο(ν) και κατωκιcεν εκει Ιουδαιουc και οcα επιτηδια ην προc τη τουτων επανορθωcει εθετο εν αυταιc	**14.34** and he fortified Joppa (which *is* close by the sea) and Gezer (which *is* on the appointed boundaries of Ashdod, in which the warring *people* had previous*ly* been dwelling), and he settled Judeans there, and placed in them all *the thing*s that were suitable to set them up again;

14.31 εκτιναι S[ca] V A 64[+]236 La[109] La[146] | εκκλιναι S* • **14.32** οπλοδοτηcεν V A 64[+]236 La[109] La[146] | + αυτου S • **14.33** το S[cb1] V A 64[+]236 | των S* • **14.34** Γαζαραν S[cb1] V A [-ζηρα 64[+]236] La[146] | Γαραζαν S* •

14.29 The document records the mighty deeds done by **Simon the son of Mattathias, priest of the sons of Joiarib** (2.1), **and his brothers,** in a time of **wars** (1.24, 30, etc.) and **danger.** They did not spare their lives (Mark 8.35; Acts 20.24; 21.13; Rom 16.3–4; Php 2.30), but **gave themselves to the danger** (see on 11.23; 13.5), **and stood against the opponents of their nation**—as all forces of evil must be "stood against" (1 Pet 5.9; Jas 4.7; Eph 6.13). They labored not for themselves, but **so that their holy places and the Law would be established** (see on 2.26–27; 3.21, 43; 4.36; 13.3). And by their labors, **they glorified their nation with great glory** (see on 3.3; 14.35).

14.30–31 After **Jonathan** had brought together **his nation,** and had become **high priest** (10.20–21), and had died (had **been added to his people,** as in Gen 25.8, etc.), there had been a time of special danger: Israel's **enemies** had sought to invade **their district** and defile **their holy places** (see 12.53–13.1).

14.32 That was the time when **Simon rose up against** the enemies, **and made war for his nation** (as described in 13.1–10).

Like David (1 Kgs 9.4; 1 Chr 29.3), and like the Lord's faithful servants under the new covenant (Acts 4.34–37; 2 Cor 8.1–7), Simon gave his own self to the Lord (13.5), and also the things that he possessed: **he spent much money of his own** in the Lord's work. "Whoever may have the world's means of life, and see his brother having a need, and shut up his bowels from him—how does the love of God remain in him?" (1 Jn 3.17). So Simon provided **the men of** his nation's military **force** with what they needed: **weapons** (cf. 4.6) and **payments** (cf. 3.28–31).

14.33–34 Simon also **fortified the cities of Judea** (13.10, 33), including cities that had previously been in the power of their enemies, such as **Bethzur** (v 7; 11.65–66), **Joppa** (v 5; 12.33–34; 13.11; 15.28, 35) and **Gezer** (v 7; 13.53; 15.28, 35). He **settled**[373] them instead with **Judeans** (people who "would do the Law," 13.48; 11.66; 12.34), and provided them with **all the things** that would help **to set them up again**[374] (cleansing whatever was unclean, 13.47–48, 50; restoring whatever had fallen, 12.37; 13.10, 33).

14.35 και ⸂ιδεν ο λαος⸃ την πιcτιν	**14.35** and the people saw Simon's
του Cιμωνοc κ(αι) την δοξαν	faithfulness, and the glory that he
ην εβουλευcατο ποιηcαι τω εθνι	took counsel to provide for his nation,
αυτου και ⸂εθεντο⸃ αυτον	and they placed him
ηγουμενον αυτων και αρχιερεα δια	*as* their leader and high priest,
το αυτον πεποιηκεναι παντα ταυτα	because he *had* done all these *things*,
και την δικαιοcυνη(ν) και την πιcτιν	and the righteousness and faithfulness
η(ν) cυνετηρηcεν τω εθνι αυτου	that he kept toward his nation,
και εξεζητηcεν παντι τροπω	and *how* he sought out every way
υψωcαι τον λαον αυτου	to raise his people high;

14.35 ιδεν ο λαος S^{ca} V A 64^{+}236 La^{109} La^{146} | > S • εθεντο V A 64^{+}236 La^{109} La^{146} | εθετο S •

[373] **He settled.** The Greek is *katōkisen,* "he caused to dwell," as also in v 37.

[374] **Set them up again** (*epanorthōsei;* compare *orthōs,* 11.43): restore *(an-)* them to an upright *(orthos)* condition (like someone who has been bent over, Luke 13.13); "set them on their feet" (NJB); in Spanish, *enderezamientos* (Jünemann). "I will rebuild the fallen tent of David ... and I will rebuild its ruins and set it up again [*anorthōsō*]" (Acts 15.16).

In this clause, the use of *pros* with the dative (*pros tē toutōn epanorthōsei,* **to set them up again**) is unusual. Abel (258; *Grammaire,* §50*k*) regards it as equivalent to the accusative (although no truly analogous instance has been found), and Grimm (215) as a textual error for the accusative (although the accusative is found here only in two inferior manuscripts—98 and 731—whereas S, V, A, and *f*$^{64+19}$ are united in favor of the dative). Muraoka (589, §II.3) gives the sense here as "in addition to," a common meaning of *pros* with the dative (e.g., Gen 28.9, LXX; cf. BDAG 874, §2b); but if so, the addition would awkwardly dislocate the principal subject ("and as many things as were suitable, in addition to setting them up again, he placed in them"). Perhaps it is best to regard the dative here as expressing close commitment to the task (Schwyzer, 2.513; LSJ 1497, §B.II), as in *pros tō eirēmenō logō ēn* ("he was occupied with [*pros*] the thing that had been said," Plato, *Phaedo,* 84c).

14.36 και εν ταις ημεραις αυτου ευοδωθη εν ταις χερσιν αυτου του εξαρθηναι τα εθνη εκ της χωρας αυτω(ν) και τους εν τη πολι Δα(υι)δ τους εν Ι(ερουσα)λημ ‹οι εποιησαν› ‹εαυτοις› ακραν εξ ης ‹εξεπορευοντο› και εμιαινο(ν) κυκλω των αγιω(ν) και εποιουν πληγην μεγαλην εν τη αγνια	**14.36** and in his days it prospered in his hands *for* the nations to be put away out of their district, and the *people* in the city of David who *were* in Jerusalem (who had made for *them*-selves a citadel, out of which they had been going and had been polluting round about the holy *places*, and had done a great injury to *their* purity);
14.37 και κατωκισεν εν αυτη ανδρας Ιουδαιους και ωχυρωσεν αυτην προς ασφαλιαν της χωρας και της πολεως και υψωσεν τα τειχη της Ι(ερουσα)λημ	**14.37** and he settled Judean men in it, and fortified it for *the* security of the district and of the city, and raised high the walls of Jerusalem;

14.36 οι εποιησαν S^{ca} V A 64^{+}236 | εποιησεν S* • εαυτοις V A 64^{+}236 | αυ- S • εξεπορευοντο S^{ca} V A 64^{+}236 La^{146} | επ- S* •

14.35 The people of Judea **saw** Simon's good works (cf. Matt 5.16; 1 Tim 5.25; Psa 119.74): his **faithfulness**[375] and **righteousness** (unlike Alcimus, 7.14–17) in serving **his nation; the glory that he took counsel to provide**[376] **for his nation** (v 29); and his ceaseless striving **to raise his people high,** uplifting those who had been brought low (v 14; 3.51). In all these ways, "he sought good things for his nation" (v 4; see the notes there). Recognizing what he had **done,** the people **placed him as their leader and high priest** (v 41; 13.8, 42).

14.36–37 Certain people **in Jerusalem . . . had made for themselves a citadel,** and had been **polluting** the area **round about the holy places,** injuring the **purity** of those places (see 1.32–37; 13.50). But in Simon's **days** it became possible (**it prospered**)[377] to **put away** those people (13.50), settling[378] the citadel instead with **Judean men,** and fortifying it (as described in 13.52). Similarly, Simon was able to **put away** the foreigners (**nations**) who had been causing trouble elsewhere in the **district** of Judea (cf. v 13).

---

[375] **Faithfulness** *(pistin)* occurs twice in this verse according to S and A (supported by La[109] and La[146]). Instead of the first occurrence, 64^{+}236 have "activity" *(praxin).* V has "faithfulness and activity" *(pistin kai praxin)* at that point.

[376] **To provide.** The Greek is *poiēsai* ("to do" or "to make").

[377] **It prospered** *(euodōthē):* that is, it "went [*hodoō*] well [*eu-*]" (*ging es . . . gut voran,* LXX.D). As always, the Maccabean History avoids explicitly naming the One (4.55) who made it go well (Rom 1.10; 3 Jn 2). Compare: "May our God and Father himself, and our Lord Jesus, make straight [*kateuthunai*] our way [*hodon*]" (1 Thes 3.11).

[378] **He settled.** As in v 34, the Greek is *katōkisen,* "he caused to dwell."

14.38 και ο βαϲιλευϲ Δημητριοϲ εϲτηϲε(ν) αυτω την αρχιεροϲυνην κατα ταυτα	**14.38** and King Demetrius established the high priesthood for him in accordance with these *things*,
14.39 και εποιηϲεν αυτο(ν) των φιλων αυτου και εδοξαϲεν αυτον δοξη μεγαλη	**14.39** and made him *one* of his Friends, and honored him with great honor:
14.40 ηκουϲεν γαρ οτι προϲηγορευνται οι Ιουδαιοι υπο Ρωμαιων φιλοι και ϲυμμαχοι και αδελφοι και οτι απηντηϲαν τοιϲ πρεϲβευταιϲ ‹Ϲιμωνοϲ› ενδοξωϲ	**14.40** for he had heard that the Judeans had been publicly declared by *the* Romans *to be* friends and military allies and brothers, and that they had met the ambassadors of Simon with honor;
14.41 και οτι οι Ιουδαιοι και οι ιερειϲ ευδοκηϲαν του ειναι ‹αυτων› Ϲιμωνα ηγουμενον και αρχιερεα ειϲ τον αιωνα εωϲ του αναϲτηναι προφητην πιϲτον	**14.41** and that the Judeans and the priests had been well pleased *for* Simon to be their leader and high priest to lasting time, until a faithful prophet *should* rise up,
14.42 και του ειναι ‹επ› αυτων ϲτρατηγον και οπωϲ μελη αυτω περι των αγιων καθιϲταναι ‹δι αυτου› επει των εργων αυτων και επι τηϲ χωραϲ και επι των οπλω(ν) και επι των οχυρωματων	**14.42** and to be army commander over them, and that he should take care of the holy *places*, *and* through him *people would be* established over their works, and over the district, and over the weapons, and over the fortresses;
14.43 και οπωϲ μελη αυτω περι τω(ν) αγιων και οπωϲ ‹ακουηται› υπο παντων και οπωϲ ‹γραφωνται› επι τω ονοματι αυτου παϲαι ϲυγγραφαι ‹› εν τη χωρα και οπωϲ περιβαληται πορφυρα(ν) και χρυϲοφορη	**14.43** and that he should take care of the holy *places*, and that he should be heard by all *people*, and that all *the* writings in the district should be written in his name, and that he should wrap himself in purple and wear gold;
14.44 και ουκ εξεϲται ‹ουδενι› του λαου και των ιερεων αθετηϲαι τι τουτων και αντιπιν τοιϲ υπ αυτου ρηθηϲομενοιϲ και ‹επιϲυϲτρεψαι› ϲυϲτροφην εν τη χωρα ανευ αυτου και ‹περιβαλεϲθαι› πορφυραν και ενπορπουϲθαι πορπην χρυϲην	**14.44** and no one at all of the people or priests will have authority to set aside any *one* of these *things*, or to speak in opposition to the *things* said by him, or to gather a gathering in the district without him, or to wrap *him*self in purple or pin *him*self with a golden pin;

14.40 Ϲιμωνοϲ S^{ca} V A 64^{+}236 | -ν S* • **14.41** αυτων S^{ca} V A La^{146} | -τω S* | > 64^{+}236 • **14.42** επ S* V A 64^{+}236 La^{146} | ε S^{ca} | > S^{1} • δι αυτου V A La^{146} | αυτουϲ S 64^{+}236 • **14.43** ακουηται V A 64^{+}236 La^{146} | -ουονται S • γραφωνται S^{ca} V^{b} A 64^{+}236 La^{109} La^{146} | -φον- S* V* • ϲυγγραφαι V A 64^{+}236 | + αι S • **14.44** ουδενι S^{cb1} V A 64^{+}236 La^{109} La^{146} | ουθεν S* • επιϲυϲτρεψαι A 64^{+}236 La^{109} La^{146} | επιϲτρ- S V • περιβαλεϲθαι S^{ca} V 64^{+}236 | -βαλλεϲ- S* A •

14.45 οϲ δ α(ν) παρα ταυτα ποιηϲη η αθετηϲη τι τουτων ενοχοϲ εϲται	**14.45** but whoever should do *anything* beyond these *things* or set aside any *one* of these *things*, he will be held *for punishment.*

14.38–39 Simon was also **honored** beyond the nation of Israel (cf. 5.63): **King Demetrius** acknowledged his **high priesthood** and **made him one of his Friends** (see 13.36). Simon had sought the glory that is from God, not from men (cf. John 5.44); yet God had honored him in ways that he had not sought (cf. 2 Chr 1.11–12).

14.40 Demetrius was aware that other people outside Israel—**the Romans**—had treated the Israelites **with honor,** accepting them as **friends and military allies and brothers** (v 18; cf. 8.17–32; 12.1, 3–4).

14.41–44 Demetrius was also aware **that** Simon had the strong support of his own people: they were **well pleased for** him **to be their leader and high priest** (contrast the irreverent Israelites who had previously been "well pleased to be enslaved to" Antiochus Epiphanes, 6.23; 1.43).

This sentence began as a list of things that Demetrius "had heard" (v 40), but the mention of **the Judeans and the priests** leads it in another, greater direction—so that it builds into a comprehensive declaration of the honors that **the Judeans and the priests** are choosing to bestow on Simon.[379] Similar changes of direction in mid-sentence are familiar to every reader of the New Testament Scriptures (see, e.g., 1 Tim 1.3–5; Acts 1.3–5; Rom 15.22–25).

The Judeans and the priests accepted Simon:

- **to be their leader and high priest** and **army commander** (as described in 13.42);
- to **take care of the holy places** (as described in v 15) and appoint officials **over their works** ("the works of the holy places," 10.44);
- to appoint officials **over the district** of Judea (cf. 9.53) **and over** its defense (its **weapons** and **fortresses;** see on v 10);
- to **be heard** (2.65)—that is, heeded, in the way that the utterance of a king was expected to be heeded (2.19, 22).

This authority was given exclusively to Simon. Only **in his name** could **the writings of the district** be issued (as illustrated in 13.42). No other person was permitted to act as a leader in Judea, e.g., by summoning a **gathering** (cf. 2 Sam 15.31, LXX; 2 Kgs 15.15, LXX) or wearing any signs of leadership (such as **purple** clothes or a **golden**

[379] Such changes of construction tend to give the closing stages of a sentence "more emphasis" (Robertson 435), like a sonata movement modulating into an unexpected key; but tidy-minded ancient copyists and modern translators have often been tempted to alter them (MHT 3.343, §3*c*). In the present passage, one manuscript (71) removed the *hoti* (**that**) at the beginning of v 41, making a new start there, and some English versions have done the same ("The Jewish people and their priest have, therefore, made the following decisions," NAB).

pin: see the notes on 10.20, 89; 4.23). And **all the people** were required to heed his authority. **No one at all of the people or priests** was exempt.

Notice the similarities with Jesus' position today. Jesus is the leader (Matt 2.6) and high priest (Heb 3.1) of the spiritual Israel, and the commander of their armies (Rev 19.11–16). He appoints those who are over them (Mark 3.14–19; Eph 4.7–11). He had the care of the earthly holy places when He was on earth (John 2.14–17; Matt 21.12–13), and He has the care of the holy places in heaven today (Heb 9.11–14, 23–24). He is to be heard by all, without exception (Acts 3.22–23; Matt 17.5), and in all respects (2 Cor 2.9). And this authority is given exclusively to Him (Matt 28.18; Eph 1.22–23; 1 Cor 8.6; Acts 4.12).

Certain rulers in the ancient world were appointed only for a specified time (8.16), or only while some other ruler was absent (3.32–33). The Judeans decreed that Simon's authority would not be limited in that way: it would continue indefinitely, **to lasting time.**[380]

Nevertheless, Simon and his family would not lead Israel forever; the prophets had declared that the kingdom would eventually be restored to a Son of David, whose rule would have "no end" (Isa 9.6–7; Jer 23.5–6; Amos 9.11). Israel was waiting **until a faithful prophet should rise up** as Moses had said: "The LORD your God will raise up for you a prophet like me from among you, from your brothers" (Deut 18.15–18).

These things came to pass through Jesus. He was the Prophet like Moses (Acts 3.22–24); He was also the prophesied Son of David (Luke 1.31–32). He brought about a change in the Law and a change in the priesthood (Heb 7.12), so that He Himself became the leader and high priest of God's people (Matt 2.6; Heb 3.1) "to lasting time" (Heb 1.8; 6.20; 7.24)—not just till the coming of some further prophet, but eternally, without end (Luke 1.33; 1 Cor 15.25–26).

14.45 Whoever would **do anything beyond** the regulations specified in the previous verses, **or set aside any** of those regulations, would **be held** for punishment (cf. Ezra 7.26).[381] In these respects, too, Simon's leadership was a miniature model of Jesus'.

---

[380] **To lasting time** (Greek *eis ton aiōna* ≡ Hebrew *lʿwlm* [Heb 5.6 ≡ Psa 110.4] or *lʿd* [2 Cor 9.9 ≡ Psa 112.9]) describes persistence into the indefinite future (TDNT 1.198–200, §§B1a–b; NIDNTT 3.830, §2b)—not necessarily to eternity ("for ever," KJV), but as long as the situation indicated by the context continues to apply (*so lange,* Luther 1912; cf. Deut 15.17; Exod 21.6). Compare "the hill and the watchtower will be caves until lasting time [Hebrew *ʿd ʿwlm* ≡ LXX *eōs tou aiōnos*] ... until the Spirit is poured out on us from on high," after which the situation would be reversed (Isa 32.14–15). In the same way, "His holy prophets from lasting time" (*ap' aiōnos,* Luke 1.70; Acts 3.21) means that such prophets have existed not from eternity but from the remote past ("from of old," ASV).

[381] **He will be held** ("held in," *enochos*—"so that he cannot escape," Thayer 217; "held fast," TDNT 2.828). The term describes someone reserved for a punishment (e.g., death, Mark 14.64; Gehenna, Matt 5.22) that is determined by a judicial body (e.g., the Sanhedrin, Matt 5.22). Other forms of *en+echō* are used to describe a child "held in [*en ... echousa*]" a woman's

No one today has authority to go beyond the regulations of the new covenant (2 Jn 9; 1 Cor 4.6) or to set them aside (Mark 7.8–13; Heb 2.1–3; 10.28–29).

14.46 και ευδοκηϲεν παϲ ο λαοϲ θεϲθε ‹Ϲιμωνι› ποιηϲαι κατα τουϲ λογουϲ τουτουϲ	**14.46** And all the people were well pleased to assign Simon *the right* to do in accordance with these words.
14.47 και επεδεξατο Ϲιμων και ευδοκηϲεν αρχιερατευειν και ειναι ϲτρατηγοϲ και εθναρχηϲ των Ιουδαιων και ιερεων και του ‹προϲτατηϲαι› παντων	**14.47** And Simon accepted, and he was well pleased to be high priest, and to be army commander and national ruler of the Judeans and of *the* priests, and to protect all *of them*.'"

14.46 Ϲιμωνι V A 64⁺236 La[146] | -να S • **14.47** προϲτατηϲαι S[ca] V A La[109] La[146] | προϲϲτηϲαι S* | πρωτοϲτατηϲαι 64⁺236 •

14.46–47 The agreement between Simon and the people was willing on both sides: **All the people were well pleased to assign Simon the right to do** these things, **and Simon ... was well pleased to accept them.** The same terms are used of the relationship between God and His people under the new covenant: God is "well pleased" to accept them (Eph 1.5, 9; Luke 12.32; cf. Heb 10.38), and they are "well pleased" to serve under His leadership (2 Cor 12.10; Rom 15.26–27; cf. 2 Thes 2.12).[382]

14.48 και την γραφην ταυτην ειπον θεϲθαι εν δελτοιϲ χαλκαιϲ και ϲτηϲαι αυταϲ ε(ν) περιβολω των αγιων εν τοπω επιϲημω	**14.48** And they said to place this writing in bronze slabs, and to establish them in *the* surroundings of the holy *place*s in a conspicuous place,
14.49 τα δε αντιγραφα αυτων θεϲθαι εν τω γαζοφυλακιω οπωϲ εχη Ϲιμων και οι υιοι αυτου	**14.49** but to place copies of them in the storage-place, so that Simon and his sons might have *them*.

14.48 The above **writing** was to be preserved **in bronze slabs,** and displayed (cf. 11.37) **in the surroundings of the holy places** ("on stelae in Mount Zion," v 26).[383]

---

womb (Matt 1.18), a sick man "held in [*echōn en*]" his sickness (John 5.5), and a corpse "held in [*echonta en*]" its tomb (John 11.17).

[382] The inscription began in v 27. Where does it end? Some translations (e.g., ESV and NETS) end it at v 45, construing vv 46–47 as a description of subsequent events. But those verses do not report anything new; rather, they summarize what had happened when Simon was first appointed (13.1–9). Therefore, it is preferable to construe vv 46–47 as a continuation of the inscribed summary of the past (as in NAB, REB, and SAAS). Nothing in the wording of vv 48–49 indicates whether or not those verses were also part of the inscription (as indicated in NJB).

[383] Mount Zion was the site of the temple (the **holy places**), as 4.37–38; 5.54; 7.33 show. Thus, "in Mount Zion" (v 26) and **in the surroundings of the holy places** refer to the same site, not to two different sites.

14.49 Copies of the inscription were also provided for **Simon and his sons.** These copies were placed **in the storage-place** ("treasury," KJV), which was located in the temple (John 8.20; Mark 12.41–44), where Simon, being the high priest, served (cf. also 13.52).

Antiochus son of Demetrius

Antiochus son of Demetrius writes to Simon

15.1 και απεστιλεν Αντιωχος υιος	**15.1** And Antiochus son of Demetrius
Δημητριου του βασιλεως επιστολας	the king sent letters
απο των νησων της θαλασσης	from the islands of the sea to
⸤Σιμωνι⸥ ⸤αρχιερει⸥ και εθναρχη	Simon, high priest and national ruler
των Ιουδαιων και παντι τω εθνι	of the Judeans, and to all the nation;

15.1 Σιμωνι S^{ca} V A 64^{+}236 La^{109} La^{146} | -ν S* • αρχιερει 64^{+}236 La^{109} [*sacerdoti magno* La^{146}] | ιερει S V A •

15.1 Yet another member of the Seleucid royal family—**Antiochus son of Demetrius,** not previously mentioned in this book[384]—began seeking power. From his current home in **the islands of the** Mediterranean **sea** (6.29; 11.38), he **sent letters ... to Simon ... and to all the nation** of the Judeans.

15.2 και ησαν περιεχουσαι τον τροπον	**15.2** and their contents *were in* this
τουτον βασιλευς Αντιοχος Σιμωνι	way: "King Antiochus to Simon,
ιερει μεγαλω και εθναρχη	great priest and national ruler, and
και εθνει Ιουδαιων χεριν	to *the* nation of *the* Judeans: Rejoice.
15.3 επι τινες λοιμοι κατεκρατησαν	**15.3** Since some plague-bearers have
της βασιλιας των πατερων ημων	overpowered the kingdom of our
βουλομαι δε αντιποιησασθαι	fathers, but I want to take action
της βασιλιας	against *them* in regard to the king-
οπως αποκαταστησω αυτην	dom, so that I may restore it
⸤ως ην το προτερον⸥	as it was previous*ly*, and I have called
⸤εξενολογησα δε⸥ ⸤πληθη⸥ δυναμεων	together multitudes of foreign forces
και ⸤κατεσκευασα⸥ πλοια πολεμικα	and have prepared warships;

15.3 ως ην / το προτερον V A 64^{+}236 La^{109} La^{146} | ~ S • εξενολογησα δε S^{ca} V A 64^{+}236 La^{109} La^{146} | και εξενολογησα(ν) S* • πληθη 64^{+}236 La^{109} | -θος S V A La^{146} • κατεσκευασα S^{ca} V A 64^{+}236 La^{109} La^{146} | -ευασαν S* •

[384] In modern histories, **Antiochus son of Demetrius** is generally called Antiochus VII or Antiochus Sidetes. ("Sidetes," i.e., "from [the city of] Side" [cf. 15.23], is a nickname, and does not appear to have been used by the king himself; his official name was Antiochus Euergetes.) Classical historians (e.g., Appian, *Syriaca,* 68.358) report that he was the son of the first Demetrius, and the brother of the second Demetrius (who was still a prisoner in the land of Media, 14.3).

15.4 βουλομαι δε εκβηναι κατα την χωραν οπως μετελθω τους κατεφθαρκοτας τη(ν) χωραν ημων και τους ηρημωκοτας πολις πολλας εν τη βασιλεια μου	**15.4** and I want to go out through the district, so that I may go after those who have ruined our district and those who have made many cities in my kingdom desolate;
15.5 νυν ουν ιστημι σοι παντα τα ⸂αφερεματα⸃ α αφηκαν σοι οι προ εμου βασιλεις και οσα αλλα δοματα αφηκαν σοι ⸂⸃	**15.5** now therefore, I am establishing for you† all the remissions that the kings before me have set free for you†, and whatever other gifts that they have set free for you†.
15.6 και επετρεψα σοι ποιησαι κομμα ιδιον νομισμα τη χωρα σου	**15.6** And I have permitted you† to make *your* own coinage *as* legal tender for your† district,
15.7 Ι(ερουσα)λημ ⸂δε κ(αι) τα⸃ αγια ⸂ειναι⸃ ελευθερα και παντα τα οπλα οσα κατεσκευασας και τα οχυρωματα α ωκοδομησας ων κρατις μενετω σοι	**15.7** and *for* Jerusalem and the holy *place*s to be free. And *as for* all the weapons that you† have prepared, and the fortresses that you† have built *and* are holding—let them remain for you†.
15.8 και παν οφιλημα βασιλικον και τα εσομενα βασιλικα απο του νυν και εις τον απαντα χρονον αφισθω σοι	**15.8** And *as for* every king's *tax* that is owed, and the *thing*s that will be king's *taxes* from now *on* and for all time—let it be set free for you†.
15.9 ⸂ως⸃ δ α(ν) κρατησωμεν της βασιλειας ημων δοξασωμεν σε και το εθνος σου και το ιερον δοξη μεγαλη ωστε φανεραν γενεσθαι την δοξαν υμω(ν) εν παση τη γη	**15.9** And when ever we may take hold of our kingdom, we will honor you† and your† nation and the temple with great honor, so that your^{pl} honor *will* become visible in all the earth."

15.5 αφερεματα S^{ca} A 64^{+}236 La^{109} La^{146} \| αφεμ- S* V • σοι 3° S^{ca} V A 64^{+}236 La^{109} La^{146} \| + οι προ εμου βασιλεις S* • **15.7** δε κ(αι) τα S^{ca} V A 64^{+}236 La^{109} La^{146} \| δεκτα S* • ειναι S^{ca} V A 64^{+}236 La^{109} La^{146} \| > S • **15.9** ως S^{cb1} V A 64^{+}236 \| ων S* •

15.2–9 Antiochus says that he wants **to take action**[385] **in regard to** his family's **kingdom,** to defeat those[386] who **have overpowered** it, and to **restore it.** He reaffirms the

[385] **Take action against** (*antipoiēsasthai*). Its prefixed *anti-* could signify either action "against" someone else (as in Dan 4.35 [32], *θ'*) or action "counterbalancing" something else (as in Lev 24.19, LXX). In the present context, the former sense is obviously the more appropriate: "some plague-bearers have overpowered the district, but I want to take action against them." Some have taken the *anti-* to describe an act of taking "back" something from someone else (NJB), but usage of the word elsewhere does not support that (LSJ 161).

[386] Antiochus does not name the opponents, but merely refers to them as **some plague-bearers** (see the notes on 10.61). The term would certainly include Trypho and his supporters.

remissions and **gifts** that had been granted by previous **kings** (10.27–43; 11.27–36; 13.37–39), allows the Judeans to maintain their own **weapons** and **fortresses** (10.6; 13.38), and authorizes Simon **to make** his **own coinage.**[387] He also promises that when he gains possession of the **kingdom,** he will **honor** Simon, the **nation** of Judea, and their **temple.** But other kings had made such promises without keeping them (compare, e.g., 11.42), and Antiochus would not keep these promises of his (v 27).

Antiochus soon gained possession of the Seleucid kingdom (vv 10–12), but he never did **restore** *(apokatastēsō)* **it as it was previously.** "The kings were shattered in those days" (14.13); the Lord did not allow any of them to regain the power that earlier Seleucid rulers (such as Antiochus the Great, or even Antiochus Epiphanes) had possessed. Contrast the Lord's own plan to "restore [*apokatastēsei*] all things" through John the Baptist and Jesus (Matt 17.11–13; Acts 3.19–21; cf. Acts 15.16). Nothing decreed by the Lord can fail (Isa 55.10–11); nothing else can succeed (Psa 127.1).

Antiochus expels Trypho

15.10 ετουc δ´ και ο´ και ρ´ ‹εξηλθεν› Αντιοχος ειc την γην τω(ν) πατερων αυτου κ(αι) cυνηλθον προc αυτον παcαι αι δυναμειc ωcτε ολιγουc ειναι ‹τουc καταλειφθενταc› cυν Τρυφωνι	**15.10** *In the* hundred and seventy-fourth year, Antiochus came out into the land of his fathers. And all the forces came together to him, so that few *were* left to be with Trypho.

15.10 εξηλθεν S[ca] V A 64[+]236 La[109] La[146] | και ηλθεν S* • τουc καταλειφθενταc 64[+]236 La[109] La[146] | > S V A •

15.10 Antiochus arrived in Syria (the **land of his fathers**) in the **hundred and seventy-fourth year.**[388] He was supported by **all the** military **forces** there; **Trypho** was left with **few** supporters. Only a few years earlier, the military forces had gathered to Trypho, and Demetrius could find little support (11.54–55). Now that situation was reversed. The Lord raises up and casts down at His own pleasure; those who are first at one time may be last at another (Ecc 10.7; Luke 13.30). What Trypho had done to his predecessor, his successor was now doing to him (cf. Jer 50.29; Psa 137.8).

15.11 και εδιωξεν αυτον Αντιοχοc και ηλθεν ειc Δωρα φευγων την επι θαλαccηc	**15.11** And Antiochus pursued him; and he came, when *he* fled, to Dor *that is* close by *the* sea:
15.12 ηδει γαρ οτι επιcυνηκται επ αυτον τα κακα και αφηκαν αυτον αι δυναμιc	**15.12** for he knew that the evil *things* had gathered against him, and *his* forces had left him.

[387] There is no earlier record of the Judeans being permitted **to make** their **own coinage.** Antiochus soon withdrew his authorization (v 27), and there is no evidence that Simon actually did issue any coins. The earliest known Judean coins are currently believed to date from the high priesthood of Simon's successor John (Hendin [1996] 66–77).

[388] 174 SE would probably correspond to about 139–138 BCE.

15.13 και παρενεβαλε(ν) Αντιοχος επι Δωρα και συν αυτω δωδεκα ‹μυριαδες› ανδρων ‹πολεμιστων› και οκτακισχιλια ‹ιππος›	**15.13** And Antiochus camped against Dor, and with him a hundred and twenty thousand men *who were* warriors, and eight thousand horse.
15.14 και εκυκλωσεν την πολι(ν) ‹και τα πλοια απο θαλασσης συνηψαν και εθλιβεν την πολιν› απο της γης και της θαλασσης και ουκ ειασεν ουδενα εκπορευεσθε ουδε εισπορευεσθε	**15.14** And he surrounded the city, and the ships made contact from *the* sea. And he was oppressing the city from land and sea, and did not allow anyone at all to go out or come in.

15.13 μυριαδες S[ca] A 64[+]236 [-δας S*] [La[109] La[146]] | χιλιαδες V • πολεμιστων S[ca] V A 64[+]236 | -ικων S* • ιππος S[ca] V A 64[+]236 | -ον S* • **15.14** και τα πλοια απο θαλασσης συνηψαν και εθλιβεν την πολιν V A 64[+]236 La[109] La[146] | > S •

15.11–14 When **Antiochus pursued him,** Trypho **fled to** the ancient Canaanite city of **Dor,** in the former territory of Manasseh (Jdg 1.27; Josh 17.11), **close by the sea** (cf. Josh 11.2). Antiochus besieged the city by both **land** (with a large army) and **sea** (with **ships**), so that no one could **go out or come in** (see v 25).

Letters from Rome

15.15 και ηλθεν Νουμηνιος και οι παρ αυτου εκ Ρωμης εχοντες επιστολας τοις βασιλευσιν και ταις χωραις εν αις εγεγραπτο ‹ταδε›	**15.15** And Numenius, and the *people* alongside him, came from Rome, having letters to the kings and districts, in which these *thing*s were written:
15.16 Λευκιος υπατος Ρωμαιων Πτολεμαιω βασιλει χαιρι(ν)	**15.16** "Lucius, highest of *the* Romans, to Ptolemy *the* king: Rejoice.
15.17 οι πρεσβυται των Ιουδαιων ηλθον προς ημας φιλοι ημων και συμμαχοι ανανεουμενοι την εξ αρχης φιλιαν και συμμαχιαν απεσταλμενοι απο Σιμωνος του αρχιερεως και του δημου των Ιουδαιων	**15.17** The ambassadors of the Judeans have come to us *as* our friends and military allies, renewing the earlier friendship and military alliance, having been sent by Simon the high priest and by the people of the Judeans.
15.18 ηνεγκαν δε ‹ασπιδα› χρυσην απο μνων ‹͵α´›	**15.18** And they have brought a golden shield *weighing* a thousand minas.
15.19 ηρεσεν ου(ν) ημιν γραψαι ‹τοις› βασιλευσιν και ταις χωραις οπως μη εκζητησωσι(ν) ‹αυτοις κακα κ(αι) μη πολεμησωσιν› αυτους και τας πολεις αυτων και την χωραν αυτω(ν) και ινα μη συνμαχωσιν τοις πολεμουσιν προς αυτους	**15.19** Therefore it has pleased us to write to the kings and districts, so that they may not seek out evil *thing*s for them, and may not make war against them and their cities and their district; and in order that they may not be military allies with those who might be making war against them.

15.20 εδοξεν δε ημιν δεξασθαι την αcπιδα παρ αυτων	**15.20** And it has seemed *good* to us to receive the shield from them.
15.21 ει τινεc ουν λοιμοι δειαπεφευγαcιν ⸤εκ⸥ τηc χωραc αυτω(ν) προc υμαc παραδοτε αυτουc Cιμωνι τω αρχιερει οπωc εκδικηcει αυτουc κατα τον νομον αυτων	**15.21** Therefore, if any plague-bearers have fled away from their district to you^{pl}, give them up^{pl} to Simon the high priest, so that he may take vengeance *on* them in accordance with their law."
15.22 και ταυτα ⸤εγραψεν⸥ Δημητριω τω βαcιλει κ(αι) Ατταλω και Αριαραθη και Αρcακη	**15.22** And he wrote these *thing*s to Demetrius the king, and to Attalus and to Ariarathes and to Arsaces,
15.23 και ειc παcαc ταc χωραc και ⸤Cαμψακη⸥ και Cπαρτιαταιc και ειc Δηλο(ν) και ειc Μυνδον και ειc ⸤Cικυωνα⸥ και ειc την Καρια(ν) και ειc Cαμον και ειc ⸤⸥ Παμφυλιαν και ειc ⸤Λυκιαν⸥ και ειc Αλικαρναccον και ειc Ροδον και ειc Φαcηλιδα και ειc Κω και ειc Cιδην και ειc Αραδον και Γορτυνα και Κνιδον και Κυπρον και Κυρηνην	**15.23** and to all the districts, and to Sampsaces and to *the* Spartans, and to Delos and to Myndus and to Sicyon and to Caria and to Samos and to Pamphylia and to Lycia and to Halicarnassus and to Rhodes and to Phaselis and to Cos and to Side, and to Arvad and Gortyna and Cnidus and Cyprus and Cyrene.
15.24 το δε αντιγραφον τουτων εγραψαν Cιμωνι τω αρχιερει	**15.24** And they wrote a copy of these *thing*s to Simon the high priest.

15.15 ταδε A 64^{+}236 La^{109} La^{146} | ταυτα S V • **15.17** πρεcβυται S V = -βευται A 64^{+}236 • **15.18** αcπιδα S^{ca} V A 64^{+}236 La^{109} La^{146} | ανc- S* • ⸤α′ S^{ca} V A 64^{+}236 La^{109} La^{146} | α S* • **15.19** τοιc S^{ca} V A 64^{+}236 | ταιc S* • αυτοιc κακα κ(αι) μη πολεμηcωcιν S^{ca} V A La^{109} La^{146} | αυ- κακα μηδε π- 64^{+}236 | > S* • **15.21** εκ S^{ca} V A 64^{+}236 | > S* • **15.22** εγραψεν S^{ca} V A La^{109} La^{146} | -ψαν S* | -ψαμεν 64^{+}236 • **15.23** Cαμψακη A 64^{+}236 La^{109} | -ψαμη S V • Cικυωνα S^{ca} V A 64^{+}236 La^{109} La^{146} | Cυκ- S* • Παμφυλιαν V 64^{+}236 | ^ την S A • Λυκιαν S^{ca} V A 64^{+}236 La^{109} La^{146} | Τηκ- S* •

15.15–24 Simon had "sent Numenius to Rome, bearing a great golden shield with a weight of a thousand minas, to establish the military alliance with them" (14.24). Now **Numenius** returned, with **letters** in which the Romans instructed all the neighboring **kings and districts:**

- not to do **evil** to the Judeans;
- not to **make war against them;**
- not to **be military allies** of their opponents;
- to **give . . . up to Simon** any enemies who had escaped from Judea, so that they might receive punishment (**vengeance**) **in accordance with** Judean **law.** The leaders raised up by God under the old covenant were authorized by Him to **take vengeance** on evildoers in this way: see the notes on 7.24; 2.67.

One of the letters—addressed to **Ptolemy the king** of Egypt (a successor of the Ptolemy mentioned in 1.18; 10.51; 11.18)—is quoted in detail. Similar letters were addressed to other kings—**Demetrius the king**[389] of Syria, **Arsaces** the king of Media and Persia (14.2), **Attalus,** and **Ariarathes**[390]—and to other districts east of Rome, including Greek cities (**Sparta,** 12.2–23; **Sicyon**), regions on the Mediterranean north coast (**Pamphylia,** Acts 13.13; 14.24; 27.5; **Lycia,** Acts 27.5; **Cnidus,** Acts 27.7; **Myndus, Caria,**[391] **Halicarnassus, Phaselis, Side**) and south coast (**Cyrene** in Libya, Acts 2.10), and various Mediterranean islands (**Samos,** Acts 20.15; **Rhodes** and **Cos,** Acts 21.1; **Cyprus,** Acts 21.3; **Arvad** off the coast of Phoenicia, Ezek 27.8, 11; **Delos;** the city of **Gortyna** on Crete).[392] A **copy** was also provided for **Simon** himself.

This list shows impressively how far Rome's influence was already extending, and hints at the great diversity of peoples who would become components of its empire (in accordance with Daniel's prophecy, Dan 2.41–43). Yet the kingdom that would replace Rome—the kingdom of God (Dan 2.44)—would include an even greater diversity of peoples, moving outward from those mentioned here (Jer 31.10; Isa 24.15; 42.10–12; Acts 2.5–11) to "all nations," "from sea to sea, and from the River to the ends of the earth" (Psa 72.11, 8; Rev 7.9; Acts 10.35).

The letter was sent in the name of **Lucius, highest of the Romans.** The Romans had no king (8.14); **Lucius** was presumably the consul in charge of foreign policy that year (see the notes on 8.16).

In the Maccabean History, this straightforward, authoritative letter intrudes into the account of the inconclusive conflict between Antiochus and Trypho, and invites comparison with it—a narrative device that has been much admired. "On the one hand, the Romans' secure support [*respaldo*] contrasts with the struggles entangling the Seleucids; on the other hand, the faithfulness of these allies condemns the juxtaposed disloyalty of Antiochus" (Alonso Schökel, *Macabeos,* 128).

---

[389] **Demetrius the king.** At the time when the letters were written, perhaps the Romans had not yet heard of Demetrius's captivity; or perhaps they regarded him as still the rightful ruler of the region (cf. 14.1–3).

Trypho is not among the rulers listed; the Romans did not recognize him as having any authority (Diodorus 33.28a).

[390] Classical historians report that **Attalus** II was king of Pergamum at this time (Strabo 13.4.2; Polybius 32.12), and that **Ariarathes** V was king of Cappadocia (Diodorus 31.19.7–8; 31.28 [31.42]; Polybius 3.5.2; 32.1).

[391] The Carians are often identified with the Carites of 2 Kgs 11.4, 19, but this is very doubtful (ABD 1.872).

[392] Only one of the names is uncertain. **Sampsaces** *(Sampsakē)* is the reading of A and 64^{+}236 (supported by La^{109} and 7a1^{+}7h7), whereas S and V read "Sampsames" *(Sampsamē).* It might possibly be either Samsat (Samosata) on the Euphrates or Samsun on the Black Sea (ABD 5.949; Abel 267). The reading in the Clementine edition of the Vulgate, *Lampsaco* ("Lampsaces"), is merely an editor's conjecture, and has no manuscript support in any language.

Antiochus is estranged from Simon

15.25 Αντιοχος δε ο βασιλευς ‹παρενεβαλεν› επι Δωρα εν τη δευτερα προσαγων δια ‹παντος› αυτη τας χειρας και μηχανας ποιουμενος και συνεκλεισεν το(ν) Τρυφωνα του ‹μη› εκπορευεσθαι και εισπορευεσθαι	**15.25** But Antiochus the king camped against Dor, in *its* second *district,* bringing *his* hands near it at all *times* and making devices *of war.* And he shut Trypho up *from* going out or going in.

15.25 παρενεβαλεν S[ca] V A 64[+]236 La[109] La[146] | παρεβαλεν εν S* • παντος V A 64[+]236 La[146] | -των S • μη S[ca] 64[+]236 La[146] | > S* V A •

15.25 Antiochus continued to besiege the city of **Dor** (as described in vv 13–14). More details of the siege are now given. The besiegers camped **in** the city's **second district**—that is, in its "outskirts" (NJB)[393]—and kept assailing its central district closely **at all times** with the help of **devices of war** (see on 5.30; "siege-engines," REB), so that **Trypho** was unable to go **out** or **in.**

15.26 κ(αι) απεστιλεν αυτω Σιμων δισχιλιους ανδρας εκλεκτους συμμαχησαι αυτω και αργυριον και χρυσιο(ν) και σκευη ικανα	**15.26** And Simon sent him two thousand chosen men to be military allies for him, and silver and gold and a considerable *amount of* equipment.
15.27 και ουκ ηβουλετο αυτα δεξασθαι αλλα ηθετησεν πα(ν)τα οσα συνεθετο αυτω το προτερον κ(αι) ηλλοτριουτο αυτω	**15.27** And he was not willing to receive them, but set aside all *the thing*s that he had agreed with him previous*ly*; and he was becoming estranged from him.

15.26–27 Simon provided Antiochus with **military allies** and resources (**silver and gold and a considerable amount of equipment**), but Antiochus **was not willing to receive them.** Instead, he **set aside all the things that he had agreed with** Simon (as described in vv 1–9), just as previous kings had set aside their promises to the Israelites (Antiochus Eupator, 6.62; Demetrius son of Demetrius, 11.53; Trypho, 13.19).

---

393 **In its second district** *(en tē deutera)* is the reading of S*, V, and A (supported by La[146]). This expression describes the outer part of a city, the part that developed later (Zep 1.10, LXX; "the new part," HALOT 2.650, §2); see Abel 270 and Simons §1196. The besiegers had already gained possession of the outer part of Dor, and were blockading its inner part (just as Judean forces, while in possession of the rest of Jerusalem, blockaded its citadel: 12.36; 13.49). The expression is not a common one, and puzzled some readers even in ancient times (La[109] omits it altogether). It cannot mean "for the second time" (indicating either that Antiochus was besieging Dor for the second time [REB] or that the author was mentioning it for the second time [Nelis 249]). In Greek, "for the second time" would usually be *ek deuterou* (9.1; Jnh 3.1; Hag 2.20; Acts 10.15; etc.), and certainly not *en tē deutera.* The Antiochene copies read "on the second day" (*en tē hēmera tē deutera,* 64[+]236; *en tē deutera hēmera,* S[ca]), but that would not fit the context here (note especially the phrase **at all times**).

15.28 και απεcτιλεν προc αυτον	**15.28** And he sent to him
Αθηνοβιον ενα των φιλων αυτου	Athenobius, one of his Friends,
κοινολογηcομενον αυτω λεγων	to confer with him, saying: "You^{pl}
υμειc κατακρατειτε τηc Ιοππηc	yourselves^{pl} are overpowering Joppa
και Γαζαρων και τηc ακραc τηc εν	and Gezer and the citadel that *is* in
Ι(ερουcα)λημ πολιc τηc βαcιλιαc μου	Jerusalem, cities of my kingdom.
15.29 τα ορια αυτων ερημωcατε	**15.29** Their appointed boundaries
και ‹εποιηcατε› πληγην μεγαλην	you^{pl} have made desolate, and you^{pl}
επι τηc γηc	have done a great injury on the land;
και εκυριευcατε	and you^{pl} have gained dominion
‹τοπων› πολλων εν τη βαcιλια μου	over many places in my kingdom.
15.30 νυν ου(ν) παραδοτε	**15.30** Now therefore, give up^{pl} the
ταc πολιc αc ‹κατελαβεcθε›	cities that you^{pl} have taken hold of,
και τουc φορουc των τοπων	and the tributes of the places where
ων κατεκυριευcατε εκτοc	you^{pl} have gained dominion, outside
των οριων τηc Ιουδαιαc	the appointed boundaries of Judea;
15.31 ει δε μη δοτε ‹αντ αυτων›	**15.31** but if not, give^{pl} instead of them
πεντακοcια ταλαντα αργυριου	five hundred talents of silver,
και τηc καταφθοραc ηc ατεφθαρκατε	and five hundred other talents
και τω(ν) φορων των πολεω(ν)	*for* the ruin that you^{pl} have ruined
αλλα ταλαντα πεντακοcια	and *for* the tributes of the cities.
ει δε μη παραγενομενοι	But if not, when we *have* come,
‹εκπολεμηcομεν› υμαc	we will overpower you^{pl} in battle."

15.29 εποιηcατε S^{ca} V A $64^{+}236$ La^{109} La^{146} \| π- S* • τοπων V A $64^{+}236$ La^{146} \| > S • **15.30** κατελαβεcθαι V* = -θε V^{b} A $64^{+}236$ \| παρελαβετε S • **15.31** αντ αυτων S^{ca} V A La^{146} $7a1^{+}7h7$ \| αυτων S* \| > $64^{+}236$ • εκπολεμηcομεν V $64^{+}236$ La^{109} La^{146} \| -cωμε(ν) S \| -coυcιν A •

15.28–31 Antiochus sent a message to the Judeans, accusing them of **overpowering,** taking **hold of,** and gaining **dominion over** various **places** that were **outside the appointed boundaries of Judea** and belonged instead to his own **kingdom.** He specifically named the cities of **Joppa and Gezer, and the citadel that is in Jerusalem** (see on 14.5–7). He ordered the Judeans either to **give up** those cities, or to pay **five hundred talents of silver** for them (see on 13.16), plus **five hundred other talents** for the damage they had done in the area. These accusations and demands were unjust (vv 33–34).

If the Judeans refused, Antiochus declared that he would **overpower** them **in battle.** True, he had recently been successful in driving away Trypho (vv 10–11); but success against the enemies of God is no guarantee of success against God (cf. 2 Kgs 19.8–35).

15.32 και ηλθεν Αθηνοβιοc ο φιλοc	**15.32** And Athenobius the king's
του ‹βαcιλεωc› ειc Ι(ερουcα)λημ	Friend came to Jerusalem.
και ειδεν την δοξαν Cιμωνοc	And he saw the glory of Simon,
και κυλικιον μετα χρυcωματω(ν) και	and *his* cabinet with gold vessels

αργυρωματω(ν) ⸤κ(αι)⸥ παραστασιν ικανην και ⸤εξιστατο⸥ και ⸤απηγγιλεν⸥ αυτω τους λογους του βασιλεως	and silver vessels, and *the* considerable state *he kept;* and he was amazed. And he told him the king's words.

15.32 βασιλεως 1° S^{ca} V A $64^{+}236$ La^{109} La^{146} | -λευσαι S* • κ(αι) 5° S^{ca} V A $64^{+}236$ La^{109} La^{146} | > S* • εξιστατο S^{ca} V A $64^{+}236$ La^{109} La^{146} | -αντο S* • απηγγιλεν S^{ca} A $64^{+}236$ La^{109} La^{146} | -λαν S* V •

15.32 Antiochus's messenger, **Athenobius the king's Friend** (see on 2.18), brought the message **to Jerusalem.** Just as the Queen of Sheba had been amazed at the glory of Solomon (1 Kgs 10.4–5), Athenobius **was amazed** at **the glory of Simon** (see on 14.4), the **considerable state** ("attendance," KJV)[394] that he kept, and his **cabinet with gold vessels and silver vessels** (a sign of prosperity: cf. 1 Kgs 10.21; Est 1.7)—at least some of which would have come from Antiochus's predecessors (cf. 11.58).

Simon defends Judea

15.33 και αποκριθεις Σιμων ειπε(ν) αυτω ουτε γην αλλοτριαν ειληφαμεν ουτε αλλοτριων κεκρατηκαμεν αλλα της κληρονομιας των π(ατ)ρων ημων υπο δε εχθρων ημω(ν) ακριτως εν τινι κ(αι)ρω κατεκρατηθη	**15.33** And Simon, when *he* responded, said to him: "We have neither taken strangers' land nor held strangers' *property,* but *only* *that* of our fathers' inheritance. But for some period of time it had been unjustly overpowered by our enemies.
15.34 ημεις δε καιρον εχοντες αντεχομεθα της κληρονομιας των π(ατ)ρων ημων	**15.34** But we ourselves, having *the* occasion, are holding onto our fathers' inheritance.
15.35 περι δε Ιοππης κ(αι) Γαζαρων ων αιτις αυται εποιουν εν τω λαω πληγη(ν) μεγαλην και την χωραν ημων τουτων δωσομεν ταλαντα ρ´ και ουκ απεκριθη αυτω λογον	**15.35** But concerning Joppa and Gezer, for which you† are asking, they themselves were doing a great injury among the people and *in* our district; *for* these we will give a hundred talents." And he did not respond anything to him,
15.36 απεστρεψε(ν) δε μετα θυμου προς τον βασιλεα και ⟨απηγγιλεν⟩ αυτω τους λογους τουτους και την δοξαν Σιμωνος και παντα οσα ειδεν και ωργισθη ο βασιλευς οργη μεγαλη	**15.36** but returned with indignation to the king, and told him these words, and the glory of Simon, and *all* *the things* that he had seen. And the king became angry with great anger.

15.36 απηγγιλεν S^{ca} V A $64^{+}236$ La^{109} La^{146} | -λαν S* •

[394] **State** *(parastasin)* describes persons or things "stationed" (*paristēmi,* 6.35) near someone or something. The Queen of Sheba was similarly impressed by the "standing" (*stasin,* LXX) of Solomon's servants (1 Kgs 10.5).

15.33–35 Simon defended the Israelites' activities in much the same way as Jephthah had done a thousand years earlier (Jdg 11.14–27).

- Antiochus accused the Judeans of taking land "outside the appointed boundaries of Judea"—but in reality, they were merely **holding onto** their **fathers' inheritance,** the land that God had promised to Abraham (Gen 15.7, 18–21; Acts 7.4–5) and had given to Israel in the time of Joshua (Num 34.1–15; Josh 11.23). (Indeed, even if the Judeans had wished to give some of that land to an outsider, they had no authority to do so: Lev 25.23; 1 Kgs 21.3; cf. Num 36.7.)
- Antiochus accused the Judeans of "overpowering" that land—but in reality, **it had been overpowered by** their **enemies.**
- Antiochus accused the Judeans of doing "a great injury on the land"—but in reality, the enemy cities were the ones that had done **a great injury.** The Israelites' activities, which the king called ruining and injuring, were actually a cleansing and a strengthening (14.7, 34; cf. 2 Kgs 18.22). Thus Antiochus was calling evil good and good evil (Isa 5.20; Prov 17.15).

Simon not only "spent much money of his own" for his nation (14.32), but also sent much money to an enemy whom he knew to be deceitful (13.17–19). On the present occasion he responded with similar generosity. The two cities demanded by Antiochus, **Joppa and Gezer,** were part of Israel's lawful **inheritance,** belonging respectively to the tribes of Dan (Josh 19.46) and Ephraim (Josh 16.3)—so Antiochus was not entitled to any payment at all for them. Moreover, he had treated Simon's earlier gifts with gross ingratitude (vv 26–27). Nevertheless Simon willingly offered him a large sum of money, **a hundred talents** (see the notes on 13.16). He was not discouraged by unthankfulness, but continued to offer gifts to an enemy who had no right to them—just as God does with us (Luke 6.35 ≡ Matt 5.44–45).

15.36 Simon's defense silenced the king's emissary (cf. Matt 22.34; 1 Pet 2.15; Titus 2.8; Psa 63.11; 107.42). Athenobius **did not respond anything**[395] **to him;** he merely **returned with indignation** (cf. 1 Kgs 21.4) and **told** the king what he had witnessed.

Antiochus sends Cendebeus against Judea

15.37 Τρυφων δε εμβας εις πλοιο(ν) εφυγεν εις Ορθωσιαν	**15.37** But Trypho, having gone into a ship, fled to Orthosia.
15.38 και κατεστησεν ο βασιλευς το(ν) Κενδεβαιον επιστρατηγον της παραλιας και δυναμις πεζικας και ιππικας εδωκεν αυτω	**15.38** And the king established Cendebeus *as* chief army commander of the seaside, and gave him forces: footsoldiers and horse-soldiers.

[395] **He did not respond anything** *(logon),* where *logon* is presumably a statement (as in Matt 15.12; 19.11, 22; BDAG 600, §1aγ) on the subject under discussion (as in Acts 8.21; 15.6; BDAG 600, §1aε; Muraoka 434, §6). Athenobius may not have been completely wordless, but he made no attempt to answer Simon's defense.

15.39 και ενετιλατο αυτω παρεμβαλλειν κατα προcωπον της Ιουδαιας και ενετιλατο αυτω οικοδομηcαι ‹την› Κεδρων και ‹οχυρωcαι› τας πυλας ‹και› οπως ‹πολεμηcη› τον λαο(ν) ο δε βαcιλευc εδιωκε τον Τρυφωνα	**15.39** And he commanded him to camp against *the* face of Judea, and commanded him to build up Kedron and fortify the gates, and that he should make war against the people. But the king *kept* pursuing Trypho.

15.39 την V A 64⁺236 | > S • οχυρωcαι V A 64⁺236 La[109] La[146] | οικοδομηcαι S • και 4° V A La[109] La[146] 7a1⁺7h7 | > S 64⁺236 • πολεμηcη V 64⁺236 La[146] [*debellare* La[109]] | -μηcωcιν S | -μη A •

15.36–39 Antiochus, however, was still occupied with **Trypho,** who had managed to slip through the blockade **into a ship,** and had escaped from Dor to the city of **Orthosia.**[396] While Antiochus himself **kept pursuing Trypho,**[397] he instructed his army commander **Cendebeus** to **make war against the people** of **Judea.** In preparation for this war, Cendebeus was to **build up** the city of **Kedron**[398] **and fortify** its **gates.**[399]

15.40 και παρεγενηθη Κενδεβαιοc ειc Ιαμνιαν και ηρξατο του ερεθιζειν τον λαον κ(αι) ‹ενβατευειν› ειc την Ιουδαιαν και αιχμαλωτιζει(ν) τον λαον και φονευειν	**15.40** And Cendebeus came to Jabneh, and he began to stir up the people and go into Judea and take the people captive and murder *them.*
15.41 και ωκοδομηcεν την Κεδρων και απεταξεν εκει ιππειc κ(αι) δυναμειc οπωc εκπορευομενοι ‹εξοδευcωcιν› ταc οδουc τηc Ιουδαιαc ‹› καθα cυνεταξεν ‹αυτω ο βαcιλευc›	**15.41** And he built up Kedron, and he set apart there horsemen and forces, so that, when *they* went out, they would depart *on* the paths of Judea, just as the king had ordered him.

15.40 ενβατευειν S[ca] V A 64⁺236 La[109] La[146] | εκβαccευειν S* • **15.41** εξοδευcωcιν V [-ευω- A 64⁺236] La[146] | -ευcουcιν S • καθα S[ca] V A 64⁺236 La[109] La[146] | ^ και S* • αυτω / ο βαcιλευc V A 64⁺236 La[109] La[146] | ~ S[ca] | ο βαcιλευc S* •

---

[396] According to Pliny (*Natural History,* 5.17.78), **Orthosia** was situated on the coast just south of the Eleutherus River (cf. Maccabaica 11.7; 12.30).

[397] This is the last we hear of Trypho. Classical historians give conflicting stories of his end. Some say that he committed suicide (Strabo 14.5.2); others say that he was killed by his enemies (Appian, *Syriaca,* 68.358; Josephus, *Antiquities,* 13.224).

[398] **Kedron,** as this passage shows, was a city near Jabneh (v 40) and Modein (16.4). Therefore, it might possibly be Gederoth in the lowland of Judah (Josh 15.41).

[399] **The gates** *(tas pulas)* are those of the city just mentioned (as in, e.g., "Jerusalem … and the walls … and the foundations," Ezra 4.12).

15.40–41 Cendebeus did what **the king had ordered.** From bases in **Jabneh** (see on 4.15) and **Kedron,** his forces **went out** into the surrounding region (on **the paths of Judea**) and began to **take the people captive and murder them,** as Israel's enemies had been doing repeatedly since the time of Antiochus Epiphanes (1.24, 30, 32, etc.).

Simon sends his sons against Cendebeus

16.1 και ανεβη Ιωαννης	**16.1** And John went up
εκ Γαζαρω(ν)	from Gezer,
και απηγγιλεν Cιμωνι τω π(ατ)ρι	and told Simon his father
αυτου α ‹cυνετελεcεν Κενδεβαιοc›	what Cendebeus had been doing.

16.1 cυνετελεcεν Κενδεβαιοc S^{ca} 64^{+}236 La^{109} La^{146} | -λεcεν Δεβ- S* | -λεκενδεβ- V* | -λεκε Δεβ- V^{b} | -λει Κενδεβ- A •

16.1 By this time, Simon's son **John,** who lived in **Gezer,** was the Judean army leader (13.53). John now went to **Simon his father** (who lived in Jerusalem, 13.52) **and told him what Cendebeus had been doing.**

16.2 και εκαλεcεν Cιμων	**16.2** And Simon called
τουc δυο υιουc αυτου τουc	his two older sons,
πρεcβυτερουc Ιουδα(ν) και Ιωαννην	Judas and John,
κ(αι) ειπεν αυτοιc εγω και οι αδελφοι	and said to them: "I and my brothers
μ(ου) και ο οικοc του π(ατ)ρ(ο)c μου	and my father's house,
επολεμηcαμεν τουc πολεμουc	we have warred the wars of Israel
Ιc(ραη)λ απο νεοτητοc	from youth
εωc τηc cημερον ημεραc	until today's day;
και ευοδωθη εν ταιc χερcιν ημω(ν)	and it has prospered in our hands
ρυcαcθαι τον Ιc(ραη)λ πλεονακιc	to deliver Israel many times.
16.3 νυνει δε γεγηρακα	**16.3** But now I have become old,
και υμειc δε εν τω ελεει	but you[pl] yourselves[pl] also, by
ικανοι εcτε εν τοιc ετεcιν γινεcθε	the mercy, are sufficient in years.
αντ εμου και του αδελφου μου	Be[pl] in place of me and my brothers,
και εξελθοντεc ‹υπερμαχιται›	and, when *you* have gone out[pl], fight[pl]
υπερ του εθνουc ημων η δε εκ του	on behalf of our nation; and may
ου(ρα)νου βοηθεια εcτω μεθ υμων	the help from Heaven be with you[pl]."

16.3 υπερμαχιται S^{ca} V A 64^{+}236 La^{109} La^{146} | > S* •

16.2–3 Simon now appointed **his two older sons, Judas and John,** to do the work that he himself and his **brothers** had done **from youth until today's day.** Just as Simon and his brothers had **warred the wars of Israel** (3.2),[400] so his sons were now

---

[400] **We have warred the wars** [*epolemēsamen tous polemous*] **of Israel** (as in 2.66; 3.2) is the reading of S^{1}, V, A, and 64^{+}236 (supported by 7a1^{+}7h7), whereas S* (supported by La^{109} and La^{146}) reads "we have made war against the ones warring against [*epolemēsamen tous polemious*] Israel" (cf. 7.29; 14.33–34).

to **fight on behalf of** their **nation.** Likewise, under the new covenant, those who "have fought the good fight" (2 Tim 4.7) are to hand on that work to their true children in faith (1 Tim 1.2)—who in their turn will entrust the same work "to faithful people, who will be able to teach others also" (2 Tim 2.2).

Those who are well off may easily forget the Source of their blessings (Deut 8.11–18; Prov 30.8–9; Hos 13.6). But Simon did not. Looking back (like Joshua, Josh 23.1–16), in a situation of prosperity and abundance (15.32), at the mighty achievements of the past forty years, he did not ascribe them to the hands of himself and his family. On the contrary, those **hands** had been **prospered** by Heaven (4.55; 14.36) to achieve those things (Psa 115.1; 1 Cor 15.10; 2 Cor 3.5). What he now had, he had only **by the mercy** (3.44; 4.10, 24).[401] And whatever his sons might achieve, they would achieve only if they had **the help from Heaven** (3.53; 12.15). Those who fight the same fight under the new covenant can be prospered only by the same Source: by the mercy of their Lord (Rom 11.30–31; Titus 3.5; 1 Pet 1.3) and with His help (Acts 26.22; Luke 1.54; Heb 4.16; 2.16; 13.6; Psa 121.1–2; 124.8).

16.4 και επελεξε(ν) εκ της χωρας εικοςι χιλιαδας ανδρω(ν) πολεμιςτων και ιππεις και επορευθηςαν επι τον Κε(ν)δεβαιον και εκοιμηθηςαν εν Μωδιν	**16.4** And he chose from the district twenty thousand men *who were* warriors, and horsemen; and they went against Cendebeus, and slept at Modein.

16.4 The Judean forces **against Cendebeus** spent the night before the battle **at Modein.** The war against the nations was going to end in the place where it had started (2.15–28).

Cendebeus is defeated

16.5 και αναςταντες το πρωι επορευθηςαν εις το πεδιον και ιδου δυναμεις πολλη εις ςυναντηςιν αυτοις πεζικη και ιππεις κ(αι) χιμαρρους ην ανα μεςον αυτων	**16.5** And when *they* had risen up *in* the early morning, they went into the level place; and, see! a great force *was coming* to meet them— footsoldiers and horsemen; and *there* was a storm-brook between them.
16.6 και παρενεβαλε κατα προςωπον αυτω(ν) αυτος και ο λαος αυτου και ιδεν τον λαον διλουμενον διαπεραςε τον χιμαρρουν και διεπεραςεν πρωτος	**16.6** And he himself and his people camped opposite their face. And he saw the people terrified to cross over the storm-brook. And he crossed over first;

[401] **By the mercy.** As usual in the Maccabaica, the Divine Source of that mercy (cf. Eph 2.4; 1 Pet 1.3) is not named (see the introduction to this commentary). Compare the more familiar expressions "saved from the anger" and "give place to the anger" (Rom. 5.9; 12.19), where the Source of the anger is not named.

κ(αι) ειδον αυτον οι α(ν)δρες και διεπεραcα(ν) καθοπιcθεν ⸤αυτου⸥	and the men saw him, and crossed over behind him.
16.7 και διειλεν τον λαον και τουc ιππιc εν μεcω των πεζων ην δε ιπποc των υπεναντιω(ν) πολλη cφοδρα	**16.7** And he divided up the people, and the horsemen *were* in *the* midst of the footsoldiers; but *the* enemies' horse were very many.

16.6 αυτου 2° S^{ca} V A 64^{+}236 La^{109} La^{146} | -τω(ν) S* •

16.5–7 The One who had prospered the fathers (v 2) now prospered those who walked in the footsteps of the fathers. Their **enemies** were **a great force,** with **very many** horsemen, and were separated from the Judeans only by a **storm-brook** (see the notes on 5.37). At first the Judean **people** were **terrified,** but their leader[402] himself set the example, and **crossed over first** to face the enemy (as Judas had done in a similar situation, 5.43). Seeing his example, the rest of the army **crossed over behind him.** We today have a "great cloud" of such examples, and have all the more reason to be "imitators of those who by faith and perseverance inherit the promises" (Heb 12.1; 6.12; 13.7; 1 Cor 4.16; 11.1; Rom 4.12).

16.8 κ(αι) εcαλπιcαν ταιc ⸤ιεραιc⸥ cαλπιγξιν και ⸤ετροπωθη Κενδαιβεοc⸥ κ(αι) η παρεμβολη αυτου και επεcον εξ αυτων τραυματιαι πολλοι οι δε καταλιφθεντεc εφυγον ειc το οχυρωμα	**16.8** And they trumpeted with the sacred trumpets, and Cendebeus and his company were turned back. And many wounded *one*s of them fell; but the *one*s who were left fled into the fortress.
16.9 τοτε ετραυματιcθη Ιουδαc ο αδελφοc Ιωαννου Ιωαννηc δε κατεδιωξεν αυτουc εωc ηλθεν ειc Κεδρων ην ωκοδομηcεν	**16.9** Then Judas, John's brother, was wounded. But John pursued after them, until he came to Kedron, which he had built up.
16.10 και εφυγο(ν) ειc τουc πυργουc τουc εν τοιc αγροιc Αζωτου και ενεπυριcεν αυτην εν πυρι και επεcο(ν) εξ αυτων ειc ανδραc διcχιλιουc και απεcτρεψεν ειc την Ιουδαιαν μετα ειρηνηc	**16.10** And they fled into the towers *that were* in the fields of Ashdod. And he set it on fire with fire, and up to two thousand men of them fell. And he returned to Judea in peace.

16.8 ιεραιc V La^{109} La^{146} | > S A 64^{+}236 • ετροπωθη Κενδαιβεοc S^{ca} V A 64^{+}236 [La^{109}] La^{146} | -θηcαν Δαιβ- S* •

16.8–10 As in the past, the Judeans did not trust to their own power, but sought

402 **He himself crossed over.** Simon had assigned the leadership to two of his sons (Judas and John, vv 2–3); the one mentioned here is presumably John, who has been the most prominent of Simon's sons in the narrative so far (v 1; 13.53) and continues to be the most prominent in what follows (vv 9–10; cf. Grimm 231).

God's help in the way He had appointed: **they trumpeted with the sacred trumpets,** in accordance with His Law for His old covenant people ("When you go to war in your land against an oppressor who oppresses you, then you will make a noise with the trumpets; and you will be remembered before the LORD your God, and you will be saved from your enemies," Num 10.9).

Many of their enemies were **wounded** and **fell,** and the remainder **fled.** One of Simon's sons, **Judas,** was himself wounded; but the other, **John, pursued** Cendebeus **to Kedron, which he had built up** (15.39, 41). Many of the enemies fled into **towers in the fields of Ashdod,**[403] where they were burnt **with fire** (as had happened at Ashdod on a previous occasion, 10.83–85).

The Judeans were now able to return **to Judea in peace.**

THE DEATH OF SIMON

Ptolemy son of Abubus

16.11 και Πτολεμαιος ο του Αβουβου ην καθεσταμενος στρατηγος εις το πεδιον Ιερειχω κ(αι) εσχεν αργυριον και χρυσιον πολυ	**16.11** And Ptolemy the *son* of Abubus had been established *as* army commander for the level place of Jericho; and he had much silver and gold:
16.12 ην γαρ γαμβρος του αρχιερεως	**16.12** for he was a marriage-relation of the high priest.
16.13 κ(αι) υψωθη η καρδια αυτου και εβουληθη κατακρατησαι της χωρας κ(αι) εβουλευετο δολω κατα Σιμωνος και των υιων αυτου αραι αυτους	**16.13** And his heart was exalted, and he wanted to overpower the district; and he was taking counsel in deceit against Simon and his sons, to do away with them.

16.11–13 Ptolemy[404] **the son of Abubus** would appear important in the world's eyes for three reasons: he was the **army commander** for the plains around **Jericho** (cf. Josh 5.10); he was a **marriage-relation**[405] of Simon (**the high priest,** 13.42; 14.17); and **he had much silver and gold** ("those who love a rich person are many," Prov 14.20; 19.4). Yet he was not content with what he already had (Luke 12.15; Ecc 5.10; 6.7).

---

[403] **Ashdod** here is probably the ancient Philistine city (4.15), although in this context it could possibly be a geographical term for a kind of terrain, "the slopes" (9.15) in the vicinity of Kedron (v 9). The Medeba mosaic map (believed to date from the sixth century CE) depicts four unnamed towers or small fortresses on the coastal plain between Jabneh and Ashdod, but presumably the area's fortifications would have been very different eight centuries earlier.

[404] **Ptolemy** is a Greek name, and does not necessarily imply any connection with Egypt. (The first Ptolemy to rule Egypt was a Greek, not an Egyptian: 1.6, 8.)

[405] The term **marriage-relation** *(gambros)* describes a man "connected by marriage" to some specified person (Muraoka 125)—e.g., a daughter's husband (Gen 19.14, LXX) or wife's father (Exod 3.1, LXX).

His heart was exalted (like Alexander's, 1.3), **and he wanted** to gain power over the whole **district** of Judea. So he began devising a plan to **do away** with **Simon and his sons** (as Trypho had done with Jonathan, 12.40).

Ptolemy kills Simon and his sons

16.14 Σιμων δε ην εφοδευων	**16.14** But Simon was visiting
τας πολις τας εν τη χωρα κ(αι)	the cities that *were* in the district,
φροντιζων ‹› της επιμελιας αυτων	and keeping in mind the care of them.
και κατεβη εις Ιερειχω αυτος και	And he came down to Jericho,
Ματταθιας και Ιουδας ‹οι υιοι› αυτου	he and Mattathias and Judas his sons,
ετους ζ´ και ο´ και ρ´	*in the* hundred and seventy-seventh
εν μηνι ‹αι´›	year, in *the* eleventh month
ουτος ο μην Σαββατ	(this *is* the month Shebat).

16.14 της S^{ca} A La^{109} La^{146} | ^ τα S* V | ^ τα περι 64^{+}236 • οι υιοι [> οι S^{ca}] V A 64^{+}236 [*filius* La^{109} La^{146}] | αδελφος S* • αι´ S^{ca} V A 64^{+}236 La^{109} La^{146} | αιου S* •

16.14 Simon's work involved **visiting the cities that were in the district** of Judea (14.17; see on 9.24), **and keeping in mind the care of them.** "He sought good things for his nation" (14.4); "he sought out every way to raise his people high" (14.35). He was like Samuel, who journeyed annually from city to city, judging the people of Israel (1 Sam 7.15–17); and like Paul, whose "daily concern for all the churches" (2 Cor 11.28) impelled him to "look over the brethren in every city in which we proclaimed the word of the Lord, how they are holding" (Acts 15.36).

As part of this work, **in the eleventh month** (called **Shebat,** Zec 1.7) of the **hundred and seventy-seventh year**[406] Simon **came down to Jericho** with two of his sons: **Mattathias and Judas.**

16.15 και υπεδεξατο αυτους	**16.15** And the *son* of Abubus received
ο του Αβουβου εις το οχυρωματιον ‹›	them with deceit in the little fortress
το καλουμενον Δωκ μετα δολου	*that is* called Dok,
ο ωκοδομηcεν	which he had built.
κ(αι) εποιηcεν αυτοις ποτον μεγαν	And he made a great banquet
και ενεκρυψεν εκει α(ν)δρας	for them, and hid men in there.

16.15 οχυρωματιον V A 64^{+}236 La^{109} La^{146} | + εις S •

16.15 Ptolemy **the son of Abubus** acted **with deceit,** like those who arrested and killed Jesus (Matt 26.3–4 ≡ Mark 14.1). His treachery was all the worse, because he was a man whom Simon had reason to trust (Psa 55.12; 41.9 ≡ John 13.18, 26–27). He invited Simon and his sons into a **little fortress** that **he had built,** and **made a**

---

[406] 177 SE, in the reckoning of the Maccabean History, would probably be equivalent to about 135–134 BCE.

great banquet [*epoiēsen . . . poton megan*] **for them.** In itself there would be nothing sinister or unusual about that. Exactly the same Greek expression is applied to the "great feast" *(poton megan)* that Solomon "made" *(epoiēsen)* in thanksgiving after God's great promises to him at Gibeon (1 Kgs 3.15, LXX). As that passage shows, the term **banquet** *(potos)* corresponds to Hebrew *mšth,* "a word derived from *šth* 'to drink,' but meaning simply 'feast'" (LEH 510). A person invited to such a feast would therefore have no reason to expect ungodliness or drunkenness.

16.16 και οτε εμεθυcθη Cιμων και οι υιοι αυτου εξανεcτη Πτολεμαιοc και οι παρ αυτου κ(αι) ελαβον τα οπλα αυτων και επιcηλθον τω Cιμωνι ειc το cυμποcιον κ(αι) ‹απεκτειναν› αυτο(ν) και τουc δυο ϋιουc αυτου και ‹τιναc› τω(ν) πεδαριων αυτου	**16.16** And when Simon and his sons were full of drink, Ptolemy and the *men* alongside him rose up, and took their weapons, and came in on Simon, into the banquet, and killed him and his two sons and some of his servants.

16.16 απεκτειναν V A 64⁺236 | -τινον S • τιναc S[ca] V A 64⁺236 | -να S* •

16.16 By the end of the feast **Simon and his sons were full of drink.**[407] The armed men whom Ptolemy had hidden in the fortress (v 15) then **came . . . into the banquet, and killed** Simon **and his two sons and some of his servants.** Nobody knows when life will end, or how suddenly (Ecc 9.12); but blessed are those who have served the Lord faithfully, so that they are ready to face Him whenever, and however, the end may come (Matt 25.1–13; 1 Jn 2.28; 2 Pet 3.11–12; 1 Thes 5.1–10).

16.17 κ(αι) εποιηcεν αθεcιαν μεγαλην και απεδωκεν κακα α(ν)τι αγαθων	**16.17** And he did a great act of treachery, and returned evil in place of good.

[407] **Were full of drink** *(emethusthē).* This term can mean either "be drunk" (Gen 9.21, LXX) or simply "be filled" (Psa 36.8, LXX); see LEH 390; Muraoka 446, §§II.1, 2. In the present passage, some English versions adopt the former sense ("were drunk," ESV; cf. Truchet 261–62; Knabenbauer 260), some the latter ("had drunk freely," NAB; cf. Lapide 78; Pellicanus 5.331v; Drusius 56; Sacy 305). Either might perhaps fit the context. The tactic of getting people drunk in order to kill them was undoubtedly used in ancient Israel (2 Sam 13.28); in the present passage, however, the wording could indicate merely that Ptolemy waited till his guests were satisfied and comfortable (cf. Psa 104.15) before striking. At any rate there is no indication that Simon "gave way to" a "vice" on this occasion (Rawlinson, "I Maccabees," 536). Even people who are familiar with the taste of alcohol can be made intoxicated with it unawares (Gutberlet, *Erste Buch der Machabäer,* 260); and Simon would have been less likely to recognize its taste than most people. Under the old covenant Law, priests were forbidden to drink alcohol when they served in the tabernacle (Lev 10.9), and rulers were forbidden to drink alcohol under any circumstances (Prov 31.4), because it could make them "stumble in judgment" (Isa 28.7; Prov 31.5). **Simon** was both a ruler and a priest (Maccabaica 13.42), and had been notably diligent from his youth in obeying the Law (Maccabaica 2.64–65, 68; 14.14).

16.17 Ptolemy **did a great act of treachery,**[408] **and returned evil in place of good,** like the one who betrayed Jesus (Psa 109.5; cf. Prov 17.13; Psa 38.20).

"Here we can see two utterly opposite ways of life, and two men driven by utterly different spirits. One was puffed up with pride, thinking only of his own self-interest; the other was full of love for his people, thinking only of their good [14.4, 32–35]. One was ungrateful to the man whose daughter he had married, and was full of the cruel desire to dispossess his father-in-law, kill him, and lay hands on his country; the other was full of gratitude to God and Israel, who had chosen him as leader and high priest, and was devoted to the cares of watching over the safety and comfort of its cities [v 14]" (Sacy 304).

Ptolemy seeks control of the district

16.18 και εγραψεν ταυτα Πτολεμαιος και απεστιλεν ‹› τω βασιλει ‹οπως αποστιλη αυτω› δυναμις εις βοηθιαν και παραδω τας πολεις αυτω και την χωραν	**16.18** And Ptolemy wrote *about* these *things* and sent *it* to the king, so that he should send him forces for help, and give the cities and the district over to him.
16.19 και απεστιλεν ετερους εις Γαζαραν αραι τον Ιωαννην και τοις χιλιαρχοις απεστιλεν επιστολας παραγενεσθαι προς αυτον οπως δω αυτοις αργυριον και ‹χρυσιο(ν) κ(αι)› δοματα	**16.19** And he sent other *men* to Gezer, to do away with John. And he sent letters to the command- ers of thousands, *for them* to come to him, so that he might give them silver and gold and gifts.
16.20 και ετερους απεστιλεν καταλαβεσθαι τη(ν) Ι(ερουσα)λημ και το ορος του ιερου	**16.20** And he sent other *men* to take hold of Jerusalem and the mountain of the temple.

16.18 τω S^{ca} V A 64^{+}236 La^{109} La^{146} | ^ ταυτα οπως S* • οπως αποστιλη αυτω S^{ca} V A 64^{+}236 [La^{109}] La^{146} | > S* • **16.19** χρυσιο(ν) κ(αι) S^{ca} V A 64^{+}236 [La^{109}] La^{146} | > S* •

16.18–20 Ptolemy **sent** some of his men **to Gezer, to do away with** Simon's son **John** (13.53), and **other** men **to take hold of Jerusalem and the mountain of the temple.** But he would also need support from the army (cf. 11.55; 15.10–12) and, if possible, from King Antiochus (who had been at enmity with Simon, 15.27, 36). So he wrote to the main army **commanders** (offering them **silver and gold and gifts**), and also **to the king,** asking for additional military **forces** and for authority over **the cities and the district** of Judea. His victim had been diligent in pursuing good (see on v 14; cf. Prov 11.27; Rom 12.8); he himself was now being very diligent in pursuing evil (v 17).

---

[408] An **act of treachery** *(athesian)* is a "setting aside" (*atheteō,* TDNT 8.158–59) of one's obligations toward someone else—as Antiochus Eupator "set aside [*ēthetēsen*] the oath that he had sworn" (6.62; cf. Gal 3.15). To set aside our heavenly Father's covenant with us is the greatest of all treacheries (Mark 7.9; Luke 7.30; 1 Thes 4.8; Heb 10.28–29).

Ptolemy's plan to kill John fails

16.21 και προδραμων τις απηγγειλεν Ιωαννει εις Γαζαρα οτι απωλετο ο πατηρ αυτου και οι αδελφοι αυτου και οτι απεσταλκεν και σε αποκτιναι	**16.21** And a certain *man,* having run ahead, reported to John at Gezer that his father and his brothers had been destroyed, and that "he has sent to kill you† also."

16.21 But the Lord had a greater plan than Ptolemy, and His word traveled more quickly than Ptolemy's (cf. Psa 147.15). A **certain man** had **run ahead** of Ptolemy's supporters, and he warned **John at Gezer that his father and brothers had been destroyed, and that** Ptolemy was planning to **kill** John too.

16.22 και ακουσας εξεστη σφοδρα και συνελαβεν τους α(ν)δρας τους ελθοντας απολεσαι αυτον κ(αι) απεκτινεν αυτους επεγνω γαρ οτι εζητουν αυτον απολεσαι	**16.22** And when *he* had heard, he was very much amazed. And he took hold of the men who came to destroy him, and killed them: for he knew that they were seeking to destroy him.

16.22 John **was very much amazed:** like his father and his brothers, he had no prior suspicion of Ptolemy's plan. When Ptolemy's men **came to destroy him,** he was ready for them; by **seeking to destroy him,** they destroyed only themselves (Matt 26.52; Rev 11.18; Prov 11.19).

John son of Simon (16.23–24)

16.23 και τα λοιπα τω(ν) λογων Ιωαννου και των πολεμω(ν) αυτου και των ανδραγαθιων αυτου ω(ν) ηνδραγαθησεν κ(αι) της οικοδομης τω(ν) τιχων ων οικοδομησεν και των πραξεων αυτου	**16.23** And the rest of the accounts of John and his wars and his manly good deeds that he did, and the building of the walls that he built, and his activities,
16.24 ιδου ταυτα γεγραπται επι ‹βιβλιου› ημερων αρχιερωσυνης αυτου αφ ου εγενηθη αρχιερευς μετα τον π(ατε)ρα αυτου	**16.24** see! these *thing*s are written on *the* book of *the* days of his high priesthood, from *the time* that he became high priest after his father.

16.24 βιβλιου V A 64*236 | -ιω S •

16.23 John, who now became high priest (v 24), walked in the steps of his fathers, fighting **wars** (vv 2–10)—not just any wars, but the kind of wars that are coupled with **manly good deeds** (5.56; 9.22; 10.15; 8.2; the good deeds of a grownup person as opposed to a child: see on 9.10)—and **building . . . walls** to protect the Lord's people as He had appointed (Psa 51.18; Mic 7.11; Isa 58.12; Dan 9.25; Neh 2.17).[409] The

[409] John's coins (Hendin 186–89) are radically different from those of every previous Hellenistic ruler of Israel (see the footnote to 15.6; cf. Eyal, *The Hasmoneans,* 182–83). Theirs were self-

Lord's people under the new covenant are to do the same things: to "act like men" (1 Cor 16.13), to fight spiritual wars (2 Cor 10.4–5), and to build spiritual walls (Acts 15.14–18).

16.24 John's good deeds are listed only briefly in the Maccabean History, but they were **written** more fully in the **book of the days of his high priesthood,** evidently a record similar to the now lost "books of the words of the days" of many earlier rulers, both within Israel (1 Kgs 14.19; 22.45) and in other countries (Est 2.23; 6.1; 10.2).

---

aggrandizing; his are self-effacing. There is never any image of the leader, and the inscription always associates his people with himself—e.g., "John the high priest and the company of the Judeans" *(Yhwḥnn hkhn hgdl wḥbr hYhwdym)* or "John the high priest, head of the company of the Judeans" *(Yhwḥnn hkhn hgdl r'š ḥbr hYhdm).* The reverse carries no inscription, and shows a pomegranate (a reminder of the high priest's robe, Exod 28.31–35) or sometimes a helmet (a reminder of the **wars**).

COMMENTARY ON THE EIGHTEEN PSALMS

Introduction

The Eighteen Psalms describe the start of Roman rule over Judea. They therefore bear witness to the fulfillment of some of Daniel's prophecies, and show how the Romans came to have the authority described in the New Testament Scriptures (Matt 22.21; Luke 2.1; 3.1; John 11.48; 19.15; Acts 25.10–12, 21; 28.17).

The psalms are also remarkable for their understanding of the old covenant prophecies about the Messiah. They illustrate strikingly what the New Testament Scriptures tell us: at the time when Jesus arrived on earth, there were faithful people looking for the redemption of Israel (Luke 2.25, 38; 24.21) and teaching accurately the things about Christ that could be known from the previous Scriptures (cf. Acts 18.24–25).

Structure

The collection is arranged in a symmetrical, mirror-image shape:

A. The foreign invader and his end (1–2).
  B. Endurance when disciplined (3).
    C. May God remove the hypocrites (4).
      D. God will nourish every living thing (5).
  B. Endurance when disciplined (6).
A. The foreign invader (7–9).
  B. Endurance when disciplined (10).
      D. God will gather His people (11).
    C. May God remove the liars (12).
  B. Endurance when disciplined (13–16).
A. The foreign invader and the coming Messiah (17–18).

There is progression here, as well as symmetry; the subjects in the second half of the collection correspond to those in the first half, but sometimes extend further and deeper. Where Eighteen Psalms 1 and 2 look ahead from the invasion to the end of the invader, 17 and 18 look ahead to the coming of the Messiah. Where 5 speaks about God's earthly blessings for every living thing, 11 speaks about His spiritual blessings for His people. The last of the psalms about endurance under discipline (16) develops into an extended prayer for deliverance from sin.

The three A-sections contain the three largest psalms (2; 8; 17). These are the three sections that deal with the subject of the Roman invasion.

Name and Authorship

The earliest known name for these psalms—"Eighteen Psalms of Solomon" *(Psalmoi Solomōntos iē')*—is recorded in Codex Alexandrinus (probably fifth century CE).

In the surviving Greek manuscripts that contain this collection, it is entitled either "Psalms of Solomon" or "Wisdom of Solomon."[1] Moreover, in nearly all of them, the individual psalms are prefaced by superscriptions attributing them to Solomon. However, those superscriptions are presumably later additions, not part of the original text (they are not found in the Syriac manuscripts).[2]

The psalms themselves mention events that happened long after Solomon, such as the arrival of the Romans in Jerusalem. In itself, that might not rule out Solomon's authorship. After all, Isaiah lived long before the death of Jesus, and Asaph lived long before the conquest of Jerusalem, yet they wrote about those events in the past tense (Isa 53.4–12; Psa 79.1–13). Solomon, like Isaiah and Asaph, was a prophet. Under the guidance of God's Spirit, he too might possibly have written about future events in the past tense. Nevertheless, nothing in these psalms connects them with Solomon in any way. They never claim to be by Solomon. They never even mention Solomon. In none of them is there any detail suggesting that the writer lived in the time of Solomon (or at any time earlier than the Roman period).

Therefore, the name "Psalms of Solomon" is not authorized by anything in the text of these psalms themselves. It is also potentially confusing. The Psalter in the Hebrew Scriptures contains at least two items that are indeed psalms of Solomon: Psalms 72 and 127. There is also another serious source of confusion. A different collection of hymns, written around the end of the first century CE, became known in ancient times as the "Odes of Solomon." The "Odes of Solomon" and the present group of eighteen psalms ("Psalms of Solomon") were often confused in ancient times, and are sometimes confused even today.[3]

---

[1] Manuscripts of f^{253} entitle the collection *Sophia Solomōntos* ("Wisdom of Solomon"), whereas those of f^{260} entitle it *Psalmoi Solomōntos* ("Psalms of Solomon").

[2] In the Hebrew Psalter, later copyists in both Greek and Syriac tended to add superscriptions to psalms that originally did not have any. For instance, Psalm 2 of the Psalter has no superscription in the original Hebrew or in the earliest Greek and Syriac manuscripts. But in some medieval Greek manuscripts it is superscribed "a psalm of David"; and many medieval Syriac copies gave it elaborate superscriptions such as "about the calling of the Gentiles, and a prophecy of the death of the Messiah." No doubt the superscriptions to the Eighteen Psalms arose in a similar way, in order to identify their supposed author and summarize their content.

Except for the attributions to Solomon, everything in the superscriptions to the Eighteen Psalms could readily have been derived from the psalms themselves (as the footnotes in the following commentary show). By contrast, the superscriptions to the Hebrew Psalter contain much information that could never have been deduced from the psalms themselves.

[3] The name "Wisdom of Solomon" (as in f^{253}) would likewise be potentially confusing, because that name has commonly been applied since ancient times to the well-known LXX Book of Wisdom (*Liber Sapientiae,* Vg).

Because of those problems, Ryle and James (xliv, lx–lxi) proposed the name "Psalms of the Pharisees." Yet there is no more reason to connect these psalms with the Pharisees than with King Solomon. They never claim to be written by Pharisees. They never even mention Pharisees. And they conspicuously lack all the distinctive characteristics of Pharisaic writings.[4] For instance, they always adhere closely to the language and teachings of the Scriptures, never supplementing or modifying Scripture with unwritten tradition in the way that even very brief documents by the Pharisees and their heirs do (cf. Mark 7.3–13).

To avoid confusion, we will refer to these psalms simply as the "Eighteen Psalms." (No other ancient collection of psalms or hymns contains 18 items.) We will refer to the book of Psalms in the Hebrew Scriptures as the "Hebrew Psalter."

In both style and content, the Eighteen Psalms form a highly distinctive group. None of them could have been written by the same authors as (say) the so-called "Odes of Solomon," or the so-called "Psalm 151" added as a supplement to the Septuagint, or the noncanonical psalms found among the Dead Sea Scrolls. Among all known writings of the period, by far the most similar to the Eighteen Psalms are the songs uttered by Jesus' family and their friends around the time of His birth (Luke 1.46–55, 68–79; 2.29–32). Almost every line in those songs is composed partly of words and phrases that are also found in these Psalms—and in a way that suggests that the singers are not quoting from a book, but simply talking the same language and thinking the same thoughts as the Eighteen Psalms (Ryle-James lix, xci–xcii; Viteau 146–48). The chart on the next page (largely adapted from Viteau) shows some (not all) of the verbal resemblances between Mary's song of praise (Luke 1.46–55) and these Psalms. Line by line, Mary's hymn is expressed in the language and terminology of the Eighteen Psalms, without ever using one direct quotation from them—almost as if she had been brought up from childhood singing from that psalmbook (or some very similar collection), and had not formally memorized it but had simply absorbed its way of speaking.

More generally, the content of the Eighteen Psalms shows that they originated in some group of the same kind as Jesus' family and their friends—a group who were holding fast to the word of God ("walking in all the commandments and ordinances of the Lord," Luke 1.6), in contrast to the much greater numbers who had departed from it and introduced other practices ("you forsake the commandment of God and hold onto the traditions of Men," Mark 7.8; "not knowing the Scriptures, nor the power of God," Mark 12.24).

These points have even led to suggestions that the author might have been the young Simeon (Ryle-James lix). If Simeon was about 80–85 at the time of Jesus' birth, he would have been about 20–25 at the time of Pompey's arrival in Jerusalem, and about 35–40 at the time of Pompey's death.

---

[4] Delcor, "Psaumes de Salomon," 236–40. "That identification ['Psalms of the Pharisees'] must now be abandoned" (Wright 8).

Luke 1.46–55	Eighteen Psalms
My soul makes great the Lord (1.46).	Why are you sleeping, my soul, and not blessing the Lord? (3.1; cf. 12.1).
My spirit has been glad over [*epi*] God my Savior (1.47).	I will praise Your name with gladness (5.1); on [*epi*] God our Savior (17.3; cf. 3.7; 8.39).
He has looked on the humiliation of His slavewoman (1.48).	Your eyes are looking on them (18.2); to have mercy on the righteous from the humiliation (2.39); the Lord will be mindful of His slaves (10.4; cf. 2.41).
The Mighty One has done great things for me (1.49).	The Lord is kind ... to do in accordance with His mercy for His lovingkind ones (2.40); the good things ... which God will do (17.50).
Holy is His name (1.49).	He has blessed the name of the Lord (6.6–7, 2).
His mercy is ... for those who fear Him (1.50).	His mercy will be upon those who fear Him (13.11).
He has done strength with His arm (1.51).	God is ... mighty in His great strength (2.33).
He has dispersed the arrogant ones in the mind of their heart (1.51).	To utterly break the arrogance of the sinner ... to reprove the sinners in the word of their heart (17.26–27; cf. 2.35).
He has filled the hungry with good things (1.53).	If I should be hungry ... You Yourself will give ... those who fear the Lord have been glad in good things (5.10–21).
He has taken up the cause of Israel His servant, to be mindful of mercy (1.54).	May the Lord's salvation be upon Israel His servant (12.7; cf. 7.9; 17.23); the Lord will be mindful of His slaves in mercy (10.4).
Just as He spoke to our fathers, to Abraham and to his seed, to lasting times (1.55).	You Yourself have chosen the seed of Abraham ... You covenanted with our fathers concerning us (9.17–19); God has spoken good things of Israel to lasting time and still more (11.8).

But there is no special reason to think that all Eighteen Psalms were written by one person. Like the Hebrew Psalter, or the songs in Luke 1–2, they might have been composed by a number of people sharing a common faith. At any rate it is possible that Simeon may have known the author(s), as Viteau (88) observed. There cannot have been many people holding these particular beliefs in Jerusalem at that time.[5]

Contents

The Eighteen Psalms describe a disaster that happened in a time of prosperity. Jerusalem "was well off and was abounding in children," who were rich and were honored in distant lands (1.3–4). A foreigner—a person "strange to" the "race" of Israel (17.9)—came to Jerusalem "from the end of the earth" (8.16). At first he was welcomed and allowed to enter the city peacefully. "The rulers of the land met him with joy; they said to him: 'Blessed is your path; come, enter with peace.' ... They opened up the gates close by Jerusalem; they crowned her walls. He entered ... with peace; he set up his feet with great security" (8.18–20).

But once inside the city, he attacked some of those who were within. The attack happened "suddenly" (1.2). "An outcry of war" was heard (1.2), "oppression and the voice of war, the voice of a resounding trumpet, slaughter and destruction, the voice of a great people, like that of an extremely great wind" (8.1–2). "With a battering ram he began putting down fortified walls" (2.1). "He destroyed their rulers ... he poured out the blood of those who dwelt in Jerusalem" (8.23). "Young man and old man and their children together" were sent away to the distant west (17.13–14). The invaders even entered the temple: "strange nations went up on [God's] sacrificial altar" and "trampled it down ... in arrogance" (2.2). The foreign leader himself was later slain on the shore of Egypt (2.30–31).

Those attackers were "sinners" (1.1; 2.1). But so were the people of Jerusalem. "Their deeds opposed to the Law went beyond the nations who had been before them" (1.8; 8.14). "There was no one among them who did righteousness and judgment; from their ruler and the least people, they were in every sin" (17.21). We hear of sinners who "profaned the Lord's holy places with profaneness" (1.8; 8.12–13), fornicators and adulterers (2.13–15; 4.4–5; 8.10–11), slanderers and liars (12.1–5; 4.10–15), hypocrites "sitting ... in the council of the lovingkind ones" although their "heart has departed a long way from the Lord" and they are "filled with Law-breaking" (4.1, 15).[6] (On the other hand, there is no suggestion that the people of

---

[5] The testimony of Scriptural and non-Scriptural sources alike is that the majority of the religious leaders and teachers in Judea were either Pharisees or Sadducees (Acts 23.6; Matt 3.7; 22.34; Josephus, *Antiquities,* 14.288–298, etc.); and while there were many smaller groups, most of them—like those associated with the Dead Sea Scrolls—appear to have likewise left the Scriptures for one -ism or another. By contrast, the writer(s) of the Eighteen Psalms may be said to have "belonged to no sect" (cf. deSilva, *Jewish Teachers of Jesus, James, and Jude,* 149), in the sense that they taught no doctrine beyond those recorded in the Hebrew Scriptures.

[6] There is no reason to think that the Eighteen Psalms apply the term "sinners" to members of one particular sect only. These Psalms do "not accuse the sinners of heresy or of subscribing to false doctrines ... but, rather, of wrong behavior" (a point well made in an analogous situation by Heger, *Challenges to Conventional Opinions on Qumran and Enoch Issues,* 197).

Jerusalem are practicing idolatry—a sin that was prevalent there in the time of the Hebrew Scriptures.)

Those were the very sins that Jesus found at Jerusalem, when He came to earth a few decades later: profanation of the temple (Mark 11.15–17), adultery (Mark 8.38), lies and slander (John 8.44, 48), hypocrisy and departure from God's Law (Mark 7.6–13; Matt 23.27–28).

When the foreign leader came, there was a "king" in Israel—and that king was himself "Law-breaking" (Eighteen Psalms 17.22). "You Yourself, Lord, chose David king over Israel, and You Yourself swore to him concerning his seed . . . for his kingship not to cease before You." But "people to whom You did not promise . . . made desolate the throne of David" and set up a "kingship" of their own. God would punish their arrogance by casting them down when the foreign invader came (17.5–11).

Instead, God would set up "the Son of David" as King over Israel (17.23). The psalms call this King the "Anointed One" (Greek *Christos* ≡ Syriac *Mšyḥ'*) and even the "Lord" (17.36—an allusion to Psa 110.1, which indicates that He would be Lord even of His ancestor David).[7] He would be "a righteous King" (Eighteen Psalms 17.35), "clean from sin" (17.41), and would "judge the peoples and nations in the wisdom of His righteousness" (17.31), "shepherding the Lord's flock of sheep in faithfulness" (17.45). Nations would "come from the endpoint of the earth to see His glory" (17.34). He would "utterly break the arrogance of the sinner like a potter's vessels, with an iron rod" (17.26). Yet He would not overcome His enemies by earthly means—horses or riders or bows or vast armies—but solely by "the word of His mouth" (17.37, 39).[8] "Blessed will be those who come to be in those days, to see the good things of the Lord, which He will do for the coming generation!" (18.7; 17.50).

---

[7] Because Eighteen Psalms 17.36 identifies the Messiah as the Lord who is greater than David (indeed, the Syriac version of this verse uses the term *MRY',* which is applied only to Deity), pronouns referring to the Messiah are capitalized in the translations from the Eighteen Psalms in this volume. It has been argued that a hypothetical earlier form of the Eighteen Psalms did not call the Messiah "Lord" (so Atkinson, *I Cried to the Lord,* 131–32, n. 2; in rebuttal, Wright 48–49; cf. Ryle-James 141–43; Viteau 361–62). However, that question does not affect our policy. Our translations are of texts that exist, not of hypothesized earlier states of them.

[8] "Like the authors of the Psalms of Solomon, Jesus was revolutionary; unlike many of his contemporaries who shared in the hope of the restoration of the kingdom to a messiah from Israel, Jesus did not endorse violence as the means by which to pursue revolution." The Messiah foreseen in these psalms is remarkable because "the weapons are unconventional: 'He will destroy the lawless nations by the word of his mouth'" (deSilva, *Jewish Teachers of Jesus, James, and Jude,* 156, 151)—and also because he has "characteristics that might be ascribed to a preexistent angelic or divine being," since he "is described as 'a righteous king . . . the Lord Messiah' . . . 'free from sin' . . . 'powerful in the holy spirit and wise in the counsel of understanding, with strength and righteousness'" (Scott, *Jewish Backgrounds of the New Testament,* 309–10). All these characteristics are, of course, ascribed to Jesus in the New Testament Scriptures (see the commentary below on 17.27, 35, 41, 42).

Looking still further ahead, the Eighteen Psalms recognize that "those who fear the Lord will be raised up to lasting time, and their life will be in the Lord's light, and it will not cease any more"; "they will not be uprooted all the days of heaven," whereas "the sinners' inheritance will be destruction and darkness... to lasting time" (3.13–16; 14.2–7; 15.11–15; 13.9–10).

In all these respects, these psalms report faithfully what had been foretold in the Hebrew Scriptures about the Messiah and the hope of eternal life.

Like the Hebrew Scriptures, the Eighteen Psalms are mainly concerned with the people of Israel, and therefore say relatively little about God's plan for other nations. The salvation of the Gentiles was a mystery that had not been fully revealed in those days (Eph 3.4–6). Even so, like the Hebrew Scriptures, the Eighteen Psalms contain foretastes of that mystery. They foresee that the coming Messiah will rule in righteousness not only Israel, but also the foreign nations (17.31), who will be enslaved to Him (17.32, Greek) as His possession (17.32, Syriac), and who will "come from the endpoint of the earth to see His glory" (17.34).

The Eighteen Psalms fully acknowledge that the Lord is righteous in all His ways, including the punishments He bestows on the wicked and the afflictions He grants to the faithful. "We have acknowledged Your honorable name to be righteous... because You are the God of righteousness, who judges Israel with discipline" (8.31–32; 2.36–40; 7.1–10; 9.10; 10.6; 17.12). His discipline is to be cherished, because it is designed to purify and strengthen those whom He loves (13.6–9; 16.11–15; 18.4–5). "The righteous one will not think little of being disciplined by the Lord.... The righteous one has stumbled, and he has acknowledged the Lord to be righteous" (3.4–5). When we are suffering we can only cry out to our Lord and humbly ask for His mercy (5.7–10). Although "we ourselves have hardened our neck ... do not overlook us, O our God" (8.35–36).

Hasty readers have sometimes thought that the writer(s) of the Eighteen Psalms trusted in themselves that they were righteous (cf. Luke 18.9–14) and did not regard themselves as sinners. Certainly these psalmists recognized that God's people must lead holy, righteous lives, separate from all sin (Eighteen Psalms 14.1; 15.5–6). But these psalmists also fully recognized that they themselves were prone to sin (16.1–3; 9.3) and fell far short of the righteousness of God (5.14–16), and that they needed the correction and atonement that only He can provide (3.4–10; 16.3–15; 13.6–9; 10.1–2). Those who have sinned and are being scourged, in these psalms, are not only "they" but "we": "we ourselves have hardened our neck" (8.35); "in our sins, sinners stood up against us" (17.6).

The psalms never state the name or nationality of the foreign invader, but their accounts are so detailed that he is easily recognized. The key facts are as follows:

- *At the time of the invasion, Jerusalem was being ruled by a king who was not a descendant of David, and whose rule was contrary to God's Law* (17.5–8, 22). This shows that the invasion happened later than anything recorded in the Maccabean History. Until the Babylonian captivity, Jerusalem was ruled by kings descended from David, whose rule was explicitly authorized by the Lord (2 Sam 7.12–16; 2 Kgs 22.1–2; 23.30, 34; 24.6, 17; Matt 1.6–11). During the next few centuries, Jerusalem was ruled by foreign kings, who were not descended from David but whose rule was again explicitly authorized by the Lord (Dan 2.37–39; 5.18; Jer 25.9–14; 27.6–7; 28.14; 2 Chr 36.23; Ezra 1.2). And from the time when the yoke of the foreign kings "was lifted up from Israel" until the last events recorded in the Maccabean History, Jerusalem had no earthly king at all; during that time, its rulers—Simon and his son John—were high priests, not kings (Maccabaica 13.41–42; 16.23–24).

- *The invaders sent their captives away to the distant west* ("close by the sunset," 17.14). This shows that the invaders were Romans. Armies of two earlier rulers—the Babylonian king Nebuchadnezzar and the Hellenistic king of the north Antiochus Epiphanes—had occupied Jerusalem (2 Kgs 24.10–25.21; Dan 8.24–25; 11.30–33; Maccabaica 1.20–64), but neither of them had sent their captives to the west (nor could they have done so, even if they wanted, because neither of them had any authority in the west).
- *The invaders entered the temple but did not destroy it* (2.2). This further rules out Nebuchadnezzar, because his armies burned and demolished the temple (2 Kgs 25.9, 13–17). It also shows that we are not reading an account of the destruction of Jerusalem by the Romans after the time of Christ (Matt 23.35–38; 24.15–34; Luke 19.41–44; 21.20–32; 23.28–31; cf. John 11.48). On that occasion, the temple was demolished (Matt 24.1–2).
- *The foreign leader died in Egypt* (2.30–31). This further rules out Antiochus Epiphanes, who died between Persia and Babylon (Maccabaica 6.1–16).

So these psalms are describing an invasion of Jerusalem by the Romans, before the time of Christ but after the last events recorded in the Maccabean History.

The information in the Eighteen Psalms also tallies with the accounts provided by later historians. They report that, shortly after the death of the high priest John son of Simon about 104 BCE (cf. Maccabaica 16.23–24), his descendants declared themselves kings, even though they were not descended from David (Josephus, *Antiquities,* 13.301; Strabo, 16.2.40). After about thirty years, a dispute arose between two rival claimants to the throne, the brothers Aristobulus and Hyrcanus (Josephus, *Antiquities,* 14.4). Each of them appealed to the Roman leader Pompey. At first the Romans were received into Jerusalem peacefully, but then opposition broke out, especially in the temple area. The Romans' opponents were defeated (many being killed or exiled); Pompey entered the temple in defiance of the Law of Moses, and made Judea a Roman province (about 63 BCE; Josephus, *Antiquities,* 14.30–78).

Fifteen years later (about 48 BCE) Pompey himself was killed on the coast of Egypt at Mount Cassius, and his body was left drifting in the waves, just as the Eighteen Psalms described (Velleius Paterculus, *Roman History,* 2.53; Plutarch, *Pompey,* 77.4–80.1; Appian, *Civil Wars,* 2.84–86; Cassius Dio, *Roman History,* 42.4–5; Lucan, *Pharsalia,* 8.698–699).

Almost at the time when Pompey captured Jerusalem—possibly on the same day—the future Caesar Augustus (Luke 2.1) was born.[9] The Lord's hand was actively molding the world into the right shape for the coming of the Messiah (Gal. 4.4).

Date of Composition

The Eighteen Psalms appear to have been written at various times, possibly during a period of two decades or more.

Psalm 7 states that Judea has not yet been attacked ("set on," 7.1) or given into the hand of the nations (7.3), and the temple has not yet been trampled by them (7.2). This psalm, then, must have been composed before Pompey's conquest and defilement of the temple in 63 BCE—although probably not long before, because there is already a danger that those things might happen.

Psalms 1; 2; 8; 13; 17; and possibly 9 (see its commentary below) describe Jerusalem as already conquered. These psalms were apparently composed in or after 63 BCE.

The latest event undoubtedly mentioned in the past tense, in any of the psalms, is the death of Pompey about 48 BCE (Eighteen Psalms 2.30–31). Allusions to the reign of Herod the Great (who died about 4 BCE) have sometimes been suspected, but none has been established (see the commentary on 17.9).

The remaining psalms contain no allusions to the Romans, or to anything else by which their dates could be determined. Some of them might have been written substantially earlier or later than the time of Pompey, though their language and teachings show that they originated from the same cultural group as the Pompeian psalms.

In view of the accuracy of the Eighteen Psalms' teachings about the Messiah, a few writers have argued that they must have been written after the time of Christ, and therefore that the current crisis described in them cannot be Pompey's conquest of Judea.[10] However, the references to Pompey are too specific and too detailed to be brushed aside thus; and no believer who lived after the time of Christ could have written on the subject of some of these psalms without any allusion to His death and resurrection (especially in 17.23–51 and 18.6–10; cf. Ryle-James xc).

Language and Style

The Eighteen Psalms have been preserved in two versions: Greek and Syriac. The Greek version is written in a highly distinctive style, using frequently some turns of

---

[9] Ferguson, *Backgrounds of Early Christianity,* 411. According to Classical historians, Augustus was born on September 23, 63 BCE (Suetonius, *Augustus,* 5; Suerbaum, "Merkwürdige Geburtstage," 334–35). Pompey conquered Jerusalem "in the late autumn of 63 B.C." (Schürer-Vermes 1.239–40); Josephus claims that it happened on the Day of Atonement (*Antiquities,* 14.66; Goldstein, "Hasmonean Revolt," 349, n. 1)—which would have been about a week before the end of September, and therefore possibly on the day when Augustus was born (Duckworth, "Roman Provincial System," 177, n. 1).

[10] Efrón, *Studies in the Hasmonean Period,* 219–86.

phrase and syntactic constructions that are much less common elsewhere. Some of its most striking characteristics are:

- Many clauses are simply linked by *kai* ("and"), but many others, still more simply, are directly juxtaposed without any link at all.
- Short phrases consisting of *en* ("in") followed by a noun or infinitive are extremely frequent. There are eight in the first psalm alone: "in my being oppressed" (1.1), "in the setting on of sinners" (1.1), "in my being well off" (1.3), "in children" (1.3), etc.
- The wording is sometimes extremely concise, omitting material that might seem almost essential to the sense, e.g., "they did not bring" (1.6). This happens particularly often in phrases beginning with *apo* ("from"), e.g., "He turned away His face from their mercy" (i.e., from showing them mercy, 2.8); "have mercy on the righteous one from the humiliation of the sinner" (2.39).
- The so-called inverted genitive—elsewhere very rare—appears several times, e.g., "menstruation of blood" (8.13); "corruption of sleep" (16.1).

The Syriac version is less distinctive, stylistically closer to the common language of Syriac Biblical translations. It has fewer direct juxtapositions of clauses (where the Greek has a direct juxtaposition, the Syriac often has a linking *w-* ["and"]—e.g., "<u>and</u> to God," 1.1; "<u>and</u> I accounted," 1.3).[11] It has fewer "in"-phrases (where the Greek has *en* plus an infinitive, the Syriac sometimes has *kd* ["when"] plus a finite verb—e.g., "when I was oppressed" instead of "in my being oppressed," 1.1). Its genitives are never inverted (e.g., "blood of menstruation," 8.13).[12]

The Maccabean History was written during a period of peace; its Greek form is beautifully lucid and limpid (except in a few verses that describe particular crises or struggles). The Eighteen Psalms were written in and immediately around a time of war; their Greek form is much more gnarled and knotted (partly, but not only, because of the tendency to extreme conciseness noted above). At those knots the Syriac form is often smoother and easier to follow.

Even in the Greek version, the style is strongly Hebraic. Many turns of phrase are close imitations of Hebrew idioms, e.g., "was heard . . . in my presence" (1.2); "they profaned . . . with profaneness" (1.8). Therefore it is generally assumed that the Eighteen Psalms were composed in Hebrew, although there is no absolute proof of this, and some writers have suggested that the Greek text might possibly be the original.[13]

---

[11] "It is a consistent pattern for Syriac translations to add *waw*" (Williams, *Early Syriac Translation Technique,* 4).

[12] For unknown reasons, ancient Syriac translators often tended to reverse the sequence in which their source texts presented equivalent or related terms (Williams, *Early Syriac Translation Technique,* 204–35).

[13] So, most recently, Davila, *Provenance of the Pseudepigrapha,* 160–61. One further small piece of evidence may be noted. In Eighteen Psalms 15.5, the wording closely echoes the Greek

Ryle and James, writing before the discovery of the Syriac version, supplied a long list of passages where they detected possible "errors of translation" from the original Hebrew (Ryle-James lxxix–lxxxi). But in all cases, the existing Greek is fully comprehensible as it stands; and in nearly all of them, it is fully supported by the Syriac (which may possibly have been independently translated from the Hebrew—see the discussion below).

At any rate, it would be unwise to assume that all (or even most) of the unusual phrases in the existing Greek text of the Eighteen Psalms are mistranslations. The Greek of Revelation—and even of 2 Peter—is far stranger than anything in these psalms, yet nobody assumes that the peculiar expressions in those books can be explained as mistranslations.

At the other extreme, Hilgenfeld (*Messias Judaeorum,* xvi–xvii) argued that the Eighteen Psalms not only were composed in Greek, but also contained echoes of a work known to have originated in Greek: the Book of Wisdom. However, in none of the examples cited by Hilgenfeld is the similarity of wording either close or distinctive (Ryle-James lxxxv–lxxxvii; Viteau 120–22).

If indeed the Eighteen Psalms were composed in Hebrew, the original Hebrew text must have disappeared without trace very early. No ancient writer shows any sign of having seen it, or even any awareness that it had once existed. But that would not be surprising. Few ancient writers show any sign of having seen it in any language. Even in Greek, this seems to have been always a rare book.

Text

The Eighteen Psalms have been preserved complete in Greek and almost complete in Syriac. In both languages, the known manuscripts are believed to range in date from about the tenth to about the sixteenth century.

---

versions of 2 Sam 6.5, where there is no equivalent in any known Hebrew text, and the material probably arose in Greek, not as a translation of any variant Hebrew text (Driver, *Notes on ... Samuel,* 266). It is possible that the hypothetical Hebrew original of Eighteen Psalms 15.5 said something different, and that the allusion to 2 Sam 6.5 was introduced by the Greek translator—but that is unlikely, because the allusion appears to be embedded in the context (cf. Eighteen Psalms 15.3). It is also possible that the Hebrew original had a briefer allusion to 2 Sam 6.5, which the Greek translator recognized and decided to expand with additional material from the Greek rendering of that verse—but 2 Sam 6.5 has never been a widely cited passage, and the briefer an allusion to it was, the less likely a translator would have been to recognize it. Therefore, in this particular case, it would be simplest to suppose that there never was any Hebrew text, and that the Greek text of Eighteen Psalms 15.5 derives directly from the Greek of 2 Sam 6.5. Use of Greek was becoming widespread among Judeans by this period (Gundry, "Language Milieu of First-Century Palestine," 404–08; van der Horst, "Greek in Jewish Palestine," 154–76; Victor, *Colonial Education and Class Formation in Early Judaism,* 83–91).

Hebrew may indeed have been the work's original language; but it is wise to remember that the point has never been proved, and is not likely to be.

Eleven **Greek** manuscripts (complete or partial) of these psalms are known to exist. Seven of these are relevant for textual purposes;[14] they fall into two distinct groups:

- 253, 655, and 659, collectively designated f^{253}.
- 260, 336, 629, and 769, collectively designated f^{260}.

When the f^{253} manuscripts differ from each other, the reading of 253 itself is usually the one that is supported by f^{260}. When the f^{260} manuscripts differ from each other, the reading of 336 is usually the one that is supported by f^{253}. Therefore, the two Greek manuscripts likely to be closest to the common ancestor of f^{253} and f^{260} are 253 and 336.

Manuscripts 655 and 659 were copied by the same scribe, almost certainly from the same source manuscript, and are virtually identical. Manuscripts 629 and 769 are also very similar and presumably derive from a single source, although they were copied at different times and by different scribes.

Four **Syriac** manuscripts are known.[15] Two of them (14k1 and 16q7) contain only 16.6–13, as part of an anthology of prayers derived from diverse sources. The other two manuscripts (10h1 and 16h1) included the full collection of Eighteen Psalms, but both are now partly damaged, and neither preserves the last few verses of the collection (18.8–14).

The Syriac version of the Eighteen Psalms is generally closer to f^{253} than to f^{260}. There are two possible reasons for that: (i) The Syriac version may have been translated from a Greek text resembling f^{253}. (ii) The Syriac version may have been independently translated from the (hypothetical) Hebrew (in which case, f^{253} generally follows that Hebrew more closely than f^{260} does).

These two possibilities have been intensively examined in the literature on the Eighteen Psalms. Those who maintain that the Syriac version was independently translated from the Hebrew have been able to explain every variant between the Syriac and the Greek on that basis; those who maintain that it was translated from the Greek have been able to explain every variant on that basis. The most that can be said is that some variants are more *plausibly* explained if the Syriac was translated from the Hebrew, whereas other variants are more *plausibly* explained if the Syriac was translat-

---

[14] Of the other four Greek manuscripts, 149 was copied directly from 260, while 471, 606, and 3004 descend from either 260 or 149 (Gebhardt 14–25; Hann, *Manuscript History of the Psalms of Solomon,* 63–70). As 260 itself is still fully legible throughout, its descendants are not needed for textual purposes. 260 is part of the so-called "Bible of Niketas," manuscripts 90 and 719 of the prophets being its companions (Belting and Cavallo, *Bibel des Niketas;* Lowden, "An Alternative Interpretation of the Manuscripts of Niketas," 559–74). Its individual origin and textual affinities, therefore, cannot be considered in isolation from those manuscripts.

[15] In addition, Jacob of Edessa wrote a quotation of 3.1–6 in the margin of a seventh-century Syriac manuscript of the *Hymns of Severus.* But his quotation was not taken from the existing Syriac version of the Eighteen Psalms. He may have translated it directly from the Greek.

ed from the Greek. But at no point is either theory *impossible.*[16] It is of course also possible that the Syriac translator may have consulted both the original Hebrew and the Greek—as the Syriac translators of the Hebrew Psalter[17] and many other books of the Hebrew Scriptures appear to have done.

If the Syriac version was translated independently from the Hebrew, then any reading that is found both in the Syriac and in one form of the Greek text is likely to have stood in the Hebrew. On the other hand, if the Syriac was translated from a Greek text resembling f^{253}, then any reading that is found both in the Syriac and in f^{253} has no special textual importance, but any reading that is found both in the Syriac and in f^{260} is likely to have stood in the common ancestor of f^{253} and f^{260}. Therefore, whatever the origin of the Syriac version, agreements between it and f^{260} are likely to have stood in the earliest text that we can now recover.

Where the two known Syriac manuscripts differ from each other, the Greek version sometimes supports 10h1, sometimes 16h1.

In summary, the main relations between the key manuscripts may be charted thus:[18]

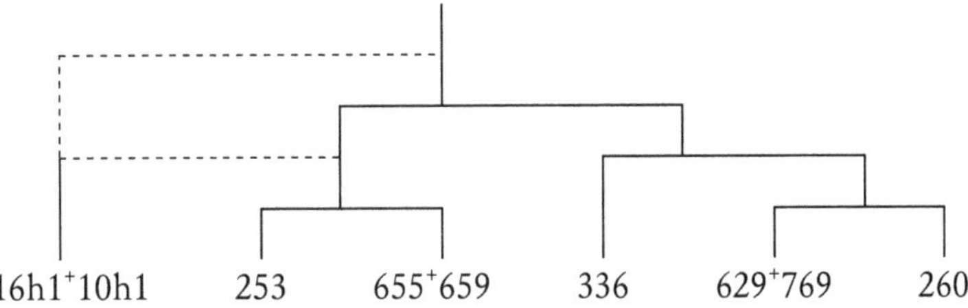

For the Greek text printed in the following pages, the copytext is 253. Our editorial principles have been:

- **Spelling** has not been standardized. Like most medieval Greek copyists, the scribe of 253 does not write iota subscripts or adscripts, sometimes treats ε as interchangeable with αι, sometimes treats η as interchangeable with ει or ι, and sometimes treats ω as interchangeable with ο (Hann, *Manuscript History of the Psalms of Solomon,* 38–39).

---

[16] See Kuhn, *Die älteste Textgestalt der Psalmen Salomos;* Begrich, "Der Text der Psalmen Salomos"; and, especially, Trafton.

[17] Carpajoso, *Character of the Syriac Version of Psalms,* 187–272, suggests that the earliest Syriac version of the Hebrew Psalter was prepared mainly from Hebrew, but was influenced at some points by the Greek; and that this was later revised to align it more closely with the Greek.

[18] The dotted lines mark the possible origins of the Syriac version (from a Greek text resembling 253, from a Hebrew text, or from both). The chart is not a full genealogical diagram (stemma); a small amount of textual cross-fertilization has occurred, at least between manuscripts of f^{253} and f^{260}. (For instance, in a few places the Syriac and 260 share one reading, whereas 253 and 336 share another; see, e.g., the apparatus on 15.9; 17.15, 39.)

In points of detail, the genealogical conclusions of Gebhardt and Hann are not entirely reliable, as some of their arguments were founded on faulty collations.

- The letter **sigma** is printed σ throughout the body of the text (even at the ends of words, as in 253), but c in the superscriptions. (In 253, the form c is occasionally used in the body of the text as well; the form ς is never used.)
- Like spelling, **accentuation** was more variable and less stereotyped in medieval times[19] and has not been standardized in this edition (except where the copytext has an ambiguously written accent or an abbreviated syllable, in which case we have printed the form that is closest to modern practice).
- Modern **word divisions** have been supplied where relevant. (The medieval manuscripts divide words only irregularly.)[20]
- **Punctuation** is that of the copytext.
- The text is printed throughout as **verse,** each verse line being separately paragraphed, as in the oldest known manuscript (336). The later Greek manuscripts generally separate the verse lines with punctuation marks. (The paragraphing of this edition has been determined by the text itself, and does not necessarily correspond to that of 336 or any other medieval manuscript.)
- **Uppercase** is used for the first letters of psalms and the first letters of proper names. Otherwise, the text is printed in **lowercase.** (The scribe of 253 also used uppercase to mark a few line-beginnings [within 2.16, 33; 3.11; 4.9; 5.9; 8.13, 27; 15.6; 17.19, 32, 50; 18.11, 12]. He occasionally used lowercase for the first letters of proper names.)
- Scribal **abbreviations** have been expanded inside curved brackets.
- Except for the points listed above, all **changes** to the copytext have been placed inside subscript angle brackets ‹thus› (the reading of the copytext being recorded underneath in a brief textual apparatus). We have, for instance, departed from 253 at points where a reading of f^{260} is supported by the Syriac version and/or by 655 or 659.

For the Syriac text printed in the following pages, the copytext is 16h1 as far as that exists (up to and including ܡܪܝܐ ܠܒܪ in 17.38), and 10h1 for the remainder (from ܡܡܠܟܗ in 17.38 to the end). Spelling, pointing, and punctuation are those of the copytext. Each verse line is printed as a separate paragraph (the Syriac manuscripts, like the Greek ones, distinguish lines of verse by punctuation). All changes to

[19] MHT 2.55–61; Robertson 229–36; Probert, *Ancient Greek Accentuation,* 48–52; Chandler, *Greek Accentuation,* xiv–xvi. A few sections of 253 contain two sets of accents (both, apparently, written during or soon after medieval times); in each such instance, we have reproduced the one that conforms to modern practice.

[20] For instance, διαπαντὸσ is found in 253 and 336 at 3.3; in 260 at 3.4; and in all three manuscripts at 2.40—whereas διὰ παντὸσ is found in 253 and 336 at 3.4, and in 260 at 3.3. We print δια παντοσ throughout, but reproduce the accentuation of our copytext (253) each time.

Many of the word divisions in Wright's edition do not follow either modern custom or the medieval manuscripts, but were evidently caused by typographical accidents (in 10.6, for instance, Wright prints αἰνέσει τῷ ὀνόματι κυρίου as αἰ νέσει τῷ ὀνόματικυρίου).

the copytext have been placed inside subscript angle brackets <thus> (the reading of the copytext being recorded underneath in a brief textual apparatus). We have, for instance, departed from 16h1 at points where a reading of 10h1 is supported by manuscripts of the Greek version.[21]

No conjectural emendations have been introduced into either the Greek text or the Syriac text.

The **textual apparatus** records all changes from 253 (Greek text) and 16h1 (Syriac text), and reports the readings at those points of 336 and 260 (Greek text) and 10h1 (Syriac text). Other witnesses to the text are cited occasionally but not regularly.

Our English versions translate the Greek and Syriac texts printed above them, but do not necessarily follow the medieval punctuation and accentuation of those texts.[22] For instance, at 2.15 the Greek manuscripts have either αὗται (f^{260}) or αὕται (f^{253}), but our English rendering construes the word as αὐταί. At 5.16 the Greek manuscripts have οὐ, but our English rendering construes the word as οὑ.

Verse Numbering

Two different systems of verse numbering are now in use.

The first system was introduced by La Cerda in the first published edition of the Eighteen Psalms (1626). This system has since been used in all editions and translations of the Syriac version (including Harris-Mingana, Baars, and Trafton) and in many editions and translations of the Greek version (including Whiston, Ryle-James, and APOT).

The second numbering system was introduced by Gebhardt in his edition of the Eighteen Psalms (1895). This system has since been used in many editions and translations of the Greek version (including Rahlfs, OTP, NETS, and Wright), but has never been applied to the Syriac.

The present volume deals with both the Greek and the Syriac texts. Therefore, it uses La Cerda's verse numbering. In the texts and translations printed on the following pages, Gebhardt's verse numbering has also been provided inside square brackets, wherever it differs from La Cerda's.

In the texts printed on the following pages, the **left** column contains the **Greek,**

---

[21] Therefore, the parallel columns on the following pages compare the form of Greek text most closely resembling the Syriac with the form of Syriac text most closely resembling the Greek. But in each language there are few manuscript variations that would significantly affect the sense; these are discussed in footnotes.

[22] The Greek version would almost certainly have had no punctuation or accents originally. The Syriac version is likely to have been written from the outset with seyame, and may or may not have been translated at a time when other points were also used; it would probably have been written from the outset with some punctuation, but not necessarily that shown in the existing copies (cf. Hatch, *Album of Dated Syriac Manuscripts,* 40–42; Segal, *The Diacritical Point and the Accents in Syriac,* 11–12; Trafton 34 n. 1).

with an English translation underneath it. The **right** column contains the corresponding **Syriac,** with an English translation underneath it.

Psalm 1

Jerusalem calls out to the Lord in wartime

1.1 [1] Ἐβόησα πρὸσ κ(ύριο)ν ἐν τῷ θλίβεσθαί με εἰσ τέλοσ· I called out to *the* Lord when I was oppressed to *the* end,	ܩܥܝܬ ܠܘܬ ܡܪܝܐ܂ ܟܕ ܐܬܐܠܨܬ ܒܚܪܬܝ܂ I called out to the LORD when I was oppressed, at my end,
πρὸ(σ) θ(εὸ)ν ἐν τῷ ἐπιθέσθαι ἁμαρτωλοὺσ· to God when sinners set on *me.*	ܘܠܘܬ ܐܠܗܐ ܟܕ ܩܡܘ ܥܠܝ ܚܛܝ̈ܐ܂ and to God when sinners set themselves over against me,
1.2 [2] ἐξάπινα ἠκούσθη κραυγὴ πολέμου ἐνώπιόν μου· Suddenly *there* was heard an outcry of war in my presence.	ܡܢ ܫܠܝܐ ܓܝܪ ܐܫܬܡܥ ܩܕܡܝ ܩܠܐ ܕܩܪܒܐ܂ for suddenly *there* was heard before me the voice of war.

1.1–2a[23] **I called out to the Lord.** The speaker is the city of Jerusalem, pictured in the form of a woman[24] "abounding in children" (v 3), as in Lamentations 1.12–22; 2.20–22 (cf. Isa 49.14; Ezek 26.2; Jer 2.2). But her identity is not revealed immediately. As often in the Scriptures (especially in psalms and other writings by prophets), we are plunged into the situation first; only afterwards do we learn its context and circumstances (cf. Psa 74.1; 77.1–2; Song 1.2).

Jerusalem has been **oppressed** by **sinners,** who attacked her (**set on** her[25]) with an **outcry of war,** like the outcry that had heralded the Babylonian invasion centuries earlier (Jer 4.19). The oppression was extreme, to the uttermost degree (**to the end**[26]).

---

[23] Only one manuscript (336) provides this psalm with a superscription: *Psalmos tō Salomōn prōtos* ("first psalm of Solomon"). Wright prints 260's *Psalmoi Solomōntos A* as a superscription to this psalm, but the layout in the manuscript shows it actually consists of the title to the whole collection (*Psalmoi Solomōntos,* "Psalms of Solomon") followed—on the next line, and in much smaller script—by the numeral *A* identifying the first item in that collection.

[24] The speaker takes feminine case-endings (*pollēn,* "abounding," v 3).

[25] **When sinners set on me.** The wording of the Greek is *en tō epithesthai hamartōlous,* "in the setting on of sinners." Compare the Lord's promise to Paul at Corinth: "No one will set on [*epithēsetai*] you to harm you" (Acts 18.10; cf. Gen. 43.18, LXX; BDAG 384, §2).

[26] **To the end** *(eis telos)* reappears in 2.5, where the sense is clearly "to the uttermost" (as in 1 Thes 2.16), "to the bitter end" (cf. Muraoka 676, §3b.iii). "The hope of the afflicted will not be destroyed to the end" (*eis telos,* Psa 9.18, LXX), but God's enemies will be destroyed "to the

And it happened **suddenly,**[27] again like the Babylonian invasion (Jer 4.20)—or like the destruction that will happen to the whole world on the last day (1 Thes 5.3).

She had thought herself righteous

ἐπακούσεταί μου ὅτι ἐπλήσθην δικαιοσύνησ· He will hearken to me, because I have been filled with righteousness:	ܢܫܡܥܢܝ ܓܝܪ ܡܛܠ ܕܐܬܡܠܝܬ ܙܕܝܩܘܬܐ. For He will hear me, because I have been filled with righteousness:
1.3 [3] ἐλογισάμην ἐν καρδία μου ὅτι ἐπλήσθην δικαιοσύνησ· I accounted in my heart that I had been filled with righteousness,	ܘܐܬܚܫܒܬ ܒܠܒܝ ܡܛܠ ܕܐܬܡܠܝܬ ܙܕܝܩܘܬܐ. and I accounted *it* in my heart, because I had been filled with righteousness,
ἐν τῷ εὐθηνῆσαί με καὶ πολλὴν γενέσθαι ἐν τέκνοισ· when I was well off and was abounding in children.	ܟܕ ܥܬܪܬ ܘܗܘܝܬ ܒܣܘܓܐ ܕܒܢ̈ܝܐ. when I was rich and *had* an abundance of sons;
1.4 [4] ὁ πλοῦτοσ αὐτῶν διεδόθη εἰσ πᾶσαν τὴν γῆν· Their riches were distributed into all the earth,	ܒܥܘܬܪܗܘܢ ܓܝܪ ܐܬܝܗܒ ܠܟܠܗ̇ ܐܪܥܐ. for their riches were given to all the earth,
καὶ ἡ δόξα αὐτ(ῶν) ἕωσ ἐσχάτου ‹› τῆσ γῆσ· and their glory to *the* end of the earth.	ܘܬܫܒܘܚܬܗ(ܘܢ) ܥܕܡܐ ܠܣܘ̈ܦܝܗ̇ ܕܐܪܥܐ. and *their* glory even to *the* ends of the earth.
1.5 [5] ὑψώθησαν ἕωσ τ(ῶν) ἄστρων· They were exalted even to the stars;	ܐܬܬܪܝܡܘ ܥܕܡܐ ܠܟܘ̈ܟܒܐ. They were exalted even to the stars,
εἶπαν οὐ μὴ πέσωσιν· they said they would certainly not fall.	ܘܐܡܪܘ ܕܠܐ ‹ܢܦܠܘܢ.› and they said that they would not fall.

1.4 ἐσχάτου 253[c+]655[+]659 336[+]260 ≡ ܠܣܘ̈ܦܝܗ̇ 16h1 10h1 | + τὴν γῆ(ν) καὶ ἡ δόξα αὐτῶν· ἕωσ ἐσχάτου 253* • **1.5** ܢܦܠܘܢ. 10h1 ≡ πέσωσιν 253 336[+]260 | > 16h1 •

end" (*eis telos,* Psa 52.5, LXX; Josh 8.24, LXX). In the present verse, the Syriac version has *b'ḥryty* (**at my end**); compare the English phrase "at the end of my tether."

[27] **Suddenly.** Greek *exapina* (as in Mark 9.8); Syriac *mn šly'* (as in Luke 9.39; TS 2.4167; SL 1564, §4d).

1.2b In her distress Jerusalem sought the Lord's help, and "called out to" Him (v 1). "God's chosen ones [are] calling out to Him day and night," and He has promised to deliver them "from all their oppressions" (Luke 18.7–8; Psa 34.17; 37.39–40; 145.19; 1 Jn 3.22). So Jerusalem was confident that her cry would be heeded: **He will hearken to me, because I am filled with righteousness.**[28] In reality, however, many of Jerusalem's inhabitants were "filled with Law-breaking" (4.15) at this time, though she herself had not been aware of that (v 7). "The LORD is far away from wicked ones, but He hears the entreaty of righteous ones" (Prov 15.29; 1 Pet 3.12 ≡ Psa 34.15–17; John 9.31). There is "one who is pure in his own eyes, and he is not washed from his filthiness" (Prov 30.12; cf. Matt 5.20; Luke 18.9–14). Such people need to "wash yourselves, make yourselves clean; turn away the evil of your deeds from before My eyes; cease to do evil, learn to do good." The Lord will not **hearken to** their prayers unless they "are willing and hearken" to Him (Isa 1.15–20).

1.3–5 The attack came at a time when God had lavished many blessings on Jerusalem:

- She **was well off** (*euthēnēsai,* Muraoka 299; **rich,** Syriac), just as she had been "well off" (prosperous) before the Babylonian captivity (Zec 7.7, LXX).
- She **was abounding in children.**[29] Jerusalem's **children** were her inhabitants (Psa 149.2; Joel 2.23; 3.6; Lam 4.2; cf. Ezek 23.10; Gal 4.25). When her inhabitants were carried away to Babylon, and when they were persecuted by Antiochus Epiphanes, Jerusalem was deprived of children (Lam 1.5; Maccabaica 1.38); but during Maccabean times, she was restored and resettled (Maccabaica 14.36–37).
- Her children had **riches** and **glory,** which had spread throughout **all the earth... to the end of the earth.** During the century before the coming of the Romans, the inhabitants of Jerusalem had prospered and flourished, so that their **glory** was spread abroad through the surrounding nations, **to the end of the earth** (v 4)—as the Maccabean History shows. Judas Maccabeus "was spreading glory wide for his people... and he was named even to the end of the earth" (Maccabaica 3.3, 9). The same applied to his brother Simon: "the name of his glory was named even to the end of the earth" (Maccabaica 14.10, 21, 29; 15.9). Their **riches,** too, **were distributed**[30] **into all** the surrounding parts of the earth. Simon

---

[28] **He will hearken to me.** The prefixed *eipa* ("I said") in Gebhardt and Rahlfs (translated in several English versions) has no manuscript support, either Greek or Syriac. In the Scriptures, a passage of quoted speech does not need any preliminary "I said," "she said," etc.: see, e.g., Psa 2.3 (the words of the wicked: "Let us tear off their bonds..."); 2.7 (the words of the LORD's Anointed: "I will recount the LORD's decree..."); Lam 1.9, 11; 2.20 (the words of Jerusalem).

[29] **I was abounding in children.** The wording of the Greek is *pollēn genesthai en teknois,* "I had become abundant in children."

[30] **Were distributed.** Hann's advocacy of the reading *dielthoi* (*Manuscript History of the Psalms of Solomon,* 62) is based on a faulty collation. In fact all manuscripts of f^{253} read *diedothē,* and so do all manuscripts of f^{260} except for 260 itself (and its four descendants).

"spent much money of his own" to provide for those around him (Maccabaica 14.32); in his days the Judeans were able to send gifts of gold and silver to both Antioch and Rome (Maccabaica 13.37; 14.24; 15.18, 26).

- Her children **were exalted** to an extreme degree (**even to the stars;** cf. Isa 14.13; Obad 4). Simon "strengthened all the lowly ones" and "sought out every way to raise his people high" (Maccabaica 14.14, 35).

Nevertheless, earthly prosperity can make people forget the Lord (Deut 6.10–12; Prov 30.8–9): those who are **exalted** by Him may exalt not Him but themselves (see on Maccabaica 1.3). While she was prospering, Jerusalem considered (**accounted**) that she **had been filled with righteousness,**[31] and her children **said they would certainly not fall** (cf. Psa 10.6; Isa 47.7). But prosperity is no proof of righteousness. God in His love often bestows His blessings on righteous and unrighteous alike (Matt 5.45). The unrighteous may be **well off** (Hos 10.1; Jer 12.1; Psa 73.12, LXX), exalted with riches and glory and many children (like Haman, Est 3.1; 5.11, LXX). Therefore "let the person who thinks he stands watch lest he should fall" (1 Cor 10.12). Even people who have received greater blessings than any of the things listed above—people "who have become sharers in the Holy Spirit, and have tasted the good word of God and the powers of the age to come"—may still **fall** (Heb 6.4–6).

Her children sinned greatly

Greek	Syriac
1.6 [6] καὶ ἐξύβρισαν ἐν τοῖσ ἀγαθοῖσ αὐτῶν	ܘܠܛܘ ܒܛܒ̈ܬܗܘܢ.
And while *they had* their good *things*, they did exorbitant wrong,	And while *they had* their good *things*, they cursed,
καὶ οὐκ ἤνεγκαν· and they did not bear.	ܘܠܐ ܝܕܥܘ. and they did not know;

1.6 ܘܠܛܘ ܒܛܒ̈ܬܗܘܢ. ܘܠܐ 10h1 [καὶ ἐξύβρισαν ἐν τοῖσ ἀγαθοῖσ αὐτῶν καὶ οὐκ 253 336⁺260] | > 16h1 •

1.6 While they had their good things, they did exorbitant wrong. The **good things** are the **riches** and **glory** described in the preceding verses (v 3–5); the same term is applied to the "many good things" owned by the rich man in Jesus' parable (Luke 12.19). All **good things** are given by God (Jas 1.17; Acts 14.17).

Yet **while they had** those **good things,**[32] Jerusalem's inhabitants **did exorbitant wrong** *(exubrisan)*. Forms of *hubrizō* are applied in the Scriptures to a great diversity

---

[31] In the Syriac, v 3 describes *why* Jerusalem believed what she asserted in v 2. In the Greek, it further describes *what* she believed.

[32] **While** [Greek *en* ≡ Syriac *b-*] **they had their good things.** While they were in the state or condition of having those things (BDAG 327, §2b); a common meaning of Hebrew *b-* (BDB 88, §I.6).

of sins (irreverence, Heb 10.29; physical injury, Matt 22.6; Acts 14.5; insulting speech, Luke 11.45; damage to property, Acts 27.21, 10; see also the comments on 2.30–31; Maccabaica 3.20). The present instance has been rendered variously as **cursed** (Syriac),[33] "injured [men]" (Whiston), and "became insolent" (APOT)—each of which would be consistent with the situation described in these psalms. At any rate, the form *exubrizō* marks a particularly extreme or intense form of behavior; it is most often applied to violently rushing water (Ezek 47.5; Gen 49.4; cf. Muraoka 255, §2). We have therefore adopted a rendering that marks an extreme kind of wrongdoing but is otherwise nonspecific: **they did exorbitant wrong.** Jerusalem's children were doing great wrong in many ways: they were spurning God (4.24), making a mockery of sin (2.13), profaning what was holy (v 8), mistreating other people (4.23), and exalting themselves (v 5). Indeed they were committing "every sin" (17.21; 8.14).

In the next clause, the Greek and Syriac texts differ.

- **They did not bear** (Greek version). In an English sentence, the thing borne would need to be specified, but this is not always necessary in Greek (see, e.g., John 2.8). The children of Jerusalem **did not bear** to God (cf. 17.34) the things that were His due: glory, honor (Psa 29.1–2; 96.7–8), and, under the old covenant, the appointed gifts and sacrifices (Psa 68.29; 76.11; cf. Mal 1.13). "They profaned the holy places of the Lord" and the gifts that should have been offered there (v 8; 2.3; 8.13; cf. Mal 2.11; Zep 3.4), instead of devoting to God the **good things** that He had given them (1 Chr 29.14; cf. Hos 2.8).[34] In the heavenly Jerusalem too, "the glory and the honor of the nations" is to be borne to God (Rev 21.24, 26).
- **They did not know** (Syriac version). The children of Jerusalem did not know the Lord (2.35; cf. Isa 44.18; Jer 10.14; 4.22). Those who reject the knowledge of God will themselves be rejected by Him (Hos 4.6; 2 Thes 1.8).[35]

---

[33] **They cursed.** Syriac *lwṭ* does not usually correspond to Greek *hubrizō* (Trafton 26), but the two terms did have some semantic overlap; *lwṭ* was a common Syriac rendering of Hebrew *qll,* which was rendered by Greek *hubrizō* in 2 Sam 19.43. Trafton was also puzzled by the absence of a direct object in the Syriac; but this too has parallels elsewhere, e.g., "in their heart they curse [*lyṭyn*]" (Psa 62.4, Syr). The children of Jerusalem should have been doing the opposite of cursing—blessing (2.37); but they were not (3.1).

[34] **Did not bear** has sometimes been taken to mean "were not able to endure": the children of Jerusalem "could not keep their ambition under control" (Ryle-James 5). But this would not fit the present context so closely, and, in Greek, would require some form of *dunamai,* "be able" (as in Jer 20.9, LXX: *ou dunamai pherein*).

[35] How did the difference between Greek **bear** and Syriac **know** arise? (i) The Greek and Syriac could be renderings of different Hebrew texts (*hby'w* and *hbynw* respectively: Gebhardt 92). (ii) The Syriac could be a rendering of a Greek text different from that of the existing Greek manuscripts (*egnōkan* instead of *ēnegkan:* APOT 2.631). (iii) The Syriac could be a rendering of the existing Greek text (if the translator was puzzled by **bear** and therefore substituted

1.7 [7] αἱ ἁμαρτίαι αὐτῶν ἐν ἀποκρύφοισ Their sins *were* in hidden *place*s,	ܚܛܗ̈ܝܗܘܢ ܓܝܪ ܒܟܣܝܐ ܗܘܘ. for their sins were in hiding,
καὶ ἐγὼ οὐκ ᾔδειν· and I myself did not know.	ܘ‹ܐܢܐ› ܠܐ ܝܕܥ ܗܘܝܬ. and I myself did not know.

1.7 ܘܐܢܐ 10h1 ≡ καὶ ἐγὼ 253 336⁺260 | ܐܢܐ 16h1 •

1.7 Their sins were in hidden places. Sin is often committed "in hidden places," in the hope that it will not be seen (4.5; Job 24.15; John 3.19–20). "The sons of Israel secretly did things that were not right against the LORD their God" (2 Kgs 17.9). However, no sin can be hidden from His knowledge (9.5–6; Psa 94.7–11). A few years after these psalms were written, the Lord came to Jerusalem and told her children: "You yourselves outwardly appear beautiful to people, but inwardly you are full of hypocrisy and opposition to the Law" (Matt 23.27–28). "People" could be deceived by their outward appearance—but He was not. "Nothing is covered up that will not be revealed, and hidden that will not be known" (Luke 12.1–2).

I myself did not know. Her children's sins were so secretive that Jerusalem herself was unaware of them—just as, many generations earlier, Israel had been unaware of the sin secretly committed by Achan (Josh 7.7–12). Yet the whole city was now suffering because of her children's sins (she was "oppressed to the end," vv 1–2)—just as all Israel had suffered because of Achan's sin ("they cannot stand before their enemies," Josh 7.12).

1.8 [8] αἱ ἀνομίαι αὐτῶν ὑπερ τα προ αὐτ(ῶν) ἔθνη· Their deeds opposed to *the* Law *went* beyond the nations *who had been* before them;	ܘ‹ܥܘܠܗܘܢ› ܝܬܝܪ ܡܢ ܥܡ̈ܡܐ ܕܩܕܡܝܗܘܢ. And their injustice abounded beyond the peoples *who had been* before them,
ἐβεβήλωσαν τὰ ἅγια κ(υρίο)υ ἐν βεβηλώσει: they profaned the Lord's holy *place*s with profaneness.	ܘܛܢܦܘ ܠܗܝܟܠܗ ܕܡܪܝܐ ܒܛܢܘܦܘܬܐ. and they made the LORD's temple unclean with uncleanness.

1.8 ܘܥܘܠܗܘܢ 10h1 [αἱ ἀνομίαι αὐτῶν 253 336⁺260] | ܘܥܒܕ̈ܝܗܘܢ 16h1 •

1.8 Their deeds opposed to the Law went beyond the nations who had been before them. Before the Israelites entered the land of Canaan, it had been occupied by other

something easier: Trafton 27). (iv) The existing Syriac could be a simple transcriptional accident (if an early copyist had been unconsciously influenced by the sight of the word *yd'*, "know," in the next verse). All four suggestions are purely speculative; nothing in the text or context would favor one rather than another.

nations. Those nations had done great evil; therefore the LORD had cast them out, and He had warned the Israelites that if they committed such deeds, He would reject them too (Lev 18.24–30).

But in spite of that warning, "Judah and the inhabitants of Jerusalem . . . did evil beyond the nations whom the LORD destroyed before the sons of Israel" in the days of King Manasseh (2 Chr 33.9), in the days of Alcimus (see the comments on Maccabaica 7.23), and again at the time described in these psalms: "they did not leave any sin that they did not do beyond the nations" (8.14).[36] They had committed **deeds opposed to** God's **Law** (see the comments on Maccabaica 2.44). If those who have come to know God do such deeds, they must expect even worse punishment than those who have never known Him (Luke 12.47–48).

They profaned the Lord's holy places with profaneness. To **profane** *(bebēloō)* something is to make it **unclean** *(ṭm',* Syriac; Ezek 43.7–8; cf. Maccabaica 1.48; Eighteen Psalms 17.51), the opposite of **holy** (Lev 10.10; Ezek 44.23). People who do **deeds opposed to** God's **Law** are profane themselves (2.13–14; 1 Tim 1.9) and are capable of profaning everything that is **holy,** including—under the old covenant—the Lord's temple (Ezek 7.21–22; 23.38–39; 44.7; Maccabaica 3.51; 4.54; cf. Acts 24.6), His sacrificial altar (Maccabaica 4.38, 44; Eighteen Psalms 2.2–3; 8.13), His Sabbaths and appointed feasts (Exod 31.14; Neh 13.17–18; Isa 56.2, 6; Maccabaica 1.43, 45), and the gifts and sacrifices that were offered to Him (Lev 22.15; 19.8; Eighteen Psalms 2.3; 8.13).

In the Greek version of the present verse, the things that are profaned are **the Lord's** *hagia,* a term that can be applied either to the **holy places** of the temple (see the comments on Maccabaica 2.12; BDAG 11, §2b) or to the "holy things" (Ryle-James) offered there (i.e., the gifts and sacrifices, Lev 22.15). However, that distinction is of little importance; in practice, profanation of the places and profanation of the offerings happened together (2.2–3; 8.12–13).[37]

Under the new covenant, God's people are themselves a holy temple (Eph 2.21; 1 Cor 3.16) offering themselves as holy sacrifices (Rom 12.1; 1 Pet 2.5); they must not be profane themselves (Heb 12.16), and they must avoid everything that is profane (1 Tim 4.7).

Psalm 2

This psalm is closely related to the previous one. The previous one described a sudden attack on Jerusalem (1.1–2); this one describes the effects of the attack: the city's fortified walls were torn down (v 1), her altar was trampled by foreign nations (v 2), her sons and her daughters were taken into captivity (v 6). Again the reasons for the disaster—the people's sins—are fully confessed (vv 3, 7–18).

---

[36] The passages cited above show that those **nations** were the pre-Israelite inhabitants of Canaan, not "the gentile invasions in the past . . . e.g., Antiochus Epiphanes" (OTP 2.651).

[37] The corresponding Syriac, *hykl',* refers unambiguously to the **temple** (Dan 5.2, MT = Syr).

Foreign nations trampled the Lord's altar

Greek	Syriac
2.0 [0] Ψαλμὸς τῷ Cαλωμῶν περὶ Ἱερουςαλήμ: A psalm belonging to Solomon, concerning Jerusalem.	
2.1 [1] Ἐν τῷ ὑπερηφανεύεσθαι τὸν ἁμαρτωλὸν· ἐν κριῷ κατέβαλλε τείχη ὀχυρὰ In the arrogance of the sinner, with a *battering* ram he *began* putting down fortified walls,	ܒܫܘܒܗܪܗ ܕܥܘܠܐ ܐܘܪܡ ܒܥܐܕܐ ܫܘܪ̈ܐ ܚܣܝܢ̈ܐ In *the* boasting of the unjust *man,* he cast *down* strong walls at the feast,
καὶ οὐκ ἐκώλυσασ· and You[†] did not prevent *him.*	ܘܠܐ ܟܠܝܬ. and You[†] did not hinder;
2.2 [2] ἀνέβησαν ἐπὶ τὸ θυσιαστήριόν σου ἔθνη ἀλλότρια Strange nations went up on Your[†] sacrificial altar;	ܘܣܠܩܘ ܥܠ ܡܕܒܚܟ ܥܡܡ̈ܐ ܢܘܟܪ̈ܝܐ and strange peoples went up on Your[†] altar,
κατεπατοῦσαν ἐν υποδήμασιν αὐτῶν ἐν υπερηφανία· they trampled *it* down with their sandals in arrogance,	ܘܕܫܝܢ ܗܘܘ ܒܡܣܢ̈ܝܗܘܢ܆ ܒܫܘܒܗܪܬܐ. and they trampled *it* with their shoes in boasting,
2.3 [3] ἀνθῶν οἱ υἱοὶ Ἰ(ερουσα)λὴμ ἐμίαναν τὰ ἅγια κ(υρίο)υ· because Jerusalem's sons stained the Lord's holy places;	ܡܛܠ ܕܒܢ̈ܝ ܐܘܪܫܠܡ ܛܢܦܘ ܒܝܬ ܡܩܕܫܗ ܕܡܪܝܐ. because Jerusalem's sons made unclean the LORD's holy house;
ἐβεβηλοῦσαν τὰ δῶρα τοῦ θ(εο)ῦ ἐν ανομίαισ· they profaned the gifts of God by deeds opposed to the Law.	ܘܡܛܢܦܝܢ ܗܘܘ ܩܘܪ̈ܒܢܘ(ܗܝ) ܕܐܠܗܐ ܒܥܘܠܬܐ. and they made unclean *the* offerings of God, in injustice.

2.1[38] Once again, as in the time of Antiochus Epiphanes (Maccabaica 1.21, 24, 31), Jerusalem has been attacked **in . . . arrogance** (vv 2, 29; 17.15, 26—the opposite of humility, Jas 4.6; 1 Pet 5.5) by a **sinner,** who **began putting down**[39] the city's **fortified**

---

[38] In the Greek copies (but not in the Syriac), the psalm is superscribed **A psalm belonging to Solomon, concerning Jerusalem.**

[39] **He began putting down** (*kateballe,* imperfect tense) is the reading of 253 and 336, whereas 260 reads **he put down** (*katebale,* aorist).

walls (cf. Maccabaica 4.60; 13.10; 14.37).[40] At times when Jerusalem had been faithful to the Lord, He had protected her from attack. That had happened in the time of Hezekiah: "from the hand of the king of Assyria I will deliver ... this city, and I will defend this city for my sake, and for my slave David's sake" (2 Kgs 20.6). But on the present occasion the Lord **did not prevent** the attacker from breaking through the walls and conquering the city (as at other times of disobedience, e.g., 2 Kgs 25.4, 10). God is opposed to the arrogant (Jas 4.6; 1 Pet 5.5), and He will ultimately destroy them (Luke 1.51); but He has sometimes given oppressors power for a while, and during the time of their power He has not prevented them from doing evil things (Psa 105.25; Isa 10.5–12; Dan 5.18–20).

2.2 Strange nations—that is, people from foreign countries (cf. Heb 11.9; Acts 7.6), who were forbidden to enter the holy place (Lam 1.10; cf. Acts 21.28)—**trampled** God's **sacrificial altar** (situated at the entrance to the temple, Exod 40.29), as in the days of Antiochus Epiphanes (Maccabaica 3.45, 51).[41]

2.3 These things were allowed to happen **because**[42] of what **Jerusalem's sons** had been doing (a point that will be developed further in vv 7–15). They themselves had been "trampling on the sacrificial altar of the Lord from every uncleanness" (8.13). In opposition to His **Law** (1.8), they had **stained** (*miainō,* as in Titus 1.15) and **profaned** (*bebēloō,* as in 1.8) what should have been **holy**[43] and belonged to **God.**

Jerusalem's children were taken captive

2.4 [4] ἕνεκεν τούτ(ων) εἶπεν ἀπορίψατε αὐτὰ μακρὰν ἀπ᾽ ἐμοῦ·	ܡܛܠ ܗܢܐ ܐܡܪ. ܕܐܪܦܘ ܘܫܕܘ ܐܢܘܢ ܡܢܝ.
On account of these *things*, He said: "Throw^pl^ them away far from Me."	Because of this, He said: "Cast^pl^ away and throw^pl^ them away from Me,"

---

[40] The Greek text states that the sinner attacked the walls **with a battering ram** *(en kriō),* as in the time of Nebuchadnezzar (Ezek 4.2; 21.22). The corresponding Syriac states that the attack occurred **at the feast** (*bʿdʾʿdʾ,* 16h1; 10h1 adds seyame, "at the feasts"). This difference could have arisen either by translation of different Hebrew texts (*kr,* "ram"; *krh,* "feast") or during the transcription of Syriac copies (*ʿrdʾ,* "pole"; *ʿdʿdʾ,* "feast"). Josephus reports that Pompey attacked Jerusalem with battering rams (*War,* 1.147 ≡ *Antiquities,* 14.62) and captured the city on one of the appointed holy days (*Antiquities,* 14.66).

[41] Classical historians state that, on capturing Jerusalem, Pompey and some of his soldiers entered the temple (Josephus, *War,* 1.152 ≡ *Antiquities,* 14.71–72; Tacitus, *Histories,* 5.9).

[42] The context shows that Greek *anthōn* here means **because** (as in vv 15, 39; Gen 22.18, LXX; BDAG 88, §4), like the Syriac *mṭl.*

[43] As in 1.8 (see the comments there), Greek *hagia* could include the **holy places** and/or the "holy things" (Ryle-James) offered there. The corresponding Syriac, *byt mqdšh* (16h1), unambiguously designates the **holy house** (in 1.8 the Syriac is different, but its sense is the same).

Greek	Syriac
οὐκ ευόδωκεν αὐτοῖσ [5] τὸ κάλλοσ τῆσ δόξησ αὐτοῦ·	ܘܠܐ ܐܬܩܢ ܒܗܘܢ ܫܘܦܪܐ ܕܬܫܒܘܚܬܗ.
He did not make the beauty of His glory to prosper for them;	and He did not establish the beauty of His glory with them;
2.5 [5] ἐξουθενώθη ἐνώπιον τοῦ θ(εο)ῦ·	ܐܣܬܠܝ ܩܕܡ ܡܪܝܐ.
it was despised in *the* sight of God;	it was rejected before the LORD,
ἠτιμώθη ἕωσ εἰσ τέλοσ·	ܘܐܦ ܠܚܪܬܗ› ܥܕܡܐ ܠܫܝܛܘܬܐ.
it was dishonored even to *the* end.	and she was dishonored even to the end.

2.5 ܘܐܦ ܠܚܪܬ 10h1 | ܘܪ- 16h1 •

2.4–5 When the children of Israel had been obedient to God, they had been "the people of His nearness" (Psa 148.14; cf. Psa 73.28; John 14.23). But now, **on account of** the **things** that they had been doing (v 3), the Lord appointed the foreign nations[44] to **throw them down far from** Him. "Every high thing raised up against the knowledge of God" must be thrown down (2 Cor 10.5). So, in the time of the Babylonian captivity, "the Lord … threw down the beauty of Israel from heaven to earth" (Lam 2.1). So also the Old Testament Babylon (Jer 51.63–64) and the New Testament Babylon (Rev 18.21) were thrown down because of their iniquities.

Jerusalem had been **the beauty of** God's **glory** (Psa 50.2; Lam 2.15). He had said to her: "Your name went out among the nations because of your beauty, for it was complete, because of My splendor that I put upon you" (Ezek 16.14). But now, because of her children's sins, **He did not make the beauty of His glory**[45] **to prosper**[46] **for them;**

[44] The instruction **Throw them down** (Greek) ≡ **Cast away and throw them down** (Syriac) is addressed to a plurality of people.

[45] **His** (God's) glory is the reading of 253 and 336⁺260 in Greek *(autou)* and of 16h1 in Syriac *(-h),* whereas "her" (Jerusalem's) glory is the reading of 10h1 in Syriac (*-h* with a supraliteral dot). ("Her" [*autēs*] is also the reading of 471 in Greek, but that is presumably a simple copyist's error, as 471 seems to be a direct descendant of 260: see Hann, *Manuscript History of the Psalms of Solomon,* 68–70.) The meaning is not significantly affected. This glory was God's because it came from Him, and Jerusalem's because He gave it to her (17.35; Ezek 16.14).

[46] **Make … to prosper** is the reading of 253 and 336 in Greek *(euodōken)* and of both Syriac manuscripts *('tqn).* Wright construes the Greek as continuing God's address to the foreign nations ("Do not give them a pleasant path," Wright mg), but that is not a possible rendering (the verb is an indicative, not an imperative). 260 reads *euōdōken,* which is presumably a variant spelling of the same word (*o* and *ō* are frequently interchanged in the manuscripts of these psalms, and in other medieval Greek manuscripts: cf. Thackeray §28; MHT 2.73–75). Its reading has sometimes been construed as a form of *euōdeō,* "be fragrant" (LSJ 740; "there is no sweet savour in them," Whiston), but that verb is not found in Biblical Greek (where *euōdiazō* is used instead). Gebhardt emended the word to *eudokō en,* and also accepted the reading *autēs*

instead, **it was despised** and **dishonored**[47] to the utmost degree (**even to the end,** cf. 1.1) in His **sight.** All things **prosper** only when they are "prospered by the will of God" (Rom 1.10); He causes all things to prosper for His people (Rom 8.28), but those who persist in sinning against Him cannot hope to prosper (Prov 28.13; Jer 2.37). When the Israelites rebelled against Him, "He rejected Israel utterly … and He delivered His strength into captivity, and His excellence into the hand of an oppressor" (Psa 78.56–61). But He promised that there would come a time when **His glory** would again be seen on Jerusalem (Isa 60.1–3, 19)—a promise that has now been fulfilled through our Lord Jesus (Luke 2.30–32; Rev 21.23).

Greek	Syriac
2.6 [6] ‹οἱ› υἱοὶ καὶ ‹αἱ› θυγατέρεσ ἐν αιχμαλωσία πονηρὰ	ܒܢܝ̈ܗ̇ ‹ܘܒܢܬ̈ܗ̇› ܒܫܒܝܐ ܡܪܝܪܐ.
Her sons and *her* daughters *were* in harmful captivity;	Her sons and her daughters *were* in bitter captivity,
ἐν σφραγίδι· ὁ τράχηλοσ αὐτῶν ἐν επισήμω ἐν τοῖσ ἔθνεσιν·	ܘܩܕܠܗܘܢ ܣܝܡ ܠܗܘܢ، ܢܝܪܐ ܚܬܝܡܐ ܕܥܡܡ̈ܐ.
their neck *was sealed* with a seal, with a conspicuous *sign,* by the nations.	and on their neck was set the sealed yoke of the peoples.

2.6 οἱ 336⁺260 | > 253 • ܘܒܢܬ̈ܗ̇ 10h1 ≡ καὶ αἱ θυγατέρεσ 336⁺260 | καὶ θ- 253 | ܘܒܢܬܗ̇ 16h1 •

2.6 So now **the sons and the daughters** of Jerusalem were punished by suffering **in harmful**[48] **captivity.** They were being scattered (8.34), carried away to the distant west

(see the previous footnote). In that case, the clauses **He did not make the beauty of His glory to prosper for them; it was despised in the sight of God** would become "I take no pleasure in them. The beauty of her glory was despised before God" (NETS). However, the emendation has no manuscript support, and creates a word sequence that would be very unnatural in Hebrew (cf. APOT 2.652; moreover, in Hebrew such a clause would normally be preceded by *w-*, which neither the Greek nor the Syriac attests here).

[47] In one of the Syriac manuscripts (10h1), **it was rejected** *('stly)* is masculine, referring to **the beauty of His glory,** whereas **and she was dishonored** *(w'ṣṭ'rt)* is feminine, referring to **Jerusalem** herself (notice the feminine **her** sons and **her** daughters in the next clause, v 6); see the comments on 1.1. In the other Syriac manuscript (16h1), the second verb is plural, "and they were dishonored" *(w'ṣṭ'rw),* referring to Jerusalem's sons and daughters. Ultimately the meaning is not affected, because the dishonor of Jerusalem (the beauty of God's glory) is the dishonor of her people.

[48] **Harmful** *(ponēra).* In the Eighteen Psalms, Greek *ponēros* often describes that which causes harm or injury (Muraoka 576, §2), either to oneself ("because his fall is harmful, then he will not be raised up," 3.13) or to others ("harmful wild animals … were plucking their flesh," 13.3; "every harmful woman … causes a mindless one to stumble," 16.7). See also the footnote to Maccabaica 1.36. The present verse is concerned, not with whether the captivity was unjust,

(as far as the sunset, 17.14). God had warned His people in advance that this would happen if they disobeyed Him (Deut 28.41). The prophesied punishment had already occurred in the time of the Babylonians (Lam 1.3, 18), and it would occur yet again, later in the time of the Romans (Luke 21.24). In this way, "the woman with many sons has languished" (1 Sam 2.5).

God had also warned them that, when these things happened, their enemy would "put a yoke of iron on your neck, until he has destroyed you" (Deut 28.48). That too was now occurring: the foreign **nations**[49] had sealed the captives' **neck with a seal.**[50] This was no secret thing. It was **conspicuous** (*episēmō,* as in 17.32; Matt 27.16; Rom 16.7; TDNT 7.267–68), manifest "in the sight of the nations . . . in the eyes of all those who pass by" (Ezek 5.8, 14), a visible sign *(sēmeion)* of God's judgment (Deut 28.45–46, LXX).

God judged them for their sins

2.7 [7] κατὰ τὰσ ἁμαρτίασ αὐτ(ῶν) ἐποίησεν αὐτοῖσ·	ܘܐܝܟ ܚܛܗܝ̈ܗܘܢ ܗܟܢܐ ܥܒܕ ܠܗܘܢ܀
In accordance with their sins, He did to them,	And in accordance with their sins, so He did to them,
ὅτι ἐγκατέλειπεν αὐτοὺσ εἰσ χεῖρασ κατισχυόντ(ων)·	ܡܛܠ ܕܐܪܦܝ ܐܢܘܢ ܒܐܝܕܐ ‹ܕ›ܡܢ ܕܥܫܝܢ ܡܢܗܘܢ܀
because He left them in *the* hands of *those* who had strength.	because He left them in the hand of *one* who *was* more powerful than they.

2.7 ܕܡܢ 10h1 ≡ 253 336⁺260 | ܡܢ 16h1 •

2.7 The judgments described in the preceding verses (vv 4–6) were **in accordance with** the people's **sins.** Indeed "all have sinned, and fall short of the glory of God" (Rom 3.23), and therefore all of us deserve such punishment (Luke 13.1–5). "If you keep watch over iniquities, LORD—Lord, who will stand?" (Psa 130.3). But in His mercy and patience, He very often deals with us "not in accordance with our sins" (Psa 103.10), "less than our iniquities" (Ezra 9.13).

---

but with its effects on the captives (*captivité rigoureuse,* Viteau; *penosa esclavitud,* AAT). It was **bitter** to them (Syriac *mryr',* as in Lam 1.4; Jer 9.15–16, Syr).

[49] The Greek phrase *en tois ethnesin* indicates that the seal was imposed **by the nations** (so the Syriac: **a sealed yoke of** [*d-*] **the peoples;** similarly Wright, "a Gentile mark"; cf. Ezek 19.4, 8–9; 26.5) and/or that it was visible "among the nations" ("a spectacle among the nations," OTP; cf. Ezek 5.8, 14).

[50] Objects were sealed to keep them securely closed (Matt 27.66; Rev 20.3) and to indicate their ownership (Rev 7.2). In the present passage, the Syriac version states that the **yoke** around the captives' **neck** was **sealed,** whereas the Greek does not specify whether the **seal** was stamped on a yoke, or directly on the flesh of the **neck** (Ryle-James 12).

He will not leave the righteous in the hands of the wicked (Psa 37.33). However, the people of Jerusalem had not listened to Him (vv 9, 11), and therefore He had **left them in the hands** of enemies more powerful than themselves (**those who had strength;** cf. Psa 38.19; Joel 2.1–10).

Greek	Syriac
2.8 [8] ἀπέστρεψεν γὰρ τὸ πρόσωπον αὐτοῦ ἀπὸ ἐλέουσ αὐτῶν· For He turned away His face from their mercy,	ܐܗܦܟ ܓܝܪ ܐܦ̈ܘܗܝ ܡܢ ܪ̈ܚܡܘܗܝ. For He turned His face from His compassions,
νέον καὶ πρεσβύτην καὶ τέκνα αὐτ(ῶν) εἰσ ἅπαξ· young *man* and old *man* and their children all alike,	ܠܛܠܝ̈ܐ ܘܣ̈ܒܐ ܘܒ̈ܢܝܗܘܢ ܐܟܚܕܐ. the youngsters and the old *ones* and their sons together,
2.9 [8] ὅτι πονηρὰ ἐποίησαν εἰσ ἅπαξ τοῦ μὴ ἀκούειν· because they did wicked *things* all alike, not hearing *Him.*	ܡܛܠ ܕܒܝܫܬܐ ܥܒܕܘ ܐܦ ܗܢܘܢ ܐܟܚܕܐ ܕܠܐ ܢܫܡܥܘܢܢܝ. because they themselves also did evil together, so that they did not hear Me.

2.8–9 God **turned away His face from their mercy**—that is, from showing mercy to them.[51] **All** of them **alike**[52] had done **wicked** deeds, not heeding Him (Neh 9.29; Isa 65.12).[53] Therefore, He withheld His mercy from **all** of them **alike—young man and old man and their children**—without partiality (v 19; cf. Deut 28.50; 2 Chr 36.17). He hides **His face** from those who provoke His anger (Deut 31.16–18; 32.19–20; Isa 59.2; Jer 33.5); but to those who seek His **mercy,** His mercy is everlasting (Isa 54.8).

---

[51] **Their mercy.** Not the mercy that they showed, but the mercy that would be shown to them. Cf. "the good work of the infirm man" (Acts 4.9), i.e., the good work done to the infirm man (BDF §163; MHT 3.210–12).

[52] In this book *eis hapax* means **all alike,** grouped into *(eis)* one *(hapax)* without any exceptions (the corresponding Syriac here is *'kḥd',* "as one," i.e., **together**); cf. Dan 2.35, *θ'*; LXX.DE 2.1915. The rendering "once again" (OTP) would not fit the use of the term in 11.3 ("those who are gathered together all alike by the Lord"—the Syriac there is *klhwn,* "all of them").

[53] **Not hearing** *(tou mē akouein)* is sometimes construed as specifying the purpose of the evildoing ("they wrought evil ... to the intent that they should not hearken unto him," Ryle-James; *pour ne pas écouter,* Viteau), but this seems implausible, especially when it involves a whole city population. In this context, **not hearing** is more likely to be simply a further description of the evildoing. For similar sentence constructions, see: "[Pharaoh] did evil to our fathers, making [*tou poiein*] them cast out their infants" (Acts 7.19); "have you also done evil against the widow ... killing [*tou thanatōsai*] her son?" (1 Kgs 17.20, LXX). Cf. BDF §400.8; MHT 1.216–18; Robertson 1066–68. The idiom corresponds to Hebrew *l-* plus infinitive, which is comparably flexible (GKC §114*f–o*).

Greek	Syriac
2.10 [9] καὶ ὁ οὐ(ρα)νὸσ ἐβαρυθύμησε κ(αὶ) ἡ γῆ ἐβδελύξατο αὐτοὺσ· And the heaven was heavily indignant, and the earth abominated them,	ܘܐܬܚܡܬ ܫܡܝܐ ܪܘܪܒܐܝܬ. ܘܐܪܥܐ ܐܣܠܝܬ ܐܢܘܢ. And the heaven became greatly indig- nant, and the earth rejected them,
2.11 [9] ὅτι οὐκ ἐποίησε πᾶσ ἄν(θρωπ)οσ ἐπ' αὐτῆσ ὅσα ἐποίησαν· because no person on her had done as much as they had done.	ܡܛܠ ܕܠܐ ܥܒܕ ܟܠ ܒܪܐܢܫ ܥܠܝܗ̇ ܐܝܟ ܕܥܒܕܘ. because no son of man on her did as they did,
2.12 [10] καὶ γνώσεται ἡ γῆ τὰ κρίματά σου πάντα τὰ δίκαια ὁ θ(εό)σ· And the earth will know all Your† righteous judgments, O God.	ܘܕܬܕܥ ܐܪܥܐ ܟܠܗܘܢ ܕܝ̈ܢܝܟ ܙܕ̈ܝܩܐ ܐܠܗܐ. and in order that the earth might know all Your† righteous judgments, God.
[11] ἔστησαν τοὺσ υἱοὺσ Ἰ(ερουσα)λὴμ εἰσ ἐμπεγμὸν ἀντὶ πορνῶν ἐν αὐτῇ· They set up Jerusalem's sons for scoffing, because of *the* fornicatresses in her;	ܐܩܝܡܘ ܠܒܢܝ̈ܗ̇ ܕܐܘܪܫܠܡ ܒܡܘܚܟܐ ܒܓܘܗ̇. ܚܠܦ ܙܢܝ̈ܬܐ. They set up Jerusalem's sons in ridicule in *the* midst of her, instead of fornicatresses,
2.13 [11] πᾶσ ὁ ‹παραπορευόμενοσ› εἰσεπορεύετο κατέναντι τοῦ ἡλίου· every*one who was* going past was going in, right in front of the sun.	ܘܟܠ ܡܢ ܕܛܥܐ ܗܘܐ. ܛܥܐ ܗܘܐ ܐܝܟ ܕܠܩܘܒܠ ܫܡܫܐ. and every*one* who was straying, was straying as *if* before the sun,
[12] ἐνέπαιζον ταῖσ ἀνομίαισ αὐτ(ῶν) **2.14 [12]** καθὰ ἐποίουν αὐτοί· They were scoffing at their deeds opposed to *the* Law, *which were* just as they themselves were doing;	ܟܕ ܡܒܙܚܝܢ ܗܘܘ ܒܥܘܠܘܬܗܘܢ. ܐܝܟ ܕܐܦ ܗܢܘܢ ܥܒܕܝܢ ܗܘܘ. when they were mocking at their injustice, *which was* as also they themselves were doing,

2.13 παραπορευόμενοσ 336⁺260 ≡ ܕܛܥܐ 16h1 10h1 | πορευ- 253 •

ἀπέναντι τοῦ ἡλίου παρεδειγμάτισαν ἀδικίασ αὐτῶν· before the sun they made a show of their unrighteous *deeds*.	ܠܩܘܒܠ ܫܡܫܐ ܦܪܣܘ ܥܘܠܗܘܢ܀ before the sun they displayed their injustice.
[13] καὶ θυγατέρεσ Ἰ(ερουσα)λὴμ βέβηλοι κατὰ τὸ κρίμα σου· And *the* daughters of Jerusalem *were* profane, in accordance with Your† judgment,	ܘܒܢܬܗ ܕܐܘܪܫܠܡ ܐܬܛܢܦܝ ܐܝܟ ܕܝܢܟ܀ And *the* daughters of Jerusalem were made unclean, in accordance with Your† judgment,
2.15 [13] ἀνθῶν αὗται ἐμιαίωσαν αὐτὰσ ἐν φυρμῷ ἀναμίξεωσ· because they themselves had stained themselves in an intermingling of mixing together.	ܡܛܠ ܕܗܢܝܢ ܠܢܦܫܗܝܢ ܛܢܦܝ ܒܚܘܠܛܢܐ ܕܙܪܝܚܘܬܐ܀ because they themselves had made their soul unclean in a mingling of overindulgence.

2.10 The heaven was heavily indignant, and the earth abominated them. The heavens and the earth were created by God and always act in obedience to His will (18.12–14; Psa 119.91; Isa 48.13). Therefore they respond to sin in the way that He ordains; when He sharpens His indignation, "the world will fight together with Him against" His enemies, because that is what He directs it to do (Wisdom 5.20; 16.17; Josh 10.11–13; Jdg 5.20). The land of Canaan "vomited out" its corrupt inhabitants (Lev 18.25, 28); the Red Sea rose to cover Israel's enemies (Exod 14.28; 15.10); the sun left off shining when Jesus was crucified (Luke 23.44–45); stones and blood have cried out in protest against human sins (Hab 2.11; Gen 4.10). **The heaven** and **the earth** likewise express their Creator's indignation and abhorrence of evil (Jer 2.12–13). "He calls the heavens … and the earth to plead the cause of His people" (Psa 50.4).

2.11–15a No person on her (the earth, v 10) **had done as much** evil **as** Jerusalem's inhabitants **had done** (see the comments on 1.8; Maccabaica 7.23). Some of those evil deeds are now described. There were **fornicatresses**[54] in Jerusalem, and **every** passer-by **was going in** (to consort with them, Ezek 23.44)[55] openly, in broad daylight (**right**

[54] **Fornicatresses** (Greek *pornōn* ≡ Syriac *znyt'*). The word is broader than the modern term "prostitutes" (OTP). In the Scriptures, it applies to all those who commit fornication (Gen 34.31; Deut 22.20–21), not only to those who seek payment for doing so (Gen 38.15).

[55] **Everyone who was going past** [*paraporeuomenos*] **was going in** [*eiseporeueto*] openly. The Syriac has an even more striking play on words: **Everyone who was** *'br* **was** *'br* openly. In Syriac, as in Hebrew, *'br* can mean both "pass" (go past, ≡ Greek *paraporeuomai;* Gen 37.28, etc.; go in, ≡ Greek *eisporeuomai;* Deut 11.11) and "trespass" (transgress, ≡ Greek *parabainō;* Num 24.13, etc.). So, in Syriac, the clause is saying both (i) "everyone who was passing by was sinning openly" ("everyone who was passing was trespassing"; "everyone who was stepping over there was overstepping") and (ii) "everyone who was sinning was doing so openly."

in front of the sun—the opposite of "secretly," 2 Sam 12.12; equivalent to "before the eyes of all Israel," 2 Sam 16.22; cf. Num 25.4). **Daughters of Jerusalem . . . stained themselves**[56] **in an intermingling of mixing together** (for instance, "son with mother and father with daughter were mingling together," 8.10). **Before the sun they made a show of** [*paredeigmatisan,* Greek ≡ *prsyw,* Syriac] **their unrighteous deeds** (cf. Isa 3.9)—in other words, they did the very thing that righteous Joseph did not want to do with the supposed fornication of Mary (*deigmatisai* ≡ *nprsyh,* Matt 1.19): they "paraded" their unrighteous deeds (AOT), "openly published" them (Whiston), instead of mourning over them as they should have done (1 Cor 5.2). Those who commit fornication make themselves **profane** (Lev 21.9, 7), i.e., unclean (see on 1.8). All such deeds were **opposed to** God's **Law** under the old covenant (Lev 19.29; Deut 22.20–21), just as they are today under the new (Acts 15.29). "Those who practice such things will not inherit the kingdom of God" (Gal 5.19–21; 1 Cor 6.9–10).

Those who committed the **deeds opposed to the Law** in Jerusalem were scoffed at by people who were doing the same things themselves. **They set up**[57] **Jerusalem's sons for scoffing, because of the fornicatresses in her.**[58] **. . . They were scoffing at their deeds opposed to the Law,**[59] **which were just as they themselves were doing.** These scoffers were the foreign invaders, as the psalm later makes clear: "they scoffed and they did not spare" (v 25). Jerusalem's inhabitants were supposed to be the LORD's people, doing righteous deeds—and yet they were doing **just** the same kinds of **deeds opposed to** God's **Law** as the scoffers **themselves were doing.** Both "Jews and Greeks . . . are all under sin" (Rom 3.9).

"We know that the judgment of God is on those who practice such things, in accordance with truth" (Rom 2.2). When His **righteous judgments** are carried out,

---

[56] The medieval manuscripts construe αυται as a demonstrative pronoun with a rough breathing, *hautai* ("these *ones*" had stained themselves). Our translation construes it as a personal pronoun with a smooth breathing, *autai* (they **themselves** had stained themselves), which matches the sense of the Syriac.

[57] **They set up** *(estēsan)* is the reading of 253 and 336 (supported by Syr), whereas 260 reads "He [God] set up" *(estēsen).*

[58] The Syriac version has **they set Jerusalem's sons in ridicule in the midst of her** [Jerusalem], **instead of** [*ḥlp*] **fornicatresses.** The nations despised Jerusalem's inhabitants, in the way that a fornicatress would be despised (Ezek 16.27). The Greek version could theoretically be construed in the same way (taking the preposition *anti* to mean "instead of"). But the immediate context (vv 13–15) talks of actual fornication in Jerusalem as a cause of scoffing. Thus it is more appropriate to render *anti* **because,** as elsewhere in this psalm (see footnote to v 3): the nations were scoffing at Jerusalem **because of** the city's fornicatresses. If God's people in any age behave wickedly, it causes others to blaspheme (Rom 2.24; 1 Tim 5.14; 6.1; Titus 2.5, 8).

[59] **They were scoffing at their deeds opposed to the Law** *(enepaizon tais anomiais autōn).* The dative *tais anomiais* indicates, not that they were scoffing "with" these deeds (NETS), but that they were scoffing **at** them (see LEH 195). Similarly, the Syriac reads **they were mocking at** (*mbzḥyn . . . b-,* TS 1.503; SL 133) **their injustice.**

those judgments will be even more manifest than the most open sins have been: **the earth will know** them **all** (vv 18, 36; and especially 8.27).

His judgments were righteous

Greek	Syriac
[14] τὴν κοιλίαν μου κ(αὶ) τὰ σπλάγχνα μου πονῶ ἐπὶ τούτοισ· *In* my belly and my inward parts, I am in pain over these *thing*s.	ܟܪܣܝ ܘܐܡܥܝ ܚܫܘ ܥܠ ܗܠܝܢ. My belly and my inward parts have been in pain over these things.
2.16 **[15]** ἐγὼ δικαιώσω σε ὁ θ(εό)σ ἐν εὐθύτητι καρδίασ· I myself will acknowledge You† to be righteous, O God, in uprightness of heart,	ܐܢܐ ܕܝܢ ܐܙܕܩܟ ܡܪܝܐ. ܒܬܪܝܨܘܬܗ ܕܠܒܝ. But I myself will acknowledge You† to be righteous, LORD, in *the* uprightness of my heart,
ὅτι ἐν τοῖσ κρίμασίν σου ἡ δικαιοσύνη σου ὁ θ(εό)σ· because in Your† judgments *is* Your† righteousness, O God,	ܡܛܠ ܕܒܕܝܢܝܟ ܙܕܝܩܘܬܟ ܐܠܗܐ. because in Your† judgments *is* your† righteousness, God,
2.17 **[16]** ὅτι ἀπέδωκασ τοῖσ ἁμαρτωλοῖσ κατὰ τὰ ἔργα αὐτ(ῶν)· because You† have repaid the sinners in accordance with their works,	ܡܛܠ ܕܦܪܥ ܐܢܬ ܠܥܘܠܐ ܐܝܟ ܥܒܕܝܗܘܢ. because You† *are* repaying the unjust *one*s in accordance with their deeds,
καὶ κατὰ τὰσ ἁμαρτίασ αὐτ(ῶν) τὰσ πονηρὰσ ‹σφόδρα› and in accordance with their sins, *which were* extremely wicked.	ܘܐܝܟ ܚܛܗܝܗܘܢ ܒܝܫܐ ܘܡܪܝܪܐ. and in accordance with their sins, *which were* evil and bitter.
2.18 **[17]** ἀνεκάλυψασ τὰσ ἁμαρτίασ αὐτ(ῶν) ἵνα φανῇ τὸ κρίμα σου· You† have uncovered their sins, in order that Your† judgment may be seen;	ܓܠܝܬ ܚܛܗܝܗܘܢ ܡܛܠ ܕܢܬܝܕܥ ܕܝܢܟ. You† have uncovered their sins so that Your† judgment might be known,
2.19 **[17]** ἐξήλιψασ τὸ μνημόσυνον αὐτ(ῶν) ἀπὸ τῆσ γῆσ· You† have wiped away their memorial from the earth.	ܘܓܠܚܬ ܕܘܟܪܢܗܘܢ ܡܢ ܐܪܥܐ. and You† have blotted out their memorial from the earth.
[18] ὁ θ(εὸ)σ κριτὴσ δίκαιοσ καὶ οὐ θαυμάσει πρόσωπον·	ܐܠܗܐ ܕܝܢܐ ܘܙܕܝܩܐ ܘܠܐ ܢܣܒ ܒܐܦܐ.

God is a righteous judge, and He will not be impressed by a face.	God *is* the judge, and righteous, and *does* not accept *people* by *their* faces.

2.17 σφόδρα 336⁺260 | -ρο(ν) 253 •

2.15b–19 Like faithful people in any age (2 Pet 2.8; Psa 119.136, 158; Ezek 9.4; Ezra 9.3–10.1; Rom 9.1–5; 10.1; Php 3.18), the psalmist suffered **pain** in the very depths of his being (**my belly and my inward parts,** Jer 4.19; Isa 16.11) as he contemplated **these things** (Jerusalem's sins and the scoffing of her enemies, vv 11–15). He recognized that God was **righteous,** and that His **righteousness** was evident **in** His **judgments** (Psa 7.11; 98.9; Acts 17.31). God was repaying **the sinners in accordance with their works,** and "it is a righteous thing" for Him to do so (2 Thes 1.6; Rev 16.5–6; 19.2). His judgments are fair to all, without any trace of partiality: **He will not be impressed**[60] **by a face,** but will look on the heart (1 Sam 16.7). "Accepting [people] by faces" is the usual Scripture term for acceptance on the basis of something outward (riches, reputation, physical appearance, etc.). God's judgments are never like that (Deut 10.17; 2 Chr 19.7; Acts 10.34–35). When He judges, "the person who does unrighteously will receive back for what he did unrighteously, and there is no acceptance of faces" (Col 3.25; Rom 2.6–11). The mightiest rulers on earth will undergo that judgment (vv 34–35), just like their lowliest subjects.

I myself[61] **will acknowledge You to be righteous** ("I will justify Thee," Whiston; Greek *dikaiōsō se* ≡ Syriac *'zdqk*). The New Testament Scriptures repeatedly state that God "justifies," i.e., "acknowledges to be righteous," those who believe in Him and obey His word (Jas 2.24–25; Rom 2.13; 3.24). That is, such people are "pronounced and treated as right" by Him (BDAG 249, §2bβ). Here a similar point is made: those people "justify" God—they **acknowledge** Him **to be righteous,** pronouncing Him to be right and treating Him as right (Luke 7.29; Rom 3.4; Eighteen Psalms 3.3, 5; 4.9; 8.7, 27, 31; 9.3; cf. 1 Tim 3.16; Matt 11.19; TDNT 2.213, §B1f; 2.214, §C2).[62]

You have uncovered their sins, in order that Your judgment may be seen. "God will bring every deed into judgment, with every hidden thing, whether good or evil" (Ecc 12.14). His **judgment** is like light, which uncovers what is hidden (1 Cor 4.5; John 3.19–21); and when **sins** are **uncovered** in that way, then His **judgment** is manifest to all: "All the nations will see My judgment that I have done … and the nations will know that the house of Israel went into exile for their iniquity" (Ezek 39.21–24).

---

[60] **Be impressed.** The Greek is unusual, and remarkably intense: *thaumasei,* "be amazed" (as in Luke 4.22, etc.). The term **accept** (Syriac *nsb,* corresponding to Greek *lambanō*) is used much more commonly in such contexts (Gal 2.6, etc.).

[61] Notice the emphatic pronoun, both in Greek and in Syriac: whatever Jerusalem's sinners may do, and however the Gentiles may scoff (v 13), still **I myself** (Greek *egō* ≡ Syriac *'n'*) will acknowledge You to be righteous. There is a similar emphatic pronoun in Josh 24.15: whatever you listeners may do, "I myself [Greek *egō* ≡ Syriac *'n'*] and my house will serve the LORD."

[62] The idea is well expressed in the Spanish and French renderings *yo reconozco tu justicia* (AAT), *je te reconnais juste* (Viteau), *je te proclamerai juste* (Prigent).

You have wiped away their memorial from the earth. God has "wiped out" the name of the wicked; "their remembrance has been destroyed" (Psa 9.5–6; cf. Prov 10.7), whereas the righteous receive a lasting name and unfading glory (Isa 56.5; Luke 10.20; Rev 3.12; see the comments on Maccabaica 2.51).

The nations dishonored Jerusalem

Greek	Syriac
2.20 [19] ὠνίδησαν γὰρ ἔθνη Ἰ(ερουσα)λὴμ ἐν καταπατήσει· For *the* nations reproached Jerusalem by trampling *her* down;	ܚܣܕܘ ܓܝܪ ܥܡ̈ܡܐ ܠܐܘܪܫܠܡ ܒܪܘܫܥܗܘܢ܆ For the peoples reproached Jerusalem in their ungodliness,
κατέσπασεν τὸ κάλλοσ αὐτῆσ ἀπὸ θρόνου δόξησ· He pulled down her beauty from a throne of glory.	ܘܐܬܦܣܩ ܦܘܪܣܗ̇ ܡܢ ܬܪܘܢܘܣ ܕܬܫܒܘܚܬܗ̇. and her book was erased from *the* throne of her glory,
2.21 [20] περιεζώσατο σάκκον ἀντὶ ἐνδύματοσ εὐπρεπείασ· She girded herself around with sackcloth, in place of clothing of good appearance;	ܘܐܬܟܣܝܬ̇ ܣܩܐ ܚܠܦ ܠܒܘܫܐ ܕܢܐܘܬܐ. and she was covered with sackcloth instead of clothing of seemliness,
σχοινίον περὶ τὴν κεφαλὴν αὐτῆσ ἀντι στεφάνου· a rope *was* round about her head in place of a crown.	ܘܚܒܠܐ ܥܠ ܪܫܗ̇ ܚܠܦ ܟܠܝܠܐ. and a rope *was* on her head instead of a crown.
2.22 [21] περιείλατο μίτραν δόξησ ἣν περιέθηκεν αὐτῇ ὁ θ(εό)σ· She put off *the* headdress of glory that God had put on her;	ܐܪܡܝܬ̇ ܡܢܗ̇ ܙܝܘܐ ܕܬܫܒܘܚܬܐ ܗܘ ܕܐܘܪܒ ܥܠܝܗ̇ ܐܠܗܐ. She took off from her*self* the splendor of glory that God had put on her;
2.23 [21] ἐν ατιμία τὸ κάλλοσ αὐτῆσ ἀπερρίφει ἐπὶ τὴν γῆν· in dishonor her beauty was thrown away on the earth.	ܒܨܥܪܐ ܫܘܦܪܗ̇ ܐܫܬܕܝ ܥܠ ܐܪܥܐ. in dishonor her beauty was thrown away on the earth.

2.20–23a The nations had **reproached** [*ōnidēsan* = *ōneidisan,* a spelling variation] **Jerusalem**—that is, they had humiliated her (Jer 15.9, LXX; Muraoka 498, §3) **by trampling her down** (v 2), just as had happened before ("God, nations have come into Your inheritance ... we have become a reproach to our neighbors," Psa 79.1, 4) during the Babylonian invasion (Lam 5.1) and again in the time of Antiochus Epiphanes (Maccabaica 4.58; 7.16–17).

In the past, Jerusalem had been a city of great **beauty** (see the comments on v 4).

Indeed, she had been "the whole of beauty" (Psa 50.2; Lam 2.15). She had worn **clothing of good appearance** (Ezek 16.13). On her head **God had put** a sign of great honor: a **crown,** a **headdress of glory** (Ezek 16.12; cf. Jer 13.18). He had seated her on a **throne of glory** (Jer 14.21). But now all these things were gone. **He pulled down**[63] **her beauty**[64] from her **throne** (Lam 2.1). She wore signs of humiliation: a garment of **sackcloth,** and a **rope round about her head** (Isa 3.24; Jer 6.26). Her glory was turned to **dishonor** (v 5).

Jerusalem was suffering these things justly, because of her sins (vv 16–17). And, indeed, what happened at this time to her will ultimately happen to all who persist in sin (God "lays arrogant ones asleep to lasting destruction in dishonor," v 35). Yet there was also a time when such humiliations were inflicted on One who never committed any sin. He was deprived of all beauty (Isa 53.2; 52.14), reproached (Matt 27.44; Heb 13.13), dishonored (John 8.49), and trampled down (Heb 10.29), not for any sin of His own, but for our sins (1 Pet 2.21–24), in order that we might sit with Him on His throne (Rev 3.21) and be crowned with glory as He is crowned (1 Pet 5.4; Heb 2.9).

Let it be enough, Lord

[22] καὶ ἐγὼ εἶδον **2.24 [22]** καὶ ἐδεήθην τοῦ προσώπου κ(υρίο)υ· καὶ εἶπον	ܘܐܢܐ ܚܙܝܬ ܘܒܥܝܬ ܐܦܘ̈ܗܝ ܕܡܪܝܐ ܘܐܡܪܬ.
And I myself saw, and I requested from the Lord's face, and I said:	And I myself saw, and I requested from the LORD's face, and I said:

---

[63] **He pulled down** *(katespasen).* The immediate context suggests that the subject (**He**) is God (v 19), although some have construed it as a reference to the nations' leader (v 1), or to Jerusalem herself ("she pulled down"; *elle a arraché,* Viteau; cf. v 21). It could also be read as a Hebrew impersonal subject, "one pulled down" (GKC §144*d;* see also the footnote to v 32a). To remove the shift from plural (**the nations reproached**) to singular (**He pulled down**), Gebhardt conjecturally emended the latter to *katespasthē* ("it was pulled down"). But such shifts are abundant in the Hebrew Scriptures and cannot all be emended out of existence (see the examples in König 4.237–38). Compare, in the original, "He has devoured [*'kl,* singular] Jacob, and they have made desolate [*hšmw,* plural] His dwelling-place" (Psa 79.7); "the horsemen set themselves [*štw,* plural] at the gates, and He took away [*wygl,* singular] the covering of Judah" (Isa 22.7–8).

[64] **He pulled down her beauty.** Both Syriac copies read **her book was erased** (*'tpsq,* a term applied to a document when it is obliterated: Didascalia 136.2; cf. SL 1212, §1i). The Scriptures depict God's records of the righteous as being kept in a **book** (Psa 56.8; Dan 12.1; Mal 3.16); those whom He rejects are erased from the book (Psa 69.28; Exod 32.32; Rev 3.5). The same image appears a few lines earlier, using a different verb: **You have blotted out** [*'ṭyt*] **their memorial** (v 19, Syriac). Harris-Mingana and Baars conjecturally emended *sprh* (**her book**) to *šwprh* ("her beauty," matching the Greek).

ἱκάνωσον κ(ύρι)ε τοῦ βαρύνεσθαι ‹χεῖρά› σου ἐπὶ Ἰ(σρα)ὴλ· ἐν επαγωγὴ ἐθνῶν	ܣܦܩ. ܐܘܩܪܬ ܐܝܕܟ ܡܪܝܐ ܥܠ ܐܝܣܪܐܝܠ. ܒܡܝܬܝܘܬܐ ܕܥܡ̈ܡܐ.
"Let *it* be enough, Lord—the weighing down of Your† hand on Israel by bringing *the* nations against *it*,	"*Let it* be enough; You† have made Your† hand heavy, LORD, on Israel, by bringing the peoples,
2.25 [23] ὅτι ἐνέπαιξαν καὶ οὐκ εφείσαντο· ἐν οργῇ καὶ θυμῶ μετα μηνίσεωσ	ܡܛܠ ܕܒܙܚܘ ܘܠܐ ܚܣܘ. ܒܪܘܓܙܐ ܘܒܟܐܬܐ
because they scoffed and they did not spare, in anger and indignation with wrath;	because they mocked and they did not spare, in anger and in rebuke;
2.26 [23] καὶ συντελεσθήσονται· ἐὰν μη σὺ κ(ύρι)ε ἐπιτιμήσειϲ αὐτοῖϲ ἐν ὀργή σου·	ܡܫܠܡܝܢ. ܐܠܐ ܐܢ ܐܢܬ ܡܪܝܐ ܬܟܐܐ ܒܗܘܢ ܒܪܘܓܙܟ.
and they will be brought to an end unless You† Yourself†, Lord, shall rebuke them in Your† anger;	*they were* bringing them to an end, unless You† Yourself‡, LORD, will rebuke them in Your† anger;

2.24 χεῖρά 336⁺260 ≡ ܐܝܕܟ 16h1 10h1 | -ρασ 253 •

23b–26 Seeing the sufferings described above, the psalmist prayed: **Let it be enough, Lord—the weighing down of your hand on Israel.**[65] The Lord's **hand** was heavy on the people (cf. Psa 32.4; 1 Sam 5.6), **weighing** them **down** with afflictions (cf. 2 Cor 1.8) **by bringing** the foreign **nations on** them. Those nations **scoffed** at Israel (see on vv 12–13) and **did not spare** (17.14; cf. Acts 20.29), like the king of Babylon, who destroyed Jerusalem in an earlier generation and did not spare or have compassion (Jer 21.7). They acted mercilessly, **in anger and indignation with wrath** (cf. Eph 4.31).

If such things were allowed to continue, **they** (the Israelites) **will be brought to an end** (the nations will "swallow us up," 8.36). Therefore the psalmist pleads: **Let it be enough, Lord** (cf. 2 Sam 24.16). Amos and David likewise begged the Lord to withdraw His hand before the destruction was complete: "Lord GOD, please cease; how can Jacob stand? for he is small" (Amos 7.5); "Remove Your plague from me; I have been brought to an end by the blow of Your hand . . . . Turn Your gaze from me . . . before I go away and am no more" (Psa 39.10, 13). So also, when the Romans destroyed Jerusalem in the lifetime of those who heard Jesus, "unless the Lord had cut short the days, no flesh would have been saved; but because of the chosen ones whom He chose, He cut short the days" (Mark 13.20; cf. Isa 1.9 ≡ Rom 9.29).

---

[65] **Israel** is the reading of 253 and both Syriac copies, whereas 336⁺260 read "Jerusalem."

The destruction of Israel would be complete **unless You Yourself, Lord, shall rebuke them** (the foreign nations) **in Your anger** (cf. Psa 2.5). Those who have acted **in anger** (vv 25, 28) will themselves reap **anger** from Him—to **rebuke them** (Psa 2.1, 5 ≡ Acts 4.25), to put an end to their evil deeds (Psa 7.6, 9), and to punish them (Rom 2.8).

2.27 [24] ὅτι οὐκ ἐν ζήλει ἐποίησαν ἀλλ' ἐν επιθυμία ψυχῆσ· because *it was* not in zeal *that* they did *it*, but in *the* desire of *their* soul,	ܡܛܠ ܕܠܐ ܗܘܐ ܒܛܢܢܐ ܥܒܕܘ. ܐܠܐ ܐܢ ܒܪ ܡܢ ܪܓܬܐ ܕܢܦܫܐ. because it was not in zeal *that* they did *it*, unless in *the* desire of *their* soul,
2.28 [24] ἔκχεαι τὴν ὀργὴν αὐτ(ῶν) εἰσ ἡμᾶσ ἐν αρπάγματι· to pour out their anger onto us by plundering.	ܕܢܫܕܘܢ ܪܘ ܠܚܡܬܗܘܢ ܥܠܝܢ ܒܚܛܘܦܝܐ. so that they might pour out their anger onto us by plundering.

2.27–28a The nations deserve God's anger (v 26) **because** they opposed Jerusalem's sinners **not in zeal** for the Lord (as Jesus did when He cleansed the temple, John 2.13–17), but rather **in the desire of their soul,**[66] **to pour out their anger onto us** (v 25) **by plundering** (e.g., from the temple, 8.12; cf. Maccabaica 13.34; Heb 10.34).

[25] καὶ μη χρονήσησ ὁ θ(εό)σ τοῦ ἀποδοῦναι αὐτοῖσ εἰσ κεφαλὰσ· And do not wait† a long time, O God, to repay them onto *their* heads,	ܐܢܬ ܕܝܢ ܡܪܝܐ ܠܐ ܬܘܚܪ. ܬܦܪܘܥ ܐܢܘܢ ܒܪܫܗܘܢ. But You†, LORD, may You† not delay; repay† them onto their head,
2.29 [25] τοῦ εἰπεῖν τὴν ὑπερηφανίαν τοῦ δράκοντο(σ) ἐν ‹ἀτιμία›· to say *that* the arrogance of the serpent *is* in dishonor."	‹ܠܡܐܡܪ› ܫܘܒܗܪܗ ܕܬܢܝܢܐ ܒܨܥܪܐ. to say *that the* boasting of the dragon *is* in dishonor."

2.28 μὴ 336⁺260 | ^ καὶ 253 • **2.29** ܠܡܐܡܪ 10h1 ≡ τοῦ εἰπεῖν 253 336⁺260 | ܠܡܐܡܪܘܗ 16h1 • ἀτιμία 260 ≡ ܒܨܥܪܐ 16h1 10h1 | ἀτιμία μιᾶ 336 | αἰτία μία 253 •

2.28b–29 Therefore the psalmist asks God **not** to **wait a long time … to repay.** "Run, LORD, to bring me to safety; LORD, hasten for my help … my God, do not delay"

[66] A **desire** (*epithumia,* Greek ≡ *rgt',* Syriac) for a good thing is good (1 Tim 3.1; Php 1.23; Luke 22.15), but a **desire** to please one's own **soul** (Rev 18.14) with this world's possessions "is a root of all evil things" (1 Tim 6.9–10). The Syriac text states that these sinful nations had no zeal **unless** *('l' 'n)* it was merely a **desire** of their own **soul.** The Greek states that they had no zeal (i.e., for the Lord), **but** rather *(all')* merely a **desire** of their own **soul.** Although the phrasing differs, the point is the same.

(Psa 40.13, 17; 22.19; 38.21–22; Rev 6.10). God's salvation does not delay (Isa 46.13). He acts on behalf of His chosen ones "quickly" (Luke 18.7–8); He helps Jerusalem at the earliest possible moment, "at the turning of the morning" (Psa 46.5). The Lord says, "Behold, I come quickly" (Rev 22.12).

God repays evildoers **onto their** own **heads:** His repayment is directed at the people who have done the wrong. "I have poured out on them My indignation; in the fire of My anger I have brought them to an end; I have rendered their way against their own head" (Ezek 22.31; 11.21; Psa 7.16; Jdg 9.57). "The soul that sins, it shall die ... the wickedness of the wicked one shall be upon him" (Ezek 18.20).

Do not wait a long time ... to say that the arrogance of the serpent is in dishonor.[67] Ever since the creation of the world, God has brought things to pass by "saying" them: whatever He chooses **to say** happens. "God said, "Let there be light"; and there was light" (Gen 1.3). "He said, and it was; He commanded, and it stood" (Psa 33.9). "My word that comes from My mouth will not return to Me empty, but it will do what I delight in, and it will prosper in what I sent it to do" (Isa 55.11; Num 23.19; Ezek 24.14). So this verse entreats the Lord to **say** that what the psalmist desires is so (cf. "Say to my soul, 'I am your salvation,'" Psa 35.3). Until now, the **arrogance** of the evildoer has been triumphant (v 1) and Jerusalem has been in dishonor (vv 5, 23); but at God's decree, the evildoer himself would be **in dishonor** (v 32).

The evildoer is described as a **serpent** or **dragon** (Greek *drakontos;* Syriac *tnyn'*), like Satan himself (Rev 12.9; 20.2) and earthly leaders who follow Satan (e.g., Pharaoh, Ezek 32.2; Nebuchadrezzar, Jer 51.34). Here the reference is specifically to the arrogant sinner mentioned in verse 1, the leader of the foreign nations against Jerusalem, as the following verses (vv 30–33) show.

---

[67] **To say [that] the arrogance of the serpent [is] in dishonor** *(eipein tēn huperēphanian tou drokontos en atimia).* The Greek syntax has puzzled commentators, but there are close structural parallels elsewhere, e.g., "to say [that] a person [is] profane or unclean" (*koinon hē akatharton legein anthrōpon,* Acts 10.28). **To say** something is X is to designate it as X (cf. BDAG 590, §4).

In dishonor is the reading of both Syriac copies *(bṣ'r')* and of 260 in Greek *(en atimia),* whereas 336 reads "in one dishonor" *(en atimia mia)* and 253 reads "in one cause" *(en aitia mia).* Wright mistakenly gives the reading of 253 as *en ai tiamia;* the manuscript's scribe split *aitia* across a page-break (as he did also with *hēmartēkosi* in 9.14), but his accentuation shows that he expected it to be read as one word. The same reading (not broken across a page) occurs in 253's nearest relatives, 655 and 659.

To say is the reading of all Greek copies *(tou eipein)* and of 10h1 in Syriac *(lm'mr),* whereas 16h1 reads "to throw" *(lmrmyw).* The latter difference could have originated (i) in Syriac, either accidentally or if a copyist assumed that *lm'mr* must be a transcriptional error for *lmrmyw;* or (ii) in Greek, if the source of 16h1 was translated from a Greek text that read *tapeinoun* ("make low") or *tou rhiptein* ("to throw") instead of *tou eipein.* Wellhausen (*Die Pharisäer und die Sadducäer,* 133) conjecturally emended the text, proposing that the original Hebrew read *lhmyr* ("to change") instead of *l'mr* ("to say"); this suggestion has no manuscript support in either Greek or Syriac.

The arrogant one is destroyed

Greek	Syriac
2.30 [26] καὶ οὐκ ἐχρόνησα ἕωσ ἔδειξέν μοι ὁ θ(εὸ)σ τὴν ὕβριν αὐτοῦ· And I did not wait a long time until God showed me his disgrace,	ܘܠܐ ܐܫܬܘܚܪܬ ܒܙܒܢܐ ܕܚܘܝ ܠܝ ܡܪܝܐ ܨܥܪܗ. And I was not delayed until the LORD showed to me his dishonor,
ἐκκεκεντημένον ἐπι τ(ῶν) ὀρέων Αἰγύπτου· pierced close by the mountains of Egypt	ܟܕ ܡܡܚܐ ܥܠ ܛܘܪ̈ܐ ܕܡܨܪܝܢ. when *he was* being smitten close by the mountains of Egypt,
ὑπερ ελαχίστου ἐξουδενωμενον ἐπὶ γῆσ καὶ θαλάσσησ· on behalf of *the* least *person,* despised on earth and sea,	ܘܝܬܝܪ ܡܢ ܒܨܝܪܐ ܡܣܠܝ ܥܠ ܐܪܥܐ ܘܥܠ ܝܡܐ. and being rejected more than *the* least *thing* on the earth and on the sea,
2.31 [27] τὸ σῶμα αὐτοῦ ‹διαφερόμενον› ἐπι κυμάτ(ων) ἐν ὕβρει πολλῇ· his body being carried about on *the* waves with much disgrace,	ܘܦܓܪܗ ܕܝܢ ܟܕ ܐܬܐ ܥܠ ܓܠ̈ܠܐ ܒܨܥܪܐ ܣܓܝܐܐ. but when his body *was* going upon the rolling waves with much dishonor,
καὶ οὐκ ἦν ὁ θάπτων· **2.32 [27]** ὅτι ἐξουθένωσεν αὐτὸν ἐν ατιμία· and *there* was no *one* *who was* burying *him,* because he despised him in dishonor.	ܘܠܝܬ ܕܩܒܪ. ܡܛܠ ܕܐܣܠܝܘܗܝ ܒܨܥܪܐ. and there was no *one* who buried *him,* because they rejected *him* in dishonor,

2.31 διαφερόμενον 336 | -μιενον 253 | διεφθαρμένον 260 •

2.30–32a God acted speedily, as He had been asked to do (v 28); the psalmist **did not wait a long time**[68] to see the result. The Lord's people have to wait only "a little time" for their prayers to be answered (Rev 6.11); "before they call, I will answer; while they are yet speaking, I will hear" (Isa 65.24). Then **God showed me**[69] **his** [the

[68] **And I did not wait a long time** (*kai ouk echronēsa,* Greek) ≡ **And I was not delayed** (*wl' 'štwḥrt,* Syriac). Harris-Mingana and Trafton render the Syriac "and I did not delay"; however, intransitive forms of *'ḥr* can mean "be delayed" as well as "delay" (1 Tim 3.15; Acts 20.16; SL 29), and "be delayed" suits the present context better. Greek *chronizō* commonly has such meanings as "spend time," "take time" (LSJ 2008, §§1, 4); Muraoka (737, §3b) suggests that it is here equivalent to "be made to wait long."

[69] **God showed** *(edeixen).* In the Scriptures this expression usually describes a revelation, either by instruction (Exod 25.9 ≡ Heb 8.5; Gen 12.1; Zec 1.9) or in a vision (Gen 41.25; Amos 7.1;

serpent's, v 29] **disgrace**[70]—that is, the **disgrace** that happened to him (as v 31 shows). Those who have dishonored others will themselves be dishonored (4.21, 23; Jer 50.15, 29). "They poured out the blood of the holy ones and the prophets, and blood You have given them to drink" (Rev 16.5–6).

The serpent's **disgrace** consisted of being **pierced close by**[71] **the mountains of Egypt . . . his body being carried about on the waves with much disgrace, and there was no one who was burying him.** Compare the Lord's judgments on Jezebel ("the dogs will eat Jezebel in the allotted inheritance of Jezreel, and there will be none to bury her," 2 Kgs 9.10, 30–37) and on Jehoiakim ("with a donkey's burial he will be buried, dragged and cast out beyond the gates of Jerusalem," Jer 22.18–19; "his corpse will be cast out to the heat by day and to the frost by night," Jer 36.30). At the time of his death, **no one** would be willing to bury him, **because he** (any such person—any potential burier) **despised him with dishonor.**[72] His **body** would simply be left adrift **on the waves,** to be disposed of by anyone who might happen to find it.

The Greek version states that the evildoer was despised **on behalf of the least person.** If even the **least** of God's people should be oppressed, their Master will act on

---

Acts 10.28; Rev 4.1—in which case the things shown tend to be reported in apparent past tenses, since they are shown to the viewer as completed events, even if their fulfillment is still future: Mussies, *Morphology of Koine Greek,* §12.3.3.4; Fanning, *Verbal Aspect in New Testament Greek,* 271–74 and n. 163; Joosten, *Verbal System of Biblical Hebrew,* 208; Rogland, *Alleged Non-Past Uses of Qatal,* §3.4.4). Nowhere else does "God showed me X" appear to be simply equivalent to "X happened."

[70] **Disgrace** *(hubrin).* The word is here used in its passive sense ("shame, insult, mistreatment," BDAG 1022, §2; *ignominie,* Viteau). Its meaning is discussed further in the notes to 1.6. The active sense ("insolence," OTP) would not match Syriac *ṣʿrh* (**dishonor**) here or Greek *atimia* (**dishonor**) in v 32, and would not fit well in v 31 (where even OTP has the passive sense: "shame").

[71] Since the evildoer's body is deposited at sea ("carried about on the waves," v 31), Greek *epi tōn oreōn* ≡ Syriac *ʿl ṭwrʾ* cannot here mean "upon the mountains" ("slain on the mountains of Egypt," APOT), but rather "over against the mountains," **close by the mountains.** Both *epi* and *ʿl* are very frequently used in that sense (examples are listed in Muraoka 263, §I.3; BDAG 363, §2a; TS 2.2886, §1). Compare, e.g., "he sent them away until they were close by the sunset" (17.14); "they camped close by the water" (Maccabaica 9.33; 11.67); "close by the sea . . . on the shore" (John 21.1, 4). Classical historians report that Pompey was killed in a boat offshore near Mount Cassius in Egypt, and that his headless body was unceremoniously thrown out of the boat into the water (it was later burned on the beach): Plutarch, *Pompey,* 79–80; Cassius Dio 42.5.

[72] **Because he** (any such person; see KG 2.1, §352) **despised him with dishonor.** Syriac (like English) uses the plural to convey the same sense: **because they rejected him in dishonor.** The rendering "because He [God] had rejected him with dishonor" (APOT) is much less natural; it would make the verb refer back to a distant subject, skipping over three potential subjects mentioned more recently (**the least person; his body;** and **one who was burying**).

their behalf, and punish the oppressor. "You shall not afflict any widow or orphan ... If, crying, he cries out to Me, hearing, I will hear his cry, and My anger will be kindled, and I will kill you with the sword" (Exod 22.23–24). "Whoever causes one of these little ones who believe in Me to stumble, it is better for him that a donkey's millstone be hung about his neck, and that he be sunk in the depth of the sea .... It is not the will of your Father in the heavens that one of these little ones should be destroyed" (Matt 18.6–14; cf. Eph 6.9; Jas 5.4; Ecc 5.8).

The corresponding Syriac states that the evildoer was rejected **more than the least thing.**[73] The man who had sought to be "lord of earth and sea" (v 33) was degraded below even the **least thing** on earth (cf. Ecc 9.4).

He did not know the greatness of God

Greek	Syriac
[28] οὐκ ελογίσατο ὅτι ἄν(θρωπ)όσ ἐστιν· He did not take account of *the fact* that he was a human being,	ܠܐ ܓܝܪ ܐܬܚܫܒ ܕܒܪܐܢܫܐ ܗܘ̇. for he did not take account that he was a son of man,
καὶ τὸ ὕστερον οὐκ ἐλογίσατο· and he did not take account of *what would be* afterwards.	ܘܚܪܬܐ ܠܐ ܐܬܕܪܟ. and he did not know the end,
2.33 [29] εἶπεν ἐγὼ κ(ύριο)σ γῆσ καὶ θαλάσσησ ἔσομαι He said: "I myself will be lord of earth and sea,"	ܐܡܼܪ ܓܝܪ <ܕܐܼܢܐ> ܐܗܘܐ ܡܪܗ ܕܐܪܥܐ ܘܕܝܡܐ. for he said: "I myself will be lord of the earth and the sea,"

2.33 ܕܐܼܢܐ 10h1 ≡ ἐγὼ 253 336^{+}260 | ܕܐܼܠܐ 16h1 •

2.32b–33a The leader of the nations **did not take account of** his limitations. He thought it was in his own power to **be lord of earth and sea.** (Both in Greek and in Syriac, there is an emphatic pronoun here: **I myself will be** this.) He did not reflect **that he was** merely **a human being,** and he did not consider what future every human being must face (**what would be afterwards**). Someone who receives great blessings (power, security, wealth) may easily forget the Source of those blessings, and think they are due to "my power and the strength of my hand" (Deut 8.7–18; Prov 30.8–9; Hos 13.6; Isa 10.13–14). That was the mistake made by ancient Babylon: "You said, 'I will be a queen'; you did not take these things to heart, you did not remember its end" (Isa 47.7). It was the mistake made by the ruler of Tyre: "Your heart is lifted up, and you have said, 'I am a god, I sit in the seat of God.' ... You are a human being and not a god, but you have placed your heart as the heart of God .... Will you say, 'I am God,' before the face of those who kill you? But you are a human being, and not a

[73] **On behalf of the least person** is Greek *huper elachistou.* **More than the least thing** is Syriac *ytyr mn bṣyr',* which would correspond to Greek *huper elachiston.*

god, in the hand of the one who pierces you" (Ezek 28.2, 9). It was the mistake made even by Israel: "You became fat, you became thick, you became covered with flesh; and he abandoned the God who made him, and scorned the God of his salvation .... Oh that they were wise, understood this, discerned their end!" (Deut 32.15, 29). "In all your words, remember your end, and to lasting time you will not sin" (Sir 7.36).

Greek	Syriac
καὶ οὐκ ἐπέγνω· ὅτι ὁ θ(εὸ)σ μέγασ and he did not know that God *is* great,	ܘܠܐ ܝܕܥ ܕܡܪܝܐ ܗܘ ܐܠܗܐ. and he did not know that the LORD is God,
κραταιὸσ ἐν ἰσχύει αὐτοῦ τῇ μεγάλῃ· mighty in His great strength.	ܪܒܐ ܘܚܣܝܢܐ ܘܫܠܝܛܐ. great and powerful and strong,
2.34 [30] αὐτὸσ βασιλεὺσ ἐπὶ τ(ῶν) οὐ(ρα)νῶν He *is* King over the heavens,	ܘܗܘܝܘ ܡܠܟܐ ܥܠ ܫܡܝܐ ܘܥܠ ܐܪܥܐ. and He is the King over the heaven and over the earth,
καὶ κρίνων βασιλεῖσ καὶ ἀρχᾶσ· and *is* judging kings and rulers,	ܘܕܐܶܢ ܡ̈ܠܟܘܬܐ ܘܪ̈ܫܢܐ. and *is* judging the kingdoms and the rulers,
2.35 [31] ὁ ἀνιστῶν ἐμὲ εἰσ δόξαν the *One* who raises me up to glory,	ܗܘ ܕܡܩܝܡ ܠܝ ܒܬܫܒܘܚܬܐ. the *One* who raises me up in glory,
καὶ κοιμίζων ὑπερηφάνουσ· εἰσ ἀπώλιαν αἰῶνοσ ἐν ατιμία and who lays arrogant *ones* asleep to lasting destruction in dishonor,	ܘܡܕܡܟ ܠܫܒܗܪ̈ܢܐ. ܠܐ ܒܫܥܬܐ ܐܠܐ ܠܥܠܡ ܒܨܥܪܐ. and who makes boastful *ones* sleep, not in a moment but to lasting time, in dishonor,
ὅτι οὐκ ἔγνωσαν αὐτὸν· because they did not know Him.	ܡܛܠ ܕ‹ܠܐ› ܝܕܥܘܗܝ. because they did not know Him.

2.35 ܕܠܐ ܝܕܥܘܗܝ 10h1 ≡ οὐκ ἔγνωσαν αὐτὸν 253 336⁺260 | ܕܝܕܥܘܗܝ 16h1 •

2.33b–35 He did not know that God is great (Greek), **that the LORD is God** (Syriac).[74] What is known about God is evident to all (Rom 1.19, 21)—yet many people do "not think fit to have God in their knowledge" (Rom 1.28; 1 Cor 15.34; Job 21.14). "Do you not know? Do you not hear? Has it not been told to you from the beginning? Have you not understood from the foundations of the earth? He is the

[74] Wright transposed the line *kratаios en ischu[e]i autou tē megalē* (**mighty in His great strength**) to the end of v 32 (immediately following **he did not take account of what would be afterwards**). This emendation has no basis in any of the manuscripts (Greek or Syriac) and is probably a typographical accident.

One who sits above the circle of the earth, and its inhabitants are like grasshoppers ... who sets rulers for nothing, and makes the earth's judges as emptiness" (Isa 40.21–23). He is the One who is truly **Lord of earth and sea,** and **King over the heavens (and over the earth,** Syriac). "You rule over the lifting up of the sea .... The heavens are Yours, also the earth is Yours; the world and its fullness, You Yourself have founded them" (Psa 89.9, 11; Job 38.4–38; Mark 4.41). "I know that the LORD is great, and our Lord beyond all gods. The LORD has done all that He has pleased, in the heavens and in the earth, in the seas and all the depths" (Psa 135.5–6).

He is the "King of kings" (1 Tim 6.15), the **King ... judging** all lesser **kings and rulers** (a power that He has given to His Son, John 5.22; Acts 17.31; Rev 17.14). "God is the judge; this person He makes low, and this person He raises on high" (Psa 75.4–7). He **raises me**[75] **up to glory,** as He raised up His servants David (Acts 13.22), Solomon (1 Kgs 8.20), and Jesus Himself (Acts 3.22, 26), whereas He **lays arrogant ones asleep**[76] **to lasting destruction in dishonor, because they did not know Him.** "Those who do not know God ... will pay the penalty of lasting destruction, away from the face of God and from the glory of His strength" (2 Thes 1.8–9; Psa 79.6).

See the Lord's judgment, and bless Him

Greek	Syriac
2.36 [32] καὶ νῦν ἴδετε οἱ μεγιστάνεσ τῆσ γ(ῆ)σ τὸ κρίμα τοῦ κ(υρίο)υ·	ܘܗܫܐ ܚܙܘ ܪ̈ܘܪܒܢܝܗ̇ ܕܐܪܥܐ ܕܝܢܗ ܕܡܪܝܐ.
And now, O great men of the earth, see[pl] the Lord's judgment,	And now, great *one*s of the earth, see[pl] the LORD's judgment,
ὅτι μέγασ βασιλεὺσ καὶ δίκαιοσ κρίνων τὴν ὑπ' ουρανὸν·	ܡܛܠ ܕܡܠܟܐ ܗܘ ܙܕܝܩܐ. ܘܕܐܢ ܠܕܠܬܚܬ ܡܢ ܟܠܗ̇ ܫܡܝܐ.
because *He is* a great King and righteous, judging the *earth* under heaven.	because He is the righteous King, and *is* judging what *is* beneath all of heaven.

2.36 One of the earth's great men has suffered a terrible judgment (vv 30–35); now all other **great men of the earth** are urged to **see the Lord's judgment,** so that they may fear (v 37) to do what their predecessor did (Ezek 18.14; Psa 52.5–6; 40.1–4; 58.10–11; 64.9; Wis 6.2–10). If they are **great,** He is not only **great** but also **righteous** (Rev 15.3; Psa 9.4); and if they are great in the **earth,** He is the One **judging** that **earth.**[77]

---

[75] **Me** may be the collective voice of God's people (as in the previous psalm), since it stands in contrast with the **arrogant ones** as a whole. See the preliminary comments on this psalm.

[76] **Who lays ... asleep** (Greek *koimizōn* ≡ Syriac *mdmk*) is "a striking word" (Ryle-James 27). Those who sin become spiritually sick and die ("fall asleep," *koimōntai* ≡ *ddmkyn,* 1 Cor 11.30). To be cleansed of our sins, it is necessary to "wake" from spiritual sleep "and rise up from the dead" (Eph 5.14; Rom 13.11–12; 1 Thes 5.6).

[77] **The [earth] under heaven** *(tēn hup' ouranon).* The subject of the feminine singular article *tēn* is the feminine singular noun *gēs* ("earth") in the line above (*die [Erde] unter dem Himmel,* Zöckler)—as in Job 1.7, LXX (*tēn gēn . . . tēn hup' ouranon,* "the earth . . . the [earth] under heaven").

"He has set up His throne for judgment, and He Himself judges the world in righteousness" (Psa 9.7–8; Rev 19.1–2).

2.37 [33] εὐλογεῖτε τὸν θ(εό)ν οἱ φοβούμενοι τὸν κ(ύριο)ν ἐν επιστίμη· Bless[pl] God, O *those* who fear the Lord with understanding,	ܒܪܟܘ ܠܡܪܝܐ ܗܘܢ ܕܕܚܠܝܢ ܡܢ ܡܪܝܐ ܒܐܣܟܡܐ. Bless[pl] the LORD, those who fear the LORD in the *right* manner,
ὅτι τὸ ἔλεοσ κ(υρίο)υ ἐπὶ τοὺσ φοβουμένουσ αὐτὸ(ν)· μετα κρίματο(σ) because the Lord's mercy *is* on those who fear Him with judgment,	ܡܛܠ ܕܪ̈ܚܡܘܗܝ ܕܡܪܝܐ ܥܠ ܕܕ̈ܚܠܘܗܝ ܒܕܝܢܐ. because the LORD's compassion *is* on *those* who fear Him with judgment,
2.38 [34] τοῦ διαστεῖλαι ἀνα μέσων δικαίου καὶ ἁμαρτωλοῦ· to make a distinction between *the* righteous *one* and *the* sinner,	ܠܡܦܪܫ ܒܝܬ ܙܕܝ̈ܩܐ ܘܥܘ̈ܠܐ. to make a separation between the righteous *ones* and the unjust *ones*,
ἀποδοῦναι ἁμαρτωλοῖσ εἰσ τὸν αἰῶνα κατὰ τὰ ἔργα αὐτ(ῶν)· to repay sinners to lasting time in accordance with their works,	ܠܡܦܪܥ ܠܥܘ̈ܠܐ ܠܥܠܡ ܐܝܟ ܥܒ̈ܕܝܗܘܢ. to repay the unjust *ones* to lasting time in accordance with their deeds,
2.39 [35] καὶ ἐλεῆσαι δίκαιον ἀπὸ ταπεινώσεωσ ἁμαρτωλοῦ· and to have mercy on the righteous one from the humiliation of the sinner,	ܘܠܡܚܣ ܠܙܕܝ̈ܩܐ ܡܢ ܡܘܟܟܐ ܕܥܘ̈ܠܐ. and to have mercy toward the righteous *ones* from the humiliation of the unjust *ones*,
καὶ ἀποδοῦναι ἁμαρτωλῶ ἀνθῶν ἐποίησεν δικαίω· and to repay the sinner because of what he did to the righteous one,	ܘܠܡܦܪܥ ܠܥܘ̈ܠܐ ܚܠܦ ܕܥܒܪ ܙܕܩܐ. and to repay the unjust *ones* because he transgressed righteousness,

2.37 As in the Psalter 135.20, **those who fear the Lord** are commanded to **bless** Him (*eulogeite,* "speak well of" Him; v 41). Their **fear** of Him is a fear **in the right manner** (Syriac),[78] **with understanding** (Greek) and **with judgment:** "The fear of the LORD is the beginning of wisdom, and the knowledge of the Holy One is understanding" (Prov 9.10; Psa 111.9–10). Those who fear Him with **understanding** and **judgment**

[78] **In the right manner** (Syriac *b'skm'*) ≡ Greek *euschēmonōs,* "in a good manner," "fittingly" (Rom 13.13; TS 1.308, §2; SL 74, §1b).

hate evil and turn away from it (Prov 14.16; 8.13; 16.6), walking instead in uprightness (Prov 14.2). "Having therefore these promises, beloved ones, let us cleanse ourselves from every defilement of flesh and spirit, completing holiness in the fear of God" (2 Cor 7.1).

The Lord's mercy is on those who fear Him, in every generation (Luke 1.50; Psa 103.11, 17); He takes pleasure in them (Psa 147.11) and saves their soul from death (Psa 33.18–19).

2.38–39 The Lord's mercy (v 37) is not "to kill the righteous with the wicked" (Gen 18.25) but **to make a distinction between**[79] them (Mal 3.18): **to have mercy on the righteous one,** but **to repay sinners to lasting time in accordance with their works** (Rom 2.5–8), including the works that they have done **to the righteous one** ("it is a righteous thing, with God, to repay affliction to those who afflict you," 2 Thes 1.6–7). Both blessing the righteous and punishing the wicked are acts of God's mercy (He saved His people Israel "because His lovingkindness is to lasting time," and He destroyed their enemies "because His lovingkindness is to lasting time," Psa 136.13–18).

The humiliation of the sinner *(tapeinōseōs hamartōlou)* is often taken to be the humiliation inflicted by the sinner (Ryle-James 29); but in Biblical Greek *tapeinōsis* always takes the genitive of the person who suffers the humiliation, not the person who inflicts it (Luke 1.48; Neh 9.9; Psa 22.21; etc.). Therefore, **the humiliation of the sinner** must be the humiliation suffered by the sinner (cf. Jas 1.10: let the rich man exult "in his humiliation [*tapeinōsei autou*], because like a flower of grass he will pass away"). The righteous one is shown mercy **from** *(apo)* that humiliation, i.e., he is shown mercy by being separated from it—as, conversely, the sinner is punished by being separated from *(apo)* the face and glory of God (2 Thes 1.9; cf. BDAG 105, §1e; Buttmann 277).

2.40 [36] ὅτι χρηστὸ(σ) ὁ κ(ύριο)σ τοῖσ ἐπικαλουμένοισ αὐτὸν ἐν ὑπομονῇ· because the Lord is kind to those who call on Him with endurance,	ܡܛܠ ܕܒܣܝܡ ܗ̇ܘ ܡܪܝܐ ܠܐܝܠܝܢ ܕܩܪܝܢ ܠܗ ܒܡܣܝܒܪܢܘܬܐ. because the LORD is kind to those who call to Him with endurance,
ποιῆσαι κατὰ τὸ ἔλεοσ αὐτοῦ τοῖσ ὁσίοισ αὐτοῦ· to do in accordance with His mercy to His lovingkind ones,	ܠܡܥܒܕ ܐܝܟ ܪ̈ܚܡܘܗܝ ܠܚܣ̈ܝܘܗܝ. to do in accordance with His compassion to His lovingkind *ones*,

[79] **Between.** *Ana mesōn* (the reading of 253) is simply a spelling variant of *ana meson* (336*260). The Greek letters *o* and *ō* are often treated as interchangeable in manuscripts of this period (see the introduction to this commentary).

παρεστάναι δια παντὸσ ἐνώπιον αὐτοῦ ἐν ἰσχύει·	ܠܡܩܡ ܩܕܡܘܗܝ ܒܟܠܙܒܢ ܒܚܝܠܐ.
for them to stand nearby through all time in His sight with strength.	for them to stand before Him in every time with power.

2.40 The Lord is kind to those who call on Him with endurance. When God's people suffer affliction from evildoers (v 39), "the one who endures to the end ... will be saved" (Matt 10.22). He will bless those who patiently endure hardship (Rom 2.7; 2 Thes 1.4–5; Heb 10.36; Jas 5.11) while they **call on Him** without ceasing (Luke 18.1–8; Eph 6.18). He will **do in accordance with His mercy to His lovingkind ones** (Greek *hosiois* ≡ Syriac *ḥswhy;* see the comments on Maccabaica 2.42; 7.17): "with a lovingkind one You show Yourself lovingkind" (Psa 18.25); "the merciful . . . shall receive mercy" (Matt 5.7). The result is that they will **stand nearby**[80] **through all time** ("to lasting time and still more," 9.20; 11.9) **in His sight** (those who endure will "stand in the sight of" the Lord Jesus, Luke 21.36) **with strength.** "The LORD gives strength to His people" (Psa 29.11); that is what enables them to endure (Col 1.11; Isa 40.29–31; Eph 6.10).

2.41 [37] εὐλογητὸσ κ(ύριο)σ εἰσ τὸν αἰῶνα ἐνώπιον δούλων αὐτοῦ:	ܒܪܝܟ ܗܘ ܡܪܝܐ ܠܥܠܡ ܡܢ ܥܒܕܘܗܝ.
Blessed *be the* Lord to lasting time in *the* sight of His slaves.	Blessed is the LORD to lasting time by His slaves.

2.41 Blessed is the Lord to lasting time in the sight [*enōpion*] **of His slaves** (Greek)—**by** [*mn*] **His slaves** (Syriac). In His sight, angels and elders and living creatures are constantly saying: "Blessing ... be to our God to lasting times of lasting times" (Rev 7.12). And His **slaves** on earth (see the footnote to Maccabaica 4.30) are called to join with them (Psa 111.1) in blessing Him at all times, now (Psa 34.1; 146.1–2) and always (Psa 145.1–2; 1 Thes 4.17; Rev 7.9–17). He is "blessed from lasting time and to lasting time" (Psa 41.13; 2 Cor 11.31).

Psalm 3

This psalm is very closely linked with the last section of its predecessor (2.36–41). It begins where that psalm ends, with an exhortation to bless God (v 1) for the righteousness of His judgments (vv 3–4), which distinguish between the righteous person and the sinner (vv 14–16).

---

[80] **Stand nearby** (*parestanai,* an intransitive use of the verb: see TDNT 5.837–41; BDAG 778–79, §2; Muraoka 535, §II); the Syriac rendering is **stand before** *(mqm qdm)*. Under the old covenant, the Levites were appointed "to stand [*-estanai*] nearby [*par-*] before the Lord to serve" Him (Deut 10.8, LXX; *nqwm qdm,* Syr). God "will raise us up with Jesus, and will set us nearby Himself [*parastēsei*] together with you" (2 Cor 4.14), just as Gabriel is "standing nearby [*parestēkōs*] in the sight of God" (Luke 1.19; *q'm qdm,* Syr).

In the Greek, Psalm 3 starts by addressing the psalmist's soul (**are you sleeping** [*hupnois,* singular] **. . . and not blessing** [*eulogeis,* singular], v 1), then speaks to a plurality (**Psalm** [*psalate,* plural] **a new hymn,** v 2), then returns to the singular (**Psalm** [*psalle,* singular] **. . . be alert** [*grēgorēson,* singular], v 2). In view of the close connection with Psalms 1–2, this suggests that the one addressed may again be Jerusalem—a collective entity, both singular and plural (see the preliminary comments on Psalm 2). Similarly, the following verses speak of God's people in collective terms, sometimes as **the righteous one** [*dikaios,* singular], sometimes as **righteous ones** [*dikaioi,* plural] (vv 3–8).[81]

The present psalm is constructed like Psalm 1 of the Hebrew Psalter. It describes the way of the **righteous one** (vv 3–10; cf. Psa 1.1–3), and then, more briefly, the way of the **sinner** (vv 11–14; cf. Psa 1.4–5), finishing with a description of their contrasting futures (vv 15–16; cf. Psa 1.6). In the closing lines, even the wording of the two psalms becomes similar: "Wicked ones will not stand in judgment" (Psa 1.5) ≡ **the sinner . . . will not be raised up** (v 13). "The LORD knows the way of righteous ones" (Psa 1.6) ≡ **He shall watch over the righteous ones** (v 14). "The way of wicked ones is destroyed" (Psa 1.6) ≡ **the destruction of the sinner will be to lasting time** (v 13). The fourteenth of these Eighteen Psalms has a similar structure (see the headnote to its commentary).

Sing to the Lord

3.0 [0] Ψαλμὸϲ τ(ῷ) Cωλωμῶν περι δικαίω(ν): A psalm belonging to Solomon, concerning *the* righteous ones.	
3.1 [1] Ἵνα τί ὑπνοῖσ ψυχὴ καὶ ‹οὐκ εὐλογεῖσ› τὸν κ(ύριο)ν· Why are you† sleeping, *my* soul, and not blessing† the Lord?	ܠܡܢܐ ܕܡܟܬܝ ܢܦܫܝ ܘܠܐ ܡܒܪܟܬܝ ܠܡܪܝܐ. Why *are* you† sleeping, my soul, and not blessing to the LORD?

3.1 οὐκ εὐλογεῖσ 253^{c} $336^{+}260$ ≡ ܠܐ ܡܒܪܟܬܝ 16h1 10h1 | οὐλογεῖσ 253* •

3.1[82] The psalmist rebukes his **soul** for **sleeping** (see the footnote on 2.35) instead of **blessing the Lord.** "Let us not sleep, just as the rest do, but let us keep alert and be sober" (1 Thes 5.6; Eph 5.14). "To wake out of sleep" is to "cast off the works of

---

[81] Compare, e.g., "And now, Israel, hear [Hebrew *šmʿ* ≡ Greek *akoue,* singular] . . . that you may live [Hebrew *tḥyw* ≡ Greek *zēte,* plural]" (Deut 4.1; and see König 4.232–37). In the Syriac version of this psalm there are the same fluctuations between singular and plural in vv 3–8, but all the verbs in vv 1–2 are singular.

[82] In the Greek copies (but not in the Syriac), the psalm is superscribed **A psalm belonging to Solomon, concerning the righteous ones.**

darkness" and "put on the armor of light" (Rom 13.11–12)—in contrast to the watchmen described by Isaiah, who "are blind; all of them do not know; all of them are silent dogs; they cannot bark—dreaming, lying down, loving to sleep" (Isa 56.10). We have good reason to "bless the Lord at every time . . . continually" (Psa 34.1), "all the day" (Psa 71.8), "every day . . . to lasting time and continuing time" (Psa 145.1–2). "Let us offer up a sacrifice of praise to God continually, the fruit of lips that confess His name" (Heb 13.15), "giving thanks always for all things" to Him (Eph 5.20).

Greek	Syriac
3.2 [1] ὕμνον ‹καινὸν› ‹ψάλατε› τῷ θ(ε)ῷ τῷ αἰνετῷ· Psalm[pl] a new hymn to the God *who is* praiseworthy.	ܬܫܒܘܚܬܐ ܚܕܬܐ ܠܐܠܗܐ. A new hymn to God:
[2] ψάλλε καὶ γρηγόρησον ἐπι τὴν γρηγόρησιν αὐτοῦ· Psalm† and be alert† to attain His alertness,	ܙܡܪ، ܘܐܬܬܥܝܪ، ܒܬܥܝܪܘܬܗ. sing† and be awakened† in His wakefulness,
ὅτι ἀγαθὸσ ψαλμὸσ τῷ θ(ε)ῷ ἐξ αγαθῆσ καρδίασ· because a good psalm to God *is* out of a good heart.	ܡܛܠ ܕܙܡܝܪܬܐ ܛܒܬܐ ܠܐܠܗܐ ܡܢ ܠܒܐ ܛܒܐ. because a good psalm to God *is* from a good heart.

3.2 καινὸν 336⁺260 ≡ ܚܕܬܐ 16h1 10h1 | καὶ αἶνον 253 • ψάλατε 336⁺260 | ψάλλετε 253 •

3.2 Psalm a new hymn. God's people are commanded constantly to "sing a new song to the LORD" (Psa 96.1–2; 98.1; Isa 42.10; Rev 14.3); "He has set a new song in my mouth, praise to our God" (Psa 40.3). The song is not **new** in the sense that its words have never been sung before (if so, how could the command be obeyed when the song was sung for the second time?). Rather, just as the Lord's mercies "are new every morning" (Lam 3.23; Zep 3.5), so we are to offer new praise (**a new hymn**)[83] to Him continually.[84] No one can sing thus except those who have a **good heart:** "no one was able to learn" the "new song" except those who were purchased by the Lamb (Rev 14.3). "The good person, out of the good treasure of his heart, brings forth good, and the evil person, out of the evil treasure, brings forth evil; for out of the abundance of his heart, his mouth speaks" (Luke 6.45). So **out of a good heart** will come a **good psalm**—whereas out of a sinful heart will come curses (v 11).

[83] Greek *humneō* (**hymn**) and Syriac *šbḥ* correspond to Hebrew *hll,* "praise" (Heb 2.12 ≡ Psa 22.22).

[84] "A new song implies the continual recurrence of fresh reasons and occasions for the praise of God" (Alexander, *Psalms,* 1.261). "Every new deliverance requires 'a new song'" (Horne, *Psalms,* 1.266).

God's people are not to sleep in spirit (v 1) but to **be alert** (1 Thes 5.6) in blessing Him (cf. "Persevere earnestly in prayer, being alert in it with thanksgiving," Col 4.2). In that way, they will **attain**[85] **His alertness. His alertness** is both the alertness that He requires, and the alertness that He possesses: He Himself is always alert ("the One who keeps Israel does not slumber, and does not sleep," Psa 121.4), and He requires His people to be like Himself in that respect (Col 4.2; 1 Pet 5.8; etc.). He has "pierced" them "like a goad of a horse" to make them alert (16.4).

God is **praiseworthy** in all things (Rev 4.11; 1 Chr 29.11–13; Rom 11.36): His judgments are to be received "with confession and acknowledgement of His righteousness," as the following verses show (vv 3–5).

The righteous one looks to God and is cleansed from sin

Greek	Syriac
3.3 [3] δίκαιοι μνημονεύσουσιν δια παντὸσ τοῦ κ(υρίο)υ· Righteous *one*s will be mindful of the Lord through all *time;*	ܘܙܕܝ̈ܩܐ ܒܟܠܙܒܢ ܢܬܕܟܪܘܢ ܠܡܪܝܐ. At every moment the righteous *one*s will be mindful of the LORD;
ἐν ἐξομολογήσει καὶ δικαιώσει τὰ κρίματα τοῦ κ(υρίο)υ· with confession and acknowledgement of *His* righteousness *they will be* *mindful of* the Lord's judgments.	ܒܬܘܕܝܬܐ ܘܒܙܕܝܩܘܬܐ ܕܝ̈ܢܘܗܝ ܕܡܪܝܐ. with confession and with righteousness *they will be* *mindful of* the LORD's judgments.

3.3 Righteous ones will be mindful of the Lord through all time, day and night (Psa 1.2; Josh 1.8); they do not forget His dealings (Psa 103.2) or His word (Psa 119.16).

With confession and acknowledgement of His righteousness they will be mindful of the Lord's judgments.[86] A **confession** (Greek *exomologēsis* ≡ Syriac *twdyt'*) is a

---

[85] **Be alert** *epi* **His alertness** means "be alert for the purpose of His alertness," "be alert in order to attain His alertness," as the corresponding phrase in 16.4 shows. (Cf., e.g., "he was led as a sheep *epi* [for the purpose of] slaughter," Acts 8.32; BDAG 366, §11; Muraoka 267, §III.4f.) "Be alert because of His alertness" ("keep awake for he is awake," Wright) is not a possible rendering (it would require *epi* plus dative [BDAG 365, §6c; Muraoka 266, §II.6]—not *epi* plus accusative). Nor is "be aware of how he is aware of you" (OTP)—which also misses the contrast with **sleeping** (v 1). The Syriac rendering is **be awakened in** [*b*-] **His wakefulness.**

[86] In the Greek, the verb **will be mindful** *(mnēmoneusousin)* has two objects (Muraoka 465, §1). The first, **of the Lord** *(tou kuriou),* is genitive (as usual; e.g., Luke 17.32; Heb 13.7; BDAG 655, §1a), but the second, **judgments** *(ta krimata),* has to be accusative (as, e.g., in Matt 16.9; 1 Thes 2.9; BDAG 655, §1b; BDF §175; KG 2.1, §417.5), because a genitive would naturally be misread as "acknowledgement of the righteousness of the Lord's judgments." The Syriac is somewhat similar. The verb's first object is marked by the preposition *l*-, but in the second clause, the preposition as well as the verb is omitted (cf., e.g., "You have trodden in the sea with Your horses, and [You have trodden in] the gathering of many waters," Hab 3.15, Syr).

"public declaration" (9.12)—in this context, a declaration that God's dealings are righteous (as in 10.7, 16.5; Rom 15.9), i.e., an act of "praise" or "thanksgiving" (APOT). The next few clauses restate and develop the point. The righteous one **will be mindful**—that is, he "will not think little"—**of the Lord's judgments**—that is, "of being disciplined by the Lord." When he has been thus disciplined, "he has acknowledged the Lord to be righteous" (vv 4–5). Those who have suffered under the Lord's hand declare: "I know, LORD, that Your judgments have been in righteousness, and in faithfulness You have afflicted me" (Psa 119.75); "You have been righteous in all that has come upon us; for You have done faithfulness, and we have done evil" (Neh 9.33; Ezra 9.13; Dan 9.7, 14; Lam 1.18; 2 Chr 12.6). That acknowledgement is made repeatedly in these psalms: "I myself will acknowledge You to be righteous, O God… because in Your judgments is Your righteousness" (2.16); "may lovingkind ones acknowledge the judgment of their God to be righteous" (4.9); "I acknowledged God to be righteous in His judgments" (8.7); "God was acknowledged to be righteous in His judgments" (8.27); "we have acknowledged Your honorable name to be righteous… because You are the God of righteousness, who judges Israel with discipline" (8.31–32); Israel was scattered among the nations "in order that You might be acknowledged to be righteous, O God… because You are the righteous judge" (9.3–4); "our Lord is righteous and lovingkind in His judgments… and Israel will praise the name of the Lord with gladness, and lovingkind ones will confess it" (10.6–7).

3.4 [4] οὐκ ὀλιγορήσει δίκαιοσ	ܠܐ ܢܒܣܪ ܙܕܝܩܐ
παιδευόμενο(σ) ὑπὸ τοῦ κ(υρίο)υ·	ܕܡܬܪܕܐ ܡܢ ܡܪܝܐ.

(On the presence or absence of *l-* in such cases, see Nöldeke §§288, 290; Duval §342.) Biblical Syriac, unlike Greek, had no noun meaning specifically **acknowledgement of righteousness** ("justification"), so the translator used here the simpler term *zdyqwt'* (**righteousness**) instead.

Several other ways of construing the verse have been proposed. (i) The second clause has been construed as "in confession and acknowledgment of [His] righteousness [are] the Lord's judgments" (cf. Harris-Mingana). But in such a construction, the confession would have to be the Lord's own confession, not anyone else's (compare, e.g., "in faithfulness [is] all His work," Psa 33.4). (ii) Alternatively, *dikaiōsei* has been construed as a verb, in which case the verse would read: "Righteous ones will be mindful of the Lord through all time with confession, and he will acknowledge the Lord's judgments to be righteous" (cf. Geiger, *Psalter Salomo's,* 35, 108). The shift from plural (they "will be mindful") to singular ("he will acknowledge") may look strange, but it certainly occurs by the start of the next verse ("The righteous one will not think little…"). However, this is not a possible way of construing the corresponding Syriac. (iii) The second clause has been construed as "with confession and acknowledgement of the righteousness [of] the Lord's judgments" (cf. APOT). But in that case **judgments** would have to be genitive (like *hēmōn* in Rom 4.25); and again the Syriac cannot be construed thus.

253⁺655⁺659 read *mnēmoneusousin* (**will be mindful**); 336⁺260⁺629⁺769 read *mnēmoneuousi[n]* ("are mindful"). The error arose in minuscule script, in which the extra *-s-* is very easily missed (indeed, no previous modern collator has noticed it). The future tense is confirmed by v 4.

The righteous *one* will not think little of being disciplined by the Lord;	The righteous *one* will not regard lightly that he is disciplined by the LORD,
ἡ εὐδοκία αὐτοῦ διὰ παντὸσ ἔναντι κ(υρίο)υ·	ܡܛܠ ܕܨܒܝܢܗ ܒܟܠ ܙܒܢ ܩܕܡ ܡܪܝܐ.
his good pleasure *will be* before *the* Lord through all *time.*	because his good pleasure *will be* before the LORD in every time.

3.4 The righteous one will not think little of being disciplined [*paideuomenos*] **by the Lord.** To be **disciplined** is to be trained by correction, in the way that a child *(pais)* is trained by correction (Heb 12.10; Acts 22.3; 7.22; Eph 6.4). "When we are judged, we are disciplined by the Lord, in order that we may not be condemned with the world" (1 Cor 11.32). "Do not think little of the discipline of the Lord, nor faint when you are reproved by Him, for one whom the Lord loves He disciplines" (Heb 12.5–6 ≡ Prov 3.11–12; Rev 3.19; cf. Job 5.17).

His discipline is to be prized (2 Cor 12.10); only a fool would ignore or reject it (Prov 15.5; 17.10; 27.22).

His good pleasure [Greek *eudokia* ≡ Syriac *ṣbynh*] **will be before the Lord through all time.** Instead of slighting or scorning the Lord's discipline, the righteous person is "well pleased" *(eudokō ≡ ṣb')* with it (2 Cor 12.10), and he maintains this **good pleasure** in everything he does **before the Lord** (Luke 1.6, 8) at **all** times.[87] He does not seek his own pleasure (Hebrew *ḥpṣ*), but always delights (Hebrew *'ng*) in the Lord (Isa 58.13–14).

3.5 [5] προσέκοψεν ὁ δίκαιοσ καὶ ἐδικαίωσεν τὸν κ(ύριο)ν·	ܐܬܬܩܠ ܙܕܝܩܐ ܘܙܕܩ ܠܐܠܗܐ.
The righteous *one* has stumbled, and he has acknowledged the Lord to be righteous;	The righteous *one* has stumbled, and he has acknowledged God to be righteous;
ἔπεσεν καὶ ἀποβλέπει τί ποιήσει αὐτῷ ὁ θ(εό)σ·	ܢܦܠ ܘܡܣܟܐ <> ܕܡܢܐ ܢܥܒܕ ܠܗ ܡܪܝܐ.
he has fallen, and he is looking toward what God will do for him;	he has fallen, and *he is* awaiting what the LORD will do for him,

3.5 ܘܡܣܟܐ 10h1 ≡ καὶ ἀποβλέπει 253 336⁺260 | + ܐܝܟܐ 16h1 •

[87] The clause cannot be rendered "his desire is to be always in the Lord's presence" (OTP); that would require at least one verb, and preferably two (e.g., *eudokei stathēnai*). **His good pleasure** might theoretically describe the Lord's good pleasure toward the righteous one (as in Luke 2.14), but that could hardly be the sense here; could the Lord's own **good pleasure** be said to be **before** Himself (cf. Ryle-James 33)?

3.6 [5] ἀποσκοπεύει ὅθεν ἥξει σωτηρία ⸤αὐτοῦ⸥·	ܘܡܣܟܪ ܕܢܚܙܐ ܐܝܟܐ ܢܐܬܐ ܦܘܪܩܢܗ.
he is watching toward *the place* where his salvation will come from.	and looking *to see* which *place* his salvation will come from.

3.6 αὐτοῦ 336⁺260 ≡ 16h1 \| αὐτῶ 253 •

3.5–6 The righteous one has stumbled . . . he has fallen—that is, he has sinned (vv 9, 11–13). "There is no righteous man in the earth who does good and never sins" (Ecc 7.20); "all have sinned and fall short of the glory of God" (Rom 3.23). Indeed, "in many things we all stumble" (Jas 3.2). We stumble when we walk in the darkness, and do not see where we are going (John 11.9–10; 1 Jn 2.10–11); we fall when we do not watch (*blepetō,* "see"; 1 Cor 10.12).

Both a righteous person and a sinner, therefore, may stumble and fall. But after it has happened, the sinner continues sinning and does not get up again (vv 11–13), whereas the **righteous one . . . has acknowledged the Lord to be righteous** (see the comments on v 3). **He is looking toward** [*apoblepei*] **what God will do for him** (cf. 1 Sam 22.3) and **is watching toward** [*aposkopeuei*] **the place where his salvation will come from.** Moses was willing to suffer ill treatment and reproach because "he was looking toward [*apeblepen*] the reward" (Heb 11.25–26); contrast the sinners at the time of the Babylonian captivity, who "watched [*apeskopeusamen*] for a nation that does not save" (Lam 4.17, LXX). To look toward any human for salvation "is worthlessness"; only God can deliver us from evil (Psa 60.11–12; Matt 6.13). When "the steps of a man have been established by the LORD . . . he falls but he is not cast out; for the LORD supports his hand" (Psa 37.23–24; 94.17–18).

3.7 [6] ἀλήθια τ(ῶν) δικαίων παρὰ θ(εο)ῦ σ(ωτῆ)ρ(ο)σ αὐτ(ῶν)·	ܫܪܪܐ ܕܙܕܝ̈ܩܐ ܡܢ ܩܕܡ ܐܠܗܐ ܦܪܘܩܗܘܢ.
The faithfulness of the righteous *ones* *is* from God their Savior;	The faithfulness of the righteous *ones* *is* from before God their Savior;
οὐκ αυλίζεται ἐν οίκω δικαίου ἁμαρτία ἐφ αμαρτίαν·	ܠܐ ܓܝܪ ܒܒܝܬܐ ܕܙܕܝ̈ܩܐ. ܚܛܝܬܐ ܥܠ ܚܛܝܬܐ.
in *the* house of *the* righteous *one,* sin upon sin does not find lodging.	for in the house of the righteous *ones*, sin on sin *is* not being housed,

3.7 In this verse, repeated sin (**sin upon sin,** Isa 30.1; Sir 5.5) is contrasted with **faithfulness** ("steadfastness" [APOT], enduring reliability). **Righteous ones** have the **faithfulness** that comes **from God their Savior,** who saves them (vv 5–6) and cleanses them from their sin (v 10). Therefore, repeated sin (**sin upon sin**) **does not find lodging** with them ("one who practices deceit does not dwell in my house," Psa 101.2–7)—whereas sinners provide a home for multiplied evils (Matt 12.43–45). Having refused **God** as **their Savior**, they pile one **sin upon** another (Rom 1.28–32; Gal 5.19–21; 2 Tim 3.1–5; Sir 34.25–26), increasing in wrongdoing (2 Tim 3.13).

The **righteous one** is concerned not only about his own deeds, but also about those that happen **in his house** (see the comments on v 8). If a sin happens in a region that is under our authority, where we could have prevented it, we ourselves will be held guilty (1 Sam 3.13; cf. Ezek 3.18–19; 2 Jn 10–11; Rev 18.4).

3.8 [7] ἐπισκέπτεται διὰ παντὸσ τὸν οἶκον αὐτοῦ ὁ δίκαιοσ· Through all *time* the righteous *one* is watching over his house,	ܡܛܠ ܕܒܟܠ ܙܒܢ ܚܐܪ ܒܒܝܬܗ ܕܙܕܝܩܐ. because at every time *He is* looking on *the* house of the righteous *one,*
τοῦ ἐξάραι ἀδικίαν ἐν παραπτώματι αὐτοῦ· to take away unrighteousness in his transgression.	ܠܡܚܛܐ ܚܛܗܐ ܕܣܘܪܚܢܘܬܗ. to blot out *the* sins of his transgressions,

3.8 Because all of us commit **transgression** "in many things" (see the comments on vv 5–6), constant watchfulness is necessary **to take away unrighteousness.** The Syriac version speaks of God's watchfulness (**He is looking on the house of the righteous one, to blot out transgressions**); the Greek version speaks of the righteous person's watchfulness (**the righteous one is watching over his house, to take away transgression**). Both statements are true. God is constantly watching over His people to remove their sins: "The eyes of the LORD are toward righteous ones, and His ears toward their cry for help" (Psa 34.15 ≡ 1 Pet 3.12); "if we confess our sins, He is faithful and righteous to forgive us the sins, and cleanse us from all unrighteousness" (1 Jn 1.9). At the same time, the righteous themselves are watching constantly to remove sin, both from themselves (one who "has watched, and has turned away from all transgression … will live," Ezek 18.28; Lam 3.40; 2 Cor 13.5) and from their households (Gen 18.19; 35.2; Job 1.5; Josh 24.15; Deut 6.6–7; Eph 6.4).

3.9 [8] ἐξιλάσατο περι ἀγνοίασ ἐν νηστεία· καὶ ταπεινώσει ψυχὴν ‹αὐτοῦ·› He has made atonement concerning *his* ignorance with fasting, and he will humble his soul,	ܘܦܪܩ ܢܦܫܗ. ܒܡܕܡ ܕܚܛܐ ܒܠܐ ܝܕܥܬܐ ܒܨܘܡܐ ܘܒܡܟܝܟܘܬܐ. and he has saved his soul in *the* thing that he sinned without knowing *it,* by fasting and by humiliation,
3.10 [8] καὶ ὁ κ(ύριο)σ καθαρίζει· πᾶν ἄνδρα ὅσιον καὶ τὸν οἶκον αὐτοῦ· and the Lord is cleansing every lovingkind man and his house.	ܘܡܪܝܐ ܡܕܟܐ ܟܠ ܓܒܪ ܚܣܝܐ. ܘܠܒܝܬܗ. and the LORD *is* cleansing every lovingkind man and his house.

3.9 αὐτοῦ· 336⁺260 ≡ 16h1 | > 253 •

3.9 No sin can ever be cleansed without **atonement.** This applies even to a deed of **ignorance**—that is, a sin committed when the sinner "did not know it" (Lev 5.18) and "it was hidden from" his eyes (Lev 4.13; Psa 19.12). "If a soul sins, and does any of all the commands of the LORD that shall not be done, and does not know it, then he is guilty, and shall bear his iniquity" unless atonement is made for him (Lev 5.17–19). It is God who makes atonement for sin (Psa 78.38; 79.9; 65.3; Deut 21.8); people too can make atonement, when they have been "given" the means of atonement by Him (Lev 17.11). Under the old covenant the Lord provided His people with various means of **atonement,** including certain types of animal sacrifices (only if the worshipers were faithful and obedient to the Lord, Mal 1.9–10) and prayer and **fasting** (again, only if the worshipers were faithful and obedient to the Lord, Zec 7.2–10).[88]

Fasting is a way to **humble** one's **soul** (Psa 35.13)[89] by avoiding all food and drink for a time (Est 4.16; Jnh 3.5, 7; Acts 27.33), devoting oneself instead to seeking the Lord in prayer (Dan 9.3; Ezra 8.23; 2 Sam 12.16). Jesus Himself humbled His soul by fasting (Matt 4.2), and after the coming of the new covenant His disciples also fasted (Acts 13.2–3; 14.23), as He had directed (Matt 6.17–18; cf. Luke 5.35). Like any act of obedience to the Lord, fasting is of no value if it is done to be seen by men (Matt 6.16), or in a vain attempt to suppress the flesh (Col 2.20–23), or by people who fail to serve God from the heart (Isa 58.3–7). But people who faithfully sought Him in prayer while humbling their souls with **fasting** obtained **atonement** for sin, both under the old covenant (Dan 9.3, 20–23; Ezra 8.23) and under the new (Acts 9.8–11).

---

[88] This passage certainly says "that piety, through confession, penance [repentance], and fasting can atone for sin"; but it does not say that they can atone for sin "in place of sacrifice" (Atkinson, *I Cried to the Lord,* 195–96). No sin has ever been atoned for without sacrifice (1 Jn 2.2). Like the Eighteen Psalms, the book of Isaiah teaches that confession in prayer could atone for sin (Isa 6.5–7); but we cannot therefore deduce that prayer could atone for sin "in place of" sacrifice (on the contrary, see Isa 19.21; 53.10), or that either prayer or sacrifice could atone for sin without obedience to God's other commands as well (Isa 1.11–20; 66.3–4). This point applies equally to the New Testament Scriptures. When Peter told his hearers to "repent and be baptized . . . for the forgiveness of your sins" (Acts 2.38), he was certainly teaching that repentance and baptism can atone for sin; but he was not teaching that they can atone for sin "in place of" faith (Rom 4.5–7) and the blood of Jesus (Eph 1.7) and a willingness to forgive others (Matt 6.12, 14–15). No single statement about atonement ever encompasses every aspect of the subject; nor could it reasonably be expected to do so.

[89] The two clauses **he has made atonement . . . with fasting** and **he will humble** [*tapeinōsei*] **his soul** refer to the same event, despite the apparent difference in tenses; in the second clause, the Greek future is used like a Hebrew *wayyiqṭol* (as occasionally happens even in passages not translated from Hebrew, e.g., Rev 4.9–10; cf. MHT 3.86). *Tapeinōsei* could theoretically be construed as a noun ("humiliation," as in the Syriac), but in the Greek version that would leave **his soul** floating (a problem that does not arise in the Syriac, where **his soul** is placed as the object of the verb in the first half of the verse). Gebhardt and Rahlfs emended *psuchēn* (**his soul**) to *psuchēs* ("of his soul"), but that has no manuscript support in either Greek or Syriac.

3.10 The Lord is cleansing every lovingkind man and his house (provided that his **house** has turned away from sin, as described in v 7). The Lord is a God “who takes away iniquity and passes over transgression for the remnant of His inheritance . . . . He will tread our iniquities underfoot, and You will cast all their sins into the depths of the sea” (Mic 7.18–19; Jer 33.8; 1 Jn 1.9; Psa 51.2). **Every** one who is **lovingkind** will receive lovingkindness from Him (see the comments on 2.40).

The sinner stumbles and is destroyed to lasting time

3.11 [9] προσέκοψεν ἁμαρτωλὸσ	ܐܬܬܩܠ ܓܝܪ ܥܘܠܐ
καὶ καταρᾶται ζωὴν αὐτου·	ܘܠܛ ܠܚܝܘܗܝ.
The sinner has stumbled,	For the unjust *one* has stumbled,
and he curses his life,	and he has cursed his life,
τὴν ἡμέραν γενέσεωσ αὐτοῦ·	ܘܠܝܘܡܐ ܕܐܬܝܠܕ ܒܗ.
καὶ ὠδίνασ μ(ητ)ρ(ό)σ·	ܘܠܚܒܠܐ ܕܐܡܗ.
the day of his birth,	and the day in which he was born,
and *his* mother’s birthpangs.	and his mother’s birthpangs.
3.12 [10] πρὸσέθηκεν ἁμαρτίασ	ܘܐܘܣܦ ܚܛܗܐ
ἐφ’ ‹ἁμαρτίασ› τῇ ζωῇ αὐτοῦ·	ܥܠ ܚܛܗܐ ܠܚܝܘܗܝ.
He has added sins	And he has added sins
upon sins to his life.	upon sins to his life;

3.12 ἁμαρτίασ 2° 336⁺260 | -τίαισ 253 • |

3.11–12 Like the righteous person, the **sinner has stumbled** and fallen (v 13; Psa 27.2). But his reaction is quite different. Whereas the righteous person “has acknowledged the Lord to be righteous” and has turned to the Lord for help (3.5–6), the sinner does not; he **curses his life, the day of his birth, and his mother’s birthpangs,** and continues to do evil, adding **sins upon sins to his life.**

The term here translated **curses** (Greek *kataratai* ≡ Syriac *lṭ*) is the opposite of blessing (Rom 12.14; Jas 3.9), and has no reference to foul language. Jesus cursed (*katērasō* ≡ *lṭt*) the barren fig tree when He said: “Never again to lasting time may anyone eat fruit from you” (Mark 11.21, 14). Job “cursed his day” when he said: “May the day perish when I was born” (Job 3.1, 3); nevertheless Job acknowledged the Lord to be righteous (Job 1.21), and was later approved by Him for doing so (Job 42.8). Thus the error described in this passage is not simply that the sinner **curses** (righteous Job and Jesus did so), but that he commits **sins** in his cursing (which righteous Job and Jesus did not) and, instead of making atonement for his sins, persists in them, adding **sins upon sins** (2 Tim 2.16; Matt 12.43–45; Isa 1.5; 30.1; Psa 78.17; 2 Chr 28.22; Ezek 23.14; Hos 13.2; Sir 3.27). Cain added the sin of murder to the sin of unacceptable sacrifice (Gen 4.3–8). Judas Iscariot added the sin of betraying the righteous to the sin of theft (John 12.4–6; 18.2–5). In the book of Revelation, the fourth bowl of God’s wrath caused sinners to curse Him and add still more to their sins:

"they blasphemed God who has power over these plagues, and they did not repent to give Him glory" (Rev 16.8–9).

Greek	Syriac
3.13 [10] ἔπεσεν ὅτι πονηρὸν τὸ πτῶμα αὐτοῦ· καὶ οὐκ ἀναστήσεται He has fallen. Because his fall *is* ruinous, then he will not be raised up.	ܢܦܠ ܘܡܛܠ ܕܒܝܫܐ ܡܦܘܠܬܗ ܘܠܐ ܢܩܘܡ. he has fallen, and because his fall *is* ruinous, then he will not stand.
[11] ἡ ἀπώλεια τοῦ ἁμαρτωλοῦ εἰσ τὸν αἰῶνα· The destruction of the sinner *will be* to lasting time,	ܐܒܕܢܗ ܓܝܪ ܕܥܘܠܐ ܠܥܠܡ ܗܘ. For *the* destruction of the unjust *one* will be to lasting time,
3.14 [11] καὶ οὐ ₍₎ μνησθήσεται ὅταν ἐπισκέπτηται δικαίουσ· and He will not be mindful of *him,* whenever He shall watch over *the* righteous *ones*.	ܘܠܐ ܢܬܕܟܪ ܐܡܬܝ ܕܣܥܪ ܙܕܝܩܐ. and He will not be mindful of *him,* when *He is* looking on the righteous *one.*

3.14 οὐ 336⁺260 | + μὴ 253 •

3.13 The sinner's **fall** is permanent:[90] **he will not be raised up** again (Psa 36.12; 18.38; Amos 8.14), like a stone dropped into a river (Jer 51.63–64). His "inheritance will be Hades and darkness and destruction" (14.6), and that **destruction** will endure **to lasting time** (2.35). "Those who do not know God ... will be punished with judgment—lasting destruction, away from the face of God and from the glory of His strength" (2 Thes 1.8–9; Psa 49.19; Dan 12.2; Matt 25.41, 46).

3.14 Righteous ones suffer discipline at present (v 4), but there will come a time when God will **watch over** *(epi-)* them. The term **watch over** can be used either positively or negatively: God is "watching over" everyone, to bless the righteous and punish the wicked (9.8–10; 10.5; 15.13–15). But in the present context, the term refers specifically to the fact that **He shall watch over the righteous** to do good to them (as in v 8, Syr; 11.2, 7; Luke 1.68, 78; 7.16; Acts 15.14). That will happen because He will **be mindful of** them (5.18): "I know them ... and I give them lasting life" (John 10.27–28; cf. Job 23.10). But **He will not be mindful of** the sinner. "I never knew you; depart from Me, you who work deeds opposed to the Law" (Matt 7.23; 25.12). "The LORD knows the way of righteous ones, but the way of wicked ones is destroyed" (Psa 1.6).

---

[90] The sinner **will not be raised up** because his fall is *ponēron* (Greek) ≡ *byš'* (Syriac), i.e., "grievous" (APOT), "injurious" to the sinner (Muraoka 576, §2; cf. Matt 21.41, Syr)—in this case, injurious beyond remedy (*fatale,* Viteau; cf. Muraoka 576, §2b).

Lasting destruction and lasting life

Greek	Syriac
3.15 [12] αὕτη ἡ μερὶσ τ(ῶν) ἁμαρτωλῶν εἰσ τὸν αἰῶνα·	ܗܕܐ ܗ̇ܝ ܡܢܬܗܘܢ ܕܥܘ̈ܠܐ ܠܥܠܡ.
This *will be* the sinners' portion to lasting time,	This will be *the* unjust *ones*' portion to lasting time,
3.16 [12] οἱ δὲ φοβούμενοι τὸν κ(ύριο)ν ἀναστήσονται εἰσ ζωὴν αἰώνιον·	ܐܝܠܝܢ ܕܝܢ ܕܕܚܠܝܢ ܡܢ ܡܪܝܐ. ܢܩܘܡܘܢ ܠܚܝ̈ܐ ܕܠܥܠܡ.
but *those* who fear the Lord will be raised up to lasting life,	but those who fear the LORD will stand to the life of lasting time,
καὶ ἡ ζωὴ αὐτ(ῶν) ἐν φωτὶ κ(υρίο)υ ‹καὶ› οὐκ ἐκλείψη ἔτι:	ܘܚܝ̈ܝܗܘܢ ܒܢܘܗܪܗ ܕܡܪܝܐ. ܘܠܐ ܬܘܒ ܢܬܛܠܩ ܗܠܠܘܝܐ
and their life *will be* in *the* Lord's light, and it will not cease *any* more.	and their life *will be* in the LORD's light, and it will never again be ended. Hallelujah.

3.16 καὶ 2° 336⁺260 ≡ ܘ- 16h1 | > 253 •

3.15–16 The destruction described in verses 13–14 **will be the sinners' portion**[91] **to lasting time, but those who fear the Lord will be raised up to lasting life** (Matt 25.46; John 3.36; 5.24; 12.25; Rom 2.7–8; 6.23, Gal 6.8), a life that **will not cease any more.** "The one who believes in Me will live even if he dies; and everyone who lives and believes in Me will not die at all to lasting time" (John 11.25–26). "I give them lasting life, and they will not be destroyed at all to lasting time, and no one will snatch them out of My hand" (John 10.28).

This **life**[92] **will be in the Lord's light.** "God is light" (1 Jn 1.5; Isa 60.19). "Everyone who does evil hates the light, and does not come to the light, lest his works should be exposed; but the one who does faithfulness comes to the light" (John 3.21; 1 Jn 2.10–11), passing "out of darkness into His marvelous light" (1 Pet 2.9; Eph 5.8; Isa 60.1–2; John 8.12; Rev 22.5).[93]

---

[91] The term **portion** *(meris)* is applied to part of something (e.g., part of a geographical region, Acts 16.12)—in this context, the part that each person will receive from God (as in Col 1.12; Luke 10.42; Psa 11.6, LXX; Job 27.13, LXX).

[92] In the Syriac, **their life** (*ḥyyhwn,* a plural noun referring to a singular concept) takes a singular verb (**will ... be ended,** *ntṭlq*), as in John 1.4, Syr. This type of construction is well documented in Syriac (Arayathinal §303, n. 2; it is not as rare as the comments of Harris-Mingana 2.106–07 and Trafton 57–58 might suggest). It is seen also in Hebrew (JM §150*g*).

[93] In the Syriac manuscript (16h1), but not in any of the Greek copies, this psalm ends with **Hallelujah** *(hllwy')*. Similarly, the copyist of 10h1 initially wrote "Hallelujah" at the end of

Psalm 4

This psalm rebukes Israel's **hypocrites** (vv 7, 22, 25) only a few decades before Jesus did, and in similar terms. The hypocrite acts **as if in zeal** (v 3) and **as if he is innocent** (v 6); he is **among the first** to **condemn sinners in judgment** (vv 2–3). But he is **speaking the Law with deceit,** and merely **to please Men** (vv 10, 8, 21, 27). His **heart has departed far from the Lord** (v 1); inwardly he is **filled with Law-breaking** (vv 15, 1, 27) and is seeking to destroy whole **houses** (vv 11–15, 23).

God "wants all people to be saved and come to the knowledge of the truth" (1 Tim 2.4); He is "not willing for any to be destroyed, but for all to come to repentance" (2 Pet 3.9). Nevertheless He will punish dreadfully those who persist in rejecting His mercy, and "it is a righteous thing" for Him to do so (2 Thes 1.6–9). Under both the old covenant and the new, God's people have prayed that unrepented evil may not be allowed to continue unpunished, but may incur the Lord's judgment. Such prayers are explicitly approved in the New Testament Scriptures (Psa 69.23 ≡ Rom 11.10; Psa 109.8–11 ≡ Acts 1.16–20); indeed, they are explicitly approved by Jesus Himself (Luke 18.7–8; cf. Rev 6.10). God "will not justify the wicked" (Exod 23.7), and He requires His people to have the same attitude (Prov 17.15; 24.24). So the present psalm prays that the hypocrite may suffer **dishonor** (v 16, 18, 21), **corruption of his flesh, poverty, childlessness** in **old age,** and a **house** empty of anything that might satisfy **his soul** (vv 7, 19–20); that **God** may **uncover his** evil **works with laughter and mockery** (v 8); and when he is dead, that his unburied body may be **scattered by wild animals** and scavenged by the birds of the heavens (vv 21–22). Again the severity of these words resembles the severity of the punishments for hypocrisy proclaimed by Jesus a few decades later (Matt 23.13–38).

The hypocrite among the lovingkind ones

4.0 [0] Διαλογὴ τοῦ Cαλωμῶν τοῖc ἀνθρωπαρέcκ(οιc): A reasoning of Solomon, in regard to those who please Men.	
4.1 [1] Ἵνα τί σύ βέβηλε κάθησαι ἐν συνεδρίῳ ‹ὁσίων›· Why are you† sitting, you† profane *one,* in *the* council of *the* lovingkind *one*s,	ܠܡܢܐ ܐܢܬ ܪܫܝܥܐ ܝܬܒ ܐܢܬ ܒܟܢܘܫܬܐ ܕܙܕܝܩܐ. Why *are* you† sitting, you† ungodly *one,* in the assembly of the righteous *one*s,

---

Eighteen Psalms 1, but later deleted it. In both 10h1 and 16h1, the Eighteen Psalms follow immediately on from the 42 so-called "Odes of Solomon," each of which does indeed end with "Hallelujah"; therefore, copyists would have had an instinctive tendency to add the word at the ends of the ensuing items (Harris-Mingana 2.414).

καὶ ἡ καρδία σου μακρὰν ἀφέστηκεν
ἀπὸ τοῦ κ(υρίο)υ·
and your† heart has departed
far from the Lord,

ܘܠܒܟܝ ܦܪܝܫ
ܡܢ ܐܠܗܐ.
and your† heart *has* departed
from God,

ἐν παρανομίαισ
παροργίζων τὸν θ(εὸ)ν Ἰ(σρα)ήλ·
with Law-breakings
making the God of Israel angry?

ܘܒܥܘܠܟܝ
ܡܪܓܙ ܐܢܬܝ ܠܐܠܗܗ ܕܐܝܣܪܐܝܠ.
and in your† injustice you†
are making *the* God of Israel angry?

4.1 ὁσίων 336 [ܕܙܕܝ̈ܩܐ 16h1] | ὁσίω 253 | > 260 •

4.1[94] The psalm's opening verses describe someone who is "living . . . with lovingkind ones" (v 7) and **sitting in the council** [*sunedriō*] **of the lovingkind ones.** A **council** is a gathering *(sun-)* of people (the Syriac uses the term *knwšt'*, **assembly**), often to decide matters requiring judgment (as in v 2; cf. Matt 5.22; 10.17; Mark 15.1; Acts 5.21, 27).

It is a good thing to be **sitting** in good company. "Blessed is the man who . . . has not sat in the seat of scorners" (Psa 1.1); "one who walks with wise people will be wise, but one who accompanies fools will suffer evil" (Prov 13.20). But not everyone who sits in good company is a good person (Matt 26.21–24; Acts 20.30; 2 Pet 2.1; 1 Jn 2.19). Although the person described in these verses is sitting with **the lovingkind ones,** he himself is **profane** (unclean: see the notes on 1.8). His **heart has departed far from the Lord** (Mark 7.6; Ezek 33.31; Psa 58.2), and his deeds **break** God's **Law** (see on Maccabaica 1.11)—so that he is **making the God of Israel angry.** "All irreverence and unrighteousness" makes God angry (Rom 1.18). No one can **break** His **Law** and hope to escape His anger (Rom 2.5–6).

4.2 [2] περισσὸσ ἐν λόγοισ·
περισσὸσ ἐν σημειώσει ὑπερ πάντασ·
Overflowing in words,
overflowing in a signal,
more than all *people*—

ܡܬܝܬܪܐ ܒܡ̈ܠܝܟܝ. ܘܡܬܝܬܪܐ
ܒܐܬܘ̈ܬܟܝ ܝܬܝܪ ܡܢ ܟܠ ܐܢܫ.
Abounding in your† words
and abounding in your† signals,
more than every man,

ὁ σκληρὸσ ἐν λόγοισ
κατακρίναι ἁμαρτωλοὺσ ἐν κρίσει·
the *one who is* hard in *his* words
to condemn sinners in judgment,

ܗܘ ܕܩܫܐ ܒܡ̈ܠܘܗܝ
ܠܡܚܝܒܘ ܠܚ̈ܛܝܐ ܒܕܝܢܐ.
one who *is* hard in his words
to condemn the sinners in judgment,

---

[94] In the Greek copies (but not in the Syriac), the psalm is superscribed **A reasoning of Solomon, in regard to those who please Men** (cf. vv 8, 10, 21). From a purely grammatical standpoint, the dative could also be translated "with" ("conversation . . . with the men-pleasers," APOT); but the rendering **in regard to** ("discourse . . . pertaining to the men-pleasers," NETS; *Betrachtung . . . über die Menschendiener,* Holm-Nielsen; cf. 17.0) suits the content better.

Greek	Syriac
4.3 **[3]** καὶ ἡ χεὶρ αὐτοῦ ἐν πρώτοισ ἐπ' αὐτὸν ὡσ ἐν ζήλει· and his hand *is* among *the* first upon him, as *if* in zeal,	ܘܐܝܕܗ ܠܩܕܡ ܥܠܘܗܝ ܐܝܟ ܕܒܛܢܢܐ. and his hand *is* first upon him as *if* in zeal,
καὶ αὐτὸ(σ) ἔνοχοσ ἐν ποικιλία ἁμαρτωλῶν ἐν ακρασίαισ· and he himself *is* held *for punishment* with a diversity of sinners in self-indulgent deeds.	ܘܗܘ ܡܚܝܒ ܒܣܘܓܐܐ ܕܡܪܚܘܬܐ ܕܚܛܝܐ. and he is condemned with a multitude of overindulgence of sinners.

4.2–3 When a **judgment** is pronounced, the evildoer is **overflowing** [*perissos*] . . . **beyond all people,** both in the **words** he utters (which are notably **hard**) and in the **signal**[95] he makes (he is **among the first** to lift his **hand** against the offender; the old covenant regulations on this subject are given in Deut 17.7).

To human eyes—which can see these outward things, but cannot look into the heart (v 1)—the man might seem to be motivated by **zeal** for the Lord (cf. 2.27). But in reality **he himself is held for punishment** (Greek; see the comments on Maccabaica 14.45)—in other words, he is **condemned** (Syriac) because of his **self-indulgent deeds,**[96] just like the **diversity of sinners**[97] on whom he sits in judgment (v 2). "With what judgment you judge, you will be judged; and with what measure you measure, it will be measured to you" (Matt 7.1–5; cf. Sir 28.3–5; 18.20). So, "in the matter in which you are judging the other person, you are condemning yourself" if, like this hypocrite, "you yourself are doing the same things" (Rom 2.1).

---

[95] **Signal** (*sēmeiōsei,* Greek); **signals** (*'twt,* Syriac). Both the Syriac and the Greek are used in Psa 60.4 to translate the Hebrew term *ns* ("signal," "banner"; cf. BDB 651). Moreover, the Syriac is linguistically equivalent to the Hebrew term *'wt* ("sign," "signal," cf. BDB 16–17; contrasted with "word": "Aaron spoke all the words . . . and did the signs," Exod 4.30, where the LXX rendering is *sēmeia*).

The sign or signal can be anything that signifies some piece of information: a mark on the body (Gen 17.11), a mark on the doorpost (Exod 12.13), a banner or standard (Psa 74.4); an act done by a person (Isa 20.3), an act done by God (2 Kgs 20.9–11). In the present context the **signal** is a hand gesture (*geste,* Viteau; *Gesten,* LXX.D): plural **words** and singular **signal** in v 2a correspond to plural **words** and singular **hand** in vv 2b–3. Most English translators have rendered it "appearance," but that is neither a possible meaning of the Syriac (cf. TS 1.412–13; SL 109) nor a probable meaning of the Greek (it would be "a strange word to use in this connexion," Ryle-James 41).

[96] **Self-indulgent deeds** (*akrasiais,* as in Matt 23.25; 1 Cor 7.5): deeds that lack *(a-)* control or power *(kratos)*. The absolute opposite of self-control (*egkrateia,* power over what is within, cf. 1 Cor 7.9; 9.25).

[97] **Sinners** *(hamartōlōn)* is the reading of 253 (supported by the Syriac), whereas 336^{+}260 read **sins** *(hamartiōn)*.

4.4 [4] οἱ ὀφθαλμοὶ αὐτοῦ ἐπι πᾶσαν γυναῖκα ἄνευ διαστολῆσ· His eyes *are* upon every woman without distinction;	ܥܝܢܘܗܝ ܥܠ ܟܠ ܐܢܬܬܐ ܕܠܐ ܢܟܦܘܬܐ. His eyes *are* on every woman, with no shame,
ἡ γλῶσσα ‹αὐτοῦ› ψευδὴσ ἐν συναλλάγματι μεθ ὅρκου· his tongue *is* lying when *he makes* an agreement with an oath.	ܘܠܫܢܗ ܕܓܠ ܒܗܘܦܟܐ ܕܡܘܡܬܐ. and his tongue *is* speaking falsehood in the dealings of oaths.
4.5 [5] ἐν νυκτὶ καὶ ἐν ἀποκρύφοισ ἁμαρτάνει ὡσ ‹οὐχ› ὁρώμενοσ· At night and in hidden *place*s he is sinning, as *if he is* not being seen;	ܒܠܠܝܐ ܘܒܚܫܘܟܐ ܐܝܟ ܕܠܐ ܡܬܚܙܐ. In the night and in the darkness, as *if he is* not looked on,
ἐν ὀφθαλμοῖσ αὐτοῦ λαλεῖ πάσῃ γυναικὶ ἐν συνταγῇ κακίασ· with his eyes he is speaking to every woman with an assignation of evildoing;	ܒܥܝܢܘܗܝ ܡܡܠܠ ܥܡ ܟܠ ܐܢܬܬܐ ܒܢܟܠܐ ܕܒܝܫܬܐ. with his eyes *he is* speaking with every woman in a scheme of evil;
4.6 [5] ταχὺσ εἰσόδῳ εἰσ πᾶσαν οἰκεῖαν ‹ἐν ἱλαρότητι› ‹ὡσ ἄκακοσ›· *he is* quick in entering into every house with cheerfulness, as *if he is* innocent.	ܘܩܠܝܠ ܠܡܥܠ ܒܟܠ ܒܝܬܐ ܒܚܕܘܬܐ. ܐܝܟ ܗܘ ܕܠܝܬ ܒܗ ܒܝܫܬܐ. and *he is* quick to enter in every house with joy, like *one* in whom there is no evil.

4.4 αὐτοῦ 2° 336⁺260 ≡ 16h1 | > 253 • **4.5** οὐχ 336⁺260 | ὀχ' 253 • **4.6** ἐν ἱλαρότητι 336⁺260 | ἱλαρότι 253 • ὡσ ἄκακοσ 336⁺260 ≡ ܐܝܟ ܗܘ ܕܠܝܬ ܒܗ ܒܝܫܬܐ 16h1 | ὡσάκκοσ 253 •

4.4–5 His eyes are upon every woman (cf. 2 Pet 2.14) in a way that "speaks" to them (cf. Prov 6.13), urging them to do evil (**an assignation of evildoing**). Job "made a covenant with [his] eyes" that he would not "pay attention to a virgin" (Job 31.1; cf. Sir 9.8); but David fell into sin when he "saw a woman washing herself… and the woman was extremely good of appearance" (2 Sam 11.2). "Everyone who looks at a woman to desire her has already committed adultery with her in his heart" (Matt 5.28).

The Greek text says that the secret sinner does this **without distinction** *(diastolēs)*. This is usually taken to mean that he pursues women "indiscriminately" (APOT). However, the corresponding Syriac says that he does it **with no shame** *(nkpwt')*, disobeying the Lord's command "to make a distinction [*diasteilai*] between the holy and the profane, and between the unclean and the clean" (Lev 10.10, LXX). God's people must always "be separate" from corruption and cleanse themselves "from all defilement of flesh and spirit, perfecting holiness in the fear of God" (2 Cor 6.14–7.1).

The sinner commits his sins **at night and in hidden places . . . as if he is not being seen.** "The eye of the adulterer keeps watching for twilight, saying, 'No eye will see me'" (Job 24.15; Prov 7.9). He may even think that the Lord does not notice him (Ezek 8.12; Psa 94.7; Isa 29.15). But he is thinking only of outward appearances, trying to "appear righteous outwardly to Men," while his inside is full of rottenness (Matt 23.27–28). "There is a person who goes astray from his bed, saying in his soul, 'Who sees me? Darkness is surrounding me, and the walls are hiding me, and no one sees me.' . . . Human eyes are his fear, and he does not know that the Lord's eyes are ten thousand times brighter than the sun, and are looking into the hidden parts" (Sir 23.18–19). "'Can a man hide himself in secret places, and I will not see him?' says the LORD" (Jer 23.24; Prov 15.3; Psa 139.7–16).

Whether it speaks with the **tongue** or the **eyes,** a bad heart cannot produce good speech—any more than a bad tree can produce good fruit (Matt 12.33–35). The secret sinner's **tongue is lying when he makes an agreement,** even when he swears a solemn **oath** about it (like the people described in Hos 10.4).[98] "Everyone will deceive his companion, and will not speak the truth; they have taught their tongue to speak lies" (Jer 9.5; 7.9–10; Hos 4.2; Ezek 17.18). God's people under the old covenant were commanded not to break their word when they made an oath (Num 30.2; Psa 15.4), and under the new covenant are commanded to go even further than that: "You have heard that it was said to the people of old, 'You shall not commit perjury, but shall repay your oaths to the Lord.' But I say to you: Do not swear an oath at all . . . but let your word be 'Yes, yes' and 'No, no'; but what surpasses these things is from the evil one" (Matt 5.33–37; Jas 5.12).

4.6 He is quick in entering into every house in a way that appears **innocent (with cheerfulness**—seemingly like the righteous, 16.12; compare the foreign invader who came into Jerusalem "as a father into the house of his sons, with peace," 8.20). The secret sinner is among the "lovers of pleasure rather than lovers of God," who have a "form of reverence" but have "denied its power," and "who slip into houses and capture little women heaped with sins, being led away by various desires" (2 Tim 3.4–6). Those who "are slaves not of our Lord Christ but of their own bellies . . . through good words and blessings deceive the hearts of the innocent" (Rom 16.18).

May God remove the hypocrites

4.7 [6] ἐξάραι ὁ θ(εὸ)σ τοὺσ	ܐܪܝܡ ܐܠܗܐ ܠܐܝܠܝܢ
ἐν υποκρίσει ζῶντασ μετὰ ὁσίων·	ܕܒܡܣܒ ܒܐܦ̈ܐ ܕܝܢܝܢ.
May God remove those *who are* living in hypocrisy with lovingkind *ones*;	God has taken away *those* who *are* judging by playing *the* hypocrite,

[98] In this context, the **oath** may be specifically an oath that he is innocent (v 6) of adultery (vv 4, 5), like the oath described in Num 5.19–22; see the comments on 8.11.

ἐν φθορᾷ σαρκὸ(σ) αὐτοῦ καὶ πενίᾳ τὴν ζωὴν αὐτοῦ· in corruption of his flesh and *in* poverty *may God remove* his life.	ܢܚܐ ܕܝܢ ܥܡ ܬܪܝܨܐ ܒܚܒܠܗ ܕܦܓܪܗ ܘܒܡܣܟܢܘܬܐ ܕܚܝ̈ܘܗܝ. but *may He* live with the upright *one* in the corruption of his body and in the reproach of his life.
4.8 [7] ἀνακαλύψαι ὁ θ(εὸ)σ τὰ ἔργα ἀν(θρώπ)ων ἀνθρωπαρέσκων· May God uncover the works of *the* Men who please Men,	ܢܓܠܐ ܐܠܗܐ ܥܒ̈ܕܘܗܝ ܕܐܢܫܝܢ ܕܫܦܪܝܢ ܠܒ̈ܢܝܢܫܐ. God will uncover *the* deeds of those who please sons of men,
ἐν καταγέλωτι καὶ μυκτηρισμῷ τὰ ἔργα αὐτοῦ· with laughter and mockery *may God uncover* his works.	ܒܓܘܚܟܐ ܘܒܒܙܚܐ ܥܒ̈ܕܘܗܝ. with laughter and with mockery *God will uncover* his deeds.

4.7–8 People of the kind described in the previous verses are **living in hypocrisy.**[99] Their **works** are done only to **please Men** (the term applied in Eph 6.6; Col 3.22 to those who do "eye service"—who labor, not "from the heart" and "for the Lord," but to impress the eye and "for Men"). Hypocrites "do all their works to be seen by Men" and "so that they may be honored by Men" (Matt 23.5, 25–28; 6.2, 5, 16).

The psalm prays that God may **uncover the works** of such people. Not all evil **works** are evident at first (1 Tim 5.24; see the comments on Maccabaica 12.46); only God can look into the heart (1 Sam 16.7; Heb 4.12–13) and **uncover** its true contents. "God will bring every work into judgment, with every hidden thing—whether it is good, or whether it is evil" (Ecc 12.14). Then He "will bring to light the hidden things of darkness, and will reveal the purposes of the hearts" (1 Cor 4.5; Rom 2.15).

With laughter and mockery may God uncover his works.[100] "The One who dwells in the heavens laughs; the Lord mocks at" His enemies (Psa 2.4; 37.13; 59.8). "It is a righteous thing" (2 Thes 1.6) that those who have mocked at Him (Luke 16.14; 23.35–36; Acts 2.13; 17.32) should reap as they have sown (Gal 6.7) and be repaid in accordance with their deeds (Prov 1.24–31; Psa 109.17–18; Rev 18.6, 20). "He scorns the scorners" (Prov 3.34).

The Greek and Syriac versions of verse 7b differ.

- In the Greek version, this line is a further prayer that God may remove the **life** of the evildoer **in corruption of his flesh and in poverty.** Those who rejected Jesus

---

[99] **Living** (*zōntas,* Greek); the Syriac version has **judging** *(dynyn).* **In hypocrisy** (*en hupokrisei,* Greek) ≡ **by playing the hypocrite** (*bms'b b'p',* "by acceptance of faces," Syriac; see the comments on 2.19, and the footnotes to vv 10 and 25; cf. Jas 2.1–4).

[100] Note the shift from plural (the works of the **Men**) to singular (**his** works). Such fluctuations are common in these psalms, as in the Hebrew Scriptures (see the footnote to 2.20).

suffered both **corruption of** the **flesh**[101] and **poverty,** in accordance with David's prophecies: "May their eyes be darkened from seeing, and make their loins stoop continually" (Psa 69.23 ≡ Rom 11.10). "May his days be few . . . . May a usurer snare all that belongs to him, and may strangers plunder his labor" (Psa 109.8–11 ≡ Acts 1.16–20).

- In the Syriac version, the line describes God's dealings with the righteous in contrast to the evildoers: may God remove the wicked (v 7a), but may He **live with the upright one in the corruption of his** [the upright one's] **body and in the reproach**[102] **of his life.** Constantly "our outer person is being corrupted," and if we serve God we must expect to suffer reproach (Matt 5.11; Luke 6.22; 2 Cor 4.16–17, 8–11; Heb 11.25–26; 1 Pet 4.14; cf. Rom 15.3). But in spite of these adversities, "if we have died with Christ, we believe that we will also live with Him" (Rom 6.8; 2 Tim 2.11; 2 Cor 13.4), in accordance with His promise: "I will not leave you at all, nor will I forsake you at all" (Heb 13.5; Isa 41.17; Deut 31.6).

The psalm's prayers for judgment on the evildoer are continued and extended in verses 16–22 (see the comments there).

4.9 [8] καὶ δικαιώσαισαν ὅσιοι τὸ κρίμα τοῦ θ(εο)ῦ αὐτῶν·	ܘܢܘܕܘܢ ܚܣ̈ܢܐ ܕܝܢܗ ܕܐܠܗܗܘܢ.
And may lovingkind *ones* acknowledge the judgment of their God to be righteous	And the fortresses will acknowledge *the* judgment of their God to be righteous,
ἐν τῷ ἐξαίρεσθαι ἁμαρτωλοὺσ ἀπο προσώπου δικαίου·	ܟܕ ܡܬܬܪܡܝܢ ܪ̈ܫܝܥܐ ܡܢ ܩܕܡ ܙܕ̈ܝܩܐ.
when sinners are removed from *the* face of *the* righteous *one,*	when the ungodly *ones* are cast *down* from before the righteous *ones*,

4.9 When sinners are removed by God (v 7), **may lovingkind ones**[103] **acknowledge the judgment of their God to be righteous.** See the comments on 2.16; 3.3.

The hypocrite's deluding words

4.10 [8] ἀνθρωπάρεσκον λαλοῦντα ‹νόμον› μετα ‹δόλ(ου)›·	ܢܣܒ ܒܐ̈ܦܐ ܕܡܡܠܠ ܢܡܘܣܐ ܒܢܟܠܐ.

[101] **Corruption of the flesh** is a punishment for corruption of life (Gal 6.7–8; 2 Pet 2.12, 18–19).

[102] **And in the reproach** *(wbmksnwt')* is the reading of the only known Syriac manuscript (16h1). Both Harris-Mingana and Baars emended it to *wbmsknwt'* ("and in the poverty," matching the Greek version).

[103] **Lovingkind ones.** The only known Syriac manuscript (16h1) reads *ḥsn'* (**the fortresses,** as in 2 Chr 32.1; Psa 89.40). Both Harris-Mingana and Baars emended it to *ḥsy'* ("the lovingkind ones," matching the Greek version).

Greek	Syriac
one who is pleasing Men, who is speaking *the* Law with deceit.	*one who is* playing *the* hypocrite, who *is* speaking the Law with deceit.
4.11 [9] καὶ οἱ ὀφθαλμοὶ αὐτ(ῶν) ἐπ οἶκον ἀνδρὸσ ἐν ευσταθία· ὡσ ὄφισ And their eyes *are* on a man's house *that is* in stability—like *the* snake,	ܘܥܝܢܘܗܝ ܥܠ ܒܝܬܐ ܒܫܠܝܘܬܐ ܐܝܟ ܚܘܝܐ. And his eyes *are* on a house *that is* at peace, like the snake,
διαλύσαι σοφίαν ἀλλήλων ἐν λόγοισ παρανόμων· breaking apart each other's wisdom with Law-breakers' words.	ܠܡܫܪܐ ܚܟܡܬܐ ܕܚܕ ܚܕ. ܒܡ̈ܠܐ ܕܥܘܠܘܬܐ. to undo each one's wisdom with words of injustice.
4.12 [10] οἱ λόγοι αὐτοῦ παραλογισμοὶ εἰσ πρᾶξιν ἐπιθυμίασ ‹ἀδίκου›· His words *are* deluding words, for *the* working of an unrighteous *one*'s desire;	ܦܬ ܡ̈ܠܘܗܝ ܒܚܘܫܒܐ ܒܝܫܐ ܐܝܬܝܗܘܢ. ܠܦܘܠܚܢܐ ܕܪ ܪܓܬܐ ܕܥܘܠܐ. His words are in evil reasonings, for the working of the desire of injustice,
4.13 [10] οὐκ ἀπέστη ἕωσ ἐνίκησεν σκορπίσαι ὡσ ἐν ορφανία· he did not depart until he had conquered *so as* to scatter *them,* as *if* with *the* loss of children,	ܘܠܐ ܦܪܩ ܥܕܡܐ ܕܒܕܪ ܒܡܘܬܐ. and *he did* not depart until he scattered *them* in death,
[11] καὶ ἠρήμωσεν οἶκον ἕνεκεν ἐπιθυμίασ παρανόμου· and he made a house desolate on account of *the* Law-breaker's desire;	ܘܐܚܪܒ ܒܝܬܐ ܡܛܠ ܪ ܪܓܬܐ ܕܥܘܠܐ. and he made a house desolate because *of his* desire of injustice,
4.14 [11] παρελογίσατο ἐν λόγοισ ὅτι οὐκ ἔστιν ὁρῶν καὶ κρίνων· he deluded with words, *saying* that *there* was no *one* seeing and judging.	ܘܐܬܚܫܒ ܒܡ̈ܠܐ ܕܠܝܬ ܡܢ ܕܚܙܐ ܘܕܐܢ. and he considered with words that there was no *one* who *was* seeing and judging.
4.15 [12] ἐπλήσθη ἐν παρανομία ἐν ταύτη He became filled with Law-breaking by this,	ܘܐܬܡܠܝ ܒܗܢܐ ܥܘܠܐ. And he became filled with this injustice,

4.10 νόμον 336^{+}260 ≡ ܢܡܘܣܐ 16h1 | μόνον 253 • δόλ(ου) 336^{+}260 ≡ ܒܢܟܠܐ 16h1 | δόυλου 253 • **4.12** ἀδίκου 336^{+}260 | -κων 253 •

καὶ οἱ ὀφθαλμοὶ αὐτοῦ· ἐπ οἶκον ἕτερον and his eyes *were* upon a different house	ܘܥܝ̈ܢܘܗܝ ܥܠ ܒܝܬܐ ܐܚܪܢܐ and his eyes *were* on another house
ὀλεθρεῦσαι ἐν λόγοισ ἀναπτερώσεωσ· to destroy *it* with words of flight.	ܠܚܘܪܒܢܗ ܒܡ̈ܠܐ ܕܦܪܚܘܬܐ for its desolation with words that *were* making *it* to fly,
[13] οὐκ εμπιπλαται ἡ ψυχὴ αὐτοῦ ὡσ ἅδησ ἐν πᾶσι τούτοισ· His soul, like Hades, is not filled with all these *things*.	ܘܠܐ ܡܬܡܠܝܐ ܢܦܫܗ ܐܝܟ ܫܝܘܠ. ܒܗܠܝܢ ܟܠܗܝܢ and *yet* his soul, like Sheol, *is* not filled with all these *things*.

4.10–15 The evildoer sets his **eyes** on a **house** that is **in stability** (Greek; cf. Prov 3.29; Jdg 18.7, 27), **at peace** (Syriac; cf. Psa 35.20). He uses **deluding words** (Col 2.4), **speaking the Law** of God **with deceit** (cf. 12.1; Mark 14.1) in order to impress **Men,**[104] so that he can corrupt the innocent (v 25) by **breaking apart** *(dialusai)* their **wisdom**[105]—separating and scattering it (as a band of men is separated and scattered, Acts 5.36). In every age Satan seeks to disrupt and divide the singlemindedness and steadfastness of wisdom (2 Cor 11.3; Eph 4.14; Matt 6.22; Acts 2.46; cf. Matt 12.25).

The evildoer is **like the snake,** because he acts with a poisoned mouth and a sharpened tongue (Psa 58.4) and a skill at deceiving (2 Cor 11.3; Gen 3.1, 13; Rev 12.9). He is **unrighteous,** and he desires to accomplish the **desire** of an **unrighteous one** (Gal 5.16–24; 1 Cor 10.6; John 8.44).

He is confident that there is **no one seeing and judging** (as described in v 5), so he has no fear of punishment. He perseveres with his scheme: he does **not depart** from it

[104] **One who is pleasing Men** (*anthrōpareskon,* Greek) ≡ **one who is playing the hypocrite** (*nsb b'p',* Syriac; see the comments on 2.19, and the footnotes to vv 7 and 25). The renderings in Harris-Mingana ("the acceptor of persons") and Trafton ("the one who shows partiality") are incorrect. Syriac *nsb b'p'* here refers not to those who show partiality (i.e., accept by face; SL 923, §9a) but to those who are hypocritical (i.e., are accepted by face; SL 923, §9b), as in Matt 22.18, Syr.

[105] **Breaking apart each other's** [*allēlōn*] **wisdom.** *Allēlōn* often means "mutually," "reciprocally" (cf. LSJ 69), but not always (non-reciprocal uses are found in Classical writers from Homer onward: DGE 2.159, §B). "They will betray each other" (Matt 24.10) means only that some of them will betray others; "the dead had already fallen on each other" (Wis 18.23) means only that some of them had fallen on others (further examples are listed in Viteau 274–75). In the same way, **breaking apart each other's wisdom** means only that some of them will destroy the wisdom of others. There is therefore no reason to emend the text (it is supported by the Syriac).

until he has **conquered so as to scatter**[106] his victims, like a shepherd who neglects the sheep (Jer 23.1; 10.21; 50.6) or a wolf who attacks them (John 10.12).[107] In this way he makes the victims' **house desolate** (as Jerusalem itself would soon be, Matt 23.37–38). "Insubordinate people, empty talkers, and mind-deceivers . . . overthrow whole houses, teaching things that they ought not" (Titus 1.10–11).

He became filled with Law-breaking by this.[108] A little leaven leavens the whole lump (1 Cor 5.6–8). Those who "did not think fit to have God in their knowledge" become "filled with all unrighteousness" (Rom 1.28–29; Matt 23.25–28; Acts 13.10). (The converse is equally true: those who "abound still more and more in the knowledge" of God become "filled with the fruit of righteousness that comes through Jesus Christ": Php 1.9–11; Jas 3.17; Acts 9.36; 11.24.) So one success is not enough for this evildoer. After it is accomplished, he sets his **eyes . . . upon a different house, to destroy it** too.[109] One sin leads to another. He enters "every house" (v 6) and makes "many houses desolate" (v 23). And even so, **his soul . . . is not filled with all these** deeds.[110] It is **like Hades** (the realm of the dead, 14.6), "never filled" (Prov 30.15–16).

---

[106] **He had conquered so as to scatter** *(enikēsen skorpisai).* "The foll[owing] inf[initive] . . . indicates what the victory enables the victor to do" (BDAG 673, §1a), as in Rev 5.5.

[107] The Greek version states that he scatters them **as if with loss of children,** like the nation during the Babylonian captivity, "bereaved of children and barren, exiled and wandering" (Isa 49.21). The Syriac version states that he scatters them **in death,** like the sufferers described in Psa 141.7: "our bones have been scattered at the mouth of Sheol."

[108] **By this** *(en tautē).* The feminine *tautē* looks back to the preceding feminine noun *paranomia,* **Law-breaking:** "he became filled with Law-breaking by this [Law-breaking]." Compare the Syriac: **he became filled with this injustice.** Doing evil, he became filled with evil.

[109] He seeks **to destroy it with words of flight** (*anapterōseōs,* Greek ≡ *dprḥwt',* Syriac). "Both [the Greek and the Syriac] are rare words, and both have at their roots the basic notion of flying" (Trafton 68). Other forms of Greek *anapteroō* (DGE 2.262) often mean "frighten, excite fear," but can also mean "be flighty" (≡ Hebrew *hmh,* "be tumultuous," Prov 7.11; Chrysostom, PG 57.368) or "incite to flight" (Sir 34.1; Herodotus 2.115). Other forms of Syriac *prḥ* (SL 1236) can mean "disperse, squander" (Luke 15.13, 30) or "make to fly" (≡ Hebrew *prḥ,* Ezek 13.20). In the present passage, the meaning "words that incite to flight," corresponding to some form of Hebrew *prḥ,* would suit both the Greek and the Syriac and would fit the context: the hypocrite's deluding words incite his victims to depart from their stability (vv 11–13), i.e., they are *verführenden Worten* (Holm-Nielsen). "Words of prodigality" (Harris-Mingana) would also suit the Syriac (although not the Greek); "agitating words" (OTP) would also suit the Greek (although not the Syriac). "Clamorous words" (NETS) derives from an assumption that *anapteroō* in Prov 7.11 (LXX) means "be loud" rather than "be tumultuous, unruly" (LSJ 118); but that is extremely unlikely, as nowhere else is any form of *anapteroō* (or *prḥ*) used in any such sense. The entry for *anapterōsis* in LSJ 118 confused Sir 34.1 with the present verse, and that error misled DGE 2.262 to omit the noun entirely.

[110] The punctuation of the Syriac manuscript (16h1) attaches **with all these things** to the following sentence.

May he fall in dishonor

4.16 [14] γένοιτο κ(ύρι)ε ἡ μερὶσ
αὐτοῦ ἐν ατιμία ἐνώπιό(ν) σου·
Lord, may his portion be
with dishonor in Your† sight;

ܬܗܘܐ ܡܪܝܐ
ܒܨܥܪܐ ܩܕܡܝܟ.
LORD, may it be
in dishonor before You†—

ἡ ἔξοδοσ αὐτοῦ ἐν στεναγμοῖσ
καὶ ἡ εἴσοδοσ αὐτοῦ ἐν αρὰ·
may his departing *be* with groans
and his entering with cursing,

ܡܦܩܗ ܒܬܢܚܬܐ
ܘܡܥܠܗ ܒܠܘܛܬܐ.
his going out with groans
and his entering with curses,

4.17 [15] ἐν οδύναισ καὶ πενία
‹καὶ› ἀπορία ἡ ζωὴ αὐτοῦ·
his life with griefs and poverty
and perplexity,

ܒܟܐܒܐ ܘܒܡܣܟܢܘܬܐ
ܘܒܚܣܝܪܘܬܐ ܚܝܘܗܝ,
his life with pains and with poverty
and with lack,

κ(ύρι)ε ὁ ὕπνοσ αὐτοῦ ἐν λύπαισ·
καὶ ἡ ἐξέγερσισ αὐτοῦ ἐν απορίαισ·
Lord, his sleep with sorrows
and his rising with perplexities.

ܡܪܝܐ ܢܗܘܐ. ܫܢܬܗ ܒܥܩܬܐ
ܘܥܝܪܘܬܗ ܒܐܘܠܨܐ.
LORD, may his sleep be with sorrows
and his waking with oppressions,

4.18 [16] ἀφαιρεθείη ὕπνοσ
ἀπο κροτάφων αὐτοῦ ἐν νυκτὶ·
May sleep be removed
from his temples at night;

ܘܬܬܪܝܡ ܫܢܬܐ
ܡܢ ܨܕܥܘܗܝ ܒܠܠܝܐ.
and may sleep be taken away
from his temples at night;

‹ἀποπέσοι› ἀπὸ παντὸσ ἔργου
χειρῶν αὐτοῦ ‹ἐν ἀτιμία·
may he fall away from every work
of his hands in dishonor.

ܢܦܠ ܡܢ ܟܠ ܥܒܕܐ
ܕܐܝܕܘܗܝ ܒܨܥܪܐ.
may he fall from every work
of his hands in dishonor.

4.19 [17] κενὸσ χερσὶν αὐτοῦ
εἰσέλθοι εἰσ τὸν οἶκον αὐτοῦ›·
With his hands empty
may he come into his house,

ܘܟܕ ܣܦܝܩܢ ܐܝܕܘܗܝ
ܢܥܘܠ ܠܒܝܬܗ.
And when his hands have been emptied, may he enter into his house,

---

καὶ ἐλλειπησ ὁ οἶκοσ αὐτοῦ ἀπὸ
παντὸσ οὗ ἐμπλήσει ψυχὴν αὐτοῦ·
and *may* his house *be* lacking from any
thing with which his soul will be filled.

ܘܢܗܘܐ ܚܣܝܪ ܒܝܬܗ ܡܢ
ܟܠ ܡܕܡ ܕܡܣܒܥ ܢܦܫܐ.
and may his house be lacking from any
thing that *would* satisfy the soul.

4.17 καὶ 2° 336⁺260 ≡ 16h1 | > 253 • **4.18** ἀποπέσοι 336⁺260 ≡ ܢܦܠ 16h1 | -σοιεν 253 • **4.18–19** ἐν ἀτιμία· κενὸσ χερσὶν αὐτοῦ εἰσέλθοι εἰσ τὸν οἶκον αὐτοῦ 336⁺260 ≡ 16h1 | > 253 •

4.16–19 The prayers for judgment on the evildoer, which began in verses 7–8, are now continued and extended. The psalm prays that the evildoer's **portion**[111] may ultimately **be**[112] **with dishonor** (cf. Psa 83.16). God "lays asleep arrogant ones to lasting destruction in dishonor" (2.35). Indeed, anyone who persists in sin "finds dishonor, and his reproach is not wiped out" (Prov 6.33; 18.3).

In the Law of Moses, the Israelites had been warned that if they did not hearken to the Lord and keep all His commands, they would be cursed wherever they went, and in whatever they did: "cursed shall you be in your coming in, and cursed shall you be in your going out" (Deut 28.15–19).

The same curse is proclaimed in this psalm: **may his departing be with groans, and his entering with cursing . . . his sleep with sorrows and his rising with perplexities.**[113] "The wicked are like the driven sea; for it is not able to rest . . . . There is no peace, says my God, for the wicked" (Isa 57.20–21; cf. Job 27.13–23). Even **at night,** when people would normally find rest, **may sleep be removed from his temples.**[114] "All his days are sorrows, and his work is a vexation; even at night his heart does not rest" (Ecc 2.23). **His life** is to be afflicted **with griefs and poverty,** and no **work of his hands** is to succeed (**may he fall away from every work of his hands in dishonor**), so that he returns to **his house** each day **with his hands empty** ("much seed shall you carry out to the field, and little shall you gather," Deut 28.38–42; Hag 1.6).

4.20 [18] ἐν ‹μονώσει› ἀτεκνίασ τὸ γῆρασ αὐτοῦ εἰσ ἀνάλημψιν·	ܘܟܠ ܒܝܠܕܗ ܚܕ: ܢܩܪܒܝܘܗܝ.
May his old age *be* in solitariness of childlessness, until he *is* taken up.	And may *each* one from his begetting make war with him.

4.20 μονώσει 336⁺260 | μονία 253 •

[111] **His portion.** What he will receive from the Lord (see the footnote on 3.15).

[112] **Lord, may his portion be.** The Greek verb is *genoito,* "come to be." The Syriac manuscript (16h1) reads simply **Lord, may it be** *(thw' mry');* the feminine verb form puzzled Trafton (68), but it must refer back to **his soul** (*npšw,* feminine) in the previous clause (so that the sense is "Lord, may his soul be . . ."). Editors have conjecturally emended the Syriac to *thw' mnth mry'* ("Lord, may [his] portion be"; Harris-Mingana) or *thw' mnth dmry'* ("May [the] portion of [the] Lord be"; Baars—highly improbable, because *mnth dmry'* would mean not "the sinner's portion from the Lord," but "the Lord's own portion": see Išoʿdad of Merv, *Psaumes,* 170.1 [discussing Psa 119.57]; cf. *mnth dyʿqwb,* Jer 10.16, Syr).

[113] **Perplexities** (Greek *aporiais,* as in Luke 21.25) ≡ **oppressions** (Syriac *twk'* ≡ Hebrew *tk,* Psa 10.7).

[114] **Temples** (Greek *krotaphōn* ≡ Syriac *ṣdʿw,* the part of Sisera's head that Jael pierced, Jdg 4.21, LXX B ≡ Syr; the "side of the forehead," Muraoka 414; "the part of the head between the eye and the ear," TS 2.3366). The Syriac word is equivalent to Hebrew *ṣd* ("side," Num 33.55; Josh 23.13).

4.20 The Greek and Syriac versions of this line differ.

- In the Greek version, the line is a prayer that the evildoer's **old age** until his death[115] may be solitary and childless (like Babylon, Isa 47.8–9; the opposite of the blessings bestowed on the righteous, 1 Sam 2.5; Psa 127.3–5; Isa 49.20–22; Mark 10.29–30). "They will become of no account, and their old age will be without honor at last" (Wis 3.17).
- In the Syriac version, the line is a prayer that **each one** of the evildoer's children (each person who is **from his begetting**)[116] may **make war with him.**[117] In the Scriptures, not only nations but also individuals are said to **make war** with one another (Jas 4.1; Psa 56.1–2), for instance by using "their tongue as a sword" (Psa 64.3; 57.4). Those who have afflicted others in that way will reap as they themselves have sown (cf. Ezek 35.5–6; Matt 26.52), even from their own families (cf. 2 Chr 32.21).

Greek	Syriac
4.21 [19] σκορπισθείησαν σάρκεσ ἀνθρωπαρέσκων ὑπὸ θηρίων· May *the* flesh of *those* who please Men be scattered by wild animals,	ܢܬܒܕܪ ܡܢ ܚܝ̈ܘܬܐ ܒܣܪܐ ܕܢܣ̈ܒܝ ܒܐܦ̈ܐ. May the flesh of *those* who accept *people* by *their* faces be scattered by living creatures,
καὶ ὀστᾶ παρανόμων κατέναντι τοῦ ἡλίου ἐν ατιμία· and *the* bones of Law-breakers, right in front of the sun in dishonor.	ܘܓܪ̈ܡܐ ܕܥܘ̈ܠܐ ܩܕܡ ܫܡܫܐ ܒܨܥܪܐ. and the bones of the unjust *ones*, before the sun in dishonor.
4.22 [20] ὀφθαλμοὺσ ἐκκόψαισαν κόρακεσ ὑποκρινομένων·	ܢܢܩܪ̈ܘܢ ܥܘܪ̈ܒܐ ܕܐܝܠܝܢ ܕܙܩܦܝܢ ܠܒ̈ܢܝܢܫܐ.

[115] **Until he is taken up** *(analēmpsin)* from the earth (Luke 9.51; cf. Acts 1.2); not necessarily into heaven (see BDAG 67).

[116] **From his begetting** *(mn yldh).* The Greek rendering **childlessness** raises the possibility that the Syriac might be construed "without [*mn*] his begetting offspring, may each one make war with him" (cf. "without [*mn*] oil," Psa 109.24, Syr; Arayathinal §127.II). However, the presence of **each one** *(ḥd)* favors the much commoner partitive sense of *mn,* "each one from among those whom he has begotten," as in "any one [*ḥd*] from [*mn*] your brothers" (Deut 15.7, Syr; cf. Duval §320*e;* Nöldeke §249C). Baars incorrectly prints seyame on *yldh.*

[117] **May each one make war with him** *(ḥd nqrbywhn).* In this clause, Harris-Mingana construed the verb as a Peal form of *qrb* and conjecturally emended the text by prefixing *l'* ("not"), giving the translation "let not one draw near to him." Baars accepted this emendation, but Trafton (69) rightly pointed out that a Peal form of *qrb* would require a preposition (SL 1400; TS 2.3722), and that in the present clause the verb must be an Aphel form, **make war with** (SL 1401, Af. §1a).

May crows cut out *the* eyes of hypocrites,	May the ravens pluck out *the eyes* of those who *are* pleasing sons of men,

4.21–22 Even the dead bodies of the **hypocrites** (**those who please Men**) are to suffer the **dishonor** that happened to Jezebel (2 Kgs 9.35–37) and to those who perished at the time of the Babylonian captivity: "They shall not be lamented, and they shall not be buried .... Their dead bodies shall be food for the flying creatures of the heavens, and for the animals of the land" (Jer 16.4; 7.33; 8.1–2; Deut 28.26; cf. Psa 79.2 ≡ Maccabaica 7.17). Their **flesh** and **bones** are to lie unburied in broad daylight (**right in front of the sun**), **scattered by wild animals,** and with **crows** pecking at their **eyes** (as in Prov 30.17).

4.23 [20] ὅτι ‹ἠρήμωσαν› οἴκουσ πολλοὺσ ἀν(θρώπ)ων ἐν ατιμία·	ܡܛܠ ܕܐܚܪܒܘ ܒ̈ܬܐ ܣܓܝ̈ܐܐ ܕܐܢܫܐ ܒܨܥܪܐ.
because they have made many persons' houses desolate in dishonor,	because they have made many houses of man desolate in dishonor,
καὶ ‹ἐσκόρπισαν ἐν› ἐπιθυμία·	ܘܒܕܪܘܗܝ ܒܪܓܬܐ.
and they have scattered *them* in *their* desire,	and they have scattered him in *their* desire,
4.24 [21] καὶ οὐκ ‹ἐμνήσθησαν θ(εο)ῦ›·	ܘܠܐ ܐܬܕܟܪܘ ܠܐܠܗܐ.
and they have not been mindful of God,	and they have not been mindful of God,
καὶ οὐκ εφοβήθησαν τὸν θ(εὸ)ν ἐν ἅπασι τούτοισ	ܘܠܐ ܕܚܠܘ ܡܢ ܐܠܗܐ ܒܗܠܝܢ ܟܠܗܝܢ
and they have not feared God in any of these *things*,	and they have not feared God in any of these *things*,

4.23 ἠρήμωσαν 336^{+}260 ≡ ܕܐܚܪܒܘ 16h1 | -σεν 253 • ἐσκόρπισαν ἐν 336^{+}260 ≡ ܘܒܕܪܘܗܝ ܒ- 16h1 | ἐσκόρπισεν 253 • **4.24** ἐμνήσθησαν θ(εο)ῦ 336^{+}260 ≡ ܐܬܕܟܪܘ ܠܐܠܗܐ 16h1 | εμνήσθησ ἀν(θρώπ)ου 253 •

4.23–24 The hypocrites will suffer dishonor (v 21) for two reasons:

- **because** they have dishonored **many** others and **scattered** them (as described in verses 13, 15) **in their desire** (v 12; see the comments on 2.27);
- because **they have not been mindful of God** (Isa 1.3; Rom 1.28) and **have not feared** Him (Jer 5.23–24; Psa 36.1; 55.19; Luke 23.40).

"The fear of the LORD is to hate evil" (Prov 8.13; Exod 18.21) and turn aside from evil (Prov 16.6). But hypocrites, being Men-pleasers (vv 8, 21), are more fearful of people's actions than of God's (Prov 29.25; Luke 12.4–5).

4.25 **[21]** καὶ παρώργησαν τὸν θ(εὸ)ν· and they have made God angry	ܘܐܪܓܙܘ ܠܐܠܗܐ. and they have made God angry,
καὶ παρώξυνεν **[22]** ἐξάραι αὐτοὺσ ἀπὸ τ(ῆ)σ γῆσ· and He has sharpened *His anger* to remove them from the land,	ܘܐܬܚܡܬ ܠܡܘܒܕܘ ܐܢܘܢ ܡܢ ܐܪܥܐ. and He has become indignant to destroy them from the land,
ὅτι ψυχὰσ ἀκάκων παραλογισμῷ ὑπεκρίνοντο· because with deluding words they have been playing *the* hypocrite to souls of innocent *one*s.	ܡܛܠ ܕܠܢ̈ܦܫܬܐ ܬܡܝ̈ܡܬܐ. ܒܡܚܫ̈ܒܬܐ ܗܦܝ̈ܟܬܐ ܢܣܒܘ ܒܐܦ̈ܝܗܝܢ. because, with perverse reasoning, they have been playing *the* hypocrite to the innocent souls.

4.25 By their evil deeds, the hypocrites **have made God angry** (Deut 31.29; Jdg 2.12), **and He has sharpened**[118] **His anger to remove them from the land.** Those who provoke the LORD to anger will be destroyed by Him (Psa 2.12; Deut 9.18–19; 1 Kgs 15.29–30) **because** of their sins—**because with deluding words** (v 12) **they have been playing the hypocrite to souls of innocent ones.**[119] The New Testament Scriptures warn us to take care "that no one may delude you with persuasive words" (Col 2.4); there are many hypocrites who "by kind words and blessings deceive the hearts of the innocent" (Rom 16.17–18).

---

[118] **He has sharpened** *(parōxunen)* is the reading of 253, supported by the Syriac (16h1), whereas 336+260 read "they have sharpened" (*parōxunan,* which could easily be an accidental copying error, since the previous clause has a plural verb ending in *-an*).

The same word is used to describe God's anger in Deut 32.41, LXX ("I will sharpen [*paroxunō*] My sword"). In the present passage the verb has no object, and therefore the sense "hasten" (LSJ 1343, §III) is possible ("He has hastened to remove them from the land"), but the corresponding Syriac (**He has become indignant,** *'tḥmt*) and the parallel with Deut 32.41 favor the sense **He has sharpened [His anger],** the implied object being found in the previous clause. Such implied objects are very common in these psalms (cf., most recently, "they have scattered [the victims mentioned in the preceding clause]," v 23) and in the Hebrew Scriptures (GKC §117*f*).

[119] **They have been playing the hypocrite to** [*hupekrinonto*] **souls of innocent ones.** Trafton took the Syriac in an opposite sense—"they showed partiality to [*nsbw b'pyhyn*] innocent souls"—although he recognized that this did not fit the context (Trafton 71). Syriac *nsbw b'pyhyn* can indeed mean "showed partiality," but it can also mean "were hypocritical" (see the footnotes to vv 7 and 10). The context and the equivalent Greek show that the latter is the sense here ("they had played the hypocrite with innocent souls," Harris-Mingana).

God will deliver those who fear Him

4.26 [23] μακάριοι οἱ φοβούμενοι τὸν κ(ύριο)ν ἐν ἀκακίᾳ αὐτ(ῶν)· Blessed *are those* who fear the Lord in their innocence;	ܛܘܒܝܗܘܢ ܠܐܝܠܝܢ ܕܕܚܠܝܢ ܡܢ ܡܪܝܐ ܒܬܡܝܡܘܬܗܘܢ. Blessed *are* those who fear the LORD in their wholeheartedness;
4.27 [23] καὶ ὁ κ(ύριο)σ ῥῦσεται αὐτοὺσ ἀπὸ ἀν(θρώπ)ων δολίων καὶ ἁμαρτωλῶν· and the Lord will deliver them from deceitful and sinful human beings,	ܘܡܪܝܐ ܢܦܪܘܩ ܐܢܘܢ ܡܢ ܓܒܪ̈ܐ ܢܟܘܠܬܢܐ ܘܥܘ̈ܠܐ. and the LORD will save them from the men who speak falsehood and *are* unjust,
καὶ ῥύσεται ἡμᾶσ ἀπὸ παντὸσ σκανδάλου παρανόμου· and He will deliver us from every stumblingblock of *the* Law-breaker.	ܘܢܦܪܘܩ ܡܢ ܟܠ ܡܟܫܘܠܐ ܕܥܘ̈ܠܐ. and He will save us from every stumblingblock of the unjust *one*s.

4.26–27 Despite all the evils that the **Law-breaker** does, **those who fear the Lord in their innocence** are richly **blessed** (Psa 112.1; 128.1, 4; 115.13). "To fear the LORD" is "for our good always, that He may make us live" (Deut 6.24), and **He will deliver us from every stumblingblock** set in our path by the enemy (Matt 13.41; Psa 119.165; 141.9, LXX). "The angel of the LORD camps around those who fear Him, and delivers them" (Psa 34.7). For earthly Israel, that involved earthly blessings (Deut 6.1–2); for today's spiritual Israel, it involves spiritual blessings (Col 3.22–24; Rev 11.18).

4.28 [24] ἐξάραι ὁ θ(εὸ)σ τοὺσ ποιοῦντασ ἐν υπερηφανίᾳ πᾶσαν ἀδικίαν· May God take away those who do all unrighteousness in arrogance,	ܐܘܒܕ ܐܠܗܐ ܟܠ ܕܥܒ̈ܕܝܢ ܛܠܘܡܝܐ ܒܫܘܒܗܪܬܐ. God has destroyed all *those* who do wrongfully in pride,
ὅτι κριτὴσ μέγασ καὶ κραταιὸσ **4.29 [24]** κ(ύριο)σ ὁ θ(εὸ)σ ἡμῶν ἐν δικαιοσύνῃ· because a great and mighty judge in righteousness *is the* Lord our God.	ܡܛܠ ܕܕܝܢܐ ܚܣܝܢܐ ܡܪܝܐ ܗܘ ܐܠܗܢ. ܒܙܕܝܩܘܬܐ because the powerful judge in righteousness is the LORD our God.
[25] γένοιτο κ(ύρι)ε τὸ ἔλεόσ σου ἐπι πάντασ τοὺσ ἀγαπῶντάσ σε: Lord, may Your† mercy come to be on all those who love You†.	ܢܗܘܘܢ ܡܪܝܐ ܪ̈ܚܡܝܟ ܥܠ ܟܠܗܘܢ ܐܝܠܝܢ ܕܪܚܡܝܢ ܠܟ. LORD, may Your† compassion be on all those who love You†.

4.28–29 May God take away[120] **those who do all unrighteousness in arrogance** (Deut 29.20–21; Isa 13.11; Psa 5.4–6), whereas **may Your mercy come to be on all those who love You.** "God is not unrighteous to forget … the love that you have shown for His name" (Heb 6.10); those who are merciful will themselves receive **mercy** (Matt 5.7; 2 Tim 1.16–18; Matt 25.34–40).

A great and mighty judge in righteousness is the Lord our God (Rev 16.5–7; Psa 98.9; 47.2; 92.15; 7.11). "The LORD … is righteous; He will not do unrighteousness; morning by morning He gives forth His judgment" (Zep 3.5). "Your righteousness is like the mountains of God; Your judgment is like the great deep" (Psa 36.6). His judgments are so great that they are beyond searching (Rom 11.33).

Psalm 5

This psalm has a symmetrical A-B-C-B-A structure:

- A. **Praise** the **name** of the **Lord** with **gladness** because He is **kind** (vv 1–3).
  - B. Each person's **portion** is **from** God, and he cannot **increase it beyond** God's **judgment** (vv 4–6).
    - C. In our **oppression,** we **will call on** God **for help,** and He **will hearken** (vv 7–17).
  - B. The Lord's **blessing** is a **due measure of sufficiency;** someone who has an **overabundance … sins** (vv 18–20).
- A. His people are **glad** because His **kindness is on** them; **blessed** is the **glory** of the **Lord** (v 21–22).

Lord, You are kind and merciful

5.0 [0] Ψαλμὸς· τῷ Σαλωμῶν: A psalm belonging to Solomon.	
5.1 [1] Κ(ύρι)ε ὁ θ(εό)σ αἰνέσω τῷ ὀνόματί σου ἐν ἀγαλλιάσει· Lord, O God, I will praise Your† name with gladness,	ܡܪܝܐ ܐܠܗܝ ܐܫܒܚ ܫܡܟ ܒܪܢܝܐ. LORD my God, I will glorify Your† name with delight,
ἐν μέσῳ ἐπισταμένων τὰ κρίματά σου τὰ δίκαια· in *the* midst of *those* who understand Your† righteous judgments,	ܒܝܢܬ ܐܝܠܝܢ ܕܝܕܥܝܢ ܕܝܢܝ̈ܟ ܙܕܝܩܐ. among those who know Your† righteous judgments,
5.2 [2] ὅτι ‹σὺ χρηστὸσ› καὶ ἐλεήμων ἡ καταφυγὴ τοῦ πτωχοῦ·	ܡܛܠ ܕܐܢܬ ܒܣܝܡ ܘܡܪܚܡܢ. ܘܒܝܬ ܓܘܣܗ ܕܡܣܟܢܐ.

[120] **Take away** *(exarai)*. Mistaking the medieval scribe's ligature, Wright incorrectly gives the reading of 253 as *xarai*.

because You† *are* kind and merciful, the refuge of the poor *one;*	because You† *are* kind and compassionate, and *the* house of refuge of the poor *one;*
5.3 [2] ἐν τῷ κεκραγέναι με πρὸσ σὲ μὴ παρασιωπήσησ ἀπ᾽ ἐμοῦ· when I have cried out to You†, do† not pass by me in silence.	ܟܕ ܐܩܥܐ ܠܘܬܟ ܠܐ ܬܫܬܘܩ ܡܢܝ. when I call out to You†, do not be silent† from me.

5.2 σὺ χρηστὸσ 336⁺260 ≡ ܕܐܢܬ ܒܣܝܡ 16h1 | εὔχρηστο(σ) 253 •

5.1–2[121] **Lord, O God, I will praise Your name with gladness ... because You are kind and merciful.** "All the earth" has reason to "serve the LORD with joy," praising and giving thanks to Him, "for the LORD is good; His lovingkindness is to lasting time" (Psa 100.1–5; 32.11–33.5; cf. Luke 19.37). "Let me praise Your name to lasting time and continuing time .... The LORD is favorable and compassionate, long to anger and great of lovingkindness; the LORD is good to all, and His compassions are over all His works" (Psa 145.1–2, 8–9; Joel 2.13; Psa 86.5).

He is **the refuge**[122] **of the poor one** (see on 15.2), "a secure height for the crushed one, a secure height at times of oppression" (Psa 9.9; 14.6; 35.10), "a stronghold for the poor one, a stronghold for the needy one in his oppression, a refuge from the storm" (Isa 25.4).

5.3 When I have cried out to You (v 7), **do not pass by me in silence.** The Lord is silent when He is "far away from" people (Psa 35.22) and does not hearken to their entreaties (Psa 39.12; cf. Psa 28.1; 83.1–2; 109.1–2). He does **not pass by ... in silence** when He takes action to deliver the righteous (Psa 50.3–6, LXX) and to punish the wicked (Isa 65.6–7).

Who will take from You, unless You give?

5.4 [3] οὐ γὰρ λήψεται σκύλα παρὰ ἀνδρὸσ δυνατοῦ· For *one* will not take plunder from a powerful man;	ܡܛܠ ܕܠܐ ܢܣܒ ܓܒܪ ܒܪܢܫܐ ܫܒܝܬܐ ܡܢ ܓܒܪܐ ܓܢܒܪܐ. Because a son of man *will* not take *any* captured *thing* from the powerful man;

[121] In the Greek copies (but not in the Syriac), the psalm is superscribed **A psalm belonging to Solomon.**

[122] **Refuge** (Greek *kataphugē*) ≡ **house of refuge** (Syriac *byt ʿrwqyh*); a place to flee (*pheugō* ≡ *ʿrq*). "We have fled for refuge [*kataphugontes*]" so that we may "take firm hold of the hope set before us" (Heb 6.18).

5.5 [3] κ(αὶ) τίσ λήψεται ἀπὸ πάντ(ων) ὧν ἐποίησασ ἐὰν μη σὺ δῶσ·	ܐܘ ܡܢܘ ܢܣܒ ܡܢ ܟܠ ܡܕܡ ܕܥܒܕܬ. ܐܠܐ ܐܢ ܐܢܬ ܬܬܠ ܠܗ.
and who will take from all *things* that You† have made, unless You† Yourself† should give?	indeed, who *will* take from any thing that You† have made, unless You† Yourself† should give *it* to him?

5.4–5 No one can **take plunder**[123] from anyone who is more **powerful** (Mark 3.27). **Who** among us, therefore, can **take** anything from God, **unless** He Himself, in His good pleasure, chooses to **give** it to us (Rom 11.35–36; 1 Chr 29.11–12; 1 Cor 4.7; Jas 1.17, 5)?

5.6 [4] ὅτι ἄν(θρωπ)οσ καὶ ἡ μερὶσ αὐτοῦ παρὰ σοῦ ἐν σταθμῷ·	ܡܛܠ ܕܒܪܐܢܫܐ ܘܡܢܬܗ ܠܘܬܟ ܗܝ ܒܡܬܩܠܐ.
Because a person and his portion *are* from You† in a balance;	Because a son of man and his portion is from You† in the balance,
οὐ προσθήσει τοῦ πλεονάσαι παρὰ τὸ κρίμα σου ὁ θ(εό)σ·	ܘܠܐ ܢܘܣܦ ܠܡܬܝܬܪܘ ܠܒܪ ܡܢ ܕܝܢܟ. ܐܠܗܐ.
he will not proceed to increase *it* beyond Your† judgment, O God.	and he will not proceed to increase *it* beyond Your† judgment, God.

5.6 **A person and his portion are from** God: He is the One who determines what each one of us is (Exod 4.11; Rom 9.20–21; 1 Cor 12.18), and what each one of us has (our **portion:** see on 3.15). He has weighed out our **portion** precisely, as if **in a balance** (Wis 11.20; Psa 39.4–5; cf. Ezek 4.10), and we cannot **proceed to increase it** (Matt 6.27; Ecc 3.14) **beyond** His allotted **judgment.** "A person cannot receive anything at all, unless it has been given to him from Heaven" (John 3.27; Psa 127.1). See also the footnote to 9.7b.

In our oppression we will call on You

5.7 [5] ἐν τῷ θλίβεσθαι ἡμᾶσ ἐπικαλεσόμεθα ‹σε› εἰσ βοήθειαν·	ܒܐܘܠܨܢ ܩܪܝܢܟ ܠܥܘܕܪܢܢ.
In our oppression we will call on You† for help,	In our affliction we will call on You† for our help,
καὶ σὺ οὐκ ἀποστρέψη τὴν δέησιν ἡμῶν	ܘܐܢܬ ܠܐ ܐܗܦܟܬ ܒܥܘܬܢ.

[123] The Syriac version has *šbyt'*, a term usually applied to a captured people (e.g., Isa 45.13, Syr) but sometimes, as here, to a **captured thing** (TS 2.4020–21, §2; Begrich, "Text der Psalmen Salomos," 145–46); note *mqm* (**thing**) in the next line.

and You† Yourself‡ will not turn away our request,	and You† Yourself‡ have not turned away our request,
ὅτι σὺ ὁ θ(εὸ)σ ἡμῶν εἶ· because You† Yourself‡ are our God.	ܡܛܠ ܕܐܢܬ ܗܘ ܐܠܗܢ. because You† Yourself‡ are our God.

5.7 σε 336⁺260 ≡ 16h1 | > 253 •

5.7 We can receive nothing unless God gives it (vv 5–6), so in any time of distress (**oppression**), we must **call on** Him (6.1) **for help** (Isa 43.11; 45.22; Acts 4.12). None of us, however mighty, can deliver ourselves from trouble (Amos 2.14–15; Ecc 9.11).

We can call on Him only if He is **our God** (Exod 6.7; Zec 13.9; Isa 41.10). "We know that God does not hear sinners; but if anyone is God-fearing and does His will, He hears him" (John 9.31; Psa 66.18; Prov 28.9; 15.29; 1 Jn 3.22). That is His consistent promise: "The LORD's face is against those who do evil," but "the LORD's eyes are toward righteous ones, and His ears are toward their cry for help .... They have cried out, and the LORD has heard, and from all their oppressions He has brought them to safety" (Psa 34.15–17 ≡ 1 Pet 3.12).

5.8 [6] μη βαρύνησ τὴν χεῖρά σου ἐφ' ἡμᾶσ· Do not weigh down† Your† hand on us,	ܠܐ ܬܫܬܘܚܪܝ ܐܝܕܟ ܡܢܢ. Do not let Your† hand delay away from us,
ἵνα μὴ δι ἀνάγκην ἁμαρτωμεν· in order that we may not sin because of compulsion.	ܕܠܐ ܢܬܥܫܢ ܕܢܚܛܐ. so that we may not be overcome so that we may sin.

5.8 Do not weigh down Your hand on us,[124] **in order that we may not sin because of compulsion.** God does not compel anyone to sin; those who sin, sin by their own choice (Jas 1.13–15; Eighteen Psalms 9.7–9; Ezek 33.11). Sin cannot rule over those whom God protects (1 Cor 10.13) and who obey Him (1 Jn 3.6–9). Those who act in the integrity of their heart, God can withhold from sinning (Gen 20.6). But those who disobey Him, God will give over to sin (Psa 81.11–12; John 12.37–40; Rom 1.24,

[124] **Do not weigh down Your hand on us** (Greek). The Syriac manuscript (16h1) has **Do not let Your hand delay** [*tštwḥry*] **away from us** (cf. "LORD, do not delay," Psa 40.17, Syr; Dan 9.19; "away from [*mn*]," 2 Thes 1.9, Syr). A Hebrew text *ʿl tʾḥr ydk ʿlynw* could be read either as "Do not let Your hand linger upon us" (using *ʿl* "of what rests heavily *upon* a person," BDB 753, §II.1b; cf. Greek) or as "Do not let Your hand linger opposed against us" (using *ʿl* "in a hostile sense ... *against,*" BDB 757–58, §II.7d; cf. Syriac).

Kuhn (*Die älteste Textgestalt der Psalmen Salomos,* 19) and Trafton (75–76) proposed that the Syriac originally had *twqr* ("weigh down"), which was changed accidentally to *twḥr* and then consciously to *tštwḥry;* but the second step would be hard to explain, especially as it left such an unusual construction. Why would anyone make such an alteration without also altering *mn* to the usual *l-* plus infinitive (as in "my lord delays to [*l-*] come," Matt 24.48 [Syr], etc.)?

26; 11.8; 2 Thes 2.11); and if we persist in disobeying Him, He may give us over to sin so that we have no power to repent—we **sin because of compulsion,** and are incapable of doing otherwise (Heb 6.4–6). Therefore we must entreat Him **not** to subject us to that terrible punishment, but to deliver us from evil (Matt 6.13; Psa 19.13; 119.133; Prov 30.7–9) and to correct us with His **hand** gently and mercifully, not heavily (Psa 38.1–2; 6.1; Jer 10.24; Hab 3.2).

5.9 [7] καὶ ἐὰν μὴ ἐπιστρέψησ ἡμᾶσ οὐκ αφεξόμεθα And if You† should not turn us back, we will not be far away,	ܘܠܐ ܬܗܦܘܟ ܐܦ̈ܝܟ ܡܢܢ: ܕܠܐ ܢܪܚܩ ܡܢܟ. And do not turn† Your† face from us, so that we may not be far off from You†,
ἀλλ' ἐπι σὲ ἥξομεν· but to You† we will come.	ܐܠܐ ܠܘܬܟ ܢܐܬܐ. but to You† we will come.

5.9 And if You should not turn us back, [125] **we will not be far away, but to You we will come.** The expression **turn us back** *(epistrepsēs hēmas)* has often been interpreted "turn us back to You," "restore us to You" (cf. Psa 80.7, 19), resulting in such translations as: "Even if you do not restore us, we will not stay away, but will come to you" (OTP). But that would hardly make sense. How could any of us return to God if God Himself did not restore us (vv 4–7)? In the present context, therefore, **turn us back** must mean "turn us back to our former state" ("to the point of origin," Muraoka 282, §Ia), as in Gal 4.9. We will come to God unless He Himself turns us back by turning His face **from us** (Syriac) and weighing down His hand on us so that we cannot escape from our sin (v 8). "LORD, I will seek Your face ... do not turn away Your servant in anger" (Psa 27.8–9; 22.24). Jesus has promised: "All that the Father gives Me will come to Me; and the one who comes to Me I will certainly not cast out" (John 6.37).

5.10 [8] ἐὰν γὰρ πινάσω πρὸσ σὲ κεκράξομαι ὁ θ(εό)σ For if I should be hungry, to You† I will cry out, O God,	ܐܢܓܝܪ ܐܟܦܢ ܡܪܝܐ ܠܘܬܟ ܐܩܪܐ ܐܠܗܐ For if I should be hungry, LORD, to You† I will call, God,
καὶ σὺ δώσεισ μοι· and You† Yourself† will give to me.	ܘܐܢܬ ܬܬܠ. and You† Yourself† will give.

5.10 To Him we must look for all our needs: **if I should be hungry, to You I will cry out, O God** (as Jesus instructed us to do, Matt 6.11), **and You Yourself will give to me** (Psa 107.4–9; Luke 1.53). The principle is not limited to bodily hunger: "Blessed

[125] The corresponding Syriac reads **And do not turn Your face from us** (as in: "LORD, do not turn Your face from me, and do not afflict Your servant in anger, and do not cast me out," Psa 27.9, Syr).

are those who hunger and thirst for righteousness, for they shall be filled" (Matt 5.6; Isa 55.1–2). "Those who seek the LORD do not lack any good thing" (Psa 34.10).

You nourish all creatures

5.11 [9] τὰ πετεινὰ καὶ τοὺσ ἰχθύασ σὺ τρέφεισ· The flying creatures and the fishes You† Yourself‡ nourish	ܠܦܪܚܬܐ ܓܝܪ ܘܠܢ̈ܘܢܐ ܐܢܬ ܡܪܒܐ ܐܢܬ. For the flying creature and the fishes You† Yourself‡ make to grow
ἐν τῷ διδόναι σε ὑετὸν ἐρήμοισ εἰσ ἀνατολὴν χλόησ· when You† give rain to deserts for *the* rising of green growth,	ܟܕ ܡܬܠ ܡܛܪܐ ܒܡܕܒܪܐ ܠܡܦܩܢܘܬܐ ܕܬܕܐܐ. when You† give rain in the desert for the bringing forth of the green sprout,
[10] ἑτοιμάσαι χορτάσματα ἐν ἐρήμω παντὶ ζῶντι· to prepare food in *the* desert for every*thing* that is living;	ܠܡܛܝܒܘ ܡܐܟܘܠܬܐ ܒܡܕܒܪܐ ܠܟܠ ܚܝܘܬܐ. to prepare food in the desert for every living creature;
5.12 [10] καὶ ἐὰν πινάσωσιν πρὸσ σὲ ἀροῦσιν πρόσωπον αὐτῶν· and if they should be hungry, to You† they will lift up their face.	ܘܐܢ ܢܟܦܢܘܢ ܠܘܬܟ ܢܪܝܡܘܢ ܐܦ̈ܝܗܘܢ. and if they should be hungry, to You† they will lift up their faces.

5.11–12 The Lord loves everything that He has made (Wis 11.24–26) and provides nourishment **for everything that is living,** whether plant or animal;[126] in their hunger, **they will lift up their face** to Him, just as we ourselves are to do (v 10). "The eyes of all hope for You, and You give them their food in the time" (Psa 145.15–16; 104.27–28, 10–15). If God provides for the birds and the fishes, how much more will He provide for those who fear Him (Luke 12.24)?

5.13 [11] τοὺσ βασιλεῖσ καὶ ἄρχοντασ καὶ λαοὺσ σὺ ‹τρέφεισ› ὁ θ(εό)σ· The kings and rulers and peoples You† Yourself‡ nourish, O God,	ܠܡ̈ܠܟܐ ܘܠܪ̈ܘܪܒܢܐ ܘܠܥܡ̈ܡܐ ܐܢܬ ܗܘ ܡܬܪܣܐ ܐܠܗܐ. The kings and the great *one*s and the peoples You† Yourself‡ nourish, God,

5.13 τρέφεισ 336⁺260 ≡ ܡܬܪܣܐ 16h1 | στρ- 253 •

[126] **You give rain . . . to prepare** [*hetoimasai*] **food in the desert for everything that is living.** Gebhardt and Rahlfs conjecturally emended the infinitive to *hētoimasas* ("You prepare"), without any manuscript support in either Greek or Syriac.

καὶ πτωχοῦ καὶ πένητοσ ἡ ἐλπὶσ τίσ ἐστιν εἰ μη σὺ κ(ύρι)ε	ܘܣܒܪܗ ܕܡܣܟܢܐ ܘܕܒܝܫܐ. ܡܢܘ. ܐܠܐ ܐܢ ܐܢܬ ܡܪܝܐ.
and who is the hope of a poor *one* and of an impoverished *one,* except You†, Lord?	and who is *the* hope of the poor *one* and of the wretched *one,* except You†, LORD?

5.13 He also provides nourishment for all people, from **kings and rulers** to the **poor** and **impoverished**[127] (Gen 1.29–30; 9.3; Psa 136.25; Acts 14.16–17). What other **hope** do any of us have (Job 27.8–9; Psa 146.3–5; 1 Tim 6.17)?

The kindness of God

5.14 [12] καὶ σὺ ‹ἐπακούσῃ› ὅτι τίσ χρηστὸ(σ) καὶ ἐπιεικὴσ ἀλλ ἢ σύ·	ܘܬܥܢܝܘܗܝ، ܡܛܠ ܕܐܢܬ ܗܘ ܒܣܝܡܐ ܘܢܝܚܐ.
And You† Yourself† will hearken, because who *is* kind and tolerant but You†,	and You† will answer, because You† are kind and gentle,
εὐφράναι ψυχὴν ταπεινοῦ ἐν τῷ ἀνοίξαι χεῖρά σου ἐν ελέει·	ܘܬܣܒܥ ܢܦܫܗ ܟܕ ܬܦܬܚ ܠܗ ܐܝܕܟ ܒܪܚܡܐ.
making *the* soul of *the* humble *one* glad by the opening up of Your† hand in mercy?	and his soul will be satisfied, when You† open Your† hand to him in compassion.

5.14 ἐπακούσῃ 336 [-ηι 260] | -ησ 253 •

5.14 God's people can be confident that, when they seek Him in the way He has appointed, He **will hearken** as He has promised (see the comments on v 7)—not because of their merit, but **because** He is merciful (Dan 9.18; Titus 3.5). He, and He alone, **is kind and tolerant** (Matt 11.30; Luke 6.35; Rom 2.4), opening up His **hand in mercy** to gladden **the soul of the humble one** (Acts 14.17; cf. Psa 4.7). "You, Lord, are good, and forgiving, and great of lovingkindness to all those who call on You" (Psa 86.4–5). **Who** else is like that? "There is no one holy like the LORD; for there is no one righteous like our God" (1 Sam 2.2, LXX). "No one is good except one: God" (Mark 10.18).

5.15 [13] ἡ χρηστότησ ἀνθρώπου ἐν φειδῷ καὶ ἡ αὔριον·	ܠܒܣܝܡܘܬܗ ܓܝܪ ܕܒܪܢܫܐ. ܒܚܘܣܢܐ ܗܝ.. ܝܘܡܢ ܘܡܚܪ.
The kindness of a human being *is done* sparingly and the next day,	For *the* goodness of a son of man is *done* sparingly, today and tomorrow,

[127] Greek **impoverished** *(penētos)* ≡ Syriac **wretched** *(byš')*, i.e., badly off—a common meaning of this word (TS 1.440; SL 144). In French, Prigent neatly renders it *miséreux*.

Greek	Syriac
καὶ ἐὰν δευτερώσῃ ἄνευ γογγυσμοῦ καὶ τοῦτο θαυμάσιασ· and if he should do *it* twice without grumbling, then You† might be amazed at this;	ܘܐܢ ܗܘ ܕܬܢܐ ܠܡܬܠ ܘܠܐ ܪܛܢ. ܘܗܢܐ ܬܡܗܐ ܗܘ. and if he *is* giving again and not murmuring, then this is an astonishing thing;
5.16 [14] τὸ δὲ δόμα σου πολὺ μετα χρηστότητοσ καὶ πλούσιον· but Your† gift *is* great with kindness, and rich,	ܡܘܗܒܬܟ ܕܝܢ ܕܝܠܟ ܣܓܝܐܐ ܒܛܝܒܘܬܐ ܘܒܒܥܘܬܐ. but Your† own gift *is* great with goodness and with a request,
καὶ οὐκ ἐστιν ἡ ἐλπὶσ ἐπὶ σὲ οὐ φείσεται ἐν δόματι· and *there* is no hope on You† when he will be sparing with a gift.	ܘܠܝܬ ܣܒܪܐ ܕܠܘܬܟ ܕܚܝܣ ܒܡܘܗܒܬܐ. and there is no hope with You† when he will be sparing with gifts,

5.15 Human **kindness** is a rare commodity (cf. Rom 3.12), administered only in tiny doses (**sparingly,** 2 Cor 9.6; cf. Sir 20.15), seldom **without grumbling** (1 Pet 4.9; cf. 2 Cor 9.7), and perpetually put off till tomorrow (not now, but **the next day**).[128] Instead, we should be predisposed to give when the need arises: "You shall not hold back good ... when it is in the power of your hand to do it. You shall not say to your companion, 'Go away, and come back, and tomorrow I will give,' when it is there with you" (Prov 3.27–28; cf. Luke 6.30, 34–36; Deut 15.7–10).

5.16 By contrast, God's giving is generous (**rich**)[129] and abundantly kind (**great with kindness**). "The LORD is favorable and compassionate, long to anger and great of lovingkindness" (Psa 145.8). "His compassions have never ended; they are new at each of the mornings" (Lam 3.22–23).

God does not approve the person described in the previous verse (**he**)[130]—the person who **will be sparing with a gift** (v 15). If we are ungenerous and unmerciful to others, **there is no hope** that God will be generous and merciful to us (Matt 18.21–35; 6.12–15; Jas 2.13; Sir 28.3–5).[131] Only those who are themselves kind and

---

[128] **Sparingly and the next day** is the reading of the Greek text. The Syriac (16h1) reads **sparingly, today and tomorrow,** i.e., for a short time only (Luke 13.32).

[129] **Rich.** The Syriac (16h1) reads **with a request** *(bb'wt');* the Lord gives His good gifts to those who ask Him (Matt 7.7–11; Jas 1.5–7; Psa 145.18–19; 86.5). Harris-Mingana and Baars emended the Syriac to *b'wtr'* ("with wealth").

[130] **He will be sparing** (Greek *pheisetai* ≡ Syr *nḥws*). The subject of the verb is the same as the subject of **he should do it twice** (*deuterōsē*, Greek) ≡ **he** [*hw*] **is giving again** (Syr) in the previous verse—i.e., the ungenerous **human being** *(anthrōpou,* Greek) ≡ **son of man** (*br'nš',* Syr).

[131] **There is no** [*ouk*] **hope on You when** [*hou,* in a situation where] **he will be sparing with a gift.** The same Greek construction is seen in Rom 4.15: there is no transgression "when [*hou,*

generous (2 Cor 8.1–5) will reap kindness and generosity from the Lord: "One who sows sparingly will also reap sparingly, and one who sows with blessings will also reap with blessings" (2 Cor 9.6–11). "A person who shows favor to a weak one lends to the LORD, and He will repay him his dealing" (Prov 19.17).

5.17 [15] ἐπι πᾶσαν τὴν γῆν τὸ ἔλεόσ σου κ(ύρι)ε ἐν χρηστότητι· Your† mercy, Lord, *is* upon all the earth in kindness.	ܥܠ ܟܠܗ̇ ܐܪܥܐ ܓܝܪ ܪ̈ܚܡܝܟ ܡܪܝܐ ܒܛܝܒܘܬܐ. for Your† compassions, LORD, *are* upon all the earth in goodness.

5.17 The Lord's **mercy . . . in kindness** is not localized or limited in extent (as human mercy is, Sir 18.13). Instead, it extends **upon all the earth.** Humans may do small-scale deeds of mercy and kindness for a good person or a friend, but God has lavished deeds of boundless mercy and kindness on everyone—even on His enemies (Rom 5.7–8; Matt 5.44–48; Luke 6.34–35). "The LORD is good to all, and His compassions are over all His works" (Psa 145.9).

A due measure is enough

5.18 [16] μακάριοσ οὗ μνημονεύει ὁ θ(εὸ)σ ἐν συμμετρία αὐταρκίασ· Blessed *is the one* of whom God is mindful with a due measure of sufficiency;	ܛܘܒܘܗ̱ܝ ܠܒܪܢܫܐ ܕܡܬܕܟܪܘܗ̱ܝ ܡܪܝܐ ܒܡܣܟܢܘܬܐ. Blessed *is the* son of man of whom the LORD is mindful in poverty;
5.19 [16] ἐὰν ὑπερπλεονάση ὁ ἄν(θρωπ)οσ ἐξαμαρτάνει· if a person should have an overabundance, he sins.	ܕܣܦܩܘܬܗ ܓܝܪ ܡܬܝܬܪ ܒܪܢܫܐ ܕܢܚܛܐ ܠܗ. for a son of man will have an overabundance of his sufficiency, so that he will sin because of it.
5.20 [17] ἱκανὸν τὸ μέτριον ἐν δικαιοσύνῃ· *An amount* in measure with righteousness *is* enough,	ܦܘܫܐ ܡܣܟܢܘܬܐ ܒܙܕܝܩܘܬܐ. Poverty with righteousness *is* profitable.

in a situation where] there is no law" (BDAG 733, §2). In 253 *hou* is given a smooth breathing *(ou),* and our printed Greek text reproduces that, but no breathings would have been marked in the earliest manuscripts; *ou* makes no sense in this context ("there is no hope on You that will not [*ou*] be sparing with a gift"), and *hou* is confirmed by the Syriac (16h1), which reads **there is no hope with You when** [*d-*] **he will be sparing with gifts** (Nöldeke §347; or ". . . which will be sparing with gifts" [Trafton]). The reading of 260 is "the one whose [*hou*] hope is on You will not [*ou*] be sparing with a gift"—which does not materially change the point of the line. The sparing giver has no hope (253 and 16h1); the unsparing giver has hope (260).

καὶ ἐν τούτω ἡ εὐλογία κ(υρίο)υ
εἰσ πλεισμονὴν
ἐν δικαιοσύνη·
and in this *is* the Lord's blessing
for full satisfaction
with righteousness.

5.18–20 To have **a due measure of sufficiency** (*autark[e]ias,* an amount **in measure,**[132] not an **overabundance**) is a **blessing** from **the Lord.** Such an amount, **with righteousness,** is **enough** for **full satisfaction.**[133] "Reverence with sufficiency [*autarkeias*] is great gain. For we carried nothing into the world, for neither are we able to carry anything out; but having nourishment and clothing, with these things we will be sufficed [*arkesthēsometha*]" (1 Tim 6.6–8; cf. Php 4.11–12). "Good is a little, with the fear of the LORD, beyond much treasure and tumult with it" (Prov 15.16–17; 16.8). That **blessing** was what the Lord gave His people in the wilderness: "the one gathering much had no excess, and the one gathering little had no lack; a man gathered according to the mouth of his eating" (Exod 16.18 ≡ 2 Cor 8.15; cf. Deut 12.15; 16.17). Under the new covenant, likewise, "God is able to make all favor abound to you, so that in everything, always having all sufficiency [*autarkeian*], you may abound to every good work" (2 Cor 9.8).

But **if a person should have an overabundance, he sins.** "Those who want to be rich fall into temptation and a snare and many senseless and harmful desires, which plunge people into ruin and destruction" (1 Tim 6.9–10). "How hard it is for those who have riches to go into the kingdom of God!" (Mark 10.23–25; cf. Luke 16.19–25). Therefore we are to pray: "Do not give me destitution or riches; tear for me the bread of my allowance, lest I am filled, and act falsely, and say 'Who is the LORD?', or lest I lose my possessions and steal, and violate the name of my God" (Prov 30.7–9; cf. Matt 6.11).

Your kindness will be on Israel

5.21 [18] ηὐφράνθησαν
οἱ φοβούμενοι κ(ύριο)ν ἐν ἀγαθοῖσ·
Those who fear *the* Lord
have been glad in good *things*,

ܐܬܒܣܡܘ ܓܝܪ
ܕܕ̈ܚܠܘܗܝ ܕܡܪܝܐ ܒܛܒ̈ܬܗ
For *those* who fear the LORD
have been glad in His good things,

[132] **Due measure** *(summetria)* . . . **measure** *(metrion).* The terms indicate a severely limited amount (Ezek 4.11, 16, LXX); the corresponding Syriac is **poverty** (*msknwt',* TS 2.2633; SL 791), the opposite of riches (Prov 10.15, Syr).

[133] The sentence **and in this is the Lord's blessing for full satisfaction with righteousness** is not present in the Syriac manuscript (16h1). As the previous line also ends **with righteousness,** a copyist's eye might easily have skipped over it.

καὶ ἡ χρηστότησ σου ἐπι Ἰ(σρα)ὴλ ‹ἐ(ν)› τῇ βασιλεία σου· and Your† kindness *will be* upon Israel in Your† kingdom.	ܘܛܝܒܘܬܟ ܥܠ ܐܝܣܪܝܠ ܒܡܠܟܘܬܟ. and Your† goodness *will be* upon Israel in Your† kingdom.
[19] εὐλογημένη ἡ δόξα κ(υρίο)υ ὅτι αὐτὸσ βασιλεὺσ ἡμῶν: Blessed *be* the glory of *the* Lord, because He *is* our King.	ܡܒܪܟܐ ܗܝ ܬܫܒܘܚܬܗ ܕܡܪܝܐ. ܡܛܠ ܕܗܘܝܘ ܡܠܟܢ Blessed is *the* glory of the LORD, because He is our King.

5.21 ἐ(ν) 2° 260 \| > 253 •

5.21 The Lord's **kindness will be on Israel** (Deut 32.9–14); those **who fear** Him are those whom He blesses with **good things.** "The LORD's eye is toward those who fear Him . . . to bring their soul to safety from death, and to keep them alive in hunger" (Psa 33.18–19; 112.1–3; 128.1–4). Indeed, "there is no lack for those who fear Him . . . those who seek the LORD do not lack any good thing" (Psa 34.9–10). "The LORD's lovingkindness is from lasting time and to lasting time on those who fear Him" (Psa 103.17). Under the new covenant, those people of every nation who keep God's commands are His **Israel** (Rom 2.26–29) and receive the blessings of His **kindness** (Rom 11.22; Titus 3.4–7). He may sometimes deprive them of earthly food (Php 4.12; 1 Cor 4.11; 2 Cor 11.27), and sooner or later He inevitably deprives them of earthly life (Heb 9.27), but He always gives them a sufficiency of whatever He knows them to need—whatever He knows to be **good** for them (2 Cor 12.9–10; Psa 84.11; Matt 6.31–33; 7.11). Even when He deprives them of life, He gives them something that is "very much better" (Php 1.23).

God's people **have been glad in** these **good things** (Psa 126.3; John 16.22; Acts 2.46; Phil 4.4; 1 Pet 1.5–8),[134] and bless[135] His glory **because He is** their **King.** "The sons of Zion will rejoice in their King" (Psa 149.2; Zec 9.9). "I will exalt You, my God, O King, and let me praise Your name to lasting time" (Psa 145.1).

Blessed be the glory of the Lord (Ezek 3.12). The **glory of the Lord** was manifested to the eyes of a few chosen people at Mount Sinai (Exod 24.16–17) and in His tabernacle (Exod 40.34) and temple (1 Kgs 8.10–11), and is now revealed to the understanding of everyone in the world who receives Jesus (Isa 40.5; John 1.12–14), for Jesus is "the brightness of His glory" (Heb 1.3; 2 Cor 4.6). That **glory** is **blessed** "above all blessing and praise" (Neh 9.5) "to lasting time" (Psa 72.19).

---

[134] **Those who fear the Lord have been glad** (*ēuphranthēsan,* 253 ≡ *euphranthēsan,* 260 [a common spelling variant: Thackeray §5, 68; §16.4] ≡ *'tbsmw,* 16h1). Gebhardt and Rahlfs conjecturally emended the Greek text to *euphrantheiēsan* ("May those who fear the Lord be glad"), but that has no manuscript support in either Greek or Syriac. The past tense is emphasized even more strongly in Psa 126.3 (*egenēthēmen euphrainomenoi,* LXX, "we have become glad").

[135] **Blessed is the glory of the Lord.** In this verse, **blessed** translates *eulogēmenē,* "spoken well of [*eu*-]" by His servants (Luke 1.64; 24.53; 1 Cor 14.16; Rev 5.13; 7.11–12; cf. Jas 3.9).

Psalm 6

The man who calls on the name of the Lord will be saved

6.0 [0] Ἐν ελπίδι τῷ Σολομῶν:	
In hope; belonging to Solomon.	

6.1 [1] Μακάριοσ ἀνὴρ οὗ ἡ καρδία αὐτοῦ ἑτοίμη ἐπικαλέσασθαι τὸ ὄνομα κ(υρίο)υ·	ܛܘܒܘܗܝ ܠܒܪܢܫܐ ܕܡܛܝܒ ܠܒܗ ܠܡܩܪܐ ܒܫܡܗ ܕܡܪܝܐ.
Blessed *is the* man whose heart *is* prepared to call on the name of *the* Lord;	Blessed *is the* son of man whose heart *is* prepared to call in *the* name of the LORD,
6.2 [1] ἐν τῷ μνημονεύειν αὐτὸν τὸ ὄνομα κ(υρίο)υ σωθήσεται·	ܘܟܕ ܡܬܕܟܪ ܫܡܗ ܕܡܪܝܐ ܡܬܦܪܩ.
when he is mindful of the Lord's name, he will be saved.	and when he is mindful of the LORD's name, he will be saved,

6.1–2[136] **Blessed is the man whose heart is prepared** [*hetoimē*] **to call on the name of the Lord**—the man whose heart is "set" (AOT) in such a way as to call on His name, not with the joyful enthusiasm of a moment (Mark 4.5, 16–17), but with thoughtful preparation and patient endurance (Luke 8.15; 14.28–30). "Blessed is the man who fears the LORD . . . . His heart is set [Hebrew *nkwn* ≡ LXX *hetoimē*]; he is confident in the LORD" (Psa 112.1, 7). To **call on the name of the Lord** is not simply to call Him "Lord" but to obey His word (Matt 7.21–27); similarly, to be **mindful** of His **name** is to keep His law (Psa 119.55). "Whoever" thus calls on His name **will be saved** (Joel 2.32 ≡ Rom 10.13), whether they lived before the old covenant (Gen 12.7–8), under the old covenant (Psa 99.6–7), or under the new covenant today ("Arise, and be baptized, and wash away your sins, calling on His name," Acts 22.16; 2.21, 38).

6.3 [2] αἱ ὁδοὶ αὐτοῦ κατευθύνονται ὑπὸ κ(υρίο)υ·	ܘܐܘܪܚܬܗ ܡܬܬܪ̈ܨܢ ܡܢ ܩܕܡ ܡܪܝܐ.
His paths are being directed by *the* Lord,	and his paths *are* being directed from before the LORD,
καὶ πεφυλαγμένα ἔργα χειρῶν αὐτοῦ ὑπὸ κ(υρίο)υ θ(εο)ῦ αὐτοῦ·	ܘܡܬܢܛܪ ܥܒܕܐ ܕܐܝܕܘܗܝ ܡܢ ܐܠܗܗ.
and *the* works of his hands *are* guarded by *the* Lord his God.	and the deed of his hands *is* watched over by his God.

6.3 Such a person's **paths** are **directed by the Lord,** and his **works** are **guarded**

[136] In the Greek copies (but not in the Syriac), the psalm is superscribed **In hope** [cf. v 8]; **belonging to Solomon.**

(**watched over,** Syriac) by Him (cf. 12.6). We cannot direct our own **paths** (Jer 10.23); the Lord must show us where to walk ("Teach me Your way, LORD, and lead me in the path of straightness," Psa 27.11; Isa 48.17)—and He has done this by the plain light of His word, so that we can see exactly where to place our feet: "Your word is a lamp to my foot, and a light to my path" (Psa 119.105; cf. 1 Jn 2.11; 1.7; John 12.35). "Know Him in all your ways, and He Himself will direct your paths" (Prov 3.6). If a person lives in this way, God will establish and bless his **works** (Deut 28.8; Psa 1.1–3; 1 Cor 15.58; Psa 90.17; Prov 16.3; Isa 26.12).

His soul will not be terrified

Greek	Syriac
6.4 [3] άπο όράσεωσ πονηρῶν ἐνυπνίων αὐτοῦ οὐ ταραχθήσεται· From *the* sight of his harmful dreams, he will not be distressed;	ܘܚܙܘܬܗ ܒܝܫܬܐ ܕܒܠܠܝܐ ܠܐ ܬܬܥܝܪ܂ ܡܛܠ ܕܕܝܠܗ ܗܘ܂ And his harmful vision in the night will not be stirred up, because he is His,
6.5 [3] ἡ ψυχὴ αὐτοῦ ἐν διαβάσει ποταμῶν καὶ σάλον θαλασσῶν οὐ πτωηθήσεται· when *he is* going through rivers and *the* shaking of seas, his soul will not be terrified.	ܘܢܦܫܗ ܒܥܡܠܐ ܕܢܗܪܘܬܐ܂ ܘܒܫܓܫܐ ܕܝܡܡܐ ܠܐ ܬܬܪܗܒ܂ and in the toil of a river and the stirring up of seas, his soul will not be agitated.
6.6 [4] ἐξανέστη ἐξ ὕπνου αὐτοῦ καὶ ηὐλόγησεν τῷ ὀνόματι κ(υρίο)υ· He has risen up out of his sleep, and he has blessed the name of *the* Lord,	ܩܡ ܓܝܪ ܡܢ ܫܢܬܗ ܘܫܒܚ ܠܫܡܗ ܕܡܪܝܐ܂ For he has risen from his sleep, and he has glorified *the* name of the LORD,
6.7 [4] ἐπ ευσταθία καρδίασ αὐτοῦ ἐξύμνησεν τῷ ὀνόματι τοῦ θ(εο)ῦ· in *the* stability of his heart, he has hymned to the name of God,	ܘܒܢܝܚܘܬܐ ܕܠܒܗ ܙܡܪ ܠܫܡܗ ܕܡܪܝܐ܂ and in the restfulness of his heart, he has sung to *the* name of the LORD,

6.5 σάλον 253 = -λων 260 •

6.4–7a No harm can ever come to the righteous (Prov 12.21; Psa 91.10; Wis 3.1; Rom 8.31–39). On every side he may be faced with troubles—he may be assailed with **harmful dreams** (Job 7.13–15), he[137] may have to pass **through rivers**[138] **and the**

[137] In the Greek version, **his soul** is placed between v 4 and v 5, so that it could be construed as the subject of either. In the Syriac version, it is unambiguously the subject of v 5.

shaking of seas (Isa 43.2; Psa 66.12; 2 Cor 11.25; Matt 7.25)—but in all such situations **his heart** remains in a condition of **stability**[139] because he knows that his troubles are fleeting like a dream (Isa 29.5, 8), whereas the God on whom he has set his hope is eternal (Psa 102.12).

Therefore he continues to **bless** and **hymn** the name of God. He "will not fear from the dread of night ... for You, LORD, are my refuge" (Psa 91.5, 9). "God is a refuge and strength for us ... therefore we do not fear when the land changes, when the mountains fall into the heart of the seas; its waters are in a tumult," but "the LORD of hosts is with us; God of Jacob is a secure height for us" (Psa 46.1–3, 7). God "stills the uproar of the seas, the uproar of their rolling waves, and the tumult of the peoples" (Psa 65.7). "In the world you have tribulation," Jesus told His disciples, but "in Me you may have peace" (John 16.33; Isa 26.3; Php 4.7).

He has risen up out of his sleep, and he has blessed the name of the Lord. "God, You are my God; I seek You at dawn" (Psa 63.1); "at the midpoints of night I rise to give thanks to You" (Psa 119.62). "Let me bless the LORD at every time; His praise will be in my mouth continually" (Psa 34.1)—"always," and "for all things" (Eph 5.20).

The Lord fulfills every request of those who fear Him

Greek	Syriac
[5] καὶ ἐδεήθη τοῦ προσώπου κ(υρίο)υ περὶ παντὸσ τοῦ οἴκου αὐτοῦ·	ܘܒܥܐ ܡܢ ܩܕܡ ܐܦܘ̈ܗܝ ܕܡܪܝܐ. ܥܠ ܟܠܗ ܒܝܬܗ.
and he has requested from the Lord's face concerning all his house,	and he has requested from the LORD's face on behalf of all his house,

---

[138] **When he is going through rivers** (*en diabasei potamōn,* Greek). The corresponding Syriac (16h1) reads **in the toil of a river** (*bʿbd' dnhrwt',* its customary activity; cf. Psa 93.3; 65.7). Baars emended this to *bʿbr' dnhrwt'* with seyame ("in the crossing of rivers").

[139] The Greek states that the righteous person will have **harmful dreams** but **will not be distressed** by them. The Syriac (16h1) states that no **harmful vision** will **be stirred up** within him (Ettaphal forms of *zwʿ* are used to describe something or someone being stirred up; cf. Acts 21.31). The Greek is speaking about dreams that are frightening but do not involve any evil to the dreamer (like some of Daniel's visions: Dan 7.15; 8.27). The Syriac is speaking about dreams that tell of an evil coming to the dreamer (like the dream of Pharaoh's baker, Gen 40.16–19, 22).

Trafton (82–83) suggested that the Syriac originally read "he [the righteous person] will not be stirred up," but this would leave the preceding phrase **his harmful vision in the night** dangling awkwardly (cf. Harris-Mingana).

After this, the Syriac has an additional clause, **because he is His.** "The Lord knows those who are His" (2 Tim 2.19), and He will not allow them to be destroyed by any danger (John 10.14, 27–29). The only ones who can harm us are ourselves (Eighteen Psalms 9.7, 9).

Stability (*eustath[e]ia;* for the verb, cf. Jer 49.31, LXX) is the condition of standing *(histēmi)* well *(eu-);* the Syriac has **restfulness** (*nyḥt',* as in Psa 95.11, Syr).

6.8 [5] καὶ κ(ύριο)σ εἰσήκουσεν πρὸσευχὴν παντὸ(σ) ἐν φόβω θ(εο)ῦ· and *the* Lord has heard *the* prayer of every*one who is* in *the* fear of God,	ܘܡܪܝܐ ܫܡܥ ܒܥܘܬܐ ܕܟܠ ܕܒܕܚܠܬܗ ܗܘ. and the LORD hearkens at the request of every*one* who *is* in *the* fear of Him,
[6] καὶ πᾶν αἴτημα ψυχῆσ ἐλπιζούσησ πρὸσ αὐτὸν ἐπιτελεῖ ὁ κ(ύριο)σ· and every request of a soul who is hoping toward Him, the Lord fulfills.	ܘܟܠ ܫܐܠܬܐ ܕܢܦܫܐ ܕܡܣܒܪܐ ܒܗ ܘܡܫܡܠܐ ܡܪܝܐ. and every thing asked by the soul who *is* hoping in Him, then the LORD fulfills.

6.7b The person who fears the Lord **has requested** the Lord's mercy for **all his house** (both for his household in the flesh, and for his household in the Lord: Gen 48.15–16; Job 1.5; Lev 16.6; 1 Sam 12.23; 1 Chr 16.43; Rom 9.1–3; 10.1; Col 1.9–12; 4.12; 1 Jn 5.16).

6.8 The Lord hears and fulfills **every request** of **everyone who is in the fear of God** and **who is hoping toward Him.** "He does the good pleasure of those who fear Him, and He hears their cry for help, and saves them" (Psa 145.19; 34.15, 17). "Ask, and it shall be given you . . . for everyone who asks receives" (Matt 7.7–8). "If we ask anything in accordance with His will, He hears us; and if we know that He hears us in whatever we may ask, we know that we have the asked things which we asked from Him," provided that "we keep His commands and do the things that are pleasing before Him" (1 Jn 5.14–15; 3.22). "If you abide in Me, and My words abide in you, ask whatever you will, and it will come about for you" (John 15.7; Mark 11.24). If we ask and do not receive, it is because we are asking in a way that is not good (Jas 4.2–3) and/or for a thing that is not good (2 Cor 12.8–10).

6.9 [6] εὐλογητὸσ κ(ύριο)σ ὁ ποιῶν ἔλεοσ τοῖσ ἀγαπῶσιν αὐτὸν ἐν αληθεία: Blessed *be the* Lord, the *One* who does mercy to those who love Him in truth.	ܒܪܝܟ ܗܘ ܕܥܒܕ ܪ̈ܚܡܐ. ܥܠ ܐܝܠܝܢ ܕܪܚܡܝܢ ܠܗ <> ܒܫܪܪܐ. Blessed is the *One* who does compassions upon those who love Him in truth.

6.9 ܠܗ ≡ αὐτὸν 253 260 | + ܠܗ 16h1 •

6.9 The Lord always **does mercy to those who love Him in truth** (10.4; 14.1; not merely in word or tongue, but in action, 1 Jn 3.18: "this is the love of God, that we keep His commandments," 1 Jn 5.3; cf. Matt 22.36–40). "All the paths of the LORD are lovingkindness and faithfulness for those who keep His covenant" (Psa 25.10). "To those who love God, He works all things together for good" (Rom 8.28).

Psalm 7

This psalm refers to a time when the Lord's **holy place** was not yet being trampled by the **nations,** but there was a danger that it might happen (vv 1–3; cf. Ryle-James 68; Atkinson, *I Cried to the Lord,* 110–11). It is therefore appropriately placed before the next psalm, which describes the occurrence of the threatened disaster (8.16–24; cf. 2.1–2; 17.25).

Do not let our enemies trample Your holy place

Greek	Syriac
7.0 [0] Τῶ Cολομῶν ἐπιcτροφῆc: Belonging to Solomon; of turning back.	
7.1 [1] Μὴ ἀποσκηνώσησ ἀφ' ἡμῶν ὁ θ(εό)σ· Do not move† Your† tent away from us, O God,	ܠܐ ܬܪܚܩ ܡܫܟܢܟ ܡܢܢ ܐܠܗܐ. Do not take away† Your† tent from us, God,
ἵνα μὴ ἐπιθῶνται ἡμῖν οἳ ἐμίσησαν ἡμᾶσ δωρεὰν· in order that they may not set on us— those who have hated us for nothing;	ܕܠܡܐ ܢܩܘܡܘܢ ܥܠܝܢ ܐܝܠܝܢ ܕܣܢܐܘܢ ܡܓܢ. lest they rise over against us— those who hate us for nothing;
7.2 [2] ὅτι ἀπώσω αὐτοὺσ ὁ θ(εό)σ because You† have rejected them, O God;	ܡܛܠ ܕܕܚܝܬ ܐܢܘܢ ܐܠܗܐ. because You† have driven them away, God,
μὴ πατισάτω ὁ ποὺσ αὐτ(ῶν) κληρονομίαν ἁγιάσματόσ σου· do not let their foot trample *the* inheritance of Your† holy place.	ܕܠܐ ܬܕܘܫ ܪܓܠܗܘܢ ܝܪܬܘܬܐ ܕܩܘܕܫܟ. so that their foot might not trample the inheritance of Your† holy place.

7.1–2[140] Under the old covenant, God met with His people in an earthly **tent** (tabernacle; Greek *skēnē* ≡ Syriac *mškn';* Acts 7.44, 46–47; Heb 9.8; Lev 26.11)—first in the wilderness, later at Shiloh, and finally at Jerusalem. But when the people were disobedient, in the days of Eli "He departed from … the tent" at Shiloh (Psa 78.60), and in the days of the Babylonian captivity "He did violence to His tent, He destroyed His appointed place" at Jerusalem (Lam 2.6). The present psalm prays that such things might not happen again: **Do not move Your tent** ["tabernacle," Whiston] **away from us, O God.**

[140] In the Greek copies (but not in the Syriac), the psalm is superscribed **Belonging to Solomon; of turning back** (either by God ["Turn back, O God, Your mercy to us, and have compassion on us," 8.33], or by His people ["when You discipline me, it is to turn me back," 16.11]).

If the Lord moved His **tent away from** His people, "many evils" would come upon them (Deut 31.17; cf. Num 14.42). Their enemies[141] would **set on** them ("assail" them, APOT) and **trample**[142] **the inheritance of** God's **holy place.** Those things did indeed happen in that generation: "sinners set on" Jerusalem (1.1), and "strange nations... trampled down" God's sacrificial altar (2.2).

At the end of the old covenant, God "pitched His tent" *(eskēnōsen)* among His people in the form of Jesus (John 1.14). "The tent of God is with humans, and He will pitch His tent [*skēnōsei*] with them, and they will be His peoples, and God Himself will be with them as their God" (Rev 21.3). "We ourselves are the sanctuary of the living God, as He has said: 'I will dwell among and walk among them, and I will be their God, and they themselves will be My people'" (2 Cor 6.16). But "what agreement does God's sanctuary have with idols?" (2 Cor 6.16). If anyone does not let the Word of Christ and the Spirit of God dwell in him, he does not belong to Him (Rom 8.9; cf. 1 Jn 4.12–13; Col 3.16 ≡ Eph 5.18).

Discipline us mercifully

7.3 [3] σὺ ἐν θελήματί σου παίδευσο(ν) ἡμᾶσ Discipline† us Yourself‡ by Your† *own* will,	ܐܢܬ ܒܝ ܒܨܒܝܢܟ ܪܕܝܢܝ Discipline† me Yourself‡ in Your† good pleasure,
καὶ μη δῶσ ἔθνεσιν· and do not give† *us* to *the* nations;	ܘܠܐ ܬܫܠܡܢ ܠܥܡܡܐ. and do not deliver† us to the peoples;
7.4 [4] ἐὰν γὰρ ἀποστείλησ θάνατον for if You† should send death,	ܐܢ ܓܝܪ ܬܫܕܪ ܡܘܬܐ. for if You† send death,
σὺ ἐντέλῃ αὐτῷ περὶ ἡμ(ῶν)· You† Yourself‡ will command it concerning us;	ܐܢܬ ܦܩܘܕ ܠܗ ܥܠܝܢ. You† Yourself‡ *will* set it over us,
[5] ὅτι σὺ ἐλεήμων· because You† *are* merciful,	ܡܛܠ ܕܐܢܬ ܗܘ ܡܪܚܡܢܐ. because You† are compassionate,
καὶ οὐκ οργισθήσῃ τοῦ συντελέσαι ἡμᾶσ· and You† will not be angry *so as* to bring us to an end.	ܘܠܐ ܬܪ ܠܢ ܐܝܟ ܕܠܡܓܡܪܘܬܢ. and You† will not be angry so that we are brought to an end.

7.3–4 Discipline [*paideuson*] **us.** "Those whom the Lord loves, He disciplines [*paideuei*]" for their benefit (Heb 12.6–11 ≡ Prov 3.12): see the comments on 8.32, 35 ("You

---

[141] The enemies in this psalm are people whom God has **rejected** (cf. Psa 53.5) and **who have hated** His people **for nothing** (cf. John 15.25 ≡ Psa 69.4).

[142] **Trample** *(patisatō).* Wright incorrectly gives the reading of 253 as *patisantō.*

are the God of righteousness, who judges Israel with discipline .... You Yourself are our discipliner"). His **discipline** is painful (*lupēs,* Heb 12.11). Nevertheless He is **merciful** to all those who fear Him (Luke 1.50; Rom 9.23), and though He may **send** them **death** (Gen 3.19; 1 Sam 2.6; Heb 9.27), He will not **bring** them **to an end** (Lam 3.22): "In Your many compassions You did not make an end of them or forsake them, for You are a God merciful and compassionate" (Neh 9.31). "The one who believes in Me, even if he should die, shall live" (John 11.25; Heb 11.13–16; Rom 8.38–39). It is better to receive **discipline** and **death** from the hand of God,[143] than to be given over **to the nations**—or to any human power. "Let me fall into the hand of God, for His compassions are great, and let me not fall into the hand of humanity" (2 Sam 24.14; Ptolemaica 6.10; Sir 2.18); see the comments on 5.15–16.

It pleases God when His people humbly submit to the painful discipline He sends them. Jesus Himself accepted the Father's **will** rather than His own (Matt 26.39), leaving an example to those who follow Him (1 Pet 2.19–23). And God promised to show favor to His disobedient people if they would "accept the punishment of their iniquity" (Lev 26.41), as David (2 Sam 15.26) and the thief on the cross (Luke 23.40–41) did.

7.5 [6] ἐν τῷ κατασκηνοῦν τὸ ὄνομά σου ἐν μέσῳ ἡμῶν ἐλεηθησόμεθα· As Your† name *is* dwelling in our midst, we will be shown mercy,	ܡܛܠ ܫܡܟ ܒܝܢ ܕܥܡܪܐ ܫܟܝܢܬܟ ܢܗܘܘܢ ܥܠܝܢ ܪ̈ܚܡܐ. For, because Your† name *is* dwelling among us, compassions will be upon us,
7.6 [6] καὶ οὐκ ἰσχύσει πρὸσ ἡμᾶσ ἔθνοσ and no nation will have strength against us,	ܘܠܐ ܢܫܟܚܘܢ ܥܡ̈ܡܐ ܠܡܬܚܝܠܘ ܥܠܝܢ. and the peoples will not find *a way* to be powerful over against us,
[7] ὅτι σὺ ὑπερασπιστῆσ ἡμῶν· because You† *are* *the One* who holds a shield over us,	ܡܛܠ ܕܐܢܬ ܗܘ ܚܝܠܢ. because You† are our power,

7.5 If God's **name is dwelling in our midst, we will be shown mercy.** Under the old covenant, God chose "to make His name dwell" in Jerusalem (Deut 12.11, 5; 1 Kgs 11.36; 8.29). He promised that "if I send death among My people, if My people, on whom My name is called, will humble themselves, and pray and seek My face and turn back from their evil ways, then I will hear from the heavens, and forgive their

---

143 **Death** may here refer specifically to death by disease ("pestilence," Ryle-James), as it certainly does in 13.2 (see the comments there). The renderings "if you send Death away, it will be because you, yourself, have told him what to do about us" (Wright) and "if ever you dispatch Death, you give him orders about [avoiding] us" (Wright mg) fail to recognize the passage's allusion to 2 Sam 24.13–15.

sin, and heal their land; now My eyes shall be open and My ears attentive to the prayer of this place [the Jerusalem temple]" (2 Chr 7.13–15). However when the people defiled His dwelling place with their sins, He departed from it and cast them out (Jer 7.3–15). Under the new covenant, God's name dwells "to lasting time" in the heavenly Jerusalem, among those who have put away their sins (Ezek 37.26–28; 43.7–9; John 14.23; Rev 21.2–3; Heb 12.22–23).

7.6 If God dwells among His people (v 5), **no nation will have strength against** them (Deut 11.22–25; 28.10). "You have overcome them, because greater is the One in you than the one in the world" (1 Jn 4.4; Rom 8.37; 1 Cor 15.57). The Lord **holds a shield over** them, protecting them from "tens of thousands" of enemies (Psa 3.3, 6–8). "He is a shield to all who seek refuge in Him" (Psa 18.30; 7.10; 84.11; 115.9–11).

We will call on You, and You will hearken

7.7 [7] καὶ ἡμεῖσ ἐπικαλεσόμεθά σε καὶ σὺ ἐπακούσῃ ἡμῶν· and we ourselves will call upon You†, and You† Yourself† will hearken to us,	ܘܚܢ ܢܩܪܐ ܠܘܬܟ ܘܐܢܬ ܬܥܢܝܢ. and we ourselves will call to You†, and You† Yourself† will answer us,
7.8 [8] ὅτι σὺ οἰκτειρήσειϲ τὸ γένοσ Ἰ(σρα)ὴλ εἰσ τὸν αἰῶνα because You† Yourself† will have compassion on the race of Israel to lasting time,	ܡܛܠ ܕܐܢܬ ܬܚܘܣ ܠܙܪܥܗ ܕܐܝܣܪܐܝܠ ܠܥܠܡ because You† Yourself† will have mercy on *the* seed of Israel to lasting time,
καὶ οὐκ απώσει· and You† will not reject,	ܘܠܐ ܬܛܥܝܘܗܝ. and You† will not lead it astray.
[9] καὶ ἡμεῖσ ὑπο ζυγόν σου τὸν αἰῶνα and we *will be* under Your† yoke *to* lasting time,	
καὶ μάστιγα παιδίασ σου· and the scourge of Your† discipline.	

7.7 We ourselves will call upon You, and You Yourself will hearken to us. See the comments on 6.1, 8 ("The Lord has heard the prayer of everyone who is in the fear of God, and every request of a soul who is hoping toward Him, the Lord fulfills").

7.8 You Yourself will have compassion on the race of Israel to lasting time, and You will not reject.[144] "The LORD will not forsake His people" (1 Sam 12.22; Psa 94.14;

---

[144] **You will not reject** Israel (Greek); **you will not lead** Israel **astray** (Syriac). Human guides and teachers may lead astray (Jer 23.32; Isa 9.16), but the Lord never leads His people astray

Jer 31.36–37; Rom 11.1–2). "I will not destroy the house of Jacob, says the LORD .... All the sinners of My people will die," but "I will raise up the tent of David that has fallen, and I will wall up its breaches, and raise up its ruins, and build it up as in lasting time" (Amos 9.8–11)—a promise that has now been fulfilled through the gospel (Acts 15.14–18), so that "He might make known the riches of His glory on ... us whom He called, not only from the Jews, but also from the Gentiles" (Rom 9.23–24), who are Jews inwardly, circumcised in heart (Rom 2.28–29). So, in that way, "all Israel shall be saved" (Rom 11.26). Not one of them will be lost (John 6.39); "they will never be destroyed" (John 10.28–29; Luke 21.18–19).

We will be under Your yoke to lasting time, and the scourge of Your discipline.[145] Yokes are bars (Lev 26.13) set on the necks of oxen (Num 19.2; 1 Kgs 19.19, 21) so that their master can control them (cf. 1 Kgs 12.4; Jer 27.12), especially when plowing (Hos 10.11). The compassions of the wicked are cruel (Prov 12.10), and so Israel was often oppressed and afflicted by her human masters. The Babylonians did not show mercy, and "very heavily laid [their] yoke" on the aged (Isa 47.6). Rehoboam declared, "I will add to your yoke ... I will discipline you with scorpions" (1 Kgs 12.14). But God is like the righteous man who cares for his animal (Prov 12.10), and He scourges His sons with love (Heb 12.6). "My yoke is kind, and My burden is light" (Matt 11.28–30), because it is laid on His people in mercy and in love, to do them good in the end (Deut 8.16). Therefore "it is good for a man to bear the yoke," because the Lord will "have compassion according to the multitude of His lovingkindnesses" (Lam 3.27, 31–32).

7.9 [10] κατευθύνεισ ἡμᾶσ ἐν καιρῷ ἀντιλήψεώσ σου· You† will direct us in *the* time of Your† help,	ܐܬܩܢ ܒܙܒܢܐ ܕܡܥܕܪܢܘܬܟ. Establish† us in the time of Your† help,
τοῦ ἐλεῆσαι τὸν οἶκον Ἰακὼβ· εἰσ ἡμέραν ἐν ‹ῇ› ἐπηγγείλω αὐτοῖσ: to have mercy on the house of Jacob for *the* day in which You† have promised to them.	ܠܡܚܢ ܠܒܝܬܗ ܕܝܥܩܘܒ. ܠܝܘܡܐ ܗܘ ܕܡܛܝܒ ܠܗܘܢ. to have mercy toward *the* house of Jacob for the day that *is* prepared for them.

7.9 ῇ 260 | ῷ 253 •

7.9 You will direct [*kateuthuneis*] **us in the time of Your help** [*antilēpseōs*], **to have mercy on the house of Jacob for the day in which You have promised to them.** The

---

(cf. Titus 1.2; Heb 6.18; Num 23.19). Rather, "He leads [them] in the paths of righteousness" (Psa 23.3; Isa 49.10).

[145] **And we will be under Your yoke to lasting time, and the scourge of Your discipline.** These clauses are not present in the Syriac manuscript (16h1).

Lord had **promised** through His prophets that there would come a **time** (a **day**) when "the crooked things will be made straight [*eutheian*]" (Isa 40.3–4). That day was now at hand; those prophecies were about to be fulfilled through the coming of John the Baptist and Jesus (Luke 3.4–5), when "He has given help [*antelabeto*] to Israel His servant, to be mindful of mercy, just as He spoke to our fathers" (Luke 1.54–55). "He has raised up a horn of salvation for us ... just as He spoke through the mouth of His holy prophets from lasting time ... to do mercy with our fathers ... to direct [*kateuthunai*] our feet into the way of peace" (Luke 1.68–79). From that straight *(-euth-)* way we must be careful not to depart (2 Pet 2.15; Acts 13.10).

Psalm 8

The previous psalm had asked that the nations might not "trample the inheritance of Your holy place" (7.1–3). Now the foreseen danger has actually happened: an enemy **from the end of the earth** has **entered** Jerusalem, **destroyed** many of the inhabitants, and **led away** others into captivity (vv 1–6, 15–24). In the architecture of the Eighteen Psalms, these two psalms are connected like the first two: in each case a shorter preliminary psalm leads to a longer, fuller one that gives a more detailed account of the disaster.

The voice of war in Jerusalem

8.0 [0] Τῶ Coλoμῶν εἰc νίκοc: Belonging to Solomon; for victory.	
8.1 [1] Θλίψιν καὶ φωνὴν πολέμου ἤκουσεν τὸ οὖσ μου· My ear heard oppression and *the* voice of war,	ܐܘܠܨܢܐ ܘܩܠܐ ܕܩܪܒܐ ܫܡܥ̈ܝ ܐܕ̈ܢܝ. My ears heard affliction and the voice of war,
φωνὴν σάλπιγγοσ ἠχούσησ σφαγὴν καὶ ὄλεθρον· *the* voice of a resounding trumpet, slaughter and destruction,	ܩܠܐ ܕܩܪܒܐ ܘܪܘܓܫܐ ܕܩܛܠܐ ܘܕܐܒܕܢܐ. the voice of war and the uproar of killing and destruction,
8.2 [2] φωνὴ λαοῦ πολλοῦ ὡσ ἀνέμου πολλοῦ σφόδρα· *the* voice of a great people, like *that* of an extremely great wind,	ܩܠܐ ܕܥܡܐ ܣܓܝܐܐ ܐܝܟ ܪܘܚܐ ܚܣܝܢܬܐ ܘܣܓܝܐܬܐ. the voice of a great people, like a powerful and great wind,
ὡσ καταιγὶσ πυρὸσ πολλοῦ φερομένου δι ἐρήμου· like a stormwind of a great fire that is brought through *the* desert.	ܐܝܟ ܥܠܥܠܐ ܕܢܘܪܐ ܕܐܬܝܐ ܒܠ ܡܕܒܪܐ. like a whirlwind of fire that is coming through the desert.

Greek	Syriac
8.3 [3] καὶ εἶπα τῇ καρδίᾳ μου And I said to my heart:	ܘܐܡܪܬ ܠܠܒܝ. And I said to my heart:
ποῦ ἄρα κρινεῖ αὐτὸν ὁ θ(εό)σ· “Where then will God judge him?”	ܕܐܝܟܐ ܗܘ ܕܐܢ ܠܗ. “Where then *will He* judge him?”
8.4 [4] φωνὴν ἤκουσα εἰσ Ἰερουσαλὴμ πόλιν ἁγιάσματοσ· I heard a voice in Jerusalem, *the* city of *the* holy place;	ܩܠܐ ܫܡܥܬ ܒܐܘܪܫܠܡ ܡܕܝܢܬܐ ܡܩܕܫܬܐ. I heard a voice in Jerusalem, the city of the holy place;

8.1–4[146] The psalmist has **heard** a **voice in Jerusalem.**[147] It is a **voice of war** (1.2, Syr), the **voice of a resounding trumpet** (which was used to announce war, 1 Cor 14.8; Num 10.9; Neh 4.18–20),[148] the **voice of a great** number of **people** (the invaders came from a plurality of nations, 2.2, 24; 17.25), an **uproar** (Syriac) of **slaughter and destruction** (described further in v 23). Similar terms had been used to describe the Babylonian invasion (Jer 4.19; Zep 1.14–16). The sound is **like that of an extremely great wind, like a stormwind of a great fire** sweeping **through the desert.** Previous times of destruction had been described this way in the Hebrew Scriptures (Jer 4.11–13; 51.1–2; Isa 21.1; Dan 11.40).

I said to my heart:[149] **“Where then will God judge him?”** The pronoun **him** (*auton,* masculine singular) refers back to the **people** (*laou,* masculine singular) in the previous verse.[150] Where is God going to **judge** this destroyer? If he is allowed to triumph even in Jerusalem, the **city of the holy place** (cf. Isa 64.10–11; Psa 79.1–7), then **where** can God possibly do justice on him by punishing him? (For this sense of **judge,** cf. Acts 7.7; Rev 19.2.)

---

[146] In the Greek copies (but not in the Syriac), the psalm is superscribed **Belonging to Solomon; for victory.** The phrase **for victory** *(eis nikos)* is used in θ′ to translate Hebrew *lmnṣh,* “for the overseer [of song]” (Psa 12.0, etc.).

[147] **I heard ... in** [Greek *eis* ≡ Syriac *b-*] **Jerusalem.** *Eis* is often equivalent to *en* (BDAG 289, §1aδ). In this sentence *eis* unambiguously indicates the direction of the voice (it was heard *eis* Jerusalem, in the direction of Jerusalem), whereas *en* would be ambiguous (it might indicate the location of the hearer, as in Jer 4.5, LXX: “let it be heard in [*en*] Jerusalem”).

[148] Both the Israelites and their enemies used trumpets in battle (Maccabaica 9.12).

[149] **I said to my heart** *(eipa tē kardia mou).* As often in the Scriptures (BDAG 588, §1bγ), the dative indicates the one **to** whom this is **said:** the psalmist is saying it **to** his **heart.** Compare, e.g., “they do not say to their heart” (Hos 7.2), and Maccabaica 6.11. The existing Greek text is supported by the Syriac. There is therefore no reason to accept the conjectural insertion *en* (Hilgenfeld, Gebhardt, and Rahlfs), which would turn the statement into “I said in my heart.”

[150] **Him** is sometimes taken to be Israel (AOT), but there is no such antecedent in the context (the next verse mentions **Jerusalem,** but Jerusalem would be treated as feminine, not masculine; cf. 1.3). The rendering “us” (APOT) assumes a textual error, and is not supported by any known manuscript, either Greek or Syriac.

8.5 [5] συνετρίβη ἡ ὀσφύσ μου ἀπο ἀκοῆσ· my loins were broken down from hearing *it;*	ܘܐܫܬܪܝ̈ ܚܘܩܝ̈ ܚܨܝ̈ ܡܢ ܫܡܥܬܐ. and the joints of my loins became loose from what was heard,
παρελύθη γόνατά μου· **8.6 [6]** ἐφοβήθη ἡ καρδία μου· my knees were paralysed, my heart feared,	ܘܒܘܪ̈ܟܝ ܙܓܠ and my knees trembled,
ἐταράχθη τὰ ὀστᾶ μου ὠσ λινόν· my bones were unsettled, like flax.	ܘܐܬܬܙܝܥܘ ܓܪ̈ܡܝ ܐܝܟ ܟܬܢܐ. and my bones shook like flax.

8.5–6 Hearing this noise, the psalmist was appalled (**my loins were broken down . . . my knees were paralysed, my heart feared, my bones were unsettled like flax**[151]), like the prophets who contemplated earlier destructions ("my heart is disquieted in me," Jer 4.19; "my loins are filled with pain . . . my heart strays, horror has terrified me," Isa 21.3–4).

8.7 [6] εἶπα κατευθύνουσιν ‹ὁδοὺσ› αὐτῶν ἐν δικαιοσύνη· I said: "They will direct their paths in righteousness."	ܘܐܡܪܬ ܢܬܪܨܘܢ ܐܘܪ̈ܚܬܗܘܢ ܒܙܕܝܩܘܬܐ. And I said: "They will direct their paths in righteousness."

8.7 ὁδοὺσ 260 ≡ ܐܘܪ̈ܚܬܗܘܢ 16h1 | δοὺσ 253 •

8.7a I said: "They will direct their paths[152] **in righteousness."**[153] At the time when he **said** this, the psalmist "did not know" the truth about the secret iniquities of Jerusalem's inhabitants (cf. 1.7, 3); he hoped that they would walk in the paths of

---

[151] **Flax** is proverbially feeble (Jdg 15.14).

[152] **They will direct their paths.** The subject of the plural verb is Jerusalem (v 4), a collective (one city composed of many people) which can therefore take either singular or plural verbs (BDF §134.1; Robertson 404; Nöldeke §318; Duval §354*d*). (Jerusalem's opponent is also a collective and can also take either singular or plural verbs: v 18; 17.13–14.) In both Greek *(kateuthunousin)* and Syriac *(ntrṣwn),* the verb could be construed either as future (**they will direct**) or as present ("they are directing"). The past tense rendering in OTP ("they directed," with the marginal gloss: "Jerusalem had supposedly always done what is right") is incorrect: the statement is concerned with what Jerusalem's inhabitants are currently doing and/or will do in the future, not what they had done in the past.

[153] **They will direct their paths in righteousness.** This is sometimes treated as "an ironic rhetorical question," "Are not these people righteous?" (Wright; cf. Viteau). But such a question would normally require a preliminary *mē* (MHT 3.283; Robertson 917–18) or some other marker (cf. Viteau, *Verbe,* §53*c*); and the very next verse (v 8) shows that the people's sins had not been apparent.

righteousness appointed by God (Acts 13.10; see the comments on 7.9). "The righteousness of a perfect person directs his way" (Prov 11.5; that is the way of wisdom, Prov 8.20). However, God would soon expose their hidden sins (vv 8–9).

Nevertheless, the psalmist's hope was not ignorant or naïve. God Himself expresses the hope that people will walk in righteousness, even in situations where He must already know that they will not: "I said, 'Surely you will fear Me; you will receive discipline . . . .' But they rose early, they corrupted all their deeds" (Zep 3.7; cf. Isa 63.8–10). Love "hopes all things" (1 Cor 13.7).

God has uncovered the people's sins

Greek	Syriac
[7] ἀνελογησάμην	ܘܐܬܕܟܪܬ
τὰ κρίματα τοῦ θ(εο)ῦ	ܕܝ̈ܢܘܗܝ ܕܡܪܝܐ.
ἀπο κτίσεωσ οὐρανοῦ καὶ γῆσ·	ܕܡܢ ܟܕ ܐܬܒܪܝܘ ܫܡܝܐ ܘܐܪܥܐ.
I took careful account of God's judgments from *the* creation of heaven and earth;	And I was mindful of the LORD's judgments that *have been* from *the time* when the heaven and the earth were created,
ἐδικαίωσα τὸν θ(εὸ)ν ἐν τοῖσ	ܘܙܕܩܬ ܠܐܠܗܐ
κρίμασιν αὐτοῦ τοῖσ ἀπ' αἰῶνοσ·	ܒܟܠܗܘܢ ܕܝ̈ܢܘܗܝ ܕܡܢ ܥܠܡ.
I acknowledged God to be righteous in His judgments that have been from lasting time.	and I acknowledged God to be righteous in all His judgments that *have been* from lasting time.

8.7b In reality, the One who has acted in righteousness (v 7a) is not Jerusalem but the Lord. **From lasting time** (Psa 119.52; 103.17)—from the time when **heaven and earth** were created—He has always been **righteous in His judgments:** see the comments on 3.3. "His work is perfect, for all His ways are judgment; a God of faithfulness and without iniquity, righteous and upright is He" (Deut 32.4). And in the present situation, the righteousness of His judgment on Jerusalem has been demonstrated by the sins He has revealed (vv 8–14).

Greek	Syriac
8.8 **[8]** ‹ἀνεκάλυψεν› ὁ θ(εὸ)σ τὰσ	ܓܠܐ ܕܝܢ ܐܠܗܐ ܥܒ̈ܕܝܗܘܢ
ἁμαρτίασ αὐτῶν ἐναντίον τοῦ ἡλίου·	ܩܕܡ ܫܡܫܐ.
God has uncovered their sins before the sun;	But God has uncovered their deeds before the sun,
ἔγνω πᾶσα ἡ γῆ	ܘܐܬܝܕܥ ܠܟܠܗ ܐܪܥܐ
τὰ κρίματα τοῦ θ(εο)ῦ τὰ δίκαια·	ܕܝ̈ܢܘܗܝ ܕܡܪܝܐ ܙܕܝ̈ܩܐ.
all the earth has known the righteous judgments of God.	and the righteous judgments of the LORD became known to all the earth.

8.8 ἀνεκάλυψεν 260 | ἀνακάλ- 253 •

8.9 [9] ἐν καταγαίοισ κρυφίοισ αἱ παρανομίαι αὐτῶν ἐν παροργισμῷ· Their Law-breakings *were* in underground hidden *place*s, making *Him* angry.	ܒܛܫܝܬܐ ܓܝܪ ܕܐܪܥܐ ܡܥܘܠܝܢ ܗܘܘ For they were doing injustice in hiding places of the land.

8.8–9 The **Law-breakings** of Jerusalem's inhabitants (v 7a) had occurred secretly, **in underground hidden places,** where they would not be seen by human eyes (see the comments on 1.7; 4.5). But God saw them (9.5; Jer 23.24), and they made Him **angry**[154] (4.1, 25; Deut 31.29). Now He **has uncovered their sins** (see the comments on 2.18), so that they are evident in broad daylight (**before the sun,** 2 Sam 12.12). (God is Himself light, and this light exposes the evil deeds of those who love darkness: 1 John 1.5–6; John 3.19–21; Eph 5.13.) As a result, **all the earth** could see what the sinners had done, and could know[155] that God's **judgments** against Jerusalem were **righteous** (vv 7b, 27; cf. Jer 5.7–9, 26–29; 9.8–9).

8.10 [9] υ(ἱὸ)σ μετὰ μ(ητ)ρ(ὸ)σ· καὶ π(ατ)ὴρ μετα θυγατρὸσ συνεφύροντο· Son with mother and father with daughter were mingling together;	ܒܪܐ ܥܡ ܐܡܗ. ܘܐܒܐ ܥܡ ܒܪܬܗ ܡܬܚܠܛܝܢ ܗܘܘ. The son with his mother and the father with his daughter were intermingling,
8.11 [10] ἐμοιχῶντο ἕκαστο(σ)· τὴν γυναῖκα τοῦ πλησίον αὐτοῦ· they were committing adultery, each *one* with his neighbor's wife.	ܘܟܠܗܘܢ ܓܝܪܝܢ ܗܘܘ ܢܫ̈ܐ ܕܚܒܪ̈ܝܗܘܢ. and all of them were committing adultery with their companions' wives.
συνέθεντο αὐτοῖσ συνθήκασ μετὰ ὅρκου **8.12** περι τούτων· They agreed an agreement among them*selves* with an oath concerning these *thing*s.	ܘܐܬܩܝܡܘ ܒܝܢܬܗܘܢ ܩܝ̈ܡܐ ܥܠ ܗܠܝܢ. And they covenanted a covenant among themselves concerning these things.
[11] τὰ ἅγια τοῦ θ(εο)ῦ διηρπάζωσαν They were plundering the holy *place*s of God,	ܒܝܬ ܩܘܕܫܗ ܕܐܠܗܐ ܡܒܙܙܝܢ ܗܘܘ. They were plundering *the* holy house of the LORD,

[154] **Making [Him] angry.** The wording of the Greek is *en parorgismō,* "in [the] making of anger" ("in provocation," NETS).

[155] **Became known** *('tyd'),* Syriac. The reading printed by Baars, *'tyr',* is a typographical error.

Greek	Syriac
ὡσ μὴ ὄντοσ κληρονόμου λυτρουμένου· as *if there* were no heir who redeemed.	ܐܝܟ ܗܘ̇ ܕܠܝܬ ܕܝܳܪܬ ܘܦܳܪܘܩ. as *if* there was no one who *was* inheriting and saving.
8.13 [12] ἐπατοῦσαν τὸ θυσιαστήριον κ(υρίο)υ ἀπὸ πάσησ ἀκαθαρσίασ· They were trampling on the sacrificial altar of *the* Lord from every uncleanness,	ܘܕܳܝܫܝܢ ܗ̱ܘܘ ܗܰܝܟܠܗ ܒܟܠܗ̇ ܛܡܐܘܬܗܘܢ. And they were trampling His shrine in all their uncleanness,
καὶ ἐν αφεδρῷ αἵματο(σ) ἐμίαναν τὰσ θυσίασ ὡσ κρέα βέβηλα· and with menstruation of blood they stained the sacrifices like profane meats.	ܘܒܕܡܐ ܕܟܣܝܬܐ ܛܡܐܘ ܕܒ̈ܚܐ ܐܝܟ ܒܣܪܐ ܛܡܐܐ. and with the blood of menstruation they made the sacrifices unclean like unclean flesh.

8.10–13 Some of the people's sins (vv 8–9) are now specified.

- **Son with mother and father with daughter were mingling together; they were committing adultery, each one with his neighbor's wife** (cf. 2.15). For such deeds, the people of Canaan had fallen before the Israelites (Lev 18.6–8, 20, 24–25); for such deeds, the people of Judah had fallen before the Babylonians (Jer 5.7–8; 29.21–23; cf. Ezek 23.37).
- **They agreed an agreement among themselves with an oath concerning these** sins. Compare 4.4, where the hypocrite, seeking to commit fornication with "every woman ... is entering into every house ... as if he is innocent," while "his tongue is lying in an agreement with an oath." Not only did Jerusalem's inhabitants commit sin, but they made a mutual **agreement** to do it (as in Psa 31.13; Luke 22.3–6); and not only did they agree to do it, but they even took an **oath** to do it (like the people who "made a conspiracy and bound themselves with a curse" to do evil in Acts 23.12). (The **oath** is often assumed to be an oath that no adultery has taken place, as in Num 5.19–22; but it is not clear how the procedure described in that law could be called an **agreement among themselves.**)
- **They were plundering the holy places**[156] **of God** (as foreign conquerors had done, 1 Kgs 14.25–26; 2 Kgs 24.11–13; Maccabaica 1.21–24), **as if there were no heir who redeemed.**[157] Under the old covenant Law, property that had been

[156] **The holy places.** As in 1.8 and 2.3, Greek *ta hagia* could include the **holy places** and/or the "holy things" (Ryle-James) offered there. The corresponding Syriac, *byt qwdšh* (16h1), unambiguously designates the **holy house.**

[157] **As if there were no heir who redeemed.** In both Greek and Syriac, the wording recalls Psa 7.2, "lest ... there is no one who redeems" (*mē ontos lutroumenou,* LXX; *lyt dprq,* Syr). In the present passage, the conditional **as if** (*hōs,* 253 ≡ *'yk,* 16h1) implies that Jerusalem does indeed

taken over by someone else could be bought back (**redeemed**) by a rightful **heir** (either the original possessor, Lev 25.26–27, or his nearest relative, Lev 25.25). The land of Israel was the Lord's inheritance (Lev 25.23; Psa 79.1), which He had given to the children of Israel (Gen 15.18; 35.12); but other nations sometimes disregarded this and tried to seize it for themselves. For example, during the Babylonian captivity the Ammonites had seized possession of the land of Gad, as if Israel had no heir to redeem it: "Are there no sons to Israel? Is there no heir to him? Why has Milcom taken possession of Gad, and his people are dwelling in its cities?" (Jer 49.1). In the situation described here, the plunderers were acting in the same way—**as if** they could take whatever they liked from God's temple, and there was **no heir** to get it back (v 36).

Yet the prophets had promised that Israel would indeed have an **heir who redeemed.** The LORD "saw that there was no man, and was astonished that there was no one to intercede; and His own arm saved for Him, and His righteousness supported Him . . . and a Redeemer will come to Zion" (Isa 59.16–20). This promise was soon to be fulfilled through Jesus (Rom 11.26), who "made redemption for His people . . . salvation from our enemies, and from the hand of all those who hate us" (Luke 1.68–71).

- **They were trampling on the sacrificial altar of the Lord from**[158] **every uncleanness,** just as the foreign invaders "trampled [the sacrificial altar] down with their sandals," and so defiled it (2.2, 20; 17.25). Under both the old covenant and the new, God's holy things must not be approached by any person in a state of uncleanness (Lev 10.3; 15.31; 22.2–7; Isa 1.12–13; 1 Pet 2.1–3; 1 Cor 11.27–29; 2 Cor 6.14–7.1).
- **With menstruation of blood they stained the sacrifices,** treating the holy offerings as if they were merely **profane** (unholy, 1.8) **meats.** Under the old covenant Law, anyone who came into contact with menstrual blood was in a state of fleshly defilement (Lev 15.19–24) and, while in that state, could not come into contact with the appointed sacrifices (Lev 22.2–7).

---

have an heir to redeem—presumably "the Davidic Messiah plainly announced in 17.3 ff." (Prigent 969 n. 11), since nothing in the Eighteen Psalms anticipates redemption from any other direction (see also the comments on v 34).

[158] The Greek version states that Jerusalem's inhabitants were trampling on the altar **from** *(apo)* **every uncleanness.** This would most naturally mean that they were coming **from** a condition of defilement to the altar (Ryle-James 79; Holm-Nielsen 79; cf. "they will come from [*m*-] the cities of Judah . . . bringing burnt offerings . . . to the house of the LORD," Jer 17.26; Zep 3.10), although it could possibly indicate that the trampling was caused by (arose **from**) the uncleanness (BDAG 106, §5c; Viteau 295; cf. "from his joy he goes and sells," Matt 13.44; "sleeping from the sorrow," Luke 22.45).

The Syriac version states that the inhabitants were trampling the holy place **in** [*b*-] **all their uncleanness.**

8.14 [13] οὐ παρέλειπον ἁμαρτίαν ἣν οὐκ ἐποίησαν ὑπὲρ τὰ ἔθνη· They did not leave *any* sin that they did not do beyond the nations.	ܘܠܐ ܫܒܩܘ ܚܛ̈ܗܐ ܕܠܐ ܥܒܕܘ ܘܝܬܝܪ ܡܢ ܥܡ̈ܡܐ. And they did not leave *any* sins that they did not do even beyond the peoples.

8.14 The people of Israel had greater advantages than any other nation, because "they were entrusted with the words of God" (Rom 3.1–2; Deut 4.7–8; Neh 9.13–14) and knew "His will . . . being instructed out of the Law" (Rom 2.18; 2 Tim 3.15–17). Yet, at this time, **they did not leave any sin that they did not do beyond the nations:** see the comments on 1.8 and Maccabaica 7.23.

Because of this, God brought war on them

8.15 [14] δια τοῦτο ἐκέρασεν αὐτοῖσ ὁ θ(εὸ)σ πν(εῦμ)α πλανήσεωσ· Because of this, God mixed for them a spirit of going astray;	ܡܛܠܗܕܐ ܡܙܓ ܠܗܘܢ܆ ܐܠܗܐ ܪܘܚܐ ܕܛܥܝܘܬܐ. Because of this, God mixed for them the spirit of going astray,
ἐπότισεν αὐτοὺσ ποτήριον οἴνου ἀκράτου εἰσ μέθην He gave them to drink a cup of unmixed wine, to *the point of* drunkenness.	ܘܐܫܩܝ ܐܢܘܢ܆ ܟܣܐ ܚܝܐ ܠܪܘܝܘܬܐ. and He made them drink the living cup to *the point of* being drunk.

8.15 Because of their sins, **God mixed** (*ekerasen,* Isa 5.22, LXX; Rev 14.10; 18.6) a drink for the inhabitants of Jerusalem, and **gave them to drink a cup of** exceptionally strong drink, **unmixed wine** (as in Rev 14.10), the sort of drink that would cause **drunkenness.**[159] The same picture is used repeatedly in the Scriptures to describe God's judgments: against "all the wicked ones of the land" (Psa 75.8); against "all the nations . . . all the kingdoms of the land, which are on the face of the earth," including those conquered by Babylon, and finally Babylon itself (Jer 25.15–29; 51.7); against Judah at the time of the Babylonian conquest (Isa 51.17; Ezek 23.31–34); against "the great city that reigns over the kings of the land" (Rev 18.3–6; 17.18); against anyone who worships the beast (Rev 14.9–11). In the present passage the drink consists of **a spirit of going astray,** like the spirit sent by God in punishment against Ahab (1 Kgs 22.20–23), against false prophets (Ezek 14.9), and against "all those who did not believe the truth, but were well pleased with unrighteousness" (2 Thes 2.11–12). If we reject God and go **astray** *(planēseōs)* from Him (Heb 3.10), He may punish us by allowing us the very thing we desire (Prov 1.29–31; Psa 81.11–12).

---

[159] **To [the point of] drunkenness** *(eis methēn).* The preposition *eis* indicates that the drinking *(methuō)* continues "up to" (BDAG 289–90, §3) the condition of **drunkenness**—as in "you will drink blood to [the point of] drunkenness" (Ezek 39.19, LXX; cf. Tobit 4.15).

8.16 [15] ἤγαγεν τὸ(ν) ἀπ αισχάτου τῆσ γῆσ τὸν παίοντα κραταιῶσ· From the end of the earth He brought the *one* who was striking mightily;	ܐܝܬܝ ܠܗܘ ܕܡܢ ܣܘ̈ܦܝܗ ܕܐܪܥܐ ܕܐܠܨ ܡܥܫܢܐܝܬ From *the* ends of the earth He brought the *one* who *was* oppressing harshly
8.17 [15] ἔκρινεν τὸν πόλεμον ἐπι Ἰερουσαλὴμ καὶ τ(ὴν) γῆν αὐτῆσ he decided the war against Jerusalem and her land.	ܘܕܐܢ. ܩܪܒܐ ܥܠ ܐܘܪܫܠܡ ܘܥܠ ܐܪܥܗ. and deciding war against Jerusalem and against her land.

8.16–17 God also punished the disobedient people by bringing **against** them someone **from the end of the earth,** someone **who was striking** the land with warfare (just as Assyria had done: Isa 14.29, LXX). Moses had forewarned the Israelites that, "because you did not serve the LORD your God with joy . . . then you will serve your enemies whom the LORD will send against you . . . . The LORD will raise up a nation against you from far away, from the end of the earth . . . and he will besiege you in all your gates until your high and fortified walls, in which you trust, come down" (Deut 28.47–52). So, in the days of Isaiah, "because this people has refused the waters of Shiloah . . . then for this, behold, the Lord will bring against them . . . the king of Assyria and all his glory" (Isa 8.6–8). In the time of the Eighteen Psalms the Israelites were once again rejecting their God, and once again He brought an enemy against them. The new enemy's military activity (his **striking**) was powerful (he struck **mightily**) and conclusive: **he decided the war**—in other words, he brought the war to a decisive outcome.[160] That too was in accordance with Moses' prophecies: "You will be struck before your enemies . . . and you will be given into the hand of the enemy" (Lev 26.17, 25).[161]

[160] **He decided the war** *(ekrinen ton polemon).* This expression is fairly common in the writings of Hellenistic historians, and always means that the outcome of the conflict is settled, whether by victory or by defeat. So, for instance, we read of situations where people did not want "to decide the war [*krinein ton polemon*] in battle" at times when defeat was likely (Diodorus 17.10.6; 20.109.5). The definitions "win a battle" (LSJ 996, §2c) and "resolve a military conflict by winning it" (Muraoka 413, §7) are therefore too restrictive. The subject of the verb can be either God ("The Deity most righteously decided the battle," Cassius Dio 44.45.1) or a human ("the struggle was equally poised for a long time, but the king came heavily down on the part opposed to him, and decided the battle," Appian, *Mithridatica,* 13.85). Other passages helpfully illustrating the usage of the expression include Diodorus 18.17.3; 20.113.5; Polybius 3.117.11. Such renderings as "he decreed war" (APOT, doubtfully), "he determined upon war" (AOT), and "he declared war" (OTP) are inconsistent with Greek usage; they would require *krinō* plus an infinitive (e.g., *ekrinan polemēsai,* Plutarch, *Parallela minora,* 3).

[161] In vv 16–17 our rendering of the Syriac follows the punctuation of the Greek (so also Harris-Mingana). The only known Syriac manuscript (16h1) punctuates this passage so that the major sense break follows *wd'n* (**deciding**). This would leave the rest of v 17 without a verb,

8.18 [16] ἠπάντησαν αὐτῷ οἱ ἄρχοντεσ τ(ῆ)σ γῆσ μετα χαρᾶσ· The rulers of the land met him with joy;	ܘܐܪܥܘܗܝ ܕܝܢ̈ܘܗܝ ܕܐܪܥܐ ܒܚܕܘܬܐ And *the* judges of the land met him with joy,
εἶπαν αὐτῷ ἐπευκτὴ ἡ ὁδόσ σου δεῦτε εἰσέλθατε μετ ειρήνησ· they said to him: "Blessed *is* your† path; come, enter[pl] with peace."	ܘܐܡܪܘ ܠܗ. ܬܬܩܢ ܐܘܪܚܟ. ܬܐ ܥܘܠ ܒܫܠܡܐ. and they said to him: "Your† path will be established; come†, enter† with peace."

8.18 The rulers of the land met this enemy **with joy.** They should have received the LORD their King **with joy** (Deut 28.47, just cited), but they were not willing for Him to reign over them (Luke 19.14; cf. 1 Sam 8.7). The welcome that should have been given to Him, they gave instead to their future destroyer (v 23).[162] So, a generation or two later, their successors rejected the Messiah their King, and said, "We have no king but Caesar" (John 19.15)—who would destroy them (cf. John 11.48).

They said to the enemy: **"Blessed is your path;**[163] **come, enter**[164] **with peace."** But

---

but the missing verb would be the one supplied by the immediate context (Nöldeke §§332, 382), i.e., *d'n,* so the sense would be essentially the same: "From the ends of the earth He brought one who was oppressing harshly and deciding—[deciding] war against Jerusalem and against her land" (cf. Trafton). However, this would be a very strange way to say what could be said more simply in exactly the same words by punctuating them more conventionally. Presumably the punctuation was misplaced by a scribe who did not recognize that **war** was the thing decided (see the previous footnote).

[162] Classical historians reported that the Roman general Pompey came to Judea because of a dispute between rival rulers of the land. Those who favored one side welcomed Pompey and his army into the city, but those who favored the other side then fortified the temple area and resisted him (Strabo 16.2,40; Josephus, *War,* 1.142–143 ≡ *Antiquities,* 14.58–59).

[163] The Greek version has **Blessed** [*epeuktē*] **is your path.** In non-Biblical Greek, forms of *epeuchomai* generally mean "pray" or "vow," which might suggest that the destroyer's path was "prayed for" or "longed for" (cf. LSJ 619); but in the LXX *epeuchomai* and *epeuktos* invariably correspond to Hebrew *brk* and mean "bless" (Deut 10.8; 1 Chr 23.13; Jer 20.14), so this is more likely to be the sense here. Moreover, **blessed** is closer to the Syriac (16h1), which has **Your path will be established** (*ttqny,* as in Prov 4.26, "all your paths will be established"; Psa 37.23; in such contexts it corresponds to Hebrew *kwn*). Compare vv 19–20, "they made level the paths that were rough, for his entry... and he set up his feet with great faithfulness" (Syr). **Blessed** and **established** are overlapping concepts in the Scriptures ("Solomon will be blessed [*bryk*], and the throne of David will be established [*nkwnh*]," 1 Kgs 2.45).

[164] Notice the shift in the Greek between singular (*sou,* **your** path, addressed to one) and plural (*eiselthate,* **enter,** addressed to more than one). The enemy, like Jerusalem herself, is a collective, a singular entity consisting of a plurality ("a great people," v 2), and is therefore grammatically both singular and plural (see the footnote on v 7a).

in fact he was entering with the opposite of peace (vv 16–17). They were "saying 'Peace, peace,' when there is no peace" (Jer 6.14); they were saying to their destroyer what was to be said to their Redeemer ("Blessed is the King who comes in the name of the Lord; peace in heaven, and glory in the highest regions," Luke 19.38).

8.19 [17] ὡμάλισαν ὁδοὺσ τραχείασ ἀπο εἰσόδου αὐτοῦ·	ܘܐܫܘܝܘ ܐܘܪ̈ܚܬܐ ܕܥܣܩܐ ܠܡܥܠܢܘܬܗ.
They leveled *the* rough paths away from his entering;	And they leveled the paths that *were* rough, for his entry;
ἤνοιξαν πύλασ ἐπὶ Ἰ(ερουσα)λὴμ· ἐστεφάνωσαν τείχη αὐτῆσ·	ܘܦܬܚܘ ܬܪ̈ܥܐ ܥܠ ܐܘܪܫܠܡ ܘܟܠܠܘ ܫܘܪ̈ܝܗ̇.
they opened up *the* gates close by Jerusalem, they crowned her walls.	they opened the gates close by Jerusalem, and they crowned her walls.

8.19 Jerusalem's rulers **leveled the rough paths**[165] **away from his entering**[166] and **opened up** the **gates,**[167] again doing for their destroyer what was to be done for their Redeemer (Luke 3.4–6 ≡ Isa 40.3–5). Contrast Nehemiah, who, being a wise governor, was meticulously careful to guard the city's gates against her enemies (Neh 7.3). God's people must guard their gates carefully against evil (cf. Prov 4.23; Psa 34.13), but open them freely to their King (Psa 24.7; Rev 3.20; Luke 12.36).

They crowned the city's **walls** to adorn it, in the way that was done at times of "very great gladness" (Maccabaica 4.57–58). What should have been a cause of great sorrow, they treated as a cause of rejoicing (cf. 1 Cor 5.2, 6).

8.20 [18] εἰσῆλθεν ὡσ πατὴρ εἰσ οἶκον υἱῶ(ν) αὐτοῦ μετ εἰρήνησ·	ܘܥܠ ܐܝܟ ܐܒܐ ܠܒܝܬܐ ܕܒ̈ܢܘܗܝ ܒܫܠܡܐ.

[165] In the Syriac manuscript (16h1) **paths** is plural (with seyame), but **rough** is singular. This presents **paths** as a plural noun denoting a singular entity (**his entry,** singular, could occur only by a single route); cf. Arayathinal §303, n. 2. (Here and elsewhere in the manuscript, the seyame might, of course, have been allocated by a later scribe, rather than the initial Syriac translator.) Harris-Mingana and Baars emended **rough** to plural (matching the Greek).

[166] The phrase **away from his entering** *(apo eisodou autou)* is clearly adapted from the common expression *apo tēs hodou,* "from the way," "out of the way" (e.g., "lift up the stumblingblock from the way [*apo tēs hodou*] of My people," Isa 57.14, LXX). Most English translators have interpreted it as "before his entering" (AOT), but such renderings are not supported by Greek usage.

[167] **The gates close by** [*epi*] **Jerusalem.** The gates of the city itself (i.e., those situated in its walls) would not normally require a preposition (Neh 7.3; Psa 87.2; etc.). Ryle-James may therefore be correct in suggesting that the **gates close by Jerusalem** "are the approaches to Jerusalem; the passes and roads, which admitted an army to the capital" (Ryle-James 82; see also the footnote to 2.30).

He entered like a father into *the* house of his sons, with peace;	And he entered like a father into the house of his sons, with peace,
ἔστησεν τοὺσ πόδασ αὐτοῦ μετα ἀσφαλείασ πολλῆσ·	ܘܐܩܝܡ ܪ̈ܓܠܘܗܝ ܒܫܪܪܐ ܣܓܝܐܐ.
he made his feet stand with great security.	and he made his feet stand with great faithfulness.

8.20 The destroyer **entered . . . with peace** (see the comments on v 18)—in the way that a **father** would enter the **house of his sons**—and **set up his feet** inside the city **with great security,** the security of foot that God would provide for His Messiah (Psa 18.33, 36).

8.21 [19] κατελάβετο τὰσ πυργοβάρεισ αὐτῆσ καὶ τὸ τεῖχοσ Ἱερουσαλὴμ·	ܘܐܚܕܘ ܡܓ̈ܕܠܝܗ̇ ܘܫܘܪ̈ܝܗ̇ ܕܐܘܪܫܠܡ.
He took hold of her towers and the wall of Jerusalem,	And they took hold of her towers and *the* walls of Jerusalem,
8.22 [19] ὅτι ὁ θ(εὸ)σ ἤγαγεν αὐτὸν μετα ἀσφαλείασ ἐν τῇ πλανήσει αὐτῶν·	ܡܛܠ ܕܐܠܗܐ ܐܝܬܝܗܝ ܒܬܘܩܢܐ ܥܠ ܛܥܝܘܬܗܘܢ.
because God led him with security, as they *had* gone astray.	because God brought him with stability, on *account of* their going astray.

8.21 Once he was inside the city, the trouble started: **he took hold of**[168] Jerusalem's **towers** and **wall.**[169] A century earlier, Antiochus Eupator had entered Jerusalem with a promise "to be at peace"—but when he was inside it, "he set aside the oath which he had sworn, and commanded to pull down the wall" (Maccabaica 6.60–62). When an enemy "shows favor with his voice, you will not believe him, for seven abominations are in his heart" (Prov 26.24–25).

8.22 The enemy was able to accomplish this **because God** allowed it, because Jerusalem's inhabitants **had gone astray.** Similarly, the Babylonian conquest of Jerusalem happened "because they sinned against the LORD," because "their shepherds caused

---

[168] **He took hold of her towers . . . he destroyed their rulers . . . he poured out the blood** (vv 21–23). The Syriac version (16h1) has plural verbs here (like the plural verb in the Greek version in v 18: see the footnote there): **they took hold of her towers . . . they destroyed their rulers . . . they poured out the blood.**

[169] Classical historians report that Pompey's troops forcibly broke down the **wall** around the temple area and its **towers,** and then slaughtered or captured the opponents within (Strabo 16.2.40; Josephus, *War,* 1.149–151 ≡ *Antiquities,* 14.69–71).

them to go astray" (Jer 50.6–7); and a century later, Jesus told the city that it would be besieged and destroyed "because you did not know the time of your being looked on" (Luke 19.41–44).

8.23 [20] ἀπώλεσεν ἄρχοντασ αὐτ(ῶν) καὶ πᾶν σοφὸν ἐν βουλῇ· He destroyed their rulers and every*one who was* wise in counsel;	ܘܐܘܒܕܘ ܫ̈ܠܝܛܢܝܗܘܢ ܡܛܠ ܕܚܟܝܡ ܒܡܠܟܐ. And they destroyed their rulers, because he was wise in counsel,
ἐξέχεεν τὸ αἷμα τ(ῶν) οἰκούντων Ἰ(ερουσα)λὴμ ὡσ ὕδωρ ἀκαθαρσίασ· he poured out the blood of those who dwelt in Jerusalem like water of uncleanness.	ܘܐܫܕܘ ܕܡܐ ܕܥܡܘܪ̈ܝܗ ܕܐܘܪܫܠܡ ܐܝܟ ܡ̈ܝܐ ܕܛܢܦܘܬܐ. and they poured out the blood of *the* dwellers of Jerusalem like the waters of uncleanness.

8.23 He destroyed their rulers and everyone who was wise[170] **in counsel**—the kinds of people who had been seized in the Babylonian invasion (2 Kgs 25.6, 18–21, 12).

He poured out the blood of those who dwelt in Jerusalem, treating it as if it were mere filthy water—**water of uncleanness**—just as previous oppressors had done (Psa 79.2–3 ≡ Maccabaica 7.17).

8.24 [21] ἀπήγαγεν τοὺσ υἱοὺσ καὶ τὰσ θυγατέρασ αὐτ(ῶν)· ἃ ἐγέννησαν ἐν βεβηλώσει· He led away their sons and daughters who had been fathered in profaneness.	ܘܐܘܒܠ ܒ̈ܢܝܗܘܢ ܘܒ̈ܢܬܗܘܢ ܗܢܘܢ ܕܗܘܘ ܒܛܡܐܘܬܐ. And he led *away* their sons and their daughters, those who were in uncleanness.
8.25 [22] ἐποίησαν κατὰ τὰσ ἀκαθαρσίασ αὐτ(ῶν) καθὼσ οἱ π(ατέ)ρεσ αὐτ(ῶν)· They did in accordance with their uncleannesses, just as their fathers *had done;*	ܘܥܒܕ ܠܛܡܐܘܬܗܘܢ ܐܝܟ ܕܐܦ ܐܒ̈ܗܝܗܘܢ. And he did their uncleannesses, as also their fathers *had done;*
8.26 [22] ἐμίανεν Ἰερουσαλὴμ καὶ τὰ ἡγιασμένα τῷ ὀνόματι τοῦ θ(εο)ῦ·	ܘܛܡܐܬ ܐܘܪܫܠܡ ܐܦ ܠܐܝܠܝܢ ܕܡܩܕܫܝܢ ܗܘܘ ܠܫܡܗ ܕܐܠܗܐ.

[170] **And every[one who was] wise** is the reading of the Greek text *(kai pan sophon)*. The Syriac manuscript (16h1) has *mṭl dḥkym,* **because he** [their ruler] **was wise,** although Harris-Mingana suggested that this could be a textual error for *wkl dḥkym* ("and every[one who was] wise"), which would match the Greek.

Jerusalem also stained
the *things* that had been made holy
to the name of God.

and Jerusalem also made unclean
those *things* that had been made holy
to *the* name of God.

8.24–26 He led away their sons and daughters into captivity far away (see the comments on 2.6; 17.14). The people who suffered these things **had been fathered in profaneness** (uncleanness; see on 1.8). They had been born to sinful parents (Psa 51.5) and into a sinful world (1 Jn 5.19; Gal 1.4); and they themselves had walked in the steps of their sinful parents (cf. Matt 23.31–32; Num 32.14): **they did in accordance with their uncleannesses,**[171] **just as their fathers had done.** "They rebelled against God . . . and acted treacherously, like their fathers" (Psa 78.56–57). Moreover, like previous generations, **Jerusalem also stained the things that had been made holy**[172] **to the name of God.** Before the Babylonian conquest, the Lord had declared that the city's priests "have profaned My holy things; they have made no distinction between the holy and the profane, and they have not taught the difference between the unclean and the clean" (Ezek 22.26, 8). The latest generation had done the same deeds—and was therefore suffering the same penalty.

God judges in righteousness

8.27 [23] ἐδικαιώθη ὁ θ(εὸ)σ
ἐν τοῖσ κρίμασιν αὐτοῦ
ἐν τοῖσ ἔθνεσιν τῆσ γῆσ·

ܘܐܙܕܕܩ ܐܠܗܐ
ܒܕܝ̈ܢܘܗܝ
ܒܥܡ̈ܡܐ ܕܐܪܥܐ.

God was acknowledged to be
righteous in His judgments
among the nations of the earth,

And God was acknowledged to be
righteous in His judgments
among the peoples of the earth,

8.28 [23] καὶ οἱ ὅσιοι τοῦ θ(εο)ῦ ὡσ
ἀρνία ἐν ακακία ἐν μέσω αὐτ(ῶν)·

ܘܚܣܝ̈ܘܗܝ ܕܐܠܗܐ ܐܝܟ
ܐܡܪ̈ܐ ܬܡܝ̈ܡܐ ܒܝܢܬ ܗܘܢ.

and God's lovingkind *ones were* like
lambs in innocence
in *the* midst of them.

and God's lovingkind *ones were* like
innocent lambs
among them.

---

[171] **They did in accordance with their uncleannesses.** They were in a state of **uncleanness,** and **they did in accordance with** that state. Those who are righteous do what is righteous; those who are unclean do what is unclean (1 Jn 3.7–10; John 8.44). The Syriac (16h1) reads **he did their uncleannesses,** i.e., the one "who was oppressing harshly" (v 16) did the same evil deeds as the people whom he conquered (see the comments on 2.13); however, Harris-Mingana and Baars conjecturally emended *w'bd* (**and he did**) to *w'bdw* ("and they did," matching the Greek).

[172] **Jerusalem also stained** [*emianen Hierousalēm kai*] **the things that had been made holy** is the reading of 253 (supported by 16h1), whereas 336⁺260 read: "they stained Jerusalem and [*emianan Hierousalēm kai*] the things that had been made holy." Jerusalem herself is depicted as sinning in 17.16 Syr, and repeatedly in the Hebrew Scriptures (e.g., Lam 1.8).

8.27 God was acknowledged to be righteous in His judgments (2.16) **among the nations of the earth** (vv 7b–8). Because of what God has "shown" to his people and what their "eyes have seen" concerning His judgments, they "have acknowledged Your honorable name to be righteous" (vv 30–32)—and even the surrounding **nations,** seeing Jerusalem's sins now uncovered (vv 8–14), would **acknowledge** that she had been punished rightly (cf. Deut 29.24–28; 1 Kgs 9.8–9; Jer 22.8–9). He had provided comparable evidence to earlier generations also: "you will see their way and their doings, and you will know that I have not done without cause all that I have done in" Jerusalem (Ezek 14.23). In the time of Moses, not only could the Israelites see God's judgments and acknowledge His righteousness (Deut 10.20–21; 11.2–7; 4.3; 3.21), but even their mightiest enemy saw it too, and was forced to acknowledge that "the LORD is righteous" (Exod 9.25–27). "The LORD ... has revealed His righteousness to the eyes of the nations" (Psa 98.2).

8.28 God's lovingkind ones (see on Maccabaica 2.42; 7.17) **were like lambs in innocence in the midst of them**—like Jeremiah (Jer 11.19), Jesus (Acts 8.32–35 ≡ Isa 53.7–8), and His disciples (Matt 10.16–18; Rom 8.36 ≡ Psa 44.11, 22).

Greek	Syriac
8.29 [24] αἰνετὸσ κ(ύριο)σ ὁ κρίνων πᾶσαν τὴν γῆν ἐν δικαιοσύνη αὐτοῦ·	ܡܫܒܚ ܗܘ ܐܠܗܐ ܕܕܐܢ ܠܟܠܗ ܐܪܥܐ ܒܙܕܝܩܘܬܗ.
Praiseworthy *is the* Lord, the *One* who judges all the earth in His righteousness.	Glorified *is* God, He who judges all the earth in His righteousness.

8.29 Praiseworthy is the Lord, the One who judges all the earth in His righteousness (vv 7b, 27). "Glory and power are our God's, for true and righteous are His judgments....Give praise to our God, all His slaves, those who fear Him" (Rev 19.1–5).

Greek	Syriac
8.30 [25] ἰδοὺ δὴ ὁ θ(εό)σ ἔδειξασ ἡμῖν τὸ κρίμα σου ἐν τῇ δικαιοσύνῃ σου·	ܗܐ ܐܢܬ ܐܠܗܐ ܚܘܝܬܢ ܙܕܝܩܘܬܟ.
See! Indeed, O God, You† have shown us Your† judgment in Your† righteousness;	Now, God, You† Yourself‡ have shown us Your† righteousness;
8.31 [25] εἴδοσαν οἱ ὀφθαλμοὶ ἡμῶν τὰ κρίματά σου ὁ θ(εό)σ·	ܘܚܙܝ ܥܝܢܝܢ ܕܝܢܝܟ. ܐܠܗܐ.
our eyes have seen Your† judgments, O God.	and our eyes have seen Your† judgments, God.
[26] ἐδικαιώσαμεν τὸ ὄνομά σου τὸ ἔντιμον εἰσ αἰῶνασ·	ܘܙܕܩܢ ܫܡܟ ܡܝܩܪܐ ܠܥܠܡܝܢ.

We have acknowledged Your† honorable name to be righteous to lasting times,	And we have acknowledged Your† honorable name to be righteous to lasting time,
8.32 [26] ὅτι σὺ ὁ θ(εὸ)σ ‹τῆσ δικαιοσύνησ›· κρίνων τὸν Ἰ(σρα)ὴλ ἐν παιδείᾳ·	ܡܛܠ ܕܐܢܬ ܗܘ ܐܠܗܐ ܕܙܕܝܩܘܬܐ. ܕܕܐܢ ܐܢܬ ܠܝܣܪܐܝܠ ܒܡܪܕܘܬܐ.
because You† *are* the God of righteousness, who judges Israel with discipline.	because You† are the God of righteousness, You† who judge Israel with discipline.

8.32 τῆσ δικαιοσύνησ 336⁺260 ≡ ܕܙܕܝܩܘܬܐ 16h1 | τὴν -ύνην 253 •

8.30–31 God, You have shown us Your judgment … our eyes have seen Your judgments, and as a result **we have acknowledged Your honorable name to be righteous:** see the comments on v 27.

8.32 You are the God of righteousness, who judges Israel with discipline (see on v 35; 3.4; 7.3). He disciplines them "on account of iniquity" (Psa 39.11), because He loves them (Rev 3.19), so that they may not be condemned (1 Cor 11.32; cf. Psa 118.18).

God, have compassion on us

8.33 [27] ἐπίστρεψον ὁ θ(εό)σ τὸ ἔλεόσ σου ἐφ' ἡμᾶσ	ܐܗܦܟ ܥܠܝܢ ܪ̈ܚܡܝܟ
Turn back†, O God, Your† mercy upon us,	Turn† Your† compassions upon us,
καὶ οἰκτείρησον ἡμᾶσ·	ܘܚܘܢܝܢ.
and have compassion† on us.	and have mercy† on us.

8.33 Turn back, O God, Your mercy upon us, and have compassion on us. "The LORD is compassionate and favorable, long to anger and great of lovingkindness," and therefore He is merciful to His people: "He has not done to us in accordance with our sins" (Psa 103.8–10). He "will not cast off to lasting time; for if He has afflicted, then He will have compassion, in accordance with the abundance of His lovingkindnesses" (Lam 3.31–32). Acknowledging that His judgments have been righteous, we can therefore appeal to Him for **mercy** and **compassion** (Psa 119.75–76), "not on account of our righteousnesses, but on account of Your abundant compassions" (Dan 9.18).

8.34 [28] συνάγαγε τὴν διασπορὰν Ἰ(σρα)ὴλ μετὰ ἐλέουσ καὶ χρηστότητοσ·	ܘܟܢܘܫ ܒܕܪܗ ܕܐܝܣܪܝܠ. ܒܪ̈ܚܡܐ ܘܒܒܣܝܡܘܬܐ.
Gather† together the scattering of Israel with mercy and kindness,	And gather† *the* scattering of Israel with compassions and goodness,

8.35 **[28]** ὅτι πίστισ σου μεθ’ ἡμῶν because Your† faithfulness *is* with us,	ܡܛܠ ܕܗܝܡܢܘܬܟ ܥܡܢ. because Your† faithfulness *is* with us.
[29] καὶ ἡμεῖσ ἐσκληρύναμεν ‹τὸν› τράχηλον ἡμῶν· and we ourselves have hardened our neck,	ܘܚܢܢ ܩܫܝܢ ܩܕ̈ܠܢ. And we ourselves have hardened our necks,
καὶ σὺ παιδευτὴσ ἡμῶν εἶ and You† Yourself‡ are our discipliner.	ܘܐܢܬ ܪܕܘܢ ܐܢܬ. and You† Yourself‡ *are* disciplining us.

8.35 τὸν 336⁺260 | > 253 •

8.34 Gather together the scattering of Israel, because the people had been dispersed in distant lands (v 24; 2.6; 17.14; see the comments on 9.2). The Eighteen Psalms recognize that this gathering would take place through the Messiah (see the comments on 17.28, 34)—and so indeed it came to pass: He died "in order that He might gather into one the children of God who were scattered abroad" (John 11.52), bringing them all home "to the city of the living God, the heavenly Jerusalem" (Heb 12.22), as described in Acts 2.6–11, 36–41; 10.34–35 (cf. Eph 2.13–18).

8.35 Your faithfulness is with us. God "will not do falsehood in [His] faithfulness," and will not defile His covenant with His people: He will discipline them, but not abolish His promises to them (Psa 89.30–37; Jer 33.20–21); rather, because of His **faithfulness,** He will protect and deliver them ("the Lord is faithful, who will establish you, and will keep you from the evil one," 2 Thes 3.3; 1 Thes 5.23–24; 1 Cor 10.13). "If we are faithless, He Himself remains faithful: for He is not able to deny Himself" (2 Tim 2.13); and so, when we **have hardened our neck** (by not hearkening to Him, believing in Him, and obeying Him, 2 Kgs 17.14; Neh 9.16–17, 29; Jer 17.23), then He **is our discipliner** to correct that hardening. Discipline (v 32; 3.4; 7.3) is contrasted with destruction (Prov 19.18; 23.13–14; Psa 118.18; cf. Jer 10.24; 30.11); God disciplines His people not to destroy them, but to teach them His Law (Psa 94.12)—so that "one who loves discipline loves knowledge" (Prov 12.1)—and to deliver their souls from Sheol (Prov 23.13–14)—so that "corrections of discipline are the way of life" (Prov 6.23). "Take a firm hold on discipline; do not let it go; guard it, for it is your life" (Prov 4.13).

8.36 **[30]** μὴ ὑπερίδησ ἡμᾶσ ὁ θ(εὸ)σ ἡμῶν· Do not overlook† us, O our God,	ܠܐ ܬܗܘܐ ܡܢܢ ܐܠܗܢ. Do not look† away from us, our God,
ἵνα μὴ καταπίωσιν ἡμᾶσ ἔθνη ὡσ μὴ ὄντοσ λυτρουμένου·	ܕܕܠܡܐ ܢܒܠܥܘܢ ܥܡ̈ܡܐ ܐܝܟ ܗܘ ܕܠܝܬ ܕܦܪܘܩ.

in order that *the* nations may not swallow us up, as *if there* were no *one* who redeems.	lest the peoples devour us, as *if* there were no *one* who *is* saving.

8.36 Do not overlook[173] us, O our God, in order that the nations may not swallow us up. "If the LORD had not been for us, when humanity stood against us, then they would have swallowed us as living things" (Psa 124.2). But when "the Lord is my helper, I will not be afraid; what will humanity do to me?" (Heb 13.6 ≡ Psa 118.6).

The nations would be able to destroy God's people completely if there were **no one who redeems.** But His people do have a Redeemer (see the comments on v 12): "the LORD will redeem you from the hand of your enemies" (Mic 4.10; Luke 1.68, 71).

We will not keep away from You

8.37 [31] καὶ σὺ ὁ θ(εὸ)σ ἡμ(ῶν)· ἀπ αρχῆσ And You† *are* our God from *the* beginning,	ܘܐܢܬ ܐܠܗܢ ܐܢܬ ܡܢ ܒܪܫܝܬ. And You† *are* our God Yourself† from in *the* beginning,
καὶ ἐπὶ σὲ ἡ ἐλπὶσ ἡμῶν κ(ύρι)ε· and our hope *is* on You†, Lord.	ܘܥܠܝܟ ܗܘ ܣܒܪܢ. ܡܪܝܐ and our hope is on You†, LORD.
8.38 [32] καὶ ἡμεῖσ οὐκ ἀφεξόμεθά σου And we ourselves will not keep away from You†,	ܘܚܢܢ ܠܐ ܢܪܚܩ ܡܢܟ. And we ourselves will not keep away from You†,
ὅτι χρηστὰ τὰ κρίματά σου ‹ἐφ'› ἡμᾶσ· because kind *are* Your† judgments upon us.	ܡܛܠ ܕܛܒܝܢ ܐܢܘܢ ܕܝܢܝܟ. because good are Your† judgments

8.38 ἐφ' 336⁺260 [16h1] | εἰσ 253 •

8.37–38 You are our God from the beginning (Psa 22.9–10; 71.5–6; 90.1), **and our hope is on You.** "My hope is from Him; He only is my rock and my salvation" (Psa 62.5–6); no one else can redeem us from our enemies (Psa 60.11). Therefore, whatever anyone else may choose to do (cf. Josh 24.15), **we ourselves** (emphatic, *hēmeis*) **will not keep away from You** (5.9), **because kind are Your judgments upon us.** People come to Him from the ends of the earth because of the kindness of His judgments (5.2, 14–17, 21), because "He brings to safety the needy one who cries for help.... He redeems their soul from fraud and from wrong" (Psa 72.10–14; Mic 7.18).

---

[173] Greek *huperidēs* (**overlook**) ≡ Syriac *thm' mn* (**look away from**), as in "Do not overlook [*huperidēs* ≡ *thm' mn*] my request" (Psa 55.1, in a similar context). Baars prints *tmh',* a typographical error, instead of *thm'.*

8.39 [33] ἡμῖν καὶ τοῖσ τέκνοισ ἡμ(ῶν) ἡ εὐδοκία εἰσ τὸν αἰῶνα· To us and to our children *is* *Your* good pleasure to lasting time;	ܥܠܝܢ ܘܥܠ ܒܢܝܢ. ܨܒܝܢܟ ܠܥܠܡ upon us and upon our sons; Your† good pleasure *is* to lasting time,
κ(ύρι)ε σ(ωτ)ὴρ ἡμῶν οὐ σαλευθησόμεθα ἔτι τὸν αἰῶνα χρόνον· Lord our Savior, we will not be shaken *any* more *to* lasting time.	ܡܪܝܐ ܐܠܗܐ ܦܪܘܩܢ. ܘܬܘܒ ܠܐ ܢܬܬܙܝܥ ܠܥܠܡ. LORD God our Savior, and we will never again be shaken, to lasting time.

8.39 To us and to our children[174] **is Your good pleasure** [*eudokia*] **to lasting time.** "The LORD's lovingkindness is from lasting time and to lasting time on those who fear Him, and His righteousness is to sons of sons, to those who keep His covenant" (Psa 103.17–18). But if someone "draws back, My soul is not well pleased [*eudokei*] with him"; let us therefore not be among "those who draw back to destruction, but those of faith to the preservation of the soul" (Heb 10.38–39): **Lord our Savior, we will not be shaken** [*saleuthēsometha*] **any more to lasting time.** "Everyone who comes to Me and hears My words and does them ... is like a person building a house, who dug and went deep and laid the foundation on the rock; and a flood came, and the river burst onto that house and did not have the strength to shake [*saleusai*] it, because it was well built" (Luke 6.47–48).

8.40 [34] αἰνετὸσ κ(ύριο)σ ἐν τοῖσ κρίμασιν αὐτοῦ ἐν στόματι ὁσίων· Praiseworthy *is the* Lord in His judgments in *the* mouth of lovingkind *ones*,	ܡܫܒܚ ܗܘ ܡܪܝܐ ܒܕܝܢܘܗܝ ܒܦܘܡܐ ܕܚܣܝܘܗܝ. Glorified is the LORD in His judgments in the mouth of His lovingkind *ones*,
8.41 [34] καὶ εὐλογημένοσ Ἰ(σρα)ὴλ ὑπὸ κ(υρίο)υ εἰσ τὸν αἰῶνα: and blessed *be* Israel by *the* Lord to lasting time.	ܘܡܒܪܟ ܗܘ ܐܝܣܪܐܝܠ ܡܢ ܡܪܝܐ ܠܥܠܡ. and blessed is Israel by the LORD to lasting time.

8.40–41 Praiseworthy is the Lord in His judgments in the mouth of lovingkind ones (see on v 29)—and conversely, **blessed be Israel by the Lord to lasting time.** "He blesses the house of Israel ... He blesses those who fear the LORD, the little ones

---

[174] The Greek mentions **us** both in v 38 (God's judgments are kind **upon us**) and in v 39 (His good pleasure is **to us**). The Syriac manuscript (16h1) mentions **us** only once (God's judgments are good **upon us**), although a copyist might have accidentally omitted a second instance ("good [are] Your judgments upon us; upon us and upon our sons [is] Your good pleasure to lasting time"; cf. Trafton 98, n. 84).

with the great ones" (Psa 115.12–13), and His greatest blessing to them was the sending of His Son "to bless you, by turning each one of you from your wicked ways" (Acts 3.26), so that they might be blessed "with every spiritual blessing" (Eph 1.3) **to lasting time** (those "who are blessed of My Father" will ultimately inherit the kingdom prepared for them from the foundation of the world, Matt 25.34).

Psalm 9

The opening lines of this psalm describe a time when the people of Israel **were cast out from** their **inheritance** (the land of Canaan) and were **led away in exile into a strange land,** so that they were scattered **in every nation** (vv 1–2). Taken in isolation, the wording would fit equally the carrying away to Babylon under Nebuchadnezzar (so, e.g., Ryle-James 89) and the carrying away to Rome under Pompey (so, e.g., Schüpphaus, *Psalmen Salomos,* 50–51). Nevertheless, in their present context these lines immediately follow the appeal to "gather together the scattering of Israel" in the time of Pompey, "in order that the nations may not swallow us up" (8.33–41); clearly they were placed here as a continuation of the same subject.[175] The two psalms also have many other similarities of wording. In the final collection of Eighteen Psalms, therefore, 9 continues a subject raised in the closing stages of the large-scale psalm 8, just as 3 and 18 continue subjects raised in the closing stages of the other two large-scale psalms, 2 and 17.

Israel was exiled because of its sins

Greek	Syriac
9.0 [0] Τῷ Σαλομῶν εἰς ἔλεγχον: Belonging to Solomon; for reproof.	
9.1 [1] Ἐν τῷ ἀπαχθῆναι Ἰ(σρα)ὴλ ἐν αποικεσία εἰσ γῆν ἀλλοτρίαν· When Israel was led away in exile into a strange land,	ܟܕ ܢܦܩ ܐܝܣܪܐܝܠ ܒܫܒܝܐ ܠܐܪܥܐ ܢܘܟܪܝܬܐ. When Israel went out in captivity to a strange land,
ἐν τῷ ἀποστῆναι αὐτοὺσ ἀπὸ κ(υρίο)υ του λυτρωσαμένου αὐτούσ· when they departed from *the* Lord who had redeemed them,	ܟܕ ܐܪܚܩܘ ܡܢ ܡܪܝܐ ܦܪܘܩܗܘܢ. when they went far off from the LORD their Savior,
9.2 [1] ἀπερίφησαν ἀπο κληρονομίασ ἧσ ἔδωκεν αὐτοῖσ κ(ύριο)σ· they were cast out from *the* inherit- ance that *the* Lord had given to them.	ܐܫܬܕܝܘ ܡܢ ܝܪܬܘܬܐ ܗܝ ܕܝܗܒ ܠܗܘܢ ܐܠܗܐ. they were cast down from the inherit- ance that God had given to them.

175 Atkinson (*I Cried to the Lord,* 191) has objected that the clause **the scattering of Israel was in every nation** (v 2) would not suit the Pompeian deportation. The objection, if valid, would apply equally to the Babylonian deportation. But it is not valid; see the comments on the verse.

Greek	Syriac
[2] ἐν παντὶ ἔθνη ἡ διασπορᾶ τοῦ Ἰ(σρα)ὴλ κατὰ τὸ ῥῆμα τοῦ θ(εο)ῦ In every nation *was* the scattering of Israel, in accordance with the word of God,	ܒܟܠܗܘܢ ܥܡܡܐ ܗܘܐ ܒܘܕܪܗ ܕܝܣܪܝܠ. ܐܝܟ ܡܠܬܗ ܕܐܠܗܐ. In all the peoples *was the* scattering of Israel, in accordance with *the* word of God,
9.3 [2] ‹ἵνα δικαιωθῇσ› ὁ θ(εό)σ ἐν τῇ δικαιοσύνῃ σου ἐν ταῖσ ἀνομίαισ ἡμῶν· in order that You† might be acknowledged to be righteous, O God, in Your† righteousness, in our deeds opposed to *the* Law,	ܡܛܠ ܕܬܙܕܕܩ ܐܠܗܐ ܒܙܕܝܩܘܬܟ. ܒܥܘܠ ܕܝܠܢ. in order that You† might be acknowledged to be righteous, God, in Your† righteousness, in our injustice,
9.4 [2] ὅτι σὺ κριτὴσ δίκαιοσ ἐπὶ πάντασ τοὺσ λαοὺσ τῆσ γῆσ· because You† *are the* righteous judge over all the peoples of the earth.	ܡܛܠ ܕܐܢܬ ܗܘ ܕܝܢܐ ܙܕܝܩܐ. ܥܠ ܟܠܗܘܢ ܥܡܡܐ ܕܐܪܥܐ. because You† are the righteous judge over all the peoples of the earth.

9.3 ἵνα δικαιωθῇσ 336⁺260 ≡ ܡܛܠ ܕܬܙܕܕܩ 16h1 | ἵν δικαιόσησ 253 •

9.1–2[176] When Israel was enslaved in Egypt, the **Lord** had **redeemed** them (see the comments on 8.12, 36) "from the hand of the enemy" (Psa 106.10; 78.42; "from the house of slaves, from the hand of Pharaoh," Deut 7.8; 13.5). He provided such redemption also for later Israelites (Mic 4.10; Jer 15.21). But in spite of this, Israel repeatedly **departed** [*apostēnai*] **from the Lord who had redeemed them** (cf. Deut 32.15, LXX). This happened, for instance, in the time of the Babylonians (Dan 9.5), and again in the time of Antiochus Epiphanes (Maccabaica 1.15). It was happening yet again in the time of the Eighteen Psalms (4.1). Later believers are warned against the same danger: "Watch, brothers, lest there shall be in any of you an evil, unbelieving heart, in departing [*apostēnai*] from the living God" (Heb 3.12).

Because of[177] the Israelites' departure from the Lord, **they were cast out from the inheritance that the Lord had given to them.** That **inheritance** was the land of

[176] In the Greek copies (but not in the Syriac), the psalm is superscribed **Belonging to Solomon; for reproof** *(elegchon)*. All those who sin are "reproved [*elegchomenoi*] by the Law as transgressors" (Jas 2.9; 1 Tim 5.20). The present psalm reproves Israel for its "deeds opposed to the Law" (v 3): only by confessing these sins can the soul be cleansed and forgiveness obtained (vv 12–15).

[177] **When they departed.** The Greek is *en tō apostēnai autous,* "in their departing," which could indicate both time (**when they departed;** cf. the previous clause, **when Israel was led away**) and causation ("because they departed," Ryle-James; cf. BDF §219(2); MHT 3.253). The corresponding Syriac, *kd 'rḥqw,* refers unambiguously to time (**when they went far off**).

Canaan; and the Lord had provided it for Israel by casting out the nations who had previously dwelt in it (Psa 78.55). When the Israelites sinned like those previous nations, they too were cast out, **led away in exile into a strange land,** and scattered among the nations. This happened in the time of the Babylonians (2 Kgs 24.14–15; 25.11, 21; Jer 20.4; Lam 1.3), and it was happening again in the time of the Eighteen Psalms (2.6; 8.24, 34; 17.14). Nor was that the last. A further terrible exile would happen later in the Roman period, during the lifetime of the generation who heard Jesus (Luke 21.24, 32).

The scattering of Israel was in every nation. ("In every nation" has a similar meaning in Col 1.6, 23.) Those captured in the time of the Babylonians had been taken to Babylon (2 Kgs 24.15–16; 2 Chr 36.20; Jer 39.9), and those captured in the time of the Eighteen Psalms were taken to the "sunset" (17.14)—but in both cases they would have been dispersed widely after that. Captives taken by one nation were sold later to other nations (Joel 3.6, 8; Ezek 27.13; Maccabaica 3.41), and those who remained with their captors might go wherever those captors went (armies often journeyed widely, e.g., Maccabaica 1.17; 3.37; the captor in the time of the Eighteen Psalms eventually ended his life "close by the mountains of Egypt," 2.30).

The punishment happened **in accordance with the word of God.** Both the Law of Moses and the prophets had warned the Israelites that, if they disobeyed God, they would be taken into captivity and scattered among the nations (Lev 26.33; Deut 28.64; Jer 9.16; Ezek 12.14–15). What His **word** had proclaimed, He had done (Zec 7.12–14), just as He always does. "Has He said, and will He not do it? and has He spoken, and will He not set it up?" (Num 23.19). "My word that goes out of My mouth will not return to Me empty, but it will do what I desire, and it will succeed in the thing for which I sent it" (Isa 55.10–11).

9.3 The punishment happened **in order that You might be acknowledged to be righteous, O God, in Your righteousness, in our deeds opposed to the Law.** See the comments on 2.16 ("I myself will acknowledge You to be righteous . . . because You have repaid the sinners in accordance with their works") and 8.7. The two phrases **in** [*en*] **Your righteousness** and **in** [*en*] **our deeds opposed to the Law** are grammatically parallel: the punishment has happened "by reason of" (cf. APOT) these two things, "because of" these two things.[178] Because of God's **righteousness,** and because of the people's **deeds opposed to the Law,** God punished the people; and therefore He can **be acknowledged to be righteous**—whereas a judge who left sin unpunished would clearly not be righteous (cf. Jer 30.11; Exod 23.7; Prov 17.15). Thus "our unrighteousness brings out plainly the righteousness of God": "Let God come out to be true,

---

[178] **In** (Greek *en* ≡ Syriac *b-*) has here a causal meaning, "because of" (Muraoka 232, §11; TS 1.431–32, §6), as in, e.g., "because of [*en* ≡ *b-*] this, we believe that You came out from God" (John 16.30); "I am not declared righteous because of [*en* ≡ *b-*] this" (1 Cor 4.4); "Judah went into exile to Babylon because of [*en,* LXX ≡ *b-*, Syr] their transgression" (1 Chr 9.1).

but every person a liar, just as it is written: 'In order that You may be acknowledged to be righteous in Your words'" (Rom 3.4–5). So God's judgment would **be acknowledged to be righteous,** both by the Israelites themselves ("You are righteous in regard to all that has come upon us; for You have done faithfulness, and we have been evil," Neh 9.33; Psa 58.10–11) and by foreign nations ("all the nations will see My judgment . . . and all the nations will know that the house of Israel went into exile in [because of] their iniquity," Ezek 39.21–23; Jer 40.3).

9.4 You are the righteous judge over all the peoples of the earth. He will judge not only Israel (v 1), but also **all** people of all nations (17.4, 31b); "He judges the world in righteousness, and the peoples in His faithfulness" (Psa 96.13; Acts 17.31). No one "will escape the judgment of God . . . who will give back to everyone in accordance with his works," whether they are Jew or Gentile (Rom 2.3–12).

No one is hidden from Your knowledge

9.5 [3] οὐ γὰρ κρυβήσεται ἀπὸ τῆσ γνώσεώσ σου πᾶσ ποιῶν ἄδικα· For *there* will not be hidden from Your† knowledge any*one* who is doing unrighteous *deeds*,	ܡܛܠ ܕܠܐ ܡܬܛܫܝܐ ܐܢܫ ܡܢ ܬܪܥܝܬܟ ܟܠ ܡܢ ܕܥܒܕ ܥܘܠܐ. For *there will* not *be* hidden from Your† thought any*one* who *is* doing injustice;
9.6 [3] καὶ αἱ δικαιοσύναι τ(ῶν) ὁσίων σου ἐνώπιόν σου κ(ύρι)ε· and the righteous deeds of Your† lov- ingkind *ones are* in Your† sight, Lord,	ܘܙܕܝܩܘܬܐ ܕܝܢ ܕܬܪ̈ܝܨܝܟ ܡܪܝܐ ܩܕܡܝܟ. but the righteousness of Your† upright *ones*, LORD, *is* before You†,
καὶ ποῦ κρυβήσεται ἄν(θρωπ)οσ ἀπὸ τῆσ γνώσεώσ σου **9.7 [3]** ὁ θ(εό)σ· and where will a person be hidden from Your† knowledge, O God?	ܘܠܐܝܟܐ ܢܬܛܫܐ ܒܪܐܢܫܐ ܡܢ ܬܪܥܝܬܟ ܐܠܗܐ. and where will the son of man be hidden from Your† thought, God?

9.5 God is able to judge righteously every person on earth (v 4), **for** no one **who is doing unrighteous deeds** can ever **be hidden from** His **knowledge.** His "eyes are open on all the ways of the sons of Man, to give each man in accordance with his ways, and in accordance with the fruit of his deeds" (Jer 32.19; 16.17; Psa 90.8; Sir 17.19–20; 23.19); and He even "knows the concealed things of the heart" (Psa 44.21; Jer 17.10).

9.6–7a Similarly, **the righteous deeds**[179] of God's **lovingkind ones** are not hidden from His knowledge (cf. v 5)—quite the contrary: they are not merely "known to"

[179] The plural *hai dikaiosunai* here means **the righteous deeds** (as in Matt 6.1), matching "unrighteous deeds" in the previous verse. The Syriac manuscript (16h1) has the singular, *zdyqwt'*, without seyame (**the righteousness**—or perhaps, in view of the Greek, "the righteous deed," as in Tobit 12.8–9, Syr 12a1).

Him (cf. Wright), but are actually **in** His **sight** (*enōpion,* "in full view of" Him, Muraoka 243, §II.2), in the place where we must all stand for our deeds to be judged (Rev 20.12). "There is no creature unrevealed in His sight, but all things are naked and exposed to the eyes of Him to whom is our account" (Heb 4.13).

Then **where will a person be hidden from Your knowledge?** His eyes are "in every place" (Prov 15.3), whether that place is as far up as the heavens, as far down as Sheol, or as far away as the "ends of the sea" (Psa 139.7–12). We can never hide from the One who fills heaven and earth (Jer 23.23–24) and extends beyond them (1 Kgs 8.27).

Our soul can choose to do righteousness or unrighteousness

[4] τὰ ἔργα ἡμῶν ἐν εκλογὴ καὶ ἐξουσία τῆσ ψυχῆσ ἡμῶν· Our works *are* in *the* choosing and authority of our soul	ܥܒ̈ܕܝܢ ܓܝܪ ܒܚܐܪܘܬܐ ܘܒܓܒܝܘܬܐ ܕܢܦܫܢ For we are doing *what is* in the freedom and the choosing of our soul,
τοῦ ποιῆσαι δικαιοσύνην κ(αὶ) ἀδικίαν ἔργοισ χειρῶν ἡμῶν· to do righteousness or unrighteous- ness by *the* works of our hands;	ܠܡܥܒܕ ܛܒܬܐ ܘܒܝܫܬܐ ܒܥܒܕܐ ܕܐܝ̈ܕܝܢ. to do good or evil in the deed of our hands;
9.8 [4] καὶ ἐν τῇ δικαιοσύνῃ σου ἐπισκέπτῃ υἱοὺσ ἀνθρώπων· and in Your† righteousness You† are watching over *the* sons of Men.	ܘܒܙܕܝܩܘܬܟ ܚܐܪ ܐܢܬ ܒܒܢ̈ܝܢܫܐ. and in Your† righteousness You† *are* looking on *the* sons of men.

9.7b Our works are in the choosing and authority of our soul to do righteousness or unrighteousness by the works of our hands. If we **do** unrighteous deeds (v 5), we cannot excuse ourselves by claiming that God has caused us to do them (see on v 9). He has given our souls **authority** to choose either **righteousness or unrighteousness.** The Israelites were offered that choice by the Law of Moses: "I have set before your face life and good, and death and evil . . . . Then choose life, in order that you will live" (Deut 30.15–19, 1; 11.26; Sir 15.15–17). Some people "did evil in My eyes, and chose what I did not delight in" (Isa 65.12; 66.4; Prov 1.29). Others "choose the things that please Me, and take hold in My covenant" (Isa 56.4), such as Moses ("choosing rather to be ill-treated with the people of God, than to have the pleasure of sin for a time," Heb 11.25) and Mary of Bethany ("Mary has chosen the good part, which will not be taken away from her," Luke 10.42). "I have chosen keeping the threshold in the house of my God, beyond dwelling in tents of wickedness" (Psa 84.10). In these matters God has given us **freedom** (*ḥ'rwt',* Syriac, as in 1 Cor 10.29; Gal 5.1; 1 Pet 2.16).[180]

---

[180] Atkinson (*Intertextual Study of the Psalms of Solomon,* 199–200) argues that the views expressed in this passage "contradict" those expressed in 5.6 ("A person and his portion are from

9.8 In Your righteousness You are watching over [*episkeptē;* "visit," APOT; "oversee," OTP] **the sons of Men.** "The LORD has looked from the heavens; He has seen all the sons of Man . . . the One who molds their heart, the One who understands all their works" (Psa 33.13–15; 11.4–5). And He not only sees these things, but responds **in** His **righteousness,** caring for those who are afflicted ("the Lord their God has watched over [*epeskeptai*] them, and He will turn back their captivity," Zep 2.7, LXX; Ezek 34.11–16; cf. Psa 9.4–9; 94.9–10), and scourging those who are disobedient ("with a rod I will watch over [*episkepsomai*] their deeds opposed to the Law," Psa 89.32, LXX; Jer 44.13). Above all, He "has watched over [*epeskepsato*] and redeemed His people" by sending Jesus to save them from their sins (Luke 1.68; Acts 15.14).

9.9 [5] ὁ ποιῶν δικαιοσύνην θησαυρίζει ζωὴν αὐτῷ παρα κ(υρί)ω·	ܗܘ ܓܝܪ ܕܥܒܕ ܙܕܝܩܘܬܐ. ܣܝܡܬܐ ܕܚܝܐ ܣܐܡ ܠܗ ܠܘܬ ܡܪܝܐ.
The *one* who does righteousness is treasuring up life for him*self* with *the* Lord,	For one who does righteousness *is* treasuring up the treasure of life for him*self* with the LORD,
καὶ ὁ ποιῶν ἀδικίαν αὐτὸσ αἴτιοσ τῆσ ψυχῆσ εν ἀπωλεῖα·	ܘܗܘ ܕܥܒܕ ܥܘܠܐ ܗܘ ܚܐܒ ܕܕܝܢܐ ܕܢܦܫܗ ܒܐܒܕܢܐ.
and the *one* who does unrighteousness—he *is the* cause of *his* soul *being* in destruction,	and one who does injustice is guilty of the judgment of his soul in destruction,
9.10 [5] τὰ γὰρ κρίματα κ(υρίο)υ ἐν δικαιοσύνη κατ ἄνδρα καὶ οἶκον	ܕܕܝܢܘܗܝ ܓܝܪ ܒܙܕܝܩܘܬܐ ܥܠ ܟܠ ܒܪܐܢܫ ܘܒܝܬܗ.
for the Lord's judgments *are* in righteousness on each man and house.	for His judgments *are* in righteousness on every son of Man and his house.

9.9 The one who does righteousness is treasuring up life for himself with the Lord. "Treasure up for yourselves treasures in heaven" (Matt 6.20); people who do so are "treasuring away for themselves a good foundation for the coming time, so that they may take hold of what is really life" (1 Tim 6.19). "A person who pursues righteousness and lovingkindness finds life" (Prov 21.21; Rom 2.7; 6.22–23; Matt 25.46; Gal 6.8–9). But if people "obey unrighteousness," "in accordance with your hardness and unrepentant heart you are treasuring up anger for yourself in the day of anger and revelation of God's righteous judgment" (Rom 2.5, 8–9). So **the one who does unrighteousness . . . is the cause of his soul being in destruction.** "The soul that sins, it

You in a balance; he will not proceed to increase it beyond Your judgment, O God"). In fact there is no more contradiction here than there is in the Hebrew Scriptures. Eighteen Psalms 5.6 (like, e.g., Prov 19.21) states that the Lord's decree will stand; Eighteen Psalms 9.7–9 (like, e.g., Ezek 18.20–24) discusses the basis on which He has decreed it.

shall die .... The righteousness of the righteous one shall be upon himself, and the wickedness of the wicked one shall be upon himself" (Ezek 18.20; Prov 9.12; 14.14). We cannot blame God for our **destruction** if we do **unrighteousness** (Jas 1.13–14); we have no one to blame but ourselves. "God our Savior ... wants all people to be saved and come to the knowledge of the truth" (1 Tim 2.3–4); He is "not wanting any to be destroyed, but all to come to repentance" (2 Pet 3.9). "I have no delight in the death of one who dies, says the Lord GOD; then turn back, and live!" (Ezek 18.32, 23; Lam 3.33). So, only a few decades after the composition of the Eighteen Psalms, Jesus said to Jerusalem: "I wanted [*ēthelēsa*] to gather your children together ... and you did not want [*ēthelēsate*] it" (Matt 23.37). Their **destruction** came because their own will was contrary to their Lord's will.

9.10 The Lord's judgments are in righteousness (vv 3–4) **on each man**[181] **and house.** "The Lord is cleansing every lovingkind man and his house" (3.10); His "deeds of mercy will be on the house of Israel to lasting time" (v 20)—whereas "sins will make the houses of sinners desolate, and sinners will be destroyed in the day of the Lord's judgment" (15.13). To both of those groups, the **Lord's judgments** are carried out **in righteousness:** it is righteous for the lovingkind to receive mercy (Gen 18.25; Psa 11.7), and it is righteous for the sinners to receive destruction (2 Thes 1.6; Rev 16.5–6).

God will be kind to those who call on Him

9.11 [6] τίνι χρηστεύσῃ ὁ θ(εό)σ εἰ μὴ τοῖσ ἐπικαλουμένοισ τὸν κ(ύριο)ν·	ܠܡܢܘ ܓܝܪ ܢܛܐܒ ܐܠܗܐ. ܐܠܐ ܐܢ ܠܗܢܘܢ ܕܩܪܝܢ ܠܡܪܝܐ.
To whom will You[†] be kind, O God, except to those who call upon the Lord?	For to whom will God be good, except to those who call to the LORD?

9.11 To whom will You be kind, O God, except to those who call upon the Lord? "The Lord is kind to those who call on Him" (2.40; 5.7; 7.7); see the comments on 6.1–2. But to those who "despise the riches of His kindness" (Rom 2.4), and to those who do not "continue in His kindness," He will show not kindness but the opposite of kindness: severity (*apotomia,* Rom 11.22; cf. Psa 18.25–26).

---

[181] **The Lord's judgments are ... on each man and house** [*kat' andra kai oikon*]. Here *kata* followed by an accusative noun *(andra, oikon)* has a distributive sense, "indicating repetition of [the] same process with multiple entities" (Muraoka 366, §II.8). The Lord's judgments are dealt out man by man and house by house, to each one, as the Syriac version explicitly indicates: **His judgments are ... on every** [*ʿl kl*] **son of Man and his house.** Compare *kata polin kai komēn* ("through each city and village," Luke 8.1), *kata polin* ("in each city," Titus 1.5; Maccabaica 11.3), *kata mian sabbatou* ("on each first day of the week," 1 Cor 16.2), etc. "Come down on man" (Wright) misunderstands the idiom.

9.12 [6] καθαρίσει ἐν ἀμαρτίαισ ψυχὴν ἐν ἐξομολογήσει ἐν ἐξαγορίαισ· He will cleanse *the* soul *that is* in *its* sins, by confession, by public declarations,	ܡܕܟܐ ܓܝܪ ܚܛܗ̈ܝܗ ܕܢܦܫܐ ܒܬܘܕܝܬܐ. For *He will* cleanse *the* sins of the soul, by his confession,
9.13 [6] ὅτι αἰσχύνη ἡμῖν καὶ τοῖσ προσώποισ ἡμῶν περι απάντ(ων)· because *there is* shame to us and to our faces on account of all *things*.	ܡܛܠ ܕܒܗܬܬܐ ܗܝ ܠܢ ܘܠܐܦܝ̈ܢ ܥܠ ܟܠܗܝܢ ܗܠܝܢ. because *there* is shame to us and to our faces on *account of* all these things.

9.12 The Lord **will cleanse**[182] **the soul that is in its sins by confession, by public declarations.** "If we confess our sins, He is faithful and righteous to forgive us our sins and to cleanse us from all unrighteousness" (1 Jn 1.9). "One who covers his transgressions does not prosper; but one who confesses and leaves them has obtained compassion" (Prov 28.13). Such confessions are **public declarations** (10.7), made "with the mouth" (Rom 10.9–10) in the hearing of other people (Jas 5.16; Acts 19.18), as happened under the old covenant on the Day of Atonements ("Aaron will put his two hands on the head of the living goat, and confess over it all the iniquities of the sons of Israel, and all their transgressions, and all their sins," Lev 16.21) and on many other occasions when sin offerings were presented ("when he is guilty for any of these things, then he shall confess that he has sinned concerning it, and he shall bring his guilt penalty to the LORD for his sin which he has sinned, a female from the flock... and the priest shall make atonement for him from his sin," Lev 5.5–6).[183]

---

[182] **He will cleanse** [*katharisei*]. Gebhardt and Rahlfs conjecturally emended this to *katharieis* ("You will cleanse"), but the third person (**He**) is the reading of all manuscripts, both Greek and Syriac. Alternations between second person (**You,** v 11) and third person are extremely common in the Hebrew Scriptures (e.g., "He overturns peoples beneath me... You raise me aloft," Psa 18.47–48), especially in appeals to God and to human superiors, where a shift to the third person is often a mark of special deference ("let your maidservant, I ask, speak in your ears, and hear the words of your maidservant; let not my lord, I ask, set his heart to this man," 1 Sam 25.24–25; "far be it from You to do such a deed as this... behold, I ask, I have undertaken to speak to the Lord," Gen 18.25–27; "if I have found favor in your eyes, O king, and if it is good to the king," Est 7.3).

[183] The present verse (like Psa 32.5) mentions only the **confession,** not the offerings—but this does not mean that confession alone would be enough to **cleanse the soul,** if the appointed offerings were neglected (as argued by Wright 10: "piety had become a substitute for sacrifice"). Conversely, passages that describe atonement by sacrifice with no mention of confession (e.g., 2 Chr 29.24; Neh 10.33) do not imply that sacrifice alone could make atonement if sins remained unconfessed (cf. Isa 1.11–17). Under the new covenant, confession is the only requirement for cleansing mentioned in 1 Jn 1.9; but who would deduce from this that confession alone can

9.13 The Lord's cleansing is needed (vv 11–12), **because there is shame to us and to our faces on account of all things.** "To You, Lord, is righteousness, but to us shame of face . . . because we have sinned against You" (Dan 9.7–8). "I am ashamed and humiliated to lift up my face to You, my God, because our iniquities have increased over our head" (Ezra 9.6). Contrast the hardened sinner: "the forehead of a woman who fornicates was yours; you refused to be ashamed" (Jer 3.3; 6.15). Such people glory in what should shame them (Phil 3.19; 1 Cor 5.2, 6).

9.14 [7] καὶ τίνι ἀφέσει ἁμαρτίασ εἰ μὴ τοῖσ ἡμαρτηκόσι· And to whom will He forgive sins, except to those who have sinned?	ܠܡܢܘ ܓܝܪ ܢܫܒܘܩ ܚܛܗܐ. ܐܠܐ ܐܢ ܠܗܠܝܢ ܕܚܛܘ. For to whom will He forgive sins, except to those who have sinned?

9.14 To whom will He forgive[184] sins, except to those who have sinned? Repentant sinners need not despair of receiving God's forgiveness, because they are exactly the people whom God has forgiven and will forgive (1 Tim 1.15–16). Jesus said, "I did not come to call righteous ones, but sinners to repentance" (Luke 5.32; 15.7; 18.13–14). The Lord's forgiveness is available to those who have sinned (v 14) and who regret their sins (v 15) and confess them (v 12), calling on the Lord in the way He has appointed (v 11; cf. Viteau 306). "All have sinned" (Rom 3.23; 1 Jn 1.10; Psa 143.2), and therefore all need this forgiveness (Psa 130.3–4).

9.15 [7] δικαίουσ εὐλογήσεισ καὶ οὐκ ευθύνεισ περι ὧν ἡμάρτοσαν· You† will bless righteous *ones*, and You† will not punish *them* on account of *the things* *in* which they have sinned,	ܠܙܕܝܩܐ ܓܝܪ ܡܒܪܟ. ܘܠܐ ܡܚܣܕ ܐܢܬ ܠܗܘܢ ܥܠ ܡܕܡ ܕܚܛܘ. For You† *are* blessing righteous *ones*, and You† *do* not reproach them on *account of* the *things* *in* which they have sinned,
καὶ ἡ χρηστότησ σου περι ἁμαρτάνοντασ ἐν μεταμελεῖα· and Your† kindness *is* concerning *those* who sin with regret.	ܛܝܒܘܬܟ ܓܝܪ ܥܠ ܐܝܠܝܢ ܕܚܛܘ ܡܐ ܕܬܒܘ ܐܢܬ ܗܝ. for Your† goodness is concerning those who have sinned, when they have turned back.

"cleanse us from all unrighteousness," without faith (Rom 10.9–10) and baptism (Matt 3.6; Acts 2.37–38)? We cannot demand that every sentence should mention every individual component of God's plan for atonement of sin. What sentence anywhere in the Scriptures does?

[184] **Will He forgive** (*aphesei,* 253 ≡ *aphēsei,* 336⁺260, a spelling variation: cf. Thackeray §6.14; the form in 253 is influenced by the customary spelling *aphesei* for the dative of "forgiveness"). Gebhardt and Rahlfs conjecturally emended it to *aphēseis* ("will You forgive"), but see the footnote to v 12.

9.15 You will bless righteous ones (Psa 5.12; 128.1–6), **and You will not punish**[185] **them on account of the things in which they have sinned.** In His lovingkindness, the Lord "has not done to us in accordance with our sins, and He has not dealt with us in accordance with our iniquities"; on the contrary, "He has put our transgressions far away from us" (Psa 103.10–12).

Your kindness is concerning[186] **those who sin with regret** (*metameleia,* Greek)—that is, **those who have sinned** and then **have turned back** (*tbw,* Syriac), like the son whose father told him to work in the vineyard, and who "answered and said, 'I will not'; but afterward he regretted [*metamelētheis*] and went" (Matt 21.29). Our heavenly Father will show kindness not to those who sin without regret (Deut 29.19–20; Prov 23.35; 30.20; Hos 12.8), and not even to those who merely regret their sins (Matt 27.3–5; John 17.12), but He will show kindness to those whose **regret** has caused them to **turn back** (2 Cor 7.9–10). King Saul and King David both said "I have sinned"; but David repented, and therefore was forgiven (2 Sam 12.13), whereas Saul "rejected the word of the LORD" and continued to do evil, and therefore was himself rejected (1 Sam 15.24–26; cf. Matt 21.28–32). Esau, "wanting to inherit the blessing, was rejected, for he found no place for repentance, though he sought for it with tears" (Heb 12.16–17). All who sin will likewise be rejected, unless they repent and turn away from sin (Luke 13.2–3; John 5.14). But "when a wicked one turns back from his wickedness that he has done, and does justice and righteousness, he will save his soul alive; and when he perceives, and turns back from all his transgressions that he did, living, he will live; he will not die" (Ezek 18.27–28).

Have compassion, because You have chosen Israel

9.16 [8] καὶ νῦν σὺ ὁ θ(εό)σ	ܘܗܫܐ ܐܢܬ ܗܘ ܐܠܗܢ.
καὶ ἡμεῖσ λαόσ σου ὃν ἠγάπησασ·	ܘܚܢܢ ܥܡܟ ܗܘ ܕܐܚܒܬ.
And now, You† *are* God,	And now, You† are our God,
and we *are* Your† people	and we are Your† people
whom You† have loved;	whom You† have loved;

[185] **You will not punish** [*euthuneis*]. The usual meaning of *euthunō* is "make straight" (John 1.23; Jas 3.4), but that is clearly not the sense here; God does indeed "make straight [*kateuthunai*] the man who makes peace in his house" (12.6; 18.9). In non-Biblical Greek *euthunō* sometimes means "call to account" (LSJ 715, §III.2), i.e., bring to judgment to determine whether punishment should be imposed (Plutarch, *Cicero,* 9.4), but here the context requires a still stronger sense, **punish** (Muraoka 300, §2), "exact the full penalty" (Ryle-James 93), as in "Do not take vengeance on [*ekdikēsēs*] us ... nor punish [*euthunēs*] us" (Ptolemaica 2.17). The Syriac version has **reproach** (*mks,* as in Jer 6.15, Syr; Luke 3.19; John 3.20).

[186] **Concerning** *(peri)* here has the same meaning as in v 19: "with regard to" (BDAG 798 §2d), as in 1 Tim 6.4, 21. In both verses the Syriac rendering is *l* (cf. the footnote to 11.9). In the present verse Gebhardt and Rahlfs emended the Greek *peri* to *epi* ("on"), although in v 19 they left *peri* unaltered.

ἴδε καὶ οἰκτείρησον ὁ θ(εὸ)σ	ܚܙܝ ܘܐܬܪܚܡ ܐܠܗܗ
Ἰ(σρα)ὴλ ὅτι σοὶ ἐσμὲν·	ܕܝܣܪܐܝܠ. ܡܛܠ ܕܕܝܠܟ ܚܢܢ.
see†, and have compassion†, O God of Israel, because we are Yours†,	see†, and have compassion†, God of Israel, because we are Yours†.
καὶ μὴ ἀποστήσησ ἔλεόσ σου ἀφ'	ܠܐ ܬܥܒܪ ܪ̈ܚܡܝܟ ܡܢܢ.
ἡμῶν ἵνα μὴ ἐπιθῶνται ἡμῖ(ν)·	ܕܠܐ ܢܪܕܘܢ ܥܠܝܢ ܥܡ̈ܡܐ
and do not cause Your† mercy to depart† from us, in order that they may not set on us,	Do not take away† Your† compassions from us, that the peoples may not set on us,

9.16 You are God, and we are Your people whom You have loved. God's repeated promise to those whom He has saved is: "I will be their God, and they will be My people" (Jer 31.33 ≡ Heb 8.10; Rev 21.7; 2 Cor 6.16; Ezek 11.20; 36.28; Zec 8.8; 13.9; Hos 2.23 ≡ Rom 9.25–26). He **loved** Abraham and Isaac and Jacob (Deut 4.37; 10.15; Isa 41.8; 2 Chr 20.7; Jas 2.23; Rom 9.13); He **loved** their descendants, the nation of Israel, "all His lovingkind ones" (Deut 33.3; 7.6–8; Hos 11.1–4), including all those "whom He also called, not from the Jews only, but also from the Gentiles" (Rom 9.22–26).

See, and have compassion, O God of Israel, because we are Yours, and do not cause Your mercy to depart from us. "Do not be angry, LORD, to the utmost, and do not remember iniquity to continuing time; behold, look now, we are all Your people" (Isa 64.9). Even when He sent afflictions on His people (vv 1–2) and caused them to suffer shame (v 13), He continued to **have compassion** on them: "Ephraim is a precious son to Me … for as often as I have spoken against him, remembering, I still remember him. Therefore My inward parts are moved for him; having compassion, I will have compassion on him, says the LORD" (Jer 31.20). "The mountains will depart and the hills will move, but My mercy will not depart from you, and the covenant of My peace will not be moved, says the LORD, who has compassion on you" (Isa 54.10; 49.14–16); see also the comments on 16.6.

In order that they may not set on us. See the comments on 1.1. To God alone can His people turn for help against the oppressor (Psa 60.11–12; 2 Chr 20.12–13). The appeal that was made at the beginning of this group of three psalms (7.1) is thus repeated at the close.

9.17 [9] ὅτι σὺ ἡρετίσω	ܡܛܠ ܕܐܢܬ ܓܒܝܬ
τὸ σπέρμα Ἀβραὰμ	ܠܙܪܥܗ ܕܐܒܪܗܡ.
παρα πάντα τὰ ἔθνη·	ܝܬܝܪ ܡܢ ܟܠܗܘܢ ܥܡ̈ܡܐ.
because You† Yourself† have chosen the seed of Abraham beyond all the nations,	because You† Yourself† have chosen *the* seed of Abraham beyond all the peoples,

9.18 [9] καὶ ἔθου τὸ ὄνομά σου ἐφ' ἡμᾶσ κ(ύρι)ε and You† have placed Your† name on us, Lord,	ܘܣܡܬ ܥܠܝܢ ܫܡܟ ܡܪܝܐ. and on us You† have set Your† name, LORD,
καὶ οὐ καταπαύσεισ ‹εἰσ› τὸν αἰῶνα· and You† will not rest to lasting time.	ܘܠܐ ܬܫܠܐ ܥܕܡܐ ܠܥܠܡ. and You† will not rest even to lasting time.

9.18 εἰσ 336⁺260 16h1 \| > 253 •

9.17 You Yourself have chosen the seed of Abraham beyond all the nations. "The LORD set His affection on your fathers to love them, and He chose their seed after them—you, beyond all the nations" (Deut 10.15). Therefore He did for **the seed of Abraham** what He did not do for any other nation, giving them His Law (Psa 147.19–20; Rom 3.1–2) and setting them "high above all the nations" (Deut 26.19).

9.18 You have placed Your name on us. A mark of God's special favor, given to those whom He blesses (Num 6.23–27; Jer 14.9; Rev 3.12; 22.4).

You will not rest[187] **to lasting time.** "For Jerusalem's sake I will not rest until her righteousness goes out as brightness, and her salvation as a burning torch" (Isa 62.1). He **will not rest** until His work is finished (Gen 2.2; John 5.17; cf. Isa 62.6–7), just as a diligent human worker will not rest until his work is finished (Ruth 3.18; John 9.4).

9.19 [10] ἐν διαθήκῃ διέθου τοῖσ πατράσιν ἡμῶν περὶ ἡμ(ῶν)· With a covenant You† covenanted with our fathers concerning us,	ܒܩܝܡܐ ܐܩܝܡܬ ܠܐܒܗ̈ܬܢ ܥܠܝܢ. With a covenant You† covenanted with our fathers concerning us,
καὶ ἡμεῖσ ἐλπιοῦμεν ἐπὶ σὲ ἐν ἐπιστροφῇ ψυχῆσ ἡμῶν· and we ourselves will hope on You† in *the* turning back of our soul.	ܘܚܢܢ ܡܣܒܪܝܢ ܒܟ. ܒܬܝܒܘܬܗ ܕܢܦܫܢ. and we are hoping in You† in *the* turning back of our soul.

9.19 With a covenant You covenanted with our fathers concerning us. God established His covenant with Abraham "to be a God to you and to your seed after you" (Gen 17.7), and gave help to later generations because He "was mindful of His covenant with Abraham" (when He delivered His people from Egypt, Exod 2.24; when He delivered them from later enemies, Lev 26.44–45; when He delivered them from sin

---

[187] **You will not rest** is the reading of 253 *(ou katapauseis),* supported by the Syriac *(l' tšl');* some other Greek manuscripts have the third person, "it [His name] will not rest" (*ou katapausei,* 336 ≡ *ou katapausē,* 260, a spelling variation). Gebhardt and Rahlfs conjecturally emended to *ouk apōsē* ("let You not reject").

through Jesus, Luke 1.71–75). "To lasting time He has been mindful of His covenant, the word He commanded to a thousand generations, which He covenanted with Abraham" (Psa 105.8–9, LXX).

We ourselves will hope on You. "In hope we were saved; but hope that is seen is not hope; for who hopes for what he sees? But if we hope for what we do not see, with patience we eagerly wait for it" (Rom 8.24–25). So God's people in all ages—Abraham (Rom 4.18), the twelve tribes of Israel (Acts 26.7), all nations (Matt 12.21; Rom 15.12)—have placed their **hope** in His promises.

In[188] the turning back of our soul. The people of God "were like sheep that are going astray; but you have turned yourselves back onto the Shepherd and Overseer of your souls" (1 Pet 2.25; Acts 3.19; 26.18). "When You discipline me, it is to turn me back" (16.11).

9.20 [11] τοῦ κ(υρίο)υ ‹ἡ› ‹ἐλεημοσύνη› ἐπ οἶκον Ἰ(σρα)ὴλ εἰσ τὸν αἰῶνα καὶ ἔτι:	ܕܡܪܝܐ ܐܘܦ ܪ̈ܚܡܐ ܥܠ ܒܝܬܐ ܕܐܝܣܪܝܠ ܗܫܐ ܘܠܥܠܡ.
May the Lord's work of mercy *be* upon *the* house of Israel to lasting time and still more.	The LORD's compassions *will be* on the house of Israel now and to lasting time.

9.20 ἡ 336⁺260 | > 253 • ἐλεημοσύνη 336⁺260 [655] 659 | ἐλεμ- 253 •

9.20 May the Lord's work of mercy[189] be upon the house of Israel to lasting time and still more (11.9; "through all time," 2.40).[190] "The LORD's lovingkindness is from lasting time and to lasting time on those who fear Him, and His righteousness is to sons of sons, to those who keep His covenant and are mindful of His assigned instructions, to do them" (Psa 103.17–18). So "Israel will be saved by the LORD with a lasting salvation; you will not be ashamed and will not be humiliated to lasting time of continuing time" (Isa 45.17).

---

[188] **In** [Greek *en* ≡ Syriac *b*-] **the turning back of our soul.** In this context (in both Greek and Syriac), the preposition **in** certainly involves the thought that God's people will hope on Him at the time "when our soul is turned unto thee" (Ryle-James; cf. 1.1). Yet it may go beyond that; it may also include the thought that their hope is expressed **in** the turning of their souls ("as our souls turn to thee," AOT; cf. "they themselves had stained themselves in [*en* ≡ *b*-] an intermingling of mixing together," 2.15; "the nations reproached Jerusalem by [*en* ≡ *b*-] trampling her down," 2.20).

[189] A **work of mercy** [*eleēmosunē*] is a good work bestowed out of the giver's mercy *(eleos),* like those done by Dorcas (Acts 9.36) and Cornelius (Acts 10.2). The Syriac manuscript (16h1) has the plural, **compassions** (*rḥm',* with seyame).

[190] **To lasting time and still more** (Greek *eis ton aiōna kai eti*) generally corresponds to Hebrew *l'lm w'd* ("to lasting time and continuing time"), as in Exod 15.18; Dan 12.3.

Psalm 10

Blessed is the man whom the Lord scourges

Greek	Syriac
10.0 [0] Ἐν ὕμνοις τῷ Σαλωμῶν: In hymns; belonging to Solomon.	
10.1 [1] Μακάριοσ ἀνὴρ οὗ ὁ κ(ύριο)σ ἐμνήσθη ἐν ελεγμῷ· Blessed *is the* man of whom the Lord has been mindful with reproof,	ܛܘܒܘܗܝ ܠܓܒܪܐ ܕܐܬܕܟܪܗ ܐܠܗܐ ܒܡܣܟܢܘܬܐ. Blessed *is* the man of whom God has been mindful in poverty,
καὶ ἐκυκλώθη ἀπὸ ὁδοῦ πονηρὰσ ἐν μάστιγι· and he has been surrounded from *the* wicked path with a scourge,	ܘܟܠܝܗܝ ܡܢ ܐܘܪܚܐ ܕܒܝܫܬܐ. ܒܢܓܕܐ. and he has restrained him from the path of evil with scourges,
καθαρισθῆναι ἀπὸ ἁμαρτίασ τοῦ μη πληθύναι· to be cleansed from sin *for it* not to multiply.	ܠܡܬܕܟܝܘ ܡܢ ܚܛܝܬܗ ܕܠܐ ܬܣܓܐ. to be cleansed from his sin so that it may not increase.
10.2 [2] ὁ ἑτοιμάζων νῶτον εἰσ μάστιγασ καὶ καθαρισθήσεται· The *one* who prepares *his* back for scourges will also be cleansed,	ܗܘ ܓܝܪ ܕܡܛܝܒ ܚܨܗ ܠܢܓܕܐ. ܐܦ ܢܬܕܟܐ. For he who prepares his back for scourgings will also be cleansed,

10.1–2a[191] **Blessed is the man of whom the Lord has been mindful with reproof** [*elegmō*].[192] "There are blessings for the man whom You discipline, LORD, and You make him learn from Your Law" (Psa 94.12). Therefore "do not despise the discipline of the Lord, nor faint when you are reproved [*elegchomenos*] by Him; for whom the Lord loves He disciplines, and He scourges [*mastigoi*] every son whom He receives." Such reproof brings blessings because it is provided "for our benefit, for us to share His holiness. All discipline seems for the present to be not joyful but sorrowful; but later it gives back the peaceful fruit of righteousness to those who have been exercised by it" (Heb 12.5–11; Rev 3.19; Deut 8.5–6).

And he has been surrounded from the wicked path with a scourge [*mastigi*]. The Lord is often described in the Scriptures as chastising His people with a **scourge,** a

---

[191] In the Greek copies (but not in the Syriac), the psalm is superscribed **In hymns; belonging to Solomon.**

[192] **With reproof** (Greek). The Syriac manuscript (16h1) has **in poverty** [*bmsknwt'*]. "The LORD is a house of refuge for the poor [*skn'*], and their helper in times of oppression .... He does not forget the cry of the poor [*skn'*]" (Psa 9.9, 12, Syr). Harris-Mingana and Baars emended it to *bmksnwt'* ("with reproach").

whip that lashes the **back** (see, e.g., Heb 12.6, in the preceding paragraph). "If his sons leave My Law ... with a rod I will attend to their deeds opposed to the Law, and with a scourge [*mastixin*] to their sins" (Psa 89.30–32, LXX). Certainly we should be willing to accept God's scourging of our spirit, when we consider that our Master, who committed no sin, accepted scourging of His flesh on our behalf (Luke 18.33; John 19.1). "Corrections of discipline are the way of life" (Prov 6.23), delivering the soul from Sheol (Prov 23.13–14) and from the condemnation incurred by the world (1 Cor 11.32), keeping it **from the wicked path,** and cleansing it **from sin.**

By the Lord's discipline, a person is **surrounded** (*ekuklōthē,* Greek)—that is, shielded on all sides, and hence **restrained** (Syriac) **from** straying onto the **path** of evil.[193] "Lovingkindness will surround [*kuklōsei*] the one who is confident in the LORD" (Psa 32.10, LXX; Deut 32.10); "His faithfulness will surround [*kuklōsei*] you with a shield" (Psa 91.4, LXX; the corresponding Hebrew reads: "a shield and a surround [*sḥrh*] is His faithfulness").

Being kept from the path of evil, he is **cleansed from sin for it not to multiply.** People who are not restrained from sin "will go forward to the worse" (2 Tim 3.13), "will go forward to greater irreverence" (2 Tim 2.16). So "our transgressions have been multiplied before You, and our iniquities have testified against us ... transgressing and acting falsely against the LORD, and turning away from following our God" (Isa 59.12–13). We need discipline to keep us back from sin (Prov 22.15; Jer 31.18–19), but some people refuse to receive discipline (Jer 2.30; 5.3; Zep 3.2; Isa 1.4–5; 9.13). The person who will be **cleansed** is **the one who prepares his back for scourges** (cf. Sir 2.1), as our Master did: "I was not rebellious; I did not turn back; I gave my back to those who struck Me, and my cheeks to those who pulled out the hair; I did not hide My face from shame and spitting" (Isa 50.5–6). He said to His disciples, "If anyone wants to come after Me, let him deny himself, and lift up his cross, and follow Me; for whoever may want to save his life will lose it, and whoever may lose his life for My sake will find it" (Matt 16.24–25). Those who thus "share in the sufferings of Christ" (1 Pet 4.13) **will ... be cleansed** by a process of refining, like the refining of silver in a furnace (Mal 3.2–3; Isa 1.25; 48.10; Psa 66.10–12; Zec 13.9).

The Lord is kind to those who love Him

χρηστὸ(σ) γὰρ ὁ κ(ύριο)σ	ܛܒ ܗܘ ܓܝܪ
τοῖσ ὑπομένουσιν παιδείαν·	ܠܐܝܠܝܢ ܕܡܩܒܠܝܢ ܡܪܕܘܬܐ.
for the Lord *is* kind	for He is good
to those who endure under discipline.	to those who *are* accepting discipline.

[193] **Surrounded from** involves a strikingly forceful compression of sense, as if the act of surrounding is itself sufficient to keep the soul **from** sin, and no additional action (verb) is needed. Compare "hold power ... from," 16.7; "have mercy ... from," 2.39; "be destroyed from," 12.5; "warred away from," Maccabaica 14.26 (see the comments and footnote there). The Syriac rendering is **restrained** (*klyhy,* as in 2 Pet 2.16, Pococke ≡ Harklean) **from.**

10.2b The Lord is kind to those who endure under discipline. "Blessed is the man who endures under trial" (the one who is "faithful up to death," Rev 2.10), "because he will receive the crown of life" (Jas 1.12) and will find "favor with God" (1 Pet 2.20). "We hold blessed those who have endured. You have heard of the endurance of Job, and you have seen the Lord's end, that the Lord is very apt to be inwardly moved, and is compassionate" (Jas 5.11). "If He has afflicted, then He will have compassion, in accordance with the abundance of His lovingkindnesses" (Lam 3.32; Psa 30.5; 1 Pet 1.6–7; 5.8–10; Rom 8.18).

10.3 [3] ὀρθώσει γὰρ ὁδοὺσ δικαίων For He will make *the* paths of righteous *ones* straight,	ܬܪܝܨܝ ܗܝ ܓܝܪ ܐܘܪܚܗ ܕܙܕܝܩܐ. For *the* path of the righteous *one* is straight,
κ(αὶ) οὐ ‹διαστρέψει› ἐν παιδεία· and He will not turn *them* aside by discipline,	ܘܠܐ ܡܦܬܠܐ ܠܗ ܡܪܕܘܬܐ. and discipline *will* not make it twisted,
10.4 [3] καὶ τὸ ἔλεοσ κ(υρίο)υ ἐπὶ τοὺσ ἀγαπόντασ αὐτὸν ἐν ἀληθεία· and the mercy of *the* Lord *will be* upon those who love Him in truth;	ܘܚܙܬܗ ܓܝܪ ܕܡܪܝܐ ܥܠ ܗܢܘܢ ܕܪܚܡܝܢ ܠܗ ܒܫܪܪܐ. for *the* sight of the LORD *will be* upon those who love Him in truth,
[4] καὶ ‹μνησθήσεται› κ(ύριο)σ τῶν δούλων αὐτοῦ ἐν ελέει· and *the* Lord will be mindful of His slaves in mercy,	ܘܢܬܕܟܪ ܡܪܝܐ ܠܥܒܕܘܗܝ ܒܪ̈ܚܡܐ. and the LORD will be mindful of His slaves in compassion,
10.5 [4] ἡ γὰρ μαρτυρία ἐν νόμω διαθήκησ αἰωνίου· for *His* testimony *is* in *the* Law of *the* lasting covenant—	ܣܗܕܘܬܐ ܓܝܪ ܒܢܡܘܣܐ ܕܩܝܡܐ ܕܠܥܠܡ. for the testimony *is* in the Law of the covenant that *is* to lasting time,
ἡ μαρτυρία κ(υρίο)υ ἐπὶ ὁδοὺσ ἀν(θρώπ)ων ἐν επισκοπῆ· the Lord's testimony upon *the* paths of Men in *His* watching over *them*.	ܣܗܕܘܬܗ ܕܡܪܝܐ ܒܐܘܪ̈ܚܬܐ ܕܒܢ̈ܝ ܐܢܫܐ ܒܣܘܥܪ̈ܢܐ. the LORD's testimony *is* in the paths of *the* sons of Men in *His* looking on *them*.

10.3 διαστρέψει 336⁺260 ≡ ܡܦܬܠܐ 16h1 | διαπρ- 253 • **10.4** μνησθήσεται 336⁺260 | μνήσεται 253 •

10.3 By discipline, the Lord **will make the paths of righteous ones straight,** and **will not turn** those paths **aside.** "The Lord will give you the bread of oppression and the water of affliction, but your Teacher will not hide Himself any more ... and your ears will hear a word from behind you, saying, 'This is the way, go in it,' when you turn to the right, and when you turn to the left" (Isa 30.20–21); thus they will have "lasting rightmindedness" (v 9). The Lord's **discipline** will not **turn aside** the **paths** of **righteous ones,** He "will not allow you to be tempted above what you are able; but with the temptation He will make also the way of escape, so that you may be able to endure" (1 Cor 10.13). No trial can separate righteous people from God; instead, "in all these things we are more than conquerors" (Rom 8.35–39). "I will lead the blind in a way they did not know, and I will make them go in paths they did not know; I will turn darkness to light before them, and crooked places straight" (Isa 42.16).

10.4 The mercy of the Lord will be upon those who love Him in truth (see on 6.9)—those who are **His slaves.** (Those who "have received mercy" are to live "as slaves of God," 1 Pet 2.10, 16.) **He will be mindful of** them: "He has not forgotten the outcry of afflicted ones" (Psa 9.12; 136.23–24; Heb 6.10). His mindfulness of His slaves, and His mercy on them, were demonstrated above all by His sending of Jesus: "He has looked on the lowliness of His slavewoman .... He has taken up the cause of Israel His servant, to be mindful of mercy" (Luke 1.46–55).

10.5 Testimony to the Lord's mercy (v 4) is found in the **Law** of His **covenant:**[194] the **Law** testifies repeatedly that God "keeps covenant and lovingkindness to those who love Him and who keep His commandments" (Deut 7.9; Dan 9.4; Neh 1.5; cf. Psa 119.159). And this **testimony** to His mercy is displayed constantly **in** His **watching over** their **paths**—in the fact that "God has had mercy on Israel in His watching over them" (11.2).

10.6 [5] δίκαιοσ καὶ ὅσιοσ κ(ύριο)σ ἡμ(ῶν) κρίμασιν αὐτοῦ εἰσ τὸν αἰῶνα Our Lord *is* righteous and lovingkind in His judgments to lasting time,	ܙܕܝܩ ܗܘ ܘܬܪܝܨ ܐܠܗܢ ܒܟܠܗܘܢ ܕܝܢܘܗܝ. Our God is righteous and upright in all His judgments,
καὶ Ἰ(σρα)ὴλ αἰνέσει τῷ ὀνόματι κ(υρίο)υ ἐν εὐφροσύνῃ· and Israel will praise the name of *the* Lord with gladness,	ܘܐܝܣܪܝܠ ܢܫܒܚ ܠܫܡܗ ܕܡܪܝܐ ܒܚܕܘܬܐ. and Israel will glorify *the* name of the LORD with joy,

[194] God's **covenant** with Israel was a **lasting** [*aiōniou*] **covenant,** because any covenant established by Him is a **lasting** one (with Abraham, Gen 17.7; with David, 2 Sam 23.5; Jer 33.20–21; with His new covenant people, Heb 13.20; Jer 32.40). The people themselves might break it (Isa 24.5; Jer 31.32), but He would not (Psa 89.34; Lev 26.44). The old covenant with Israel was replaced by the new covenant through Christ, not because God destroyed the old covenant, but because He brought it to fulfillment in Christ (Matt 5.17; Luke 16.17; Gal 3.24–25; Rom 10.4). *Aiōniou* is here feminine (as in Heb 13.20; 9.15; cf. MHT 2.157; BDF §59(2); KB 1.1, §147b).

10.7 [6] καὶ ‹ὅσιοι› ἐξομολογήσονται ἐν ἐκκλησίᾳ λαοῦ· and lovingkind *ones* will confess *it* in *the* assembly of *the* people;	ܘܚܣܝܐ ܢܘܕܘܢ ܒܥܕܬܐ ܕܥܡܐ. and the lovingkind *ones* will confess *it* in the assembly of the people.
καὶ πτωχοὺσ ἐλεήσει ὁ θ(εὸ)σ ἐν ευφροσύνῃ Ἰ(σρα)ὴλ· and the Lord will have mercy on poor *ones* in *the* gladness of Israel,	ܘܥܠ ܡܣܟܢܐ ܢܚܘܢ ܡܪܝܐ ܒܚܕܘܬܗ ܕܐܝܣܪܝܠ. And the LORD will have compassion on the poor *ones* in *the* gladness of Israel,
10.8 [7] ὅτι χρηστὸσ καὶ ἐλεήμων ὁ θ(εὸ)σ εἰσ τὸν αἰῶνα· because God *is* kind and merciful to lasting time,	ܡܛܠ ܕܒܣܝܡ ܗܘ ܘܡܪܚܡܢ ܐܠܗܐ ܠܥܠܡ. because God is kind and compassionate to lasting time,
καὶ συναγωγαὶ Ἰ(σρα)ὴλ δοξάσουσιν τὸ ὄνομα κ(υρίο)υ· and *the* gatherings of Israel will glorify the name of *the* Lord.	ܘܟܢܘܫܬܐ ܕܐܝܣܪܝܠ ܢܫܒܚܘܢ ܠܫܡܗ ܕܡܪܝܐ. and the gatherings of Israel will glorify *the* name of the LORD.

10.7 ὅσιοι 253^{c} 336^{+}260 ≡ ܚ̈ܣܝܐ 16h1 10h1 | ὅτιοι 253* •

10.6–8 Because **our Lord** is always **righteous and lovingkind in His judgments** (2.19; 8.7, 38; 9.10; 18.3; Psa 119.75–76, 137; Jer 9.24), **Israel will praise** His **name with gladness** (5.1; 15.5; Psa 97.8; 13.5; 107.21–22), **and lovingkind ones will confess it**[195] publicly (9.12), **in the assembly,** in the **gatherings of Israel** where "a great number of people" are gathered together (Psa 35.18)—just as Jesus Himself did (Heb 2.12 ≡ Psa 18.49; 22.22; 40.9–10), and as people of all nations on earth are to do (Rom 15.9 ≡ Psa 18.49).

The Lord will have mercy on poor ones … because it is His nature always to do so: He is **kind and merciful to lasting time.** "In our lowliness He has been mindful of us, for His lovingkindness is to lasting time, and He has torn us away from our oppressors, for His lovingkindness is to lasting time" (Psa 136.23–24; Luke 1.50; cf. Isa 41.17–18; 2 Cor 8.9; Jas 2.5).

10.9 [8] τοῦ κ(υρίο)υ ἡ σωτηρία ἐπὶ οἶκον Ἰ(σρα)ὴλ ‹εἰσ σωφροσύνην› αἰώνιον:	ܕܡܪܝܐ ܗܘ ܓܝܪ ܦܘܪܩܢܐ ܥܠ ܒܝܬܐ ܕܐܝܣܪܝܠ. ܠܡܠܟܘܬܐ ܕܠܥܠܡ.

[195] **Will confess it** [*exomologēsontai*]: both "acknowledge" (NETS) and "give thanks" (APOT); see the comments on 3.3.

May the Lord's salvation *be*	For the LORD's salvation is
on *the* house of Israel	on the house of Israel
to lasting soundness of mind.	to the kingdom that *is* to lasting time.

10.9 εἰσ σωφροσύνην 260 655⁺659 ≡ ἐισωφροσύνην 253 | εἰσ εὐφ- 336 •

10.9 May the Lord's salvation be on the house of Israel (3.6–7; 16.4–5). "The LORD is strength to His people, and He is the protection of salvations to His Anointed One" (Psa 28.8–9).

This **salvation** will lead **to** [*eis*] **lasting** blessings, which are variously described in the available manuscripts:[196]

- Lasting **soundness of mind** (*sōphrosunēn,* the opposite of incorrect thinking: Rom 12.3; Acts 26.25; 2 Cor 5.13). "The Lord's lovingkind ones will live in [His Law] to lasting time" and "go in the righteousness of His orders" (14.1–2); "He will make the paths of righteous ones straight" (see the comments on v 3). "I will give them one heart and one way, to fear Me all the days, for their good and their sons' good, and I will make a lasting covenant with them" (Jer 32.39–40; cf. Ezek 36.25–27), a promise fulfilled under the new covenant through Jesus (Heb 8.10–11). "God has given us a spirit ... of power and love and soundness of mind [*sōphronismou*]" (2 Tim 1.7; cf. 1 Pet 4.7).
- Lasting gladness (cf. vv 6–7). "The Lord's lovingkind ones will inherit life in gladness" (14.7). "The LORD's redeemed ones will return and come to Zion with singing, and lasting joy will be on their head; gladness and joy will overtake them; sorrow and sighing will flee" (Isa 51.11). Jesus promised that blessing to His disciples: "your heart will rejoice, and no one takes your joy away from you" (John 16.22; Rev 21.4).
- A lasting **kingdom.** "The kingdom of our God will be to lasting time" (17.4). Daniel had foretold that, in the days of the kingdom after Greece, "the God of the heavens will set up a kingdom that will not be destroyed to lasting time" (Dan 2.44; 7.27). That prophecy too was fulfilled in Jesus: "He will be king over the house of Jacob to lasting time, and of His kingdom there will be no end" (Luke 1.33); and those who receive forgiveness of sins under the new covenant have been transferred into His kingdom (Col 1.13).

---

[196] *Sōphrosunēn* (**soundness of mind**) is the reading of 253 and 260, whereas 336 reads *euphrosunēn* ("gladness"). The reading of 16h1 is *mlkwt'* (apparently **kingdom;** but compare *mlwkwt'* "advice," "counsel" [TS 2.2142; SL 766], which might possibly correspond to Greek *sōphronsunēn*). In this context the expected term would be *euphrosunēn* rather than *sōphrosunēn* (Ryle-James 100)—but precisely for that reason, *sōphrosunēn* would be more likely to have been altered by a copyist (either through accidental misreading after vv 6–7, or through attempted correction).

In 253 a single *s* does double duty as both the last component of the preposition *eis* and the first component of the noun *sōphrosunēn* (Thackeray §9.1); cf. the footnote to Maccabaica 12.2.

Psalm 11

Baruch 5	Eighteen Psalms 11
5.1 Jerusalem ... clothe yourself† with the excellence of the glory that *is* from God to lasting time.	**11.8** Clothe yourself†, Jerusalem, with the clothes of your† glory; prepare† the robe of your† holy place.
......	......
5.5 Stand up†, Jerusalem, and stand† on high, and look around† to *the* sunrise, and see† your† children who are gathered together from *the* sun's setting even to *its* rising at the word of the Holy *One,* rejoicing at the mindfulness of God....	**11.3** Stand†, Jerusalem, on high, and see† your† children from *the* sunrise and *the* sunset, *those* who are gathered together all alike by *the* Lord. **11.4** From *the* north they are coming to the gladness of their God....
5.7 For God has ordained *for* every high mountain to be made low, and *the* lasting hills, and *the* valleys to be filled to level the land, in order that Israel may proceed securely in the glory of God.	**11.5** High mountains He has made low into a leveling, for them; **11.6** the hills have fled away from their entering.
5.8 And the forests have cast shadows and every tree of fragrance for Israel by the command of God.	The forests have cast shadows for them when they *were* passing through; **11.7** God has made every tree of fragrance to rise for them,
5.9 For God will lead Israel with gladness by the light of His glory	in order that Israel may go past in *the* watching over *them* of *the* glory of their God....
with *the* mercy and righteousness that *are* from Him.	**11.9** *May* the Lord's mercy *be* on Israel to lasting time and still more.

This psalm looks forward to the gathering of God's people who had been scattered abroad ("in every nation," 9.1–2; 8.24; 2.6; 17.14), which the Messiah would accomplish (17.28, 34). Most of the psalm's material is derived from the final section of the book of Baruch;[197] the above chart shows the main points of similarity.

---

[197] The resemblance is far too close for the two passages to have been derived independently from the Hebrew Scriptures (as suggested by Kneucker, *Baruch,* 43–45). Some researchers formerly suggested that the book of Baruch derived this material from the Eighteen Psalms (Ryle-James lxxii–lxxvii; APOT 1.573). However, the reverse was demonstrated by Pesch, "Die Abhängigkeit des 11 salomonischen Psalms vom letzten Kapitel des Buches Baruch," 251–63, who showed that the final section of Baruch is inseparably linked to the preceding parts of the

Proclaim the good message of God's mercy on Israel

Greek	Syriac
11.0 [0] Τῷ Cολομῶν εἰc προcδοκίαν: Belonging to Solomon; for looking ahead.	
11.1 [1] Σαλπίσατε ἐν Σιὼν ἐν σάλπιγγι σημασίασ ἁγίων· Trumpet[pl] in Zion with *the* holy *ones*' trumpet of signaling;	ܩܥܘ ܒܨܗܝܘܢ ܒܩܪܢܐ ܝܕܝܥܬܐ ܕܩܕܝܫܐ. Call[pl] in Zion with the holy *ones*' known trumpet;
11.2 [2] κηρύξατε ἐν Ἰ(ερουσα)λὴμ φωνὴν εὐαγγελιζομένου· proclaim[pl] in Jerusalem *the* voice of *one* who declares a good message,	ܐܟܪܙܘ ܒܐܘܪܫܠܡ ܩܠܐ ܕܡܣܒܪܢܐ. proclaim[pl] in Jerusalem the voice of the preachers,
ὅτι ἠλέησεν ὁ θ(εὸ)σ Ἰ(σρα)ὴλ ἐν τῇ ἐπισκοπῇ αὐτῶν· because God has had mercy on Israel in *His* watching over them.	ܡܛܠ ܕܐܬܪܚܡ ܐܠܗܐ ܥܠ ܐܝܣܪܐܝܠ ܒܣܘܥܪܢܗ because God has had compassion on Israel in His looking on *them.*

11.1–2[198] God's people **in Jerusalem** (**Zion**) are here instructed to **proclaim . . . the voice of one who declares a good message** (*euaggelizomenou,* the term applied to those who declared the good message [gospel] of Jesus: e.g., angels, Luke 1.19; 2.10; John the Baptist, Luke 3.18; Jesus Himself, Luke 4.17–21; 8.1; His disciples, Acts 8.4, 12; 11.20; 13.32; 14.7). This proclamation is to be made **because**[199] God has watched over Israel (v 7) and **has had mercy on** them (in the way that will be described in vv 3–7). "He has watched over and made redemption for His people . . . to do mercy" (Luke 1.68–72), "because of the inward parts of mercy of our God, by which the Sunrise from the height will watch over them, to make light visible to those who sit in darkness and the shadow

---

book (see also Assan-Dhôte and Moatti-Fine, *Baruch,* 123–26). In Baruch 4.5–30, Jerusalem clothes herself in sackcloth when her children are taken away (4.19–20); in Baruch 4.31–5.9, she clothes herself in glory when her children return with gladness in the glory of God (which is already stated explicitly in 4.23–24).

[198] In the Greek copies (but not in the Syriac), the psalm is superscribed **Belonging to Solomon; for looking ahead** (*prosdokian;* "expectation," APOT). This is a psalm that looks ahead to the near future. Compare John the Baptist's question to Jesus: "Are you the One who is coming, or should we look ahead for [*prosdokōmen*] another?" (Luke 7.19).

[199] In the Greek version, *hoti* could be construed either as describing the proclamation of the good message **because** the Lord has had mercy on Israel, or as describing the proclamation of the good message "that" He has had mercy on Israel (AOT). In the Syriac version there is no ambiguity: it has *mṭl d-,* **because.**

of death, to make straight their feet into the path of peace" (Luke 1.78–79).

The proclamation is to be accompanied by the sound of the **trumpet of signaling,**[200] which God's **holy** people, under the old covenant, were commanded to use "to praise and glorify the LORD" (2 Chr 5.12–13; Psa 98.4–6) and to be remembered by Him (Num 10.10; Maccabaica 4.40).

The Lord is gathering Israel together

11.3 [2] στήθι Ἰ(ερουσα)λὴμ ἐφ υψηλοῦ κ(αὶ) ἴδε τα τέκνα σου· Stand†, Jerusalem, on high, and see† your† children	ܩܘܡܝ ܐܘܪܫܠܡ ܒܪܘܡܐ. ܘܚܙܝ ܠܒܢܝܟܝ Stand†, Jerusalem, in the height, and see† your† sons
ἀπὸ ἀνατολῶν καὶ δυσμῶ(ν) συνηγμένα εἰσ ἅπαξ ἀπὸ κ(υρίο)υ· from *the* sunrise and *the* sunset, *those* who are gathered together all alike by *the* Lord.	ܕܡܢ ܡܕܢܚܐ ܘܡܢ ܡܥܪܒܐ ܡܬܟܢܫܝܢ ܟܠܗܘܢ ܡܢ ܡܪܝܐ. who *are* gathered from the sunrise and from the sunset, all of them, by the LORD,
11.4 [3] ἀπὸ βορρᾶ ἔρχονται τῇ εὐφροσύνῃ τοῦ θ(εο)ῦ αὐτῶν· From *the* north they are coming to the gladness of their God;	ܘܡܢ ܓܪܒܝܐ ܐܬܝܢ ܠܚܕܘܬܗ ܕܐܠܗܗܘܢ. and from the north they are coming to *the* joy of their God,
ἐκ νήσων μακρόθεν συνήγαγεν αὐτοὺσ ὁ θ(εό)σ· out of *the* islands far away God has gathered them together.	ܘܡܢ ܓܙܪ̈ܬܐ ܪ̈ܚܝܩܬܐ ܟܢܫ ܐܢܘܢ ܐܠܗܐ. and from the islands far away God has gathered them.

11.3–4 Jerusalem's inhabitants (her **children,** 1.3; 2.6; 8.24) have been scattered "in every nation" (see the comments on 9.2). Now she is invited to **stand** on a **high** place, where she will have a clear view (like Moses on Mount Nebo, Deut 34.1–4; cf. Rev 21.10) in all the directions where her children have been scattered.

All her children are being **gathered together . . . by the Lord** from the lands in all those directions: the east (the **sunrise**) and the west (the **sunset**), the **north** and the **islands,** just as had been prophesied (Psa 107.1–3; Isa 11.11–12; 27.12–13; 43.5–7; 49.12; 66.19–20). "Behold, I will take the sons of Israel from among the nations where they have gone; and I will gather them from round about, and bring them to their own land . . . and David My Servant will be their Ruler to lasting time, and I will make a covenant of peace with them; it will be a lasting covenant; and I will establish

[200] **Of signaling.** Greek *sēmasias,* corresponding to Hebrew *trw'h* ("outcry," "loud sound," Num 31.6; 10.5–6). The Syriac rendering here is *ydy't'* (**known**); the signal of the trumpet makes its proclamation **known** (1 Sam 4.5–6, Syr; 1 Cor 14.8–9; Psa 89.15).

and multiply them, and will set My holy place in their midst to lasting time; and My dwelling place will be with them, and I will be their God, and they will be My people" (Ezek 37.21–27).

Those prophecies had not been fulfilled at the end of the Babylonian captivity. (No Davidic king arose at that time.) They had not yet been fulfilled at the time when the Eighteen Psalms were written. But they would be fulfilled very soon afterwards, under the new covenant. Jesus said: "Many will come from the sun's rising and setting, and they will recline with Abraham and Isaac and Jacob in the kingdom of heaven" (Matt 8.11); and He instructed His disciples "that repentance and forgiveness of sins should be proclaimed in His name to all the nations, beginning from Jerusalem" (Luke 24.47; Mark 16.15; Matt 28.19). By that means, "exiles of the dispersion" in far distant places (e.g., "Pontus, Galatia, Cappadocia, Asia, and Bithynia") have now been "fathered again … for an inheritance incorruptible and unstained and unfading, which is kept in heaven for you" (1 Pet 1.1–4; Jas 1.1). Israelites according to the flesh have come into this new, spiritual Jerusalem from the sunrise ("Parthians and Medes and Elamites and those dwelling in Mesopotamia"), from the sunset ("the parts of Libya near Cyrene … Rome"), from the north ("Cappadocia … Pontus and Asia … Phrygia and Pamphylia"), and from the islands ("Cretans," Acts 2.9–11). And, in addition, people of all nations—even though they are not Israelites according to the flesh—have now been reckoned as spiritual Israelites (Rom 2.29; Php 3.3; Col 2.11) and "have come to Mount Zion, and to the city of the living God, the heavenly Jerusalem" (Heb 12.22; Gal 4.26; cf. Mal 1.11).

They are coming to the gladness of their God.[201] "Enter into the joy of your Lord" (Matt 25.21, 23), in whose presence there is "fullness of joys" (Psa 16.11). When "the LORD's redeemed ones return and come to Zion … lasting joy will be on their head; gladness and joy will overtake them; sorrow and sighing will flee" (Isa 51.11; cf. Jer 31.9–14).

11.5 [4] ὄρη ὑψηλὰ ἐταπείνωσεν εἰσ ὁμαλισμὸν αὐτοῖσ· High mountains He has made low into a leveling, for them;	ܛܘܪ̈ܐ ܪ̈ܡܐ ܡܟܟ ܘܫܦܠ ܠܗܘܢ܇ The lofty mountains He has abased, and He has put them down,
11.6 [4] οἱ βουνοὶ ἐφύγοσαν ἀπο εἰσόδου αὐτ(ῶν)· the hills have fled away from their entering.	ܘܪ̈ܡܬܐ ܥܪ̈ܩܘ ܡܢ ܡܥܠܢܗܘܢ܇ and the lofty hills have fled away from their entering.

[201] **They are coming to the gladness** [*erchontai tē euphrosunē*] **of their God.** A dative following *erchomai* indicates that **to** which one comes (Matt 21.5; Rev 2.5, 16; Hos 10.12, LXX; cf. KG 2.1, §423.17; BDAG 394, §1ↄ; BDF §192). The Syriac version expresses the same idea by means of the preposition *l*- (**to**).

[5] οἱ δρυμοὶ ἐσκίασαν αὐτοῖσ
ἐν τῇ παρόδῳ αὐτῶν·
The forests
have cast shadows for them
when they *were* passing through;

ܐܪ̈ܙܐ ܛܠܠ ܥܠܝܗܘܢ܆
ܟܕ ܥܒܪܝܢ ܗ̇ܘܘ.
He has caused the cedars
to cast shadow over them
when they were passing through,

11.7 [5] πᾶν ξύλον εὐωδίασ
ἀνέτειλεν αὐτοῖσ ὁ θ(εό)σ·
God has made every tree of fragrance
to rise for them,

ܘܟܠ ܩܝܣܐ ܕܪܝܚܐ ܒܣܝܡܐ
ܐܪܝܚ ܠܗܘܢ܆ ܐܠܗܐ.
and God has scented every pleasant
tree for them,

---

[6] ἵνα παρέλθῃ Ἰ(σρα)ὴλ ἐν
επισκοπὴ δόξησ θ(εο)ῦ αὐτῶν·
in order that Israel may go past in
the watching over *them*
of *the* glory of their God.

ܡܛܠ ܕܢܥܒܪ ܐܝܣܪܐܝܠ. ܒܣܘܥܪܢܐ
ܕܬܫܒܘܚܬܗ ܕܐܠܗܗܘܢ܆.
in order that Israel may go past
in the looking on *them*
of *the* glory of their God.

11.5–7 In order that Israel may return (vv 3–4), the **glory of their God** has been **watching over them,** making a pleasant path for them—just as He watched over those who journeyed from Egypt through the wilderness (Psa 78.52–54), and those who returned to Jerusalem with Ezra (Ezra 8.31).

- The **high mountains** have been **made low** and leveled, and **the hills have fled away,** so that there are no obstacles in His people's path (Isa 57.14). This was the work that John the Baptist did by "proclaiming the baptism of repentance for the forgiveness of sins" and preparing the Lord's way (Luke 3.3–6 ≡ Isa 40.3–5). It was the work that Jesus' apostles continued after Him, "pulling down . . . every high thing that is raised up against the knowledge of God" (2 Cor 10.5; cf. Isa 2.12–14).
- **The forests have cast shadows** to protect His people from the heat of the sun (Psa 121.5–8; Isa 4.5–6)—that is, from "tribulation or persecution" (Matt 13.6, 21), from "those who are terrifying" (Isa 25.4–5).
- **Every tree of fragrance** has risen for them, so that their path is not through a wilderness, but through a glorious and fruitful region (Isa 41.19–20; 55.13; 60.13). John saw "a river of water of life ... coming out of the throne of God and of the Lamb ... and from this side and that side of the river, the tree of life, producing twelve fruits, giving back its fruit in each month; and the leaves of the tree were for the healing of the nations" (Rev 22.1–2). Wisdom's "ways are ways of pleasantness, and all her paths are peace" (Prov 3.17). Indeed, God's people are themselves to be fruitful trees (Psa 92.12–15; Isa 61.3; cf. John 15.6; Heb 6.7–8) yielding fragrance for Him (Ezek 20.41; 2 Cor 2.14–16).

God has spoken good things of Israel

11.8 [7] ἔνδυσαι Ἰ(ερουσα)λὴμ
τὰ ἱμάτια τῆσ δόξησ σου·

ܐܬܠܒܫܝ ܐܘܪܫܠܡ
ܡܐ̈ܢܐ ܕܬܫܒܘܚܬܟܝ.

Clothe yourself†, Jerusalem, with the clothes of your† glory;	Put on†, Jerusalem, the clothes of your† glory,
ἑτοίμασον τὴν στολὴν τοῦ ἁγιάσματόσ σου· prepare† the robe of your† holy place,	ܘܛܝܒܝ ܐܣܛܠܐ ܕܩܘܕܫܬܟܝ. and prepare† the robe of your† holiness,
ὅτι ὁ θ(εὸ)σ ἐλάλησεν ἀγαθὰ Ἰ(σρα)ὴλ εἰσ τὸν αἰῶνα καὶ ἔτι· because God has spoken good *things* of Israel, to lasting time and still more.	ܡܛܠ ܕܐܠܗܐ ܡܠܠ ܛܒܬܐ ܠܐܝܣܪܐܝܠ ܗܫܐ ܘܠܥܠܡ. because God has spoken good things *in regard* to Israel, now and to lasting time.

11.8 God has spoken good things about **Israel** (see on 17.50) **to lasting time.** He has promised His people: "The mountains will depart and the hills will move, but My mercy will not depart from you, and the covenant of My peace will not be moved" (Isa 54.10–17). Indeed He always gives **good things** to His children (Matt 7.11). In "the holy city, the new Jerusalem," "they will reign to lasting times of lasting times" (Rev 21.1–22.5).

To make ready for those things, **Jerusalem** is told to **clothe** herself **with the clothes of** her **glory** (which God had given her before she was dishonored, 2.20–23), and to **prepare the robe of** her **holiness** (Syriac; her **holy place,** Greek). These are the kinds of garments that God Himself wears (Isa 59.17; Psa 93.1; 104.1). Like Him, His people are to be clothed with the glorious clothing of righteous deeds (Rev 19.7–8; Job 29.14–17) and salvation (Psa 132.9, 16; Isa 61.10); they are to be holy like Him, and to glorify Him (1 Pet 1.15–16; 2.9; Eph 1.12; Isa 43.7, 21). "Clothe yourself in your strength, Zion; clothe yourself in the garments of your beauty, Jerusalem, the holy city; for the uncircumcised and the unclean will no longer proceed to come into you" (Isa 52.1; Rev 21.2, 27).

May the Lord raise up Israel

11.9 [8] ποιῆσαι κ(ύριο)σ ἃ ἐλάλησεν ἐπὶ Ἰ(σρα)ὴλ καὶ Ἰερουσαλὴμ· May *the* Lord do *the things* that He has spoken concerning Israel and Jerusalem;	ܢܥܒܕ ܡܪܝܐ ܡܕܡ ܕܡܠܠ ܥܠ ܐܝܣܪܐܝܠ ܘܥܠ ܐܘܪܫܠܡ. May the LORD do *the* thing that He has spoken concerning Israel and concerning Jerusalem;
ἀναστῆσαι κ(ύριο)σ τὸν Ἰ(σρα)ὴλ ἐν ονόματι δόξησ αὐτοῦ· may *the* Lord raise up Israel by *the* name of His glory;	ܢܩܝܡ ܡܪܝܐ ܠܐܝܣܪܐܝܠ ܒܫܡܐ ܕܬܫܒܘܚܬܗ. may the LORD lift up Israel by the name of His glory.

[9] τοῦ κ(υρίο)υ τὸ ἔλεοσ ἐπὶ τὸν Ἰ(σρα)ὴλ εἰσ τὸν αἰῶνα καὶ ἔτι:	ܪ̈ܚܡܘܗܝ ܕܡܪܝܐ ܥܠ ܐܝܣܪܐܝܠ ܗܫܐ ܘܠܥܠܡ.
may the Lord's mercy *be* on Israel to lasting time and still more.	*May* the LORD's compassions *be* on Israel now and to lasting time.

11.9 The psalm ends with a prayer that the Lord may **do the things that he has spoken** (v 8) about **Israel and Jerusalem,**[202] and may **raise up Israel** in His **mercy** (9.20; 7.8; 17.51; 18.1) **to lasting time and still more** (9.20). Within a few decades, this prayer was to be answered by the coming of the new covenant, when God fulfilled His promise to the fathers by raising up Jesus (Acts 13.32–33) and raising up His people together with Him (Col 2.12; 3.1), so that the fallen tent of David was again built up and set upright (Acts 15.16–17 ≡ Amos 9.11–12).

He has done these things **by the name of His glory.** His name is a **name** of **glory** (Isa 63.14; Psa 72.19), and for the sake of the glory of His name, He acts to save His people (Psa 79.9; 106.8; Isa 48.9–11).

Psalm 12

Lord, deliver my soul from a lying tongue

12.0 [0] Τῶ Cαλωμῶν ἐν γλώccῃ παρανόμων:	
Belonging to Solomon; against *the* tongue of *the* Law-breakers.	
12.1 [1] Κ(ύριε) ῥῦσαι τὴν ψυχήν μου ἀπὸ ἀνδρὸσ παρανόμου καὶ πονηροῦ·	ܡܪܝܐ ܦܨܝ ܗ̇ ܠܢܦܫܝ ܡܢ ܓܒܪܐ ܗܦܝܟܐ ܘܥܘܠܐ.
Lord, deliver† my soul from a man *who is* Law-breaking and harmful,	LORD, deliver† my soul from the man *who is* opposed and unjust,
ἀπὸ γλώσσησ παρανόμου καὶ ψιθύρου	ܘܡܢ ܠܫܢܐ ܡܠܫܢܢܐ ܘܥܒܪ ܢܡܘܣܐ.
from a tongue *that is* opposed to *the* Law, and *that is* whispering,	and from the tongue *that is* whispering and transgressing the Law,
καὶ λαλούσησ ψευδῆ καὶ δόλια·	ܕܡܠܠ ܕܓܠܘܬܐ ܘܢܟܠܐ.
and that speaks lying *words* and deceitful *words*.	that has spoken falsehood and deceit.

[202] **The things that He has spoken concerning** [Greek *epi* ≡ Syriac ܥܠ] **Israel and Jerusalem.** The same preposition is used in the same sense ("on the subject of") in Jer 30.4; 33.14, LXX ≡ Syr.

12.1[203] **Lord, deliver my soul from a man who is Law-breaking** [4.1] **and harmful** [16.7]. "Deliver me from the hand of a wicked one" (Psa 71.4; 140.1); "pray for us ... that we may be delivered from improper and bad people" (2 Thes 3.1–2; Rom 15.30–31). In the present psalm, the prayer is specifically for deliverance from the sort of evildoer who sins with the **tongue** by uttering things that are **opposed to the Law ... lying words and deceitful words** (cf. Psa 120.2; 64.2–3)—like the things spoken by those who opposed Jesus (Mark 14.55–56) and His disciples (Acts 6.11–14; 24.5–6, 13; 25.7).

The evil talker is also described as **whispering** (*psithurou,* Greek ≡ *mlḥšn',* Syriac), a term that can describe any soft, insidious utterance (Ecc 10.11, LXX ≡ Syr) but is most often applied to falsehoods whispered by someone "double-tongued" (Sir 28.13) "against" a victim because of hatred and a desire to do evil (Psa 41.7).

Greek	Syriac
12.2 [2] ἐν ποικιλία στροφῆσ οἱ λόγοι τῆσ γλώσσησ ἀνδρὸσ πονηροῦ· In a diversity of turning *are* the words of a harmful man's tongue,	ܒܗܘܦܟܐ ܓܝܪ ܕܡ̈ܠܐ. ܐܝܬܘܗ(ܝ) ܠܫܢܗ ܕܓܒܪܐ ܥܒܪ ܢܡܘܣܐ. For in turnings of words is *the* tongue of the man who transgresses the Law,
ὥσπερ ἐν λαῷ πῦρ ἀνάπτον καλλονὴν αὐτοῦ· just like a fire among a people, setting alight its beauty.	ܡܬܚܙܐ ܓܝܪ ܕܐܝܟ ܗܘ ܕܫܦܝܪ ܥܒܕ. ܘܡܚܝܕ ܢܘܪܐ ܒܥܡܐ. for *he* appears like one who *is* doing beautifully, and *he* makes a fire take hold among the people.
12.3 [3] ἡ παροικία αὐτοῦ ἐμπλῆσαι οἴκουσ ἐν γλώσσῃ ψευδεῖ· His visit *is* to fill houses with *his* lying tongue,	ܡܥܡܪܗ ܓܝܪ ܠܡܡܠܐ ܒ̈ܬܐ ܒܡܡܠܠܐ ܕܓܠܐ. For his dwelling *is* to fill houses with false speech;
ἐκκόψαι δένδρα εὐφροσύνησ φλογιζούσησ παρανόμουσ· to cut down *the* trees of gladness that sets aflame Law-breakers,	ܦܣܩ ܐܝ̈ܠܢܐ ܕܒܣܝܡܘܬܗ ܒܝܩܕܢܐ ܕܥܒܪ ܢܡܘܣܐ. he has cut down the trees of his gladness in the burning of transgressing the Law.
12.4 [3] σὺνχέαι οἴκουσ παρανόμουσ ἐν πολέμῳ χείλεσιν ψιθύροισ· to set in turmoil Law-breaking houses by warfare with whispering lips.	ܐܘܒܕ ܒ̈ܬܐ ܕܥܒ̈ܕܝ ܥܠ ܢܡܘܣܐ ܒܩܪܒܐ. ܘܒܣܦ̈ܘܬܐ ܡܠܚܫܢܝ̈ܬܐ He has destroyed the houses of those who do *deeds* opposed to the Law, by warfare and whispering lips.

[203] In the Greek copies (but not in the Syriac), the psalm is superscribed **Belonging to Solomon; against the tongue of the Law-breakers.**

12.2–4a In a diversity of turning are the words[204] **of a harmful man's tongue.** God is one (Mark 12.29 ≡ Deut 6.4) and His truth is one (Eph 4.3–6; Rom 15.5–6; Php 2.2; 1 Cor 1.10). With Him there is "no change or shadow of turning" (Jas 1.17) from age to age (Heb 1.12; 13.8). Falsehoods, however, are varied ("diverse and strange teachings," Heb 13.9; "diverse lusts and pleasures," Titus 3.3) and changeable ("carried about by every wind of teaching," Eph 4.14; "crooked in their pathways, and devious in their tracks," Prov 2.15; Sir 27.11; Jas 1.6–8; 2 Pet 2.17). They are constantly shifting. "Evildoers are like the driven sea; for it cannot rest, and its waters drive up mire and mud" (Isa 57.20).

In the subsequent clauses, the **diversity of turning** is compared to a complex jumble of concepts, vividly evoking erratic change, instability, and confusion (as in 2 Pet 2.14–17 ≡ Jude 12–13).[205] Even in ancient times this jumble was evidently difficult to understand, since copyists' transcriptions vary to an unusual extent. (The text discussed below is that of manuscript 253.) Modern readers should not be surprised if they likewise find it difficult. We need not expect a portrait of **lying things and deceitful things** to be plain and straightforward in all respects.

The evildoer's **words** are **just like a fire among a people.** "The tongue is a fire . . . setting aflame the course of creation, and being set aflame by hell" (Jas 3.6; Prov 16.27; 26.18–21; Sir 28.9–13). That fire is destructive, **setting alight its beauty.** An evildoer's "word will devour away [*nomēn hexei*] like gangrene" (2 Tim 2.17). In the Greek text, **its** [*autou*] **beauty** could refer either to the beauty of the **people** [*laō*] or to that of the **fire** itself [*pur*].[206] (For the beauty of the people, cf. 2.20, 23, 4; for the beauty of what is evil, cf. 16.8.) Evil destroys its own beauties (Jas 5.3; 2 Pet 2.1) as well as the beauties of others (Isa 64.11; Psa 74.7).

---

[204] **In a diversity of turning [are] the words** *(en poikilia strophēs hoi logoi)* is the reading of 253 and 336, whereas 260 reads "in the doing of perversity [are] the words" *(en poiēsei diastrophēs hoi logoi).* In most ancient Greek scripts, *-lia* and *dia-* would have looked very similar (and there would have been no spaces between the words).

The Syriac has no equivalent to either *poikilia* or *poiēsei;* it reads **for in turnings of words** *(bhwpk' gyr dml').*

[205] **Turning** also pictures instability and confusion (this time using the noun *tropēs*) in Jas 1.17—another passage whose linguistic complexity evidently puzzled ancient copyists, resulting in a remarkable range of variant texts (and, as in the passage under discussion, many modern commentators feel uncomfortable with all the options: see, e.g., Adamson, *Epistle of James,* 96–97; Davids, *Epistle of James,* 87–88; Martin, *James,* 29–30).

[206] In the Syriac, the beauty is unambiguously that of the evildoer: **he appears like one who is doing beautifully, and he makes a fire take hold among the people.** In Greek, 260 reads *halō* ("threshing floor") instead of *laō* (**people**), and *kalamēn* ("reed," "straw"; cf. Joel 2.5, LXX) instead of *kallonēn* (**beauty**)—yielding the sense "just like a fire in a threshing floor, setting alight its straw." But **people** and **beauty** are attested in both Greek and Syriac by all manuscripts except 260 and those copied from it.

The evildoer visits people's **houses,** and the purpose of his **visit** (*paroikia;* "sojourn," AOT) is **to fill**[207] those **houses with a lying tongue,** as described in 4.11–15, 23. "I will punish all . . . those who fill their masters' houses with injustice and deceit" (Zep 1.9). "There are many insubordinate people, empty talkers, and mind-deceivers . . . who overturn whole houses, teaching things that they should not" (Titus 1.10–11).

The evildoer does these things to righteous and unrighteous alike.

- Righteous people are here pictured as **trees of gladness** (just as they are called "trees of life" a little later, 14.2–3; cf. Matt 3.10; 7.17–19; Ezek 31.3–18). The evildoer seeks to **cut down** those **trees,** because their gladness **sets** him **aflame,** provoking him and causing him to burn inwardly (Psa 112.9–10; Est 6.11–12; Neh 2.10; Acts 13.44–45).[208] When Judas Maccabeus and his companions "were warring the war of Israel with gladness . . . all the workers of opposition to the Law were utterly unsettled" and sought "to shatter and do away with the strength of Israel' (Maccabaica 3.2–7, 10, 20, 35).
- Unrighteous households (**Law-breaking**[209] **houses**) are also attacked by the evildoer. He seeks **to set** them too **in turmoil** by means of **warfare with whispering lips** (1 Tim 5.13; Prov 20.19). Satan's house is divided against itself (cf. Matt 12.25–26), with the result that his servants often hate and destroy their own allies (Rev 17.16; Isa 19.2; 2 Chr 20.22–24). Foolishness tears her house down with her own hands (Prov 14.1).

---

[207] **To fill** (*emplēsai,* accented ἐμπλῆσαι) is the reading of 260 and is supported by the Syriac. In 253 and 336 the accentuation is ἐμπλῆσαι ("that he may fill," optative), in which case the sense would be: "just like a fire among a people, setting alight its beauty, [is] his visit, that he may fill houses with [his] lying tongue." Hilgenfeld and various subsequent editors conjecturally emended the Greek text to *emprēsai* ("to set on fire").

[208] **The trees of gladness that sets aflame Law-breakers** *(paranomous)* is the reading of 253. Instead of the last word, 336⁺260 have *paranomou,* which is difficult to construe unless it means something like "the trees of Law-breaking gladness that sets aflame" (cf. Ryle-James 104–05). The Syriac version has **he cut down the trees of his gladness in the burning of transgressing the Law.** In that text, **the trees of his gladness** (v 3) would apparently be equivalent to **the houses of those doing deeds opposed to the Law** (v 4), and both would describe unrighteous victims—although the rendering "the trees of His [God's] gladness" could not be ruled out entirely; everywhere else in the Eighteen Psalms, in either Greek or Syriac (5.1, 14, 21; 10.6, 7, 9 [336 only]; 11.4; 14.7; 15.5; 17.40), **gladness** is an attribute of the righteous (Ryle-James 104).

[209] Rahlfs omitted **Law-breaking,** which had been questioned by previous editors on the grounds that "people do not disturb Law-breaking houses" (Viteau 317). In reality the Scriptures teem with cases of Law-breakers harming other Law-breakers (Jdg 2.11–15; 18.1–31; Luke 13.1; etc.). If the Lord does not always protect the households of the righteous from the depredations of evildoers, how much less reason would He have to protect the households of Law-breakers (cf. Jer 25.29; Prov 11.31 ≡ 1 Pet 4.18)? The reading in the text is attested by all known manuscripts (both Greek and Syriac).

[4] μακρύναι ὁ θ(εὸ)σ ἀπὸ ἀκάκων
χείλη παρανόμων ἐν απορία·
May God keep far
from innocent *ones* *the* lips
of Law-breakers with perplexity,

ܐܪܚܩ ܐܠܗܐ ܡܢ ܬܡܝܡܐ.
ܣܦܘܬܐ ܕܥܒܪ̈ܝ ܢܡܘܣܐ.
God has put far off
from the innocent *ones* the lips
of those who transgress the Law,

καὶ σκορπισθείησαν ὀστὰ ψιθύρων
ἀπο φοβουμένων κ(ύριο)ν·
and may *the* bones
of whispering *ones* be scattered
away from *those* who fear *the* Lord;

ܘܢܬܒܕܪܘܢ ܓܪ̈ܡܐ ܕܡܠܚܫ̈ܢܐ.
ܡܢ ܐܝܠܝܢ ܕܕܚܠܝܢ ܡܢ ܡܪܝܐ.
and may the bones
of the whispering *ones* be scattered
from those who fear the LORD;

12.5 [4] ἐν πυρὶ φλογὸσ
γλῶσσα ψιθύροσ ἀπόλοιτο
ἀπο ὁσίων·
in a fire of a flame, may *the*
whispering tongue be destroyed
from *the* lovingkind *ones*.

ܒܢܘܪܐ ܕܡܫܬܠܗܒܐ
ܢܐܒܕ ܠܫܢܐ ܠܚܘܫܬܐܢܐ
ܡܢ ܬܡ̈ܝܡܐ. ܘܒ̈ܬܝܗܘܢ.
in a fire that *is* flaming, may the
whispering tongue be destroyed from
the innocent *ones* and their houses.

12.4b–5 May God keep evil talkers (vv 1–3) **far from innocent ones,** smiting them **with perplexity** ("confusion," OTP),[210] scattering their **bones** (Psa 53.5), and destroying (v 8) their tongues **in a fire of a flame.** The "tongue of deceit" will be punished with "hot coals" (Psa 120.4–5); he has been like a fire to others (v 2), so it is fitting for him to be burned with fire himself (cf. Matt 26.52; Ezek 35.6; Wis 11.16), both in this life (the gladness of the righteous sets him aflame, v 3) and in the age to come ("all liars … will be in the lake of fire and sulfur, which is the second death," Rev 21.8; Matt 13.40–42; 25.41; cf. Psa 140.10–11; 11.6). Even in this life, the Lord protects the righteous from the wicked: "You keep them hidden in Your shelter from the contention of tongues" (Psa 31.20; 121.7; John 17.15). And after death, "there is a great gulf fixed" to separate the two groups (Luke 16.26). No one "who does abomination or lying" is ever allowed to enter the heavenly Jerusalem (Rev 21.27).

May the Lord's salvation be on Israel

12.6 [5] ‹› φυλάξαι κ(ύριο)σ
‹ψυχὴν ἡσύχιο(ν) μισοῦσαν ἀδίκουσ
May *the* Lord guard
the quiet soul
that hates unrighteous *ones*,

ܘܢܛܪ ܡܪܝܐ ܠܢܦܫܐ ܕܙܕ̈ܝܩܐ.
ܕܣܢܝܐ ܠܥ̈ܘܠܐ.
And may the LORD watch over
the righteous *ones*' soul
that hates the unjust *ones*,

---

[210] **Perplexity** *(aporia)*. The term is applied to the perplexity of Herod when he heard the message of John the Baptist (Mark 6.20), and the perplexity of the generation warned by Jesus, when Jerusalem was "trampled by the nations" (Luke 21.24–25, 32).

καὶ κατευθύναι κ(ύριο)σ, ‹ἄνδρα ποιοῦντα, εἰρήνην ἐν οἴκω·	ܘܢܬܩܢ ܡܪܝܐ ܠܓܒܪܐ ܥܒܕ ܫܠܡܐ ܒܒܝܬ ܡܪܝܐ.
and may *the* Lord direct *the* man who makes peace in *his* house.	and may the LORD direct the man who makes peace in the LORD's house.

12.6 φυλάξαι 336⁺260 ≡ ܘܢܛܪ 16h1 10h1 | ^ συνχέαι οἴκουσ καὶ 253 • ψυχὴν … κατευθύναι κ(ύριο)σ 336⁺260 ≡ ܢܦܫܐ … ܢܬܩܢ ܡܪܝܐ 16h1 10h1 | > 253 • ἄνδρα ποιοῦντα 336⁺260 ≡ ܠܓܒܪܐ ܥܒܕ 16h1 10h1 | -ρὸσ -τασ 253 •

12.6 May the Lord[211] **guard** His people ("from the evil one," 2 Thes 3.3; John 17.12; **watch over** them, Syriac) and **direct** them (see the comments on 6.3). Jesus came "to direct our feet into the way of peace" (Luke 1.79)—and not our feet only, but even our hearts (2 Thes 3.5; Acts 8.21).

The quiet[212] **soul … the man who makes peace in his house** is the one who suffers patiently without retaliating, and who stills his soul and waits for the Lord to save him (Psa 37.7; 62.5–6; 1 Pet 2.19–23). "If possible, from your part, live in peace with all people" (Rom 12.18). "My soul has dwelt much with one who hates peace. I am peace; but when I speak, they are for war" (Psa 120.6–7). "Live in peace, and the God of love and peace will be with you" (2 Cor 13.11; Heb 12.14; Matt 5.9; Jas 3.17–18; 1 Pet 3.10–12). To say that such a soul **hates unrighteous ones** (Psa 139.21–22; 26.5; 119.158; Rev 2.6) may sound paradoxical, but it is perfectly true. No one has any love for peace—or for anything that is good—unless they hate what is evil (Psa 97.10; Amos 5.15; Rom 12.9); someone who loves or accepts an evil is actually a hater of good (Mic 3.2; John 15.19; 7.7; 2 Tim 3.3–4). "Those who leave the Law praise a wicked one, but those who keep the Law contend with them" (Prov 28.4). One of the wisest kings of Judah was rebuked on one occasion for that error. "Do you help the wicked one, and love those who hate the LORD? Then because of this, anger is upon you from the face of the LORD" (2 Chr 19.2). "Whoever therefore may want to be a friend of the world, he is seating himself as an enemy of God" (Jas 4.4).

12.7 [6] τοῦ κ(υρίο)υ ἡ σωτηρία ἐπὶ Ἰ(σρα)ὴλ παῖδα αὐτοῦ εἰσ τὸ(ν) αἰῶνα·	ܕܡܪܝܐ ܗܘ ܦܘܪܩܢܐ ܥܠ ܐܝܣܪܝܠ ܥܒܕܗ ܠܥܠܡ.
May the Lord's salvation *be* upon Israel His servant to lasting time,	*May* the LORD's salvation *be* on Israel His slave to lasting time,

---

[211] Wright's textual apparatus indicates that both instances of *kurios* (**Lord**) are missing from 253, 655*, and 659, but in fact *kurios* appears once in this verse in all three of those manuscripts (including both states of 655).

[212] **Quiet.** *Hēsuchion* is here feminine (cf. MHT 2.157; Thackeray §12.1), like *aiōniou* in 10.4 (see the footnote there).

12.8 [6] καὶ ἀπόλοιντο οἱ ἁμαρτωλοὶ ἀπὸ προσώπου κ(υρίο)υ ἅπαξ· and may the sinners be destroyed from *the* face of *the* Lord once *for all,*	ܘܢܐܒܕܘܢ ܚ̈ܛܝܐ ܐܟܚܕܐ. ܡܢ ܩܕܡ ܐܦ̈ܘܗܝ ܕܡܪܝܐ. and may the sinners be destroyed together from before *the* face of the LORD,
καὶ ὅσιοι κ(υρίο)υ κληρονομίσαισαν ἐπαγγελείασ ‹κ(υρίο)υ›: and may *the* Lord's lovingkind *ones* inherit *the* Lord's promises.	ܘܚܣܝ̈ܘܗܝ ܕܡܪܝܐ ܢܐܪܬܘܢ ܡܘ̈ܠܟܢܘܗܝ ܕܡܪܝܐ. and may the LORD's lovingkind *ones* inherit the LORD's promises.

12.8 κ(υρίο)υ 3° 336⁺260 ≡ ܕܡܪܝܐ 16h1 10h1 | > 253 •

12.7 May the Lord's salvation be upon Israel His servant to lasting time. "Israel will be saved by the LORD with a lasting salvation; you will not be put to shame, and you will not be humiliated, until lasting times of continuing time" (Isa 45.17). This will be accomplished by the inclusion of both Jews and Gentiles in the Israel of God (Rom 2.28–29), "and so all Israel will be saved" (Rom 11.25–26).

12.8 May the sinners be destroyed from the face of the Lord once for all. At the final judgment, those who are disobedient will be punished with "lasting destruction from the face of the Lord and from the glory of His strength" (2 Thes 1.9; Psa 68.1–2). This will happen **once for all** (*hapax,* as in Heb 10.2): it will be just as permanent and unalterable as the salvation of His faithful servants (see v 7; Matt 25.46). "The life of the righteous ones will be to lasting time; but sinners will be taken to destruction, and their memorial will not be found any more" (13.9–10).

And may the Lord's lovingkind ones inherit the Lord's promises. The Lord's **promises** were addressed "to Abraham and to his seed" (Gal 3.16; Heb 11.17–18; Rom 9.4), and are made available through Jesus to both Jews and Gentiles (Rom 15.8–10), to those who have faith and persevere to the end in that faith (Heb 6.11–12; 1 Pet 1.3–5; 2 Pet 1.3–4).

Psalm 13

The arm of the Lord has saved us

13.0 [0] Τῷ Σαλωμὼν ψαλμὸς παράκλησις τῶ(ν) δικ(αί)ω(ν): Belonging to Solomon, a psalm, an encouragement; of the righteous *ones*.	
13.1 [1] Δεξιὰ κ(υρίο)υ ἐσκέπασέν με *The* right hand of *the* Lord has covered me,	ܝܡܝܢܗ ܕܡܪܝܐ ܟܣܝܬܢ. *The* right *hand* of the LORD has covered us,

Greek	Syriac
δεξιὰ κ(υρίο)υ ἐφείσατο ἡμῶν· *the* right hand of *the* Lord has spared us;	ܝܡܝܢܗ ܕܡܪܝܐ ܚܣܬ ܥܠܝܢ. *the* right *hand* of the LORD has spared us;
13.2 [2] ὁ βραχίων κ(υρίο)υ ἔσωσεν ἡμᾶσ ἀπὸ ῥομφαίασ διαπορευομένησ· the arm of *the* Lord has saved us from *the* sword that passed through,	ܘܕܪܥܗ ܕܡܪܝܐ <ܦܪܩܢ> ܡܢ ܪܘܡܚܐ ܕܡܗܠܟܐ. and *the* arm of the LORD has saved us from the sword that *was* going around,
ἀπο λιμοῦ καὶ θανάτου ἁμαρτωλῶν from hunger and *the* death of sinners.	ܘܡܢ ܟܦܢܐ ܘܡܘܬܐ ܕܚܛܝ̈ܐ. and from hunger and the death of the sinners.
13.3 [3] θηρία ἐπεδράμοσαν αὐτοῖσ πονηρᾶ· Harmful wild animals ran on them;	ܐܪܗܛ ܥܠܝܗܘܢ ܚܝ̈ܘܬܐ ܒܝ̈ܫܬܐ. He brought quickly on them harmful living creatures,
ἐν τοῖσ ὀδοῦσιν αὐτ(ῶν) ἐτίλλοσαν σάρκασ αὐτ(ῶν)· with their teeth they were plucking their flesh,	ܘܒܫܢ̈ܝܗܘܢ ܡܒܬ̈ܩܝܢ ܗܘܘ ܒܣܪܗܘܢ. and with their teeth they were tearing their flesh,
καὶ ἐν ταῖσ μύλαισ ἔθλων ὀστᾶ αὐτ(ῶν)· and with *their* grinders they were crushing their bones.	ܘܒܪ̈ܚܝܬܐ <ܡܦܫܚܝܢ ܗܘܘ> ܠܓܪ̈ܡܝܗܘܢ. and with *their* grinders they were breaking their bones.
[4] καὶ ἐκ τούτων ἁπάντ(ων) ἐρρύσατο ἡμᾶσ κ(ύριο)σ· And out of all these *things* *the* Lord has delivered us.	ܠ ܕܝܢ ܡܢ ܗܠܝܢ ܟܠܗܝܢ ܦܪܩ ܡܪܝܐ. But from all these *things* the LORD has saved us.

13.2 ܦܪܩܢ 10h1 ≡ ἔσωσεν ἡμᾶσ 253 336⁺260 \| ܦܪܩܢܝ 16h1 • **13.3** ܡܦܫܚܝܢ ܗܘܘ 10h1 ≡ ἔθλων 253 336⁺260 \| ܗܘܘ ܡܦܫܚܝܢ 16h1 •

13.1–3[213] In Babylonian times, God had sent "four harmful judgments—sword, and hunger, and a harmful beast, and death—against Jerusalem, to cut off from it person and animal"; but He had also promised that a remnant of the inhabitants would be spared (Ezek 14.13–22).

[213] In the Greek copies (but not in the Syriac), the psalm is superscribed **Belonging to Solomon, a psalm, an encouragement; of the righteous ones.**

In the time of this psalm, the people of Jerusalem had again been exposed to those four judgments: the **sword that passed through,**[214] **hunger, death,** and **harmful wild animals.**[215] Both here and in Ezekiel 14, **death** refers specifically to death by disease ("plague," Ryle-James), and is distinguished from death inflicted by human agency or some other visible cause (so also in, e.g., 15.8; 2 Sam 24.13–15; Rev 6.8; BDAG 443, §3). Some of the **sinners** had perished from the disease;[216] others had been attacked by the **wild animals,** which **ran on them** and devoured them with their **teeth.**[217]

But again God had allowed a remnant to escape: **out of all these** judgments **the Lord has delivered us.** The Lord's **right hand** and **arm** had **covered** and **spared** them, saving them **from** the four judgments, just as His **hand** and **arm** had **covered** His people in the past (Exod 33.22; Isa 49.2; 51.16), **spared** them (Deut 33.3, LXX; Isa 63.9; Psa 72.13), and **saved** them (Psa 98.1–3; 44.3; 17.7; 20.6; 138.7; cf. Isa 59.1)—and just as His **hand** and **arm** would soon save "Israel His servant" through Jesus (Luke 1.51–54, 66; John 10.29; Acts 4.28, 30; 11.21).

The irreverent one is unsettled

Greek	Syriac
13.4 [5] ἐταράχθη ὁ ἀσεβὴσ δια παραπτώματα αὐτοῦ·	ܐܬܬܙܝܥ ܕܝܢ ܪܫܝܥܐ ܡܛܠ ܫܘܪ̈ܥܬܗ.
The irreverent *one* was unsettled because of his transgressions,	But the ungodly *one* was disturbed because of his transgressions,

---

[214] **The sword that was going around** is the corresponding Syriac. The term *hlk* here means "go around" (as the devil himself does, 1 Pet 5.8, Syr), and although *rwmḥ'* most often means "spear," its resemblance to Greek *romphaia* made it also a natural equivalent for **sword** (as in Luke 2.35, Syr; Maccabaica 2.9, 7h7; etc.). Compare the common LXX practice of using Greek *allophulos,* "foreigner," to translate the similar-sounding Hebrew *Plšty,* "Philistine."

[215] **Harmful** [*ponēra,* Greek ≡ *byšt',* Syriac] **wild animals.** Animals that are harmful to humans (*féroces,* Viteau). The term *ponēros* ≡ *byš'* is applied not only to things that are sinful (the opposite of righteous, Matt 13.49), but also to things that are physically harmful or painful (e.g., painful sores, *ponēron, byš',* Rev 16.2 ≡ *ponōn, k'byhwn,* Rev 16.11; cf. Muraoka 576, §2). The Scriptures sometimes describe hostile people as animals (Psa 7.1–2; 22.12–13, 16), but here (as in Ezek 14.13–22) the **wild animals** and the hostile people are two separate groups.

[216] Wright paraphrases **the death of sinners** as "death at the hands of sinners," but this neither suits the context nor is consistent with Biblical idiom. The **them** *(autois)* in the next clause, on whom the animals **ran,** must grammatically be the same group, the **sinners;** and in vv 4–6 the **sinners** are **taken** and overturned (**taken to destruction,** v 10). Moreover, **the death of** a person, in Biblical usage, is the death experienced by that person: "the death of the wicked" (Ezek 18.23), "the death of the high priest" (Num 35.25), "the death of His lovingkind ones" (Psa 116.15), "the death of His Son" (Rom 5.10).

[217] In both Greek and Syriac, the term **grinders** (*mulais* ≡ *rḥwt'*) can be applied (a) to millstones and (b) to millstone-like teeth (not "fangs" [AOT] but "molars" [APOT]): LSJ 1152, §V; SL 1455, §4. In this context the meaning is the latter.

Greek	Syriac
μήποτε συμπαραληφθῇ μετὰ τ(ῶν) ἁμαρτωλῶν· lest he should be taken along with the sinners,	ܕܕܠܡܐ ܢܬܬܒܪ ܥܡ ܥܘܠܐ. lest he should be crushed with the unjust *one,*
13.5 [6] ὅτι δινὴ ἡ καταστροφὴ τοῦ ἁμαρτωλοῦ· because the overturning of the sinner *is* terrible,	ܡܛܠ ܕܒܝܫܐ ܗܝ ܡܦܘܠܬܗ ܕܥܘܠܐ. because *the* fall of the unjust *one* is ruinous;

13.4 By contrast, the **irreverent** person[218] **was unsettled**[219] **because of his transgressions** (cf. Isa 59.11–13; Ezek 7.16–18), realizing that he too might **be taken** (**be crushed,** Syriac) by God, **along with the sinners** already mentioned (those who had already perished, vv 2–3). The deaths of past sinners by the hand of God warn all of us that we are in danger of sharing their doom. "Do you think that these sinners were sinners beyond all the Galileans, because they suffered these things? No, I say to you; but unless you repent, you will all likewise be destroyed" (Luke 13.2–3; Num 16.26; Jer 51.6; Rev 18.4–5).

13.5a The overturning of the sinner is terrible. "It is a fearful thing to fall into the hands of the living God" (Heb 10.31). Let those who hear of it (2 Kgs 21.12; Acts 5.11; Rev 18.9–10) "fear, and never proceed to do an evil thing like this" (Deut 13.11; 17.13; 19.20; cf. 1 Tim 5.20).

The righteous are disciplined but spared

Greek	Syriac
καὶ οὐχ ἅψεται δικαίου οὐδὲν ἐκ πάντ(ων) τούτων· and nothing at all out of all these *things* will touch *the* righteous *one;*	ܠܙܕܝܩܐ ܕܝܢ ܚܕܐ ܡܢ ܗܠܝܢ ܠܐ <ܬܬܩܪܒ>. but not one out of these *things* will touch the righteous *one;*
13.6 [7] ὅτι οὐχ ὁμοῖα ἡ παιδεία τ(ῶν) δικαίων ἐν αγνοία· because not alike *are* the discipline of *the* righteous *ones* in *their* ignorance	ܡܛܠ ܕܠܐ ܦܚܡܐ ܡܪܕܘܬܐ ܕܙܕܝܩܐ ܕܕܠܐ ܒܝܕܥܬܐ. because not comparable *is* the discipline of the righteous *ones* who *are* not in knowledge

13.5 ܬܬܩܪܒ 10h1 ≡ ἅψεται 253 336⁺260 | ܬܬܩܪܒܝ, 16h1 •

---

218 **The irreverent one** *(ho asebēs)* is the reading of all Greek manuscripts, supported by the Syriac *(ršy")*. Wellhausen and subsequent editors conjecturally emended it to *ho eusebēs* ("the reverent one").

219 **Was unsettled** (*etarachthē*, Greek ≡ *'ttzy'*, Syriac). The same term is used to describe Herod's response to the work of God's hand (Matt 2.3).

καὶ ἡ καταστροφὴ ‹τῶν ἁμαρτωλῶν› **13.7 [8]** ἐν περιστολῇ and the overturning of the sinners in *their* arrayment.	ܠܗܘܦܟܐ ܕܥܘ̈ܠܐ ܕܒܝܕܥܬܐ. to the overthrow of the unjust *one*s who *are* in knowledge.
παιδεύεται δίκαιοσ· ἵνα μὴ ἐπιχαρῇ ὁ ἁμαρτωλὸσ τῷ δικαίῳ· *The* righteous *one* is disciplined in order that the sinner may not rejoice over the righteous *one;*	ܡܬܪܕܐ ܓܝܪ ܙܕܝܩܐ. ܐܝܟ ܕܠܐ ܢܚܕܐ ܠܗ ܥܘܠܐ. For the righteous *one is* disciplined so that the unjust *one* may not rejoice *in regard* to him;
13.8 [9] ὅτι νουθετήσει δίκαιον ὡσ υἱὸν ἀγαπήσεωσ· because He will admonish *the* righteous *one* as a son of love,	ܡܛܠ ܕܢܪܬܝܘܗܝ ܓܝܪ ܙܕܝܩܐ ܐܝܟ ܕܠܒܪܗ ܪܚܝܡܐ. because He will admonish the righteous *one* as His son of love,
καὶ ἡ παιδεία αὐτοῦ ὡσ πρωτοτόκου· and his discipline *will be* like *that* of a firstborn,	ܘܡܪܕܘܬܗ ܐܝܟ ܕܒܘܟܪܐ. and his disciplining *will be* like *that* of a firstborn,
13.9 [10] ὅτι φείσεται κ(ύριο)σ τ(ῶν) ὁσίων αὐτοῦ· because *the* Lord will spare His lovingkind *one*s,	ܡܛܠ ܕܚܣ ܙܕܝܩܐ ܥܠ ܚܣ̈ܝܕܘܗܝ because the Righteous *One* will spare over His lovingkind *one*s,
καὶ τὰ παραπτώματα αὐτ(ῶν) ἐξαλείψει ἐν παιδείᾳ· and He will wipe out their transgressions with discipline;	ܘܣܟܠܘ̈ܬܗܘܢ ܢܛܠܐ ܒܡܪܕܘܬܐ. and He will blot out their transgressions with discipline.

13.6 τῶν ἁμαρτωλῶν 336⁺260 ≡ ܕܥܘ̈ܠܐ 16h1 10h1 | τοῦ -λοῦ 253 •

13.5b Nevertheless, **nothing at all out of all these** judgments (vv 1–3) **will touch the righteous one**—a highly emphatic statement *(ouch… ouden ek pantōn).* All such judgments "will be a long way off from the righteous ones" (see the comments on 15.8). "The righteous, and the wise, and their works, are in the hand of God" (Ecc 9.1), and no one is able to snatch them out of that hand (John 10.28–29).

13.6–9a In this life, both **righteous ones** and **sinners** may suffer greatly. But their sufferings are **not alike.**

- Those who are **righteous** commit sins of **ignorance,** which require correction by God (Psa 19.12; cf. 1 Cor 4.4; Lev 5.17–19). Therefore, the **righteous** must suffer as a form of **discipline,** to **wipe out their transgressions** and keep them from sin (16.11; 1 Cor 11.32; Heb 12.7–11; cf. 2 Cor 12.7). "It is good for me that I have been afflicted, in order that I learn Your decrees" (Psa 119.71; 94.12). God

will admonish the righteous one as a son of love (Deut 8.5; Heb 12.6–7; Rev 3.19), as a **firstborn** ("Israel is my son, my firstborn," Exod 4.22; all those "who are enrolled in heaven" are "firstborn ones," Heb 12.23; cf. Jas 1.18; Rev 14.4). When the **righteous one** suffers in this way, the **sinner** has no reason to **rejoice over** him. "Do not rejoice against me, my enemy; though I have fallen, I will arise .... I will bear the anger of the LORD, for I have sinned against Him, until He pleads my cause and does judgment for me; He will bring me out to the light, I will see His righteousness" (Mic 7.8–10; Psa 30.1).

- But people who sin willfully—**in** the **knowledge** of the truth—must suffer a final **overthrow** (Syriac) from which there will be no recovery (v 10). If "we are willfully sinning after receiving the knowledge of the truth, there no longer remains a sacrifice for sins, but a certain fearful expectation of judgment, and the zeal of a fire that is going to devour the adversaries" (Heb 10.26–29; cf. Deut 29.19–20; Heb 6.4–6; 12.15–17; Num 15.28–31).

The Greek version describes these **sinners** as transgressing **in their arrayment** *(peristolē),*[220] a term applied in Biblical Greek to fine clothing (Exod 33.6, LXX; Sir 45.7; "ornamental garment," Muraoka 553; "adornment," LEH 488; compare, in these psalms, "array [*peristeilon*] my tongue and my lips in words of truth," 16.10). In the Scriptures, the fine clothing of sinners is worn to draw attention to themselves, and to make what is really corrupt appear outwardly attractive and impressive: "When you clothe yourself in scarlet, when you adorn yourself with ornaments of gold ... in vain you beautify yourself" (Jer 4.30). That was true of Babylon the harlot (who "was wrapped in purple and scarlet, and gilded with gold and precious stone and pearls," Rev 17.4); of the woman of folly (Prov 7.10, 16–17); of the daughters of Zion denounced by Isaiah (Isa 3.16–24); of Herod (Acts 12.21–23); of the Pharisees ("they do all their deeds to be seen by people; for they broaden their phylacteries and lengthen their fringes," Matt 23.5; cf. 1 Tim 2.9; 1 Pet 3.3).[221]

---

[220] Most commentators have connected the phrase *en peristolē* not with this clause but with the next one (in which case it would describe the discipline suffered by the righteous, not the sin of the sinners), and they have assigned it the meaning "in secret" (Ryle-James) rather than **in arrayment.** This is grammatically implausible (**the sinners ... in their arrayment** is structurally parallel to **the righteous ones in their ignorance**—as the Syriac version confirms); it assigns a rare meaning to *peristolē;* and it produces a dubious statement ("The fact that righteous men like Job had suffered, and that not secretly, was well known to the writer, so that we hesitate to credit him with an assertion of the contrary here," Ryle-James 109).

[221] This difference between the versions might have arisen if the Syriac translator was puzzled by the unusual phrase **in arrayment** (either as it stands in the existing Greek, or in its underlying Hebrew), and simply decided to render it in a way that suited the context. A textual error is improbable but not impossible. In Hebrew, **in knowledge** would almost certainly have been *bd't* (Exod 35.31; Prov 13.16); and if the Greek translator had worked from a manuscript with accidentally transposed letters—*b'dt*—he might well have concluded that it was best understood as *b'd[w]t* ("in ornamenting").

The basic point in this passage is also made in the New Testament Scriptures: the righteous “are disciplined by the Lord,” whereas the people of this world “are condemned” (1 Cor 11.32; cf. Wis 11.10; 16.4–6).

The righteous will live for ever, but sinners will be destroyed

[11] ἡ γὰρ ζωὴ τ(ῶν) δικαίων εἰσ τὸν αἰῶνα· for the life of the righteous *ones* *will be* to lasting time;	ܚܝ̈ܝܗܘܢ ܓܝܪ <ܕܙܕܝ̈ܩܐ> ܠܥܠܡ ܐܢܘܢ܀ For *the* life of the righteous *ones* *will be* to lasting time;
13.10 [11] ἁμαρτωλοὶ δὲ ἀρθήσονται εἰσ ἀπώλειαν· but sinners will be taken to destruction,	ܚ̈ܛܝܐ ܕܝܢ ܢܬܬܪܡܘܢ ܠܐܒܕܢܐ. but the sinners will be cast down to destruction,
κ(αὶ) ‹οὐχ› ευρεθήσεται μνημόσυνον αὐτ(ῶν) ἔτι· and their memorial will not be found *any* more.	ܘܠܐ ܢܫܬܟܚ ܬܘܒ ܕܘܟܪܢܗܘܢ܀ and their memorial will never again be found.

13.9 ܕܙܕܝ̈ܩܐ 10h1 ≡ δικαίων 253 336⁺260 | ܕܙܕܝܩܐ 16h1 • **13.10** οὐχ 336⁺260 | οὐκ 253 •

13.9b–10 The life of the righteous ones will be to lasting time. “In the pathway of righteousness is life, and in the way of its path is no death” (Prov 12.28; John 11.26; Psa 16.10–11; Rom 2.7). At the final judgment, “the righteous ones” will go away “into lasting life” (Matt 25.46).

But sinners will be taken to destruction (see on 2.35; 3.13; 12.5, 7–8), **and their memorial will not be found any more.** “The memory of a righteous one is for a blessing, but the name of wicked ones rots” (Prov 10.7). “You have wiped out their name to lasting time and continuing time . . . their memorial has been destroyed” (Psa 9.5–6; 109.13–15). It is wiped out “from under heaven” (Deut 29.20) and “from the book of life” (where the names of the righteous are written, Psa 69.28)—so that when the books are finally opened for the dead to be judged, the sinner’s name is “not found written in the book of life,” and he is “cast into the lake of fire” (Rev 20.11–15; cf. Rev 3.5).

13.11 [12] ἐπι δὲ τοὺσ ὁσίουσ τὸ ἔλεοσ κ(υρίο)υ· But the Lord’s mercy *will be* upon the lovingkind *ones*,	ܥܠ ܚܣ̈ܝܐ ܕܝܢ ܢܗܘܘܢ ܪ̈ܚܡܘܗܝ ܕܡܪܝܐ. But *the* LORD’s compassions will be upon the lovingkind *ones*,

καὶ ἐπὶ τοὺσ φοβουμένουσ ⸤αὐτὸν⸥	ܥܠ ܟܠܗܘܢ ܕ̈ܚܠܘܗܝ
τὸ ἔλεοσ αὐτοῦ:	ܢܪܚܦ
and His mercy *will be* upon those who fear Him.	and He will hover over all those who fear Him.

13.11 αὐτὸν 336⁺260 ≡ 16h1 10h1 | > 253 •

13.11 But the Lord's mercy will be upon the lovingkind ones, and His mercy will be upon those who fear Him.[222] "Blessed are the merciful, for they will receive mercy" (Matt 5.7; 2 Tim 1.16–18); "through all time" they will be "in His presence" (2.40). "His mercy is to generations and generations for those who fear Him" (Luke 1.50; see the notes on 2.37).

Psalm 14

To an even greater extent than Eighteen Psalms 3, the present psalm is constructed like Psalm 1 of the Hebrew Psalter, as the following comparison shows:

Eighteen Psalms 14	**Hebrew Psalter 1**
Threefold description of the Lord's lovingkind ones (v 1)	Threefold description of the righteous man (1.1)
They **live** in His **Law . . . to lasting time** (vv 1–2)	"In the law of the LORD is his desire . . . daytime and night" (1.2)
They are **trees** that will never be **uprooted to lasting time** (vv 2–3)	"He is as a tree" whose "leaf will not fade away" (1.3)
Not so are the sinners (vv 4–5)	"Not so are the wicked ones" (1.4)
Their inheritance will be . . . destruction, and they will not be found in the day of mercy (v 6)	They "will not stand in the judgment"; their way "will be destroyed" (1.5–6)
The Lord's lovingkind ones will inherit life (v 7)	The LORD knows the way of the righteous ones (1.6)

---

222 **His mercy** [*eleos*] **will be on those who fear Him** (Greek). The Syriac has **He will hover over** [*nrḥp*] **all those who fear Him,** using the picturesque verb *rḥp,* "hover over," "cherish" (TS 2.3886–87; SL 1458). God cares for His people "as an eagle . . . hovers over [*mrḥp,* Syr ≡ *yrḥp,* Hebrew] its young" (Deut 32.11).

In the present verse there is no need to think that the Syriac version was prepared from a different textual source than the existing Greek. Other Syriac translators also used forms of *rḥp* to render words for mercy or compassion, in contexts where Greek translators used forms of *eleos* (e.g., Isa 9.17; 30.18; Ezek 24.14).

The Lord is faithful to those who love Him in truth

14.0 [0] Ὕμνος τῷ Σαλωμῶν: A hymn belonging to Solomon.	
14.1 [1] Πιστὸσ κ(ύριο)σ τοῖσ ἀγαπῶσιν αὐτὸν ἐν αληθείᾳ· *The* Lord *is* faithful to those who love Him in truth,	ܡܗܝܡܢ ܡܪܝܐ ܠܐܝܠܝܢ ܕܪܚܡܝܢ ܠܗ ܒܫܪܪܐ. The LORD *is* faithful to those who love Him in truth,
τοῖσ ὑπομένουσιν παιδείαν αὐτοῦ· to those who endure under His discipline,	ܠܗܢܘܢ ܕܡܣܝܒܪܝܢ ܡܪܕܘܬܗ. to those who bear His discipline,
[2] τοῖσ πορευομένοισ ἐν δικαιοσύνῃ προσταγμάτ(ων) αὐτοῦ· to those who go in *the* righteousness of His decrees.	ܠܗܢܘܢ ܕܡܗܠܟܝܢ ܒܟܐܢܘܬܐ ܒܦܘܩܕܢܘܗܝ. to those who go about in righteousness in His commands.

14.1a[223] **Those who love** the Lord **in truth** (i.e., not merely in word; see the comments on 6.9) are **those who endure under His discipline** (10.2), because love "endures all things" (1 Cor 13.7; cf. Jas 1.12; 2 Thes 3.5), and are also **those who go in the righteousness of His decrees,** because "the one who has My commands and keeps them—that is the one who loves Me" (John 14.21–23, 6). Indeed, "this is the love of God, that we keep His commands" (1 Jn 5.3). Anyone who does not keep His commands does not love Him (John 14.24).

The Lord is faithful to His people, protecting them from the evil one (2 Thes 3.3), and delivering them from temptation (1 Cor 10.13). "He is God, the faithful God, keeping His covenant and lovingkindness to those who love Him and who keep His commands" (Deut 7.9).

They will never be uprooted

ἐν νόμῳ ἐνετείλατο ἡμῖν εἰσ ζωὴν ἡμῶν· In *the* Law, He has commanded us for our life;	ܢܡܘܣܐ ܝܗܒ ܠܢ ܠܚܝܝܢ. He gave us the Law for our life,
14.2 [3] ὅσιοι κ(υρίο)υ ζήσονται ἐν αὐτῷ εἰσ τὸν αἰῶνα· *the* Lord's lovingkind *ones* will live in it to lasting time.	ܘܚܣܝܘܗܝ ܕܡܪܝܐ ܢܚܘܢ ܒܗ ܠܥܠܡ. and the LORD's lovingkind *ones* will live in it to lasting time.

[223] In the Greek copies (but not in the Syriac), the psalm is superscribed **A hymn belonging to Solomon.**

ὁ παράδεισοσ τοῦ κ(υρίο)υ τὰ ξύλα τῆσ ζωῆσ ὅσιοι αὐτοῦ· The Paradise of the Lord, the trees of life, *are* His lovingkind *one*s;	ܦܪܕܝܣܗ ܕܡܪܝܐ ܐܝ̈ܠܢܐ ܕܚ̈ܝܐ. ܕܐܝܬܝܗܘܢ ܚܣܝ̈ܕܘܗܝ. *The* Paradise of the LORD, the trees of life, are His lovingkind *one*s,
14.3 [4] ἡ φυτεία αὐτῶν ἐρριζομένη εἰσ τὸν αἰῶνα· their plant *is* rooted to lasting time;	ܘܒܝ ܨܒܬܗܘܢ ܡܫܪܪܐ ܠܥܠܡ. and their adornment *is* set firmly to lasting time,
οὐκ εκτειλήσονται πάσασ τὰσ ἡμέρασ τοῦ οὐ(ρα)νοῦ· they will not be uprooted all the days of heaven,	ܘܠܐ ܢܬܥܩܪܘܢ ܟܠܗܘܢ ܝܘ̈ܡܬܐ ܕܫܡܝܐ. and it will not be uprooted all the days of heaven,
[5] ὅτι ἡ μερὶσ καὶ κληρονομία τοῦ θ(εο)ῦ ἔστὶν Ἰ(σρα)ήλ· because God's portion and inheritance is Israel.	ܡܛܠ ܕܡܢܬܗ ܕܡܪܝܐ ܘܝܪܬܘܬܗ ܐܝܣܪܝܠ. because the LORD's portion and His inheritance *is* Israel.

14.1b–3 In the Law, He has commanded us for our life.[224] "If you are wanting to enter into life, keep the commands" (Matt 19.17); "do this, and you will live" (Luke 10.25–28; Lev 18.5; Deut 32.46–47). "Attend to my words ... for they are life to those who find them" (Prov 4.20–22; 3.1–2). That **life** is promised not for this age only, but **to lasting time** (Luke 10.25, 28; Rom 2.7), and it is obtained **in the Law,** not anywhere else: **the Lord's lovingkind ones will live ... to lasting time,** and they will do so **in it**—in the Law, not in any other way of life. The person who "will be blessed" is not the person who glances briefly at God's Law and then turns away, but the person who "has endured" in it (Jas 1.22–25; Rom 2.13), repenting of all sin (opposition to that Law, 1 Jn 3.4; 1.9), and "walking in all the Lord's commands and righteous decrees, without blemish" (Luke 1.6). "If you endure in My word, you are truly My disciples" (John 8.31; 15.4–9). "Let no one lead you astray: the one who does righteousness is righteous" (1 Jn 3.7).

The trees of life are His lovingkind ones; their plant is rooted to lasting time; they will not be uprooted all the days of heaven. "A righteous one flourishes like a

---

[224] **In the Law** [*en nomō*], **He has commanded us** is the reading of 253. Other Greek manuscripts read *en nomō ō* (629⁺769), *en nomō hōs* (260), or *en nomō hon* (336), connecting this clause with the previous one ("those who go in the righteousness of His orders, in the Law that He commanded us for our life," 629⁺769; " ... in the Law, as He commanded us for our life," 260). However, the Syriac supports 253 in connecting this clause with the next one, and the clause structure—in all Greek texts—also favors that (as noted by Trafton 132): **will live** corresponds to **for our life,** and **in it** refers directly back to **in the Law.**

palm tree; he increases like a cedar in Lebanon" (Psa 92.12–14). Such a person is a tree of **life** because he lives **to lasting time ... all the days of heaven:** "The man who trusts in the LORD ... will be like a tree planted next to streams of waters," which "will not cease from making fruit" (Jer 17.7–8; Psa 1.3), "flourishing ... to lasting time and continuing time" (Psa 52.8). "The root of righteous ones will never be moved" (Prov 12.3, 12), whereas the ax is laid at the root of every unrighteous tree: it will be cut down and destroyed (Matt 3.10; Psa 92.7).

A **Paradise** (Greek *paradeisos* ≡ Syriac *prdys'* ≡ Hebrew *prds*) is a "garden" (TDNT 5.765–73). The word can refer even to an earthly garden, park, or forest (in all three languages: Ecc 2.5; Neh 2.8), but is applied particularly to the future abode of the righteous (Luke 23.43)—the garden where the tree of life grows (Rev 2.7).

God's portion (see on 3.15) **and inheritance is Israel.** "The LORD's portion is His people; Jacob is the allotment of His inheritance" (Deut 32.9). They are the people whom He "has chosen for Himself ... for His personal property" (Psa 135.4)—a promise inherited by all those who are in Christ (1 Pet 2.9–10; cf. Isa 19.23–25).

Not so are the sinners

Greek	Syriac
14.4 [6] καὶ οὐχ οὕτωσ οἱ ἁμαρτωλοὶ καὶ παράνομοι· But not so *are* the sinners and Law-breakers	ܘܠܐ ܗܟܢܐ ܚܛܝ̈ܐ ܘܥܘ̈ܠܐ. ܗ̇ܢܘܢ܆ But not so are the sinners and the unjust *ones*
οἳ ἠγάπησαν ἡμέραν ἐν μετοχῇ ἁμαρτίασ αὐτ(ῶν)· who have loved a day in *the* participation of their sin.	ܕܐܚܒܘ ܝܘܡܐ ܒܩܘܒܠܐ ܕܚܛܝܬܐ. who have loved a day in the acceptance of sin.
[7] ἐν μικρότητι σαπρίασ ἡ ἐπιθυμία αὐτ(ῶν)· Their desire *is* in the littleness of worthlessness,	ܒܙܥܘܪ̈ܘܬܗ ܓܝܪ ܕܒܝܫܬܐ ܪ̈ܓܬܗܘܢ܀ For their desire *is* in *the* littlenesses of evil,
14.5 [7] καὶ οὐκ ἐμνήσθησαν τοῦ θ(εο)ῦ and they have not been mindful of God,	ܘܠܐ ܐܬܕܟܪܘ ܠܐܠܗܐ. and they have not been mindful of God,
[8] ὅτι ὁδοὶ ἀν(θρώπ)ων· γνωσταὶ ἐνώπιον αὐτοῦ δια παντὸσ· that *the* paths of Men *are* known in His sight through all *time,*	ܕܐܘܪ̈ܚܬܗܘܢ ܕܒ̈ܢܝ ܐܢܫܐ ܓ̈ܠܝܢ ܐܢܝܢ ܩܕܡܘܗܝ ܒܟܠܙܒܢ. that *the* paths of *the* sons of Men have been uncovered before Him in all time,

καὶ ταμεῖα καρδίασ ἐπίσταται προ τοῦ γενέσθαι· and He understands *the* inner rooms of *the* heart before they come to be.	ܘܬܘܘ̈ܢܐ ܕܠܒܐ ܝܕܥ ܡܢ ܩܕܡ ܕܢܗܘܘܢ܀ and *He* knows the inner rooms of the heart, from before they are.

14.4–5 Not so (Psa 1.4)—not like the righteous ones—**are the sinners and Law-breakers.** They are different in almost every respect:

Righteous ones:	**Sinners:**
love the Lord (v 1)	**have loved** a day in the participation of their sin; their **desire** is in the littleness of worthlessness (v 4)
love **the Lord** (v 1)	have not been mindful of **God** (v 5)
live in God's **Law** (v 2)	are **Law**-breakers (v 4)
live in it to **lasting time** (v 2)	participate in sin for a **day,** a **little** time (v 4)

To the righteous, even a single day in God's courts is better than a thousand days anywhere else (Psa 84.10). But **sinners** have the opposite attitude. They "hate the good, and love the evil" (Mic 3.2). They **have loved** "the enjoyment of sin for a time-period" (Heb 11.25; cf. Prov 10.23)—a **little**[225] time, a **day,** participating in **sin** and **worthlessness**[226]—rather than an eternity of life in God's Law (v 2). "The world is passing away, and its desire; but the one who does the will of God endures to lasting time" (1 Jn 2.17). Yet these people find **worthlessness** so much more desirable than God, that a day of sin seems better to them than an eternity in God's courts.

They have not been mindful of God (Psa 78.42; 106.7). "They did not think fit to have God in their knowledge" (Rom 1.28). "They have not said in their heart, 'Now let us fear the LORD our God'" (Jer 5.23–24).

In particular, the sinners **have not been mindful . . . that**[227] **the paths of Men are**

---

[225] **Littleness** *(mikrotēti),* Greek; **littlenesses** *(z'wrwth),* Syriac. In each of those languages, forms of this word are commonly applied both to time ("briefness," AOT; cf. Heb 10.37; Rev 6.11) and to quality (*Niedrigkeit* ["baseness"], Holm-Nielsen; cf. Matt 11.11). Here both connotations may be involved. Both are stated explicitly in the vicinity (**a day** and **worthlessness**), which would naturally prompt a reader to think of both at this point.

[226] **Worthlessness** *(saprias).* Not necessarily "corruption" (APOT) or "decay" (OTP), but extremely poor quality (BDAG 913), like worthless fish (even when freshly caught, Matt 13.48) or a worthless tree (Matt 7.17–18); see also the footnote on 16.14. The corresponding Syriac is **evil** (*byšt',* as in Mark 7.21–23).

[227] **That.** Greek *hoti* could mean either **that** (as in 1.3; 2.32b) or "because" (as in 1.2; 2.32a). In the latter case, the sense would be that the sinners should have been mindful of God, because He knows all things. Syriac *d-* supports the rendering **that,** and so does Sir 23.19, on which the

known in His sight (Prov 5.21; Jer 16.17) at **all** times (Sir 17.15), **and He understands the inner rooms of the heart** (the "concealed things of the heart," Psa 44.21) **before they come to be** (Isa 42.9; John 13.19; Jer 1.5). "There is no creature unrevealed in His sight, but all things are naked and exposed to the eyes of Him with whom is our account" (Heb 4.13).

The inheritance of the sinners and the righteous

14.6 [9] δια τοῦτο ἡ κληρονομία αὐτῶν ᾅδησ καὶ σκότοσ καὶ ἀπώλεια·	ܡܛܠܗܕܐ ܝܪܬܘܬܗܘܢ܇ ܫܝܘܠ ܘܐܒܕܢܐ ܘܚܫܘܟܐ.
Because of this, their inheritance *will be* Hades and darkness and destruction,	Because of this, their inheritance *will be* Sheol and destruction and darkness,
καὶ οὐχ ευρεθήσονται ἐν ἡμέρα ἐλέουσ δικαίων·	ܘܒܝܘܡܐ ܕܚܢܢܐ ܕܙܕ̈ܝܩܐ ܠܐ ܢܫܬܟܚܘܢ܆.
and they will not be found in *the* day of mercy of *the* righteous *ones*;	and in the day of mercy of the righteous *ones* they will not be found;
14.7 [10] οἱ δὲ ὅσιοι κ(υρίο)υ κληρονομήσουσιν ζωὴν ἐν ευφροσύνῃ:	ܚܣܝ̈ܕܘܗܝ ܕܝܢ ܕܡܪܝܐ ܢܐܪܬܘܢ ܚ̈ܝܐ ܒܚܕܘܬܐ.
but the Lord's lovingkind *ones* will inherit life in gladness.	for the LORD's lovingkind *ones* will inherit life in gladness.

14.6 Because the sinners have loved evil and have not been mindful of God (vv 4–5), **their inheritance will be:**

- **Hades** (Greek) ≡ **Sheol** (Syriac), the Greek and Semitic names for the abode of the dead (*das Totenreich,* Holm-Nielsen), a realm of torment for the wicked (Luke 16.23; in that sense, contrasted with heaven, Matt 11.23). Sinners' evil deeds "will pursue them even to Hades below" (15.11). The righteous are redeemed from the hand of Sheol (Psa 49.15; Prov 15.24); but the wicked will pass from it only into the final lake of fire (Rev 20.13–14).
- **Darkness.** The righteous are delivered out of the power of darkness (Col 1.13) into God's marvelous light (1 Pet 2.9); but the wicked "will be cast out into the outer darkness" (Matt 8.11–12; 22.13; 25.30); "the gloom of darkness has been kept to lasting time" for them (2 Pet 2.17, 4).
- **Destruction.** The wicked are "bringing on themselves quick destruction" (2 Pet 2.1, 3; Matt 7.13); "they will be punished with eternal destruction from the face of the Lord" on the last day (2 Thes 1.9).

---

present passage was based (the sinner "does not know that [*hoti* ≡ *d-*] the Lord's eyes are ten thousand times brighter than the sun, looking on all the paths of Men, and perceiving into the hidden parts").

They have loved darkness (John 3.19) and destruction (Rom 3.15–16), and those are the very things that they will receive (cf. Psa 109.17).

The **day of mercy of the righteous ones** is the day when **mercy** is shown to the **righteous ones** (15.15—just as "their mercy," 2.8, is the mercy shown to them, and "the anger of unrighteous ones," 15.6, is the anger shown to unrighteous ones). **In** that **day** (2 Tim 1.18), the sinners **will not be found.** Sinners "will not stand in the judgment" (Psa 1.5–6). They may flourish for a little while (v 4), but there will come a time when they will no longer be found (Psa 37.36), like Antiochus the Great (Dan 11.19) and the proud city of Tyre: "you will not be; and you will be sought for, and you will not be found any more to lasting time" (Ezek 26.21).

14.7 But the Lord's lovingkind ones will inherit the opposite of Hades and destruction—namely **life** (cf. Psa 16.10–11). They "have passed out of death into life" even in the present age (1 Jn 3.14; John 5.24), and "in the age to come" they "will inherit lasting life" (Mark 10.30; Matt 19.29).

In gladness. "Lasting joy will be on their head; gladness and joy will overtake them; sorrow and sighing will flee" (Isa 51.11). Even in the present age they "are glad with a joy that cannot be spoken and that is glorified" (1 Pet 1.6, 8; Php 3.1; 4.4); and "at the revelation of His glory" they will "rejoice gladly" even more (1 Pet 4.13; Jude 24). On that day every "good and faithful servant" will "enter into the joy" of the Lord (Matt 25.21, 23), as Jesus Himself did (Heb 12.2; Acts 2.28).

Psalm 15

Like its two predecessors, this psalm contrasts the inheritances of the sinners and the righteous. The relationship between the three psalms is particularly close in their concluding lines:

Eighteen Psalms 13	Eighteen Psalms 14	Eighteen Psalms 15
Sinners will be taken to **destruction** (13.10)	The sinners' inheritance will be **Hades** and **darkness** and **destruction** (14.6)	The sinners' inheritance will be **destruction** and **darkness**; their sins will pursue them even to **Hades** below (15.11)
The **life** of the righteous ones will be to lasting time, and the Lord's **mercy** will be on the lovingkind ones... on those who fear Him (13.9, 11)	In the day of **mercy** of the righteous ones... the Lord's lovingkind ones will inherit **life** (14.6–7)	Those who fear the Lord **will receive mercy** in the day of judgment; they **will live** by their God's **deeds of mercy** (15.15)

God is the hope of the poor

15.0 [0] Ψαλμὸς τῷ Cαλωμῶν μετα ᾠδῆς: A psalm belonging to Solomon, with a song.	
15.1 [1] Ἐν τῷ θλίβεσθαί με ἐπεκαλεσάμην τὸ ὄνομα κ(υρίο)υ· In my oppression I called on the name of *the* Lord;	ܒܐܘܠܨܝ ܓܝܪ ܩܪܝܬ ܫܡܗ ܕܡܪܝܐ. In my oppression I called on *the* name of the LORD,
εἰσ βοήθειαν ‹ἤλπισα› τοῦ θ(εο)ῦ Ἰακὼβ καὶ ἐσώθην· I hoped for *the* help of the God of Jacob, and I was saved,	ܘܠܡܥܕܪܢܝ ܩܪܝܬ ܠܐܠܗܗ ܕܝܥܩܘܒ. ܘܐܬܦܪܩܬ and for my help I called to *the* God of Jacob, and I was saved,
15.2 [1] ὅτι ἐλπὶσ καὶ καταφυγὴ τ(ῶν) πτωχῶν σύ ὁ θ(εό)σ· because You†, O God, *are the* hope and refuge of the poor *ones*.	ܡܛܠ ܕܣܒܪܐ ܘܒܝܬ ܓܘܣܐ ܕܡܣܟ̈ܢܐ ܐܢܬ ܗ̣ܘ ܐܠܗܐ. because You†, God, are the hope and house of refuge of the poor *ones*.

15.1 ἤλπισα 336⁺260 ≡ 16h1 10h1 \| ἐσώθην 253 •

15.1–2[228] The **poor** (Greek *ptōchōn* ≡ Syriac *mskn'*) are those who are lacking (18.2–3) and in need, whether they are "poor as to the world" (e.g., in need of food or clothing, Jas 2.5, 15) or "poor in spirit" (Matt 5.3). **God** is their **hope** and **refuge** (their "place to flee": see the footnote on 5.2), because they are the very people whom He saves (Psa 18.27; 35.10; 72.4, 12–14; 147.6).

So, **in** the time of **oppression** when the Eighteen Psalms were written (1.1), God's people **called on the name of the Lord** (see on 6.1) and **hoped**[229] **for** His **help** (5.13), and they were **saved** from their oppression (as described in 13.2; cf. Psa 34.6). "Every request of a soul who is hoping toward Him, the Lord fulfills" (6.8). "The LORD . . . brings a poor one to safety from the one who is stronger than him" (Psa 35.10)—as He did when Christ saved His people from the devil (Psa 72.12–14; Luke 11.20–22).

Those who confess God's name will never be shaken

15.3 [2] τίσ γὰρ ἰσχύει ὁ θ(εό)σ εἰ μὴ ἐξομολογήσασθαί σοι ἐν αληθεία·	ܡܢܘ ܓܝܪ ܕܡܫܟܚ ܢܘܕܐ ܠܟ ܒܫܪܪܐ.

[228] In the Greek copies (but not in the Syriac), the psalm is superscribed **A psalm belonging to Solomon, with a song** (cf. v 5).

[229] **I hoped** (Greek) apparently corresponds to Hebrew *qwyty,* while **I called** (Syriac) in the same clause corresponds to Hebrew *qryty.* The two occur together in Psa 130.1, 5: "I have called on You [*qr'tyk*], LORD . . . . I have waited for [*qwyty*] the LORD."

For who has strength, O God, except to confess to You† in truth?	For who that *is* powerful will confess to You† in truth?
15.4 [2] καὶ τί δυνατὸσ ἄν(θρωπ)οσ εἰ μὴ ἐξομολογήσασθαι τῷ ὀνόματί σου·	ܘܡܢܘ ܚܝܠܗ ܕܒܪܐܢܫܐ. ܐܠܐ ܕܢܘܕܐ ܠܫܡܟ.
and why *is* a person powerful, except to confess to Your† name?	and what *is the* might of a son of man, except to confess to Your† name?

15.3–4 The term **confess** (Greek *exomologēsasthai* ≡ Syriac *nwdʾ*) refers sometimes to public declaration of sin (9.12), sometimes, as here, to acknowledgement and praise of God's righteousness and lovingkindness (see the comments on 3.3; 10.6–7). The present passage is concerned particularly with confession presented to God in song ("a new psalm with a song," v 5); we are "to glorify God for His mercy, just as it is written, 'Therefore I will confess [*exomologēsomai* ≡ *ʾwdʾ*] to You among the nations, and I will psalm to Your name'" (Rom 15.9 ≡ Psa 18.49). **Who has strength . . . except** to do that?[230] Whatever **strength** we have has been given to us by God (1 Chr 29.12; Psa 18.32), and He has given it to us "so that in all things God may be glorified" (1 Pet 4.11; 2.9; Isa 43.7)—not for us to remain inactive and ungrateful (asleep, 3.1). "You shall love the Lord your God . . . with all your strength" (Mark 12.30), and we are to sing praises to Him with all our strength (2 Sam 6.5, LXX ≡ 1 Chr 13.8).

The confession is to be uttered **in truth:** not in pretence (Php 1.18; 1 Tim 2.7) or with the tongue only (1 Jn 3.18), but from the heart (v 5). "Those who worship Him must worship Him in spirit and truth" (John 4.24).

15.5 [3] ψαλμὸν καινὸν μετὰ ᾠδῆσ ἐν εὐφροσύνῃ καρδίασ·	ܘܬܫܒܚܬܐ ܚܕܬܐ ܒܩܠܐ ܒܚܕܘܬܐ ܕܠܒܐ.
A new psalm with a song in gladness of heart,	A new song with the voice in gladness of the heart,
καρπὸν χειλέων ἐν οργάνω ἡρμοσμένω γλώσσησ·	ܦܐܪܐ ܕܣܦܘܬܐ ܒܡܐܢܐ ܕܡܬܩܢ ܒܠܫܢܐ.
the fruit of lips with *the* matched instrument of *the* tongue,	the fruit of the lips with an instrument that *is* set in order, with the tongue,

[230] **Who has strength . . . except to confess to You?** is the reading of the Greek. The existing Syriac text reads **Who that is powerful will confess to You?** Kuhn (*Die älteste Textgestalt der Psalmen Salomos,* 39) suggested that the term "except" had been accidentally omitted from the Syriac, since it is present in the next line (v 4) in both Greek and Syriac. Even so, the existing Syriac text still makes sense: those who are **powerful** are indeed prone to "forget the LORD" (Deut 8.10–14; 6.10–12; Hos 13.6; Prov 30.8–9).

ἀπαρχὴν χειλέων ἀπὸ καρδίασ ὁσίασ καὶ δικαίασ·	ܪ̈ܫܝܬܐ ܕܣܦ̈ܘܬܐ ܡܢ ܠܒܐ ܢܟܦܐ ܘܙܕܝܩܐ.
the firstfruits of lips from a heart lovingkind and righteous—	the firstfruits of the lips from a heart lovingkind and righteous—

15.5 Every **psalm** offered to God by His people is to be a **new psalm:** see the comments on 3.2. It is to be offered **in gladness of heart** (5.1; 10.6; "with all my heart," Psa 9.1–2) **from a heart lovingkind and righteous.** An evil heart cannot bring forth utterances that are acceptable to God (Matt 12.34–35; 15.18–20). "Those who are crooked of heart are an abomination to the LORD" (Prov 11.20), even when they worship Him (Prov 28.9; 15.29; Psa 66.18); they must first have their hearts cleansed with the cleansing that He provides (Acts 2.37–38; 15.9; 8.21–23), and only then will they be able to offer worship that is acceptable to Him (Psa 51.19; Heb 10.22).

A psalm is the **fruit of lips,** given to God as an offering of **firstfruits.** Under the old covenant, His people were commanded to present Him with an offering "from the first of all the fruit of the land" (Deut 26.2; 18.4; Num 18.12): "Glorify the LORD from your possessions, and from the firstfruits of all your produce" (Prov 3.9)—as Abel did (Gen 4.4), and as Eli's sons did not (1 Sam 2.29). Those who sing psalms, similarly, "offer up to God a sacrifice of praise continually—that is, the fruit of lips that confess to His name" (Heb 13.15). In this activity the **lips** and **tongue** are to be **matched** (Greek)—that is, **set in order** (Syriac) **with** one another, "tuned" to match one another (OTP).[231] A human body is not to be "double-worded" (*dilogous,* 1 Tim 3.8), speaking both good and bad (Jas 3.9–12). Its members are to act in harmony (1 Cor 12.14–26) and speak in harmony (Sir 5.9–10), like the members of Christ's body (1 Cor 12.12), "so that singlemindedly with one mouth you may glorify the God and Father of our Lord Jesus Christ" (Rom 15.6).

15.6 [4] ὁ ποιῶν ταῦτα οὐ σαλευθήσεται εἰσ τὸν αἰῶνα ἀπὸ κακοῦ·	ܟܠ ܕܥܒܕ ܗܠܝܢ ܠܐ ܢܬܬܙܝܥ ܠܥܠܡ ܡܢ ܒܝܫܐ.
the *one* who does these *things* will not be shaken to lasting time by evil;	every*one* who does these *things* will not be disturbed to lasting time by evil.
φλὸξ πυρὸσ καὶ ὀργὴ ἀδίκων ‹οὐχ› ἅψεται αὐτοῦ·	<ܫܠܗܒܝܬܐ> ܕܢܘܪܐ ܘܪܘܓܙܐ ܕܥܘ̈ܠܐ ܠܐ ܢܬܩܪܒ ܠܗܘܢ.
the flame of fire and *the* anger of unrighteous *ones* will not touch him,	The flame of fire and the anger of unrighteous *ones* will not touch them,

[231] **Matched** (*hērmosmenō,* Greek) ≡ **set in order** (*mtqn,* Syriac). As in verse 3, the wording is based on that of 2 Sam 6.5, LXX (B = f^{93} = A), where David and his companions sang praises to the Lord "with matched instruments with all their strength." The Jacobite Syriac rendering there is *mlḥm'* ("fitted," "harmonized").

15.7 [5] ὅταν ἐξέλθῃ ‹ἐπὶ› ἁμαρτωλοὺσ ἀπὸ προσώπου κ(υρίο)υ·	ܐܡܬܝ ܕܢܦܘܩ ܥܠ ܚܛܝܐ ܡܢ ܩܕܡ ܡܪܝܡܐ.
whenever it shall go out against sinners from *the* Lord's face	when it goes out against sinners from before the High *One*
ὀλεθρεῦσαι πᾶσαν ὑπόστασιν ἁμαρτωλῶν·	ܠܡܥܩܪ ܟܠܗܘܢ ܥܩܪܝܗܘܢ ܕܥܘܠܐ.
to destroy every foundation of sinners,	to uproot all *the* roots of unjust *ones*,

15.6 ܒܠܗܒܝܬܐ 10h1 [φλὸξ 253 336⁺260] | ܕܒ- 16h1 • οὐχ 336⁺260 | οὐκ 253 • **15.7** ἐπὶ 336⁺260 | ἐφ 253 •

15.6–7 The one who does these things—the person who offers acceptable sacrifices of praise to God (vv 3–5)—**will not be shaken to lasting time by evil.** He "will not fall to lasting time" (Psa 15.5; 112.6), because the LORD will support him (Psa 37.23–24). **Anger**[232] and a **flame of fire** will eventually **go out**[233] **against sinners from the Lord's face to destroy every foundation** (Psa 82.5) **of sinners:** "the LORD will swallow them in His anger, and fire will devour them" (Psa 21.9; Rev 14.10). But that anger, that fire, and that destruction **will not touch** the righteous (13.5; just as the destruction of the firstborn in Egypt "did not touch them," Heb 11.28). When the wicked "depart . . . into the lasting fire," the righteous will be blessed with eternal life in the Father's kingdom (Matt 25.31–46).

15.8 [6] ὅτι τὸ σημεῖον τοῦ θ(εο)ῦ ἐπι δικαίουσ εἰσ σωτηρίαν·	ܡܛܠ ܕܐܬܗ ܓܝܪ ܕܡܪܝܐ ܥܠ ܙܕܝܩܐ ܠܦܘܪܩܢܐ.
because the sign of God *is* upon righteous *one*s for salvation;	because *the* sign of the LORD *is* upon the righteous *one*s for salvation;
[7] λιμὸσ καὶ ῥομφαία καὶ θάνατοσ· ἀπο δικαίων μακρὰν·	ܡܘܬܐ ܓܝܪ ܘܪܘܡܚܐ ܘܟܦܢܐ ܡܢ ܙܕܝܩܐ ܢܪܚܩܘܢ.
hunger and sword and death *will be* far from *the* righteous *one*s,	for death and the sword and hunger will be far off from the righteous *one*s,

[232] The context shows that this **anger of unrighteous ones** is the anger that will **go out against** unrighteous ones (not the anger that unrighteous ones direct against the righteous)—just as "the mercy of righteous ones" (14.6; 2.8) is the mercy shown to righteous ones (not the mercy that righteous ones show to others).

[233] **It shall go out** (*exelthē,* Greek ≡ *npwq,* Syriac). The subject of the singular verb may be either the **flame** plus **anger** in the preceding clause (they are two descriptions of a single entity; cf. 1 Cor 15.50; John 1.17; Viteau, *Sujet,* §141*b;* MHT 3.314, §4(vii); Nöldeke §322), or else the **evil** mentioned in the clause before that. The sense is not affected; the **evil** (i.e., harm) that God brings on evildoers (Isa 31.2; Josh 23.15) *is* the **flame** of His **anger** (Psa 78.48–49).

15.9 [7] φεύξονται γὰρ ὡσ διωκόμένου ‹› λιμοῦ ἀπὸ ὁσίων· for they will flee from *the* lovingkind *one*s, like those who are being pursued by hunger,	ܢܥܪܩܘܢ ܓܝܪ ܡܢܗܘܢ. ܐܝܟ ܕܥܪܩ ܡܘܬܐ ܡܢ ܚܝܐ. for they will flee from them, like death fleeing from living *one*s,

15.9 λιμοῦ 260 [ܡܘܬܐ 16h1 10h1] | ^ ἀπὸ 253 336 •

15.8–9a In the day when the Lord judges sinners, **righteous ones** will not be touched by His anger (v 6), **because the sign** [*sēmeion*] **of God is upon** them **for salvation.** In the Babylonian era, God set a **sign** (*sēmeion,* LXX) on the foreheads of the righteous people in Jerusalem; those people would be spared, when all the others were destroyed (Ezek 9.4–10). During the present age also, the servants of God are sealed on their foreheads; those people will not be harmed, when destruction falls upon the others (Rev 7.3; 9.4; cf. Eph 4.30).

The Lord's terrible judgments—**hunger and sword and death** (disease), as described in 13.2—**will be far from the righteous ones.** Yes, many righteous people have suffered in the flesh from hunger (2 Cor 11.27) and the sword (Heb 11.37) and death by disease (2 Kgs 13.14). Yet none of those things "will touch" them (see the comments on 13.5); all such things will remain **far from** them. "By God's power they are being guarded through faith for salvation" (1 Pet 1.5; 2 Pet 2.9; 2 Cor 1.8–10). Jesus, similarly, promised His disciples that, even though "they will put some of you to death" in the flesh, "not a hair of your head will be destroyed at all" (Luke 21.16–18). "Many evils" will afflict a "righteous one, but from all of them the LORD will bring him to safety," without allowing any part of him to be harmed (Psa 34.19–20; 91.5–12; Rom 8.35–39; Sir 33.1). The Scripture teaching on this subject is faithfully summarized in the book of Wisdom: "The souls of the righteous are in the hand of God, and no torment will touch them at all. In the eyes of the thoughtless they seemed to have died, and their departure was reckoned as an evil thing ... but they are in peace, for ... their hope is full of immortality" (Wis 3.1–4). Jesus promised, "The one who believes in Me, even if he shall die ... shall certainly not die, to lasting time" (John 11.25–26).

God's judgments are so terrible that birds and animals, mountains and islands, and even heaven and earth flee from them (Jer 4.23–25; 9.10; Rev 16.20; 20.11)—yet, amazingly, those judgments will themselves **flee from** the righteous (cf. Lev 26.7–8; Deut 28.7). The Lord's judgments inescapably pursue their victims (v 9b; Jer 29.18)—yet in the presence of the righteous, it will be as if those judgments **are** themselves **being pursued.**

Here the Greek and Syriac versions differ somewhat in detail, although the basic point is the same in both.

The similarities and differences are best seen in a rendering that attempts to follow the word order of each text:

Hunger and sword and death ... will flee,
like those pursued by hunger, from lovingkind ones (Greek).
Death and the sword[234] **and hunger ... will flee,**
like fleeing death, from living ones (Syriac).

This shows (i) that Greek **lovingkind ones** corresponds to Syriac **living ones,**[235] and (ii) that in each language the first named of the three notorious pursuers is the one named in the final clause (**hunger,** Greek; **death,** Syriac). The main difference is that the Greek pictures **hunger**[236] as the pursuer in that final image,[237] whereas the Syriac pictures **death** as the pursuee. Even so, in both languages the dreaded destroyer is evoked only to emphasize that it, and all its associates, **will flee from** those whom God protects. That is a startling paradox—but no more startling than the familiar paradox that death will itself undergo death (Rev 20.14).

Sinners will be destroyed in the day of judgment

[8] καταδιώξονται δὲ ἁμαρτωλοὺσ καὶ καταλήμψονται· but they will pursue after *the* sinners and take hold of *them,*	ܢܪܕܦܘܢ ܕܝܢ ܒܬܪ ܥܘܠܐ ܘܢܕܪܟܘܢ ܐܢܘܢ܀ but they will pursue after the unjust *one*s and overtake them,
καὶ οὐκ εκφεύξονται οἱ ποιοῦντεσ ἀνομίαν τὸ κρῖμα κ(υρίο)υ· and those who are doing a deed opposed to *the* Law will not escape the Lord's judgment;	ܘܐܝܠܝܢ ܕܥܒܕܝܢ ܥܘܠܐ ܠܐ ܢܥܪܩܘܢ ܡܢ ܕܝܢܗ ܕܡܪܝܐ and those who *are* doing injustice will not flee away from the LORD's judgment,

[234] **Sword.** For this rendering of Syriac *rwmḥ',* see the footnote on 13.2.

[235] Syriac *ḥy'* could also be translated "life" (Trafton), but comparison with the Greek suggests the rendering **living ones** (as in 2 Tim 4.1, Syr). The word was emended by Harris-Mingana to *ḥsy'* (≡ Greek *hosiōn,* **lovingkind ones**). The conjectural reconstruction "famine, sword, and death ... will flee from the devout and pestilence from the living" (Wright) suffers from two problems: (a) it fails to recognize that "the devout" (Greek) and "the living" (Syriac) are renderings of the same term (as the word order shows); (b) it fails to account for the presence of **like** in all existing texts (Greek *hōs* ≡ Syriac *'yk*).

[236] **Hunger** (*limou,* 260; *apo limou,* 253 and 336) has been conjecturally emended by some editors to "war" (*polemou,* Gebhardt and Rahlfs; *apo polemou,* Perles and Viteau). The emendation loses symmetry (in the existing text, hunger is forced to do what it proverbially makes others do), and it gains nothing (in the Scriptures, hunger is just as deadly a pursuer of victims as war is, Jer 29.18).

[237] The rendering "as famine being pursued by the holy ones" (Trafton) is grammatically impossible; those who are **being pursued** are plural *(diōkomenoi).* At this point the Syriac could not be merely a free translation of the existing Greek; it must derive from a slightly different text (either in Greek or in Hebrew).

[9] ὡσ ὑπὸ πολεμίων ἐμπείρων καταλημφθήσονται· they will be taken hold of, as *if* by *one*s well-tried in making war,	ܐܝܟ ܝ̈ܕܥܝ ܩܪܒܐ ܢܕܒܪܘܢ ܐܢܘܢ܀ for like *one*s who know war they will go before them,
15.10 [10] τὸ γὰρ σημεῖον τῆσ ἀπωλείασ ἐπι τοῦ μετώπου αὐτ(ῶν)· for the sign of destruction *is* on their forehead.	ܡܛܠ ܕܐܬܐ ܕܐܒܕܢܐ ܥܠ ܐ̈ܦܝܗܘܢ܀ because the sign of destruction *is* on their faces.

15.9b Although **hunger and the sword and death** will flee from righteous ones (vv 8–9a), **they will pursue after sinners** (Jer 29.18; Prov 13.21) **and take hold of them** (cf. 1 Thes 5.4)—in accordance with Moses' prophecy that, if Israel did not obey the Lord, "all these curses . . . will pursue after you and overtake you" (Deut 28.45; Psa 7.3–5, LXX ≡ Syr). The forces that **take hold of** the sinners will be expert and strong, like a horde of soldiers **well-tried in making war,** relentlessly pursuing after and overtaking a fleeing victim (2 Kgs 25.5, LXX ≡ Syr); none of those who disobey God's **Law** will **escape** His **judgment.** "Not an escapee of them will escape; if they dig through into Sheol, from there My hand will take them; and if they go up to the heavens, from there I will bring them down" (Amos 9.1–2). "Sudden destruction will come upon them . . . and they will not at all escape" (1 Thes 5.2–3).

15.10 "The sign of God is on righteous ones for salvation" (v 8), but sinners are marked in the opposite way: **the sign of destruction is on their forehead.** In John's prophecy, "a mark on their right hand, or on their forehead," is given to all those who worship the beast that is speaking blasphemies against God (Rev 13.16–17); and "if anyone . . . receives the mark of the beast on his forehead, or on his right hand, he himself also will drink from the wine of God's anger . . . and he will be tormented with fire and sulfur . . . and the smoke of their torment goes up to lasting times of lasting times" (Rev 14.9–11).

15.11 [10] καὶ ἡ κληρονομία τῶν ἁμαρτωλῶν ἀπολεία καὶ σκότοσ· And the sinners' inheritance *will be* destruction and darkness,	ܘܝܪܬܘܬܗܘܢ ܕܚ̈ܛܝܐ ܐܒܕܢܐ ܘܚܫܘܟܐ: And *the* sinners' inheritance *will be* destruction and darkness,
καὶ ‹αἱ› ἀνομίαι αὐτῶν διώξονται αὐτοὺσ ἕωσ ᾅδου κάτω· and their deeds opposed to *the* Law will pursue them even to Hades below.	ܘܥܘܠܗܘܢ ܢܪܕܘܦ ܐܢܘܢ ܥܕܡܐ ܠܫܝܘܠ ܬܚܬܝܬܐ. and their injustice will pursue after them even to Sheol below;
15.12 [11] ἡ κληρονομία αὐτ(ῶν)· οὐχ ευρεθήσεται τοῖσ τέκνοισ αὐτῶν·	ܘܝܪܬܘܬܗܘܢ ܠܐ ܢܫܬܟܚ ܠܒ̈ܢܝܗܘܢ܀

Their inheritance will not be found for their children,	and their inheritance will not be found for their sons,
15.13 [11] αἱ γὰρ ἁμαρτίαι ‹ἐξερημώσουσιν› οἴκουσ ἁμαρτωλῶν· for sins will make sinners' houses desolate,	ܣܟܠܘ̈ܬܗܘܢ ܓܝܪ ܡܚܪܒܢ ܒ̈ܬܐ ܕܚ̈ܛܝܐ. for sins will make the sinners' houses desolate,
[12] καὶ ἀπολοῦνται ἁμαρτωλοὶ ἐν ἡμέρα κρίσεωσ κ(υρίο)υ εἰσ τὸν αἰῶνα· and sinners will be destroyed in *the* day of *the* Lord's judgment to lasting time,	ܘܢܐܒܕܘܢ ܚ̈ܛܝܐ ܒܝܘܡܐ ܕܕܝܢܗ ܕܡܪܝܐ ܠܥܠܡ. and the sinners will be destroyed in the day of the LORD's judgment to lasting time,
15.14 [12] ὅτ᾽ ἂν ἐπισκέπτηται ὁ θ(εὸ)σ τὴν γῆν ἐν κρίματι αὐτοῦ· whenever God shall watch over the earth in His judgment;	ܐܡܬܝ ܕܣܥܪ ܐܠܗܐ ܐܪܥܐ ܒܕܝܢܗ. when the LORD *is* looking on the earth in His judgment;

15.11 αἱ 336⁺260 | > 253 • **15.13** ἐξερημώσουσιν 336⁺260 | -μώσωσιν 253 •

15.11–14 Under the old covenant, God promised every family in Israel an earthly **inheritance** in the promised land (Num 26.51–56) provided they obeyed Him faithfully (Deut 4.40; 16.20). Generation by generation, this inheritance would be handed down to the family's **children** or nearest relatives (Num 27.8–11). But if the people disobeyed the Lord, they would be deprived of their inheritance (Lev 20.22–26; Deut 28.58, 63; Lam 5.2). "A good person makes his sons' sons inherit" (Prov 13.22), whereas **sins** would **make sinners' houses desolate,**[238] and they would leave no **inheritance . . . for their children** (Psa 109.8–11). Their sins would **pursue them** even after the present life—**even to Hades below,** the realm of the dead (14.6), as in the case of the rich man described by Jesus (Luke 16.23).

The fire of the Lord's anger "burns even to the lowest Sheol" (Deut 32.22); those who have provoked His indignation do not escape from Him there (Amos 9.2; Psa 139.8). Their only **inheritance** will be everlasting **destruction and darkness** (as described in 14.6) in the **day of the Lord's judgment** (Matt 10.15; Rom 2.5; Acts 17.31), the "day of judgment and of destruction of irreverent people" (2 Pet 3.7) when **God shall watch over the earth in His judgment.**

Under the new covenant, God's people inherit salvation (Heb 1.14) and eternal life

---

[238] **Sins will make sinners' houses desolate.** What they have done to other people's houses (4.13; 12.4; Mic 2.2) will be done to them. God rewards us in accordance with what we have done (Psa 28.4); if someone has done evil to others, "evil is not removed from his house" (Prov 17.13).

(Matt 19.29) in His kingdom (Matt 25.34). Like the earthly inheritance under the old covenant, it will be inherited only by those who serve Him faithfully (Acts 20.32; 26.18; Heb 6.12); those who sin will have no inheritance in the kingdom of God unless their sins have been washed away (1 Cor 6.9–11; Gal 5.19–21; Eph 5.5; Rev 21.7–8).

15.15 [13] οἱ δὲ φοβούμενοι τὸν κ(ύριο)ν ἐλεηθήσονται ἐν αὐτῇ· but those who fear the Lord will receive mercy in it,	ܘܥܠ ܐܝܠܝܢ ܕܕܚܠܝܢ ܡܢ ܡܪܝܐ ܢܗܘܘܢ ܪ̈ܚܡܐ. ܒܗ̇ and upon those who fear from the LORD, *there* will be compassions in it,
καὶ ζήσονται ἐν τῇ ἐλεημοσύνῃ τοῦ θ(εο)ῦ αὐτ(ῶν)· and they will live by their God's deeds of mercy;	ܘܢܐܚܘܢ ܒܪ̈ܚܡܘܗ̇ܝ ܕܐܠܗܢ. and they will live by our God's compassion;
καὶ ἁμαρτωλοὶ ἀπολοῦνται εἰσ τὸν αἰῶνα χρόνον: and sinners will be destroyed to lasting time.	ܘܚ̈ܛܝܐ ܢܐܒܕܘܢ ܠܙܒܢܐ ܕܠܥܠܡ. and sinners will be destroyed to *the* time of lasting time.

15.15 Yet for **those who fear the Lord,** the day of the Lord's judgment (vv 13–14) will be a day of **mercy** (14.6; cf. 1 Jn 4.17; 2 Tim 4.8). On that day, they will not **be destroyed** like the **sinners,** but **will live** (14.7)—"not because of works that we have done in righteousness, but in accordance with His own mercy" (Titus 3.4–5). He is "a God of forgiveness, merciful and lovingkind, long to anger and abundant in loving-kindness" (Neh 9.17), and is "rich in mercy," (Eph 2.4); His **deeds of mercy** are "many" (Neh 9.28, 31), and they are lavished to all nations (Rom 11.30–32; 9.23–24; 15.9) and all generations: "His mercy is to generations and generations for those who fear Him" (Luke 1.50).

Psalm 16

The basic situation described in this psalm resembles that in Psalm 73 of the Hebrew Psalter. The psalmist has **little short of slipped** (v 1; Psa 73.2), has suffered chastise-ment (**He pierced me like a horse's goad,** v 4; "I have been struck," Psa 73.14), and gives thanks **because You have helped me for salvation** (v 5; "You have taken hold of my right hand," Psa 73.23).

A tendency toward condensation of language can be seen in many of the Eighteen Psalms (especially in their Greek version). In the present psalm, that tendency reaches its peak, resulting in an exceptional number of abrupt transitions and startling images: **dozed from the Lord** (v 1—not "dozed and fell away from the Lord"); **pierced me like a horse's goad** (v 4—not "pierced me as if with a horse's goad"); **hold power over me… from harmful sin** (v 7) and its antithesis, **placed underneath from useless sin** (v

8); **array my tongue and my lips in words of truth** (v 10); **reproved by the hand of his worthlessness** (v 14); the unexpectedly compressed datives *tō makran* (**when it was far,** v 2) and *eudokia* (**in good pleasure,** v 12). Editors have tended to emend these features, and translators have tended to smooth them out, but we suggest that they are peculiarly appropriate to the psalm's subject matter: of all the Eighteen Psalms, this is the one most intimately concerned with the deepest and most disturbing upheavals of the soul, with personal sin and personal suffering.

I almost slipped, but the Lord helped me

16.0 [0] Ὕμνος τῷ Σαλωμῶν εἰς ἀντίληψιν ὁσίοις: A hymn belonging to Solomon, for help to *the* lovingkind *one*s.	
16.1 [1] Ἐν τῷ νυστάξαι ψυχήν μου ἀπὸ κ(υρίο)υ· When my soul dozed from *the* Lord,	ܟܕ ܐܬܡܗܝܬ ܢܦܫܝ ܩܠܝܠ ܡܢ ܡܪܝܐ. ܟܕ ܩܠܝܠ When my soul looked away from the LORD a little,
παρα μικρὸν ὠλίσθησα ἐν ‹καταφθορᾶ› ὕπνου· I little short of slipped in *the* corruption of sleep;	ܗܘܐ ܗܘܝܬ ܒܨܪ ܡܦܠܬܐ ܕܫܢܬܐ ܕܚܒܠܐ. I was little short of *being* in the downfalls of the sleep of corruption;
16.2 [1] τῷ μακρὰν ἀπὸ θ(εο)ῦ when *it was* far from God,	ܘܟܕ ܐܪܚܩܬ ܡܢ ܡܪܝܐ. and when *I had* gone far off from the LORD,
[2] παρ ολίγον ἐξεχύθη ἡ ψυχή μου εἰσ θάνατον· my soul was little short of poured out to death	ܟܕ ܩܠܝܠ ܡܬܐܫܕܐ ܗܘܬ ܢܦܫܝ ܠܡܘܬܐ my soul was little short of poured out to death
σύνεγγυσ πυλῶν ᾅδου μετὰ ἁμαρτωλοῦ· near *the* gates of Hades with *the* sinner,	ܠܘܬ ܬܪܥܐ ܕܫܝܘܠ ܥܡ ܚܛܝܐ. beside the gates of Sheol with the sinners,
16.3 [3] ἐν τῷ διενεχθῆναι ψυχήν μου ἀπὸ κ(υρίο)υ θ(εο)ῦ Ἰ(σρα)ὴλ· when my soul was carried away from *the* Lord God of Israel,	ܘܟܕ ܐܬܪܟܢܬ ܢܦܫܝ ܡܢ ܐܠܗܗ ܕܐܝܣܪܝܠ. even when my soul sank down from *the* God of Israel,

16.1 καταφθορᾶ 336⁺260 [ܕܚܒܠܐ 16h1] | -φόρα 253 •

εἰ μὴ ὁ κ(ύριο)σ ἀντελάβετό μου τῷ ἐλέει αὐτοῦ εἰσ τὸν αἰῶνα·	ܐܠܘܠܐ ܡܪܝܐ ܥܕܪܢܝ ܒܪ̈ܚܡܘܗܝ ܕܠܥܠܡ.
if the Lord had not helped me by His mercy, *which is* to lasting time.	if the LORD had not helped me by His compassions that *are* to lasting time.

16.1–3[239] The psalmist's **soul** has **dozed**[240]—that is, he has nearly (**little short of**) **slipped** into the **sleep** that consists of **corruption;**[241] his **soul** has nearly perished (it **was little short of poured out to death**). These things are the sleep, corruption, and death that happen when the **soul** is **far from God** (Luke 15.13; Jer 2.5; Matt 15.8 ≡ Isa 29.13), and they are far worse than the mere death and corruption of the body. "Do not fear those who kill the body but are not able to kill the soul; but rather, fear the One who is able to kill both body and soul in hell" (Matt 10.28). That is the death that the **sinner** will ultimately face after he has passed through the **gates of Hades** (the realm of the dead; see on 14.6; 15.11): "The soul that sins . . . will die . . .

[239] In the Greek copies (but not in the Syriac), the psalm is superscribed **A hymn belonging to Solomon, for help to the lovingkind ones** (cf. vv 3–5).

[240] The Greek has **dozed** (*nustaxai,* like the virgins in Jesus' parable, Matt 25.5) **from the Lord.** Notice the characteristically forceful compression of sense in **dozed from** ("dozed and fell away from" might have been expected); compare "hold power over me from," v 7; "placed underneath from," v 8; "surrounded from," 10.1; "destroyed from," 12.5; "warred away from," Maccabaica 14.26 (see the comments and footnote there). The Syriac has **looked away** (*'hmyt,* as in Deut 22.1) **from the LORD** (the opposite of looking toward the Lord: cf. Luke 12.36; Heb 12.2).

[241] **Corruption** *(kataphthora)* is the reading of 336⁺260, and is supported by the Syriac *(ḥbl')* and by the parallel with **death.** The reading of 253 is "sinking" *(kataphora).* Like **death,** the term **corruption** is applied in the Scriptures sometimes to the perishing of the body (Psa 49.9, LXX ≡ Syr; 1 Cor 15.42), sometimes (as here) to the perishing of the soul because of sin (Gen 6.11–12, LXX ≡ Syr; Gal 6.8; 2 Pet 2.12).

Corruption of sleep (Greek) ≡ **sleep of corruption** (Syriac); the construction is inverted but the sense is equivalent. Similarly, "menstruation of blood" (Greek) ≡ "blood of menstruation" (Syriac) in 8.13; "beauty of his anger" (Greek) ≡ "anger of his beauty" (Syriac) in 17.14. In some cases, such inversions occurred in Hebrew: "flint of rock" (Deut 32.13) ≡ "rock of flint" (Deut 8.15); "the flood of waters" (Gen 6.17) ≡ "waters of the flood" (Gen 7.7); "repetition of silver" (Gen 43.15) ≡ "silver of repetition" (Gen 43.12). In other cases, the inversion was introduced during translation into Greek: "end of time" (θ') ≡ "time of the end" (MT) in Dan 8.17; "in a fire of flame" (LXX) ≡ "in a flame of fire" (Hebrew) in Sir 8.10; 45.19. See Schulz, "Der Status constructus in der Geschichte der Exegese," 270–77.

Gebhardt and Rahlfs conjecturally emended Greek *hupnou tō* to *hupnountōn,* turning **in the corruption of sleep; when I was far from God** into a single clause: "in the corruption of those who sleep far from God." However, the Syriac version supports the Greek in this respect (indeed, it separates the two clauses with the conjunction *w-*), and the psalm's opening clause confirms that the psalmist himself has departed **from the Lord.**

but if the wicked one turns back from all his sins that he did, and keeps all of My assigned instructions, and does justice and righteousness—living, he will live; he will not die" (Ezek 18.20–21). "Those who are far away from You are destroyed" (Psa 73.27). Even in the present life, to be **far from** God is to be already close to (**little short of**) that death. Someone who has departed from the Lord is already dozing spiritually, and needs to wake out of that sleep (v 4; Rom 13.11; Eph 5.14; 1 Thes 5.6; 1 Cor 15.34) before it is too late.

The psalmist was being **carried away** (*dienechthēnai,* like the helpless ship heading for disaster in Acts 27.27); he had no power to save himself (cf. Psa 89.48), and would certainly have perished **if the Lord had not helped me by His mercy** (as He helped that ship, Acts 27.21–24). "If the LORD had not been for us ... the waters would have swallowed us"; He, and He alone, has been "our help" (Psa 124.1–4, 8; see also the comments on v 13). "He will bring to safety the needy one who cries for help ... and there is no helper for him" (Psa 72.12; Rom 7.24; 8.2). And His **mercy** exists **to lasting time** (Psa 136.1–26): it is available **at every time** (v 4). "His mercy is to generations and generations for those who fear Him" (Luke 1.50); it is "from lasting time and to lasting time" (Psa 103.17).

16.4 [4] ἔνυξέν με ὡσ κέντρον ἵππου ἐπὶ τὴν γρηγόρησιν αὐτοῦ· He pierced me like a horse's goad to attain His alertness;	ܕܩܪܢܝ ܐܝܟ ܥܘܩܬܐ ܕܣܘܣܝܐ ܠܥܝܪܘܬܗ. He pierced me like a horse's goad to attain His wakefulness;
ὁ σωτὴρ καὶ ἀντιλήπτωρ μου ἐν παντὶ καιρῷ ἔσωσέν με· my Savior and Helper at every time saved me.	ܦܪܘܩܝ ܘܡܥܕܪܢܝ ܒܟܠܙܒܢ ܗܘ. ܐܚܝܢܝ. He is my Savior and my Helper at every time; He made me to live.

16.4 The Lord **pierced me, like a horse's goad,**[242] **to attain His alertness**—the alertness that He requires, and that He Himself possesses (as in 3.2: see the comments there). An animal like a horse is not easily trained: "there is no making it to understand" without unpleasant constraints (Psa 32.9)—and in that respect a human fool requires similar treatment (Prov 26.3; cf. Jer 31.18). In all situations we ought to keep alert (*grēgoreō,* Matt 25.1–13; Mark 13.34–37; 1 Thes 5.6; 1 Pet 5.8) and be quick to hear and respond to our Master (Jas 1.19; Psa 119.60; Acts 22.16). But far too often we humans are slow to grasp what even those who are under our authority—the dumb animals—know (Isa 1.3; Jer 8.7). How many times the Lord has had to rouse

---

[242] **He pierced me like a horse's goad.** The juxtaposition of **pierced** and **goad** (*kentron,* accusative) is unsettlingly direct, imitating the act itself; normally the accusative would be reserved for the thing pierced, and the implement would be treated as a dative (e.g., "pierced his side [*pleuran,* accusative] with a spear [*logchē,* dative]," John 19.34). In English, similarly, we would find it more comfortable to say "as if <u>with</u> a horse's goad."

up His people (Psa 106.43; Neh 9.28, 31)! How much labor we have caused Him, and often with how little result (Jer 7.25–26; Luke 20.10–15)!

By that means **My Savior . . . saved me.** God's words are goads (Ecc 12.11). We may try "to kick against the goads," as Saul the Pharisee did (Acts 26.14), but they have the power to save us (Acts 11.14; Jas 1.21), just as the people who "were pierced to the heart" on the Day of Pentecost were **saved** when they "accepted the word" (Acts 2.37–41).

16.5 [5] ἐξομολογήσομαί σοι ὁ θ(εό)σ ὅτι ‹ἀντελάβου› μου εἰσ σωτηρίαν:	ܐܘܕܐ ܠܟ ܐܠܗܐ. ܡܛܠ ܕܥܕܪܬܢܝ ܒܦܘܪܩܢܟ.
I will confess to You†, O God, because You† have helped me for salvation,	I will confess to You†, God, because You† have helped me with Your† salvation,
καὶ οὐκ ‹ἐλογίσω με› μετὰ τ(ῶν) ἁμαρτωλῶν εἰσ ἀπώλειαν·	ܘܠܐ ܚܫܒܬܢܝ ܥܡ <> ܚܛ̈ܝܐ ܠܐܒܕܢܐ.
and You† have not counted me with the sinners for destruction.	and You† have not counted me with the sinners for destruction.

16.5 ἀντελάβου 260 ≡ ܕܥܕܪܬܢܝ 16h1 | -βετό 253 • ἐλογίσω με 260 = ελογήσωμαι 253 = ἐλογήσομαι 336 ≡ ܚܫܒܬܢܝ 16h1 • ܥܡ ≡ μετὰ 253 $336^{+}260$ | + ܥܡ 16h1 •

16.5 Because God has helped and saved me (vv 3–4), **I will confess to You**—that is, "acknowledge" You (NETS), "give thanks to" You (APOT): see the comments on 3.3. **You have not counted me with the sinners** (cf. Rom 4.8), those who are appointed **for destruction** (see the comments on 14.6). The righteous have indeed sinned (9.15), but they have been "cleansed from sin" (10.1; 9.12, 14; 13.9) and turned back from sin (v 11), and therefore they are no longer **counted** (Greek *elogisō* ≡ Syriac *ḥšbtny*) among the **sinners:** "Blessed is the man to whom the Lord will not count sin" because his sins have been "forgiven" and "covered" (Rom 4.7–8 ≡ Psa 32.1–2). "God was in Christ reconciling the world to Himself, not counting to them their trespasses" (2 Cor 5.19).

Keep me from sin

16.6 [6] μὴ ἀποστήσησ τὸ ἔλεόσ σοῦ ἀπ' ἐμοῦ ὁ θ(εό)σ·	ܠܐ ܬܥܒܪ ܪ̈ܚܡܝܟ ܡܢܝ ܐܠܗܐ.
Do not cause Your† mercy to depart† from me, O God,	Do not take away† Your† compassions from me, God,
μὴ δὲ τὴν μνήμην ‹› σου ἀπὸ καρδίασ ‹μου› ἕωσ θανάτου·	ܘܠܐ ܢܥܒܪ ܕܘܟܪܢܟ ܡܢ ܠܒܝ ܥܕܡܐ ܠܡܘܬܐ.

nor the mindfulness of You† from my heart until death.	and do not let mindfulness of You† depart† from my heart even until death.

16.6 μνήμην 336⁺260 \| + περι 253 • μου 336⁺260 ≡ ,- 16h1 \| > 253 •

16.6 Do not cause Your mercy to depart from me (see the comments on 9.16). "The Lord's mercy is on those who fear Him with judgment" (2.37; 13.11; 15.15; "those who love Him in truth," 4.29; 10.4; 6.9) "from lasting time and to lasting time" (Psa 103.17). But He takes it away from those who reject Him (as He took it away from King Saul, 2 Sam 7.15). Therefore His people pray, "LORD, I seek Your face; do not hide Your face from me; do not turn away Your servant in anger" (Psa 27.8–9; 51.11).

If the Lord's **mercy** is not to **depart from** us, then **mindfulness of** Him (v 9) must not depart from our **heart.** "Be mindful of His marvelous things that He has done, His wonders, and the judgments of His mouth" (Psa 105.5). His word is to be remembered, delighted in, and obeyed (Psa 119.16, 52, 55); His lovingkindness and faithfulness are to be written "on the slab of your heart" (Prov 3.3) and kept there constantly **until death,** because the person "faithful until death" is the one who will receive the crown of life (Rev 2.10; Matt 10.22). "If indeed we hold the beginning of our assurance firm until the end" (Heb 3.14, 6), He "will also establish you even to the end" (1 Cor 1.8; 1 Thes 3.13).

16.7 [7] ἐπικράτησόν μου ὁ θ(εό)σ ἀπὸ ἁμαρτίασ πονηράσ· Hold power† over me, O God, from harmful sin,	ܦܪܘܩܢܝ ܡܪܝܐ ܡܢ ܚܛܝܬܐ ܒܝܫܬܐ. Save† me, LORD, from harmful sin,
καὶ ἀπὸ πάσησ γυναικὸσ πονηρὰσ σκανδαλιζούσησ ἄφρονα· and from every harmful woman who causes a mindless *one* to stumble,	ܘܡܢ ܟܠ ܐܢܬܬܐ ܒܝܫܬܐ ܕܡܟܫܠܐ ܠܫܒܪܐ. and from every harmful woman who makes the childish *one*s to stumble,
16.8 [8] καὶ μὴ ἀπατησάτω με κάλλοσ γυναικὸ(σ) παρανομούσησ· and do not let *it* deceive me— *the* beauty of a woman who breaks *the* Law,	ܘܠܐ ܢܪܡܝܢܝ ܫܘܦܪܗ ܕܐܢܬܬܐ ܥܘܠܬܐ. and let it not make me fall— *the* beauty of the unjust woman,
καὶ παντὸσ ὑποκειμένου ἀπὸ ἁμαρτίασ ἀνοφελοὺσ· and of any*thing* that is placed underneath from useless sin.	ܐܦܠܐ ܟܠ ܚܛܗܐ ܕܐܝܬ. nor indeed any sin that there is.

16.7–8 While we are in our sins, we are enslaved to sin (John 8.34; Rom 6.16–17), held captive by it (Rom 7.23), and ruled over by it (Rom 5.21; 6.12). In that state, we "cannot cease from sin" (2 Pet 2.14); we have no power in ourselves to escape from its slavery, captivity, and tyranny. "Can the Ethiopian change his skin, or the leopard his spots? Then also you may be able to do good, who are accustomed to do evil" (Jer 13.23). Only God has the power to free us from our slavery to sin (Rom 6.17–18; 7.24; 8.2); only to Him can we appeal for the help we need (vv 3–5): **Save me, LORD, from harmful** [*byšt'*] **sin** (Syriac; "save us from the evil [*byš'*] one," Luke 11.4, Syr). The corresponding Greek is **hold power over** [*epikratēson*] **me,** a startlingly vivid expression. *Epikrateō* is the term applied to a ruler who has power (*kratos,* 17.3) over (*epi*) his subjects (Ezra 4.20, LXX; Maccabaica 10.52; 14.17), overpowering all opposition (cf. Ecc 4.12, LXX; Gen 47.20). All power belongs to God (1 Tim 6.15–16); His people are in subjection to Him, protected "under the powerful [*krataian*] hand of God" (1 Pet 5.6; cf. Psa 89.13, LXX) and "strengthened … according to the power of His glory" to endure patiently and withstand all trials (Col 1.11). "He will deliver us from every stumblingblock of the Law-breaker" (4.27).[243]

"Keep watching … in order that none of you may be hardened by the deceitfulness of sin" (Heb 3.12–13). Sin is particularly likely to **deceive** if it appears to us in an outwardly good guise (2 Cor 11.3–4, 13–15), disguised by the **beauty … of anything**[244] **that is placed underneath from useless sin** (such as the **beauty of a woman who breaks the Law;** another example is outwardly "good words and blessings," Rom 16.18). Such things may **cause a mindless one** (*aphrona,* as in Prov 7.7, LXX) **to stumble** and may "deceive the hearts of the innocent" (Rom 16.18), but they are mere tools and vassals of sin, **underneath** (*hupo-*) it ("subject to" it, OTP), and are therefore the exact antithesis of the righteous, **over** (*epi-*) whom God is to **hold power.**[245] "Sin shall not be lord over you …. Just as you presented your members as slaves to uncleanness and opposition to the Law … so now present your members as slaves to righteousness" (Rom 6.14, 19). Sin's tools can hold no power over those who are in God's power.

God, in His faithfulness, provides a "way out" (an *ekbasin,* 1 Cor 10.13) from the temptations of sin. He provides this in at least two ways: by withholding people from opportunities to sin (1 Sam 25.34; Gen 20.6; cf. Psa 19.13), and by giving them His corrective word to guard against sin: "Set up my footsteps in Your saying, and do not

---

[243] **Hold power over me … from** involves another compression of sense (see the footnote on "dozed from," v 1, and the comments and footnote on Maccabaica 14.26). A second verb might have been expected (e.g., "Hold power over me … withholding me from").

[244] *Pantos* could possibly mean "anyone" (OTP), but **anything** suits the sentence structure (note the ABBA pattern in vv 7–8: **sin … woman … woman … anything**) and is supported by the Syriac rendering (**any sin that there is**).

[245] **Placed underneath from** (*hupokeimenou apo*). Proposals to interpret this as "placed under [the eyes] by" (Viteau) or "existing from" (Trafton 151), or to emend *apo* to *hupo* (Muraoka 702, §3), overlook the contrast between *epikratēson … apo hamartias* (v 7) and *hupokeimenou apo hamartias* (v 8). This is the third pregnant construction involving *apo* in the psalm (see the footnotes to vv 1 and 7).

let any iniquity have dominion over me" (Psa 119.133); "the command is a lamp, and the Law a light, and corrections of discipline are the way of life, to keep you from the woman of evil" (Prov 6.23–24). "All Scripture is ... useful [*ōphelimos*] for teaching, for reproof, for straightening, for discipline in righteousness" (2 Tim 3.16)—unlike **sin,** which is **useless** (*anōphelous,* Titus 3.9). There is no usefulness in what leads only to disaster (Luke 9.25). "Therefore do not be mindless [*aphrones*], but understand what the will of the Lord is" (Eph 5.17).

16.9 [9] τὰ ἔργα τ(ῶν) χειρῶν μου κατεύθυνον ἐν τόπῳ σου· Make the works of my hands straight† in Your† place,	ܘܐܬܩܢ ܥܒܕ ܐܝܕܝ ܩܕܡܝܟ. And direct† *the* work of my hands before You†,
καὶ τὰ διαβήματά μου ἐν τῇ μνήμῃ σου διαφύλαξον· and guard† my steps in the mindfulness of You†.	ܘܗܠܟܬܝ ܢܛܪ ܒܕܘܟܪܢܟ. and watch† over my steps in *the* mindfulness of You†.
16.10 [10] τὴν γλῶσσάν μου καὶ τὰ χείλη μου ἐν λόγοισ ἀληθείασ περίστειλον· Array† my tongue and my lips in words of truth;	ܠܫܢܝ ܘܣܦܘܬܝ ܒܡܠܐ ܕܫܪܪܐ ܐܬܩܢ. Direct† my tongue and my lips in words of truth;
ὀργὴν καὶ θυμὸν ἄλογον μακρὰν ποίησον ἀπ ἐμοῦ· anger and unreasoning indignation, set† far from me;	ܪܘܓܙܐ ܘܚܡܬܐ ܕܠܐ ܡܠܬܐ ܐܪܚܩ ܡܢܝ. anger and indignation that *is* not reasoned, keep† away from me;
16.11 [11] γογγυσμὸν καὶ ὀλιγοψυχίαν ἐν θλίψει μάκρυνον ἀπ' ἐμοῦ· grumbling and faintheartedness in oppression, keep† far from me;	ܪܛܢܐ ܘܒܘܪܘܬ ܢܦܫܐ ܒܐܘܠܨܢܐ ܐܪܚܩ ܡܢܝ. murmuring and littleness of soul in affliction, keep† away from me;
ἐὰν ἁμαρτήσω ἐν τῷ σὲ παιδεύειν εἰσ ἐπιστροφήν· if I should sin, when You† discipline *me, it is* to turn *me* back.	ܐܢ ܓܝܪ ܐܚܛܐ ܟܕ ܪܕܐܢܬ ܠܬܝܒܘܬܐ. for if I sin, when You† discipline *me, it is* to turn *me* back.

16.9 Make the works of my hands straight in Your place (Greek) ≡ **direct the work of my hands before You** (Syriac). "In all your ways know Him, and He Himself will make your paths straight" (Prov 3.6); He has the power to "establish you in every good work" (2 Thes 2.17; John 15.4–5; Psa 90.17). His people and all their **works** are present constantly **before** Him (9.6; 14.5; 2.40) in His **place**[246]—the holy place (Psa 24.3; 68.3; 76.2, LXX) where He dwells constantly with them (John 14.23; 1 Cor 6.19; 2 Cor 6.16; Eph 2.22) in accordance with His promise ("I will be with you all the days, even to the end of the age," Matt 28.20).[247]

Guard my steps in the mindfulness of You (see also the comments on verse 6). "Teach me to do Your good pleasure, for You are my God; Your good Spirit will lead me in a land of uprightness" (Psa 143.10). His Spirit provides that guidance through His word (Eph 5.18 ≡ Col 3.16; Eph 6.17); therefore, the way to **guard** our **steps** from sin is to store up His word as a hidden treasure within our heart (Psa 17.4–5; 119.11, 133).

16.10–11 Array [*peristeilon;* "clothe," Muraoka 552–53; "cover," LEH 488] **my tongue and my lips in words of truth.** When God removes iniquity from people, He takes away their filthy garments and arrays them in new, clean clothing (Zec 3.3–5; Rev 7.13–14; Gal 3.27; cf. Matt 22.11–13), which consists of righteous deeds (Rev 19.8; Isa 61.10); they are "to put away from you … the old person, which is being corrupted in accordance with the desires of deceit … and to clothe yourselves with the new person, which in accordance with God is being created in righteousness and loving-kindness of the truth" (Eph 4.22–24)—a transformation that is to affect "whatever you do, in word or deed" (Col 3.5–17; 2 Thes 2.17; cf. Rom 15.18; 2 Cor 10.11).

Anger and **indignation** are among the components of the old clothing that is laid aside when God provides the new (Col 3.8; Eph 4.31). "Man's anger does not accomplish God's righteousness" (Jas 1.19–20); it is **unreasoning** *(alogon),* "thoughtless" (OTP), like an irrational animal (2 Pet 2.12).

In a time of **oppression** it is also possible to fall into **faintheartedness** (*oligopsuchian,* "discouragement" [OTP]—the opposite of encouragement, 1 Thes 5.14) and **grumbling** (*goggusmon,* the sin committed by those in the wilderness who "were destroyed by the destroyer," 1 Cor 10.10; cf. Exod 16.2–3; Num 14.2–4). All this too is part of the old clothing and must be laid aside (Php 2.14). God's people are not to droop in a day of oppression (Prov 24.10; Matt 13.21), but to endure it patiently (Rom 12.12; 2 Thes 1.4). "Through many oppressions we must enter into the kingdom of God" (Acts 14.22).

---

[246] **In Your place** *(en topō sou):* both the place that He has (Psa 24.3, LXX) and the place that He provides (cf. Rev 12.6)—as "God's righteousness" is both the righteousness that He has (Rom 3.5, 26) and the righteousness that He provides (Rom 3.21–22, 26). APAT 2.144 suggested the conjectural emendation *enōpion sou* ("in Your sight," as in 2.40; 9.6; 14.5), which would match the Syriac.

[247] Notice that **in Your place** is parallel to **in the mindfulness of You.** God's dwelling place is with those who are mindful of Him—those who love Him and keep His commands (John 14.23; Psa 24.3–6; 2 Cor 6.16–18).

The psalmist asks God to **set** all these things **far from** him (Prov 30.8). The sinner is in the opposite position: as described at the start of this psalm, he is "far from God" (verse 2).

If I should sin, when You discipline me, it is to turn me back (13.8–9). "We are disciplined by the Lord in order that we may not be condemned" (1 Cor 11.32); He disciplines us "for our benefit, to share His holiness" (Heb 12.10), as He did when He provided the apostle Paul with a "thorn in the flesh" (2 Cor 12.7–10), and as He does when He provides all of us with His word (2 Tim 3.16–17; Isa 30.21). "It is good for me that I have been afflicted, in order that I learn Your decrees" (Psa 119.71; 94.12–13). See also the comments on 8.35.

The righteous one is disciplined and endures

16.12 [12] εὐδοκίᾳ δὲ μετὰ ἱλαρότητο(σ) στήρισον τὴν ψυχήν μου· But in good pleasure, with cheerful- ness, make my soul steadfast†;	ܒܨܒܝܢܐ ܕܝܢ ܕܚܕܘܬܐ ܥܫܢ ܢܦܫܝ. But with good pleasure of joy make my soul strong†,
ἐν τῷ ἐνισχύσαι σε τὴν ψυχήν μου ἀρκέσει μοι τὸ δοθὲν· when You† strengthen my soul, what has been given will be enough for me;	ܘܟܕ ܕܝܢ ܬܚܝܠ ܠܢܦܫܝ. ܢܣܦܩ ܠܝ ܡܕܡ ܕܐܬܝܗܒ. and when You† strengthen my soul, what has been given will be sufficient for me;
16.13 [13] ὅτι ἐὰν μη σὺ ‹ἐνισχύσησ›· because if You† Yourself† should not strengthen,	ܡܛܠ ܕܐܢ ܐܢܬ ܠܐ ܬܚܝܠ. because if You† will not strengthen,
τίσ ὑφέξεται πεδίαν ἐν πενίᾳ· who will bear discipline in poverty?	ܡܢܘ ܢܣܝܒܪ ܡܪܕܘܬܐ ܒܡܣܟܢܘܬܐ. who will bear discipline in poverty?

16.13 ἐνισχύσησ 336 [-ύσηισ 260] | -ύσαισ 253* | -ύσαησ 253[c] •

16.12 The weak soul may fall into faintheartedness *(oligopsuchian)* and grumbling in a time of affliction (v 11). But the **soul** *(psuchēn)* that is made **steadfast** (*stērison,* standing firm under trial: 1 Pet 5.9; cf. 2 Tim 2.19) responds in the opposite way: with **good pleasure** (2 Thes 1.11) and **cheerfulness** (not grudging, 2 Cor 9.7; Prov 18.22, LXX). For a soul that has been **strengthened** *(enischusai)* by God in that way, **what has been given** by God **will be enough** (2 Cor 12.9; Heb 13.5)—even if it is poverty (vv 13–14). "I have learned, in whatever circumstances I am, to be content .... In everything and in all things I have learned the secret both of being well-fed and of being hungry, both of having abundance and of lacking. I have strength [*ischuō*] for all things in the One who empowers me" (Php 4.11–13).

16.13 The power to remain steadfast and cheerful in all circumstances (v 12) must come from God. **If** God should **not strengthen** people, **who will bear discipline in poverty?** With that strength, we can bear "all things" (Php 4.13, cited in the preceding paragraph); without it, we can do nothing (John 15.5; Psa 124.1–5; cf. 2 Cor 3.5).

16.14 [14] ἐν τῷ ἐλέγχεσθαι ψυχὴν ἐν χειρὶ σαπρίασ αὐτοῦ· When a soul is reproved by *the* hand of his worthlessness,	ܟܕ ܬܬܟܘܢ When it is rebuked
ἡ δοκιμασία σου ἐν σαρκὶ αὐτοῦ καὶ ἐν θλίψει πενίασ· *it is* Your† testing in his flesh and in *the* oppression of poverty.	ܒܒܣܪܗ ܘܒܐܘܠܨܢܐ ܕܡܣܟܢܘܬܗ. in *the* flesh and in the affliction of its poverty,

16.14 A **soul** who is disciplined with poverty (v 13) **is reproved by the hand of** ("by means of," APOT)[248] the **worthlessness** of his condition,[249] and so is subjected to **testing** by God **in his flesh and in the oppression of poverty.** This **testing** *(dokimasia)* is like a fire ("the furnace of oppression," Isa 48.10), and it refines the soul as a fire refines gold or silver: impurities are burned away, and the precious metal is purified (1 Pet 1.7; Psa 66.10; Zec 13.9). In this way, by being subjected to weakness (**worthlessness ... poverty**) the soul is **strengthened** (vv 12–13; cf. Heb 11.34; 2 Cor 12.9–10).[250]

---

[248] **By the hand of.** "By the activity of" (BDAG 1082, §2a), "by means of" (Thayer 667). Compare "ordained ... by the hand of a mediator" (Gal 3.19); "destroy the land ... by the hands of strangers" (Ezek 30.12, LXX; Josh 20.9; 1 Chr 20.8). The rendering "in the hand of" (NETS) is also possible (cf. Prov 18.21; Gen 16.6), but does not suit the verb **reproved.**

[249] **His worthlessness.** Even though the **soul** is feminine in Greek *(psuchēn),* it takes here a masculine pronoun, **his** *(autou),* in 253 and 336, because the subject is considered as a (generic) masculine (Holm-Nielsen 97; MHT 3.312, §2*b*). Compare *tēn kephalēn ex ou* ("the Head [feminine], from whom [masculine]"), Col 2.19. The **worthlessness** *(saprias)* described here is not "corruption" (APOT) or "mortality" (OTP), which do not fit the present context, but the **oppression of poverty**—a condition "of such poor quality as to be of little or no value" (BDAG 913, *sapros,* §1; see the footnote to 14.4, where the meaning of the word is discussed).

[250] In this verse, the Syriac manuscript 16h1 has a much shorter text (**When it is rebuked in the flesh and in the affliction of its poverty**), which has nothing equivalent to any of the Greek words from *psuchēn* to *hē dokimasia sou.* This is evidently the result of an accidental omission (the copyist had also accidentally skipped the first half of v 11, but he detected that mistake and corrected it). The other Syriac manuscript (10h1) is here fragmentary and difficult to read; the first half of the verse is missing, but the second half certainly has something extra before **in the flesh** (Baars reads the letters *ṣbynk,* "Your good pleasure"—which might correspond to Greek *eudokia sou* rather than *dokimasia sou*). Nevertheless, as the text of 16h1 stands, the subject of the feminine verb *ttkwn* (**it is rebuked**) would still be the feminine noun *npšy* ("my soul") in v 12, so the basic sense of the passage remains the same.

16.15 [15] ἐν τῷ ὑπομεῖναι δίκαιον ἐν τούτοισ ἐλεηθήσεται ὑπὸ κ(υρίο)υ: When the righteous *one* endures in these things, he will be shown mercy by *the* Lord.	ܘܟܕ ܢܣܝܒܪ ܙܕܝܩܐ ܒܗܠܝܢ. ܢܗܘܘܢ ܥܠܘܗܝ، ܪ̈ܚܡܐ ܡܢ ܡܪܝܐ. and when the righteous *one* bears with these things, compassions from the LORD *will be* upon him.

16.15 When the righteous one endures in these things, he will be shown mercy by the Lord. "Blessed is the man who endures under trial, because, having been tested, he will receive the crown of life" (Jas 1.12; 5.11; 1 Pet 2.20; 2 Tim 2.12; Matt 10.22). Jesus Himself illustrates that. He, "for the joy that was laid before Him, endured the cross, having despised the shame, and has sat down at the right hand of the throne of God" (Heb 12.2).

Psalm 17

This psalm, the largest of the Eighteen Psalms and the one with the greatest breadth of subject matter, balances Psalm 2 at the start of the collection and Psalm 8 in the middle. Like them, it deals with Jerusalem's sins and her punishment at the hands of a foreign enemy (vv 6–22); but it goes further than they do, and looks ahead to the days of the coming Messiah, the Son of David (vv 23–51)—a topic that will be discussed again in the final psalm of the collection.

We will hope on God

17.0 [0] Ψαλμὸϲ τῷ Ϲαλωμῶ(ν) μετα ᾠδῆϲ τῷ βαϲιλεῖ: A psalm belonging to Solomon, with a song; in regard to *the* King.	
17.1 [1] Κ(ύρι)ε σὺ ‹αὐτὸσ› βασιλεὺσ ἡμῶν εἰσ τὸν αἰῶνα καὶ ἔτι· Lord, You† Yourself† *will be* our King to lasting time and still more,	ܡܪܝܐ ܐܢܬ ܗܘ ܡܠܟܢ. ܗܫܐ ܘܠܥܠܡ. LORD, You† Yourself† *will be* our King now and to lasting time,
ὅτι ἐν σοί ὁ θ(εό)σ ‹› καυχήσεται ἡ ψυχὴ ἡμῶν· because in You†, O God, our soul will boast.	ܡܛܠ ܕܒܟ ܐܠܗܐ ܬܫܬܒܗܪ، ܢܦܫܢ. because in You†, God, our soul will boast.

17.1 αὐτὸσ 336⁺260 ≡ ܗܘ 16h1 10h1 | > 253 • θ(εό)σ 336⁺260 ≡ ܐܠܗܐ 16h1 10h1 | + ἡμῶν 253 •

17.1[251] Lord, You Yourself will be our King to lasting time and still more. "The

[251] In the Greek copies (but not in the Syriac), the psalm is superscribed **A psalm belonging to Solomon, with a song; in regard to the King.** Comparison with 18.0 ("again of the Christ the

LORD is King to lasting time and continuing time" (Psa 10.16; 146.10). Moreover, this King is **our** King (Isa 33.22); we are not among those who "do not want this one to be king over us" (Luke 19.14). "This God is our God; to lasting time and continuing time, He Himself leads us" (Psa 48.14). And the same can be said of the King appointed by Him—the Son of David (v 23): His rule, too, will continue "to lasting time" (v 39). "He will be King over the house of Jacob to lasting time; and of His kingdom there will be no end" (Luke 1.33; Heb 1.8).

In You, God, our soul will boast. "Let not the wise one boast in his wisdom, and let not the mighty one boast in his might, and let not the rich one boast in his riches; but let the one who boasts boast in this—in understanding and knowing Me, that I am the LORD, doing lovingkindness, justice, and righteousness in the land" (Jer 9.23–24). "Let the one who boasts, boast in the Lord" (1 Cor 1.31). Again, this can also be said of the Son of David: "May it never come about that I should boast, except in the cross of our Lord Jesus Christ" (Gal 6.14). "We ourselves are the circumcision—the ones who worship in the Spirit of God and boast in Christ Jesus" (Php 3.3).

17.2 [2] καὶ τίσ ὁ χρόνοσ ζωῆσ ἀν(θρώπ)ου ἐπὶ τῆσ γῆσ· And what *is* the time of a Man's life on the earth?	ܘܡܢܐ ܐܝܬ ܚܝ̈ܘܗܝ ܕܒܪܐܢܫܐ ܥܠ ܐܪܥܐ. And what is a son of Man's life on the earth?
κατὰ τὸν χρόνον αὐτοῦ καὶ ἡ ἐλπὶσ αὐτοῦ ἐπ' αὐτὸν· As *is* his time, *so* also his hope *is* on him.	ܐܝܟ ܙܒܢܗ ܗܟܢܐ ܐܦ ܦܓܪܗ. For as *is* his time, so also *is* his flesh.

17.2 What is the time of a Man's life on the earth? "What is your life? for you are a vapor that becomes visible for a little, and then disappears" (Jas 4.14). "His days are like a shadow that passes away" (Psa 144.4; 102.11), "like the grass that changes: in the morning it flowers and changes, in the evening it is cut off and dries up" (Psa 90.5–10; 103.15–16; Isa 40.6–7 ≡ 1 Pet 1.24; Job 14.1–2). "You have set my days as handbreadths, and my lifetime is as nothing before You" (Psa 39.5).

As fleeting **as is his time,** so fleeting **also** is Man's **hope,** which is placed **on** himself (on **Man**).[252] "Our days on the earth are like a shadow, and there is no hope" (1 Chr

Lord") shows that the **King** mentioned in this inscription is not the Father (v 1) but His Anointed (vv 23, 35–36, 47). The psalm could scarcely be said to be "for the king" (Wright) or addressed "to the King" (OTP); rather, the dative *tō basilei* indicates that it is written **in regard to the King** ("of the King," APOT; "pertaining to the king," NETS; cf. 4.0).

[252] **As is his time, so also his hope is on him.** The contrast between hope **on him** and hope **on God** (v 3) shows that **on him** *(ep' auton)* refers to hope on **Man** (*anthrōpou,* in the previous clause). Other proposed renderings include: (i) "throughout his time, also his hope is on him" (Viteau), taking *kata* as "throughout the period of" (Muraoka 365, §4b; KG 2.1.478,

29.15; cf. 1 Thes 4.13; Eph 2.12; Prov 11.7; Wis 2.1–9), not even the amount of hope that a tree has when it is cut down (Job 14.7–12).

17.3 [3] ἡμεῖσ δὲ ἐλπιοῦμεν ἐπὶ τὸν θ(εὸ)ν σ(ωτῆ)ρα ἡμῶν· But *as for* us, we will hope on God our Savior,	ܚܢܢ ܕܝܢ ܡܣܟܝܢܢ ܥܠ ܐܠܗܐ ܦܪܘܩܢ. But we are hoping on God our Savior,
ὅτι τὸ κράτο(σ) τοῦ θ(εο)ῦ ἡμῶν εἰσ τὸν αἰῶνα μετ ελέουσ· because the might of our God *will be* to lasting time with mercy,	ܡܛܠ ܕܐܘܚܕܢܗ ܕܐܠܗܢ ܠܥܠܡ ܒܪ̈ܚܡܐ. because *the* dominion of our God *will be* to lasting time with compassions,
17.4 [3] καὶ ἡ βασιλεία τοῦ θ(εο)ῦ ἡμῶν εἰσ τὸν αἰῶνα ἐπι τὰ ἔθνη ‹ἐν κρίσει›· and the kingdom of our God *will be* to lasting time over the nations in judgment.	ܘܡܠܟܘܬܗ ܕܐܠܗܢ ܠܥܠܡ ܥܠ ܥܡ̈ܡܐ ܒܕܝܢܐ. and *the* kingdom of our God *will be* to lasting time over the peoples in judgment.

17.4 ἐν κρίσει 336[+]260 ≡ ܒܕܝܢܐ 16h1 10h1 | > 253 •

17.3–4 But we ourselves have a better hope: **we will hope on God our Savior** (Psa 146.3–5; 62.5–8), **because** His **might** (*kratos,* 1 Tim 6.16) and His **kingdom** are not fleeting, as earthly human life is (v 2); on the contrary, they will continue **to lasting time.** "To the One who sits on the throne, and to the Lamb, be … the might [*kratos*], to lasting times of lasting times" (Rev 5.13). "The kingdom of the world has become that of our Lord and of His Christ; and He will be king to lasting times of lasting times" (Rev 11.15).

God's **might** and **kingdom** are exercised with both **mercy** and **judgment.** "Your judgments are on all the earth with mercy" (18.3). "Sinners will be destroyed in the day of the Lord's judgment … but those who fear the Lord will receive mercy in it" (15.13–15). His **judgment** is exercised not only over Israel, but over all the **nations** (v 31b; cf. Matt 12.18–21); and His **mercy** is available not only to Israel (v 51), but to all the **nations** (v 38; cf. Rom 15.9–12).

---

§433β.II.2a), as in Judith 16.21; (ii) "according to his time and his hope on him" (NETS)—but the statement that a person's time is "according to his time" would yield little sense (and would be stylistically uncharacteristic of these psalms).

The Syriac reads **as is his time, so also is his flesh,** i.e., his body ends when his life does (1 Cor 6.13; 15.50; Ecc 12.7); Harris-Mingana emended *bsrh* (**his flesh**) to *sbrh* ("his hope"), matching the Greek.

You swore that David's kingship would not cease

17.5 [4] σὺ κ(ύρι)ε ἡρετήσω τὸν Δα(υὶ)δ βασιλέα ἐπι Ἰσραὴλ· You† Yourself†, Lord, chose David king over Israel,	ܐܢܬ ܡܪܝܐ ܓܒܝܬ ܠܕܘܝܕ: ܡܠܟܐ ܥܠ ܐܝܣܪܝܠ. You† Yourself†, LORD, chose David *as* the king over Israel,
καὶ σὺ ὤμοσασ αὐτῷ περὶ τοῦ σπέρματοσ ‹αὐτοῦ› εἰσ τὸν αἰῶνα· and You† Yourself† swore to him concerning his seed to lasting time	ܘܐܢܬ ܝܡܝܬ ܠܗ ܥܠ ܙܪܥܗ. and You† Yourself† swore to him concerning his seed
τοῦ μὴ ἐκλείπειν ἀπέναντί σου βασίλειον αὐτοῦ· *for* his kingship not to cease before You†.	ܕܠܐ ܬܬܥܛܐ ܡܢ ܩܕܡܝܟ ܡܠܟܘܬܗܘܢ. that their kingship will not be blotted out from before You†.

17.5 αὐτοῦ 1° 336⁺260 ≡ 16h1 \| > 253 •

17.5 The **Lord chose David** as **king over Israel** (Psa 78.70–72), and **swore** an oath **to him concerning his seed** (his "offspring," NETS), promising that David's **kingship** was **not to cease before** the Lord. This promise was not made only for David's own lifetime, or for one or two generations thereafter; it would stand **to lasting time.** "I have sworn to David my servant: 'To lasting time I will set up your seed, and I will build your throne to a generation and a generation.' . . . I will set up his seed to continuing time, and his throne as the days of the heavens" (Psa 89.34, 29, 35–37; 2 Sam 7.12–16).

That promise would never fail (1 Kgs 9.5). Even the greatest of all kings of Israel—the Prince of Peace, the Messiah—would be a descendant of David (John 7.42; Jer 23.5–6), and "there will be no end to the increase of His government . . . on the throne of David and on his kingdom" (Isa 9.6–7).

But sinners, to whom You did not promise, set up kingship

17.6 [5] καὶ ἐν ταῖσ ἁμαρτίαισ ἡμῶν ἐπανέστησαν ἡμῖν ἁμαρτωλοί· But in our sins, sinners stood up against us;	ܘܒܚܛܗܝܢ ܕܝܢ ܩܡܘ ܥܠܝܢ ܚܛܝܐ. But in our sins, sinners rose up over against us,
ἐπέθεντο ἡμῖν καὶ ‹ἔξωσαν› ἡμᾶσ οἷσ οὐκ ἐπηγγείλω· they set on us, and they drove us out—*people* to whom You† did not promise;	ܘܣܡܘ ܥܠܝܢ ܘܐܪܚܩܘܢܝ ܗܢܘܢ ܕܠܐ ܦܩܕܬ ܠܗܘܢ. and they set on us, and they themselves took me away; *things* that You† did not command them,

μετα βίασ ἀφείλαντο· by force they took *it* away,	ܒܩܛܝܪܐ ܢܣܒܘ by force they took,
17.7 [5] καὶ οὐκ εδόξασαν τὸ ὄνομά σου τὸ ἔντιμον· **[6]** ἐν δόξῃ and they did not glorify Your† honorable name with glory.	ܘܠܐ ܫܒܚܘ ܠܫܡܟ ܡܝܩܪܐ ܒܬܫܒ̈ܚܬܐ. and they did not glorify Your† honorable name with glories.
ἔθεντο βασίλειον ἀντὶ ὕψουσ αὐτ(ῶν)· They set kingship in place of their high condition;	ܘܣܡܘ ܡܠܟܘܬܐ ܚܠܦ ܪܘܡܗܘܢ܆ They set kingship instead of their high position;
17.8 [6] ἠρήμωσαν τὸν θρόνον Δα(υὶ)δ ἐν υπερηφανίᾳ ἀλλάγματο(σ)· they made desolate the throne of David in *the* arrogance of *that* exchange.	ܐܚܪܒܘ ܟܘܪܣܝܗ ܕܕܘܝܕ ܒܫܘܒܗܪܐ ܕܫܘܚܠܦܗܘܢ܆. they made desolate *the* throne of David in the boastfulness of their exchange.

17.6 ἔξωσαν 336⁺260 | -αντο 253 •

17.6 The promise of kingship had been given to David and to his seed (v 5). **But** in the time of the Eighteen Psalms, **sinners . . . to whom You did not promise**[253] had arisen. They **stood up against** God's people, **set on us** (cf. 1.1; 7.1; 9.16), and **drove us out,**[254] just as David (1 Sam 26.19) and Jephthah (Jdg 11.7) were driven away by the sinners around them. In the time of Jeremiah, the Lord had rebuked "the shepherds who shepherd My people" for similar practices: "you have scattered My flock, and you have driven them away, and you have not watched over them" (Jer 23.2).

---

[253] **People to whom You did not promise** (Greek) describes the **sinners,** whereas **things that You did not command to them** (Syriac) describes the things that the sinners seized. The meaning of the passage is not affected. The sinners were not promised the kingship (Greek), and when they seized the kingship, they seized what was not promised to them (Syriac).

[254] **They set on us, and they drove us out.** The singers of the psalm are including themselves (**us**) among those who were driven out. (The Syriac version is even more specific: the evildoers took **me** away.) This does not mean that those responsible for the Eighteen Psalms were "the legitimate line of the High Priesthood" (Ryle-James 130) displaced by the family of Mattathias (the psalm is not objecting to that family's priesthood, but to its **kingship**). Nor does it mean that they were "Hyrcanus and his Pharisee supporters" (Viteau 342) displaced by Aristobulus and the Sadducees (Hyrcanus had no more **promise** from God than Aristobulus). In this context, **us** must be either the house of David (deSilva, *Jewish Teachers of Jesus, James, and Jude,* 287 n. 12) displaced by the unauthorized kings, or else, more generally, those who remained faithful to God, displaced by those who did not (cf. vv 18–20).

By force they took it away (*apheilanto,* as in Gen 21.25, LXX). In the Greek, the verse ends with an abruptness befitting its topic. The object—the thing that is taken away—is not specified, and has to be deduced from the context. The following verses (vv 7–8) show that what was taken away was the **kingship** (v 5). The sinners seized **by force** (*bias,* as in Exod 1.13–14; Isa 52.4) what was not rightfully theirs (cf. Mic 2.2).

17.7–8a To **glorify** God's **name** is to glorify God Himself (Isa 24.15)—to acknowledge and fear the glory that is His (Psa 22.23; Rev 15.4; Isa 25.3). Those who serve the Lord faithfully are glorifying Him (John 17.4; 1 Cor 10.31); those who do not respect His Law are dishonoring and failing to **glorify** Him (Rom 2.17, 24; 1.21–32).[255] That is what these sinners were doing. God had given them a **high condition** (as He often did for Israel, Acts 13.17; Maccabaica 1.40). But they were not satisfied with that. In **arrogance,** they made an **exchange,** and replaced their **high condition**[256] with a **kingship** that was contrary to God's Law (vv 5–6). When they did this, they rejected the **throne of David** and **made** it **desolate** (like a land that has been "overthrown by foreigners," Isa 1.7). In fact, they did to the **throne of David** what the sinners at Mount Sinai had done to God Himself, when "they exchanged their Glory for the shape of an ox" (Psa 106.20). The tent of David had now fallen and was ruined (Amos 9.11)—and its ruins could be raised up only by a Son of David (v 23; Acts 15.14–16).

Before Jesus, the last Judean king descended from **David** had been Zedekiah, who was captured by the Babylonians and died in prison in Babylon (Jer 52.1–11). After that, the land was ruled by foreign kings authorized by God (Jer 27.12–13; Dan 2.37–40), who appointed local governors in Judea (2 Kgs 25.22; Ezra 5.14–16; Hag 1.1; Neh 5.14). When the yoke of the nations was taken away during the Maccabean period, Judea was ruled by Simon and then by his son John; but neither of them was a king; they were simply high priests and leaders of the Judeans (Maccabaica 13.41–42; 16.23–24). Thus, during the whole time from the Babylonian period to the Maccabean period, no one **to whom** God **did not promise** had set up a **kingship by force.**

That happened during the following half century—the time between the high priesthood of John and the coming of the Romans. Classical historians and ancient coins testify that one of John's sons assumed the title "king," and that his successors did the same.[257] Their family was not descended from David, but from Aaron (see the comments on Maccabaica 2.1); they were authorized by God's Law to be high

---

[255] **They did not glorify Your honorable name with glory.** Compare "they profaned the Lord's holy places with profaneness" (1.8). **With glory** has sometimes been taken with the following clause ("they set up in glory" their kingship, NETS), although that is not a possible way of construing the Syriac text.

[256] **In place of** [*anti*] **their high condition.** In this passage *anti* is sometimes rendered "because of" (OTP). However, the sense **in place of** (as in 2.21) is confirmed by the term **exchange** *(allagmatos)* in the next clause, and is supported by the Syriac version.

[257] Josephus, *Wars,* 1.70 ≡ *Antiquities,* 13.301; Strabo 16.2.40; Hendin 190–216.

priests,[258] but when they declared themselves kings, they were acting contrary to God's promises to David (v 5).

In any age, those who have received a **high condition** may easily become **arrogant** and reach out for more than God has given them, instead of giving **glory** to Him. That was the error of Korah and his fellow Levites, who had been raised up by God to serve at His tabernacle (Num 16.8–10), and of Uzziah (2 Chr 26.18), who had been raised up by God to be king. "God sets Himself against arrogant ones, but He gives favor to lowly ones. Make yourselves lowly, therefore, under the mighty hand of God, in order that He may lift you high" (1 Pet 5.5–6).

You will put them down when a foreigner arises

[7] καὶ σὺ ὁ θ(εό)σ καταβαλεῖσ αὐτοὺσ καὶ ἀρείσ σπέρμα αὐτῶν ἀπὸ τῆσ γῆσ· But You†, O God, You† will put them down, and You† will take their seed from the earth;	ܘܐܢܬ ܕܝܢ ܬܣܚܘܦ ܐܢܘܢ܆. ܘܬܥܒܪ ܙܪܥܗܘܢ ܡܢ ܐܪܥܐ. But You† Yourself† will overthrow them, and You† will remove their seed from the earth;
17.9 [7] ἐν τῷ ἐπαναστῆναι αὐτοῖσ ἄν(θρωπ)ον ἀλλότριον γένουσ ἡμῶν· when *there* rises up against them a person strange to our race,	ܘܟܕ ܢܩܘܡ ܥܠܝܗܘܢ܆ ܓܒܪܐ ܢܘܟܪܝܐ ܡܢ ܫܪܒܬܐ ܕܝܠܢ. and when *there* rises up against them a man strange to our kindred,
17.10 [8] κατὰ τὰ ἁμαρτήματα αὐτῶν ἀποδώσεισ αὐτοῖσ ὁ θ(εό)σ· in accordance with their sins You† will repay them, O God,	ܐܝܟ ܚܛܗܝܗܘܢ܆ ܬܦܪܘܥ ܐܢܘܢ܆ ܐܠܗܐ. In accordance with their sins You† will repay them, God,
εὑρεθῆναι αὐτοῖσ 17.11 [8] κατὰ τὰ ἔργα αὐτ(ῶν)· *for it* to be found to them in accordance with their works.	ܘܬܫܬܟܚ ܠܗܘܢ ܐܝܟ ܥܒܕܝܗܘܢ܆. and it will be found to them in accordance with their deeds.
[9] οὐκ ελεήσει αὐτοὺσ ὁ θ(εό)σ· God will not have mercy on them;	ܘܠܐ ܬܪܚܡ ܥܠܝܗܘܢ܆ ܐܠܗܐ. And do not have compassion† on them, God;

[258] Ryle and James mistakenly wrote that the Maccabean leaders "usurped the High Priesthood," and that the current passage rebukes them for doing so (Ryle-James 130). In fact their family belonged to the very first course of priests descended from Aaron, so their right to be high priests under the old covenant Law is beyond question (see the comments on Maccabaica 10.21). Moreover, this passage says nothing against their high priesthood. It talks only of an unauthorized **kingship.**

ἐξερεύνησεν τὸ σπέρμα αὐτῶν καὶ οὐκ αφῆκεν αὐτ(ῶν) ἕνα·	ܦܩܘܕ ܙܪܥܗܘܢ ܘܠܐ ܬܫܒܘܩ ܡܢܗܘܢ ܘܠܐ ܚܕ.
He has searched out their seed, and He has not left one of them.	punish† their seed, and do not leave† *any* out of them, not even one.

17.8b "Everyone who raises himself up will be brought low" (Luke 14.11) by the Lord (Dan 4.37; Psa 18.27; 52.5; 75.4–7; Luke 1.52). God would **put ... down** the arrogant sinners who had set themselves up contrary to His Law (vv 7–8a). The kingship would be taken away from them and their **seed** (cf. Psa 109.8–10), because it was for David and his seed (v 5), and their **seed** would be removed **from the earth** (see the comments on v 11).

17.9 This would happen **when there rises up against them a person strange to our race**—that is, someone who is not an Israelite (Deut 17.15; cf. Maccabaica 15.33; 1.44).[259] The Lord had warned the Israelites long ago that, if they persisted in disobeying Him, He would give them into the power of "a people whom you have not known ... a nation whom neither you nor your fathers have known" (Deut 28.33, 36).

Who was this foreigner (**person strange to our race**) who would **put ... down** the family of unauthorized kings? There have been two main suggestions: (i) the Roman leader Pompey, who entered Jerusalem in 63 BCE and deposed the last of the Maccabean kings; (ii) the Idumean leader Herod the Great, who captured Jerusalem in 37 BCE and subsequently had several members of the Maccabean family killed. Most of this passage would fit both options, but the earlier incident is favored by the description of large-scale deportation to the distant west (v 14) and by the resemblance between vv 13–14 and 8.23–24 (where the reference is undoubtedly to Pompey).[260]

17.10–11 At that time, **God** would **repay** the sinners **in accordance with their sins ... in accordance with their works** (see the comments on 2.17), as he will do with "every person" (Matt 16.27; Rom 2.6; 2 Cor 5.10; Jer 17.10; 32.19; Psa 28.4–5).

When that happened, it would **be found to them**[261] **in accordance with their works.** The term **be found** (Greek *heurethēnai* ≡ Syriac *tštkḥ*) indicates not only that

---

[259] **When there rises up against them a person strange to our race.** The Syriac version prefaces this line with *w-* (**and**), which separates it from the preceding clause; therefore, it can only be construed with the following clause. In the Greek version, the line could be construed either with the preceding or with the following clause. The meaning is not affected.

[260] Atkinson initially identified the **person strange to our race** with Herod ("Herod the Great, Sosius, and the Siege of Jerusalem (37 B.C.E.) in Psalm of Solomon 17," 313–22), but he later abandoned this position and accepted the identification with Pompey (*I Cried to the Lord,* 135–39).

[261] **Be found to them.** The dative *autois* could mean either that this would be found [in regard] to them (as in Deut 21.17, LXX) or else that it would be found by them (as in Isa 65.1, LXX). The former meaning is better suited to the context here.

the repayment of their works would "befall" (AOT) or "happen to" (Wright) them, but that it would become manifest ("be shown to be" this, BDAG 412, §2; NIDNTT 3.529, §1c) when God judged them—just as the outcome of God's judgment on the righteous will also one day **be found,** i.e., be manifest. "Be diligent to be found by Him in peace, unspotted and unblemished" (2 Pet 3.14), "in order that I may gain Christ and be found in Him" (Php 3.8–9), "in order that the appraisal of your faith ... may be found to praise and glory and honor at the revelation of Jesus Christ" (1 Pet 1.7); then, "being clothed, we will not be found naked" (2 Cor 5.3).

"God is kind and merciful to lasting time" (10.8); His mercy "is over all the earth in kindness" (5.17); His King, the Son of David, "will have mercy on all the nations" (v 38). But these false kings had shown no mercy; they had driven out God's people and seized by force what did not belong to them (v 6). On those who act without mercy **God will not have mercy** (Jas 2.13; cf. Matt 5.7). They will be repaid **in accordance with their works** (Sir 16.12); as they themselves have sown, so shall they reap (Gal 6.7–8; Prov 22.8; Matt 7.1–2). These false kings had made desolate the throne of David (v 8), and therefore God would make their throne desolate: **He has searched out their seed, and He will not leave one of them.**[262] He would put an end to their lineage just as surely as He had put an end to the lineage of other disobedient kings (1 Kgs 14.10–11; 16.11–13; 21.21–22). "The seed of wicked ones has been cut off" (Psa 37.28).[263]

---

[262] **God will not have mercy on them; He has searched out their seed, and He has not left one of them.** Gebhardt and Rahlfs conjecturally emended *eleēsei* (**will not have mercy**) to *ēleēsen* ("has not had mercy"), but that would still leave future tenses in the previous lines (**You will put them down ... You will take ... You will repay,** vv 8–10). In fact shifts between apparent past and apparent future are common in the Hebrew prophets (Klein, "Prophetic Perfect," 45–60; Joosten, *Verbal System of Biblical Hebrew*, 207–08; Rogland, *Alleged Non-Past Uses of Qatal*, §3.4), and they cannot all be textual errors. Compare the tense shift in: "She has fallen, she has fallen, Babylon the great! ... So will Babylon the great city be thrown down" (Rev 18.2, 21 ≡ Jer 51.8, 64). The future condemnation has already occurred in God's determination (2 Pet 2.3). In the present passage the apparent Greek "past tenses" (aorists) correspond to Syriac imperatives: **Punish their seed, and do not leave any out of them, not even one.** (The converse is seen in 4.7: Greek "May God remove those" ≡ Syriac "God has taken away those.")

[263] Atkinson makes the strange claim that "the Hasmoneans [the descendants of Mattathias] were not all removed from the earth as the author predicted" (*I Cried to the Lord*, 156). There is certainly no sign of them today; indeed, their male line disappeared without trace from historical records within a few decades after the Roman conquest. The majority of the family's leading members were killed by the Romans and/or by Herod (Josephus, *Antiquities*, 15.8–10, 53–56, 164–181; Plutarch, *Antony*, 36; Cassius Dio 49.22.6). They did not all die immediately, and they did not all die by violence; but no passage in the Eighteen Psalms suggests that they did. God's judgment on the house of Eli (1 Sam 2.30–36) was likewise carried out gradually over several generations (1 Sam 4.11, 17–20; 22.17–20; 1 Kgs 2.27). His promise to "wipe away

17.12 [10] πιστὸ(σ) ὁ κ(ύριο)σ ἐν πᾶσι τοῖσ κρίμασιν αὐτοῦ οἷσ ποιεῖ ἐπὶ τὴν γῆν·	ܡܗܝܡܢ ܡܪܝܐ ܒܟܠܗܘܢ ܕܝܢܘܗܝ ܕܥܒܕ ܥܠ ܐܪܥܐ.
The Lord *is* faithful in all His judgments which He does on the earth.	The LORD *is* faithful in all His judgments which He has done on the earth.

17.12 The Lord is faithful (14.1) **in all His judgments**—that is, all His judgments are righteous (Psa 19.9). Not only is He faithful when He judges His people and shows mercy on them (8.34–35, 38), but He is also faithful when He judges His enemies and deals out condemnation to them (Rev 19.11–15). All His dealings with all people on earth are consistent. "If we are faithless, He remains faithful, for He cannot deny Himself" (2 Tim 2.13).

The Law-breaker made our land desolate

17.13 [11] ἠρήμωσεν ὁ ἄνομοσ ‹› τὴν γῆν ἡμῶν ἀπὸ ἐνοικούντων αὐτὴν·	ܐܚܪܒ ܥܘܠܐ ܐܪܥܢ ܡܢ ܟܠ ܕܝܬܒ ܥܠܝܗ.
The *one who is* opposed to *the* Law made our land desolate from *those who were* dwelling in it;	The unjust *one* made our land desolate from every*one* who *was* dwelling on it;
ἠφάνισαν νέον καὶ πρεσβύτην καὶ τέκνα αὐτ(ῶν) ἅμα·	ܣܚܦܘ ܛܠܝ̈ܐ ܘܣܒ̈ܐ ܘܒܢܝ̈ܗܘܢ ܐܟܚܕܐ.
they wiped out young man and old man and their children together.	they destroyed young *ones* and old *ones* and their sons together.
17.14 [12] ἐν οργῇ κάλλουσ αὐτοῦ ἐξαπέστειλεν αὐτὰ ἕωσ ἐπι δυσμῶν·	ܒܫܘܦܪܐ ܕܪܘܓܙܗ ܫܕܪ ܐܢܘܢ ܥܕܡܐ ܠܡܥܪܒܐ.
In *the* anger of his beauty he sent them away until *they were* close to *the* sunset,	In the beauty of his anger he sent them even to the sunset,
καὶ τοὺσ ἄρχοντασ τῆσ γῆσ εἰσ ἐμπεγμὸν καὶ οὐκ εφείσατο·	ܘܠܫܠܝܛܗ ܕܐܪܥܐ ܠܡܘܝܩܐ ܘܠܐ ܚܣ.
and *he set* the rulers of the land for scoffing, and he did not spare.	and *he set the* ruler of the land for derision, and he did not spare.

17.13 τὴν γῆν $336^{+}260$ | ^ ἐπὶ 253 •

the memory of Amalek from under the heavens" because of what the Amalekites did in the time of Moses (Exod 17.14) was carried out "from generation to generation" (Exod. 17.16) over a still longer period (at least several hundred years: 1 Sam 15.2–3; 2 Sam 8.11–12; 1 Chr 4.43). He is longsuffering toward us, and therefore His punishment for sin is not always executed speedily (cf. Ecc 8.11); but it is certain and unerring (Hab 2.3 ≡ Heb 10.37; 2 Pet 3.9–10).

17.13–14 Someone **opposed to the Law** (an **enemy,** v 15) has done evil in **our land** (and specifically **in Jerusalem,** v 16). He **made our land desolate,** depriving it of its inhabitants (**those who were dwelling in it**)[264] by killing some and sending others[265] away to the distant west (**until they were close to the sunset**).

This **enemy** cannot be a local Judean ruler (e.g., one of the arrogant sinners who usurped the kingship, vv 6–8, or one of the Herods), because he sent his captives far to the west. For the same reason, he cannot be one of the Seleucids (e.g., Antiochus Epiphanes); they had authority in the north and east, but certainly not in the distant west (Maccabaica 8.6–8). The only ancient enemy of Israel that fits the description in this passage is Rome.

As in 8.18, the enemy is not an individual (e.g., Pompey) but a collective group (the Roman invading force), because it is described in both singular and plural terms (singular: he **made ... desolate;** plural: **they wiped out**).[266]

In the time of Moses, God had warned the Israelites that, if they did not obey Him, "I will make the land desolate" (Lev 26.31–33). That had already happened repeatedly (in the time of the Babylonians: Jer 25.11, 17–18; Lam 5.18; in the time of Antiochus Epiphanes: Maccabaica 1.39, 2.12). Now it was happening again. And Jesus prophesied that Jerusalem would again be made **desolate** during the lifetime of the generation that rejected Him (Luke 13.34–35; 21.20, 32).

The enemy **wiped out** (*ēphanisan,* "made to dis[*a*-]appear[-*phanizō*]") people of all ages (2.8), as had also been foretold by Moses (Deut 28.50) and had been done by previous conquerors (the Babylonians: 2 Chr 36.17; Lam 2.21; Antiochus Epiphanes: Maccabaica 2.9).

The enemy **set the rulers of the land for scoffing** (see the comments on 2.12–13, 25). That too had happened when Jerusalem was made desolate by the Babylonians (Jer 24.8–9; Lam 5.12; 4.16) and in the Maccabean period (Maccabaica 7.34; 9.26). God raises up, and He brings low; at His own pleasure He "pours out contempt on nobles" (Psa 107.40).

The enemy did these things **in the beauty of his anger** (Syriac)[267]—one of the

---

[264] He **made our land desolate from those who were dwelling in it.** A characteristic condensation, the preposition *apo* (**from**) appearing to imply a second verb (e.g., "taking it away"); see the comments on v 42.

[265] **He sent them** [*auta*] **away.** The pronoun *auta* is neuter because its closest antecedent (*tekna,* **children**) is neuter, without necessarily excluding the earlier masculine nouns **young man** and **old man** (cf. BDF §135(3)).

[266] See the footnote to 8.7a. Similarly, the enemy is both singular and plural in Psa 74.3–10; 106.10–11; and "Rome" is both singular and plural in Maccabaica 8.17, 24 (as is "Egypt" in Psa 105.38).

[267] The Greek version reads **in the anger of his beauty,** an inverted genitive (see the footnote to 16.1), which expresses the same idea (it is equivalent to "in his beautiful anger," just as "the throne of His glory" [Matt 19.28; 25.31] is equivalent to "His glorious throne"; see BDF §165;

Eighteen Psalms' characteristic paradoxes, like the pursued pursuer (15.8–9), the mercy of death (7.4), and the command imposed by the slave (18.14). "The beauty of a woman who breaks the Law" (16.8) is actually just as paradoxical, and in the same way; if it seems less startling, that is only because it is familiar from other writings. The enemy came in splendor and glory, like other mighty conquerors ("clothed in splendor . . . all of them desirable young men," Ezek 23.12; "clothed in fine linen and purple and scarlet, and gilded with gold and precious stone and pearl," Rev 18.16; 17.4). But like theirs, his **beauty** was deceptive; it was the beauty of someone who came in **anger.**[268] Moses had warned the Israelites that, when God brought a nation to punish them, that nation would be "a hard-faced nation," one that would show no compassion for **old** or **young** (Deut 28.50). That was what the kingdom of Rome was like: as Daniel had foretold, it was "feared and awesome and surpassingly powerful . . . devouring and pulverizing and treading down" its opponents (Dan 7.7). The Roman forces "scoffed and they did not spare, in anger and indignation with wrath" (Eighteen Psalms 2.25, 28).

17.15 [13] ἐν ἀλλοτριότητι ὁ ἐχθρὸσ ἐποίησεν ‹ὑπερηφανίαν›· In *his* estrangement the enemy did arrogance,	ܒܢܘܟܪܝܘܬܐ ܡܫܬܒܗܪ ܒܥܠܕܒܒܐ. In *his* estrangement the enemy *was* boasting,
καὶ ἡ καρδία αὐτοῦ ἀλλοτρία ἀπὸ τοῦ θ(εο)ῦ ἡμῶν· and his heart *was* estranged from our God,	ܘܠܒܗ ܢܘܟܪܝ ܗܘ ܡܢ ܐܠܗܢ. and his heart was estranged from our God.
17.16 [14] καὶ πάντα ὅσα ἐποίησεν ἐν Ἰ(ερουσα)λὴμ· and all *things*, as many as he did in Jerusalem,	ܘܟܠܡܕܡ ܥܒܕܬ ܐܘܪܫܠܡ. And Jerusalem did everything
καθὼσ καὶ τὰ ἔθνη ἐν ταῖσ πόλεσι ‹τοῖσ θεοῖσ› αὐτ(ῶν)·	ܐܝܟ ܕܐܦ ܥܡ̈ܡܐ ܥܒܕܘ ܒܡܕ̈ܝܢܬܗܘܢ ܠܐܠܗ̈ܝܗܘܢ.

MHT 3.214). In the present passage, Ryle-James suggested that the original Hebrew text read "the anger of his indignation [*'pyw*]," which was mistranscribed or misread as "the anger of his beauty [*ypyw*]." But there is no textual evidence for that, and such an error has no plausibility; "anger" and "indignation" are associated in many Scripture passages, in none of which has any process of transcription or translation substituted a word for "beauty."

[268] **His anger** is sometimes taken to be God's anger (APOT); but the subject of the immediately preceding and following verses (vv 13, 15) is undoubtedly the enemy, and the "anger" in the closely parallel passage 2.25 is certainly the enemy's, not God's.

were just as also the nations *did*	as also the peoples did
in the cities to their gods.	in their cities to their gods.

17.15 ὑπερηφανίαν 260 ≡ ܒܫܘܒܗܪܗ 16h1 10h1 | ἐν υπερηφανία 253 336 •
17.16 τοῖσ θεοῖσ 336⁺260 ≡ ܠܐܠܗ̈ܝܗܘܢ 16h1 10h1 | τοὺσ θεουσ 253 •

17.15 The enemy was not only a stranger to "our race" (v 9), but also a stranger to **our God,** like the Gentiles generally ("estranged from the citizenship of Israel and foreigners from the covenants of promise, having no hope, and without God in the world," Eph 2.12). **In his estrangement the enemy did arrogance** (see on 2.1–2), one of the many sins committed by those who have no knowledge of God (Rom 1.28, 30). Israel's sinners had acted in arrogance (v 8), and therefore God punished them by the hand of an enemy who also committed **arrogance.** The enemy's "deeds opposed to the Law . . . were just as [the people of Jerusalem] themselves were doing" (2.13–14; see the comments there); when he arrogantly defiled and trampled on the Lord's holy things, he was doing only what the sinners in Jerusalem had already been doing (2.1–3; 8.13).

17.16 Here the Greek and Syriac versions are significantly different.[269]

- **All** the things that the enemy **did in Jerusalem were just as also the nations did in the cities to their gods** (Greek version).[270] In his ignorance of Israel's God (v 15), the enemy did not see any difference between the LORD and the gods of other nations (a sin of **arrogance:** 2 Kgs 18.33–35; 19.28). He thought he could do **in Jerusalem** all the things that any nation could do in any other city to any of **their** false **gods,** such as entering the holy place and walking around there (in **arrogance,** 2.1–2). (That was exactly the attitude of Ptolemy Philopator, as described in the Ptolemaic History: he saw no reason why he should not enter the holy place in Jerusalem, when he was allowed to enter the holy places of all other cities' gods; Ptolemaica 1.13.)
- **Jerusalem did everything as also the peoples did in the cities to their gods** (Syriac version). The people of Jerusalem, who ought to have known God (Rom 2.17–20), had done the same sins as the nations that were estranged from God (v 15; 2.14). Indeed, "they did not leave any sin that they did not do beyond the nations" (see the comments on 8.14; 1.8).

---

[269] Whichever form is original, the difference evidently arose in Greek. The existing Greek manuscripts have *epoiēsen en,* but the Syriac version has been translated either from a Greek text reading simply *epoiēsen* or from a Hebrew source of the latter.

[270] **As also the nations did in the cities to their gods** [*tois theois*] is the reading of 336⁺260 (supported by the Syriac), whereas 253 reads "as also the nations made their gods [*tous theous*] in their cities." Gebhardt and Rahlfs conjecturally emended the text to read "as also the nations did in the cities of their vigor [*tou sthenous*]," i.e., in the [other] cities that their vigor had conquered.

Those who were faithful fled

17.17 [15] καὶ ἐπεκρατοῦσαν αὐτῶν ‹οἱ› υἱοὶ τῆσ διαθήκησ ἐν μέσω ἐθνῶν συμμίκτ(ων)· But the sons of the covenant held power over them in *the* midst of *the* mixed nations.	ܘܐܚܝܕܝܢ ܗܘܘ ܠܗܘܢ ܒܢ̈ܝܗ̇ ܕܕܝܬܩܝ ܒܝܢܬ ܥܡ̈ܡܐ ܚ̈ܠܝܛܐ. But *the* sons of *the* covenant held power over them among the mingled peoples;
οὐκ ἦν ὁ ποιῶν ἐν μέσω ἐν αὐτοῖσ ἐν Ἰ(ερουσα)λὴμ ἔλεοσ καὶ ἀλήθειαν· *There* was no *one* who did mercy and truth in the midst among them, in Jerusalem.	ܘܠܝܬ ܗ̇ܘܐ ܒܝܢܬܗܘܢ ܕܥܒܕ ܪ̈ܚܡܐ ܘ<ܫܪܪܐ> ܒܐܘܪܫܠܡ. and there was no *one* among them who did compassion and truth in Jerusalem;

17.17 οἱ 336⁺260 | > 253 • ܘܫܪܪܐ 10h1 ≡ ἀλήθειαν 253 336⁺260 | ܘܫܪܪܢ 16h1

17.17 The **sons of the covenant** (the faithful Israelites, Acts 3.25)—those who kept God's **covenant** (Psa 132.12) and **loved the gatherings of lovingkind ones** (v 18)—were now **in the midst of the mixed nations** (the Gentiles, Jer 25.24, LXX), and were surrounded everywhere by evil: **there was no one who did mercy and truth**[271] anywhere among them[272] (vv 21–22), just as had been the case in the Babylonian period (Jer 5.1) and at other times of great trouble in Israel ("the lovingkind one has perished from the earth, and there is no one upright among humanity," Mic 7.2; Psa 12.1).

But the evildoers did not overcome the sons of the covenant. On the contrary, **the sons of the covenant** overcame them (**held power over them;** cf. 16.7). They **fled from them** (v 18), and so **their souls** were **saved from** the **evil** around them (v 19). In every generation, those who keep God's covenant and flee from all forms of evil (1 Cor 6.18; 10.14; 1 Tim 6.11; 2 Tim 2.22) "are more than conquerors" (Rom 8.37) and "have overcome the world" (1 Jn 5.4). "You are of God, little children, and have overcome them, because greater is the One who is in you than the one who is in the world" (1 Jn 4.4).

Such people remain "blameless and uncontaminated, children of God unblemished in the midst of a crooked and twisted generation, among whom you are shining as

---

[271] **And truth.** The Syriac manuscript 16h1 reads *wšrrnn.* In 10h1 the first part of the word is difficult to read in photofacsimile, but the visible traces are fully consistent with *wšrr',* and the ending is certainly -', not *-nn.* Trafton (167) misread the text of 16h1 as *wšrryn,* and regarded *wšrr'* as a conjectural emendation.

[272] The Greek text (of 253) emphasizes the full extent of the corruption by a threefold repetition: **in** [*en*] **the midst among** [*en*] **them in** [*en*] **Jerusalem.** Wherever one looks, **in** every direction (cf. "in the streets of Jerusalem … in her wide places," Jer 5.1), **no one** righteous can be seen. Gebhardt and Rahlfs conjecturally deleted **in the midst** *(en mesō).*

lights in the world" (Php 2.15). "The light shines in the darkness, and the darkness does not take hold of it" (John 1.5; Dan 12.3).[273]

17.18 [16] ἐφύγοσαν ἀπ’ αὐτ(ῶν) οἱ ἀγαπῶντεσ συναγωγὰσ ὁσίων· Those who loved *the* gatherings of lovingkind *ones* fled from them;	ܥܪܩܘ ܡܢܗܘܢ ܐܝܠܝܢ ܕܪܚܡܝܢ ܗܘܘ ܠܟܢܫܬܐ ܕܚܣܝܐ. those who loved the gathering of the lovingkind *ones* fled from them,
ὡσ στρουθία ἐξεπετάσθησαν ἀπο κοίτησ αὐτῶν· like birds they flew from their bed.	ܘܦܪܚܘ ܐܝܟ ܨܦܪܐ ܕܦܪܚܝܢ ܡܢ ܩܢܝܗܘܢ. and flew like birds that fly from their nests.

17.18 Those who serve God faithfully have always **loved the gatherings of lovingkind ones.** "I have been joyful with those who say to me, 'We will go to the house of the LORD'" (Psa 122.1). But at the time described here, such people did not gather with those around them (those around them were doing evil, v 17). Instead, they **fled from them** and hurriedly left (**flew from**) their homes (**their bed**) like birds[274]—just as the

[273] In the above discussion, verse 17 is taken as the start of a new section—the section describing those who remained faithful (vv 17–20). If this is correct, the conjunction rendered **But** at the start of verse 17 (Greek *kai* ≡ Syriac *w-*) marks a contrast with the preceding section (exactly like the **But** at the start of v 6; cf. Muraoka 353, §4; TS 1.1057, §3).

Often, however, the new section is regarded as starting only at verse 18. On that view, the **sons of the covenant** in verse 17 would be sinful Israelites (cf. v 7), who, living **in the midst of the mixed nations,** were corrupted by those nations, so that they themselves also no longer **did mercy and truth.** "Do not be led astray: evil companionships corrupt good morals" (1 Cor 15.33; 5.6). "Someone who walks with wise ones will be wise, but someone who accompanies fools will suffer evil" (Prov 13.20).

The major difficulty with that view is the statement that **the sons of the covenant held power over them.** The usual explanation is that the Judean sinners **held power over** the Romans when they told the Romans to enter and occupy Jerusalem (Viteau 347), as described in 8.18–22: "The rulers of the land met [the enemy] with joy; they said to him: 'Your path is blessed; come, enter with peace.'" But that passage is describing an invitation, not a victory of superior power **over** *(epi-)* an inferior. The Judeans had no such power over the Romans.

Alternatively, the Greek verb *epekratousan* has been interpreted as meaning, not that the unfaithful Israelites **held power over** anyone, but that they "laid hold on" the gods mentioned in verse 16 (i.e., "clave unto" them, Ryle-James mg; cf. 1 Kgs 9.9), or else that they "surpassed" the Gentiles in doing evil (Ryle-James; cf. 1.8; 8.14). But no form of Greek *epikrateō* appears to be used anywhere else in either of those senses (Viteau 347; cf. LSJ 640; Muraoka 275). And the word certainly means **held power over** in the previous psalm (16.7).

[274] **They flew** *(exepetasthēsan).* The Greek verb has often been rendered "they were scattered" (NETS), but in Biblical Greek it always depicts aerial motion (Muraoka 214), as the comparison with **birds** here confirms; and the corresponding Syriac unambiguously means **they flew**

faithful had been forced to flee hastily in the time of Antiochus Epiphanes, when "the evil things pressed hard upon them" (see the comments on Maccabaica 2.27–30; 1.38), and just as the faithful would be forced to flee hastily during the Roman destruction of Jerusalem prophesied by Jesus (Matt 24.15–21).

17.19 [17] ἐπλανῶντο ἐν ερήμοισ· σωθῆναι ψυχὰσ αὐτ(ῶν) ἀπο κακοῦ·	ܘܛܥܝܢ ܗ̈ܘܘ ܒܡܕܒܪܐ. ܠܡܦܪܩ ܢܦܫܗܘܢ ܡܢ ܒܝܫܐ.
They were straying in deserts *for* their souls to be saved from evil,	And they *were* straying in the desert to save their soul from evil,
καὶ τίμιον ἐν ὀφθαλμοῖσ παροικίασ ψυχῆ σεσωσμένη ἐξ αὐτ(ῶν)· ‹›	ܘܝܩܝܪܐ ܗܘܬ ܒܥܝ̈ܢܝܗܘܢ ܬܘܬܒܘܬܗ̇ ܕܢܦܫܐ ܕܐܬܦܪܩܬ ܗܘܬ ܡܢܗܘܢ.
and *the* soul saved from them *was* valuable in *the* eyes of *the* sojourning group.	and *the* sojourning of the soul that was saved from them was valuable in their eyes.

17.19 αὐτ(ῶν) 2° 336⁺260 ≡ 16h1 10h1 | + ἐφύγοσαν ἀπ αὐτ(ῶν) οἱ ἀγαπῶντεσ συναγωγὰσ ὁσίων· 253 •

17.19 For their souls to be saved from the **evil** around them, those who served God faithfully were now **straying in deserts** (Heb 11.38)—desolate, uninhabited regions (in contrast to **gatherings,** v 18), regions where they would be relatively safe from the enemy (Rev 12.6, 14; 1 Sam 23.14; Maccabaica 2.29). "Who will give me a travelers' lodging place in the desert? Then I will leave my people and go away from them, for they are all adulterers, an appointed gathering of treacherous people" (Jer 9.2).

The soul saved from them[275] **was valuable in the eyes of the sojourning group** (Greek version).[276] Whenever a soul escapes from the power of evil, this is precious in the eyes of all God's servants—including those who are in heaven, His angels (Luke 15.10, 7), as well as those who are **sojourning** (dwelling temporarily, *paroikias*)[277] on

---

(prḥw). The faithful needed the freedom of airborne creatures in their escape (Psa 55.6–7; Rev 12.14; cf. Psa 139.9). **Birds** could also be construed as the subject of this verb, but in that case a present tense ("as birds fly from their bed") or a participle ("like birds flying from their bed") would be expected.

[275] The first half of this verse describes the **soul** as **saved from evil;** the second half of the verse describes the **soul** as **saved from** the evildoers (**them,** i.e., those described in vv 13–17).

[276] **The soul saved from them was valuable in the eyes of the sojourning group** (Greek version). The Syriac version construes this statement in a slightly different way: **The sojourning** (in the desert, v 19a) **of the soul saved from** the evildoers **was valuable in their eyes** (in the eyes of the escapees described in v 18). The basic point is the same.

[277] **Sojourning** (*paroikias)*. Dwelling temporarily "in a foreign land" (Acts 7.6; Heb 11.9; cf. Luke 24.18). All of us are merely sojourners on earth (1 Pet 1.17; 2.11; Psa 119.19; 1 Chr

earth, His people. "I rejoice . . . that you were grieved to repentance; for you were grieved in accordance with God . . . for grief in accordance with God works repentance to salvation" (2 Cor 7.9). "I rejoiced greatly that I found some of your children walking in the truth" (2 Jn 4; 3 Jn 4; Rom 16.19; Acts 11.23).

17.20 [18] εἰσ πᾶσαν τὴν γῆν ἐγενήθη σκορπισμὸσ αὐτ(ῶν) ὑπὸ ἀνόμων· Into all the land was their scattering by *those who were* opposed to *the* Law,	ܒܟܠܗ ܐܪܥܐ ܗܘܐ ܒܘܕܪܗܘܢ ܡܢ ܥܘ̈ܠܐ. In all the land was their scattering by the unjust *ones*.
ὅτι ἀνέσχεν ὁ οὐ(ρα)νὸσ τοὺ στάξαι ὑετὸν ἐπὶ τὴν γῆν· because heaven withheld the falling of rain on the land;	ܡܛܠܗܕܐ ܐܬܬܚܝܕܘ ܫܡܝܐ ܕܠܐ ܢܫܒܘܩܘܢ ܡܛܪܐ ܥܠ ܐܪܥܐ. Because of this, the heaven was held back, so that it should not send down rain on the land,
17.21 [19] πηγαὶ συνεσχέθησαν αἰώνιοι ἐξ αβύσσων ἀπο ὀρέων ὑψηλῶν· lasting wellsprings were held back, out of *the* depths, from *the* high mountains,	ܘܡܒ̈ܘܥܐ ܕܡܢ ܥܠܡ. ܘܐܬܬܚܝܕܘ ܡܢ ܬܗ̈ܘܡܐ ܘܡܢ ܛܘ̈ܪܐ ܪ̈ܡܐ. and the watersprings that *were* from lasting time also were held back, from the abysses and from the lofty mountains,
ὅτι οὐκ ἦν ἐν αὐτοῖσ ποιῶν δικαιοσύνην καὶ κρίμα· because there was no *one* among them who did righteousness and judgment.	ܡܛܠ ܕܠܝܬ ܗܘܐ ܒܗܘܢ ܕܥܒܕ ܙܕܝܩܘܬܐ ܘܕܝܢܐ. because there was no *one* among them who did righteousness and judgment.
[20] ἀπο ἄρχοντοσ αὐτῶν καὶ λαοῦ ἐλαχίστου ἐν πάσῃ ἁμαρτίᾳ· From their ruler and *from* *the* least people *they were* in every sin,	ܡܢ ܪ̈ܝܫܢܝܗܘܢ ܘܥܕܡܐ ܠܙܥܘܪ̈ܝܗܘܢ. ܐܝܬܝܗܘܢ ܒܟܠ ܚܛ̈ܗܝܢ. From their rulers and even to their little *ones* they were in all sins;

29.15), merely "foreigners and temporary residents on the earth" (Heb 11.13), "for we do not have here an enduring city, but we are seeking the one that is to come" (Heb 13.14); "our citizenship is in heaven" (Php 3.20).

In the present passage the term has a collective sense (**sojourning group**), as in Sir 16.8 (Muraoka 536, §3b; BDAG 779, §2).

17.22 [20] ὁ βασιλεὺσ ἐν παρανομία· καὶ ὁ κριτὴσ ἐν απειθεία· καὶ ὁ λαὸσ ἐν αμαρτία·	ܡܰܠܟܳܐ ܒܥܘܠܐ ܐܝܬܘ(ܗܝ). ܘܕܝܢܐ ܒܡܪܚܘܬܐ. ܘܥܡܐ ܒܚܛܝܬܐ.
the king in Law-breaking, and the judge in disobedience, and the people in sin.	the king was in injustice, and the judge in anger, and the people in sin.

17.20–22 The faithful sons of the covenant fled in all directions: there was a **scattering** of them **into all the land**—as happened again a few decades later: there was "a great persecution against the church that was in Jerusalem, and they were all scattered throughout the regions of Judea and Samaria, except the apostles" (Acts 8.1; 11.19).

In the time of Moses, God had told the Israelites that if the nation obeyed Him, He would bless them abundantly with rain (Deut 28.12), but that if they disobeyed Him, "He will shut up the heavens, and there will be no rain, and the land will not yield its fruit" (Deut 11.17; 28.23–24; Psa 107.33–34; 1 Kgs 8.35). That punishment had already been imposed repeatedly (in the time of Elijah: Luke 4.25; in the Babylonian period: Jer 14.4; in the Persian period: Hag 1.6–11). Now it was happening again. **Heaven withheld the falling of rain on the land,**[278] and **wellsprings** that had provided water in every generation (**from lasting time,** Syriac) were now **held back** in all parts of the region (from the **depths** to the **high mountains**).

This punishment happened **because there was no one among them who did righteousness and judgment** (cf. v 17). **Every** kind of **sin** was being committed ("they did not leave any sin that they did not do beyond the nations," 8.14),[279] and the whole nation was implicated, "from the least of them even to the greatest of them" (Jer 6.13).[280] Even those who ought to have led the people in doing right—the **king**

---

[278] In the Greek version, v 20 states that this drought was what caused the faithful to be scattered so widely: **Into all the land was their scattering, because** [*hoti*] **heaven withheld the falling of rain.** In the Syriac version, the corresponding passage states that the drought was the result of their scattering: **In all the land was their scattering .... Because of this** [*mṭlhn'*], **the heaven was held back ....** Looking further back, the drought was ultimately the result of the sins that had caused their scattering (v 21, in both Greek and Syriac).

[279] **Law-breaking, and ... disobedience, and ... sin** emphasize the extent of the problem not by listing three different conditions, but by describing the condition in three different ways (cf. "iniquity and transgression and sin," Exod 34.7; "My commands, My assigned instructions, and My laws," Gen 26.5).

[280] Syriac **from their rulers and even to their little [one]s** describes the range of people involved in the **sin** (like Jer 6.13, cited above). Greek **from their ruler and [from the] least people** describes the originators of the **sin:** it came alike **from** (*apo,* BDAG 106–07, §5d; cf. Jas 1.13; Gen 6.13, LXX) all sections of society. The difference could have arisen either in Hebrew (the Greek version would correspond to Hebrew *w'm,* the Syriac to Hebrew *w'd*) or, even more plausibly, in Syriac (if the original Syriac rendering was *wd'm'* [corresponding to the Greek], and this was later altered to the more usual *w'dm'*).

(Deut 17.18–20; Prov 16.10, 12; 1 Kgs 10.9) and the **judge** (Deut 16.18–20; 2 Chr 19.5–7)—were doing wrong. And where they led, the **people** were willing to follow (Prov 29.12; Jer 5.31; 2 Tim 4.3–4). No matter what other people may go astray—however many they may be, or however illustrious they may be—we are not to be influenced by them. "My son, if sinners entice you, do not consent. If they say, 'Walk with us . . .' do not walk in the way with them; hold your foot back from their path" (Prov 1.10–15).

Raise up the Son of David to be King over Israel

17.23 [21] ἴδε κ(ύρι)ε καὶ ἀνάστησον αὐτοῖσ τὸν βασιλέα αὐτ(ῶν) υἱῶ Δα(υὶ)δ·	ܚܙܝ ܡܪܝܐ ܘܐܩܝܡ ܠܗܘܢ ܠܡܠܟܗܘܢ ܠܒܪܗ ܕܕܘܝܕ.
See[†], Lord, and raise up[†] for them their King, *the* Son of David,	See[†], LORD, and lift up[†] for them their King, *the* Son of David,
εἰσ τὸν καιρὸν ὃν ἴδεσ σὺ ὁ θ(εό)σ· τοῦ βασιλεῦσαι ἐπὶ Ἰ(σρα)ὴλ παῖδα σου·	ܒܙܒܢܐ ܗܘ ܕܚܙܐ ܐܢܬ ܐܠܗܐ. ܕܢܡܠܟ ܥܠ ܐܝܣܪܝܠ ܥܒܕܟ.
for the period of time which You[†] Yourself[‡] have seen, O God, to be King over Israel Your[†] servant,	in the time that You[†] Yourself[‡] *are* seeing, God, so that he may be King over Israel Your[†] slave,

17.23 Raise up for them their King, the Son of David . . . to be King over Israel. Later (in verse 36), this **King** is also called the Christ (Greek) ≡ Messiah (Syriac).

Five hundred years earlier, during the Babylonian period, the Lord had taken away the last of the kings descended from David. But when He did so, He promised that He would give **Israel** another, and greater, **King** descended from **David:** "Behold, the days are coming, says the LORD, that I will raise up for David a righteous Branch; and He will reign as King, and act wisely, and do judgment and righteousness in the land. In His days Judah will be saved, and Israel will dwell with security" (Jer 23.5–6). "To the increase of His government and to peace there will be no end, on the throne of David and over His kingdom, to establish it and to uphold it in judgment and in righteousness, from now on and until lasting time" (Isa 9.6–7). These things would happen in **the period of time which You Yourself have seen.**[281] The Lord, who knows the end from the beginning (Isa 46.10; 45.21), has already **seen** every day that will come (Psa 37.13; 139.16).

Only a few decades after this prayer was made, it was answered "when the fullness of the time had come" (Gal 4.4; Mark 1.15; cf. Dan 9.24–27; Rom 5.6) by the birth of Jesus: "The Lord God will give Him the throne of His father David, and He will be

[281] **Have seen** (Greek *ides* ≡ Syriac *ḥz'*). Gebhardt and Rahlfs conjecturally emended the Greek text to *eilou* ("have chosen").

King over the house of Jacob to lasting times; and of His kingdom there will be no end" (Luke 1.31–33; Acts 13.23; Rev 22.16).

17.24 [22] καὶ ὑπόζωσον αὐτὸν ἰσχὺν τοῦ θραῦσαι ἄρχοντασ ἀδίκουσ· and undergird† Him with strength to shatter *the* unrighteous rulers;	ܘܐܣܘܪܝܗܝ ܒܚܝܠܐ. ܕܢܡܟܟ ܪ̈ܝܫܢܐ ܕܥܘܠܐ. and bind† round about Him with strength, so that He may abase the rulers of injustice,
17.25 [22] καθάρισον Ἰ(ερουσα)λὴμ ἀπὸ ἐθνῶν καταπατούντων ἐν απωλεία· cleanse† Jerusalem from *the* nations who are trampling *her* down in destruction,	ܕܢܕܟܝܗ̇ ܠܐܘܪܫܠܡ ܡܢ ܥܡ̈ܡܐ ܕܡܕܝܫܝܢ ܠܗ̇ ܠܐܒܕܢܐ. so that He may cleanse Jerusalem from the peoples who *are* trampling her to destruction,
[23] ἐν σοφία ἐν δικαιοσύνη· **17.26** ἐξῶσαι ἁμαρτωλοὺσ ἀπο κληρονομίασ· in wisdom in righteousness to drive out *the* sinners from *the* inheritance,	ܠܡܘܒܕܘ ܥ̈ܘܠܐ ܡܢ ܝܪܬܘܬܟ. to destroy the unjust *ones* from Your† inheritance,
ἐκτρίψαι ὑπερηφανίαν ἁμαρτωλοῦ ὡσ σκεύη κεραμέωσ· to utterly break *the* arrogance of *the* sinner like a potter's vessels,	ܠܡܬܒܪܘ ܫܘܒܗܪܐ ܐܝܟ ܚܨܦܐ ܕܦܚܪܐ. to shatter boastfulness like the potter's potsherd,
[24] ἐν ῥάβδω σιδηρὰ συντρίψαι πᾶσαν ὑπόστασιν αὐτ(ῶν)· with an iron rod to break down every foundation of them,	ܠܡܬܒܪܘ ܒܫܒܛܐ ܕܦܪܙܠܐ ܟܠܗ ܥܘܫܢܗܘܢ. to shatter with an iron rod all their strength,
17.27 [24] ὀλοθρεῦσαι ἔθνη παράνομα ἐν λόγω στόματο(σ) αὐτοῦ· to destroy *the* Law-breaking nations with *the* word of His mouth,	ܠܡܘܒܕܘ ܥܡ̈ܡܐ ܥ̈ܘܠܐ ܒܡܠܬ ܦܘܡܗ. to destroy the unjust peoples with *the* word of His mouth;
[25] ἐν απειλῆ αὐτοῦ φυγεῖν ἔθνη ἀπὸ προσώπου αὐτοῦ· at His rebuke *for the* nations to flee from His face,	ܒܟܐܬܗ ܢܥܪܩܘܢ ܥܡ̈ܡܐ ܡܢ ܩܕܡ ܐܦܘ̈ܗܝ. at His reproof the peoples will flee from before His face;

καὶ ἐλέγξαι ἁμαρτωλοὺσ	ܘܠܡܟܣܘ ܠܚ̈ܛܝܐ
ἐν λόγῳ καρδίασ αὐτῶν·	ܒܡܠܬܐ ܕܠܒܗܘܢ܂
and to reprove *the* sinners	and to correct the sinners
in *the* word of their heart.	in the word of their heart,

17.24–27 Undergird Him (Greek) ≡ **bind round about Him** (Syriac) **with strength.** The Lord had undergirded with **strength** His creature Behemoth ("the first of the works of God," Job 40.15–19), but His Anointed would be girded with even greater **strength** (Psa 18.32). By that **strength** He would:[282]

- **Shatter the unrighteous rulers.** By His **strength** He would "rule in the midst of [His] enemies," placing them as a footstool underneath His feet (Psa 110.1–2; 18.39–40). That promise is being fulfilled today through Jesus (Eph 1.22; 1 Cor 15.25–26; Matt 21.44). The same strength enables His people, whose loins are "girded with truth," to stand firm against all spiritual forces of wickedness (Eph 6.10–14).
- **Cleanse**[283] **Jerusalem from the nations who** were **trampling her down** (v 13; 2.20) and **drive out** (Joel 2.20; Prov 2.22) **the sinners from the inheritance** (the land of Israel, 9.2)—in the way that the sinful nations who possessed the land before Israel had been driven out (Psa 78.55). The Son of David would accomplish these things **in wisdom in righteousness** (Isa 11.1–4).[284] The prophets had foretold that, under the new covenant, there would be no unclean person or foreigner in Jerusalem (Isa 52.1; Joel 3.17; Zec 14.21). That promise too is fulfilled through Jesus, "who became for us wisdom from God and righteousness" (1 Cor 1.30). Concerning "the holy city, the new Jerusalem," it is written: "nothing unclean will enter into it at all ... but only those written in the Lamb's book of life"

---

[282] Most of the Greek verbs in vv 25–27 could also possibly be construed as optatives ("May He drive out ... may He utterly break ... may He break down ... may He destroy"). However, **to shatter** (*tou thrausai,* v 24) and **to flee** (*phugein,* v 27) are unambiguously infinitives. The Syriac version presents most of them as infinitives (preceded by *l-*), but not all.

[283] **Cleanse Jerusalem.** In the Greek text, the Lord is entreated to undergird *(hupozōson)* the Messiah with strength and to **cleanse** *(katharison)* Jerusalem. In the Syriac, the Messiah Himself is to **cleanse** *(dndkyh)* Jerusalem through the strength supplied by the Lord. What the Lord does, He does through the Messiah (John 3.35; 5.22; 17.2; Matt 28.18), and what the Messiah does, He does from the Lord (John 5.19, 30; 10.37–38; Acts 10.38). Gebhardt and Rahlfs conjecturally emended the Greek text to the infinitive *katharisai* ("to cleanse," referring to the Messiah).

[284] **In** [*en*] **wisdom in** [*en*] **righteousness** (Greek version; these phrases are not found in the Syriac version) counterbalances **in destruction** at the end of the previous line (the nations are tearing down; the Wisdom of God will build up, Prov 14.1; 2 Cor 10.8; 13.10). The repeated *en* is stylistically characteristic of these psalms (as noted by Ryle-James 138; see the footnote to v 17). Gebhardt and Rahlfs conjecturally deleted the second *en* (turning the phrases into "in wisdom of righteousness").

(Rev 21.2, 27). Only those who "were washed . . . were made holy . . . were made righteous in the name of the Lord Jesus Christ" are able to inherit His kingdom (1 Cor 6.9–11; Matt 25.34–36, 41–43; Eph 5.5).

- **Utterly break the arrogance of the sinner like a potter's vessels,** and **break down every foundation of them with an iron rod,** as the Lord had prophesied centuries earlier: "I will give the nations as Your inheritance . . . . You will crush them with a rod of iron; You will shatter them like a potter's vessel" (Psa 2.8–9). Again the promise is fulfilled in Jesus (Rev 12.5; 19.15) and in His people (Rev 2.26–27).
- **Destroy the Law-breaking nations with the word of His mouth** (cf. v 39). The prophets had foretold that the Son of David "will smite the earth with the rod of His mouth, and with the breath of His lips He will kill the wicked" (Isa 11.4). This too is now being accomplished through Jesus: "Out of His mouth comes out a sharp sword, in order that with it He may smite the nations" and kill the wicked (Rev 19.15, 21; 2.16; 2 Thes 2.8). The **word of His mouth** is a message of life for the faithful, but it is also a message of death for the disobedient (2 Cor 2.15–17; John 12.48).
- Force the **nations** to **flee from His face** at **His rebuke** (Psa 104.7). When God arises, "those who hate Him flee for refuge from His face" (Psa 68.1–2). The **nations** will **flee** in vain to hide themselves "from the anger of the One who sits on the throne, and from the anger of the Lamb" (Rev 6.15–17). Even the ruler of this evil world flees from Him and His servants (Jas 4.7).
- **Reprove the sinners in the word of their heart** (the word that they utter in their heart, Psa 4.4; 10.6; Matt 24.48). When the message of Jesus reproves **sinners,** it pierces our **heart** and reveals the secrets of our heart, so that our own heart speaks against our sins (1 Cor 14.24–25; Rom 2.15; Acts 2.37). His reproof is "living and active, and sharper than any two-mouthed sword, and piercing until the division of soul and spirit, of both joints and marrow, and judging the ideas and thoughts of the heart" (Heb 4.12).

Whatever forces may oppose the Lamb, "the Lamb will overcome them, because He is Lord of lords and King of kings" (Rev 17.14). "Every high thing raised up against the knowledge of God" is cast down before Him (2 Cor 10.5). "At the name of Jesus every knee shall bow, of those in heaven and on earth and under the earth, and every tongue shall confess that Jesus Christ is Lord" (Php 2.10–11).

He will lead a holy people

17.28 [26] καὶ συνάξει λαὸν ἅγιον οὗ	ܕܢܟܢܫ ܥܡܐ ܩܕܝܫܐ ܗܘ
ἀφηγήσεται ἐν δικαιοσύνῃ·	ܕܢܫܬܒܗܪ ܒܙܕܝܩܘܬܐ.
And He will gather together	to gather
a holy people whom	the holy people who
He will lead away in righteousness,	will boast in righteousness,

καὶ κρινεῖ φυλὰσ λαοῦ ἡγιασμένου ὑπὸ κ(υρίο)υ θ(εο)ῦ αὐτοῦ· and He will judge *the* tribes of *the* people that is made holy by *the* Lord His God.	ܘܢܕܘܢ ܫܪ̈ܒܬܐ ܕܥܡܐ ܕܡܩܕܫ ܡܪܝܐ ܐܠܗܗ. and He will judge the kindreds of the people whom the LORD His God makes holy.

17.28 At the time when the Eighteen Psalms were written, "those who loved the gatherings of lovingkind ones" had been scattered and were straying in desolate regions (see the comments on vv 18–19). But the future Son of David would **gather together a holy people,** and would **lead** them **away** from *(ap-)* their former dwelling places to be with Him. The prophets had foretold that when He came, the Lord "will gather together the outcasts of Israel, and the scattered ones of Judah He will assemble together from the four ends of the earth" (from everywhere between Elam and Ethiopia, Isa 11.10–12), a promise that began to be fulfilled on the Day of Pentecost (Acts 2.5–11, 39) and will be completed when the righteous are finally gathered together at the end of the age (Matt 13.30, 40, 43). His people are **made holy** (Eph 5.26; cf. v 33; Heb 9.13–14) **by the Lord His God** (John 17.17; 1 Cor 6.11; Acts 26.18; Heb 2.11), and **He will judge** them ("all judgment" has been given to Jesus, John 5.22; see the comments on v 48).

17.29 [27] καὶ οὐκ αφήσει ἀδικίαν ἐν μέσω αὐτ(ῶν) αὐλισθῆναι ἔτι· And He will not leave unrighteousness to find lodging in their midst *any* more,	ܘܠܐ ܬܘܒ ܢܫܒܘܩ ܕܬܒܘܬܝ ܣܟܠܘܬܐ ܒܝܢܬܗܘܢ. And He will never again leave *any* sin that *is* lodging among them,
καὶ οὐ κατοικήσει πᾶσ ἄν(θρωπ)οσ μετ' αὐτ(ῶν) εἰδὼσ κακίαν· and *there* will not dwell with them any person who knows evildoing;	ܘܠܐ ܬܘܒ ܢܥܡܪ ܒܝܢܬܗܘܢ ܓܒܪܐ ܕܝܕܥ ܒܝܫܬܐ. and *there* will never again dwell among them a man who knows evil;

17.29 In the **midst** of His holy people (v 28), **He will not leave** any **unrighteousness,** or **any person who knows evildoing** (v 36). Those who do not know God "are wise to do evil, but they do not know to do good" (Jer 4.22—the opposite of God's people, Rom 16.19). The prophets had foretold that all Jerusalem's people would be righteous (Isa 60.21) and holy (Isa 4.3; Zec 14.20–21). "Do you not know that unrighteous ones will not inherit the kingdom of God? Do not be led astray; neither fornicators, nor idolaters, nor adulterers, nor soft ones, nor homosexuals, nor thieves, nor greedy ones, nor drinkers, nor revilers, nor swindlers, will inherit the kingdom of God" (1 Cor 6.9–10). All such people are "outside" the city of God, the new Jerusalem (Rev 22.14–15). "All those who do deeds opposed to the Law" will be cast out of His kingdom; only the righteous can remain within it (Matt 13.41–43).

17.30 [27] γνώσεται γὰρ αὐτοὺσ ὅτι πάντεσ υἱοὶ θ(εο)ῦ εἰσὶν αὐτῶν· for He will know them, that they are all sons of their God.	ܢܕܥ ܐܢܘܢ ܓܝܪ ܡܛܠ ܕܟܠܗܘܢ ܒܢܝܐ ܐܢܘܢ ܕܐܠܗܐ. because *He will* know them, that all of them are the sons of God,
[28] καὶ καταμερίσει αὐτοὺσ ἐν ταῖσ φυλαῖσ αὐτ(ῶν) ἐπὶ τῆσ γῆσ· And He will divide them in their tribes over the land,	ܘܢܦܠܓ ܐܢܘܢ ܒܫܪܒܬܗܘܢ ܒܐܪܥܐ. and He will divide them in their kindreds in the land,
17.31 [28] καὶ πάροικοσ καὶ ἀλλογενὴσ οὐ παροικήσει αὐτοῖσ ἔτι· and a sojourner and a foreigner will not sojourn with them *any* more.	ܘܬܘܬܒܐ ܘܢܘܟܪܝܐ ܠܐ ܢܥܡܪ ܥܡܗܘܢ. and the sojourner and the stranger will not dwell with them,

17.30 There would be no evildoers among His people (v 29); instead, **all** of them would be **sons of their God,** as the prophets had foretold (Hos 1.10), and as has now been fulfilled through Jesus (Rom 9.26). Those who have been baptized into Christ "are all sons of God through faith in Christ Jesus" (Gal 3.26–27; Rom 8.14); but no one who does unrighteousness is a son of God (1 Jn 3.10).

He will know the sons of God. Jesus said, "I know My own" (John 10.14, 27; cf. Rev 2.19)—whereas to the unrighteous He will say, "I never knew you" (Matt 7.23). "The Lord ... knows those who take refuge in Him" (Nah 1.7), those who love Him (1 Cor 8.3), those who follow Him (John 10.27).

He will divide them in their tribes over the land, as Ezekiel had foretold would happen in the day when God would send the river of living water (Ezek 47.13). All those "out of all nations and tribes" who "have washed their robes and made them white in the blood of the Lamb" are guided by Him "to springs of living water" (Rev 7.9–17), where they receive an inheritance in His dwelling place (Rev 21.7). "Blessed are the meek, for they will inherit the land" (Matt 5.5).

17.31a No **sojourner** or **foreigner** will live, even temporarily (**sojourn:** see the footnote on v 19), **with** His people **any more;** instead, He will "cleanse Jerusalem from the nations" and "drive out the sinners from the inheritance" (see the comments on vv 25–26).

He will rule the nations in righteousness

[29] κρινεῖ λαοὺσ καὶ ἔθνη ἐν σοφίᾳ δικαιοσύνησ αὐτοῦ: διάψαλμ(α): He will judge *the* peoples and nations in *the* wisdom of His righteousness. Selah.	ܡܛܠ ܕܕܐܢ ܥܡܡܐ ܘܐܡܘܬܐ ܒܚܟܡܬܐ ܕܙܕܝܩܘܬܗ. because *He will be* judging the peoples and the nations in the wisdom of His righteousness.

17.32 [30] καὶ ἕξει λαοὺσ ἐθνῶν δουλεύειν αὐτῶ ὑπὸ τὸν ζυγὸν αὐτοῦ·	ܘܢܩܢܐ ܥܡܐ ܡܢ ܥܡܡܐ. ܕܢܦܠܚܘܢܗܝ ܬܚܝܬ ܢܝܪܗ.
And He will have *the* peoples of *the* nations to be enslaved to Him under His yoke,	And He will possess a people from the peoples, who will work for Him under His yoke,
καὶ τὸν κ(ύριο)ν δοξάσει ἐν επισήμω πᾶσησ τῆσ γῆσ·	ܘܢܫܒܚܘܢܗܝ ܠܡܪܝܐ ܓܠܝܐܝܬ ܒܟܠܗ ܐܪܥܐ.
and He will glorify the Lord in a conspicuous *place* of all the earth,	and they will glorify the LORD openly in all the earth,

17.31b The Son of David **will judge** not only His holy people (v 28), but also all **peoples and nations** (see the comments on v 49), as the prophets had foretold (Isa 2.4). "All the nations" will be gathered before Jesus for judgment on the last day (Matt 25.31–33; "all everywhere," Acts 17.30–31). He will judge them **in the wisdom of His righteousness** (foretold by the prophets, Isa 2.4; 11.1–4; fulfilled in Jesus, Rev 19.11; Acts 17.31).[285]

17.32 All **nations** will **be enslaved to Him under His yoke,** as the prophets had foretold (Psa 72.11; Dan 7.27). In the days when God appointed the king of Babylon as king of kings over the nations (Dan 2.37–38), "all the nations" were commanded to "put their neck under the yoke of the king of Babylon" and "serve him" (Jer 27.5–8). Today Jesus is King of kings over the **nations** (Rev 17.14; Matt 28.18–19). All nations are to **be enslaved to Him** (Gal 1.10; Eph 6.6; Rom 6.16–22), and He commands them all to "lift up My yoke upon you ... for My yoke is kind, and My burden is light" (Matt 11.29–30).

The Greek version states that the Son of David **will glorify the Lord in a conspicuous place** (*en episēmō,* as in 2.6),[286] one that stands out above **all the earth.** Jesus "glorified [the Father] on earth, having completed the work that You gave Me to do" (John 17.4; 13.31; cf. Heb 1.3), and the new Jerusalem established by Him is set on "a mountain great and high" (Rev 21.10; cf. Heb 12.22), as the prophets had foretold

---

[285] At the end of this verse the Greek copies (but not the Syriac) add *diapsalma* (≡ Hebrew **Selah**). The term might have been added to the Greek by the person who added the superscriptions (Ryle-James 140), or it might have been removed from the Syriac (Syriac translators also tended to omit "Selah" when rendering the Hebrew Psalter: Trafton 175).

[286] **In a conspicuous place.** The term *episēmos* describes anything marked out *(-sēmos)* above *(epi-)* others: a notable place (Maccabaica 11.37), a notable sign of captivity (see on 2.6), a notable day (Est 5.4, LXX), a notable person (Matt 27.16; Rom 16.7; Ptolemaica 6.1). Its opposite is *asēmos,* "inconspicuous," "undistinguished" (Gen 30.42, LXX; Acts 21.39). The renderings "at the centre of all the earth" (AOT) and "in a place to be seen of all the earth" (APOT, doubtfully) are not supported by the usage of *episēmos* elsewhere.

("the mountain of the LORD's house will be established at the head of the mountains, and will be raised up above the hills," Isa 2.2).

The Syriac version states that the people under His yoke **will glorify the LORD openly,** as the prophets had also foretold ("all nations . . . will bow themselves down before the LORD, and will glorify Your name," Psa 86.9). Those whom God has adopted as sons through Jesus have been created "for the praise of His glory" (Eph 1.5–6, 12; Isa 43.21).

17.33 [30] καὶ καθαριεῖ Ἰ(ερουσα)λὴμ ἐν ἁγιασμῶ ὼσ καὶ τὸ ἀπ αρχῆσ·	ܘܢܕܟܝܗ̇ ܠܐܘܪܫܠܡ ܒܡܩܕܫܘܬܐ ܐܝܟ ܕܡܢ ܩܕܝܡ.
and He will cleanse Jerusalem by making *her* holy, as also the *way she was* from *the* beginning,	and He will cleanse Jerusalem in holiness, as *it was* before,
17.34 [31] ἔρχεσθαι ἔθνη ἀπ ἄκρου τ(ῆ)σ γῆσ ἰδεῖν τὴν δόξαν αὐτοῦ·	ܕܢܐܬܘܢ ܥܡ̈ܡܐ ܡܢ ܣܘܦ̈ܝܗ̇ ܕܐܪܥܐ. ܠܡܚܙܐ ܠܫܘܒܚܗ.
for nations to come from *the* endpoint of the earth to see His glory,	so that the peoples will come from *the* ends of the earth to see His glory,
φέροντεσ δῶρα τοὺσ ἐξησθενηκότασ υἱοὺσ αὐτῆσ·	ܟܕ ܡܝܬܝܢ ܐܒܦܪ̈ܐ ܠܒ̈ܢܝܗ̇. ܗܢܘܢ ܕܐܬܒܕܪܘ ܡܢܗ̇.
bearing gifts, her sons who have become utterly weak,	when *they are* bringing gifts to her sons who have been scattered from her,
17.35 [31] καὶ ἰδεῖν τὴν δόξαν κ(υρίο)υ ἣν ἐδόξασεν αὐτὴν ὁ θ(εό)σ·	ܘܠܡܚܙܐ ܠܫܘܒܚܗ ܕܡܪܝܐ. ܗܘ ܕܫܒܚܗ̇ ܐܠܗܐ.
and to see the glory of *the* Lord *with* which God has glorified her.	and to see *the* glory of the LORD *with* which God has glorified her.

17.33 He will cleanse Jerusalem by making her holy (see the comments on vv 25, 28), **as also the way she was from the beginning.** In earlier times "Israel was holy to the LORD"; but the nation had "gone far from" God and had become guilty (Jer 2.2–3; cf. Hos 2.15), and therefore she needed to be restored to her former state (Isa 1.25–26; cf. Rev 2.4–5).

17.34–35a The queen of Sheba "came from the ends of the earth to hear the wisdom of Solomon" (Matt 12.42). Similarly, in the kingdom of the Son of David, **nations** would **come from the endpoint of the earth to see His glory . . . and to see the glory of the Lord with which God has glorified** Jerusalem. The prophets had foretold that, through Him, "the glory of the LORD will be revealed, and all flesh will see it together" (Isa 40.5), a prophecy that was fulfilled through the coming of Jesus (Luke 3.6; John 1.14; cf. 2 Cor 4.4–6). At that time the **nations** would **see,** not only the glory of God, but also the glory **with which God has glorified** Jerusalem (foretold in the prophets: Isa 62.2; fulfilled through Jesus: Rev 21.10–11, 23); and by what they saw, "all the nations" would themselves receive mercy (v 38) and be made holy (v 49), just like the people of Israel (v 48).[287]

The nations would **come . . . bearing gifts,** and those gifts would be Jerusalem's **sons.**[288] This too had been foretold: "All nations ... will come and see My glory ... and they will bring your brothers from all the nations, a gift to the LORD, on horses, and in chariots, and in litters, and on mules, and on camels, to My holy mountain Jerusalem" (Isa 66.18–20; 60.3–4).

At the time when the Eighteen Psalms were written, Jerusalem's **sons** had **become utterly weak** (Greek) and **scattered** (Syriac), having suffered first at the hands of those who unjustly seized the kingship (v 6), and then at the hands of the foreign enemy (vv 13–20). But God had promised through the prophets that He would care for His afflicted and scattered people: "I will bring them out from the peoples, and gather them together from the lands . . . . I will seek the lost, and I will bring back the scattered, and I will bind up the injured, and I will strengthen the weak" (Ezek 34.13–16). Jesus said, "They will come from east and from west and from north and from south, and will recline at table in the kingdom of God; and behold, there are last ones who will be first" (Luke 13.29–30). In Christ "God has chosen the weak things of the world, in order that He may shame the strong things" (1 Cor 1.27). "When I am weak, then I am strong" (2 Cor 12.10).

[32] καὶ αὐτὸσ βασιλεὺσ δίκαιοσ διδακτὸσ ὑπὸ θ(εο)ῦ ἐπ' αὐτοὺσ· And He *is* a righteous King taught by God over them,	ܘܗܘ ܡܠܟܐ ܙܕܝܩܐ ܡܠܦ ܡܢ ܐܠܗܐ ܥܠܝܗܘܢ܀ And He *is* a righteous King taught by God over them,
17.36 [32] καὶ οὐκ ἔστιν ἀδικία ἐν ταῖσ ἡμέραισ αὐτοῦ ἐν μέσῳ αὐτ(ῶν)· and *there* is no unrighteousness in His days in their midst,	ܘܠܝܬ ܥܘܠܐ ܒܝܘܡܬܗ ܒܝܢܬܗܘܢ܀ and there is no injustice in His days among them,

[287] Cf. Kaiser, *Mission in the Old Testament,* 29: "In the blessing of Israel all the nations of the earth might be drawn to receive the message of God's salvation as well"—which was fulfilled supremely through the coming of the Messiah.

[288] The Greek version reads **bearing gifts, her sons;** the Syriac reads **bringing gifts for** [*l*-] **her sons** (cf. Psa 45.12; 72.10; Matt 2.11).

ὅτι πάντεσ ἅγιοι καὶ βασιλεὺσ αὐτ(ῶν) χ(ριστὸ)σ κ(ύριο)σ·	ܡܛܠ ܕܟܠܗܘܢ ܩܕܝܫܝܢ. ܘܡܠܟܗܘܢ ܡܫܝܚܐ ܡܪܝܐ.
because all *of them are* holy *ones*, and their King *is the* Christ, *the* Lord.	because all of them *are* holy, and their King *is* the Messiah, the LORD.

17.35b The Son of David **is a righteous King taught by God.** "In righteousness a throne is established" (Prov 16.12), as Jesus' throne is (Heb 1.8–9; Jer 23.5). He said, "I do nothing from Myself; but just as the Father taught Me, these things I speak" (John 8.28; 7.16–18; 5.19; 12.49–50; 14.10, 24).

17.36 There is[289] **no unrighteousness** among His people, **because all of them are holy** (see the comments on vv 28–29).

Their King is the Christ (*Christos,* Greek) ≡ **the Messiah** (*Mšyḥ',* Syriac; compare John 1.41; 4.25). In both languages the term means "Anointed." Every king of Israel was anointed (1 Sam 15.1; 2 Sam 12.7), and the prophets had foretold that the future Son of David would likewise be anointed by God as King of Israel (Psa 2.2; 45.7; Isa 61.1). Those prophecies were fulfilled in Jesus of Nazareth (Acts 4.26–27; Heb 1.8–9; Luke 4.18, 21), because "God anointed Him with the Holy Spirit and with power" (Acts 10.38).

This **King,** this Anointed One, would be the **Lord.**[290] The term **Lord** *(kurios)* can be applied to any master (Matt 6.24), from a human being in authority ("masters [*kuriois*] according to the flesh," Eph 6.5) to God (the "Master [*kurios*] . . . in heaven," Eph 6.9). Every king is the lord (master) of his subjects (1 Sam 26.16; Gen 40.1; 2 Sam 3.21; 1 Kgs 2.38; 12.27; 18.8; etc.), and so the future Son of David, who would be **King** of Israel, had been called **Lord** by the prophets (David calls Him "Lord" in Psa 110.1 [*kuriō,* LXX]).[291] It is therefore no surprise to find Him called **Lord** in this passage also. When Jesus was born, shepherds in the vicinity of Bethlehem were told that He was "Christ the Lord" (Luke 2.11); and thirty years later, Peter told the

[289] **There is.** Greek *estin* (present tense) here depicts "a future occurrence as if it were occurring already" (Fanning, *Verbal Aspect in New Testament Greek,* 225–26), "differing from the future tense mainly in the tone of assurance that is imparted" (MHT 1.120; Porter, *Verbal Aspect in the Greek of the New Testament,* 230–32; BDF §323). Death, the last enemy, "is destroyed' already (*katargeitai,* present; 1 Cor 15.25). Often, as in the passage under discussion, present and future verbs occur side by side (e.g., Rev 9.6; John 3.36). Syriac *lwt* is used in both present and future situations (Nöldecke §§301, 270).

[290] **The Christ, the Lord** *(christos kurios).* Carrière and Rahlfs conjecturally emended the Greek text to *christos kuriou* ("the Christ of the Lord"). The Syriac version unambiguously supports the existing Greek here.

[291] The Pharisees of Jesus' time clearly accepted that the Messiah was called "Lord" in Psa 110.1. Otherwise Jesus could not have silenced them by asking them why David called the Christ his Lord (Matt 22.42–46). They could simply have replied that David never did call the Christ his Lord.

crowd on the Day of Pentecost "that God has made Him both Lord and Christ—this Jesus whom you crucified" (Acts 2.36).[292]

He will not wage war by earthly power

17.37 [33] οὐ γὰρ ἐλπιεῖ ἐπι ἵππο(ν) καὶ ἀναβάτην καὶ τόξον·	ܡܛܠ ܕܠܐ ܗܢܐ ܢܣܒܪ ܥܠ ܣܘܣܝܐ ܘܠܐ ܥܠ ܪܟܒܐ. ܘܠܐ ܥܠ ܩܫܬܐ.
For He will not hope on a horse and a rider and a bow,	Because *He will* not hope on a horse, nor on a rider, nor on a bow,
οὐδὲ πληθυνεῖ αὐτῷ χρυσίον οὐδὲ ἀργύριον εἰσ πόλεμον·	‹ܘܐܦܠܐ› ܡܣܓܐ ܠܗ ܕܗܒܐ ܘܣܐܡܐ ܠܩܪܒܐ.
nor will He multiply for Himself gold, nor silver, for war,	nor *will He* make for Him*self* many *things* of gold and silver for war,
καὶ πολλοῖσ οὐ συνάξει ἐλπίδασ εἰσ ἡμέραν πολέμου·	ܘܠܐ ܢܣܒܪ ܥܠ ܣܓܝܐܐ ܒܝܘܡܐ ܕܩܪܒܐ.
and He will not gather together hopes by many for a day of war.	and He will not hope on many in the day of war.

17.37 ܘܐܦܠܐ 10h1 ≡ οὐδὲ 253 336^{+}260 | ܐܦܠܐ 16h1 •

17.37 The future King of Israel (v 36) would not be like earthly kings. When preparing **for a day of war,** earthly kings might put their trust in earthly things: their military equipment (**a horse or a rider or a bow;** cf. Deut 17.16; Psa 33.16–17; 20.7), their finances (**gold** or **silver;** cf. Deut 17.17), and/or the size of their army (**many**).[293] But this King would not. The outcome of a battle is determined only by God (Prov 21.31; Isa 31.1–3), and the Son of David would place His **hope** only on God (v 38),

[292] The Syriac version describes **the Messiah** as **the Lord** (*MRY'*), a form applied only to God the Father and Christ (TS 2.2204–05)—although, like Greek *kurios,* it can translate either Hebrew *'dny* (a term applicable to any master) or Hebrew *YHWH* ("Jehovah," the special name of the true God). It is hypothetically possible that the original Hebrew might have been less specific than either the existing Greek or Syriac texts (it might possibly have read something like *mšyḥ YHWH,* which could be construed either as "the Messiah, the Lord" or as "the Messiah of the Lord"; cf. LXX.DE 2.1937). But it is unwise to rewrite a text on the basis of presuppositions about what it might or might not have originally said. And even if the Hebrew original had explicitly identified the Messiah as God, that would still not be surprising, because previous prophecies had done the same (Isa 9.6; Psa 45.6 ≡ Heb 1.8). As Jesus pointed out, even lesser human masters had been termed "gods" in the Hebrew Scriptures (John 10.34–36).

[293] **Many** (Greek *pollois* ≡ Syriac *sgy'*). The term is derived from 1 Sam 14.6, where "many" (*pollois* ≡ *sgy',* in all Greek and Syriac texts of the verse) again occurs without any accompanying noun. In the present passage Gebhardt and Rahlfs conjecturally added *laois* ("peoples") to the Greek text.

not on any earthly aid to victory. "There is no hindrance to the LORD to save by many or by few" (1 Sam 14.6; Psa 44.3; Hos 1.7; see the comments on Maccabaica 3.18).

Jesus' "kingdom is not of this world," and He commanded His servants not to fight in a worldly way (John 18.36; Matt 26.52; Luke 6.29; 2 Tim 2.24). "The weapons of our warfare are not of the flesh" (2 Cor 10.3–5); on the contrary, they are spiritual (e.g., truth, righteousness, and faith, Eph 6.12–17).

He will smite the land with His word

17.38 [34] κ(ύριο)σ αὐτὸσ βασιλεὺσ αὐτοῦ ἐλπὶσ ‹τοῦ› δυνατοῦ ἐλπίδι θ(εο)ῦ·	ܡܪܝܐ ܓܝܪ ܗ̇ܘ ܡܠܟܗ̇ ܗܘܝ ܣܒܪܗ. ܘܚܝܠܗ ܥܠ ܣܒܪܗ ܕܐܠܗܗ.
The Lord Himself *is* His King, *the* hope of the *One who is* powerful in *the* hope of God,	For the LORD Himself *is* His King; His hope and His might *are* on *the* hope of His God,
καὶ ἐλεήσει πάντα τὰ ἔθνη ἐνώπιον αὐτοῦ ἐν φόβῳ·	ܘܥ ...ܡ ܠܥ̈ܝܢܘܗܝ، ܥܠ ܟܠܗܘܢ... ܠܬܐ
and He will have mercy on all the nations *that are* in His sight in fear.	and … before His eyes on all of… fear.

17.38 τοῦ 336^{+}260 \| αὐτοῦ 253 •

17.38[294] On earth, greater kings ruled over lesser kings. King Solomon, for instance, "ruled over all the kings from the River even up to the land of the Philistines, and up to the border of Egypt" (2 Chr 9.26). A great king, to whom all lesser kings were subject, was a "king of kings" (Dan 2.37–38; Ezra 7.12). The future Son of David would be a King (v 36)—indeed, He would be the "King of kings" (Rev 17.14), because "all kings will bow themselves down to Him" (Psa 72.11; 2.10–12). But even He would still have one **King** over Him: **the Lord Himself** would be **His King.** "The head of Christ is God" (1 Cor 11.3). Jesus said, "The Father is greater than I" (John 14.28); He was, and is, subject to the Father (1 Cor 15.27–28), and always submitted obediently to the Father's commands (John 8.29; 5.30; 6.38; 14.31; 15.10).

The Lord (the Father) is **the hope of the One who is powerful in the hope of God.** The future Son of David would be **powerful,** but His power would not come from earthly sources (v 37). Instead, He would place His **hope** only in **God,** and His power would be given to Him by God (v 42). This too was fulfilled in Jesus: "God anointed Him with the Holy Spirit and with power" (Acts 10.38), so that "the power of the Lord was with Him" (Luke 5.17; 4.14, 36; 6.19).

By His power, the Son of David would "destroy the Law-breaking nations" (v 27),

---

[294] The only known Syriac manuscript of this section (10h1) is partly fragmentary; hence the intermittent gaps in the Syriac text from this point onwards.

but He would **have mercy on all the nations that are in His sight in fear,**[295] i.e., on all those who come before Him with the reverence and awe that a ruler deserves (Prov 24.21)—not in disobedience, as Law-breakers (v 27), but in obedience, as subjects (v 32). "The LORD has mercy on those who fear Him" (Psa 103.13; Eighteen Psalms 13.11; 15.15). Non-Israelites ("the peoples") as well as Israelites ("the tribes of the people") would be "made holy" under the rule of the coming Son of David (vv 48–49). The prophets had foretold that the nations would turn to Him (Isa 11.10; 42.4), and those prophecies are fulfilled in the present age, when people from **all the nations** turn to Jesus (Rom 15.12; Matt 12.18–21) and live "in the fear of Christ" (Eph 5.21; 6.5; 1 Pet 3.14–15 ≡ Isa 8.12–13), receiving **mercy** from Him and from His Father (2 Jn 3; Jude 21), in accordance with the prophecies (Hos 2.23 ≡ Rom 9.25; 1 Pet 2.10). But those who shrink away from His sight (Heb 10.38–39; John 3.19–20), or who do not fear Him (Col 3.22; Php 2.12; cf. Rom 3.18), cannot expect His mercy (John 5.22–29).

17.39 [35] ‹πατάξει› γὰρ γῆν τῷ λόγῳ τοῦ στόματοσ αὐτοῦ εἰσ αἰῶνα· For He will smite *the* land with the word of His mouth to lasting time;	ܢܡܚܝܗ̇ ܓܝܪ ܠܐܪܥܐ ܒܡܠܬ ܦܘܡܗ ܠܥܠܡ. For He will smite the land with *the* word of His mouth to lasting time,
17.40 [35] εὐλογήσει λαὸν κ(υρίο)υ ἐν σοφίᾳ μετ ευφροσύνησ· He will bless *the* people of *the* Lord in wisdom with gladness.	ܘܢܒܪܟ ܠܗ ܠܥܡܗ ܕܡܪܝܐ ܥܡ...ܒܚܕܘܬܐ. and He will bless *the* people of the LORD with … gladness.

17.39 πατάξει 260 ≡ ܢܡܚܝܗ̇ 10h1 | κατ- 253 336 •

17.39 He will smite the land, not with a horse or a bow or a huge army (v 37), but merely **with the word of His mouth** (see the comments on v 27). His **word** has greater **strength** than any ruler on earth (cf. Ecc 7.19); it can even **do away with sinners** (v 41; John 12.48). Jesus' followers "do not wage war in accordance with the flesh; for the weapons of our warfare are not fleshly, but are powerful to God for the tearing down of strongholds—tearing down reasonings, and every high thing raised up against the knowledge of God, and taking every thought captive into the obedience

---

[295] **And He will have mercy.** The traces in 10h1 probably represent the Syriac equivalent *wn[rḥ]m* ("and He will have compassion"). The next word has seyame. It was read by Harris-Mingana as *lḥšhy* (≡ *lḥšwhy*, "for his sufferings") and by Baars as *lḥwhy*, but we are skeptical of the supposed *ḥ;* its strokes are too far apart (more like two letters than one) and the right stroke is longer than the left, contrary to this scribe's practice elsewhere. The two strokes are written over an erasure, which may have affected their shape. We read *l'[y]nwhy,* **before His eyes** (the slope of this scribe's ' tends to be influenced by the slope of a preceding *l;* cf. his writing of *l'lm* at the end of v 39). "For his sufferings" would be grammatically awkward, and would not correspond to the Greek.

of Christ" (2 Cor 10.3–5). They fight and overcome their spiritual enemies not with a sword or a spear, but with "the sword of the Spirit, which is the word of God" (Eph 6.17; Rev 12.11; 19.15). All "the kings of the earth and their armies" who are "gathered together against" Jesus and His followers will be "killed by the sword … that came out of His mouth" (Rev 19.19–21).

17.40 He will bless the people of the Lord (those who come before Him in fear, verse 38). "The God and Father of our Lord Jesus Christ … has blessed us with every spiritual blessing in the heavenly regions in Christ" (Eph 1.3). God had promised Abraham that "in your Seed all the nations of the earth will be blessed" (Gen 22.18 ≡ Acts 3.25; Gal 3.8, 16); and Jesus was the fulfillment of that promise, as Peter explained to the people of Jerusalem: "To you first God, having raised up His Servant, sent Him to bless you by turning each one from your iniquities" (Acts 3.26; Gal 3.14). He did this **in wisdom** (see on vv 25, 31, 42) **with gladness:** His birth was a message of "great joy, which will be for all the people" (Luke 2.10–11; Rom 15.10; Gal 4.27). When the Lord opens up His hand in mercy, it makes "the soul of the humble one glad" (5.14; 10.7).

17.41 [36] καὶ αὐτὸ(σ) καθαρὸσ ἀπὸ ἁμαρτίασ· τοῦ ἄρχειν ⸂λαοῦ μεγάλου⸃·	ܘܗܘ ܕܟܝ ...ܗܘܐ ܪܫܐ ܠܥܡܐ ܪܒܐ.
And He *will be* clean from sin to rule a great people,	And He will be clean … ruler to a great people,
ἐλέγξαι ἄρχοντασ· καὶ ἐξᾶραι ἁμαρτωλοὺσ ἐν ἰσχύει λόγου·	ܠܡܟܣܘ ܠܪ̈ܫܢܐ ܘܠܡܘܒܕܘ ܠܚ̈ܛܝܐ ܒܡܠܬܗ.
to reprove rulers, and to do away with sinners in *the* strength of *His* word.	to correct the rulers, and to destroy the sinners with His word.

17.41 λαοῦ μεγάλου 336[+]260 ≡ ܠܥܡܐ ܪܒܐ 10h1 | λαοὺσ μεγάλουσ 253 •

17.41 He will be clean from sin. "All have sinned and fall short of the glory of God" (Rom 3.23; Ecc 7.20; 1 Jn 1.8, 10)—but the Son of David, the Messiah, would be different. Jesus, uniquely, "did no sin" (Isa 53.9 ≡ 1 Pet 2.22; 1 Jn 3.5; 2 Cor 5.21; Heb 4.15; 7.26), and therefore He is uniquely able **to rule a great people.** The ruler of a **great people** must have "an understanding heart . . . to discern between good and evil" (1 Kgs 3.8–9); he must be "one who rules over people righteously, ruling in the fear of God" (2 Sam 23.3); he must "judge the people with righteous judgment" (Deut 16.18). Being without sin Himself, Jesus is able **to rule** His **people** with perfect righteousness (Isa 11.4–5; 32.1; Jer 23.5; Zec 9.9; Psa 45.6 ≡ Heb 1.8). Being without sin Himself, He is also uniquely able **to reprove rulers and to do away with sinners in the strength of His word** (see the comments on vv 27, 39). Only one who is **clean from sin** is in a position to judge others for sin (Matt 7.1–5; Rom 2.1–3; cf. John

8.7). And even the **rulers** are subject to His reproof, for He is King even over them (Rev 17.14; Psa 72.11).

17.42 [37] καὶ οὐκ ἀσθενήσει ἐν ταῖσ ἡμέραισ αὐτοῦ ἐπι θ(ε)ῷ αὐτοῦ· And He will not become weak in His days on His God,	ܘܠܐ ܢܬܒܨܪ ܒܝܘܡܬܗ ܡܢ ܐܠܗܗ. And He will not decrease in His days from His God,
ὅτι ὁ θ(εὸ)σ κατηργάσατο αὐτὸν δυνατὸν ἐν πν(εύματ)ι ἁγίω· because God has made Him powerful in *the* Holy Spirit	ܡܛܠ ...ܕܝܫܐ. because ... Holy ...
καὶ σοφὸ(ν) ἐν βουλῇ συνέσεωσ μετα ἰσχύοσ καὶ ‹δικαιοσύνησ›· and wise in *the* counsel of understanding with strength and righteousness,	ܘܚܟܝܡܐ ܒܡܠܟܐ ܕܣܟܠܐ. ܒܚܝܠܐ ܘܒܙܕܝܩܘܬܐ and wise in the counsel of foolishness with power and with righteousness,
17.43 [38] καὶ εὐλογία κ(υρίο)υ μετ᾽ αὐτοῦ ἐν ἰσχύει and *the* Lord's blessing *will be* with Him in strength,	ܘܒܒܘܪܟܬܗ ܕܡܪܝܐ ܥܡܗ. ܒܚܝܠܐ and with the LORD's blessing with Him in might,
καὶ οὐκ ασθενήσει· and He will not become weak;	ܘܠܐ ܐܬܒܪܗ. and He has not become weak;
17.44 [39] ἡ ἐλπὶσ αὐτοῦ ἐπὶ κ(ύριο)ν His hope *is* on *the* Lord,	...ܡܪܝܐ ܗ̤ܘ ... is the LORD,
καὶ τίσ δύναται πρὸσ αὐτὸν· and who is able *to prevail* against Him?	ܘܡܢܘ ܢܩܘܡ ܠܘܩܒܠܗ. and who will rise to face Him?
[40] ἰσχυρὸσ ἐν ἔργοισ αὐτοῦ· καὶ κραταιὸσ ἐν φόβω θ(εο)ῦ· Strong in His works, and mighty in *the* fear of God,	ܡܚܝܠ ܓܝܪ ܒܥܒܕܘܗܝ. ܘܥܫܝܢ ܒܕܚܠܬܗ ܕܐܠܗܗ. For *He will be* mighty in His works, and powerful in *the* fear of His God,

17.42 δικαιοσύνησ 336[+]260 ≡ ܒܙܕܝܩܘܬܐ 10h1 | -νην 253 •

17.42–44 The Son of David, the Messiah, **will not become weak … on His God,** an expressively condensed statement (see the footnote to Maccabaica 14.26), which is presented more fully in the following lines: **He will not become weak; His hope is on the Lord.** God is always faithful in His promises, and therefore no one who fixes their **hope** steadfastly on Him will be put to shame (Heb 10.23; 6.18; 3.6; Rom 5.5; Psa 25.3).

Far from becoming **weak,** the Messiah would be "powerful in the hope of His God" (see the comments on v 38), **because** God **made Him powerful in the Holy Spirit** ("God anointed Him with the Holy Spirit and with power," Acts 10.38; Luke 4.14).[296] **The Lord's blessing will be with Him in strength** (Luke 19.38), so that He would be **strong in His works** (as described in Acts 2.22), **wise in the counsel of understanding**[297] **with strength and righteousness** (as described in Isa 11.2; cf. Ecc 7.19) and **mighty in the fear of God** (as described in Isa 11.3). "In the fear of the LORD is confidence of strength" (Prov 14.26).

Not only would the Messiah have strength Himself, but He would also give strength to His people (see the comments on v 45).

Who is able to prevail against Him? If God is with someone, no one is able to prevail against them (Jer 1.19; 15.20; 20.11; Rom 8.31–39). Not even the gates of Hades can prevail against the work of Jesus (Matt 16.18); not even the combined forces of wickedness can stand against Him (Rev 17.14; 19.19–21).

17.45 [40] ποιμαίνων τὸ ποίμνιον κ(υρίο)υ ἐν πίστει καὶ δικαιοσύνῃ·	ܪܥܐ ܡܪܥܝܬܗ ܕܡܪܝܐ ܒܙܕܝܩܘܬܐ ܘܒܗܝܡܢܘܬܐ.
shepherding the Lord's flock of sheep in faithfulness and righteousness,	shepherding the LORD's flock in righteousness and faithfulness,
κ(αὶ) οὐκ ἀφήσει ἀσθενῆσαι ἐν αὐτοῖσ ἐν τῇ νομῇ αὐτ(ῶν)·	ܘܠܐ ܢܫܒܘܩ ܕܐܢܫ ܢܬܟܪܗ ܒܡܪܥܝܬܗ.
and He will not leave *any* among them to become weak in their pasture.	and He will not let a man become weak in His flock of sheep.

17.45 Like David (Psa 78.70–72), the Son of David would be a Shepherd, **shepherding the Lord's flock of sheep in faithfulness and righteousness,** as the prophets had foretold (Ezek 34.23; 37.24). Jesus said, "I am the good Shepherd; and I know My own, and My own know Me, just as the Father knows Me, and I know the Father; and I lay down My life for the sheep" (John 10.11–15).

He will not leave any among them to become weak (see the comments on v 34). Israel had suffered from "shepherds who were feeding themselves .... The weak ones you have not strengthened, and the diseased ones you have not healed, and the injured ones you have not bound up ... and on all the face of the earth My flock was scattered ... from there being no shepherd, and My shepherds did not seek My flock" (Ezek 34.1–8). But the Lord would "bring back the scattered, and I will bind up the

[296] **Holy Spirit** *(pneumati hagiō)*. The present passage is based on Isa 11.2, where the word **Spirit** appears four times, the first of which is explicitly "the Spirit of the LORD;" we have therefore capitalized the term here.

[297] **Understanding** *(suneseōs)* is the reading of the Greek text. The Syriac manuscript (10h1) has *pt'',* **foolishness** (cf. 1 Cor 1.21–24, 27), although Harris-Mingana and Baars conjecturally emended this to *ptn',* "understanding," matching the Greek.

injured, and I will strengthen the weak" by sending the Son of David to shepherd them (Ezek 34.13–16, 23). Jesus said, "My sheep … follow Me, and I Myself give them lasting life, and to lasting time they will not at all be destroyed; and no one will snatch them out of My hand" (John 10.27–28).

17.46 [41] ἐν ἰσότητι πάντασ αὐτοὺσ ἄξει· In equality He will lead them all,	ܠܟܠܗܘܢ ܢܟܢܫ ܒܫܘܝܘܬܐ. He will gather all of them in equality,
καὶ οὐκ ἔσται ἐν αὐτοῖσ ὑπερηφανία· τοῦ καταδυναστευθῆναι ἐν αὐτοῖσ· and there will not be *any* arrogance among them, *for* *any* among them to be overpowered.	ܘܠܐ ܬܫܬܟܚ ܒܗܘܢ ܫܒܗܪܘܬܐ ܕܬܬܥܫܢ ܥܠܝܗܘܢ. and boasting will not be found among them, so that it might be powerful over them.

17.46 In equality He will lead them all. Under His leadership "there is neither Jew nor Greek, there is neither slave nor free man, there is neither male nor female; for you are all one in Christ Jesus" (Gal 3.28; Col 3.11). In accordance with His own example (Matt 20.25–28; Php 2.3–6), no member of the flock is to "lord it over" any other, but all are to "wrap yourselves in lowliness of mind, because God sets Himself against arrogant ones, but He gives favor to lowly ones" (1 Pet 5.3–5). So **there will not be any arrogance among them, for any among them to be overpowered** by it (*katadunasteuthēnai,* as in Acts 10.38). They are not under sin's power, but under their Master's (vv 32, 44; 16.7–8; Rom 6.14, 22).

17.47 [42] αὕτη ἡ εὐπρέπεια τοῦ βασιλέωσ Ἰ(σρα)ὴλ ἣν ἔγνω ὁ θ(εό)σ· This *will be* the good appearance of the King of Israel whom God has known,	ܗܕܐ ܗܝ ܐܝܩܘܬܗ ܕܡܠܟܗ ܕܐܝܣܪܐܝܠ. … This is *the* beauty of *the* King of Israel …
ἀναστῆσαι αὐτὸν ἐπ' οἶκον Ἰ(σρα)ὴλ παιδεῦσαι αὐτὸν· to raise Him up over *the* house of Israel to discipline it.	…ܩܡܘ ܥܠ ܒܝܬܗ ܕܐܝܣܪܐܝܠ ܠ…ܗ. … raise over *the* house of Israel to … it.

17.47 David had been a person of **good appearance** (1 Sam 16.12). The Son of David, the future King of Israel, would be "beautiful beyond the sons of Man" (Psa 45.2–3)—not with fleshly beauty (quite the contrary: Isa 53.2), but with **this,** with the spiritual qualities that have just been described (wisdom, vv 42; purity from sin, v 41; righteousness, vv 42, 45; power in the Holy Spirit, vv 42–44; fear of God, v 44; faithfulness, v 45). "The LORD … beautifies [*yp'r*] the meek with salvation" (Psa 149.4).

God has known this **King** (just as this King knows His flock, v 30; John 10.14–15), and God would set Him up **over the house of Israel to discipline it** (*paideusai,* to “correct” [APOT] and “educate” [AOT] it by training it in righteousness, 2 Tim 3.16; Heb 12.11), as described in 18.8–9.

Greek	Syriac
17.48 [43] τὰ ῥήματα αὐτοῦ πεπυρωμένα ὑπερ χρυσίον τὸ πρῶτον τίμιον· His words *will be* refined by fire beyond the most valuable gold;	ܦܬܓܡܘ̈ܗܝ ܒܩܝܢ ܠܥܠ ܡܢ ܕܗܒܐ. ܘܡܝܩܪܐ His words *will be* tested beyond gold, and honorable,
ἐν συναγωγαῖσ διακρίνει λαοῦ φυλὰσ ἡγιασμένου· in *the* gatherings He will judge *the* tribes of *the* people that is made holy;	ܒܟܢܘ̈ܫܬܐ ܠܟܘ... ܫܪ̈ܒܬܐ ܡܢ ܥܡܐ ܩܕܝܫܐ. in the gatherings to ... the kindreds from the holy people;
17.49 [43] οἱ λόγοι ‹αὐτοῦ› ὡσ λόγοι ἁγίων ἐν μέσω λαῶν ἡγιασμένων· His words *will be* like *the* words of *the* holy *ones*, in *the* midst of *the* peoples who are made holy.	ܦܬܓܡܘ̈ܗܝ ܐܝܟ ܦܬܓܡ̈ܐ ܕܩܕ̈ܝܫܐ ܒܝܢܬ ܥܡܐ ܩܕܝܫܐ. His words *will be* like the words of the holy *ones* among the holy people.

17.49 αὐτοῦ 336⁺260 ≡ 10h1 | αὐτ(ῶν) 253 •

17.48–49 Just as the Son of David would be able to conquer His enemies with His word (vv 27, 39, 41), so He would be able to discipline His flock (v 47) with **His words,** because those words would be outstandingly precious—they would be more **refined**[298] than **the most valuable gold,** and they would be comparable to the **words of the holy ones** (the holy angels and/or holy people who spoke the word of God).[299] The Wisdom of God says, “Receive My discipline, and not silver; and knowledge, beyond choice gold” (Prov 8.10). “Every word of God is refined” (Prov 30.5), like precious metal (Psa 12.6; Prov 10.20; 25.11–12), and Jesus always spoke the words that God gave him to speak (John 8.26; 12.49; 14.10; cf Deut 18.18–19).

---

[298] **Refined by fire.** The Greek has *pepurōmena* (“put through fire,” as in Rev 3.18); the Syriac has *bqyn* (**tested,** as in 1 Pet 1.7). Both are applied to the words of God (e.g., Psa 18.30, LXX ≡ Syr).

[299] The term **holy ones** *(hagiōn)* can refer to both holy people (v 36; Rom 1.7; 12.13) and holy angels (Psa 89.5, 7, LXX); therefore, the **words of the holy ones** can encompass both the words of holy angels (“the word of the holy ones,” Dan 4.17) and the words of holy people (“the words that were spoken beforehand by the holy prophets,” 2 Pet 3.2). In this context the two groups do not need to be distinguished, because both the holy angels and the holy prophets spoke the same thing—the word of God (Heb 2.2; 2 Pet 1.21). The word of the Messiah would be **like** theirs: it too would be the word of God (v 35; John 12.49–50).

The Son of David would "gather a holy people" (v 28); **in the gatherings He will judge**[300] **the tribes of the people that is made holy** (v 28), and declare **His words . . . in the midst of the peoples who are made holy.** "The Father . . . has given all judgment to the Son" (John 5.22; Acts 10.42; 17.30–31); and He will judge by means of the word that He has spoken (John 12.48). Not only Israelites (**tribes of the people**),[301] but also peoples of other nations (**peoples**), would be **made holy** under His government: all nations are able "to receive forgiveness of sins and an inheritance among those who are made holy by faith in" Jesus (Acts 26.18; Rom 15.16). Only those who have thus been **made holy** have a place in His kingdom (1 Cor 6.9–11).

May God quickly bring about His mercy

17.50 [44] μακάριοι οἱ γενόμενοι ἐν ταῖσ ἡμέραισ ἐκείναισ· Blessed *will be* those who come to be in those days,	ܛܘܒܝܗܘܢ ܠܐܝܠܝܢ ܕܗܘܝܢ ܒܝܘܡܬܐ ܗܢܘܢ. Blessed *will be* those who are in those days,
ἰδεῖν τὰ ἀγαθὰ Ἰ(σρα)ὴλ ἐν συναγωγῇ φυλῶ(ν) ‹ἃ ποιήσει› ὁ θ(εό)σ· to see the good *things* of Israel, which God will do in *the* gathering of *the* tribes.	ܠܡܚܙܐ ܛܒܬܐ ܕܐܝܣܪܝܠ ܒܟܢܘܫܬܐ ܕܥܡܐ. ܕܥ... ܐܠܗܐ to see the good *things* of Israel, which God . . . in the gathering of the people,

17.50 ἃ ποιήσει 260 [ܕܥ... 10h1] | ποιῆσαι 253 336 •

17.50 Blessed will be those who come to be in the **days** of the Son of David, the Messiah. Jesus said to those who lived in His days: "Blessed are your eyes, because you see; and your ears, because you hear. For, amen, I say to you that many prophets and righteous people desired to see the things that you see—and they did not see; and to hear the things that you hear—and they did not hear" (Matt 13.16–17; 1 Pet 1.10–12; cf. Eph 3.4–5; Heb 11.39–40).

To see the good things of Israel, which God will do in the gathering of the tribes. "How great is Your goodness, which . . . You have done for those who seek refuge in You!" (Psa 31.19). "God has spoken good things of Israel to lasting time and still more" (11.8). Under the new covenant, both Jews and Gentiles according to the flesh have been gathered into His **Israel** (Rom 2.28–29; 9.6–8; Php 3.3) and receive the

---

[300] **He will judge.** Here the Greek is *diakrinei;* in v 28 it is simply *krinei.* The two forms are often used to describe the same act of judgment (e.g., in 1 Cor 6.1–6). "As I judged [*diekrithēn*] your fathers in the desert of the land of Egypt, so I will judge [*krinō*] you" (Ezek 20.36, LXX—where both forms translate Hebrew *špt*).

[301] **The tribes of the people** *(laou phulas)* is the reading of 253, supported by the Syriac (10h1), whereas 336*260 have "the peoples, the tribes" *(laous phulas).*

good things that God has bestowed on His people (Matt 7.11). Indeed "all things work together for good to those who love God" (Rom 8.28).

17.51 [45] ‹ταχύναι› ὁ θ(εὸ)σ ἐπι Ἰ(σρα)ὴλ τὸ ἔλεο(σ) αὐτοῦ· May God quickly bring about His mercy on Israel;	ܠܡܣܪܗܒܘ ܪ̈ܚܡܘܗܝ ܥܠ ܐܝܣܪܝܠ to hasten His compassions on Israel,
ῥύσεται ἡμᾶσ ἀπὸ ἀκαθαρσίασ ἐχθρῶ(ν) βεβήλων· He will deliver us from *the* uncleanness of profane enemies.	ܕܢܦܨܐ ܠܢ ܡܢ ܛܡܐܘܬܐ ܕܥܡ̈ܡܐ ܡܣܝ̈ܒܐ. so that He may deliver us from the uncleaness of the polluted peoples.
[46] κ(ύριο)σ αὐτὸ(σ) βασιλεὺσ ἡμ(ῶν) εἰσ τὸν αἰῶνα καὶ ἔτι: *The* Lord Himself *will be* our King to lasting time and still more.	ܡܪܝܐ ܗܘ ܓܝܪ ܡܠܟܢ. ܗܫܐ...ܠܥܠܡ. For the LORD is our King now ... to lasting time.

17.51 ταχύναι 336⁺260 | -νη 253 •

17.51 May God quickly bring about His mercy on Israel (see on 11.8–9); **He will deliver**[302] **us from the uncleanness of profane enemies.** God is never slow concerning His promises (2 Pet 3.9). In this case, the answer came particularly **quickly**—within a few decades, when "the Lord, the God of Israel ... raised up a horn of salvation for us in the house of David His servant ... to show mercy with our fathers ... to grant for us to serve Him without fear, being delivered out of the hand of enemies" (Luke 1.68–74, 78, 54). Jesus delivers His people from all **enemies** (even from sin, death, and the devil: 1 Jn 3.8; Heb 2.14–15; Rom 8.2–3; 6.17–18); "He must reign until He has put all His enemies under His feet" (1 Cor 15.25).

The psalm ends as it began: **The Lord Himself will be our King to lasting time and still more** (v 1).

Psalm 18

As at the beginning and in the middle of the Eighteen Psalms, a long psalm is followed by a short one that continues and develops some of its themes (compare Eighteen Psalms 17 and 18 with 2 and 3, and with 8 and 9).

Lord, your mercy will be on Israel

18.0 [0] Ψαλμὸϲ τῶ Cαλωμὼν
ἔτι τ(ο)ῦ χ(ριϲτο)ῦ κ(υρίο)υ:

[302] **He will deliver** *(rhusetai).* Gebhardt and Rahlfs conjecturally emended to *rhusaito* ("may He deliver").

A psalm belonging to Solomon;
again of Christ *the* Lord.

18.1 [1] Κ(ύρι)ε τὸ ἔλεόσ σου
ἐπι τὰ ἔργα τ(ῶν) χειρῶν σου
εἰσ τὸν αἰῶνα·

ܡܪܝܐ ܪ̈ܚܡܝܟ
ܥܠ ܥܒܕ ܐܝ̈ܕܝܟ
ܠܥܠܡ.

Lord, Your† mercy *will be*
on the works of Your† hands
to lasting time;

LORD, Your† compassions *will be*
on *the* work of Your† hands
to lasting time,

18.2 [1] ἡ χρηστότησ σου ‹μετὰ›
δόματοσ πλουσίου ἐπὶ Ἰσραὴλ·

ܘܛܝܒܘܬܟ ܒܡܘܗܒܬܐ
ܥܬܝܪܬܐ ܥܠ ܐܝܣܪܝܠ.

Your† kindness *will be* with
a rich gift on Israel.

and Your† goodness *will be* with
a rich gift on Israel.

---

[2] οἱ ὀφθαλμοί σου ἐπιβλέποντεσ
ἐπ᾽ αὐτὰ·
καὶ οὐχ ὑστερήσει ἐξ αὐτ(ῶν)·

ܥ̈ܝܢܝܟ ܚܙܝܢ
ܟܠ.
ܘܠܝܬ ܡܕܡ ܕܛܫܐ ܡܢܗܘܢ

Your† eyes *are* looking on them,
and not *one* out of them
will lack *anything;*

Your† eyes *are* seeing every*thing,*
and there is nothing
that *is* hiding from them;

18.3 [2] τὰ ὦτα σου ἐπακούει·
εἰσ δέησιν πτωχοῦ ἐν ελπίδι·

ܘܐܕ̈ܢܝܟ ܫ̈ܡܥܢ
ܠܣܒܪܗ ܕܡܣܟܢܐ (ܐ).

Your† ears are hearkening
to *the* request of *the* poor *one* in hope.

and Your† ears *are* hearkening
to *the* hope of *the* poor *one.*

---

[3] τὰ κρίματά σου
ἐπι πᾶσαν τὴν γῆν μετὰ ἐλέουσ·

ܕ̈ܝܢܝܟ
ܥܠ ܟܠܗ ܐܪܥܐ ܒܪ̈ܚܡܐ.

Your† judgments *are*
on all the earth with mercy,

Your† judgments *are*
on all the earth in compassions,

18.4 [3] καὶ ‹ἡ› ἀγάπη σου ἐπι
σπέρμα Ἀβραὰμ υἱοῦ Ἰ(σρα)ὴλ·

ܘܚܘܒܟ ܥܠ
ܙܪܥܗ ܕܐܝܣܪܝܠ ܒܪܗ ܕܐܒܪܗܡ.

and Your† love *is* on *the*
seed of Abraham, *on the* son of Israel.

and Your† love *is* on *the*
seed of Israel, *the* son of Abraham.

---

[4] ἡ παιδία σου ἐφ᾽ ἡμᾶσ
ὡσ υ(ἱὸ)ν πρωτότοκον μονογενῆ·

ܡ ... ܥܠܝܢ
ܐܝܟ ܕܠܒܪܐ ܒܘܟܪܐ ܝܚܝܕܝܐ.

Your† discipline *is* on us
as a firstborn son, an only *one,*

... on us
as to a firstborn son, an only one,

18.2 μετὰ 336⁺260 10h1 | ἐπι 253 • **18.4** ἡ 1° 336⁺260 | > 253 •

Greek	Syriac
18.5 [4] ἀποστρέψαι ψυχὴν εὐήκοον	ܠܡܗܦܟܘ ܢܦܫܐ ܕܡܫܬܡܥܐ.
ἀπο ἀμαθίασ ἐν αγνοία·	ܕܠܐ ܡܠܦܐ ܘܠܐ ܝܕ̈ܥܐ
to turn back a soul	to turn back a soul
that is willing to hear	*that has* hearkened, which
from being unlearned in ignorance.	*had* not *been* taught and *did* not know,

18.1–5[303] Always (**to lasting time**) the Lord shows **mercy** in His **judgments ... on all the earth,** on all **the works of** His **hands** (Psa 138.8). "The LORD is good to all, and His compassions are on all His works"; He is "lovingkind in all His ways" (Psa 145.9, 17). Even when we reject Him, and sin against Him, He continues to do lovingkindness toward us and send us His good gifts (Matt 5.45; Acts 14.17; cf. Wis 11.24–26). His **judgments ... on all the earth** have been "less than our iniquities" (Ezra 9.13; Psa 103.10), because of His **mercy** (Psa 78.38–39; Lam 3.22; Acts 14.16–17; 17.30).

But especially the Lord bestows His **kindness** and **love** on His chosen people—the **seed of Abraham,** the people descended from **Israel** (5.21; 9.20; 11.9).[304] "I will recount the lovingkindnesses of the LORD ... in accordance with all that the LORD has bestowed on us, and the abundance of goodness toward the house of Israel that He has bestowed on them in accordance with His compassions and the abundance of His lovingkindnesses; and He said, 'Surely they are My people ...'; and He was a Savior for them" (Isa 63.7–8). His favor toward them is a **rich gift** ("the riches of His kindness," Rom 2.4; "the riches of His favor in kindness," which "is the gift of God," Eph 2.7–8). He treats Israel as His **firstborn son** (Exod 4.22), indeed His *monogenē* son ("only-begotten" [APOT], the **only** [*mono-*] one of this origin [*-genēs*]; TDNT 7.737–41).

God's **eyes are** constantly **looking on** His people, and His **ears are hearkening to** their **request** (1 Pet 3.12 ≡ Psa 34.15; 33.18; Prov 15.29). In particular, He will hear-

---

303 In the Greek copies (but not in the Syriac), the psalm is superscribed **A psalm belonging to Solomon; again of Christ the Lord** (cf. vv 6–10; 17.0).

304 **On the seed of Abraham, [on] the son of Israel** *(epi sperma Abraam huiou Israēl).* **The seed of Abraham** and **the son of Israel** are obviously parallel phrases, in which the words **seed** and **son** both describe the nation descended from **Abraham** and Jacob (**Israel**)—as the next line confirms. Therefore, the preposition *epi* (**on**) must govern both phrases, the first in the accusative *(sperma),* the second in the genitive *(huiou).* Compare, e.g., Matt 25.21, where again *epi* governs two matched terms, the first in the accusative (*epi oliga,* "over a few things"), the second in the genitive (*epi pollōn,* "over many things"). Such constructions depend on the fact that *epi* can take either the accusative or the genitive, even when referring to the same thing (*epi* with accusative, Matt 14.25 ≡ *epi* with genitive, Mark 6.48). In the present passage Fabricius and many later editors conjecturally emended *huiou* to *huious* ("sons"), but the singular is necessary here because the whole nation is being viewed as an **only** *(monogenē)* son (as the next line indicates). The Syriac supports the singular in both lines.

As often in the Eighteen Psalms, the Syriac word order—**on the seed of Israel, the son of Abraham**—differs here from the Greek (so, e.g., Greek "in faithfulness and righteousness" ≡ Syriac "in righteousness and faithfulness," 17.45).

ken to **the request of the poor one**—the person who **lacks** either worldly goods or spiritual goods (see the comments on 15.2). No problem, and no request, ever passes unnoticed by Him (**nothing** is **hiding from** His sight, Syriac; see 9.5–6; Heb 4.13); and therefore **not one out of** His chosen people will ever **lack anything** (Greek; 1 Cor 1.7; Psa 34.10). They will always have all the earthly things that He knows them to need (Matt 6.31–33), and they will always have all the spiritual things that He knows them to need (Eph 1.3; Php 4.19; 2 Cor 9.8–11).

Even the righteous can commit sins in **ignorance** (see the comments on 13.6; 3.9). But because God has set His **love** on Israel (Heb 12.5–10), He subjects them to His **discipline** (His correction), in order **to turn** them **back ... from being unlearned in ignorance,** so that they understand His Law (Psa 94.12; 2 Tim 3.16; see the notes on 8.35; 16.11). To turn back from ignorance, a **soul** must be **willing to hear** (Greek *euēkoon,* "well-hearing")—that is, it must have **hearkened** (Syriac) to the correction. "One who shuns discipline rejects His own soul, but one who hearkens to correction obtains understanding" (Prov 15.32; 19.20, 27; 8.33). If we do not hearken to the Lord (v 5), He will not hearken to us (v 3; Zec 7.13; Jer 7.16, 28–29).

The King of Israel, Christ (v 6), was the Seed of Abraham (singular, Gal 3.16), the firstborn (Heb 1.6; Col 1.15) and only (*monogenēs,* John 1.14) Son of God. Through Him, both Jews and Gentiles can belong to **Israel** and receive the blessings promised to the new covenant Israel by the prophets (see on 5.21). "If you are Christ's, then you are the seed of Abraham, heirs in accordance with the promise" (Gal 3.29, 7).

May God cleanse Israel for the day of His Christ

18.6 [5] ‹καθαρίσαι› ὁ θ(εὸ)σ Ἰ(σρα)ὴλ εἰσ ἡμέραν ἐλέουσ ἐν εὐλογίᾳ· May God cleanse Israel for *the* day of mercy with blessing,	ܠܡܕܟܝܘ ܠܐܝܣܪܝܠ ܠܝܘ... ܒܒܘܪܟܬܐ. to cleanse Israel for *the* day ... with blessing,
εἰσ ἡμέραν ἐκλογῆσ ἐν ἀνάξει χ(ριστο)ῦ αὐτοῦ· for *the* day of *His* choosing in *the* raising up of His Christ.	ܠܝܘܡܗ ܠ... for *the* day of ....

18.6 καθαρίσαι 260 | καθαρίσῃ 253 •

18.6 There would come a **day of mercy with blessing** when God would raise up[305] **His Christ** (see the comments on 17.23), who would "bless the people of the Lord"

---

[305] **Raising up.** In this context, *anaxei* presumably means "bringing up," "raising up" (LEH 41; compare *anagagein,* Rom 10.7) rather than "bringing back," "restoration" (Muraoka 43). The Son of David would be raised from His situation at birth (Php 2.7) up to the situation of being King of Israel (Php 2.11).

and "have mercy on all the nations" that come before Him in fear (see the comments on 17.40, 38). This would be a **day of** God's **choosing**—a day that He had foreseen and had selected long beforehand as the right time for the Christ to come (see the comments on 17.23).

The psalm prays that God may **cleanse Israel** in preparation **for** that day. No one who is unclean can have any place in His kingdom (Eph 5.5; Gal 5.19–21; 2 Cor 6.17; 7.1). The Lord had promised Israel that, before their King came, "I will send out My messenger, and he will prepare the way before My face .... And he will turn back the heart of the fathers to the sons, and heart of the sons to the fathers, lest I come and smite the land with a curse" (Mal 3.1; 4.6). That promise was fulfilled in the sending of John the Baptist, who did indeed "turn back many of the sons of Israel to the Lord their God" and "prepare for the Lord a people equipped" for Him (Luke 1.16–17). "All the Judean region, and all the people of Jerusalem, were going out to him and were being baptized by him in the Jordan River, confessing their sins" (Mark 1.5). But not everyone accepted this cleansing (Matt 21.32); and the wrath of God came upon those who remained unclean, as it always does (Col 3.5–6).

18.7 [6] μακάριοι οἱ γενόμενοι ἐν ‹ταῖσ› ἡμέραισ ἐκείναισ· Blessed *will be* those who come to be in those days,	..ܛܘܒܝܗܘܢ ܠܐܝܠܝܢ ...ܡܬܐ ...ܢ Blessed *are* those ....
ἰδεῖν τὰ ἀγαθὰ κ(υρίο)υ ἃ ποιήσει γενεὰ τῇ ἐρχομένῃ· to see the good *things* of *the* Lord, which He will do for the coming generation,	ܠ...ܐ ... to ....
18.8 [7] ὑπὸ ῥάβδον παιδείασ χ(ριστο)ῦ κ(υρίο)υ ἐν φόβῳ θ(εο)ῦ αὐτοῦ· under *the* rod of discipline of Christ *the* Lord in *the* fear of His God,	... .
ἐν σοφίᾳ πν(εύματο)σ καὶ δικαιοσύνησ καὶ ἰσχύοσ· in *the* wisdom of *the* Spirit and of righteousness and of strength,	... .
18.9 [8] κατευθύναι ‹ἄνδρα› ἐν ἔργοισ δικαιοσύνησ φόβῳ θ(εο)ῦ· to direct a man in works of righteousness in *the* fear of God,	... .

καταστῆσαι πάντασ αὐτοὺσ ἐνώπιον κ(υρίο)υ·	...
to set up all of them in *the* sight of *the* Lord,	....
18.10 [9] γενεὰ ἀγαθὴ ἐν φόβω θ(εο)ῦ ἐν ἡμέραισ ἐλέουσ: διάψαλμ(α):	...
a good generation in *the* fear of God in days of mercy. Selah.	....

18.7 ταῖσ 260 | > 253 • **18.9** ἄνδρα 260 | -ρασ 253 •

18.7 Blessed will be those who come to be in the **days** of the Christ, **to see the good things of the Lord** (see the comments on 17.50), **which He will do for the coming generation**[306] (cf. John 4.21, 23; Luke 23.29).

18.8 That generation would live **under the rod of discipline of Christ the Lord**[307] (see on 17.47–49). A **rod** is an instrument that was used to **discipline** a child (Prov 13.24; 22.15; 23.13–14). Christ's **rod** is His word ("the rod of His mouth . . . the breath of His lips," Isa 11.4). With that **rod** He shatters sinners (see the comments on 17.26), and with that **rod** He governs His people in uprightness (Heb 1.8 ≡ Psa 45.6; cf. Gen 49.10). He administers His **discipline:**

- **In the fear of His God.** He is "mighty in the fear of God" (see on 17.44), and His discipline is guided by that fear (John 8.26–29); and His discipline teaches them to fear God (v 9). "The fear of the LORD is a fountain of life, to turn aside from the snares of death" (Prov 14.27; Psa 34.11–14).
- **In the wisdom of the Spirit.**[308] "God has made Him powerful in the Holy Spirit" (see on 17.42), and His discipline is guided by the wisdom of that Spirit (Isa 11.2; Col 3.16; 1.9; Eph 1.17).
- **In the wisdom . . . of righteousness.** He is righteous (see the comments on 17.35), and His discipline is guided by "the wisdom of His righteousness" (see on 17.31; John 5.30).
- **In the wisdom . . . of strength.** He is "strong in His works," so strong that no one can prevail against Him (see on 17.43–44), and His discipline is guided by the wisdom of that strength (Col 1.28–29).

---

[306] **The coming generation** *(genea tē erchomenē).* As often in Biblical Greek, the participle has the article but the preceding noun does not (BDF §412(3); Robertson 778).

[307] In this verse the phrase *christou kuriou* could also be rendered "of the Lord's Christ"; but comparison with 17.36 (where the wording is unambiguous, *christos kurios*) favors the translation **of Christ the Lord.**

[308] **Spirit** *(pneumatos).* The same Spirit as in 17.42 (see the footnote there).

18.9–10 Christ's discipline is guided by the fear of God (v 8), and it teaches people the **fear of God** (Luke 12.5; 2 Cor 7.1), directing them **in works of righteousness in** that **fear.** "I will teach you the fear of the LORD .... Turn aside from evil, and do good" (Psa 34.11–14 ≡ 1 Pet 3.10–11). "By the fear of the LORD one turns away from evil" (Prov 16.6; 8.13). **To direct** *(kateuthunai)*[309] people is to make them "straight" (*euthus;* Psa 7.9–10, LXX); those who heed God's wisdom and are guided by His discipline "walk in paths of straightness" (Prov 4.11; 3.6; Heb 12.11, 13).

His discipline would **set up all of** His people as a **good generation** in **the sight of the Lord.** The people of this world are "an evil generation" (Deut 1.35; Luke 11.29), but Christ's people are the opposite: "blameless and uncontaminated, children of God unblemished in the midst of a crooked and twisted generation" (Php 2.15). Only thus can anyone stand **in the sight of the Lord.** "God is with the righteous generation" (Psa 14.5), whereas the generation that does not know His ways cannot enter into His rest (Heb 3.10–11).

The days of Christ's rule would be **days of mercy** for Israel (17.51) and for all nations (17.38).[310]

Great is our God, who has commanded the lights

18.11 [10] μέγασ ἡμῶν ὁ θ(εὸ)σ ...
καὶ ἔνδοξοσ· ἐν ὑψίστοισ κατοικῶν·
Great *is* our God and glorious, ...
dwelling in *the* highest *place*s,

18.12 [10] ὁ διατάξασ ἐν πορία ...
φωστῆρασ εἰσ καιροὺσ·
ὡρῶν ἀφ ἡμερῶν εἰσ ἡμέρασ·
the *One* who ordered *the* lights ....
in *their* journey for times
of hours from days to days,

καὶ οὐ παρέβησαν ἀπο ...
ὁδοῦ ἧσ ἐνετείλω αὐτοῖσ·
and they have not turned away from ....
the path that You† commanded them.

18.13 [11] ἐν φόβω θ(εο)ῦ ἡ ὁδὸσ ...
αὐτ(ῶν) καθ' ἑκάστην ἡμέραν·

[309] **To direct** (*kateuthunai,* accented κατευθῦναι, infinitive) is the reading of 769, whereas 253 and 260 have the accentuation κατευθύναι ("may He direct," optative). In the next clause, all three manuscripts have the accentuation καταστῆσαι (**to set up,** infinitive).

[310] At the end of this verse the Greek copies add *diapsalma* (≡ Hebrew **Selah**), as in 17.31. No Syriac text of this section has been discovered.

In *the* fear of God *is* their path in each day,	....
ἀφ’ ἧσ ἡμέρασ ἔκτισεν αὐτοὺσ ὁ θ(εὸ)σ καὶ ἕωσ αἰῶνοσ·	...
from *the* day God created them, and until lasting time.	....
18.14 [12] καὶ οὐκ επλανήθησαν ἀφ ἧσ ἡμέρασ ἔκτισεν αὐτούσ·	...
And they have not gone astray from *the* day when He created them;	....
ἀπὸ γενεῶν ἀρχαίων· οὐκ ἀπέστησαν ὁδῶν αὐτῶν·	...
from old generations they have not departed from their paths,	....
εἰ μὴ ὁ θ(εὸ)σ ἐνετείλατο αὐτοῖσ ἐν επιταγὴ δούλων αὐτοῦ:	...
except *when* God commanded them by *the* order of His slaves.	....

18.11 Great is our God and glorious, dwelling in the highest places. "The LORD is raised aloft over all nations; His glory is over the heavens" (Psa 113.4), "the One seated above the circle of the earth, and those who live on it are like grasshoppers; the One stretching out the heavens like thin cloth, and spreading them out like a tent to live in" (Isa 40.22). This is not a description of His physical location (1 Kgs 8.27), but of His spiritual location. Spiritually, He is located far above even the mightiest things in the heavens (Psa 8.1; cf. Psa 97.9); all of them are subject to His commands (as described in vv 12–14).

18.12–14 God **ordered the lights** (the sun, moon, and stars, Psa 136.7–9) **in their journey** "for appointed times" (Psa 104.19; Gen 1.14–16), so that their journeys measure **times of hours from days to days** (an expression that means "from year to year" [APOT], as in Exod 13.10, LXX—see Muraoka 320, §3f—and not "from day to day" [OTP]).

From the day when God created them, and until lasting time,[311] these lights **have not gone astray,** and **have not turned away** from the tasks that the Lord **commanded**

---

[311] **Until lasting time** *(eōs aiōnos).* Not "unto eternity" (AOT) or "forever" (OTP), but into the indefinite future (like the high priesthood of Mattathias's descendants; see the footnote to Maccabaica 14.41). The sun, moon, and stars will continue in their paths into the indefinite future (cf. Jer 31.35–36), but they will certainly not continue forever (Psa 102.25–26; Isa 51.6; Luke 21.33; 2 Pet 3.7–12).

them. Instead, **in the fear of God** they have constantly obeyed Him (Sir 16.28; 42.23). "Because of His abundance of might and strength of power, not one" of the things that He has set in the heights "is missing" (Isa 40.26). "All things are Your servants" (Psa 119.91).

The collection of psalms finishes with one of its great paradoxes. Suddenly it looks down from the heights to the depths. **Slaves** are the lowest and most powerless of all people (cf. Luke 1.48), in bondage under a "yoke" (17.32; Gal 5.1; Lev 26.13, LXX). Yet so greatly does God favor **His slaves** (2.40–41; 10.3–4; see the footnote to Maccabaica 4.30) that the heavenly objects on high, which have never faltered for any other reason, have **departed from their paths** at the **order of** such **slaves** as Joshua (Josh 10.12–14) and Isaiah (2 Kgs 20.9–11; Sir 48.23). He has made the highest things in His creation low, for those who are utterly subservient to Him (11.5).

The ending is startling not only because of the sudden change of direction, but also because the collection simply stops in mid-flight, without any apparent conclusion. Sudden mid-flight endings may have been particularly favored in books written around this time (Acts 28.30–31 and Wisdom 19.22 are famous examples), although somewhat similar endings can be found in some books written in earlier centuries (e.g., Isa 66.24; Lam 5.22).

THE PTOLEMAIC HISTORY

The Ptolemaic History describes a persecution of the Jews during the latter stages of Greek rule, about two hundred years before the birth of Christ.

Authorship and Date of Composition

The book was certainly composed in Greek (its syntax is very strongly Hellenic rather than Hebraic). Most of it is set in Alexandria, and its vocabulary and syntax strikingly resemble those of other writings associated with Alexandria (details are given in APOT 1.156–58), so its author had almost certainly lived there or somewhere nearby.

The book describes events that happened during and shortly after the battle of Raphia, which is estimated to have occurred around 217 BCE. It might conceivably have been written at any time during the following two centuries. Attempts have been made to date it more precisely by comparing its language with that of other Hellenistic documents,[1] but nothing conclusive can be deduced from such comparisons, because only a very small proportion of accurately datable Hellenistic writings have been preserved.[2] Besides, the author of the Ptolemaic History was exactly the sort of person who does not conform to current fashions (OTP 2.514); his language use might well have been different from most of his contemporaries'.

Names

In ancient times the book was sometimes called the *Ptolemaika* ("Ptolemaic Matters," i.e., "Ptolemaic History").[3] That name accurately describes its contents, which take place in the Ptolemaic kingdom during the reign of Ptolemy IV.

More often, even in ancient times, it was called the "Third Book of the Maccabees." This name is obviously both incorrect and seriously misleading, and has often been

---

[1] At the time of writing, the most recent survey of these attempts is Modrzejewski, *Troisième Livre des Maccabées,* 118–23, who cautiously concludes that the strongest available evidence tends to favor a date of composition around 100 BCE.

[2] King, *Hebrew and Hellenistic Thought in the Wisdom of Solomon,* 26.

[3] In all the complete Antiochene manuscripts (f^{64}), the book is either superscribed or subscribed *Ptolemaika ē Makkabaika* ("Ptolemaic Matters or Maccabean Matters"). The name *Ptolemaika* also appears to be assigned to it in the Pseudo-Athanasian *Synopsis,* although there the text is uncertain.

criticized.[4] The book never mentions Judas Maccabeus or any member of his family, and all the events recounted in it happened over 50 years before Maccabean times.

Content

The book is in two main sections.

The Attempt to Enter the Temple. After Ptolemy [IV] Philopator defeated Antiochus [III, the Great] at Raphia (1.1–5), he visited Jerusalem and sought to enter the temple, contrary to the Law of Moses (1.6–15). The people of the city rushed to the temple (1.16–29) and prayed to the Lord for help (2.1–20). Ptolemy then fell down, temporarily paralysed and unable to speak, and had to be carried away (2.21–24).

The Persecution in Egypt. When Ptolemy returned to Egypt, he decreed first that all the Jews there be enslaved unless they abandoned their religion (2.25–33), and then that they be brought to Alexandria and put to death (3.1–30).

The Jews were imprisoned in the city's hippodrome (4.1–21) and the king commanded that they be trampled to death by elephants (5.1–10). But they were delivered three times: on the first occasion because God struck the king with a deep sleep (5.11–22), on the second because He erased the king's memory of the command (5.23–35), and on the final occasion because two angels appeared, terrifying the unbelievers and causing the elephants to trample the king's own forces (5.36–6.21).

After this, Ptolemy ordered the Jews to be released (6.22–29). The Jews appointed a festival of thanksgiving for their deliverance (6.30–41). The king issued a formal decree absolving them (7.1–9), and authorized them to punish those who had departed from the faith (7.10–15). The Jews returned to their homes in joy, and were treated with greater respect thereafter (7.16–23).

Reliability

On a first reading, the book's reliability is easily underestimated—partly because it recounts improbable incidents, and partly because it recounts them in an elaborate Hellenic manner, which may look strange to readers accustomed to the Hebraic narrative style of the history books in the Hebrew Scriptures and the Gospels. Nevertheless, various key points—including some of those that seem most improbable—are independently attested by other ancient sources.

The book's description of the battle of Raphia tallies closely with that in Polybius (5.79.1–5.86.7), even though neither account can have been derived from the other. The two present their material quite differently (e.g., Polybius 5.80.3 mentions Arsinoe's presence before the battle, whereas Ptolemaica 1.4 describes her actions during the battle); they show no traces of each other's wording; and each contains details that could not have been deduced from the other.

---

[4] "It ought rather to be entitled 'Ptolemaic Matter' [*Ptolemaikon*]" (superscription to Greek minuscule 19). "Indeed, the applicability of the title of 'Maccabees' even to the other books so named is dubious" (Hadas, *Third and Fourth Books of Maccabees,* 5).

The fact that the victorious king visited the cities in his newly regained territories and entered their temples (Ptolemaica 1.6–7, 13) is recorded in the Raphia Decree issued at the time by the Egyptians (cf. Polybius 5.86.11). Jerusalem would certainly have been one of the places visited—it was the major city nearest to Raphia—and we know that, under the old covenant, the Lord did take action (more than once) to punish unauthorized people who tried to come into contact with His holy things (1 Sam 6.19; 2 Sam 6.6–7; 2 Chr 26.16–20).

Ptolemy Philopator's bizarre unpredictability and constant reveling, as described in the Ptolemaic History, also tally closely with the accounts of his character in Polybius and Plutarch. "Secure in his present circumstances, he devoted his time to the ostentatious revels available to a sovereign, showing himself inattentive and gruff toward those of his court and the others who were governing Egypt, and displaying contempt and indifference toward those who were appointed to deal with foreign matters" (Polybius 5.34.3–4; cf. 15.34.5; Plutarch, *Agis and Cleomenes,* 33.1–35.2). A modern historian, looking only at the surface, might reflect merely that a king who has spent the previous night reveling (Ptolemaica 5.3) is likely to oversleep the next day (5.11–12), and that a chronic heavy drinker can tend to suffer unpredictable memory lapses (5.27–28) and episodes of sudden collapse or loss of consciousness (2.22). In each case the writer of the Ptolemaic History sees more deeply, and recognizes that all such incidents, great or small, occur to suit the purposes of God (cf. Isa 14.24, 27; Rom 8.28; Gen 50.20).[5]

During the persecution in Alexandria, all Jews who consented to the king's registration were to be branded *(charassesthai)* with the mark of Dionysus (Ptolemaica 2.29). This incident is probably referred to in Revelation 13.16–17, where only those who receive the mark *(charagma)* of the beast are allowed to buy or sell.[6]

The festival commemorating the deliverance from the elephants is also documented elsewhere, and was still being celebrated in Alexandria late in the first century CE (Josephus, *Against Apion,* 2.55). Writers on Esther often point out that the existence of the feast of Purim is itself evidence of the incident it commemorates. Writers on the Ptolemaica make the same point about this feast. It was instituted for the very purpose of ensuring that later generations would continue to know what had happened.

---

[5] It is also noteworthy that, according to the Ptolemaic History, the king never does repent or confess his wickedness; instead, he denies it and puts the blame on his advisers (7.1–9). Such an ending is alien to the art of Hellenistic fiction writers, and certainly could not have been invented by this particular book's writer (he makes his points by direct emphasis, not obliquely by irony). It must surely be based on fact.

[6] Swete, *Apocalypse of St. John,* 173. Similar practices are reported by some Classical writers (e.g., Herodotus 2.113; 7.233), but the book of Revelation is unlikely to be alluding to them. It derives nearly all its source material from the Hebrew Scriptures and other Jewish religious documents; and no other incident of the kind is found either in the Hebrew Scriptures or in any other known Jewish writing of the period.

On two points the Ptolemaic History disagrees with other ancient sources, but in each case it is likely to have been better informed than the others.

Josephus places the elephant incident in a later era, that of Ptolemy VIII (*Against Apion,* 2.53–55); but he quite often misplaces Hellenistic events chronologically (some instances are listed in the chapter on Josephus). The Ptolemaic History, written much closer in time to the incident and probably in the very city where it had happened, is most unlikely to be in error here.[7]

The Ptolemaic History gives the number of Ptolemy's elephants as 500 (5.2). This used to be doubted, because Polybius says that Ptolemy had only 73 elephants at the battle of Raphia (5.79.2; 5.82.7) and that "most of them" *(autōn hoi pleious)* were captured by the enemy during the battle (5.86.6). But more recently the statement in the Ptolemaic History has been supported by two different lines of evidence.

First, evidence has been produced that the term "five hundred" may not be a precise figure in this context, but simply an Indian idiom for "a very large number,"[8] which passed into Hellenistic use in relation to elephants (Strabo 15.2.9), no doubt because it was part of the terminology used by the elephants' Indian trainers (cf. Maccabaica 6.37). In the same way, in modern English such military terms as "myriad" (originally 10,000), "legion" (originally 3,000), and "cohort" (originally one-tenth of a legion) have lost their precise significance and have come to mean simply "a large number."

Secondly, the Raphia inscription states that, far from losing his elephants to the enemy at Raphia, Ptolemy captured "all of" *(ḏr=w)* the enemy's (Raphia Decree M.14). Presumably this statement is at least broadly correct—not only because a resoundingly defeated, hastily fleeing army would be much more likely to lose its own elephants than to gain its vanquishers', but also because the inscription was set up at the time and was meant to be read by people who would know whether its claims were true or false. Polybius, by contrast, wrote a century later and derived his information from Seleucid sources, i.e., from the side defeated at Raphia. It is well documented that, before a battle, ancient military leaders sometimes scaled down the estimated size of the opposing forces in order not to alarm their own troops; and that, after a battle, the losing side frequently underreported the extent of the defeat and even falsely claimed offsetting successes. So Polybius's sources may have underestimated the number of Ptolemy's elephants before the battle, and were almost certainly wrong in claiming to have captured most of them during the action.[9]

Therefore, the unarmed Jews in Alexandria are likely to have faced many more elephants than had been deployed against the full might of the Seleucid army at Raphia.

The Ptolemaic History also deserves respect for the reliability of its teachings. "The keenest heresy-hunter could have found no fault with its uncompromising orthodoxy" (APOT 1.162); "our author may best be pictured as a staunch conservative, swimming

---

[7] King, *Hebrew and Hellenistic Thought in the Book of Wisdom,* 48.

[8] Modrzejewski, *Troisième Livre des Maccabées,* 57–58, 155.

[9] Walbank, *Historical Commentary on Polybius,* 1.615.

against the stream of the more radical tendencies of his time" (OTP 2.514).[10] It accurately declares that the Lord needs nothing (2.9; cf. Acts 17.25), that His dwelling is unapproachable by people (2.15; cf. 1 Tim 6.16), that all things are in His power (5.28), and that He is eager to forgive (5.13). It accurately summarizes material found in many different parts of the Hebrew Scriptures: the Flood (2.4), the destruction of Sodom (2.5), the deliverance from Egypt (2.6–8; 6.4), the commandments and promises given through Moses (1.11; 6.15), the promises given in the time of Solomon (2.10), the deliverance of Jonah (6.8), the destruction of Sennacherib's army (6.5), the deliverance of Daniel and his companions (6.6–7).

[10] Only by seeing differences where none exist, would it be possible to imagine that the book's writer "appears as an ardent champion of the old Deuteronomic orthodoxy, which at the risk of oversimplification may be described as the conviction that God rewards the righteous and punishes the wicked, and against which the author of Job registers a vehement protest" (OTP 2.514). In reality the doctrine of the Ptolemaic History is no different from that of Job (or, for that matter, Deuteronomy). Exactly like Job, the Alexandrian Jews in the Ptolemaic History are subjected to extreme and seemingly unreasonable (*alogiston,* 6.12) sufferings, the causes of which they can only guess at (6.10); and exactly like Job's, their faithfulness is indeed rewarded by God in the end (7.22).

THE EPITOME OF THE ACTS OF JUDAS MACCABEUS

The Epitome of the Acts of Judas Maccabeus contains a historical narrative summarizing "the matters relating to Judas Maccabeus and his brothers, and the cleansing of the greatest temple, and the dedication of the altar, and also the wars against Antiochus Epiphanes and his son Eupator" (2.19–20). Most of this narrative (4.7–15.37) covers the same period as the first half of the Maccabean History (Maccabaica 1.10–7.50), from the accession of Antiochus Epiphanes to Judas's final victory over Nicanor.

The narrative is preceded by two letters from Jews in Judea to those in Egypt (Epitome 1.1–2.18), urging them to observe the Feast of the Dedication (1.9, 18; 2.16).

Authorship and Date of Composition

The compiler of the historical narrative does not name himself, but he says that his work is an abridgement of an earlier history on the same subject, which had been written in five books by Jason of Cyrene. Jason and his work are otherwise unknown; no other ancient allusion to them has ever been discovered.

The Epitome is written in a strongly Hellenic style and was undoubtedly composed in Greek by "a writer well trained in the writing of Greek, who knows the technical terms of Greek historiographical writing." He was probably living outside Judea,[11] and his principal source (the work of Jason of Cyrene) also seems to have originated outside Judea.

The latest date given in the Epitome is 188 SE, the date of its opening letter (1.10). This would correspond to about 124 BCE, ten years later than any event mentioned in the Maccabean History. Like the Maccabean History, it contains no reference to the Roman conquest of Jerusalem about 63 BCE; indeed, it claims that "the city has been held by the Hebrews" ever since the time of Judas Maccabeus (15.37). Therefore, it is usually believed to have been completed some time between about 120 and 65 BCE. The initial stage (the work of Jason of Cyrene) could possibly have been written several decades earlier.

Names

In ancient times, the book was known as the "Epitome of the Acts of Judas Maccabeus" (*Iouda Makkabaiou praxeōn epitomē,* subscribed to Codex Venetus), or, more briefly, the "Epitome of Maccabean Matters" (*tēn tōn Makkabaikōn epitomēn,* Clement

[11] Doran, *2 Maccabees,* 15–17 (the quotation is from 16); Schwartz, *2 Maccabees,* 45–55.

of Alexandria, *Stromata,* 5.14.97). That describes the book accurately and unambiguously: its main subject is "the matters related to Judas Maccabeus" (Epitome 2.19), and it is abridged *(epitemein)* from an earlier work (2.23).

When the Maccabean History came to be reckoned as the "First Book" on its subject, the Epitome came to be called the "Second [Book] of Maccabean Matters" (*Makkabaikōn deuteron,* superscribed to Greek minuscule 93), and then, less accurately, the "Second Book of the Maccabees," a name it has retained to the present day.

The First Letter (1.1–10a)

The first letter, dated 188 SE (1.10),[12] briefly encourages the Jews in Egypt to observe the feast in the month Chislev (1.9). This was the feast commemorating the dedication of the altar, which had been instituted forty years earlier, in the time of Judas Maccabeus (Maccabaica 4.52–59; Epitome 10.5–8).

The Second Letter (1.10b–2.18)

The second letter is undated. It informs the Jews in Egypt that the Judeans had just been saved from great dangers: the enemies fighting against the holy city had been driven away (1.12), and their king, Antiochus, had been killed in a Persian temple that he was trying to rob (1.13–17). Now the Judeans are going to celebrate the cleansing of the holy place, in the month Chislev, and they write encouraging their brethren in Egypt to do the same (1.18; 2.16).

The bulk of the letter consists of two long stories about past events. According to the first story, when the temple was rebuilt after the return from Babylon, its sacrifices were ignited under the supervision of Nehemiah by a supply of inflammable liquid that had been discovered in a hidden place (1.19–36). According to the second story, the ark of the covenant had previously been hidden by Jeremiah on Mount Nebo just before the Babylonian captivity (2.1–8).

The Historical Narrative (2.19–15.39)

The historical narrative consists of two main parts, framed by short introductory and concluding passages.

Introduction (2.19–32). The writer explains the nature and purpose of his work.

The Oppression of the Faithful (3.1–7.42). According to the Epitome, King Seleucus (IV, the predecessor of Antiochus Epiphanes) sent his officer Heliodorus to Jerusalem to plunder the temple, but this was prevented by heavenly messengers (3.1–4.6). When Antiochus Epiphanes became king, some Judeans got his permission to introduce Greek customs in their nation (4.7–50). After his second invasion of Egypt, Antiochus himself entered Jerusalem, defiled and plundered the temple, and killed many of the people (5.1–27). He then issued laws commanding the Judeans to worship idols and forbidding the worship of God (6.1–11). The Epitome describes in

---

[12] Letters were customarily dated at the end, not the start (Epitome 11.21, 33, 38).

detail the torture and death of a wise old man named Eleazar and a mother and her seven sons because they remained faithful to God (6.12–7.42).

The Triumph of the Faithful (8.1–15.37). Judas Maccabeus and his companions opposed the king's laws and defeated the armies that were sent against them (8.1–36). Antiochus Epiphanes himself died after failing to plunder a temple in Persia (9.1–29). Maccabeus and his companions cleansed the temple in Jerusalem (10.1–8). Antiochus Eupator became king, and the evils continued (10.9–13). Nevertheless the faithful Judeans were victorious over their enemies not only within Judea itself, but also in surrounding regions (10.14–12.45). Eventually the king himself invaded Judea and established a peace treaty with the people (13.1–26). The next king, Demetrius, renewed the war against the Judeans (14.1–46), but his army was defeated by Judas, and its leader, Nicanor, was killed in the battle (15.1–37).

Conclusion (15.38–39). The author briefly sums up his approach to his task.

As noted above, the section of the Epitome from the accession of Antiochus Epiphanes to the death of Nicanor (4.7–15.37) covers the same time period as the first half of the Maccabean History (Maccabaica 1.10–7.50). Nevertheless, neither book shows any sign of the other's influence, or even any awareness of the other's existence. Even when the two are describing the same event, they always present and arrange the material in completely independent ways. There are not even any indications that either has borrowed from the other's wording. (Contrast the striking similarities between the Gospels, or between the books of Kings and Chronicles—or, for that matter, between Josephus and his source material in the Maccabean History, or between Livy and his source material in Polybius.)

Like nearly all ancient history books—including the Maccabean History—the Epitome is arranged mainly in chronological sequence, but sometimes on the basis of subject matter rather than chronology. As a result, the Epitome and the Maccabean History do not always present incidents in the same order (just as the different Gospels do not always present the incidents of Jesus' life in the same order).

The table on the following page shows how material in the Epitome corresponds to that in the Maccabean History.

In this table:

- **Boldface** marks material found at the same place in the Epitome as in the Maccabean History.
- Ordinary Roman type marks material found at this point in the Maccabean History, but somewhere elsewhere (or not at all) in the Epitome.
- *Italics* mark material found at this point in the Epitome, but somewhere else (or not at all) in the Maccabean History.
- Angle brackets < > enclose a passage describing the same event in a different section of the narrative. If it is uncertain whether the event is the same or not, the passage is marked with a query thus: ? < >.

Events	Maccabaica	Epitome
Heliodorus stricken in the temple	—	3.1–4.6
Antiochus Epiphanes becomes king	1.10	4.7
Judeans allowed to follow foreign laws	1.11–15	4.7–50
The king invades Egypt	1.16–19	5.1–10
He enters and plunders the temple	1.20–28	5.11–21
Massacre in Jerusalem	1.29–40	5.22–26
Judas Maccabeus flees	<2.1–28>	5.27
The king commands idol worship	1.41–64	6.1–10
Mattathias rebels and flees	2.1–28	<5.27>
Massacre on the Sabbath	2.29–41	6.11
Death of Eleazar	—	6.12–31
Death of seven sons and their mother	—	7.1–42
The deeds and death of Mattathias	2.42–70	—
The victories of Judas	3.1–9	8.1–7
Victories over Apollonius and Seron	3.10–26	—
Antiochus leaves for Persia	3.27–37	—
Victory at Emmaus	3.38–4.25	8.8–36
Victory over Lysias at Bethzur	4.26–35	? <11.1–15>
Death of Antiochus Epiphanes	<6.1–16>	9.1–28
Philip attempts to gain power	<6.55–63>	9.29
Cleansing of the temple	4.36–61	10.1–8
Antiochus Eupator becomes king	<6.17>	10.9–13
Victory in Idumea	5.1–5	10.14–23
Victory over Timothy	5.6–8	10.24–38
Victory over Lysias at Bethzur	? <4.26–35>	11.1–15
Letters from Lysias, the king, and Rome	—	11.16–38
Victory at Joppa and Jabneh	—	12.1–9
Victories in Gilead and Galilee	5.10–54	12.10–31
Battles in the south	5.55–68	12.32–45
Death of Antiochus Epiphanes	6.1–16	<9.1–28>
Antiochus Eupator becomes king	6.17	<10.9–13>
Siege of the citadel	6.18–27	—
The king invades Judea	6.28–31	13.1–13
Battle at Bethzechariah	6.32–47	13.14–17
The king makes peace	6.48–63	13.18–26
Demetrius becomes king	7.1–4	14.1–2
Alcimus goes to the king	7.5–7	14.3–11
Bacchides and Alcimus in Judea	7.8–25	—
The king sends Nicanor to Judea	7.26–38	14.12–36
Death of Razis	—	14.37–46
Death of Nicanor	7.39–50	15.1–37

There are two main differences in the arrangement of the material:

- In the Epitome, the death of Antiochus Epiphanes is placed *before* the cleansing of the temple. In the Maccabean History, it is placed *after* those events. (The king must have been alive when the cleansing of the temple began, because he heard about it shortly before his death; but the cleansing may not have been completed until around the time of his death, or even slightly later. See the notes on Maccabaica 6.7.)
- In the Maccabean History, the separate campaigns in Galilee, Gilead, and Judea are placed under the reign of Antiochus Epiphanes. In the Epitome, they are placed under the next reign—that of Antiochus Eupator. (Antiochus Epiphanes was still alive at this stage, but he had departed for Persia; in effect, therefore, his young son Antiochus Eupator was already the ruler in the regions where the battles took place.)[13]

The three largest blocks of material found in the Epitome but not in the Maccabean History are the stories of Heliodorus's attempt to plunder the temple (3.1–40), the death of Eleazar (6.12–31), and the death of the seven sons and their mother (7.1–42).

Reliability of the Epitome

The writer frankly acknowledges that his work may be inadequate in some respects: "If I have done it well and to the point, that is what I myself wanted; but if in a way that is shoddy and mediocre [*eutelōs kai metrōs*], that was all I could attain" (15.38). He has tried to do his best; but he does not claim that he has achieved perfection.

Different sections of the book give different, and contradictory, accounts of the death of Antiochus Epiphanes in Persia.[14] According to the first account, Antiochus and his soldiers were trapped inside a temple and beheaded there:

---

[13] In addition, Maccabaica 4.26–35 states that Judas defeated Lysias at Bethzur during the reign of Epiphanes, whereas Epitome 11.1–15 states that Judas defeated Lysias at Bethzur during the reign of Eupator. However, the accounts differ in various details (the enemy dead are given as 5,000 in the Maccabaica, 27,000 in the Epitome), so these may possibly have been two different battles (Knabenbauer 390–91). Bethzur was strategically vital for the Seleucids' control of Judea (Maccabaica 6.7, 26; 9.52), so it was natural for them to rush to its defense. We know that Lysias fought the Judeans there twice in the time of Epiphanes (Maccabaica 4.29; 6.31); if he had fought them on yet another occasion in the time of Eupator, it might well have happened in the same neighborhood.

[14] Presumably this mistake arose because the book's final compiler incorporated documents from different sources and failed to notice the conflict between them. The second and more accurate account is in the main body of the book, and therefore probably derives from Jason of Cyrene. The first account claims to have been written by the Judean leaders shortly after the event—but this is highly dubious, as its writer has obviously confused Antiochus Epiphanes with Antiochus the Great. What contemporary would have confused Thermopylae with Marathon, or the death of John F. Kennedy with that of Abraham Lincoln? Such mistakes are indeed *possible* at the time, but become *likely* only after the lapse of many years.

> When the priests of the temple of Nanea had set out the treasures, and he had come with a small number [of people] inside the wall of the sacred precinct, they shut the temple as soon as Antiochus had come in. Opening the hidden door of the ceiling, they threw stones and struck down the leader and his companions, and cut off their heads and threw them to the people outside. [1.15–16.]

According to the second account, he escaped from a temple but later, in another city, was struck down by a fatal illness:

> He had entered into the city called Persepolis, and he set out to rob the temple and seize hold of the city. So multitudes with weapons rushed to help, and it came about that Antiochus was put to flight by the people of the region, and was forced to retreat in shame. But while he was in Ecbatana ... the all-seeing Lord, the God of Israel, struck him down with an incurable and invisible blow . . . . And so worms swarmed from the body of the irreverent man, and, while he was still alive in anguish and pain, his flesh rotted away. [9.2–5, 9.]

The independent testimonies of the Maccabean History (6.1–16), Polybius (31.9.1–3), and other Classical historians, show that the second account is closer to the truth: they all agree that Antiochus was driven away from a temple and died later of disease. The writer of Epitome 1.11–16 has confused Antiochus Epiphanes, who persecuted the Judeans, with his father Antiochus the Great, who did indeed perish while robbing a temple (Diodorus 28.3; 29.15; Strabo 16.1.18).[15]

The later sections of the Epitome also contain some undoubted errors. For instance, its report of the death of Nicanor ends:

> This, then, was how the history of Nicanor turned out; and as the city has been held [*kratētheisēs*] by the Hebrews from those times onward, I will end my account here also [15.37].

In fact, Jerusalem was "held by the Hebrews" after the death of Nicanor for only "a few days" (cf. Maccabaica 7.50). Within a month after Nicanor's death, Judas Maccabeus was also dead (Maccabaica 7.1, 43; 9.3, 18); and when he died, the region—including Jerusalem—deserted to the Syrians, in whose possession it remained until at least the following year (Maccabaica 9.23–24, 50–54).

It is impossible that Jason's five books could have been not only completed, but also

---

[15] The writer is certainly *intending* to describe the death of Epiphanes, because he says that this Antiochus was severely persecuting the Judeans—which Antiochus Epiphanes did (Epitome 1.11–12; 2.18), whereas Antiochus the Great did not (3.1–3). See Fillion, *Sainte Bible,* 6.794; Knabenbauer 285–86 (in reply to Vigouroux, *Livres saints,* 4.156–69). Others (e.g., Lapide 82–83) have suggested that the Antiochus mentioned in Epitome 1.11–16 is Antiochus VII, son of Demetrius. But Antiochus VII was not killed in a temple; he died, perhaps by suicide, in a battle against the Parthians (Diodorus 35.16–17; Appian, *Syriaca,* 68.359; Justin 38.10).

abridged by the writer of the Epitome, within a month of the death of Nicanor. By the time the Epitome was written, Jerusalem must certainly have fallen back into enemy hands at least once—and possibly more than once.

Since the Epitome is demonstrably in error at some points where its testimony can be checked, it is clear that its unsupported testimony is not to be trusted at any point where it cannot be checked. This affects such points as the following:

- Epitome 1.19–36 claims that the sacrifices in the rebuilt temple after the return from Babylon were ignited under the supervision of Nehemiah by a supply of inflammable liquid that had been discovered in a hidden place. No such incident is recorded anywhere in the Scriptures.[16]
- Epitome 2.1–8 claims that the ark of the covenant was stored on Mount Nebo by Jeremiah before the Babylonian captivity. Again, there is no record of this anywhere in the Scriptures (even in the writings of Jeremiah).
- Epitome 3.1–40 says that King Seleucus sent his officer Heliodorus to take money from the temple at Jerusalem; but as he approached the treasury, he was struck down and scourged by heavenly messengers. Heliodorus is mentioned by other ancient sources (*OGIS* 247; Appian, *Syriaca,* 45.233), but none of them says that he visited Jerusalem or saw any apparitions there. The incident is possible—similar incidents undoubtedly did happen at times, under the old covenant (see the previous chapter)—but as the Epitome contains false and dubious matter elsewhere, its unsupported testimony here is not sufficient reason to credit it.
- Epitome 12.39–45 claims that Judas Maccabeus arranged for sin offerings to be made on behalf of idolaters who had died in battle. No such practice is reported in the Maccabean History or authorized by the Hebrew Scriptures.
- Epitome 14.37–46 claims that a man named Razis committed suicide rather than fall into the hands of his enemies, and praises the "nobleness" *(eugeneia)* of his act. This incident is not reported elsewhere, and this doctrine is not taught anywhere in the Scriptures.

For the above reasons, those who have measured both books by the standard of Scripture have generally seen a marked difference between the Maccabean History and the Epitome. Luther, for instance, in his 1533 prefaces to both books, observed that the Maccabean History, "in its statements and its wording, adopts virtually the same style as the other books of Holy Scripture, and would not have been unworthy to class among them," whereas the Epitome "should be cast out" from that class because it contains some material that "is neither instructive nor commendable [*taugt nicht und*

---

[16] Moreover, Epitome 1.18–20 appears to state that the temple was not rebuilt, or any sacrifices offered on it, until Nehemiah was sent to Jerusalem by the king of Persia. This suggests that the writer had confused the Nehemiah who lived in the time of Zerubbabel (Ezra 2.2 ≡ Neh 7.7), when sacrifice was offered and the temple partly rebuilt (Ezra 3.1–4.5), with the famous Nehemiah who was sent to Jerusalem by King Artaxerxes of Persia a century later (Neh 2.1–10), long after the temple had been completed (Ezra 6.15). See Nelis, *II Makkabeeën,* 61.

ist nicht zu loben]."[17] Those who regard the two books as similar in quality are not using the standard of Scripture to measure them.

Nevertheless, the unreliability of the Epitome should not be exaggerated (Luther went on to remark that "there is some good in it" as well). As the table above shows, many of the incidents and events reported in the Epitome are independently attested by the Maccabean History. Some of them are also attested by Classical historians (especially Polybius and/or writers dependent on Polybius).

Even Epitome 6.12–7.42 (the account of the deaths of Eleazar and the mother and her seven sons) appears to have some historical foundation. These incidents were not recorded in the Maccabean History or by any Classical historian. However, there seems to be an allusion to them in Hebrews 11.35: "Others were tortured [*etumpanisthēsan*], not accepting their release, in order that they might obtain a better resurrection." In English translation this may not look much like the narratives in the Epitome, but in the Greek the similarity is much stronger; the term *tumpanon* is applied to the torture of Eleazar in Epitome 6.19, 28, and the remaining clauses of Hebrews 11.35 resemble the declarations of the sons and their mother in Epitome 7.9, 14, 23, 29.[18] Of course, while this may confirm that the incidents are basically historical, it does not prove that everything said about them in the Epitome is reliable. Moreover, Hebrews 11.35 might have been referring not to the existing Epitome, but to its underlying source material (e.g., in the work of Jason of Cyrene).[19]

---

[17] Prideaux reached the same conclusions: the Maccabean History "is a very accurate and excellent history, and comes the nearest to the style and manner of the sacred historical writings of any extant," whereas some of the material in the Epitome is "fabulous and absurd .... This Second Book of the Maccabees doth by no means equal the accurateness and excellency of the First" (*Historical Connection of the Old and New Testaments,* 2.162–64). Elsewhere (2.102) he also compared the Epitome unfavorably with the Ptolemaic History. There is another classic analysis of the difference in quality between the Maccabean History and Epitome in Pellicanus 5.332r–v.

[18] McClister, *Commentary on Hebrews,* 432–34; King, *Hebrews,* 402–03; Bruce, *Epistle to the Hebrews,* 337–38; Delitzsch, *Epistle to the Hebrews,* 2.282–83; Spicq, *Épître aux Hébreux,* 2.364–65.

[19] The deaths of Eleazar and the mother and her seven sons are also described in a philosophical work known in ancient times as *Peri autokratoros logismou* ("On the Sovereign Power of Reason"; Eusebius, *History,* 3.10), which is nowadays usually called "4 Maccabees." It was probably written in the first or early second century CE (deSilva, *4 Maccabees,* xiv–xvii; van Henten, *Maccabean Martyrs,* 73–78). This account has no independent historical value, as it derived its information directly from the Epitome (or, less probably, from the latter's source material in Jason of Cyrene; see van Henten, *Maccabean Martyrs,* 70–73; de Silva, *4 Maccabees,* xxx–xxxi; Freudenthal, *Ueber die Herrschaft der Vernunft,* 72–90; Hadas, *Third and Fourth Books of Maccabees,* 92–94; Klauck, *4 Makkabäerbuch,* 654–57). The deaths of the seven sons and their mother were also recorded in Rabbinic tradition, which placed them several centuries later, during the reign of the Roman emperor Hadrian (Gittin 57b; Midrash Rabbah, Lam 1.50).

Similar comments may be made about the doctrines taught in the Epitome. Some of them are not supported by Scripture, and all of them need to be measured against the Scriptures (1 Jn 4.1–6; Acts 17.11; 2 Tim 3.16–17; Isa 8.20). But in this area too, the book's errors should not be exaggerated.

The Maccabean Epitome reminds us that the Lord is "Almighty" (*pagkratē,* 3.22), "the King of kings" (13.4), "the Lord of spirits and of all authority" (3.24), whose judgments are always righteous (12.6; 13.8). Even the mightiest evildoer is subject to Him, and if He allows evil to be done, it is only to serve His own good purpose. That was why He allowed Antiochus Epiphanes to inflict evil on Jerusalem: "Because of the sins of those who dwelt in the city, the Sovereign was angered for a short time, and therefore His disregard of the Place came about" (5.17). "But although He disciplines us with calamity, He does not forsake His people" or withdraw His mercy from them (6.16; cf. 11.9; 13.12). Those who perished at the hands of Antiochus Epiphanes are represented as looking forward to "the God-given hopes of being raised up again by Him" (7.14) "to a lasting renewal of life" (7.9), and as saying: "We ourselves are suffering because of our sins; but if our living Lord has been angered for a short time, for our rebuke and discipline, then He will again be reconciled with His own slaves" (7.32–33; cf. 7.18). In all those respects, the Epitome's teachings are fully in accordance with Scripture.

The Epitome also states that Eleazar was commanded to eat food that was contrary to the Law of Moses. However, "those who were in charge of the Law-breaking sacrificial meal … encouraged him to bring meat of his own providing, fit for him to eat, and pretend to be eating meat from the sacrifice commanded by the king, so that by doing this he might be delivered from death." But Eleazar refused even to pretend to eat meat sacrificed to idols, lest "many of the young … might be led astray through my pretense" (6.21–25). This too is consistent with the teachings of Scripture. "If food causes my brother to stumble, I will eat no meat to lasting time, in order that I may not cause my brother to stumble" (1 Cor 8.13).

Here as elsewhere, every saying that is trustworthy can be affirmed confidently, because "these things are good and profitable for people" (Titus 3.8).

JOSEPHUS

Flavius Josephus wrote his histories of Israel—*The Jewish War* and *Jewish Antiquities*—during the last decades of the first century after Christ. Both of them contain some material dealing with the period between Malachi and Jesus.

The Jewish War *(Peri tou Ioudaikou polemou)*

The *Jewish War* (completed about 75–79 CE) begins by describing briefly the deliverance of Israel through Mattathias and his sons and the rule of their descendants (1.31–130). It then narrates, in more detail, the conquest of Judea by Pompey and the reign of Herod the Great (1.131–673). Josephus may possibly have adapted much of this material from an earlier history (now lost) by Nicolaus of Damascus, which he certainly used when preparing his *Antiquities* (see below).

The main body of the book deals with the Roman war against Judea under the leadership of Vespasian and Titus (about 66–70 CE).

The Jewish Antiquities *(Ioudaikē archaiologia)*

Josephus's other main historical work, the *Jewish Antiquities,* was completed about 93–94 CE. Its first eleven books are mainly a paraphrase of the historical narratives in the Hebrew Scriptures, from the creation to the Persian period. Books 12 through 14 discuss the history of Israel in the Greek period and under the descendants of Mattathias, and the start of Roman rule. This section of Josephus's work consists of four main blocks of material, derived from different sources:

- ***Antiquities* 12.11–153** paraphrase the so-called **Letter of Aristeas,** a story about the translation of the Septuagint in Egypt in the time of Ptolemy II.
- ***Antiquities* 12.154–236** contain an extended story about the **Tobiad** family from Gilead across the Jordan. Josephus's source for this material is unknown.
- ***Antiquities* 12.242–13.214** paraphrase **Maccabean History 1.10–13.42** (from Antiochus Epiphanes to the deliverance from Greek rule in the time of Simon).[20]
- ***Antiquities* 13.225–14.486** revise and expand Josephus's own ***War* 1.51–356** (from the high priesthood of Simon to the establishment of Herod as king).

[20] Perhaps Josephus was working from a copy of the Maccabean History in which the final chapters were missing or damaged (ancient scrolls tended to become most worn at the ends). More likely, however, he simply wished to save work by using material he had already written (in the *War*) as early in the narrative as he could reasonably do so, i.e., at the end of Greek rule. The *Antiquities* was a huge and demanding task; why should he add to his labors by doing anew what he had done already?

Josephus supplemented his four major sources with material drawn mainly from world histories by Gentile writers, especially Nicolaus of Damascus (named as a source at *Antiquities,* 12.126–127; 13.250, 347; 14.9, 68, 104) and Strabo (named as a source at 13.285, 319, 347; 14.35, 68, 104, 111, 138; 15.9). He also seems to have had access to a source of information about the high priests who lived during this period. There are no signs that he used (or even knew of the existence of) the Ptolemaic History or the Maccabean Epitome.

The remaining books of the *Antiquities* (books 15–20) continue the history of Judea from the reign of Herod until the outbreak of rebellion against Rome (about 66 CE).

Reliability

The reliability of these sections of Josephus's work varies considerably, depending mainly on the reliability of his sources.

The **Letter of Aristeas** professes to be a report of the translation of the Septuagint in Alexandria at the time of Ptolemy (II) Philadelphus, written by a Greek official who was personally involved in the proceedings. However, the document has obviously been forged by a Jew living at a later time. No unbelieving Greek would speak of Israel's God and priesthood with such invariable reverence (Aristeas 3, etc.),[21] or would issue uncorrected such mockery of the Greek gods and wise men (Aristeas 134–137). Twice he uses language indicating that he lives at a much later date than the events he is describing: "for everything used to be administered by these kings through decrees and with great care" (Aristeas 28); "for such was the arrangement decreed by the king, which may be seen even to the present time" (Aristeas 182). The document, therefore, shows us what one Jewish writer in later Hellenistic times wanted people to believe about the origin of the Septuagint. But the true origin of the Septuagint may have been very different.[22]

Josephus's paraphrase of Aristeas does not always represent accurately the sense of the original.[23] Sometimes, indeed, his alterations actually reverse the sense (contrast Aristeas 311 with *Antiquities,* 12.109).

Where the **Tobiad** story can be tested against other sources of information, it too proves unreliable.[24] According to Josephus, the Tobiads maintained close relations

---

[21] When reproducing the description of the high priest's garments from the Law of Moses, he carefully avoids transcribing the name of the LORD (Aristeas 98).

[22] Wright, "The *Letter of Aristeas* and the Reception History of the Septuagint," 47–67.

[23] Meecham, *Letter of Aristeas,* 331–32. Some of the differences may have been due to negligence (the later books of the *Antiquities* seem to have been more carelessly prepared than the earlier ones: Schürer-Vermes 1.58). Others may have been made deliberately, e.g., for stylistic reasons (Pelletier, *Flavius Josèphe,* esp. 251–61).

[24] Gera, "On the Credibility of the History of the Tobiads," 21–38; *Judaea and Mediterranean Politics 219 to 161* B.C.E., 36–58; Grabbe, *History of the Jews and Judaism,* 2.75–78.

with Ptolemy (V) Epiphanes in Alexandria throughout his reign (*Antiquities,* 12.154, 158–187, 196–221)—yet by that time, the whole of Syria-Palestine was under the control of Ptolemy's enemy Antiochus the Great (Dan 11.15–17; Polybius 3.2.4, 8). According to Josephus, the Tobiad leader Hyrcanus built a fortress east of the Jordan and carved out caves in the nearby mountain (*Antiquities,* 12.229–232). Papyri of the period do indeed refer to a fortress built by the Tobiad family (CPJ 1.1), and its ruins have almost certainly been located at ʿIraq al-Amir, where one of the nearby caves is inscribed with the name "Tobiah" (*Ṭwbyh,* CIJ 868)—but both the papyri and the archeological evidence indicate that the fortress had been built at least a century before the time specified by Josephus.[25]

The **Maccabean History,** of course, provided Josephus with source material of greatly superior nature. Where errors exist in this part of the *Antiquities,* they have often been caused by haste or carelessness in reading that source. "The king sent a chief collector of tribute . . . and he came into Jerusalem" (Maccabaica 1.29) is misread as saying that the king himself came (*Antiquities,* 12.248); "Seron and his men were shattered . . . and about 800 men of them fell" (Maccabaica 3.23–24) is misread as saying that Seron himself fell (*Antiquities,* 12.292); Jazer's "daughters" (i.e., villages; Maccabaica 5.8) are misinterpreted as "wives and children" (*Antiquities,* 12.329); and so on.

There is also a fundamental difference in viewpoint between the *Antiquities* and the Maccabean History. In the Maccabean History, the Judeans repeatedly ascribe their victories and successes solely to the power of God, never to their own merit or skill (Maccabaica 3.18–22, 60; 4.10; 7.42). But when each of those passages is paraphrased in the *Antiquities,* the reference to God's power is either omitted or replaced by a reference to the fighters' virtues and abilities (*Antiquities,* 12.290–291, 304, 307, 409).[26] In this respect, Josephus's account resembles those of modern historians, who invariably attribute the successes of the Maccabean period to the Judeans' own capacities and resources rather than to the will of God.

After Josephus leaves the Maccabean History to describe **Simon and his successors,** the standard of accuracy drops once more. The names and succession of the rulers appear to be basically correct, but most of the stories about them do not appear in any other surviving source, and the few details that can be checked are not always consistent with other records. According to Josephus, John's son Aristobulus "transformed the government into a kingship, and was the first to put on a diadem" (*Wars,* 1.70 ≡

[25] Ji, "A New Look at the Tobiads of ʿIraq al-Amir," 417–40.

[26] "Josephus shifts the focal point from God's unconditional power of deliverance to a stress on the fighters' character and the goals for which they have taken up arms" (Gafni, "Josephus and I Maccabees," 119–22). A similar policy can be seen elsewhere in his *Antiquities.* "In an effort to place greater stress on the human characters in his history, Josephus de-emphasizes, in general, the Divine role" by comparison with the Scriptures (Feldman, *Studies in Josephus' Rewritten Bible,* 568).

Antiquities, 13.301), but according to Strabo, Aristobulus's brother and successor Alexander Janneus "was the first to declare himself king instead of high priest" (16.2.40). As far as it goes, the evidence of the coinage tends to support Strabo: no known coin of Aristobulus designates him as king, whereas many coins of Alexander Janneus do (Hendin 190–216). Assumption of kingship was no trivial matter in ancient times—especially in Judea, where only descendants of David were authorized to be kings—so it is surprising that there should have been any disagreement as to when, and under which ruler, it happened.

In fact, much of Josephus's account of this period was clearly taken from allusions in historical works by non-Judean (Gentile) writers.[27] Probably he relied mainly on the world history written by Nicolaus of Damascus, since Nicolaus is the author cited most often in this section of Josephus's narrative.[28] If so, that may explain some of the problems. Nicolaus was a friend and supporter of Herod the Great during the last decade of Herod's life. Therefore, his sources of information about the family displaced by Herod—the descendants of Simon—may have been sparse or untrustworthy, and he may not have made fair use of them; Josephus says elsewhere (with plausible supporting evidence) that Nicolaus was often inclined to vilify and misrepresent Herod's opponents (*Antiquities,* 16.183–185). The various negative stories about Simon's descendants in the *Antiquities* should be considered in that light.[29]

The account of **Pompey's conquest of Judea** seems to be of a markedly higher standard. This series of events was well documented in ancient times, so Josephus would have had excellent sources available to him, and his detailed narrative compares well with the other surviving sources. When he wrote the *War,* soon after the troubles of 66–70 CE, he had to be careful to avoid adverse criticism of the Romans, but he had more freedom when preparing the *Antiquities* two decades later. In the earlier work he says that, during Pompey's attack on the temple area, "most [of those slain] were killed by their hostile fellow countrymen" (*War,* 1.150). In the later work, that statement becomes "some of the Judeans were killed by the Romans, and some by one another" (*Antiquities,* 14.70).

The information about the **high priests** contains some serious errors, and should not be trusted except where it is confirmed by independent sources. The extreme example is Josephus's statement that Judas Maccabeus became high priest after the death of Alcimus (*Antiquities,* 12.414, 434)—which cannot be correct (Alcimus died at

---

[27] "His meagre comments on the reign of John Hyrcanus are either, where they concern external political history, borrowed from Greek historians, or, where they relate to internal affairs, partly legendary in character. There is not the slightest evidence for the use of a contemporary Jewish source" (Schürer-Vermes 3.1.185).

[28] Wacholder, Nicolaus of Damascus, 59–61.

[29] Stern, "דרכו של יוסף בן מתתיהו בכתיבת ההיסטוריה," 22–28; "ניקולאוס איש-דמשק כמקור לתולדות ישראל בימי בית הורדוס ובית חשמונאי," 375–94.

least twelve months after Judas: Maccabaica 9.3, 54–56), and is inconsistent with what Josephus himself says elsewhere (*Antiquities,* 20.237).[30]

[30] Another conspicuous mistake is his statement that Simon became high priest after the victory over Cendebeus: *nikēsas... archiereus apodeiknutai* (*War,* 1.53; contrast Maccabaica 13.42; 14.17, 35, 38; 16.2–10; cf. VanderKam, *From Joshua to Caiaphas,* 284, n. 119). We have fewer sources of information about earlier Hellenistic high priests, but the little that we do have suggests that Josephus's material may be similarly unreliable there. It is usually believed that he "wrongly identified" the high priest at the start of the Greek period with the Jaddua mentioned in an earlier context in Neh 10.21; 12.11, 22 (Yamauchi, "Ezra-Nehemiah," 582). Similarly, his story of intermarriage between the high priest's family and Sanballat's (*Antiquities,* 11.303–312) has several undoubted errors (Rowley, *Men of God,* 246–76) and is apparently "a garbled variant of that found in" Neh 13.28 (see the carefully reasoned discussion in Williamson, *Ezra, Nehemiah,* 400–01). His account of the alleged two high priests both called Simon, son of Onias, is also inconsistent with other ancient documents and is unlikely to be fully correct (as is conceded even by its principal defenders, e.g., VanderKam, *From Joshua to Caiaphas,* 137–57).

DANIEL

The overthrow of Persia by Greece, the Maccabean rebellion against the Greek kings, and the replacement of Greece by another world kingdom—these things did not happen unprepared or unannounced. They were the accomplishment of long-established plans, which God had revealed through His prophets hundreds of years earlier.

The prophet Daniel lived during the Babylonian and early Persian periods, more than five hundred years before the birth of Christ. He came to Babylon as a youth in the reign of one of the final kings of Judah (Dan 1.1–6), and he served the LORD faithfully until the reign of the first king of Persia (Dan 1.21; 10.1). He was greatly beloved by the LORD (Dan. 9.23; 10:11, 19), and the LORD revealed to him many things that were yet future. Some of these came to pass within Daniel's own lifetime, such as the madness of Nebuchadnezzar (Dan 4.1–37) and the conquest of Belshazzar's kingdom by the Medes and Persians (Dan 5.17–31). But most of Daniel's visions were not fulfilled until long after his death.

God revealed through Daniel that four successive earthly kingdoms would rule the world from the time of the Babylonian empire onwards. Then God would set up His own kingdom, which would put an end to all the earthly kingdoms, and would remain forever.

This message was revealed through Daniel twice:

- **Daniel 2** records a vision dreamed by the Babylonian king Nebuchadnezzar. The king himself could not understand his dream, but Daniel was able to interpret it. The king dreamed of a "great image," a statue in four parts: its head was gold, its breast and arms of silver, its belly and loins of bronze, its legs and feet of iron and clay (2.31–33). This represented Nebuchadnezzar's own kingdom and the three world kingdoms that would succeed it (2.37–43). The statue was destroyed by a stone, which became a great mountain (2.34–35)—indicating that "in the days of those kings, the God of the heavens will set up a kingdom that will never be destroyed .... It will pulverize and put an end to all these kingdoms, and it will itself stand forever" (Dan 2.44).
- **Daniel 7** records a vision seen by Daniel himself, much later in the Babylonian period. In the vision, he saw "four great living creatures": one like a lion, one like a bear, one like a leopard, and "a fourth living creature" that is not compared to any specific animal (7.3–7). Like the four parts of Nebuchadnezzar's statue, these four creatures represented the four successive world kingdoms (7.17). Again God promised that, after these things, He would set up "a lasting dominion that will not pass away," a kingdom "that will not be destroyed" (7.13–14, 18).

Later still, Daniel was given two further visions, which described two of the kingdoms in more detail.

- **Daniel 8** records a vision of two living creatures: a ram and a goat (8.3–8). These two creatures represented two successive world kingdoms: the Medo-Persian kingdom (8.20) and the Greek kingdom that would conquer it (8.21–22). The vision foretold that the Greek kingdom would break into four (8.8, 22), and that a king from one of those four parts would oppress God's people, defile the temple, and abolish the appointed sacrifices for several years, after which the temple would be cleansed (8.9–14, 23–26).
- **Daniel 11** records a vision about the future kings of Persia and Greece. At first, the kings of Persia would prosper and would seek to attack Greece (11.2), but later the king of Greece would become supreme (11.3). His kingdom would break into four (11.4). For a while, the kings of the South would be strong, repeatedly defeating the kings of the North (11.5–11); but later, the kings of the North would defeat the South (11.12–27). One king of the North would oppress the land of God's people, defile the temple, and replace the appointed sacrifices with an "abomination"; but in the end he would perish (11.28–45).

The chart on the facing page shows the correspondence between these various prophecies.

The following discussion presents the prophecies of Daniel that relate to the time between the end of the Persian empire and the coming of Christ. It juxtaposes Daniel's words with the words of later historians who described these events as they unfolded, or who were able to piece them together from earlier documents. Some of those historians were Gentile writers who did not know the Scriptures or the power of God, and whose testimony is fallible and incomplete. Nevertheless, even they are able to give names to the people, places, and incidents in the inspired history of Daniel, and unwittingly show that not one jot or tittle of the word of God falls to the ground or fails to prosper in the thing for which he sent it (Josh 23.14; Isa 55.11; John 10.35).

The First King of Greece
[Alexander III of Macedon, 336–323 BCE]

Daniel's fullest account of the end of the Persian empire, and its overthrow by the king of Greece, is given in chapter 8. He sees a **ram** with **two horns** (named later in the chapter as **the kings of Media and Persia**), and a **he-goat** with one conspicuous **horn** (named as **the first king** of Greece). The he-goat (the king of Greece) comes **from the west**, runs against the ram, and defeats it:

> **8.3** And I lifted up my eyes, and saw. And behold, a ram *was* standing next to the watercourse; and it *had two* horns. And the *two* horns *were* high; and one *was* higher than the other; and the high *one* came up last.

8.4 I saw the ram butting seaward and northward and southward. And no living things *could* stand before his face, and there was no one who *could* rescue from his hand. And he did just as *he* pleased, and made *himself* great....

8.5 And behold, a he-goat of the goats came from the west, over *the* face of *the* whole earth, and without touching *the* earth. And the he-goat *had* a visible horn between his eyes.

8.6 And he came up to the ram with the *two* horns, which I saw standing next to the watercourse. And he ran at him in *the* fury of his power.

8.7 And I saw him arriving beside the ram. And he became embittered at him, and struck down the ram, and broke his two horns. And there was no power in the ram to stand before his face. And he threw him down to *the* earth, and trampled him; and there was no one who rescued *the* ram from his hand.

Daniel 2 **Image**	**Daniel 7** **Four creatures**	**Daniel 8** **Two creatures**	**Daniel 11** **Kings**
Head of gold (2.32) ≡ you (king of Babylon, 2.37–38)	Like a lion (7.4)		
Breast and arms of silver (2.32) ≡ second kingdom (2.39)	Like a bear raised to one side (7.5)	Ram with one horn higher (8.3–4) ≡ kings of Media and Persia (8.20)	Kings of Persia (11.2)
Belly and loins of bronze (2.32) ≡ third kingdom (2.39)	Like a leopard with four heads (7.6)	Goat with great horn, replaced by four (8.5–12) ≡ king of Greece, replaced by four (8.21–22)	Kingdom of Greece, divided into four (11.3–45)
Legs and feet of iron and clay (2.33) ≡ fourth kingdom (2.40–43)	Fourth creature (7.7)		
Stone that became a mountain (2.34–35) ≡ kingdom of God (2.44)	One like a Son of Man (7.13–14) ≡ holy ones receive kingdom (7.18)		

Later in the chapter, Daniel is given the following explanation:

> **8.20** The ram that you saw, with the *two* horns—*these are the* kings of Media and Persia.
> **8.21** And the hairy goat *is the* king of Greece. And the great horn that *is* between his eyes—he *is* the first king.

The historical fulfillment of these events is reported in the Maccabean History and many other ancient histories. Darius (known to modern historians as Darius III) was defeated by Alexander of Macedon (later known as Alexander the Great):

> Darius set up his army at Gaugamela by the River Bumodus, about 600 stadia from the city of Arbela....
>
> And for some little time the battle became hand-to-hand; but when the horsemen who were with Alexander, and also Alexander himself, attacked fiercely, both pushing against the Persians and striking their faces with their spears, and the Macedonian phalanx came at them, tightly packed and bristling with pikes, then Darius, who had already been afraid a long time, saw terrors all together everywhere, and he himself was the first to turn and flee. [Arrian 3.8.7; 3.14.3]

> This having been the outcome of the battle, the sovereignty of the Persians was considered to be altogether dissolved, and Alexander, who was proclaimed king of Asia, offered great sacrifices to the gods and gave his friends wealth and houses and provinces. [Plutarch, *Alexander,* 34.1]

The extent of the ram's downfall in the eyes of the world can be seen from a speech made far away in Athens shortly afterwards (about 330 BCE):

> Is there anything strange or unexpected that hasn't happened in our time? For we haven't lived a human life; instead, we were born to be a tale of wonder to those who come after us. Isn't the king of the Persians— ... he who dared to write in his letters that he was the ruler of people everywhere from the sun's rising to its setting—nowadays isn't he struggling desperately, no longer to be lord over others, but by this time to save his own skin? [Aeschines, *Against Ctesiphon,* 132]

So Alexander became supreme ruler over many countries:

> And it came about that Alexander the Macedonian, the son of Philip, came out of the land of Kittim and defeated Darius king of the Persians and Medes. And after he had defeated him, then he reigned in place of him, as he had previously reigned over Greece. And he fought many battles, and took possession of fortresses, and killed kings of the earth, and went through to the ends of the earth, and took plunder from a multitude of nations. And the earth was quiet before him. And his heart was exalted and lifted up. And he gathered together a very strong army, and ruled countries, nations, and monarchs; and they became tributary to him. [Maccabaica 1.1–4]

Modern historians estimate that Alexander became king of Macedon about 336 BCE, and defeated Darius about 331 BCE.[31]

The Division of the Kingdom of Greece [The Successors of Alexander, 323–305 BCE]

Daniel 8 describes how **the first king** of **Greece** perished in the midst of his greatness. His **nation** then was divided into **four kingdoms,** but those kingdoms did not have the **strength** that he had:

> **8.8** And *the* he-goat of the goats made *himself* great, until *he was* extremely *so.* And when he was powerful, the great horn was broken; and four visible *horns* came up in its place, to *the* four winds of *the* heavens....
> **8.21** And the hairy goat *is the* king of Greece. And *as for* the great horn that *is* between his eyes—he *is* the first king.
> **8.22** And *as for its* being broken, and four stood in its place—four kingdoms will stand from the nation, but not with his strength.

There is another account of the same events in Daniel 11:

> **11.3** And a mighty king will stand, and rule a great realm, and do as *he* pleases.
> **11.4** And when he *is* standing, his kingdom will be broken. And it will be divided to *the* four winds of the heavens, and not to his posterity.

Again the historical fulfillment is reported in the Maccabaica and many other ancient histories. Alexander died after a reign of only 12 years. At that time, his kingdom was divided among his closest followers (honored "servants ... who had been brought up with him from his youth"). Those followers later declared themselves kings ("put on diadems"), and their kingdoms were inherited by their descendants "for many years":

> And after these things he fell upon his bed, and he knew that he was dying. And he called his servants, who were honored, who had been brought up with him from his youth; and he divided his kingdom among them, while he was still alive. And Alexander reigned 12 years, and he died.
>
> And his servants began to rule, each one in his own place. And they all put on diadems after he was dead, and so did their sons after them, for many years: and they multiplied evils in the earth. [Maccabaica 1.5–9]

According to modern calculations, Alexander died, and his kingdom was divided, around 323 BCE; his successors officially designated themselves kings, and began wearing the royal diadem, around 306–304 BCE.[32]

---

[31] Shipley, *Greek World after Alexander,* 36–38; Pfeiffer, *Between the Testaments,* 67–70.

[32] Errington, *History of the Hellenistic World,* 43–44; Shipley, *Greek World after Alexander,* 43; Bevan, *House of Seleucus,* 1.57; Holbl, *History of the Ptolemaic Empire,* 20.

The Kings of the South and North
[Ptolemy I Soter and Seleucus I Nicator, 305–283 BCE]

Daniel 11 continues with a long, remarkably detailed prophecy of the rivalry between two of the divided Greek kingdoms: the kings of the **South** (the Ptolemies, based in Egypt) and the kings of the **North** (the Seleucids, based in Syria), whose realms are shown in the map on the facing page. Those were the two kingdoms directly relevant to the history of Israel, which lay between them and was ruled first by the South, then by the North. The other portions of Alexander's empire were much more distant, and had very little contact with the land of Israel.

Daniel foretells that, in the earliest years, the **king of the South** would **become strong.** But one of his important officials (**commanders**) would become even **stronger,** and would gain possession of **a great realm** (in the next verse, this commander receives the title **king of the North:** Dan 11.6).

> 11.5 And *the* king of the South will become strong. But *one* of his commanders will become stronger than he, and will rule; his realm *will be* a great realm.

Ancient historians report that the rise of these kings was a long and complex process, as first one, then another, gained the upper hand and became **strong.**

In the initial division of Alexander's empire, the province of Egypt, in the **South,** was given to Ptolemy (Diodorus 18.3.1)—who soon established himself in a position of great power there. A year or two later, one of Alexander's former military leaders, Antipater,

> divided up the provinces afresh; but to Ptolemy he allocated what was already in his power, for it was impossible to displace him, because he appeared to be holding Egypt by his own valor, as if it had been conquered in battle .... He was exceptionally gentle and forgiving, and also a doer of good deeds [*euergetikos*]; and this was the very thing that most increased his power and made many people want to share his friendship. [Diodorus 18.39.4–5; 19.86.3]

Thus Ptolemy, in the **South,** became **strong** very rapidly. The future king of the North, Seleucus, was in a much weaker position at first. In fact, for a while was forced to seek refuge under Ptolemy's authority. In Antipater's division of the provinces, he had been given the province of Babylonia [Diodorus 18.39.6] But several years later, when a conflict arose there,

> Seleucus ... fled with 50 horsemen, planning to retreat into Egypt to Ptolemy .... By condemning himself to flee, Seleucus had given up his province without any struggles or risks. [Diodorus 19.55.4–6]

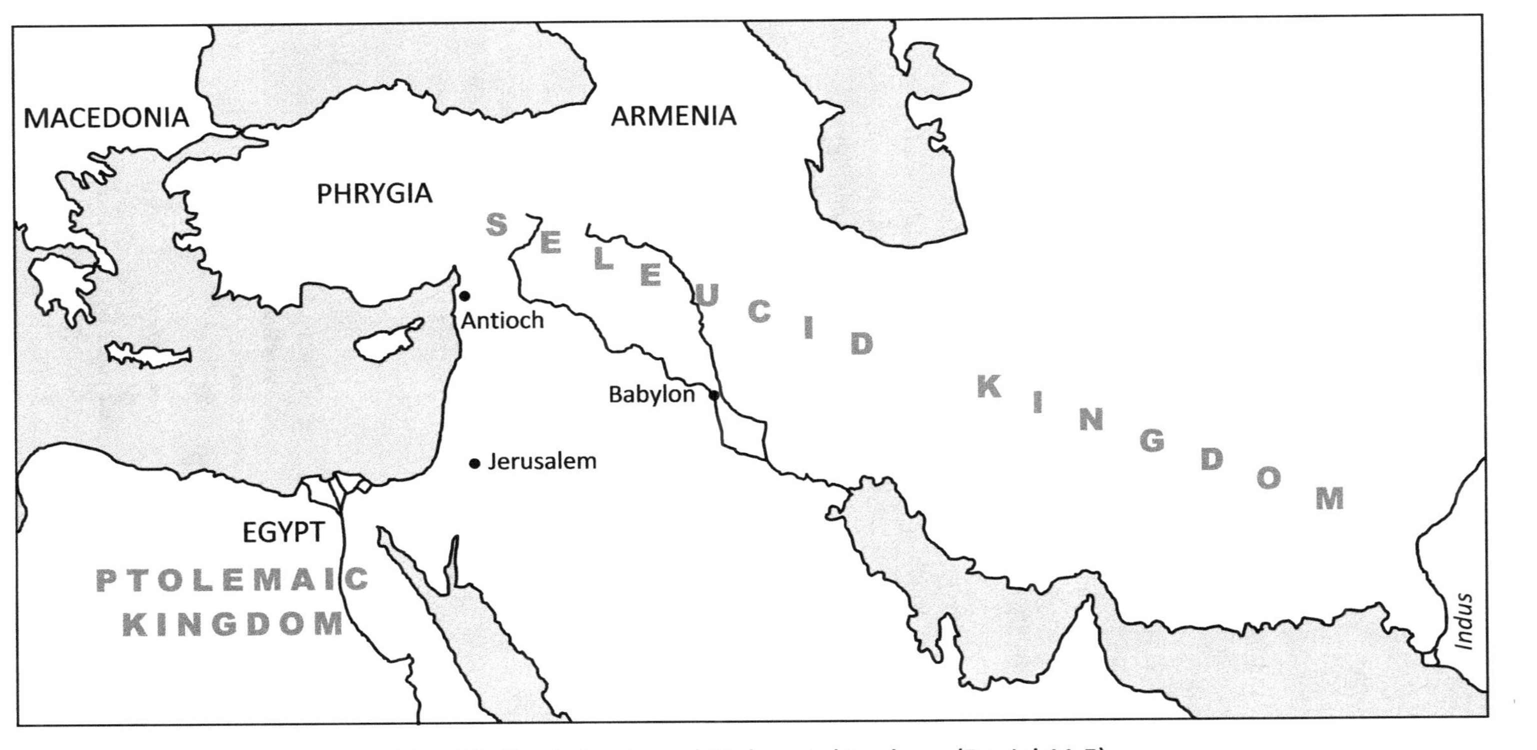

Map 25: The Seleucid and Ptolemaic kingdoms (Daniel 11.5)

So Seleucus resorted to Ptolemy for help, and regained his position in Babylon with Ptolemy's backing:

> Ptolemy . . . sent Seleucus to Babylon to regain his authority; and he gave him 1,000 footsoldiers for this purpose, and 300 horse. And with such small numbers Seleucus recovered Babylon, whose men joined together in accepting him eagerly; and before long he greatly extended his authority . . . . Always lying in wait for the nearby nations, and having power to compel and persuasiveness in diplomacy, he gained authority over Mesopotamia and Armenia and what is called Seleucid Cappadocia, and the Persians and Parthians and Bactrians and Areians and Tapyrians and Sogdianians and Arachosians and Hyrcanians and all the other adjoining peoples as far as the River Indus, where Alexander's spear had conquered—so that the boundaries of his rule in Asia extended further than those of any ruler except Alexander, for the whole area from Phrygia to the Indus was subject to Seleucus. [Appian, *Syriaca,* 54.273–274; 55.281–282]

Eventually, therefore, Seleucus managed to establish an even larger and **stronger** kingdom in the **North** than Ptolemy had in the South. "Of those who succeeded Alexander as rulers, Seleucus became the greatest king, was the most kingly in mind, and ruled over the greatest amount of land after Alexander himself" (Arrian 7.22).

The chart on the facing page shows the successive kings of the North and South during the next century and a half (about 323–164 BCE), and the prophecies in Daniel 11 that relate to them.

An Unsuccessful Alliance
[Ptolemy II Philadelphus and Antiochus II Theos, 252 BCE]

Daniel foretells that, after much time had passed (**at the end of the years**), the rival rulers of the **South** and the **North** would attempt to **join together** in an **equitable arrangement:** the Southern king's **daughter** would go to the **king of the North** (in marriage; cf. Jdg 1.14; 12.9). But the arrangement would fail. She would not maintain her **strength.** Instead, she and her supporters would be **given over** to death. Her husband **and his offspring** would also **not stand.**

> **11.6** And at *the* end of *the* years, they will join together, and *the* daughter of *the* king of *the* South will come to *the* king of the North to make an equitable arrangement. But she will not retain *the* strength of *her* arm; and he and his offspring[33] will not stand. And she will be given *over,* and *those* who brought her *there,* and her father, and *the one* who supported her in *those* times.

---

[33] **His offspring** *(zrʿw).* The Hebrew text could be read either *zarʿô* (**his offspring,** as in Gen 48.19; Num 14.24; 24.7; Psa 25.13; 37.25, 26; Jer 22.28) or *zᵉrōʿô* ("his arm," as in Deut 11.2; Isa 17.5; 40.10; 48.14; Jer 48.25; Ezek 31.17). In ancient times, *θ′* and Vg took the former view, whereas the Masoretic scribes and LXX took the latter. Either would fit the context.

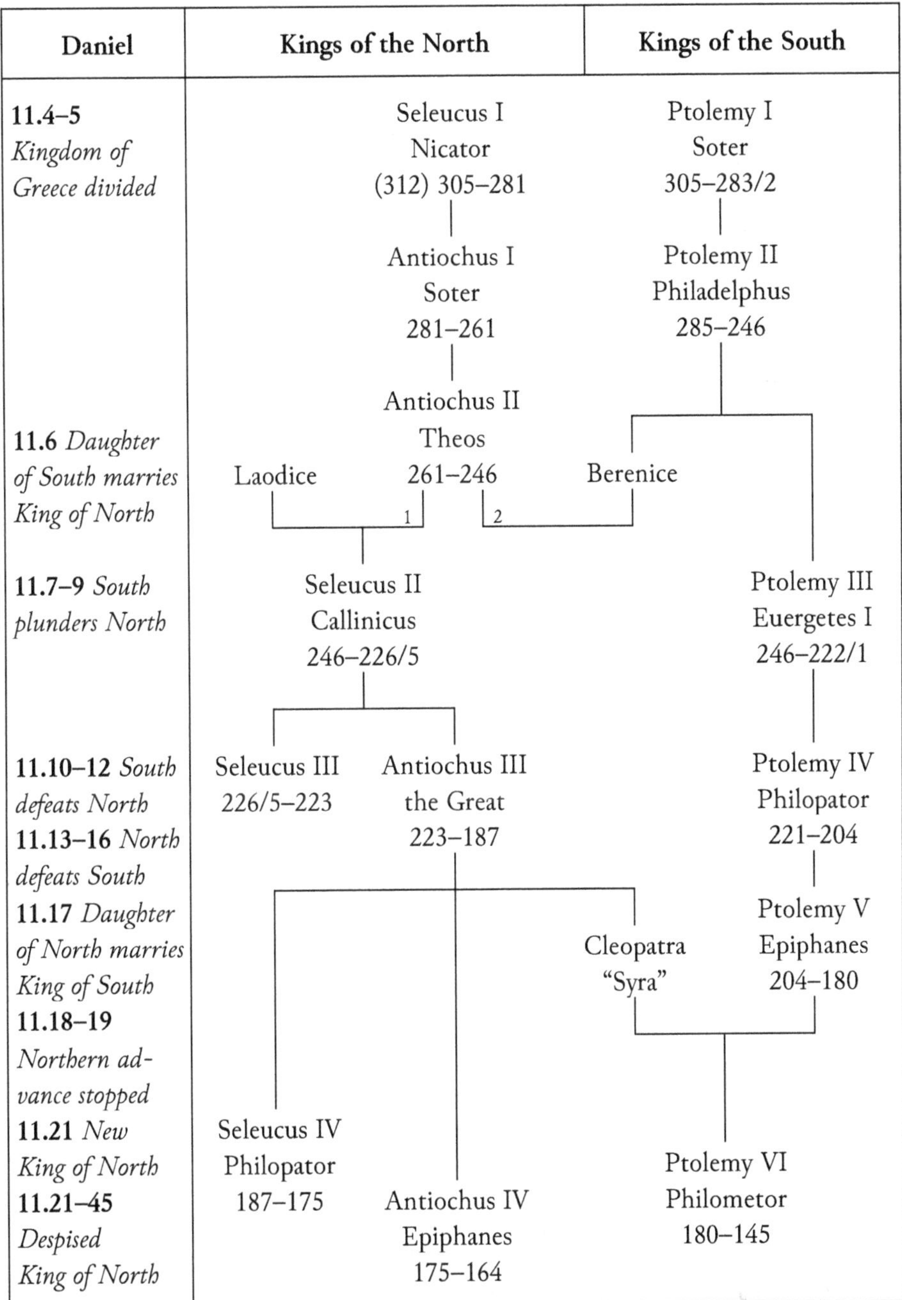

Daniel	Kings of the North	Kings of the South
11.4–5 *Kingdom of Greece divided*	Seleucus I Nicator (312) 305–281	Ptolemy I Soter 305–283/2
	Antiochus I Soter 281–261	Ptolemy II Philadelphus 285–246
11.6 *Daughter of South marries King of North*	Laodice (1) — Antiochus II Theos 261–246 — (2)	Berenice
11.7–9 *South plunders North*	Seleucus II Callinicus 246–226/5	Ptolemy III Euergetes I 246–222/1
11.10–12 *South defeats North* **11.13–16** *North defeats South*	Seleucus III 226/5–223 Antiochus III the Great 223–187	Ptolemy IV Philopator 221–204
11.17 *Daughter of North marries King of South* **11.18–19** *Northern advance stopped*		Cleopatra “Syra” Ptolemy V Epiphanes 204–180
11.21 *New King of North* **11.21–45** *Despised King of North*	Seleucus IV Philopator 187–175 Antiochus IV Epiphanes 175–164	Ptolemy VI Philometor 180–145

When Alexander’s original successors died, their kingdoms passed to their descendants (Maccabaica 1.9). After many years (around 253–252 BCE, according to modern calculations), a marriage alliance between the two realms was arranged: the current **king of the North** (Antiochus II Theos) married Berenice, the **daughter** of the current **king of the South** (Ptolemy II Philadelphus). The marriage was an important event, long remembered for the lavish gifts that accompanied the bride (Porphyry, *FGrH* 260.43), and many surviving ancient documents refer to it. There even exists a private letter written on papyrus at the time by a member of Berenice's entourage, a physician named Artemidorus ("We have just come into Sidon after going with the queen as far as the borders," *P. Cair. Zen.* 2.59251).

Yet those who formed the alliance did **not stand.** A few years later (about 246 BCE), Antiochus died. Then his previous wife Laodice arranged for Berenice, their young child, and most of Berenice's attendants to be killed. (Some ancient sources say that Laodice was also responsible for the death of Antiochus; very likely even the earliest historians did not know the truth about that.) About the same time, Ptolemy Philadelphus died in Egypt. (No ancient record indicates the cause, or whether there was any direct connection between his death and the others.) The main surviving accounts differ in some points of detail, so each of them is printed below:

> Ptolemy Philadelphus gave his daughter named Berenice in marriage to Antiochus, who had already had two sons ... by a previous wife named Laodice .... Antiochus ... much later restored Laodice to royal status, together with her children; but she was afraid that her husband might change his mind and restore Berenice to favor, so she had him killed by her servants with poison; and she handed over Berenice and the son whom she had borne by Antiochus ... to be killed, and set up her elder son, Seleucus Callinicus, as king in his father's place .... After the murder of Berenice and the death of her father Ptolemy Philadelphus in Egypt, her brother—who was the Ptolemy called Euergetes—succeeded as the third ruler of the kingdom. [Porphyry, *FGrH* 260.43]

> The Antiochus called Theos married Laodice, his sister on his father's side, by whom he had a son, Seleucus. He formed a second marriage with King Ptolemy's daughter Berenice, by whom he had a son, whom he left an infant when he died. He left his kingdom to Seleucus. Laodice had Berenice's son put to death .... [The conspirators] fell upon Berenice and killed her; and most of the women with her, who were defending her, were killed with her. [Polyaenus 8.50]

> This Theos his wife killed by poison .... Laodice killed him, and then Berenice and Berenice's child. [Appian, *Syriaca,* 65.344–345]

> On the death of Antiochus, king of Syria, his son Seleucus succeeded in his place, and began his reign by murdering members of his family; and his mother Laodice, who ought to have opposed this, encouraged it. He killed his stepmother Berenice—who was the sister of Ptolemy, [the new] king of Egypt—together with her child, his little brother. [Justin 27.1]

All those directly involved in the alliance were now dead. The throne of Syria passed to Laodice's son Seleucus (II Callinicus), and the throne of Egypt to Berenice's brother Ptolemy (III Euergetes I).

The South Plunders the North
[Ptolemy III Euergetes and Seleucus II Callinicus, 246–226 BCE]

Next Daniel foretells that after the king of the South and his daughter had died (Dan 11.6), there would arise **in his place** a new king—one of her relatives (**one from the shoots of her roots,** i.e., one of the descendants of her ancestors). The new king would attack the **fortress of the king of the North,** and would be successful (**gain power**), taking idols and costly objects of **silver and gold** back to **Egypt.**

Some time later, the **king of the North** would try to **come into** the **kingdom** in the **South;** but he would be obliged to **return** home.

> **11.7** And *one* from *the* shoots of her roots will stand *in* his place. And he will come against the army, and come into *the* fortress of *the* king of the North. And he will take action against them and gain power.
> **11.8** And also their gods, with their molten *images,* with their desirable articles—silver and gold—he will bring into exile *in* Egypt. And *for some* years he himself will stand *away* from *the* king of the North.[34]
> **11.9** And he will come in*to the* kingdom of *the* king of the South, and return to his *own* ground.

Classical historians report that, after the deaths described in the previous section, the new king of Egypt, Berenice's brother, "invaded Syria and advanced to Babylon" (Appian, *Syriaca,* 65.346). It was claimed that "he despoiled the kingdom of Seleucus, and carried off in plunder 40,000 talents of silver and some 2,500 precious vessels and images of gods" (Porphyry, *FGrH* 260.43). A contemporary inscription at Adulis on the Red Sea, celebrating this victory, has been preserved:

> The Great King Ptolemy... having received from his father the kingdom of Egypt and Libya and Syria and Phoenicia and Cyprus and Lycia and Caria and the Cyclades, marched out into Asia with forces of footsoldiers and horsemen and a naval array and elephants.... And, having become lord of all the region on this side of the Euphrates, and of Cilicia and Pamphylia and Ionia and the Hellespont and Thrace, and of all the forces in these regions and of Indian elephants, and having made the monarchs in all these places his subjects, he crossed the Euphrates River. And, having brought under his control Mesopotamia and Babylonia and Susiana and Persia and Media and all the remaining regions as far as Bactria, and having sought

---

[34] **He himself will stand away from** [Hebrew *m-*] **the king of the North.** The Hebrew text could mean either "he will refrain from [attacking] the king of the North" (NASB; "stand away from" means "refrain from" in Gen 29.35) or possibly "he will stand secure... against the king of the North" (Stone; cf. Psa 43.1). Both would fit the report in Justin (27.2) that Ptolemy III successfully defended his realm against Seleucus II, after which there was peace between them for ten years. The rendering "he shall continue more years than the king of the North" (KJV) is grammatically possible but does not suit the context of vv 8–9.

> out whatever sacred things had been carried away by the Persians from Egypt, and having brought them back, with other treasures from these places, to Egypt, he sent his forces through the river canals. [*OGIS* 54]

Some time later, according to Justin, Seleucus (the **king of the North**) "made war on Ptolemy, believing that he now matched his strength; but ... he was defeated ... and fled trembling to Antioch" (Justin 27.2; cf. Eusebius, *Chronicle,* 251b–c).

The South Defeats the North
[Ptolemy IV Philopator and Antiochus III the Great, 225–217 BCE]

As we have seen, the king of the North described in Daniel 11.9 would be driven back by the South—but in the next generation, his **sons** would **stir themselves up** to renew the struggle. One of those sons would muster a **great multitude**, powerful enough to **engulf and pass over.** Yet the **king of the South** would **come out and make war with him,** and the Northern **multitude** would be defeated (**given into his hand**) in an immense battle (when **tens of thousands** would **fall**).

> **11.10** And his sons will stir themselves up and gather a multitude of great forces. And he will come, coming; and he will engulf and pass over. And he will return and stir himself up even to his fortress.
> **11.11** And *the* king of the South will be embittered, and will come out and make war with him, with *the* king of the North. And he will set up a great multitude; but the multitude will be given in*to* his hand.
> **11.12** And the multitude will be carried away; and his heart will be exalted, and he will cause tens of thousands to fall; but he will not be strong.

According to the Classical historians, Seleucus II was succeeded as **king of the North** by two of **his sons:** Seleucus (III) Soter, who reigned for only two or three years, and then Antiochus (III) the Great (Polybius 2.71.3–5; Appian, *Syriaca,* 66.347–348). Both sons actively tried to strengthen and extend the kingdom's boundaries in war. Soon after Antiochus became **king of the North** (around 223–222 BCE), he was already trying to capture the regions between Syria and Egypt from the **king of the South** (Polybius 5.42.8–5.46.5). He would ultimately be successful (see the next section), but only after about twenty years.

The first major clash between Antiochus and the new **king of the South,** Ptolemy (IV) Philopator, took place about 217 BCE. The **great multitude** of Antiochus's soldiers advanced south to the border of Egypt, but there Ptolemy defeated them, after a close-fought, fluctuating battle near the town of Raphia. The conflict is described briefly in the Ptolemaic History:

> Having learned ... that Antiochus had seized the places that he himself had controlled, Philopator gave orders to all his forces, both footsoldiers and horsemen. And taking with him his sister Arsinoe, he set out as far as the regions near Raphia, where Antiochus's forces were camped....

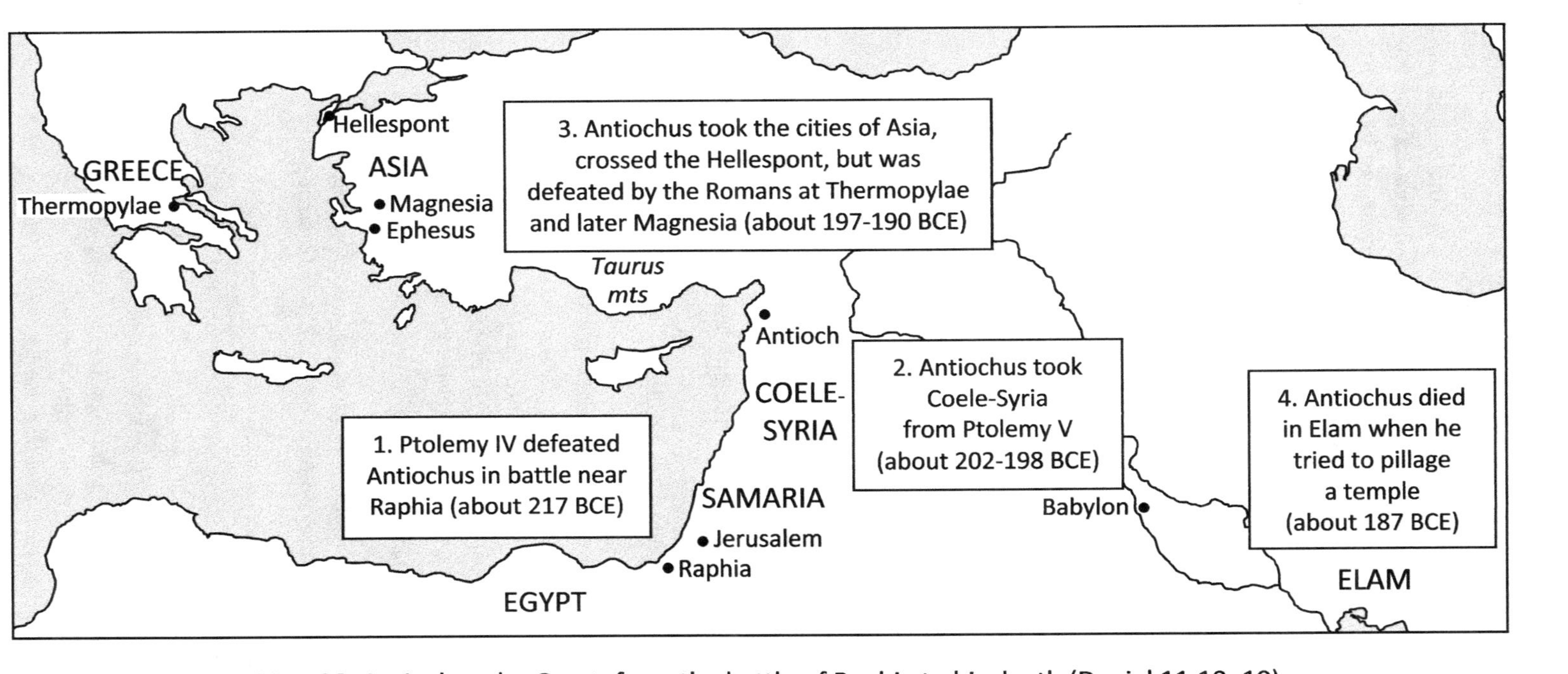
Hellespont
GREECE
ASIA
Thermopylae
Magnesia
Ephesus
3. Antiochus took the cities of Asia, crossed the Hellespont, but was defeated by the Romans at Thermopylae and later Magnesia (about 197-190 BCE)
Taurus mts
Antioch
COELE-SYRIA
2. Antiochus took Coele-Syria from Ptolemy V (about 202-198 BCE)
4. Antiochus died in Elam when he tried to pillage a temple (about 187 BCE)
1. Ptolemy IV defeated Antiochus in battle near Raphia (about 217 BCE)
SAMARIA
Babylon
Jerusalem
Raphia
EGYPT
ELAM

Map 26: Antiochus the Great: from the battle of Raphia to his death (Daniel 11.10–19)

> But when an intense battle had begun, and matters were turning out rather in favor of Antiochus, Arsinoe went about encouraging the forces with wailing and tears, her hair loose, and urged them to help themselves and their children and wives, boldly promising to give them each two minas of gold if they were victorious. And so it happened that their enemies were destroyed in hand-to-hand combat, and many captives were also taken. [Ptolemaica 1.1, 4–5]

Polybius gives a detailed account of the battle (5.79.1–5.86.8) and provides estimates of the casualties (presumably from a Seleucid source, which probably understates Antiochus's losses; see the chapter on the Ptolemaic History):

> On Antiochus's side, nearly 10,000 footsoldiers and more than 300 horsemen had perished, and more than 4,000 had been captured . . . . And on Ptolemy's side, about 1,500 footsoldiers and 700 horsemen had perished. [Polybius 5.86.5–6]

An Egyptian inscription commemorating Ptolemy's victory has also been preserved:

> It came about, in Year 5 [of his reign], month 1 of summer, day 1, he went out from Pelusium. He fought with Pharaoh Antiochus[35] at a certain town that is called Raphia, which is close to the border district of Egypt, which is to the east of the town of Bethelea and Pasinefer.
>
> On day 10 of the abovenamed month, he overpowered him in a great and glorious manner . . . . He forced Antiochus to throw his diadem and his cloak <down to the ground>, and to flee . . . while only a few men were with him, in a wretched and contemptible manner . . . .
>
> Pharaoh [Ptolemy] captured many men and all the elephants. He acquired much gold and silver, and the other valuable things that were found in the towns that Antiochus had been holding, having been brought there for him from his own borders. He caused them all to be sent to Egypt.
>
> He journeyed through the other places that were inside his borders. He went into the temples that were there. He performed burnt offerings and drink offerings, and all the men who were in the towns welcomed him with joyful hearts and held festivities. [Raphia Decree, M.10–16][36]

The **king of the South** took great pride in this victory (**his heart** was **exalted**)—but, just as Daniel had prophesied, he would **not be strong.**

---

[35] Antiochus is accorded remarkable honor in the Raphia inscription. Not only is his name written in a royal cartouche, but he is also given the title "Pharaoh" *(Pr-ʿꜣ),* a most surprising designation for a non-Egyptian king.

[36] The decree was issued in hieroglyphic, demotic, and Greek. The translation is mainly from the demotic text (the only form that has been well preserved); supplementary material inside angle brackets has been taken from the hieroglyphic text.

The North Defeats the South

[Antiochus III the Great and Ptolemy V Epiphanes, 202–198 BCE]

The defeat foretold in Daniel 11.11–12 would not stop the king of the North. He would return later (at the end of the times) against the king of the South, with an even greater multitude. With the help of a raised mound, he would capture an inaccessible city, and the forces of the South would not stand against him.

After that, the king of the North (**the one who comes against** the king of the South) would have possession of the land of Israel (the **Land of Beauty;** cf. Jer 3.19), and **no one** would be able to oppose him.

> **11.13** And *the* king of the North will return and set up a multitude *that will be* greater than the former *one*. And at *the* end of the times, *the* years, he will come, coming, with great force*s* and many goods.
> **11.14** And in those times, many *people* will stand against *the* king of the South. And *the* sons of ravagers of your people will raise themselves up, to establish *the* vision; but they will stumble.
> **11.15** And *the* king of the North will come, and cast up a raised mound, and capture an inaccessible city. And *the* arms of the South will not stand, and *the* people of his choosing; and there will be no strength *for them* to stand.
> **11.16** And the *one* who comes against him will do as *is* his good pleasure, and there will be no *one* standing against his face. And he will stand in *the* Land of Beauty; and all of it[37] *will be* in his hand.

Polybius reports that, when Ptolemy Philopator died, the kingdom of the **South** passed into the hands of his infant son, Ptolemy (V) Epiphanes. Both Antiochus the Great and the king of Macedonia (Philip V) seized this opportunity to gain control of some of Ptolemy's territories.

Around 202–198 BCE, Antiochus defeated Ptolemy's general, Scopas, and conquered Coele-Syria (the region between Syria and Egypt; see the commentary on Maccabean History 10.69).[38]

> Antiochus and Ptolemy Philopator quarreled, and finally went to war with each other over Coele-Syria . . . .
>
> When Ptolemy passed away from life, Antiochus and Philip plotted together to divide the realms left to his infant son, and they began doing mischief [*kakopragmonein*], Philip laying hands on Egypt and Caria and Samos, and Antiochus on Coele-Syria and Phoenicia. [Polybius 3.2.4, 8]

---

[37] **And all of it** *(wklh)*. The Hebrew text could be read either *w^ekullāh* (**and all of it**) or *w^ekālāh* ("and a full end," as in Jer 4.27). In ancient times the LXX (88) took the former view, the Masoretic scribes the latter.

[38] Grainger, *Hellenistic Phoenicia,* 99–105.

> Ptolemy's army leader Scopas set out for the upper regions and overthrew the Judean nation in the winter.... When Scopas was conquered by Antiochus, Antiochus took possession of Batanea and Samaria and Abela and Gadara; and after a short time, the Judeans dwelling near the holy place named Jerusalem surrendered to him. [Polybius 16.39.1, 3–4 ≡ Josephus, *Antiquities,* 12.135–136]

This important change is also mentioned in Livy 33.19.8: "Antiochus ... subjugated [*redactis*] all the cities of Coele-Syria from Ptolemy's power to his own." For the next sixty years (until the end of Greek rule), Judea, Samaria, Galilee, and the regions beyond the Jordan were always ruled by the kings of the **North** (Polybius 28.1.2–5).

Another Unsuccessful Alliance
[Antiochus III the Great and Ptolemy V Epiphanes, 194–193 BCE]

Daniel foretells that the king of the North would **come with all the power of his kingdom** and **give** the king of the South his **daughter** on **equitable terms.** In this way he would seek to undermine his rival's kingdom (**destroy it**). But, like the earlier marriage alliance between these two kingdoms (verse 6), it would not be successful (it would **not stand,** and would **not come about** to suit the Northern king).

> **11.17** And he will set his face to come with *the* power of all his kingdom, and *bringing* equitable *terms* with him, and will take action. And he will give him a daughter of women, to destroy it. But it will not stand, and will not come about for him.[39]

According to Livy and Appian, Antiochus the Great had hoped to gain possession of Egypt. At one time (probably around 196 BCE), when he heard rumors that young Ptolemy V was dead, he actually started preparing to invade the country (Livy 33.41.3; 33.44.7; Appian, *Syriaca,* 4.15). But the rumors were false. Instead "King Antiochus... gave his daughter in marriage to Ptolemy king of Egypt, at Raphia in Phoenicia," probably around 194–193 BCE (Livy 35.13.4; cf. Polybius 18.51.10; 28.20.9). Appian says that Antiochus did it "to cajole the boy" (*Syriaca,* 5.18).

Yet the alliance did not actually give Antiochus any further power over Egypt. When Ptolemy V died (around 180 BCE; Polybius 24.6.7), his widow was left in control of the country, but she did not transfer it to her Syrian relatives; instead, she continued to rule Egypt herself as a Ptolemaic sovereign,[40] and after her death it was handed down to the children whom she had borne to Ptolemy.

---

[39] **It will not stand, and will not come about for him.** The alliance "shall not stand or be to his advantage" (ESV). Alternatively, the subject could be the **daughter** just mentioned: "she will not take a stand [for him] or be on his side" (NASB); but this is less likely (in view of Isa 7.7, on which the present passage is modeled). Either way, the meaning is much the same.

[40] During this period, coins were issued bearing her name and image, and in official documents her name stood first, sometimes with the title "the Goddess Epiphanes" (*P. Freib.* 3.12; *P. Ryl.* 4.589).

The Northern Advance is Stopped [Antiochus III the Great, 197–190 BCE]

The kingdom of the North was now reaching its maximum extent. Daniel prophesies that its king would **turn** his attention toward the **coastal regions** on the shores of the Mediterranean (Jer 25.22; 2.10), and **capture many** of them. But at this point, an opposing **leader** would **put an end to** the great king's **insolence.**

> **11.18** And he will turn his face back to *the* coastal regions, and capture many. But a leader will put an end to his insolence for him; he will not turn his insolence back onto him.[41]

Antiochus the Great's westward advance through the **coastal regions** of the northern Mediterranean is documented at great length in Polybius and Livy. Around 197 BCE, "he himself set out with 100 decked naval vessels and 200 lighter ships ... to win over the cities that had been under Ptolemy's control along the whole shore of Cilicia and Lycia and Caria" (Livy 33.19.10–11). By the end of that year, all the regions as far as Ephesus, on the west coast of Asia, had submitted to him. "After wintering at Ephesus, King Antiochus tried to subject all the cities of Asia to their former sovereignty." One of those cities then appealed for help to Rome, but Antiochus "left Ephesus with his ships and sailed to the Hellespont, ordering his land forces to be transported from Abydos to the Cheronesus" in Europe (Livy 33.38.1–8). During the next few years he advanced south to Greece, but was driven back at Thermopylae and then defeated decisively (around 190 BCE) at Magnesia, northeast of Ephesus, by Roman forces who received significant assistance from King Eumenes II of Pergamum (Livy 37.37.9–37.44.3).

The subsequent treaty required Antiochus to withdraw from all his western provinces, and to pay the Romans an immense annual tribute and give them hostages:

> There shall be friendship between Antiochus and the Romans for all time if he does what is in accord with this agreement:
>
> King Antiochus and his subjects shall not allow through their territory any army that would make war on the Romans or their allies, nor shall he give it any supplies; and the Romans and their allies will also do likewise toward Antiochus and those who are under his rule.
>
> And Antiochus shall not make war on those who are in the islands or in Europe. And he shall evacuate the cities and territories <and villages and fortresses on this

---

[41] **He will not** [*blty*] **turn his insolence back onto him.** Such renderings as "Indeed, he shall turn his insolence back upon him" (ESV) are grammatically impossible: Hebrew *blty* always has a negative meaning (BDB 116–17; HALOT 1.136). The idea may be either that the king **will not** be able to **turn** any of **his insolence back onto** the opposing leader (cf. NAB), or else that the opposing leader **will not turn ... back onto** the king any of the kind of **insolence** that the king himself had displayed (*ohne dass er sein Schmähen ihm vergelten wird,* König 3, §388*k*).

side of the Taurus mountains as far as the River Tanais, and from the Taurus valley as far as the heights where it turns toward Lycaonia; from these towns and fields and fortresses> he shall take nothing except the weapons borne by his soldiers, and if anything happens to have been taken away, it shall be restored to its own city....

And Antiochus shall give the Romans 12,000 talents of the finest Attic money over 12 years, giving 1,000 each year—the talent not weighing less than 80 Roman pounds—and 540,000 modii of wheat....

And Antiochus shall give <the Romans 20> hostages not younger than 18 years of age or older than 45, and he shall replace them every three years.

And if anything should be lacking from the amounts paid back, he shall pay it back the following year.

And if any of the cities or nations against which Antiochus is forbidden by this document to make war should act first in starting a war against him, Antiochus may make war on them, but he himself shall neither have sovereignty over those nations and cities nor accept them as friends.

And any disputes that arise between the parties shall be submitted to judicial decision. And if both parties wish to add anything to this agreement or take anything away from it by common decree, it shall be allowed. [Polybius 21.43.1–27 ≡ Livy 38.38.2–18][42]

The Death of the King of the North [Antiochus III the Great, 187 BCE]

After his advance into the coastal regions had been stopped (Daniel 11.18), the king of the North would **turn . . . back** eastward to **his own land,** but he would perish (**stumble and fall** and **not be found;** cf. Psa 37.35–36).

11.19 And he will turn his face back to *the* fortresses of his *own* land; and he will stumble and fall, and will not be found.

Various ancient documents report that Antiochus died around 187 BCE, in Elam, one of the eastern provinces of his kingdom (CM §4.29; see the comments on Maccabean History 6.1).

When Antiochus the Great tried to pillage the temple of Bel, the barbarians in the neighborhood set upon him all by themselves, and killed him. [Strabo 16.1.18]

King Antiochus, being burdened with a heavy tribute by the Romans who had defeated him... attacked at night, with his army, the temple of Jupiter in Elam. When this was known, the local inhabitants came running and killed him with all his soldiers. [Justin 32.2; cf. Diodorus 29.15 [29.18]; 28.3]

[42] The translation is mainly from Polybius; material inside angle brackets is taken from Livy, at points where there are gaps in the extant text of Polybius.

A New King of the North
[Seleucus IV Philopator, 187–175 BCE]

Daniel foretells that the next king of the North would **send . . . an oppressor** through his **kingdom.** But his reign would last only a short time (**a few days**).

> **11.20** And in his place will stand *one* who will send through an oppressor of *the* splendor of *the* kingdom.[43] And in a few days he will be broken, but not in anger and not in war.

"On the death of Antiochus the Great, his son Seleucus [IV] succeeded him" (Appian, *Syriaca,* 45.232). The **oppressor** whom he sent may be the Heliodorus mentioned in the Epitome of the Acts of Judas Maccabeus and in several inscriptions on Delos ("Heliodorus son of Aeschylus, who was brought up with King Seleucus and is also over his affairs of state, and is of his family," *OGIS* 247). According to the Epitome, Seleucus was told

> about the indescribable sums of money filling the treasury in Jerusalem—so much so that the immensity of the funds was beyond counting; and . . . it was possible for these sums to fall under the king's authority . . . . And he chose Heliodorus, who was over his affairs of state; and, having given him commands, he sent him to perform the removal of the aforesaid sums of money. [Epitome 3.6–7]

Daniel's prophecy contrasts the new king with his predecessor. Antiochus the Great was king for 35 years and died fighting (**in anger** and **in war**), whereas his successor reigned for only 12 years (CM §4.23) and perished in peacetime—reportedly at the instigation of the very Heliodorus who had been his principal minister of state (see the next section).

The Despised King of the North
[Antiochus IV Epiphanes, 175 BCE]

Daniel foretells that the next king of the North would be a **despised** person who would not be given the **kingship** by his people, but would gain it by **smooth words.**

> **11.21** And in his place a despised *one* will stand. And they will not give him *the* honor of kingship; but he will come in *a time of* ease, and take *the* kingship strongly by smooth *words*.

"When Seleucus passed away from life . . . Antiochus, who was called Epiphanes, received the kingdom" (Epitome 4.7; CM §4.25). At the time, Antiochus was in

[43] **The splendor of the kingdom** could describe either the region that is oppressed (the king "will send an oppressor through the Jewel of his kingdom," NASB) or the purpose of the oppression (the king "shall send an exactor of tribute for the glory of his kingdom," ESV).

Athens, where he had risen to an important position in a remarkably short time (his name appears as chief magistrate, with an elephant emblem, on Athenian coins of 176–175 BCE). He himself later said that he was "beloved" in the days of his authority (Maccabaica 6.11), and various ancient sources comment on his deceitfulness in later diplomacy (Diodorus 30.18.2 [30.22b]; Livy 45.11.1, 8; etc.).

The surviving documents say little about the circumstances of his accession, except for a story told by Appian:

> Seleucus . . . gave his own son Demetrius as a hostage to the Romans, in place of his brother Antiochus. When Antiochus had been released from being a hostage and was still in Athens, Seleucus died as a result of a plot by Heliodorus, one of the court officials. But when Heliodorus tried to seize control of the government, he was cast out by Eumenes and Attalus, and they restored it to Antiochus so that the man would be their ally. [Appian, *Syriaca,* 45.232–233]

Eumenes was the influential king of Pergamum who opposed Antiochus the Great at Magnesia (see above); his brother Attalus was often closely associated with him.

The King's Power
[Antiochus IV Epiphanes, 175–164 BCE]

The remainder of Daniel 11 continues to describe the despised king of the North (v 21). In some places it foretells specific events (his invasions of Egypt, vv 25–28, 29–30, 40–43; his defilement of the temple, v 31; his death, v 45), but mostly it surveys his deeds in general. Powers (**arms**) that opposed him would **be broken** before him (as described in more detail in vv 25, 40–42). Even though he set out with only a small number of supporters (**a little nation**), he would **come** into the richest regions (the **fat places**) unchallenged and **in a time of ease,** gathering **plunder and loot and goods,** and would **scatter** what he gained, distributing it **for** those round about him (as described in vv 28, 38–39, 43). Yet there would be a deceptive side to his apparent generosity: those who became his allies (**joined themselves with him**) would be treated with **deceit** (as described in v 27).

> **11.22** And arms, being engulfed,[44] will be engulfed before his face, and will be broken; and also a leader of *the* covenant.[45]

---

[44] **Arms, being engulfed.** The Masoretic scribes construed *hšṭp* as a noun, *haššeṭep* ("engulfing"). This is not impossible (at one stage, the opposing **arms** were "a force that is extremely great and powerful," v 25); but the infinitive absolute *hiššāṭōp* (**being engulfed**) forms a much commoner Hebrew construction (GKC §113*l–n;* JM §123*d–e*) and fits the immediate context better: **being engulfed,** these forces would **be engulfed.** (So also ESV: "Armies shall be utterly swept away before him.")

[45] **A leader of the covenant.** The Hebrew term *ngyd* (**leader**) can be applied to the ruler of a country ("leader of Tyre," Ezek 28.2; "leader over My people Israel," 1 Sam 9.16), an officer

11.23 And after they join themselves with him, he will act deceitfully. And he will come, and will become powerful with a little nation.
11.24 He will come in *a time of* ease even in*to the* fat *place*s of *the* province, and he will do what his fathers have not done, and his fathers' fathers. He will scatter plunder and loot and goods to them. And against inaccessible *place*s he will plan his plans, even until a time.

The North Defeats the South
[Antiochus IV Epiphanes and Ptolemy VI Philometor, 170 BCE]

Daniel foretells that the king of the North would oppose the **king of the South.** The two kings would wage **war,** with **great** forces on both sides; and the **king of the South** would **not stand:** his **force** would **be engulfed.** Afterwards, the two kings would meet and **speak lies at one table;** but their designs would **not prosper.**

11.25 And he will rouse up his strength and his heart against *the* king of the South, with a great force. And *the* king of the South will stir himself up even to war, with a force *that is* great and extremely powerful; but he will not stand, for they will plan plans against him.
11.26 And *those* who eat his delicacies will break him, and his force will be engulfed; and many wounded will fall.
11.27 And *the* two kings—their heart *will be* for evil, and they will speak lies at one table. But it will not prosper; for *the* end *will* yet *be* at *the* appointed *time.*

The Maccabean History describes Antiochus's success in the South as follows:

> And the kingdom was prepared in the sight of Antiochus, and he determined to reign over the land of Egypt, so that he might reign over the two kingdoms. And he entered into Egypt with a great multitude, with chariots and elephants and a great array; and he made war against Ptolemy king of Egypt; and Ptolemy turned back before him, and fled; and many fell wounded. And they took possession of the strong cities in the land of Egypt; and he took the plunder of the land of Egypt. [Maccabaica 1.16–19]

---

under him ("heads of the thousands and the hundreds . . . every leader," 1 Chr 13.1; 2 Chr 32.21), or a priest of the LORD ("leader of the house of God," 1 Chr 9.11; Neh 11.11). A **covenant** can be either an agreement between two people (e.g., Hiram and Solomon, 1 Kgs 5.12) or God's covenant with His people (Exod 19.5; 24.7–8; the "covenant of holiness," Dan 11.28, 30, 32).

Thus the **leader of the covenant** could be either the king of the South who was defeated by Antiochus (v 25) and entered into a covenant with him (v 27), or else Onias, the high priest of Israel (Epitome 3.1) who is said to have been killed by his enemies in the time of Antiochus (Epitome 4.34). The latter view seems less likely; Antiochus reportedly had nothing to do with the death of Onias, and punished his murderer (Epitome 4.27–38).

After these victories (about 170 BCE), according to the Classical historians, Antiochus posed as a friend of the young Egyptian king Ptolemy VI (Philometor), but "he deceived and sought to overthrow completely the one who trusted him" (Diodorus 30.18.2 [30.22b]; Livy 45.11.1, 8; cf. Polybius 30.26.9).

Action against the Holy Covenant
[Antiochus IV Epiphanes, 170 BCE]

On his **return** from his victories in the South, the king of the North would take action **against the covenant of holiness.**

> **11.28** And he will return to his *own* land with a great *amount* of goods. And his heart *will be* against *the* covenant of holiness; and he will take action, and return to his *own* land.

The Maccabean History describes what Antiochus did **against the covenant of holiness** at this time (in the year 143 SE ≡ about 170 BCE). He visited Jerusalem, entered the holy place, and plundered the temple:

> And after he had defeated Egypt, Antiochus returned in the 143rd year, and went up against Israel. And he went up against Jerusalem with a great multitude, and entered arrogantly into the holy place, and took the golden altar, and the lampstand of the light, and all its vessels, and the table of the showbread, and the cups for drink offerings, and the bowls, and the golden incense vessels, and the veil, and the crowns, and the golden adornment that was on the face of the temple, and he scaled off everything. And he took the silver and the gold and the precious vessels; and he took the hidden treasures that he found.
>
> And when he had taken everything, he went away into his own land. [Maccabaica 1.20–24]

The North is Driven Back from the South
[Antiochus IV Epiphanes and Ptolemy VI Philometor, 168 BCE]

Later the king of the North would **return . . . into the South.** But this **last** invasion would not be as successful as the **first** one (described in vv 25–28). This time, he would be opposed and **defeated** by **ships** sent from the Mediterranean coastal region (**Kittim;** see the comments on Maccabaica 1.1).

> **11.29** And at *the* appointed *time* he will return, and come in*to the* South. But as *it was the* first *time,* it will not also be so *the* last.
> **11.30a** But ships of Kittim will come against him, and he will be defeated.

According to Classical historians, Antiochus was back in Egypt around 168 BCE, two years after his initial success; but an ambassador sent by the Roman senate forced him to withdraw from the country:

He was victorious in a naval battle at Pelusium, and, having crossed the Nile with his army on a hastily made bridge, was striking terror at Alexandria with his siege; he seemed to be not far from gaining possession of an extremely rich kingdom. [Livy 44.19.9]

When the senate learned that Antiochus had become lord of Egypt and almost of Alexandria, they considered that the aforesaid king's increasing status affected them, and appointed Gaius Popilius as their ambassador to end the war....

When the king greeted him loudly from a distance and held out his right hand, Popilius, the Roman commander, handed him a copy of the senate's decree .... Having at hand a staff of vinewood, he drew a circle with it around Antiochus, and ordered him to stay in this circle until he gave his decision about the things written there. And the king, disoriented by this proceeding and air of superiority, replied after a short time that he would do everything demanded by the Romans .... The document ordered him to end the war with Ptolemy at once. Therefore, as a fixed number of days had been given to him, he led his forces away to Syria, deeply hurt and complaining, but yielding to the situation for the present. [Polybius 29.2.1–3; 29.27.2, 5–8.]

The Holy Place Defiled
[Antiochus IV Epiphanes, 168–167 BCE]

After the king of the North left the South, he would again **return** homewards, and would again **take action** against God's covenant (the **covenant of holiness**), defiling the **holy place,** abolishing the **continual offering** appointed by the old covenant Law (Exod 29.38–42; Num 28.3–6), and setting up a **desolating abomination** in its place.

11.30b And he will return, and have indignation against *the* covenant of holiness, and take action. And he will return and pay heed to *those* who forsake *the* covenant of holiness.
11.31 And arms from him will stand and defile the holy place, the fortress. And they will put away the continual *offering,* and set up the desolating abomination.
11.32a And with smooth *words* he will pollute those who do wickedness against *the* covenant.

Again the Maccabean History describes what Antiochus did **against the covenant of holiness,** two years after his previous intrusion (i.e., in the year 145 SE ≡ about 168 BCE). His officers first seized military control of Jerusalem, and then commanded the people to **forsake** the Law of God. The **holy place** was defiled, and a **fortress** was set up there. Any **offering** to God was forbidden. A **desolating abomination** (a "heathen altar") was placed on the sacrificial altar in the Jerusalem temple, and sacrifices were offered to idols there and elsewhere in the land:

And after two years, the king sent a chief collector of tribute into the cities of Judah. And he came into Jerusalem with a great multitude, and spoke words of peace to

> them deceitfully; and they believed him. And he fell upon the city suddenly, and struck it with a great calamity, and destroyed many people out of Israel.... And they took possession of the city of David, and built *it* up with a great and strong wall, with strong towers; and it became a citadel for them. And they put there a sinful nation... and it became a place of ambush against the holy place, and an evil accuser to Israel continually. And they shed innocent blood round about the holy place, and defiled the holy place....
>
> And many people of Israel were well pleased with his way of worship, and sacrificed to idols and profaned the Sabbath. And the king sent letters by the hand of messengers to Jerusalem and the cities of Judah, that they should follow laws strange to the land, and should forbid burnt offerings and sacrifices and drink offerings in the holy place; and should profane the Sabbaths and feasts, and pollute the holy place and those who were holy; that they should build heathen altars and temples, and shrines for idols, and should sacrifice swine's flesh and unclean beasts.... And he appointed overseers over all the people, and commanded the cities of Judah to sacrifice, city by city. And many of the people gathered together to them—everyone who forsook the Law; and they did evil things in the land.... And on the 15th day of Chislev, in the 145th year, they built an abomination of desolation on the sacrificial altar.... And on the 25th day of the month they sacrificed on the heathen altar that was on the sacrificial altar. [Maccabaica 1.29–30, 32–37, 44–52, 54, 59]

The next chapter in the Maccabean History contains a sample of the **smooth words** employed to **pollute** the people of Judah and turn them **against** God's **covenant:**

> And the king's officers answered and spoke to Mattathias, saying, "You are a ruler and an honored and great man in this city, and strengthened with sons and brothers. Now, come first and do the king's command, as all the nations have done, and the men of Judah, and those who remain in Jerusalem. And you and your sons will be counted among the king's Friends, and you and your sons will be honored with silver and gold and many gifts." [Maccabaica 2.17–18]

Those who Know God Take Action
[Antiochus IV Epiphanes, 167–164 BCE]

Daniel foretells that, when the holy place was defiled and the offerings were abolished, the **people who know their God** would stand firm (**hold on strongly**). Many of them would perish in war and its consequences (**stumble by sword and by flame, by exile and by plunder**), but this would **refine** and **purify** them. Others would **join with them** deceitfully (**with smooth words**).

> **11.32b** But *the* people who know their God will hold on strongly, and take action.
> **11.33** And *those* of the people who are discerning will cause many to take heed. But they will stumble by sword and by flame, by exile and by plunder, *for some* days.
> **11.34** And in their stumbling they will be helped *with* a little help. And many will join with them with smooth *words*.

> **11.35** And *some* of the *one*s who are discerning will stumble, to refine and to purify and to make *them* white, until *the* time of *the* end; for *it is* yet for *the* appointed *time.*

The Maccabean History describes how some people in Israel remained faithful to God during this time of persecution:

> And many in Israel were strong, and they determined within themselves not to eat unclean things. And they chose to die, so that they might not be defiled with the foods, and might not profane the holy covenant; and they died....
>
> And Mattathias cried out in the city with a loud voice, saying, "Whoever is zealous for the Law and maintains the covenant, let him come out after me." And he and his sons fled into the mountains.... Then many who were seeking justice and judgment went down into the desert, to settle there.... And all those who fled from the evils were added to them, and became a support for them. And they brought together an army, and struck down sinners in their anger, and transgressors in their wrath. ... And the work prospered in their hand. [Maccabaica 1.62–63; 2.27–29, 43–44, 47]

Many of the faithful perished during this struggle and its aftermath, including all five of Mattathias's sons (Maccabaica 2.50; 6.43–46; 9.5–21, 35–42; 12.39–48; 13.3–5, 23; 16.13–16).

The King's Good Pleasure
[Antiochus IV Epiphanes, 175–164 BCE]

Daniel foretells that the **king** of the North[46] would **prosper** for a while, **until** the time

---

[46] Some commentators consider that the final section of Daniel 11 continues to refer to Antiochus Epiphanes ("in the smallest details this prophecy manifestly fits the history of Antiochus's reign," Fabre d'Envieu, *Livre du prophète Daniel,* 2.2.1435–40; Barnes, *Notes ... on ... Daniel,* 451–52; King, *Daniel,* 728–29). Others believe that this section refers partly to Antiochus Epiphanes, and partly to matters yet future ("the writer is never speaking only about one era of history, even though the prediction was to be applied to Antiochus as the first of many oppressors," Baldwin, *Daniel,* 198–202; Longman, *Daniel,* 282–83; Duguid, *Daniel,* 203–04). And still others hold that this section has no reference to Antiochus, but refers solely to matters yet future ("it is most likely that the author never intended 11:36–45 to be about Antiochus," Steinmann, *Daniel,* 535–40; Wood, *Commentary on Daniel,* 304–05; Leupold, *Exposition of Daniel,* 510–12).

A full discussion of this subject would be out of place in the present book, which is solely concerned with the history of Israel between Malachi and Jesus. We have continued to trace parallels with the career of Antiochus Epiphanes throughout the final section of Daniel 11, because no obvious change of subject is marked in the text of the passage itself (on the contrary, the "time of the end" mentioned in v 35 must surely be the same as the "time of the end" mentioned in v 27 and in v 40, as noted by Keil, *Daniel,* 384–85). Readers who believe that we are mistaken on this point may still find our discussion useful. Even if Daniel 11 does shift from the time of Antiochus Epiphanes to a future time, this must indicate that there is a close of God's **indignation** had **ended** (cf. Dan 8.19). During his prosperity he would **exalt himself... over against every god,** and would **speak** against the true God (the **God of gods,** Dan 2.47; Deut 10.17). He would set up **inaccessible ... fortresses,** and would lavish great **honor** on his favorites (**those whom he recognizes**).

> **11.36** And the king will do as *is* his good pleasure. And he will exalt himself, and make himself great, over against every god. And against *the* God of gods he will speak marvelous *things*. And he will prosper until *the* indignation is ended; for what is inscribed will be done.
> **11.37** And he will not pay heed to *the* gods of his fathers and *the* desire of women, and he will not pay heed to any god. For he will make himself great over all.
> **11.38** And in his place he will glorify a god of fortresses, and will honor a god that his fathers did not know, with gold and silver and valuable stones and desirable things.
> **11.39** And he will take action in regard to *the* inaccessible *places* of *the* fortresses, with *the help of* an alien god. He will multiply honor *to those* whom *he* recognizes,[47] and he will make them rule over many, and he will also divide *the* land for a price.

The full title that Antiochus gave himself on his coins was "Antiochus, god made visible" (*Antiochou Theou Epiphanous:* SC 2.1476, etc.). As the Maccabean History records, he was quite prepared to desecrate and plunder the temples of other gods—including the true God—in order to aggrandize himself:

> And he went up against Jerusalem with a great multitude, and entered arrogantly into the holy place, and took the golden altar, and the lampstand of the light, and all its vessels, and the table of the showbread, and the cups for drink offerings, and the bowls, and the golden incense vessels, and the veil, and the crowns, and the golden adornment that was on the face of the temple, and he scaled off everything. And he took the silver and the gold and the precious vessels; and he took the hidden treas-

---

kinship or similarity between the two periods—a "tight parallel between the actions of Antiochus IV" and those of his future successor(s) (Steinmann, *Daniel,* 544–45). We today are beset by "many antichrists" (1 Jn 2.18); on any view of the subject, it is good for us to see how closely Antiochus Epiphanes paralleled the antichrists of the present age—and how, by the grace of God, a small band of faithful believers was able to resist and overcome him.

There is a similar disagreement about the final section of Daniel 8. Some commentators believe that Dan 8.23–25 refers to Antiochus Epiphanes (Steinmann, *Daniel,* 418–21); others maintain that certain aspects of it do not fit Antiochus and must refer to matters still future (Wood, *Commentary on Daniel,* 225–28). Again, and for similar reasons, we have continued to note parallels with the career of Antiochus throughout that section.

[47] **[Those] whom he recognizes** *(ʾšr hkyr)*. The Hebrew phrase could also be construed as "[the one] who recognizes [him]" ("whosoever acknowledgeth [him]," ASV); but in that case, the following **he will multiply... and he will make them rule** *(yrbh... whmšylm)* would involve an awkward change of both subject and number.

> ures that he found. And when he had taken everything, he went away into his own land....
>
> And he heard that in Elam in Persia there was a city renowned for riches, for silver and gold; and that the temple in it was extremely rich.... And he came and sought to capture the city and pillage it. [Maccabaica 1.21–24; 6.1–3]

While he was oppressing Judea, he issued commands to **honor** his supporters and **divide the land for a price:** "to make foreigners dwell in all their boundaries, and to give away their land as an inheritance" (Maccabaica 3.36). He built a **fortress** adjacent to the temple at Jerusalem (Dan 11.31),[48] and garrisoned it with foreigners:

> And they took possession of the city of David, and built it up with a great and strong wall, with strong towers; and it became a citadel for them. And they put there a sinful nation, transgressors, and they strengthened themselves in it.... And the holy place was trodden down, and foreigners' sons were in the citadel—the nations were lodging there. [Maccabaica 1.32–34; 3.45]

He was famous for "the expense and the gifts that he had given... with a lavish hand" (Maccabaica 3.30), and those who supported him were promised great **honor** ("Do the king's command... and you and your sons will be counted among the king's Friends, and you and your sons will be honored with silver and gold and many gifts," Maccabaica 2.18).

The End of the King of the North [Antiochus IV Epiphanes, 164 BCE]

In both chapter 8 and chapter 11, Daniel pauses just before describing the final catastrophe, and reminds his readers just what ambitious and audacious deeds this king would perform.

> **8.25** And he will make *himself* great in his heart, and in *a time of* ease he will destroy many; and he will stand against *the* Leader of leaders. But without a hand he will be broken.

He would be highly exalted and immensely destructive; he would even oppose the **Leader of leaders** ("against the God of gods he will speak marvelous things," 11.36)—yet he would ultimately **be broken.**

The point is developed again, at greater length, in chapter 11: just before the king's **end** is described, the full scale of his achievements is recalled. At the height of his

---

[48] According to one source, Antiochus issued orders "to pollute the sanctuary in Jerusalem and call it by the name of Olympian Zeus" (Epitome 6.2). That might perhaps be the **god of fortresses... a god that his fathers did not know.** The wording in Daniel does not imply that **his fathers** had never heard of this **god** (cf. Lebram, "König Antiochus im Buch Daniel," 755–56), but that they had never set up any such policy for worshiping it.

career, he would defeat the **king of the South,** enter the **Land of Beauty** (Israel; see above, on 11.16), and **rule over . . . all the desirable things of Egypt**—as described already (11.25, 28).[49] Even people living west of Egypt (**Libyans**) and south of Egypt (**Cushites**) would be subject to him at that time. He would also set out **to destroy** many people at the other end of his kingdom, in the **east** and the **north.** The greatest of all his audacities would be to **plant** his **tents** at the **mountain of holiness** (Jerusalem: Dan 9.16), defying the God of gods without any immediate harm (see the discussion of 11.28 above). A king who could accomplish such things might seem utterly invincible.

Yet this king would still **come to his end,**[50] and would have **no one** to rescue him then. The man who was seeking **to destroy** many would be destroyed himself.

> **11.40** And at *the* time of *the* end, *the* king of the South will butt against him. And *the* king of the North will sweep against him with chariots and with horsemen and with many ships; and he will come in*to the* lands, and engulf and pass over.
> **11.41** And he will come in*to the* Land of Beauty. And many will stumble; but these will be delivered from his hand: Edom and Moab and *the* head of *the* sons of Ammon.
> **11.42** And he will send out his hand against *the* lands, and *the* land of Egypt will not be delivered.
> **11.43** And he will rule over *the* treasures of gold and silver, and over all *the* desirable things of Egypt. And Libyans and Cushites *will be* at his heels.

---

[49] One ancient commentator on Daniel claimed that this passage refers to a further invasion of Egypt by Antiochus a year before his death: "In the eleventh year of his reign he again fought against his sister's son, Ptolemy Philometor. For when Ptolemy heard that Antiochus was coming, he gathered many thousands of his people, but Antiochus stormed out against many countries . . . and devastated them all as he passed through them. And he came into the glorious land, that is, Judea . . . and then he proceeded to Egypt . . . . Antiochus, while hastening against Ptolemy . . . did not touch the Idumeans, Moabites, and Ammonites who were on the border of Judea, lest by becoming involved in another war he should cause Ptolemy to become stronger" (Porphyry, *FGrH* 260.55). However, the story cannot be accepted on the basis of a single unsupported source (cf. 2 Cor 13.1)—especially as that source might simply have deduced it from this very passage in Daniel. If Antiochus had indeed visited Judea at this time, the Maccabean History would certainly have mentioned it. (For the view that Dan 11.40–45 describes a further invasion of Egypt, see Stuart, *Commentary on . . . Daniel,* 354–58. For the view that it summarizes Antiochus's career as a whole, see Fabre d'Envieu, *Livre du prophète Daniel,* 2.2.1418–35; Barnes, *Notes . . . on . . . Daniel,* 467–74; King, *Daniel,* 732–42.)

[50] Careless readers sometimes assume Daniel predicted that this king would **come to his end** in Jerusalem (**at the mountain of the beauty of holiness**). The passage says nothing of the kind—any more than it says that the king would come to his end in Egypt or Libya or Cush. It mentions his success over all those regions, and it mentions **his end;** but it does not connect that **end** with any of those regions.

11.44 But reports from *the* east and from *the* north will disturb him, and he will come out with great fury, to destroy and to give over many.
11.45 And he will plant *the* tents of his palace between *the* seas at *the* mountain of *the* beauty of holiness. But he will come to his end, and no one will help him.

The Maccabean History describes how, at the end of his life, Antiochus Epiphanes took half his army eastward across the Euphrates and into Persia (the "upper districts").[51] But he was put to flight by the people there, and on the way back to Babylon he fell ill, dying after "many days" of suffering, in the year 149 SE (164 BCE):

> And he took counsel to go into Persia, and take the tributes of the districts, and gather much money .... And the king took ... half of the forces, and moved away from Antioch, his royal city, in the 147th year. And he crossed over the river Euphrates, and went through the upper districts ....
>
> And King Antiochus was journeying through the upper districts; and he heard that in Elam in Persia there was a city renowned for riches .... And he came and sought to capture the city and pillage it; and he was not able, because the thing had become known to the people of the city, and they rose up against him for battle, and he fled. And he moved away from there with great sorrow, to return to Babylon .... And he fell on his bed, and fell into an illness from the sorrow, because it had not come about for him as he had desired. And he was there many days, because his great sorrow was renewed upon him, and he realized that he was dying .... And King Antiochus died there in the 149th year. [Maccabaica 3.31, 37; 6.1–4, 8–9, 16]

This episode is also reported in the Maccabean Epitome (9.1–28), and by Appian (*Syriaca,* 76.352) and Polybius:

> King Antiochus, wanting to furnish himself with funds, set out in war against the temple of Artemis in Elam. But when he came to those parts, his hopes were disappointed, because the barbarians living near the place would not submit to this transgression; and while he was retreating, he died at Tabae in Persia. [Polybius 31.9.1–3]

---

[51] The **reports ... from the east and from the north** are, of course, not mentioned in the Maccabean History, which is concerned solely with Antiochus's dealings with Israel (even his illness and death are discussed only in that light). At least some of those **reports** evidently concerned trouble in Armenia. "Artaxias, the king of Armenia, rebelled against Antiochus ... and gathered a powerful army; but Antiochus, who was mightier in those days than any of the other kings, went to war against him and conquered him, forcing him to do homage to him" (Diodorus 31.25 [31.17a]; Appian, *Syriaca,* 46.236). Fragmentary astronomical diaries for 147 SE probably also refer to this episode; they say something about Antiochus in relation to the land of Ḫabigalbat in northern Mesopotamia (SH 2.496–97, §-164; Gera and Horowitz, "Antiochus IV in Life and Death," 243–49). However, the course of Antiochus's eastern expedition cannot be fully reconstructed from the fragmentary evidence available (Gruen, *Hellenistic World and the Coming of Rome,* 2.661–62, n. 237; cf. Shayegan, *Arsacids and Sasanians,* 161–65).

Whereas his father perished fighting (see the comments on 11.19) and his brother reportedly was murdered (see the comments on 11.20), Antiochus Epiphanes was **broken without** any human **hand,** just as Daniel had prophesied.

The Cleansing of the Holy Place
[Antiochus Epiphanes, 165–164 BCE]

Daniel 11 leaves one important question unanswered. It foretells that the holy place would be defiled and the continual offering would be taken away (11.31), and it says that God's people would "take action" against those things (11.32–35)—but it does not explicitly state whether their action would be successful. That question is explicitly answered in Daniel 8: the defilement of the **holy place,** and the removal of the **continual offering,** would last only for a few years (**2,300 evenings and mornings**). After that, the **holy place** would be **made right** once more.

> **8.11** The continual *offering* was taken away, and *the* established foundation of His holy place was thrown down....
> **8.13** And I heard a holy *one* speaking. And another holy *one* said to *the* certain *one* who spoke: "Until when *will* the vision *be*—the continual *offering* and the desolating transgression, giving both *the* holy place and the host *to be* trampled?"
> **8.14** And he said to me: "Until 2,300 evenings *and* mornings; and *then* the holy place will be made right."

The Maccabean History records that the temple was cleansed by the sons of Mattathias—Judas Maccabeus and his brothers—in the year 148 SE (about 165–164 BCE):

> But Judas and his brothers said, "Behold, our enemies have been shattered; let us go up to cleanse the holy places and dedicate them." ... And he chose unblemished priests, who were willing to obey the Law; and they cleansed the holy places....
>
> And they rose up at dawn, early in the morning, on the 25th day of the ninth month, which is the month Chislev, in the 148th year, and offered sacrifice according to the Law on the new altar of burnt offerings that they had made.... And all the people fell on their faces, and bowed down, and gave blessings to Heaven, the One who had prospered them. [Maccabaica 4.36, 42–43, 52–55]

Before the Fourth Kingdom
[164–63 BCE]

After the cleansing of the temple, Judas Maccabeus and his brothers continued the work foretold in Daniel 11.32–35 (discussed above):

> **11.32b** But *the* people who know their God will hold on strongly, and take action.
> **11.33** And *those* of the people who are discerning will cause many to take heed. But they will stumble by sword and by flame, by exile and by plunder, *for some* days.
> **11.34** And in their stumbling they will be helped *with* a little help. And many will

join with them with smooth *words*.
11.35 And *some* of the *ones* who are discerning will stumble, to refine and to purify and to make *them* white, until *the* time of *the* end; for *it is* yet for *the* appointed *time*.

Antiochus Epiphanes died around this time (Maccabaica 6.16), but the faithful Judeans still suffered oppression under the reigns of his immediate successors, his son Antiochus (V) Eupator (Maccabaica 6.17) and Demetrius (I Soter) son of Seleucus (Maccabaica 9.1). Not until the year 170 SE (approximately 142 BCE), in the time of the last surviving son of Mattathias—Simon—was complete freedom from foreign control attained:

> In the 170th year, the yoke of the nations was lifted up from Israel, and the people began to write in their writings and contracts: "In the first year of Simon, great high priest and army commander and leader of the Judeans." ...
>
> And the land of Judah had rest all the days of Simon; and he sought the good of his nation; and his authority and his glory pleased them, all his days .... He made peace in the land, and Israel rejoiced with great joy. And everyone sat under his vine and his fig tree, and there was no one to terrify them; and those who made war against them in the land ceased; and the kings were shattered in those days. And he strengthened all those of his people who had been brought low; he sought out the Law, and put away everyone who was committing transgression and wicked. And he glorified the holy places, and multiplied the vessels of the holy places. [Maccabaica 13.41–42; 14.4, 11–15]

This time of obedience and prosperity continued under the leadership of Simon's son John (Maccabaica 16.23–24), who is estimated to have died about 104 BCE.

However, later generations of Maccabean rulers did not remain faithful to God's Law. God had commanded that only descendants of David could be appointed kings of Israel (2 Sam 7.12–16; 1 Kgs 9.5). Therefore, Simon and his son John never claimed to be kings, they were simply priests and leaders of the people (Maccabaica 13.42; 16.24). But John's descendants—people "to whom [God] made no promise" of kingship—seized the kingship "by force":

> You, Lord, chose David as king over Israel, and You swore to him concerning his seed for ever, that his kingdom would not cease before You.
>
> But in our sins, sinners rose up against us; they—those to whom You made no promise—fell upon us and drove us out; they took it away by force, and they did not glorify Your honorable name with glory. They put kingship in place of their exaltation; in the arrogance of that exchange, they made the throne of David desolate. [Eighteen Psalms 17.5–8]

This seizure of kingship is also recorded by Josephus (*Wars* 1.70 ≡ *Antiquities* 13.301) and Strabo (16.2.40). On coins of this period, the first known Judean ruler who called himself king was John's son Alexander Janneus (Jonathan), who ruled about 103–76 BCE (Hendin 193–201).

The Fourth Kingdom
[Rome, 63 BCE]

The next incident foretold by Daniel is the coming of an unnamed **fourth kingdom** after the kingdom of Greece. This would correspond to the **iron** and **clay legs** and **feet** of the statue described in Daniel 2:

> **2.31** You, O king, were looking, and behold, a great image. This image *was* great, and its brightness *was* surpassing. *It was* standing before you, and its appearance *was* feared.
> **2.32** This image—its head *was* of good gold; its breast and its arms of silver; its belly and its loins of bronze;
> **2.33** its legs of iron; its feet—*part* of them *was* of iron, and *part* of them *was* of clay....
> **2.40** And *there* will be a fourth kingdom, powerful as iron—because iron pulverizes and shatters all *things,* and like iron that crushes all these *things*, it will crush and pulverize.
> **2.41** And *as for* what you saw—the feet and the toes, *part* of potter's clay, and *part* of iron—*the* kingdom will be divided. And *some* of the sturdiness of iron will be in it, because you saw the iron mixed with *the* clay of the mud.
> **2.42** And *the* toes of the feet, *part* of iron and *part* of clay—*part* of the kingdom will be powerful, and *part* of it will be brittle.
> **2.43** *As for* what you saw—the iron that was mixed with *the* clay of the mud—they will be mixed with *the* seed of man, and they will not join this with this, just as iron *is* not mixed with clay.

It would also correspond to the **fourth living creature** described in Daniel 7:

> **7.7** After this I was looking in *the* visions of the night, and behold, a fourth living creature, *one* that was feared and awesome and surpassingly powerful. And *there were* great iron teeth to her. And *she was* devouring and pulverizing and treading down the remainder with her feet. And she *was* different from all the living creatures that *were* before her.

In those prophecies, Daniel foretold that the **fourth kingdom** would be **surpassingly powerful,** capable of **devouring and pulverizing and treading down** its predecessors.

Daniel gave no name to the fourth kingdom. In fact, the kingdom after Greece arose from a region that had no Hebrew name—Rome. (There was no word for "Rome" in classical Hebrew. Whenever the early Hebrew Scriptures referred to the Romans, they always had to describe them in roundabout ways.)[52]

---

[52] Because Daniel gave no name to this kingdom, its identity has been questioned by various writers.

The view that this kingdom was Rome is the most ancient recorded view, and was held by nearly all readers who lived in the time of the Roman empire itself (Josephus, *Antiquities,* 10.276; 2 [4] Esdras 12.10–16; Barnabas 4.5; Irenaeus 5.26.1; Origen, PG 12.60; Hippolytus, *Daniel,* 2.12.6; 4.5.1–2; etc.). "How could we not understand the things formerly prophesied in Babylon by Daniel, and now currently being fulfilled in the world?" (Hippolytus, *Daniel,* 2.12.1). Moreover, although Jesus Himself left no specific comment on the four-kingdom prophecies, He certainly taught that Daniel had prophesied about Rome (Matt 24.15 ≡ Luke 21.20).

The unbeliever Porphyry (third century) and various later writers have suggested that Daniel's fourth kingdom might itself be the Greek kingdom. But if so, what were its three predecessors? According to most advocates of this view, they were the kingdoms of Babylonia, Media, and Persia. That, however, faces the following objections: (i) There never were separate, successive Median and Persian world empires. All through their period of sovereignty—from the time when they defeated the Babylonians until the time when they were defeated by the Greeks—the Medes and Persians always ruled together, in alliance. (ii) Furthermore, the person who compiled the book of Daniel certainly knew that the Medes and Persians jointly ruled a single kingdom; he said so several times (Dan 5.28; 6.8, 12, 15; 8.20). (iii) The second creature of Daniel 7, which was "raised on one side" (7.5), corresponds to the goat with one horn higher in 8.3, which is explicitly identified as "the kings of Media and Persia" (8.20). The third creature of Daniel 7, which had "four heads" (7.6), corresponds to the goat with four horns in 8.8, which is explicitly identified as the kingdom of Greece (8.21–22). (The Persian kingdom never broke into four parts. The only ancient world empire that did so was the Greek kingdom.) (iv) Therefore, the second kingdom of Daniel 7 cannot be a fictitious separate Median kingdom; it must be the Medo-Persian kingdom. The third kingdom of Daniel 7, which was in four parts, cannot be the Persian kingdom; it must the Greek kingdom. And so the fourth kingdom of Daniel 7 must be a kingdom following the Greek kingdom.

Recently, some writers have suggested that Daniel's four kingdoms were not intended to predict specific kingdoms at all, but were simply general symbols expressing "the fact that evil kingdoms (of an unspecified number) will succeed one another" (Longman, *Daniel,* 190; similarly Duguid, *Daniel,* 111). The main difficulties with that view are as follows: (i) If the new theory is correct, the beasts of Daniel 7 would have a completely different meaning from the beasts of the very next vision—which are explicitly identified as specific kingdoms (Dan 8.20–21), and which closely parallel two of the beasts described in Daniel 7 (see point iii of the previous paragraph). (ii) In Daniel 2, the first kingdom is demonstrably not a general symbol; it is explicitly identified as a specific kingdom (that of Nebuchadnezzar, Dan 2.37–38), while the second one is explicitly identified as the kingdom that would follow Nebuchadnezzar's (2.39). (iii) The new theory depends on a characteristically modern—not ancient—way of reading such prophecies. Indeed, it assumes that the meaning of these sections of Daniel was never discerned by any known person until our own day (see the historical survey of interpretations in Rowley, *Darius the Mede,* 70–137); all previous generations "missed the point" of them and adopted "a wrong strategy" ("people miss the point when they spend time arguing who the kingdoms were," Duguid, *Daniel,* 37; "it is a wrong strategy to . . . associate the different stages of the statue [in Daniel 2] with particular empires," Longman, *Daniel,* 82).

By the time of Judas Maccabeus (about 165 BCE), Rome was already becoming more powerful than any of the existing Greek kingdoms. The two mightiest kings of the North (Seleucids) had both been forced to submit to Rome: Antiochus the Great after the battle of Magnesia, and Antiochus Epiphanes after his conquest of Egypt (see above). The Romans had been equally powerful in the west, defeating the kings of Macedonia (Philip V and Perseus) and the Greek states south of Macedonia:

> They had shattered in battle and conquered Philip, and Perseus king of Kittim .... The people of Greece had taken counsel to come and destroy them, and the thing had become known to them, and they had sent an army leader against them, and made war against them, and many wounded men of them fell; and they had taken captive their wives and children, and pillaged them, and conquered their land, and pulled down their fortresses, and pillaged them, and enslaved them, until this day. [Maccabaica 8.5, 10]

A quarter of a century later, the Romans professed to have some influence over the kings of the South (Ptolemy), the North (Demetrius), Medo-Persia (Arsaces), Pergamum (Attalus), and Cappadocia (Ariarathes), as well as the Spartans in Greece and a great number of districts north of the Mediterranean, in the Mediterranean, and south of the Mediterranean: "Delos and Myndos and Sicyon and Caria and Samos and Pamphylia and Lycia and Halicarnassus and Rhodes and Phaselis and Cos and Side, and Arvad and Gortyna and Cnidus and Cyprus and Cyrene" (Maccabaica 15.16–23).

According to ancient historians, Judea itself came under Roman rule as a result of a dispute over the kingship between Hyrcanus and Aristobulus, two sons of Alexander Janneus. Both sides appealed to Rome for support. Around 63 BCE, the Roman general Pompey arrived in the region, captured Jerusalem, and made Judea part of the Roman province of Syria:

> So when Judea came to be openly ruled by monarchs, the first to proclaim himself king instead of priest was Alexander, and this man had two sons, Hyrcanus and Aristobulus. But when they began quarreling about the sovereignty, Pompey came over and deposed them, and pulled down their defenses, and, most important of all, took Jerusalem itself by force. [Strabo 16.2.40]

> Without fighting, the Romans took possession of Cilicia and both inland Syria and Coele-Syria, and Phoenicia and Philistia, and all the other regions called Syria, from the Euphrates as far as Egypt and the Sea. And as one region, the people of the Judeans, was still resisting, Pompey crushed them powerfully, and sent their king Aristobulus to Rome, and demolished their greatest and, to them, holiest city, Jerusalem. [Appian, *Syriaca,* 50.251–252]

According to Josephus, Pompey was consulted not only by the two rivals for the kingship, but also by people who wanted neither of them to be king:

> He came to Damascus, and there he heard the case of the Judeans and their leaders, Hyrcanus and Aristobulus, who were quarreling with one another. And the nation was against them both, asking not to be ruled by kings, because their ancestral custom was to obey the priests of the God whom they honored, whereas these two, who were priests' descendants, were seeking to change the nation's form of government so that it might be enslaved. [Josephus, *Antiquities,* 14.40–41]

When Pompey reached Jerusalem, he was welcomed into the city by the supporters of Hyrcanus, but the supporters of Aristobulus (whom Pompey had imprisoned) occupied the temple area and resisted him. When Pompey's army finally managed to break through and enter the area, many of their opponents were slaughtered, while Pompey and some of his companions arrogantly entered the Holy of Holies itself:

> But there was a disagreement among the people within the city, who were not of one mind about their situation. To some it seemed best to deliver the city to Pompey; but Aristobulus's supporters were advising that they should shut him out, because he was keeping their leader imprisoned. And the latter ones acted first, and took possession of the temple and cut off the bridge from it to the city, and prepared themselves for a siege; but the others accepted the army in, and handed over to Pompey both the city and the king's palace.
>
> And Pompey sent his subordinate officer Piso with an army to guard both the city and the king's palace, and fortified the houses next to the temple and all the places around the temple outside. And first he offered conciliatory terms to those within; but when they would not listen to what he was asking, he walled up the surroundings, with Hyrcanus willingly assisting in every way. And at dawn Pompey pitched his camp on the north side of the temple, where it was open to attack .... When he had brought near and set up siege engines and instruments of war transported from Tyre, he began battering the temple with his catapults ....
>
> But when the siege engine was brought close, the largest of the towers was shaken and fell down, and made a breach in the fortifications, and the soldiers poured in .... And the whole area was full of slaughter, for some of the Jews were killed by the Romans, and some by one another .... And a transgression of no small extent was done in regard to the sanctuary, which in former times had been inviolate and invisible, for Pompey and not a few of his companions went into it, and saw everything that was unlawful for any people except the high priests to see .... And he made Jerusalem tributary to the Romans ....
>
> The causes of this suffering that came on Jerusalem were Hyrcanus and Aristobulus, by their mutual dissension; for we lost our freedom and became subject to the Romans, and were forced to give back to the Syrians the region that we had won by our arms and taken away from the Syrians; and the Romans exacted more than 10,000 talents from us in a short time. [Josephus, *Antiquities,* 14.58–62, 69–74, 77–78]

The Romans' peaceful entry into Jerusalem, their forcible capture of the fortified areas, their slaughter of their opponents, and their desecration of the temple, are all recorded in the Eighteen Psalms:

> God ... brought from the end of the earth one who strikes severely; he decided the war against Jerusalem and her land. The rulers of the land met him with joy; they said to him, "Blessed is your path; come, enter with peace." They smoothed the rough paths away from his entrance; they opened the gates near Jerusalem; they crowned her walls. He entered ... with peace; he set up his feet with great security. He seized Jerusalem's towers and wall .... He destroyed their rulers and everyone who was wise in counsel; he poured out the blood of Jerusalem's inhabitants. [Eighteen Psalms 8.15–23]

> When the sinful man became arrogant, he cast down the fortified walls with a battering ram, and You did not hinder. Strange nations went up on Your altar; they trampled it arrogantly with their feet. [Eighteen Psalms 2.1–2]

> The transgressor made our land desolate from its inhabitants; they destroyed the young man and the old man and their children together .... He sent them away far to the west, and he set the rulers of the land for a mockery, and did not spare. [Eighteen Psalms 17.13–14]

In the New Testament Scriptures, we no longer hear anything about the family of Mattathias. By that time, Judea was entirely under Roman control (Luke 2.1; 3.1; Mark 12.14–17; John 19.15; 11.48; Acts 16.21; 17.7; 25.10–12).

The Kingdom of God

In Nebuchadnezzar's dream of the image (Daniel 2), its four parts, representing the four successive world kingdoms, were finally destroyed by a **stone** that was **cut out** without **hands:**

> **2.34** A stone was cut out, which *was* not *done* by hands. And it struck against the image on its feet of iron and clay; and it pulverized them.
> **2.35** Then the iron, the clay, the bronze, the silver, and the gold were pulverized as one. And they became like chaff from summer threshing-floors. And the wind lifted them up, and *there* was not found any place for them. And the stone that struck against the image became a great mountain, and filled all the earth.

Daniel then explained the meaning of this dream. After the fourth world kingdom had appeared, **God** would set up His own **kingdom,** which would **stand** forever:

> **2.44** And in *the* days of those kings, *the* God of the heavens will set up a kingdom that to lasting time will not be destroyed; and the kingdom will not be left to another people. It will pulverize and put an end to all these kingdoms, and it will itself stand to lasting time.

The arrival of this kingdom is recorded in the New Testament Scriptures.

> And in the 15th year of the reign of Tiberius Caesar, Pontius Pilate being governor of Judea, and Herod being tetrarch of Galilee, and his brother Philip tetrarch of the region of Iturea and Trachonitis, and Lysanias tetrarch of Abilene, in the high priesthood of Annas and Caiaphas, the word of God came to John the son of Zacharias. [Luke 3.1–2]

> And in those days John the Baptist comes, preaching in the wilderness of Judea, saying: "Repent, for the kingdom of God has come near." [Matt 3.1–2]

> And after John was delivered up, Jesus came into Galilee, preaching the good message of God, and saying: "The time period has been fulfilled, and the kingdom of God has come near; repent, and believe in the good message." [Mark 1.14–15]

> These twelve Jesus sent out, having commanded them, saying: . . . "Go . . . to the destroyed sheep of the house of Israel; and as you go, preach, saying that 'the kingdom of God has come near.'" [Matt 10.5–7]

So in year 15 of the Roman emperor Tiberius Caesar (about 27 CE), and shortly afterwards, the **kingdom** of **God** was already near. John the Baptist said so; Jesus said so; Jesus taught His twelve apostles to say so. And up to the time when Jesus died on the cross several years later, the situation remained the same: even on that day, His disciples were still "looking for the kingdom of God" (Luke 23.51).

But when Jesus had risen from the dead, and His disciples began to preach the good message of the kingdom—"both in Jerusalem, and in all Judea and Samaria, and to the end of the earth" (Acts 1.8)—they no longer said that the kingdom of God was near. By that time, Jesus' followers had already been transferred into His kingdom:

> The Father . . . has delivered us out of the authority of darkness, and has transferred us into the kingdom of the Son of His love. [Col 1.13]

> The One who loved us, and released us from our sins by His blood . . . has made us a kingdom, priests to His God and Father. [Rev 1.5–6]

> You were slain, and bought for God with Your blood people out of every tribe and tongue and people and nation; and You have made them a kingdom, priests to our God and Father. [Rev 5.9–10]

> And the great dragon was thrown down, the ancient serpent, the one who is called the devil and Satan, who leads astray the whole inhabited world. He was thrown down to the earth, and his angels were thrown down with him. And I heard a great voice in heaven, saying, "Now has come about the salvation and the power and the kingdom of our God, and the authority of His Christ, because the accuser of our brothers has been thrown down, the one who accuses them before our God day and

> night; and they have conquered him because of the blood of the Lamb, and because of the word of their testimony." [Rev 12.9–11]

The final stage of world history foretold by Daniel had now begun. The **kingdom** of **God** had arrived, and was proceeding to fill **all the earth** ("all the world," Col 1.6; "all creation," Col 1.23; "all the nations," Rom 16.26).

> The kingdom of the world has become that of our Lord and of His Christ; and He shall be king to lasting times of lasting times. [Rev 11.15]

JOEL 3.4–8 AND ZECHARIAH 9.1–16

In Joel 3.4–8, the LORD speaks to some of the nations adjoining Israel: **Tyre and Sidon** on the coast in the north, near Galilee (Luke 6.17; Mark 7.31; Ezra 3.7), and **Philistia** on the coast in the south, near Judea (Zep 2.4–7; Josh 13.2–4; Isa 11.14).

The Lord rebukes those nations for two deeds:

- They **have taken** the LORD's **silver** and **gold,** His **good and desirable things,** and put them in their own idolatrous **temples** (v 5).
- They **have sold** people of Judea (**sons of Judah and sons of Jerusalem**) into the hand of **Greeks,** with the result that those Judeans have been transported **far away from** their land (v 6).

The Lord promises that He will rouse up the sold Judeans **from the place to which you sold them** (v 7), and that the nations who committed those deeds will suffer the same fate themselves. The LORD will deliver them **into the hand of the sons of Judah,** who will then **sell them ... to a nation far away** (the **people of Sheba,** very far south of Judah: Matt 12.42 ≡ 1 Kgs 10.1).

3.4 And also, what *are* you^{pl} to Me, Tyre and Sidon, and all *the* circuits of Philistia? *Are* you^{pl} repaying^{pl} Me *for* a deed? And if you^{pl} *are* repaying^{pl} Me, I will return your^{pl} deed lightly and promptly upon your^{pl} *own* head,
3.5 because you^{pl} have taken My silver and My gold, and you^{pl} have brought My good *and* desirable *things* to your^{pl} temples,
3.6 and you^{pl} have sold sons of Judah and sons of Jerusalem to *the* sons of the Greeks, in order to put them far away from their border.
3.7 Behold, I *am* rousing them up from the place to which you^{pl} sold them; and I will return your^{pl} deed upon your^{pl} *own* head;
3.8 and I will sell your^{pl} sons and your^{pl} daughters in*to the* hand of *the* sons of Judah; and they will sell them to *the* people of Sheba, to a nation far away: for *the* LORD has spoken.

There is a strikingly similar prophecy in Zechariah 9.1–16. Again God warns that He will punish the people of **Tyre and Sidon** and the **Philistines:**[53]

9.1 *The* word of *the* LORD against *the* land of Hadrach, and Damascus, its resting-place ...

---

[53] In Zechariah 9, the Lord also lists some other places in the vicinity of Tyre and Sidon—**Hadrach, Damascus,** and **Hamath**—and mentions some of the individual Philistine cities by name: **Ashkelon, Gaza, Ekron,** and **Ashdod.**

> **9.2** and also Hamath is bordering on her; *and* Tyre and Sidon—for she has been very wise.
> **9.3** And Tyre has built a fortress for herself, and she has heaped up silver like dust, and gold like mud of *the* streets.
> **9.4** Behold, *the* Lord will dispossess her, and will strike down her strength into *the* sea; and she herself will be devoured by fire.
> **9.5** Ashkelon will see and fear, and Gaza, and she will writhe greatly in pain, and Ekron, for her expectation has been put to shame; and *the* king will be destroyed from Gaza, and Ashkelon will not dwell *any more,*
> **9.6** and *the* ill-begotten person will dwell in Ashdod; and I will cut off *the* pride of *the* Philistines....

And again the LORD promises that He **will rouse up** the people of **Judah** and **save them** from the **sons** of **Greece:**

> **9.13** *As* a bow for *Myself* I have bent Judah, I have set Ephraim. And I will rouse up your† sons, Zion, over against your† sons, Greece; and I will set you† as a sword of a mighty *man.*
> **9.14** And *the* LORD will be seen over them, and his arrow will go out like a lightning-flash; and *the* Lord GOD will sound *the* trumpet, and he will go in *the* stormwinds of *the* south.
> **9.15** *The* LORD of armies will shelter them...
> **9.16** and *the* LORD their God will save them in that day as *the* flock of his people.

In both of these passages, the promises to deliver **Judah** from **Greece** show that the prophecies are foretelling the persecution of Judea during the Greek era, and its deliverance through Judas Maccabeus and his brothers.

In those days, "the kingdom of the Greeks was utterly enslaving Israel with slavery" (Maccabaica 8.18). When Antiochus began persecuting the Judeans, his officers "took the plunder of the city" and "took captive the women and children and livestock" (1.29–32). Antiochus himself plundered the temple: "he took the silver and the gold and the precious vessels; and he took the hidden treasures that he found" (1.21–24). Mattathias lamented: "Her vessels of glory have been carried away into captivity.... What nation has not taken an inheritance in her kingdom, and taken possession of her plunder? All her adornment has been taken away; instead of a free woman, she has become a slavewoman" (2.9–11). A little later, "forces from Syria and from the land of the foreigners" came "to take the sons of Israel for servants" (3.41); in this context, "the land of the foreigners" (4.22) is the "land of the Philistines" (3.24; 5.68). Later still, Israelites living in Gilead wrote that "all our brothers who were in the land of Tubias have been put to death, and they have taken captive their wives and children and equipment" (5.13), and "people from Ptolemais and Tyre and Sidon, and all Galilee of the foreigners, were gathered against" those who remained faithful (5.15). And even later, another Greek king refers to "every soul of the Judeans who has been taken captive from the land of Judah into any part of my kingdom" (10.33).

All this is exactly what the prophets had foretold. Oppressors from the kingdom of the **Greeks,** including forces from **Tyre and Sidon** and the land of the **Philistines,** had taken captive people from **Judah,** who had been sold into slavery and/or transported far away ("into any part" of the kingdom). God's **silver** and **gold** and **desirable things** had also been **taken away** during this tribulation.

But the deliverance from these troubles also came to pass exactly as the prophets had foretold. In the days of Jonathan, Bacchides "gave back to him the captives whom he had taken captive previously from the land of Judah" (Maccabaica 9.72). Jonathan's successor Simon continued this work: "he gathered together a great number of captives" (14.7). In his days "the yoke of the nations was lifted up from Israel" (13.41). Instead, the people of **Tyre and Sidon** and the **Philistines** themselves became subject to the Judeans (Tyre and Sidon, 5.15, 22; 11.59; Ashdod, 10.83–84; 14.34; 16.10; Gaza, 11.61–62; 13.43–48; Ashkelon, 10.86; 11.60; Ekron, 10.89), and the Judeans deported some of them from their homelands to places elsewhere (13.47–48).[54] All these things happened, not because of the Judeans' own power, but because **the LORD their God** chose to **save** them (3.18–21; 4.9–11, 24–25, 55; 12.15).

In between the two sections of Zechariah 9 cited above, the prophet also foretells that the deliverance would extend even further. Not only would the foreign oppression be reversed, but Jerusalem's own **King** would also come, speaking **peace to the nations,** and ruling **even to the ends of the earth:**

> **9.9** Rejoice† greatly, daughter of Zion; cry out†, daughter of Jerusalem. Behold, your† King is coming to you†. He *is* righteous and saved, lowly, and riding on a donkey, and on a colt, *the* son of a she-ass.
> **9.10** And I will cut off *the* chariot from Ephraim, and *the* horse from Jerusalem; and *the* bow of war will be cut off. And He will speak peace to *the* nations. And His rule *will be* from sea even to sea, and from *the* River even to *the* ends of *the* earth.

So the fulfillment of these prophecies was accomplished gradually over a span of two centuries.[55] It began when the Lord roused up Judas Maccabeus and his earliest

---

[54] Of course, the punishment of **Tyre and Sidon** and the **Philistines** had begun earlier. But the earlier punishments had not been inflicted **because** those nations had **sold the sons of Judah... to the Greeks.** Sale to the Greeks began only after Greece made contact with this part of the world. (Indeed, there is no record of it happening under any Greek ruler earlier than Antiochus Epiphanes. Most of the earlier Greek rulers had reportedly treated the Judeans with respect [Epitome 3.1–3].)

[55] The close relation between its start in Maccabean days and its completion through Christ was traced by Theodoret. "These things did indeed also receive fulfillment under the Maccabees, when Judas and Jonathan and Simon were army commanders; for after the conquest, when they had reduced the cities of the Philistines to subjection, and had settled them with Judeans instead [Maccabaica 13.47–48], then they also converted many of those people to godliness. But the culmination of the prophecy was seen after the coming of our Savior; for

companions against the sons of Greece in the Judean wilderness; it continued during the following generations, as He overthrew those enemies and cleansed their cities for His people to dwell in; and it was completed when His Son came speaking **peace to the nations** (Eph 2.13–18; Acts 10.36), and setting up a kingdom that extends **even to the ends of the earth** (Acts 1.8; Col 1.6, 13, 23; Rom 16.26). The things prophesied in Zechariah 9.9 "were written of Him" (John 12.14–16; Matt 21.4–5).

---

nowadays the Ashkelonites and Ekronites and the other Philistines have rejected the error of idolatry, and have accepted the light of the knowledge of God [Acts 8.40] .... [In Zec 9.13,] He calls 'Judah' and 'Ephraim' those who are descended from them [Gal 3.6, 29], whom He has sent to fight against the children of the Greeks, having given them weapons that are not of the flesh, but are powerful to God for the tearing down of fortresses, to tear down human reasonings and every high thing raised up against the knowledge of God, and taking every thought captive to the obedience of Christ [2 Cor 10.4–5] .... Yet this prophecy also had its accomplishment under the Macedonians, as in a type. For the children of Zion attacked those of the Greeks, and put to flight many ten thousands of them, and, having come back victorious, raised up a trophy, and raised up the altar that had been cast down [Maccabaica 4.36–51]" (PG 81.1291, 1295).

BIBLIOGRAPHY

Texts

Baars, Willem (ed.). "Psalms of Solomon." In *The Old Testament in Syriac*. Part 4, Fascicle 6. Leiden: Brill, 1972.

Benedictine Abbey of St. Jerome (eds.). *Libri I–II Macchabaeorum*. Biblia Sacra iuxta latinam vulgatam versionem. Rome: Libreria Editrice Vaticana, 1995.

Cañas Reillo, José Manuel (ed.). *Glosas marginales de* Vetus Latina *en Biblias Vulgatas Españolas*. Madrid: CSIC, 2000.

—— (ed.). "Un testimonio inédito de *Vetus Latina* (1 Macabeos 1,1–6,40): el Codex Hubertianus (Londres, British Museum, Add 24142)." *Sefarad* 61 (2001): 57–82.

Ceriani, A. M. (ed.). *Translatio Syra Pescitto Veteris Testamenti ex codice Ambrosiano*. 2 vols. Milan: Pogliani, 1876–1883.

Codex Sinaiticus: A Facsimile Edition. Peabody, MA: Hendrickson, 2010.

de Bruyne, Donatien, and Bonaventure Sodar (eds.). *Les Anciennes Traductions latines des Machabées*. Anecdota Maredsolana. Maredsous: Abbaye de Maredsous, 1932.

Fritzsche, O. F. (ed.). *Libri apocryphi Veteris Testamenti graece*. Leipzig: Brockhaus, 1871.

Gebhardt, Oscar von (ed.). ΨΑΛΜΟΙ ΣΑΛΟΜΩΝΤΟΣ*: Die Psalmen Salomo's*. Leipzig: Hinrichs, 1895.

Hanhart, Robert (ed.). *Maccabaeorum liber III*. 2nd ed. Göttingen: Vandenhoeck & Ruprecht, 1980.

Harris, Rendel, and Alphonse Mingana (eds.). *The Odes and Psalms of Solomon*. 2 vols. Manchester: Manchester University Press, 1916–1920.

Holmes, Robert, and James Parsons (eds.). *Vetus Testamentum graecum cum variis lectionibus*. Vol. 5. *Apocrypha*. Oxford: Clarendon, 1827.

Kappler, Werner (ed.). *Maccabaeorum liber I*. 3rd ed. Göttingen: Vandenhoeck & Ruprecht, 1990.

—— and Robert Hanhart (eds.). *Maccabaeorum liber II*. 3rd ed. Göttingen: Vandenhoeck & Ruprecht, 2008.

Kenyon, Frederick G. (ed.). *Codex Alexandrinus in Reduced Photographic Facsimile. Old Testament*. 4 vols. London: British Museum, 1915–1956.

Lagarde, Paul Anton de (ed.). *Libri Veteris Testamenti apocryphi syriace*. Leipzig: Brockhaus, 1861.

Penna, Angelo, Dirk Bakker, and K. D. Jenner (eds.). "1–2 Maccabees." In *The Old Testament in Syriac*. Part 4, Fascicle 4. Leiden: Brill, 2013.

Rahlfs, Alfred (ed.). *Septuaginta*. (1935.) Revised by Robert Hanhart. Stuttgart: Deutsche Bibelgesellschaft, 2006.

Sievers, Joseph (ed.). *Synopsis of the Greek Sources for the Hasmonean Period: 1–2 Maccabees and Josephus.* Rome: Pontifical Biblical Institute, 2001.

Swete, H. B. (ed.). *The Old Testament in Greek.* 4th ed. 3 vols. Cambridge, England: Cambridge University Press, 1912.

Tischendorf, Constantin von (ed.). *Bibliorum Codex Sinaiticus Petropolitanus.* 4 vols. St. Petersburg, Russia: n. p., 1862.

Wright, Robert B. (ed.). *The Psalms of Solomon: A Critical Edition of the Greek Text.* New York: T. & T. Clark, 2007.

English Versions (in Chronological Order)

The Holy Bible... in the Earliest English Versions. (Wycliffite Early and Later Versions.) Ed. Josiah Forshall and Frederic Madden. 4 vols. Oxford: Oxford University Press, 1850.

The Bible and Holy Scriptures. (Geneva Bible.) Geneva: Rowland Hall, 1560.

The Holie Bible Faithfully Translated... out of the Authentical Latin. (Douai Version.) 2 vols. Douai: Laurence Kellam, 1609–1610.

The Holy Bible ... Newly Translated out of the Originall Tongues. (King James Version.) London: Robert Barker, 1611.

———. *Newly Translated out of the Original Tongues.* (Ed. Benjamin Blayney.) 2 vols. Oxford: Oxford University Press, 1769.

———. *The Cambridge Paragraph Bible of the Authorized English Version.* Ed. F. H. Scrivener. 2nd ed. Cambridge, England: Cambridge University Press, 1873.

———. *With the Marginal Readings Adopted by General Convention.* New York: Nelson, 1903.

A Collection of Authentick Records Belonging to the Old and New Testament. Tr. William Whiston. 2 vols. London: Whiston, 1727.

The Holy Bible, Translated from the Latin Vulgate. (Ed. Richard Challoner. Douai-Rheims-Challoner Version. 1749–1750. Haydock Second Quarto Series.) New York: Dunigan, 1859.

The Five Books of Maccabees. Tr. Henry Cotton. Oxford: Oxford University Press, 1832.

The Apocrypha ... Revised A.D. 1894. (Revised Version.) Oxford and Cambridge, England: Oxford University Press and Cambridge University Press, 1895.

The Apocrypha: An American Translation. Tr. Edgar J. Goodspeed. Chicago, IL: University of Chicago Press, 1938.

The Jerusalem Bible. London: Darton, Longman & Todd, 1966.

The New English Bible with the Apocrypha. Oxford and Cambridge, England: Oxford University Press and Cambridge University Press, 1970.

The New American Bible. Paterson, NJ: St. Anthony Guild, 1970.

———. *Revised Edition.* New York: Catholic Book Publishing, 2011.

The Apocrypha of the Old Testament: Revised Standard Version: Expanded Edition. Ed. Bruce M. Metzger. New York: Oxford University Press, 1977.

Good News Bible with Deuterocanonicals/Apocrypha: The Bible in Today's English Version. Ed. Robert G. Bratcher. New York: American Bible Society, 1979.

The Apocryphal Old Testament. Ed. H. F. D. Sparks. Oxford: Clarendon, 1984.

The New Jerusalem Bible. London: Darton, Longman & Todd, 1985.

The Old Testament Pseudepigrapha. Ed. James H. Charlesworth. 2 vols. New York: Doubleday, 1985.

The Revised English Bible with the Apocrypha. Oxford and Cambridge, England: Oxford University Press and Cambridge University Press, 1989.

The Holy Bible: New Revised Standard Version... with the Apocryphal/Deuterocanonical Books. New York: Oxford University Press, 1989.

A New English Translation of the Septuagint. Ed. Albert Pietersma and Benjamin G. Wright. New York: Oxford University Press, 2007.

The Orthodox Study Bible. (St. Athanasius Academy Septuagint.) Nashville, TN: Thomas Nelson, 2008.

The English Standard Version Bible . . . with Apocrypha. Oxford: Oxford University Press, 2009.

The Old Testament. Vol. 2. *The Historical Books.* Tr. Nicholas King. Stowmarket, Suffolk: Kevin Mayhew, 2012.

Other Modern Language Versions (in Chronological Order)

Biblia: das ist die gantze Heilige Schrift Deudsch. Tr. Martin Luther. Wittenburg: Hans Lufft, 1545.

La Biblia... Revista... por Cypriano de Valera. (Versión Reina-Valera.) Amsterdam: Lorenzo Jacobi, 1602.

La Sacra Bibbia tradotta in lingua Italiana. Tr. Giovanni Diodati. 2nd ed. Geneva: Pierre Chouet, 1641.

La Sainte Bible interpretee par Iean Diodati. Geneva: Pierre Chouet, 1644.

Biblia, dat is de gantsche H. Schrifture... door last der Hoogh Mog Heeren Staten Generael der Vereenighde Nederlanden. 2nd ed. Amsterdam: Ravesteyn, 1657.

La Sainte Bible. Tr. David Martin. Revised by Pierre Roques. 2 vols. Basel: Im-Hoff, 1744.

La Sagrada Biblia traducida... de la Vulgata latina. Tr. Felipe Scio de San Miguel. Revised by José Palau. 10 vols. Barcelona: Pons, 1846.

Die Bibel... nach der in Zürich kirchlich eingeführten Uebersetzung. Zurich: Evangelischen Gesellschaft, 1868.

Die Apocriefe Boeken des Ouden Verbonds. Tr. Johannes Dyserinck. Haarlem, Netherlands: Erven Loosjes. 1874.

Библия . . . в русском переводе. (Russian Synodal Version.) Moscow: Синодальная типография, 1876.

Die Bibel... nach der deutschen Übersetzung D. Martin Luthers. Durchgesehen nach dem von der Deutschen evangelischen Kirchenkonferenz genehmigten Text. Stuttgart: Württembergische Bibelanstalt, 1912.

Die Heilige Schrift des Alten und des Neuen Testaments. (1931.) Zurich: Verlag der Zürcher Bibel, 1955.

Apócrifos del Antiguo Testamento. Ed. Alejandro Díez Macho and Antonio Piñero Sáenz. 6 vols. Madrid: Ediciones Cristiandad, 1982–2009.

La Bible: Écrits intertestamentaires. Ed. André Dupont-Sommer and Marc Philonenko. Bibliothèque de la Pléiade. Paris: Gallimard, 1987.

La Sagrada Biblia: Versión de la Septuaginta al español. Tr. Guillermo Jünemann Beckschaefer. Santiago: Centro de Exalumnos del Seminario Conciliar, 1992.

Septuaginta Deutsch. Ed. Wolfgang Kraus and Martin Karrer. 2nd ed. Stuttgart: Deutsche Bibelgesellschaft, 2010.

La Biblia Griega Septuaginta. Ed. Natalio Fernández Marcos and Victoria Spottorno Díaz-Caro. Vols. 1–2. Salamanca: Sígueme, 2008–2011.

Other Ancient Sources

Appian. *Appien: Histoire romain.* Collection Budé. Vol. 6. *Le Livre syriaque.* Ed. Paul Goukowsky. Paris: Belles Lettres, 2007.

Arrian. *Flavii Arriani quae exstant omnia.* Ed. A. G. Roos and G. Wirth. 2 vols. Leipzig: Teubner, 1967–1968.

Boffo, Laura (ed.). *Iscrizioni greche e latine per lo studio della Bibbia.* Brescia: Paideia, 1994.

Cassius Dio. *Cassii Dionis Cocceiani Historiarum romanarum quae supersunt.* Ed. U. P. Boissevain. 5 vols. Berlin: Weidmann, 1895–1931.

Curtius Rufus, Quintus. *Q. Curtius Rufus: Historiae.* Ed. Carlo M. Lucarini. Berlin: de Gruyter, 2009.

Diodorus Siculus. *Diodori Bibliotheca historica.* Ed. Ludwig Dindorf. 5 vols. Leipzig: Teubner, 1866–1868.

——. *Diodore de Sicile: Bibliothèque historique: Fragments.* Collection Budé. Vols. 1–3. Ed. Paul Goukowsky. Paris: Belles Lettres, 2006–2012.

Dittenberger, Wilhelm (ed.). *Orientis Graeci Inscriptiones Selectae.* 2 vols. Leipzig: Hirzel, 1903–1905.

—— (ed.). *Sylloge Inscriptionum Graecarum.* 3rd ed. 4 vols. Leipzig: Hirzel, 1915–1924.

Eusebius. *Eusebius Werke.* Vol. 3. Part 1. *Das Onomasticon der biblischen Ortsnamen.* Ed. Erich Klostermann. Der griechischen Christlichen Schriftsteller der ersten drei Jahrhunderte. Leipzig: Hinrichs, 1904.

Frey, Jean-Baptiste (ed.). *Corpus Inscriptionum Judaicarum.* 2 vols. Rome: Pontificio Istituto di Archeologia Cristiana, 1936–1952.

Gauthier, Henri, and Henri Sottas (eds.). *Un Décret trilingue en l'honneur de Ptolémée IV.* Cairo: Service des Antiquités, 1925.

Glassner, Jean-Jacques (ed.). *Mesopotamian Chronicles.* Ed. Benjamin R. Foster. Atlanta, GA: Society of Biblical Literature, 2004.

Jacoby, Felix (ed.). *Fragmente der griechischen Historiker.* 3 vols. in 15 fascicles. Berlin: Weidmann, 1923–1958.

Josephus, Flavius. *Flavii Iosephi opera.* 7 vols. Ed. Benedict Niese. Berlin: Weidmann, 1885–1895.

Justin. *M. Iuniani Iustini Epitoma historiarum Philippicarum Pompei Trogi*. Ed. Otto Seel. 3rd ed. Stuttgart: Teubner, 1985.

Kroll, Wilhelm (ed.). *Historia Alexandri magni (Pseudo-Callisthenes)*. Vol. 1. *Recensio vetusta*. Berlin: Weidmann, 1926.

Livy. *Titi Livi Ab urbe condita libri XXXI–XLV*. Ed. John Briscoe. 3 vols. Stuttgart: Teubner, 1986–1991.

——. *Titi Livi Ab urbe condita*. Oxford Classical Texts. Vol. 6. *Libri XXXVI–XL*. Ed. P. G. Walsh. Oxford: Oxford University Press, 1999.

Moretti, Luigi (ed.). *Iscrizioni agonistiche greche*. Rome: Signorelli, 1953.

Pliny the Elder. *C. Plinii Secundi Naturalis historia*. Ed. Karl Mayhoff. 6 vols. Leipzig: Teubner, 1892–1909.

Plutarch. *Plutarchus: Alexander et Caesar*. Ed. Konrat Ziegler. 2nd ed. Leipzig: Teubner, 1994.

Polybius. *Polybii Historiae*. Ed. Theodor Büttner-Wobst. 5 vols. Leipzig: Teubner, 1882–1905.

Robert, Louis and Jeanne. *Fouilles d'Amyzon en Carie*. Vol. 1. Paris: De Boccard, 1983.

Sachs, Abraham, and Hermann Hunger (eds.). *Astronomical Diaries and Related Texts from Babylonia*. 6 vols. Vienna: Österreichische Akademie der Wissenschaften, 1988–2006.

Simpson, R. S. (ed.). "Raphia Decree." In *Demotic Grammar in the Ptolemaic Sacerdotal Decrees*. Oxford: Griffith Institute, 1996. 242–57.

Strabo. *Strabons Geographika*. Ed. Stefan Radt. 10 vols. Göttingen: Vandenhoeck & Ruprecht, 2002–2011.

Tcherikover, Victor A., Alexander Fuks, and Menahem Stern (eds.). *Corpus Papyrorum Judaicarum*. 3 vols. Cambridge, MA: Harvard University Press, 1957–1964.

Valerius, Julius. *Iuli Valeri Alexandri polemi*. Ed. Bernard Kuebler. Leipzig: Teubner, 1888.

Secondary Works

Abel, F.-M. *Grammaire du grec biblique*. Études Bibliques. Paris: Gabalda, 1927.

——. *Géographie de la Palestine*. Études Bibliques. 2 vols. Paris: Gabalda, 1933–1938.

——. *Les Livres des Maccabées*. Études Bibliques. Paris: Gabalda, 1949.

—— and Jean Starcky. *Les Livres de Maccabées*. Bible de Jérusalem. 3rd ed. Paris: Cerf, 1961.

Adamson, James. *The Epistle of James*. New International Commentary. Grand Rapids, MI: Eerdmans, 1976.

Adrados, Francisco R. (ed.). *Diccionario Griego-Español*. Vols. 1–7. Madrid: CSIC, 1980–2009.

Alexander, J. A. *The Psalms Translated and Explained*. New York: Scribner, 1852.

Alonso Schökel, Luis (commentary). *Macabeos*. Nueva Biblia Española. Madrid: Ediciones Cristiandad, 1976.

André, L. E. Tony. *Les Apocryphes de l'Ancien Testament*. Florence: Paggi, 1903.

Arayathinal, Thomas. *Aramaic Grammar*. 2 vols. Mannanam, India: St. Joseph's Press, 1957–1959.

Assan-Dhôte, Isabelle, and Jacqueline Moatti-Fine. *Baruch, Lamentations, Lettre de Jérémie.* La Bible d'Alexandrie. Paris: Cerf, 2005.

Atkinson, Kenneth. "Herod the Great, Sosius, and the Siege of Jerusalem (37 B.C.E.) in Psalm of Solomon 17." *Novum Testamentum* 38 (1996): 313–22.

——. *I Cried to the Lord: A Study of the Psalms of Solomon's Historical Background and Social Setting.* Leiden: Brill, 2004.

——. *An Intertextual Study of the Psalms of Solomon.* Lewiston, NY: Edwin Mellen, 2000.

Avi-Yonah, Michael. *The Madaba Mosaic Map.* Jerusalem: Israel Exploration Society, 1954.

——. *The Holy Land: A Historical Geography from the Persian to the Arab Conquest (536 B.C. to A.D. 640).* 2nd ed. Ed. Anson F. Rainey. Jerusalem: Carta, 2002.

Baldwin, Joyce G. *Daniel: An Introduction and Commentary.* Tyndale Old Testament Commentaries. Leicester: Inter-Varsity Press, 1978.

Bar-Kochva, Bezaleel. *Judas Maccabaeus.* Cambridge, England: Cambridge University Press, 1989.

Barnes, Albert. *Notes, Critical, Illustrative, and Practical, on the Book of Daniel.* New York: Leavitt & Allen, 1853.

Barotti, Lorenzo. *Lezioni sacre.* Vol. 2. *Su i libri de' Maccabei.* Parma: Stamperia Reale, 1786.

Bartlett, John R. *The First and Second Books of the Maccabees.* Cambridge Bible Commentary. Cambridge, England: Cambridge University Press, 1973.

——. *1 Maccabees.* Guides to Apocrypha and Pseudepigrapha. Sheffield: Sheffield Academic Press, 1998.

Bauer, Walter. *A Greek-English Lexicon of the New Testament and Other Early Christian Literature.* Tr. W. F. Arndt and F. W. Gingrich. 3rd ed. Revised by F. W. Danker. Chicago, IL: University of Chicago Press, 2000.

Begrich, J. "Der Text der Psalmen Salomos." *Zeitschrift für die Neutestamentliche Wissenschaft* 38 (1939): 131–64.

Belting, Hans, and Guglielmo Cavallo. *Die Bibel des Niketas.* Wiesbaden: Reichert, 1979.

Bergsträsser, Gotthelf. *Hebräische Grammatik.* 2 vols. Leipzig: Hinrichs, 1918–1922.

Bevan, E. R. *The House of Seleucus.* 2 vols. London: Edwin Arnold, 1902.

Bévenot, Hugo. *Die beiden Makkabäerbücher.* Bonn: Peter Hanstein, 1931.

——. "The Armenian Text of Maccabees." *Journal of the Palestine Oriental Society* 14 (1934): 268–83.

Bickerman(n), Elias. "La Coelè-Syrie: Notes de géographie historique." *Revue Biblique* 56 (1947): 256–68.

——. *The God of the Maccabees.* (1937.) Tr. Hoerst R. Moehring. Leiden: Brill, 1979.

——. *The Jews in the Greek Age.* Cambridge, MA: Harvard University Press, 1988.

Blass, Friedrich, and Albert Debrunner. *A Greek Grammar of the New Testament and Other Early Christian Literature.* Revised by Robert W. Funk. Chicago, IL: University of Chicago Press, 1961.

Bogaert, P.-M. "Septante et versions grecques." *Supplément au Dictionnaire de la Bible* 12/68 (1993): 536–692.

Bosworth, A. B. *The Legacy of Alexander*. Oxford: Oxford University Press, 2002.

Botterweck, G. Johannes, Helmer Ringgren, and Heinz-Josef Fabry (eds.). *Theological Dictionary of the Old Testament*. Vols. 1–15. Grand Rapids, MI: Eerdmans, 1974–2006.

Bringmann, Klaus. *Hellenistische Reform und Religionsverfolgung in Judäa. Eine Untersuchung zur jüdisch-hellenistischen Geschichte (175–163 v.Chr.)*. Göttingen: Vandenhoeck & Ruprecht, 1983.

Bromiley, Geoffrey W. (ed.). *The International Standard Bible Encyclopedia*. 3rd ed. 4 vols. Grand Rapids, MI: Eerdmans, 1979–1988.

Brown, Colin. *New International Dictionary of New Testament Theology*. 3 vols. Grand Rapids, MI: Zondervan, 1975–1978.

Brown, Francis, S. R. Driver, and Charles A. Briggs. *A Hebrew and English Lexicon of the Old Testament*. Oxford: Clarendon, 1907.

Bruce, F. F. *The Epistle to the Hebrews*. New International Commentary. Grand Rapids, MI: Eerdmans, 1964.

Buttmann, Alexander. *A Grammar of the New Testament Greek*. Tr. J. H. Thayer. Andover, MA: Draper, 1873.

Calmet, Augustin. *Les Maccabées*. Commentaire Littéral. Paris: Emery, 1712.

Carpajosa, Ignacio. *The Character of the Syriac Version of Psalms*. Leiden: Brill, 2008.

Chandler, Henry W. *A Practical Introduction to Greek Accentuation*. 2nd ed. Oxford: Clarendon, 1881.

Charles, R. H. (ed.). *The Apocrypha and Pseudepigrapha of the Old Testament*. 2 vols. Oxford: Clarendon, 1913.

Cohen, Getzel M. *The Hellenistic Settlements in Syria, the Red Sea Basin, and North Africa*. Berkeley, CA: University of California Press, 2006.

Cowe, S. P. "La versión armenia." In *El Texto Antiqueno de la Biblia griega*. Ed. Natalio Fernández Marcos and José Ramón Busto Saiz. Vol. 1. *1–2 Samuel*. Madrid: CSIC, 1989. lxxi–lxxix.

Curchin, Leonard A. *Roman Spain: Conquest and Assimilation*. London: Routledge, 1991.

Dancy, J. C. *A Commentary on I Maccabees*. Oxford: Blackwell, 1954.

Davids, Peter H. *The Epistle of James*. New International Greek Testament Commentary. Grand Rapids, MI: Eerdmans, 1982.

Davila, James R. *The Provenance of the Pseudepigrapha*. Leiden: Brill, 2005.

de Bruyne, Donatien. "Le Texte grec des deux premiers livres des Machabées." *Revue Biblique* 31 (1922): 31–54.

Delcor, Mathias. "Psaumes de Salomon." *Supplément au Dictionnaire de la Bible* 9/48 (1973): 214–45.

Delitzsch, Franz. *A Commentary on the Epistle to the Hebrews*. Tr. T. L. Kingsbury. 2 vols. Edinburgh: T. & T. Clark, 1871.

deSilva, David A. *4 Maccabees: An Introduction and Commentary on the Greek Text in Codex Sinaiticus*. Leiden: Brill, 2006.

——. *The Jewish Teachers of Jesus, James, and Jude: What Earliest Christianity Learned from the Apocrypha and Pseudepigrapha.* Oxford: Oxford University Press, 2012.

Dionysius Cartusianus. *Enarrationes in lib. Iob ... I Machabaeorum, II Machabaeorum.* Cologne: Petrus Quentell, 1534.

Doran, Robert. "The Persecution of Judeans by Antiochus IV: The Significance of 'Ancestral Laws.'" In D. C. Harlow, K. M. Hogan, M. Goff, and J. S. Kaminsky (eds.). *The "Other" in Second Temple Judaism.* Grand Rapids, MI: Eerdmans, 2011. 423–33.

——. *2 Maccabees.* Hermeneia. Minneapolis, MN: Fortress, 2012.

Driver, S. R. *Notes on the Hebrew Text and the Topography of the Books of Samuel.* 2nd ed. Oxford: Clarendon, 1913.

Drusius, Johannes. *Liber Hasmonaeorum, qui vulgo prior Machabaeorum.* Franeker: Gillis van den Rade, 1600.

Duckworth, H. T. F. "The Roman Provincial System." In *The Beginnings of Christianity.* Part 1. *The Acts of the Apostles.* Vol. 1. Ed. F. J. Foakes Jackson and Kirsopp Lake. London: Macmillan, 1920. 171–217.

Duguid, Iain M. *Daniel.* Reformed Expository Commentary. Phillipsburg, NJ: P&R Publishing, 2008.

Dušek, Jan. *Aramaic and Hebrew Inscriptions from Mt. Gerizim and Samaria Between Antiochus III and Antiochus IV Epiphanes.* Leiden: Brill, 2012.

Duval, Rubens. *Traité de grammaire syriaque.* Paris: Vieweg, 1881.

Efrón, Joshua. *Studies on the Hasmonean Period.* Leiden: Brill, 1987.

Elitzur, Yoel. *Ancient Place Names in the Holy Land.* Jerusalem: Magnes, 2004.

Engelbrecht, Edward A. (ed.). *The Apocrypha: The Lutheran Edition with Notes.* St. Louis, MO: Concordia, 2012.

Errington, R. Malcolm. *A History of the Hellenistic World.* Chichester: Wiley, 2008.

Eyal, Regev. *The Hasmoneans: Ideology, Archaeology, Identity.* Göttingen: Vandenhoeck & Ruprecht, 2013.

Fabre d'Envieu, Jules. *Le Livre du prophète Daniel.* 4 vols. Paris: Thorin, 1888–1891.

Fairweather, William, and J. Sutherland Black. *The First Book of Maccabees.* Cambridge Bible for Schools and Colleges. Cambridge, England: Cambridge University Press, 1897.

Fanning, Buist M. *Verbal Aspect in New Testament Greek.* Oxford: Clarendon, 1990.

Feldman, Louis H. *Studies in Josephus' Rewritten Bible.* Leiden: Brill, 1998.

Fernández Marcos, Natalio. *The Septuagint in Context.* Tr. Wilfred G. E. Watson. Leiden: Brill, 2001.

——. "The Antiochene Edition in the Text History of the Greek Bible." In *Der Antiochenische Text der Septuaginta in seiner Bezeugung und seiner Bedeutung.* Ed. Siegfried Kreuzer and Marcus Sigismund. Göttingen: Vandenhoeck & Ruprecht, 2013. 57–73.

Fillion, Louis-Claude. *La Sainte Bible commentée.* Vol. 6. Paris: Letouzey & Ané, 1899.

Finkelstein, Israel. "The Territorial Extent and Demography of Yehud/Judea in the Persian and Early Hellenistic Periods." *Revue Biblique* 117 (2010): 39–54.

Fischer, B. "Lukian-Lesarten in der Vetus Latina der vier Königsbücher." In *Miscellanea Biblia et Orientalia R. P. Athanasio Miller ... oblatus.* Rome: Herder, 1951. 169–77.

Fischer, Thomas. *Seleukiden und Makkabäer.* Bochum: Studienverlag Brockmeyer, 1980.

Freedman, D. N. (ed.). *The Anchor Bible Dictionary.* 6 vols. New York: Doubleday, 1992.

Freudenthal, Jacob. *Die Flavius Josephus beigelegte Schrift Ueber die Herrschaft der Vernunft (IV Makkabäerbuch).* Breslau: Schletter (H. Skutsch), 1869.

Frey, J. B. (ed.). *Corpus inscriptionum Judaicarum.* 2 vols. Rome, Pontificio Istituto di Archeologia Cristiana: 1936–62.

Gafni, Isaiah M. "Josephus and I Maccabees." In *Josephus, the Bible, and History.* Ed. Louis H. Feldman and Gohei Hata. Leiden: Brill, 1988. 116–31.

Geier, Martin. *Commentarius in Psalmos Davidis.* 3rd ed. Dresden: J. J. Winckler, 1697.

Gera, Dov. "On the Credibility of the History of the Tobiads." In *Greece and Rome in Eretz Israel.* Ed. A. Kasher, U. Rappoport, and G. Fuks. Jerusalem: Yad Izhak Ben-Zvi, 1990. 21–38.

——. *Judaea and Mediterranean Politics 219 to 161 B.C.E.* Leiden: Brill, 1998.

—— and Wayne Horowitz. "Antiochus IV in Life and Death: Evidence from the Babylonian Astronomical Diaries." *Journal of the American Oriental Society.* 117 (1997): 240–52.

Gillet, Henri-Joseph. *Les Machabées.* Paris: Lethielleux, 1884.

Ginsburg, Christian D. *Introduction to the Massoretico-Critical Edition of the Hebrew Bible.* With a Prolegomenon by Harry M. Orlinsky. New York: Ktav, 1966.

Goldstein, Jonathan A. *I Maccabees.* Anchor Bible. Garden City, NY: Doubleday, 1976.

——. *II Maccabees.* Anchor Bible. Garden City, NY: Doubleday, 1983.

——. "The Hasmonean Revolt and the Hasmonean Dynasty." In *The Cambridge History of Judaism.* Vol. 2. *The Hellenistic Age.* Ed. W. D. Davies and Louis Finkelstein. Cambridge, England: Cambridge University Press, 1989. 292–351.

Grandclaudon, Marcel. *Les Livres des Macchabées.* Bible Pirot-Clamer. Paris: Letouzey & Ané, 1951.

Grabbe, Lester L. "Maccabean Chronology: 167–164 or 168–165 B.C.E.?" *Journal of Biblical Literature* 110 (1991): 59–74.

——. "Were the Pre-Maccabean High Priests 'Zadokites'?" In *Reading from Right to Left: Essays on the Hebrew Bible in Honour of David J. A. Clines.* Edited by J. Cheryl Exum and H. G. M. Williamson. London: T. & T. Clark, 2003. 205–15.

——. *A History of the Jews and Judaism in the Second Temple Period.* Vols. 1–2. London: T. & T. Clark, 2004–2008.

Grainger, John D. *Hellenistic Phoenicia.* Oxford: Clarendon, 1991.

——. *The Roman War of Antiochos the Great.* Leiden: Brill, 2002.

——. *A Seleukid Prosopography and Gazetteer.* Leiden: Brill, 1997.

Gray, Rebecca. *Prophetic Figures in Late Second Temple Jewish Palestine: The Evidence from Josephus.* New York: Oxford University Press, 1993.

Grayson, Albert Kirk. *Assyrian Rulers of the Early First Millenium BC.* Vol. 2. *858–745 BC.* Toronto: University of Toronto Press, 1996.

Grimm, C. L. W. *Das erste Buch der Maccabäer.* Kurzgefasstes exegetisches Handbuch zu den Apokryphen. Leipzig: Hirzel, 1855.

——. *Das zweite, dritte und vierte Buch der Maccabäer.* Kurzgefasstes exegetisches Handbuch zu den Apokryphen. Leipzig: Hirzel, 1857.

——. *A Greek-English Lexicon of the New Testament.* Revised by J. H. Thayer. 4th ed. Edinburgh: T. & T. Clark, 1901.

Gruen, Erich S. *The Hellenistic World and the Coming of Rome.* 2 vols. Berkeley, CA: University of California Press, 1984.

Gundry, R. H. "The Language Milieu of First-Century Palestine." *Journal of Biblical Literature* 83 (1964): 404–08.

Gutberlet, Constantin. *Das erste Buch der Machabäer.* Münster: Aschendorff, 1920.

——. *Das zweite Buch der Machabäer.* Münster: Aschendorff, 1927.

Hackett, H. B. (ed.). *Dr. William Smith's Dictionary of the Bible.* 4 vols. New York: Hurd & Houghton, 1868–1870.

Hadas, Moses. *The Third and Fourth Books of Maccabees.* Jewish Apocryphal Literature. New York: Harper, 1957.

Hann, Robert R. *The Manuscript History of the Psalms of Solomon.* Atlanta, GA: Scholars Press, 1982.

Harrington, Daniel J. *The Maccabean Revolt.* Wilmington, DE: Michael Glazier, 1988.

Hatch, W. H. P. *An Album of Dated Syriac Manuscripts.* Boston: American Academy of Arts and Sciences, 1946.

Heger, Paul. *Challenges to Conventional Opinions on Qumran and Enoch Issues.* Leiden: Brill, 2012.

Hendin, David. *Guide to Biblical Coins.* 3rd ed. New York: Amphora, 1996.

——. *Guide to Biblical Coins.* 5th ed. New York: Amphora, 2010.

Hilgenfeld, Adolf. *Messias Judaeorum.* Leipzig: Reisland, 1869.

Hölbl, Günther. *A History of the Ptolemaic Empire.* Tr. Tina Saavedra. London: Routledge, 2001.

Holm-Nielsen, Svend. *Die Psalmen Salomos.* Jüdische Schriften aus hellenistisch-römischer Zeit. Gütersloh: Gerd Mohn, 1977.

Horne, George. *A Commentary on the Book of Psalms.* 3rd ed. Perth, Scotland: Morison, 1794.

Houghton, Arthur, and Catherine Lorber. *Seleucid Coins: A Comprehensive Catalogue.* 2 parts in 4 vols. New York: American Numismatic Society, 2002–2008.

Hrabanus Maurus. "Commentaria in libros Machabaeorum." In *Patrologia Latina* 109. Ed. J.-P. Migne. Paris: Migne, 1864. 1125–1256.

Hunt, Alice. *Missing Priests: The Zadokites in History and Tradition.* New York: T. & T. Clark, 2006.

Išoʿdad of Merv. *Commentaire . . . sur l'Ancien Testament.* Vol. 6. *Psaumes.* Ed. Ceslas van den Eynde. Corpus Scriptorum Christianorum Orientalium. Louvain: Peeters, 1981.

Jastrow, Morris. *Dictionary of the Targumim, the Talmud Babli and Yerushalmi, and the Midrashic Literature.* 2 vols. London: Luzac, 1903.

Jenni, Ernst, and Claus Westermann (eds.). *Theological Lexicon of the Old Testament.* Tr. M. E. Biddle. 3 vols. Peabody, MA: Hendrickson, 1997.

Ji, Chang-Ho C. "A New Look at the Tobiads of 'Iraq al-Amir." *Liber Annuus* 48 (1998): 417–40.

Joosten, Jan. *The Verbal System of Biblical Hebrew.* Jerusalem: Simor, 2012.

Kampen, John. *The Hasideans and the Origin of Pharisaism: A Study in 1 and 2 Maccabees.* Atlanta, GA: Scholars, 1988.

Kaiser, Walter C., Jr. *Mission in the Old Testament: Israel as a Light to the Nations.* 2nd ed. Grand Rapids, MI: Baker, 2012.

Kasher, Aryon. *Jews and Hellenistic Cities in Eretz-Israel.* Tübingen: Mohr (Siebeck), 1990.

Kautzsch, Emil (ed.). *Die Apokryphen und Pseudepigraphen des Alten Testaments.* 2 vols. Tübingen: Mohr (Siebeck), 1900.

—— (ed.). *Gesenius' Hebrew Grammar.* Revised by A. E. Cowley. 2nd ed. Oxford: Clarendon, 1910.

Keil, Carl Friedrich. *Biblischer Commentar über den Propheten Daniel.* Leipzig: Dörffling & Franke, 1869.

——. *Commentar über die Bücher der Makkabäer.* Leipzig: Dörffling & Franke, 1875.

Kilpatrick, G. D. "I–III Maccabees." In *Studies in the Septuagint.* Ed. Sidney Jellicoe. New York: Ktav, 1974. 418–33.

King, Daniel H., Sr. *The Book of Daniel.* Truth Commentaries. Bowling Green, KY: Guardian of Truth, 2012.

——. *The Book of Hebrews.* Truth Commentaries. Bowling Green, KY: Guardian of Truth, 2008.

——. *Hebrew and Hellenistic Thought in the Book of Wisdom.* Bowling Green, KY: Guardian of Truth, 2005.

Kirkpatrick, A. F. *The Book of Psalms.* Cambridge Bible for Schools and Colleges. 3 vols. Cambridge, England: Cambridge University Press, 1895–1901.

Kittel, Gerhard, and Gerhard Friedrich (eds.). *Theological Dictionary of the New Testament.* Tr. Geoffrey W. Bromiley. 10 vols. Grand Rapids, MI: Eerdmans, 1964–1976.

Klauck, Hans-Josef. *4 Makkabäerbuch.* Jüdische Schriften aus hellenistisch-römischer Zeit. Gütersloh: Gerd Mohn, 1989.

Klein, G. L. "The 'Prophetic Perfect.'" *Journal of Northwest Semitic Languages* 16 (1990): 45–60.

Knabenbauer, Josephus. *Commentarius in duos libros Machabaeorum.* Cursus Scripturae Sacrae. Paris: Lethielleux, 1907.

Kneucker, J. J. *Das Buch Baruch.* Leipzig: Brockhaus, 1873.

Koehler, Ludwig, Walter Baumgartner, and J. J. Stamm. *The Hebrew and Aramaic Lexicon of the Old Testament.* Ed. M. E. J. Richardson. 5 vols. Leiden: Brill, 1994–2001.

König, Friedrich Eduard. *Historisch-kritisches Lehrgebäude der hebräischen Sprache.* 3 vols. Leipzig: Hinrichs, 1881–1897.

——. *Stilistik, Rhetorik, Poetik in Bezug auf die biblische Litteratur.* Leipzig: Dieterich, 1900.

Kraus, Wolfgang, and Martin Karrer (eds.). *Septuaginta Deutsch: Erläuterungen und Kommentare.* 2 vols. Stuttgart: Deutsche Bibelgesellschaft, 2011.

Kuhn, K. G. *Die älteste Textgestalt der Psalmen Salomos insbesondere auf Grund der syrischen Übersetzung neu untersucht.* Stuttgart: Kohlhammer, 1937.

Kühner, Raphael. *Ausführliche Grammatik der grieschischen Sprache.* 3rd ed. Teil 1. Revised by F. W. Blass. 2 vols. Hanover: Hahn, 1890–1892.

——. *Ausführliche Grammatik der grieschischen Sprache.* 3rd ed. Teil 2. Revised by Bernhard Gerth. 2 vols. Hanover: Hahn, 1898–1904.

Lapide, Cornelius a. *Commentarius in Esdram … et Machabaeos.* Antwerp: Meursius, 1645.

Lebram, Jürgen C. H. "König Antiochus im Buch Daniel." *Vetus Testamentum* 25 (1975): 737–72.

Leupold, H. C. *Exposition of Daniel.* Columbus, OH: Wartburg, 1949.

Liddell, H. G., and Robert Scott. *A Greek-English Lexicon.* Revised by Henry Stuart Jones. 9th ed. (1940.) With revised Supplement. Oxford: Clarendon, 1996.

Longman, Tremper, III. *Daniel.* NIV Application Commentary. Grand Rapids, MI: Zondervan, 1999.

Lowden, John. "An Alternative Interpretation of the Manuscripts of Niketas." *Byzantion* 53 (1983): 559–74.

Lust, Johan, Erik Eynikel, and Katrin Hauspie. *Greek-English Lexicon of the Septuagint.* 2nd ed. Stuttgart: Deutsche Bibelgesellschaft, 2003.

Martin, Ralph P. *James.* Word Biblical Commentary. Waco, TX: Word Books, 1988.

Meecham, H. G. *The Letter of Aristeas.* Manchester: Manchester University Press, 1931.

Merrill, Eugene H. *An Historical Survey of the Old Testament.* 2nd ed. Grand Rapids, MI: Baker, 1991.

Meyer, Rudolf, and Herbert Donner (eds.). *Wilhelm Gesenius' Hebräisches und aramäisches Handwörterbuch über das Alte Testament.* 18th ed. Vols. 1–3. *Alef-mem.* Berlin: Springer, 1987–2005.

Michaelis, Johann Michaelis. *Deutsche Uebersetzung des ersten Buchs der Maccabäer.* Göttingen: Huber, 1778.

Mittag, P. F. *Antiochos IV. Epiphanes.* Berlin: Akademie Verlag, 2006.

Modrzejewski, Joseph Mélèze. *Troisième Livre des Maccabées.* Bible d'Alexandrie. Paris: Cerf, 2008.

Momigliano, Arnaldo. "The Date of the 1st Book of Maccabees." In *Sesto contributo alla storia degli studi classici e del mondo antico.* 2 vols. Rome: Editione di Storia e Letteratura, 1980. 2.561–66.

Moulton, J. H., W. F. Howard, and Nigel Turner. *A Grammar of New Testament Greek.* 4 vols. Edinburgh: T. & T. Clark, 1906–1976.

Mørkholm, Otto. *Antiochus IV of Syria.* Copenhagen: Gyldendal, 1966.

Muccioli, Federicomaria. "Antioco III e la politica onomastica dei Seleucidi." In *New Studies on the Seleucids.* Ed. Edward Dąbrowa. Cracow: Jagiellonian University Press, 2011. 81–96.

Muraoka, Takamitsu. *A Greek-English Lexicon of the Septuagint.* Louvain: Peeters, 2009.

Mussies, Gerard. *The Morphology of Koine Greek as Used in the Apocalypse of St. John.* Leiden: Brill, 1971.

Nelis, J. T. *I Makkabeeën*. Roermond: Romen & Zonen, 1972.

———. *II Makkabeeën*. Bussum: Romen, 1975.

Nodet, Étienne. "*Asidaioi* and Essenes." In *Flores Florentino: Dead Sea Scrolls and Other Early Jewish Studies in Honour of Florentino García Martínez*. Ed. Anthony Hilhorst, Émile Puech, and Eibert Tigchelaar. Leiden: Brill, 2007. 63–87.

Nöldeke, Theodor. *Compendious Syriac Grammar*. Tr. James A. Crichton. (1904.) With Appendix ed. Anton Schall. Winona Lake, MI: Eisenbrauns, 2001.

O'Brien, David. "Between the Testaments." In Leon J. Wood, *A Survey of Israel's History*. 2nd ed. Grand Rapids, MI: Zondervan, 1986. 351–81.

Payne Smith, Robert. *Thesaurus Syriacus*. 2 vols. Oxford: Clarendon, 1879–1901.

Pearson, Lionel. "The Diary and Letters of Alexander the Great." *Historia* 3 (1954–1955): 429–39.

Pelletier, André. *Flavius Josèphe, adapteur de la lettre d'Aristée*. Paris: Klincksieck, 1962.

Pellicanus, Conradus. *Commentaria Bibliorum*. Vol. 5. *Libri veteris instrumenti qui sunt extra canonicum Hebraicum*. Zurich: Froschover, 1535.

Pesch, Wilhelm. "Die Abhängigkeit des 11 salomonischen Psalms vom letzten Kapitel des Buches Baruch." *Zeitschrift für die Alttestamentliche Wissenschaft* 26 (1955): 251–63.

Pfeiffer, Charles F. *Between the Testaments*. Grand Rapids, MI: Baker, 1959.

Pina Paolo, Francesco. *The Consul at Rome*. Cambridge, England: Cambridge University Press, 2011.

Pomykala, Kenneth E. "The Convenant with Phinehas in Ben Sira." In *Israel in the Wilderness*. Ed. Kenneth E. Pomykala. Leiden: Brill, 2008. 17–36.

Porter, Stanley E. *Verbal Aspect in the Greek of the New Testament, with Reference to Tense and Mood*. New York: Peter Lang, 1989.

Prideaux, Humphrey. *An Historical Connection of the Old and New Testaments*. Revised by J. Talboys Wheeler. 2 vols. London: Tegg, 1858.

Probert, Philomen. *Ancient Greek Accentuation: Synchronic Patterns, Frequency Effects, and Prehistory*. Oxford: Oxford University Press, 2006.

Pusey, E. B. *Daniel the Prophet*. 2nd ed. Oxford: Parker, 1868.

Rahlfs, Alfred. "Die Kriegselephanten im I. Makkabäerbuche," *Zietschrift für die Alttestamentliche Wissenschaft* 52 (1934): 78–79.

Rawlinson, George. "I Maccabees" and "II Maccabees." In *Apocrypha*. (Speaker's Commentary.) Ed. Henry Wace. 2 vols. London: John Murray, 1888. 2.373–648.

Robertson, A. T. *A Grammar of the Greek New Testament in the Light of Historical Research*. 5th ed. New York: Harper, 1931.

Rogland, Max. *Alleged Non-Past Uses of Qatal in Classical Hebrew*. Assen, Netherlands: Van Gorcum, 2003.

Rowley, H. H. *Darius the Mede and the Four World Empires in the Book of Daniel*. 2nd ed. Cardiff: University of Wales Press, 1959.

——. *Men of God: Studies in Old Testament History and Prophecy*. London: Nelson, 1963.

Ryle, Herbert E., and Montague R. James. ΨΑΛΜΟΙ ΣΟΛΟΜΩΝΤΟΣ*: Psalms of the Pharisees*. Cambridge, England: Cambridge University Press, 1891.

(Sacy, Louis-Isaac LeMaistre de, and Pierre Thomas du Fossé.) *Les Machabées.* Paris: Desprez & Desessartz, 1695.

Sakenfeld, K.D. (ed.). *The New Interpreter's Dictionary of the Bible.* 5 vols. Nashville, TN: Abingdon, 2006–2009.

Sanctius, Gaspardus. *In libros Ruth… Machabaeorum commentarii.* Lyon: Cardon, 1628.

Sartre, Maurice. "La Syrie-Creuse n'existe pas." In *Géographie historique au Proche-Orient.* Ed. Pierre-Louis Gatier, Bruno Helly, and Jean-Paul Rey-Coquais. Paris: CNRS, 1988. 15–40.

Saulcy, Félicien de. *Histoire de l'art judaïque.* 2nd ed. Paris: Didier, 1864.

Schmidt, Gottfried. "Die beiden Syrischen Übersetzungen des 1. Maccabäerbuches." *Zeitschrift für die Alttestamentliche Wissenschaft* 17 (1897): 1–47, 233–62.

Schulz, Alfons. "Der Status constructus in der Geschichte der Exegese." *Zeitschrift für die Alttestamentliche Wissenschaft* 54 (1936): 270–77.

Schürer, Emil. *A History of the Jewish People in the Age of Jesus Christ.* Tr. John Macpherson, Sophia Taylor, and Peter Christie. 5 vols. Edinburgh: T. & T. Clark, 1890.

——. *A History of the Jewish People in the Age of Jesus Christ.* Revised by Geza Vermes, Fergus Millar, and Martin Goodman. 3 vols. in 4. Edinburgh: T. & T. Clark, 1973–1987.

Schwartz, Daniel R. "Hasidim in 1 Maccabees 2:24?" *Scripta Classica Israelica* 13 (1994): 7–18.

——. *2 Maccabees.* Berlin: de Gruyter, 2008.

Schwartz, Seth. "Israel and the Nations Roundabout: 1 Maccabees and the Hasmonean Expansion." *Journal of Jewish Studies* 42 (1991): 16–38.

Schwyzer, Eduard. *Griechische Grammatik.* 4 vols. Leipzig: Beck. Vol. 1, 6th ed., 1990; vol. 2, 5th ed., 1988; vol. 3, 2nd ed., 1980; vol. 4, 3rd ed., 1994.

Scott, J. Julius, Jr. *Jewish Backgrounds of the New Testament.* 2nd ed. Grand Rapids, MI: Baker, 2000.

Scurlock, Joan. "167 BCE: Hellenism or Reform?" *Journal for the Study of Judaism in the Persian, Hellenistic and Roman Period* 31 (2000): 125–61.

Segal, J. B. *The Diacritical Point and the Accents in Syriac.* London: Oxford University Press, 1953.

Shayegan, M. Rahim. *Arsacids and Sasanians.* Cambridge, England: Cambridge University Press, 2011.

Sherwin-White, Susan, and Amélie Kuhrt. *From Samarkhand to Sardis: A New Approach to the Seleucid Empire.* Berkeley, CA: University of California Press, 1993.

Shipley, Graham. *The Greek World after Alexander.* London: Routledge, 2000.

Simons, J. J. *The Geographical and Topographical Texts of the Old Testament.* Leiden: Brill, 1959.

Smith, G. A. *The Historical Georgraphy of the Holy Land.* 4th ed. London: Hodder & Stoughton, 1897.

Sokoloff, Michael. *A Dictionary of Jewish Palestinian Aramaic of the Byzantine Period.* 2nd ed. Ramat-Gan, Israel: Bar Ilan University Press, 2002.

——. *A Syriac Lexicon.* Winona Lake, IN, and Piscataway, NJ: Eisenbrauns and Gorgias, 2009.

Spicq, Ceslaus. *L'Épître aux Hébreux.* Études Bibliques. 2 vols. Paris: Gabalda, 1952–1953.

Stanley, A. P. *Sinai and Palestine.* 2nd ed. London: Murray, 1864.

Steinmann, Andrew E. *Daniel.* Concordia Commentary. St. Louis, MO: Concordia, 2008.

——. *The Oracles of God: The Old Testament Canon.* St. Louis, MO: Concordia, 1999.

Stern, Menaḥem. "דרכו של יוסף בן מתתיהו בכתיבת ההיסטוריה [Josephus ben Mattathias's Method of Writing History]." In היסטוריונים ואסכולות היסטוריות *(Hisṭoryonim we-Askolot Hisṭoriyyot).* Jerusalem: Ha-Ḥevrah ha-Hisṭorit ha-Yiśra'elit, 1962. 22–28.

——. "ניקולאוס איש-דמשק כמקור לתולדות ישראל בימי בית הורדוס ובית חשמונאי [Nicolaus of Damascus as a Source for Jewish History in the Herodian and Hasmonean Periods]." In המקרא ותולדות ישראל *(Ha-Miqra we-toldot Yiśra'el).* Ed. Binyamin Uffenheimer. Tel Aviv: Universiṭat Tel Aviv, 1972. 375–94.

Suerbaum, Werner. "Merkwürdige Geburtstage." *Chiron* 10 (1980): 327–55.

Stuart, Moses. *A Commentary on the Book of Daniel.* Boston, MA: Crocker & Brewster, 1850.

Swete, H. B. *The Apocalypse of St. John.* 4th ed. London: Macmillan, 1911.

Täubler, Eugen. *Imperium Romanum: Studien zur Entwicklungsgeschichte des Römischen Reichs.* Vol. 1. Leipzig: Teubner, 1913.

Tcherikover, Victor. *Hellenistic Civilization and the Jews.* Tr. S. Applebaum. Philadelphia, PA: Jewish Publication Society, 1959.

Tenney, Merrill C. (ed.). *The Zondervan Encyclopedia of the Bible.* 2nd ed. Revised by Moisés Silva. 5 vols. Grand Rapids, MI: Zondervan, 2009.

Thackeray, Henry St. John. *A Grammar of the Old Testament in Greek.* Vol. 1. Cambridge, England: Cambridge University Press, 1909.

Threatte, Leslie. *The Grammar of Attic Inscriptions.* 2 vols. Berlin: de Gruyter, 1980–1996.

Trafton, Joseph L. *The Syriac Version of the Psalms of Solomon.* Atlanta, GA: Scholars Press, 1985.

Trench, R. C. *Synonyms of the New Testament.* 9th ed. London: Macmillan, 1880.

Tsafrir, Yoram, Leah Di Segni, and Judith Green. *Tabula Imperii Romani Iudaea-Palaestina: Eretz Israel in the Hellenistic, Roman and Byzantine Periods: Maps and Gazetteer.* Jerusalem: Israel Academy of Sciences and Humanities, 1994.

van der Horst, Pieter W. "Greek in Jewish Palestine in Light of Jewish Epigraphy." In *Hellenism in the Land of Israel.* Ed. John J. Collins and G. E. Sterling. Notre Dame, IN: University of Notre Dame Press, 2001. 154–74.

VanderKam, James C. *From Joshua to Caiaphas: High Priests After the Exile.* Minneapolis, MN: Fortress, 2004.

VanGemeren, Willem A. (ed.). *New International Dictionary of Old Testament Theology and Exegesis.* 5 vols. Grand Rapids, MI: Zondervan, 1997.

van Henten, Jan Willem. *The Maccabean Martyrs as Saviours of the Jewish People.* Leiden: Brill, 1997.

Victor, Royce M. *Colonial Education and Class Formation in Early Judaism.* London: T. & T. Clark, 2010.

Vigouroux, Fulcran. *Les Livres saints et la critique rationaliste.* 5 vols. 3rd ed. Paris: Roger & Chernoviz, 1890–1891.

Viteau, Joseph. *Étude sur le grec du Nouveau Testament . . . . Sujet, complément et attribut.* Paris: Bouillon, 1896.

——. *Étude sur le grec du Nouveau Testament: Le Verbe: Syntaxe des propositions.* Paris: Bouillon, 1893.

——. *Les Psaumes de Salomon.* Paris: Letouzey, 1911.

Wacholder, Ben Zion. *Nicolaus of Damascus.* Berkeley, CA: University of California Press, 1962.

Walbank, F. W. *A Historical Commentary on Polybius.* 3 vols. Oxford: Clarendon, 1957–1979.

Wellhausen, Julius. *Die Pharisäer und die Sadducäer.* Griefswald: Bamberg, 1874.

Werline, Rodney A. "Robert B. Wright, ed., *The Psalms of Solomon: A Critical Edition of the Greek Text.*" *Review of Biblical Literature* 11 (2009): 203–07.

Williams, P. J. *Early Syriac Translation Technique and the Textual Criticism of the Greek Gospels.* Piscataway, NJ: Gorgias Press, 2013.

Williamson, H. G. M. *Ezra, Nehemiah.* Word Biblical Commentary. Waco, TX: Word Books, 1985.

Wilson, Robert Dick. *Studies in the Book of Daniel.* 2 vols. New York: Putnam, 1917.

Winer, G. B. *A Treatise on the Grammar of New Testament Greek.* Tr. W. F. Moulton. 3rd ed. Edinburgh: T. & T. Clark, 1882.

Wood, Leon. *A Commentary on Daniel.* Grand Rapids, MI: Zondervan, 1973.

Wordsworth, Christopher. *The Holy Bible.* Vol. 6. *Daniel, the Minor Prophets, and Index.* London: Rivingtons, 1872.

——. *The Church of England and the Maccabees.* 2nd ed. London: Rivingtons, 1876.

Wright, Benjamin G., III. "The *Letter of Aristeas* and the Reception History of the Septuagint." *Bulletin of the International Organization of Septuagint and Cognate Studies* 39 (2006):47–67.

Wright, N. T. *Christian Origins and the Question of God.* Vol. 1. *The New Testament and the People of God.* London: SPCK, 1992.

Yamauchi, Edwin. "Ezra-Nehemiah." In *The Expositor's Bible Commentary.* Ed. Frank E. Gaebelein. Grand Rapids, MI: Zondervan, 1988. 563–771.

Zeitlin, Solomon (commentary). *The First Book of Maccabees.* Jewish Apocryphal Literature. New York: Harper, 1954.

——. *The Second Book of Maccabees.* Jewish Apocryphal Literature. New York: Harper, 1954.

Zöckler, Otto. *Die Apokryphen.* Kurzgefasster Kommentar zu den heiligen Schriften Alten und Neuen Testamentes. Munich: C. H. Beck, 1891.

www.ingramcontent.com/pod-product-compliance
Lightning Source LLC
Chambersburg PA
CBHW070858140426
R18135300001B/R181353PG42812CBX00008B/15
9781936341696